SAGE
vantage

Course tools done right. Built to support your teaching. Designed to ignite learning.

SAGE vantage is an intuitive digital platform that blends trusted SAGE content with auto-graded assignments, all carefully designed to ignite student engagement and drive critical thinking. With evidence-based instructional design at the core, **SAGE vantage** creates more time for engaged learning and empowered teaching, keeping the classroom where it belongs—in your hands.

- **3-STEP COURSE SETUP** is so fast, you can complete it in minutes!

- Control over assignments, content selection, due dates, and grading **EMPOWERS** you to **TEACH YOUR WAY**.

- Dynamic content featuring applied-learning multimedia tools with built-in assessments, including video, knowledge checks, and chapter tests, helps **BUILD STUDENT CONFIDENCE**.

- eReading experience makes it easy to learn by presenting content in **EASY-TO-DIGEST** segments featuring note-taking, highlighting, definition look-up, and more.

- Quality content authored by the **EXPERTS YOU TRUST**.

⑤SAGE vantage™
engage. learn. soar.

sagepub.com/vantage

The
Hallmark
Features

Entrepreneurship: The Practice and Mindset catapults students beyond the classroom by helping them develop an entrepreneurial mindset so they can create opportunities and take action in uncertain environments.

- A new chapter on **DEVELOPING YOUR CUSTOMERS** helps students gain a deeper understanding of market segmentation, customer personas, and the customer journey.

- **2 MINDSHIFT ACTIVITIES PER CHAPTER** challenge students to take action outside the classroom and do entrepreneurship.

- **15 NEW CASE STUDIES** and **16 NEW ENTREPRENEURSHIP IN ACTION PROFILES** highlight a diverse range of entrepreneurs and start-ups.

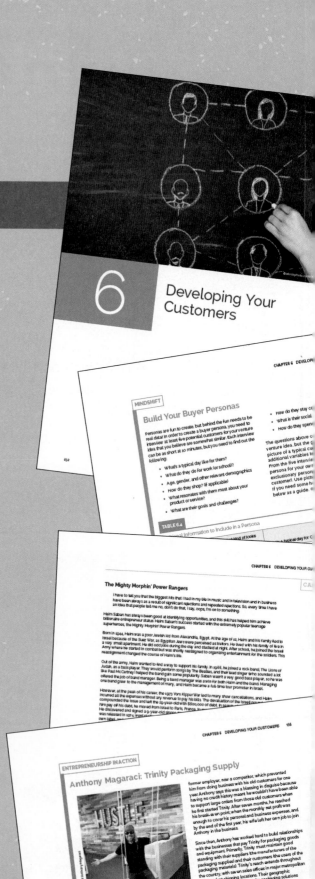

SAGE Publishing:
Our Story

At SAGE, we mean business. We believe in creating evidence-based, cutting-edge content that helps you prepare your students to succeed in today's ever-changing business world. We strive to provide you with the tools you need to develop the next generation of leaders, managers, and entrepreneurs.

- We invest in the right **AUTHORS** who distill research findings and industry ideas into practical applications.

- We keep our prices **AFFORDABLE** and provide multiple **FORMAT OPTIONS** for students.

- We remain permanently independent and fiercely committed to **QUALITY CONTENT** and **INNOVATIVE RESOURCES**.

Entrepreneurship

Second Edition

We dedicate this book to future entrepreneurs of all types across the globe who will create opportunities and take action to change their world and the world of others. Embrace the journey and the learning, and take pride in knowing that you are moving society forward.

Entrepreneurship

The Practice and Mindset

Second Edition

Heidi M. Neck
Babson College

Christopher P. Neck
Arizona State University

Emma L. Murray

Los Angeles | London | New Delhi
Singapore | Washington DC | Melbourne

FOR INFORMATION:

SAGE Publications, Inc.
2455 Teller Road
Thousand Oaks, California 91320
E-mail: order@sagepub.com

SAGE Publications Ltd.
1 Oliver's Yard
55 City Road
London EC1Y 1SP
United Kingdom

SAGE Publications India Pvt. Ltd.
B 1/I 1 Mohan Cooperative Industrial Area
Mathura Road, New Delhi 110 044
India

SAGE Publications Asia-Pacific Pte. Ltd.
18 Cross Street #10-10/11/12
China Square Central
Singapore 048423

Printed in Canada

Library of Congress Cataloging-in-Publication Data

Names: Neck, Heidi M., author. | Neck, Christopher P., author. | Murray, Emma L., author.

Title: Entrepreneurship : the practice and mindset / Heidi M. Neck, Babson College, Christopher P. Neck, Arizona State University, Emma L. Murray.

Description: Second Edition. | Thousand Oaks : SAGE Publishing, 2020. | Revised edition of the authors' Entrepreneurship, [2018] | Includes bibliographical references and index.

Identifiers: LCCN 2019031105 | ISBN 9781544354620 (paperback) | ISBN 9781544354637 (epub) | ISBN 9781544354644 (epub) | ISBN 9781544354651 (pdf)

Subjects: LCSH: Entrepreneurship.

Classification: LCC HB615 .N43297 2020 | DDC 658.4/21—dc23
LC record available at https://lccn.loc.gov/2019031105

Acquisitions Editor: Maggie Stanley
Content Development Editor: Lauren Gobell
Editorial Assistant: Janeane Calderon
Production Editor: Veronica Stapleton Hooper
Copy Editor: Diana Breti
Typesetter: C&M Digitals (P) Ltd.
Proofreader: Talia Greenberg
Indexer: Beth Nauman-Montana
Cover Designer: Scott Van Atta
Marketing Manager: Sarah Panella

This book is printed on acid-free paper.

20 21 22 23 24 10 9 8 7 6 5 4 3 2 1

BRIEF CONTENTS

DETAILED CONTENTS

© Peshkova/Shutterstock

CHAPTER 3: Creating and Recognizing New Opportunities 56

CHAPTER 4: Using Design Thinking 78

©iStockphoto.com/oatawa

©iStockphoto.com/marrio31

©iStockphoto.com/Gerasimov174

©iStockphoto.com/ipopba

©iStockphoto.com/utah778

©iStockphoto.com/PeopleImages

©iStockphoto.com/Gearstd

©iStockphoto.com/AndreyPopov

©iStockphoto.com/kongxinzhu

©iStockphoto.com/Weedezign

©iStockphoto.com/South_agency

Organic Valley (with permission)

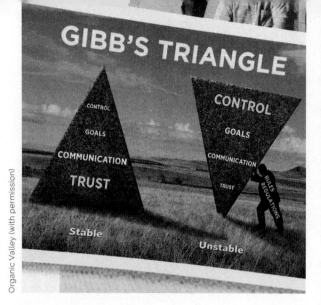

Organic Valley (with permission)

AP Photo/ Manish Swarup

PREFACE

Entrepreneurship: The Practice and Mindset (2nd ed.) catapults students beyond the classroom to think and act more entrepreneurially in order to create opportunities and take action in uncertain environments. Based on the world-renowned Babson program, this text emphasizes practice and learning through action.

Entrepreneurship has historically and narrowly been defined as starting a new business, with little attention given to the individuals—the entrepreneurs of all types—who have the mindset, skillset, and toolset to create change, improve the world, and make a difference in their lives as well as the lives of others. The most current view of entrepreneurship is represented in this text. This is a view that entrepreneurship today is not reserved for the chosen few but is a life skill needed by all. The world will benefit not only from those who start new ventures but also from those who act entrepreneurially in all that they do. We are living in the entrepreneurial generation, and all students must get comfortable with creating and testing new ideas, navigating uncertain environments, and acting in order to learn rather than learning in order to act.

Entrepreneurship: The Practice and Mindset is a practice-based, realistic, and inclusive approach to entrepreneurship. It is a core textbook for college-level undergraduate and graduate students seeking methods for starting and running something new: a new business for-profit or nonprofit, inside a large corporation, or within a family business. Four points guide the philosophy of this book:

First, every student should be exposed to the practice of entrepreneurship regardless of major, discipline, or chosen career path. The life skill developed through the discipline of entrepreneurship is both necessary and differentiating. We have the innate ability to build, problem solve, lead, reflect, experiment, improvise, and empathize, but sometimes we lack the mindset (or have lost the mindset at some point) to do so in creative and ingenious ways. Our education system has deemphasized critical thinking in favor of right and wrong. In short, we have educated the human race to be less entrepreneurial than ever before. It's time to get those entrepreneurship skills back.

Second, students cannot simply read about entrepreneurship; they must *do* entrepreneurship. The text requires a lot of "doing" and, as a result, students develop courage to take action in highly ambiguous environments. Our vision in writing this book was to create a practice-based text that promotes active learning and engagement with the realities of entrepreneurship, encouraging students to think like entrepreneurs rather than passively learn about them.

Third, this textbook approaches learning entrepreneurship as a method that goes beyond simply understanding and knowing; it requires using, applying, and acting. We treat entrepreneurship as a method that demands practice. In fact we call it "the Entrepreneurship Method" throughout the book. Traditionally, entrepreneurship is taught as a process that typically involves traversing a linear pathway of identifying an opportunity, understanding resource requirements, acquiring resources, writing a business plan, implementing the plan, and then exiting the business at some point. In reality, entrepreneurship isn't that clean or clear cut. Additionally, the word *process* assumes known inputs and known outputs, as in a manufacturing process; it implies you will get to a specific destination. For example, building a car on an assembly line is a manufacturing process. You have all the parts; you know how they fit together; and you know the type of car you will have at the end because it was planned that way. A process is quite predictable. Entrepreneurship is not predictable and, therefore, cannot adequately be taught as a process. It's too messy for that and we need to embrace the messiness.

Fourth, students completing this text will be thinking and acting more entrepreneurially than when they started. Every action students take in this text will aid in building their entrepreneurial mindset. Every action is designed with intention so that students can experience and practice creative and nimble thinking, leading to a heightened level of experimentation where numerous iterations represent stages of learning rather than successes and failures or right and wrong answers. This text is a journey that encourages students to act their way into learning and knowing. It's about getting comfortable with uncertainty and developing the courage to act and find all the pieces of the puzzle.

It's about *being* entrepreneurial!

NEW TO THIS EDITION

We have made several enhancements to this edition while retaining the unique mindset approach. In addition to updating the chapter references, we have updated all end of chapter case studies, provided new Entrepreneurship Meets Ethics features, new Research at Work features, new Mindshift features, new profiles for Entrepreneurship in Action features, and added new entrepreneurial research supported by the latest studies. Additionally, we have added a new chapter on developing your customers.

Chapter 1: Practicing Entrepreneurship

- Chapters 1 (A Global Social Movement) and 2 (Practicing Entrepreneurship) from the first edition have been combined to create a new chapter

- New Entrepreneurship in Action: Juan Giraldo, Waku

- Expanded discussion on deliberate practice, including a new section on how deliberate practice shapes the brain

- New Entrepreneurship Meets Ethics: When to Practice Entrepreneurship

- New Case Study: Gyan-I Inc.

Chapter 2: Activating an Entrepreneurial Mindset

- Chapter 3 (Developing an Entrepreneurial Mindset) from the first edition was retitled and renumbered as Chapter 2

- New Entrepreneurship in Action: Franklin Yancey, WME Entertainment and Yancey Realty

- Further detailed discussion on mindset featuring U.S. senator Corey Booker

- New Mindshift: Building Entrepreneurial Habits

- New Entrepreneurship Meets Ethics: Family and Friends Along for the Ride

- Expands on the dysfunctional side of passion by describing a recent Stanford study

- New Case Study: Doctory

Chapter 3: Creating and Recognizing New Opportunities

- Chapter 5 (Generating New Ideas) from the first edition was retitled and renumbered as Chapter 3

- Added one new figure on increasing complexity and unknowingness in opportunity creation

- Added two new tables on discovering new opportunities and the IDEATE model for opportunity recognition

- New Entrepreneurship in Action: Jazmine Valencia, JV Agency

- New section on the four pathways to opportunity identification

- New Entrepreneurship Meets Ethics: The Ethics of Taking Someone's Idea

- New Mindshift: Practicing Identify in the IDEATE Model
- Research at Work: Testing IDEATE in the Entrepreneurial Classroom
- New Case Study: Yoee Baby

Chapter 4: Using Design Thinking

- Chapter 6 from the first edition was renumbered as Chapter 4
- Added one new figure on insight statements
- Added three new tables on skills of designers, three phases of design thinking, and design thinking as a social technology
- New discussion of the four approaches of design company IDEO
- New Entrepreneurship in Action: Shaymaa Gaafar, Shay Jaffar
- New Mindshift: Needs Are Verbs; Solutions Are Nouns
- New example (Clean Team Ghana) to illustrate the three phases of design thinking in action
- New section explaining the four different types of observation
- Research at Work: Design Thinking Is a Social Technology
- Expanded discussion on preparing for an interview
- Expanded discussion on empathy using new IDEO example
- Detailed description of the interviewing process

Chapter 5: Building Business Models

- Discussion of Massive Open Online Courses (MOOCs) and the Imitation Model as examples of different types of business models
- New Entrepreneurship in Action: Brandon Steiner, Steiner Sports
- New Entrepreneurship Meets Ethics: The Rights of Research Participants
- Discussion of business author Doug Hall's Three Laws of Marketing Physics: overt benefit, real reason to believe, and dramatic difference
- New Mindshift: The Overt Benefit, Real Reason to Believe, and Dramatic Difference
- Research at Work: Overt Benefit, Real Reason to Believe, and Dramatic Difference
- New Case Study: NatureBox

Chapter 6: Developing Your Customers

- New Entrepreneurship in Action: Anthony Magaraci, Trinity Packaging Supply
- Expanded discussion on creating an end user profile, including psychographics
- New section Crossing the Chasm and explanation of "beachhead market"
- New example to illustrate customer journey mapping
- New Entrepreneurship Meets Ethics: Can You Sell Customer Information?
- New Mindshift: Build Your Buyer Personas
- New Mindshift: Creating a Customer Journey Map
- Research at Work: Emotional Motivators

- New example to illustrate market sizing
- New Case Study: The Mighty Morphin' Power Rangers

Chapter 7: Testing and Experimenting With New Ideas

- New introduction featuring the benefits of experimentation
- New Entrepreneurship in Action: Karima Mariama-Arthur, WordSmithRapport
- New section explaining different types of experiments
- New section exploring prototypes in greater depth
- New Entrepreneurship Meets Ethics: When Links Break
- New example illustrating the six steps of scientific experimentation
- New example to explain the rules of experimentation in relation to stakeholders
- New Mindshift: Creating a Mockup
- New Research at Work: Why Overconfident Entrepreneurs Fail
- Introduces the five-dimensional model of curiosity created by Todd B. Kashan at George Mason University
- New section on building curiosity strength
- New Case Study: Stitch Fix

Chapter 8: Developing Networks and Building Teams

- New Entrepreneurship in Action: Markesia Akinbami, Ducere Construction Services
- Introduces new research by the Economist Intelligence Unit on the benefits of informal professional networks and communities
- Introduction to the concept of implicit bias
- Adapted table: Top Organizations for Entrepreneurs
- New section on incubators and accelerators
- New Entrepreneurship Meets Ethics: Developing Networks and Building Teams
- New Mindshift: Building My Network
- Adapted table: LinkedIn Groups Dedicated to Entrepreneurs
- Adapted table: Facebook Groups for Entrepreneurs
- Discussion of Google's research on shared vision and management behaviors
- Research at Work: Don't Pitch Like a Girl
- New Case Study: AmeriCan Packaging

Chapter 9: Creating Revenue Models

- New Entrepreneurship in Action: Kathey Porter, Porter Brown Associates
- Discussion on data brokers
- New Entrepreneurship Meets Ethics: How to Make an Ad
- New Mindshift: Revenue Model Pivot Practice
- Research at Work: The Dark Side of Entrepreneurship
- Provides detailed explanation of break-even analysis
- New Case Study: Invento Robotics

Chapter 10: Planning for Entrepreneurs

- New Entrepreneurship in Action: Dr. Emmet C. (Tom) Thompson II, AFC Management
- New Entrepreneurship Meets Ethics: When to Be Transparent With Investors
- New section introducing the concept statement as an important part of planning
- New Mindshift: What Do You Know About Your Competition?
- Research at Work: Can We Think Ourselves Into (and out of) Planning?
- Additional tips for writing any type of business plan
- New Case Study: IoMob

Chapter 11: Anticipating Failure

- New Entrepreneurship in Action: David James, K12 Landing
- Adapted table: Entrepreneurs Share Their Reasons for Failure
- Explores a study by CBI Insights on the number one reason for startup failure
- New Entrepreneurship Meets Ethics: From Tech Hero to Zero Net Worth
- New Mindshift: Go Get Rejected
- Research at Work: Overcoming the Stigma of Failure
- Updated figure: Fear of Failure Rates Around the World
- Updated figure: GEM Global Report
- New Case Study: Petwell Supply Co.

Chapter 12: Bootstrapping and Crowdfunding for Resources

- New Entrepreneurship in Action: Bryanne Leeming, Unruly Studios
- Adapted table: Common Bootstrapping Strategies
- New Entrepreneurship Meets Ethics: When to Proclaim a Product Is Ready
- New Mindshift: Bootstrapping for Your Business
- Research at Work: The Informational Value of Crowdfunding for Music Entrepreneurs
- New Case Study: FUBU

Chapter 13: Financing for Startups

- New Entrepreneurship in Action, Joel Barthelemy: GlobalMed
- Expanded discussion on splitting the ownership pie
- New section: The Age of the Unicorn
- Adapted table: Why Angels and Entrepreneurs Are Good for Each Other
- Updated table: Most Active Angel Groups in the U.S.
- Additional advice from the Angel Capital Association (ACA)
- Research at Work: Why Most Entrepreneurs Can't Access Capital
- Adapted table: Guidelines for Finding the Right VC for Your Startup
- New section: What About a Bank Loan?
- New section: The Due Diligence Process for VCs

- New Entrepreneurship Meets Ethics: Replacing the Founder CEO
- New Mindshift: Watch *Shark Tank* as an Investor
- New Case Study: Gravyty

Chapter 14: Navigating Legal and IP Issues

- New Entrepreneurship in Action: Cameron Herold, 1-800-GOT JUNK? & COO Alliance
- Adapted table: Useful Online Legal Resources
- New section: The Founders' Agreement
- Adapted table: Resources for IP Information
- New section: Nondisclosure Agreement
- Updated Research at Work: Patent Trolls
- New Mindshift: Patent Battles
- New Entrepreneurship Meets Ethics: The Danger of Going on *Shark Tank*
- Expanded discussion of unpaid internships referencing the "primary beneficiary test" adopted by the Department of Labor
- New case: LULA

Chapter 15: Engaging Customers Through Marketing

- Expanded introduction detailing how entrepreneurial marketing is different
- New Entrepreneurship in Action: Charlie Regan, Nerds on Site
- New Section: Marketing Trends
- Discusses new ideas for entrepreneurs to engage consumers through creating content
- New Section: How to Build Your Personal Brand
- Adapted table: Tips for Building Your Personal Brand
- New Entrepreneurship Meets Ethics: How Social Media Can Provide Marketing Headaches
- New Mindshift: What "About Us"?
- Research at Work: How a Pitch Can Help Build Your Brand
- New Case Study: RealPlay

Chapter 16: Supporting Social Entrepreneurship

- New Entrepreneurship in Action: Organic Valley
- Discussion on the climate crisis drawing from studies from the University of Hawaii and information from the Intergovernmental Panel on Climate Change
- New Entrepreneurship Meets Ethics: How Social Entrepreneurs Can Be Unethical
- New Mindshift: How Entrepreneurship Is Saving the Planet
- Research at Work: United Nations Sustainable Development Goals
- Adapted table: Examples of Impact Investment Funds
- Expanded discussion on CSR initiatives drawing from the latest research

- New section: Social Entrepreneurship and Audacious Ideas
- Updated figure: Global Entrepreneurship Monitor Measuring Entrepreneurial Activity
- Updated figure: Global Entrepreneurship Monitor Measuring Rates by Gender
- New Case Study: 1854 Cycling Company

What Makes Our Book Unique

- A focus on the **entrepreneurial mindset** helps students develop the discovery, thinking, reasoning, and implementation skills necessary to thrive in highly uncertain environments.

- An emphasis on the **Entrepreneurship Method**, in which entrepreneurship is approached as a method that requires doing. It's not a predictive or linear process. It's messy, but clarity comes with action and practice.

- Each chapter includes two **Mindshift activities** in which students take action outside the classroom in order to practice various aspects of entrepreneurship.

- Instructors are provided with **experiential learning activities** to use inside the classroom.

- A unique chapter on **learning from failure** helps students anticipate setbacks, develop grit, and understand the value of experimentation and iteration.

- A new chapter on **developing your customers** helps students gain a deeper understanding of their customers and explains how this knowledge is essential for early business success.

- **Cutting-edge topics** such as design thinking, business model canvas, bootstrapping, and crowdfunding are covered in depth, exposing students to the latest developments in the field.

An Inclusive Approach

The media often exaggerate the meteoric rise of "overnight global sensations" such as Bill Gates (Microsoft), Steve Jobs (Apple), Mark Zuckerberg (Facebook), Elon Musk (Tesla), and Travis Kalanick (Uber). These stories have perpetuated the myth of the "tech entrepreneurial genius" and have captured the public imagination for decades. Although Bill Gates and his peers are certainly inspirational, we would argue that few can personally identify with the stories surrounding them, and they do little to represent the reality of entrepreneurship.

In *Entrepreneurship: The Practice and Mindset*, we deconstruct the myths and stories, which we believe limit others from becoming entrepreneurs. Dominant myths include that entrepreneurship is reserved for startups; that entrepreneurs have a special set of personality traits; that entrepreneurship can't be taught; that entrepreneurs are extreme risk takers; that entrepreneurs do not collaborate; that entrepreneurs devote large periods of time to planning; and that entrepreneurship is not a life skill.

With the support of extensive research, we show that the traditional view of the startup is not the only path for entrepreneurs; that there is no scientific evidence to suggest that entrepreneurs are any different from the rest of us in terms of personality traits or behaviors; that entrepreneurship can, indeed, be taught; that entrepreneurs are more calculated (rather than extreme) risk takers; that they collaborate more than they compete, act more than they plan, and perceive entrepreneurship as a life skill.

We also show that entrepreneurs do not have to come from a technology background to succeed. In *Entrepreneurship: The Practice and Mindset*, we include personal accounts of entrepreneurs from all types of disciplines, in the United States and around the world, including those in the fields of recruitment, science, food and beverage, tourism, engineering, finance, clothing, industrial design, pet services, fitness, costume design, sports, and promotional marketing.

These personal stories are intended to illustrate the realities of being an entrepreneur, detailing the unpredictability of entrepreneurship together with the highs and the lows; like famous U.S. entrepreneur computer designer Adam Osborne, we believe that "the most valuable thing you can make is a mistake—you can't learn anything from being perfect."

Entrepreneurship is all around us; everyone has the ability to think and act entrepreneurially, transform opportunity into reality, and create social and economic value. But as we show, practice is key to success, and learning is inseparable from doing.

A Mindset and Action Approach

Mindset is the precursor to action. The work of researcher and Darden School of Business professor Saras D. Sarasvathy has added a new dimension to the field in understanding the entrepreneurial mindset. Sarasvathy discovered patterns of thinking, a theory she calls *effectuation,* which is the idea that the future is unpredictable yet controllable. In other words, because thinking can be changed and altered, we all have the ability to think and act entrepreneurially, and this thinking can be learned and taught. Moreover, entrepreneurship is not only about altering the way we think—it is about creating mindshifts to take action that yield significant change and value. And creating these mindshifts takes practice and experimentation.

We believe that it is very important to emphasize the mindset in the early development of entrepreneurship students. Often the mindset is either ignored or considered to be too difficult to teach. We introduce entrepreneurial mindset very early in the text, and then the mindset is further developed throughout the book based on the actions that students take and are required to practice throughout the book.

Knowing that an entrepreneurial mindset is needed is not sufficient for a strong entrepreneurship education. Practicing the mindset and helping students develop it over time are essential components of learning the discipline of entrepreneurship today. In her previous book, *Teaching Entrepreneurship,* Heidi Neck and her coauthors Candy Brush and Patti Greene encouraged educators to build classroom environments that encouraged students to play, create, experiment, empathize, and reflect in order to build a bias toward action and become more entrepreneurial. These elements are emphasized throughout this text.

FEATURES

In each chapter, we include the following features that help students think and act like entrepreneurs:

- **Entrepreneurship in Action** at the beginning of each chapter includes interviews with entrepreneurs from many different businesses and disciplines both in the United States and around the world, demonstrating how the concepts discussed in the chapter are applied in real situations.

- Two **Mindshift** activities in each chapter provide instructors with exercises that encourage students to think and act outside of their comfort zones. These activities can be performed inside or outside the classroom, and the accompanying critical thinking questions promote further comprehension and analysis.

- **Entrepreneurship Meets Ethics** provides students with examples of ethical dilemmas and challenges related to topics discussed in the chapter. These real-world scenarios and the accompanying critical thinking questions guide students to think about how they would take action if confronted with a similar situation.

- **Research at Work** highlights recent seminal entrepreneurship studies and explores their impact on and application to the marketplace.

- Short **Case Studies** tell the stories of real companies from various sectors and markets to illustrate chapter concepts and encourage further exploration of these topics.
- **Summaries** and **Key Terms** recap important chapter information to aid with studying and comprehension.
- Topical **Supplements** offer greater depth of practice:
  - **Financial Statements and Projections for Startups** demonstrate how students can build financial projections based on sound data, using different types of financial statements.
  - **The Pitch Deck** provides an in-depth description of the pitch deck, includes sample slides, walks students through the preparation of their own pitch deck, and advises students on how to predict and prepare for the question-and-answer period that usually follows a pitch presentation.
- **VentureBlocks** simulation
  - In the VentureBlocks simulation, students start from scratch, with no resources or business ideas, and must explore a new, unknown market of bearlike pets called nanus. On their journey through the simulation, students learn how to interview customers to identify business opportunities based on their needs. Most students will complete VentureBlocks in 30 to 60 minutes. The simulation includes tutorials so they know what to do and how to navigate at all times. The simulation ends when they identify business opportunities that meet the needs of nanu owners.

CONTENT AND ORGANIZATION

Part I. Entrepreneurship Is a Life Skill

Chapter 1: Practicing Entrepreneurship describes the skills most important to the Entrepreneurship Method, how entrepreneurship is more of a method than a process, and the concept of deliberate practice.

Chapter 2: Activating an Entrepreneurial Mindset outlines the effectiveness of mindset in entrepreneurship and explains how to develop the habits of self-leadership, creativity, and improvisation.

Part II. Creating and Developing Opportunities

Chapter 3: Creating and Recognizing New Opportunities explores the four pathways (design, effectuate, search, and find) toward explaining how entrepreneurs identify and exploit opportunities.

Chapter 4: Using Design Thinking describes the importance of design thinking in understanding customers and their needs, explains the four different types of observation, emphasizes the role of empathy in design thinking, and illustrates the key parts of the design thinking process and their relevance to entrepreneurs.

Chapter 5: Building Business Models examines the core areas of a business model, explores the importance of customer value propositions (CVPs), and illustrates the components of the business model canvas.

Chapter 6: Developing Your Customers explores different types of customers, customer segmentation, customer personas, the customer journey mapping process, and market sizing.

Chapter 7: Testing and Experimenting With New Ideas explains the benefits of experimentation, illustrates the six steps of scientific experimentation and how they apply to entrepreneurs, demonstrates how to test hypotheses, and discusses the five-dimensional model of curiosity.

Chapter 8: Developing Networks and Building Teams explains the importance of networks for building social capital, identifies the benefits of professional informal networks and communities, describes different ways of building networks, and describes how networking can help build a founding team.

Part III. Evaluating and Acting on Opportunities

Chapter 9: Creating Revenue Models describes the different types of revenue models used by entrepreneurs and identifies different strategies entrepreneurs use when pricing their products and calculating prices.

Chapter 10: Planning for Entrepreneurs explains vision as an important part of entrepreneurial planning, the different types of plans used by entrepreneurs, and the types of questions to answer during planning, and provides advice for writing business plans.

Chapter 11: Anticipating Failure explores failure and its effect on entrepreneurs; the consequences of fear of failure; how entrepreneurs can learn from failure; and the significance of "grit" and its role in building tolerance for failure.

Part IV. Supporting New Opportunities

Chapter 12: Bootstrapping and Crowdfunding for Resources describes the significance of bootstrapping and bootstrapping strategies for entrepreneurs and also discusses crowdfunding as a form of investment for entrepreneurial ventures.

Chapter 13: Financing for Startups outlines the stages of equity financing, explains the roles of angel investors and venture capital investors in financing entrepreneurs, and describes the due diligence process.

Chapter 14: Navigating Legal and IP Issues outlines the most common types of legal structures available to startups; describes IP, IP theft, and some IP traps experienced by entrepreneurs; and discusses the founders' agreement and nondisclosure agreements.

Chapter 15: Engaging Customers Through Marketing explores the principles of marketing and how they apply to new ventures, describes branding and how to build a personal brand, explains the value of social media for marketing opportunities, and discusses the different types of marketing tools available to entrepreneurs.

Chapter 16: Supporting Social Entrepreneurship defines social entrepreneurship, discusses the different types of social entrepreneurship, and explains how it can help to resolve wicked problems around the world that are connected to the United Nations Sustainable Development Goals.

DIGITAL RESOURCES

A Complete Teaching and Learning Package

Engage, Learn, Soar with **SAGE vantage**, an intuitive digital platform that delivers *Entrepreneurship: The Practice and Mindset, Second Edition*, textbook content in a learning experience carefully designed to ignite student engagement and drive critical thinking. With evidence-based instructional design at the core, SAGE vantage creates more time for engaged learning and empowered teaching, keeping the classroom where it belongs—in your hands.

Easy to access across mobile, desktop, and tablet devices, SAGE vantage enables students to engage with the material you choose, learn by applying knowledge, and soar with confidence by performing better in your course.

Highlights Include:

- **eReading Experience.** Makes it easy for students to study wherever they are—students can take notes, highlight content, look up definitions, and more!

- **Pedagogical Scaffolding.** Builds on core concepts, moving students from basic understanding to mastery.

- **Confidence Builder.** Offers frequent knowledge checks, applied-learning multimedia tools, and chapter tests with focused feedback to assure students know key concepts.
- **Time-saving Flexibility.** Feeds auto-graded assignments to your gradebook, with real-time insight into student and class performance.
- **Quality Content.** Written by expert authors and teachers, content is not sacrificed for technical features.
- **Honest Value.** Affordable access to easy-to-use, quality learning tools students will appreciate.

Favorite SAGE vantage Features

- **3-step course setup** is so fast you can complete it in minutes!
- **Control over assignments**, content selection, due dates, and grading empowers you to teach your way.
- **Quality content** authored by the experts you trust.
- **eReading experience** makes it easy to learn and study by presenting content in easy-to-digest segments featuring note-taking, highlighting, definition look-up, and more.
- **LMS integration provides single sign-on** with streamlined grading capabilities and course management tools.
- **Auto-graded assignments** include:
  - formative **knowledge checks** for each major section of the text that quickly reinforce what students have read and ensure they stay on track;
  - dynamic, hands-on **multimedia activities** that tie real world examples and motivate students to read, prepare for class;
  - summative **chapter tests** that reinforce important themes; and
  - **helpful hints and feedback** (provided with all assignments) that offer context and explain why an answer is correct or incorrect, allowing students to study more effectively.
- **Compelling polling questions** bring concepts to life and drive meaningful comprehension and classroom discussion.
- **Short-answer questions** provide application and reflection opportunities connected to key concepts.
- **Instructor reports** track student activity and provide analytics so you can adapt instruction as needed.
- **A student dashboard** offers easy access to grades, so students know exactly where they stand in your course and where they might improve.
- **Honest value** gives students access to quality content and learning tools at a price they will appreciate.

⑤SAGE coursepacks

SAGE Coursepacks for Instructors

The **SAGE coursepack** for *Entrepreneurship: The Practice and Mindset, Second Edition* makes it easy to import our quality instructor materials and student resources into your school's learning management system (LMS), such as Blackboard, Canvas, Brightspace by D2L, or Moodle. Intuitive and simple to use, **SAGE coursepack** allows you to integrate only the content you need, with minimal effort, and requires no access code. Don't use an LMS platform? You can still access many of the online resources for *Entrepreneurship: The Practice and Mindset, Second Edition* via the **SAGE edge** site.

Available SAGE content through the coursepack includes:

- Pedagogically robust **assessment tools** that foster review, practice, and critical thinking and offer a more complete way to measure student engagement, including:
  - Diagnostic **coursepack chapter quizzes** that identify opportunities for improvement, track student progress, and ensure mastery of key learning objectives.
  - **Test banks** built on Bloom's taxonomy that provide a diverse range of test items.
  - **Activity and quiz options** that allow you to choose only the assignments and tests you want.

- Editable, chapter-specific **PowerPoint®** slides that offer flexibility when creating multimedia lectures so you don't have to start from scratch but can customize to your exact needs.

- **Instructions** on how to use and integrate the comprehensive assessments and resources provided.

⑤SAGE edge™

SAGE edge is a robust online environment featuring an impressive array of tools and resources for review, study, and further exploration, keeping both instructors and students on the cutting edge of teaching and learning. SAGE edge content is open access and available on demand. Learning and teaching has never been easier!

SAGE edge for Students at **https://edge.sagepub.com/neckentrepreneurship2e** provides a personalized approach to help students accomplish their coursework goals in an easy-to-use learning environment.

- **Learning objectives** reinforce the most important material

- Mobile-friendly **eFlashcards** strengthen understanding of key terms and concepts, and make it easy to maximize your study time, anywhere, anytime.

- Mobile-friendly practice **quizzes** allow you to assess how much you've learned and where you need to focus your attention.

- Carefully selected video resources bring concepts to life, are tied to learning objectives, and make learning easier.

SAGE edge for Instructors at **https://edge.sagepub.com/neckentrepreneurship2e** supports teaching by making it easy to integrate quality content and create a rich learning environment for students.

- The **Test bank**, built on Bloom's taxonomy (with Bloom's cognitive domain and difficulty level noted for each question), is created specifically for this text.

- **Sample course syllabi** provide suggested models for structuring your course.

- Editable, chapter-specific **PowerPoint®** **slides** offer complete flexibility for creating a multimedia presentation for the course, so you don't have to start from scratch but can customize to your exact needs.

- **Lecture Notes** features chapter summaries and outlines, providing an essential reference and teaching tool for lectures.

- Sample **answers to questions in the text** provide an essential reference.

- **Case notes** include summaries, analyses, and sample answers to assist with discussion.

- **Entrepreneurial exercises** written by Heidi Neck and other faculty from Babson College can be used in class to reinforce learning by doing.

- **Mindset Vitamins** are brief, fun, daily activities that can help you practice developing your entrepreneurial mindset every day

- **Suggested projects, experiential exercises, and activities** help students apply the concepts they learn to see how the work in various contexts, providing new perspectives.

- A set of all the **graphics from the text**, including all the maps, tables, and figures in PowerPoint formats are provided for class presentations.

- **Excel spreadsheets** accompany the supplement on financials.

- **Sample pitch decks** serve as examples to help students formulate their own pitch.

SAGE Premium Video

Entrepreneurship offers premium video, available exclusively in the **SAGE vantage** digital option, produced and curated specifically for this text, to boost comprehension and bolster analysis.

VentureBlocks Simulation

Practice interviewing customers and identifying their needs with VentureBlocks, a game-based simulation.

Simulation Goals

1. **Develop** a better understanding of approaching opportunity creation through the identification of customer needs.

2. **Practice** interviewing potential customers:
   a. Approach strangers and start a conversation.
   b. Ask good open-ended questions to get useful and relevant information.
   c. Identify bad questions that would make real-world customer interviews unsuccessful.
   d. Feel rejection when someone does not want to engage in a conversation.

3. **Improve** listening and observation skills to identify the needs of potential customers and build strong customer insights.

4. **Cultivate** pattern recognition skills to identify potential opportunities that meet the needs of multiple customer types.

5. **Distinguish** between needs, customer insights, and solutions.

What Is VentureBlocks?

In the VentureBlocks simulation, you start from scratch, with no resources or business ideas, and must explore a new, unknown market of bear-like pets called nanus. On your journey through the simulation, you learn how to identify business opportunities based on customer needs.

Most students will complete VentureBlocks in 30 to 60 minutes. The simulation includes tutorials so you know what to do and how to navigate at all times. Take your time, though, because this is a points-based competition. You will be able to see the top five performers at all times in your class on the real-time leaderboard!

The nanu

Here's a little bit more information about the simulation.

You assume the role of a nascent entrepreneur who lives in a small town called Trepton. A few years ago, scientists in Trepton created a new pet: the nanu. These cute bear-like pets are becoming popular fast. The number of nanu owners in Trepton is growing, and a few well-known veterinarians project nanu ownership to surpass dog ownership by the year 2040. This could be disruptive! The entrepreneur (you!) believes business opportunities exist but must learn more about nanus and their owners.

VentureBlocks is completed when you identify business opportunities that meet the needs of nanu owners. In order to do this, you must complete missions across eight levels of play. In Levels 1–4 you develop empathy for nanu owners by talking with them. In Levels 5–7, you generate customer insights that lead to business opportunities. A simulation learning summary occurs in Level 8. Figure 1 details the missions.

VentureBlocks represents early-stage entrepreneurial activity, and its foundations are rooted in design thinking that was introduced in this chapter. Figure 2 should look familiar: This is the human-centered approach framework presented in the chapter. Remember, strong opportunities are found at the intersection of feasibility, viability, and desirability. Feasibility answers the question, Can it be done from a technical or organizational perspective? Viability answers the question, Can we make money doing it? Desirability answers the question, What do people need?

FIGURE 1

VentureBlocks Missions

LEVEL	MANDATORY MISSION	LOCATION
1	Start a conversation and get rejected	Trepton Park
2	Trash a bad question while talking to people	Trepton Park
3	Talk to a nanu owner and earn 75 XP (experience points)	Trepton Park
4	Talk to a nanu owner and earn 110 XP (experience points)	Trepton Park
5	Go home and build 3 good insights	Home
6	Choose your top insight	Home
7	Create 2 business ideas based on your chosen insight	Home

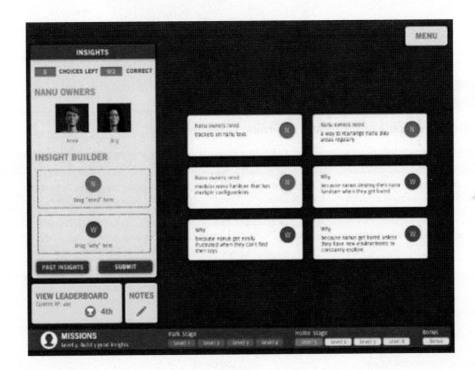

It is very common for entrepreneurship students to start with feasibility and viability. And these do represent two very important factors in building a sustainable business model, but sometimes we try to answer these questions too soon without giving adequate attention to what people need. As a result, VentureBlocks is designed to focus first on desirability: what nanu owners need.

How to Use With This Text

Although the concepts students will practice in this simulation are most directly connected to concepts in Chapter 4: Using Design Thinking, they will also practice concepts from Chapter 3: Creating and Recognizing New Opportunities and Chapter 11: Learning From Failure. Figure 3 demonstrates how the chapter Learning Objectives align with the Simulation Goals.

How to Access the Simulation

To access the VentureBlocks Simulation, visit sage.ventureblocks.com and enter your registration code. Your registration code will be available once your instructor sets up the course at sage.ventureblocks.com..

FIGURE 2

Design-Thinking Framework Revisited

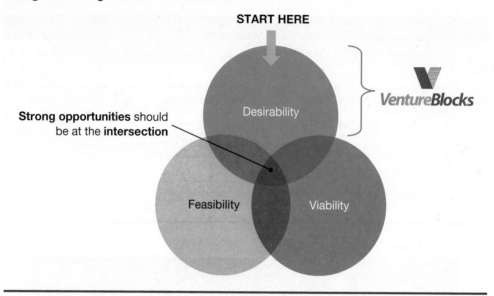

START HERE

Strong opportunities should be at the intersection

Desirability

VentureBlocks

Feasibility   Viability

FIGURE 3

Simulation Goals and Chapter Learning Objectives

SIMULATION GOALS	LEARNING OBJECTIVES
Develop a better understanding of approaching opportunity creation through the identification of customer needs.	6.2 Demonstrate design thinking as a human-centered process focusing on customers and their needs.
Practice interviewing potential customers.	6.6 Demonstrate how to interview potential customers in order to better understand their needs.
Improve listening and observation skills to identify the needs of potential customers and build strong customer insights.	6.5 Demonstrate how to observe and convert observation data to insights.
Cultivate pattern recognition skills to identify potential opportunities that meet the needs of multiple customer types.	5.4 Demonstrate how entrepreneurs find opportunities through active search and alertness. 5.3 Apply the two primary pathways to opportunity identification.
Distinguish between needs, customer insights, and solutions.	5.5 Connect idea generation to opportunity recognition.
Apply learning from unsuccessful attempts to future attempts and develop an appreciation for the necessity of iteration.	11.5 Describe the significance of "grit" and its role in building tolerance for failure.
Reflect on both successes and failures through built-in debrief questions.	11.4 Explain the different ways entrepreneurs can learn from failure.

ACKNOWLEDGMENTS

The authors would like to thank the following people for their support in writing this book.

Heidi Neck would like to thank Dale Meyer, Candida Brush, Patricia Greene, Len Schlesinger, and the late Jeffry Timmons for the inspiration behind the book—all mentors and friends. She would also like to thank her research assistant and MBA '20, Gaurav Khemka; Anton Yakushin, her partner in VentureBlocks; and Babson College for their support in writing this book. Most important, she thanks the Timmons family and other Babson donors to the Jeffry A. Timmons endowed chair. This book would not have been possible without the resources provided by the Timmons endowed chair that Heidi Neck has held since 2008.

Chris Neck thanks Dean Amy Hillman at Arizona State (W. P. Carey School of Business) and Kevin Corley (department head, Department of Management and Entrepreneurship, Arizona State University) for their encouragement of his teaching and research efforts. He thanks Duane Roen (dean of the College of Integrative Sciences and Arts at Arizona State University) for his steadfast support and encouragement to excel in the classroom. He also thanks Mike Goldsby, Jeff Houghton, Stuart Mease, and Jay Heiler for their steadfast support for the book and other projects over the years.

He'd also like to thank those behind-the-scenes individuals who assisted in the research, development, and/or editing of various parts of this book. Specifically, he thanks Alex Stanley, Kevin Murphy, Tristan Gaynor, George Heiler, Rose Mary Sanders, and Sarah Hohmann. Their contributions to this book made the book even better.

We'd also like to thank Shyam Devnani, Brad George, Patti Greene, Candy Brush, Dennis Ceru, Matt Allen, Andrew Corbett, and Erik Noyes for their contributions to the experiential exercises featured on the instructor website.

We are indebted to the entrepreneurship faculty at Babson College and the University of Arizona's McGuire Center for Entrepreneurship, who were some of the earliest supporters of this book. Thank you Carlos J. Alsua, Randy M. Burd, K. Krasnow Waterman, Mark Peterson, Tristan Reader, and Richard Eric Yngve for your insightful feedback on the test bank. Your comments have helped us develop a better product, and for that we are very grateful. Additionally, we thank the countless adopters of the first edition who gave us both accolades and critical feedback to make the second edition an even better product. Special gratitude is given to Dan Cohen at Wake Forest University, who allowed us to build his IDEATE methodology into the book.

We also want to thank Ronda Taylor Bullock, Carly Erickson, April Kensington, Alex Smereczniak, Mark Aznavourian, Dana and Dave Lafleur, and Kevin Keller, who graciously allowed us to feature them in the new videos accompanying the second edition.

Writing a textbook is a huge undertaking that extends far beyond the author team. We would like to thank the incredibly committed team at SAGE for their constant encouragement, endless patience, and thoughtful suggestions. Their passion and enthusiasm has helped to deliver a textbook of which we are extremely proud.

Maggie Stanley, our acquisitions editor, has championed this book every step of the way, and we are enormously grateful for her considerate input and constant support. Content development editor Lauren Gobell has been a welcome driving force, encouraging us to explore and consider new ideas. Our talented editor Elsa Peterson helped clarify and refine the material and has significantly contributed to the quality of this textbook. Diana Breti, our copy editor, has been meticulous in her work, for which we are very appreciative. Veronica Stapleton Hooper, our production editor, oversaw the entire production process and, thanks to her, the whole project was kept on track. We'd also like to thank marketing manager Sarah Panella and marketing associate Kerstin Christiansen for their efforts promoting the book, editorial assistant Janeane Calderon for handling a number of tasks during development and production, permissions assistant Tyler Huxtable for his work helping secure permission to use a number of items included in the text, and senior graphic designer Scott Van Atta for creating a stunning interior and cover design.

For their thoughtful and helpful comments and ideas on our manuscript, we sincerely thank the following reviewers. Our book is a better product because of their insightful suggestions.

Jay A. Azriel, York College of Pennsylvania

Henry Balfanz, Alma College

Melissa S. Baucus, Texas State University

Sara Bliss Kiser, Alabama State University

Robert H. Epstein, University of Central Oklahoma

Mary Goebel-Lundholm, Peru State College

Jim Jindrick, University of Arizona Research, Discovery, and Innovation

Lori K. Long, Baldwin Wallace University

Vincent E. Mangum, Atlanta Metropolitan State College

Elizabeth A. McCrea, Stillman School of Business, Seton Hall University

Wallace W. Meyer Jr., University of Kansas

Mark B. Mondry, Virginia Polytechnic Institute and State University

Vitaliy Skorodziyevskiy, Texas Tech University

Jeffrey D. Stone, California State University Channel Islands

Sam Vegter, Western Piedmont Community College

Bill Wales, University at Albany, SUNY

We are also enormously grateful for the reviewers who provided valuable feedback on the first edition:

Anuradha Basu, San Jose State University

Susan Berston, City College of San Francisco

Constant D. Beugre, Delaware State University

Martin Bressler, Southeastern Oklahoma State University

Candida Brush, Babson College

Jacqueline H. Bull, Immaculata University

Kimble Byrd, Rowan University

C. S. Richard Chan, Stony Brook University

Shih Yung Chou, The University of Texas of the Permian Basin

Diane Denslow, University of North Florida

Art Diaz, University of Texas at El Paso

Robert S. D'Intino, Rowan University

Steven Edelson, Walsh University

Kevin Ernst, Ohio Northern University

Frances Fabian, University of Memphis

David J. Gavin, Marist College

Ranjan George, Simpson University

Peter Gianiodis, Duquesne University

Amy R. Gresock, University of Michigan—Flint

Maurice Haff, University of Central Oklahoma

Sheila Hanson, University of North Dakota

Lerong He, State University of New York at Brockport

Kirk Heriot, Columbus State University

Laurent Josien, SUNY Plattsburgh

Ryan Kauth, University of Wisconsin—Green Bay

Ram Kesavan, University of Detroit Mercy

Sara Kiser, Alabama State University

Rebecca Knapp, Saddleback College

Jon Krabill, Columbus State Community College

Nancy Kucinski, Hardin-Simmons University

Thomas Lachowicz, Radford University

Denise Lefort, Arapahoe Community College

Ada Leung, Penn State Berks

Martin Luytjes, Jacksonville University

Michele K. Masterfano, Drexel University

Sue McNamara, SUNY Fredonia

Stuart Mease, Virginia Tech

Wallace W. Meyer Jr., University of Kansas

John Edward Michaels, California University of Pennsylvania

Erik Monsen, University of Vermont

Charlie Nagelschmidt, Champlain College

David M. Nemi, Niagara County Community College

Laurel F. Ofstein, Western Michigan University

Bill Petty, Baylor University

Jonathan Phillips, Belmont University

Marlene Reed, Baylor University

Maija Renko, University of Illinois at Chicago

Rodney Ridley, Wilkes University

Timothy Ritter, Western Kentucky University

Robert W. Robertson, Independence University

Linda Wabschall Ross, Rowan University

Jacqueline Schmidt, John Carroll University

Darrell Scott, Idaho State University

Sally Sledge, Norfolk State University

Frank R. Spitznogle, Northern Arizona University

Joseph R. Stasio Jr., Merrimack College

Sunny Li Sun, University of Missouri—Kansas City

Lauren Talia, Independence University

Keith Ward, St. Edward's University

Paula A. White, Independence University

Lei Xu, Texas Tech University

Bill Zannini, Northern Essex Community College

Thanks are also due to the individuals who developed the digital resources that accompany this book: Steven Edelson, Jordan Jensen, Eva Mika, Colette Rominger, Sally Sledge, Tristan Gaynor, Paula A. White, and Cecilia Williams.

ABOUT THE AUTHORS

HEIDI M. NECK, PHD

Heidi M. Neck, PhD, is a Babson College professor and the Jeffry A. Timmons Professor of Entrepreneurial Studies. She has taught entrepreneurship at the undergraduate, MBA, and executive levels. She is the academic director of the Babson Academy, a dedicated unit within Babson that inspires change in the way universities, specifically their faculty and students, teach and learn entrepreneurship. The Babson Academy builds on Neck's work starting the Babson Collaborative, a global institutional membership organization for colleges and universities seeking to increase their capability and capacity in entrepreneurship education, and her leadership of Babson's Symposia for Entrepreneurship Educators (SEE), programs designed to inspire faculty from around the world to teach more experientially and entrepreneurially as well as build world-class entrepreneurship programs. Neck has directly trained more than 3,000 faculty around the world in the art and craft of teaching entrepreneurship. An award-winning teacher, Neck has been recognized for teaching excellence at Babson for undergraduate, graduate, and executive education. She has also been recognized by international organizations, the Academy of Management and USASBE, for excellence in pedagogy and course design. Most recently, in 2016 The Schulze Foundation awarded her Entrepreneurship Educator of the Year for pushing the frontier of entrepreneurship education in higher education.

Her research interests include entrepreneurship education, entrepreneurship inside organizations, and creative thinking. Neck is the lead author of *Teaching Entrepreneurship: A Practice-Based Approach* (Elgar), a book written to help educators teach entrepreneurship in more experiential and engaging ways. Additionally, she has published 40+ book chapters, research monographs, and refereed articles in such journals as *Journal of Small Business Management*, *Entrepreneurship Theory & Practice*, and *International Journal of Entrepreneurship Education*. She is on the editorial board of the *Academy of Management Learning & Education* journal.

Neck speaks and teaches internationally on cultivating the entrepreneurial mindset and espousing the positive force of entrepreneurship as a societal change agent. She consults and trains organizations of all sizes on building entrepreneurial capacity. She is the cofounder of VentureBlocks, an entrepreneurship education technology company, and was co-owner of FlowDog, a canine aquatic fitness and rehabilitation center that was located just outside of Boston. Heidi earned her PhD in strategic management and entrepreneurship from the University of Colorado at Boulder. She holds a BS in marketing from Louisiana State University and an MBA from the University of Colorado, Boulder.

CHRISTOPHER P. NECK, PHD

Dr. Christopher P. Neck is currently an associate professor of management at Arizona State University, where he held the title "University Master Teacher." From 1994 to 2009, he was part of the Pamplin College of Business faculty at Virginia Tech. He received his PhD in management from Arizona State University and his MBA from Louisiana State University. Neck is author of the books *Self-Leadership: The Definitive*

Guide to Personal Excellence (2016, SAGE); *Fit to Lead: The Proven 8-Week Solution for Shaping up Your Body, Your Mind, and Your Career* (2004, St. Martin's Press; 2012, Carpenter's Sons); *Mastering Self-Leadership: Empowering Yourself for Personal Excellence* (6th ed., 2013, Pearson); *The Wisdom of Solomon at Work* (2001, Berrett-Koehler); *For Team Members Only: Making Your Workplace Team Productive and Hassle-Free* (1997, Amacom Books); and *Medicine for the Mind: Healing Words to Help You Soar* (4th ed., 2012, Wiley). Neck is also the coauthor of the principles of management textbook *Management: A Balanced Approach to the 21st Century* (2013, 2017, Wiley); the introductory entrepreneurship textbook *Entrepreneurship* (2017, SAGE); and the introductory organizational behavior textbook *Organizational Behavior* (2016, SAGE).

Dr. Neck's research specialties include employee/executive fitness, self-leadership, leadership, group decision-making processes, and self-managing teams. He has more than 100 publications in the form of books, chapters, and articles in various journals. The outlets in which Neck's work has appeared include *Organizational Behavior and Human Decision Processes, The Journal of Organizational Behavior, The Academy of Management Executive, Journal of Applied Behavioral Science, The Journal of Managerial Psychology, Executive Excellence, Human Relations, Human Resource Development Quarterly, Journal of Leadership Studies, Educational Leadership,* and *The Commercial Law Journal.*

Due to Neck's expertise in management, he has been cited in numerous national publications, including *The Washington Post, The Wall Street Journal, The Los Angeles Times, The Houston Chronicle,* and the *Chicago Tribune.* Additionally, each semester Neck teaches an introductory management course to a single class of anywhere from 500 to 1,000 students.

Dr. Neck was the recipient of the 2007 *Business Week* Favorite Professor Award. He is featured on www.businessweek.com as one of the approximately 20 professors from across the world receiving this award.

Neck currently teaches a mega section of Management Principles to approximately 500 students at Arizona State University. Neck received the Order of Omega Outstanding Teaching Award for 2012. This award is granted to one professor at Arizona State by the Alpha Lambda chapter of this leadership fraternity. His class sizes at Virginia Tech filled rooms up to 2,500 students. He received numerous teaching awards during his tenure at Virginia Tech, including the 2002 Wine Award for Teaching Excellence. Also, Neck was the 10-time winner (1996, 1998, 2000, 2002, 2004, 2005, 2006, 2007, 2008, and 2009) of the Students' Choice Teacher of The Year Award (voted by the students for the best teacher of the year within the entire university). Also, the organizations that have participated in Neck's management development training include GE/Toshiba, Busch Gardens, Clark Construction, the United States Army, Crestar, American Family Insurance, Sales and Marketing Executives International, American Airlines, American Electric Power, W. L. Gore & Associates, Dillard's Department Stores, and Prudential Life Insurance. Neck is also an avid runner. He has completed 12 marathons, including the Boston Marathon, the New York City Marathon, and the San Diego Marathon. In fact, his personal record for a single long-distance run is 40 miles.

EMMA L. MURRAY, BA, HDIP, DBS IT

Emma L. Murray completed a bachelor of arts degree in English and Spanish at University College Dublin in County Dublin, Ireland. This was followed by a higher diploma (Hdip) in business studies and information technology at the Michael Smurfit Graduate School of Business in County Dublin, Ireland. Following her studies, Emma spent nearly a decade in investment banking before becoming a full-time writer and author.

As a writer, Emma has worked on numerous texts, including business and economics, self-help, and psychology. Within the field of higher education, Emma worked with Dr. Christopher P. Neck and Dr. Jeffery D. Houghton on *Management* (2013, Wiley) and is the coauthor of the principles of management textbook *Management: A Balanced Approach to the 21st Century* (2013, 2017, Wiley) and the coauthor of *Organizational Behavior* (2017, SAGE).

She is the author of *The Unauthorized Guide to Doing Business the Alan Sugar Way* (2010, Wiley-Capstone) and the lead author of *How to Succeed as a Freelancer in Publishing* (2010, How To Books). She lives in London.

An Open Letter to All Students

Dear Student,

We suspect you are reading this now because you are on a journey—a journey in search of meaning, a desire to make a significant impact on the world, an itch to bring something new to market, a yearning not simply to find yourself but also to create yourself. Many believe that entrepreneurship can be a path to all of this. For some it can be, but it takes a lot of dedication and a lot of practice. That's what this book is all about: practicing entrepreneurship.

You are going to hear about the concept of practice throughout this entire book, and we want to take a minute to put this word in perspective. Think about a sport you're pretty good at or a musical instrument you have mastered. Even if you love the idea of playing the piano, it's very difficult to sit at the piano and start playing a piece that others really want to hear. You may be a very good soccer player today, but when you started playing, we're sure the coach didn't put you in the game immediately and say, "Go play, kid!" Similarly, you could destroy a golf course if you didn't know the basics of hitting that little white ball. Before we play the music piece in front of others, or play in our first competitive soccer game, and before we tee up on the first hole of a prestigious golf course, we have to practice.

Rarely do we perform the entire piece of music, or play the actual game, or get on the actual golf course before practicing parts of the experience. You practice scales on the piano, then you learn how to read the music, then you play simple pieces, then more complex compositions, and so on. In soccer, you work on fundamentals of kicking the ball, foot coordination, passing, heading, and tackling. A golfing instructor will make you swing different clubs for hours before you are allowed to try to hit the golf ball. Yes, just swinging. No hitting! You may also recognize in practicing these different experiences that you have to take action. We don't just read about playing the piano or soccer or golf. We have to do in order to learn. We have to take action in order to practice, and it is through practice that we can progress.

By practicing entrepreneurship, you will hone your skills and become proficient so that you can take action to reach your goals. Whether you have a concrete plan to bring something new to market or just a passion for finding ways to make the world a better place, we hope this book will help you on your journey.

Enjoy the journey and don't forget to practice!

The Authors

PART I

Entrepreneurship Is a Life Skill

CHAPTER 1:
Practicing Entrepreneurship

CHAPTER 2:
Activating an Entrepreneurial Mindset

1 Practicing Entrepreneurship

"The best way to predict the future is to create it."

—Peter Drucker

Chapter Outline

Learning Objectives

1.1   Explain the importance of action and practice in entrepreneurship.

1.2   List the seven lesser-known truths about entrepreneurship.

1.3   Compare and contrast the different forms of entrepreneurship in practice today.

1.4   Distinguish between entrepreneurship as a method and as a process.

1.5   Compare and contrast the prediction and creation approaches to entrepreneurship.

1.6   Illustrate the key components of the Entrepreneurship Method.

1.7   Assess the role of deliberate practice in achieving mastery.

1.8   Propose different ways in which this book can help you practice entrepreneurship.

There's no doubt that we are living in unpredictable times: High schools and colleges are struggling to keep up with the ever-changing job market; underemployment rates are skyrocketing, especially among younger people; those halfway through their careers are asking what else is possible; mature workers are wondering what comes next; and seniors are postponing their retirement to stay relevant. The traditional concept of staying in one job for your entire working life is a thing of the past, especially when people are being asked to reinvent themselves every 5 years. In a world full of uncertainty, rapid change is the only constant.

Although the future of the traditional workplace may be unclear, the climate is ripe for entrepreneurship. Traditionally, entrepreneurship has been associated with launching new businesses. However, many individuals and institutions are beginning to think of entrepreneurship as a vital life skill that extends far beyond the ability to launch a venture, a life skill that prepares individuals to deal with an ambiguous and uncertain future. In other words, you don't need to build your own company to think and act like an entrepreneur! Entrepreneurship embodies methods for thinking, acting, identifying opportunities, and approaching problems that enable people to manage change, adjust to new conditions, and take control of actualizing personal goals, aspirations, and even dreams. It's also a vehicle for developing a set of skills—financial, social, communication, marketing, problem solving, and creative thinking, to name a few—that are applicable across many fields. Taken together, these are mindsets and skillsets that not only enable you to start a venture, but will also distinguish you in a variety of traditional and nontraditional life paths. To be entrepreneurial is to be empowered to create and act on opportunities of all kinds for yourself.

1.1 ENTREPRENEURSHIP REQUIRES ACTION AND PRACTICE

>> **LO 1.1 Explain the importance of action and practice in entrepreneurship.**

Entrepreneurship is a way of thinking, acting, and being that combines the ability to find or create new opportunities with the courage to act on them.

The pursuits of entrepreneurs have touched every corner of our lives, affecting every aspect of the way we live—from electricity, to music, to transport, to agriculture, to manufacturing, to technology, and many more. Although it can be difficult to see

Entrepreneurship: a way of thinking, acting, and being that combines the ability to find or create new opportunities with the courage to act on them.

Master the content at **edge.sagepub.com/ neckentrepreneurship2e**

Sam Hood via Wikimedia Commons.

The first automatic dishwasher, invented by Josephine Cochrane

entrepreneurial possibilities in the midst of unemployment, economic recession, war, and natural disasters, it is this sort of turbulence that often pushes us into creating new opportunities for economic progress. History shows us that in spite of the obstacles in their paths, all kinds of entrepreneurs have consistently taken action to change the world. For instance, Benjamin Franklin successfully invented the lightning rod (1749); George Crum created the potato chip (1853); and Josephine Cochrane invented the first automatic dishwasher (1893). This text is about creating the next page of history. It's time to bring the voices of today's entrepreneurs into the conversation. It's also time to bring *your* voice into the conversation. What kind of entrepreneur do you want to be?

1.2 ENTREPRENEURSHIP MAY BE DIFFERENT FROM WHAT YOU THINK

>> LO 1.2   List the seven lesser-known truths about entrepreneurship.

Our belief is that by taking action and putting ideas into practice, everyone "has what it takes" to be an entrepreneur. However, this is not necessarily the same message that is delivered by popular media. Let's examine some popular images of entrepreneurs. What is the truth behind these images?

Media Images of Entrepreneurs

The media often exaggerate the meteoric rise of "overnight global sensations" such as Bill Gates (Microsoft), Steve Jobs (Apple), Mark Zuckerberg (Facebook), Elon Musk (Tesla), Jack Ma (Alibaba), Oprah Winfrey (Harpo Group), and Travis Kalanick (Uber). The likes of Bill Gates and his peers are certainly inspirational, but we would argue that few can personally identify with the stories surrounding them, and they do little to represent the reality of entrepreneurship.

The truth is there is no such thing as an overnight success.

Debunking the Myths of Entrepreneurship

Rather than focusing on the myth of the overnight success story, let's take a look at some truths, illustrated in Table 1.1. Separating truth from fiction can be difficult, especially when some of these truths collide with the stories we read about in the media. Let's explore these truths in more detail to further understand how entrepreneurship can be a path for many.

TABLE 1.1

The Truths About Entrepreneurship

Truth 1	Entrepreneurship is not reserved for startups.
Truth 2	Entrepreneurs do not have a special set of personality traits.
Truth 3	Entrepreneurship can be taught (it's a method that requires practice).
Truth 4	Entrepreneurs are not extreme risk takers.
Truth 5	Entrepreneurs collaborate more than they compete.
Truth 6	Entrepreneurs act more than they plan.
Truth 7	Entrepreneurship is a life skill.

Juan Giraldo, Waku

Photo Courtesy of Juan Giraldo

Juan Giraldo, founder of Waku

Entrepreneurs are seeing many opportunities in the market for health drinks: no sugar, low sugar, vitamin-infused waters, carbonated, not carbonated, healthy teas, fermented teas, drinkable yogurt, cold brew coffees, smoothies—it seems that we are all craving tasty yet healthy replacements for soda. Dozens of new beverages have emerged in the marketplace to satisfy the latest health trends, serving consumers' needs to feed mind, body, and spirit. We are in the midst of a generational shift that has created an industry with exponential growth. Take kombucha tea, for instance: This fermented tea, which is claimed to provide significant health benefits, is expected to be a $5 billion industry by 2025.

Juan Giraldo, an Ecuador-born entrepreneur, has been capitalizing on these trends with his company, Waku. Waku produces and sells wellness teas made with 20 super herbs from the Andes Mountains. They compete directly with kombucha-style drinks, but, Juan claims, "Waku tastes much better." Traditional kombucha is a lightly fermented beverage that boasts great health benefits derived from various probiotics. "Waku's wellness teas are also delicious and nutritious, but the health benefits stem from the medicinal benefits of the herbs used in the ingredients. The drinks are not fermented and are excellent for one's digestive system."

Juan has been an entrepreneur since he was 19 years old. His first company was an advertising firm that he sold to his business partner, and his next venture was an online fashion outlet, which went bankrupt within 18 months. After that, he became CEO of a small IT consulting firm before founding Waku. The idea for Waku arose when Juan and his friend, Nicolas Estrella, exchanged fond memories of the "wellness tea" they used to drink in their homeland of Ecuador. After both moved to Boston, they decided to produce their own version of this beverage and sell it in the Boston area. The initial production of the tea helped support the businesses of approximately six independent Andes farmers who grew the medicinal herbs and flowers used to produce the product. What exactly is Waku? It is a filtered water brew blend of 20 herbs and flowers. The name comes from the Quechua word *wanku* (together), which represents the combining of the ingredients as well as the team effort that goes into the production of the product.

Juan's first step was to travel to Ecuador to source the right ingredients in order to test his concept. Back in the United States, the Waku team began developing prototypes. At the same time he was developing Waku, Juan was also earning his MBA at Babson College. Thinking that millennials were his target market, he felt surrounded by his potential customers and used them as resources. Juan would buy rival tea products and conduct countless taste tests to compare his Waku recipes to the competition. By developing early prototypes and conducting taste tests, he was able to interact with potential customers and get valuable feedback. Juan quickly learned that his target customers were not millennials who were well educated and well traveled, but women between the ages of 40 and 60 who wanted to live a healthier lifestyle.

The early growth of Waku created supply challenges. As the company grew from shipping one pallet of ingredients from Ecuador to ordering one full container (11 pallets) a month, Waku altered its strategy for paying its suppliers. Originally, Juan was expected to pay for all ingredients at the time of purchase, but that required a lot of cash up front. At the same time, Waku needed the ingredients from its suppliers to effectively meet forecasted demand. To find a solution, Juan traveled to Ecuador to work out a deal with the suppliers. After building trust with his suppliers, he proposed that they give Waku 180 days of credit to pay for ingredients. This would allow Waku the time to get the ingredients, produce the teas, sell the teas, and then pay its suppliers. As Juan explains, "At first the suppliers were hesitant, but after I showed them Waku's plans for payment and how important the suppliers were to the brand, they agreed."

With $200,000 in annual revenues, Juan believes the product has the potential to be a legitimate contender for market share as the business grows. Although Juan is certainly concerned with profits, that is not his only motive. His business offers beverages that he grew up with, and

(Continued)

(Continued)

he truly believes in the brand because of how much it hits home. "I want to provide opportunities for the people back in Ecuador. Producing top-quality ingredients is what we are known for in the rural parts of my country." Today, Waku has four full-time employees, an intern, and a strategic consultant. It also provides steady, reliable business to many farmers throughout rural Ecuador. As Waku continues to grow, many people in Ecuador will reap the benefits through an influx of capital and job creation.

Although he has been an entrepreneur for a long time, Juan admits that he didn't know much about the healthy beverage sector and needed a lot of advice. "I sent out emails to the top competitors in the industry, simply asking for advice. And many were more than willing to offer it!" Juan recalled. His advice to other entrepreneurs? "Don't be shy to ask for help. Mentors can have huge impacts on your performance. Reach out to the superstars in your industry.

You will be amazed how many people will want to help a young entrepreneur who has the burning desire to succeed."

Critical Thinking Questions

1. What differentiates Waku from other health beverages on the market today?

2. Why was Juan able to approach his suppliers with the request he made regarding payment?

3. Does Waku have a responsibility to the region of the world in which it sources its ingredients and finds its inspiration? ●

Sources:

Juan Giraldo (interview with author, October 22, 2018).
https://www.grandviewresearch.com/press-release/global-kombucha-market
https://livewaku.com/
https://www.bostonglobe.com/lifestyle/food-dining/2018/10/15/waku-wellness-tea-with-roots-ecuador/23cPv5lwSkwLrkdhcNSrnN/story.html

Truth 1: Entrepreneurship Is Not Reserved for Startups

The term *startup* came into vogue during the 1990s dot-com bubble, when a plethora of web-based companies were born. The term has various meanings, but we subscribe to Steve Blank's definition of **startup**: a temporary organization in search of a scalable business model.[1] In the traditional view of startups, anyone who starts a business is called an entrepreneur. The entrepreneur creates a business based on research to assess the validity of an idea or business model. The business may be partially funded by seed money from family members or investors, but usually the majority is funded by the entrepreneurs themselves.

If the business is successful, the startup does not remain a startup. It can develop into its own formal organization, be merged with another organization, or be bought by another company. This traditional view of the startup, however, is not the only path for entrepreneurs. The truth is that entrepreneurs are everywhere, from corporations to franchises, to for-profit and nonprofit organizations, to family enterprises. We will explore these different types of entrepreneurs in more detail later in the chapter.

> **Startup:** a temporary organization in search of a scalable business model.

Truth 2: Entrepreneurs Do Not Have a Special Set of Personality Traits

There is no evidence to suggest that entrepreneurs have a special set of personality characteristics that distinguishes them from the rest of us.

Early research identified four main traits that are ascribed to entrepreneurs: a need for achievement, an innate sense of having the ability to influence events, a tendency to take risks, and a tolerance for ambiguity. Yet there is no scientific evidence to confirm whether these traits are a result of nature or nurture or any proven patterns in the behavior of entrepreneurs versus nonentrepreneurs.[2] Academics researching traits of entrepreneurs seem to have a prevailing fascination with defining "who" the entrepreneur is, rather than what he or she does.

However, over the last couple of decades, researchers have moved away from the traits perspective in favor of examining how entrepreneurs think and act and have discovered that there are patterns in how entrepreneurs think. This means we can change how we think and that all of us have the ability to act and think entrepreneurially with practice.

In particular, the work of researcher Saras Sarasvathy has added a new understanding of the entrepreneurial mindset. Through a study involving serial entrepreneurs—entrepreneurs who start several businesses, either simultaneously or consecutively—Sarasvathy discovered patterns of thinking and developed a theory she calls **effectuation**, which is the idea that the future is unpredictable yet controllable. Entrepreneurs create and obtain control by taking actions to learn, collecting information, and reducing risk and uncertainty, and they are able to take action with resources that are available at a particular point in time.[3] In other words, it's about starting small with what you have, rather than what you think

> **Effectuation theory:** an entrepreneurial approach to taking quick action using resources you have available to get early traction on new ideas.

you need. As the entrepreneur starts, very small actions lead to other actions and new resources. See Research at Work for more on effectuation theory.

Sarasvathy believes that effectual entrepreneurs focus on creating a future rather than predicting it. This means they create new opportunities, make markets rather than find them, accept and learn from failure, and build relationships with a variety of stakeholders. Effectual entrepreneurs use their own initiative and resources to fulfill their vision of the future.

We strongly believe that the mindset is the precursor to action. To us, it makes sense that if entrepreneurs are in the right frame of mind, there is greater confidence, intentionality, and vision to bring ideas from the whiteboard to the real world. We are not born with an entrepreneurial mindset; we have to work to develop it. As a result, and because it's so important, we devote a whole chapter to it (see Chapter 2).

Truth 3: Entrepreneurship Can Be Taught (It's a Method That Requires Practice)

Because so many people tend to believe that "entrepreneurs are born and not made," those same people question whether entrepreneurship can be taught. If it were true that entrepreneurs have a certain set of innate personality traits, then entrepreneurship could not be taught. But, remember, there is no proven set of traits. What has been proven, instead, is that entrepreneurs exhibit common patterns in how they think, and our thinking can be changed and altered.[4] As a result, entrepreneurship can be taught. Furthermore, it's being taught everywhere around the globe. It would be difficult to find a college or university not offering at least one entrepreneurship course today (see Figure 1.1). Many of these courses teach entrepreneurship as a linear process, which involves identifying an opportunity, understanding resource requirements, acquiring resources, planning, implementing, and harvesting (exiting a business).[5] But the word *process* assumes known inputs and known outputs—a process is quite predictable.

Entrepreneurship is not predictable and, therefore, cannot adequately be taught as a process. Instead, approaching entrepreneurship as a method, as advocated in this text, results in a body of skills that—when developed through practice over time—constitute a toolkit for entrepreneurial action.[6] The entrepreneurial method requires consistent practice so that knowledge and expertise can be continuously developed and applied to future endeavors. More on this a bit later in the chapter!

Truth 4: Entrepreneurs Are Not Extreme Risk Takers

Contrary to the stereotype that entrepreneurs like to gamble when the stakes are high, there is no evidence to suggest that entrepreneurs take more risks than anyone else. In fact, entrepreneurs with gambling tendencies are usually not successful, simply because they are leaving too much to chance.[7] Risk is very personal and relative. Things always seem more risky from the outside looking in because we really don't know what calculations were made to take the first step, then the second, then the third, and so on. In fact, most entrepreneurs are very calculated risk takers and gauge what they are willing to lose with every step taken. They practice a cycle of act-learn-build that encourages taking small actions in order to learn and build that learning into the next action (see Figure 1.2).[8] Entrepreneurship should never be a zero-sum game; it's never an all-or-nothing decision. It's not about ascending the summit of Mount Everest without ropes or oxygen. It just looks that way from the outside!

Steve Jobs and Bill Gates collaborated on the Apple Mac despite being fierce competitors.

Truth 5: Entrepreneurs Collaborate More Than They Compete

Community and networking play important roles in entrepreneurship. No entrepreneur is an island and building strong connections with others is key to business success. Networking is so important to entrepreneurship that we have devoted an entire chapter

FIGURE 1.1

Millennials—A Highly Educated and Entrepreneurial Generation

Change in the Percentage of 25- to 29-Year-Olds With Selected Levels of Educational Attainment, 2007–2013

Entrepreneurship Courses Offered

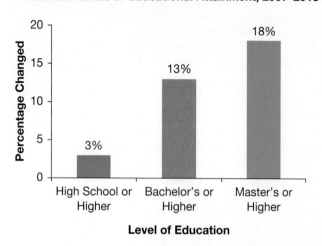

Business School Alumni Who Began Businesses After Graduation

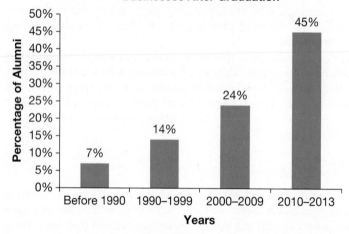

FIGURE 1.2

Act-Learn-Build

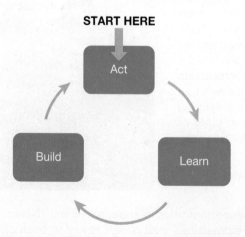

to it (see Chapter 8). Entrepreneurs draw on shared experiences and desire to learn from others facing similar challenges. It can be hard to know what entrepreneurship is all about until you are actually in the throes of it, so it becomes very important to have a support group of like-minded entrepreneurs willing to help one another out with a "pay it forward" attitude—collaborating for the greater good.[9]

Not only do successful entrepreneurs collaborate with other entrepreneurs, they also collaborate with their target customers to test new ideas, potential investors to build trust, and family and friends for support. In fact, recent studies have shown that collaboration and information sharing are more important in entrepreneurship than skills like determination or opportunity recognition.[10]

Truth 6: Entrepreneurs Act More Than They Plan

Does every entrepreneur need a business plan to succeed? Not necessarily. Research revealed that fewer than half of Inc. 500 founders wrote formal business plans prior to launching their companies, and nearly 30% had only basic plans.[11] So, how did they do it? They acted: They went out and talked to other people, connected with their customers, generated buzz about their product or service, and built a strong network. With every action, they collected real data that informed the next step. In short, they each practiced being an entrepreneur.

Today's investors want to know what the entrepreneur has done, milestones met, action completed, customers sold, and overall traction. Planning and research is important but the creation of a formal business plan is not. Spending too much time writing a business plan means you are not spending enough time taking action on your idea in order to really learn whether it can work.

Truth 7: Entrepreneurship Is a Life Skill

As we discussed in the introduction to this chapter, traditionally, entrepreneurship has been associated mostly with launching new businesses. However, these days, the meaning of entrepreneurship has transcended into something more than just the ability to begin a new business. Many individuals and institutions perceive entrepreneurship as

---

MINDSHIFT

Tell Me Your Story

Every entrepreneur has a story. What beliefs and expectations do you have about entrepreneurs' stories? To what extent do you think they conform to media images of entrepreneurs? In what ways might you expect them to be different? Here is an activity to help you examine your beliefs and expectations.

Find and introduce yourself to an entrepreneur—any type of entrepreneur is fine. Ask for 20 minutes of his or her time, and simply start with the opening question: *Tell me the story of how you became an entrepreneur.*

As the story unfolds, you may want to ask other questions, such as

What worried you the most as you started the venture?

What excited you most about starting the venture?

What resources did you use to start? Where did they come from?

What moments do you remember most?

Who helped you most along the way?

How do you describe yourself to others?

What advice do you have for me as a student of entrepreneurship?

After having this 20-minute conversation, reflect on the beliefs and expectations you started with and answer the Critical Thinking Questions.

Critical Thinking Questions

1. In what ways did your chosen entrepreneur confirm your beliefs and expectations?

2. In what ways did the story motivate you (or not)?

3. What did you learn that was most unexpected? ●

a life skill that helps people to deal with an uncertain future by providing them with the methods to think, act, identify opportunities, approach problems in a specific way, adapt to new conditions, and take control of personal goals and ambitions. It also provides people with a set of skills that can be applied to many other fields. Being entrepreneurial empowers us to create opportunities and reach our goals.[12] Remember the definition of entrepreneurship: a way of thinking, acting, and being that combines the ability to find or create new opportunities with the courage to act on them.

Now that we have separated the truths from the myths, it is time to create a new narrative. Our economic future depends on entrepreneurs, and the traditional, narrow definition has stifled what it really means to be an entrepreneur. But to create a new story, we need to know more about the different types of entrepreneurs in the workplace today.

1.3 TYPES OF ENTREPRENEURSHIP

>> **LO 1.3** **Compare and contrast the different forms of entrepreneurship in practice today.**

Now that we have explored the truths about entrepreneurship, let's take a look at the types of entrepreneurship that are most commonly in practice today.

Corporate Entrepreneurship

Corporate entrepreneurship (or intrapreneurship): a process of creating new products, ventures, processes, or renewal within large organizations.

Corporate entrepreneurship (also known as **intrapreneurship**) is a process of creating new products, ventures, processes, or renewal within large corporations.[13] It is typically carried out by employees working in units separate from the mainstream areas of the corporation who create and test innovations that are then assimilated into the broader corporation.

Corporate entrepreneurs tend to explore new possibilities and seek ways in which the organization's current structure and process can enable innovation. Similar to external entrepreneurs, corporate entrepreneurs identify opportunities, build teams, and create something of value in order to enhance competitive position and organizational profitability. Deloitte-owned design consultancy Market Gravity, based in the United Kingdom, celebrates the achievement of corporate entrepreneurs by holding an annual Corporate Entrepreneur Awards (CAE) ceremony.[14] Categories include awards for those who dare to "throw out the rule book" to achieve their goals; those with a proven concept who have succeeded in making their goals a reality; and those who have turned an idea into something groundbreaking. Past winners for corporate entrepreneurship have included employees from LEGO, Reebok, and Xerox.

Corporations like Google, Apple, Virgin, and Zappos are also known for encouraging an entrepreneurial spirit. However, not all corporations are as enthusiastic about employees acting entrepreneurially inside the company. Some companies fear that if employees are encouraged to be more entrepreneurial, they will leave the company and start their own business. This is really an outdated view, though. Most corporations realize that they no longer have long-term employees.

LEGO is an example of a company that embraces entrepreneurship.

© Helen H. Richardson/Contributor/Getty Images

Entrepreneurship Inside

Entrepreneurs inside: entrepreneurs who think and act entrepreneurially within organizations.

Entrepreneurs inside are employees who think and act entrepreneurially within different types of organizations. Although this sounds similar to corporate entrepreneurs (employees who work for large corporations), there is an important difference: Entrepreneurs inside can exist and function in any type of organization, big or small, including government agencies, nonprofits, religious entities, self-organizing entities, and cooperatives.[15] These types of entrepreneurs often need inside support from senior managers or other team members for their initiatives, which can be difficult if those people tend to resist new ideas or are keen to simply "stick to the company brief" rather than push boundaries. Building a tribe of willing supporters is essential for getting buy-in to their ideas and proving there is a market for them.

The headquarters of MITRE in McLean, Virginia

What inside entrepreneurs have in common with other entrepreneurs is the desire to create something of value, be it a groundbreaking initiative or a new department, product, service, or process. When this happens, there is very little separation between who they are and what they do. Peter Modigliani is a defense department acquisition analyst at Massachusetts-based MITRE, a not-for-profit organization that provides guidance to the federal government. He breaks the traditional boundaries set by the chain of command by liaising with people inside and outside the organization to generate different perspectives. He says, "The more you can regularly connect with folks from other divisions, skillsets, and customers, the increased chances someone can offer you a fresh perspective or connection."[16]

Franchising

A **franchise** is a type of license purchased by an individual (franchisee) from an existing business (franchisor) that allows the franchisee to trade under the name of that business.[17] In this type of entrepreneurship, both the franchisor (the founder of the original business) and the franchisee are entrepreneurs. Franchising can be a beneficial way for entrepreneurs to get a head start in launching their own businesses, as they do not have to spend the same amount of time on marketing, building the brand, developing processes, and sourcing product.

A 7-Eleven franchise location

Franchise: a type of license purchased by a franchisee from an existing business called a franchisor to allow them to trade under the name of that business.

Royalties: a share of the income of a business paid by a franchisee to the franchisor.

A franchise is often referred to as a "turnkey operation." In other words, the franchisee turns the key to open the door and is ready for business. A franchisee not only pays the franchisor a lump sum to buy the franchise but also has to pay **royalties**, which are calculated as a percentage of monthly sales revenue. According to results of *Entrepreneur* magazine's annual Franchise 500, announced in 2017, 7-Eleven, McDonald's, Dunkin' Donuts, and the UPS Store are among the most popular franchises in the United States.[18] Today there are more than 740,000 franchise establishments in the United States. Table 1.2 describes the pros and cons of owning a franchise.[19]

Buying a Small Business

Buying a small business is another way to enter the world of entrepreneurship. In this arrangement, the entrepreneur is buying out the existing owner(s) and taking over operations. For some entrepreneurs this is a less risky approach than starting from scratch.[20] Chris Cranston was the owner of FlowDog, a canine aquatic and rehabilitation center outside of Boston. In 2009 she bought the business, which was called Aquadog at the time, from the previous owner. Cranston changed the name but subsumed a loyal customer base, pool equipment, location, some employees, and a favorable lease. In Cranston's words, "Starting from a blank slate was too overwhelming for me. I needed something that I could build upon. That I could handle!"[21] And handle it she has. FlowDog grew an average of 20% each year between 2009 and 2018, when Chris sold it to a large animal hospital in Boston.

TABLE 1.2

Pros and Cons of Owning a Franchise

PROS	CONS
Ready-made business systems to help the franchise to become operational right away.	Franchise fee to be paid upfront.
Formal training program (online modules, formal training class) after franchise agreement signed.	Royalties (percentage of sales) to be paid to franchisor every month.
Technology designed to help manage customers and administrative processes.	Strict franchisors' rules with no wiggle room.
Marketing/advertising already in place to help launch your franchise.	Requirement to pay a percentage of gross sales into the franchisor's marketing fund.
Excellent support systems (in-house personnel, field reps, etc.).	Most products and supplies need to be purchased from the franchisor.
Real estate resources to help source best location for franchise.	Sale of franchise requires approval from the franchisor.
A whole franchisee network to reach out to for help and advice.	Potential competition from other franchisees in the network.

Source: Based on material in Libava. J. (2015, February 16). The pros and cons of owning a franchise. *Entrepreneur.* Retrieved from https://www.entrepreneur.com/article/242848. Originally appeared at http://www.thefranchiseking .com/franchise-ownership-pros-cons

Social Entrepreneurship

Since the beginning of the 21st century, social entrepreneurship has become a global movement, with thousands of initiatives launched every year to improve social problems such as water shortages, lack of education, poverty, and global warming.

There has been considerable debate as to how to define social entrepreneurship. Some argue that all types of entrepreneurship are social, while others define it as purely an activity of the nonprofit sector. These blurred lines imply that entrepreneurs are forced to choose between making a social or an economic impact. We contend that social entrepreneurs can do both. It is possible to address a social issue and make a profit—keeping a company economically stable ensures its capability to consistently meet the needs of its customers without relying on fundraising or other methods to keep it afloat.[22] We therefore define **social entrepreneurship** as the process of sourcing innovative solutions to social and environmental problems.[23]

A subcategory of social entrepreneurship is the **benefit corporation,** or **B Corp**. This is a form of organization certified by the nonprofit B Lab that ensures that strict standards of social and environmental performance, accountability, and transparency are met.[24] The voluntary certification is designed for for-profit companies aiming to achieve social goals alongside business ones. To be certified as a B Corp, the organization is rated on how its employees are treated, its impact on the environment, and how it benefits the community in which it operates.[25] B Corp certification ensures that the for-profit company fulfills its social mission, and the certification protects it from lawsuits from stakeholders that may claim that the company is spending more time or resources on social issues rather than maximizing profit.

B Corp members include Betterworld Books, which donates a book to someone in need every time a book is purchased; Revolution Foods, which provides affordable, freshly prepared meals to school children from low-income households; and the UK-based Toast Ale, which is tackling food waste by making beer from leftover bread from bakeries and supermarkets that would otherwise have been thrown away.[26]

Social entrepreneurship: the process of sourcing innovative solutions to social and environmental problems.

Benefit corporation (or B Corp): a form of organization certified by the nonprofit B Lab that ensures strict standards of social and environmental performance, accountability, and transparency are met.

Family Enterprising

A **family enterprise** is a business that is owned and managed by multiple family members, typically for more than one generation. What makes family enterprising part of the portfolio of entrepreneurship types is that each generation has an opportunity to bring the organization forward in new, innovative ways.[27] Family-owned businesses are hugely important for the U.S. economy and account for 60% of employment, 78% of new jobs, and 65% of total wages (see Figure 1.3).[28]

An entrepreneurial agenda to move the family business forward is essential to business survival, as demonstrated by their low survival rate: For instance, approximately 70% of family businesses fail or are sold before the second generation reaches a position to take over.[29]

Many leading organizations that are family businesses are generally considered to be more stable, not only because of their history and experience, but because of their ability to take a long-term view, which inspires commitment and loyalty from their employees. Yet a long-term view that becomes stagnant is detrimental and can lead the company into a downward spiral.

Widely known businesses such as Walmart in the United States, auto company Volkswagen in Germany, and health care company Roche in Switzerland are all long-standing family businesses that continue to go from strength to strength. To continue their cycle of growth and continuity, family members must pass on their entrepreneurial mindsets as well as their business ethos. It is this mindset that ensures the survival of the family business for many years to come.

Family enterprise: a business that is owned and managed by multiple family members, typically for more than one generation.

Serial Entrepreneurship

Serial entrepreneurs, also known as **habitual entrepreneurs**, are people who start several businesses, either simultaneously or consecutively. Not satisfied with just focusing on one business, serial entrepreneurs are constantly looking out for the next big thing or

Serial entrepreneurs (or habitual entrepreneurs): entrepreneurs who start several businesses, either simultaneously or consecutively.

FIGURE 1.3

Percentage of Family-Owned Businesses

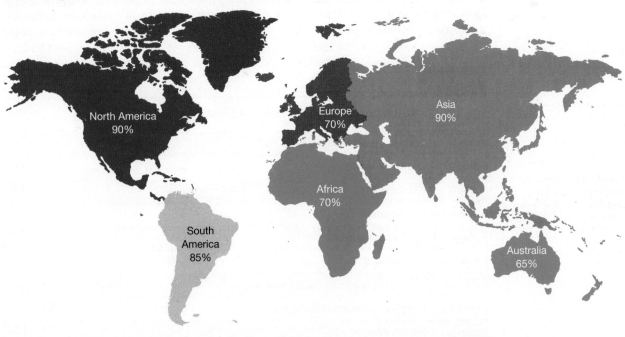

Natalie Campbell, founder of Morgan de Toi and cofounder of A Very Good Company

exploring ways to implement their diverse range of ideas. Natalie Campbell is a good example of a serial entrepreneur. While at university, she started her first venture running a franchise of fashion chain Morgan de Toi before going on to cofound social innovation agency A Very Good Company.[30]

1.4 ENTREPRENEURSHIP IS A METHOD, NOT A PROCESS

>> **LO 1.4   Distinguish between entrepreneurship as a method and as a process.**

A method is a systematic way of approaching a task, whereas a process is a series of steps taken to achieve a particular end. Traditionally, entrepreneurship has been viewed as a process of sequential steps that lead to a successful business (as in Table 1.3).

The process approach to entrepreneurship emphasizes planning and prediction—from firm creation right up until firm exit. It suggests that if you follow the 10 steps correctly, your new venture is more likely to succeed and that if you use proven business models, your risk of failure is reduced. There is no doubt that such a process works for larger organizations and corporations—but entrepreneurial ventures are not just smaller versions of large corporations.[31] The 10-step process isn't enough for entrepreneurial ventures. Why? Because it relies too much on history to predict the future, and a new venture with a new innovation does not have any history to draw from. And, simply stated, there are no steps or rules; it's just not that clean!

Entrepreneurship is nonlinear and unpredictable; it is ill-defined, unstructured, and complex. In fact, some statistics show that more than 50% of startups fail after 5 years of business.[32] There are several reasons for the extraordinary failure rate, such as lack of entrepreneurship education and not developing the ability to work through the messiness, accept ambiguity, and take action even when you are not really sure what to do. The interesting side of failure is that research has shown that if entrepreneurs who have failed

TABLE 1.3

The Entrepreneurship Process: An Outdated View

Step 1	Think of a product or service to sell
Step 2	Do market research
Step 3	Get some financial projections
Step 4	Find a partner/team
Step 5	Write a business plan
Step 6	Get financing
Step 7	Find space, build a prototype, hire people
Step 8	Bring your product/service to market
Step 9	Manage the business
Step 10	Plan an exit

try again, they are far more likely to be successful in their second venture—even if the second venture is completely different from the first. The point of these statistics is not to scare you but to show you how unpredictable, complex, and chaotic entrepreneurship can be. The environment for entrepreneurship is fluid, dynamic, uncertain, and ambiguous. Doesn't it make sense that the way we learn entrepreneurship needs to help us manage such "craziness"? The good news is there is a way to manage the chaos and craziness, and we call this the Entrepreneurship Method. Viewing entrepreneurship as a method does not guarantee success or a fixed outcome, but it does help guide you through the craziness of entrepreneurship and increase your chances of success. Table 1.4 illustrates some key points about the Entrepreneurship Method.[33]

From this we can see that entrepreneurship is less an aptitude than it is a practice and mindset, and realizing that entrepreneurship is more of a method than a process is the first step in this journey we call entrepreneurship. Viewing entrepreneurship as a method caters to its uncertain and unpredictable nature. It represents a body of skills that together comprise a toolkit for entrepreneurial action.[34] Table 1.5 summarizes the differences between entrepreneurship as a method and entrepreneurship as a process.

Approaching entrepreneurship as a method gives us comfort and direction, but it is not a recipe. Part of the Method is learning and practicing as you go and consciously reflecting on events as and when they take place. Part of the Method is iterative. The entire Method, however, is action based and, of course, requires practice.

TABLE 1.4

Assumptions Underlying the Entrepreneurship Method

It applies to novices and experts regardless of experience levels.
It is inclusive, which means it works for any organization at any stage of business.
It requires continuous practice with a focus on doing in order to learn.
It is designed for an unpredictable environment.
It changes how we think and act in ambiguous situations.
It helps you get unstuck when you are trying to start something new.

Source: Adapted from Neck, H. M., & Greene, P. G. (2011). Entrepreneurship education: Known worlds and new frontiers. *Journal of Small Business Management, 49*(1), 55–70. Reprinted with permission from John Wiley & Sons.

TABLE 1.5

Method Versus Process

ENTREPRENEURSHIP AS A METHOD	ENTREPRENEURSHIP AS A PROCESS
A set of practices	Known inputs and predicted outputs
Phases of learning	Steps to complete
Iterative	Linear
Creative	Predictive
Action focus	Planning focus
Investment for learning	Expected return
Collaborative	Competitive

Source: Neck, H. M., Greene, P. G., & Brush, C. (2014). *Teaching entrepreneurship: A practice-based approach.* Northampton, MA: Edward Elgar.

1.5 THE METHOD INVOLVES CREATING THE FUTURE, NOT PREDICTING IT

>> **LO 1.5**   **Compare and contrast the prediction and creation approaches to entrepreneurship.**

Earlier, we examined the truths behind some common images of entrepreneurs. As we just discussed, entrepreneurship is no longer about a path of starting and growing a venture using a linear, step-by-step process. Instead, it is a much messier, ongoing method of creating opportunities, taking smart action, learning and iterating, and using a portfolio of skills to navigate an ever-changing world.

The skills and mindset presented in this book are essential to the Entrepreneurship Method. There is no magic formula for success, but if you develop the skills and mindset, you will learn to work smarter and faster and be able to make decisions based on reality instead of guesses. As we will repeat many times throughout this book, entrepreneurship is a method that requires practice, and action trumps everything. The Method starts with the mindset. Even though our next chapter is devoted to the entrepreneurial mindset, let's do a quick lesson now on entrepreneurial thinking.

This chapter's Entrepreneurship in Action feature describes how Juan Giraldo, founder of Waku, created opportunities and took action to get his venture off the ground. How can Giraldo predict that his wellness tea business is going to succeed? The truth is, he can't; his focus is on creating a future rather than predicting it. But, by creating what he wants and what he believes his customers need, he's in control.

Managerial Versus Entrepreneurial Thinking

Entrepreneurial ventures are not smaller versions of large corporations. Take this a little further and think about this: Managers lead corporations but entrepreneurs lead startups. Leading in a corporate environment is very different from leading a startup environment. Why? Because there is a lot more uncertainty and risk in the startup environments *and* a lot less information and data.

Managerial thinking works best in times of certainty and when there is access to information and data on which to base decisions. Managerial thinking is the dominant logic of large, established organizations, where goals are predetermined, issues are transparent, and information is reliable and accessible. Under these circumstances, it is relatively straightforward to analyze a situation, define problems and opportunities, and diagnose and find solutions. Big organizations can use sophisticated planning tools to analyze past and present data in order to predict any shifts in the business landscape. Yet this process is by no means foolproof, as demonstrated by many well-planned initiatives backed by large companies that do not succeed. Those same companies want to be more entrepreneurial.

An early entrepreneurial venture is unlikely to have access to sophisticated predictive tools, nor does it have access to the data.[35]

A simple dinner party example can quickly illustrate the difference between entrepreneurial and managerial thinking. If you are throwing a dinner party for a group of friends, you might choose a recipe or draw up a menu, buy the ingredients, and cook the meal according to a set of instructions provided to you in the cookbook. Here you are approaching the dinner party as a manager. In contrast, you might invite some friends over and ask each person to bring one ingredient but not tell them what to bring. Let's say 10 people show up and the ingredients are French bread, fresh pasta, potatoes, spinach, a few different types of cheeses, steak, salmon, romaine lettuce, avocado, and kale. These ingredients plus the ingredients you already have in your kitchen are what you have to cook with. Now, the group must come together, use the ingredients, and create dinner! This is an example of entrepreneurial thinking—creating something without a concrete set of instructions. Though the two ways of thinking—managerial and entrepreneurial—seem polar opposites, the goal is the same: to cook a meal for your group of friends. It's how you approach the challenge and with what resources that is different.

In reality, entrepreneurs should and do employ both ways of thinking, but, in general, most of us possess the managerial skills depicted in Table 1.6. This is not surprising;

TABLE 1.6

Managerial Versus Entrepreneurial Thinking

MANAGERIAL	ENTREPRENEURIAL
Big planning	Small actions
Wait until you get what you need	Start with what you have
Expected return	Acceptable loss
Linear	Iterative
Optimization	Experimentation
Avoid failure at all costs	Embrace and leverage failure
Competitive	Collaborative
Knowable	Unknowable
Plan to act	Act to learn

Source: Sarasvathy, S. D. (2008). *Effectuation: Elements of entrepreneurial expertise.* Cheltenham, UK and Northampton, MA: Edward Elgar; Schlesinger, L., Kiefer, C., & Brown, P. (2012). *Just start: Take action, embrace uncertainty, create the future.* Cambridge, MA: Harvard Business School Press. http://www.e-elgar.com/

the fact is we have been honing these skills for years throughout primary school, then secondary, and now college. We actually did think more entrepreneurially when we were babies—a time when everything around us was a mystery and uncertain. The only way we learned as a baby was by trial and error. Traditional education, the need to find the correct answer, and the constant need for measurement and assessment have inhibited our entrepreneurial nature. So if you ever feel like you can't get unstuck and you're not really sure how to solve a problem, just remember that we were all born with the ability to think and act entrepreneurially. As social entrepreneur and Nobel Prize winner Muhammad Yunus says,

> We are all entrepreneurs. When we were in the caves we were all self-employed . . . finding our food, feeding ourselves. That's where the human history began. . . . As civilization came we suppressed it, and made into labor. . . . Because you stamped us, we are labor. We forgot that we are all entrepreneurs.[36]

Although managerial thinking has its advantages and is necessary, it is not enough in today's uncertain, complex, and chaotic business environment. Ideally, new ventures need both entrepreneurs and managers in order to function. And most of the time the manager and the entrepreneur are one and the same, so you need to develop skills in both entrepreneurial and managerial thinking. The secret is understanding when to act and think like an entrepreneur and when to act and think like a manager. In the beginning of anything new, you'll need to be thinking like an entrepreneur. You'll need to take small actions to collect your own data. You'll need to use the resources you have rather than wait for lots of resources to come to you. You'll need to fail in order to make progress, experiment with new ideas, collaborate with others, share your ideas, and realize that you might be in uncharted territory. And all of this is ok. Just keep moving forward and take smart action.

Entrepreneurial and Managerial Thinking in Action

To further examine entrepreneurial and management thinking, here is an example based on a thought experiment called "Curry in a Hurry" devised by Darden School of Business professor Saras D. Sarasvathy.[37] Say you want to start an Indian restaurant in your

Kumar Sriskandan/Alamy Stock Photo

Customers dining in a small Indian restaurant

hometown. You could begin by assessing your market through questionnaires, surveys, and focus groups to separate those people who love Indian food from those who don't. Then you could narrow the "love it" segment down to the customers whom you might be able to approach when your restaurant opens.

This approach would help you predict the type of diners who might become regulars at your restaurant. You could then continue your information-gathering process by visiting other Indian restaurants to gauge their business processes and contacting vendors to gauge prices and availability of goods. Having spent months acquiring all this knowledge, you could formulate a business plan, apply for bank loans and loans from investors, lease a building and hire staff, and start a marketing and sales campaign to attract people to your restaurant.

This is one way to go about starting a new business, but it is based on two big assumptions: (1) you have the finances and resources for research and marketing, and (2) you have the time to invest in intensive planning and research. Typically, this is the sort of path taken by novice entrepreneurs who navigate worlds that they perceive as certain; they spend huge amounts of time on planning and analysis and allow the market to take control while they take a back seat. In short, they spend lots of time and money taking a managerial approach to predict the future.

Given that the managerial approach to opening a new restaurant is time-consuming and expensive, what other approach could novice entrepreneurs take to carrying out the same task? If you followed the entrepreneurial approach to starting your Indian restaurant, you would be going down a very different path. To learn more about the entrepreneurial approach and the corresponding effectuation theory, see the *Research at Work* feature below.

To implement the entrepreneurial approach, first, you would take a look at what means you have to start the process. Let's assume you have only a few thousand dollars in the bank and very few other resources. You could start by doing just enough research to convince an established restaurateur to become a strategic partner, or persuade a local business owner to invest in your restaurant, or even create some dishes to bring to a local Indian restaurant and persuade them to let you set up a counter in their establishment to test a selection there.

Second, you could contact some of your friends who work in nearby businesses and bring them and their colleagues some samples of your food, which might lead to a lunch delivery service. Once the word is out and you have a large enough customer base, you might decide to start your restaurant.

Getting out in your community, meeting new people, and building relationships with customers and strategic partners can lead to all sorts of opportunities. Someone might suggest that you write an Indian cookbook and introduce you to a publishing contact; someone else might think you have just the right personality to host your own cooking show and connect you with someone in the television industry. Others might want to learn more about Indian culture and inspire you to teach classes on the subject; or they might express an interest in travel, inspiring you to organize a food-themed tour of different regions around India. Suddenly you have a wealth of different business ideas in widely varied industries. Your original goal of starting a restaurant has evolved and multiplied into several different streams, demonstrating how it is possible to change, shape, and construct ideas in practice through action (see Figure 1.4).

But who knows what the actual outcome will be? Let's say the majority of people just don't like your cooking, even though your close friends rave about it. If you are really determined to reach your initial goal, you could use their feedback to work hard at improving your recipes and try again. However, if you silently agree with your customer base, you haven't lost too much time and money in your idea—which means you have resources left over to focus on your next entrepreneurial pursuit.

FIGURE 1.4

The Creation Approach in Action

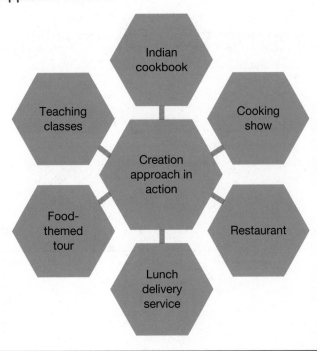

Sources:

Adapted from Schlesinger, L., Kiefer, C., & Brown, P. (2012). Just start: Take action, embrace uncertainty, create the future. Cambridge, MA: Harvard Business School Press.

Sarasvathy, S. D. (2008). Effectuation: Elements of entrepreneurial expertise. Northampton, MA: Edward Elgar.

Neck, H. M. (2011). Cognitive ambidexterity: The underlying mental model of the entrepreneurial leader. In D. Greenberg, K. McKone-Sweet, & H. J. Wilson (Eds.), The New entrepreneurial leader: Developing leaders who will shape social and economic opportunities (pp. 2442). San Francisco: Berrett-Koehler.

The creation approach to entrepreneurship is based on how entrepreneurs think. They navigate uncertain worlds to create rather than find opportunities; they make markets, learn from failure, and connect with a variety of stakeholders to fulfill their vision of the future.

1.6 THE KEY COMPONENTS OF THE ENTREPRENEURSHIP METHOD

>> LO 1.6   Illustrate the key components of the Entrepreneurship Method.

The Entrepreneurship Method provides a way for entrepreneurs to embrace and confront uncertainty rather than to avoid it. It emphasizes smart action over planning. It emphasizes moving quickly from the whiteboard to the real world. It's a method that can be learned and should be repeated. There is no guarantee for success, but it does offer a few powerful assurances:

- You will act sooner, even when you don't know exactly what to do.

- Those things you can do, you will, and those things you can't, you will try.

- You will try more times because trying early is a low-cost experiment.

- You will fail sooner—enabling better, higher-quality information to be incorporated into the next iteration.

- You'll likely begin experimenting with many new ideas simultaneously.

The Method includes the two approaches that have already been addressed: prediction and creation. Prediction requires thinking about and analyzing existing information in order to predict the future, and creation is most concerned with acting and collecting

FIGURE 1.5

The Entrepreneurship Method

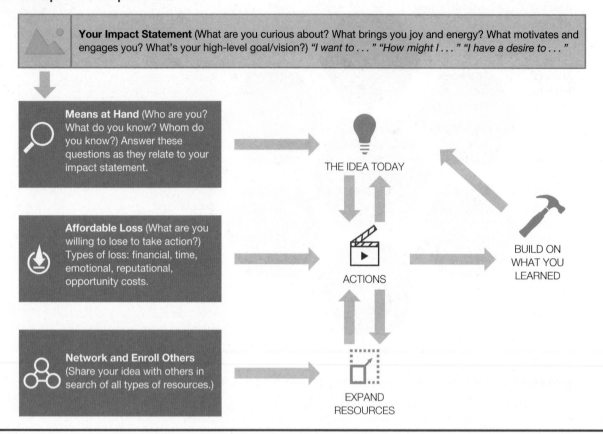

Adapted from the following sources:

Neck, H. M. (2011). Cognitive ambidexterity: The underlying mental model of the entrepreneurial leader. In D. Greenberg, K. McKone-Sweet, & H. J. Wilson (Eds.), *The new entrepreneurial leader: Developing leaders who will shape social and economic opportunities* (pp. 24–42). San Francisco, CA: Berrett-Koehler.

Sarasvathy, S. D. (2008). *Effectuation: Elements of entrepreneurial expertise.* Northampton, MA: Edward Elgar.

Schlesinger, L., Kiefer, C., & Brown, P. (2012). *Just start: Take action, embrace uncertainty, create the future.* Cambridge, MA: Harvard Business School Press.

new data—real and relevant data—in order to create the future. The prediction logic is better suited when we can deduce the future from the past, while the creation logic is the only choice under conditions of extreme uncertainty.

Eight Components of the Entrepreneurship Method

Now that we understand the difference between a method and a process of entrepreneurship, it is time to take a deeper dive into the components of the Method, as illustrated in Figure 1.5. Let's examine each of them in more detail.

1. **Identify your desired impact on the world** (see the Ted Talk at https://www .ted.com/talks/simon_sinek_how_great_leaders_inspire_ action?language=en). This is a simple statement that connects to your curiosity, drive, and motivation. To be successful at creating and building a new business, a new strategy, a new product, or anything radically new requires desire—you have to have a strong feeling to achieve something larger than yourself. Rarely is entrepreneurship about the money or the profit. Granted, fast-growth companies are primarily concerned with wealth creation, but the general reasons people start businesses go much deeper. Some pursue what they love, others value their autonomy and ability to control their work experience, and others have a strong desire to bring something new to

market.[38] The profit motive is simply not sustainable in the long run because entrepreneurship is hard work and requires satisfaction and desire that is derived from deep within. Ask yourself: What's my why?

2. **Start with the means at hand**.[39] Answer the following questions: Who am I? What do I know? Whom do I know? The composite answer will help you understand your current resource base—the resources you have available today that you can use for immediate action.

3. **Describe the idea today.** The idea is identified by connecting your means to your impact statement. What can you start to do today with what you have today?

4. **Calculate affordable loss.**[40] Leaving one's comfort zone is always perceived as risky, but risk is relative. What is considered high risk to one may not seem high risk to another; therefore, it can be quite difficult to calculate risk and use it as a valid decision-making criterion. Rather than calculating risk, think about taking action in terms of what you are willing to lose. What are you truly willing to give up in terms of money, reputation, time, and opportunity cost? By answering these questions, you take control rather than allowing yourself to be controlled by risk or the fear of failure.

5. **Take small action.** Nothing drastic . . . the first action is just a small start to get you going. No excuses here. You can do it. Once you calculate your affordable loss, you control all the risk.

6. **Network and enroll others in your journey.** The Entrepreneurship Method is about collaboration and cocreation rather than competition. Sharing your ideas and enrolling others in your journey will increase your resource base, expand the possibilities available, and validate your idea.

7. **Build on what you learn.** Assess performance of your action. Keep in mind that assessment is not about "killing" your new idea; it's about making the idea better. There is no right or wrong answer at this stage, just better. Expect and embrace setbacks, and celebrate the learning. When Thomas Watson, the founder of IBM, was asked about the key to success he responded, "Increase the rate of failure."

8. **Reflect and be honest with yourself.** One question always arises: How do I know when I should stop or keep going? The answer is easy. Quit only if you no longer have the desire inherent in your impact statement or if you have exceeded your affordable loss. Otherwise, the real question you have to answer now is "What are you going to do next?"

As you continue with the Entrepreneurship Method, you'll find that your affordable loss changes (usually increases) with each action. Why? Your idea receives greater validation, you have a solid and growing knowledge base, more people have joined your team, resource stocks increase, and your overall confidence in your ability to act grows. By practicing the Entrepreneurship Method, you will manage to deal with extreme uncertainty, control it, and use it to help you create what others cannot.

1.7 ENTREPRENEURSHIP REQUIRES DELIBERATE PRACTICE

>> **LO 1.7** Assess the role of deliberate practice in achieving mastery.

In this section, we will explore the word *practice* so you better understand why we refer to the Entrepreneurship Method as both a mindset and a practice. We are surrounded by heroes in athletics, music, business, science, and entertainment who appear to exhibit astoundingly high levels of performance. How do they do it? How do musicians play complex pieces of music from memory, and how do professional sports players perform

The 3-Hour Challenge

You may or may not have given a lot of thought to your entrepreneurial plans and goals. Either way, this activity will challenge you to clarify what plans and goals you have and why.

You can commit to doing a lot of things for only 3 hours, so give this Mindshift challenge a try. The 3 hours do not have to be spent in one continuous period. Doing it all at a stretch is probably not practical, so it is fine to spread out the time in 1-hour increments, but don't take longer than 3 days.

Hour 1: Write down your impact statement. Keep in mind that this is something that drives your curiosity, motivation to engage, and enthusiasm. Your impact statement is not an idea; it's a statement that expresses the type of impact you want to make as an entrepreneur. The following are examples of impact statements:

- I have a desire to help people age more gracefully.
- I have a desire to use video games to effect positive change.
- I have a desire to build greater community among different populations on my college campus.
- I have a desire to design clothes that help teenagers feel more confident.
- I have a desire to create healthy snack foods.

Take a full hour to write down your impact statement. Give it deep thought and really ask yourself, "What excites me?" Write it as clearly, sincerely, and completely as you can.

Hour 2: Share your impact statement with your classmates or others in your life, and try to find someone who shares a similar vision. Your goal is to find just one other person with a similar vision, but if you find more, that's great too!

Hour 3: Once you find your person, schedule a 1-hour meeting. Meet someplace unusual, not in the same coffee shop or restaurant where you always go. Share where your desired impact is coming from, and identify three potential business ideas that the two of you could pursue together to fulfill your desired impact. For example, if you both have a desire to create healthy snack foods, you may come up with an idea for vending machines that hold only fresh fruit and vegetables.

That's it . . . just craft your impact statement, find someone who shares your desire, and identify three potential business ideas. Don't judge the quality of your ideas at this point. There will be plenty of time for that.

Critical Thinking Questions

1. What assumptions and beliefs did you have before starting the 3-hour challenge?

2. In what ways did the 3-hour challenge confirm your assumptions and beliefs? In what ways did it change them?

3. What did you learn about yourself that was unexpected or surprising? ●

---

seemingly unbelievable acts? And how do entrepreneurs move from being novices to expert serial entrepreneurs? The answer lies in a certain type of practice.

We have all heard the expression "practice makes perfect," but what does this really mean? We often associate practice with repetition and experience; for example, we picture a violinist playing a piece of music for hours every day or a basketball player shooting hoops for prolonged periods. However, research has shown that people who spend a lot of time simply repeating the same action on a regular basis reach a plateau of capability regardless of how many hours they have put in.[41] A golf enthusiast who spends a couple of days a week playing golf will reach a certain level, but she is unlikely to reach professional status solely through this form of practice. Performance does not improve purely as a result of experience. Similarly, as studies have shown, there is no evidence to suggest that world-class chess champions or professional musicians and sports players owe their success to genes or inheritance. How, then, do people advance from novice level to top performer?

Researchers have found that it all depends on *how* you practice. To achieve high levels of performance, high performers engage in **deliberate practice**, which involves carrying out carefully focused efforts to improve current performance.[42] The Mindshift features throughout this text are a useful way of deliberately practicing entrepreneurship. Table 1.7 lists the components of deliberate practice.

Deliberate practice: carrying out carefully focused efforts to improve current performance.

TABLE 1.7

Components of Deliberate Practice

• Requires high levels of focus, attention, and concentration.
• Strengthens performance by identifying weaknesses and improving on them.
• Must be consistent and be maintained for long periods of time.
• Must be repeated to produce lasting results.
• Requires continuous feedback on outcomes.
• Involves setting goals beforehand.
• Involves self-observation and self-reflection after practice sessions are completed.

Source: Baron, R. A., & Henry, R. A. (2010). How entrepreneurs acquire the capacity to excel: Insights from research on expert performance. *Strategic Entrepreneurship Journal, 4,* 49–65. Reprinted with permission from John Wiley & Sons.

Although aspects of deliberate practice exist in activities such as sport, chess, and music, it is also present in such diverse pursuits as typing, economics, and medicine. One study explored the use of deliberate practice by identifying the study habits of medical students when learning clinical skills. Researchers found that over time, students who used deliberate practice were able to make more efficient use of their time, energy, and resources.[43] In short, they seemed to "learn how to learn."

You might not be conscious of it, but chances are you probably already use some of the elements of deliberate practice. Think of when you first played a sport or picked up a musical instrument. You may have played the instrument for only 15 minutes a few times a week, or played football for 30 minutes twice a week, but without knowing it, during those short sessions, you were fully focused on what you were doing and intentionally repeating the activity, with a goal of improving your performance.

World-renowned sushi chef Jiro Ono has engaged in deliberate practice all his life by mastering the art of making sushi.[44] Of course, Ono cannot do it all by himself, so he has a number of apprentices under his careful watch. He starts off each apprentice with a small part of the sushi-making process—how to use a knife, how to cut fish, and so on. The apprentices are only permitted to move on to the next stage of the process once they have mastered each task. To put this into context, one of Ono's apprentices was only allowed to cook eggs for the first time after training under Ono for 10 years. Not only has Ono perfected the art of sushi making, but his commitment to deliberate practice has almost certainly benefited his brain.

Deliberate Practice Shapes the Brain

Engaging in deliberate practice is even more worthwhile when you consider the effect it has on the brain.[45] When certain brain cells sense a lot of focused repeated activity, chemicals are produced to create myelin—a fatty, white tissue that increases the speed and strength of neural impulses, thereby improving performance. In contrast, regular practice without focused effort, consistent feedback, and guidance only reinforces mindless, automatic habits. For example, when you first learned to drive, you probably really concentrated on how to control the car, but after many instances of driving, you will find that you perform every step of the process without even thinking about it. You may think regular practice is sufficient for completing certain tasks, but you will have little chance of mastering them without systematic, deliberate practice. There is a big difference between practicing out of habit and using your head. For instance, virtuoso violinist Nathan Milstein was concerned that he wasn't practicing enough—everyone else seemed to be practicing all day long but he wasn't.[46] When he asked his professor for advice, Milstein was told, "It really doesn't matter how long. If you practice with your fingers, no amount is enough. If you practice with your head, two hours is plenty."

Deliberate Practice and Entrepreneurs

What does deliberate practice mean for entrepreneurs? Sustained effort, concentration, and focus have important cognitive benefits such as enhancing perception, memory, intuition, and the way in which we understand our own performance (or metacognition). Expert entrepreneurs who engage in deliberate practice are generally more skilled at perceiving situations, understanding the meaning of complex patterns, and recognizing the differences between relevant and irrelevant information.

Entrepreneurs who engage in deliberate practice are better at storing new information and retrieving it when they need to, which helps them to plan, adapt, and make decisions more quickly in changing situations. Deliberate practice also enables entrepreneurs to realize what they know and don't know. Among the most common mistakes entrepreneurs make are getting blindsided by passion, which makes them overly optimistic and overconfident in their skills and abilities, and underestimating their resources—mistakes that often lead to unnecessary risk and failure.[47] Although passion is an important quality to possess, it is best guided by awareness of your own capabilities and knowledge. These sorts of mistakes can be overcome by receiving continual feedback on your performance from an expert in the field.[48] This is why it is so important for entrepreneurs to seek out mentors, coaches, or even a good friend whose business sense you admire and who will work with you, offer feedback, and help guide you in your decision making.

Finally, expert entrepreneurs who have consistently used deliberate practice over a number of years tend to have a higher sense of intuition, which enables them to make decisions more speedily and accurately based on knowledge and experience.

"Years of deliberate practice" may sound daunting, but you probably already have a head start! The cognitive skills that you developed through deliberate practice (e.g., by playing a musical instrument or sport, creative writing, or anything else that requires strong focus and effort) are all transferable to entrepreneurship. You have the capability to enhance your skills and become a lifelong learner—and you can demonstrate this by creating your own entrepreneurship portfolio.

RESEARCH AT WORK

How Entrepreneurs Think

The Entrepreneurship Method in this text aligns with the work of Dr. Saras Sarasvathy and her theory of effectuation,[49] which is based on the idea that because the future is unpredictable yet controllable, entrepreneurs can affect the future. Sarasvathy believes it is futile for entrepreneurs to try to predict the future.

In 1997, Dr. Sarasvathy traveled to 17 states across the United States to interview 30 entrepreneurs from different types and sizes of organizations and from a variety of industries to assess their thinking patterns. The aim of her research was to understand their methods of reasoning about specific problems. Each entrepreneur was given a 17-page problem that involved making decisions to build a company from a specific product idea. By the end of the study, Sarasvathy discovered that 89% of the more experienced, serial entrepreneurs used more creative, effectual thinking more often than its contrary—predictive or causal thinking.[50]

Until Dr. Sarasvathy's study, we really didn't know how entrepreneurs think—at least, previous research didn't identify such salient patterns as her work. She found that entrepreneurs, especially those entrepreneurs who had started businesses multiple times, exhibited specific thinking patterns. Thus, we are able to demonstrate that entrepreneurship can be taught because we can train ourselves to think differently—and how we think is the antecedent to how we act.

Critical Thinking Questions

1. What strengths and weaknesses do you see in Sarasvathy's effectuation theory of entrepreneurship? Give some examples that would apply to real life.

2. If you were asked to participate in Dr. Sarasvathy's study, how might she classify your ways of thinking and problem solving?

3. What additional research questions can you suggest that would shed light on how entrepreneurs think and solve problems? ●

1.8 HOW THIS BOOK WILL HELP YOU PRACTICE ENTREPRENEURSHIP

>> **LO 1.8** **Propose different ways in which this book can help you practice entrepreneurship.**

By now, we hope that we have proved to you that becoming an entrepreneur is a pathway for many and that the world needs more entrepreneurs of all kinds. To reinforce our message, the following are some fundamental beliefs that form the main ethos of this book.

We believe that you as the student must take action and practice entrepreneurship at every opportunity. In each chapter of this book, you will find the following features, which are designed to challenge you to do just that.

- Entrepreneurship in Action: In entrepreneurship, there is no one right answer. Role models are very important because, by learning from others, you can develop empathy for entrepreneurs around the world who may be doing the same as you someday. Entrepreneurship in Action includes interviews with entrepreneurs from many different businesses and disciplines in the United States and around the world.

ENTREPRENEURSHIP MEETS ETHICS

When to Practice Entrepreneurship

Becoming great at any skill requires a considerable deal of practice. Psychology writer Malcolm Gladwell believes it takes 10,000 hours of practice to become great at any skill. However, in the course of acquiring those 10,000 hours, burgeoning entrepreneurs must find a way to support themselves, and that often means having a conventional, full-time job.

Is it ethical to work on entrepreneurial ventures during company time? Can your performance at your current workplace be hampered because of your dedication to personal ventures?

These questions must be addressed for any entrepreneur to become an effective manager of employees upon starting a new business. According to a CareerBuilder survey, 29% of workers have a side job, and that number grows for younger workers.

For entrepreneurial-spirited workers, a close review of the employment contract and company handbook should be the first step, to make sure there are no specific policies against having a side business or job, especially a noncompetition clause. If there is no language barring an additional business pursuit, then a worker is in the clear to act on different pursuits. Nevertheless, that does not mean an employer or supervisor will be wholly happy to hear of a side venture.

Thus, an entrepreneurial employee is left with two options: disclose the nature of a side venture or do not.

Understanding a company's culture may be the first step in solving this conundrum, which takes time and relationship building to figure out. There is a possibility that an employer may be particularly interested in how an employee's entrepreneurial venture may help that employee grow with regard to the primary job. If there could be any potential conflict down the road, disclosing basic information to a human resources representative could be the best form of action.

Critical Thinking Questions

1. Should workers devote all of their energy to their primary paid job? Can the mere existence of a side job hurt a worker's performance in a primary job?

2. Is it unethical to hide a side job from an employer, even if it is legal?

3. Can employers benefit from having an employee who wishes to become an entrepreneur? Could this be a sought-after trait for recruiters? ●

Sources:

Baer, D. (2014, June 2). Malcolm Gladwell explains what everyone gets wrong about his "10,000 hour rule." *Business Insider*. Retrieved from http://www.businessinsider.com/malcolm-gladwell-explains-the-10000-hour-rule-2014-6

Bitte, R. (2018). 4 questions smart people ask about side gigs (so they don't lose their jobs). *The Muse*. Retrieved from https://www.themuse.com/advice/4-questions-smart-people-ask-about-side-gigs-so-they-dont-lose-their-jobs

Morad, R. (2016, September 29). Survey: More than one-third of working millennials have a side job. *Forbes*. Retrieved from https://www.forbes.com/sites/reneemorad/2016/09/29/survey-more-than-one-third-of-working-millennials-have-a-side-job/#180359d6132f

- Mindshift: Because entrepreneurship requires action, there are two Mindshift features in each chapter that require you to close the textbook and go and act. This is when you will deliberately practice entrepreneurship.

- Entrepreneurship Meets Ethics: Entrepreneurs sometimes face complex ethical challenges that cause conflict. Peppered with situations faced by real-world entrepreneurs, the Entrepreneurship Meets Ethics feature challenges you to think about how you would take action if you were confronted with a similar ethical dilemma.

- Research at Work: This feature highlights recent seminal entrepreneurship studies and their impact on and application to the real world. This will allow you to view how the latest research applies to real-life settings.

- Case Study: Finally, witness the content of the chapter come alive in a short case study presented at the end of each chapter. These case studies are based on real companies of all kinds—for-profit, nonprofit, technology, social, product-based, service-based, online, and others—that have been started by entrepreneurs of all types.

Entrepreneurship is all around us—everyone has the ability to think and act entrepreneurially, to transform opportunity into reality, and to create social and economic value. But remember, practice is key—learning is inseparable from doing. So, let's get started! ●

$SAGE edge™

Get the tools you need to sharpen your study skills. SAGE edge offers a robust online environment featuring an impressive array of free tools and resources.

- Access practice quizzes, eFlashcards, video, and multimedia at **edge.sagepub.com/neckentrepreneurship2e**

SUMMARY

1.1   Explain the importance of action and practice in entrepreneurship.

Practice and action make it possible to achieve success. Many of the successful entrepreneurs behind major corporations today established their companies by acting, learning, and building what they learned into their next actions. Many entrepreneurs have learned entrepreneurship by doing entrepreneurship, but this text is designed to help you practice the essentials in the hope that you can avoid some of the more common pitfalls.

1.2   List the seven lesser-known truths about entrepreneurship.

There are seven lesser-known truths about entrepreneurship: (1) entrepreneurship is not reserved for startups; (2) entrepreneurs do not have a special set of personality traits; (3) entrepreneurship can be taught and it is a method that requires practice; (4) entrepreneurs are not extreme risk takers; (5) entrepreneurs collaborate more than they compete; (6) entrepreneurs act more than they plan; (7) entrepreneurship is a life skill.

1.3   Compare and contrast the different forms of entrepreneurship in practice today.

Corporate entrepreneurship (or intrapreneurship) is entrepreneurship within large corporations. Inside entrepreneurs are similar to corporate entrepreneurs, but they can be found in any type of organization, large or small, nonprofit or for-profit, and even among governing bodies. Franchising and buy-outs are popular ways to start relatively near the ground level. Social entrepreneurship—entrepreneurship focused on making the world a better place—is manifested in nonprofit and large, for-profit firms alike. A form of social entrepreneurship is the Benefit Corporation, or B Corp, which designates for-profit firms that meet high standards of corporate social responsibility. Family enterprises, entrepreneurship started within the family, remain a dominant form of business development in the United States and abroad. Serial entrepreneurs are so committed to entrepreneurship that they're constantly on the move creating new businesses.

1.4   Distinguish between entrepreneurship as a method and as a process.

The Entrepreneurship Method outlines the tools and practices necessary to take action. Entrepreneurship as a process, instead, guides would-be creators along a thorough but static path from inception to exit.

1.5   Compare and contrast the prediction and creation approaches to entrepreneurship.

The two main perspectives on entrepreneurship are the predictive logic, the older and more traditional view; and the creation logic, which has been developed through recent advances in the field. Prediction is the opposite of creation. Whereas prediction thinking is used in situations of certainty, the creation view is used when the future is unpredictable.

1.6   Illustrate the key components of the Entrepreneurship Method.

The Entrepreneurship Method is designed so entrepreneurs can embrace and confront uncertainty rather than avoid it. The eight components are identify your desired impact on the world; start with the means at hand; describe the idea today; calculate affordable loss; take small action; network and enroll others in your journey; build on what you learn; and reflect and be honest with yourself.

1.7   Assess the role of deliberate practice in achieving mastery.

Practice doesn't make perfect; rather, deliberate practice makes perfect. Starting with specific goals, deliberate practice involves consistent, targeted efforts for improvement. Feedback and self-reflection are necessary for meaningful improvement, and repetition is required to achieve lasting results.

1.8   Propose different ways in which this book can help you practice entrepreneurship.

The tools for success and methods to hone entrepreneurial skills will be available in every chapter. Thought and action exercises alike will be employed, and research and testimonials from proven academics and entrepreneurs will be provided as we move through the text. As a final test of application, case studies will follow every chapter, giving you the opportunity to employ what you've learned, a chance for entrepreneurship within a unique and real-world context.

KEY TERMS

Benefit corporation
  (or B Corp)   12

Corporate entrepreneurship (or
  intrapreneurship)   10

Deliberate practice   22

Effectuation theory   6

Entrepreneurs inside   10

Entrepreneurship   3

Family enterprise   13

Franchise   11

Inbound marketing   28

Outbound marketing   28

Royalties   11

Serial entrepreneurs (or habitual
  entrepreneurs)   13

Social entrepreneurship   12

Startup   6

CASE STUDY

Saurbh Gupta, founder, Gyan-I Inc.

> Before you start your entrepreneurship journey, make sure you validate your reason and motivation for doing so. If you are convinced that you are doing this for the right reasons, whatever it may be, you shall be able to take on whatever comes your way.
>
> —Saurabh Gupta, founder of Gyan-I Inc.

The name of Saurabh Gupta's company, Gyan-I, means "knowledgeable one" in Hindi. Having always wanted to be his own boss, Saurabh's entrepreneurship journey began when he came across an opportunity while working for a very large charitable foundation called Daniels Fund. Daniels Fund is headquartered in Denver, Colorado, and is dedicated to providing grants, scholarship programs, and ethics education in Colorado, New Mexico, Utah, and Wyoming. As vice president of IT, Saurabh oversaw the end-to-end management of the organization's entire IT infrastructure. This included vendor negotiations, department budgeting, project planning, and execution. Daniels Fund manages assets of more than 1 billion dollars, but Saurabh realized that smaller, less wealthy nonprofit organizations faced similar IT issues and technological challenges. He identified a real unmet need: IT services for nonprofit organizations that did not have the infrastructure or money to support a full-time IT staff. Saurabh felt that meeting this need would fit perfectly with his skillset and experience and would be a good way to finally fulfill his dream of becoming an entrepreneur.

Though he toyed with the idea of starting Gyan-I Inc. for years, he could only take the leap after he received his U.S. green card in 2011. The CEO of Daniels Fund was supportive of Saurabh's decision to start his own company and was also his first customer! His former CEO continues to be his mentor and a pillar of support today.

Gyan-I Inc. provides technology consulting and managed IT services primarily for nonprofit and small-business organizations. As Saurabh explains it,

> For an organization with 10 to 100 people, it doesn't really make sense to hire a techie. What we do is that we run the basics around the network, website, online infrastructure, and even consult

companies to give them new ideas and improve overall operations using IT. Most of the work is remote and our clients sometimes like us to operate out of their offices. While the five-member team usually works out of Denver, people are all over the country. Recently, however, we have pivoted the business to focus on cybersecurity, and all the services I just mentioned are offered only to legacy clients.

Over the past 2 years, with the increasing number of cyber incidents, crime, and malware, cybersecurity in business infrastructure has gained significant importance.

The hacking of the 2016 U.S. elections was a watershed moment for us. While cybersecurity is a space that I personally really enjoyed, it is also a space that is gaining significant importance and is here to stay. The IT infrastructure around the world is changing with more offerings coming on the cloud, increasing exposure to the Internet, making cybersecurity even more necessary and relevant. We saw this as an opportunity to evaluate the strength of our team and internal resources, focus our offerings towards cybersecurity and move up the pecking order in our niche market segment.

Gyan-I Inc. now offers three services that help small businesses manage their cyber risk. First, they do an initial risk assessment and give a report on the risk businesses are likely to face and consult on how to overcome the risk. Second, they extend offerings by hand-holding the company and providing the necessary support to protect the companies from risk, analyze their security, and train employees on an ongoing basis. The third service is related to fast responses to cyber breaches. The response to these higher-margin services, Saurabh says, has been "good."

In 2011, when Saurabh started, he was alone and "bootstrapped" the business. Bootstrapping is entrepreneurship lingo for starting a business with very limited resources without outside investment. Saurabh believes his bootstrapping approach helped him start small but grow with intention. As people joined the team, the company began to grow organically and slowly, not to mention being profitable from Day 1. Bootstrapping the company presented Saurabh with its own sets of constraints. He felt that it would not be possible to deliver the services to his clients at a low cost and on time if he developed his own resources (IT infrastructure). Instead, he adopted existing software-as-a-service (SaaS) solutions that were not only tried and tested but also readily available (e.g., SaaS for payroll, project management software). Using these existing solutions allowed him to bundle and customize his offerings to address the specific needs of his customers, improving customer satisfaction.

Inbound marketing: bringing potential customers to your business by creating online content that addresses their needs, in order to build trust and brand awareness.

Outbound marketing: promoting your product or service through traditional activities such as advertising, trade shows, and cold calling.

Bootstrapping also meant that other overhead costs had to be minimized. His first office was in a co-op workspace in Denver. "Everything is an operational expense when you're bootstrapped," he quipped. The business developed organically and mostly through word of mouth. Because most of the leads resulted from inbound marketing, their sales cycles were extremely short, so they could contact the customer, pitch the product, and close the sale in less than one day. This enabled them to grow 30% every year. Gyan-I Inc. currently has 45 to 50 customers, and they have expanded their marketing efforts to include outbound marketing. They have recently hired a marketing professional to help grow the company base and brand.

Not everything was smooth sailing for Saurabh. He recalls an early misstep in the business around 2013, when he decided to focus on developing a SaaS product called Applyd (http://applyd.co/) from scratch. He noticed many of his nonprofit clients followed a paper-based approach to file requests for scholarships. He thought it was possible to streamline this process electronically, reducing the time spent on redundant activities for these 500 potential clients. Building a product from scratch was different from what Gyan-I had done so far. Saurabh, however, felt that he understood the problem and that the product he would build would be adopted by potential users almost immediately. He decided to dive in with both feet, allocated a budget, and spent a lot of time building and working on the concept. His budget was running out and he was spending more than he wanted to on building the product. He was able to scrape through and finished the software in 2014, but the product did not achieve expected sales. It reached only 2–3% of the addressable market. The clients simply didn't use it. He quickly realized that his clients were not early adopters and couldn't see the value in automation. Saurabh stopped pursuing Applyd in 2015.

Saurabh realized that the company successfully worked as an outsourced model. His customers needed IT support and not new IT products. Gyan-I worked because it had internal resources—knowledgeable people who offered quality service and attention. Clients knew their IT was in good, capable hands. Today Saurabh is confident that his boutique business has a sustainable model that is scalable. The small staff size of the company also positions it well to provide high-quality services.

When a client approaches us, the team is able to be nimble and efficient. We are able to fine-tune our offerings in real-time based on the feedback and requirements of the client. Some clients are hard pressed for time and want work to be completed within the week, while some don't mind spreading it over a few months. We are able to manage those expectations, a big advantage in this space.

Added to this is the awareness that Gyan-I Inc. has of the events affecting its industry, especially those related to cybersecurity. This nimble attitude has allowed it to pivot effectively and leverage and build on the existing strengths of the team.

Saurabh's journey as an entrepreneur has not been without a struggle. He says that starting and running a company has been a spiritual and philosophical journey for him. It has not only helped him become more observant and disciplined in his personal life, but he has also developed a sense of self-awareness—something that he is very thankful for. Although he's not able to spend as much time with his family as he would like, he has been able to strike a meaningful balance between family life and work life. The technology industry is constantly evolving, and Saurabh points out that he is always concerned about the company's ability to remain relevant to customer needs and wants as the managed IT services industry is experiencing a tectonic shift toward cloud-based computing and consumption. This means that he is continuously learning in order to stay ahead of the game.

Critical Thinking Questions

1. How risky is it to start a technology services company today when technology is changing at such a rapid pace?

2. The Entrepreneurship Method is about taking action and trying new things. Do you see evidence of the Method during the creation of Gyan-I?

3. As you think about doing something entrepreneurial, today or someday, what is your motivation for doing so?

Source: Saurabh Gupta (interview with Babson MBA graduate assistant Gaurav Khemka, September 09, 2018.)

2 Activating an Entrepreneurial Mindset

"If you want something you've never had, you must be willing to do something you've never done."

—Thomas Jefferson

Chapter Outline

Learning Objectives

2.1 THE POWER OF MINDSET

>> **LO 2.1   Appraise the effectiveness of mindset in entrepreneurship.**

In Chapter 1, we learned about the Entrepreneurship Method. Part of the Method is being in the right mindset to start and grow a business. The words from "Rise and Shine" in Figure 2.1 have been transcribed from an athlete motivation video on YouTube. It is a good description of how our mindset operates. When we wake up in the morning we have a choice between the "easy" way and the "right" way. Depending on our mindset, we will choose one path or the other. In this chapter's Entrepreneurship in Action feature, we describe how Franklin Yancey's entrepreneurial mindset encouraged him to start his own business selling comfortable stadium seats for sporting events. Yancey credits his early entrepreneurial experiences, his college education, and supportive family for his success.

But what motivated Yancey to start his own business? After all, he was still in college and had plenty of time to think about what he wanted to do afterward. We could say that Yancey was in the right mindset to start a business. He saw a problem that needed to be fixed and he was curious about finding solutions. Thanks to prior experiences, he had the confidence to take action by knocking on doors and gaining support for his idea. He also believed enough to persist with his idea, even in the face of high financial risk. It was Yancey's entrepreneurial mindset that kept him on the right track and ultimately led to success in multiple businesses.

2.2 WHAT IS MINDSET?

>> **LO 2.2   Define "entrepreneurial mindset" and explain its importance to entrepreneurs.**

We emphasized mindset in Chapter 1 and it's also in the subtitle of this text, so perhaps it is time we stopped to examine what it actually means. It has traditionally been defined as "the established set of attitudes held by someone."[1] It's really our lens for viewing the world, interpreting what we see, and reacting or responding to what we hear. Our mindset subconsciously guides our reactions and decisions. Sometimes it's really hard to define mindset, so perhaps a quick story will better illustrate.[2,3] Corey Booker, a U.S. senator for the state of New Jersey, was a law student in 1997. He had great passion for the city of Newark, which at the time was one of the most

$SAGE edge™

Master the content at **edge.sagepub.com/neckentrepreneurship2e**

Franklin Yancey, WME Entertainment and Yancey Realty

Photo courtesy of Franklin Yancey

Franklin Yancey, Founder of College Comfort and Yancey Realty

As a young child growing up in Blackstone, Virginia, Franklin Yancey used to go out to the woods, dig up trees, pot them, and sell them to neighborhood families. He also sold stickers by cutting pictures out of skateboard magazines. You could say that Franklin developed an entrepreneurial mindset very early on. His father certainly helped. As Franklin said, "My father was a hard worker who came up from little means working in tobacco fields at a very early age. Later he started his own pharmacy. My strong work ethic comes from both of my parents." You could also say that athletics also contributed to his mindset. From a young age, Franklin, his brother, and his sister played sports at competitive levels and they all were inducted into their high school hall of fame. His brother even played golf on the PGA Tour.

While in college at Virginia Tech University in the mid-1990s, Franklin enrolled in a management course, which jumpstarted his interest in entrepreneurship. "I realized that I didn't want to work for someone else," Franklin said. While walking to the Virginia Tech football stadium for a game, Franklin noticed a pile of portable, dilapidated stadium seats. These were seat cushions with a back support that fans could rent for a sporting event to make sitting in the stadium more comfortable. "They were made from cheap material and had been badly maintained," recalled Franklin. Teaming up with his roommate, John Hite, he decided to make a better product to rent to the university. And so the two became the founders of College Comfort: a company that manufactured and rented comfortable stadium seats for sporting events and large stadium events.

To produce the seats, they found a local former Levi's plant and asked for quotes to stitch high-quality material with school colors onto the rental stadium seats. Their first high-stakes deal came shortly after when Franklin pitched contracts with both East Carolina University and Virginia Tech for stadium seat cushion rentals. It was essential to get both schools to sign on, in order to get cash to produce the product and build credibility for College Comfort. Luckily, they both signed.

Franklin worked hard to market the product in new places. The next year they signed eight additional customers. Thanks to friends and family, they didn't have lodging expenses while they traveled around the country sourcing more customers. In their third year of business, College Comfort signed on 12 more schools and the business has continued to grow ever since.

In early 2008, a large privately owned, multibillion-dollar entertainment company called WME-IMG Entertainment acquired College Comfort. Today, Franklin still works on this part of the business as a vice-president with WME-IMG. He leads a team of 10 people and has contracts with more than 100 universities, NASCAR, Major League Baseball, and others to provide thousands of rental stadium seat attachments for events.

While truly enjoying his work with WME-IMG, he still felt the entrepreneurship "itch" to start something else from scratch. So in 2016, he created a real estate company in Charlotte, N.C., called Yancey Realty that focuses on commercial real estate, residential real estate, and property management. He now has more than 30 agents in three locations. Franklin feels the autonomous nature of his WME-IMG job, combined with the use of technology, allows him to do both "jobs" well. He feels the secret sauce in his real estate business is his ability to empower his agents to get the job done by providing them with the resources they need to perform.

Franklin credits his entrepreneurial mindset for his ability to work hard. "I hear 'work smart, not hard,' and I understand the logic behind it. But the real mission is to work smart *and* to work longer and harder than others. You have to lead yourself before you can lead others, too!" Even after all of his success and at the age of 42, he still works many long nights, but it is all worth it to him. As he sees it, "There is only one title that matters: owner. Being an entrepreneur is about being an owner."

Critical Thinking Questions

1. In what ways does his mindset play a role in Franklin's success?

2. What is the one key trait that all entrepreneurs must possess, according to Franklin?

3. Have you considered any products or services as solutions to problems while walking through your own college campus? If so, describe them. ●

Source: Franklin Yancey (interview with author, December 31, 2018)

FIGURE 2.1

Rise and Shine

Athletes use a motivational mindset to achieve goals on the field.

It's six am and your hand can't make it to the alarm clock fast enough before the voices in your head start telling you that it's too early, too cold, and too dark to get out of bed. Aching muscles lie still in rebellion pretending not to hear your brain commanding them to move. A legion of voices are shouting their permission for you to hit the snooze button and go back to dream land. But you didn't ask their opinion. The one voice you're listening to is a voice of defiance. The voice that says there's a reason you set that alarm in the first place. So sit up, put your feet on the floor, and don't look back—because we've got work to do.

Source: Red Productions. (2012, February 16). *TCU baseball 2012—The grind* [Video file]. Retrieved from https://www .youtube.com/watch?v=MNL_DAI19_I

economically depressed cities in the country. In his final year of Yale law school, he began working as a tenants' rights advocate in Newark—even moving to the harshest area of the city called the Central Ward. There he met Virginia Jones, the president of the Brick Towers tenants' association—a slum in the Central Ward. Corey expressed to Virginia his interest in helping the community. As the story goes, Virginia took Corey to the middle of the busy street outside of the Brick Towers. She told Corey to look around and describe what he saw. Corey looked around and responded with such things as, "I see a playground overgrown with weeds and the equipment is rusty. I see trash on the sides of the road. I see houses with their windows boarded up. I saw a drug deal happening on that corner last night. I see so many people out of work." The list could go on but Virginia Jones stopped Corey Booker and simply said, "You can't help this area." She paused. The petite Virginia Jones looked up at the broad-shouldered and tall young Corey Booker and said, "Boy, you need to understand that the world outside of you is a reflection of what you have inside of you, and if you're one of those people who only sees darkness, despair, that's all there's ever gonna be." This is an example of mindset—the mindset Corey had but also the mindset Corey needed. His life and mindset forever changed on that day.

Fortunately our mindset is not static; it can change, as evidenced by the Corey Booker story above. Research has shown that our mindset needn't be "set" at all. Stanford University psychologist Carol Dweck proposes that there are two different types of mindset: a fixed mindset and a growth mindset (see Figure 2.2).[4]

FIGURE 2.2

What Kind of Mindset Do You Have?

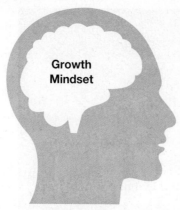

Growth Mindset

I can learn anything I want to.
When I'm frustrated, I persevere.
I want to challenge myself.
When I fail, I learn.
Tell me I try hard.
If you succeed, I'm inspired.
My effort and attitude determine everything.

Fixed Mindset

I'm either good at it, or I'm not.
When I'm frustrated, I give up.
I don't like to be challenged.
When I fail, I'm no good.
Tell me I'm smart.
If you succeed, I feel threatened.
My abilities determine everything.

Source: Created by Reid Wilson @wayfaringpath.

Fixed mindset: the assumptions held by people who perceive their talents and abilities as set traits.

In a **fixed mindset**, people perceive their talents and abilities as set traits. They believe that brains and talent alone are enough for success, and they go through life with the goal of looking smart all the time. They take any constructive criticism of their capabilities very personally and tend to attribute others' success to luck (see Research at Work, below, for a study about luck) or some sort of unfair advantage. People with a fixed mindset will tell themselves they are no good at something to avoid challenge, failure, or looking dumb.

Growth mindset: the assumptions held by people who believe that their abilities can be developed through dedication, effort, and hard work.

On the other hand, in a **growth mindset**, people believe that their abilities can be developed through dedication, effort, and hard work. They think brains and talent are not the key to lifelong success, but merely the starting point. People with a growth mindset are eager to enhance their qualities through lifelong learning, training, and practice. Unlike people with fixed mindsets, they see failure as an opportunity to improve their performance and to learn from their mistakes. Despite setbacks, they tend to persevere rather than give up.

Recent studies have found that being praised simply for our intelligence can create a fixed mindset. For example, using a series of puzzle tests, Dweck discovered that 5th-grade children who were praised for their hard work and effort on the first test were far more likely to choose the more difficult puzzle the next time. In contrast, children who were praised for being smart or intelligent after the first test chose the easy test the second time around.[5]

It seems that the children who had been praised for being smart wanted to keep their reputation for being smart and tended to avoid any challenge that would jeopardize this belief. Yet the children who had been praised for how hard they had worked on the first test had more confidence in their abilities to tackle a more challenging test and to learn from whatever mistakes they might make.[6]

Dweck observes the growth mindset in successful athletes, business people, writers, musicians—in fact, anyone who commits to a goal and puts in the hard work and practice to attain it. She believes that people with growth mindsets tend to be more successful and happier than those with fixed mindsets.[7]

Although many of us tend to exhibit one mindset or the other, it is important to recognize that mindsets can be changed. Even if your mindset is a fixed one, it is possible to learn a growth mindset and thereby boost your chances for happiness and success. How can you do this? By becoming aware of that "voice" in your head that questions your ability to take on a new challenge, by recognizing that you have a choice in how you interpret what that voice is telling you, by responding to that voice, and by taking action.

For example, say you want to start a new business, but you're a little unsure of your accounting skills. Following are some messages you might hear from the "voice" in your head and some responses you might make based on a growth mindset.[8]

FIXED MINDSET: "Why do you want to start up a business? You need accounting skills. You were always terrible at math at school. Are you sure you can do it?"

GROWTH MINDSET: **"I might not be any good at accounting at first, but I think I can learn to be good at it if I commit to it and put in the time and effort."**

FIXED MINDSET: "If you fail, people will laugh at you."

GROWTH MINDSET: **"Give me the name of one successful person who never experienced failure at one time or another."**

FIXED MINDSET: "Do yourself a favor; forget the idea and hang on to your dignity."

GROWTH MINDSET: **"If I don't try, I'll fail anyway. Where's the dignity in that?"**

Next, suppose that you enroll in an accounting course, but you score very low marks on your first exam. Once again, you're likely to hear messages from the "voice" in your head and respond to them as follows.

FIXED MINDSET: "Dude! This wouldn't have happened if you were actually good at accounting in the first place. Time to throw in the towel."

GROWTH MINDSET: **"Not so fast. Look at Oprah Winfrey and Jack Ma—they suffered lots of setback along the way, yet they still persevered."**

Now suppose that a friend who hears about your low exam score makes a joke about your performance.

FIXED MINDSET: "Why am I being criticized for doing badly in the accounting exam? It's not my fault. I'm just not cut out for accounting, that's all."

GROWTH MINDSET: **"I can own this setback and learn from it. I need to do more practicing, and next time, I will do better."**

If you listen to the fixed mindset voice, the chances are you will never persevere with the accounting process. If you pay attention to the growth mindset voice instead, the likelihood is that you will pick yourself up, dust yourself off, start practicing again, and put the effort in before the next exam.

Over time, the voice you listen to most becomes your choice. The decisions you make are now in your hands. By practicing listening and responding to each of these voices, you can build your willingness to take on new challenges, learn from your mistakes, accept criticism, and take action.

As we have explored, our mindset is not dependent on luck, nor is it fixed: We each have the capability to adjust our mindset to recognize and seize opportunities and take action, even under the most unlikely or uncertain circumstances, but it takes practice. This is why the mindset is essential to entrepreneurship.

Study on Luck

In the early 1990s, British psychologist and researcher Richard Wiseman carried out an experiment on luck to determine what defines a lucky or unlucky person. Over several years, using advertisements in newspapers and magazines, Wiseman sought out people who felt consistently lucky or unlucky. He interviewed them and identified 400 volunteers whom he asked to participate in the following experiment.

The 400 participants were divided into two groups: those who considered themselves lucky and those who considered themselves unlucky. Both groups were given a newspaper and asked to count how many photographs it contained.

In took approximately 2 minutes, on average, for the unlucky people to count all the photos, but it only took a few seconds for the lucky people. Why? Because the lucky people spotted a large message occupying more than half of the newspaper's second page that stated, "Stop counting. There are 43 photographs in this newspaper." The unlucky people had missed this instruction because they were too focused on what they thought they were *supposed* to look for.

Wiseman concluded that unlucky people tend to miss opportunities because they are too focused on something else, whereas lucky people tend to be more open to recognizing opportunities.

Wiseman's overall findings have revealed that "although unlucky people have almost no insight into the real causes of their good and bad luck, their thoughts and behaviors are responsible for much of their fortune" (or misfortune).

Critical Thinking Questions

1. Identify a successful entrepreneur. Do you believe luck played a role in their success? Why or why not?

2. Do you consider yourself a particularly lucky or unlucky person? Or do you fall somewhere in the middle? Give some reasons to support your answer.

3. Can you think of an opportunity that came your way because you were open to it? How might you make yourself more open to "lucky" opportunities in the future? ●

Sources

Wiseman, R. (2003, January 9). Be lucky—it's an easy skill to learn. *The Telegraph*. Retrieved from https://www.telegraph.co.uk/technology/3304496/Be-lucky-its-an-easy-skill-to-learn.html
Wiseman, R. (2003). *The luck factor: The four essential principles*. New York, NY: Hyperion.

The Entrepreneurial Mindset

The growth mindset is essential to a mindset for entrepreneurship. In Chapter 1, we discussed the Entrepreneurship Method and how it requires a specific mindset so that entrepreneurs have the ability to see the endless possibilities in the world. Although there is no single definition of mindset and how it relates to entrepreneurs, we believe the most accurate meaning of an **entrepreneurial mindset** is the ability to quickly sense opportunities, take action, and get organized under uncertain conditions.[9] This also includes the ability to persevere, accept and learn from failure, and get comfortable with a high level of discomfort!

Many successful entrepreneurs appear to be very smart, but it is often the way they use their intelligence that counts. Cognitive strategies are the techniques people use to solve problems, such as reasoning, analyzing, experimenting, and so forth. The entrepreneurial mindset employs various cognitive strategies to identify opportunities, consider alternatives, and take action. Because working in uncertain environments "goes with the territory" in entrepreneurship, the entrepreneurial mindset requires constant thinking and rethinking, adaptability, and self-regulation—the capacity to control our emotions and impulses.

In Chapter 1 we touched on the concept of **metacognition**, which is our ability to understand and be aware of how we think and the processes we use to think (see Figure 2.3). For example, say you are reading through a complex legal document; you might notice that you don't understand some of it. You might go back and re-read it, pause to think it through, note the elements that don't make sense to you, and then either come back to it later or find a way to clarify the parts you don't understand. In this example, you are using your metacognitive skills to monitor your own understanding of the text, rather than simply plowing through the document without having much comprehension at all.

Entrepreneurial mindset: the ability to quickly sense, take action, and get organized under uncertain conditions.

Metacognition: our ability to understand and be aware of how we think and the processes we use to think.

FIGURE 2.3

Metacognition

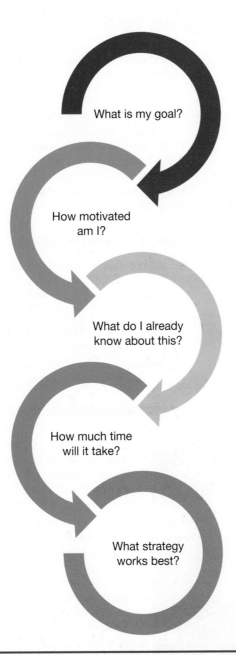

What is my goal?

How motivated am I?

What do I already know about this?

How much time will it take?

What strategy works best?

Entrepreneurs regularly engage in metacognitive processes to adapt to changing circumstances by thinking about alternative routes to take and choosing one or more strategies based on these options. Metacognitive awareness is part of the mindset, and it is not something that we are born with. It can be developed over time through continuous practice.

Passion and Entrepreneurship

Among many elements of the entrepreneurial mindset, one of the most talked about is the element of passion. The entrepreneurial mindset is about understanding who you are and how you view the world. It deeply connects to your *desired impact* (described in Chapter 1), which some people equate with passion. In the past, researchers tended to use passion as a reason to explain certain behaviors displayed by entrepreneurs that were

What Does Your Mindset Say About You?

Visit a place that you are unfamiliar with. It can be a park, somewhere on campus you haven't explored, a neighborhood, a new restaurant—really just about anywhere, provided you are not already familiar with the place. Bring with you a paper notepad and pen. Yes, real paper!

For 10 minutes, just look around and write down a description of what you observe. Make sure that when you write your observations, you use adjectives to describe what you see. For example, you may see a swing set in a park, but you need to describe that swing set. The swing set may be rusty, shiny, empty, broken, vibrant, or dull. A dog you see in the park may be big, cute, dirty, ugly, friendly, or hostile.

You must record your notes in writing, and you must observe for 10 minutes.

After you've finished, sit down and look at the list of words you've written. Circle all words that have a positive connotation. Using the park example above, you would circle shiny, vibrant, cute, and friendly. Now place a square around all words that have a negative connotation. In our park example, this could be rusty, broken, dull, dirty, ugly, and hostile.

What's the point of all of this? Remember the Corey Booker story! What you see on the outside is a reflection of your mindset on the inside. If what you see in the world is predominantly negative, then your mindset for entrepreneurship needs to be further developed. If what you see in the world is more positive, it will be much easier for you to identify opportunities and make a difference.

Critical Thinking Questions

1. In what ways did this 10-minute observation exercise confirm your existing assumptions and beliefs about your way of looking at the world? In what ways did it change them?

2. Did you learn anything about yourself that was unexpected or surprising?

3. What do you think would happen if you repeated this exercise in a different location? ●

© Bloomberg/Bloomberg/Getty Images

Pierre Omidyar, founder of eBay

Passion: an intense positive emotion, which is usually related to entrepreneurs who are engaged in meaningful ventures, or tasks and activities, and which has the effect of motivating and stimulating entrepreneurs to overcome obstacles and remain focused on their goals.

thought to be unconventional, such as perceived high risk taking, intense focus and commitment, and a dogged determination to fulfill a dream.[10] Indeed, many well-known entrepreneurs, such as Mark Zuckerberg (Facebook founder), Jeff Bezos (Amazon founder), and Pierre Omidyar (eBay founder), credit passion for their success.[11]

But what is passion, and is it really that important to entrepreneurial success? In the context of entrepreneurship, **passion** can be defined as an intense positive emotion, which is usually related to entrepreneurs who are engaged in meaningful ventures, or tasks and activities, and which has the effect of motivating and stimulating entrepreneurs to overcome obstacles and remain focused on their goals.[12] This type of passion is aroused by the pleasure of engaging in activities we enjoy. Studies have found that passion can also "enhance mental activity and provide meaning to everyday work,"[13] as well as fostering "creativity and recognition of new patterns that are critical in opportunity exploration and exploitation in uncertain and risky environments."[14]

Passion has also been associated with a wide range of positive effects, such as strength and courage, motivation, energy, drive, tenacity, strong initiative, resilience, love, pride, pleasure, enthusiasm, and joy—all of which can occur as part of the entrepreneurship process.

Passion is not all that is needed to be successful, but research has shown that positive feelings motivate entrepreneurs to persist and engage in tasks and activities in order to maintain those pleasurable emotions.[15]

However, there can also be a dysfunctional side to passion. As we explored in Chapter 1, it is possible to become blinded by passion and so obsessed by an idea or new venture that we fail to heed the warning signs or refuse to listen to negative information or feedback. This type of negative passion can actually curb business growth and limit the ability to creatively solve problems. Furthermore, a recent Stanford study carried out by postdoctoral fellow Paul O'Keefe and psychologists Carol Dweck and Gregory Walton shows that people who follow the old adage "find your passion" are less likely to try new things and tend

Consumers are more likely to get into a "habit loop" of toothbrushing when the reward (the "tingling, clean feeling") is advertised.

to give up easily when they encounter obstacles. The researchers found that "develop your passion" through a growth mindset is a much more powerful approach to persevering in a particular area. As Dweck said, "My undergraduates, at first, get all starry-eyed about the idea of finding their passion, but over time they get far more excited about developing their passion and seeing it through. They come to understand that that's how they and their futures will be shaped and how they will ultimately make their contributions."[16]

Entrepreneurship as a Habit

So far, we have discussed the meaning of mindset, the different types, and the importance of passion and positive thinking for success. As we have learned, mindset is not a predisposed condition; any one of us can develop a more entrepreneurial mindset, but how do we do it?

A good approach is to consider developing new habits. A **habit** is a sometimes unconscious pattern of behavior that is carried out often and regularly. Good habits can be learned through a "habit loop"—a process by which our brain decides whether or not a certain behavior should be stored and repeated. If we feel rewarded for our behavior, then we are more likely to continue doing it. For example, toothpaste companies instigate a habit loop in consumers by not just advertising the hygiene benefits of brushing teeth, but also the "tingling, clean feeling" we get afterwards—the reward. People are more likely to get into a toothbrushing habit loop as a result.[17]

In the sections that follow, we present three helpful habits to develop to build an entrepreneurial mindset: self-leadership, creativity, and improvisation. As with all good habits, they require practice.

Habit: a sometimes unconscious pattern of behavior that is carried out often and regularly.

2.3 THE SELF-LEADERSHIP HABIT

≫ LO 2.3   Explain how to develop the habit of self-leadership.

In the context of entrepreneurship, **self-leadership** is a process whereby people can influence and control their own behavior, actions, and thinking to achieve the self-direction and self-motivation necessary to build their entrepreneurial business ventures.[18] Entrepreneurship requires a deep understanding of self and an ability to motivate oneself to act. You cannot rely on someone else to manage you, get you up in the morning, or force you to get the work done. It can be lonely, and often no one is around to give you feedback, reprimand you, or reward you! As a result, self-leadership is required. It consists of three main strategies: behavior-focused strategies; natural reward strategies; and constructive thought pattern strategies.

Self-leadership: a process whereby people can influence and control their own behavior, actions, and thinking to achieve the self-direction and self-motivation necessary to build their entrepreneurial business ventures.

FIGURE 2.4

Elements of Self-Leadership

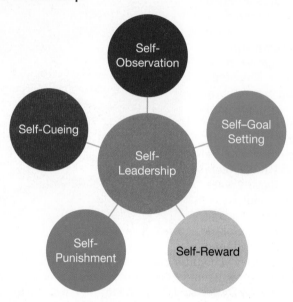

Behavior-focused strategies: methods to increase self-awareness and manage behaviors, particularly when dealing with necessary but unpleasant tasks. These strategies include self-observation, self–goal setting, self-reward, self-punishment, and self-cueing.

Self-observation: a process that raises our awareness of how, when, and why we behave the way we do in certain circumstances.

Self–goal setting: the process of setting individual goals for ourselves.

Self-reward: a process that involves compensating ourselves when we achieve our goals. These rewards can be tangible or intangible.

Self-punishment (or self-correcting feedback): a process that allows us to examine our mistakes before making a conscious effort not to repeat them.

Self-cueing: the process of prompting that acts as a reminder of desired goals and keeps your attention on what you are trying to achieve.

Natural reward strategies: types of compensation designed to make aspects of a task or activity more enjoyable by building in certain features or by reshaping perceptions to focus on the most positive aspects of the task and the value it holds.

Behavior-focused strategies help increase self-awareness to manage behaviors, particularly when dealing with necessary but unpleasant tasks. These strategies include self-observation, self–goal setting, self-reward, self-punishment, and self-cueing (see Figure 2.4).

Self-observation raises our awareness of how, when, and why we behave the way we do in certain circumstances. For example, twice a day, you could stop and deliberately ask yourself questions about what you are accomplishing; what you are not accomplishing; what is standing in your way; and how you feel about what is happening. This is the first step toward addressing unhelpful or unproductive behaviors in order to devise ways of altering them to enhance performance.

There has been much study regarding the importance of setting goals as a means of enhancing performance. **Self–goal setting** is the process of setting individual goals for ourselves. This is especially effective when it is accompanied by **self-reward**—ways in which we compensate ourselves when we achieve our goals. These rewards can be tangible or intangible; for example, you might mentally congratulate yourself when you have achieved your goal (intangible), or you might go out for a celebratory meal or buy yourself a new pair of shoes (tangible). Setting rewards motivates us to accomplish our goals.

Ideally, **self-punishment** or **self-correcting feedback** is a process that allows us to examine our mistakes before making a conscious effort not to repeat them. However, many of us have the tendency to beat ourselves up over perceived mistakes or failures; indeed, excessive self-punishment involving guilt and self-criticism can be very harmful to our performance.

Finally, we can use certain environmental cues as a way to encourage constructive behaviors and reduce or eliminate destructive ones through the process of **self-cueing**. These cues might take the form of making lists or notes or having motivational posters on your wall. They act as a reminder of your desired goals and keep your attention on what you are trying to achieve.

Rewarding ourselves is a beneficial way to boost our spirits and keep us committed to attaining our goals. **Natural reward strategies** endeavor to make aspects of a task or activity more enjoyable by building in certain features or by reshaping perceptions to focus on the most positive aspects of the task and the value it holds. For example, if you are working on a particularly difficult or boring task, you could build in a break to listen to some music or take a short walk outside. In addition, rather than dreading the nature of the work, you could refocus on the benefits of what you are doing and how good it will feel when it is done.

Much of our behavior is influenced by the way we think, and the habit of thinking in a certain way is derived from our assumptions and beliefs. **Constructive thought patterns** help us to form positive and productive ways of thinking that can benefit our performance. Constructive thought pattern strategies include identifying destructive beliefs and assumptions and reframing those thoughts by practicing self-talk and mental imagery.

As we observed earlier in this chapter, we can use positive self-talk to change our mindset and thought patterns by engaging in dialogue with that irrational voice in our heads that tells us when we can't do something. Similarly, we can engage in mental imagery to imagine ourselves performing a certain task or activity. In fact, studies show that people who visualize themselves successfully performing an activity before it actually takes place are more likely to be successful at performing the task in reality.[19]

These behavioral self-leadership strategies are designed to bring about successful outcomes through positive behaviors and suppress or eliminate those negative behaviors that lead to bad consequences. The concept of self-leadership has been related to many other areas, such as optimism, happiness, consciousness, and emotional intelligence. We believe self-leadership to be an essential process for helping entrepreneurs build and grow their business ventures.

©iStockphoto.com/Bobboz

Motivational posters help us to stay focused on our goals.

2.4 THE CREATIVITY HABIT

>> LO 2.4   Explain how to develop the habit of creativity.

Creativity is a difficult concept to define, mainly because it covers such a wide breadth of processes and people—from artists, to writers, to inventors, to entrepreneurs—all of whom could be described as creative. Yet creativity can be elusive, and sometimes we spot it only after it is presented to us. Take the classic inventions, for instance. Sometimes, we look at these inventions and wonder why on Earth we hadn't thought of them ourselves. Post-it® notes, paper clips, zippers, and Velcro®—they all seem so obvious after the fact. But of course it is the simplest ideas that can change the world.

© Kim Kulish/Corbis News/Getty Images

Employees at Facebook are encouraged to take breaks and play games in the office.

Constructive thought patterns: models to help us to form positive and productive ways of thinking that can benefit our performance.

Creativity: the capacity to produce new ideas, insights, inventions, products, or artistic objects that are considered to be unique, useful, and of value to others.

Because of its elusiveness, there is no concrete or agreed definition of creativity; however, we like to define **creativity** as the capacity to produce new ideas, insights, inventions, products, or artistic objects that are considered to be unique, useful, and of value to others.[20] For example, Neide Sellin, founder of Brazilian company VixSystem, was among the winners of the 2018 Cartier Initiative Awards for creating Lysa, a robotic guide dog for the visually impaired.[21] In doing so, Sellin has created a solution that addresses the shortage of guide dogs for the millions of visually impaired people living in Brazil.

Human beings are inherently creative, but deeper creativity can be honed and developed. Studies have shown that people who are creative are open to experience, persistent, adaptable, original, motivated, self-reliant, and do not fear failure.

But what has creativity got to do with entrepreneurship? First, there is some evidence that entrepreneurs are more creative than others. A study published in 2008 found that students enrolled in entrepreneurship programs scored higher in personal creativity than students from other programs.[22] This tells us that although everyone has the capacity to

Lysa, a robotic guide dog for the visually impaired, created by Neide Sellin of VixSystem

be creative, entrepreneurs score higher on creativity simply because they are practicing the creative process more regularly.

Readers, use caution! We are about to talk about the 1980s! A classic film called *Dead Poets Society* was a huge hit in 1989. Yes, we know you weren't born yet, but the story is timeless. It is a story about a maverick English teacher named John Keating (played by Robin Williams) who challenges the strict academic structure of Welton, a traditional, exclusive all-boys college preparatory school. Mr. Keating urges his students to question the status quo, adjust their mindset, change their behaviors, live life to the fullest, and, famously, to seize the day (using the Latin phrase *carpe diem*). We feel one scene from the movie is an excellent example of unleashing creativity and especially relevant to entrepreneurs.

In one memorable scene, student Todd Anderson (played by Ethan Hawke)—a quiet, underconfident, insecure character who is full of self-doubt about his creative abilities—has not written a poem as assigned. Mr. Keating stands him at the front of the class and prods him to yell "Yawp!" like a barbarian would do, pointing to a picture on the wall of the famous poet Walt Whitman.[23] Then Keating encourages Anderson to improvise a poem by saying the first thing that pops into his head and using his imagination to describe what he sees. By doing so, Todd is able to let go of his insecurities and create in the moment.

As Mr. Keating demonstrates in this scene, creativity is something that can be unleashed even in the most reticent person. Many of us can identify with the Todd Anderson character. It is easy for us to become blocked when we are asked to do something creative, especially when we are put on the spot. Even though we know that every single one of us has the ability to be creative, like Todd, we still find ourselves stumbling against emotional roadblocks.

The Fear Factor

James L. Adams, a Stanford University professor who specialized in creativity, identified six main emotional roadblocks preventing us from practicing creativity:

Mr. Keating (played by Robin Williams) encourages underconfident student Todd Anderson (played by Ethan Hawke) to be creative.

- fear,
- no appetite for chaos,
- preference for judging over generating ideas,
- dislike for incubating ideas,
- perceived lack of challenge, and
- inability to distinguish reality from fantasy.[24]

Of these six emotional roadblocks, it is fear that has the most detrimental effect on our capacity to be creative. Fear causes self-doubt, insecurity, and discomfort even before the beginning of the creative process. It can also block us from sharing our creativity with others because of the risk of failure, negative feedback, or ridicule.

Hamdi Ulukaya, the Turkish-born founder and CEO of the yogurt company Chobani, admitted feeling afraid every single day when he was building his multibillion-dollar business: "If I had failed, a lot of lives were going to be affected by it," he said.[25]

A Creative Mind

The importance of creativity in navigating the uncharted waters of an uncertain world is also reflected in our biology. The human brain is divided into two hemispheres. Generally speaking, the left hemisphere controls movement, sensation, and perception on the right side of our body, and the right hemisphere does the same on the left side of our body. This is why an injury to the left side of the brain can result in impairment or paralysis on the right side of the body, and vice versa. In the 1960s, researchers proposed that each of the two hemispheres had its own distinct thinking and emotional functions. This idea was then further expanded to propose "left-brained" and "right-brained" orientations as though they were personality types (see Figure 2.5).

In his book *A Whole New Mind*, business and technology author Daniel Pink uses the right-brain/left-brain model to describe how today's society is moving from left-brain thinking to right-brain thinking.[26] Historically, Pink observes, people have tended to use left-brain thinking over right-brain thinking because most tasks and activities in the agricultural and industrial age demanded these attributes. Those were the times when jobs were more methodical and predictable. Today, many of the methodical tasks have been outsourced or have been taken over by computers. Pink holds that we now live in a "conceptual age" that requires us to use both the left and right sides of the brain to create new opportunities and possibilities—in other words, to succeed in today's world, we need a different way of thinking.

However, it is important to recognize that there has been little scientific support for the model of people being "left-brained" or "right-brained." In a 2012 study, researchers at the University of Utah analyzed brain scans from more than 1,000 people between the ages of 7 and 29. They found no evidence to suggest that one side of the brain was more dominant than the other in any given individual: "Our data are not consistent with a whole-brain phenotype of greater 'left-brained' or greater 'right-brained' network strength across individuals."[27] Study researcher Jared Nielsen, a graduate student in neuroscience at the university, concludes, "It may be that personality types have nothing to do with one hemisphere being more active, stronger, or more connected."[28]

Although personality traits are not "left-brained" or "right-brained," the idea of two different types of thinking can still be helpful in understanding how to foster creativity. A study carried out by psychology professor Mihaly Csikszentmihalyi between 1990

FIGURE 2.5

Left-Versus Right-Brain Orientation

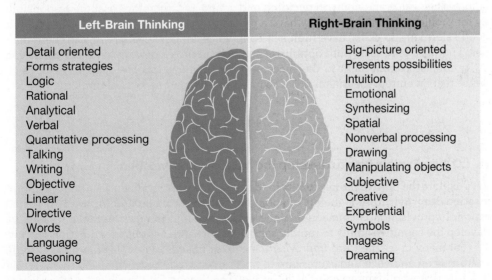

Left-Brain Thinking	Right-Brain Thinking
Detail oriented	Big-picture oriented
Forms strategies	Presents possibilities
Logic	Intuition
Rational	Emotional
Analytical	Synthesizing
Verbal	Spatial
Quantitative processing	Nonverbal processing
Talking	Drawing
Writing	Manipulating objects
Objective	Subjective
Linear	Creative
Directive	Experiential
Words	Symbols
Language	Images
Reasoning	Dreaming

Source: Neck, H. M. (2010). Idea generation. In B. Bygrave & A. Zacharakis (Eds.), *Portable MBA in entrepreneurship* (pp. 27–52; figure on p. 38). Hoboken, NJ: Wiley.

TABLE 2.1

Csikszentmihalyi's Polarity of Creative Individuals

High energy ●···●	Often quiet and at rest
Smart ●··●	Naïve
Disciplined ●···●	Playful
Strong sense of reality ●···●	Imagination and fantasy
Extroversion ●···●	Introversion
Proud ●···●	Humble
Traditionalist ●···●	Rebellious and independent
Masculine/feminine ●·································●	Feminine/masculine
Objective ●···●	Passionate
Joy and bliss ●···●	Suffering and pain

Source: Adapted from Neck, H. M. (2010). Idea generation. In B. Bygrave & A. Zacharakis (Eds.), *Portable MBA in entrepreneurship* (pp. 27–52; figure on p. 40). Hoboken, NJ: John Wiley & Sons; and adapted from Csikszentmihalyi, M. (1996). *Creativity: Flow and the psychology of discovery and invention.* New York: HarperCollins.

and 1995 shows an interesting paradox in the personality traits of creative people.[29] Csikszentmihalyi and a team of researchers identified 91 people over the age of 60 whom they considered highly creative, or "exceptional," in the fields of science, art, business, and politics. They discovered that although conflicting traits are not commonly found in the same person—for example, a person is typically introverted or extroverted, not both— they were present in many of the study participants. They exhibited seemingly polarized traits like discipline and playfulness, a strong sense of reality and a vivid imagination, and pride and humility (see Table 2.1). Csikszentmihalyi referred to these highly creative individuals as having "dialectic" personalities and concluded that for people to be creative, they need to operate at both ends of the poles.

If you compare the "polarized" traits in Table 2.1 with the left- and right-brain characteristics in Figure 2.5, you will see striking similarities, suggesting that creativity involves integrating "both sides" of the brain. In this sense, Csikszentmihalyi's study is consistent with Pink's argument that we are living in a conceptual age that requires us to tap into our creative potential and be "whole-brained" thinkers and doers.

Although successful entrepreneurs definitely do not fit into a single profile, there is some commonality in their mindset. They envision success while also preparing for failure. They value autonomy in deciding and acting and, therefore, assume responsibility for problems and failures. They have a tendency to be intolerant of authority, exhibit good salesmanship skills, have high self-confidence, and believe strongly in their abilities. They also tend to be both optimistic and pragmatic. They work hard and are driven by an intense commitment to the success of the organization. Here again, we see evidence that an entrepreneurial mindset requires more than one kind of thinking.

2.5 THE IMPROVISATION HABIT

>> **LO 2.5   Explain how to develop the habit of improvisation.**

Let's explore the third of the key habits for developing an entrepreneurial mindset: improvisation. **Improvisation** is the art of spontaneously creating something without preparation. Improvisation is connected to the entrepreneurial mindset because it helps us develop the cognitive ability to rapidly sense and act as well as change direction quickly.

For many of us, the word *improvisation* evokes images of people standing on stage in front of an audience under pressure to make them laugh or to entertain them. While it is true that world-famous comedy clubs like The Second City in Chicago offer classes in improvisation to aspiring actors—including Tina Fey, Stephen Colbert, and Jordan Peele—improvisational skills can be very useful to entrepreneurs of all types.

Improvisation: the art of spontaneously creating something without preparation.

The ability to function in an uncertain world requires a degree of improvisation. Entrepreneurs may begin with a certain idea or direction, but obstacles such as limited resources, unforeseen market conditions, or even conflicts with team members can prevent them from executing their initial plans. This means they need to find a way to quickly adapt to their circumstances, think on their feet, and create new plans to realize their vision. A recent study showed that entrepreneurs starting new ventures who displayed more signs of improvisational behavior tended to outperform those who did not have the same tendencies.[30]

Comedic improvisers in action

There is a long tradition of improvisation techniques in theater and in music styles such as jazz, but improvisation has also been growing in popularity in business and entrepreneurship. For example, many major business schools, such as UCLA's Anderson School of Management, Duke University's Fuqua School of Business, MIT's Sloan School of Management, and Columbia Business School, offer business students courses on improvisation to teach skills such as creativity, leadership, negotiation, teamwork, and communication. Indeed, Columbia takes business students to a jazz club so they can engage with professional musicians regarding how they use improvisation on stage.[31]

Robert Kulhan, an assistant professor at Duke University's Fuqua School of Business, teaches improvisation to business students and executives. Kulhan asserts that "improvisation isn't about comedy, it's about reacting—being focused and present in the moment at a very high level."[32] In the world of business, teams from The Second City are often brought in to teach improvisation skills to staff working at the Chicago branch of Deloitte Consulting.[33]

Improvisation is especially relevant to the world of entrepreneurship when uncertainty is high and the ability to react is essential (see Table 2.2).

For those of you who may feel a little apprehensive about engaging in spontaneous creation, it may comfort you to know that anyone can improvise. In fact, you may not realize it, but each one of us has been improvising all our lives. Think about it: How could any one of us be prepared for everything life has to throw at us? Often, we are forced to react and create on the spot in response to certain events. There is simply no way we can prepare for every situation and every conversation before it takes place. We are naturally inclined to deal with the unexpected; now all we have to do is deliberately practice that ability.

TABLE 2.2

Improvisation Guidelines

• Improvisation is not just for actors or musicians.
• There's no such thing as being wrong.
• Nothing suggested is questioned or rejected (no matter how crazy it might sound!).
• Ideas are taken on board, expanded, and passed on for further input.
• Everything is important.
• It is a group activity—you will have the support of the group.
• You can trust that the group will solve a certain problem.
• It's about listening closely and accepting what you're given.
• It's about being spontaneous, imaginative, and dealing with the unexpected.

Source: http://iangotts.files.wordpress.com/2012/02/using-improv-in-business-e2-v1.pdf

However, many of us are apprehensive about sharing our ideas for fear of being shot down. One of the most useful improvisation exercises to address this fear is the "Yes, and" principle. This means listening to what others have to say and building on it by starting with the words, "Yes, and." Consider the following conversation among three friends.

Peter: "I have a great idea for a healthy dried fruit snack for kids that contains less sugar than any other brand on the market."

Teresa: "Hasn't this been done already? The market is saturated with these kinds of products."

Sami: "I think it's an interesting idea, but I've heard that these products cost a fortune to manufacture and produce."

In this conversation, Peter has barely touched on his idea before it gets shot down by the others. Peter may not be conscious of it, but the reaction from his friends changes his mindset from positive to negative, instantly limiting his freedom to expand the idea further. Rather than helping Peter to build on his idea, Sami and Teresa rely on judgment and hearsay.

Now let's take a look at how the "Yes, and" principle can completely change the tone and output of the conversation.

Peter: "I have a great idea for a healthy dried fruit snack for kids that contains less sugar than any other brand on the market."

Teresa: "*Yes, and* each snack could contain a card with a fun fact or maybe some kind of riddle."

Sami: "*Yes, and* if enough cards are collected, you could go online and win a small prize."

By using "Yes, and," Peter and his friends have managed to expand on his original idea and inject a bit of positivity into the conversation.

Why don't we practice improvisation more often? Self-doubt is the most common barrier to improvisation: "I don't want to pitch my idea. I hate speaking in public"; "What if I freeze up?"; and even worse, "What if I make a fool of myself?" The fear underlying the self-doubt is the fear of failure, which stems from not being able to plan in advance.

Yet people who engage in improvisation are actually more tolerant of failure because it helps us to break free of traditional structured thinking, releases our need for control, opens our minds, improves our listening skills, and builds our confidence by encouraging us to think quickly under pressure. Originally actors were trained in improvisational techniques so they could overcome forgetting their lines on stage during a performance.

Improvisation has a significant effect on our brain activity. Scientists studied the effects of improvisation on brain activity by asking six trained jazz pianists to play a combination of learned and improvised pieces of music while lying in an MRI machine with a miniature electronic keyboard. When it came to analyzing the brain scans, the scientists found that the musicians tended to switch off the self-censoring part of the brain, which gave them the ability to freely express themselves without restriction (see Figure 2.6).[34]

FIGURE 2.6

MRI Scans From Jazz Improvisation

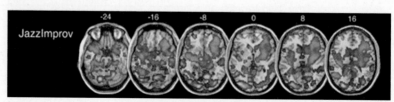

Source: Limb, C. J. Neural substrates of spontaneous musical performance: An fMRI study of jazz improvisation. *PLOS One.* Retrieved from http://journals.plos.org/plosone/article?id=10.1371/journal.pone.0001679

MINDSHIFT

Building Entrepreneurial Habits

There are four tips to building new habits:

1.   Start with a small habit.

Make the habit so small you can't say no. Make the habit so easy you can get it done without a ton of motivation. Make the habit so small that you don't have to psych yourself up each day to do it. For example, say you want to start a habit of doing push-ups every day. Start with 5 push-ups a day instead of 50 per day.

2.   Increase your habit in very small ways.

After you start small, you need to gradually improve your habit. Even a 1% improvement can add up fairly quickly. With our push-up example, you could do five push-ups a day for a week, then go to six push-ups a day the following week.

3.   As you gradually build up your habit, break the habit into small chunks.

It is critical to keep each habit reasonable. Why? You need to keep momentum going and to make the behavior as easy as possible to accomplish. When you get your push-ups to 20 a day, you may want to do 10 push-ups, twice a day. This makes it an easier physical and mental challenge.

4.   Plan to fail.

The boxer Mike Tyson said, "Everyone has a plan until they get punched in the mouth." Understand that you probably will get punched in the face at times and fail. But you need to realize that this is ok in terms of practicing your new habit. Research shows that failing to do your habit once has very little impact on the long-term progress of performing your new habit. Even the best performers fail. The difference is that the best get back on the horse, so to speak, and keep riding, keep trying to do their new habit. So, if you don't have the motivation to do your push-ups one day, then don't think, "I've missed one day; I might as well miss the whole week." This is habit-defeating thinking. Instead say, "I missed today but it's no big deal; I'm going to get back on track tomorrow and do my 20 push-ups."

Now it's time to apply the four tips to an entrepreneurial habit of your choice. This could be looking at problems with a growth mindset or looking beyond what you are supposed to look at, as in the Research at Work feature Study on Luck. It could also be getting out of your comfort zone once a day or once a week. It could even be getting more comfortable with rejection or perhaps learning one impressive new piece of information every day. The possibilities are limitless, so use your imagination.

What amazing entrepreneurial habit do you want to build?

_____

How can you break it down into a smaller habit? What are you committing to do *this* week?

_____

_____

How can you increase the habit next week?

_____

_____

Is the habit "chunkable"? In what ways?

_____

_____

Critical Thinking Questions

1.   At what point will you feel the habit has actually become a habit?

2.   At what moment did you experience failure, and how did the learning inform your next attempt?

3.   How can you apply the tips for building a habit to also breaking a habit? ●

Source: Clear, J. (2018). *Atomic habits: An easy & proven way to build good habits & break bad ones.* New York, NY: Avery.

In other words, we have a brain that is designed to generate unpredictable ideas when the self-monitoring part is suppressed.[35]

As we have learned, developing an entrepreneurial mindset requires practice in the areas of self-leadership, creativity, and improvisation. However, all this practice is meaningless unless your mindset is geared toward action.

2.6 THE MINDSET AS THE PATHWAY TO ACTION

>> LO 2.6   Relate the mindset for entrepreneurship to entrepreneurial action.

The mindset is the pathway to action. There is no entrepreneurship without action, and the mindset is antecedent to action. As we have seen in the preceding sections, the entrepreneurial mindset requires the habits of self-leadership, creativity, and improvisation. These habits create an emotional platform for entrepreneurial actions. You can have the best idea in the world, but without a mindset with a bias for action, there is nothing—no new venture, product, organization, or anything else. Taking action is the only way to get results. Even the process of changing and expanding your mindset involves taking action through deliberate practice.

But taking action requires a degree of confidence and belief in our abilities—an attribute known as self-efficacy. Let's take a look at how self-efficacy supports entrepreneurial activity.

Self-Efficacy and Entrepreneurial Intentions

Entrepreneurial self-efficacy (ESE): the belief that entrepreneurs have in their own ability to begin new ventures.

There have been an increasing number of studies on **entrepreneurial self-efficacy (ESE)**, which is the belief entrepreneurs have in their ability to begin new ventures. Self-efficacy is an essential part of the entrepreneurial mindset, and it is thought to be a good indicator of entrepreneurial intentions as well as a strong precursor to action.[36] In fact, recent research suggests that entrepreneurial self-efficacy can enable the entrepreneur to more effectively confront demands or stressors and thus improve entrepreneurial performance.[37] In other words, the research suggests that when we believe in our ability to succeed in something, we are more likely to actively take the steps to make it happen.

However, sometimes there is a fine line between self-confidence, self-efficacy, and arrogance. Arrogance leads a person to believe that he or she achieved success without help from others; further, the arrogant person may feel entitled to success and entitled to "bend the rules" to get ahead.

Kevin Plank, the CEO of the fitness apparel company Under Armour, believed in his vision so deeply that he invested all his savings—about $20,000—and took on an additional $40,000 of credit card debt just to fund the company. Thanks to his high degree of self-efficacy, Under Armour has taken in almost $2 billion in sales and has almost 6,000 employees.[38]

Like many other factors of entrepreneurship, researchers have found that ESE can be heightened through training and education.

In general, research shows that people with high levels of self-efficacy tend to put in more effort, persist with an idea, and persevere with a task more than those people who possess low levels of self-efficacy. For example, The General Self-Efficacy Scale (GSES; see Table 2.3) was designed by researchers to assess the degree to which we believe our actions are responsible for successful results.[39] It measures the belief we have in our ability to carry out difficult tasks, cope with adversity, persist in reaching our goals, and recover from setbacks.

The GSES has been used all over the world since the 1990s to measure the self-efficacy levels of a whole range of ages, nationalities, and ethnicities. It is thought to be an accurate way of testing self-efficacy levels. It consists of 10 items, takes 4 minutes to complete, and is scored on a range from 10 to 40; the higher the score, the stronger the belief in your ability to take action. Take 4 minutes and complete the scale.

Keep in mind that self-efficacy can change over time. The more you practice something, such as entrepreneurship, the greater the likelihood that your self-efficacy related to entrepreneurial action will increase.

The Role of Mindset in Opportunity Recognition

As our mindset grows and expands through practicing self-leadership, creating, and improvising, we are more inclined to recognize and create opportunities. In fact, Richard Wiseman's study of luck, described in the Research at Work feature, shows us that people who consider themselves lucky are more open to recognizing opportunities.

TABLE 2.3

The General Self-Efficacy Scale (GSES)

1	I can always manage to solve difficult problems if I try hard enough.
2	If someone opposes me, I can find the means and ways to get what I want.
3	It is easy for me to stick to my aims and accomplish my goals.
4	I am confident that I could deal efficiently with unexpected events.
5	Thanks to my resourcefulness, I know how to handle unforeseen situations.
6	I can solve most problems if I invest the necessary effort.
7	I can remain calm when facing difficulties because I can rely on my coping abilities.
8	When I am confronted with a problem, I can usually find several solutions.
9	If I am in trouble, I can usually think of a solution.
10	I can usually handle whatever comes my way.

Response Format

1 = Not at all true. 2 = Hardly true. 3 = Moderately true. 4 = Exactly true.

Source: Schwarzer, R., & Jerusalem, M. (1995). Generalized self-efficacy scale. In J. Weinman, S. Wright, & M. Johnston (Eds.), *Measures in health psychology: A user's portfolio. Causal and control beliefs* (pp. 35–37). Windsor, UK: NFER-NELSON. Scale retrieved from http://userpage.fu-berlin.de/~health/engscal.htm

---

ENTREPRENEURSHIP MEETS ETHICS

Family and Friends Along for the Ride

Switching to the realm of the entrepreneur means giving up the mindset of being an employee. Significant risks come with the change in lifestyle, and most notably, your steady paycheck disappears. For the avid entrepreneur, the risk to one's finances are often calculated, but what of the risk to those who are financially dependent on the entrepreneur, or even those who will be financially dependent in the future?

Conventional wisdom states that 9 out of 10 startups will fail (although the jury is still out on the accuracy of that number), and with such a high risk of failure, entrepreneurs face the daunting prospect of bankruptcy and poor credit before the businesses even take off. Taking precautions against the possibility of failure is a necessary step for any entrepreneur. Before beginning, it is important to decide just how much personal investment an entrepreneur should commit to, whether by using family savings or taking out loans.

It is easy to overlook the heavy financial risks for young entrepreneurs who have nobody financially dependent on them. But, the financial ruin of a failed venture has the capacity to follow an entrepreneur for many years to come. A poor credit situation and accumulated debt can take a toll on any future partner or child.

On the other side of the issue, perhaps financial stability and security do not build the strongest families. Children who grow up with an entrepreneur for a parent might develop a stronger ability to overcome adversity and cope with hardship. Although the situation may be difficult in the short term, those children could grow into stronger adults.

Critical Thinking Questions

1. How much patience should a spouse, child, or anyone financially dependent on an entrepreneur be forced to have during dire financial situations? How many failed ventures are too many for them to endure?

2. Is it fair to risk your family's financial security to pursue a dream?

3. Are the benefits of being an entrepreneur worth the heavy risk involved? Is the probability of failure too high to bet a family's future upon? ●

Sources:

Dholakiya, P. (2014, July 29). Don't fail when your business fails: Tips for bouncing back. *Fast Company*. Retrieved from https://www.fastcompany.com/3033622/dont-fail-when-your-business-fails-tips-for-bouncing-back

Griffith, E. (2017, June 27). Conventional wisdom says 90% of startups fail. Data say otherwise. *Fortune*. Retrieved from http://fortune.com/2017/06/27/startup-advice-data-failure/

Helmen, J. (2016, October 8). 3 things I learned growing up in a family of entrepreneurs. *Forbes*. Retrieved from https://www.forbes.com/sites/jillienehelman/2016/10/08/3-things-i-learned-growing-up-in-a-family-of-entrepreneurs/#6fefcb6b78c0

Think back to how Franklin Yancey started his original business, College Comfort. Alongside his friend John Hite, he identified an opportunity to make more comfortable stadium seating at a lower price than the competition by simply observing how the product was used. Through creativity and improvisation, both men succeeded in providing high-quality cushions to the sports and entertainment industry.

It is so easy to miss opportunities if we are not in the right mindset. Yancey and Hite could just as easily have casually exchanged remarks about the drabness of the seat cushions available and then simply moved on to a new topic of conversation, forgetting all about their initial observations. Even worse, one of them might have pointed out the opportunity to design new cushions, but the other could have discouraged him from persevering with the idea by saying that creating a new set of cushions would be time-consuming, expensive, and so on. Fortunately, both men were in the right mindset to identify a need for practical seating cushions and to support each other in their pursuit of the goal.

As we have explored, in order to develop an entrepreneurial mindset, we need to recognize its importance and consciously take the steps to nurture it through the practices of self-leadership, creativity, and improvisation. Working on those areas helps build higher levels of self-efficacy, which give us the confidence to create, share, and pursue our ideas. By building an entrepreneurial mindset, we are better able to identify exciting opportunities and to take action to begin new initiatives, start new businesses, and create new products and services. A continuously improving mindset is the key to successful entrepreneurship. ●

$SAGE edge™

Get the tools you need to sharpen your study skills. SAGE edge offers a robust online environment featuring an impressive array of free tools and resources.

- Access practice quizzes, eFlashcards, video, and multimedia at
  edge.sagepub.com/neckentrepreneurship2e

SUMMARY

2.1   Appraise the effectiveness of mindset in entrepreneurship.

Part of the Entrepreneurship Method is having the right mindset (or mental attitude) to start and grow a business. Entrepreneurs who have the right mindset are more likely to persist with ideas and act on potential opportunities.

2.2   Define "entrepreneurial mindset" and explain its importance to entrepreneurs.

An entrepreneurial mindset is the ability to quickly sense, take action, and get organized under certain conditions. Of the two mindsets proposed by Carol Dweck, the growth mindset represents a fundamental belief that failure is something to build on, and a learning mindset is essential for personal and professional growth.

2.3   Explain how to develop the habit of self-leadership.

Self-leadership is a process of self-direction that is developed by using behavior strategies, reward strategies, and constructive thought patterns.

2.4   Explain how to develop the habit of creativity.

Creativity is defined as the capacity to produce new ideas, insights, or inventions that are unique and of value to others. Developing the habit of creativity requires engaging in new experiences, making new associations, and letting go of fears and insecurities.

2.5   Explain how to develop the habit of improvisation.

Improvisation is the art of creating without preparation. Improvisation is recognized as a key skill not just for budding entrepreneurs, but for business practitioners of all types. Developing the habit of improvisation requires practice to quickly adapt to changing circumstances, think on your feet, and build on the ideas of others.

2.6   Relate the mindset for entrepreneurship to entrepreneurial action.

As entrepreneurship demands practice to achieve success, the right mindset is necessary for that practice to be successful. When people believe they can succeed, they're more likely to pursue the right activities to make that happen.

Behavior-focused strategies 40

Constructive thought patterns 41

Creativity 41

Entrepreneurial mindset 36

Entrepreneurial self-efficacy
   (ESE) 48

Fixed mindset 34

Growth mindset 34

Habit 39

Improvisation 44

Metacognition 36

Natural reward strategies 40

Passion 38

Self-cueing 40

Self-goal setting 40

Self-leadership 39

Self-observation 40

Self-punishment (or self-
   correcting feedback) 40

Self-reward 40

Maliha Khalid, founder and CEO, Doctory

Before the inception of Doctory.pk, Maliha Khalid was accustomed to the regular routine of having a stable job in the corporate sector; however, she eventually found her work to be unfulfilling. "Sending emails to people on the same floor did not seem like the best way to spend the rest of my life," she recalled. She needed to see the impact of her actions. And her journey began. . . .

"The context in which we are working is of deprivation. There is still a large number of people in Pakistan that do not have access to proper health care," says Ayyaz Kiani, one of the three cofounders and CHO (chief health officer) of Doctory (www.doctory.pk), a platform that connects those with little or no access to the appropriate doctors, resources, and health care specialists all throughout the country of Pakistan. Maliha Khalid, the cofounder and CEO of Doctory, says, "Pakistan is a diverse country in terms of the socio-economic backgrounds of the health care consumers and in terms of diversity in geography and languages. There are a lot of people who cannot access quality health care, primarily due to financial reasons and the lack of access to the right information. This wide range of population belong in different categories and have different needs and Doctory is working towards serving them all."

Doctory's service aims to improve access among these people. It provides a free database of doctors segmented based on specialization and location on their website. People can look for a doctor or a specialist in their locality and reach out accordingly. However, 70% of the population live in non-urban areas and need to navigate unfamiliar territory to obtain health care. Doctory points toward the fact that because every person in the country has a mobile phone with an SIM card installed in it to call Doctory health centers, services such as food delivery and cab hailing have been able to take advantage of this. However, delivery of basic services such as health has been quite late in this regard, which seems quite surprising. By taking several doctors on board, Doctory has been able to tap this market by providing consultation services to the common person on the phone. The service is free of charge and doctors answer phone calls 12 hours a day for 5 days a week.

Public health indices (data regarding health indicators created and measured by the WHO wing of the UN) of Pakistan are not particularly favorable when compared to public health indices of its South Asian counterparts. Mother and infant mortality are pretty high even when the average income is steadily increasing. The rising middle class in big cities has also led to many big "5-star hospitals" opening up for those who can afford them. People travel long distances to cities like Islamabad (the capital of Pakistan) to get quality treatment. However, not everyone can afford to travel or use the services of these hospitals.

"There are three reasons why people don't go to doctors for treatment. One, they don't have the money required to access hospitals—they can't afford the trip, the fees of the doctor, the medicines. Two, people live in far-flung areas and health services networks set up in the early 1980s are now dysfunctional. You might find a primary health center in these areas but with no doctor or medicines. Lastly, people prefer to go to a religious or a traditional healer as doctors speak a difficult language," explains Ayyaz.

Lack of trust in the system is another hurdle. When Maliha was 17, she suffered from a mysterious series of symptoms. However, arriving at the right diagnosis of her condition was a "long and frustrating experience." The lack of information became a hurdle in her way of getting an adequate diagnosis. Even the information that she received from her personal network was incomplete and sometimes outdated and irrelevant. Each consultation with the doctor led her to another doctor resulting in more questions than answers. Maliha believes she is not alone in her experience, which causes millennials in Pakistan to avoid doctors altogether.

Maliha's journey into health care started with some insight from her uncle, Ayyaz Kiani. Having worked in consumer protection for a better part of his professional life, Ayyaz asked Maliha for her feedback on a consumer protection model in health care adopted from the United States (something similar to ZocDoc). She found this intriguing and started discussing this with her family and friends in order to understand the problem better. She was not only able to relate to her own experience but every new conversation got her more excited about solving this problem of access to health care professionals and resources.

"When we started, we never thought that this was going to be a startup or a social enterprise. We just started one day because we knew that there was a need and that we needed to work on it. It then turned into a social enterprise. It was exciting to imagine using technology to work for common good and solve a real-world problem," says Maliha. She cofounded Ezpz Sehat with Ayyaz in August 2014 with the vision to allow for informed decision making for those seeking health care.

Ezpz Sehat was aimed at addressing the problem Maliha had faced when she was unwell; it was a database giving details of all doctors in the vicinity along with a system to provide feedback on the services provided. It aimed to bridge the gap between doctors and patients by improving the quality of information provided. Maliha strived to address the disparity between the access to health care and the population distribution in Pakistan, and the culture that surrounded seeing health care services. "It is common in Pakistan for patients to visit specialists instead of General Physicians to seek consultation. Since people don't necessarily know what they need, they usually spend 80% of their time and money looking for the right doctor (usually the sixth doctor they meet)," Maliha explains. This approach found its roots in the lack of trust in public health services, making access to private health care very important. Maliha and Ayyaz are working to address the problem of accessibility and affordability through multiple prototypes they built over 3 years.

However, they ultimately realized that a technology product, such as a mobile or web app, would likely alienate a big portion of the population that were not comfortable browsing on the Internet. It was around this time (March to April 2018) at a startup accelerator program in Berlin that they met Mike LaVigne, the third cofounder and CPO (Chief Product Officer) of what then came to be called Doctory.pk. Having been the cofounder and CPO of Clue, a health app for women all over the world with over 10 million downloads, Mike had research, product design, and development experience that could prove crucial to Doctory's technological development.

The focus of Doctory shifted from not only providing access to information but providing access to high-quality health care while improving accountability. It aims to serve those people that are not properly served. With pockets of the populations not being able to afford even $0.70 in doctor's fees to treat their child, the team at Doctory demand accessibility to all. In the future, the team would also like to leverage the platform to review the services being provided by doctors. They believe that these reviews could be effective in altering the level of service provided by doctors as well as build greater trust between patients and doctors. "Once doctors and health care providers know that reviews might affect careers and business, it might affect their operations for the better," says Ayyaz. "If the doctor's practice suffers because of the negative comments received, he/she is likely to be motivated to provide a better service to the consumer. This sense of responsibility and empowerment of the consumer might help transform the industry for the better."

Since November 2017, Doctory has received a great response from its customers. Its first interaction with the market was through being featured on a radio program in Pakistan. The market reaction exceeded expectations. They received 500 calls the day they went on air, a busy day for the one doctor that they had employed then! This was a good start for Doctory and it has grown extensively by word of mouth, except for the occasional SMS campaigns. The number of calls received in the first 4 weeks was around 5,000. Doctory now employs six doctors who take calls based on their availability. Usually, a call is transferred to a doctor within 5 minutes. The act of talking to a professional over the phone not only provides the necessary counseling but even helps the patients navigate the health care system in Pakistan. Through their experience, the team has learned that 60–70% of all calls received usually require nonpharmaceutical remedies and that a simple conversation can help fix the problem. Their trained doctors provide valuable, accurate, and relevant advice for their patients' health concerns—everything from advice on the common cold, to diabetes, to sexual health.

Doctory's vision is one of creating maximum social impact. The databases of doctors are available for free online and are expected to remain free in the future. In the long run, Doctory is looking to provide a host of paid services, including concierge services to help generate revenue to fund the business while reaching as many people in Pakistan as possible. All in all, the people at Doctory have found their experience to be humbling. They are able to successfully direct their callers in ways that have not only saved patients money but also helped them avoid unnecessary medical procedures.

Maliha is very optimistic about the role the next generation can play in shaping the world as we know today. She says, "Millennials can create that impact and change that is needed to take the world to the next level!"

Critical Thinking Questions

1. In your own words, how would you explain Maliha's entrepreneurial journey?

2. In what ways does Maliha Khalid's approach to life exemplify the entrepreneurial mindset advocated in this chapter? Does her approach differ in any ways?

3. Can you think of limitations you are placing on yourself that may be restricting your ability to achieve your goals? Name some specific examples.

4. How can you apply an entrepreneurial mindset to your life to help you break through these limitations in order to reach success?

Source: Maliha Khalid and Ayyaz Kiani (interview with the author, January 15, 2019)

PART II

Creating and Developing Opportunities

3 Creating and Recognizing New Opportunities

"Entrepreneurs see trends where others just see data; they connect dots when others just see dots. This ability to consistently recognize and seize opportunity does not develop overnight. It takes deliberate practice."

—Dan Cohen, entrepreneur and educator

Chapter Outline

Learning Objectives

3.1   Explain how the entrepreneurial mindset relates to opportunity recognition.

3.2   Employ strategies for generating new ideas from which opportunities are born.

3.3   Apply the four pathways to opportunity identification.

3.4   Demonstrate how entrepreneurs find opportunities using alertness, prior knowledge, and pattern recognition.

3.5   Connect idea generation to opportunity recognition.

3.1 THE ENTREPRENEURIAL MINDSET AND OPPORTUNITY RECOGNITION

>> **LO 3.1   Explain how the entrepreneurial mindset relates to opportunity recognition.**

In Chapter 2, we explored the concept of mindset and its importance to identifying opportunities. Applying what we have learned about mindset, it is evident that an entrepreneurial mindset positions you to identify opportunities and to take action. Entrepreneurship is all about openness to new ideas, new opportunities, and new ways of acting on them. Indeed, this is demonstrated time and again by countless entrepreneurs' stories, regardless of the diversity of their industries, whether for-profit or nonprofit, whether a startup or within an existing corporation. All the entrepreneurs featured throughout this text, including Juan Giraldo, founder of Waku; Saurabh Gupta, founder of Gyan-I; and Maliha Khalid, founder of Doctory, have found ways to identify new opportunities that address unmet needs in the marketplace. Let's take a closer look at what *opportunity* really means.

What Is an Opportunity?

There are many definitions of opportunity, but most include references to three central characteristics: potential economic value, novelty or newness, and perceived desirability.[1] We define **opportunity** as a way of generating value through unique, novel, or desirable products, services, and even processes that have not been previously exploited in a particular context. Jazmine Valencia is a good example of an entrepreneur who found an opportunity to provide personalized services for musicians. For an opportunity to be viable, the idea must have the capacity to generate value.

Value can take many forms. The most common form of value is economic value: the capacity to generate profit. Two other forms of value—social value and environmental value—are less understood but equally important. An opportunity has social value if it helps to address a social need or creates social good. Environmental value exists if the opportunity protects or preserves the environment. We address this further in Chapter 16 on social entrepreneurship. Startup Bios Urn, headquartered in Spain, created a biodegradable urn in which to grow trees from human ashes, to address the environmental problems of a growing population (many people don't have the land to bury their loved ones) and the polluting effects of traditional burials.[2] All forms of value, however, are predicated on the assumption that there is a market populated with enough people to buy your product or service. This does not mean that a large market is required; there are countless examples of successful businesses that run on a small scale, catering to a market that is limited in one way or another. The key is to scale the business and its costs

Opportunity: a way of generating profit through unique, novel, or desirable products or services that have not been previously exploited.

Master the content at
**edge.sagepub.com/
neckentrepreneurship2e**

Jazmine Valencia, JV Agency

Photo courtesy of Jazmine Valencia

Jazmine Valencia, founder, JV Agency

Jazmine Valencia operates at the heart of one of the most disrupted and fastest-changing industries of the past decade. She has been on the cutting edge of the music industry since the beginning of her career. In 2012, she started from the bottom at the Island Def Jam Music Group label as an intern, working her way to director of digital marketing. During her 7 years at Island Def Jam, she witnessed the dawn of social media as an effective marketing tool before it was consolidated into the handful of platforms we have today, such as Facebook, YouTube, and Instagram. Jazmine saw the changes and she saw the possibilities. "In the beginning people didn't yet know exactly what social media could do for music marketing as it had yet to establish itself as a mainstream medium and it was not clear if major players would, but I wanted to be ready."

In 2014, Island Def Jam Music Group split into multiple labels and Jazmine's entire client list was shaken up. As Jazmine said, "It was like going through a divorce and we were all confused kids." Although her job was secure, her day-to-day had changed drastically, and many of the artists she had spent years building relationships with were no longer hers. But Jazmine had skills that the artists needed, especially in this time of uncertainty. What those artists needed was help with marketing in this new world of music distribution. As a result, she left Island Def Jam in 2015 and started consulting with her clients who had been displaced in the split. She soon realized she was offering a little too much help for free. It was time, she thought, to "jump head first into starting my own music marketing agency."

It was an organic transition from Def Jam to her own business because it was easy to sell herself based on what she had already accomplished. There was no question of what she was capable of doing for musicians, and this made it easy to attract clients she had previously worked with as well as new ones. "It didn't seem like a risk to me; it felt easy and it happened by accident. I said to myself, 'Let me just go with this and see where it gets me.'"

Today, JV Agency is a marketing company handling campaigns for all levels of musicians from all genres. Jazmine leads and advises some of music's biggest artists, from indie rock band The Killers to Canadian singer-songwriter Shawn Mendes. She helps grow careers for some of the most talented musicians today using an artist-focused marketing approach to growth. This means she handles their digital marketing, social media, brand strategy, international distribution, and many other aspects of an artist's business. She credits her success in the industry to her creativity, confidence, and ability to thrive under pressure, all things she honed early on while at Island Def Jam. One thing Jazmine wishes everyone would do is replace the word "failure" with "lesson" because she feels that failure has such negative connotations. "I wish we could use a positive word for failure so people would be less afraid of making mistakes and more capable of learning lessons from their experiences." Jazmine knows that without failure and the associated learning, it's hard to see new opportunities. "Sometimes you have to learn lessons and pay the price in the short term and to realize that setbacks can be opportunities in disguise."

Critical Thinking Questions

1. Why did Jazmine start her own business?

2. Why does she recommend doing what you are passionate about?

3. What is Jazmine's perspective on failure? ●

Source: Jazmine Valencia (interview with author, January 15, 2019)

to the size of the market—to balance supply with demand. Here again, the entrepreneurial mindset is what enables us to envision how a new product or service can generate value for a niche, an age group or interest segment, a geographic area, or a larger population.

In addition, a new idea that constitutes an opportunity, whether it is a product, service, or technology, must be new or unique or at least a variation on an existing theme that you are confident people will accept and adopt. The idea must involve something that people need, desire, and find useful or valuable. Or there must be a significant problem to solve. Finding solutions to problems and meeting customer needs are the essence of opportunity recognition.

Innovation, Invention, Improvement, or Irrelevant?

Of course, all ideas are not created equal and not all ideas are venture opportunities. Part of recognizing an opportunity is the ability to evaluate ideas and identify those with the highest likelihood of success. One framework for doing this is to rate an idea on four different dimensions: The idea may be an *innovation*, an *invention*, an *improvement*, or *irrelevant*. Of these, innovations and inventions are high in novelty, while improvements and irrelevant ideas are low in novelty (see Figure 3.1).

A successful idea scores highly as an *innovation* if the product or service is novel, useful, and valuable. Today's smartphone, and the basic cellular phone of the 1980s, are both good examples of a product that meets all the requirements of a successful innovation.

Innovations and inventions are often paired together, but the difference between them lies in demand. *Inventions*, by definition, score highly for novelty, but if an invention does not reach the market or appeal to consumers, then it will be rendered useless. Inventions that succeed in finding a market move to the innovation stage.

FIGURE 3.1

Idea Classification Matrix

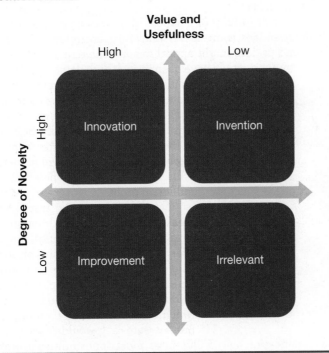

Source: Neck, H. M. (2010). Idea generation. In B. Bygrave & A. Zacharakis (Eds.), *Portable MBA in entrepreneurship* (pp. 27–52). Hoboken, NJ: John Wiley & Sons.

Post-it® notes

As an example of an invention that developed into an innovation, consider the story of Dr. Spencer Silver, the inventor of Post-it® notes.[3] More than 35 years ago, Silver was a scientist working for 3M. His task was to devise a new adhesive, something stronger and tougher that had never been seen before. During his experiments, he discovered an adhesive that was none of those things—although it did stick to surfaces, it didn't bond tightly to them. For years, Silver tried to persuade his colleagues that he had found something meaningful—the only problem was that he had no idea what the adhesive could be used for. Art Fry, another 3M scientist, had a problem of his own. Every time he tried to bookmark particular pages of the hymn book for choir practice with pieces of paper, they would fall out. Fry remembered Silver's discovery and they ended up working together to develop what we now know as the Post-it® note.

The Post-it® note took off because it was novel, useful, and practical—but it became an innovation of high value only when it hit the market. Yet ideas do not always need to be unique or novel to appeal to customers. There are many ideas that focus on *improvement* of existing products. Take folding sunglasses, serrated ice cream scoops, or liquid paper, for instance. Each product has been revisited and improved on. The products may not be high in novelty, but there is still a strong market for these products, as many people will find them useful to a degree.

Finally, there are ideas that fall into the *irrelevant* category, scoring low on both novelty and usefulness. The food and beverage industry, in particular, has experimented with some changes over the years that have failed to meet consumer expectations. Pepsi introduced a morning pick-me-up drink called Pepsi A.M., beverage giant Coors started selling mountain spring water, and soup company Campbell's combined soup and a sandwich into one frozen microwaveable meal—all of these are arguably examples of irrelevant ideas.[4]

However, it is difficult to fully pigeonhole ideas into neat categories. How can we really predict whether an idea is inventive, innovative, or irrelevant? Something we perceive as irrelevant and useless might appeal to someone else. For example, who would have thought fidget spinners would have been in such high demand? Or that Mood Rings would turn into such a trendy fashion item?[5] Or that the Slinky would make more than $3 billion?[6]

Fidget Spinners.

Even the most apparently bizarre inventions can find a home. Take Billy Bob Teeth, invented in the 1990s. Fake rotting teeth might seem absolutely ludicrous to some, but more than 20 million units have been sold, generating more than $50 million in profit.[7]

Opportunities spring from ideas, but not all ideas are opportunities. Although we all have the capability to generate a huge range of ideas, not everyone knows how to turn an idea into a valuable, revenue-generating opportunity. Making an idea a reality is a process that requires time, resources, commitment, and a great deal of work, which can seem a little daunting to many of us. But if it were easy, wouldn't everyone do it?

As the idea classification matrix illustrates, most opportunities in entrepreneurship demand high value and some degree of novelty. But how do we identify the right opportunities? The first step in the opportunity identification process is generating as many ideas as we can, for it is out of thousands of ideas that opportunities are born.

3.2 OPPORTUNITIES START WITH THOUSANDS OF IDEAS

>> **LO 3.2** **Employ strategies for generating new ideas from which opportunities are born.**

> The way to get good ideas is to get lots of ideas and throw the bad ones away. Different strategies can be employed and not all will work for you.
>
> —Linus Pauling, Nobel Laureate in Chemistry

The first step in creating and identifying opportunities is idea generation; the more ideas we generate, the greater the likelihood we will find a strong opportunity. At this stage, it's important to embrace the openness of an entrepreneurial mindset to consider ideas that might seem impractical, obvious, wild, or even silly. On the surface, you never know what may turn out to be a good or bad idea.

The Myth of the Isolated Inventor

Here's a quick exercise: Take a minute, close your eyes, and think of an idea for a new business. Ready? Think hard. How many ideas did you come up with? If you have come up with very few or no ideas at all, you are in good company. Ideas don't just spring fully formed into our minds, although the myth of the isolated inventor, working tirelessly from his or her workshop or laboratory, may lead us to think so.

In fact, as recent literature shows, history's greatest inventions occurred very differently from what we may have been taught. For instance, most of us learned in history class that Eli Whitney invented the cotton gin in 1793—except he didn't, really. In fact, he simply improved existing cotton gins by using coarse wire teeth instead of rollers. In other words, he took an existing product and enhanced it to make it more useful. The cotton gin was actually a result of the work of a group of different people who made improvements over a number of years, which finally resulted in a popular marketable innovation.[8]

Similarly, Thomas Edison did not invent the lightbulb—in fact, electric lighting and lightbulbs existed before he came along. Edison's discovery was a filament made of a certain species of bamboo that had a higher resistance to electricity than other filaments. Again, he took an existing product and made it more useful and valuable. Edison's biggest contribution to the lightbulb was making it more marketable.[9]

Many of the best-known inventions exist because of both a substantial number of people working on them simultaneously and improvements made by groups over the years or even centuries. Many sewage treatment plants and irrigation systems today use a rotating corkscrew type of pump known as Archimedes' screw, which dates back to the 3rd century BC. Although its invention is attributed to the Greek scientist Archimedes, chances are he did not devise it on his own—and even if he did, it has been modified and adapted in a multitude of ways around the world. Other inventions with long and varied histories include concrete (developed by the Romans around 300 BC); optical lenses (another ancient Roman discovery, made practical in 13th-century Europe); gunpowder (invented in the 9th century in China); and vaccination (first developed in the 1700s but not widely implemented until more than a century later). As history shows, there is very little reason to credit just one person for the creation of a novel product or service.[10]

Regardless of who is responsible for inventions and innovations, we can safely say that each of those successful products or services began with an idea. Opportunities emerge from thousands of ideas, but how can we learn to generate thousands of ideas? Let's take a look at some strategies we can use for idea generation. Keep in mind, however, that all ideas are equal! Later in the chapter, and certainly later in the text, we'll talk more about assessing whether good ideas are entrepreneurial opportunities.

The Ethics of Taking Someone's Idea

Consider this scenario: You're on a public Internet forum or social networking site and someone has posted an idea for a really innovative new product. Despite the enthusiastic responses, the person tells the forum that he wants to work on the idea as a hobby rather than turn it into a business. You are one of those people who sees huge potential in the idea, but what do you do next? If you take the idea and run with it, would you consider this ethical?

The answer to this really depends on your own personal code of ethics, which varies from one person to another. In general, your personal code of ethics are the principles used to guide your decision making and identify what is right or wrong. One person's code could justify that if something is posted on a public forum, then the poster does not mind other people knowing about the idea and therefore the opportunity is there for the taking. Another person's code could be exactly the opposite. Still another person's code could be somewhere in the middle.

But what would happen if the message was posted on a private forum set up specifically for entrepreneurs to swap ideas in a secure environment based on trust? What do you do then? Using someone else's idea in this scenario may not be illegal, but exploiting an idea from one of those members could be considered a breach of trust and therefore unethical.

The online world is ripe with ethical quandaries. One way to make the right decision is to examine your own ethical standards and ask, If the situation were reversed, what would you think? Sometimes looking at your dilemma from the other person's point of view creates greater clarity in terms of right and wrong. Seeking advice from mentors you trust and respect are ways to test the efficacy of your actions. One rule of thumb to help you handle online ethical dilemmas is this: Ask yourself if your behavior was to be published on the front page of the *Wall Street Journal*, would you be ok with this?

Critical Thinking Questions

1. Put yourself in the shoes of the poster on the private forum. When they post, is there a risk of the idea being taken by others?

2. Sharing ideas with others is part of the Entrepreneurship Method in this book. Is it possible to share new ideas and protect them at the same time?

3. What other rules of thumb (besides the *Wall Street Journal* front page test) could be used to help you navigate ethical situations? ●

Seven Strategies for Idea Generation

There are countless different ways to generate ideas—from the informal (but not very effective) type illustrated above, such as "close your eyes and think of an idea!" to more structured idea generation techniques, which we describe below.

Researchers have defined many formal methods for idea generation. Out of these, we have chosen seven main strategies that we believe are effective in the generation of entrepreneurial ideas:

- analytical strategies
- search strategies
- imagination-based strategies
- habit-breaking strategies
- relationship-seeking strategies
- development strategies
- interpersonal strategies[11]

Analytical strategies: actions that involve taking time to think carefully about a problem by breaking it up into parts, or looking at it in a more general way, to generate ideas about how certain products or services can be improved or made more innovative.

Although not all of the strategies may suit everyone, each can help us forge new connections, think differently, and consider new perspectives in different ways. Let's take a closer look at each.

Analytical strategies involve taking time to think carefully about a problem by breaking it up into parts, or looking at it in a more general way, to generate ideas about how certain products or services can be improved or made more innovative. In some cases, you may see very little correlation between problems until you think about them analytically. For example, in one study, a group was asked to think about different ways of stacking certain items. The ideas they came up with were then considered as ways to park cars. In another study, researchers found that artists who carried out critical analysis before they started their work, as well as during the task, were more successful than those who did not use the same analysis.

Search strategies involve using a stimulus to retrieve memories in order to make links or connections based on personal experience that are relevant to the current problem. For example, say you were asked to design a door hinge. Here, the door hinge is a stimulus—a starting point for searching for solutions to the problem. Although you may not have any prior experience of designing door hinges, you could search your memory to see if you can think of anything that you can associate with a door hinge to support the design process. For example, the search process may stimulate your memory of the opening and closing of a clam shell. By drawing on this memory, you could use your knowledge of the clam shell and apply it to the hinge design. This strategy illustrates our ability to be resourceful in generating associations between objects that at first appear to have no apparent relationship with each other.

Credit: ©IStockphoto.com/Gizmo

Designing a door hinge may require use of search strategies as a stimulus.

Search strategies: actions that involve using a stimulus to retrieve memories in order to make links or connections based on personal experience that are relevant to the current problem.

Imagination-based strategies involve suspending disbelief and dropping constraints in order to create unrealistic states or fantasies. For example, the Gillette team used imagination to come up with a new shampoo by imagining themselves as human hairs. Though playful and even absurd, such freeing behavior allows our minds to think in ways we never thought possible.

One of the remarkable things about generating ideas, especially ideas that come from imagination-based strategies, is that one idea can lead to another, yielding a pipeline of great ideas that may impact the world. For example, scientists at NASA have needed to use a great deal of imagination to come up with tools, protective clothing, personal care items, foodstuffs, and other inventions that can be used in outer space. Along the way, these ideas led to other inventions that have changed many people's lives here on Earth; some of them are shown in Figure 3.2.

To think creatively, our mind needs to break out of its usual response patterns. **Habit-breaking strategies** are techniques that help to break our minds out of mental fixedness in order to bring about creative insights. One strategy is to think about the opposite of something you believe, in order to explore a new perspective. Another method focuses on taking the viewpoint of someone who may or may not be involved in the situation. A popular habit-breaking strategy is to take the role of a famous or admired individual and think about how he or she would perceive the situation. This is sometimes called the Napoleon technique, as in "What would Napoleon do?"

Relationship-seeking strategies involve consciously making links between concepts or ideas that are not normally associated with each other. For example, you could make a list of words that are completely unrelated to the problem you are trying to solve, then list the characteristics of each item on the list. Next, apply those characteristics to the problem in order to come up with ideas to solve the problem. The purpose of this exercise is to stimulate the mind into making connections that would otherwise have gone unnoticed.

Imagination-based strategies: actions that involve suspending disbelief and dropping constraints in order to create unrealistic states or fantasies.

Habit-breaking strategies: actions that involve techniques that help to break our minds out of mental fixedness in order to bring about creative insights.

Relationship-seeking strategies: plans of action that involve consciously making links between concepts or ideas that are not normally associated with each other.

FIGURE 3.2

Everyday Spinoffs From NASA

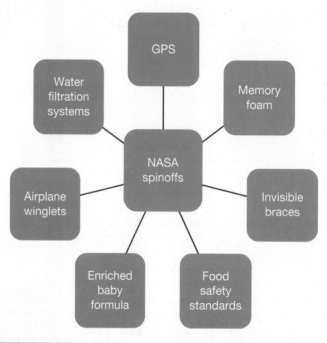

Source: Chino, M. (2014). You won't believe how many world-changing inventions came from NASA. *Inhabitat.* Retrieved from http://inhabitat.com/infographic-you-wont-believe-how-many-world-changing-inventions-came-from-nasa/; National Aeronautics and Space Administration. (2016). *Spinoff.* Retrieved from https://spinoff.nasa.gov/Spinoff2016/pdf/2016_Brochure_web.pdf

Development strategies: actions that involve enhancing and modifying existing ideas in order to create better alternatives and new possibilities.

Interpersonal strategies: actions that involve group members generating ideas and building on each other's ideas.

Development strategies are employed to enhance and modify existing ideas in order to create better alternatives and new possibilities. A common exercise in idea enhancement is to gather a group of four to six people together. Each person writes down three ideas, which are then passed around the group. Then every member spends 5 minutes suggesting improvements to the ideas to make them more feasible and effective. Group brainstorming is a good example of a development strategy.

Interpersonal strategies require group interaction; ideas are generated as a group and the group builds on each other's ideas. Brainstorming is a very common interpersonal tool for generating ideas that emphasize the creativity of the group over the individual.

The point of these seven strategies is to focus on generating enough ideas to eventually create pathways to new opportunities. Not all approaches will work for every person. Try a few and see what happens. As you try, you are training your brain to think more creatively!

3.3 FOUR PATHWAYS TO OPPORTUNITY IDENTIFICATION

>> LO 3.3   Apply the four pathways to opportunity identification.

When the famous explorer George Leigh Mallory was asked why he climbed Mount Everest, he answered, "Because it's there."[12] This indicates that Mallory took the opportunity to climb Everest simply because it was there for the taking. But how do entrepreneurs know when "the mountain" is there and when or if they should start to climb? In the case of Mallory, the idea was climbing Mount Everest, but it really wasn't an opportunity until he convinced himself that (1) the mountain was climbable and (2) he could do it. In previous sections we've talked about where ideas come from. Now it's time to shift our attention to turning ideas into marketable and valuable opportunities.[13]

In Love With Your Idea?

Find some classmates and practice this quick brainstorming exercise. It's best to have a group of five or more. The more people you have, the more powerful the exercise will be. You'll need a few materials before you begin:

1. A sheet of paper for every group member
2. A pen or pencil for every group member
3. A paper clip that will not be used—or a picture of a paper clip, if you are working with a large group
4. A timer

Here are your instructions. They are quite simple: You have 5 minutes to brainstorm as many uses as you can for a paper clip. Yes, a paper clip!

Go for quantity, do not judge your ideas, and keep in mind that wild ideas are just as acceptable as are mundane ideas. Start the timer and go.

After 5 minutes have passed, stop brainstorming uses for a paper clip and count how many ideas each person has generated. Identify the person with the most ideas—the winner!

Ask the winner to identify his or her first and second idea. Then ask the other group members to raise their hands if their list included at least one of these two ideas. Usually most of the group will raise their hands.

The point of the exercise is you shouldn't fall in love with the first ideas that pop into your mind because most people will come up with those same ideas.

Now ask the winner to share an idea from the very bottom of his or her list. Typically, you will find that not many people in the room have that idea on their lists. The thoughts we

Paper clips

Credit: ©iStockphoto.com/Photoevent

generate when we keep "digging," prodding ourselves to think of more and more ideas, are the ones that tend to be the most original and novel.

Brainstorming takes practice and it also takes energy, as it requires pushing beyond the easiest, most obvious ideas. Don't fall in love with the ideas at the top of your list. They won't be novel. Instead, keep going to get the most innovative ideas.

Critical Thinking Questions

1. Reflect on your own idea generation methods. Do you tend to fall in love with your early ideas? Why or why not?
2. Which of the seven idea generation strategies was applied in this Mindshift?
3. In what ways did the exercise challenge your previous assumptions and beliefs? Did you learn anything that surprised you? ●

An opportunity can be a new product or service, new markets, new channels of distribution, new means of production or supply, or new ways of organizing.[14] Favorable opportunities are those that are valuable, rare, costly to imitate, and fit the capabilities of the entrepreneur.[15] *Valuable* means there is a market of customers; *rare* means they offer some novelty that doesn't currently exist for customers; *costly to imitate* creates barriers to entry to other entrepreneurs; and *fit* aligns with the skills and knowledge of the entrepreneur or founding team. In this section, we focus on different pathways that entrepreneurs use to identify opportunities. Think of these pathways as steps, and as you travel the steps, reflect on how the opportunity identified is a bit more complicated and the environment in which it's identified is a bit more uncertain. The increase in complexity and uncertainty may yield more valuable opportunities (see Figure 3.3).

FIGURE 3.3

Increasing Complexity and Unknowingness in Opportunity Creation

I wanted to create something innovative. I started looking around, observed, and talked to some people and identified new, unmet needs. Then I created something to meet those needs.

I thought about what I knew, my skills, experiences, and abilities and developed an idea that matched "me." I created something and just started testing it.

I knew I wanted to start a business but was unsure what business to start. I intentionally searched for different opportunities.

I saw a clear problem and developed a solution.

Source: Neck, H. (2019). *Beyond the entrepreneurial mindset.* Keynote presentation for the Kern Entrepreneurial Engineering Network Annual Conference, January 5, 2019, Dallas, TX.

Find pathway: a pathway that assumes that opportunities exist independent of entrepreneurs and are waiting to be found.

Finding opportunities is the least complicated and perhaps most common way to identify new opportunities. The **find pathway** assumes that opportunities exist independent of entrepreneurs and are waiting to be found. Generally, an opportunity is found when the entrepreneur sees a clear problem and develops a solution. The problem is known to most, but the entrepreneur is the one who acts on the potential solution. Jason Craparo saw a clear problem. Paper business cards are passé. Most people forget to carry them or lose the ones they are given by others. However, connecting to new people at events in order to follow up with them later is essential to business and networking. He founded Contap, an online platform that enables users to connect and share information. Users can connect with one another by tapping the Contap logo on their phones when they meet. They can instantly share numbers, email addresses, websites, and any other connected social media accounts. Jason found a solution to the business card problem.

Search pathway: a pathway used when entrepreneurs are not quite sure what type of venture they want to start, so they engage in an active search to discover new opportunities.

The **search pathway** is used when entrepreneurs are not quite sure what type of venture they want to start, so they engage in an active search to discover new opportunities.[16] We all possess certain information sets or knowledge bases.[17] By actively searching these sets, we can access a wealth of information and uncover new opportunities. Typically, entrepreneurs find an area that they are interested in and then start searching for business opportunities. For example, Jen Gutman and Liz King met in the International Culinary Center pastry program. During their program, they would travel around Chinatown and other areas of New York City, tasting everything. They knew they wanted to start a pastry business together but were not sure what they wanted to do. They knew New York City didn't need another bon bon, but they wanted to turn the beloved Snickers bar into candy that capitalized on the artisanal food trend. Their idea? Recreate and make better Snickers and similar candy using high-quality, local, and organic ingredients.[18] They each had independent jobs until Liz discovered the Brooklyn Flea, a flea market for new food products. They began selling at the Brooklyn Flea in 2009 on weekends.[19] Then they set up a pop-up store for a month, and soon their business, Liddabit Sweets, was growing!

CONTAP

Contap founder Jason Craparo found a solution to paper business cards with his online platform that allows people to share their information virtually.

They developed an online store and even built a storefront in Brooklyn. Passion led their search, and their search led them to start Liddabit Sweets.

Effectuating opportunities involves using what you have (skills, knowledge, abilities) to uncover an opportunity that uniquely fits you. The opportunity builds on your experience, abilities, networks, and your confidence to act under conditions of uncertainty. Unlike finding and searching, the **effectuate pathway** is more about *creating* opportunities rather than simply uncovering them. To identify opportunities, this approach advocates using what you know, whom you know, and who you are. Your role as an entrepreneur is to take action and see how the market responds, recognize patterns, and learn from iteration to define the opportunity as it evolves. FlowDog, a canine aquatic and physical therapy facility for dogs, is a clear example of effectuation. Chris Cranston had deep knowledge of physical therapy, given her 13 years of practicing as a sports medicine physical-therapist. She also had a deep love for animals. Tired of dealing with the human side of medicine, she enrolled in a canine physical therapy course at the University of Tennessee. Armed with her extensive knowledge in sports medicine and her newfound knowledge in canine physical therapy, she began testing the market in the Boston area. She started a mobile practice to treat dogs in their homes, then she started a physical therapy clinic for an animal hospital outside of Boston, and she eventually bought a dog swimming facility and converted it to a therapeutic and physical therapy clinic for dogs. Each iteration of her business helped her create more experience, build deeper networks, and take confident action. In 2017, after 10 years of operating the clinic, she sold it to a large animal hospital in New England.

The final pathway, the **design pathway**, is one of the most complex, yet it can be the most value-creating approach. It can uncover high-value opportunities because the entrepreneur is focusing on unmet needs of customers—specifically, latent needs (needs we have but don't know we have). Design is at the top of the staircase in Figure 3.3 and is considered the most complicated pathway because of the practice and imagination it takes to uncover true unmet needs. As a matter of fact, we devote an entire chapter (Chapter 4) to this pathway! Design is another way to create opportunities because by identifying unmet needs, the entrepreneur is creating a new market. The most iconic example of using the design pathway to create a new market is the iPhone. The introduction of the iPhone (even though the BlackBerry existed) created a new global market of communication and connection. When we look back we can ask ourselves, did we need an iPhone? If the answer is "Well, I can't imagine living without one today," then you now understand what a latent need is!

The four pathways can be classified as either a discovery approach or a creation approach (see Table 3.1).[20] The discovery approach assumes that opportunities exist and we rely on entrepreneurs to discover them. Creating, on the other hand, assumes that the entrepreneur creates the opportunity rather than simply uncovering it.

Effectuate pathway: a pathway that involves using what you have (skills, knowledge, abilities) to uncover an opportunity that uniquely fits you.

Design pathway: a pathway that can uncover high-value opportunities because the entrepreneur is focusing on unmet needs of customers, specifically latent needs.

TABLE 3.1

Discovering or Creating Opportunities

	DISCOVERY	CREATION
Opportunity pathways	Find and Search	Effectuate and Design
Assumptions	The opportunity exists and is waiting to be identified	The entrepreneur creates the opportunity
Role of the entrepreneur	Be alert to and scan the environment	Take action, build, iterate
Level of experience and prior knowledge needed to identify	Low	High
Potential value of opportunity	Lower	Higher
Action orientation	Risky	Uncertain

Source: Alvarez, S. A., & Barney, J. B. 2007. Discovery and creation: Alternative theories of entrepreneurial actions. *Strategic Entrepreneurship Journal.* 1(1–2): 11–26.

3.4 ALERTNESS, PRIOR KNOWLEDGE, AND PATTERN RECOGNITION

>> **LO 3.4**   **Demonstrate how entrepreneurs find opportunities using alertness, prior knowledge, and pattern recognition.**

As we have discussed, access to the right information is one of the key influences of opportunity identification. However, access to information is not enough—it is how this information is used that makes the real impact.

Alertness

Alertness: the ability some people have to identify opportunities.

To address the question of why some people spot opportunities and some don't, researchers have suggested that opportunities are everywhere waiting to be discovered, but discovery is made only by those entrepreneurs who have **alertness**, which is the ability to identify opportunities in their environment.[21] This means that entrepreneurs do not necessarily rationally and systematically search their environment or their particular information sets for opportunities. Rather, they become alert to existing opportunities through their daily activities—in some instances, they are even taken by surprise by what they observe.

Think back to Dr. Spencer Silver, the inventor of Post-its®, mentioned earlier in this chapter. Silver was not actively searching for an opportunity to invent a specific adhesive to create sticky notes, but he became alert to the idea through his scientific experiments. He then collaborated with a colleague to create a product that would prove to be a huge market success. Silver's experience adheres to this concept of alertness that suggests that we are capable of recognizing opportunities even when we are not looking for them.

The origin of the rugby football is another interesting example of alertness.[22] Until 1860, footballs were made of animal bladders, which were blown up into a plum or pear shape, then tied and sealed. Because the bladders were constantly exploding, shoemakers were often called upon to encase the bladders in leather to protect them from bursting so easily. A young shoemaker in the town of Rugby, England, named Richard Lindon was employed in this trade, and he enlisted the help of his wife to inflate the bladders by blowing air into them. However, after his wife died from an illness attributed to contact with infected pigs' bladders, Lindon started to look for a safer option. He found a way to replace the bladders with inflated rubber tubes and used a pump to inflate the footballs without any contact with the mouth. He is credited with inventing the oval rugby football we know today, as well as the hand air pump. The point is that although Lindon had not started out looking to revolutionize the football, he was able to recognize an opportunity when it appeared.

Credit: Wikimedia Commons/Public Domain

Richard Lindon with enhanced rugby balls

Some researchers believe that entrepreneurs may be more adept at spotting opportunities than non-entrepreneurs for several reasons:

- They have access to more information.

- They may be more prone to pursuing risks than avoiding them.

- They may possess different cognitive styles from those of non-entrepreneurs.

These reasons can be attributed to an entrepreneur's level of alertness as well as their persistence and optimism. Persistence helps entrepreneurs power through obstacles and optimism helps drive persistence.[23] The combination of persistence and optimism encourages a state of alertness and readiness to identify and act on new opportunities that others may miss or just don't see.

Building Opportunities: Prior Knowledge and Pattern Recognition

There has been a great deal of research on measuring how entrepreneurs recognize opportunities. We have explored the importance of actively searching for opportunities, alertness to recognizing opportunities when they arise, and the importance of taking action to support the formation of opportunities. But once entrepreneurs have identified opportunities, how do they go about building on them?

Allen Lim was able to use his prior knowledge to build his company, Skratch Labs.

Researchers have identified two major factors in the building of opportunities: prior knowledge and pattern recognition.[24] As described in our earlier discussion of the finding approach, **prior knowledge** is information gained from a combination of life and work experience. Many studies indicate that entrepreneurs with knowledge of an industry or market, together with a broad network, are more likely to recognize opportunities than those who have less experience or fewer contacts.[25] Successful entrepreneurs often have prior knowledge with respect to a market, industry, or customers, which they can then apply to their own ventures.[26]

Prior knowledge: the information gained from a combination of life and work experience.

Allen Lim, founder of Skratch Labs, a company that provides tasty, natural hydrated food and drinks to athletes, was able to apply the knowledge he gained while working as a sports scientist and coach for professional cycling teams.[27]

Similarly, Sara Blakely, founder of Spanx, spent weeks researching the shapewear industry before using the knowledge she gained to create her seamless pantyhose product. Steve Sullivan, founder of functional and fashionable outdoor clothing company Stio, spent a number of years working in outdoor retailing before launching his venture.

These are just a few examples of how prior knowledge can be crucial in an entrepreneur's ability to build on an opportunity.

Another key factor in building and recognizing opportunities is **pattern recognition:** the process of identifying links or connections between apparently unrelated things or events. Pattern recognition takes place when people "connect the dots" in order to identify and then build on opportunities.[28] The "nine-dot exercise" (Figure 3.4) illustrates the limitations of our thinking. The challenge is to connect nine dots by drawing four

Pattern recognition: the process of identifying links or connections between apparently unrelated things or events.

FIGURE 3.4

Nine-Dot Exercise

Puzzle: Copy the above image to paper. Draw no more than four straight lines (without lifting the pencil) and connect all nine dots. No back-tracking either.

Source: Raudsepp, E., & Hough, G. (1977). *Creative growth games*. New York, NY: Jove. The nine-dot exercise is referred to as "Breaking Out" and is found on page 29. The solution is on page 113.

straight lines without lifting your pen from the paper and without backtracking. If you have difficulty completing the task, your mind may be blocked by the imaginary "box" created by the dots. Try to look beyond that imaginary constraint.

In a recent study, highly experienced entrepreneurs were asked to describe the process they used to identify opportunities.[29] Each entrepreneur reported using prior knowledge to make connections between seemingly unrelated events and trends. In cognitive science, pattern recognition is thought to be one of the ways in which we attempt to understand the world around us.

Some of the simplest ideas are born from making links from one event to the other. For example, keen travelers Selin Sonmez and Niko Georgantas were fed up with hauling their baggage around with them while waiting to check in to their accommodation. Sonmez said, "Niko and I always ended up schlepping our luggage around on the first and last days of our Airbnb stays. Similarly, we oftentimes wished to go to an event or go shopping but decided against it to because carrying bags around is a hassle. We hoped someone would find a solution to rid us of the burden. For months we wished. In the beginning of 2017, we decided to CREATE the solution."[30]

To solve this problem, Sonmez and Georgantas cofounded luggage storage company Knock Knock City, which partners with different shops to allow people to drop off their luggage for $2 an hour. Not only do travelers have the opportunity to explore new cities baggage-free, but the shops get to earn revenue by renting out unused space.

Moving from the idea to identifying an opportunity may seem like a daunting prospect, but we can all train ourselves to get better at recognizing opportunities. We do so by identifying changes in technology, markets, and demographics; engaging in active searches; and keeping our mind open to recognizing trends and patterns. And always look beyond the imaginary box!

3.5 FROM IDEA GENERATION TO OPPORTUNITY RECOGNITION

>> LO 3.5   Connect idea generation to opportunity recognition.

As we have explored, for an opportunity to be viable, the idea must be new or unique or at least a variation on an existing theme that you are confident people will accept and adopt. It must involve something that people need, desire, find useful, or find valuable, and it must have the capacity to generate profit. We cannot credit divine intervention as the source of new ideas, nor is every idea an opportunity. The best ideas are based on knowledge and the ability to transform the idea into a viable opportunity.

Let's take a look at the process that connects idea generation to opportunity recognition (see Figure 3.5). Typically, entrepreneurs go through three processes before they are able to identify an opportunity for a new business venture: idea generation, creativity, and opportunity recognition.

FIGURE 3.5

Idea Generation, Creativity, and Opportunity Recognition

Idea Generation	Creativity	Opportunity Recognition
Production of ideas for something new.	Production of ideas for something new that is also potentially *useful*.	Recognition that ideas are not only new and potentially useful, but also have the potential to generate economic value.

————— Increasing Relevance to Founding New Ventures ————►

Source: Baron, R. A., & Shane, S. A. (2008). *Entrepreneurship: A process perspective* (p. 69). Mason, OH: Thomson/South-Western Educational, a part of Cengage Learning, Inc. Reproduced by permission. www.cengage.com/permissions

The journey from idea to opportunity is important to recognize because the difference between someone who comes up with an idea and an entrepreneur is that the entrepreneur turns this idea into an actionable opportunity that has the potential to become a viable business and generate profit. Figure 3.5 illustrates the journey from idea to opportunity. Though the goal is recognizing a value opportunity, the journey starts with lots of ideas—let's say 100 ideas. These ideas can be generated in many ways, potentially through the strategies we discussed earlier in the chapter. Of those 100 ideas, you need to determine which ones are the most useful for potential customers. Let's say, then, that the original 100 are narrowed to 25. Of the remaining 25 ideas, you then need to determine which ones can generate economic value, which is profit. Finally, the entrepreneur is the one who acts on the opportunity.

Along this continuum of idea generation to creativity to opportunity recognition depicted in Figure 3.5, educators and entrepreneurs Dan Cohen and Greg Pool have developed an empirically proven method for identifying and selecting high-potential ideas that can be converted to new opportunities. Their approach is called IDEATE: Identify, Discover, Enhance, Anticipate, Target, and Evaluate (see Table 3.2).[31]

Let's apply the IDEATE method to the evolution of the modern-day gourmet food truck.

The mobile food business is not a new concept, but traditionally street food has been associated with fast food such as burgers, hot dogs, and ice cream; these are the menu items often sold from food trucks, kiosks, and food carts. Yet in the past decade, the nature of the mobile food business has changed as the street food industry has become increasingly upscale and popular with "foodies." Using the Identify stage, we could observe that food trucks are popular but customers really want more healthy options. A possible concept could be a food truck that serves fresh seasonal salads and healthy grain bowls, with a menu that changes with the seasons.

Building on this food truck concept in the Discover stage, the opportunity could morph into an entirely different concept that takes into consideration social, demographic, political, or other environmental changes. For example, given that waste management is a significant issue in the world, and islands of plastic are forming in our oceans, the salad food truck mentioned above could promote itself not only as healthy for people but also healthy for the planet.[32] All plates, cups, and utensils would be compostable—even the straws! (see https://www.ecoproducts.com/compostable_straws.html). Note how the idea of the food truck has become a bit more innovative and meets the needs of customers, too.

TABLE 3.2

The IDEATE Model for Opportunity Recognition

Identify	Identifying problems that customers are currently trying to solve, are spending money to solve, but are still not solved to the customers' satisfaction. Also identifying the underlying causes of the problem.
Discover	Actively searching for ideas in problem-rich environments where there is social and demographic change, technological change, political and regulatory change, and/or change in industry structure.
Enhance	Taking the ideas and expanding to new applications or adding innovative twists. Or simply enhancing existing ideas.
Anticipate	Studying change and analyzing future scenarios as they relate to social, technological, and other global changes and trends.
Target	Defining and understanding a particular target market, validating new ideas with early adopters.
Evaluate	Evaluating whether the solution solves a problem, size of target market, degree of personal interest by the entrepreneur, and skills and abilities of the entrepreneur.

Source: Adapted from Cohen, D. Hsu, D. & Shinnar, R. (2018) Enhancing Opportunity Identification Skills In Entrepreneurship Education: A New Approach and Empirical Test (forthcoming); and Ideate: An empirically proven method for identifying and selecting high potential entrepreneurial ideas. Workbook.

Practicing "Identify" in the IDEATE Model

Important to the IDEATE methodology is the ability to identify "headache problems." They are called headache problems because when one has a headache one usually buys aspirin. Consumers don't buy products or services; they buy solutions. In the case of a headache, the solution is an aspirin, so they buy aspirin. But other solutions could exist as well. What's important is your ability to identify headache problems *before* thinking about solutions. In this Mindshift, you are to identify five headache problems and then create five solutions per problem. We give you an example to help you get started:

Example headache problem: It's not easy to quickly exchange contact information and younger people don't carry business cards.

Possible solutions:

1. Contap (discussed in this chapter)

2. Phone bump attachment so when you bump phones the information is transferred automatically

3. QR code that can quickly be scanned

4. I look at my friend's phone and it recognizes me using iris recognition technology

5. Something connected to LinkedIn that recognizes all the people in your immediate vicinity and will send them requests to connect

At this point, we are not evaluating the ideas above. We are just helping you practice finding headache problems.

Critical Thinking Questions

1. How difficult was it to identify headache problems?

2. How will you analyze whether some of your solutions have customers who are willing to buy?

3. Do a quick Google search for your solutions. How many already exist? What does that tell you? ●

PriceM./Shutterstock

Food truck

As you enter the Enhance stage, you could morph the food truck opportunity again. Enhancing the idea requires you to expand concepts to new applications or add innovative twists. Maybe the food truck turns into "fresh food" vending machines that are in strategic urban locations and the machines are restocked daily. Or maybe they could be placed in airports, where more and more people want access to healthy food to bring on their flights. Notice now that with the twists, our market just got bigger! We gain more customers by solving more headaches.

Applying the original food truck concept to the Anticipate stage could result in an entirely new concept. Here we are forced to think about future scenarios. Food deserts are becoming a serious problem. A food desert is an area that lacks access to affordable healthy food such as fruit, vegetables, grain, and other nonprocessed food. Most of these food deserts are in rural, minority, and low-income neighborhoods with very little access to supermarkets and fresh produce—places where there are more convenience stores than grocery stores.[33] Ultimately the health of these populations is at risk. How can we morph the food truck concept and anticipate the future? Now we can perhaps think about creating a fleet of food trucks that act as "mini" produce markets. These trucks travel through low-income areas selling healthy food at reasonable prices while also educating the public on how to eat healthy on tight budgets.

In the Target stage, you could take the food-truck-in-food-deserts concept and choose a low-income urban area in which to test the idea before investing in trucks. Or you could take the original food truck concept of seasonal salads and test it in downtown Denver, Colorado—one of the healthiest cities in the United States. The idea here is to find that niche market of early adopters who will help validate your idea.

RESEARCH AT WORK

Testing IDEATE in the Entrepreneurial Classroom

Researchers Cohen, Shinnar, and Hsu (2019) set out to study the impact of the IDEATE method (discussed in Section 3.5 above) versus more traditional methods of opportunity identification. To compare the quality of ideas generated by each method, they took a group of U.S. undergraduate students enrolled in six sections of an Introduction to Entrepreneurship course. Out of the six sections of the course, three sections were taught the IDEATE method while the other three sections (the control group) learned a more traditional opportunity recognition method. Using the IDEATE method, the students were required to generate 100 high-quality ideas, or 25 ideas per IDEATE stage (see Mindshift: Practicing "Identify" in the IDEATE Model).

Because the IDEATE method is rooted in deliberate practice, the researchers hypothesized that this approach was more likely to sharpen students' skills in opportunity identification. When the experiment was complete, the researchers found "a significant correlation between the IDEATE teaching method and the innovativeness of the opportunities students identified"; they also discovered that "the students taught in sections using the IDEATE approach identified opportunities that were more innovative than the opportunities identified by students in the control sections." Overall, the researchers concluded that the IDEATE approach proved to be more effective in opportunity identification than any other of the methods tested.

Critical Thinking Questions

1. What are the benefits of the IDEATE method versus the traditional methods of opportunity identification?
2. Which method would you choose to generate your ideas, and why?
3. What would you do with your ideas after you generated them? ●

Source: Cohen, D., Shinnar, R. S., & Hsu, D. K. (2019). *Enhancing opportunity recognition skills in entrepreneurship education: A new approach and empirical test.* 2019 Babson College Entrepreneurship Research Conference, Babson Park, MA.

Finally, the Evaluate stage encourages you to take all of the ideas and begin to "size" the problem:

1. food truck with salads and bowls
2. food truck (same as #1) that only uses compostable packaging and utensils
3. fresh food vending machine
4. fleet of trucks that offer "mini" produce markets in food deserts

For each concept, what is the size of the market? Is the customer reachable? Do I have the ability to reach the customer? Do I even want to work on any of these opportunities? Do I have the skills and ability to execute them? Do I know people who can help me? These are all questions we will be answering throughout this text.●

Get the tools you need to sharpen your study skills. SAGE edge offers a robust online environment featuring an impressive array of free tools and resources.

- Access practice quizzes, eFlashcards, video, and multimedia at **edge.sagepub.com/neckentrepreneurship2e**

SUMMARY

3.1 Explain how the entrepreneurial mindset relates to opportunity recognition.

Having the right entrepreneurial mindset is essential to identifying opportunities and taking action to start new ventures. It gives entrepreneurs the confidence to network and find unmet needs in the marketplace and the ability to persist with ideas and build on opportunities.

3.2 Employ strategies for generating new ideas from which opportunities are born.

Of the nearly countless ways of generating ideas, seven strategies have been outlined by researchers: analytical strategies, search strategies, imagination-based strategies, habit-breaking strategies, relationship-seeking strategies, development strategies, and interpersonal strategies.

3.3 Apply the four pathways to opportunity identification.

The four pathways (design, effectuate, search, and find) are useful for explaining how entrepreneurs identify and exploit opportunities.

3.4 Demonstrate how entrepreneurs find opportunities using alertness, prior knowledge, and pattern recognition.

To find opportunities, entrepreneurs need to be alert to random opportunities when they arise, possess knowledge based on past experience, and identify connections between seemingly unrelated things or events through pattern recognition.

3.5 Connect idea generation to opportunity recognition.

IDEATE (identify, discover, enhance, anticipate, target, and evaluate) is an empirically proven method for identifying and selecting high-potential ideas that can be converted to new opportunities.

KEY TERMS

Alertness 68

Analytical strategies 63

Design pathway 67

Development strategies 64

Effectuate pathway 67

Find pathway 66

Habit-breaking strategies 63

Imagination-based strategies 63

Interpersonal strategies 64

Opportunity 57

Pattern recognition 69

Prior knowledge 69

Relationship-seeking strategies 63

Search pathway 66

Search strategies 63

CASE STUDY

Jillian Lakritz, founder, Yoee Baby

Jillian Lakritz's first job, after earning her MBA in 1997 from the University of Colorado–Boulder, was working on the national expansion of a chain of early childhood development centers called Crème de la Crème. These centers provide early education and childcare services for children up to 6 years old and after-school services for students between 5 and 12 years old. From her work at Crème de la Crème, Jillian learned that the most important window for cognitive development in children is the first 3 years of life, as a great deal of brain architecture is shaped during this period. This contributes directly to cognitive, linguistic, social, emotional, and motor development. Additionally, the earliest months of a baby's life also lay the foundation for all future learning, behavior, and health. Furthermore, Jillian said, "I also learned that playtime contributes significantly to this development and that it is important to make every moment count. These early play moments help build healthy brain architecture in babies, setting them up for a healthy future."

In 2009, Jillian gave birth to her daughter, Yoe. Of course, Jillian recalled her learnings during her time at Crème de la Crème and she knew that Yoe's early development needed help! "Yoe had lots of toys, but none that were really age appropriate," Jillian recalled. "Most toys are not meant for newborns. They are for children who can sit up and grab things." Jillian found herself looking for new ideas so she and Yoe could play, bond, and develop together.

Jillian started searching for play activities on popular websites and portals like babycenter.com. As she searched, she learned body awareness and sensory development are important in the first 6 months of life. One post on babycenter.com suggested that she take a feather or a piece of silk or velvet and gently caress her baby's body with it. When Jillian tried it for the first time, Yoe started laughing and smiling in a way Jillian had not seen before. "It was a really transformative moment for me because it was so joyful to see my new little baby smile. As new parents, we live for that smile—it makes your heart melt. Not only that, it was something we could do together," recalled Jillian. She also knew that while Yoe enjoyed the activity, it was also contributing to her body awareness and sensory development. Vision and hearing are the first sensory pathways that develop in a child. These are followed by early language skills and cognitive development. Sensory development is an important foundation for lifelong learning, behavior, and health. Feather playing became Jillian and Yoe's favorite pastime, but when Yoe turned 6 months old and started putting the feather in her mouth, Jillian said, "I was afraid that she would choke and this amazing activity that we did together could kill her!"

Jillian didn't want to put Yoe in danger, but she also didn't want to stop playing! That's when the "Aha!" moment occurred. She knew that if she could create a soft, irresistibly touchable baby-safe feather out of fabric, she could keep playing with her child and also share the same joy with as many new parents as possible around her. This is what inspired her to invent the product now called Yoee Baby.

After leaving Crème de la Crème in the early 2000s, Jillian worked as a product innovation, consumer insight, and brand strategy consultant for a consumer packaged goods company. Although she did not have any experience in designing and making toys, her experience in concept development enabled her to flesh out the idea. She first sketched the idea on paper, noting all the value she hoped the toy would capture. She then developed prototypes of the toy and looked long and hard for a toy designer. The initial idea was to create a character—a plush animal that had a feather-like tail. However, based on ongoing customer feedback, she made more than 15 prototypes that each tested different additions, like a handle or a teething ring. But, as Jillian says, "The feather had always been our 'holy grail.' How do you replicate nature's perfection and the gentle caress of the feather on your skin through manmade materials?"

After multiple brainstorming sessions, trying 50 types of fabrics and iterations, and early consumer testing, Jillian finally had a prototype ready to test with her consumers. Jillian also reached out to many other stakeholders to incorporate their feedback. She spoke to other manufacturers and distributors at trade shows, pediatricians, occupational therapists, neuroscientists, preschool teachers, and every other early childhood development expert she could find to help her get to a market-ready product (see image below).

High-Contrast Colors for **VISUAL STIMULATION**

Gentle Rattle & Crinkle Inside for **HEARING DEVELOPMENT**

Easy to grasp for small hands. Excellent for **FINE & GROSS MOTORSKILL PRACTICE & PLAY**

Playful Plush Character for Storytelling and **LANGUAGE DEVELOPMENT**

MACHINE WASHABLE

Soft, Feather-Like Tail for Caressing & Building **BODY AWARENESS & SENSORY DEVELOPMENT**

IRRESISTIBLY TOUCHABLE

Soft handle on the back makes it easy to pick up & **PLAY**

Silicone **TEETHER** Soothes Aching Gums

Photo courtesy of Yoeebaby.com

The Yoee Baby toy

Around the fall of 2016, Jillian finally had a working prototype that she felt good about. She had invested close to $100,000 of her own money in product development. She raised a total of $535,000 from friends and family through convertible debt. An accelerator program in Colorado also invested $30,000. Also around this time, Jillian brought her Yoee Baby product to a trade show by the American Specialty Toy Retailers Association in Denver. The trade show further validated her idea. The show had many small, independent stores, and they all loved the product. She left the trade show with 40 orders for Yoee Baby.

With greater confidence in the product, she visited a factory in China that could produce the product while also launching a $25,000 Kickstarter campaign to raise additional funds. It became one of the highest funded baby toys in Kickstarter history as of 2016, surpassing her goal and raising almost $36,000. But Kickstarter was both a blessing and a curse. She was working to fulfill her Kickstarter promises during December 2016 when there was a major fabric failure: Big plugs of fabric were pulling out of the tail of the toy. She immediately started getting emails from Kickstarter backers complaining that Yoee Baby was a safety hazard. Jillian quickly recalled all products, hired a safety consultant to figure out what the issue was, and switched factories in China—twice—all in the first year of operations. Jillian said, "It was a huge challenge that took almost a year to work through. It was one of the most difficult times at Yoee Baby."

Jillian attributes her success, in general and on Kickstarter, to her network. She reached out to people for introductions and support. Jillian passionately believes that "People are everything!" She reached out to everyone she knew to help back her project. She has assembled a very impressive board of directors, including people from Mattel, Fisher Price, and Sesame Street. Jillian hopes to raise additional capital very soon, and she is quite hopeful about the future success of Yoee Baby. "The feedback we get from new parents is off the charts! Parents love the product and are writing to us every day, sending pictures and videos of how their babies are reacting to the product. It's amazing! I love it!" Jillian exclaims.

The journey continues for Jillian and Yoee Baby. "If you really want to do this," notes Jillian, "the P-words are the most important: persistence, passion, perseverance, patience." Today, Yoee Baby has a 4.5 average rating on Amazon. Jillian has positioned Yoee Baby as a product that enables bonding through play because she feels that bonding is one of the most important parts of a parent and child relationship. New products are on the horizon!

Critical Thinking Questions

1. What strategy or strategies did Jillian employ to identify the Yoee Baby opportunity?

2. What headache problem is Jillian solving with the Yoee Baby toy?

3. What's more important, the idea or the network, to help you act on the idea?

Sources:

Jillian Lakritz (interview with Babson MBA graduate assistant Gaurav Khemka, September 28, 2018).

Center on the Developing Child at Harvard University. (2007). *The science of early childhood development*. Retrieved from http://www .developingchild.harvard.edu

Center on the Developing Child at Harvard University. (2013). *Early childhood mental health*. Retrieved from http://www.developingchild .harvard.edu

Center on the Developing Child at Harvard University. (2016). *8 things to remember about child development*. Retrieved from http://www .developingchild.harvard.edu

4

Using Design Thinking

"Design can help to improve our lives in the present. Design thinking can help us chart a path into the future."

—Tim Brown, *Change by Design: How Design Thinking Transforms Organizations and Inspires Innovation*

Chapter Outline

Learning Objectives

4.1   Differentiate between design and design thinking.

4.2   Demonstrate design thinking as a human-centered process focusing on customers and their needs.

4.3   Describe the role of empathy in the design-thinking process.

4.4   Illustrate the key phases of the design-thinking process.

4.5   Demonstrate how to observe and convert observation data to insights.

4.6   Demonstrate how to interview potential customers in order to better understand their needs.

4.7   Identify and describe other approaches to design thinking.

4.1 WHAT IS DESIGN THINKING?

>> LO 4.1   Differentiate between design and design thinking.

What pops into your mind when you hear the word *design*? You might think of fashion design or graphic design or architectural design or industrial design. All of these types of "design" represent crafts that require specialized skills and deep knowledge of materials, visualization, user interface, and front-end development. For example, a graphic designer needs deep knowledge of typography, color theory, and even brain science. Architects need skills in drawing, math, engineering, and software. But there is a certain skillset held by designers that can apply to *all* disciplines—especially entrepreneurship. These skills constitute design thinking (see Table 4.1).[1] Design thinking is a toolkit for an entrepreneur to solve complex problems *for* people. Specifically, **design thinking** is a human-centered approach to innovation that brings together what people need with what is technologically feasible and economically viable. It also allows people who aren't trained as designers to use creative tools to address a vast range of challenges. Today, design thinking has taken a prominent role in entrepreneurship education. However, use caution! Design thinking is a tool of entrepreneurs. Design thinking is not entrepreneurship. This chapter will introduce you to some of the most commonly used design-thinking tools and profile some of the biggest pioneers of this groundbreaking approach. For instance, IDEO, a global design company, has popularized the use of design thinking over the past 20 years.

Thinking like a designer can transform the ways organizations develop products, services, process, and strategy. This approach brings together what is desirable from a human point of view with what is technologically feasible and economically viable. It also allows people who aren't trained as designers to use creative tools to address a vast range of challenges.[2]

Design thinking works best at the fuzzy front end of creating something new—products, services, processes, whatever. It focuses on the people you are designing for, developing empathy for them, testing solutions on them—and, overall, creating something to meet their needs.

Design thinking: a human-centered approach to innovation that brings together what people need with what is technologically feasible and economically viable.

Master the content at
**edge.sagepub.com/
neckentrepreneurship2e**

TABLE 4.1

Seven Skills of Designers That Entrepreneurs Should Have

1. Observation
Designers are curious. They observe, always looking at the world through different lenses and making notes of things others overlook.
2. Listening
Designers develop active listening skills so they are able to identify what really matters to others. The best designers never assume they know what is best for the user.
3. Desire Change
Designers seek to solve problems and improve upon what may already exist. New products, services, and processes lead to change.
4. Context and Integration
Designers design in context. Context helps us create meaning and understanding. Attention to context brings more relevance to a solution. For example, you design a chair for a room; a room for a house; a house for a neighborhood.
5. Solution-driven
The goal of any designer is to solve a problem that was identified through observing and listening.
6. Consideration
Good designers consider their impact of their work on people, the environment, and economies.
7. Unbound
Great designers are unbound by the past and are open to the less-than-obvious solutions to problems. They ask "Why not?" when other people say it can't be done.

Source: Adapted from Gibbons, W. (2016). 9 traits of a great designer. *Creative Bloq*. Retrieved from https://www.creativebloq.com/career/9-traits-great-designer-71613188

Need: a lack of something desirable, useful, or required that is uncovered through the design process.

Needs are a lack of something desirable, useful, or required that are uncovered through the design thinking process. Entrepreneurs who succeed in identifying and satisfying the needs of customers have a better chance of gaining traction in a market. Don't fall into the trap of "if you build it they will come." It's better to create something that people need because they are more likely to pay for something they need! Fashion entrepreneur Shaymaa Gaafar, featured in Entrepreneurship in Action, used design thinking to create a brand that encourages women to express themselves while staying true to their personal values.

For entrepreneurs, design thinking is a tool that focuses on different ways to solve problems to best meet the needs of the people for whom you are designing. In other words, how do you identify new solutions that meet the needs of a market? That is the essence of design thinking, and it can be taught to entrepreneurs.[3]

The concept of design thinking aligns with many of the facets of the Entrepreneurship Method, described in Chapter 1. Design thinking applies to everyone, regardless of experience levels; it involves getting out of the building and taking action; it requires continuous practice with a focus on doing in order to learn; and it works best in unpredictable environments. Design thinking incorporates the core elements of the Method and helps put the Method into action because it requires you to collaborate, cocreate, accept and expect setbacks, and build on what you learn.

One of the biggest obstacles to trying new things or generating new ideas is the fear of failure. What if the idea doesn't work out? What if the prototype fails to meet expectations? Design thinking does not see failure as a threat as long as it happens early and is used as a springboard for further learning—in other words, "Fail early to succeed sooner."[4] Design thinking is an iterative and often messy process that uses observation,

Shaymaa Gaafar, Shay Jaffar

Photo courtesy of Shaymaa Gaafar

Shaymaa Gaafar, founder of Shay Jaffar

Fashion trends are ever-evolving and in the 21st century, some women have found themselves at odds with the modern, free-spirited, and revealing look that adorns social media and the front pages of fashion magazines. Although Western culture emphasizes individual expression, it also paradoxically encourages assimilating one's personal values into the current fashion trends in order to stay relevant. Times like this tend to give rise to independent thinkers who see things differently. This is Shaymaa Gaafar. She is a fashion entrepreneur who firmly believes that women can fully express themselves in fashion while remaining true to their personal values.

Born in Egypt and raised in the United Arab Emirates, Shaymaa grew up in a predominantly Muslim culture, where women were expected to dress modestly. As a little girl, Shaymaa never resented her culture; rather, it gave her a different lens through which beauty could be interpreted. She recalled, "As a little girl I would use all the colors to draw beautiful dresses and one day I asked my mother to help me make one." Together they sewed beautiful dresses for friends and family. Shaymaa started wearing her creations to school, and as she got older, she became aware that other girls didn't seem to have access to the same types of clothes. It was while she was studying computer science at Ain Shams University in Cairo, Egypt, that it really dawned upon Shaymaa that the fashion market was not reflecting what the women of the Middle East wanted. There was simply nothing available for women who wanted to dress modestly but also fashionably.

Although her enthusiasm for fashion never waned, Shaymaa's early career took her in a different direction. After college, she worked for IBM for more than 7 years. From there she landed an executive position at Pepsi. "People said I was crazy to leave that job," said Gaafar. "Corporate is great, but I had an inkling that maybe it wasn't for me."

After she left Pepsi, Shaymaa applied for a Fulbright Scholarship, which led her to the United States to pursue her MBA at Babson College in Massachusetts. This enabled her to seize the opportunity she had observed years before: to set up a clothing business catering to women seeking modest fashion.

While at Babson, she started her entrepreneurial fashion venture Shay Jaffar, now based in New York City.

Although Shaymaa had the idea and the passion necessary to start her own business, she admitted "that will only get a new venture so far." She received a small amount of seed money through a Babson incubator and used that money to start designing the type of fashion she dreamed of selling. However, she quickly faced challenges related to her target market. She said, "Shay Jaffar is a clothing line made for the global woman, and the end goal is to make it affordable for the everyday woman." Yet, at this stage in her startup, cash was very limited and she needed cash to fund operations. So she shifted her target market to more affluent women who had more money to spend: "A professional, accomplished woman. A woman that attends evening events and wants to be modest for any reason." Once the business is profitable, she intends to return to her original plan: "I'll design casual wear for the everyday hustle and bustle while staying true to my vision that you can be covered and be beautiful. There is no need to compromise if you want to remain modest."

Shaymaa initially tried to launch her startup in Egypt, but she soon found that the resources necessary for success were simply not as prevalent as they were in the United States. Additionally, the center of the fashion world is New York City, so Shay Jaffar is technically based in New York City, even though most of her work is done outside of Boston and sold online. Shay Jaffar is a lean operation that is very conscious of its cash. Shaymaa is not only the founder but the only employee: She relies on 22 different independent contractors to work with her on fabric and designs. This allows Shaymaa to keep costs to an absolute minimum while maintaining the quality she demands.

All in all, Shay Jaffar is a great example of a passion-turned-business. "This definitely wasn't easy. If you want to

(Continued)

(Continued)

be an entrepreneur, you need to learn to take action. It's always good to open some reports and understand your markets before doing something, but don't expect the reports and the textbooks to teach you everything. You will learn the most by taking action."

Even though most of today's fashion trends seem to veer in the opposite direction, Shaymaa understands the needs of her customers and is creating a new and growing fashion segment for women in the United States and around the world. As Shaymaa notes on her website,

> Shay Jaffar is the dream that I have been carrying for years. Today it is in full bloom. It is not only a brand, but a unique identity. An outspoken voice and an agent of change that will always challenge limitations of conventions, while cherishing the value of modesty.

Critical Thinking Questions

1. Who is Shay Jaffar's target customer?

2. What are the benefits of Shay Jaffar's current operating model?

3. For an entrepreneur, what are things that can hinder action? ●

Sources

Shaymaa Gaafar (interview with author, November 19, 2018).

Curran, S. (2019). Shay Jaffar: A brand born at Babson. *Babson Thought & Action.* Retrieved from http://entrepreneurship.babson.edu/shay-jaffar-a-brand-born-at-babson/

Shay Jaffar. (2019). Retrieved from https://shayjaffar.com/pages/our-story

interviewing, data synthesis, searching for and generating alternatives, critical thinking, feedback, visual representation, and creativity to yield valuable and innovative solutions. By using design thinking, entrepreneurs will be better able to identify and act on unique venture opportunities, solve complex problems, and create value across multiple groups of customers and stakeholders.

How do we become successful design thinkers? The first step is to focus on, even become obsessed with, who you are designing for.

4.2 DESIGN THINKING AS A HUMAN-CENTERED PROCESS

>> **LO 4.2**   **Demonstrate design thinking as a human-centered process focusing on customers and their needs.**

Tim Brown, CEO of the design firm IDEO

Typically, when new ideas are being vetted, we often jump to answer two questions: Can it be done? and Will it make money? But human-centered design thinking involves a different starting point in the creation process. The starting question focuses on humans: What do people need?[5]

As previously mentioned, IDEO has popularized design thinking and is featured several times in this chapter to illustrate design thinking in action. IDEO takes on all sorts of diverse design challenges—from developing new ways to optimize health care, to designing advertising campaigns, to finding different approaches to education, to designing new businesses. The CEO of IDEO, Tim Brown, credits one key phrase for sparking the design-thinking process: "How might we?" The "how" part presumes that the solutions to the problems already exist and they just need to be unearthed; the "might" part suggests that it is possible to put out ideas that may or may not work; and the "we" part means that the process will be a fruitful and collaborative one.[6] In short, "How might we?" encourages the design thinker to believe that anything is possible.

FIGURE 4.1

Intersection of Desirability, Feasibility, and Viability

Human-Centered Approach

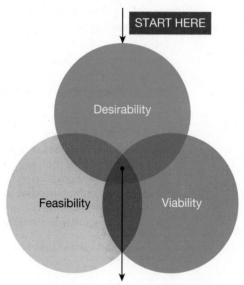

Final solutions should be at the intersection.

Source: IDEO. (2015). *The field guide to human-centered design.* San Francisco, CA: Author. Retrieved from http://d1r3w4d5z5a88i.cloudfront.net/assets/guide/Field%20Guide%20to%20Human-Centered%20Design_IDEOorg_English-ee47a1ed4b91f3252115b83152828d7e.pdf

Design thinkers welcome constraints and see them as opportunities to identify innovative solutions. An idea is deemed successful if it strikes a balance among three main criteria (see Figure 4.1):

- Feasibility—what can possibly be achieved in the near future?

- Viability—how sustainable is the idea in the long term?

- Desirability—who will want to use or buy the product or service?

The starting point is desirability—what do people need? It's not about building a new product and service and then searching for customers. It's about going to customers first, determining their needs, and then creating something to meet their needs. Even if you don't know who your customers are yet, find an opportunity space, a space that you are interested in, and watch and learn from people in this space to uncover needs. Remember, if you meet the needs of people, you are more likely to have customers.

Because design thinking is human centered, the focus is on what designers call "users." Users are those you are designing for. They are called "users" more often than "customers" because the users are not necessarily the buyer of the solution. For example, when IDEO was tasked by a medical device manufacturer to design a new device nurses could use to enter data before a surgical procedure, the client visualized an iPad-style device that the nurses would hold with two hands. Yet, when the IDEO team observed nurses (the users, in this case) during a standard medical procedure, they realized immediately that a two-handed device would not work because most nurses tend to hold the hand of patients who are anxious about undergoing surgery. Handling a two-handed device would not allow them to offer this comfort.[7] This is what's meant by design thinking being human centered. The IDEO team observed the nurses—the humans or users—to uncover the real need.

Design Thinking Is a Social Technology

Professor Jeanne Liedtka at the Darden School of Business calls design thinking a "social technology" (see Table 4.2) because design thinking is leading to significant improvements in how we work and innovate. Liedtka evaluated 50 projects from a range of sectors and types of businesses (startups, NGOs, corporations) over a 7-year period. She discovered that from business and health care to social services, design thinking was changing how organizations approached and participated in innovation. She found that design thinking unleashed the creativity and imagination of people in ways she had not seen before. Design thinking and the tools associated with design thinking (user research, empathy, testing, and experimentation) helped teams break free of the fears and biases associated with working in new spaces. The structure of design thinking creates a system to explore problems in a human-centric way as well as permission to participate at all levels of the innovation process. As Liedtka concludes,

> Recognizing organizations as collections of human beings who are motivated by varying perspectives and emotions, design thinking emphasizes engagement, dialogue, and learning. By involving customers and other stakeholders in the definition of the problem and the development of solutions, design thinking garners a broad commitment to change. And by supplying a structure to the innovation process, design thinking helps innovators collaborate and agree on what is essential to the outcomes at every phase. *That* is social technology at work. (p. 79)

Source: Liedtka, J. (2018, September-October). Why design thinking works. *Harvard Business Review*, 72–79.

TABLE 4.2

Design Thinking as a Social Technology

PROBLEM	DESIGN THINKING	IMPROVED OUTCOME
Entrepreneurs are either trapped by their own expertise and experience or they have no expertise and experience.	Provides immersion in the user's experience	A better understanding of their customer and who they are designing for
Entrepreneurs are overwhelmed by the amount of data.	Makes sense of the data by organizing it into themes, patterns, and surprises	Leads to new insights, possibilities, and opportunities
Entrepreneurs are divided by different perspectives on the team.	Builds alignment because data and insights from actual users or customers don't lie	Convergence around what matters most to users and what their needs are
Entrepreneurs are confronted by too many ideas or ideas that are not innovative.	Encourages the emergence of fresh ideas and approaches, given the focus on customer inquiry and empathic understanding	A diverse set of potential new solutions that would not otherwise have been developed
Entrepreneurs lack feedback from users and may have the mentality of "if you build it they will come."	Offers user testing through very rough and early prototypes	Accurate feedback at a low cost that conveys what's most important to users
Entrepreneurs are afraid of uncertainty and ambiguity.	Delivers learning in action as experiments engage all stakeholders	A shared commitment and confidence in the desirability, viability, and feasibility of the idea

Source: Liedtka, Jeanne (2018). Why Design Thinking Works. Harvard Business Review, September-October. pp. 72–79.

Critical Thinking Questions

1. Given the definition of social technology provided above, can you identify other examples of social technology that emerged before or during your lifetime?

2. Why has design thinking helped so many people engage in the creative process?

3. Why are entrepreneurs, in particular, benefiting from design thinking as a social technology? ●

Rise Science, a sleep analytics startup that empowers elite performance from athletes, approached IDEO to help scale and rebrand the business and optimize its sleep training system for its customers.[8] The IDEO team collaborated with the Rise Science team to identify opportunities for change, particularly when it came to Rise Science's impersonal approach to onboarding customers to the new system. By the end of the process, IDEO had come up with the following strategy: A Rise Science employee introduces players and coaches to the value of sleep training. Players who agree to take part in the program receive a sleep-training kit, which includes a personalized sleep plan (designed according to their age, game schedule, and training load); a part-human, part-machine sleep coach that monitors progress and provides feedback; and sleeping products such as sleep masks and bed sensors. After just 1 week of using the freshly designed program, 97% of players reported getting almost an extra hour of quality sleep at night. Thanks to the new approach, the Chicago Bulls, Miami Dolphins, and the University of West Virginia have since signed up to Rise Science. By introducing a human element to the system, Rise Science was able to engage its target customer base from the very beginning.

The human approach ethos is not based just on thinking about what people need, but on exploring how they behave, asking them what they think, and empathizing with how they feel. By truly understanding the emotional and cultural realities of the people for whom you are designing, you will be more able to design a better solution with real value. This is why empathy is so important to the design process.

4.3 DESIGN THINKING REQUIRES EMPATHY

>> LO 4.3   Describe the role of empathy in the design-thinking process.

Empathy is an essential skill for design thinkers and connects to both observation and listening. Developing our empathic ability allows us to better understand not only *how* people do things but *why*; their physical and emotional needs; the way they think and feel; and what is important to them.[9] In other words, to create meaningful solutions that people will buy, we need to know and care about the people who are using them.

We all have the ability to practice empathy, but how do we actually do it? The answer lies in observation, engaging people in conversation or interviewing, and watching and listening.[10] When the design thinkers at IDEO were approached by Dean Logan, county clerk for Los Angeles, to redesign the voting system, they jumped at the challenge. Los Angeles is the biggest voting jurisdiction in the United States, with a voter population that speaks more than a dozen languages. Logan wanted to make the voting system more accessible and to encourage more people to come to the ballot box.[11]

IDEO quickly realized that this wasn't a case of simply redesigning the voting system; it had more to do with using empathy to understand the complex social networks underlying the act of voting. To that end, the IDEO team spent hundreds of hours observing, listening to, and interviewing people in an effort to understand the motivations behind voting. They met with people who suffered disabilities that prevented them from going to the ballot box and sought solutions to making voting more accessible—even Stevie Wonder took part in the testing and offered his advice. But the IDEO team didn't just stop with the voting community; they observed the people who delivered the voting machines to almost 5,000 polling locations and interviewed the volunteers who assembled the

©Rob Crandall/Shutterstock

Old voting booth that IDEO is working to replace.

Empathy as an Ethical Challenge

Embrace baby warmer sleeping bag for babies, created by Stanford students

The practice of design thinking is fundamentally human centered and requires the innovator to uncover the feelings and actions of users as they experience a particular problem. These elements of empathy and user engagement make design thinking an inherently ethical endeavor. What could arouse more empathy than the death of an infant? Yet in developing countries, many premature and low-birthweight babies die from lack of warmth, or hypothermia. Is it ethical to turn a blind eye to these tragic deaths?

As a class project, Stanford graduate students Rahul Panicker, Jane Chen, Linus Liang, and Naganand Murty had been designing an intervention for at-risk babies that was low enough in cost to be used in developing countries. Their specific challenge was to create one that cost less than 1% of the cost of a state-of-the-art neonatal incubator. But when they created a prototype, collaborative field testing in Nepal with village families proved that the incubators were impractical because the families for whom the design was created lacked electricity. During their field testing, the students determined that the cold Nepal winters and limited heat sources resulted in frequent incidents of fatal hypothermia for low-birthweight babies.

Consequently, the students abandoned their electricity-powered incubator design. Instead, they began brainstorming creative solutions for a baby-warming device that didn't require electricity. The students eventually designed what looks like an infant-size sleeping bag. The bag is made of phase-change material that, after being heated, maintains its warmth for up to 6 hours, helping parents in remote villages give their vulnerable infants a chance to survive. Within 2 years of its pilot in 2011, the Embrace baby warmer had helped some 39,000 at-risk babies.

Critical Thinking Questions

1. How can you design collaboratively and inclusively when resources are highly unequal?

2. Design thinking requires incorporation of user feedback and possibly scrapping your original designs. Have you ever had to throw away work you've spent weeks or months on and start over? Would you perceive this as progress or failure?

3. Provide an example of a time when empathy, or an emotional desire to help solve a problem, prompted you to think creatively. What did you do? What were the results? ●

Sources

Bajaj, H. (2014, March 13). *How to boost your innovation and stand out from the competition.* Retrieved from http://yourstory.com/2014/03/design-thinking-entrepreneurs/

Burnette, C. (2013, September 2). *The morals and ethics of a theory of design thinking.* Retrieved from http://www.academia.edu/4390557/The_Morals_and_Ethics_of_A_Theory_of_Design_Thinking

Embrace. (2019). *About us.* Retrieved from http://embraceglobal.org/about-us/

Fabian, C., & Fabricant, R. (2014, August 5). The ethics of innovation: An ethical framework can bridge the worlds of startup technology and international development to strengthen cross-sector innovation in the social sector. *Stanford Social Innovation Review.* Retrieved from http://ssir.org/articles/entry/the_ethics_of_innovation

Rodriguez, D., & Jacoby, R. (2007, May 16). *Embracing risk to grow and innovate.* Retrieved from http://www.bloomberg.com/bw/stories/2007-05-16/embracing-risk-to-grow-and-innovatebusinessweek-business-news-stock-market-and-financial-advice

Soule, S. A. (2013, December 30). How design thinking can help social entrepreneurs. *Stanford Business Graduate School.* Retrieved from http://www.gsb.stanford.edu/insights/sarah-soule-how-design-thinking-can-help-social-entrepreneurs

machines when they arrived, identifying any obstacles along the way. They combined all their findings with a review of issues relating to security and privacy and the complex nature of the regulatory environment.

Based on this research, the team created a working model based on a set of design principles guided by a single philosophy: One machine for all. IDEO will find out during the 2020 elections whether its new and improved voting devices will encourage more people to vote.

Although rationalism and analytical techniques are important when creating products and services, as we have seen, design thinking is very much a human-centered approach and looks at the emotional as well as the functional side of problems. For example, it allows us to put ourselves in the shoes of people who live with disabilities and think about how to make the voting experience a little easier. There are many ways in which we can use empathy to relate to the people around us. To encourage students to empathize with older people, researchers at the Massachusetts Institute of Technology (MIT) created the AGNES suit (Age Gain Now Empathy Suit), which is designed for the wearer to experience the physical discomfort that many elderly people have to deal with every day, such as joint stiffness, poor posture, bad eyesight and hearing, and lack of balance.[12] This is a very powerful means to encourage people to empathize with older people, in order to identify their needs. Given that our aging population is growing, there is ample opportunity for entrepreneurs to consider ways in which they can make the lives of the elderly more comfortable. This is yet another example of how empathy is one of the key elements of the design-thinking process used to solve complex problems and identify needs. As the previous examples have demonstrated, to develop empathy, design thinkers make use of two primary tools, interviewing and observation, which we will explore in greater depth later in this chapter. But first, let's take a look at the key phases of the design-thinking process.

4.4 THE DESIGN-THINKING PROCESS: INSPIRATION, IDEATION, IMPLEMENTATION

>> **LO 4.4** **Illustrate the key phases of the design-thinking process.**

In this section, we explore IDEO's version of the design-thinking process and its effectiveness in designing solutions. IDEO looks at the design-thinking process as a system of overlapping phases, rather than a linear process of going from step 1 to step 2 to step 3 and so on. The IDEO approach combines the power of empathy, creativity, and action and consists of three main phases: inspiration, ideation, and implementation (see Table 4.3).

The design-thinking process is based on two main types of thinking: divergence and convergence. **Divergent thinking** allows us to expand our view of the world to generate as many ideas as possible without being trapped by traditional problem-solving methods or predetermined constraints. This is a concept similar to the practice of play, which frees the imagination, opens up our minds to a wealth of opportunities and possibilities, and helps us to become more innovative. In fact, IDEO builds its whole culture around play and creating a fun environment for people to work in.[13]

The second type of thinking, **convergent thinking**, allows us to narrow down the number of ideas generated through divergent thinking in an effort to identify which ones have the most potential. These ways of thinking allow us to move from openness to understanding, from abstract to concrete, and from what is to what can be. Figure 4.2 incorporates these two types of thinking with the three phases of design thinking.

Let's explore the three phases of design thinking—inspiration, ideation, and implementation—in further detail.

Inspiration

The **inspiration** phase involves two primary tasks: defining the design challenge and learning about the users you are designing for. The design challenge is the problem that stimulates the quest for a solution. It starts with a problem that is neither too narrow

Divergent thinking: a thought process that allows us to expand our view of the world to generate as many ideas as possible without being trapped by traditional problem-solving methods or predetermined constraints.

Convergent thinking: a thought process that allows us to narrow down the number of ideas generated through divergent thinking in an effort to identify which ones have the most potential.

Inspiration: the first phase of design thinking, when you develop the design challenge and acquire a deeper understanding of users.

TABLE 4.3	

Design Thinking Phases and Outcomes

DESIGN THINKING PHASE	OUTCOME
Inspiration	Design challenge and user needs
Ideation	Potential solutions to meet needs
Implementation	Prototyping and testing solutions

FIGURE 4.2

IDEO's Three Phases of Design Thinking

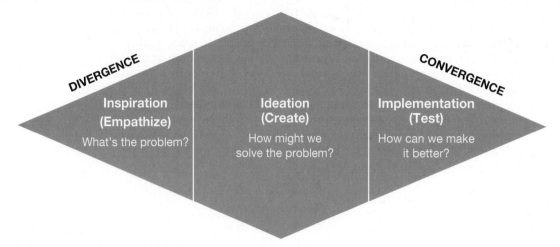

DIVERGENCE

CONVERGENCE

**Inspiration
(Empathize)**

What's the problem?

**Ideation
(Create)**

How might we
solve the problem?

**Implementation
(Test)**

How can we make
it better?

Reaching is considered
a need while *a ladder* is
considered a solution.

nor too broad and is framed in "How might we?" terms. We say neither too narrow nor too broad because a problem that is too narrow will not give you the freedom to create something innovative. Conversely, if the problem is too broad, there are no boundaries and it can be unwieldy or difficult to get started. Finding this sweet spot between broad and narrow is difficult, so some examples are offered.

Think about completing the "How might we?" question as you develop your design challenge statement. Here are some examples:

- How might we enhance the entrepreneurship education experience of students?

- How might we improve how the elderly live independently?

- How might we redesign how adults learn in virtual worlds?

- How might we reimagine how people get around in a town without cars?

Note that each of the design challenges above focus on a human, such as students, elderly people, adult learners, or people living in high-traffic, urban areas. Again, they are called "users." But in addition to defining the design challenge, we need to learn something about the users we hope to design for.

Let's imagine we are working on the following design challenge: How might we improve the customer experience in grocery stores? One way of understanding the users better is to observe and interview store customers while they are actually shopping in a grocery store. We'll talk more about observation and interviewing shortly, but for now let's imagine that you see a woman in a grocery store trying to reach something on a high shelf. You might conclude, "Hey, this woman needs a ladder." If you're thinking incrementally, next you may think about the type of ladder she needs. What if the woman is 80 years old? What does that ladder look like?

Now let's look at this from a broader perspective and help you think more creatively. Rather than simply saying the woman needs a ladder, what if we said, "How might we help customers reach products on a high shelf?"[14] Focusing on the needs that were uncovered through observing sets the stage for thinking creatively. By observing that woman trying to reach a high shelf in the store and not jumping too soon to solutions, we might come up with much more innovative ideas, such as robots, mini-elevators, or moving shelves. A simple way to think about needs versus solutions is that needs are verbs and solutions are nouns.[15] *Ladder* is a noun but *to reach* is a verb. In this phase of design thinking, we are *only* concerned with needs. No solutions at this point, please! It's too soon in the process.

Designers actively observe people in their environments to identify their real needs. By observing the actual experiences of real people as they go through their daily lives, entrepreneurs are able to imagine themselves in the shoes of the people for whom they are designing. This gives them an opportunity to develop empathy to better identify needs and, ultimately, develop solutions. It is also an excellent way to see the world differently in order to capitalize on potential opportunities that others have not yet recognized. This relates to the concept of alertness introduced in Chapter 3.

The inspiration phase of the design-thinking process is particularly useful for uncovering latent needs. **Latent needs** are needs we have but don't know we have. For example, we didn't know we needed an iPad or an iPhone until we held one. The late Steve Jobs, Apple CEO, was very good at identifying latent needs of customers, and he possessed great observation skills, yet he was often criticized for not talking to his customers. Latent needs are more easily identified by observing rather than talking because people can't always articulate what they really need. Additionally, if you can create solutions to meet latent needs, they are sometimes the most innovative, market-creating solutions.

Latent needs: needs we don't know we have.

MINDSHIFT

Needs Are Verbs; Solutions Are Nouns

Entrepreneurs too quickly jump to solutions without first considering the needs of customers. The example used in this chapter of the woman reaching something on a high shelf immediately makes us think she needs a ladder. If we jump to the solution too fast, we might miss something really innovative. Below are some examples of needs versus solutions:

NEED (VERB)	SOLUTIONS (NOUNS)
Relieve my aching back.	massage, better chair, shoes with special soles
Expand my professional network.	attend a conference, LinkedIn, set up informational interviews
Feed my dog when I'm not at home.	robot, professional pet sitter, auto-feeder

As you can see from these examples, one need can lead to multiple solutions. Now it's time for you to practice writing needs as verbs and solutions as nouns.

Walk around a place for 30 minutes (no more and no less!). You can walk around campus, a mall, in the city, around a farm, wherever you want. You are to only look for needs in the form of verbs! To complete this Mindshift you need to record five needs and at least five solutions (existing or new) to meet those needs.

Critical Thinking Questions

1. How did reframing a need as a verb impact how you viewed the world?

2. Why do we jump to solutions so quickly without first considering needs? ●

Ideation

The second phase of the design-thinking process is **ideation**, which involves generating and developing new ideas to address needs (or latent needs), based on observations made during the inspiration process. Ideation is where empathy and creativity interact to generate solutions!

Ideation: a creative process that involves generating and developing new ideas to address needs.

The ideation process is in line with the creation view described in Chapter 1 as it requires a general openness to the world and involves using our creative ability to solve problems. This is also a period of divergent thinking in the design-thinking process. Remember, it is up to you to come up with the big ideas; you cannot depend on the people you have been observing to generate them for you. Instead, you use your observation data (see 4.5 Pathways Toward Observation and Insights, below) as a basis for coming up with ideas. During the ideation phase, ideas are often generated in collaboration with a diverse group of people whose experience spans many different disciplines. Within IDEO, it is not uncommon for a design team to consist of architects, psychologists, artists, and engineers, most of whom have also had some kind of experience in business or marketing, or who have completed an MBA. By combining different viewpoints, the team can generate a wide variety of ideas and engage in productive debates about competing ideas.

Here we will talk about brainstorming as a pathway to generating solutions to the needs identified in the inspiration phase, but also don't forget what you learned in Chapter 3 on generating new opportunities. Those skills can come in handy here. But for now, it's all about brainstorming in this phase. Though an old tool, it's still very good when the rules are followed! Brainstorming was created in the 1950s by writer and advertising executive Alex Osborne, who wrote about creativity in his text *Applied Imagination*. One of the key factors of brainstorming, in Osborne's model, was to "hold back criticism until the creative current has had every chance to flow." He considered the following four ground rules for brainstorming as pivotal to divergent thinking:

- suspending all judgment;

- being open to wild suggestions;

- generating as many ideas as possible; and

- putting ideas together and improving on them.[16]

Thus, the ideation phase uses brainstorming as a way to generate as many ideas as possible to meet the needs identified in the inspiration phase. Similarly, IDEO follows a set of rules for brainstorming (see Table 4.4); many of these are based on Osborne's four rules.

TABLE 4.4

IDEO's Brainstorming Rules

1.	Avoid judging others. The whole idea of brainstorming is to make everyone comfortable enough to say whatever springs to mind. Remember, the more ideas out there, the more chance there is of building on those ideas to create the right solution.
2.	Let the creativity flow. Always encourage ideas—no matter how outlandish they may be. Seemingly "crazy" ideas can often give rise to real solutions.
3.	Be open to developing the ideas of others. However unlikely the idea may be, using positive language (use "and" rather than "but") when investigating an idea can achieve real breakthroughs.
4.	Stay on topic. Keep your attention on the topic being discussed; otherwise, you risk exploring different paths that may go far beyond the scale of the project.
5.	Follow the "one at a time" rule. There is more chance of the team developing ideas when full attention is focused on one person speaking at a time.
6.	Use visuals. Visuals such as sticky notes or rough sketches are powerful ways to get an idea across to an audience.
7.	Generate as many new ideas as possible. Try for up to 100 ideas in a 60-minute session, and then choose the ones worth developing.

Source: Adapted from IDEO. (2015). *The field guide to human-centered design.* San Francisco, CA: Author. Retrieved from http://www.designkit.org/methods/28

Implementation

Once you have used inspiration and ideation to identify some ideas that you think may have potential, it's time to enter the third phase of the design-thinking process: implementation.

Implementation seeks to answer the questions, "I have an idea, so how do I get feedback, how do I test it, how do I iterate, and how do I learn as quickly as possible whether there is a potential market?" During the implementation phase, ideas generated in the ideation phase are transformed into concrete actions that require user interaction. Note that the inspiration phase requires human interaction, but so does this phase. Again, design thinking is human centered and obsessed with users!

At the heart of the implementation process is low-cost experimentation through rapid prototyping, which creates an actual model of the product or service, which is then repeatedly tested for strengths and weaknesses until it leads from the project stage into people's lives. Prototypes need not be sophisticated or expensive.

For example, in a project with the German airline Lufthansa, to understand the growing demands of business class travelers, IDEO designers built a rapid prototype—a cheap mock-up of a plane using sturdy foam board for the plane business class seats.[17] Real passengers and crew were then invited to test them out and share their experiences, which provided the designers with valuable feedback that they could use in the next iteration of the prototype. Rapid prototypes are a time-saving, cost-effective way to learn how customers experience a product before too much money is spent on development.[18] From this example, it's clear that experimentation is relevant to the implementation phase, as it involves acting in order to learn, trying something new, learning from the attempt, and building that learning into the next iteration. This should sound familiar to the Entrepreneurship Method!

Rather than executing the ideas generated in the inspiration and ideation phases, the implementation phase focuses on early, fast, cheap testing to strengthen ideas and ensure that the design team is on the right path toward meeting the needs of the people for whom they are designing. This part is so important that we've devoted Chapter 7: Testing and Experimenting With New Ideas to this topic. Let's take a look at a real-life example of the three phases of design thinking in action.

Implementation: a process involving the testing of assumptions of new ideas to continuously shape them into viable opportunities.

The Three Phases of Design Thinking in Action

Millions of Ghana's urban poor live without indoor toilets. IDEO partnered with Unilever and Water and Sanitation for the Urban Poor (WSUP) and developed Clean Team Ghana, a waste removal service that delivers and maintains standalone rental toilets to low-income Ghanaians.[19] They used the three phases of design thinking to understand the design challenge.

During the *inspiration* phase, the IDEO team set out to define the problem and to identify any constraints. They interviewed sanitation experts, shadowed a toilet operator, and talked to many Ghanaians about how the new sanitation system might look. Early on, the team discovered an important historical fact: For a long time, night soil collectors used to collect waste from bucket latrines, but some of these collectors dumped the waste in the street. As a consequence, night soil collection was banned. By finding out this important fact, IDEO was able to learn more about in-home waste removal while ensuring that their new model didn't allow for illegal waste dumping. During the *ideation* phase, the team brought together what they had learned from their interviews and began to brainstorm. They developed several prototypes based on modifications of existing portable toilets and gave them to the Ghanaians for their input. During this phase, they learned about the technical limitations

Woman in Ghana with a working toilet

of their prototypes; for instance, the flush function would not work to full capacity due to water scarcity. The *implementation* phase focused on testing the design of the new toilet using parts from off-the-shelf cabin toilets to reduce costs. Since 2012, thousands of Ghanaians have been able to install indoor toilets in their homes

As we mentioned, the design-thinking process is not linear. It is not unusual to loop back through the three phases of inspiration, ideation, and implementation when exploring and testing new ideas. An initially successful idea, too, may need to be revisited. The concept might need a new round of inspiration, ideation, and implementation to identify key weaknesses and devise ways to remedy them. Because design thinking does not follow a strict pattern, it may at first seem like a chaotic process; however, there is structure in the chaos that serves to produce creative, meaningful results. The design challenge gives us direction, but through observation, we begin to uncover the real problems and needs. We will explore ideation and implementation in greater detail in later chapters, but here let's take a closer look at what happens during the inspiration phase.

4.5 PATHWAYS TOWARD OBSERVATION AND INSIGHTS

>> **LO 4.5**   **Demonstrate how to observe and convert observation data to insights.**

Two of the most important techniques that entrepreneurs use during the inspiration phase are observation and insight or need development. **Observation** is the action of closely monitoring the behavior and activities of users/potential customers in their own environment for greater empathic understanding. Many of us are so very accustomed to just seeing or simply talking to (or *at*) other people that we don't necessarily know how to observe. Because we are so used to our own environment, we tend to lose sight of the bigger picture or the things we miss seeing every day. It can be difficult to consciously stop and simply observe, yet observation is essential for gathering facts and identifying those latent needs previously discussed.

Observation leads to insight development, and insights are where we begin to articulate the needs of users. First, let's start with what an insight is *not*. The term is quite often misused. It is important to understand that insights and observations are not the same thing. Observations focus on the raw data that you have consciously recorded from all the things you have heard and seen, without any interpretation. An insight comes later: It is an interesting, nonobvious piece of information derived from interview or observation data that drives opportunities.

An insight is *not* just reporting what you heard in the conversations. An insight is *not* an idea. An insight *is* a statement that identifies a customer need and explains why. In other words, an **insight** is an interpretation of an observation or a sudden realization that provides us with a new understanding of a human behavior or attitude that results in some sort of action—for example, a new product or service to meet customer needs or even a new process to increase employee satisfaction.[20] Remember the grocery story example from earlier in the chapter? The need was to reach something on a higher shelf, but we didn't really address why she needed to reach something on a higher shelf. The insight in this case can be phrased as, *Grocery store customers need to reach products on higher shelves in a way that keeps them safe.* In general, an insight statement can be written using the following equation: User + Need + Why. Some useful "fill-in-the-blanks" to create powerful insight statements from your observations can be found in Figure 4.3.

Observations represent *what* we see and insights help us better understand *why* we are seeing what we are seeing. Insights are the patterns we observe; they help us identify the needs of the people we are observing. Probably one of the best ways to remember the definition of an insight is the following:

Q: "Why is a good insight like a refrigerator?"

A: "Because the moment you look into it, a light comes on."[21]

Observation: the action of closely monitoring the behavior and activities of users/potential customers in their own environment.

Insight: an interpretation of an observation or a sudden realization that provides us with a new understanding of a human behavior or attitude that results in the identification of a need.

FIGURE 4.3

Fill in the Blank for Insight Statements

_____(users)_____ need __(verb)__ because____(insert why)____.

Example: Surfers need to conveniently travel with their board because they like to explore new surfing areas.

____(users)____ need __(verb)__ in a way that ____(insert why)____.

Example: City drivers need to reduce their speed in a way that protects pedestrians and bikers.

____(users)____ need __(verb)__ so ____(insert why)____.

Example: College professors need to teach more experientially so that students are more engaged with course content.

In Chapter 3, we discussed pattern recognition, a process by which people identify links or connections, or "connect the dots," in order to identify and then build on opportunities between apparently unrelated events. You may remember Knock Knock City founders Selin Sonmez and Niko Georgantas, who connected the dots between hauling baggage around with them and empty, unused retail space.

Recognizing patterns generates *insights* that enable us to see everyday things in a new light. These insights can often take us by surprise. For example, in an effort to understand why bicycle helmets were so unpopular in Sweden, two Swedish students, Anna Haupt and Terese Alstin, spent years observing and gathering information from a whole range of adult cyclists. Their research showed that, on the surface, people attributed their reluctance to wear bicycle helmets to lack of safety, but the real reason lay in the aesthetics. It was this insight that led the women on a quest for a bicycle helmet that would be safe, comfortable, and aesthetically pleasing—a quest that led to their creation of the invisible bicycle helmet.

Insights are not ideas, but they help us generate innovative ideas, sometimes for new products or services that we didn't even know we needed. For example, how many of us have thought aloud, "Do you know what I really need? An invisible bicycle helmet!" Yet some of the greatest innovations of today have fulfilled a need that we had no idea we had—a latent need—such as the Internet or the iPhone. Instead of simply observing, Haupt and Alstin asked *why,* and they continued to ask why until they came up with a meaningful insight that led them to identify the primary need and to create the solution to meet the need. In other words, they had spotted the gap between where the customers are today and where they want to be.[22]

Model wearing invisible bicycle helmet made by Hövding, showing how the "air bag" mechanism looks when deployed.

Hövding/Splash News/Newscom

Observation Techniques

Developing keen observation skills requires practice. Some may argue that we observe every day, so we already have strong observation skills. Observation requires looking *and* seeing. Although we look every day, we may not really be seeing. Seeing is an ability to understand more deeply what we are looking at. Seeing helps us make sense of what is in front of us, what it's about, and how it relates to other things in the environment. Looking isn't sufficient for observation. You need to also see. The more we practice observation, the greater the likelihood of our developing new, meaningful insights that can lead to

TABLE 4.5

Four Types of Observation

1. Complete Observer
A complete observer is someone who is either hidden from view or is observing in plain sight but is not noticed by participants. For instance, you might go to a shopping mall to observe people's shopping habits. Other public places for this type of observation include airports, subway stations, or even public bathrooms. Although this observation technique is useful for noting how people behave—they are more likely to act naturally when they don't know they are being observed—consider the ethical implications of this approach. After all, how would you feel if you found out you were being watched without your consent?
2. Observer as Participant
In this case, the observer is known to the participants but maintains a neutral stance throughout. This type of observation may be useful to understand how people carry out certain activities, for instance, observing how people use certain software to achieve their goals.
3. Participant as Observer
Here, researchers are not only known by the participants, but considered more of a friend or a colleague. This method is often used when researchers visit remote indigenous populations or inner-city cultures to gather information on different cultural habits.
4. Complete Participant
A complete participant is almost like an undercover spy. The researcher fully engages with the participants and joins in with their activities, but they have no idea they are being observed. This technique is often used in customer research, such as the secret shopper role in the show *Undercover Boss.* It is a useful way to gather firsthand experience of how consumers operate.

Source: Adapted from Sauro, J. (2015). 4 Types of Observational Research. Retrieved from https://measuringu.com/observation-role/

AEIOU framework:
acronym for *activities, environments, interactions, objects,* and *users*—a framework commonly used to categorize observations during fieldwork.

innovative solutions. There are four types of observation that can help us to focus on the things that are not necessarily visible or obvious at first glance (see Table 4.5).[23]

Another technique used to guide observation efforts is the **AEIOU framework**: an acronym for *activities, environments, interactions, objects,* and *users.*[24] This is a framework commonly used to categorize observations during fieldwork to help you make sense of what you are seeing. AEIOU is also the focus of the Mindshift exercise. Table 4.6 defines the five AEIOU dimensions.

TABLE 4.6

The Five AEIOU Dimensions

Activities are goal-directed sets of actions—pathways toward things that people want to accomplish. What activities and actions do people engage in when carrying out tasks?
Environments include the entire arena where activities take place. What is the function of the individual, shared, and overall space? Taking photographs or drawing sketches of the environment is also a useful way to record environmental cues.
Interactions take place between a person and something or someone else. What is the nature of these exchanges? Can you observe what the person enjoys the most or the least?
Objects are the building blocks or physical items that people interact with. What are the objects and devices that people use, and how do they relate to their activities?
Users are the people whose behaviors, needs, and preferences are being observed. What are their goals, values, motivations, roles, prejudices, and relationships? Who are they?

Source: AEIOU framework. (n.d.). Retrieved from http://help.ethnohub.com/guide/aeiou-framework

In addition to the observations frameworks, there are small adjustments you can make to your own lifestyle to increase your powers of observation.[25] For example, you could deliberately change your routine. Do you always take the same route to class? Or go to the same grocery stores? If so, then try to take a different route or go to a different store, and see if you can make any observations based on these changes. Imagine you are seeing things for the first time, and see if you can discover anything new. Furthermore, the act of observation doesn't have to be a solitary activity. Bringing along someone else to help spot something you didn't notice before or offer a different point of view can be invaluable in developing new insights.

Here's a direct challenge. Once a day, stop and observe the ordinary. Look and see those everyday things that you normally take for granted, as if really seeing them for the first time. Why are manhole covers round, for instance? Why do we use forks? Why is a toothbrush the best tool for dental hygiene? Not only will this exercise improve your observation skills, but it will make you a better design thinker, for good design thinkers observe, but great design thinkers observe the ordinary in extraordinary ways.[26]

4.6 INTERVIEWING AS A USEFUL TECHNIQUE FOR IDENTIFYING NEEDS

>> **LO 4.6** **Demonstrate how to interview potential customers in order to better understand their needs.**

Interviewing is an important part of the inspiration phase, second only to observation, to understand users and identify needs. It can be an alternative and/or complement to observation. It's simply another way to collect real and valuable data. A skilled interviewer is open minded, flexible, patient, observant, and a good listener. Like observation, interviewing is a skill that improves with practice.

It's very common for entrepreneurs to interview customers after they have purchased a product or service. This is called a **feedback interview**. But it's also common to use interviewing much earlier in the process to develop insights and identify needs. This is called a **need-finding interview**. Both follow similar protocols but their purposes are different. Regardless of the type of interview you are conducting, the following sections will help you develop your interviewing skills for maximum impact.

Feedback interview: an interview conducted to get feedback on an existing product or service.

Need-finding interview: an interview conducted to better understand the problems or needs of people or validate what you think a need or problem may be.

Preparing for an Interview

First, think about whom you want to interview. Whom do you really want to learn from? Because we are still trying to identify needs, think about those people in the space you are interested in. For example, let's say you are interested in pet owners and whether there are unmet needs in this space. You might find people to talk to at a dog park or in a pet store or at a dog show. Try to stay away from people you know, even at this phase. Talking to strangers, which can be intimidating, will produce much better data than talking to people you already know. Now you need to consider why you want to talk to pet owners. What is the purpose of the conversation? In the need-finding phase you are trying to understand their lives with their pets. It's a very general goal, but that's the starting point with a need-finding interview. You should not walk into an interview thinking you already know what they need. This is the time for listening!

If the goal is to better understand pet owners' lives with their pets, then consider creating three very broad and open-ended questions to ask, such as,

1. Tell me about an average day with Fluffy.

2. Why did you adopt Fluffy?

3. How do other people in your life interact with Fluffy?

4. Tell me about some recurring "headaches" (problems) you have with Fluffy.

These four questions represent broad categories of the need-finding interview: day in the life, values related to pet ownership, connections to others, and pain points. Your role as an interviewer is to ask one broad question, listen, then probe. That's the formula: question—listen—probe!

Observations to Insights

Now it's time to practice a little design thinking. When talking about observation as a core tenet of design thinking, it's easy to say, "I've observed all my life. I don't need to practice observing." Well, you haven't been observing your entire life; you've just been looking. When we observe with purpose and intention, we often see new things.

This Mindshift is about getting outside of the classroom, observing, and then building insights from your observation data. The AEIOU framework is a tool to help you do this.

First, identify an area of curiosity for you. This could be fitness, video gaming, food, travel, education—any human activity you are curious about. Once you have identified an area of curiosity, find a space that is related to this area. For example, if you are interested in food, you could observe waiters at a local restaurant. If you are interested in education, you could observe students in a class. If you are interested in travel, you could observe people in an airport or at a highway rest stop. What's most important is that you must observe *people*. Remember, design thinking is human centered, and desirability comes first. By observing people, you can identify what they need.

Observe for 2 hours and record your notes using a table like the one below. Using the AEIOU framework helps you organize your notes.

OBSERVATION WORKSHEET
AEIOU FRAMEWORK

Activities
What are people doing?
Environment
How are people using the environment? What's the role of the environment?
Interactions
Do you see any routines? Do you observe special interactions between people? Between people and objects?
Objects
What's there and being used or not used? Describe engagement with objects. Are there any work-arounds you can identify?
Users
Who are the users you are observing? What are their roles? Are there any extreme users?

Source: Doblin, Inc. by Rick Robinson and Stef Norvaisis Available at http://help.ethnohub.com/guide/aeiou-framework

Now think about any insights arising from your observations. Remember, an insight is not an idea; it's a statement that drives your idea and identifies the needs of users. Use the fill-in-the-blank from Figure 4.3 to help you!

Critical Thinking Questions

1. Do you agree that observing and seeing are two different skills? In what ways, if any, are they different?

2. In the AEIOU framework, which aspect of observation did you find the most useful? The most challenging? Explain your answers.

3. What insight can you identify for the space you observed in this exercise? Does your insight relate to a need or a solution? Remember, insights are not solutions—they lead you to solutions. Why is separating needs and solutions important? ●

For example, let's say you were interviewing a college student who had a cocker spaniel dog and she lived in an apartment off campus. You may ask, "Why did you adopt Fluffy?" The student's response may be, "Because Fluffy helps me focus." Don't just move on to the next question. Now it's time to probe by saying, "Why does Fluffy help you focus?" From this probing question, you may learn that the student suffers from high anxiety that leads to an inability to focus on schoolwork. She doesn't want to take medication with side effects, and she learned that pets, specifically trained dogs, are very good at reducing anxiety in young people. The probing question is very important. How would you have learned the rest of the story without asking, "Why"? Always ask why! This method is called "peeling the onion," which is a way of delving into a problem one layer at a time. Begin with the challenges the person faces, and then continue to dig deeper in order to understand the root of the problem. Simply asking, "Why?" or saying, "Tell me more about _____" will help you gain a deeper understanding.

Conducting the Interview

Once you have a short list of broad questions and you have thought about how you will probe, it's important to have an approach, especially when trying to talk to strangers. When you approach strangers, they do not want to be sold anything and they don't want to spend a lot of time with you. But, you will be surprised how many are willing to talk with you when they are interested. A good tip when approaching is simply saying, "Do you have 2 minutes to talk about….?" Don't say "Do you have time?" or "Do you have a few minutes?" Strangers will find it hard to say no to 2 minutes. For example, if you walk up to someone in a dog park, you might consider asking, "I'm trying to better understand the needs of pet owners. Do you have 2 minutes to talk about your dog?" Then you jump into your first question. Usually the stranger will give you more time, but if not, be thankful for the data you got in 2 minutes and then go find another stranger.

Take notes throughout, and if you are intending to also audio record the interview, make sure you ask permission first. Remember to use your questions as a guide only—it's best to keep the tone conversational and relaxed, but directed. The golden rule of interviewing is to actively listen to the other person. Practice a technique called parroting, which is repeating back what the person has said. Two things can happen with parroting.[27] The person may correct you because you have misrepresented what they said. Or, when the person hears what they actually said, they may change their answer a bit or provide more detail. In general, don't become so focused on your prepared questions that you neglect to pay attention to what the other person is telling you. Furthermore, when you reflect back or paraphrase what the other person has said, this shows that you are listening. However, do not interrupt or try to guess the answers. If there is a pause in the conversation, don't feel obliged to rush in and fill the space—your interviewee may be thinking about something or planning what to say next.

Finally, make sure you also record some basic facts about the person (gender, occupation, age, profession, industry, affluence). There is no need to ask these questions directly, as they can be offensive. Do your best to make some reasonable guesses.

Remember, your goal here is to learn as much as possible—you're not selling to the person (although, keep in mind that this person might well be a future customer of yours). The focus should be on the people you interview, getting to know them, the problems they have experienced and how they have tried to solve them (or not), and the outcome. If you are unclear about something or have a question, don't be afraid to seek clarification. In this way, you will come away from the interview with as much concise information as possible.

One of the most common interviewing mistakes is to seek validation for your ideas. Remember, at this stage, you either have a very early idea or may not even have an idea at all. Overall, you are trying to better understand the needs of various users. For example, let's say you have an idea to schedule and source a vast array of food trucks for corporate events. During an interview with a young financial analyst at an investment bank you learn that he and his colleagues think that food trucks are not high-end enough for corporate events. Don't get defensive and argue why you think food trucks are trendy and will appeal to a newer generation of professions. The aim here is to listen and understand why he doesn't think food trucks would be that appealing. His answers may not be the ones you are looking for, and sometimes the truth hurts, but his feedback may lead to new insights and ideas. Figure 4.4 provides examples of "bad" interview question types to avoid and "good" interview question types that are often helpful.

After the Interview

As soon as the interview finishes, take some time to go through your notes and write down any additional observations or thoughts while the interaction is fresh in your mind.

FIGURE 4.4

Bad Questions to Avoid and Good Questions to Remember

BAD QUESTION REMINDERS	GOOD QUESTION REMINDERS
Too Soon: Asking a stranger for commitment or personal information before it's appropriate in the conversation	**Ask Permission:** Getting the customer's permission to conduct a short interview
Leading: Making assumptions about your customer that may be false and bringing your own biases into the conversation	**Customer Pain:** While exercising sensitivity, encouraging the customer talking about a problem or pain that they have
Dead End: Asking questions that can be answered with a "yes" or "no" and don't give your customer a chance to tell you anything meaningful	**Existing Alternatives:** Learning what the customer has tried to do to solve his or her problem in the past
Poor Listener: Showing that you clearly didn't listen to your customer's earlier responses	**Prioritize Pain:** Clarifying that alleviating the customer's pain is one of your top priorities
Sales Pitch: Asking your customer if they're interested in a product or service instead of listening and learning about them	**Dig Deep:** Following up a question to learn more
Insulting: Offending your customer so much that they end the conversation	**Get a Story:** Asking the customer to tell you a story about his or her situation

Source: Heidi Neck & Anton Yakushin, 2015 VentureBlocks Teaching Note.

Try to craft insights from your notes by looking for themes and patterns based on responses to questions, body language, and tone of voice, and make note of any other questions or findings that have emerged. Develop your reflection skill; reflection is useful here, as it helps you to make sense of your feelings, the knowledge you have gained, what questions you may have, and what you need to consider as a result. Reflecting on the interview also gives you the opportunity to come up with new perspectives and conclusions. Also think about how you could improve the interview the next time. Practice makes perfect!

The Empathy Map

One of the most useful ways to efficiently record the information from an interview is by completing an empathy map. An empathy map is a tool that helps you collate and integrate your interview data in order to discover surprising or unanticipated insights. It also enables you to uncover unmet needs, find the source of any frustrations, discover areas for improvement, explore different perspectives, and question your own assumptions and beliefs. In other words, empathy mapping gets you out of your head and into someone else's.[28]

Figure 4.5 is a template that illustrates the type of content that goes into an empathy map—you can either use this one or draw your own. The map contains four main components that help you organize data from people you interview: Say, Do, Think, and Feel.[29]

Drawing from the observations you have made during your interviews, write down the following:

Say: What sort of things did the person say? What struck you as being particularly significant? Are there any interesting quotes you can use?

Do: What sorts of actions and behavior were displayed by the person? Any particular body language that you noticed?

Think: What might the person be thinking? What sort of beliefs or attitudes might be relevant?

Feel: What sort of emotions do you think the person is experiencing?

FIGURE 4.5

Empathy Map

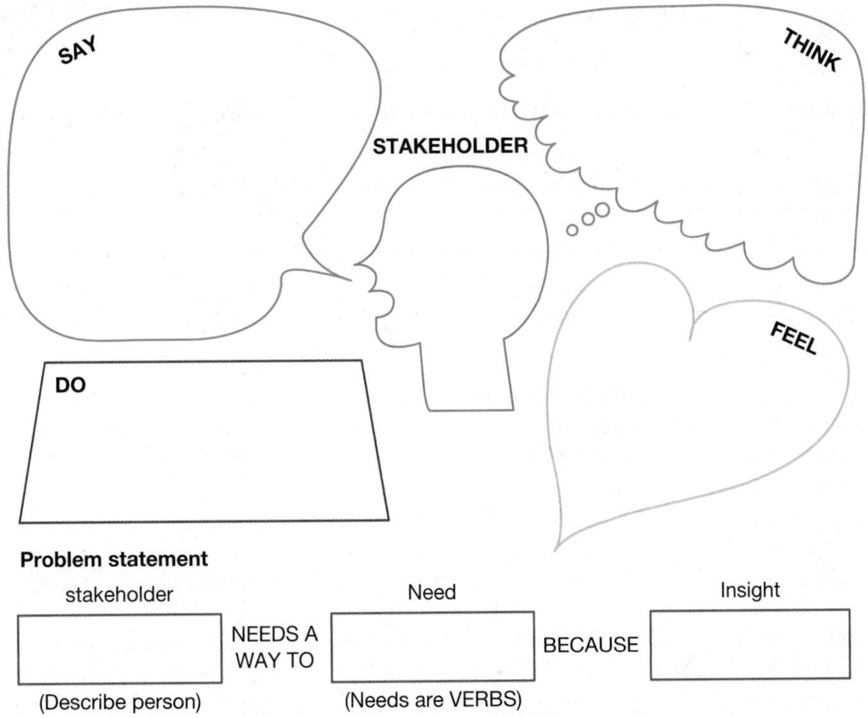

SAY

THINK

STAKEHOLDER

FEEL

DO

Problem statement

stakeholder		Need		Insight
	NEEDS A WAY TO		BECAUSE	
(Describe person)		(Needs are VERBS)		

Source: The empathy map worksheet was part of the instructional materials for the Stanford University online course Design Thinking Action Lab, taught by Leticia Britos Cavagnaro in 2013 on the NovoEd platform (https://novoed.com/designthinking/). Credit to David Grey for the original empathy map framework. More context on the use of empathy map as part of a design thinking toolkit can be found at http://dschool.stanford.edu/use-our-methods/

When complete, the empathy map is a useful way for you to spot contradictions and certain tensions that can spark a whole host of interesting insights. Sometimes we have a tendency to say one thing and mean. Anna Haupt and Terese Alstin spotted this disconnect when people at first claimed lack of safety as the reason for not wearing bicycle helmets when the real reason was vanity. This triggered an idea to create a helmet that addressed both safety and aesthetics.

4.7 VARIATIONS OF THE DESIGN-THINKING PROCESS

>> **LO 4.7** **Identify and describe other approaches to design thinking.**

Earlier in the chapter, we described IDEO's three phases of design thinking (inspiration, ideation, and implementation), but it is important to recognize that there are also other schools of design thought. The authors of *Designing for Growth* suggest four questions that are useful to ask during the design-thinking process—all of which have periods of divergence and convergence:

- What is?
- What if?
- What wows?
- What works?[30]

TABLE 4.7

The Stanford Design School Five Phases of Design Thinking

• *Empathy* is getting out and talking to your customers directly
• *Define* is defining a problem statement from that empathy work
• *Ideate* is brainstorming lots of ideas that could help you solve the problem you identified
• *Prototype* is building a crude version of the solution that you want to test with users
• *Test* is getting out and testing with users

Source: Hasso Plattner Institute of Design at Stanford. (n.d.). *An introduction to design thinking: Process guide.*

What is encourages the entrepreneur to explore the current reality of the problem; *What if* encourages you to imagine all of the possibilities without regard to the reality of the ideas; *What wows* focuses on making decisions about what the customer really wants; and *What works* tests these solutions in the marketplace.

Another variation on the design-thinking process is from the Stanford Design School. Rather than IDEO's three phases or the four questions suggested by *Designing for Growth,* the Stanford Design School uses five phases: empathy, define, ideate, prototype, and test (see Table 4.7).

Finally, the Google Design Sprint method draws on design thinking by using its tools to develop hypotheses, prototype ideas, and run low-cost tests in a real environment.[31] Based on the Stanford Design School and IDEO methodology, the design sprint model aligns Google teams under a shared vision to move faster toward product launch.

Regardless of the variations inherent in design-thinking approaches, the themes and goals are similar. Each approach focuses on the importance of people and their needs; encourages entrepreneurs to get in front of real people in order to understand them; emphasizes the identification of needs before developing solutions; and recommends testing and experimentation, not for the purposes of killing an idea but to shape it and make it stronger.

Design thinking can be used to develop new products and services and also to build organizations, design strategy, and improve processes that all bring value and deliver meaningful results. By adopting some of the methods designers use when approaching problems, entrepreneurs will be better able to find effective solutions to complex problems.

So far, we have explored the different processes of design thinking, the power of design thinking in solving complex problems, and the importance of empathy, observation, and interviewing in the creation of successful design. In the next chapter, we will apply some of the concepts we have learned from design thinking to building business models. ●

$SAGE edge™

SUMMARY

4.1 Differentiate between design and design thinking.

Many types of design are related to fashion, graphic, architectural design, or industrial design. Similar to the Entrepreneurship Method in many ways, design thinking is ultimately a constructive and collaborative process that merges the power of observation, synthesis, searching and generating alternatives, critical thinking, feedback, visual representation, creativity, problem solving, and value creation. There are seven design skills relevant to entrepreneurs: observation, listening, desire change, context and integration, solution-driven, consideration, and unbound.

4.2 Demonstrate design thinking as a human-centered process focusing on customers and their needs.

Before business feasibility and economic sustainability are considered in the design process, entrepreneurs discover what people need. Products that achieve all three are bound to be the most successful, but the product or service must first be designed to provide a desired solution, or fulfill a need, for the design process to be considered human centered.

4.3 Describe the role of empathy in the design-thinking process.

To create meaningful ideas and innovations, we need to know and care about the people who are using them. Developing our empathic ability enables us to better understand the way people do things and the reasons why; their physical and emotional needs; the way they think and feel; and what is important to them.

4.4 Illustrate the key phases of the design-thinking process.

The design-thinking process consists of three main overlapping phases: inspiration, ideation, and implementation.

4.5 Demonstrate how to observe and convert observation data to insights.

An insight, in this sense, is an interpretation of an event or observation that, importantly, provides new information or meaning. There are four different types of observation, and, like entrepreneurship, the ability to discern trends and patterns from each dimension is a skill that can be practiced and improved.

4.6 Demonstrate how to interview potential customers in order to better understand their needs.

Interviews should be done for two reasons: (1) to develop a better understanding of user needs during the inspiration phase of design thinking and (2) to get feedback on ideas during the implementation phase. The interview must be well-prepared, the customer must be listened to and intelligent questions asked, and the interview must be evaluated when it is over.

4.7 Identify and describe other approaches to design thinking.

The authors of *Designing for Growth* suggest four questions that are useful to ask during the design-thinking process, all of which have periods of divergence and convergence: What is? What if? What wows? What works?[33] Another variation on the design-thinking process is from the Stanford Design School, which uses five phases: empathy, define, ideate, prototype, and test. Finally, the Google Design Sprint method draws on design thinking by using its tools to develop hypotheses, prototype ideas, and run low-cost tests in a real environment.

KEY TERMS

AEIOU framework 94	Ideation 89	Need 80
Convergent thinking 87	Implementation 91	Need-finding interview 95
Design thinking 79	Insight 92	Observation 92
Divergent thinking 87	Inspiration 87	
Feedback interview 95	Latent needs 89	

CASE STUDY

Anton Yakushin, cofounder and CEO, VentureBlocks

Anton Yakushin is the cofounder of an education technology (EdTech) startup called VentureBlocks. Founded in March of 2014, VentureBlocks is a game-based online simulation that teaches student entrepreneurs how to interview customers and identify their needs (VentureBlocks is described in more detail below).

A self-confessed "lifelong tech nerd," Anton began coding at a young age. After high school, he sought out roles that involved building software. For several years he worked as a software engineer for a variety of employers. During this time, Anton was also working on his degree at Babson College. He signed up for an entrepreneurship course, which he hoped would help him achieve his goal to be a tech entrepreneur. He was also keen to learn the business skills he felt he needed to capitalize on his vast range of tech knowledge.

After graduating from Babson in 2008, Anton had a variety of stints in consulting and startups, but in 2014, he returned to meet with his old entrepreneurship professor, Heidi Neck. He told Professor Neck that he wanted to make a difference in the way students were taught, specifically in the area of simulations. He says,

"When I was at college, I was always surprised how limited the simulations we used were. They were limited both in terms of topics covered and with what actions you could take while playing. More often than not, you could figure out a set of buttons to click consistently and win!"

He presented an idea to create a multiplayer online game in which students would compete with each other while operating retail businesses.

Professor Neck told him that although she wouldn't use it, he should interview some other professors to find out whether they were interested. Anton reflects, "After about a dozen initial conversations with professors at various business schools, I couldn't get one person to say they would use (and much less pay or have their students pay for) such a simulation."

However, the interviews had given Anton some valuable feedback, which he shared with Professor Neck, who ultimately signed on as a cofounder. Upon assessing this feedback, Neck introduced Anton to the idea of game-based learning in education. The first step was to identify how game-based simulations could be enhanced for learning purposes and who would use them. To do this, Anton needed to identify his target users and how to address their needs.

Anton started by interviewing hundreds of people in education, including students, professors, administrators, and high school students. It was during his interviews with a hundred entrepreneurship professors from different business schools that he quickly discovered a pattern. The biggest and most consistent pain point for most of the entrepreneurship professors was teaching students to identify customer needs. The reason was that each student had a different approach: Some were not listening to their customers and were asking the wrong questions, while others were being negatively influenced by existing biases. This made it very difficult for professors to teach customer development and need finding, especially when this topic was typically restricted to one or two classes.

This feedback from entrepreneurship professors would eventually lead to the creation of VentureBlocks, a tool that would prepare students to effectively interview customers in order to identify their needs. In addition, VentureBlocks provides a safe and fun space for students to compete with each other. Through the simulation, students also learn how to develop empathy and build stronger customer insights. Because students receive instant feedback as they are playing, they learn quickly from their mistakes.

Although Anton had not originally set out to create a simulation to sell to professors to aid student learning in this area of entrepreneurship, the interview feedback showed that there was potential to provide a solution to this pain point and create a business. Building on this knowledge, Anton created a low-cost prototype to demonstrate to professors and to give them something tangible to play, themselves.

Before writing a single line of code, Anton built the simulation as a paper prototype, which underwent about 50 iterations over the course of 6 months. Anton said, "Since we wanted to build a software simulation, we prototyped with a paper card–based one where I took on the role of the computer, doing what the simulation would have done. We found, through iteration, how to engage groups of players and how to embed the lessons most crucial to professors in a fun way."

In testing the prototype, Anton regularly went to the Babson College library, cafeteria, student center, and graduate school to play with undergraduate and MBA students as well as professors to get their feedback. He also contacted other colleges within driving distance to do the same and used Craigslist to find students willing to playtest the prototype during school vacation. He took time to complete the Business Model Canvas on several occasions, in order to prove that he had a product that people would buy before he went any further. After months of testing and feedback, Anton finally knew when he had a viable product to market. Though Anton did most of the coding himself using a platform called Unity, he coordinated a team of contractors to help with 3D graphics, scriptwriting, and user-interface design.

> We decided that our product met customer needs when students confirmed (1) that they learned what we set out teach them and (2) that the process of playing was engaging to them. We knew we achieved the first goal when a group of students told me that they were going to change their approach to identifying customer needs after playing the simulation in class. We knew we achieved our second goal when a group of professors was so engaged playing that they lost track of time and became quite competitive for top score!

Although the outlook seemed positive, Anton suffered an unexpected setback in the initial stages of launching the product. During the official launch at an entrepreneurship educators' conference, the product attracted the attention of a few early adopters, but the overriding response was quite negative. When Anton asked why, he was told that most professors were impressed by the quality of the simulation, but almost everyone was unhappy with the price for student access. Anton discovered that professors, though keen to use the product, were restricted by college budgets.

> The mistake we made with pricing was that we set it based on analyzing the competition (other simulations) and by talking to professors at a handful of private, relatively expensive colleges. We realized that we had set a price that limited the number of early adopters, and in doing so hurt our opportunity to grow and scale our user base—something critical for a brand new product in the market.

The idea itself has been completely overhauled many times in the first 6 months through customer interviews and prototypes. We completely overhauled the software simulation after the first year because of how much we learned from our early adopters. We also pivoted with our revenue model and our channels. We changed pricing and revenue type along the way and also changed how we reach potential customers and what we do when we reach them.

For Anton, VentureBlocks has been a labor of love, but his passion for the product is reflected in its success. To date, VentureBlocks is used by more than 10,500 students in 100 colleges and universities and is even available bundled with the textbook that you are reading. "It's great that a textbook publisher actually sees the value in VentureBlocks, and it will be helpful for the company to extend its reach both in the U.S. and around the world."

Critical Thinking Questions

1. The three core components of design thinking are inspiration, ideation, and implementation. Can you identify these components in the evolution of VentureBlocks?

2. The journey of VentureBlocks is populated with many tests, experiments, and prototypes. Where do you think VentureBlocks would be today if Anton had simply written a business plan and started the business? Why?

3. How might you apply design thinking to your own academic endeavors to maximize your potential for success after graduation?

Sources

Anton Yakushin (interview with the author, April 22, 2019)

VentureBlocks website (http://ventureblocks.com/)

5 Building Business Models

"Startups have finite time and resources to find product/market fit before they run out of money. Therefore startups trade off certainty for speed, adopting "good enough decision making" and iterating and pivoting as they fail, learn, and discover their business model."

—Steve Blank, Silicon Valley entrepreneur

Chapter Outline

Learning Objectives

5.1   Define the business model.

5.2   Identify the four core areas of a business model.

5.3   Explain the importance of the Customer Value Proposition.

5.4   Describe the different types of Customer Value Propositions and learn how to identify customer segments.

5.5   Identify the nine components of the Business Model Canvas.

5.1 WHAT IS A BUSINESS MODEL?

>> **LO 5.1   Define the business model.**

In Chapter 1, we defined entrepreneurship as a way of thinking, acting, and being that combines the ability to find or create new opportunities with the courage to act on them. So far, we've focused on the finding and creating part of the definition, but now it's time to start thinking about the plausibility of some of your ideas. What additional actions do we need to take to convince ourselves and others that not only do we have something that customers need (see Chapter 4: Using Design Thinking) but also something that has economic feasibility and viability? Feasibility answers the question, "Can we do it?" Viability answers the question, "Can we make money doing it?" To begin answering these two questions, we must explore possible business models.

In this chapter, we will look at the different components of a business model and how each component represents assumptions and hypotheses that need further exploration. The business model as presented in this chapter is a journey to gather evidence and prove that the startup can be a sustainable business. Steve Blank, Silicon Valley entrepreneur, defines a startup as a temporary organization in search of a scalable business model. To move from temporary startup to scalable and sustainable venture requires evidence that is gathered from talking to people, investigating and asking lots of questions, testing assumptions, iterating, and learning continuously. In other words, it's a practice of hypothesizing, testing, and validating, just like the Entrepreneurship Method introduced in Chapter 1. The difference now is that we are using the Method to develop the business model. A business model is not created in a vacuum; it's built over time by collecting evidence that what you are creating works, has value for customers, is profitable, and is sustainable over the long term. This practice of hypothesizing, testing, and validating is often called **evidence-based entrepreneurship**. So, let's dig in and see if we can get beyond startup and to a scalable business model!

A **business model** describes the rationale of how a new venture creates, delivers, and captures value.[1] It includes a network of activities and resources that interact to deliver value to customers. Working through the components of a business model helps entrepreneurs better understand what they are doing, how they are doing it, for whom, and why. Value is better understood and generated in several ways: by fulfilling unmet needs in an existing market, by delivering existing products and services to existing customers but with unique differentiation, or by serving customers in new markets.

As Figure 5.1 illustrates, business models can create a whole new market in which new customers are offered a new product or service. Social media sites such as Facebook illustrate a type of business model known as Innovation. Business models can also disrupt existing markets by creating something entirely new for customers.

Evidence-based entrepreneurship: the practice of hypothesizing, testing, and validating to create a business model.

Business model: describes the rationale of how a new venture creates, delivers, and captures value.

Master the content at **edge.sagepub.com/neckentrepreneurship2e**

FIGURE 5.1

Market Entry Strategies

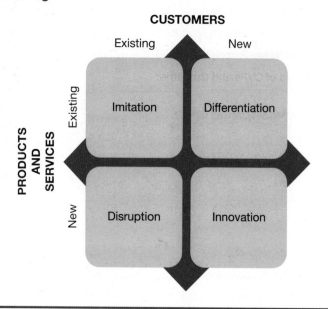

The emergence of MOOCs—Massive Open Online Courses—disrupted higher education when students opted for these free courses rather than paying tuition at colleges and universities. MOOCs are an example of the Disruption business model. Fulfilling unmet needs of customers using an existing product or service is called Differentiation. A good example of Differentiation is Quip, an electric toothbrush created by entrepreneur and inventor Simon Enever. Though there are plenty of electric toothbrushes available today, Quip differentiates itself by being simple, convenient, affordable, and portable.

Entrepreneurs like Enever use Differentiation to encourage existing customers to switch to their product or attract new customers to the product category. Finally, the Imitation business model should really be avoided. Imitation without Differentiation is not the greatest form of flattery. If you are going to offer something similar to an existing set of customers, the product needs to be better or not currently available to customers. Just because a Starbucks exists in your town does not mean that a new coffee shop would fail. Don't try to be Starbucks. Be uniquely you, in your own way, meeting customer needs not met by Starbucks. That's how you quickly move from Imitation to Differentiation.

Quip electric toothbrushes

Entrepreneurs like Brandon Steiner, profiled in the Entrepreneurship in Action feature, have the freedom to create, test, and adapt their business models until they find a compelling value proposition that meets the needs of most customers.

Because new businesses tend to be small in the beginning, it is much easier to be agile and make quick, efficient changes to the business model during the startup stage. Then, if successful, the business can scale as the young business model is tested and validated through early action. Equally, if the changes don't seem to work, then it is easy to spot the flaws and adjust them accordingly before large-scale investments are made. The most important thing before actually starting a business is to think through the business model,

Brandon Steiner, Steiner Sports

Photo courtesy of Brandon Steiner

Brandon Steiner, founder of Steiner Sports

Entrepreneurs are often the first people who are willing to look at a fragmented industry and think about how to enter the industry and stand out among the fragments (other players), so to speak. Many facets of the sports industry have proven to be fragmented failures that entrepreneurs have tried to consolidate and conquer, most of them failing in their attempts. Brandon Steiner, founder of Steiner Sports, was successful in his attempt to bring some order to the sports memorabilia market and has, in turn, built a sports collectables empire worth hundreds of millions of dollars.

Brandon Steiner grew up in Flatbush, a neighborhood in the New York City borough of Brooklyn. He is the second of three brothers and his family did not come from money. After attending Syracuse University in upstate New York, Brandon started a traditional 9 to 5 job at Hyatt, in Baltimore. In 1984, he moved back to New York City and worked at the newly opened Hard Rock Cafe. Brandon made some close friends, with whom he started his own sports bar called Sporting Club. The bar proved to be a massive success, and it attracted the attention of some very prominent figures in the sports world who wanted to emulate its success. Professional superstar athletes like Mickey Mantle and Lawrence Taylor consulted Steiner, hoping to open their own successful sports bars. As he continued to build relationships in the sporting community, Steiner started to hire athletes to make appearances at the Sporting Club. This would obviously bring in a ton of business, but it ultimately helped him identify an opportunity to monetize a need.

After observing that athletes needed professional help marketing themselves as valuable business assets, Steiner used $8,000 in savings and started the sports marketing company Steiner Associates. The company employed a relatively new type of business model at the time, one that lacked formal agreements. Although Steiner did have a great idea and vision for his new

company, he had to employ the "learn as you go" approach. According to Brandon,

> I thought we were doing really good in our first year, but we soon realized that we were about to go out of business. We didn't have formal compensation agreements with key staff members and almost half of them left. We were sprinting in the wrong direction. We were not placing enough emphasis on cash and we weren't managing our margins well. This was a wakeup call. I took out another mortgage on my house and adjusted.

Steiner now places a huge emphasis on something that is often overlooked by entrepreneurs: margins. He defines margins as the difference between revenues and expenses, and these are key indicators of success and excellent benchmarks to use when planning, according to him. Also, he feels that cash on hand is essential to ensure that the operations of a business do not cease. His view is that companies have the responsibility to pay their employees, and if they are unable to do that, the company needs to investigate whether it should close up shop, improve upon its existing business model, or follow a new model. Luckily for Steiner, he soon got his company back on track. He improved his new business model to focus on the company's financial viability; that is, he focused on the business's revenue and cost structures needed to meet its operating expenses and financial obligations.

By 1993, Steiner Sports was maintaining profits upwards of $5 million using a commission-based business model. In this model, Steiner Sports would act on the athlete's behalf and help him or her find endorsement deals, sell his or her authentic merchandise, or arrange public appearances and autograph signings. Steiner would then collect a percentage of the revenue paid to the athletes, often between 10% and 20%.

Today, Steiner Sports has 70 full-time employees and focuses most of its energies on the sports collectables market, as opposed to endorsement deals/appearances for athletes. It remains the largest sports memorabilia retailer in the world. As consumer preferences shift and demand changes, Steiner sports has been able to adapt well. Now it works with celebrities, not just athletes. For example, it will organize an auction to sell props from a certain film or sell clothes worn by a certain artist from a concert. Brandon maintains that his greatest difficulty is educating his clients on their own worth.

(Continued)

(Continued)

It's hard to get the clients to understand that "hey, these shoes might be worth something to someone; I should probably hold onto them." For celebrities and athletes it needs to become second nature for them because eventually their playing days will end, but that does not mean they can't still make money off of their performances.

From humble beginnings, Brandon Steiner created a sports empire. By 2005, Steiner Sports had reached deals with the University of Notre Dame, the New York Yankees, and the Dallas Cowboys. Per the deals, Steiner Sports has the license to sell a wide range of products including hats, game-used memorabilia, and jerseys. In 2009, in its most widely publicized deal, Steiner came to an agreement with the New York Yankees to be the chief broker of memorabilia from the old Yankee stadium. The road to get to this point was not an easy one for Brandon, but his business model was new and it brought a great amount of organization to a fragmented space. In his own words to aspiring entrepreneurs,

Don't necessarily try to be exclusively an inventor; try to be an improver. More often than not, people will try something and fail and then the next guy will come along and try that same thing and get rich. Opportunities to improve things are everywhere. The best entrepreneurs are able to make money by taking some invention and making it better.

Critical Thinking Questions

1. Consider Brandon's progression as an entrepreneur. Identify times when he jumped into a new opportunity and times when he pivoted and did something different.

2. Why should entrepreneurs be cash conscious?

3. Describe the Steiner Sports business model. ●

Sources:

Brandon Steiner (interview with author, November 20, 2018)
Van Riper, T. (2009). The selling of old Yankee Stadium. *Forbes.* Retrieved from https://www.forbes.com/2009/07/21/yankees-stadium-memorabilia-business-sports-jackson.html#2fad30ef3359

iterate, and gather evidence. However, the ability to tweak and change business models is not as quick or as efficient for larger or more established organizations, and some of them have ultimately failed because of their inability to change their business models. Consider BlackBerry, which stormed the business, government, and consumer markets with its smartphone technology in the early 2000s. Within a decade, BlackBerry failed to adapt to new competitors who were offering sleeker smartphones with additional functions such as touch interface and video/photo transmission, putting the company on the decline.[2] Similarly, Kodak failed to adapt to the digital camera revolution quickly enough, and Blockbuster did not respond in time to the growing threat of online media services provider Netflix. The point is that the business model in any company (big, small, new, old) must always be poised for adjustment and changes as new information is received and markets change.

But who says business models have to be reinvented at all? U.S.-based food company General Mills is entrepreneurial but also stays true to its business model by manufacturing food that meets the needs of its customers.[3] For instance, in response to the demand for less sugar and simpler ingredients, the company has introduced a new yogurt brand called YQ, which is targeted at key health influencers.

YQ may be considered a new innovation in yogurt products, but General Mills didn't need to change its business model to accommodate it—in fact, the product fit squarely within its existing business model of selling nutritional foods. As this example shows, the key to a successful business model is focusing on what customers want and where they are going.

5.2 THE FOUR PARTS OF A BUSINESS MODEL

≫ LO 5.2   Identify the four parts of a business model.

Let's begin a deeper exploration of the business model by breaking it down into its four major components. The business model consists of four main interlocking parts that together create "the business": the *offering*, the *customers*, the *infrastructure*, and the *financial viability*.[4] Without these four parts, there is no business, no company, no opportunity. All must coexist, and none can be ignored; however, each can be a source of innovation and advantage over the competition. In other words, competitive advantage doesn't always come from the product or service you are offering. It can come from the other areas of the business as well.

The Offering

The first part of the business model is the **offering**, which identifies what you are offering to a particular customer segment, the value generated for those customers, and how you will reach and communicate with them. The offering includes the **customer value proposition (CVP)**, which describes why a customer should buy and use your product or service. The "value" part of the CVP means how much your product or service is worth to your customers. For instance, it might only cost a plumber $40 to fix a burst pipe at a customer's house ($5 for travel, $5 for materials, and $30 for an hour's labor), but the value to the customer for having the problem fixed is far greater, which is why the plumber can afford to charge more.[5]

The CVP explains how you can help customers do something more inexpensively, easily, effectively, or quickly than before. We will explore the concept of the CVP in greater detail later in this chapter.

Offering: what you are offering to a particular customer segment, the value generated for those customers, and how you will reach and communicate with them.

Customer value proposition (CVP): a statement that describes why a customer should buy and use your product or service.

The Customers

Customers are the people who populate the segments of a market that your offering is serving (see Chapter 6: Developing Your Customers). They are the individuals or businesses willing to pay for what you are offering. Entrepreneurs typically can't serve everyone in a market, so you have to choose who you will target. In addition, you have to determine how you will reach those segments and how you will maintain a relationship with the customer. Bryan Bitticks is an entrepreneur and franchise owner of Great Clips hair salons, headquartered in Minneapolis.[6] Bitticks created a virtual online experience that enabled its customers to check in online and explore wait times. This approach has attracted thousands of younger tech-savvy customers who are more accustomed to booking appointments online. The convenience and comfort that Great Clips provides customers *before* they walk through the Great Clips door is all part of the customer experience and tied to the offering.

Customers: people who populate the segments of a market served by the offering.

The Infrastructure

The **infrastructure** generally includes all the resources (people, technology, products, suppliers, partners, facilities) that an entrepreneur must have in order to deliver the CVP. For example, Justin Gold, founder of the nut butters brand Justin's, started off using limited resources, such as his own food processor, to make his nut butter in his own kitchen.[7] When he tried to scale his business, he realized that he could not afford the types of peanut butter mills used by manufacturers. The mills turn the peanuts or other nuts into the actual buttery product. Gold went out and bought the oldest food processors he could and started to produce perfect peanut butter that was impossible for the traditional manufacturers to mimic. By being resourceful, Gold was able to build competitive advantage and uniqueness into his infrastructure to create a successful business.

Infrastructure: the resources (people, technology, products, suppliers, partners, facilities) that an entrepreneur must have in order to deliver the CVP.

Financial Viability

Financial viability defines the revenue and cost structures a business needs to meet its operating expenses and financial obligations: How much will it cost to deliver the offering to our customers? How much revenue can we generate from customers? And, of course, the difference between revenue and cost is profit.

For example, when Brandon Steiner, founder of Steiner Sports, realized the business wasn't managing its margins or meeting its financial obligations, he took out another mortgage on his house and made some changes to his business model to meet the needs of his customers (see Entrepreneurship in Action).

People often make a mistake in thinking that the business model is just about revenue and costs, but a business model is more than a financial model. It has to describe more than how you intend to make money; it needs to explain why a customer would give you money in the first place and what's in it for the customer. This is where the CVP comes in.

Financial viability: defines the revenue and cost structures a business needs to meet its operating expenses and financial obligations.

The Rights of Research Participants

Credit: MARICE COHN BAND/Newscom

Leanna Archer with her hair product

Leanna Archer started her entrepreneurial venture when she was only 9 years old. Archer used her grandmother's homemade hair care products and received numerous compliments on the softness of her hair. Motivated to investigate starting her own hair care business, Archer obtained her grandmother's recipe, which used only natural, nonchemical ingredients. Her parents provided funding, and Archer began experimenting with different ingredients. Once several prototypes had been created, Archer sent samples to neighbors to get feedback. With the success of her trials and with family helping with bookkeeping and other administrative tasks, she launched the Leanna's Hair product lines. By the time she was ready to graduate from high school, her company was bringing in a six-figure income and the story of her "teenpreneurial" success had been featured in *Forbes*, *TIME*, and *INC Magazine*, among other international publications.

Entrepreneurs often conduct focus groups to see whether they are, in fact, providing value to customers. Before beginning testing and experimentation, the entrepreneur must consider some ethical concerns related to market research and the rights of research participants. Most notably, people participating in experiments have the right to informed consent; the right to be treated with dignity regardless of racial or ethnic background, sexual preference, or socioeconomic status; the right to privacy and confidentiality; and the right not to be deceived or harmed as a consequence of research participation. In addition, there are legal requirements for testing food items and personal care products that come into contact with the human body, as well as regulations on the use of animals in product testing.

As long as the researcher is able to conduct the market research ethically and laws are followed, research doesn't have to be expensive. For example, entrepreneurs may enlist a group of people to try out free samples of a product in exchange for submitting an evaluation or attending a focus group afterward. There are also many laboratories that perform testing for regulatory compliance, with various price structures to suit different budgets.

Critical Thinking Questions

1. How would you find out what kinds of testing are required for an entrepreneurial product or service?

2. If your product or service was suitable for nonprofessional testing in people's homes or at a focus group, whom would you recruit to participate in your test? Explain how you would choose your best customer types to participate.

3. How would you ensure that the participants in your experiments were treated ethically and had their rights protected? ●

Sources

Al Smadi, S. (n.d.). *Ethics in market research: Concerns over rights of research participants.* Retrieved from http://wbiconpro.com/Marketing/Sami.pdf

Entrepreneur Media Inc. (2016). *Small business encyclopedia: Market testing.* Retrieved from http://www.entrepreneur.com/encyclopedia/market-testing

Snepenger, D. J. (2007, April 5). Marketing research for entrepreneurs and small business managers. *Montguide.* Retrieved from http://msucommunitydevelopment.org/pubs/mt9013.pdf

Tumati, P. (2010). Market research tips for startups. *Go4Funding.* Retrieved from http://www.go4funding.com/Articles/Market-Research-Tips-For-Startups.aspx

5.3 THE CUSTOMER VALUE PROPOSITION (CVP)

>> **LO 5.3** **Explain the importance of the Customer Value Proposition.**

The CVP is perhaps the most important part of your business model. The key word in CVP is *customer*. The focus should always be on the value generated for the customer and how this value is then captured by the business in the form of profit.[8]

For your CVP to be truly effective, it needs three qualities:

- It must offer better value than the competition.

- It must be measurable in monetary terms (i.e., you must be able to prove that your CVP is better value than other offerings on the market).

- It must be sustainable (i.e., you must have the ability to execute it for a considerable length of time).[9]

In Chapter 4, we explored the concept of design thinking and the phases entrepreneurs go through to identify needs and develop solutions to meet those needs. As we have learned, design thinking is ultimately an iterative and collaborative process that combines the skills of observation, synthesis, searching and generating alternatives, critical thinking, feedback, visual representation, creativity, problem solving, and need finding. Design thinking helps you create a CVP that is unique and differentiating.[10] As with design thinking, the CVP means thinking about your business from the customer's viewpoint rather than from an organizational perspective. Your CVP must demonstrate that you are meeting the needs of various customer segments.

Jobs, Pain Points, and Needs

The key to a successful CVP is a deep understanding of what the customer really wants or needs—not just how the customer does things now. It is an exciting opportunity to meet the needs of a real customer who wants to accomplish a goal, to get the job done.[11] Creating your CVP does not begin with trying to persuade customers to buy your product or service. Rather, it's about finding a goal—a job that the customer needs done—and then proposing a way to achieve that goal.[12] It's about uncovering what your customer needs and providing solutions to meet those needs. It's about relieving pain points. So, the CVP is that message that screams to a customer, "Hey! I can help you get a job done, relieve a pain point, or fulfill a need!" It's a promise to the customer—a promise of value.

Businesses start and survive because they successfully answer three questions for customers: What's in it for me? Why should I believe you? Why should I care? Best-selling business author Doug Hall calls these the overt benefit, real reason to believe, and dramatic difference, respectively.[13] The **overt benefit** is the one big benefit for the customer. Not the list of benefits—just the one big one. The marketplace is too cluttered and customers don't have time or want to figure out what's cool about your product or service. And if it's not clearly articulated, the benefit is really invisible. This means the CVP is also invisible. **Real reason to believe** provides evidence to the customer that you will do as you promise. You have to have credibility in the eyes of the customer, and this is more important than ever with the proliferation of online reviews. If you don't deliver on your promise, word travels fast online. **Dramatic difference** relates to uniqueness and how your product or service is different from the many other options that are likely available.

For example, the Swedish home-furnishings company IKEA understood the goal of customers who needed to furnish their rooms or apartments on a tight budget but did not want to settle for unattractive, worn, secondhand pieces. By providing do-it-yourself furniture kits at a lower cost than ready-made furniture sold in major furniture stores, IKEA solved the problem of obtaining good-quality, new, stylish furniture for a low price. IKEA is in the process of revamping its business model to meet the growing needs of its customers by providing affordable home delivery, renting furniture, opening stores in city center locations (rather than out of town), and using virtual reality to help people visualize home interiors.[14]

Similarly, FedEx made the job of transporting a letter or package overnight effortless in comparison with the regular mailing and parcel delivery services that existed in the 1970s when FedEx (then called Federal Express) was launched.[15]

In creating their CVPs, both IKEA and FedEx first focused on the jobs that the customer needed to get done before coming up with a solution to meet this need. The CVP also involves identifying ways in which your company best fits into customers' lifestyles;

Overt benefit: the one big benefit for your customer.

Real reason to believe: provides evidence to the customer that you will do as you promise.

Dramatic difference: the uniqueness of your product or service in relation to other available options.

Overt Benefit, Real Reason to Believe, and Dramatic Difference

Doug Hall is a speaker, inventor, author, and researcher. He loves data and the power that data have to help startups get past the idea stage. He analyzed 4,000 concept descriptions for new products or services in order to answer the question, "What is going on in customers' minds when they are making buying decisions?" Hall and his team conceived the Three Laws of Marketing Physics, which "define and describe the universe of customer purchase behavior": overt benefit, real reason to believe, and dramatic difference. Then, by using complex statistical methods to identify patterns and recurring themes, Doug was able to model and predict the success of new products. "Success" is defined as a product or service that is actively on the market for at least 5 years.

Hall found that if the product or service had a high overt benefit, its probability of success was 38%. This is actually pretty high when compared to the probability of success with a low overt benefit, which was only 13%. If the product or service had a high reason to believe, the probability of success was 42% (versus 18% for low reason to believe). If the product or service had a high dramatic difference, the probability of success was 53% (versus 15% for low dramatic difference). According to Hall, when a strong overt benefit and real reason to believe was paired with a high dramatic difference, "sales and profits explode." ●

Source: Hall, D. (2005). *Jump start your business brain: The scientific way to make more money.* Cincinnati, OH: Eureka! Institute.

The Tata Nano, the world's cheapest car

it means analyzing the relationships you need to establish with customers versus the relationships your customers expect to establish with you; finally, it emphasizes how much customers are willing to pay for value, rather than trying to extract money from your customers.[16] To illustrate these points, let's look at an example of a successful CVP in action.

Tata Motors, an automotive manufacturing company in India previously known for building trucks and buses, created a CVP to provide radically low-cost cars for the people of India. Prior to the introduction in 2008 of Tata's highly affordable car, millions of citizens mostly used scooters to get around. Sometimes whole families would put themselves at risk by crowding onto a scooter, exposed to rain, wind, and traffic hazards. The problem was that many families could not afford to buy a car—even the cheapest car cost five times more than a scooter—so they had to make do with what they could afford.

Tata Motors created a CVP focused on providing an affordable, safer, more comfortable mode of transport for the low price of $2,500. This price was intended to make the car competitive with scooters, which its customer segments were currently buying.

Yet Tata Motors' existing business model did not allow the company to create a car at the price it wanted. Creating such a radically low-cost car would require a new business model that would support the low price point. Tata needed to find ways to cut the costs of manufacturing in order to make the car affordable for its customer segments.

How did Tata do it? First, it created a product design process that removed as much cost as possible from the car. Tata looked at eliminating everything it possibly could to reduce the number of parts used in the car. The resulting car has no air conditioning, no power steering, no power windows, no fabric covering the seats, no radio, no central locking of doors, and only the driver's seat is adjustable.[17] Tata also used 60% fewer suppliers than are needed for a typical economy car, thus giving more business to fewer suppliers and reducing coordination costs.

Tata then outsourced 83% of the car's components to find the lowest possible cost. What's more, Tata worked closely with its suppliers from the start, getting them involved in designing the components rather than merely building them to Tata's specifications. For example, instead of specifying, "build a windshield wiper X inches long with a Y diameter," Tata issued a more functional goal: "wipe water from the windshield." This allowed suppliers to come up with new, innovative, and low-cost ways to meet goals. In the case of the car's wipers, the suppliers came up with the idea of having only one wiper blade rather than the standard two wipers.

Next, Tata created a different manufacturing process that reduced the cost of final assembly. It made the innovative decision to save costs by not assembling its cars. Instead, Tata ships a "kit" with all the required parts in modules to a network of local entrepreneurs who assemble the cars on demand. The modules are designed to be glued together rather than welded because gluing is less expensive and doesn't require costly welding equipment. In addition to assembling the cars, the local entrepreneurs sell and service the cars.

By reinventing its business model to fulfill its CVP, Tata's innovative approach to the production, design, and manufacturing of cars opened up a whole new market to meet the needs of hundreds of thousands of people who previously couldn't afford cars.[18] Tata didn't simply create a low-cost car; the company created a car that delivered the value customers were willing to pay for. Tata Motors attacked the problem of affordability for its customers, but even the best-thought-out CVP is no guarantee for success. Though the Nano solved the problem of affordability, comfort, and safety, customer demand was less than expected.[19] Furthermore, increased regulation on emission requirements in India would require additional investment in production and design. Today the car will only be produced on demand.[20] Company insiders and executives suggest that marketing the Nano as the "world's cheapest car" backfired as the perception of poor quality overshadowed its value proposition.[21]

Four Problems Experienced by Customers

Typically, customers face at least one of four problems that prevent them from getting a job done: lack of time, lack of money, lack of skills, or lack of access. As an entrepreneur, if you can find a new way to solve one of these problems, you're on your way to creating a strong CVP. Let's take a look at how some companies have resolved each of these problems with their own CVPs.

Lack of Time

In the United States, people spend 1.1 billion hours obtaining medical care that equates to $52 billion in time lost. In other words, Americans are spending, on average, $43 of their own money (money that could be earned working) every time they go to the doctor.[22] Waiting to be seen by the doctor, hanging around for results, filling out paperwork, being seen by the doctor, and getting prescriptions filled takes up hours of valuable time. The ThedaCare hospital system in Wisconsin has found a solution to this time-wasting problem by ensuring that patients are seen more quickly and that results are dispatched before they leave, rather than days later. They implemented systems in which value to the patient is evaluated at every touchpoint, from check-in to discharge. From online medical records to continuous improvement processes, the patient is always their primary concern. Additionally, all levels of staff are required to innovate and experiment in ways that increase productivity and patient satisfaction.[23]

Lack of Money

Delivering previously unaffordable products or services for less money can help beat the competition and open up a whole new market. Getting a taxi used to be a luxury until Uber came along; dining out was viewed as an unnecessary expense before Groupon started to offer restaurant deals and discounts; and staying in decent accommodation seemed like an impossibility for many until Airbnb launched its hospitality service. Uber, Groupon, and Airbnb are among thousands of startups that have succeeded in democratizing services previously reserved for a small portion of the population.

Overt Benefit, Real Reason to Believe, and Dramatic Difference

Let's test Doug Hall's three laws (see p. 117): overt benefit, real reason to believe, and dramatic difference. Identify 15 products that currently exist in the food space. Go to a local grocery store but look for the lesser-known brands. In other words, look for the products of startup entrepreneurs. Whole Foods is a great place to look because they are known for carrying new and local brands, but any equivalent store will do. You can go online to Amazon and see Whole Foods offerings there because Amazon now owns Whole Foods, but it's actually more fun to go to the store ... so get away from your computer!

Don't just randomly choose 15 products. First, choose five product categories, such as chips, nutrition bars, energy drinks, frozen pizza, herbal supplements, shampoo. Choose whatever categories interest you. For each of the five categories, identify three products and score each product as high, medium, or low on overt benefit; real reason to believe; and dramatic difference. Create a chart like the one below for your analysis. Extra action points are earned if you ask someone in the store which of the products you analyzed are the best sellers!

Product Category: _____

	OVERT BENEFIT I UNDERSTAND WHAT THE OBVIOUS BENEFIT OF THIS PRODUCT IS FOR THE CUSTOMER.	REASON TO BELIEVE IT'S CLEAR WHY THIS PRODUCT CAN DELIVER ON WHAT IT PROMISES TO DO.	DRAMATIC DIFFERENCE THE OVERT BENEFIT AND REASON TO BELIEVE REPRESENT SOMETHING NEW OR NOVEL TO THE WORLD.
Product 1:	High / Med / Low	High / Med / Low	High / Med / Low
Product 2:	High / Med / Low	High / Med / Low	High / Med / Low
Product 3:	High / Med / Low	High / Med / Low	High / Med / Low

Critical Thinking Questions

1. Did Hall's Three Laws stand up to your test? Why or why not?

2. How can you improve your own idea to increase its probability of success?

3. Did you really go ask someone at the store which of your analyzed products are the best sellers? If you didn't, what is preventing you from taking such action? If you did, well done. ●

Lack of Skills

In many areas of life, people might like to accomplish a task but lack the specialized skills to get the job done. This common problem creates an opportunity to provide easy-to-use solutions that convert complex professional-level tools into consumer products.

In the mid-19th century, as fewer households had servants or custom tailors, many women wished to sew clothing for themselves and their families but lacked the skills to make a well-fitting garment based on a picture in a fashion magazine. The solution was the sewing pattern that was printed on tissue paper, sold in various sizes, and accompanied by instructions that a nonexpert could follow.

A more recent example of how ease of use transformed customers' lives is the shift from computers with arcane command-line interfaces to computers with graphical user interfaces like Apple's Macintosh or Microsoft's Windows. These new interfaces meant that you no longer had to have expertise in computer programming to use a computer. To solve another common problem—lack of writing skills—online grammar checking platform Grammarly enables users to communicate better. Since its launch in 2008, Grammarly has acquired almost 7 million daily users.[24]

Lack of Access

Finally, people struggle with lack of access, which prevents them from getting a job done. For example, most of us think nothing of traveling on public transport to get to our chosen destinations, but millions of visually impaired people lack the ability to travel independently. UK-based nonprofit organization Wayfindr aims to solve this problem by providing an open standard (software that can be used by anyone) app that gives audio instructions to help vision-impaired people to navigate their journey without a human guide (https://www.wayfindr.net). This startup has set a goal to make Wayfindr available to the 285 million blind people living in the world today, thereby increasing their access to travel.

Another example of the lack-of-access problem is solar energy. The technology for small-scale solar collectors has been available since the 1970s, but it is generally suitable only for commercial buildings and homes with a large amount of roof space—and they need to be located where they receive direct sunlight for many hours per day. Moreover, it requires a sizable investment beyond the means of low-income homeowners, let alone rental tenants. To solve this problem of access, companies like Dvinci Energy, founded by entrepreneur Walid Halty, have devised a program to make solar energy affordable and accessible to everyone.[25]

A user of the Wayfindr app

5.4 DIFFERENT TYPES OF CVPs AND CUSTOMER SEGMENTS

>> **LO 5.4** **Describe the different types of Customer Value Propositions and learn how to identify your customer segments.**

You may feel you have the greatest product or service idea in the world, but how do you convince others of its greatness? This is where many entrepreneurs fall short: They have the idea in mind but may not be so clear on the marketing or the execution. In fact, some entrepreneurs cannot even prove that customers want to buy their offering. This is where the CVP really fulfills its potential, as it delineates the value of your idea in meeting customer needs. In this section, we will explore different types of CVPs and learn how to identify your customer segments.

Types of Value Propositions

Some CVPs are better than others. Let's explore three main approaches to creating value propositions: the all-benefits, points-of-difference, and resonating-focus approaches (see Figure 5.2).[26]

The **all-benefits** approach to CVP involves identifying and promoting all the benefits of your product or service to customer segments, with little regard for the competition or any real insight into what the customer really wants or needs. This is the least impactful approach for creating a value proposition because it's overly product focused. In other words, you are promoting features and benefits that customers may not even need.

The **points-of-difference** approach produces a stronger CVP than all-benefits because it focuses on your product or service relative to the competition and recognizes that your offering is unique and different from others on the market. However, although focusing on the differences may help you differentiate your business from the competition, it still doesn't provide evidence that customers will also find the differences valuable. Simply assuming that customers will find these points of difference favorable is not evidence enough to prove they will buy from you.

A CVP that uses the **resonating-focus** approach (also called "just what the customer wants" or **product–market fit**) is the "gold standard." All-benefits and points-of-difference CVPs each provide a laundry list of the presumed benefits to the customers,

All-benefits: a type of value proposition that involves identifying and promoting all the benefits of a product or service to customer segments, with little regard for the competition or any real insight into what the customer really wants or needs.

Points-of-difference: a type of value proposition that focuses on the product or service relative to the competition and how the offering is different from others on the market.

Resonating-focus: a type of value proposition that describes why people will really like your product and focuses on the customers and what they really need and value.

Product–market fit: an offering that meets the needs of customers.

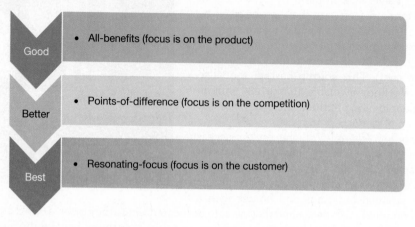

FIGURE 5.2

Three Types of Value Propositions

Good
- All-benefits (focus is on the product)

Better
- Points-of-difference (focus is on the competition)

Best
- Resonating-focus (focus is on the customer)

© Anastasia Marynych/Shutterstock

Coca-Cola Zero advertising is aimed at men while Diet Coke is aimed at women.

and the differences between your products or services in comparison with the competition, but a resonating-focus CVP drills down to what is most important to the customer. It describes why people will buy your product and focuses on the customers and what they really need and value. Your offering shows an understanding of your customers' problems and needs and describes how you intend to meet their demands.[27]

When it comes to defining your customer, you may be tempted to think that everyone will want to buy your product or service. In fact, trying to aim the CVP at "everyone" is a very common mistake made by young entrepreneurs. As a knowledgeable entrepreneur, you must realize that a major part of your business proposition is to figure out which customers to focus on and which ones to ignore. For example, if you're trying to sell luxury yachting experiences, you may target professionals between 30 and 65, with a high income, who live in a location close to water, and who have an interest in water sports. Remember, if you're not clear on your customer segment, your CVP will also not be clear.[28]

Types of Customer Segments

Many products and services are attractive to more than one customer segment. How, then, can a "gold standard" CVP be developed if the focus is supposed to center on the customer? The answer is that businesses often have different CVPs for each customer segment. This is to ensure they are meeting the needs of the customers within each segment. In this section, we will explore how businesses adjust their CVPs to cater to different types of customer segments.

Consider Diet Coke and Coca-Cola Zero. The two products have very similar ingredients, but they are aimed at different target markets. Why? Market research indicated that young men shied away from Diet Coke because they associated it with women who were trying to lose weight.[29] In response, a new CVP was created, resulting in Coca-Cola Zero, which many people believe is aimed at men.[30] By understanding the motivations, desires, and unmet needs of your customers, you are better able to create a product or service that they will be willing to buy.

Customer segments targeted by different types of businesses include mass markets, niche markets, segmented markets, diversified markets, and multisided markets. Let's take a closer look at each of these.

A **mass market** is a large group of customers with very similar needs and problems. You may have heard of the phrase "It's gone mass market," which means a product or a service is being purchased by an enormous proportion of customers all looking for the same thing. Computers, soap, cars, insurance, and health care are examples of mass market products. Coke and Pepsi are mass market products because they target a wide range of customer groups, from youths to families.

A **niche market** is a small market segment consisting of customers with specific needs and requirements. The CVP is tailored to meet these particular needs. For example, entrepreneurs Carlton and Hazel Solle created the BioScarf as an alternative to the common filtration masks used in China to protect local citizens from breathing in the polluted air (https://www.bioscarf.com). The BioScarf is a more fashionable and comfortable filtration mask made from sustainable materials and protects its user from germs, pollen, and cigarette smoke. BioScarf also operates a Plus One program that donates a BioScarf to people in need for every one sold.

A **segmented market** is divided into groups according to customers' different needs and problems. For example, a bank might provide different services to its wealthier clients than to people with an average income, or offer different products for small versus large businesses. Segmenting customers is a good way of generating more business.

A **diversified market** offers a variety of services to serve two or more customer segments with different needs and problems that bear no relationship to each other. Amazon is a good example of an organization that diversified from its retail business—selling books and other tangible products—to sell cloud computing services, online storage space, and on-demand server usage. In short, Amazon adapted its CVP to cater to a whole new wave of customers, such as web companies, that would buy these computing services.[31]

Multisided markets are markets with two or more customer segments that are linked but are independent of each other. For example, a free newspaper caters to its readers by providing commuters with newsworthy content. The newspaper also needs to prove to advertisers that it has a large readership in order to get the revenue to produce and distribute the free publication. The newspaper is dependent on both of these two distinct customer segments in order to be successful.[32]

Matching the right CVP to targeted customer segments is essential to the development of a scalable business model.

Photo courtesy of BioScarf

BioScarf, an alternative, fashionable air filtration mask

Mass market: a large group of customers with very similar needs and problems.

Niche market: a small market segment that consists of customers with specific needs and requirements.

Segmented market: a market divided into groups according to customers' different needs and problems.

Diversified market: two or more customer segments with different needs and problems that bear no relationship to each other.

Multisided markets: markets with two or more customer segments that are mutually independent of each other.

Business model canvas (BMC): a one-page plan that divides the business model into nine components in order to provide a more thorough overview.

5.5 THE BUSINESS MODEL CANVAS (BMC)

>> **LO 5.5** Identify the nine components of the Business Model Canvas.

As we have learned, there are four major parts of the business model: the offering, the customers, the infrastructure, and the financial viability. In this section, we further explore how a company creates, delivers, and captures value for customers through a more in-depth study of the **Business Model Canvas (BMC)**.[33] The BMC, introduced in 2008 by Swiss business theorist Alexander Osterwalder, divides the business model's four parts into nine components in order to provide a more thorough overview of the logic of the business model. When the four parts are divided into nine components, the result looks like this:

- The offering constitutes the (1) value proposition.
- Customers relate to (2) customer segments, (3) channels, and (4) customer relationships.

- Infrastructure includes (5) key activities, (6) key resources, and (7) key partners.
- Financial viability includes (8) cost structure and (9) revenue streams.

Figure 5.3 illustrates the nine components of a BMC using an idea for a new retail store that sells trendy T-shirts emblazoned with original designs by young, emerging artists.

Let's apply the T-shirt store example to some questions that each of the nine components must address.

1. **Customer Value Proposition:** As described earlier in this chapter, the CVP is designed to solve a customer problem or meet a need. With regard to your new T-shirt business, ask yourself the following: What value do we deliver? What bundle of products and services are we offering? What are we helping customers achieve by providing a new range of T-shirts?

2. **Customer Segments:** As defined above, a customer segment is a part of the customer grouping of a market. For example, "gluten-free" is a segment of the group of customers who buy food; another segment would be customers who are lactose intolerant. The customer segmentation questions for the T-shirt business are these: Who are your most important customers? What segment of the market would be most likely to buy your T-shirts?

3. **Channels:** The value proposition is delivered through communication, distribution, and sales channels. The core question here: What are all the ways in which you can reach your customers? For example, you could reach your customers online, through a brick-and-mortar store, and/or through word of mouth.

4. **Customer Relationships:** Relationships can be developed on a one-to-one basis in a brick-and-mortar T-shirt store and/or through a purely automated process of selling the T-shirts online. Customer relationships go beyond just buying and selling; they depend on engendering positive feelings about your business, building a sense of customer identity ("I am a so-and-so T-shirt customer"), and motivating customers to want to bring their friends into the relationship. The key here is one of the most important questions an entrepreneur can answer: How do you establish and maintain relationships with your customers?

5. **Key Activities:** What are the most important activities that the company participates in to get the job done? When running a T-shirt business, you will need to consider such activities as stock management, sales management, and T-shirt design selection.

6. **Key Resources:** Resources are what you need to develop the business, create products and services, and deliver on your CVP. Resources take many forms and include people, technology, information, equipment, and finances. How much and which resources will you need if your company has 1,000 customers or 1,000,000? What resources do you need to accomplish the key activities? If you're opening up a store, then you need to figure out the location and size; you also need people who are going to sell your T-shirts, space to store inventory, and a range of artists who will provide the designs for your T-shirts. You will also need to calculate how much money you will need to set up, as well as accumulate the skills, knowledge, and information you need to start your own business.

7. **Key Partners:** Entrepreneurs are not able to do everything by themselves, so partnering with suppliers, associates, and distributors is a logical option, not only for strategic purposes but also for efficiency. For example, you could partner with a designer who could advise you on the artwork of the T-shirts as well as provide you with a network of other designers. Could some activities be outsourced? Do you have a network of suppliers/buyers you could tap into or negotiate with?

8. **Revenue Streams:** Revenue is generated if a successful value proposition is delivered. Here you need to ask: How much are my customers willing to pay? How many customers do I need? How much cash can be generated through T-shirt sales in the store or T-shirt sales online? How much does each stream contribute to the total? (We will explore revenue models in further detail in Chapter 9.)

9. **Cost Structure:** The cost structure represents all expenses required to execute and run the business model. What are the most important costs inherent in the business model? Which resources are the most expensive to get? Which activities are the most expensive? Store rental, employee salaries, the cost of purchasing T-shirt materials and designs, and the cost of sales and marketing are all factors to consider when formulating a cost structure.

Remember, a business model is about creating, capturing, and delivering value. The BMC is a great tool to help you think about this. The right side of the BMC is about creating value and the left side is about delivering that value as efficiently as possible. Additionally, the BMC encourages you to find answers to the most important questions and think about them in a structured way, using the canvas to unlock your creativity. The process is iterative—you'll probably be moving back and forth between the boxes as you test ideas in relation to each other. Not only that, some of your ideas will need to be tested through experimentation before you have a solid answer.

To stay competitive, it is important to keep refining and revisiting your business model because, as we saw at the beginning of this chapter with the examples of BlackBerry, Blockbuster, and Kodak, leaving your model to stagnate can lead to business failure.

FIGURE 5.3

The Business Model Canvas

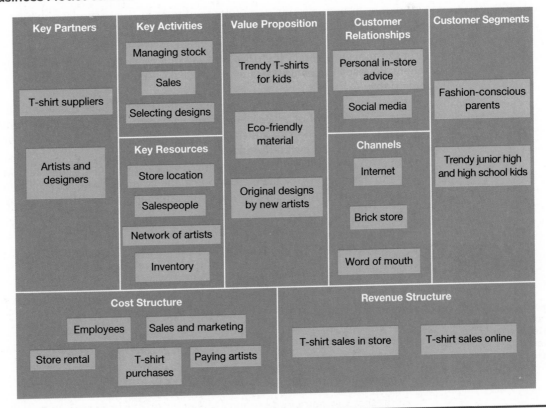

Source: Osterwalder, A., & Pigneur, Y. (2010). *Business model generation.* Hoboken, NJ: John Wiley & Sons. Retrieved from http://www.businessmodelgeneration.com/canvas/bmc

Create Your Own BMC

Download a free copy of the Business Model Canvas from http://www.businessmodelgeneration.com/canvas/bmc.

Yes, we want you to fill out the canvas with one of the many business ideas you probably have at this stage. But most students don't know where to start. Do you start with the value proposition, key resources, or customer segments?

To answer this question, fold the canvas in half so there is a crease down the middle of the page. Now open the page to its original position. The area of the canvas to the right of the crease is all about *creating* value. The area of the canvas to the left of the crease is all about *delivering* that value in an efficient way.

In order to build an innovative and sustainable business model, always focus on the right (value creation) side of the canvas first. The left (value delivery) side of the canvas is operational and process oriented. Don't spend too much time on the left until you have established something truly valuable for customers.

Again, every completed box is just a guess. Once your canvas is completed, your job is to begin testing. Start by testing the value proposition with the customer segment you've identified—the product–market fit. Are you offering something people want?

Now you are ready to complete your first canvas. Take an idea and complete a canvas using the example in Figure 5.3 as a guide.

Critical Thinking Questions

1. Why do you think this tool is called the Business Model Canvas?
2. In what ways does the division between value creation and value delivery help clarify the process of refining the business model?
3. In completing a BMC for your idea, which boxes were more difficult to fill out? Why? What are you going to do now with your completed BMC? ●

Thinking through all nine components of your business model helps you understand how the various parts work together: the value you'll create for customers, the processes you must implement to deliver value, the resources you need, and the way you'll make money. Overall, the goal is to lay out your assumptions so that you can test them. Be ready to change because your ideas will likely evolve before you get the formula right.

The common thread running through examples like IKEA, FedEx, and Tata Motors isn't that a particular set of processes is best. Each company has created its own processes and resource models to suit its CVP and industry. Tata Motors not only succeeded in creating their own tailored CVP but also gave some serious thought to how much money they would need to action their processes. Without sound financial models built into their respective business models, the companies never would have succeeded. One of the biggest considerations in building your own business model is money—it matters.

The Lean Canvas: A Business Model Canvas Alternative

Lean Canvas: an adapted version of the BMC that was created to better address the needs of startup entrepreneurs.

There have been many adaptations of the BMC, and one has emerged as very popular for entrepreneurs: the **Lean Canvas**.[34] Unlike the BMC, the Lean Canvas

- Places less emphasis on customer segments but more emphasis on likely first adopters
- Begins with a problem rather than value proposition
- Addresses key metrics and suggests focusing on one key metric to track how your business is doing
- Addresses competitive advantage and uniqueness, called "unfair advantage"

The Lean Canvas ignores some of the boxes in the BMC. Key activities and resources, customer relationships, and key partners are eliminated. Key activities in the Lean Canvas are covered in the Solutions box. Customer relationships are covered in the Channels box. Key partners in the Lean Canvas were eliminated because it may be too early for the entrepreneurs to think about strategic partners when the business is not truly functioning yet. Let's take a look at the new boxes in the Lean Canvas (see Figure 5.4) that are not included in the BMC.

Problem: Startups too often build something that doesn't solve a problem, so problem understanding and validation is essential. If you already have a product or service in mind, then what is the problem you are solving for your customers? Is it a big enough problem? Conversely, start with the problem first, validate it's an actual problem, and then create a solution. We talked a lot about this in Chapters 3 and 4!

Solution: The Solution box is where you note potential solutions to the problems identified. The Lean Canvas purposely keeps this box small so you don't fall in love too quickly with an idea and you test the solution sooner rather than later.

Key Metrics: It's easy to get dizzy from information overload and drown in the numbers. The Lean Canvas encourages identifying what is most important for your stage of business and keeping track of that. Key metrics may be the cost of acquiring a new customer, revenue, activating new users, or retention rate.

Unfair Advantage: Unfair advantage is the same thing as competitive advantage; it just sounds a bit more hip for entrepreneurs! This box is important because as you test solutions, your advantage over the competition is likely to emerge. If there is no unfair advantage, long-term success is unlikely. Sources of unfair advantage may take the form of user friendliness, product design, service experience, influence on social media, and price.

Leanstack.com is a great free resource that will walk you through an online version of the Lean Canvas. You can develop your own there!

FIGURE 5.4

The Lean Canvas

PROBLEM	SOLUTION	UNIQUE VALUE PROPOSITION	UNFAIR ADVANTAGE	CUSTOMER SEGMENTS
	KEY METRICS		CHANNELS	
EXISTING ALTERNATIVES		HIGH-LEVEL CONCEPT		EARLY ADOPTERS
COST STRUCTURE		REVENUE STREAMS		

Source: Leanstack (2019). *The Lean Canvas*. Retrieved from https://leanstack.com/leancanvas

In general, the Lean Canvas works better for those at the very early stages of a startup when a solution to a particular problem has not been chosen, or a product has not yet been developed, or few actions have been taken. If the BMC is too complex for where you are in your startup, then the Lean Canvas may be a great alternative. Just as with the BMC, however, every box is a hypothesis that needs to be tested, validated, or changed. Both the BMC and Lean Canvas are tools to help you identify a model that will help you create a sustainable business. ●

$SAGE edge™

Get the tools you need to sharpen your study skills. SAGE edge offers a robust online environment featuring an impressive array of free tools and resources.

- Access practice quizzes, eFlashcards, video, and multimedia at **edge.sagepub.com/neckentrepreneurship2e**

SUMMARY

5.1   Define the business model.

The business model is the framework for creating and delivering consumer value, while extracting value for the entrepreneur as well.

5.2   Identify the four core areas of a business model.

Each business model includes an offering, customers, infrastructure, and financial viability.

5.3   Explain the importance of the Customer Value Proposition.

The CVP outlines exactly how the firm will generate value, how it will generate it in excess of its competition, and how it will continue to do so in the future. As the true measure of any business is creating value, the true measure of a business model is its customer value proposition.

5.4   Describe the different types of Customer Value Propositions and learn how to identify your customer segments.

Businesses tend to have different CVPs for each customer segment. This is to ensure they are meeting the needs of the customers within each segment. Examples of different customer segments targeted by different types of businesses include mass market, niche market, segmented market, diversified market, and multisided markets. Types of CVPs include all-benefits, points of difference, and resonating focus.

5.5   Identify the nine components of the Business Model Canvas.

The four core elements of a business model can be expanded to nine business model components. Separating core elements into their respective components makes them easier to define and integrate with one another. The offering constitutes the (1) value proposition. Customers relate to (2) customer segments, (3) channels, and (4) customer relationships. Infrastructure includes (5) key activities, (6) key resources, and (7) key partners. Financial viability includes (8) cost structure and (9) revenue streams.

5.6   Explore the Lean Canvas as an alternative to the Business Model Canvas.

The Lean Canvas is an adapted version of the BMC and was created to better address the needs of startup entrepreneurs. The Lean Canvas replaces the BMC components of customer relationships, key activities, key resources, and key partners with unfair advantage, solution, key metrics, and problem, respectively. The focus of the Lean Canvas is problem and solution, whereas the BMC focuses more on value proposition and customer segments.

KEY TERMS

All-benefits   115

Business model   105

Business model canvas (BMC)   117

Customer value proposition (CVP)   109

Customers   109

Diversified market   117

Evidence-based entrepreneurship   105

Financial viability   109

Infrastructure   109

Lean Canvas   120

Mass market   117

Multisided markets   117

Niche market   117

Offering   109

Points-of-difference   115

Product–market fit   115

Resonating-focus   115

Segmented market   117

Gautam Gupta, cofounder, NatureBox

Gautam Gupta and his cofounder Ken Chen met during their time at Babson College and quickly became great friends. They bonded over everything related to entrepreneurship and decided to start a business together. In addition to their entrepreneurship obsession, they both had a passion for food. For Gautam, food was very personal. He struggled with obesity until he was 18 years old, when he started learning everything he could about diet and exercise. He eliminated all chips, candy, soda, and other junk food from his diet and started exercising regularly. His hard work resulted in a loss of 70 pounds before he started his first year at Babson College in August 2003.

Gautam's weight loss journey introduced him to nutrition science. He quickly discovered that snacking was one of the leading causes of obesity and the single greatest source of empty calories. He also noticed that all snacks deemed "healthy" didn't really taste very good. The market gap was clear—tasty healthy snacks. According to Gautam, "Snacking preferences differ from person to person, so we wanted to use technology to bring personalization to healthy snacking. We wanted to create a Netflix for food."

Gautam and Ken graduated from Babson and both had jobs, but they reserved time over weekends to develop NatureBox, a subscription-based healthy snack box delivery service. The part-time work on the business idea was taking too long and they were waffling on the decision to actually start a business. Gautam recalls,

> One weekend in 2011, we borrowed an office space from a friend from Babson and decided that we wouldn't leave until they made a decision about whether or not to start NatureBox. We put a box of healthy snacks together. We shot a photo of it and then we put that photo on our website and we drove some traffic through Facebook to that website.

By the end of that fateful weekend, they had 100 customers that were more than just friends and family who had actually paid for a product that didn't exist! They spent the rest of the weekend packing the 100 boxes of snacks for their first customers. When customers subscribed for more than 1 month, they knew that they were on to something.

NatureBox officially launched on January 1, 2012, providing monthly subscription boxes that included five snacks, such as nuts, trail mixes, and granola bars, under the NatureBox brand. During the early days of NatureBox, customers could not customize their snack boxes. Within the first year of operations, Gautam and Ken quickly learned that their "one size fits all" snack box did not provide a fully satisfying customer experience. When customers didn't like a snack in the box they were unlikely to keep their subscription because customers didn't want to pay for snacks that they wouldn't eat. NatureBox quickly transitioned to a more personal snacking model allowing customers to choose and customize their boxes. Over time they also learned that snacking is an impulse purchase. In 2016, customers were encouraged to purchase single, à la carte snacks in addition to the subscription option.

Gautam and Ken believe that NatureBox's most significant advantage has been their ability to understand and successfully adapt quickly to changing market conditions and customer needs. They make conscious effort to listen to the consumer and constantly gather feedback through customer reviews and online ratings. Rather than sourcing their products from other brands, their snack offerings are proprietary and developed in house. They have a membership model that allows members to subscribe to regular deliveries of snacks or make one-time purchases to try different products. They also offer a wide variety of quantities ranging from 1 ounce to 7 ounces for single serving items and bulk purchasing options of 70–80 ounces for the same snacks. Their offerings include a lot of interesting snacks such as popcorn and pretzels, cookies and bars, dried fruit, jerky, chips and crackers, trail mixes, breakfast snacks such as oatmeal and cereal, coffee, and a lot more. They also have a monthly "Discovery Box" that has a good mix of the snacks they have to offer. The January, 2019 Discovery Box, for instance, includes Crunchy BBQ Twists, Tropical Fruit Medley, Kettle Corn, Limited Edition Trail Mix Cookies, and Dark Chocolate Berry Trail Mix. Gautam and Ken want to build a brand around the healthy snacks they offer in addition to the actual box in which the snacks are contained. NatureBox links product development processes to customer feedback and their extensive network of natural product suppliers. This has helped them create more than 400 products that customers love!

A relentless customer focus has helped them understand their core customer and attract new segments. For example, the initial customer focus of NatureBox at launch was mothers looking for healthy snacking options for their children. However, they soon realized that millennial women were apt to subscribe to NatureBox for both home and work consumption. Individual, direct sales was the primary focus at NatureBox from 2011 to 2015, yet in 2016 they began selling snacking services to corporate offices. Businesses pay $20 per month per employee for an unlimited supply of snacks. This has expanded their distribution and provided a welcome new revenue stream.

In the packaged food industry, consumer feedback takes time and this lack of readily available real-time information usually extends the product innovation cycle in the perishable food industry to a few years, making both product innovation and the struggle to profitability very hard. It's not uncommon for food startups to burn through a lot of cash while channel distribution and retail partners take a huge part of the pie, making margins for food startups very thin. By successfully integrating real-time feedback into their supply chain, NatureBox has shortened the traditional multiyear product innovation roadmaps (from idea to product delivery) to 10 to 12 weeks and has constantly been adding new snacks to their product line based on consumer feedback (e.g., Sriracha Roasted Cashews, White Cheddar Caramel Popcorn, and Honey Dijon Pretzels). Developing these products in house not only enhances profitability, it also allows them to diversify the product line and therefore reach out to a broader consumer base.

Scaling NatureBox has required significant investment and most resources have come from within Gautam's network. Neither Gautam nor Ken were familiar with food manufacturing. While talking to a few of his friends in investment banking, Gautam learned of a food conference happening in Chicago. This conference introduced them to suppliers and manufacturers in the industry. Gautam's ex-employer and early-stage venture fund, General Catalyst Partners, was an early investor in NatureBox. That initial funding has led to other investors. NatureBox raised $58.5 million between 2012 and 2015. In addition to the funding, Gautam's network has been very helpful in getting NatureBox with the right people at the right time. He has leveraged his deep network of mentors and advisors to learn from their experience and expertise in order to get the business moving faster. This network has helped him hire the right people, scale up, and guide the business in the right direction.

The journey of NatureBox has been both exciting and challenging. "Making the decision to move away from only a subscription model in 2013 into one that offers both à la carte and subscription options was one of the most challenging pivots for the business," he recalls. "You can never be 100% sure as the data is never clear. It was a leap of faith!" That decision has helped the business greatly since then and has helped make the business a lot healthier. Additionally, the marketing mix has evolved over the years from only marketing on Facebook to being early adopters in channels such as podcasts. Today NatureBox is looking at narrowing down its marketing efforts back on Facebook where it has gathered over a million likes (https://www.facebook.com/NatureBox). Gautam and his team believe that the dynamic and ever-changing nature of marketing platforms makes it difficult to keep up with the trends, and a more focused approach will help make marketing activities more effective.

Gautam feels that 6 years after launching NatureBox, they are now truly delivering on its promise of a completely customizable healthy snack experience for its customers. Growth has not come easily, but Gautam says it's essential to stay calm and manage your mental state so as to not get caught up in the roller coaster ride called entrepreneurship! His advice to students and aspiring entrepreneurs is two-fold:

> First is to focus on the quality of the team, from the first person you start working with and every hire that comes on board. It is very easy to regress the quality of the team and you can only keep the bar high on talent by being personally involved. Secondly, as much fun as it is to execute the business, spend a lot of time, especially in the early stage of the business, thinking about the type of business you want to build and what it implies about the process that you need, the values of the organization. You should do as much planning on those things as much as executing. Often, entrepreneurs are quick to jump to action. The process of building a company is lot more than just offering a great product.

Critical Thinking Questions

1. Describe the NatureBox business model. Could it be improved in some way?

2. There is a lot of competition for NatureBox today. How will the company compete in the future? Are there other directions in which the team could go?

3. Do you believe that Gautam and NatureBox are delivering on their customer value proposition of a customizable healthy snack experience? Why or why not?

Sources:

Interview with Babson MBA graduate assistant Gaurav Khemka, September 28, 2018.

Anastasia. (2015). NatureBox: Interview with its CEO & founder, Gautam Gupta. *Cleverism*. Retrieved from https://www.cleverism.com/naturebox-interview-ceo-co-founder-gautam-gupta

Crunchbase. (2019). NatureBox. Retrieved from https://www.crunchbase.com/organization/naturebox#section-investors

Vernon, L. (2017). Why food startups need to keep profitability in mind right now. *Ridgeline Ventures*. Retrieved from http://ridgelinevc.com/2017/09/19/food-startups-need-keep-profitability-mind-right-now

Introducing…

 SAGE vantage™

Course tools done right.

Built to support teaching. Designed to ignite learning.

SAGE vantage is an intuitive digital platform that blends trusted SAGE content with auto-graded assignments, all carefully designed to ignite student engagement and drive critical thinking. Built with you and your students in mind, it offers easy course set-up and enables students to better prepare for class.

SAGE vantage enables students to **engage** with the material you choose, **learn** by applying knowledge, and **soar** with confidence by performing better in your course.

PEDAGOGICAL SCAFFOLDING

Builds on core concepts, moving students from basic understanding to mastery.

CONFIDENCE BUILDER

Offers frequent knowledge checks, applied-learning multimedia tools, and chapter tests with focused feedback.

TIME-SAVING FLEXIBILITY

Feeds auto-graded assignments to your gradebook, with real-time insight into student and class performance.

QUALITY CONTENT

Written by expert authors and teachers, content is not sacrificed for technical features.

HONEST VALUE

Affordable access to easy-to-use, quality learning tools students will appreciate.

©istockphoto.com/mario31

6 Developing Your Customers

"I've learned that people will forget what you said, people will forget what you did, but people will never forget how you made them feel."

—Maya Angelou

Chapter Outline

Learning Objectives

6.1   Define a customer and a market.

6.2   Describe the different types of customers entrepreneurs may encounter.

6.3   Identify your customers through segmentation.

6.4   Find your target customer.

6.5   Acquire a deeper understanding of your customer through personas.

6.6   Illustrate the customer journey mapping process.

6.7   Explain the importance of market sizing in growing your customer base.

6.1 CUSTOMERS AND MARKETS

>> LO 6.1   Define a customer and a market.

We're entering an age in which there is greater focus on the customer than ever before. Companies have realized that they must treat customers like members of a family through every stage of the journey to attract and retain their business. That means understanding and nurturing them from the very first interaction to long after the first purchase has been made. Of course, large corporations have big budgets and the staff to focus on understanding, developing, and retaining their customer base. But the good news is that even entrepreneurs with limited resources can use methods to identify and target their customers, estimate the potential of their market size, and create ways to gain a deeper understanding of exactly who is buying their products and why.

Businesses don't exist without customers, so gaining a deep understanding of your customers is absolutely essential to early business success. The truth is that no matter how great you think your product or service is, nobody will buy it unless you really understand what your customers want and need and you are providing more value than your competition. Once you have this knowledge, you can use it to attract more customers. But before the customer journey begins, let's explore what is meant by customers and markets.

Although we tend to use the terms *customer* and *consumer* interchangeably, they do not mean the same thing. A **customer** is someone who pays for a product or service. Customers become **consumers** when they actually use the product or service.

There can also be some confusion over the definition of a market.[1] Some people consider *market* to mean customers or customer demand, but that is only one part of it. A **market** is a place where people can sell goods and services (the supply) to people who wish to buy those goods and services (the demand). **Supply** refers to the sellers who compete for customers in the marketplace, while **demand** implies the prospective customers' desire for the goods and services available. A market can be a physical location, such as a farmer's market or supermarket, or a virtual one, such as the Internet or even a grouping of customers such as the "market for women's jeans." When supply meets demand, millions of successful exchanges take place every day. Generally, a market is:

- A set of actual or potential customers
- For a given set of products or services
- Who have a common set of needs or wants, and
- Who reference each other when making a buying decision[2]

Customer: someone who pays for a product or service.

Consumers: customers who actually use a product or service.

Market: a place where people can sell goods and services (the supply) to people who wish to buy those goods and services (the demand).

Supply: the sellers who compete for customers in the marketplace. There are four main elements that define a market:

Demand: prospective customers' desire for the goods and services available.

Master the content at
**edge.sagepub.com/
neckentrepreneurship2e**

TABLE 6.1

Identifying Market Opportunities: Comparisons Between Novice and Experienced Entrepreneurs

THE MAIN FOCUS OF NOVICE ENTREPRENEURS	THE MAIN FOCUS OF EXPERIENCED ENTREPRENEURS
the novelty of the idea	the degree to which their idea will solve a customer problem
the newness of the technology behind the idea	the potential for the product or service to generate cash flow
the superiority of the product or service	the speed at which revenue will be generated
the potential of the product or service to revolutionize the industry	the amount of risk involved
the tendency to make decisions based on intuition or gut feel	the people in their network who will support them in developing the venture

Source: Nijssen, E. (2014). *Entrepreneurial marketing: An effectual approach* (p. 20). London: Routledge.

Market opportunity: the degree of customer or market demand for a specific product application.

Product application: goods or services created to meet a demand, thereby providing a solution to a customer problem.

For example, family-owned dog food company The Honest Kitchen's customers are dog and cat owners who are concerned about the ingredients in their pet's food.[3] They want organic. They want natural. And they want whole food.

A big part of entrepreneurship is discovering a market opportunity for a new idea. A **market opportunity** is often identifiable by the degree of customer or market demand for a specific product application. A **product application** refers to the goods or services created to meet this demand, thereby providing a solution to a customer problem.[4] How entrepreneurs identify market opportunities very much depends on their experience. For example, novice entrepreneurs tend to focus on the novelty or newness of the idea, while experienced entrepreneurs focus on developing their idea into a viable product that will attract customers and generate money. The point is that novel ideas only go so far. If your idea doesn't solve a customer problem or meet a customer need there will be no customers at all.

Table 6.1 outlines more comparisons between novice and experienced entrepreneurs when it comes to identifying market opportunities. You will notice that the first three items listed in the table under "experienced entrepreneurs" relate to customers. This is because knowledgeable entrepreneurs realize the importance of keeping customers at the forefront of their minds from the very beginning.

In some respects, identifying a market opportunity or new venture idea is the easy part. What's most challenging is demonstrating that there is a large enough market (group of customers) willing to pay for your products and services. A logical starting point is understanding the different types of customers for your product or service. Anthony Magaraci, who is featured in Entrepreneurship in Action, works hard to evaluate the nature of the company's relationship with its customers by using a color-coding strategy.

6.2 TYPES OF CUSTOMERS

>> **LO 6.2** **Identify the different types of customers entrepreneurs may encounter.**

People often think of businesses having one type of customer, but instead of looking for a single customer, companies should identify the "chain of customers" composed of users, purchasers (buyers), and influencers.[5] Depending on the type of business you are in, the customer may play all three roles. For instance, a toy company producing toy cars may presume that its customers will be boys between the ages of 3 and 12. However, although

Anthony Magaraci, Trinity Packaging Supply

Anthony Magaraci, founder of Trinity Packaging Supply

After receiving his undergraduate degree in entrepreneurship at Rowan University in New Jersey, Anthony went to work in sales at a packaging supply company. There he discovered he had a true talent for selling, and he achieved multiple promotions during his time there. His mission was to learn as much as he could about the packaging business. As he said, "I wanted to consume as much information as I possibly could." After 3 years of great success in sales, he became a manager and learned enough to start his own company, Trinity Packaging Supply, which he founded in 2010. Today, his company brings in $30 million in annual revenue.

Trinity Packaging Supply is a wholesale supplier of packaging and shipping supplies. The company specializes in stretch film, packaging tape, corrugated boxes, void fill, shrink film, and pallets, and it offers the full spectrum of packaging material and equipment. It has more than 18,000 items in stock and provides next-day delivery in most areas of the country. Trinity specializes in national account programs, in which a company with multiple locations can spend nationally, while having the support and services of local businesses, with one streamlined point of contact nationwide. The company also offers free packaging consultations, which involve touring a company's facility and recommending ways to save on their packaging needs and processes.

The early years of Trinity Packaging Supply were the most difficult. Anthony had a noncompete agreement with his former employer, now a competitor, which prevented him from doing business with his old customers for 1 year. Anthony says this was a blessing in disguise because having no credit history meant he wouldn't have been able to support large orders from those old customers when he first started Trinity. After 7 months, he reached his break-even point, when the monthly net profit was enough to cover his personal and business expenses, and by the end of the first year, his wife left her own job to join Anthony in the business.

Since then, Anthony has worked hard to build relationships with the businesses that pay Trinity for packaging goods and equipment. Primarily, Trinity must maintain good standing with their suppliers (the manufacturers of the packaging supplies) and their customers (the users of the packaging materials). Trinity's reach extends throughout the country, with seven sales offices in major metropolitan cities and 20 shipping locations. Their geographic distribution allows them to make packaging solutions cheaper and faster for clients.

Trinity's customers are product manufacturers and distributors. Their clients have products that need to be packaged and transported, and that need crosses a lot of different industries. Having such a diverse range of customer segments tends to "flat line" or reduce the volatility of industry-specific recessions. For example, when the housing market collapsed, home improvement and building products almost ceased distribution, while fast food and alcohol distribution skyrocketed. Anthony reflected on the last recession: "Unless someone invents a way to teleport products, our industry is relatively recession-proof."

Selling to customers is essential and fundamental for any entrepreneur. "It is important to work hard, but working hard does not just mean working long hours. You have to go out and get customers. If you can do that, you're going to be successful," he says. "The key to successful selling is spending quality time with the people who can make the decision to move forward with an order." But for Anthony, his relationship with customers is not simply a transaction.

> Our relationship with our customers is crucial. For every customer, we evaluate our relationship with them in five stages, using a different color for each. We use red for a defective relationship, orange for transactional, yellow for strategic, green for partnership, and blue for "BFF." Customer service is at the heart of our company, so we will be proactive in improving and reaching

(Continued)

(Continued)

the next level of our relationship with customers. We do this by increasing the frequency of our interactions with people, either in-person or via digital platforms. Building relationships is a core value of our company, and the mentality extends to nourishing any relationship within our organization and network.

Today, Trinity has a team of 32 people; offices in Philadelphia, Atlanta, Columbus, Chicago, Dallas, Houston, and Los Angeles; and is growing at breakneck pace.

Critical Thinking Questions

1. What is Anthony's secret in terms of customer service?
2. Why is Trinity Packaging Supply recession-proof?
3. What other industries do you think are recession-proof? Why? ●

Sources:
Anthony Magaraci (interview with author, September 18, 2018)
Harris, G. (2017). We asked 169,000 workers about what makes their workplace great. Here's their take. *Inc.com*. Retrieved from https://www.inc.com/magazine/201706/greg-harris/policies-perks-methodology-best-work-places-2017.html

---

boys might certainly be the "users" of the product, they might not necessarily be the buyers; the "purchasers" might actually be the parents. Similarly, the boys' "influencers" need to be taken into account, who could be close friends or family members. Identifying how customer types overlap is important when building a target base for your product or service. Table 6.2 illustrates five different types of customers: users, influencers, recommenders, economic buyers, and decision makers.[6] Let's take a closer look at each of these types.

End users: the type of customers who will use your product. Their feedback will help you refine and tweak the product.

Influencers (or **opinion leaders**): customers with a large following who have the power to influence our purchase decisions.

- **End users:** the customers who will actually use your product. They will buy it (or not), touch it, operate it, use it, and tell you whether they love it or hate it. Gaining a deeper insight into the needs and motivations of end users is essential in the experimentation period, as their feedback will help you refine and tweak the product.

- **Influencers** (or **opinion leaders**): customers with a large following who have the power to influence our purchase decisions. Sometimes the biggest influence on the success of a service or product comes from "customers" who have no involvement in it all. Celebrities, journalists, industry analysts, and bloggers have the power to influence our purchase decisions. Yet, increasingly, it is social media influencers—those without star status who have managed to establish credibility through their online platforms—who are becoming the new face of marketing. For example, in 2017, more than 400 social media influencers, including Kendall Jenner, supermodel Bella Hadid, and actor and model Emily Ratajkowski, were paid to promote the Fyre Festival—a "luxury music festival" in the Bahamas—on their Instagram accounts.[7] Thanks to these endorsements, more than 5,000 people bought the expensive festival tickets, only to find a disaster scene when they got there. The buzz leading up to the festival and the demand for tickets (some of

TABLE 6.2

Five Types of Customers

CUSTOMER	EXAMPLE
End User	Teen playing a video game
Influencer	Celebrity endorsing the video game in a commercial
Recommender	Blogger writing positive reviews for the video game on a website
Economic buyer	Buyer for GameStop who decided to stock the video game in the company's stores
Decision maker	CEO of the gaming company who decided to buy the game from the game designer

which cost $75,000) show how powerful influencers can be. Make a list of all the outside influencers you would like to target and ways in which you can reach them, such as via social media or by attending events where your target influencers will be present.

- **Recommenders**: people who may evaluate your product and tell the public about it, such as bloggers or experts in an industry. Their opinions have the power to make or break your reputation. For example, a games blogger who recommends a new game could do wonders for a new product.

- **Economic buyers**: the customers who have the ability to approve large-scale purchases, such as buyers for retail chains, corporate office managers, and corporate VPs. Economic buyers have the power to put your product on the shelves, physically or virtually. Connecting with economic buyers brings you one step closer to the end-user customers you want to have the opportunity to buy your service or product.

- **Decision makers**: customers similar to economic buyers who have even more authority to make purchasing decisions as they are positioned higher up in the hierarchy. The ultimate decision makers do not need to be CEOs—they could also be "Mom" or "Dad," who have the power to approve purchases for their family.

Huda Kattan, founder of cosmetics line Huda Beauty, beauty blogger, and social media influencer with 23 million followers

In addition, entrepreneur and educator Steve Blank suggests that we do not ignore the *saboteurs*.[8] Saboteurs are anyone who can veto or slow down a purchasing decision—from top managers, to friends, spouses, to even children. Identify your saboteur customers and find out what's putting them off. You might learn a lot from their feedback.

6.3 CUSTOMER SEGMENTATION

>> LO 6.3   Identify your customers through segmentation.

In Chapter 5: Building Business Models, we defined customer segments as a part of the customer grouping of a market. As discussed, customer segmentation is one of the most important building blocks in the Business Model Canvas (BMC), so identifying the right customer segments for business is key to early business success.

Companies often group customers based on their common needs, common behaviors, or other attributes. This provides some insight into which customers would be more likely to buy from them. Once this has been achieved, the BMC can be tailored around the customers' needs. Customers can be divided in separate segments, if any of the following apply:

- Their needs validate an offering.

- They have different distribution channels.

- They call for different types of relationships.

- They have substantially different profitabilities.

- They are willing to pay for different aspects of the offer.

Overall, different customer segments have different needs, which require different approaches and more tailored solutions. This is why it is so important for entrepreneurs to define customer segments and become familiar with the type of customers most likely to buy their product or service.

Recommenders: people who may evaluate your product and tell the public about it, such as bloggers or experts in an industry.

Economic buyers: the customers who have the ability to approve large-scale purchases, such as buyers for retail chains, corporate office managers, and corporate VPs.

Decision makers: customers similar to economic buyers who have even more authority to make purchasing decisions as they are positioned higher up in the hierarchy.

Customer segments can be defined in four ways:[9]

1. Who are they? Find out their demographic (age, gender, education, income, etc.).

2. Where are they? Note your customers' locations.

3. How do they behave? List all behavioral or lifestyle habits demonstrated by your customers.

4. What are their needs? It is essential that you record your customers' needs to clarify your offering.

Once you have carried out the customer segmentation process, you can create an end-user profile of the person most likely to use your product or service.

Creating an End User Profile

Typically, an end user profile consists of six items: demographics, psychographics, proxy product, watering holes, day in the life, and biggest fears and motivators.[10]

Demographics: Demographics are useful data in identifying your target end user, but they may not be entirely accurate when it comes to *understanding* your end user. For example, if you find out that your end users are all men in their 30s living in a particular geographic location, it doesn't tell you much about their attitudes or likes and dislikes. It is important to analyze demographics, but don't place too much emphasis on them.

Psychographics: Psychographics is a method used to describe the psychological attributes (attitudes, values, or fears) of your target end users. Unlike demographics, which provide basic information about your users, psychographics present a more detailed overview, such as their aspirations, whom they admire, what they believe, and so on. However, it is difficult to get psychographic data and even harder to analyze for accuracy. For example, Facebook may be able to give you some information about users' likes and dislikes, but it's more difficult to pinpoint in-depth detail like fears.

Proxy product: Proxy products give you an idea of what else the user is likely to buy. For example, people who already buy from high-end fashion brands are more likely to buy an expensive piece of clothing. Proxy products can also display some demographic and psychographic characteristics. For instance, people who buy from farmer's markets rather than from potentially cheaper supermarkets may be interested in promoting sustainability. This group might also be interested in eco-friendly products, such as clothes made from recycled fabric or homemade skincare merchandise.

Watering holes: Watering holes are the places where users meet and swap information. They are also the best spots for word-of-mouth recommendations. There are many different types of watering holes, both formal and informal. Formal meeting places include work conferences or business meetings, while less formal watering holes include bars, fitness classes, and social media.

Day in the life: One of the most useful ways entrepreneurs can create a profile of their end users is to walk in their shoes for a day. This method is particularly effective after you have spent some time observing and talking to a group of end users. Creating this real-world story puts all the data into perspective and provides a deeper insight into the behavior of your potential customers. As serial entrepreneur Les Harper says, "If you can get into their shoes and see their needs from their point of view, then you can take your experience and your entrepreneurial drive and really satisfy them."[11]

Biggest fears and motivators: Find out what keeps your end users awake at night and identify their top priorities in order to understand their biggest fears and motivators. This exercise is best carried out by sitting with a group of end users, making a comprehensive list of all their concerns, and asking them to score their priorities from highest to lowest. By the end of the exercise, you will have a list of their top five priorities, which will be a useful addition to all the research you have carried out so far.

When you have created your end user profile, you will have greater insight into how real people will use your product in the real world, and this is why it is worth spending time on. Segmenting your customers, and creating an end user profile, brings you one step closer to finding your real customer base and understanding which are the most important groups to target.

6.4 TARGET CUSTOMER GROUP

>> LO 6.4   Find your target customer.

To truly understand the targeting process, you must first understand the difference between how the targeting process works in traditional marketing and how it works in entrepreneurship. In traditional marketing, the most viable customer segment is identified and a new product is developed for it. But in entrepreneurship, many entrepreneurs start with the idea of the new product and then identify the target customer segment. Testing products with customers is a valuable way for entrepreneurs to find their target customer group (see Chapter 7: Testing and Experimenting With New Ideas).[12]

But finding your target customer group is only the beginning. The success or failure of your product or service depends on the response of your potential customers in the marketplace. Typically, people respond to new innovations in different ways. Understanding how people adopt or accept new innovations is key to success. The technology adoption life cycle, introduced by communications professor Everett Rogers, is a model that describes the process of acceptance of a new innovation over time, according to defined adopter groups. The model (see Figure 6.1) divides the market into five categories of potential customers: innovators, early adopters, early majority, late majority, and laggards.

Innovators (2.5% of customers): These are the first customers to try a new product. They are people who are enthusiastic about new technology and are willing to take the risk of product flaws or other uncertainties that may apply to early versions. In general, innovators are wealthier than other adopters; in other words, they can afford to take a risk on a new innovation.

Early adopters (next 13.5% of customers): This is the second group to adopt a product. Like innovators, they tend to buy new products shortly after they hit the market. However, unlike innovators, they are not motivated by their enthusiasm for new technology. Early adopters are usually influential people from business or government who make reasoned decisions as to whether or not to exploit the innovation for competitive advantage.

Early majority (next 34% of customers): People in this category tend to take interest in a new product as it begins to have mass market appeal. They are both practical and extremely risk averse, preferring to wait and see how others view the technology before they buy it themselves. As a consequence, they look for opinions from their peers or professional contacts to support them in their decision to invest. It is essential for entrepreneurs to appeal to this group, given that it makes up more than one-third of the life cycle.

Late majority (next 34% of customers): These customers are typically skeptical, pessimistic, risk averse, and less affluent than the previous groups. However, because this group makes up such a large portion of the life cycle, they cannot be ignored. It is possible for entrepreneurs to win over this group by providing simpler products or systems at an affordable cost.

Laggards (final 16% of customers): People in this final category are the last to adopt a new innovation. They tend to have a negative attitude toward technology in general and have a strong aversion to change. Despite their best efforts, entrepreneurs may never be able to persuade this group that their innovation is worth a first glance, never mind going so far as to purchase it.

In an ideal world, all five categories of customers in the adoption life cycle would adopt the new innovation, but of course, this is not the case. As the model shows, a product tends to go through different stages of adoption over time. Some customers may rush to

FIGURE 6.1

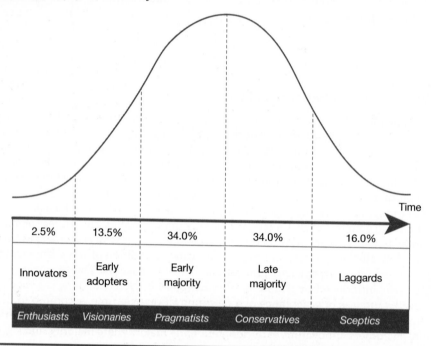

Technology Adoption Life Cycle

2.5%	13.5%	34.0%	34.0%	16.0%
Innovators	Early adopters	Early majority	Late majority	Laggards
Enthusiasts	*Visionaries*	*Pragmatists*	*Conservatives*	*Sceptics*

purchase a product as soon as it comes on the market, while others may not. Understanding this concept is essential when it comes to developing and growing your market, and it also explains why some products never really take off. Although the adoption life cycle is a useful way to win different groups of users, there are some cracks in the curve.

Crossing the Chasm

High-tech and marketing expert Geoffrey Moore identified some cracks between each phase of the adoption life cycle (see Figure 6.2). According to Moore, the biggest difficulty is making the transition between early adopters and the early majority; he calls this the "chasm." Crossing the chasm involves focusing your resources on a single, primary market first, known as a *beachhead market*, before winning over that market and then using that momentum to dominate larger markets.[13]

The beachhead market takes its name from the battle of Normandy, which took place during World War II. During the battle, the Western allies stormed the beachheads of Normandy, enabling them to control what would turn out to be one of the most important battles of World War II. The beach became a stronghold from which the allies advanced into the rest of the territory. Without the offensive in Normandy, the Germans may well have been victorious.

Focusing on one market that is the most straightforward to capture is a particularly useful way for entrepreneurs who are typically short of money, time, and human capital to establish an early following. At first, the beachhead market may be a small segment of customers, but still enough to generate the cash flow needed to strategically position the product to win over other markets.

Finding your beachhead market is key to attacking other markets, which will generate a larger following.

There are three factors that define a beachhead market:

1.   The customers in that market buy similar products.

2.   Those customers have similar expectations of value.

3.   The customers use word of mouth to communicate to others in similar regions or professional organizations.[14]

Smart Skin Care is a good example of a company that successfully discovered a beachhead market.[15] Its founder, Pedro Valencia, patented a new technology that allowed for slow-release medication. Valencia and his team spent weeks trying to find a market for the new innovation. During this time, they found that the new technology could be applied to sunscreen—the slow release of sun-blocking chemicals over a certain period of time. Yet, further research showed that the sunscreen market was too large and diverse to enter. So, Valencia continued to find a smaller segment of the market to which he could sell his product. Finally, they landed their beachhead market: a segment of people in their 30s who engaged in extreme sports such as triathlons. Not only would the athletes benefit from slow-release sunscreen, but they also had the disposable income to spend on a more expensive version. Once Valencia conquered this segment of the market, it became much easier to launch the sunscreen product in other markets. This example shows that there is more than one path to success.

Once you have identified your beachhead market, then you can use the following three steps to successfully cross the chasm:

1. Create the entire product first.

    Your early adopters may be forgiving of a few bugs and glitches, but your early majority won't. This is why it is so important to make sure your product is as whole as possible before you launch it.

2. Position the product.

    As the early majority tend to be pragmatists, it is important to position your product to this audience by emphasizing its value. This might involve showcasing the market share captured to date, sharing details of third-party support, providing professional endorsements, and mentioning any press coverage.

3. Distribute the product through the right channels.

    Penetrating the initial target segment requires direct sales and support to explain the benefits of the product. Direct sales is the least expensive and best way to create demand.

Moore has further refined these three steps by using the analogy of a bowling alley. If you hit the first pin hard enough, the others will fall. So it's important to first identify your specific market segment (the first pin), or beachhead market, and then create a plan to expand from that segment to other segments before finally reaching the broader market (knocking down all the available pins). Facebook is a good example of a company that brilliantly executed the bowling pin strategy. It first started out at Harvard before spreading to other universities and eventually across the entire world. Yelp is another good example; it began by focusing on a niche market (San Francisco) before expanding into the mass market.[16]

The Yelp app is used around the world.

© Bloomberg/Contributor/Getty Images

The Tornado

Moore suggests that if the bowling strategy is executed successfully, your product and your business may enter a tornado. Being "in the tornado" means that your product is in high demand and your business is experiencing rapid growth. During this period, it is essential to meet customer demand and ship the product efficiently.

Main Street

Following the tornado, your business is likely to enter a period of calm. Your product has proven to be a success in the market and has been widely adopted. However, there is still work to be done. Now is the time to leverage your market position by further enhancing your offering to ensure that your customers do not switch to a competitor.

FIGURE 6.2

Critical Points in the Product Adoption Cycle

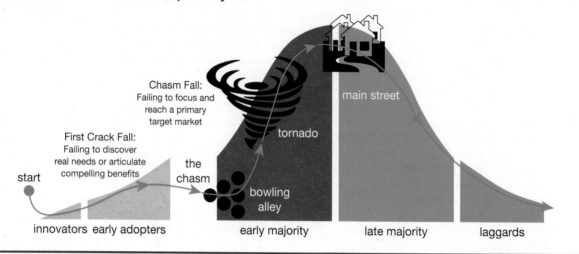

Sources:

Geoffrey A. Moore (2014) Crossing the Chasm (3rd ed). Harper Collins.

Geoffrey A. Moore (2004) Inside the Tornado. Harper Collins.

Jake Nielson (2014) https://www.ignitionframework.com/crossing-the-chasm-theory-how-to-market-sell-and-improve-your-new-invention/

6.5 CUSTOMER PERSONAS

>> **LO 6.5** Acquire a deeper understanding of your customer through personas.

Earlier in the chapter, we explored the benefits of building an end user profile for gaining insight into your customer, but going a little deeper will provide you with greater customer understanding. Today's customers make buying decisions without the input of the actual seller. Using social networks and peer reviews is more commonplace. That's why it's more important than ever to understand your customer before you try to sell to that customer. In other words, how do you sell your product without you? How do you sell your product without sales representatives? The first step is to understand your buyer personas.

Buyer personas are profiles or representations of your ideal customers based on information and market research.[17] These personas help you to create strategies to connect with your target audience and promote product and services to people who will potentially buy them.

Building personas is an important exercise in understanding your customer; as you have read, demographics and psychographics will only take you so far. In fact, combined, they really only give you a buyer profile rather than a deeper insight into customer behavior. For example, the demographics may tell you where your customer lives, his or her age range, and marital status, but that information doesn't deliver any real insight into buying behavior. Similarly, the psychographics may capture the fact that your customer is a regular church-goer and good at managing but, again, that detail doesn't say much about how, when, and why your customer makes certain purchasing decisions.

Building personas is a powerful way to predict your buyers' behavior. The personas may be based on fictional characters, but they are based on real data and information, which makes them more meaningful (see Figure 6.3). As research shows, personas have the power to engage and help us to anticipate how these fictional characters might behave in different situations.[18]

The best way to build buyer personas is through real interviews with prospective customers (see Mindshift activity). By creating your buyer's story, you will be able to

Buyer personas: profiles or representations of your ideal customers based on information and market research.

FIGURE 6.3

Cooper, the Stay-at-Home Dad

©istockphoto.com/gradyreese

LIFESTYLE

- Cooper is married to Jessica and they have three kids—2 boys (ages 8 and 10) and 1 girl (age 4)
- Jessica has a very demanding job as a lead research scientist with a biotechnology company and often works long hours.
- There are some financial pressures given that the family is living on one salary but they live in an area with strong public schools.
- Cooper gets the boys to school every day but also stays at home with his daughter. The older boys are starting to do more activities after school, which also requires a lot of scheduling and carpooling.
- Cooper, once a chef for a restaurant, also cooks all the meals.
- Cooper and Jessica love the outdoors and find themselves hiking and camping with the kids more often.

BACKGROUND

- Graduated from culinary school.
- Traveled through Italy after school to learn about Italian cuisine.
- Jessica, his wife, has a PhD in biology.
- They currently live in a suburb of Boston, Massachusetts, given that Boston is the hub of many biotech companies.

CHALLENGES/PAIN POINTS

- Jessica makes a good salary but the Boston area is expensive.
- Their youngest daughter will be in school soon, so Cooper is considering getting a job again but being a chef is not conducive to raising children given long work hours.
- Cooper is considering alternative lines of work but worries he may need to go back to school.

VALUES

- Cooper values family first. He was an acclaimed chef but when they had their first child, he knew he had to focus on the family.
- Values education and was very much attracted to Jessica because of her PhD.
- Has raised his kids to value diversity and be kind to all types of people.
- Both Cooper and Jessica are strong advocates of protecting the environment and educating their kids to do the same.

get closer to the people you are trying to influence. The information mined from those interviews, together with the data derived from your buyer profiles, will generate some key buying insights:

- The buyers who are interested in your product/service, as well as those who will never be interested, despite your best efforts

- The features of your solution that are relevant to them and those that are irrelevant

- The attitudes that put off your buyers from considering your offering. For example, perhaps they have had a negative experience with a similar product to yours, which prevents them from trying your offering.

- The kinds of resources your buyers trust when it comes to evaluating their options

- The types of buyers who are involved in the decision and the amount of influence they employ

Table 6.3 illustrates some key points for building a basic persona.

Exclusionary Personas

Buyer personas are a good representation of your ideal customer, but it is also useful to create an exclusionary persona, which is a model of who you *don't* want as a customer.[19] Building exclusionary personas saves you time and valuable resources by identifying the people who will never buy from you, regardless of how much effort you put into sales and marketing (e.g., people who are too advanced for your product or service, students who only engage with the information you provide but don't buy from you, or people who only buy from you at rock bottom prices). This is not to say that you shouldn't engage

TABLE 6.3

Key Points for Building a Persona

Demographics (age, gender, salary, location, education, family)
Goals and challenges
Value and fears
Pain points or complaints
Hobbies
Where they get their news or other information
Blogs they read
Shopping preferences
Apps used most frequently
General lifestyle description
Day in their life
Work and/or school activities
Relationship with friends
Culture
Relationship with technology
How is free time spent?
Social media usage
Views on health and well-being
Quotes from interviews

with those who fit into your exclusionary persona model (they could turn into influencers), but there is little point in trying to convert them into customers. The guidelines for creating your buyer personas also apply to creating an exclusionary persona. Identifying who your customers are *not* can actually help you further refine who your customers *are*.

Remember that a buyer profile alone will only tell you who your buyer is, but a buyer profile with buyer insights gives you a much clearer picture of the decisions you need to make to win their business.

6.6 CUSTOMER JOURNEY MAPPING PROCESS

>> **LO 6.6**   **Illustrate the customer journey mapping process.**

Customer journey map: a visual representation that captures customer experience across multiple touchpoints.

Customer journey maps are similar to personas in that they represent a typical customer experience. However, the main difference lies in the fact that personas focus on the buyer, while the customer journey map focuses on the buyer's experience. A **customer journey map** is a visual representation that captures customer experience across multiple touchpoints. It is designed to provide a holistic view of your customers' experience with your product or service while also allowing you to identify pain points. Journey mapping is a necessary process in the early stages of your startup so you can develop empathy for your customers as well as learn how to make their experience with your company or product a great one.

Build Your Buyer Personas

Personas are fun to create, but behind the fun needs to be real data! In order to create a buyer persona, you need to interview at least five potential customers for your venture idea that you believe are somewhat similar. Each interview can be as short as 10 minutes, but you need to find out the following:

- What's a typical day like for them?
- What do they do for work (or school)?
- Age, gender, and other relevant demographics
- How do they shop? (if applicable)
- What resonates with them most about your product or service?
- What are their goals and challenges?

- How do they stay connected?
- What is their social life like?
- How do they spend their free time?

The questions above can change based on your venture idea, but the goal is to get a complete picture of a typical customer (see Table 6.3 for additional variables to include in your personas). From the five interviews, create (1) a buyer persona for your own product/service and (2) an exclusionary persona (someone who should not be a customer). Use pictures as well as text. Be creative! If you need some help to get started, use Table 6.4 below as a guide. ●

TABLE 6.4

Additional Information to Include in a Persona

Is there a picture from a magazine that kind of looks like the customer you are personifying? Give the persona a name (e.g., Charlie)	What's a typical day for Charlie look like?	
Relevant demographics (age, gender, income, etc.)	What resonates with Charlie most about the product or service? What needs are being met?	What does Charlie care most about?
Job or school routines		How does Charlie spend his free time?
How does Charlie stay connected?	Describe Charlie's social life.	How does Charlie shop?

The benefits of customer journey mapping include the following:[20]

- Presents a clear picture of how your customers interact with your business, including their goals, needs, and expectations
- Clarifies what your customers think and how they feel about their experiences by identifying positive and negative emotions
- Confirms whether the customer journey is in a logical order
- Highlights the gaps between desired customer experience and the one actually experienced by your customers
- Allows you to connect to customers on an emotional level and provide the optimal customer experience by addressing and resolving key pain points

Overall, customer journey mapping is a good way to shift your perspective to your customers, to put yourself in their shoes, and think about how they can achieve their goals along their customer journey. Each touchpoint along the customer journey must be from their point of view and in the context of the goals they are trying to achieve. Then you layer on how they might be feeling when they encounter a problem. The visual

©istockphoto.com/skynesher

Thinking about the guests' journey when planning events, such as a graduation party, can help enhance the guest experience.

map charts the journey from the moment customers become aware of your product to the moment they stop being customers altogether. Customer journey mapping may sound like a lot of work, but not doing it runs the risk of unsatisfied customers and loss of opportunities to improve their experience.

For example, say you were throwing a graduation party for a group of friends.[21] You might think about the type of food and drink you will be serving, what time you would like your guests to arrive, and how many people you want to come. So far, everything is from your point of view. But now think about the party from your guests' perspective. The first touchpoint will be your guests receiving the invitation. With any luck, this will make them feel happy to be invited. But the invitation will also give rise to a number of questions: Who else is going to the party? What's the dress code? Do I need to bring snacks?

Closer to the date, you send out a reminder. That's the second touchpoint, which may prompt more questions: Where will I park? Do I need to pay for parking? Is it easy to find a parking spot?

The final touchpoint is the graduation party itself. They arrive at your house and may be asking themselves the following questions: Where do I put my coat? Where do I put the snacks I brought? How do I get a drink?

As the party host, you may have thought of some of these concerns, but not all of them because you have most likely been thinking of the party from your own perspective. This exercise is a really useful way to empathize with your customers and feel what it's like to be them.

You may wonder why journey mapping is necessary when you have already gathered lots of data on your customer base. The problem with data is that it often fails to communicate the frustrations and experiences of customers. For example, if you only analyze the data gathered from your party, you will know how much wine has been consumed, who had food and who didn't, how many guests showed up and how many didn't, but that doesn't tell you much about their experience of your party. Did they have a good time? Will they come to your next party? Will they talk to others about the party in a positive or negative way? On the other hand, a story such as the one told by a journey map is a wonderful way to engage and connect with your customers and find ways to improve their experience.

Confirming Your Findings

However, certain data are useful in confirming the findings made from your journey map. There are many sources for data about your customers, including website analytics, social media tools, and direct customer contact.[22]

Website Analytics

If your website is already up and running, then website analytics will provide you with lots of information, including your customers' location, the amount of traffic to your site, and the number of clicks on each page. Analytics also expose weaknesses in your site by showing you points in the process where your customer may have become frustrated and abandoned the site.

Social Media Tools

Social media tools are also a useful source of data. For instance, SocialMention is a tool that searches blogs, comments, and videos for mentions of your brand and advises you whether those mentions are positive or negative. This type of customer feedback provides extremely useful insights into your customers' journey. You could also consider running a survey to find out your customers' questions, feelings, and thoughts.

Direct Customer Contact

Sitting down and talking with your customers is one of the most valuable ways to get feedback about their customer experience. It can be difficult to organize but very worthwhile if you can manage it.

The customer journey map ranges from simple to extremely complicated. For fun, Google "customer journey maps" and see all the different types of maps available. We suggest you keep it simple in the beginning, using the six steps below.

Six Steps to Creating Your Customer Journey Map

1. Gather a whiteboard, sticky notes, and some felt-tip markers.

2. Identify the segment of customers you would like to map.

3. Write down as many touchpoints as you can think of for the entire journey, one on each sticky note, and post the notes on the whiteboard.

4. Identify three or four aspects of the customer journey you would like to explore (e.g., emotional needs, pain points, obstacles to satisfaction).

5. Think about how you can resolve these problems and improve the customer experience, and post these ideas on the whiteboard.

6. When you're finished, create a visual representation that shows the customer going through the process, noting the pain points, emotions, and sources of convenience.[23] The visual representation can be as crude as using stick figures or a little more sophisticated, like a cartoon, or formal, using a computer-based diagram.

Another way to think about the customer journey uses the five typical stages of customer interaction with a company: discovery, research, purchase, delivery, and after the sale.[24] For example, let's say your customer, Darnell, is going on a short business trip and is looking for a stylish overnight bag.

1. Discovery: A need has been identified by the customer. In this case, Darnell needs the right bag for his business trip.

2. Research: Once the need has been identified, the research stage begins. In trying to find the right bag, Darnell starts researching luggage online, checks prices, compares brands, reads reviews, and asks his friends for their recommendations.

3. Purchase: Darnell finds what he is looking for and makes a decision to purchase the bag.

4. Delivery: With the payment made online, Darnell receives an email confirmation and the product is delivered a few days later.

5. After sales: Darnell receives a thank you note and a discount coupon for future purchases.

Now it's time to practice your journey mapping skills with the following Mindshift.

Now you know the five stages of interaction, you can start layering some more information to find out more about your customer. Here are some factors to keep in mind while completing the journey map:[25]

Key Touchpoints: How does your user interact with your company?

Tasks: What is your customer trying to achieve?

Knowledge: What does your customer want to know?

Create a Customer Journey Map

Using your own venture idea or just a business you really like, map the journey of a typical customer. Before actually drawing the journey, it may be helpful to complete the customer journey grid below (Table 6.5). Start with the five stages of customer interaction: discovery, research, purchase, delivery, and after the sale. Then consider the key touchpoints: what the customer is doing in each stage, information needed, the pain points in each stage, what's going well in each stage, customer emotions in each stage, and customer wish list. If you are applying the journey grid below to your own venture, the source of much of the data is your own research (customer journey through competitors) and your own interviews (as suggested in Mindshift: Build Your Buyer Personas). After completing the grid, try drawing a more visual representation of the journey.

Hint: When trying to find value in your customer experience, first grid and map the journey of a customer from your closest competitor (see Table 6.5). Then show how your customer experience is better. ●

TABLE 6.5

Customer Journey Grid

	DISCOVERY STAGE	RESEARCH STAGE	PURCHASE STAGE	AFTER THE SALE STAGE
Key touchpoints (points of interaction between the customer and company)				
Tasks (what the customer is trying to get accomplished)				
Knowledge (what the customer wants or needs to know)				
Pain points (where the customer is disappointed)				
Happy points (where the customer is satisfied)				
Emotions (what the customer is likely feeling)				
Wish list (what would make the customer experience awesome)				

Pain Points: How does your company disappoint the customer?

Happy Points: How does the company satisfy the customer?

Emotions: What is your customer feeling at each stage of the process?

Wish List: What would make the customer experience awesome?

Influencers: Who or what are the key influencers in your customer's decision-making process?

Additionally, mapping a journey also uncovers areas where you can think about generating more value for the customer. For example, in the case of Darnell above, maybe he wants to receive a text message when the product is delivered. Remember that the map won't stay static; it will change over time as long as you keep revisiting it. Besides, it is worth keeping, as it serves as a good reminder that customers should always be at the forefront of your thinking.

RESEARCH AT WORK

Connecting With Customers on an Emotional Level

Researchers Scott Magids, Alan Zorfas, and Daniel Leemon suggest that connecting with the emotions of customers is integral to building sales, brand recognition, and customer loyalty. They researched hundreds of brands across a diverse group of product categories to identify "emotional motivators" that allow companies to connect on an emotional level with their customer in order to drive sales.

The researchers suggest that if companies can identify the most powerful emotional motivators for their customers, they are likely to have a competitive advantage:

> Our research stemmed from our frustration that companies we worked with knew customers' emotions were important but couldn't figure out a consistent way to define them, connect with them, and link them to results. We soon discovered that there was no standard lexicon of emotions, and so 8 years ago we set out to

create one, working with experts and surveying anthropological and social science research. We ultimately assembled a list of more than 300 emotional motivators. (p. 68)

It's complicated to measure emotion. The researchers used big customer datasets and applied extensive data analytics to identify emotional motivators. Though motivators change based on industry, brand, and customer touchpoints, the researchers were able to uncover 10 emotional motivators that crossed all the product categories and brands studied.

The research also suggests that customers who are both satisfied with the product and emotionally connected to the company or brand are 52% more valuable to the company than a customer who is only highly satisfied. ●

Source: Magids, S., Zorfas, A., & Leemon, D. (2015). The new science of customer emotions: A better way to drive growth and profitability. *Harvard Business Review*, November, 66–76.

High-Impact Motivators

EMOTIONAL MOTIVATOR	HOW ENTREPRENEURS CAN LEVERAGE THE MOTIVATOR
Stand out from the crowd	Project a unique social identity; be seen as special
Have confidence in the future	Perceive the future as better than the past; have a positive mental picture of what's to come
Enjoy a sense of well-being	Feel that life measures up to expectations and that balance has been achieved; seek a stress-free state without conflicts or threats
Feel a sense of freedom	Act independently, without obligations or restrictions
Feel a sense of thrill	Experience visceral, overwhelming pleasure and excitement; participate in exciting, fun events
Feel a sense of belonging	Have an affiliation with people they relate to or aspire to be in life; feel part of a group
Protect the environment	Sustain the belief that the environment is sacred; take action to improve their surroundings
Be the person I want to be	Fulfill a desire for ongoing self-improvement; live up to their ideal self-image
Feel secure	Believe that what they have today will be there tomorrow; pursue goals and dreams without worry
Succeed in life	Feel that they lead meaningful lives; find worth that goes beyond financial or socioeconomic measures

Source: Scott Magids, Alan Zorfas, and Daniel Leemon. The New Science of Customer Emotions: A better way to drive growth and profitability. Harvard Business Review. November 2015, pp: 66-76.

6.7 MARKET SIZING

>> LO 6.7   Explain the importance of market sizing in growing your customer base.

Market sizing: a method of estimating the number of potential customers and possible revenue or profitability of a product or service.

Once you have identified your potential market segment and gained a good understanding of your customer, it is time to assess the size of your market.

Market sizing is a method of estimating the number of potential customers and possible revenue or profitability of a product or service. It is important for investors to see that you have thought through the size of the market you intend to target. If you cannot prove that you have a good chance of penetrating the local market, then they will be unable to see the growth potential of your business.

When it comes to creating market opportunity, investors will want to see that you have thought through three important acronyms that represent different subgroups of the market: TAM, SAM, and SOM.

TAM: total available market; the total market demand for a product or service.

SAM: serviceable available market; the section of the TAM that your product or service intends to target.

SOM: share of market; the portion of SAM that your company is realistically likely to reach.

- **TAM,** or Total Available Market, refers to the total market demand for a product or service.

- **SAM,** or Serviceable Available Market, is the section of the TAM that your product or service intends to target.

- **SOM,** or Share of Market, is the portion of the SAM that your company is realistically likely to reach.

To explain these acronyms in further detail, let's take the example of an entrepreneur pitching a gourmet donut café. Let's call it The Gourmet Donut Co. The café will serve high-end coffee and tea and unique-flavored, gourmet donuts, such as maple bacon or ham and cheese, in addition to the traditional glazed and chocolate. The entrepreneur wants to locate the café in Baton Rouge, Louisiana.

The TAM is all the possible customers who visit donut shops or cafés in the United States. If you were to open coffee shops all over the United States, then you could potentially generate revenues from TAM. Although your intention is not to run your business to this scale, you could always produce this statistic to your audience as overall evidence of the popularity of donut shops and cafés.

The SAM is a little more specific than TAM as it describes the demand for your types of products within your reach; in this case, the café or donut market in the Baton Rouge area. In other words, if you had no competition in the Baton Rouge area, then you could potentially generate revenues from SAM. Keep in mind, however, that you always have competition.

The SOM describes the share of the market you can realistically reach with your café in Baton Rouge. This involves working out the percentage of SAM that you could potentially service. For example, in this case, SOM may be a particular geographic radius within the city of Baton Rouge. You would need to figure out how much market share you could capture, given the amount of competition and the geographic radius. To help your audience better visualize TAM, SAM, and SOM, you could use a graphic like Figure 6.4 in your presentation.

However, providing TAM, SAM, and SOM information to your investors is not enough; entrepreneurs need to know where this niche market is going in the future and how their business fits into it.[26] This involves understanding the deeper market dynamics at play, such as the competition and how it may evolve, any regulatory changes that might affect the product, and anything else that may impact future demand.

To really show evidence that the opportunity is a real business, entrepreneurs need to go beyond TAM, SAM, and SOM to establish a launch market.

Launch Market

Creating a launch or niche market is similar to the beachhead and bowling pin strategies. It involves proving that you already have a group of launch customers who really want to buy your product.[27] This is an essential way to convince investors that you already have a real niche customer base ready and willing to buy your product as soon as it launches.

Overall, the entrepreneur needs to assess the viability and attractiveness of the chosen segment or segments. Table 6.6 lists the key questions entrepreneurs need to answer when assessing the potential of their own customer segments.

FIGURE 6.4

TAM, SAM, and SOM

TABLE 6.6

Key Questions Relating to Customer Segments

1. What size is your customer segment?
The size of a segment is not just the number of customers, but also its potential to contribute to the growth of your company.
2. How much buying power do your customers have?
Your customers must be able to afford your product. Regardless of their enthusiasm, customers are no use to your company if they lack the resources to buy.
3. Can your customers be identified in the segment?
Although you might be able to identify your segment, you also need to be able to pinpoint and profile the people or businesses that are most likely to buy from you.
4. How accessible are the customers in your segment?
A key part of maintaining customer loyalty is being able to reach your customer base; only then will you know the most suitable marketing strategy to implement. This involves an insight to your customers' buying behavior and the types of media they might use.
5. How stable is your customer segment?
A stable customer segment is one that can be marketed to over a long period of time. Assessing the degree of stability of your customer segment is essential for the longevity of your product and your business.

Source: Adapted from Nijssen, E. J. (2017). Entrepreneurial marketing: an effectual approach. Routledge. pp 33–34.

Once you have a good idea of the market potential, then you can start to build solid strategies to calculate the market size. Determining market size is absolutely essential for any startup; without this knowledge, you may find yourself operating in a market too small to make any money. It also helps you to differentiate between your TAM and SAM, thereby clarifying the potential customer demand for your product or service offering. Table 6.7 outlines more reasons behind the importance of market sizing.

TABLE 6.7

Why Market Sizing Is Important

1. It estimates the number of sales and resulting profits of new products or customer segments.
2. It identifies growth opportunities in different product lines and customer segments.
3. It helps to pinpoint competitive threats and how to develop strategies for those threats.
4. It forces you to think about exit strategies or pivot points in the future.
5. It gives you a sense of market trends and their potential to impact your business in the future.
6. It is important for investors who want to see evidence of a large enough market to justify their investment.

Calculating Market Size

For a decent estimate of your market size, you will need to carry out the following:

1. Define your segment of the market.
    We have outlined in the sections above the importance of focusing on an initial pool of customers before you expand into other segments.

2. Conduct a top-down analysis.
    A **top-down analysis** involves determining the total market and then estimating your share of the market.[28] It typically uses demographic data like population, age, income, or location to calculate market share. For example, if your business involves selling video doorbells, you may reason that if there are 300,000 people in your area, then at least 5% of the market will buy your doorbell, in which case you will make 15,000 sales. Of course, this is just a rough estimate and further research must be carried out to produce more accurate results.

3. Conduct a bottom-up analysis.
    A **bottom-up analysis** involves estimating potential sales using calculations in order to arrive at total sales figure.[29] This type of analysis requires more effort than top-down analysis but is worth carrying out as it delivers more accurate results.

The following example illustrates how bottom-up analysis works. Let's say you have created a prototype for a new bicycle light that increases your visibility in the dark, and you want to find out if there is a profitable market for your business.[30] First, you can look at the places bicycle lights are typically sold. The lights will most likely be sold in bike shops, retailers, and online, but you decide to focus on just bike shops for now. Second, check out the number of bike shops in the United States (a quick search on the Internet should give you an idea of the number of bike shops). Third, talk to the bike shops and see if they are willing to stock your new light. Finally, check out the number of bike lights the shops usually sell in a year.

Once you have gathered all your data, remember to be conservative in your estimate. For instance, say 30 out of the 100 bike shops you have called agree to stock your product.

Top-down analysis: determining the total market using demographic data and then estimating your share of the market.

Bottom-up analysis: estimating potential sales using calculations in order to arrive at a total sales figure.

ENTREPRENEURSHIP MEETS ETHICS

Can You Sell Customer Information?

When customers buy products through an online company, they leave a lot of information behind, including their name and address and the types of products they have viewed while browsing. Partner companies often approach businesses to buy this type of data to find out more about customers' purchasing patterns. But is it right to sell customer information? And even if it is not sold, should it even be used in house?

David Hennessey, professor of marketing at Babson College, believes that using consumer information is a privacy and fairness issue if not a legal one, certainly because, in most cases, people believe they are making purchases anonymously or are somehow otherwise protected.

Hennessey suggests that companies unsure about their right to sell customer data should consult the company's code of ethics to determine how much information can be used internally and externally. He adds that the company could create its own policy to set standards around customer information and when it should or should not be shared. The American Marketing Association's set of standards are useful for determining this policy.

Overall, sometimes the most straightforward way to resolve this ethical dilemma is to put yourself in the shoes of your customers.

Critical Thinking Question

1. How would you feel if an online company you had made purchases from sold your data to a third party? Would you view it as an invasion of privacy or a betrayal? Or both? ●

Source: Di Meglio, F. (n.d.). Ethics in marketing. *Monster.* Retrieved from https://www.monster.com/career-advice/article/ethics-in-marketing

Some of those deals may not come to pass, so better to halve the number. This means it's reasonable to presume that 15% of bike shops might commit to buying your product. If there are 4,000 bike shops in the United States, then your bike lights have the potential to be sold in 600 bike shops. Similarly, from your bike shop data, you can work out the average selling price of other bike lights on the market. You can also work out the approximate number sold every year. Again, remember to be realistic: Just because the bike shop sells 200 bike lights a year doesn't mean you will sell the same amount. Simply halve the figure of sales, and that will give you a more realistic result. Better to be conservative than wildly off target.

Once you have a good idea of your potential buyers (TAM), price, and annual consumption, then you can use SAM and SOM to estimate your market potential. For instance, to get the most accurate representation, you could use SOM, and to look at the bigger market you may eventually target, you could use SAM.

4. Don't forget to do sanity checks.

You might have gathered all your data and research, but don't neglect to carry out sanity checks during the calculations process. For instance, if you calculate a market size of 350 million cyclists, but the population of the United States is only 300 million, then you know you have gone wrong somewhere.

5. Check out the competition.

Do some research on your competition. Is your industry crowded? What companies are leading the way in selling products or services similar to yours? For example, an entirely new product or service that meets a specific need is likely to capture more market share than a product in a market that is already quite saturated.

As we have explored, in order for entrepreneurs to find, build, and grow their customer base, they must take the right steps to identify the different types of customers, understand that different customers have different needs, and devise the right strategies to create the most viable marketing opportunity. Only then will entrepreneurs be able to connect with their target audience in a meaningful way and promote their products and services to people who will potentially buy them. ●

Get the tools you need to sharpen your study skills. SAGE edge offers a robust online environment featuring an impressive array of free tools and resources.

- Access practice quizzes, eFlashcards, video, and multimedia at **edge.sagepub.com/neckentrepreneurship2e**

SUMMARY

6.1   Define a customer and market.

A customer is someone who pays for a product or service. Customers become consumers when they actually use the product or service.

A market is a place where people can sell goods and services (the supply) to people who wish to buy those goods and services (the demand). *Supply* refers to the sellers that compete for customers in the marketplace, while *demand* implies the desire held by prospective customers for the goods and services available.

6.2   Describe the different types of customers entrepreneurs may encounter.

Typically, there are five different types of customers: users, influencers, recommenders, economic buyers, and decision makers.

6.3   Identify your customers through segmentation.

Different customer segments have different needs, which require different approaches and more tailored solutions. Business success depends on defining customer segments and becoming familiar with the type of customers most likely to buy the product or service.

6.4   Find your target customer.

The success or failure of a product or service depends on the response of potential customers in the marketplace. The technology adoption life cycle model divides the market into five categories of potential customers: innovators, early adopters, early majority, late majority, and laggards. Entrepreneurs can also find target customers by focusing their resources on a single, primary market first, known as a *beachhead market*.

6.5   Acquire a deeper understanding of your customer through personas.

Buyer personas are profiles or representations of your ideal customers based on information and market research. These personas help you to create strategies to connect with your target audience and promote products and services to people who will potentially buy them.

6.6   Illustrate the customer journey mapping process.

A customer journey map is a visual representation that captures customer experience across multiple touchpoints of your business. Journey mapping is a necessary process in the early stages of your startup so you can develop empathy for your customers as well as learn how to make their experience with your company or product a great one.

6.7   Explain the importance of market sizing in growing your customer base.

Market sizing is a method of estimating the number of potential customers and possible revenue or profitability of a product or service. When it comes to creating market opportunity, investors will want to see that you have thought through three important acronyms that represent different subgroups of the market: TAM, SAM, and SOM.

KEY TERMS

Bottom-up analysis   146

Buyer personas   136

Consumers   127

Customer   127

Customer journey map   138

Decision makers   131

Demand   127

Economic buyers   131

End users   130

Influencers (or opinion leaders)   130

Market   127

Market opportunity   128

Market sizing   143

Product application   128

Recommenders   131

SAM   144

SOM   144

Supply   127

TAM   144

Top-down analysis   146

Haim Saban, The Mighty Morphin' Power Rangers

I have to tell you that the biggest hits that I had in my life in music and in television and in business have been always as a result of significant rejections and repeated rejections. So, every time I have an idea that people tell me no, don't do that, I say, oops, I'm on to something.

Haim Saban has always been good at identifying opportunities, and this skill has helped him achieve billionaire entrepreneur status. Haim Saban's success started with the extremely popular teenage superheroes, the *Mighty Morphin' Power Rangers*.

Born in 1944, Haim was a poor Jewish kid from Alexandria, Egypt. At the age of 12, Haim and his family fled to Israel because of the Suez War, as Egyptian Jews were perceived as traitors. He lived with his family of five in a very small apartment. He did odd jobs during the day and studied at night. After school, he joined the Israeli Army, where he started in combat but was shortly reassigned to organizing entertainment for the soldiers. This reassignment changed the course of Haim's life.

Out of the army, Haim wanted to find a way to support his family. In 1966, he joined a rock band, The Lions of Judah, as a bass player. They would perform songs by The Beatles, and their lead singer (who sounded a lot like Paul McCartney) helped the band gain some popularity. Saban wasn't a very good bass player, so he was offered the job of band manager. Being a band manager was a win for both Haim and the band. Managing one band grew to the management of many, and Haim became a full-time tour promoter in Israel.

However, at the peak of his career, the 1973 Yom Kippur War led to many show cancellations, and Haim incurred all the expenses without any revenue to pay his bills. The devaluation of the Israeli pound compounded the issue and left the 29-year-old with $600,000 of debt. In search of a larger market to help him pay off his debt, he moved from Israel to Paris, France, to expand his scope and access a larger market. He discovered and signed a 9-year-old singer, Noam Kaniel. Noam's first record ("Difficile De Choisir"), which was released in 1974, went platinum. Riding on this success, Haim started a production company, set up his own label, and sold more than 18 million records in a period of 8 years. During these years, Haim learned how to knock on doors of distributors and piece together all that is involved in setting up a record company. He decided to continue producing and distributing music in the United States, and in the early 1980s he moved to Studio City, California.

Before moving to the United States, Haim studied how music royalties were paid in America by representative collection agencies like the American Society of Composers, Authors and Publishers (ASCAP) and Broadcast Music, Inc. (BMI). He called them to learn how the system worked and discovered that producing music for cartoons was the most profitable. He learned that sitcoms only had music that cumulatively played for 2 or 3 minutes. Cartoons, on the other hand, had wall-to-wall music that would play for the entire length of a cartoon. Collection agencies paid royalties based on the number of unit minutes on the air, making cartoon music a lot more profitable than some of the highest rated sitcoms of the time. He reached out to different cartoon producers to "make them an offer they couldn't refuse." He told them that he would compose the music for free, if he was allowed to keep both the publisher's share and the composer's share of the royalty. Producers usually had to pay composers a fee in addition to the royalties. Free compositions were unheard of, and cartoon producers found this to be a good offer.

With an innovative business model, Saban Entertainment was born. The company produced music for cartoons like *Inspector Gadget, Heathcliff, He-Man*, and other iconic TV shows. The business grew and very soon he was running 12 studios that were all producing music for cartoon TV shows.

In 1984, Haim visited Japan and happened upon the *Mighty Morphin' Power Rangers* (then called *Zyuranger*) on his hotel room TV. He really liked the show and saw another opportunity. Haim believed that the American audience would love the show and that he could produce it at a much lower cost because the action sequences, which would probably cost the most to produce, were already available to use from the Japanese show. He could shoot the same show in America, with American kids, and use existing action sequences. Once the teenagers turned into the *Power Rangers*, with their masks and spandex costumes on, they could be "kicking monster butts" anywhere, Japan or America. Haim bought the rights to the show to bring it back to America.

However, distribution cable networks were not excited about the show at all. He tried to pitch the show to people for 8 years, with no success. Networks thought the show was "cheesy" and that Haim was embarrassing himself. However, Haim was confident that if the show could run successfully in Japan for 20 years, the likelihood of it working in the United States was very high. Margaret Loesch, a Fox executive, was the only one interested in giving the show a shot and ordered it to air in 1993. The management at Fox were not happy with her decision as they did not believe in the show. Margaret decided to air the *Power Rangers* in the early morning slot, in the summer, just to test it out with little risk to the viewership. Within a week, it became the highest rated kids show ever on Fox Kids, beating out *Batman* and *Looney Tunes*. The show was immediately moved to a prime-time slot. In 1994, Fox approached Haim with an offer to buy Saban Entertainment for $400 million. The network wanted an immediate presence in television for children and

Haim had the content and the distribution network to make it happen. Saban turned down the offer, but then Chase Carey, the COO of Fox Inc. and CEO of Fox Broadcasting Company, proposed a joint venture between Saban Entertainment and Fox Kids instead. Haim agreed to give them all his cartoons and his distribution network in exchange for half of the Fox Kids network. The deal was solidified in 1995 with Saban and News Corp. each getting 49.5%.

In 2000, Haim was ready for a change. His 1995 contract with Fox Kids allowed him to sell his 49.5% share in 5 years. Haim realized that it was time to sell the network as they had started competing with firms like Disney and Warner Brothers that were 10 times their size. He knew that there were two potential buyers, CBS and Disney. Disney was very interested in the assets of the company and bought the company for $5.3 billion. Haim's share was valued at $1.5 billion. In the fall of 2001, he set up an investment fund called Saban Capital Group, which he still runs today, that allows him to invest and help other ventures grow and prosper.

Critical Thinking Questions

1. Identify and describe all the key decision makers who have influenced Haim's ventures.

2. What was most innovative about the business model of Saban Entertainment?

3. Who is the customer of Saban Entertainment? Who is the customer of the joint venture between Saban and Fox?

Sources:

Bruck, C. (2010). The influencer. *The New Yorker.* Retrieved from https://www.newyorker.com/magazine/2010/05/10/the-influencer

Dolan, K. A. (2001). Beyond Power Rangers. *Forbes.* Retrieved from https://www.forbes.com/global/2001/1126/050.html

Raz, G. (Producer). (2018, September 24). *Power Rangers: Haim Saban* [Audio podcast]. Retrieved from https://www.npr.org/templates/transcript/transcript.php?storyId=650524515

7

Testing and Experimenting With New Ideas

"What good is an idea if it remains an idea? Try. Experiment. Iterate. Fail. Try again. Change the world."

—Simon Sinek

Chapter Outline

Learning Objectives

7.1 EXPERIMENTS: WHAT THEY ARE AND WHY WE DO THEM

>> LO 7.1 Define experiments and describe why we do them.

In Chapter 4, we explored the concept of design thinking as a process that helps us identify solutions to complex problems. We also described the three phases of the design-thinking process: inspiration, ideation, and implementation—a nonlinear approach that produces creative, meaningful results. In Chapter 4 we primarily focused on inspiration and ideation; now it's time to focus on testing the solutions generated in the ideation phase. In this chapter, we will explore in further detail the processes that take place during the implementation phase, specifically with regard to experimentation. The implementation phase focuses on early, fast, low-cost testing and experimentation to strengthen ideas and ensure that entrepreneurs are on the right path to meet the needs of their potential customers.

The implementation phase also ties in with developing the skill of experimentation as part of the Entrepreneurship Method, described in Chapter 1. This involves taking action, trying something new, and building that learning into the next iteration. Experimentation requires getting out of the building and collecting real-world information to test new concepts, rather than sitting at a desk searching databases for the latest research. It involves asking questions, validating assumptions, and taking nothing for granted.

An **experiment** is defined as a test designed to help you learn and answer questions related to the feasibility and viability of your venture. In Chapter 4 we talked about design thinking, which is focused primarily on desirability. Desirability answers the question, What do people need? Feasibility answers the question, Can we do it? Viability answers the question, Can we make money doing it or is it sustainable? (See Figure 7.1.) Experiments can help validate the needs, but they are mostly designed to determine whether the solution is doable and potentially profitable.

Experiments need to have a clear purpose, be achievable, and generate reliable results. Experiments guide us toward which customer opinions to listen to, what important product or service features should take priority, what might please or upset customers, and what should be worked on next.[1] They are essential when it comes to trying out new ideas, finding solutions, and providing answers to those "What if?" questions.[2] It is through experimentation that we start to address feasibility and viability. Table 7.1 outlines the reasons why all entrepreneurs should experiment.

An experiment begins with a **hypothesis**, which is an assumption that is tested through research and experimentation. In the Entrepreneurs in Action feature, Karima Mariama-Arthur, founder of boutique consulting firm WordSmithRapport,

Experiment: a method used to prove or disprove the validity of an idea or hypothesis.

Hypothesis: an assumption that is tested through research and experimentation.

Master the content at **edge.sagepub.com/ neckentrepreneurship2e**

FIGURE 7.1

Feasibility and Viability Are Better Understood Through Experimentation

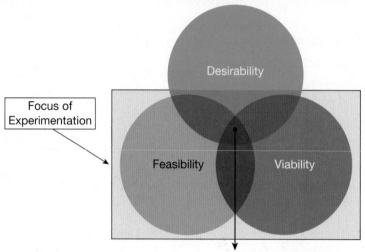

Final solutions should be at the intersection.

Source: Adapted from IDEO. (2015). *The field guide to human-centered design* (p. 14). Retrieved from http://d1r3w4d5z5a88i.cloudfront.net/assets/guide/Field%20Guide%20to%20Human-Centered%20Design_IDEOorg_English-ee47a1ed4b91f3252115b83152828d7e.pdf

TABLE 7.1

Five Characteristics of Good Experiments

1.	They are structured and follow a particular template.
2.	They are focused and don't try to test too many things at the same time. Focus on a core hypothesis.
3.	They are believable so you can trust what you learn.
4.	They are flexible so you can make changes while in the experiment if necessary.
5.	They are compact so you can learn quickly.

Source: Reprinted with permission from Testing with Humans, by Giff Constable (Copyright Owner).

used experimentation to validate her hypothesis that people want more support in leadership development and organizational performance.

As Karima discovered, there are huge benefits to experimentation for entrepreneurs. Table 7.2 outlines the reasons why all entrepreneurs should experiment.

In the next section, we will explore the different types of experimentation most commonly used by entrepreneurs.

7.2 TYPES OF EXPERIMENTS

>> LO 7.2   Identify the different types of experiments most commonly used.

Entrepreneurs have many different types of experiments and tests available to them, and some require more effort than others. Overall, the amount of effort put in tends to correlate to the believability of the information coming out. Giff Constable, author of *Testing With Humans*, illustrates this concept on his truth curve (see Figure 7.2).

ENTREPRENEURSHIP IN ACTION

Karima Mariama-Arthur, WordSmithRapport

Photo courtesy of Karima Mariama-Arthur

Karima Mariama-Arthur, founder, owner, and CEO of WordSmithRapport

Karima Mariama-Arthur was a skilled lawyer and she loved the legal profession, but she lacked "a bona fide sense of fulfillment." Thinking about what was next for her, she considered her skillset and where she excelled. "I knew what I was good at, but knowing *only* that wasn't good enough. I had to research how my skills in law, business, and academia could prove valuable in a new context. I needed to understand how my professional wheelhouse was transferrable."

Eventually WordSmithRapport, a boutique consulting firm, was born! Karima is the founder, owner, and CEO—it's a one-woman show, and it's quite successful as she works with clients in Greece, Cuba, the United States, Russia, France, and Dubai. The firm specializes in helping clients solve performance and leadership challenges. For Karima, it's all about developing the talent that exists inside companies. The mission of WordSmithRapport lies in answering one fundamental question: *How can we help advance the human condition utilizing our passion and expertise?*

Before starting a business of her own, Karima had only ever worked for large firms, academic institutions, and policy-based organizations. "I had always been the talent,

but never my own boss," she said. "I had no frame of reference for what might be required to start a business of my own." She just starting talking to people, then more people, and then more people. She prioritized educating herself on the administrative aspects of business as well, to ensure she would be operating legally and at full capacity. In addition, she committed to learning more about the consulting and professional development industries. A better understanding of the services industry (beyond legal services) was also necessary. "All of these efforts took a great deal of time, effort, and money," said Karima, "But the experiences were very illuminating and showed me gaps in my thinking and inspired me to confront any inexperience." Educating herself enabled her to avoid many pitfalls faced by entrepreneurs. She admits, "I made plenty of my own mistakes, but I could have made a ton more without taking the time to gather valuable insights from others."

Testing new service business ideas is difficult because you can't build a prototype for a service business like you can for a new app. The point of testing is to reduce risk and uncertainty and Karima did this through talking, asking, and listening to everyone she came into contact with. Karima consequently mitigated many of the tangible risks that come along with stepping away from a career to become an entrepreneur. "Any time you step outside of your comfort zone there is always the likelihood of doing poorly or simply doing worse than you thought you would. Those things I controlled as much as I could. I did good research. I was smart with money. I took my time, asked lots of questions, and followed sound advice."

Critical Thinking Questions

1. How did Karima test the idea of her consulting firm?
2. Why is it so difficult to test a service concept? ●

Source: Karima Mariama-Arthur (interview with author, November 26, 2018).

TABLE 7.2

Checklist for Experimentation

Bring people through an experience and watch their behaviors and decisions.
Test your product and the value you create for customers before you've finished the product itself. Consider what aspect of the product or service you want to test before testing the whole thing.
Prioritize what you want to learn. You don't have time to run experiments on everything. Quick testing helps you prioritize and test the most important risks and assumptions.
Create a structured plan for your experiment before you start. A chaotic experiment leads to chaotic results.
Set up success metrics before you begin so you don't rationalize your results after the fact.
Weave customer interviews into experiments, when appropriate, to maximize learning and insights.
Keep an open mind about your results, good or bad, and use good judgment when interpreting what you learn.

Source: Constable, G., & Rimalovski, F. (2018). *Testing with humans* (pp. 23–24). New York, NY: Author.

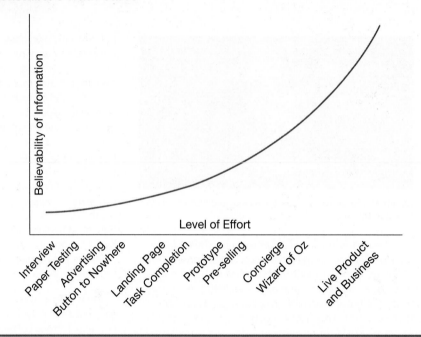

FIGURE 7.2

Giff Constable's Truth Curve

Source: Reprinted with permission from Testing with Humans, by Giff Constable (Copyright Owner).

Interview

Interviews are a fast and inexpensive way to get insights into your idea from your target customers before you begin the experiment.

Paper Testing

Creating a paper test is a simple way to outline your vision and to spot any mistakes before the process goes any further. These tests can be carried out using a range of techniques, including wireframe (or blueprint), storyboarding, or drawing the product you envision.

San Francisco–based electric skateboard manufacturer Boosted used wireframes (see Figure 7.3) to illustrate how their users would navigate their new mobile app prototype. The technique helped them to troubleshoot any problems before rolling the app out to their customers.[3]

Advertising

Advertising involves spreading the word about your business using brochures or social media directed to your relevant target market and assessing the level of response.

Button to Nowhere

Say you want to add a new feature to your website or app, but first you want to find out if your customers will click on it. Instead of spending hours building it, you could use a test called "button to nowhere."[4] This just means that when your users click on the feature, nothing happens. They might receive an "under construction" pop-up message (see Figure 7.4), but essentially, they won't be able to access anything else. The button to nowhere test is a great way to measure user interest in a new feature—the more clicks, the higher the likelihood that your new feature will attract interest.

FIGURE 7.3

Boosted Wireframe Example

Source: https://www.justinmind.com/blog/20-inspiring-web-and-mobile-wireframe-and-prototype-examples/

FIGURE 7.4

Button to Nowhere

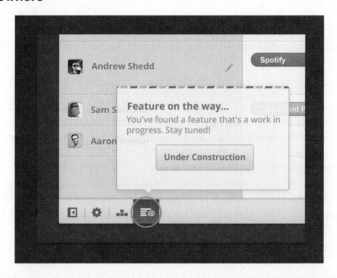

Source: Kishfy, N. (2013). Button to nowhere. *Medium*. Retrieved from https://medium.com/@kishfy/button-to-nowhere-77d911517318

Landing Page

Another useful way to gauge the level of customer response to your business's website is to include a particular call to action such as "click here for more information."

Shyam Devnani, founder of online meal service India in a Box (featured in Supplement B: The Pitch Deck), created a landing page with three different meal options to see which options the customers clicked on most. Nothing was behind the button except "thank you for visiting . . . we are still building this site."

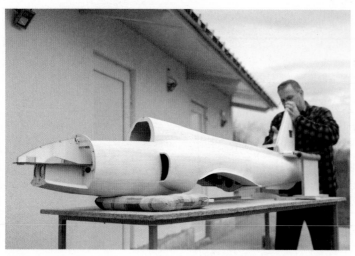
©iStockphoto.com/Slavica

Rapid prototyping

Task Completion

Task completion (also known as usability testing) involves watching someone using your product to understand what works and what doesn't. For instance, say you're creating a website to provide easier access to exam results for students. The user goal would be to look up grades, but the task would be to look up the results for a specific exam (e.g., midterms).[5]

Prototype

A prototype is an early and often crude version of a product, but there are many different types of prototypes (that we discuss later). The crudest version is called rapid prototyping: You might build a model of a product out of foam, wood, boxes, plastic, or other scrap-like material with a view to finding potential customers to interact with the physical product.

Standly was a venture idea for a standing desk that Babson students could use with their laptops in class. The first rapid prototype was made of three pieces of wood and cardboard. Students were able to test the desks in class to see if they liked to stand while using their laptops during class. Though a good experiment, the venture didn't really take off as the desk didn't generate enough sales.

Preselling

Preselling is a testing technique that involves booking orders for your product before it has been developed. This method is most commonly used on crowdfunding sites like Kickstarter. Monthly journal *Living a Great Story* used Kickstarter to launch its campaign, while Jim Poss, founder of solar-powered trash compactor company Big Belly, managed to sell one of his compactors to a ski resort in Vail, Colorado, before he had even finished the product.[6]

Concierge and Wizard of Oz

During the concierge test, the customer interfaces with the product but the "technology" is going on behind the scenes, while during the Wizard of Oz test, customers think they are interfacing with the real product, but it is actually you behind the scenes manually providing the service.

For example, VentureBlocks (featured as a case study in Chapter 4 and the game bundled with this book) used a concierge model when it was testing early versions of the game. When a user chose a question to ask in the simulated game, a live person would let them know if they were correct or incorrect and award them points in the form of poker chips.

Live Product and Business

You are up and running for real! Thanks to all the previous tests you have carried out, you have gathered enough insights and validation to launch your live product and business in the marketplace.

Some of the experiments in Constable's truth curve (Figure 7.2) also count as prototypes. For instance, a paper test or storyboard is a type of prototype. In the next section, we will explore prototypes in greater detail.

7.3 A DEEPER LOOK AT PROTOTYPES

>> **LO 7.3**   **Explore prototypes in greater depth.**

As we found in Chapter 4, prototyping is an essential part of the design process. Prototypes can be basic models or sketches that inform others and communicate what our ideas look like, behave like, and work like before the real product or service is launched.[7]

The prototype as depicted in Constable's truth curve (Figure 7.2) is really an **MVP (minimum viable product)**. An MVP is a version of a new product that allows a team to collect the maximum amount of validated learning about customers with the least effort.[8] In other words, entrepreneurs need to build products that have the most important features and benefits without overbuilding. Overbuilding a product wastes precious resources that entrepreneurs don't have in the startup stage. The MVP as prototype comes before preselling in the truth curve because it requires you to actually build the product that adds value and is meeting the needs of customers. You don't have to build a lot of them, but you do have to build it. You may even make money at the MVP stage. Barbara Baekgaard and Pat Miller, founders of luggage design company Vera Bradley, spent a couple of years at the MVP stage when they were running a small cottage operation from their hometown in Indiana and selling their bags at trade shows. In addition, search-and-discovery mobile app Foursquare began as a one-feature MVP offering their users check-ins and badges as rewards. After monitoring user responses, Foursquare enhanced the product to include recommendations and city guides. Today, Foursquare has more than 50 million monthly active users who have checked in more than 8 billion times. Finally, Instagram's MVP originally focused on photo filters only; users could use filters on their photo and save them in an album. Since then, Instagram has expanded to include videos, geolocation, and the ability to interact with other social networks.[9]

The concept of prototype covers a continuum from very rapid, low-cost early prototyping to MVP or even a pilot. Let's take a deeper look at different types of prototypes.

> **MVP (minimum viable product):** a version of a new product that allows a team to collect the maximum amount of validated learning about customers with the least effort.

Different Types of Prototypes

MVP

As described above, an MVP as prototype is the first functional and working version of your product ready for release to actual customers (see Figure 7.5).

Rapid Prototypes

Rapid prototypes are quickly created models used to visualize a product or service. Rapid prototypes could be made out of crude paper models or storyboards.

FIGURE 7.5

MVP

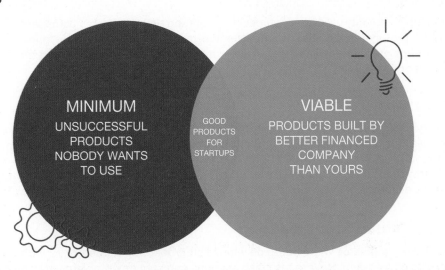

Source: S-Pro. (2018). What is a minimum viable product? *Medium.* Retrieved from https://medium.com/@sprocompany/what-is-a-minimum-viable-product-and-how-to-build-an-mvp-for-your-startup-9a02c0d4a56a

LEGO prototype

Mock-Up Prototype

A mock-up prototype is usually presented as a 2D or 3D model that looks like the finished product but lacks the right functionality. It may be used as a replica of the real product during experimentation.

High Fidelity Prototype

A high fidelity prototype is a more sophisticated version of a mock-up that has enough functionality to allow users to really interact with the product or service. An app that includes customer functions and some animation is a good example of a high fidelity prototype.[10]

LEGO Prototypes

LEGO is particularly useful for creating rough, simple prototypes of your ideas. Tim Brown, CEO of IDEO, used LEGO to build a prototype of a complex insulin injection device.

Role-Playing

Role-playing (or experiential prototyping) is a method that helps you to step into the shoes of your user by capturing their emotional experience of testing a product or service.

Wizard of Oz Prototypes

As mentioned earlier, Wizard of Oz testing can also be considered prototypes with faked functions. A common example of this type of prototype is a virtual assistant in which someone behind the scenes types out the responses to the user.

User-Driven Prototypes

This method focuses on the user creating the prototype, which in turn enables you to better understand their thinking. For example, if you have an idea about how to improve the waiting experience at airports, you might ask users to draw their own version of what this might look like, or build a LEGO prototype.[11]

Pilots and Prototypes

Although commonly used interchangeably, pilots and prototypes are not the same thing—in fact, a prototype, at least in its crude version, is often created before the pilot testing.

Pilot experiment: a small-scale study conducted to assess the feasibility of a product or service.

A **pilot experiment** is a small-scale study conducted to assess the feasibility of a product or service.

Storyboards

Storyboard: an easy form of prototyping that provides a high-level view of thoughts and ideas arranged in sequence in the form of drawings, sketches, or illustrations.

A **storyboard** is an easy form of prototyping that provides a high-level view of thoughts and ideas arranged in sequence in the form of drawings, sketches, or illustrations (see Figure 7.6).

Storyboarding may sound simple, but it is such an important part of prototyping that we have devoted the following section to it.

The Power of Storyboarding

Walt Disney animator Webb Smith developed storyboarding in the 1930s by pinning up sketches of scenes in order to visualize cartoons and spot any problems or inconsistencies before the animation went into production.[12] Since then, not only has storyboarding become standard for movies, commercials, documentaries, and advertising, but it is also

FIGURE 7.6

Storyboard

Source: Storyboards Help Visualize UX Ideas by Rachel Krause on July 15, 2018. https://www.nngroup.com/articles/storyboards-visualize-ideas/

becoming popular as a business and management tool for explaining projects or products to employees, clients, customers, stockholders, and others.[13]

What does storyboarding mean to the entrepreneur? A storyboard provides you with a better understanding of your own idea and how it interacts with customers. It is a way of compiling your thoughts and ideas into one visual, easy-to-understand, logical document or set of documents.[14] Often, it is helpful to draw a storyboard before interacting with customers or other stakeholders because it can bring clarity to the idea, better tell the story of the idea, and highlight the potential value it brings to customers. There are no hard and fast rules for storyboarding, but there must be a clear sense of what needs to be accomplished and an effort to maintain the flow or sequence of thoughts and ideas.

Remember the old adage, "A picture is worth a thousand words." Because of the visual element, a storyboard gets the main message across very quickly. It is also more likely than a lengthy, detailed, written document or speech to provoke reactions, discussion, and feedback from the people who are viewing it. As long as your storyboard flows well and is interesting and interactive, you can expect it to generate ideas and further questions.[15]

Storyboarding requires that the customer be at the center of the story. It is a way for you to draw the idea in action, which generates further questions for additional experimentation.

Basic storyboards are simple and inexpensive to create, and they do not require any artistic training or talent. They can be rough, hand-drawn sketches or simple PowerPoint slides. If you are sketching on a piece of paper, separate your page into quadrants, and then you can start to fill in each one. Your goal is not to create a work of art but to communicate: to use visual imagery to make your entrepreneurial idea more understandable.[16]

The problem-solution-benefit framework (see Figure 7.7) provides a basic structure for storyboarding. In this structure, there are three main questions to keep in mind:

- What is the problem your customer is experiencing?

- What are you offering as a solution to the problem?

- How will your customer benefit from your product/service offering?

FIGURE 7.7

The Problem-Solution-Benefit Framework

State the Problem	Show the Solution	Show the Benefit
• What is the problem your customer is experiencing?	• What are you offering as a solution to the problem?	• How will your customer benefit from your solution?

Let's apply these questions to Rent the Runway, a business founded by entrepreneurs Jennifer Fleiss and Jennifer Hyman that rents designer dresses by online subscription.[17]

The problem: Many women (even those in well-paid jobs) cannot afford designer dresses to wear to special occasions. "I want to wear a designer dress, but they are very expensive, and I would probably wear it only once."

The solution: Give women access to designer dresses by creating an online business renting designer dresses for one-tenth of the original cost. "I get access to the latest dresses, but I get to rent for the night rather than buy!"

The benefit: The rental model gives many more women the opportunity to wear designer dresses, which they could have never afforded before. It provides designers with an opportunity to build their brand because their dresses are being showcased by a larger demographic of young, fashionable women. "This service would let me feel like a movie star for my fancy party that's coming up next month."

© Astrid Stawiarz/Getty Images Entertainment/Getty Images

Rent the Runway, founded by Jennifer Fleiss and Jennifer Hyman, makes designer dresses more affordable for everyone.

Another version of a storyboard (Figure 7.8) uses a four-quadrant framework. This storyboard illustrates an idea for a new entrepreneurship course. The idea is for faculty members to create an Introduction to Entrepreneurship course in which first-year college students create, develop, operate, and launch a new business.

This storyboard shows a before-and-after scenario. The upper left quadrant shows a traditional classroom setting, with a professor standing at the top of the class, lecturing students on the theory of entrepreneurship. One student is sleeping; another student is hoping a friend will text him to give him something else to do; a third student doesn't understand the theory that the professor is teaching. The *problem* is that students are not engaged during the entrepreneurship course.

The second part of the storyboard (the upper right quadrant) suggests a *solution* to boost student engagement by separating them into teams and loaning each team $3,000 (funded by the college) as startup money for their new ventures.

In the third (lower left) quadrant, the students, armed with the money, *organize* their businesses into different function units. While they are given the freedom to create their own ideas, they are encouraged to think about how their product or service satisfies a human need. They sell their product, but they also suffer from challenges, setbacks, and great victories—as depicted in the zigzag graph illustrated with happy and unhappy faces.

The final quadrant, on the lower right, shows the *outcome*. Students pay the startup money back to the college, and the remaining profits go to charity. What are the *benefits*

FIGURE 7.8

Storyboard of an Idea to Boost Student Engagement

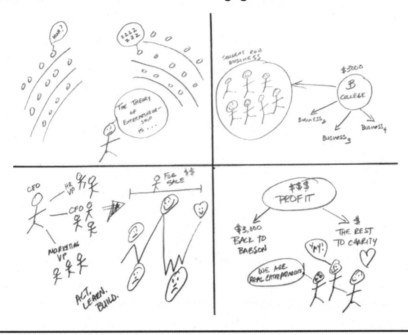

Source: Storyboards Help Visualize UX Ideas by Rachel Krause on July 15, 2018. https://www.nngroup.com/articles/storyboards-visualize-ideas/

of this idea? The students are much more engaged because they acted in order to learn. They were given the opportunity to build something real, practice entrepreneurship, and get a taste for the real entrepreneurial experience.

This storyboard generated lots of questions that needed to be answered before the course could be rolled out.

Back of a Napkin

The simplest of all entrepreneurial plans is sketching out the idea on the back of a napkin. Although this type of plan would certainly get you kicked out of a formal meeting with investors, it can be a highly effective way to gain clarity on the business idea and how it will work. There is something about sketching and pictures that makes an idea come alive. According to Dan Roam, author of *The Back of the Napkin*, we can visually solve problems with pictures. "We can use the simplicity and immediacy of pictures to discover and clarify our own ideas, and use those same pictures to clarify our ideas for other people, helping them to discover something new for themselves along the way."[18]

Sketches on a Page

Using sketches on a page to write your plan is a little more complicated than using the back of the napkin. While it is also informal, it requires a more focused approach based on how the product works or can work in the future. Sketches on a page help you think about the idea today and also what it could become in the future. You can sketch your idea by hand on blank paper, or you can do this electronically using PowerPoint, Prezi, or other software of your choosing.

A simple technique is to create a gallery sketch. With a large piece of white paper as your "canvas," use color, arrows, and labels to indicate all of the major components of the idea. Add clarifying notes as needed. Make an effort to sketch boldly, avoiding faint lines and small pictures. If the idea is for a service, try sketching a map of the events that take place when the service is provided.

Create a Storyboard and Take Action

By this point in the book, we are sure you have at least one idea, if not hundreds, floating around in your mind. We hope you've developed a practice of writing down your ideas. Now it's time to take one of your ideas and draw it in action using a storyboard format. The simplest format is the four-quadrant version depicted in Figure 7.8—the storyboard to boost student engagement.

Artistic talent is not required. Simply focus on visually representing the four aspects of your idea: problem, solution, organization, and outcomes/benefits. As you create your sketches, questions will probably arise related to your idea. Once you've completed the storyboard, write a list of all the questions that you have, now that you have envisioned your idea in action. It's okay if you have a long list. As a matter of fact, the longer the better.

Identify the three questions you want to answer first, and go answer the questions. Remember, small actions lead to quick information. Be specific: What's the question? How will you answer the question? What did you learn? How will you build this learning into the next iteration?

Critical Thinking Questions

1. At the outset of this exercise, how did you feel about being asked to create a storyboard? Do you think people with artistic training or talent have an advantage in storyboarding? Why or why not?

2. Is your list of questions longer or shorter than you expected? How easy or difficult was it to translate your top three questions into experiments?

3. What did you learn from this exercise that surprised you? ●

Taking the gallery sketch one step further, draw a "before and after" scenario. Scenarios are short stories that depict your business, or the product/service, in action. The "before" scenario shows what the lives of your customers are like today. The "after" scenario shows what their lives could be like after your venture is started. The "after" scenario represents what you dream the business could be and the impact it can have on customers in the near future.

7.4 HYPOTHESIS TESTING AND THE SCIENTIFIC METHOD APPLIED TO ENTREPRENEURSHIP

>> **LO 7.4**   **Demonstrate how to test hypotheses and explain the scientific method.**

Many types of prototypes, especially rough prototypes, are used to test hypotheses. Experiments are used to prove or disprove the validity of an idea or hypothesis. Getting out of the building and testing our hypotheses enables us to gain new insights into our target customers' wants and needs. However, testing a hypothesis is not just about gathering data—it also involves matching the results of our tests to the original hypothesis and potentially adapting our original assumptions to better understand our customer target base.[19]

When we hear the word *experiment*, we may think of scientists wearing white coats working with test tubes in laboratories or the extensive clinical trials and experiments undertaken by pharmaceutical companies when testing a new drug.[20,21] Yet the scientific method is not just limited to scientists with PhDs; it can be adapted to entrepreneurs starting new ventures. Experiments can, for example, involve observations of students studying in a library, or employees working on a group project, or consumers visiting a store. They can also involve constructing or formulating products and testing how they perform. In fact, continuous testing is an ongoing requirement for entrepreneurs.

Entrepreneurs are, by definition, experimenters, and that is why it is valuable to understand the process of experimentation—otherwise, the experiments could become disorganized and fruitless.

The scientific process of experimentation consists of the following six steps (see Figure 7.9):

1. Ask a question. For example, can tattoos be used not only on humans but in different ways?

2. Form a hypothesis. For example, tattoos are about individual expression; people are interested in "tattooing" their cars, bikes, or motorcycles.

3. Conduct research. For example, study why people tattoo their bodies. Google "car tattoos" to see if they exist. Start talking to people to better understand their perception of car tattoos.

4. Test the hypothesis. Develop a sketch of what you think a car with a tattoo could look like and share with others to get feedback.

5. Analyze the results. For example, What did you learn? What changes should be made to the original concept? Is your original hypothesis supported? If yes, what's your next question or hypothesis?

6. Communicate the results. For entrepreneurs this is really about communicating with your team and figuring out the next test![22]

FIGURE 7.9

The Scientific Method

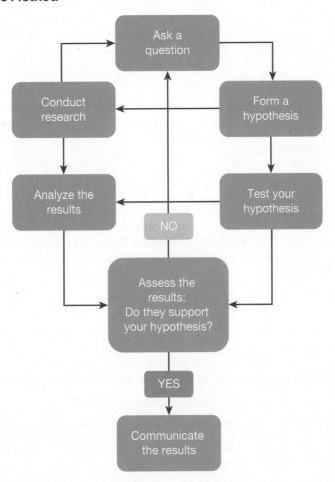

Source: Retrieved from http://generalchemistryfordson2013.weebly.com/scientific-method-flow-chart.html

The Six Steps of Scientific Experimentation in Action

Let's apply the steps of the scientific method to the initial experimentation process under-taken by robotic surgical lighting company Sybo Technology, founded by University of Utah bioengineering student Brody King.[23] King was inspired to start his company when he found himself adjusting the light for a surgeon he was shadowing during a medical procedure.

1.　Ask lots of questions

It is important to ask lots of questions to define the most specific one. For instance, when developing SpaceX, Elon Musk started out by asking, "What would most affect the future of humanity?" The answer at the time was space exploration, which has led to an even more specific question, "How can we send people to Mars?"

2.　Carry out background research

The most successful entrepreneurs become experts in their industry. How? By talking with other experts. When King started Sybo Technology, the Sybo team sought advice from more than 80 industry professionals, each of whom provided his or her perspectives on the product. The team also consulted friends, family, and social networks such as LinkedIn. Thanks to all the advice, they received much greater clarity and validation around their idea.

3.　Develop a hypothesis

Without a clear hypothesis, it is almost impossible to abandon popular assumptions in favor of new solutions. The Sybo team came up with the following hypothesis: "By automating the light adjustment process, surgeons and staff would achieve greater efficiency and enhanced focus on the patient during procedures."

4.　Test the hypothesis by running experiments

King and his team's first experiment to test the hypothesis was in the form of a simple surgeon survey consisting of only 12 questions. The response showed that 87.5% of surgeons would benefit from an automated light. These results proved to the Sybo team that they had a viable product.

5.　Analyze the data

Analyzing data and recording results is an essential part of the experimentation process. Barclay Burns, a professor of Entrepreneurship and Strategy at the University of Utah, created a method called the "Five Types of Value" (see Table 7.3) to analyze both qualitative (nonnumerical data that can be observed and recorded) and quantitative data (data that can be measured).

TABLE 7.3

Five Types of Value

1.　Value in use: Consumers enjoy using the product and will likely refer it to their friends.
2.　Value in exchange: The service is offered at a competitive price.
3.　Value in distribution: Focuses on the availability and accessibility of the product.
4.　Value in finance: Assesses the financial health of the organization and its ability to provide a high value while maintaining healthy margin.
5.　Value in fitness: Monitors the continuous process of gathering resources and innovating.

FIGURE 7.10

Sybo Technology Survey

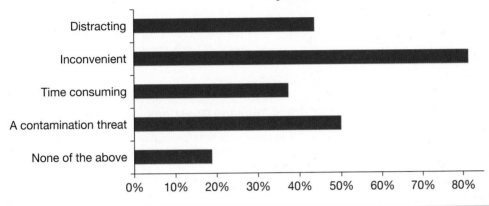

Source: Anderson, M. (2016). *The scientific method of entrepreneurship.* Retrieved from https://lassonde.utah.edu/the-scientific-method-of-entrepreneurship/

6. Assess the results

Once the accuracy of the data has been determined, it is time to draw conclusions. Figure 7.10 shows the results of a different survey sent by the Sybo team to surgeons. From these responses, the team identified "inconvenience" as the real pain point for manually adjusting lighting during surgery. Although the team's original hypothesis is still valid, it can now focus on aspects that provide a more comfortable and enjoyable experience for staff.

When you have followed the six steps, it is important to publish your results to get valuable feedback. Sybo Technology plans to do this by getting surgeons and staff to demonstrate the robotic surgical lighting product.

Although the scientific approach to experimentation is useful to entrepreneurship, keep in mind that you need to *think* like a scientist, not *act* like a scientist. Many scientific experiments take a huge amount of time, resources, and precision. As an entrepreneur, your goal is not to build the perfect experiment but to use low-cost, quick methods to shape ideas and to make them better through continual iteration. Entrepreneurial experimentation is about acting to learn, rather than getting bogged down in scientific rigor. By taking action and experimenting quickly and cheaply, you will have a better chance of refining your ideas into feasible and viable opportunities.

7.5 THE EXPERIMENTATION TEMPLATE

≫ LO 7.5 Describe the experimentation template.

A good experiment is a well-planned experiment. Early, quick experimentation is design to support or reject a hypothesis, not necessarily to support or reject the entire idea. So, it's important to answer the following questions before designing an experiment:

Experimentation Template

1. What is the hypothesis?

2. What is the pass/fail metric?

3. Who are the participants in the experiment?

4. How many participants are needed?

5. How are you going to get participants?

6. How will the experiment be run?

7. How long is the experiment?

Mockups

From the first Mindshift, you should have a storyboard. Now it's time to create a mockup—something more physical that potential customers can actually interact with. Once your mockup is complete, fill out the experimentation template, but make sure that the experiment can be conducted in 1 hour or less. Remember to start small so you can test and learn. If you are testing a service, the same rules apply. You need to simulate part of the service experience for customers.

Critical Thinking Questions

1. Was your hypothesis rejected or supported?
2. Is user interaction important at this stage? Why or why not?
3. What do you think your second experiment will be? ●

Take a group of students at Babson College, for instance. They had an early idea of creating software or some type of electronic gadget that students could use to "ping" other students when they were being distracting in the class. For example, if someone was speaking too long or spending too much time on Facebook or email, or just not staying engaged in the class, that person would be notified by his or her classmates through an app.

Rather than invest time and effort in developing the app or the software, the students obtained a professor's approval to conduct a quick, low-cost experiment. They used about $15 to buy fabric at a discount store and then purchased some wine corks. With these materials they created yellow flags similar to those used by referees in American football. Each student was given a few flags at the beginning of the class and was allowed to throw them at someone perceived to be distracting or unproductive in the class.

The hypothesis was that classmates "calling out" classmates would be a distraction. However, the exact opposite happened. Because the students knew they could be flagged, the flags actually served as a deterrent. In fact, the professor reflected at the end of the class that it had been one of the most engaging class discussions she had experienced in the entire semester. Not only was the experiment cheap, but it also generated an unexpected outcome, which led to many other interesting questions in need of testing to find answers.

Low-Cost Customer Engagement

One of the most important parts of an experiment is customer engagement with your product or service. Involving real customers in your experiment is a great way to test hypotheses, as it provides you with immediate feedback on how your product or service is received. It is also an excellent way to make connections with people who may buy your product or service when it is fully launched.

The following entrepreneurs involved real customers to test their hypothesis. Joel Gascoigne, founder of social media management platform Buffer, decided to test customer demand for his product before it was even built by creating a simple landing page and sharing it with his Twitter followers. Positive response from his potential customers gave Gascoigne the encouragement he needed to build the product. Thanks to his quick, cheap experiment, Gascoigne was able to build a relationship with his customer base before even launching Buffer online. As of 2018, more than 3 million people use the Buffer platform to schedule posts to Facebook, Twitter, LinkedIn, Instagram, and more.[24]

Christina Sembel, founder of San Francisco–based Farmgirl Flowers, also used low-cost experimentation to establish a market for her product.[25] For a year, she delivered free bouquets to city coffee shops together with a pile of 50 business cards. Sembel said, "I'd go back every week and count how many business cards were left." If most of the cards were gone, she would conclude that she'd found the right place to fill with flowers. "All the initial chatter about the company, all the inquiries, was because of those coffee shops. It was the cheapest thing I could have done," Sembel said.

We could say that Gascoigne, Sembel, and the students at Babson College used the "test and learn" approach to experimentation.[26] Test and learn is a quick, cheap way to generate knowledge about what works and what doesn't. It allows you to put your ideas and hypotheses to the test and generates results that help you to make tactical decisions. For example, because his Twitter followers gave a positive response to his Buffer product, Gascoigne was able to build and roll it out online; the students at Babson were encouraged to further test or modify their "flagging" idea after their experiment gleaned some surprising results; and the feedback Sembel gained from real customers and retailers through her low-cost experiment allowed her to grow her flower venture into a hugely successful business.

One of the major benefits of testing hypotheses is the real-time data it generates. Entrepreneurs operating a startup will be far more likely to gather evidence and data by conducting simple, low-cost experiments. Experimentation can be used to produce real and current data, as we will explore in the next section.

Low-cost experiments, such as Farmgirl Flowers making free deliveries to coffee shops, can create success for a startup.

©iStockphoto.com/Devilkae

Generating Data and the Rules of Experimentation

Organizations have traditionally relied on large amounts of historical data to gauge customer tastes and preferences. Direct mail, surveys, advertising, and catalogs are just a few of the methods that larger companies use to gather data about their customers.[27] Yet not all of these methods are reliable for entrepreneurs. Furthermore, they can be costly or they depend on feedback from existing customers that startups just don't have.

But what about when the data are lacking altogether? Often, when there are insufficient or nonexistent data, people tend to use either their intuition or their experience to make decisions. The problem with intuition is that it is often unreliable and doesn't provide the knowledge or evidence to support the feasibility of an idea.

Similarly, we can't rely wholly on experience and conventional wisdom—in fact, many innovations challenge what we thought we knew or what we thought we wanted. For example, when entrepreneur David Boehl founded his online advertising company, GraphicBomb, he defied all conventional wisdom warning him against mixing family and business by hiring two of his siblings to work for him full time.[28] Boehl has never regretted his decision, crediting his sisters with being honest, loyal, trustworthy, and forthcoming with valuable feedback. Fear of failure tends to discourage entrepreneurs from experimenting at all. Experiments can be perceived as risky and sometimes even scary, and nobody likes the idea of failing. But today's entrepreneurs are required to experiment. It's the only way they can prove a concept.

Entrepreneurial experiments are different from analytical experiments involving big data. Unlike major corporations like OfficeMax and Amazon, smaller organizations and especially startups usually do not have the resources to fund data systems analytics, nor may they even have existing data to rely on. In this case, how can entrepreneurs get the data they need if it doesn't exist?

Paul Lemley, founder of live broadcasting app Hivecast, discovered a powerful way of gathering his own data by asking at least one random person one question every day.[29] He said, "Don't stop asking people questions about your existing or future products. Even if they're hypothetical questions, people will always surprise you with their answers."

When Links Break

Should values be the first item discussed among partners before fully embarking upon a business? Perhaps an entrepreneurial venture is in the incubation phase, and the first hints of self-consciousness begin to form. *Is this a good idea? Will the public even buy this product?* After all, some initial validation would save a significant amount of time and money, if the idea turns out to be a flop.

Startups have been testing their appeal in the digital age through the use of landing pages, or early websites that offer all of the proposed services, items, experiences, of the company, without having working links that will allow the consumer to purchase those products. Developers track the number of clicks each broken link receives and gauge the general interest before too much time or money is wasted.

The moral dilemma is made clear as advertisers will market the page as genuine, essentially duping consumers into going to the website and finding they're not able to purchase any of the seemingly real products. Too much of this practice will turn consumers distrustful of whichever advertising channel led them to the fake website.

With the advent of crowdfunding sites like Kickstarter and GoFundMe, there are different avenues for gathering statistics on public appeal, while at the same time receiving a round of funding. Whether companies wish to be upfront about whether the product they are selling is real or not is up to their own ethical code. Do they care about deceiving consumers into showing preferences for products?

Critical Thinking Questions

1. How much deception is allowable in the early marketing of a venture?

2. Will consumers shy away from an advertising channel if they have been led to a website with broken product links?

3. How early into an entrepreneurial idea must values be established? ●

Sources:

Dahl, D. (2011, Sept. 6). How to assess the market potential of your idea. *Inc.* Retrieved from https://www.inc.com/guides/201109/how-to-assess-the-market-potential-of-your-new-business-idea.html

McLeod, S. (2015, Jan. 27). How to setup a landing page for testing a business or product idea. *Medium.* Retrieved from https://medium.com/early-stage-startup-validation/how-to-setup-a-landing-page-for-validating-a-business-or-product-idea-d72c35fc012c

Wilmes, L. (2018, Sept. 27). Landing pages: One giant leap for marketing. *Abstract Marketing Group.* Retrieved from https://www.abstraktmg.com/inbound-lead-generation/landing-pages-one-giant-leap-for-your-marketing-strategy/

By using this low-cost experiment, Lemley was able to identify his customer needs, generate a group of potential customers, and build brand awareness. The point is that unlike larger organizations, entrepreneurs do not need expensive systems or large amounts of cash to generate the data they need to gauge customer needs and preferences. Small-scale experiments do not need to be risky or expensive. Entrepreneurs have more freedom to experiment, as they have a lot less to lose in the beginning than larger organizations do.

The essential thing to remember about experiments, large or small, is that all results must be taken into account, even if they fail to support the hypothesis and contradict original assumptions. Ignoring data just because they tell us what we don't want to hear is detrimental to the success of any venture.

The goal of experimentation is not to conduct the "perfect" experiment but to see it as an opportunity for further learning and better decision making. Failure is also important, for if you cannot fail, you cannot learn.[30]

Though there is no one best or perfect way to conduct an entrepreneurial experiment, there are a few "rules" based on the information we have provided in this chapter so far. Table 7.4 shows some rules key to learning through experimentation. You will notice that two of the rules focus on stakeholders: the different types of stakeholders and the importance of interacting with them. Jeffrey Brown, president and CEO of Brown's Super Stores, Inc., in Philadelphia, has grown his entire business based on stakeholder interaction.[31] For instance, every day, Brown walks down the aisles of his grocery store observing his shoppers: the products they choose, whether they read the ingredients on the labels, and whether they can find everything they need. Brown even takes his lunch at a table near the store deli to encourage dialogue with his customers. Brown's store is located in one of the most impoverished areas in Philadelphia. Most of his customers live in poverty and many of them have criminal records. Yet that hasn't prevented Brown from building a highly successful business, which has since expanded to 12 supermarkets across Philadelphia. So how did he do it?

First, he asked his customers what they wanted. Most responded that they wanted to be treated with respect and to shop in a store that was clean and equipped with helpful

TABLE 7.4

The Rules of Experimentation

1.	Focus on all types of stakeholders: customers, partners, suppliers, distributors, even real estate agents.
2.	Ask lots of questions. Remember, every question you have about your idea is fertile ground for an experiment.
3.	Think like a scientist, but don't act like a scientist. In other words, it's important to think through your hypothesis, what you want to test, and how you are going to test, but don't get bogged down in the rigor.
4.	Build your learning into the next iteration. Don't ignore negative information, just as you don't want to ignore positive information. A general rule of thumb is that six pieces of information saying the same thing can be a fact!
5.	Keep track of your data. You may think a piece of information is not important, but it is essential to keep track of everything.
6.	Keep your experiments low cost and quick, and use them to shape and improve ideas.
7.	Don't just talk with stakeholders—interact with them.
8.	Don't ignore data just because you don't like what they're telling you.

staff. Second, they wanted food they could eat; for instance, some customers were North African and wanted to buy food from their country, while others were Muslim and needed a halal option. Thanks to these continuous conversations, Brown was able to provide these products and much, much more. For instance, in one conversation with a customer, a woman asked him why he wasn't employing previously incarcerated people. The outcome of this suggestion led to Brown founding Uplift, a nonprofit that trains people with criminal records to work in the grocery business. Both Uplift and Brown's Super Store team work together to run low-cost experiments to trial different ideas, such as providing onsite dietitians, cooking classes, health clinics, and mini branches of credit unions. By listening to his stakeholders and testing their feedback through experimentation, Brown has built a thriving business in a location where many others would have failed.

7.6 INTERVIEWING FOR CUSTOMER FEEDBACK

>> **LO 7.6 Explore the interviewing process for customer feedback.**

In Chapter 4, we used interviewing to help us identify needs of users. We called those need-finding interviews. Now it's time to adapt some of those interviewing skills to a different type of interview called feedback interviews. Feedback interviews are used to get feedback on prototypes—any type of prototype that has been discussed in this chapter. Feedback interviews are useful when used in conjunction with experimentation because they help you get more information on the "why" people are interacting with your product or service in different ways.

In general, a feedback interview involves the following:

1. The use of some type of prototype

2. Asking users their opinion of the product or service

3. Determining whether there is value for the user in the use of the product or service

4. Identifying ways to make the product better

5. Determining whether you are targeting the correct customers

For example, say you are looking to start your own French gourmet food truck business with a goal of selling to wealthy customers, such as business executives, at exclusive business events such as conferences and office parties. As a startup, the first step is to think about whom you know. Whom do you know who works in the business world? Or, if you don't know anyone personally, whom do you know who might know someone in the business world who can provide you with an introduction? Go through your list of contacts, or try networking sites like Facebook, Twitter, and LinkedIn. Research the companies and experts who might be able to offer you some guidance, and try to establish contacts there, too.

Think about what you want the end result of the interview to be. What is the aim of the interview? Do you need to test assumptions or learn about preferences and attitudes? What is it you want to gain from the interview?

Second, draft an introduction to the interview (four or five sentences) that lays out your intentions and the purpose of the interview. For example, say your interviewee is an events manager at a large bank. Your goal is to find out what he thinks of your gourmet French food truck business and whether it is something that the bank staff and clients would be interested in for corporate events (see Figure 7.11).

Third, prepare your interview questions. In order to get the most information from the person you are interviewing, you need to minimize yes/no questions, such as, "Do you like food trucks?" Instead, ask open-ended questions:

- "What do you think of the explosion of the food truck industry?"

- "What would motivate you, your clients, and your employees to buy from a food truck?"

- "Do you have any frustrations concerning the food from food trucks or the service provided?"

If your interviewee expresses enthusiasm for your idea, you can ask, "What do you like best about this venture concept?" If the interviewee's reaction is less than enthusiastic, you might ask, "In what ways could this venture concept be improved to have greater appeal for people like you?"

Make sure you also record some basic facts about the person (gender, occupation, age, profession, industry, affluence). There is no need to ask these questions directly, as they can be offensive. Do your best to make some reasonable guesses.

FIGURE 7.11

Sample Interview Introduction

Alex's Pictures–Moscow/Alamy Stock Photo.

Hello—I am Antonia, founder of the Le Gourmet food truck, which offers organic French food based on the finest ingredients, located in Boston, Mass. I was referred to you by Gavin Jones, head chef at the restaurant Beaujolais. I am interested in your views on my plans to sell my product at office conferences and other business events. I have a few questions that will take approximately 30 minutes. Everything you say will be treated as strictly confidential.

Why Overconfident Entrepreneurs Fail

In a recent study on confidence and accuracy, psychologist Lewis Goldberg asked experienced neurologists and their administrative assistants to identify whether patients had organic (physiological) or non-organic (distressing experiences) brain damage. Although the neurologists were more confident in their diagnoses compared to their untrained administrative assistants, the results showed that the administrative assistants were as accurate as the neurologists. The lesson? Just because we feel confident doesn't mean we are always right.

Entrepreneurs face difficult, ambiguous problems every day, but they will be less able to handle them if they have an above-average measure of confidence. Overconfident entrepreneurs are less likely to listen, learn, and change. As serial entrepreneur Mike Cassidy says, "The thing that scares me most is someone who is convinced they are right because they will never change."

However, there is a difference between overconfidence and determination. Above all, entrepreneurs need to be determined enough to identify risks, overcome obstacles, and find creative ways to bring their product to the market. Unlike overconfident entrepreneurs, determined entrepreneurs really listen, make fewer mistakes, and seek out ways to solve problems.

Critical Thinking Questions

1. Confidence is necessary, but how can you tell the difference between confidence and overconfidence?

2. Why are we talking about overconfidence in a chapter on testing and experimentation?

3. How can you be confident and curious at the same time? ●

Source: Fuur, N. (2012). Why confident entrepreneurs fail: The overconfidence death trap. *Forbes.* Retrieved from https://www.forbes.com/sites/nathanfurr/2012/11/13/why-confident-entrepreneurs-fail-the-overconfidence-death-trap/#6d68a232207c

Another useful interviewing technique is Peel the Onion, which is a way of delving into a problem one layer at a time (see Figure 7.12). Begin with the challenges the person faces, and then continue to dig deeper in order to understand the root of the problem. Simply asking, "Why?" or saying, "Tell me more about _____" will help you gain a deeper understanding.

FIGURE 7.12

Peel the Onion for Deep Understanding

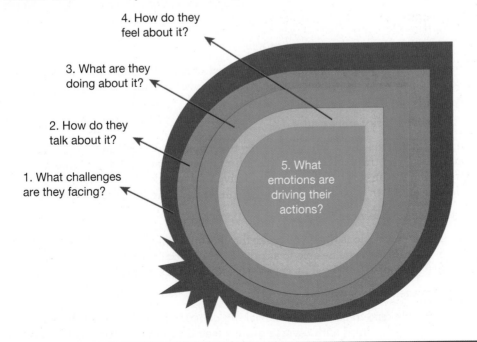

4. How do they feel about it?

3. What are they doing about it?

2. How do they talk about it?

1. What challenges are they facing?

5. What emotions are driving their actions?

TABLE 7.5

A Five-Dimensional Model of Curiosity

Deprivation Sensitivity
Recognizing a gap in knowledge, the frustration this brings, and the determination to fill it
Joyous Exploration
Delighting in the wonder of the world and the fascination it holds
Social Curiosity
Enjoying the process of learning about others by talking, listening, and observing
Stress Tolerance
Being able to handle the anxiety that comes with new experiences or uncertain situations
Thrill Seeking
Being open to taking certain social, financial, and physical risks to experience new adventures

Source: Kashdan, T. B., Stiksma, M. C. Disabato, D. J., MdKnight, P. E., Bekier, J., Kaji, J. Lazarus, R. 2018. The five-dimensional curiosity scale: Capturing the bandwidth of curiosity and identifying four unique subgroups of curious people. *Journal of Personality Research, 73*: 130–149.

The Case for Curiosity

Ask any successful entrepreneur about curiosity and they will say, "Yes, I'm a very curious person!" It's an important strength for many entrepreneurs. Experimenting, prototyping, hypothesizing, and interviewing would never come to fruition without a keen sense of curiosity. Opportunities would never be identified without curiosity. A growing body of research shows that curiosity increases perseverance and boosts performance. Todd B. Kashdan is a professor of psychology and senior scientist at the Center for the Advancement of Well-Being at George Mason University. Kashdan and his team, in conjunction with George Mason colleague Patrick McKnight, created a five-dimensional model of curiosity (see Table 7.5); the five dimensions are deprivation sensitivity, joyous exploration, social curiosity, stress tolerance, and thrill seeking. Each of these dimensions is essential to entrepreneurship.

How to Stay Curious

You may relate to most of the five dimensions, but it still takes a lot of practice and discipline to maintain and nurture curiosity. Here are some tips to help you build your curiosity strength:

1. Connect with other curious people.

Naturally curious people are keen to trade questions, explore, and collaborate. Having these people in your life will encourage you to uncover new ideas and see things from a different perspective.

2. Be a curiosity ambassador.

By asking questions and listening carefully to responses, you will encourage the people around you to do the same. Similarly, staying curious, rather than judgmental, when approaching the unknown is a more productive way to tackle tough challenges. Try not to play the expert in any room you enter. It will hinder your ambassadorship here.

3. Focus on learning.

You can only stay curious when you make the commitment to continuous learning. Only through learning will you be able to ask the right questions, find the right answers, and recognize new opportunities. Entrepreneurs are notorious for being insatiable learners.

4. Broaden your networks.

Curious people tend to be comfortable asking questions, which can lead to all sorts of productive relationships with diverse groups (see Chapter 8 for more information on networking). Entrepreneurs understand that they may not be the smartest person in the room but they need to surround themselves with the smartest people they know.

5. Ask "Why?" "What if . . . ?" and "How might we . . . ?"

Being naturally curious doesn't just mean asking questions; it also means learning to frame questions in the right way. When we were kids, asking questions was second nature, but as we grew older and more self-conscious, we tended to stop questioning in the same way. Yet by asking "Why?" "What if . . . ?" and "How might we . . . ?" we have an opportunity to challenge existing mindsets and create new ideas.

As the old saying goes, "Curiosity killed the cat, but satisfaction brought it back." In other words, without risk there is no reward. Entrepreneurs need to foster curiosity to reap the benefits of confronting new challenges and leaping into the unknown.

So, act to learn. Act to experiment. Act to test assumptions. Just be curious!

In the next chapter, we will explore the concept of evaluating opportunities through the medium of business models. ●

$SAGE edge™

Get the tools you need to sharpen your study skills. SAGE edge offers a robust online environment featuring an impressive array of free tools and resources.

- Access practice quizzes, eFlashcards, video, and multimedia at
  edge.sagepub.com/neckentrepreneurship2e

SUMMARY

7.1 Define experiments and describe why we do them.

An experiment is a test designed to help you learn and answer questions related to the feasibility and viability of your venture. Experiments need to have a clear purpose, be achievable, and generate reliable results. Experiments guide us toward which customer opinions to listen to, what important product or service features should take priority, what might please or upset customers, and what should be worked on next. An experiment begins with a hypothesis, which is an assumption that is tested through research and experimentation.

7.2 Identify the different types of experiments most commonly used.

Entrepreneurs have many different types of experiments and tests available to them, and some require more effort than others. Overall, the amount of effort put in tends to correlate to the believability of the information coming out. Giff Constable's truth curve illustrates the many different types of experiments commonly used by entrepreneurs.

7.3 Explore prototypes in greater depth.

Prototypes are basic models or sketches that inform others and communicate what our ideas look like, behave like, and work like before the real product or service is launched. An MVP as prototype is "that version of a new product which allows a team to collect the maximum amount of validated learning about customer with the least effort."

7.4 Demonstrate how to test hypotheses and explain the scientific method.

When testing hypotheses, entrepreneurs need not actually develop elaborate, extremely robust experiments; the goal is to think like a scientist, not to emulate one perfectly. Experiments are used to prove or disprove the validity of an idea or hypothesis. Getting out of the building and testing our hypotheses enables us to gain new insights into our target customers' wants and needs. The scientific process of experimentation involves the following six steps: asking lots of questions, developing hypotheses, testing hypotheses by running experiments, analyzing the data, and assessing results.

7.5 Describe the experimentation template.

The experimentation template is seven key questions for entrepreneurs to ask themselves before designing an experiment.

7.6 Explore the interviewing process for customer feedback.

Feedback interviews are used to get feedback on prototypes. Feedback interviews are useful when used with experimentation because they help you get more information on the "why" people are interacting with your product or service in different ways. Experimenting, prototyping, hypothesizing, and interviewing would never come to fruition without a keen sense of curiosity. Opportunities would never be identified without curiosity. Entrepreneurs can follow five dimensions to strengthen and maintain their curiosity: deprivation sensitivity, joyous exploration, social curiosity, stress tolerance, and thrill seeking.

KEY TERMS

Experiment 153	MVP (minimum viable product) 159	Pilot experiment 160
Hypothesis 153		Storyboard 160

CASE STUDY

Katrina Lake, CEO, Stitch Fix

Katrina Lake, at age 35, was one of the youngest female CEOs to take a company public in 2017 and one of very few females leading a tech company. Katrina Lake is the founder of Stitch Fix, a fashion e-commerce site that provides personalized styling services. It is a subscription-based model that charges $20 a month for a personal stylist. Each month, Stitch Fix mails a box with five pieces of clothing chosen by personal stylists based on customer preferences. If the customer decides to buy anything, the $20 styling fee is credited against the total purchase bill. Today, the company is valued at more than $2.5 billion.

Katrina thought the traditional e-commerce experience was plagued with ongoing customer dissatisfaction. Stitch Fix resolves two pain points for customers. First, personalized styling services can be expensive. Second, companies are experiencing too many returns of unwanted clothes purchased online. Stitch Fix revolutionizes the e-commerce fashion space by using technology to provide tools and data on shopping preferences to stylists who make recommendations to customers on clothing that fits their preferences.

"In a lot of ways, I think our value proposition is almost the opposite to a company like Amazon. It's not endless choice," Katrina explained. "In fact, it's a very select group of things that we think are highly, highly relevant for you. I think that discovery element is actually some of the hardest parts of apparel. A lot of times you're not looking for jeans that are going to ship to you fastest; you want the jeans that are going to fit your body best. That is a very different value proposition than I think what Amazon has been historically amazing at."

Katrina Lake grew up in a multicultural home in San Francisco with a Japanese mother and American dad. She studied economics at Stanford University and joined a consulting firm after graduating in 2005. She wasn't thinking of being an entrepreneur but admitted that she always had lots of ideas on how the businesses she was consulting could work better. As Katrina recalled, "We were working with a large retailer—this was in 2006. I remember asking the CEO why does every single size need to be on the floor? The customer has to walk in and find the size and take it themselves to a fitting room. I told them—how about keeping half the store as a warehouse and distribution center and the other half is like a museum? You see what you like, select them, and when you go to the fitting room everything that you wanted would be there. There would also be a few recommendations. It would be a much better experience than weeding through racks and trying to find your size. The CEO and others looked at me like I had seven heads."

Katrina left consulting in 2007 and moved to a venture capital fund, Leader Ventures. She wanted to "meet the next crazy entrepreneur with a crazy idea in retail," and she felt she was most likely to meet that person while working for a venture capital fund. If she found a company that reflected how she felt about retail, she was hoping to join that company. She met hundreds of entrepreneurs over the course of 2 years. "I realized that all of these entrepreneurs were super-unqualified normal people with lots of ideas—just like I was. A more powerful realization from my time in venture capital was that I realized that if I have all of these ideas, then I shouldn't be in the peanut gallery lobbying my ideas to people and should just do it myself and that I *could* do it myself!"

Having not quite found her big idea, she applied and was accepted to Harvard Business School in 2009. During her time in business school, Katrina started to explore different industries. The idea for Stitch Fix was based on two trends that Katrina noticed. One was that more and more dollars were moving to e-commerce, and this trend would make it harder for physical stores to survive. She noticed how Netflix was quickly replacing the Blockbuster model. The second trend related to depersonalization. With the surge of online shopping, depersonalization would increase and customer satisfaction would likely decrease—especially with apparel because it's an emotional purchase for many. Katrina decided to create a solution that used data and technology to bring a high level of personalization to the shopping experience in a way that was scalable.

A self-proclaimed mediocre student, Katrina decided to focus on her idea while at Harvard. She wanted to use her time there to get to a point where she was able to fund her new company and start paying back her student loans by the time she graduated. It was a risky entrepreneurial journey she was willing to take, though the risk wasn't that great because she would have a Harvard MBA that she could fall back on.

Katrina's entire value proposition was about making the shopping experience better online. "You could sit on your computer the entire evening with 30 browser tabs open trying to compare and contrast different jeans you want to buy. If you had a box that could get sent to you that had two pairs of jeans, or even better, one pair of jeans, and they fit you great—that is an infinitely better experience than the other alternatives out there." Katrina started exploring the idea by asking 20 of her friends and family to fill out surveys to understand the brands people liked. She realized that to scale the business, it would be very difficult to source all the clothes that customers thought they wanted. Instead, she developed a model that would send clothes to her customers from existing inventory that she would create. She used personal credit cards and bought an inventory of clothes from various retailers, kept track of their return policy (e.g., 14-day return policy), and made up personalized boxes of clothes that were relevant based on what people shared on their survey profile. If people wanted to buy the clothes, they would write her a personal check. If not, she would return the clothes within the stipulated return window. This experiment tested Katrina's assumptions. She was able to understand people's preferences based on the information they shared and their mindset while buying and trying new clothes. She also confirmed that people found value in good clothes made by brands that were not as well known.

Katrina was convinced that she wanted to pursue this idea and started looking for seed capital. Steve Anderson of Baseline Ventures was the first investor; he gave her a seed of $500,000 and is now one of the largest shareholders in Stitch Fix. However, she did find it difficult to convince other investors based on an experiment conducted with only 20 people. Her business model required a lot of investment in inventory, which deters most investors. Further complicating operations, her business model focused on using actual human designers and stylists rather than bots to process the data and personalize the experience. There was potential for too much variability and inconsistency.

After earning her MBA in 2011, Katrina moved to San Francisco. New York may have been the more obvious location for a fashion company, but Stitch Fix is really a technology company that employs many data scientists, and Silicon Valley had that type of talent. She used the seed money to set up an office, get inventory, and set up the website. Once the Stitch Fix website was running, customers signed up to use the service through an online form. Katrina sent out PayPal invoices to people who signed up because she was afraid that bots might be signing up on her website. She felt that if someone was willing to pay $20 before receiving anything, it was likely that they were real customers. The $20 fee continues to be an integral part of Stitch Fix's operations today.

Immediately following her move to San Francisco, Katrina was a CEO and personal stylist. She sourced most of her inventory at trade shows where some brands would agree to sell her only six pieces of an item. Katrina would then pick the clothes based on customers' preferences, pack, and send boxes of five items. She quickly hired her first stylist in early 2012! Katrina hired Eric Colson, the then-VP of Data Science and Engineering at Netflix, to lead the data science aspect of Stitch Fix. Since both Netflix and Stitch Fix were based on making recommendations to the customer, she felt that Eric would be a natural fit.

Word about Stitch Fix soon started to spread, with people sharing their positive customer experience with others. Katrina leveraged the chatter and started reaching out to small and medium-size social media influencers (those with around 50,000 to 100,000 followers) to help drive more traffic to the site. However, while the business was growing, raising funds was still a challenge for Katrina. Venture capitalists at the time wanted businesses that weren't human resources–heavy and were scalable to reach $1 billion. It didn't help that the hybrid model that Stitch Fix was proposing integrated both humans and data to run a company in a way that was very new to the investors. It hadn't been done before, which made it a more difficult story to tell investors. "When you're doing something that nobody else is doing, you are either the smartest or the stupidest person in the room," said Katrina.

To date, Katrina Lake has raised more than $122.4 million in six rounds of financing. Stitch Fix turned profitable in 3 years and currently has more than 5,000 employees, most of whom are stylists, and approximately 100 data scientists, and is currently valued at more than $2.5 billion. Katrina emphasizes company culture and diversity. Almost 86% of her employees are women.

Critical Thinking Questions

1. What hypotheses did Katrina have about her business and target customers?

2. How did she test those hypotheses and what did she learn?

3. What other testing or experimentation could she have done?

4. Who is the target customer for Stitch Fix? Do some research on your own!

Sources:

Crunchbase. (2019). Stitch Fix funding rounds. Retrieved from https://www.crunchbase.com/organization/stitch-fix/funding_rounds/funding_rounds_list#section-funding-rounds

Lake, K. (2017). Changing the game. *LinkedIn*. Retrieved from https://www.linkedin.com/pulse/changing-game-katrina-lake/

Recode. (2018). Full video and transcript: Stitch Fix CEO Katrina Lake at Code 2018. *Vox*. Retrieved from https://www.recode.net/2018/5/30/17397150/stitch-fix-katrina-lake-transcript-code-2018

Steinmetz, K. (2018). Stitch Fix has one of Silicon Valley's few female CEOs. *Time*. Retrieved from http://time.com/5264160/stitch-fix-has-one-of-silicon-valleys-few-female-ceos/

©iStockphoto.com/ipopba

8 Developing Networks and Building Teams

"I believe your social capital, or your ability to build a network of authentic personal and professional relationships, not your financial capital, is the most important asset in your portfolio."

—Porter Gale, author of the bestselling book, *Your Network Is Your Net Worth: Unlock the Hidden Power of Connections for Wealth, Success, and Happiness in the Digital Age*[1]

Chapter Outline

Learning Objectives

8.1   Explain the role of networks in building social capital.

8.2   Demonstrate the value of networks for entrepreneurs.

8.3   Describe different ways of building networks.

8.4   Illustrate the benefits of virtual networking.

8.5   Explain how networking can help to build the founding team.

8.1 THE POWER OF NETWORKS

>> **LO 8.1**   **Explain the role of networks in building social capital.**

Entrepreneurship is about collaboration, creating together, taking action with limited resources, and courageously navigating uncertainty. A strong network helps us do these things. Studies show that by making connections with people who share our values, we are able to achieve more than if we had acted alone.[2] In general, we have two sources of personal differentiation. We have our human capital and our social capital. Our human capital is our talent, intellect, charisma; it is what we know and who we are. Social capital, on the other hand, is our source for ideas, support, reputation, new knowledge, and resources.

The best networks can provide entrepreneurs with access to external sources of information, financing, emotional support, and expertise, and they allow for mutual learning and information exchange. Network building is a dynamic process, which expands and evolves over time; continuously making purposeful and valuable connections is essential for business success.[3]

Network building helps develops our **social capital**, which refers to our personal social networks populated with people who willingly cooperate, exchange information, and build trusting relationships with each other. Like physical capital (materials) and human capital (skills and knowledge), social capital is a productive asset. In other words, it's valuable.[4]

Social capital is less tangible than physical or even human capital because it "exists in the relationships among persons,"[5] and the value of these relationships can be difficult to assess and measure. However, in spite of its intangible nature, using social capital is a valuable way of getting work done, acquiring information, and finding resources of all types.

Social capital works through a wide range of channels. When you exchange ideas or information with someone at college, you are building social capital. Social capital can be found everywhere—in your local community, faith-based organizations, schools, clubs, online social media groups, and more. Anywhere that provides the opportunity to interact socially will help you build social capital if you recognize the value in purposeful relationships. As Bill Nye, the famous Science Guy, says, "Everyone you meet knows something you don't!"

Social capital is divided into three dimensions: the structural dimension, the relational dimension, and the cognitive dimension (see Figure 8.1). The structural dimension describes the components of your network, such as the type of social ties you may or may not have (i.e., the contacts in your network) and the degree to which these ties may be formal or informal.[6]

The relational dimension is what your contacts represent, such as a trusting relationship. When trust is present between two people, the relationship is stronger and an

Social capital: personal social networks populated with people who willingly cooperate, exchange information, and build trusting relationships with each other.

Master the content at
**edge.sagepub.com/
neckentrepreneurship2e**

Markesia Akinbami, Ducere Construction Services

Photo courtesy of Markesia Akinbami

Markesia Akinbami: owner of Ducere Construction Services

Markesia Akinbami owns a holding company called Ducere Investment Group, based in Atlanta, Georgia. The holding company offers a unique set of services, the largest being its construction services and supplier diversity consultant firm called Ducere Construction Services. Markesia, with her husband, operates Ducere Construction in Atlanta, Georgia, and Gainesville, Florida. She also operates a government health care consulting service directly out of Ducere Investment Group. Both ventures came to be through the various working relationships that Markesia has developed over the course of her professional career.

Markesia operated a residential construction business that ceased operations when the U.S. economy tanked in 2008. She and her husband agreed that they did not have the commercial construction experience expected of them, but the opportunity seemed so excellent that they moved forward with it anyway. Soon after the business closed, she met the director of Supplier Diversity at the University of Florida and was invited to participate in a mentorship program at the university where she could hone her skills as a business leader in the construction

industry. The bridges that she built and the mentoring she received through this program paved the way for her future success. As Markesia recalled, "That is often the case with bridges, which are links that go further than sharing a sense of identity and are often built through schooling and careers."

The couple worked with their mentor on multiple projects and quickly found themselves better suited to thrive in the construction industry. They started Ducere Construction services 3 years later, but it was not simply a redo for them. This company had new elements that have proven to be instrumental in its success. Along with specializing in many aspects of commercial construction, Ducere Construction also offers a powerful supplier development program for minority-run businesses. As Ducere is a minority-run business, its management is committed to advancing the mission of other diverse firms. According to the Ducere website, "The program's primary objectives are to provide opportunities and train businesses on how to capitalize on the opportunity. The competency of small and diverse suppliers is crucial to creating long-term success and competitiveness in the marketplace." It does this by subcontracting work to these firms while also providing seminars and training sessions that provide action plans that owners can use to grow their companies.

The health care consulting arm of Markesia's business stemmed from her great desire to help people struggling with mental health, behavioral health, and substance abuse issues within her community. She found that many government programs openly welcome private industry partnerships to help advance public health initiatives. The health care practice is profitable primarily through the consulting revenues it gets from working with small medical practices on things like operations and audit compliance. Yet, that is not its primary focus. Ducere also collaborates with other companies, like the Salvation Army and state agencies, on providing outpatient care to discharged mental health patients. The problem with outpatient care is that many of these people go through rehab or receive medical care, but they fall back into old habits or fail to implement the self-care practices they were taught. "These situations prove to be deadly for many folks," she says, and her partnerships aim to prevent that. From a business standpoint, these partnerships are essential for the Ducere Investment Group. "Without them, there wouldn't be a definite place for Ducere in the unorganized space of health care," says Markesia. These partnerships provide some control and clarity amidst the chaos and allow Markesia and her team to identify and seize opportunities, not just for the success of the business, but often for the betterment of many people in her community.

Ducere, like many successful ventures, was founded by entrepreneurs who developed strong social capital—that is, networks populated with people who willingly cooperate, exchange information, and build trusting relationships with one another. For Markesia, taking on a mentor was one of the most effective means of building her network because it was a relationship that connected her not just to new knowledge but also new people. Markesia quotes, "Never underestimate the power of partnerships. Your big success could be one connection away."

Critical Thinking Questions

1. Why is it important to maintain a close network?

2. How much of Markesia's success can be attributed to social capital? ●

Sources:

Markesia Akinbami (interview with author, December 19, 2018).
http://www.ducereinvestmentgroup.com/
http://ducereconstruction.com/partnership/

FIGURE 8.1

Three Dimensions of Social Capital

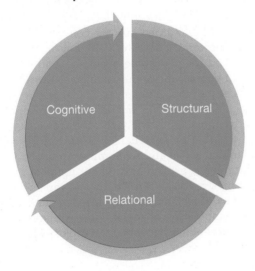

exchange of resources or overall support for your ideas or venture is greater.[7] You are more likely to convince people of your idea when they trust you. It may also be helpful to think of your social capital as an "emotional bank account."[8] You can "make conscious efforts to make meaningful deposits in your relationships"[9] by actions you take with those in your network; making these deposits builds your "balance" so that when a "withdrawal" is needed, the relationship has the necessary social capital to cover it.

The cognitive dimension describes the norms, visions, values, interpretations, and beliefs you may share with others, which provide a good foundation for working well together toward a common goal.[10]

Some observers argue that in the United States today, people are less likely to interact socially than they were in the past. Today, more time is spent at the workplace, commuting to work, and using devices like personal computers, smartphones, gaming consoles, and television, leaving less time for volunteering, joining community groups, and socializing with friends, family, and neighbors. Even spending time participating in online social networks is not as "real" as the face-to-face social interaction of the past. The decline of community networks that used to be so prevalent in the past has led to a loss of social capital.[11] However, the good news is that anyone can build social capital if they make an effort to actively and purposefully form connections with others.

The Organisation for Economic Co-operation and Development (OECD), a global organization promoting economies throughout the world, identifies three main varieties of social capital:[12]

Bonds: the connections with family, friends, and others who have a similar cultural background or ethnicity.

- **Bonds**: Connections with people who are just like us, such as family, friends, and others who have a similar cultural background or ethnicity.

Bridges: the links that go further than simply sharing a sense of identity; for example, making connections with distant friends or colleagues who may have different backgrounds, cultures, and so on.

- **Bridges**: Links that go further than simply sharing a sense of identity; for example, making connections with classmates or colleagues who may have different backgrounds, cultures, or other characteristics.

Linkages: the connections to people or groups regardless of their position in an organization, society, or other community.

- **Linkages**: Connections to people or groups regardless of their position in an organization, society, or other community.

There are many benefits to social capital. It creates a sense of shared value to the people who are connected in the network, especially when cooperation, trust, and mutual exchange are high. Our bonds with friends and family can be especially important when it comes to providing emotional, social, and economic support.

Famously, the most powerful contact in Bill Gates's network before Microsoft took off was his mother, Mary Gates. Mary Gates sat on the board of United Way with John Akers, a senior IBM executive. The relationship led to her son, Bill, pitching the Microsoft operating system to Akers, who awarded him the contract. Microsoft would eventually surpass IBM as the most powerful computer company in the world.[13] Personal bonds or "strong ties" to family and friends can be beneficial, but they can also be restrictive. Forming connections with people who are too similar to ourselves can prevent us from seeing the bigger picture, as they are less likely to challenge our ideas, which may deprive us of valuable feedback and information.[14] In addition, when bonds are too strong, social capital can have a negative impact on society. As an extreme example, members of drug cartels are often bound together by personal loyalties, and their actions go against the interests of society and inhibit social and economic progress.[15]

That's why it is important to expand beyond our range of strong ties and capitalize on the external relationships or "weak ties" in our network, such as people we meet at trade shows and exhibitions, as well as potential investors and banks, to capture a wider range of information. A combination of social bonds, bridges, and linkages is the best way to build a diverse and productive network. Let's explore why networks are so valuable in the entrepreneurship world.

8.2 THE VALUE OF NETWORKS

>> LO 8.2   **Demonstrate the value of networks for entrepreneurs.**

Building relationships and social interaction are key to starting a business. An entrepreneur is required to interact with investors, mentors, advisors, professors, potential employees, resource providers, and other stakeholders.[16] Keep in mind that in a networking group of 20 to 40 people, the number of possible referrals and leads that you could obtain is almost incalculable.

New research released by the Economist Intelligence Unit on the benefits of informal professional networks and communities, including online (Facebook, LinkedIn) and physical (parties, entrepreneurial events) networking, showed that informal networking (unstructured, free-flowing communication) was far more important to entrepreneurial success than formal networking (meeting in a formal setting).[17] Out of the 1,000 entrepreneurs surveyed across 10 cities—six cities in Asia, two in Europe, and two in the U.S.—the study found that 78% of startups benefited from active informal networking. In fact, the greater the number of networking activities, the higher the chance of greater profitability, revenue growth, and innovation.

Advantages to Networks

There are three main advantages to networks: private information, access to diverse skill-sets, and power.[18] *Private information* is the type of information that is not available to the general public. Gathering unique information from network contacts, such as the release date of a new product or what investors look for during a pitch, can give entrepreneurs the edge over the competition. The value of private information increases when trust is high in the network.

Second, networks provide *access to diverse skillsets*. A highly diverse network of contacts gives you a broader perspective of certain situations and enables you to trade information and skills with people who have different experiences and backgrounds from your own. By actively taking part in events and seeking out new contacts at meetings, you will be able to find people with complementary skills and experience to help you grow your venture. As the late Nobel Prize winner Linus Pauling said, "The best way to have a good idea is to have a lot of ideas."[19]

Finally, networks can give you access to *power*—people in senior or executive positions who can provide expert advice and introduce you to other powerful people in their network. Additionally, given the depth and breadth of your own network, you may actually have power.

Let's take a closer look at our personal networks and the different types of roles people play. First, people in your network can help you to progress by offering information and instruction, especially when you are trying to learn complex tasks. They can also refer you to others who might be able to assist you in achieving difficult tasks.[20] Second, people can help protect your venture by giving you advice when you are confronted with high-risk situations or are going through a rough patch. Third, people can provide personal and emotional support by listening to your concerns, empathizing, and offering advice when required. Finally, people become your role models. You can be inspired by their achievements, and in many cases, they represent what you would like to be when you progress as an entrepreneur. In sum, networks can provide three types of support: career support, psychosocial support, and role modeling (see Table 8.1).

Impression Management and Self-Confidence

Despite the value of networking, other research has found that students in entrepreneurship classes often don't take advantage of networking opportunities provided to them in class. Students are given access to guest speakers, other entrepreneurs, and each other, yet often they do not use these opportunities to build their networks. What stops students from networking effectively? Poor impression management and lack of confidence were the two biggest inhibiting factors identified during the study.[21]

Impression management is paying conscious attention to the way people perceive you and taking steps to be perceived in the way you want others to see you. When people interact with you, they form opinions. More and more research shows that first impressions are formed in a tenth of a second, so it pays to be mindful of how you might be perceived by others.[22] For example, the social cues that venture capitalists notice are things like the following: How much does this person believe in this idea? How confident are they when speaking? How determined are they to make this work?[23]

Impression management: paying conscious attention to the way people perceive you and taking steps to be perceived in the way you want others to see you.

TABLE 8.1

Types of Support

CAREER SUPPORT	PSYCHOSOCIAL SUPPORT	ROLE MODELING
• Sponsorship • Coaching • Exposure and visibility • Challenging assignments • Protections and preservation	• Encouragement and emotional support • Acceptance and confirmation • Counseling • Friendship • Personal feedback	• Behavior to emulate • Work ethic and values • Inspiration and motivation

Source: Murphy, W., & Kram, K. (2014). *Strategic relationships at work* (p. 23). New York, NY: McGraw-Hill.

TABLE 8.2

Gain Trust Without Saying a Word

• Don't hunch over your phone just before you are due to meet other people.
• Make the handshake more personal by keeping your elbow by your side rather than greeting with a fully extended arm.
• Lean forward and make eye contact during the conversation to show interest.
• Stand straight with your shoulders squared and your weight balanced evenly on each foot.
• Reserve your smiles for the appropriate moments rather than smiling continuously throughout.
• Try to be sensitive to what others are thinking and feeling.

Source: Shellenbarger, S. (2018). The mistakes you make in a meeting's first milliseconds. *Wall Street Journal.* Retrieved from https://www.wsj.com/articles/the-mistakes-you-make-in-a-meetings-first-milliseconds-1517322312

Research shows that entrepreneurs who display strong social competence are more likely to receive outside funding.[24]

You can manage the impressions others form of you by the way you dress, being aware of your body language, being polite and courteous, and being confident and open. Your attitude is also part of impression management; Making an effort to interact with and learn from others goes a long way toward making a positive impression. Table 8.2 lists a few ways in which you can gain trust without saying a word.

But there can be implicit bias present when forming impressions—both when we form impressions of others and when others form impressions of us. Implicit bias refers to the attitudes or stereotypes that affect our understanding, actions, and decisions in an unconscious way.[25] Implicit bias rears its head most often in issues related to gender and race; it has been referred to as stereotype confirming. "It sets people up to over-generalize, sometimes leading to discrimination even when people feel they are being fair."[26] Researchers in this area claim that everyone possesses implicit bias, even when they think they don't.[27] For example, a man may believe he and his female cofounder are equal, but he may still open the door for her when they walk into buildings. Though his intentions are good, his implicit bias is that "she needs help because I'm a man." Researchers also suggest that the implicit biases we have may not necessarily align with our declared beliefs.[28] For example, a venture capital firm led by three women claim they want to give women entrepreneurs greater access to capital. Yet when you look at their portfolio of investments, most of the deals were made with ventures led by white, male, tech entrepreneurs. The implicit bias is that men are more often successful high-growth entrepreneurs. The good news is that researchers have suggested that implicit biases are malleable and we can unlearn and de-bias ourselves. The first step is working to recognize the implicit biases we have.

Lack of confidence also plays a part in students' reluctance to make connections with others. Fear of failure, of not asking the "right" questions, and insecurity about themselves and what they want to achieve are factors that may prevent students from approaching guest speakers and asking questions. In some cases, networking is regarded negatively because some people may think of it as an insincere way of gaining a personal advantage.

While in college, or even in this course you are taking, it may not seem important to network with your classmates. However, never underestimate the value of networking with your peers. The students you sit next to in class might become your cofounders, your partners, your advisors, your employers, your stakeholders, and even your mentors one day. Interact with them, learn from shared experiences, make connections, and use them to expand your network. Keep in mind that many of the most successful ventures are built on relationships forged in college. Dropbox founders Drew Houston and Arash Ferdowsi met at MIT; Instagram founders Kevin Systrom and Mike Krieger met at Stanford; and Stacey Bendet and Rebecca Matchet,

RESEARCH AT WORK

Don't Pitch Like a Girl

A lot of research suggests that investors are biased against women entrepreneurs. Researchers Lakshmi Balachandra, Tony Briggs, Kim Eddleston, and Candida Brush wanted to dig deeper into this phenomenon. They examined how gender-stereotyped behaviors of masculinity and femininity, displayed by men or women entrepreneurs during their pitches to investors, influence investor decisions. The sample for the study included 185 elevator pitches (1 minute long) to venture capitalists during a competition; 20% of the pitches were done by women. As part of the competition, the investors decided immediately following the short pitch whether they were interested in talking more with the entrepreneur about potential investment. The table below lists the behaviors measured.

Behaviors Assessed in the Study

Masculine Characteristics	Feminine Characteristics
Forcefulness	Warmth
Dominance	Sensitiveness
Aggressiveness	Expressiveness
Assertiveness	Emotiveness

In addition to the behaviors above that were assessed, the researchers controlled for attractiveness and market potential. In other words, the results of the study were not impacted by the physical attractiveness of the entrepreneur nor the profit potential of the idea.

What they found was a bit surprising. They didn't find that investors are biased against women per se; the sex of the entrepreneur didn't impact investor preference. Rather, investors exhibited bias against the *display* of feminine behaviors during the pitch, regardless of who pitched. Investors preferred pitches in which entrepreneurs

displayed masculine behaviors because these reflected business competence, preparedness, and strong leadership. The feminine behaviors were negatively related.

The researchers contend that their findings make four important contributions to our knowledge about entrepreneurship:

1. Women are just as likely as men to have interest from investors at the pitch stage.

2. Investor bias (implicit bias) was present. Investors negatively reacted to feminine behaviors, but these behaviors were seen in both men and women.

3. Investors need to understand that such bias exists and perhaps work to change their perceptions.

4. Women who exhibited masculine behaviors were not penalized, which goes against previous research.

The authors conclude, "Our findings that investors are *not* biased against women entrepreneurs, or against women entrepreneurs who act in contrast to their gender stereotype, are unexpected and particularly noteworthy because they identify a new mechanism for gender-based discrimination in entrepreneurial finance" (p. 128).

Critical Thinking Questions

1. What "male" or "female" behaviors do you exhibit while presenting or pitching?

2. Does the list of "masculine" and "feminine" characteristics that was used in this research show implicit bias? Explain.

3. Regardless of this research, do you think there are gender differences that relate to entrepreneurship? ●

Source: Balachandra, L., Briggs, T., Eddleston, K., & Brush, C. (2019). Don't pitch like a girl!: How gender stereotypes influence investor decisions. *Entrepreneurship Theory & Practice, 43*(1): 116–137.

founders of contemporary clothing company Alice and Olivia, met at the University of Pennsylvania.[29] Without being immediately conscious of it, these founders had become self-selected stakeholders before the venture had even existed. In the next section, we will explore the concept of self-selected stakeholders and their value to entrepreneurial ventures.

Self-Selected Stakeholders

Usually, entrepreneurs do not think about stakeholders such as employees, contractors, suppliers, customers, and the like until after the business has started. However, entrepreneurs need to understand the importance of **self-selected stakeholders**.[30] These are the

Self-selected stakeholders: the people who "self-select" into a venture in order to connect entrepreneurs with resources in an effort to steer the venture in the right direction.

people who "self-select" into an entrepreneur's network in order to connect them with resources such as subject-matter expertise, funding, advice, introductions to others, new perspectives, feedback on concepts, mentors, and so on, in an effort to steer the venture in the right direction.

A stakeholder self-selects into your venture to offer some type of short-term or long-term commitment in an effort to steer your venture in the right direction. Unlike venture capitalists and other investors, your self-selected stakeholders do not need to be pitched to or sold to. They are helping you because they feel motivated to give you access to information and resources that you didn't otherwise have. When people self-select into your network without any hidden agenda or motive, there is a huge opportunity to collaborate with them to build a better business.

Stakeholders can provide valuable resources to entrepreneurs, helping cocreate and bring the venture to life. Cocreation is a strategy that focuses on bringing people together to initiate a constant flow of new ideas that help to create ventures and transform businesses for the better in an uncertain and unpredictable world. For example, Thorkil Sonne cocreated with a leading IT company and founded Denmark-based The Specialists, which focuses on finding work opportunities in technology for people with autism. Sonne has a goal to create 1 million jobs for people all over the world.[31]

Self-selection also ties in with the concept of enrolling others in your journey, as part of the Entrepreneurship Method discussed in Chapter 1. Key to building the network is the idea of enrolling people in your idea rather than selling them. You aren't asking for favors. You are sharing in hopes they want to be a part of your network. They have something to offer, and you have something of value to provide. Building your network is not a sales job. It's not about trying to convince someone to do something that he or she may not ordinarily do. Rather, people join your network because they want to. People enroll in your vision because they're moved by your enthusiasm or idea. They see something that they want to become part of.

Activities such as running clubs can help you find connections with people from a variety of backgrounds.

Peter Senge, founding chairperson of the Society for Organizational Learning, offers the following three guidelines for enrollment:

1. Be enrolled yourself. If you're not buying the future vision, opportunity, or team, others won't, either.

2. Be truthful. Don't inflate the benefits beyond what they really are.

3. Let the other person choose. Don't try hard to "convince" them—that comes across as manipulative and ultimately hurts enrollment.[32]

The first step to finding self-selected stakeholders is to think about the people you already know: your family and friends, people you have met at work, and people you encounter in school and social activities. These stakeholders may not even be part of the eventual founding team, but they are a valuable source of information and, potentially, investment.

One of the best ways to form a range of diverse connections with self-selected stakeholders is through shared activities.[33] Sports teams, clubs, community service ventures, and voluntary and charitable associations bring together all sorts of people from different experiences and backgrounds. Remember that new ventures require a variety of talents, from marketing to technology to finance, and confining yourself to a particular group whose experience mirrors yours is unlikely to expand your skillset. Your goal is to learn more about the talents of acquaintances to find areas of mutual interest.

Participating in a shared activity builds trust and passion and allows people to be themselves outside a formal environment in the attainment of a common goal. Team members can build a loyal bond that may transfer to a working relationship. For example, Ahmed El-Sharkas and Ahmed Eshra, founders of Knowledge Officer, a platform

©iStockphoto.com/skynesher

that builds personalized learning paths, met while jogging on the same running track. As they ran together, they bounced ideas off each other before agreeing to meet again to explore next steps.[34]

8.3 BUILDING NETWORKS

>> **LO 8.3   Describe different ways of building networks.**

Forging connections goes beyond striking up conversations with friends and acquaintances; a really useful network expands to meeting other individuals in your geographic location. Entrepreneurs get support and networking opportunities from so many areas, including chambers of commerce, civic organizations, seminars, incubators, accelerators, and many other organizations dedicated to supporting entrepreneurs (see Table 8.3). Check online and in the local newspaper for public calendars of local events, including public lectures.

Many cities around the world have Meetup groups—local get-togethers of people who share a passion for interests ranging from hiking to sightseeing to biking to meditation to entrepreneurship. They provide a way to find people locally who share a common interest with you. Go to Meetup.com and enter your zip code to see a wide variety of Meetups near you. One group set up in Vancouver, Canada, is for the "Extremely Shy"

TABLE 8.3

Top Organizations for Entrepreneurs

Entrepreneurs' Organization (EO)	Provides different programs aimed at specific needs and areas of focus that any entrepreneur could use
Ernst & Young Entrepreneur of the Year program	Program for entrepreneurs to compete for Entrepreneur of the Year award
Tugboat Institute	Brings purpose-driven leaders together to create businesses that have a positive impact on the world
Small Giants Community	Similar to Tugboat Institute, in that it attracts entrepreneurs who are more purpose driven than profit driven
Mastermind Talks	Invitation-only community for entrepreneurs, where members receive educational training and connections to past attendees
Kauffman Foundation	Offers entrepreneurs help ranging from educational opportunities to policy changes
Powderkeg	Growing community of more than 10,000 tech entrepreneurs and others who are building innovative companies across America
Young Entrepreneur Council (YEC)	Exclusive group of peers that offers entrepreneurs the chance to partake in monthly Q&As and join active social groups
Young Presidents' Organization (YPO)	Premier leadership organization composed of top executives from all over the world
Startup Grind	Global community of entrepreneurs that publishes helpful content and hosts conferences all over the world
Baby Bathwater Institute	Brings together a variety of entrepreneurs from across all kinds of industries and puts on unique events to keep members progressing

Sources: Hall, J. (2018). 11 entrepreneur organizations with strong communities to support you. *Forbes.* Retrieved from https://www.forbes.com/sites/johnhall/2018/04/08/11-entrepreneur-organizations-with-strong-communities-to-support-you; Rampton, J. (2015. January 2). 12 organizations entrepreneurs need to join. *Entrepreneur.* Retrieved from http://www.entrepreneur.com/article/241192

Analyzing My Network

Have you ever stopped to think about the network you already belong to?

Think about the people in your current network. First, list their names in a column on a piece of paper. Try to list 15 to 20 people that you know. Next, for each person, mark their name

- with an (A) if they help you get work done,

- with a (B) if they help advance your career or entrepreneurial ideas,

- with a (C) if they provide personal support, and

- with a (D) if they are a role model.

Now, count how many As, Bs, Cs, and Ds you have. What type of people are most plentiful in your network? What type

of people do you need more of and why? Keep in mind that entrepreneurs need all types in their network.

Critical Thinking Questions

1. How easy or difficult was it to think of 15 to 20 people in your current network? Could you think of more than 20 people?

2. Do you think the A, B, C, and D categories are a helpful way to categorize the members of your network? Would you use other categories instead or in addition?

3. How do you think others would categorize you as a member of their networks? What qualities do you possess that would be valuable to others in their networks? ●

Source: Based on Murphy, W., & Kram, K. (2014). *Strategic relationships at work.* New York, NY: McGraw-Hill.

and is the most active Meetup group in Canada, as well as being one of the top five most active groups in the world.[35] Meetups typically run from 1 hour to all day, and they can feature formal presentations or simply be free-form networking events. Many Meetup groups focus on technology (such as the SaaS consortium) or skills (such as public speaking or podcasting). As Meetups have gained traction in entrepreneurship communities around the world, they have become a powerful tool for not only networking but also recruiting new talent, building trust group to share ideas, learning new content, and meeting prospective investors.[36]

Incubators and Accelerators

Incubator: an organization that helps early stage entrepreneurs refine ideas, build out technology, and get access to resources.

Incubators and accelerators are among the best places for entrepreneurs to network and find mentors. Often the two terms are used interchangeably, but they do not mean the same thing. An **incubator** is an organization that helps early-stage entrepreneurs to refine an idea while also providing access to a whole network of other

TABLE 8.4

Top Five Incubators and Accelerators in the United States and Canada

UNITED STATES	CANADA
1. Y Combinator	1. Le Camp
2. Tech Stars	2. Creative Destruction Lab
3. 500 Startups	3. DMZ
4. AngelPad	4. Extreme Accelerator
5. Capital Factory	5. Ideaboost

Sources: The ten best startup incubators in the world. (2018). *Tendercapital.* Retrieved from https://tendercapital.com/en/the-ten-best-startup-incubators-in-the-world/; Colwell, A. (2019). The top 40 startup accelerators and incubators in North America in 2019. *Salesflare Blog.* Retrieved from https://blog.salesflare.com/top-startup-accelerators-incubators-us-canada

startups, mentors, and other valuable resources. Leading incubator 500 Startups, based in Mountain View, California, offers entrepreneurs seed funds, expert guidance, and access to investors. Recently, 500 Startups expanded into Europe and has plans to set up in Israel and Turkey.[37]

In contrast, an **accelerator** is an organization that provides tailored support for existing startups that have already built a successful product or service (usually through an incubator) by helping to develop, scale, and grow their business. Typically, accelerators offer startups free office space, feedback, and access to investors. Y Combinator, also based in Mountain View, California, is considered to be the most successful accelerator for startups, having facilitated the growth of such companies as Airbnb, Dropbox, Stripe, Reddit, Twitch, Coinbase, and Weebly.[38] Table 8.4 lists the top five incubators and accelerators in the United States and Canada.

Accelerator: an organization that provides tailored support in order to help new ventures scale and grow.

Learning How to Network

Networking is not just about collecting business cards. You may walk away from a networking event with a whole stack of business cards but with no meaningful relationships or connections forged. A business card isn't enough for someone to remember you by—you need to have meaningful conversations to maintain a relationship and provide value in a way that makes you memorable.

Networking is a two-way game. It's a targeted search, with a philosophy of contributing, giving value, sharing and exchanging information, and interacting with people.

Networking Events

Before you attend a networking event, do your research. Think about who might be there, and decide whom you would like to meet. Think of what you are going to say before you arrive. Your list of topics does not have to be solely business related. You could talk about anything from business, to sports, to weekend plans, to industry events. Remember, relationships can be forged on mutual personal interests or hobbies and not just business interests. However, it is always best to steer clear of potentially incendiary topics like politics, religion, and other issues that might elicit a strong emotional reaction.

Walking into a room full of strangers can be daunting, but the good news is that like any other skill, the skill of networking can be learned. And in keeping with the theme of this book, it takes practice. Here are some networking tips:

- Read the room: How crowded or empty is it? Is there a focal point or an activity taking place that could be a conversation starter?

- Look for potential groups to join: Look at nonverbal cues such as body language and eye contact to identify whom to approach as a likely conversant and whom to avoid.

- Commit fully to the discussion: Don't look over the shoulder of the person you're talking to as if you're hoping someone more interesting will show up.

- Be careful not to dominate the conversation: Make sure you let the other person speak and offer thoughts and opinions.

- Keep questions brief: When approaching a desired contact with a question, briefly introduce yourself, keep your question short, and explain why you are asking.

- Disengage gracefully: Look them in the eye, shake hands and say their name followed by "it's been good talking with you," or words to that effect.

- Thank people for advice: Follow up with a short note or email within 24 hours and consider connecting on LinkedIn or other professional networking sites.

Even if you consider yourself to be a confident speaker, it is worth practicing your body language. Research shows that domineering people tend to take control of the conversation and avoid eye contact a lot of the time. People who are open to making new connections generally "adopt an open stance, shoulders apart and hands at their sides, turning slightly toward newcomers to welcome them," says networking expert Kelly Decker, of Decker Communications.[39] While influential people tend to lead conversations, good networkers will listen and show interest by nodding, leaning forward, raising their eyebrows, and mirroring the speaker's gestures—for example, tilting their heads in the same way.

The Give and Take of Networking

Bear in mind that networking is a two-way street. The quid pro quo (something that is given or done in return for something) strategy is often used by networkers to initiate a business relationship.[40] The idea behind it is to first identify something your contact needs and then offer something of value. This could involve sharing some information, sending a link to an article about the subject in question, or offering your contact an introduction to someone who knows more about the subject.

Kare Anderson, author of *Mutuality Matters,* points out that when you do favors for somebody, they are more likely to repay them. Doing favors for others helps people with good ideas to find ways to capitalize on their opportunities. She provides a list of favors that may only take as little as 5 minutes and are a great way of quickly building trusting relationships:

- Use a product and offer concise, vivid, and helpful feedback.

- Introduce two people with a well-written email, citing a mutual interest.

- Read a summary and offer crisp and concrete feedback.

- Serve as a relevant reference for a person, product, or service.

- Share or comment on something on Facebook, Twitter, LinkedIn, Tumblr, Google+, or other social places.

- Write a short, specific, and laudatory note to recognize or recommend someone on LinkedIn, Yelp, or other social place.[41]

Remember that many people who are new to networking events will be as nervous as you are. If you see someone standing alone, why not approach him or her? He or she is likely to be more welcoming because you have made an effort to strike up a conversation. More important, don't assume "anyone standing alone is a loser and should be avoided."[42] This person might end up being one of your most valuable contacts. In fact, never assume that anyone—regardless of who they are or what they do—can't be a worthwhile acquaintance.

Ivan Misner, founder of business networking organization BNI, tells the story of a financial advisor friend who received a huge portion of business referred to him by a gardener on Cape Cod in Massachusetts. The gardener worked in the gardens of the grandest homes on Cape Cod and had built up good professional relationships with wealthy families living there. When the gardener heard the financial advisor was trying to get referrals in the area, he mentioned his name to his contacts in the wealthy families, and that is how the financial advisor ended up getting a huge chunk of business.[43] So the moral of the story is, never underestimate the power of the "loner" or the person with a "low wage" job, or the person sitting next to you at an entrepreneurship event. Pursue all networking opportunities—you never know where they may lead. Networking is simply about human connection and connecting with all types of people.

Finally, make a real effort to remember names (this could involve mentally writing a person's name on or above their face) and use names during conversation to fully assimilate them. Write down information soon after you meet someone.[44]

Guy Kaw4saki, author of *The Art of the Start,* provides some additional tips for networking:[45]

- Discover what you can do for someone else. Great networkers want to know what they can do for you, not what you can do for them.

- Ask good questions. The mark of a good conversationalist is to get others to talk a lot and then listen.

- Unveil your passions. Don't just talk about business—let the conversation expand into your hobbies as well.

- Read voraciously so that you have an array of information to draw on during conversations.

- Follow up with a short but personal note within 24 hours. Something like, "Nice to meet you. Hope your blog is doing well," is fine—but be sure to mention at least one personal item to show that you're not just sending a canned email.

- Prepare a self-introduction of 7 to 9 seconds (*not* a 30-second elevator speech). Tie it to why you're attending the event. This will help people figure out what to say to you.

Networking to Find Mentors

Mentors can be an invaluable resource for entrepreneurs as they offer advice based on years of experience, help you progress with your venture, and warn you of known pitfalls. They can also provide valuable connections and industry contacts. For instance, health and wellness entrepreneur Amy Backlock acknowledges the pivotal role her mentor played when she was setting up her personal training business.[46] Amy's mentor was a doctor of physical therapy who owned many rehabilitation centers. Not only was he an expert in his field but he had the contacts Amy needed to get her venture off the ground. She said, "He was a source of endless information, important contacts, and a terrific sounding board for me, all contributing to my success."

Most well-known entrepreneurs credit their mentors for their success. Steve Jobs taught Mark Zuckerberg how to build a team; Bill Gates credits Warren Buffett for his ability to deal with complex problems; and Richard Branson references British airline entrepreneur Sir Freddie Laker for his advice and guidance when trying to get Virgin Atlantic off the ground.[47] Deborah Sweeney, founder of online legal and business filing service MyCorporation, says her mentors include "my mom (full-time career woman and amazing, supportive mom), a few of my female professors, a mentor in my law practice, and colleague-mentors with whom I graduated law school."[48]

Yet entrepreneurs typically don't just have one mentor; they may build up a network of mentors over time, which can be useful when you are seeking different perspectives or guidance during particular stages of your venture. Mentors can also play a very important role in larger companies. For example, at the multinational manufacturer W. L. Gore, instead of bosses new hires are assigned mentors—people who can guide them through Gore's famously unique nonhierarchical culture and address any questions, concerns, or issues the new hire may have.[49]

How do you go about finding your mentor? Look in your personal network—the ideal mentor might be right in front of you. Sometimes the person who knows you best can be the right fit for you.

Check out your college connections, too, as they can be a valuable resource for mentors. Anywhere you have the opportunity to form connections—networking events, Meetup groups, and so forth—may be the right step toward finding the right mentor for you.[50]

However, for some entrepreneurs, asking someone to be your mentor can be daunting. Why would a successful business person or seasoned entrepreneur want to take the time to help you grow your fledgling new venture? The answer is that many mentors gain personal pleasure in sharing their experience to help others succeed. Now a mentor himself, Richard Branson is a champion of young entrepreneurial talent; he has said he gets "a real sense of pleasure from seeing talented people realize their ambitions and grow professionally and personally." Branson also believes that mentors can learn a lot from their mentees: "As I've learned, in the process you can gain new insights and discover fresh approaches to doing business by simply discussing how things work."[51]

While face-to-face networking is essential for building valuable relationships, it is also possible to network from a remote location. In the next section, we will explore the benefits of virtual networking.

Building My Network

In the first Mindshift, you analyzed your network and probably identified some gaps. Now it's time to work on filling in those gaps. For this Mindshift, you need to add three new and significant people to your network.

Step 1: Identify what types of people you want to add to your network. No names at this point, just types. For example, you may want to meet someone who has built an app or you may want to meet someone who understands commercial real estate. Write down the three types of people; you should have three *different* types written down.

Step 2: For each of the types of people, identify an event (physical and not virtual) where you could potentially meet people who fall into your category. For example, you may go to an entrepreneurship club meeting or attend a speaker event on campus.

Step 3: After you find them, send them a follow-up thank you email within 24 hours. Don't simply connect on social media; rather, email specifically why you enjoyed connecting with them, what you learned, and how you hope to stay connected. You may even want to try to set up a next meeting. Why not?

Critical Thinking Questions

1. How did you approach people at the events you attended? Did some approaches work better than others?

2. What did you learn from each person you met?

3. How will you maintain your relationship with these new people? ●

8.4 VIRTUAL NETWORKING

>> **LO 8.4   Illustrate the benefits of virtual networking.**

With the proliferation of online social networks, networking has definitely evolved! One of the speediest and simplest ways to connect with others is through social media. Twitter, LinkedIn, Facebook, Instagram, and YouTube all provide ways to connect with people who are experts in the field, potential stakeholders, or fellow entrepreneurs—anyone who can potentially help you develop, build, and grow your entrepreneurial venture. Some of these people may become self-selected stakeholders and eventually become part of your founding team. Let's explore how you can use these social media sites to build your network.

Networking Through Social Media

Twitter is one of the easiest platforms to use to find people who might become stakeholders. Signing on to Twitter is free (just choose a user name and a password) and easy (write a 280-character bio about yourself). You can upload a photo and you're ready to go.

To find others on Twitter who share your interests, you can do a keyword search (https://twitter.com/search-home) and see everyone who is using that keyword at that very instant. You can search for other people's Twitter bios and profiles at www.followerwonk.com. You can also compare users, even compare yourself to competitors, influencers, or friends. Followerwonk is also a good tool for analyzing impact, tracking followers, and retrieving "social graphs" based on Twitter statistics.

In addition to Twitter, you can interact with individuals or groups on LinkedIn (see Table 8.5). LinkedIn also has a section devoted specifically to questions and answers, which provides you with a view into the real-life challenges that business people face and the solutions that others offer. Anyone can post a question, and anyone can provide an answer. To reward helpful, quality answers, the question-asker can award a "good answer" tag. As an entrepreneur looking to build your knowledge, you can use these tags to identify the best answers from which to learn. Posting answers is a good way to show your own expertise and to demonstrate your willingness to be of help to others. When you share information with others, they will feel more inclined to reciprocate.

TABLE 8.5

LinkedIn Groups Dedicated to Entrepreneurs

Executive Suite	This group is all about connecting executives so they can share advice on leadership, decision making, and more. Members will join more than 321,000 others and gain access to their web series, discussion boards, and practical advice.
A Startup Specialists Group	With more than 281,000 members, this group, catering to startups, mentors, founders, and investors, is a great resource for entrepreneurs. It provides support, tips for building your business, crowd funding, best business practices, networking, and more.
Band of Entrepreneurs	This "non-profit organization of, by, and for entrepreneurs" group has close to 27,000 members and provides support on topics like legal help, human resources, public relations, technology, and more.
Bright Ideas and Entrepreneurs	This group facilitates discussions between entrepreneurs all over the world. With more than 22,000 members, this group invites you to share ideas and connect with other like-minded professionals.
Digital Marketing	The 1.1 million members of this group discuss areas of the digital marketing landscape, including social media marketing, mobile marketing, search engine marketing, online advertising, and more.
Entrepreneurs Meet Investors	With almost 5,500 members, this group is great for entrepreneurs seeking startup funding or for more established businesses in need of capital for further growth.
Entrepreneur's Network	Founded in 2008, this group with nearly 46,000 members aims to connect current and aspiring entrepreneurs to find answers, ask questions, and connect with similar professionals.
Future Trends	This group consists of 500,000 members and connects fellow trend hunters and visionaries from a variety of industries, such as marketing, consumer insights, strategic planning, and trend tracking.
Leadership Think Tank	With more than 263,000 members, this group aims to identify the relationship between leaders and followers through open discussions about leadership concepts and practices.
On Startups	This group of more than 644,000 members gives entrepreneurs the chance to discuss marketing, sales, finance, operations, recruiting, and other startup-related topics.

Source: Lopez. J. (2018). 20 LinkedIn groups every entrepreneur should belong to. *Business News Daily.* Retrieved from https://www.businessnewsdaily.com/7185-entrepreneur-linkedin-groups.html

Neena Dasgupta, CEO and director of Zirca Digital Solutions based in India, offers the following advice to entrepreneurs:

> Always remember to spend time making a list of people you would want to do business with in the future. These could be clients, investors, and potential partners. Next, create a highly-personalized note for each person and send them requests. When you're opening up this dialogue, don't forget to avoid hard-selling, and instead focus on how you can build a relationship.[52]

Table 8.5 lists a range of LinkedIn groups dedicated to entrepreneurs and small-business owners.

Facebook has grown from a social platform to a business platform—most businesses have a presence on Facebook. It is also useful for posting articles on Facebook pages and connecting with others who share mutual interests. Facebook groups are also beneficial for connecting with others and starting dialogues around shared interests. There

TABLE 8.6

Facebook Groups for Entrepreneurs

The Startup Chat Mastermind Group	This group is an offshoot of The Startup Chat Podcast, hosted by Steli Efti and Hiten Shah. Network with other fans of the show and get advice on topics ranging from startup growth to getting yourself into an entrepreneurial mentality.
Women in Business	This group is the virtual clubhouse of the Women In Business Club. The goal is for people to share what they're working on and get honest answers to their biggest business questions.
Intrepid Entrepreneurs	Facebook page where entrepreneurs and aspiring entrepreneurs come together to ask and answer questions, as well as give feedback on projects, ideas, and other forms of content.
The Intentional Entrepreneur	Learn how to find more (and better) clients, ace sales calls, and other must-dos when starting an online business.
Freedom Hackers Mastermind	Thriving community where entrepreneurs can gather feedback, network, discover interesting content, and help other entrepreneurs on their journey.
Savvy Business Owners	Facebook group for self-employed businesswomen.
Entrepreneurs Hustle	Group consists of a mix of seasoned business owners and new entrepreneurs, which makes for a great balance of people who are both asking for help and offering knowledge.
Small Business Connections	Group where members connect with other business owners, share events, and participate in themed discussions based on each day of the week (like Tech Tuesday and Winning Wednesday).

Source: Shah, K. (2018). 19 Facebook groups that will make you a better entrepreneur. *Gusto.* Retrieved from https://gusto.com/blog/growth/best-facebook-groups-entrepreneurs

are also specific Facebook groups for entrepreneurs (see Table 8.6) that provide a forum for entrepreneurs to meet and exchange ideas. Don't be wary of connecting with your competitors—they are a valuable source of learning and inspiration. Both Facebook and LinkedIn make it easy to find out which face-to-face conferences the people in your network are attending.

Unlike Twitter, LinkedIn, and Facebook, YouTube is not a social networking and interaction site. However, you can use YouTube as a resource for identifying experts and getting video tutorials on a specific topic. When you find an expert on YouTube, you can use other social media like Twitter and LinkedIn to establish first contact.

Instagram is also a useful networking tool. People can send short videos and photos to connect with others and showcase where they have been and what business activities they have been involved with. Lana Hopkins, founder of Mon Purse, an Australia-based leather bag and purse customization and personalization company, showcases her products during her global business travel.[53] Allowing people an insight into your professional life gives them the opportunity to get to know you and your business.

In other countries around the world, online startup support networks are becoming more popular as a means of funding early-stage ventures. VC4Africa is Africa's largest online entrepreneurship network, which brings together venture capitalists, angels, and entrepreneurs to support Africa's rapidly growing startup scene. Through its 90,000 members, the network connects entrepreneurs from 12,000 startups with the knowledge, contacts, and financing necessary to build their businesses.[54] To date, entrepreneurs have raised more than $27 million in funding through VC4Africa.[55]

Maintaining Your Network

Once you've started to build your network, it's important to maintain it—something that's easy to forget when your network is mainly virtual and you are not interacting face-to-face on a regular basis. Maintaining your network involves staying in touch through occasional interaction. Research shows we can really manage up to only 25 relationships, but we can maintain up to 150.[56]

This interaction can take the form of tweeting a useful piece of information, replying to a request for information, answering a question, or attending an event. For example, if you see an interesting video on YouTube, send a link to people in your network who might be interested. If one of your stakeholders posts a question on LinkedIn to which you know the answer (or know someone who knows the answer), answer the question or recommend an expert. Figure 8.2 lists several skills important to maintaining relationships.

If you're a member of Meetup groups, then let your network know that you're attending an upcoming meeting. You can also tweet your attendance or announce it on LinkedIn and Facebook. After the event, you can tweet or email any people with whom you talked, by thanking them for the conversation. Another way to maintain your network is to provide value back to them by writing a blog post. As an entrepreneur, you can use a blog to showcase and share your thoughts and activities with your stakeholders.

Overall, the frequency of interactions you have with your stakeholders can vary over time. There will be times when you're actively seeking advice, which means you will have more interactions. Some stakeholders will want to be involved on a daily or weekly basis. Others are fine with less frequent interactions. Overall, maintaining relationships is a skill like any other, and it pays to learn it.

By participating in social networking sites, you build credibility, transparency, and trust. If people get an insight into your professional life, see the connections you have made, and what thoughts and information you share, they will get to know you and want to build a relationship with you. Whether you're networking in person or online, it is important to look for potential candidates for your founding team. The next section focuses on how you can network to build a founding team.

Lana Hopkins, founder of Mon Purse

8.5 NETWORKING TO BUILD THE FOUNDING TEAM

>> **LO 8.5** Explain how networking can help to build the founding team.

A **founding team** is a group of people with complementary skills and a shared sense of commitment coming together in founding an enterprise to build and grow the company. The founding team usually consists of the founder and a few cofounders who possess complementary skills. There is no "right size" for the number of people on a founding team, but two to four seems to be the typical number.

Founding team: a group of people with complementary skills and a shared sense of commitment coming together in founding an enterprise to build and grow the company.

FIGURE 8.2

Skills for Maintaining Relationships

Skills for Maintaining Relationships	
• Curiosity	• Self-Management
• Questioning	• Accountability
• Deep Listening	• Intuition

Source: Adapted from Murphy, W., & Kram, K. (2014). *Strategic relationships at work*. New York, NY: McGraw-Hill.

When to Focus on Values

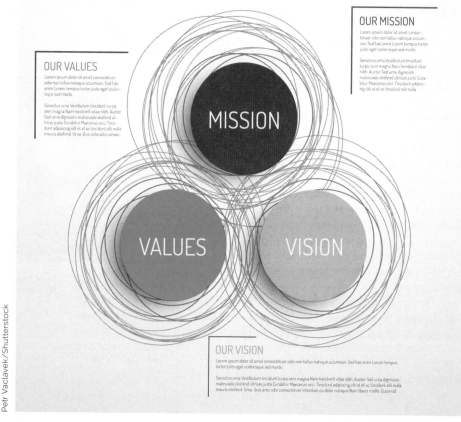

Petr Vaclavek/Shutterstock

Mission, vision, and values statements

Every well-established company has a value statement, which often goes along with a simple mission statement. For an entrepreneur in the early stages of launching a new business, time is one of the most valuable resources. An entrepreneur may be tempted to skip writing a values statement. After all, very few employees at any company would be able to recite their company's value or mission statement without pulling out the company handbook. Is it necessary to spend time on forming a values statement in the early stages of a startup? Is it even necessary to have a values statement at all?

Traditionally, a values statement allows employees to band together in their vision for how the company can change the world in a major and beneficial way. It often gives the workplace a sense of higher meaning, which can be a valuable motivational tool for employees. Additionally, having a values statement ensures that every member of the team is on the same page, and there is a written confirmation as to the direction that the business is taking.

In today's business climate, a company's brand is inherently tied to the company's culture. Workers, especially those in highly skilled industries, will be more interested in a job if they can find a higher meaning than just a paycheck. Essentially, if the values of the company are readily apparent to the business of the company, employees and candidates could be more excited to work for the company, rather than having to turn to a vague values statement. All of this suggests that the right thing for an entrepreneur to do is to create a values statement in the startup phase of his or her company. An entrepreneur can "save time" by spending time creating a sufficient values statement up front. The end result is a purposeful company culture and better motivated employees.

Critical Thinking Questions

1. Could a lack of a values statement lead a company astray?

2. Can a values statement be inherent to the operation of a company, without a need to write it down?

3. How does a values statement affect the morale of employees? ●

Sources:

Parker, M. (2016, October 18). Have company mission statements become outdated? *The Globe and Mail.* Retrieved from https://www.theglobeandmail.com/report-on-business/careers/leadership-lab/have-company-mission-statements-become-outdated/article32403376/

Smith, C. (n.d.). Can an organization have a successful strategic plan without effective mission & vision statements? *Chron.com.* Retrieved from https://smallbusiness.chron.com/can-organization-successful-strategic-plan-effective-mission-vision-statements-30779.html

The goal of the founding team is to build and grow the company and provide economic and social returns for themselves, employees, other owners, and potential investors. Research shows that more and more, new fast-growth ventures have been founded by entrepreneurial teams rather than sole entrepreneurs. In fact, overall, studies have shown that ventures started by teams typically perform better than those started by solo founders.[57] When researchers asked venture capitalists the most important factors to new venture success, their response was, "the lead entrepreneur and the quality of the team."[58]

When considering potential founding team members, it is helpful to ask yourself two questions: "Can I build the company without them?" and "Can I find someone else just like them?" If the answer to both questions is no, then you have most likely discovered a cofounder. However, if the answer to both questions is yes, then you can still keep them in your network, maintain the relationship, and potentially hire them at a later date as employees.[59]

Researchers have cited the most likely outlets where entrepreneurs find their founding teams: colleagues in organizations where they were previously employed; organizations similar to the founding firm; prior working relationships across organizations (e.g., buyers, suppliers, consultants); family members and friends; and deliberate search by the lead entrepreneur.[60]

Another way to find founding team members is through social networking sites, which enable you to find and interact with people you might otherwise never meet who share your passion and could ultimately be a resource. For example, selective networking site Cofounder's Lab (https://cofounderslab.com) provides a global forum for entrepreneurs to connect with like-minded entrepreneurs, cofounders, and advisors. Applications from entrepreneurs to join Cofounder's Lab are first screened for skillsets (50% of the members are engineers), and if the applicants are accepted, they are given access to the network for a $50 annual fee.

Overall, team members are generally found in the network of the lead entrepreneur. This means most founding teams have a lead entrepreneur (usually, but not always, the team CEO) who creates the vision; has full belief in the venture; and has the motivation and passion to persevere, inspire team members, and make judgments and decisions during difficult times.[61]

Google re:Work has done research on the importance of shared vision and good manager behaviors (https://rework.withgoogle.com/). Though founding teams are more about leadership and taking action, parts of Google's suggested group exercise are extremely important for founding teams. To create a vision, the team needs to answer three questions in the beginning, when the founding team is just forming:

Core Values: What do we believe in?

Purpose: Why do we exist?

Mission: What do we want to achieve?

During the early stages of a startup everything is constantly changing, so it's important for the group to continue to revisit these questions. As the venture gets more traction, two additional questions need to be asked:

Strategy: How will we realize our mission?

Goals: How do we plan to accomplish our strategies?

Characteristics of a Great Founding Team

Finding the right cofounders to build and scale your venture can make all the difference between your business succeeding or failing. The most successful teams are composed of members who possess the experience, skills, and abilities to manage complex problems, cope with pressure, and overcome obstacles to achieve rapid growth. Table 8.7 outlines a list of useful questions to ask potential founding team members.

Positive social relations within the team are also key when it comes to providing social and emotional support.[62] Bernd Schoner, cofounder of RFID tech startup ThingMagic, started with friends from MIT he had worked with before. They thought they knew each other well enough to start a company, but they found that "outside pressure causes people to act differently," which caused "extreme turmoil." Schoner has learned from this experience and believes that founding teams must have the right balance of personalities and characteristics in order to achieve success.[63]

Jenn Houser, a serial entrepreneur and cofounder of Upstart Bootcamp, has outlined the following useful characteristics to look for when you are evaluating potential cofounders.[64]

1. Possess the right skills.

Houser recommends identifying the top three to five business operations you need to carry out well over the next 3 years; then ask yourself who has the skills and expertise to accomplish these operations. She points out the importance of examining the track record of each candidate. Whether or not the person is a friend, she or he should be considered only if she or he has demonstrated the ability to do the job.

2. Take a hands-on approach.

During the startup stage, you and your cofounders will be doing everything—from answering the phone to ordering office supplies. Make sure your chosen cofounders are not only willing but happy to do whatever it takes to achieve goals.

For example, in 2003, former chemist and lab director Ron Holt founded the cleaning company Two Maids & A Mop, headquartered in Birmingham, Alabama. In the beginning, Holt was one of the maids with a mop: "I put my hands onto surfaces that I never thought I would," Holt says. "As a former lab director, to find yourself on a bathroom floor, cleaning up somebody's [mess]—it's not where you thought you'd be in life."[65]

Although it wasn't a glamorous start, cleaning toilets was a valuable way for Holt to learn about the cleaning business and the people he would eventually employ.

TABLE 8.7

Early Questions to Ask Potential Team Members

Who needs to be on the team at the start?
What skills does each person bring to the table?
Are there any skill gaps? Can these gaps be outsourced?
What type of work experience is related to the idea?
What is the network of each member?
Do you have ways of attracting new team members?
What are the personal and business goals of each member?
What is the role of each member, and is each role distinct?
How are you dividing ownership?

3. Use positive problem solving.

You want to choose entrepreneurial team members who are curious and driven—people who see problems not as obstacles but as challenges that must be overcome in a creative and innovative way. An entrepreneurial mindset is required for all team members.

4. Leave ego at the door.

Team success depends on collaboration and a collective willingness to work for the good of the enterprise. Cofounders with a big ego or a personal agenda are less likely to work well with others. One way to find out if potential cofounders have big egos is to ask them about a time when they achieved team success, and listen carefully to the number of times they say "I" or "we" in their response.

The Microsoft founding team

Entrepreneur John Rampton believes his ego was responsible for killing his new payments venture.[66] Rampton refused to ask for help when he needed it, missed opportunities to learn, set impossible goals, controlled all the decision making, and micromanaged his employees.

Having learned the hard way, Rampton concluded, "My business isn't about me. It's about my customers and how I can enhance their lives. If I'm not listening to their wants and needs, they won't continue to support me and my business. Focus on your customers."[67]

5. Share similar attitudes toward values, goals, and risk.

Jenn Houser advises that cofounders need to be aligned with the goals to be achieved, the values they share, and the risks they may need to take to get there. The best relationships are based on trust, and your team should feel comfortable about discussing potential ethical dilemmas and how they will be resolved. Before you commit, she recommends investing several days with your cofounders in hashing out every detail of the business and how the partnership arrangement will work.

6. Care deeply.

Although cofounders need to have the intelligence, skills, and experience to achieve goals, they also need to care deeply about the enterprise. Someone who doesn't care deeply about the success of the startup may be likely to become unavailable when things get tough, or even to jump ship at a crucial moment. Plenty of passion combined with a high degree of smarts can even compensate for limitations in experience. Finding a cofounder who has complementary skills and equal enthusiasm for your ideas can help minimize risk and increase the odds of startup success.[68]

Many startups fail because the cofounders came together too quickly rather than spending time together first. Spending time with your potential cofounders on a startup weekend or working together in a previous job allows for more bonding and building a relationship of trust and respect. The bottom line is connecting with your cofounders are like entering into a marriage on both an emotional and financial basis. Get to know each other first, before you commit, and make sure the others feel the same way about you as you do about them.

Atish Davda, founder of liquidity manager EquityZen, has created a list of attributes to look for in founding team members (see Figure 8.3).

The Value of Team Diversity

Diversity comes in many forms. We often think of diversity as referring to demographic characteristics such as age, gender, race, and ethnicity, but diversity is also found in people's career paths and goals, viewpoints, educational backgrounds, and life experiences. Most of the diversity we have in the world is composed of what we don't see. So always look below the surface! (See Figure 8.4).

FIGURE 8.3

Key Attributes of Founding Team Members

Source: Adapted from Davda, A. (2014). How you can build an incredible founding team. *Creator.* Retrieved from https://creator .wework.com/knowledge/can-build-incredible-founding-team/

FIGURE 8.4

Dimensions of Diversity

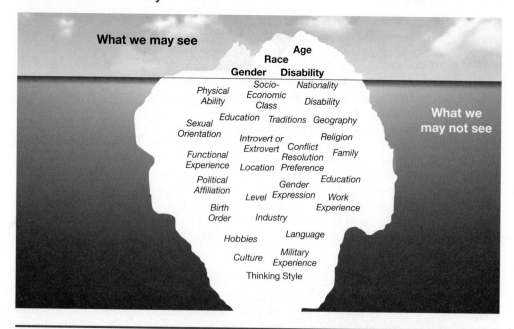

Source: Adapted by Susan Duffy, Babson College from "Turn Diversity to Your Advantage" by Salomon, Mary F and Schork, Joan M. Research Technology Management, Arlington, Vol. 46, Iss. 4, (Jul/Aug 2003): 37; http://www.brookgraham.com/WhatWeDo/Iceberg .aspx; https://spark4community.com/1043-2/

Homogeneous and Heterogeneous Teams

Which do you think is more important: homogenous teams, whose members possess the same or similar characteristics such as age, gender, ethnicity, experience, and educational background; or heterogeneous teams, meaning a group of people with a mix of knowledge, skills, and experience? Although there is no conclusive research to suggest that homogenous is better than heterogeneous or vice versa, the results of studies argue the benefits and disadvantages of both.

In homogeneous teams, members are likely to feel included because of their shared backgrounds, cultures, languages, and experiences. This helps the team to communicate more effectively and avoid misunderstandings as well as prejudices. However, sharing similarities does not mean that personality conflicts do not exist—any team, whether homogeneous or heterogeneous, is liable to have conflicts at times. Further, studies have shown that lack of diversity in homogeneous teams can stifle creativity and information processing. Indeed, it is difficult to form a homogeneous team without others feeling excluded because they do not share the same characteristics as the team members.[69]

In a heterogeneous team, there is a greater mix of experiences, skills, ethnicities, and backgrounds. A diverse set of collective characteristics can aid decision making and expand a "group's set of possible solutions and allows the group to conceptualize problems in new ways."[70] Studies have found that this type of team tends to have a higher degree of creativity and innovativeness than homogeneous teams.[71]

Researchers have argued, however, that team diversity alone will not necessarily result in better performance. What matters more than demographic diversity (age, gender, race, etc.) is team commitment and cognitive comprehensiveness, a process in which team members examine critical issues with a wide lens and formulate strategies by considering diverse approaches, decision criteria, and courses of action. Team-level cognitive comprehensiveness is positively related to entrepreneurial team effectiveness. Effective teams also tend to have a high level of member commitment, encourage each other to use different approaches, offer different perspectives on problems, and use a range of potential solutions to solve problems.[72]

Finally, there are certain drawbacks to heterogeneous teams. Groups that have a greater mix can find it more difficult to communicate and understand each other, especially if they have to navigate across different languages and cultural backgrounds. This may lead to some members feeling misunderstood or isolated, which may produce conflicts and negative emotions among members of the entrepreneurial team, resulting in poor performance.[73]

Groupthink and Healthy Conflict

A team whose members are from diverse backgrounds, hold complementary skills and experiences, and have commitment to the venture could be considered healthy. And even though conflict arising from personality difference can be destructive, there is such a thing as healthy conflict. Testing and challenging assumptions is a state that gets the team out of groupthink, a phenomenon in which people share too similar a mindset, which inhibits their ability to spot gaps or errors. Patrick Lencioni, author of *The Five Dysfunctions of a Team*, states that "productive debate over issues is good for a team." Disagreeing on issues makes things uncomfortable, but it builds clarity. "If you don't have conflict on a team, you don't get commitment," Lencioni said. "If people don't weigh in, they won't buy in."[74] Healthy conflict builds clarity; for example, if team members point out flaws in an idea, then they can work together to build it into a more robust idea.

The challenge is to ensure that constructive conflict over issues does not degenerate into dysfunctional interpersonal conflict.[75] In other words, team members need to be able to argue without taking it personally or impairing their ability to work together. In her study of teams, Stanford University professor Kathleen Eisenhardt found teams that engaged in healthy conflict shared six traits:

- developed multiple alternatives to enrich the level of debate;
- shared commonly agreed-upon goals;
- worked with more information rather than less;

Homogenous team: a group of people with the same or similar characteristics such as age, gender, ethnicity, experience, and educational background.

Heterogeneous team: a group of people with a mix of knowledge, skills, and experience.

Cognitive comprehensiveness: a process in which team members examine critical issues with a wide lens and formulate strategies by considering diverse approaches, decision criteria, and courses of action.

Groupthink: a phenomenon in which people share too similar a mindset, which inhibits their ability to spot gaps or errors.

- injected humor into the decision process;

- maintained a balanced power structure; and

- resolved issues without forcing consensus.[76]

Overall, the teams worked with more, rather than less, information and debated on the basis of facts, not emotions. When teams stay with the topic of the debate and argue their points productively, there is less chance of personal attack.

One way of preventing groupthink and promoting healthy conflict is the use of a devil's advocate to challenge assumptions and encourage different perspectives. Author and hospitality expert Paul Rutter believes that all teams should have a devil's advocate. He said, "Having an effective devil's advocate can be a guardian angel in disguise, helping your company avoid mistakes that cost time and money. This can ultimately improve employee engagement, customer loyalty, and create repeat business."[77]

However, not all teams welcome the presence of a devil's advocate. In a classic study in decision making carried out in the early 1960s, several groups of managers were formed to solve a complex problem. The groups were identical in size and composition, except that half the groups included a devil's advocate, whose role was to challenge the group's conclusions and force the others to critically assess their assumptions and the logic of their arguments. The groups with the devil's advocate performed significantly better than the other groups by generating better-quality solutions to problems.

After a short break, the groups were told to eliminate one person from their group. In each group, it was the devil's advocate whom the group chose to ask to leave. Despite the fact that the devil's advocate was the reason for the team's high performance and competitive advantage, the members chose to eliminate that member because he or she made them feel uncomfortable. "I know it has positive outcomes for the performance of the organization as a whole, but I don't like how it makes me feel personally."[78] However, as we have learned, although we may think engaging in conflict is awkward and uncomfortable, it can be valuable and constructive if it is carried out in the right way.

In sum, healthy and constructive conflict is good, provided team members are clear on the organization's goals and free of hidden agendas. Steve Jobs said it best when he stated, "It's okay to spend a lot of time arguing about which route to take to San Francisco when everyone wants to end up there, but a lot of time gets wasted in such arguments if one person wants to go to San Francisco and another secretly wants to go to San Diego."[79] ●

Credit: Cartoon Resource/Alamy Stock Vector

"Emphasize our unique differences, pass it down."

This cartoon describes the concept of groupthink.

8.1 Explain the role of networks in building social capital.

Networks provide social capital such as access to sources of financing, information, expertise, and support, and networks can be excellent sources for loyalty. They allow for learning and information exchange, and social capital enables access to a range of resources, including venture capitalists, angel investors, advisors, banks, and trade shows.

8.2 Demonstrate the value of networks for entrepreneurs.

Relationships are key to business success, and entrepreneurs in particular will need to skillfully interact with a vast array of stakeholders. Networks provide entrepreneurs with access to private information, diverse skillsets, and power. Networks can also be relied on for personal and emotional support.

8.3 Describe different ways of building networks.

Building a network extends beyond socializing with friends and acquaintances, and it often involves active participation in organized networking events. In a new relationship, it is better to give value to get value; value is a two-way game.

8.4 Illustrate the benefits of virtual networking.

Social media sites and other forms of virtual networking provide additional channels to meet or interact with stakeholders from the world over. Entrepreneurs have a number of different virtual communities in which they can participate, with many communities offering access to a specific subset of interests in entrepreneurship. Common social media platforms like Facebook also contain groups that are similar to online entrepreneurship communities.

8.5 Explain how networking can help to build the founding team.

One of the most valuable things an entrepreneur can do is connect with individuals who serve as great complements on a founding team. Research even suggests that team-started ventures are more successful than solo-founded ventures. Networking skills can often be relied on as the means to that end.

Bonds   182

Bridges   182

Cognitive comprehensiveness   201

Founding team   195

Groupthink   201

Heterogeneous team   201

Homogenous team   201

Impression management   183

Linkages   182

Self-selected stakeholders   185

Social capital   179

Jeff Goudie, AmeriCan Packaging

Jeff Goudie, cites his network as his most important resource when he launched a manufacturing company in the Dominican Republic. It was also his network that came to his rescue when things got a little murky.

After graduating with an MBA from Babson College in 2014, Jeff wanted to buy a business. At first, he and one of his classmates from Babson, Mike Cassata, wanted to buy a wood recycling factory, given the boom of the recycling industry. When that plan fell through, both Jeff and Mike started to look for jobs. Jeff joined BizCorps, a strategy advisory firm specializing in emerging markets, as a consultant. As part of his job, he had the opportunity to work in Bogotá, Colombia, for 13 months. The experience was fulfilling, fun, and rewarding; however, Jeff still wanted to do something on his own. He reached out to a childhood friend's father, who was an investment banker also looking for business opportunities in manufacturing. Together they identified an attractive opportunity for metal packaging in the Dominican Republic.

He learned that the Dominican Republic was the heart of the cigar industry, with major players such as Cohiba, Macanudo, and Swisher in the same geographic area. The issue, however, was that there were no metal packaging manufacturers in the area to support the cigar producers. "The supply chain for tobacco manufacturing was wide open. Nobody in this hemisphere was doing it!" said Jeff.

Jeff reached out to his network in Miami, his hometown, to understand the cigar manufacturing and packaging industry better. He learned that the entire supply chain for the production of cigars existed in Latin America, except for the metal packaging components. The metal packaging was sourced from China and Switzerland. If metal packaging was sourced in the Dominican Republic, Jeff knew that he could compete with China on price, compete with Switzerland on lead time, and be able to fulfill emergency production requirements and just-in-time inventory needs. Jeff concluded that the market was big enough for him to enter. It also held opportunities to diversify into other industries, such as cosmetics and promotional packaging. With data supporting his analysis, Jeff began to look for a suitable warehouse to set up his metal packaging plant close to tobacco manufacturers in the Dominican Republic.

Setting up an entire plan from scratch would be a big investment, and Jeff was having serious doubts about taking the leap. However, when he went to visit one of the prospective warehouses, all of this changed. Jeff recalled when he visited the warehouse in 2015, "Something just felt right and I ended up signing a 5-year lease to the warehouse immediately without informing my investor!" He then wrote a makeshift business plan to present to his friend's father, who was his main investor, and went on to raise $2 million in capital to set up what was now called AmeriCan Packaging.

What Jeff did not anticipate, however, was the extremely high supplier bargaining power that was a function of the mature metal packaging industry. AmeriCan Packaging needed to have a strong enough offering for the neighboring tobacco companies to switch from their established suppliers to his product, but getting his COGS low enough was proving to be difficult. He had overestimated the willingness of the metal printing suppliers to supply a small player such as AmeriCan. Because they had much bigger scales of operations, they were reluctant to work with smaller quantities of products.

To get started, Jeff needed to get a test batch of metal cans printed. "The quality of printing on tin cans and the color is an important branding component of metal packaging. Cigar companies usually need a proof of color from suppliers like AmeriCan before placing an order," Jeff explained. He was unable to find a good local printer who could match the stringent color quality requirements of the industry. "We had a lot of potential customers interested, but all of them wanted to see printing proofs, and unfortunately none of my suppliers would do so. It was a complete conundrum. These companies were mature, vertically integrated companies owned by oligarchs; they made all the cans for their other companies (beer, canned foods, paint, etc.). They didn't care about printing qualities, and they really didn't care about new customers." Jeff stated. Jeff finally found a good printer in Costa Rica, but he ran into another issue: They wouldn't print samples. In order to get a sample on an offset lithograph line, the set up and clean up time was enormous, so his suppliers said no, no, and no again! He ended up having to gamble. He had to get 20,000 tins printed as samples, as that was the minimum order quantity, only to get the sample rejected again. He was stuck with a massive stock of 20,000 and no customers.

He started to attend industry trade shows, through which he hired a consultant from Barcelona. This consultant brought in a wealth of industry knowledge and soon became indispensable to the success of the company. He reached out to universities to create an internship program for his company and was able to recruit some good talent to build on his know-how. He also leveraged LinkedIn to look for people across the supply chain. He sent more than 100 LinkedIn messages to get some of the industry experts on board as a consultant. Only 10 out of 100 replied, and he was able to hire 1 out of those 10 people. He also reached out to friends, family, professors, and others in his personal network.

Having been unable to get that first order, Jeff realized that for the established cigar industry to accept him, he needed to win their trust, which wasn't easy. Just as all hope was getting lost, the customer who had rejected the 20,000 tins he printed came in, desperate for metal cans. Their Chinese supplier had cancelled their order at the last minute. The company bought every single one of the rejected tins, and they placed an order for 300,000 more, along with an $80,000 deposit. This situation made apparent the value of Jeff's offering to the cigar manufacturer: AmeriCan could fulfill just-in-time and emergency inventory because it was a local manufacturing plant.

Jeff needed to build his reputation in the Dominican Republic, and he decided bringing on a new partner could expedite this, so he sold the majority stock position of AmeriCan to a cigar manufacturer who had a good reputation. This immediately placed AmeriCan in good standing within the industry. AmeriCan was now positioned to take bigger orders and assure people that Jeff would be able to fulfill them. The cigar manufacturer also joined the board of the company as an advisor and mentor and was successful expanding their book of business.

Jeff understood that Latin America–based cigar companies did not like dealing with suppliers from China due to differences in quality and business culture. This meant that strong relationships could be a precursor to business with smaller companies. He realized that he had been making a mistake in trying to get through to bigger companies that were driven by product prices (which were hard to compete on with China). Instead, he focused on the smaller companies that were more relationship driven, something he was good at building.

Just as the business started to grow, Jeff's business partners saw the value of the opportunity in the metal packaging industry, they started asking for more, and the team started to break down. As Jeff recalled, "The relationship soon got messy, and in August 2018 I left the company without being paid my fair share. They also fired my consultant from Barcelona and stopped the internship programs. I didn't have the money or reputation to fight to stay."

However, all the customer relationships that Jeff established were now part of his personal network. Today, he is working for one of his biggest customers from AmeriCan, running a new business unit related to metal packaging! So, the journey continues for Jeff, and his advice is, "Just do it. Even if you don't know how to do something, you can figure it out; nothing is impossible."

Critical Thinking Questions

1. Think about Jeff's journey and identify the opportunities he had to grow his network. Now think about all the opportunities he had to use his network.

2. Identify all the resources Jeff received from his network.

3. Assuming you wanted to, could you do what Jeff did with your current network?

Source: Jeff Goudie (interview with Babson MBA graduate assistant Gaurav Khemka, September 30, 2018)

PART III

Evaluating and Acting on Opportunities

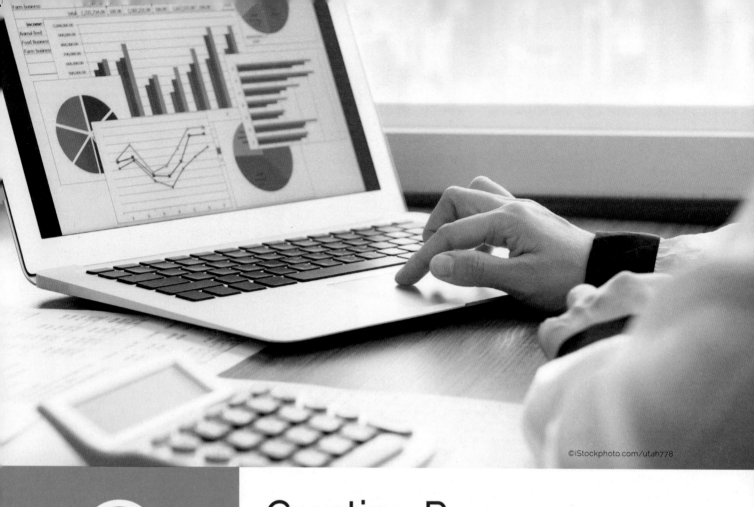

©iStockphoto.com/utah778

9 Creating Revenue Models

"My goal was never to just create a company. A lot of people misinterpret that, as if I don't care about revenue or profit or any of those things. But what not being just a company means to me is not being just that—building something that actually makes a really big change in the world."

—Mark Zuckerberg

Chapter Outline

Learning Objectives

9.1 WHAT IS A REVENUE MODEL?

>> LO 9.1   Define a revenue model and distinguish it from the business model.

Over the course of the previous chapters, we have described numerous enterprises founded by entrepreneurs from all sorts of industries and backgrounds. Diverse though the businesses may appear to be, they all have one very important thing in common: the ability to generate **revenue**, which is the income gained from sales of goods or services.

In Chapter 5, we presented several ways in which entrepreneurs use business models, but business models cannot be complete without an understanding of the underlying revenue model. In other words, how will the business earn revenue, manage costs, and produce profit?

While the terms are sometimes used interchangeably, a *business model* and a *revenue model* are not the same thing. Recall from Chapter 5 that business models fulfill three main purposes: they help entrepreneurs fulfill unmet needs in an existing market, deliver existing products and services to existing customers with unique differentiation, and serve customers in new markets. In other words, a business model describes how a venture will create, deliver, and capture value.

A **revenue model** is a key component of the business model; it identifies how the company will earn revenue and generate profits. In other words, it explains how entrepreneurs will make money and capture value from delivering on the customer value proposition (CVP) that is outlined as part of their business model. As an entrepreneur, if you have a clear strategy for generating revenue from your business, you will have a better chance of surviving. Part of this strategy is asking a few simple questions:

- How much are my customers willing to pay?

- How many customers do I need?

- How much revenue can be generated through sales?

- If I have more than one revenue stream, how much does each stream contribute to the total?

Over the course of her career, Kathey Porter, featured in Entrepreneurship in Action, used different types of revenue models for each of her businesses. In the next section, we will take a look at the different types of revenue models that are available to the startup entrepreneur.

Revenue: the income gained from sales of goods or services.

Revenue model: a key component of the business model that identifies how the company will earn income and make profits.

Master the content at **edge.sagepub.com/ neckentrepreneurship2e**

Kathey Porter, Porter Brown Associates

Photo courtesy of Kathey Porter

Kathey Porter, president and founder of Porter Brown Associates

Kathey Porter is a consultant, author, college educator, and podcaster who focuses on entrepreneurs and small-business owners. But she started in the corporate world as a marketing executive for Revlon. Using her corporate experience, she later began helping small businesses become suppliers for larger companies. She believes the key to small-business growth is to have large companies as customers, often called a B2B (business to business) model.

As president and founder of Porter Brown Associates, Kathey operates a profitable and growing consulting enterprise. She and her team service the U.S. federal government, corporations, and small businesses. They train vendors to work with the federal government, help corporations connect and partner with smaller businesses, and act as a strategy consultant to those small businesses so they can scale. According to Kathey, their mission is quite simple: "We provide tools for our clients to be successful."

Kathey's road to successfully founding and operating Porter Brown Associates included more than just a stint in corporate America. She always maintained some form of side business but held off plunging 100% into entrepreneurship until her daughter was in college. "Timing is just as important as money," says Kathey. "The fastest way to go out of business is to take on more than you can handle. Entrepreneurs tend to want to take on everything, but only say yes if it complements your skillset. You can ruin yourself, your name, and your reputation by taking on more than you can handle."

Kathey is keenly aware that skills gaps and mismanagement of priorities can drive entrepreneurs to failure. She recalls an early failure when she opened and ran a seasonal franchise retail business in a mall. Due to miscommunication with the franchisor over the allocation of revenues, the store ran into financial hardship and had to file for bankruptcy. Another time, she passed on an offer by an investor to start a hair care line and instead opted to launch a children's bedding line. After months of preparing and finding a manufacturer in China, Kathey realized the bedding market was tough, if not one of the toughest, to penetrate, and she ended up missing out on a lot of upside in the hair care market. With these setbacks, she says, "At that time, I was embarrassed and ashamed, but I see now that it set me up for success with the consultancy. The lessons I learned now help me counsel other small-business owners."

Kathey says her skillset in entrepreneurship has been developed and built over time. "Just like doctors, lawyers, and others, it takes practice."

Critical Thinking Questions

1. Kathey was a franchise owner, created a bedding line, and is now a consultant. Can you identify the revenue model she used for each?

2. Describe Kathey's path to successful business ownership. Why was corporate experience useful to her?

3. If you started a business using a professional revenue model, what service would you offer? ●

Source: Kathey Porter (interview with the author, December 2018)

9.2 DIFFERENT TYPES OF REVENUE MODELS

>> **LO 9.2**   **Illustrate the 10 most popular revenue models being used by entrepreneurs.**

As we have discussed, different types of revenue models have different revenue streams. Some companies operate using one primary revenue model while others use a combination of models.[1] Each type determines different ways in which revenue is generated, which also affects who your customers will be. For example, a retailer that generates revenue through online sales tends to attract the type of customers who prefer shopping from their computers or mobile devices rather than traveling to the local mall. Let's take a look at 10 main types of revenue models. Remember: The customer is not always your end user!

Unit Sales Revenue Model

The **unit sales revenue model** measures the amount of revenue generated by the number of items (units) sold by a company. Typically, retail businesses rely on the unit sales revenue model by selling products or service directly to consumers, whether face-to-face or online. The idea is that you earn revenue when you sell the product or service to the end user. There are two different types of unit sales: physical goods, which include clothing, food and beverages, housewares and hardware, furniture, cars, and so forth; and intangibles, which are often digital products such as music sold through iTunes or games and apps sold to smartphones and tablets. Software support may also be unit priced, meaning that customers pay by the minute or by the hour.

Another variation of the unit sales revenue model is called the razor-and-razor-blade model. This phrase was coined by Gillette, which generates huge revenue from offering a physical product like razors at no or low cost to encourage sales of the more expensive razor blades (see Figure 9.1). This has also become known as the printers-and-ink model, which most of us have encountered: The printer is sold at a low cost, but the ink or toner cartridges are priced much higher, generating ongoing revenue for the printer manufacturer. Similarly, Sony and Microsoft discount their video game consoles, but the losses incurred are more than covered by the sales of the games themselves.[2]

Unit sales revenue model: generating revenue by the number of items (units) sold by a company.

Advertising Revenue Model

The **advertising revenue model** relies on the amount of revenue gained through advertising products and services. Advertising has been around for a long time, as has this revenue model: A century ago, magazines and newspapers accepted advertisements and charged by the space or by the word, and early radio and television charged by the minute or second to broadcast ads. Today the ad revenue model has evolved from its traditional format to encompass the digital world.

Meaningful advertising revenue generated in the digital world is dependent on attracting traffic or developing a dominant niche. For example, Google AdWords is not only Google's main advertising product but also its main source of revenue. The AdWords service is a type of advertising revenue model called cost-per-click (CPC), which charges

Advertising revenue model: generating revenue by advertising products and services.

FIGURE 9.1

The Razor-and-Razor-Blade Model

a

b

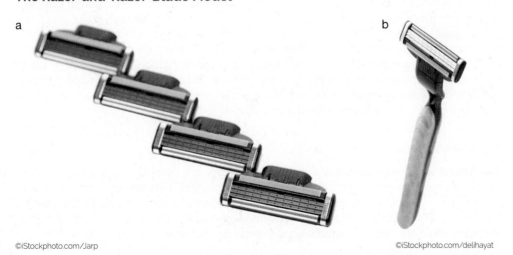

the advertiser a fee every time a user clicks on the ad. The model is intended to attract traffic to the advertiser's business while generating income for providing the AdWords service. AdWords also includes the cost-per-action (CPA) advertising model, whereby advertisers pay only when the click converts to an actual sale of a product or service. Google is an example of a business that has developed a niche by offering this form of advertising to people running businesses all over the world.

Another form of online advertising is called promoted content (also known as "sponsored" or "suggested" content), which works by having ads appear in the flow of the content that the users are reading. Often, these ads are blended in so neatly to the content that users may not even realize that they are ads. But Google isn't the only digital company with an advertising product. In 2018, Amazon became the third biggest online advertising platform behind Facebook and Google.[3] Many types of businesses use digital platforms such as Twitter, Facebook, Instagram, LinkedIn, Pinterest, Snapchat, and Yelp to publish paid ads to promote their services. For example, hand-dyed yarn startup Expression Fiber Arts uses Facebook to advertise by offering free products and downloads, discounts, and coupons. This advertising strategy has earned the company more than $1 million in annual sales over a 2-year period.[4]

Data Revenue Model

Data revenue model: generating revenue by selling high-quality, exclusive, valuable information to other parties.

Companies use the **data revenue model** when they generate revenue by selling high-quality, exclusive, valuable information to other parties. There are more than 100 data brokers operating in the United States that buy and sell third-party data. Some of these data are sold to small organizations that help landlords research potential tenants, but a large portion of it is sold to people search organizations like Spokeo, Zoominfo, PeopleSmart, Intelius, and more.[5] Data brokers tend to collect third-party information from people with whom they have no relationship, while tech giants like Facebook, Google, and Amazon collect enormous amounts of detailed data directly from their users. In 2018, Facebook came under fire for allowing British political consulting firm Cambridge Analytica to harvest the personal data of millions of users without their consent and use it for political purposes.[6] As a consequence, the industry is under pressure to evolve and balance the value of data with the privacy of its users.

Intermediation Revenue Model

Intermediation revenue model: the different methods by which third parties such as brokers (or "middlemen") can generate money.

Brokers: the people who organize transactions between buyers and sellers.

The **intermediation revenue model** describes the different methods by which third parties, such as brokers (or "middlemen"), can generate money. **Brokers** are people who organize transactions between buyers and sellers. These "middlemen" play important roles in connecting people to different services. For example, eBay acts as an auction broker as it manages the transaction between seller and buyer and generates revenue by charging a listing fee plus commission on a sale. Other common examples of intermediaries include real estate brokers who take a percentage commission each time they match a buyer and seller and credit card companies that earn revenue through the sales transaction process.

In recent years, various entrepreneurial ventures have emerged to put a new creative spin on the role of the middleman, in an effort to connect people with services in a more efficient and less expensive way. Well-known examples include Airbnb, which offers short-term accommodation that private homeowners rent out to visitors, usually tourists, at a fraction of the price of hotels, and Uber, which connects customers with drivers to provide a faster, more efficient ride-sharing service.

Licensing Revenue Model

Licensing revenue model: earning revenue by giving permission to other parties to use protected intellectual property (patents, copyrights, trademarks) in exchange for fees.

The **licensing revenue model** is a way of earning revenue by giving permission to other parties to use protected intellectual property (copyrights, patents, and trademarks) in exchange for fees. We will explore intellectual property in more detail in Chapter 14. In the technology industry, technological innovations are licensed to other users. For example, when we use our personal computers, the software is under license from the developer of that software.

Technological innovations are often sold to larger companies that have the financial and technical expertise to maximize their potential. Take apps, for instance. Many people design iPhone apps and then license them to Apple, which has the capability to market them to a wider audience. However, licensing is not just limited to technology companies. Stephen Key, cofounder of licensing company inventRight, began by licensing his ideas for novelty gifts to specialty items companies, including bathtub toys, puppets, and a red plastic arrow emblazoned with the words, "Straight from my heart."[7]

Music-streaming app Spotify generates revenue from subscriptions, licensing, and on-screen advertising.

Franchising Revenue Model

The **franchising revenue model** describes the process whereby the owner of an existing business (known as the franchisor) sells the rights to another party (known as a franchisee) to trade under the name of that business. The franchisor helps the franchisee by providing support in marketing, operations, and financing, and in return, the franchisee pays the franchisor royalties based on an agreed percentage of sales.

In Chapter 1, we explained the concept of franchising and how it can be a beneficial way for entrepreneurs to get a head start in launching their own businesses. By following an existing business model, entrepreneurs do not have to spend the same amount of time on marketing, building the brand, developing processes, and sourcing product.

Familiar franchises such as Anytime Fitness, Hampton Inns, Pizza Hut, Subway, KFC, and Supercuts regularly appear on lists of the top 500 franchises in the United States; however, some lesser-known (and somewhat quirky) franchises are also causing a bit of a stir. The Christmas Décor seasonal franchise is run by professional decorators who take the burden from homeowners by putting up Christmas decorations on their behalf. Or what about pooper scooper services franchise DoodyCalls? This franchise scoops 10 million poops from backyards and apartment complexes every year.[8]

Franchising revenue model: earning revenue by selling franchises of an existing business to allow another party to trade under the name of that business.

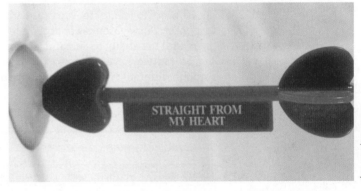

inventRight's novelty toy arrow

Source: https://www.inventright.com/index.php?option=com_content&view=article&id=107

Subscription Revenue Model

The **subscription revenue model** involves charging customers to gain continuous access to a product or service. This type of model has been traditionally applied to magazines and newspapers that charge customers a subscription fee to receive each issue of the publication. Today, a growing number of startup companies also use the subscription revenue model. For example, Blue Apron and Home Chef earn revenue by providing subscribers with a complete set of ingredients to make a meal at home; Birchbox delivers monthly beauty products to subscribers; and Barkbox charges a subscription fee to deliver a monthly box of doggy treats to dog lovers. Another type of subscription model is applied to user communities such as Angie's List, where members pay for access to a network of reviews on local businesses.

Subscription revenue model: charging customers to gain continuous access to a product or service.

Professional Revenue Model

The **professional revenue model** provides professional services on a time and materials contract. For example, consultants, lawyers, and accountants often charge by the hour for their services. Websites like Get a Freelancer, PeoplePerHour, and Elance also use this model by allowing freelancers to charge a fixed fee for projects posted online by other companies.

Professional revenue model: earning revenue by providing professional services on a time and materials contract.

Dog waste service DoodyCalls uses a franchising revenue model.

Source: https://smallbiztrends.com/2017/09/weird-franchises.html

Utility and usage revenue model: a pay-as-you-go model that charges customers fees on the basis of how often goods or services are used.

Freemium revenue model: mixing free (mainly web-based) basic services with premium or upgraded services.

Utility and Usage Revenue Model

The **utility and usage revenue model** charges customers fees on the basis of how often goods or services are used. This is also known as a pay-as-you-go model. Some mobile phone carriers use this model by charging users a fee for the number of minutes used on calls or for the volume of text messages.[9] The greater the number of minutes or volume of texts, the higher the payment. Hotels also use this model by charging customers by the night. Car rental companies also generate revenue through this model by charging per unit of time. For example, Avis and Hertz rent cars on a daily or weekly basis, while Zipcar rents cars by the hour, allowing multiple customers to use the same car at different times on the same day.[10]

Freemium Revenue Model

The **freemium revenue model** involves mixing free (mainly web-based) basic services with premium or upgraded services. In this model, businesses create at least two versions or tiers of products or services. The company gives away the low-end version of the service for free. The free "basic" version usually comes with limits on usage and functionality. The company also creates and sells higher-end versions that offer more functionality and performance. The business networking site LinkedIn gives members free access to build a profile and maintain a professional network. It charges a fee for its premium service, which further benefits job seekers and recruiters with added functions such as search filtering, sending personalized messages, and tracking visits to one's profile. Similarly, online tool SurveyMonkey allows users to create free surveys with up to 10 questions, with an allowance of up to 100 responses. SurveyMonkey charges a fee to upgrade to its premium service, which provides users with the ability to customize their survey designs and receive unlimited responses.[11]

So far, we have explored the typical ways in which businesses generate revenue through different types of revenue models. These are summarized in Table 9.1.

TABLE 9.1

Ten Types of Revenue Models

Unit Sales	The amount of revenue generated by the number of items (units) sold by a company
Advertising	The amount of revenue gained through advertising products and services
Data	The amount of revenue generated by selling high-quality, exclusive, valuable information to other parties
Intermediation	The amount of revenue generated by third parties
Licensing	The amount of revenue generated by giving permission to other parties to use protected intellectual property (patents, copyrights, trademarks) in exchange for fees
Franchising	The process whereby franchises are sold by an existing business to allow another party to trade under the name of that business
Subscription	The amount of revenue generated by charging customers payment to gain continuous access to a product or service
Professional	The amount of revenue generated by providing professional services on a time and materials contract
Utility and Usage	The amount of revenue generated by charging customers fees on the basis of how often goods or services are used
Freemium	The amount of revenue gained by mixing free (mainly web-based) basic services with premium or upgraded services

Revenue Model Pivot Practice

Your entire business can pivot if your revenue model changes. Not all revenue models fit for all business types, but it can be fun to experiment with different models just to see the possibilities. Refer to Table 9.1 and our discussion on the 10 types of revenue models. Let's say we had an idea for a new app that kept track of all the food in your house or apartment. At any given time, you could open the app and see the food inventory in your refrigerator, freezer, and pantry. The app would tell you when food was expired and could even offer recipes that use the food you have on hand. The "unit sales" revenue model would be to sell the app in the app store for $5.99. If we changed to an "advertising" revenue model, we would likely let people download the app for free and earn revenue through the sales of advertising. Potential advertisers could be grocery stores, food TV networks, publishers of food books or magazines, etc. If we then changed to a "professional" revenue model, our app may not exist at all. We may simply charge people to let us enter their homes on a weekly basis and do the inventory for them as well as cook meals. Now, the professional model may not make sense, but bringing a business through each revenue model may uncover new opportunities. What if we used a "subscription" revenue

model for the food inventory app? What would this look like? Well, maybe the original concept of the inventory app would go away, but we could offer a delivery service that would deliver the ingredients for you to cook your own meal at home. No inventory and no waste! Sound familiar? Take a look at businesses that have been started on the concept of food kits: Blue Apron, Home Chef, HelloFresh, Sun Basket, and Purple Carrot, just to name a few.

For this Mindshift, take the product or service you are working on and apply the 10 revenue models in Table 9.1 to your idea. Yes, some of them may not make sense, but many of them will. Think creatively!

Critical Thinking Questions

1. Did you notice that when you change the revenue model the customer often changes as well?

2. Did you find a revenue model that works better for your idea than your original model?

3. Did your idea change dramatically in some models versus others? Which ones and how? ●

In the next section, we take a closer look at how some companies have generated revenue by profiting from "free."

9.3 GENERATING REVENUE FROM "FREE"

>> LO 9.3   Explain how companies generate revenue by profiting from "free."

Many of us like getting a bargain, but most of us love the idea of getting something for free. But as an entrepreneur running your own business, how comfortable would you feel giving away your products and services for nothing? Unlikely as it may sound, the freemium revenue model, which offers a product or service for zero cost, is becoming more popular as a means of encouraging widespread customer adoption (see Figure 9.2).[12]

Skype is an example of a freemium model that provides the functionality to make free calls, which are fully routed through the Internet. Because of its lack of infrastructure, the costs of running Skype are minimal. It earns its revenue by charging for Skypeout, a premium service that charges users low rates for calling landlines and cell phones. In 2011, Skype was acquired by Microsoft for $8.5 billion.

The free newspaper *Metro* is another great example of a business that gives away a free product yet still makes huge profits. The *Metro* was first circulated in Stockholm, Sweden, before being made available in dozens of cities all over the world. In Britain in particular, the *Metro* has become the nation's most profitable newspaper.[13] But how does the *Metro* team make money from giving away free newspapers?

First, its readership is wealthy commuters, on average around 37 years old (described as "urbanites")—a demographic that attracts advertisers such as large supermarket chains and businesses that pay generously to reach this target audience. The *Metro* is also paid to feature major events such as Wimbledon tennis and other annual occasions. Second, the *Metro* keeps its editorial costs low by keeping its content short, punchy, and easy to read—just engaging enough for a quick 20-minute read on the train or bus to or from

How to Make an Ad

Peter Horree/Alamy Stock Photo

Red Bull paid $13 million to settle a false advertising lawsuit for its slogan, "Red Bull gives you wings."

Even if an entrepreneur does not choose an ad-based revenue model, the world of entrepreneurship is riddled with advertisements. Every new venture needs a certain amount of marketing to bridge the gap between consumer and product or consumer and service. That marketing could be in the form of sales calls, in which some persuasion must be done to pique the interest of consumers.

The inevitable ethical issue of truthfulness comes as a natural result of advertisements. Can an advertisement stretch the truth? Could it be ethical to try to convince people to buy a product that they don't need?

The Federal Trade Commission has banned any advertising that is untruthful, misleading, and unfair. However, there is an ethical gray area, which stretches beyond the prosecution of

the law. A slight exaggeration will rarely draw the ire of the law but could bring the dissatisfaction of a customer.

For the most part, consumers demand a certain level of accountability in advertising, and there are official organizations in a number of countries that vet advertisements for truthfulness. Additionally, consumers, themselves, have a tendency to respond negatively to advertisements that feel misleading, and they have developed the ability to filter out traditionally seductive advertising.

Nonetheless, the question will inevitably arise of how to market a product or service to create revenue. Entrepreneurs could find a hazardous substance in their product and choose to market their product despite the public health issue. Eventually, though, the desire for accountability from consumers tends to bring those hazardous substances to light.

Critical Thinking Questions

1. Could an advertisement be legal, yet unethical?

2. How much accountability is demanded of advertisements in the modern economy?

3. Does truthfulness matter in issues of business? ●

Sources:

Benge, V. A. (n.d.). The federal truth in advertising law. *AZCentral.* Retrieved from https://yourbusiness.azcentral.com/federal-truth-advertising-law-7108.html

Federal Trade Commission. (n.d.). Truth in advertising. *FTC.gov.* Retrieved from https://www.ftc.gov/news-events/media-resources/truth-advertising

LaMarco, N. (2018, December 3). Negative effects of false advertising. *Houston Chronicle.* Retrieved from https://smallbusiness.chron.com/negative-effects-false-advertising-25679.html

FIGURE 9.2

Freemium

©iStockphoto.com/venimo

work. Finally, it has developed its own distribution network by controlling news racks in train and bus stations where commuters can help themselves to the free publication. However, making "free" work financially is not without its risks. Obviously, if you are giving away something for nothing, you need to make sure you are still earning substantial revenues. The key to a sustainable revenue model involving "free" is earning enough money on some part of the business to pay for the costs of supporting the free side of the business.

Let's look at the two types of free financial models.

Free communication and video chat service, Skype

Direct Cross-Subsidies

Direct cross-subsidies refers to pricing a product or service above its market value to pay for the loss of giving away a product or service for free or below its market value. For example, cell phone companies lose money by giving away the phone handsets for free, but then they cover the loss by charging monthly service fees.[14] Similarly, some airlines advertise amazingly low fares, but then add fees for amenities like checked bags, additional legroom, or the ability to choose one's seat. Hotels may offer a low nightly rate but then add a mandatory "resort fee"—even if the guest doesn't use any of the hotel's "resort" facilities.

Cross-subsidization attracts customers by eliminating, or reducing, the up-front cost of a product or service. It then makes up the loss with subsequent charges, which the company expects customers to be willing to pay because they are pleased with the product or service and don't want to go through the hassle of switching. The added business gained by attracting customers with the below-market price generates more revenues for the organization through the cross-subsidy fees. Table 9.2 lists several ways of implementing direct cross-subsidies.

Direct cross-subsidies: pricing a product or service above its market value to pay for the loss of giving away a product or service for free or below its market value.

TABLE 9.2

Ideas for Direct Cross-Subsidies

• Give away services, sell products
• Give away products, sell services
• Give away software, sell hardware
• Give away hardware, sell software
• Give away cell phones, sell minutes of talk time
• Give away talk time, sell cell phones
• Give away the show, sell the drinks
• Give away the drinks, sell the show

Multiparty Markets

A **multiparty business** involves giving a product or service to one party for free, but charging the other party or parties (see Table 9.3). The classic example of a multiparty market is the ad-supported free content model so common on the Internet: Consumers get access to content for free while advertisers pay for access. Similarly, some online dating services allow women to enroll for free while men pay substantial charges to participate. Other examples include allowing job seekers to post résumés for free while charging employers for posting jobs, or giving children free admission while charging adults.

Multiparty business: giving one party a product or service free, but charging the other party (or parties).

TABLE 9.3

Ideas for Multiparty Markets

IDEA	EXAMPLE
Give away scientific articles, charge authors to publish them	Public Library of Science
Give away document readers, sell document writers	Adobe
Give away listings, sell premium search	Match.com
Sell listings, give away search	Craigslist New York Housing
Give away travel services, get a cut of rental car and hotel reservations	Travelocity
Give away house listings, sell mortgages	Zillow
Give away content, sell stuff	Slashdot/ThinkGeek
Give away résumé listings, charge for power search	LinkedIn

Source: Anderson, C. (2009). *Free: The future of a radical price.* New York, NY: Hyperion.

The challenge for the multiparty market model is to prevent costly overuse by those who get the service for free, as well as making the business valuable enough to the party that does pay.

Financially, the freemium model is often a viable option for web-based companies because of the low marginal cost of providing the service for free users: Online storage and bandwidth are cheap. However, companies running freemium models need to be constantly focused on the average cost of running the service for free users, as well as the rates at which free users convert to paying users. If the costs of supporting free customers grows too high or the number of paying customers is too low, the freemium business model will not work. Table 9.4 gives examples of some freemium ideas.

TABLE 9.4

Freemium Ideas

IDEA	EXAMPLE
Give away basic information, sell richer information in easier-to-use form	BoxOfficeMojo
Give away federal income tax software, sell state income tax software	TurboTax
Give away online games, charge a subscription to do more in a game	Club Penguin
Give away computer-to-computer calls, sell computer-to-telephone calls	Skype
Give away free photo-sharing services, charge for additional storage space	Flickr

Source: Anderson, C. (2009). *Free: The future of a radical price.* New York, NY: Hyperion.

9.4 REVENUE AND COST DRIVERS

>> **LO 9.4**   **Identify the drivers that affect revenue as well as cost.**

Now that we have explored the freemium model, let's take a look at how companies drive revenue.[15] Revenue models influence who your customers are and how you reach them. Although choosing and establishing your revenue model is an important step, it is equally important to have a deep understanding of what is driving both your revenue and your cost, in order to generate as much value (profit) as possible for your company.

Revenue Drivers

It's tempting to believe that merely selling products or services will make you money, but more factors must be taken into consideration. Drawing from the information we have provided so far in this chapter, let's apply some key revenue drivers to the idea for a new funky coffee shop. The coffee shop provides unlimited coffee for free but charges a per-minute flat fee for the amount of time your customers spend in the café.[16]

As illustrated in Figure 9.3, the first key revenue driver is your *customers*. How many customers will come into your coffee shop? How much are they willing to pay to stay? How will you attract customers to your location?

The second key driver is *frequency*. How often will your customers come into your coffee shop? What incentives can you offer to keep them coming back?

The third driver is *selling process*. How much time will you be able to sell? What kind of upselling or cross-selling opportunities can you find? For example, you might add products such as snacks to sell alongside the unlimited free coffee to generate more revenue.

The fourth driver is *price*. If you think your price per minute should be higher than what your competitors charge, what are the factors that increase the value of your product? If you raise or lower prices, what will be the impact on your customer base?[17]

But how do you determine your revenue drivers when your business hasn't even begun yet? By getting out of the building! Actively testing your assumptions and hypotheses is the best way of figuring out the underlying factors that will drive revenue for your business.

For example, let's take a look at the first key revenue driver: your customers. You might be able to sketch a brief outline of the number of customers you think will come to your coffee shop, but how do you get a more accurate estimate? You may think that customers will be attracted to your coffee shop because it is unique and trendy, but no matter how great you think your coffee shop is, people won't come if it's in the wrong location. A coffee shop situated on the outskirts of town, with very little around it, is not conducive to attracting foot traffic. Ideally, you want your coffee shop to be in a location with a high density of shoppers, which means city centers and shopping malls. If your target customer base is students, then you would want to be close to a university campus.

FIGURE 9.3

Four Key Revenue Drivers

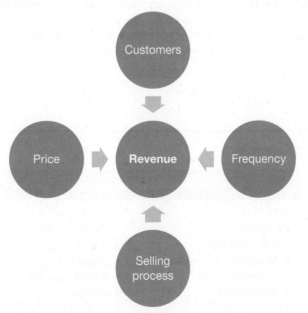

For more details about revenue drivers, see Supplement A: Financial Statements and Projections for Startups.

Renting a retail space in these shopping districts is expensive, so you need to be sure that enough people will be attracted to your coffee shop to walk in and pay to spend time there on a regular basis. How do you justify paying high rent before you even open for business?

One of the best ways to scout suitable locations for your coffee shop and determine the number of customers that might potentially buy from you is to go to your local shopping mall and watch customers as they go in and out of different coffee shops. Do this on different days, and at different times of day. Record the busy and slow periods. This will give you a better idea of the volume of customers you might expect to walk into your coffee shop and therefore the revenue you can expect to get. This, in turn, will enable you to determine whether the volume of traffic will justify the expense of the high rent you will need to pay for an advantageous location.

Cost Drivers

Understanding the factors that drive costs are just as important as your key revenue drivers.

When it comes to cost drivers, two different types of costs should be taken into consideration: **cost of goods sold (COGS)** and operating expenses. COGS and operating expenses are both types of expenses, but there are some differences between them.

Cost of goods sold (COGS): the direct cost of producing a product.

Cost of Goods Sold (COGS)

COGS occur when a sale takes place. For example, with regard to a T-shirt store, the cost is in how much money it takes to produce each T-shirt: the material, the design, the manufacturing, the packaging, and so on. Once you know how much goes into producing your T-shirts, you can think about ways to reduce costs, if you need to. For example, you might find a lower-cost manufacturer, or use less expensive material, or even negotiate with young artists to see if they can provide their designs at a lower cost. Lowering the COGS means you could potentially sell your T-shirts at a lower price to your customers.

However, there also needs to be a balance between reducing your costs and satisfying your customer. In other words, you would need to ensure that you are not devaluing your product to the extent that it would reduce your customers' willingness to buy it at all. For example, if your customers are attracted to your T-shirts because of their great quality, then it would be unwise to use cheaper material to save costs. If you can get the balance right, you can use the savings you make to invest in other areas, such as marketing or reducing debt.

Operating expenses: the costs of running your business, including your rent, utilities, administration, marketing/advertising, employee salaries, and so on.

Operating Expenses

Operating expenses are the costs of running your business, including your rent, utilities, administration, marketing/advertising, employee salaries, and so forth (see Figure 9.4). These kinds of expenses are more difficult to reduce. Cutting operating expenses can yield beneficial short-term gains, but it does not always work in the long term—for reasons we explore next.

FIGURE 9.4

Retail Operating Expenses

Operating Expenses

- Rent
- Utilities
- Administration
- Marketing/Advertising
- Salaries
- Accounting
- Insurance
- Transportation
- Taxes
- Legal Fees
- Office Supplies
- Benefits

Imagine that you have a retail store and wish to cut operating expenses. If you move your store to a cheaper but less popular location to save on rent, you will save more money. However, over time you might lose out on revenue because the new location might not attract as many customers—or the right kind of customers—compared to the more expensive location. Similarly, you will save costs if you cut out advertising and marketing expenses, but as sales depend on marketing, in the long term, you will lose customer awareness. When people don't know about your store, or start forgetting about it, your sales will suffer.

Another way to decrease operating costs is to reduce employee salaries or reduce the number of employees altogether, which has an immediate positive effect on the bottom line. However, it also might damage customer relationships if there aren't enough skilled, knowledgeable staff to help drive sales. Striking the right balance in the areas of COGS and operating expenses can be tricky, but if you know your business inside out, it becomes more manageable over time. Covering your expenses depends on sales of your product and service, and successful sales require a carefully constructed pricing strategy.

Income Statement

When your company is finally up and running, you will need some financial tools to help you measure the revenue generated and your company's profitability. The **income statement** (or **profit and loss statement**) is a financial report that shows revenue, expenses, and profit for a period of time, typically a month, quarter, or year. It subtracts the COGS and expenses (administrative, marketing, research, and other operating expenses) from the total revenue to give you a net income figure, which will be either a profit or a loss. Furthermore, every entrepreneur needs to develop a pro-forma income statement to estimate the impact of revenue and expense on the profit of the venture. While the income statement is based on measuring financial activities on a monthly or annual basis, the pro forma income statement is a projection or estimate of what the company could potentially do (see Supplement A: Financial Statements and Projections for Startups).

The income statement also reflects depreciation and amortization of your company's assets. Depreciation really means the cost of wear and tear on your physical assets such as machinery, equipment, and the building in which you operate. When you purchase an asset that has a useful life of more than 1 year, you will not include the entire cost of that asset on the income statement in the year that it is purchased. Instead, you are able to spread the cost of that asset over a predetermined period of time; therefore, you record only a portion of the cost each year until the asset is fully depreciated. Amortization works similarly to depreciation; the main difference is that amortization relates to intangible assets such as patents, trademarks, copyrights, and business methodologies. Amortization matches the useful life of an intangible asset with the revenue it generates. A sample income statement is illustrated in Figure 9.5.

Income statement (or profit and loss statement): a financial report that shows revenue, expenses, and profit for a period of time, typically a month, quarter, or year.

FIGURE 9.5

Sample Income Statement

Revenue	$200,000
(-) Cost of Goods	$100,000
Gross Profit	$100,000
(-) Sales, General and Administrative	$50,000
(-) Marketing	$5,000
(-) Research and Development	$2,000
(-) Depreciation and Amortization	$2,000
Operating Profit	$41,000
(-) Interest Expense	$1,230
(-) Taxes	$8,500
Net Income	$31,270

The Dark Side of Entrepreneurship

Entrepreneurship can be both productive and unproductive in an economy. Productive motives are those that benefit society, while unproductive motives are those that can do more harm than good. Generally, entrepreneurship focuses on positive outcomes such as job creation, economic growth, and technological progress. However, there is a darker side of entrepreneurship that can be unproductive. Unproductive entrepreneurs have been referred to as parasites that can damage the economy.

Researchers Hmieleski and Lerner wanted to study dark personality characteristics of individuals *intending* to start a business and their *motives* (productive or unproductive) for doing so. They looked at what psychologists refer to as the dark triad: narcissism, psychopathy, and Machiavellianism. *Narcissim* relates to one's self-centeredness and the need for attention and admiration from others. Those that are high in narcissism "are superior and too important to be bothered by others' needs." *Psychopathic* people demonstrate little, if any, empathy. Interestingly, those high in psychopathy do very well under stressful and uncertain conditions. Yet, they have been described as "insensitive to the needs of others and lack remorse." *Machiavellianism* relates to the need for money, power, and competition, and these types are likely to engage in deviant behaviors.

Next, Hmieleski and Lerner identified potential productive and unproductive motives for wanting to start a business.

Productive Entrepreneurial Motives

- Generate value for society
- Produce products/services that enrich the lives of people
- Develop a culture in which its employees value their work
- Be admired for the value that it adds to the community
- Attract employees who value the mission of the company as though it were their own

Unproductive Entrepreneurial Motives

- Achieve financial success, even if it is a little destructive to society
- Maximize profits, even at the cost of employees' well-being
- Grow quickly, even if it means sacrificing quality
- Earn financial profit at all costs
- Outsource work to reduce costs as much as possible

The sample included 508 undergraduate and 234 graduate students at U.S. business schools because the researchers wanted to study individuals who *intended* to start a business rather than entrepreneurs who had already started a business. Hmieleski and Lerner had two questions they wanted to answer with their data:

1. Are narcissism, psychopathy, and Machiavellianism positively associated with a person's intention to start a business?

2. How do narcissism, psychopathy, and Machiavellianism relate to motives for starting a business? Are the motives productive or unproductive?

For Question 1, researchers found that for both undergraduate and graduate students, the higher the narcissism the more likely the student was intending to start a business. When it came to psychopathy and Machiavellianism, there were no significant conclusions. Those dark personality characteristics didn't impact intention to start a business. However, narcissism played a strong role in predicting who intended to become an entrepreneur.

When examining entrepreneurial motives (Question 2), it was found that students with strong intentions to start a business had unproductive motives if they scored high on psychopathy and Machiavellianism. Conversely, students with strong intentions to start a business had productive motives if they demonstrated lower levels of psychopathy and Machiavellianism. Unlike the MBA sample, narcissistic undergraduates were more likely to have productive entrepreneurial motives. The researchers concluded that undergraduates have a "desire for attention and admiration, considering the social appeal of productive value creation—particularly among idealistic undergraduates who are currently part of a generation that has grown up with models of prosocial-oriented startups being viewed as cool by their peers."

Critical Thinking Questions

1. Can you identify examples of productive and unproductive entrepreneurship in society?

2. As you read this, you might have intentions to start a business someday. What are your motives for doing so?

3. What's your opinion on the researchers' conclusion that this generation of undergraduates wants to be a part of prosocial-oriented startups? ●

Sources:

Baumol, W. J. (1990). Productive, unproductive, and destructive. *Journal of Political Economy, 98*(5), 893–921.

Hmieleski, K. M., & Lerner, D. A. (2016). The dark triad and nascent entrepreneurship: An examination of unproductive versus productive entrepreneurial motives. *Journal of Small Business Management, 54*(S1), 7–32.

The operating profit represents the amount left over from revenue once all costs and expenses are subtracted. The interest expense is a good indicator of the company's debt, as it represents interest due in the period on any borrowed money. Taxes are the last expense item before net income. This line item includes all federal, state, and municipal taxes that are due for the period.

Net income is what is left after all costs, expenses, and taxes have been paid; it shows the company's real bottom line. Over time, you can begin to compare your company's income statements; this helps you chart trends in your company's financial performance. The trends will, in turn, help you to set financial goals and strategies.

9.5 PRICING STRATEGIES

>> **LO 9.5** **Identify different strategies entrepreneurs use when pricing their product or service.**

Startup entrepreneurs often struggle with how much to charge for their products or services. If your price is too high, you might drive customers away, but if your price is too low, then you run the risk of making very little profit. So, where do you begin?[18]

Let's say you want to start an online luxury cupcake business. You plan to make the cupcakes from fresh, natural, organic ingredients, at home with some part-time help from a friend. A courier service will deliver the beautifully packaged and personalized cupcakes up to a distance of 200 miles from your location. Your cupcake business is designed to target events such as weddings, children's parties, and corporate gatherings. If the business takes off, you aim to open a retail space in your local area and hire a couple of employees to help you run the business.

To find out how much to charge, you need to find out the going rate of cupcakes. The best place to begin is to check out your competition. Visit cupcake stores and other online cupcake companies and see how much they charge. Don't be afraid to ask people in the cupcake business direct questions about pricing and running a cupcake business; most people want to help and will be happy to give advice. Besides, making connections in this way may lead to partnerships or collaborations in the future.

In addition, talk to your friends and family to see how much they would pay, or have paid for cupcakes in the past, and ask them to share their experiences of online cupcake companies if they have used them before. You could even send out a survey to all your contacts asking them what price they would be willing to pay for a single delicious cupcake or box of premium cupcakes.

The next step is to think about your customers. What can they afford to pay? For example, you may decide to charge a higher rate for catering corporate events versus providing cupcakes for children's parties.

The key to sustaining a new business is to create consistent revenue streams. Once you have acquired new customers, your goal is to hear from them again and again. For events like weddings and children's parties, this may be difficult as they are typically one-time events. However, these customers may tell their friends how pleased they were with your service, and guests at the events may be impressed with how delicious and beautifully decorated your cupcakes were. Thus, you will rely largely on referrals and word of mouth to get more business in those areas. For corporate events, on the other hand, there are ample opportunities for repeat business. You could approach a corporation and offer a contract agreeing to provide cupcakes for all their corporate events, or a certain number of events per year. This would bring you a steady stream of revenue from a regular client.

In addition, it is helpful to compare yourself to others in the field. Do you have the right credentials to run an online cupcake business? What experience do you have in the

ZUMA Press Inc/Alamy Stock Photo

Gigi Butler built America's most successful cupcake business, with 93 outlets operating in 23 states.

bakery business? What sort of business experience do you have to operate as an online cupcake company? If you have less experience than others, then you might want to consider charging lower prices to win new clients and gain real experience. However, if you have a background in bakery and catering, already have a solid customer base, and have business qualifications to match, then you could feasibly charge higher rates.

Once you have a better idea of your competition, your target market, and how your qualifications measure up against others, it is time to plan your pricing strategy.

Pricing Products and Services

There is no right way to determine your pricing strategy, nor is there any such thing as long-term fixed pricing. As your business evolves, your prices will adjust according to demand. The best way to set a price is to base it on the information you have already gathered.

Several factors might influence your pricing strategy. For example, the positioning and brand of your product or service will affect how much it sells for. Understanding your brand is also very important when defining your business. Start defining your brand by choosing a name, logo, and design for your website. A useful exercise is to think of three to five words to describe your business that sets it apart from other competitors; for example, if very few competitors offer home delivery, you could include this in your brand description: "Luxury cupcakes delivered at home." Once you have defined your brand, you can carry the theme through your packaging, website, marketing materials, and other communications with potential customers.[19]

Using the cupcake example, think about how you are positioning your online cupcake business in the market. As you are promoting your cupcakes as a luxury product, you need to aim for a price that isn't too low. A low price on a luxury product can cause customers to doubt the quality of the item being sold.

Different Types of Pricing Strategies

There are many different pricing strategies used by different companies. Let's take a look at some common pricing strategies (see Figure 9.6).[20]

Competition-Led Pricing

Competition-led pricing: a pricing strategy that matches prices to other businesses selling the same or very similar products and services.

In **competition-led pricing**, you copy the prices suggested by other businesses selling the same or very similar products and services. However, matching a price is not generally enough to encourage customers to buy from you, especially if you're not an

FIGURE 9.6

Pricing Strategies

Source: www.learnmarketing.net

established brand. You need to find other ways to differentiate your product from your competitors to attract more customers.

Customer-Led Pricing

In **customer-led pricing**, you ask customers how much they are willing to pay and then offer your product at that price. This is a technique used by some airlines signed up to the commercial website Priceline, to offer passengers a chance to name their own price for flights. Passengers make bids—however, they don't ultimately control the fares; the airline accepts or rejects each bid depending on how acceptable it is and whether other customers are willing to pay more for the same flight. This "name your own price technique" is a useful way of attracting people to your company, and it still allows you a measure of control over your own pricing.

> **Customer-led pricing:** a pricing strategy that asks customers how much they are willing to pay and then offers the product at that price.

Loss Leader

A **loss leader** is the practice of offering a product or service at a below-cost price in an attempt to attract more customers. This involves giving special discounts and reducing prices. Loss leaders can be an effective way of competing with an established brand offering similar products and services.

Walmart and Amazon are two examples of major companies that adopt the loss leader pricing strategy to compete in the marketplace.

However, there has to be some kind of consistency to raising and lowering prices; for example, a customer who has just bought a product at full price the previous day will not be pleased if that same product is being sold at a deep discount the next day. Therefore, it is important to know how long the lower price can be sustained and to know when to readjust pricing before the business begins to lose money.

> **Loss leader:** a pricing strategy whereby a business offers a product or service at a lower price in an attempt to attract more customers.

Introductory Offer

The idea of the **introductory offer** is to encourage people to try your new product by offering it for free or at a heavily discounted price for a certain number of days or to the first 100 customers. Introductory pricing is generally used for new products or services on the market. For example, San Francisco–based ecommerce business Headsets.com, founded by CEO Mike Faith, offers new products at a lower price to attract a loyal customer base.[21]

> **Introductory offer:** a pricing strategy to encourage people to try a new product by offering it for free or at a heavily discounted price.

Skimming

Skimming is a form of high pricing, generally used for new products or services that face very little or even no competition. If your product is the first on the market, then you can sell it at a higher price and retain the maximum value upfront, until you are forced to gradually reduce your prices when competitors launch rival products. Innovative products like the iPad and Sony PlayStation 3, which were originally priced high when they were launched, are good examples of price skimming.[22]

> **Skimming:** a high pricing strategy, generally used for new products or services that face very little or even no competition.

Psychological Pricing

Customers' perceptions of price points are also important to the sale. **Psychological pricing** is intended to encourage customers to buy based on their belief that the product or service is cheaper than it really is. Flash sales, "buy one get one free," and bundled products are all methods of psychological pricing. In addition, specific prices, such as those ending in $0.99, are popular with customers, as $19.99 is a more appealing figure to most than $20. Odd though it may sound, pricing your product or service one cent lower can make a difference between selling and not selling. McDonald's, Chili's, and KFC are among dozens of fast-food restaurants that use psychological pricing to attract customers.

> **Psychological pricing:** a pricing strategy intended to encourage customers to buy on the basis of their belief that the product or service is cheaper than it really is.

Fair Pricing

Fair pricing is the degree to which both businesses and customers believe that the pricing is reasonable. Having done your financial homework as an entrepreneur, you might

> **Fair pricing:** the degree to which both businesses and customers believe that the pricing is reasonable.

FIGURE 9.7

Bundled Pricing

©iStockphoto.com/Epine_art

think your product or service is priced fairly—but that doesn't mean your customers will. Regardless of how much benefit to the customer or how valuable you think your offering is, there are some customers who are simply unwilling to pay the asking price for items or services if they do not perceive it to be fair. This is where market testing can help to define what people perceive as a fair maximum price versus an unfair price.

Bundled Pricing

Bundled pricing: a pricing strategy whereby companies package a set of goods or services together and then sell them for a lower price than if they were to be sold separately.

A form of psychological pricing, **bundled pricing** is packaging a set of goods or services together; they are then sold for a lower price than if they were to be sold separately (see Figure 9.7). The customers feel they are getting a bargain, and the increased sales generate more profit for the company. Common examples of bundled pricing include fast-food value meals, *prix fixe* meals at restaurants, snack food combos at movie theaters, cell phone packages, and cable TV packages.

Once you have decided which type of pricing is the right one for your business, then it's time to start making some proper calculations.

9.6 CALCULATING PRICE

>> LO 9.6   Explain different methods of calculating price.

Number crunching is not an exact science, but there are a few ways to calculate prices that will help you decide which one is best for your business.[23] The key to pricing is to ensure you make a profit, as well as to create value for your customers.

Break-even analysis can also help set price. Break-even is that point when your revenue equals your costs. Then, anything sold beyond break-even is considered profit.

A quick break-even analysis can help entrepreneurs quickly determine what they need to sell monthly or yearly, and in some cases daily or weekly, to cover the costs of running the business—the cost drivers we have already discussed in this chapter.

Break-even is express both in units and in dollars. For example, you may hear an entrepreneur say that her monthly break-even is 1,000 units. If the selling price of each unit is $20, then the break-even can also be said to be $20,000 (1,000 units x $20 per unit) per month.

Let's start with calculating break-even units using the following formula:

Break-even units = Fixed costs/(sales price per unit – variable cost per unit)

Fixed costs are those costs that stay the same regardless of how much revenue you are generating or how much product you produce. These costs are typically those operating expenses that are incurred outside of actually producing the product, such as rent, salaries, and utilities. Though not always suggested in the accounting textbooks, entrepreneurs should use their total operating costs as their fixed costs because it's closer to reality for a startup.[24]

The sales price per unit is the selling price, such as the $20 in our brief example above. If you have multiple products, you can simply use an average sales price per unit. For example, if you were calculating the sales price per unit for a restaurant, you would use the average sale per person.

Variable cost per unit is the COGS plus any operating expenses that actually go up and down with production of the product. These may include shipping, inventory costs, or sales commissions.

Now let's look at a simple example involving a potential smoothie café. Here's what we know based on research:

- We want to sell smoothies at an average price of $6.50.

- Monthly fixed costs include rent, payroll, advertising, insurance, taxes. These total $6,000 per month.

- The variable expenses include the fruit, milk, yogurt, juice, vegetables, ice—everything that goes into making the smoothie. Here you have to determine the cost of one smoothie. For example:

Fruit: $0.75

Milk: $0.50

Juice: $0.25

Vegetable: $1.00

Cup: $1.00

Ice: $0.10

The total variable cost per one smoothie would be $3.60.

Now we have enough information to calculate break-even units:

BEU = $6000 / ($6.50 – $3.60)

BEU = 2,069

Our smoothie café would have to sell 2,069 smoothies on a monthly basis before we start to become profitable. Now, you have to ask yourself, "Is this possible?" Additionally, you can play with the variables. What if you increased the selling price to $8.00 per smoothie? This would certainly reduce the number of smoothies to break even, but what happens if your competition is selling their smoothies closer to $6.50? You could reduce the variable costs or not include as many ingredients in each smoothie. You could also look to lower some of your fixed costs. Can you find a better location in a lower-rent area? Do you need to hire so many people in the beginning? It's best to put all of these data in an Excel spreadsheet, and you can begin playing around with the numbers. There are also break-even calculators on the Internet that you can use, but we encourage making your own spreadsheet based on your own variable and fixed costs.

Is Value the Same Thing as Price?

PRODUCT	WHAT DO I PAY, OR WHAT WOULD I PAY?	ACTUAL PRICE FOUND ONLINE (OR PRICE RANGE)	PRICE DIFFERENCE
Extra-whitening toothpaste with mouthwash in the paste (average-size tube)			
Artisan, wood-fired pizza with local ingredients (large)			
100% electric car, 4 door			
Bath soap (1 bar)			

Using the chart on this page, identify what you think you pay, or would pay, for the listed items. Then, look up the actual price on the Internet.

Critical Thinking Questions

1. What are the differences between your pricing estimates and the actual pricing? What do you believe is the source of the differences?

2. As a consumer, do you care more about the price of certain items than others? What influences your level of concern about price?

3. In this exercise, did you learn anything that surprised you? ●

Cost-Led Pricing

Cost-led pricing: a pricing strategy that involves calculating all the costs of manufacturing or delivering the product or service, plus all other expenses, and adding an expected profit or margin by predicting your sales volume to get the approximate price.

Cost-led pricing involves calculating all the costs involved in manufacturing or delivering the product or service, plus all other expenses, and adding an expected profit or margin by predicting your sales volume to get the approximate price.

For example, say it costs you a total of $2 to make a cupcake. To cover your costs, you could add a 50% markup, which would mean selling each cupcake at $3, resulting in a profit of $1 per cupcake. However, you would need to make sure that this price was competitive—too low and it will put people off by giving an impression of poor quality; too high and you may be pricing your cupcakes out of the market. You also need to ensure that you will have enough people buying the cupcakes to generate profit for your business.

Target-Return Pricing

Target-return pricing: a pricing method whereby the price is based on the amount of investment you have put into your business.

Target-return pricing involves setting your price based on the amount of investment you have put into your business. Using the cupcake business example again, you can save significant costs by working from home, but you still have expenses from investing in machinery, ingredients, paying a part-time worker, and utility and delivery costs.

Let's assume you have invested $3,000 in startup costs for your business. Your expected sales volume is 10,000 cupcakes per year. This means you need to cover your $3,000 investment from your cupcake sales as well as generate a profit. If your cupcakes sell for $3 each, that means 10,000 cupcakes sold per year will generate $30,000 in gross profit (profit before operating expenses).

However, remember that your cupcakes cost you $2 to produce, which amounts to $20,000 in production costs, leaving you with $10,000. Take away the $3,000 you have invested in the company, and you make a profit of $7,000. This means you make 70 cents profit on each $3 cupcake.

Value-Based Pricing

Value-based pricing involves pricing your product based on how it benefits the customer. Your buyers have a major influence over your pricing strategy. Think about what your product means to your buyers. Is it going to save them money or make them money? Let's say you have created a water softener suitable for homeowners to install. Because hard water is full of minerals that build up in the water lines, forcing appliances to work harder, your water softener guarantees the customer a significant saving in energy bills. On this basis, you could build in a higher price because you can assure your customers that they will make back that money within, say, 2 years of purchasing your water softener.

But what if there is no monetary benefit to your buyers? Certainly your cupcake business will not help your customers save or make money, yet there is still a value in pleasure. What is it about your cupcakes, in particular, that could appeal to customers? You may price your cupcakes the same as your competitors in the beginning, but what makes them different enough for customers to pay more? Value-based pricing would reflect whatever added value your customers perceive in your cupcakes. You could also think about different ways of generating additional revenue: selling cupcake mix, decorations, and other accessories might be ways of bringing in extra money.

In addition to the factors associated with the various pricing calculations described so far, there are two more factors your pricing calculation needs to take into consideration: your livelihood and your mistakes. For example, are you taking a salary for yourself, or do you intend to live off the profit and use any additional income to reinvest in the company? Your price also has to cover the costs of any mistakes. Say your sales volume predictions are off. You might not sell 10,000 cupcakes in a year. How much leeway have you built into your pricing to cover the costs of inaccurate estimates and other errors? Typically, you need to account for being off by a factor of two or more and still be profitable—that is, if you plan to sell 10,000 cupcakes, you need to be able to make a profit even if you end up selling only half that many, or 5,000 cupcakes. ●

> **Value-based pricing:** a pricing method that involves pricing a product based on how it benefits the customer.

Get the tools you need to sharpen your study skills. SAGE edge offers a robust online environment featuring an impressive array of free tools and resources.

- Access practice quizzes, eFlashcards, video, and multimedia at **edge.sagepub.com/neckentrepreneurship2e**

SUMMARY

9.1   Define a revenue model and distinguish it from the business model.

The revenue model specifies exactly how income and earnings will be generated from the value proposition, whereas the business model is the framework established to create value for the consumer while preserving some of that value for the entrepreneur.

9.2   Illustrate the 10 most popular revenue models being used by entrepreneurs.

There are many effective revenue models. Commonly employed models are the unit sales revenue model, advertising revenue model, data revenue model, intermediation revenue model, licensing revenue model, franchising revenue model, subscription revenue model, professional revenue model, utility and usage revenue model, and freemium revenue model.

9.3   Explain how companies generate revenue by profiting from "free."

The freemium concept has exploded in popularity in recent times. Many companies are finding that small, experience-amplifying transactions can be profitable after introducing consumers to a limited version of their product or service for free.

9.4   Identify the drivers that affect revenue as well as cost.

Revenue drivers include the customer, purchase frequency, selling process, and price.

9.5   Identify different strategies entrepreneurs use when pricing their product or service.

Pricing is critical for a product or service. Common pricing strategies include competition-led pricing, customer-led pricing, loss leader, introductory offer, skimming, psychological pricing, fair pricing, and bundled pricing.

9.6 **Explain different methods of calculating price.**

There are several methods to help you calculate the best price for your product or service, such as cost-led pricing, target-return pricing, and value-based pricing. A break-even analysis can help entrepreneurs to quickly determine what they need to sell monthly or yearly, and in some cases daily or weekly, to cover the costs of running the business.

CASE STUDY

Balaji Viswanathan, founder, Invento Robotics

> Assume that you're in the business for the long run. Building anything big and important takes a long time. Assume that 5 years of your life are going to be gone building this. Most people give up by then. (Balaji Viswanathan)

Balaji Viswanathan, the founder of Invento Robotics and the widely publicized Mitra Robot, has always seen himself as an entrepreneur. According to Balaji, "Even as a child, my goals weren't conventional. I always thought that a pushcart vendor seemed to have more freedom and liberty than someone working in an office." Balaji's father was the manager of a bank in a rural area of India and gave loans to entrepreneurs. Since there was little to do in his village, Balaji spent his early childhood with his father and among the many entrepreneurs. "The concept of creating something out of nothing fascinated me," Balaji recalled.

Balaji was an engineering student at Thiagarajar College of Engineering in Madurai, India, and, at 17 years old, caught the entrepreneurship bug during his first year. In 2000, he noticed that all professors gave handouts for students to study from. The campus had only one photocopying center, so there would always be this mad rush from students every time new material was distributed. Balaji's idea? He spoke to professors ahead of time, got their materials, and printed the handouts so that they were ready for use when the class started. The students didn't mind paying a little extra for the copies because they didn't have to waste their time getting them from the photocopying center. Balaji reached a point where he was copying close to 20,000 pages of study materials a day, and he even started helping the professors with proofreading and building content for classes. "My father was at the time making Rs. 8,000 (~$115) a month as a bank manager and I was making the same amount in college, spending just 2 hours a day. This business allowed me to pay my way through college."

Naturally curious, Balaji started researching various sectors including defense, nanotechnology, and data storage. He wrote research papers and gave many award-winning presentations that were recognized at the national level. Balaji even had the opportunity to work with then-president of India Dr. A. P. J. Abdul Kalam, a renowned aerospace scientist, and shared some of his early ideas and research. "I was quite sure that I wanted to get into academia and become a professor. I felt that as a professor, I would have the time to research and enough time otherwise to run my own company on the side."

Upon completing his undergraduate degree, Balaji left India in 2004 to earn a master's in engineering from the University of Maryland. There he started working extensively in the field of robotics. While working on his master's, he secured an internship with Cougaar Software, a robotics and AI company that now works directly with the U.S. Army. "Giving up a chance to join the company full-time right after the internship is one of my big regrets. At the time, I wanted to finish my master's and maybe even get a PhD. Now I realize that you don't necessarily need a degree." After his master's degree, Balaji worked at the Microsoft headquarters in Redmond, Washington, as a software design engineer for a little over 3 years. His passion for AI and robotics was only growing stronger. He bought a bunch of robotic kits and started building his own robots.

Balaji Viswanathan founded Invento Robotics, headquartered in Bengaluru, India, in 2016. Invento Robotics develops humanoid robots that use AI to interact with people. These robots have been piloted throughout India to handle customer interactions at banks, cinemas, hospitals, and retail outlets. Balaji recalled an early adopter, a senior executive at one of the largest public sector banks in India, Canara Bank. "The executive wanted to leave a legacy and was very excited about having robots going around the branch talking to customers. His legacy would be bringing those robots to the bank." Generally, Invento's robot prototypes were being used to help build a technology-oriented brand awareness for the companies that rented them. It helped them stand out from their competition. "We started selling the vision of the technology to these companies through our prototypes."

Balaji feels that other robotics companies, such as Honda Asimo and Boston Dynamics, have had failing business models. As Balaji explains, "These companies fail, not in terms of their technology but in terms of their value proposition to the customers. Having looked into the industry for a long time, I felt I intuitively understood how a profitable business model in this space could be created. Not just that, I felt that India as a country does not a have a visible product or a brand and that this might be a good way to help create that product! We want to make a trend-setting, cutting edge product that could be made in India for the world. That is our core vision."

Balaji cofounded Invento Robotics with his wife, Mahalakshmi, someone with complementary skillsets to his. While Balaji himself is quite technologically inclined, his wife is skilled in operations, management, and finance, something he feels has helped maintain a good balance. Not just that, Balaji tapped into his personal network of friends and family to get some initial funding to start the business. He also tapped into his very extensive network on Quora. His network on Quora is not comparable to anyone else's.

Quora is a question-and-answer website where questions are asked, answered, edited, and organized by its community of users (similar to Answers.com). Balaji is currently (and has been for a while) the most followed person on Quora, with more than 500,000 followers and close to 5,000 answers to questions that have been viewed approximately 320 million times. He was able to not only get feedback on his idea but also hired most of his team through this platform. "Finding the right people to build a hardware company was quite a challenge."

Having learned from some of his earlier startup experiences, Balaji wanted Invento to focus, from day 1, on revenue generation and building a scalable business model. He had a novel way to generate revenue in what is otherwise a highly capital- and research-intensive industry. He focused on big events because he observed that corporate clients and event organizers want something unique—a wow factor—at each event. He rented each one of his humanoid prototypes to events. Mitra (meaning "friend" in Hindi) is one of the better known of Invento's humanoids. Mitra was featured at the large, heavily attended Global Entrepreneurship Summit in 2017, in Hyderabad, India. The robot briefly interacted with Prime Minister Narendra Modi and Ivanka Trump.

Overall, the prototype rental model generated regular revenues that were used for further product development. Invento Robotics has made more than 20 prototypes and has created a revenue model that has helped fund their ongoing research. "These robot prototypes were hot off the press," noted Balaji. "As these robots were representative of what the future would look like, the incomplete functionality was not a deal breaker but a signal to competitors and customers that we are looking into the future."

Balaji warns that being a capital-intensive business with a longer-term payout than other industries creates a few challenges. "Investors were skeptical of a hardware robotics company that was operating out of India." But today the 30-member company is generating regular revenue streams and is also profitable, which has started to attract the attention of investors. Their customers include GM, Suzuki, and Accenture. In addition to funding challenges, there have also been "human" challenges because it's hard to create patience in both customers and employees—results take time. "We can't expect an iPhone to be developed on Day 1. A product like this takes time and since the industry is fairly new, it is going to take some time. We are at the same level as cars were in the 1980s." A third challenge is cash flow, given that Invento requires capital-intensive research and top talent. To keep the company nimble and forward looking, every time the company begins to get cash flow positive, they invest money to bring themselves back down to almost negative cash flow. Balaji explains, "If the company remains only cash flow positive, it would flat line and not grow. With this structure in place, the company is constantly chasing positive cash flows, helping it guide the operational and investment decisions."

Regardless of the challenges, Balaji is very strategic when attracting customers. "One of the ways we manage the risk in our business is by getting the right kind of customers. Our customers understand that they are not buying today, but buying tomorrow." Such strategic focus has created an impressive list of customers for Invento Robotics: HDFC Bank, PVR Cinemas, and Accenture—all companies invested in a vision for the future. Invento Robotics's long-term goal is to be the Apple of the robotics industry. "We are thinking about how we can put a million of our robots in business spaces over the next few years. After that, we would love to expand into homes and reach a point where every house can own a robot—our robot."

Critical Thinking Questions

1. What is unique about renting "prototypes" of robots that don't have complete functionality?

2. Look up Balaji Viswanathan on Quora. What types of questions does he answer and is there something new you can learn from him about robotics and artificial intelligence?

3. Can you identify other ways that Invento Robotics can generate revenue while they are still perfecting the product?

Sources:

Balaji Viswanathan (interview with Babson MBA graduate assistant Gaurav Khemka, April 20, 2019)

Invento website (http://www.mitrarobot.com/)

10 Planning for Entrepreneurs

"Plans are of little importance, but planning is essential."

—Winston Churchill, former British prime minister

Chapter Outline

Learning Objectives

10.1 Examine "planning" from an entrepreneurial perspective.

10.2 Explain vision as an important part of planning.

10.3 Explain the different types of plans used by entrepreneurs.

10.4 Describe the questions to ask during planning.

10.5 Debate the value of writing business plans.

10.6 Implement the tips for writing business plans.

10.1 WHAT IS PLANNING?

>> **LO 10.1** **Examine "planning" from an entrepreneurial perspective.**

Over the course of this book, we have emphasized the importance of learning by doing and acting in order to learn. Taking action in the real world, collecting data, gathering feedback, and testing business models are the most beneficial ways to develop a product or service that people actually want as well as to build a scalable business.

As we have learned, when you are first starting out as an entrepreneur, it is important to think about whom you know, what you know, and how you're going to implement your idea. This is why it is important to have a plan that helps you take the first steps on your journey to building a new venture and proving it is viable and feasible before you go any further. From an entrepreneurial perspective, **planning** is a process of envisioning the future for your business, including what you plan to do and how you plan to do it.[1]

Every business needs to start with some type of plan. Plans help you to get out of your head and see your idea for what it really is—the good, the bad, and even the ugly! They help crystalize your thoughts, allow you to clearly articulate where you want your business to go, and can be the foundation for an overall business strategy. In short, planning pushes you to move forward.

Planning is different from a plan. Planning is a verb and therefore implies action. If planning pushes you to move forward and take action, then a plan helps you organize those actions in some way. Planning is about answering the most important questions we have posed throughout the book. Dr. Emmet (Tom) Thompson, founder of AFC Management, believes that planning is the key to success.

Planning: a process of envisioning the future for a business, including what one plans to do and how one plans to do it.

10.2 PLANNING STARTS WITH A VISION

>> **LO 10.2** **Explain vision as an important part of planning.**

All planning starts with a vision. Cameron Herold, a business coach and mentor, presented the concept of vivid vision in his book *Double Double*. Vivid vision challenges the entrepreneur to imagine what a business could be 3 years into the future. Three years is a reasonable amount of time to "nail down" specific, measurable goals; vivid vision is not just fantasizing so far into the future that it becomes pure speculation. Three years makes you stretch just enough to think about how to get from today to your idea of success in Year 3.

Master the content at
**edge.sagepub.com/
neckentrepreneurship2e**

Dr. Emmet C. (Tom) Thompson II, AFC Management

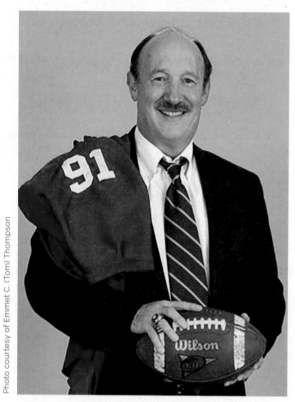

Photo courtesy of Emmet C. (Tom) Thompson

Dr. Emmet C. (Tom) Thompson, founder and president of AFC Management

Dr. Emmet "Tom" Thompson is the oldest collegiate football player in NCAA history. At the age of 61 he kicked an extra point for the 2009 Austin College football team. Though he was told being on the team would be impossible, he said, "I did all the hard work, all the running, all the things that the team did to earn my spot." For Tom, his football experience was not that much different from his entrepreneurial pursuits. "The harder things are in the beginning, the more victory you enjoy in the end."

Tom is the founder and president of AFC Management, a company founded in 1996 that serves as an umbrella for his business interests in corporate fitness management, real estate, and book production. Tom's newest business under the AFC Management umbrella is a movie development

company, 91 Kick Entertainment, and he is producing a movie based on his own life. It's clear that he is an entrepreneur in many forms—a business leader, football coach, author, motivational speaker, educator, and now movie producer!

As he reflects on his successful career, he admits there is a trend that he doesn't like. He laments that too many young entrepreneurs plan for short-term gains, rather than long-term payoffs. Tom says, "More and more, young people are more concerned with how something works than with how something lasts, in relationships and in business. Delayed gratification and patience will pay off over time." However, he also acknowledges that patience and waiting for the longer-term payoff requires planning. In fact, one of Tom's favorite quotes is by Ben Franklin, "If you fail to plan, you are planning to fail." Tom emphasizes that his secret to his success has been his long-term vision for AFE Management, including a plan for how to achieve it.

Tom reminds aspiring entrepreneurs not to wallow too much in short-term setbacks because they need to keep their eye on the big picture. "Short-term chaos can often keep people from remembering the long-term outcome they envisioned at the start, so don't lose sight of the dream," he says, "If you start thinking of all the things you need to be and do, you'll get caught up in that instead of thinking of your own vision. Planning too many things keeps you from planning the most important things."

Critical Thinking Questions

1. What is the significance of planning to the success of Tom's entrepreneurial career?

2. Do you think younger entrepreneurs only think in the short term? Do you agree with Tom's view of young people?

3. Do some research on Tom Thompson. How did he get the point where he was a 61-year-old kicker for a college football team? What is the entrepreneurial lesson from this experience? ●

Source: Emmet Thompson (interview with author, January 23, 2019).

The best way to begin the vivid vision exercise is to get out of your usual working environment (your class or your office) and go to a spot that, for you, is relaxing and peaceful—it could be a nearby park or someplace farther away such as the ocean, mountains, or a lake. Start sketching (see Chapter 7 for more on sketching) or writing and aim to create a document no more than three pages long.

TABLE 10.1

Cameron Herold's Vivid Vision

The following is an example of vivid vision elements from Cameron Herold. Herold believes that "Creating a vivid vision brings the future into the present, so we can have clarity on what we are building now. It is a detailed overview of what my business will look like, feel like, and act like 3 years out."

What I Do	Why I "do what I do" is simple and clear: I love helping CEOs turn their dreams into reality.
My Programs	My content is about my leadership and growth expertise and is designed specifically for CEOs and entrepreneurial minds. I am frequently invited to present at conferences and keynote talks at large-scale events. I set a firm limit for the number of annual speaking events I do, which increases the demand for my services, and my fees increase each year. This allows me more time with my family.
Live Programs	While on the road speaking, I book half-day and full-day workshops for groups or companies, in the same city, to teach their employees the systems to become more entrepreneurial. I run 2-day growth camps and leadership team retreats in my home city that attract companies and employees from around the globe.
Remote Programs	I leverage webinar technology, and companies book me to do remote training for their employees. Prior webinars I've done are available online for thousands of companies around the world to use—and for their employees to learn from as well.
Coaching/ Mentoring	My clients stay with me for an average of 24 months. Those who leave do so only because they've learned enough to no longer need me to guide them. I am coaching 24 clients per month by reducing the number of lower-leverage speaking events I do. My fees increase each year for new clients.
Leadership	Clients say that I hold them accountable for doing the things they need to do in order to successfully grow their company. Clients I coach love setting goals with me because our efforts directly correlate to an increase in their company's productivity. CEOs value having me on their team as a senior leader who they normally couldn't afford. Clients consistently say I've made (or saved) them millions of dollars.
Communication	People trust me because I say what's on my mind. I am respected for that. People say I'm a breath of fresh air and that I say what other people are thinking but won't say. My inner voice helps me filter my decisions.
Customer Service	My clients are very clear about what I promise them and say that I overdeliver with every interaction. My client companies feel grateful to have me helping them, as I feel grateful to play a role in their growth. I deliver incredible value. They are thrilled they have time with me consistently.
My Mentors	I connect and learn from those who have already "figured it out." I study fiercely—what the great companies do and how they do it—so I don't have to reinvent the wheel. I'm known as a "connector" because of how many people I know and regularly call on, leveraging social networks and the CEOs I meet globally. My track record of hyper-growth with my clients and honesty in my relationships is what accelerates and grows my network.
Profitability	I continue to be extremely profitable doing exactly what I love. My revenues have grown 100% in 3 years.
Balance	I choose international engagements where I'm able to add days of personal time to enjoy the country with my wife, and as our four children get older, we include them more as well.
Core Values	I live the core values that I have set for my company—and I ask people to call me on any deviation. • Do What You Love • Be Authentic • Deliver What You Promise • Balance Is Key

Source: Adapted from Herold. C. (2011). *Double double: How to double your revenue and profit in three years.* Austin. TX: Greenleaf Book Group.

The Vivid Vision Checklist

Using the vivid vision checklist, try to imagine your business or some new idea in action 3 years from now.

When you finish your own vivid vision, share it with your friends, family, and anyone else you feel would be interested in seeing it. The act of publicly sharing your picture makes your vision more real and compels you to take action in order to achieve your goals. Besides, as Herold says, "the more people who know with clarity what my company looks and feels like, the better chance there is that people will be able to help me to make it happen."[2]

Pretend you have traveled in a time machine into the future. The date is December 31, 3 years from now. You are walking around your company's offices (the startup you founded 3 years before) with a clipboard in hand.

- What do you see?
- What do you hear?
- What are clients saying?
- What do the media write about you?
- What kinds of comments are your employees making at the water cooler?
- What is the buzz about you in your community?
- What is your marketing like? Are you marketing your goods/services globally now? Are you launching new online and TV ads? What is being said on social media?

- How is the company running day to day? Is it organized and running like a clock?
- What's in the office space? Are people sitting, standing, talking? When they move from their workspace, where do they go?
- What kind of stuff do you do every day? Are you focused on strategy, team building, or customer relationships?
- What do the company's financials reveal?
- How are you funded now?
- How are your core values being realized among your employees?

Critical Thinking Questions

1. Is 3 years a useful and reasonable length of time to look ahead and envision your business? If you think 3 years is too long or too short, explain why.

2. In the vivid vision checklist, which questions did you find the most useful? The most challenging? Explain your answers.

3. Is there anything in your plans for your business that is not covered in the vivid vision checklist? Anything that is not relevant to your business? ●

Source: Herold, C. (2011). *Double double: How to double your revenue and profit in three years.* Austin, TX: Greenleaf Book Group.

An example of a gallery sketch

Once you have visualized your goals, then you can write a three-page description or draw a large sketch of these thoughts, detailing what your company will look and feel like in 3 years' time. Remember that this exercise does not involve how you are going to build the business or the steps you need to take to get there. It is simply a description of how your business might look in the future—specifically, just 3 years down the road.

Cameron Herold created his own vivid vision (see Table 10.1). Keep in mind that although Herold presented his vision in writing, the vision can also be shown as a visual such as a gallery sketch, a photo montage, or a video.

Your own vivid vision should describe what the future looks like rather than detailing how you're going to get there.

Envisioning the future is just a start. Generally the plan is the document that records the answers to questions. As this chapter will illustrate, there are many types of plans available to entrepreneurs today, including simplified plans, plans that emphasize planning with preparation, and those that flow from planning with imagination. What is most important, regardless of the type of document created, is that the questions get answered.

10.3 PLANS TAKE MANY FORMS

>> **LO 10.3 Explain the different types of plans used by entrepreneurs.**

As we discussed, plans are an important way to develop a vision, gain clarity, answer important questions, estimate timelines, and set goals. Many entrepreneurs are initially resistant to the idea of sitting down and writing a plan, or they feel that they lack the time for this task. However, this section demonstrates that there are several alternatives to choose from to help you take action and envision a future for your business—or decide, based on solid information, whether your business idea even *has* a future.

What type of plan to use when is often determined by the stage of the business. We will discuss six alternative planning tools. These include the Business Model Canvas, the business brief, the feasibility study, the pitch deck, and the business plan.

Business Model Canvas

The Business Model Canvas (BMC), introduced in Chapter 5, is a type of visual plan. It is especially useful for identifying any gaps in the business idea and integrating the various components. We say it's visual because the entire business is depicted on one page by filling in the nine blocks of the business model:

- Key partners
- Key activities
- Value proposition
- Customer relationships
- Customer segments
- Key resources
- Channels
- Cost structure
- Revenue streams

The sample BMC in Figure 10.1 illustrates the nine components using an idea for a new T-shirt store that sells trendy T-shirts emblazoned with original designs by young, emerging artists.

By thinking through all nine components of your business model, you will be able to visualize how all the various parts work together: the value created for customers, the processes you must have to deliver value, the resources you need, and the way you'll make money.

The Business Brief

The business brief is less visual than the two previous types of plans, and it requires a bit more detail and writing. Typically, a business brief is a two- to three-page document outlining the company overview, value proposition, customers, and milestones. It's something you can easily send to stakeholders that will give them an at-a-glance understanding of who you are, the business, and its potential. Creating a business brief is not too time intensive, and it indicates that you're doing your homework and thinking critically

Sample Business Model Canvas

Key Partners	Key Activities	Value Proposition	Customer Relationships	Customer Segments
T-shirt suppliers	Managing stock Sales Selecting designs	Trendy T-shirts for kids Eco-friendly material Original designs by new artists	Personal in-store advice Social media	Fashion-conscious parents Trendy junior high and high school kids
Artists and designers	**Key Resources** Store location Salespeople Network of artists Inventory		**Channels** Internet Brick store Word of mouth	

Cost Structure	Revenue Structure
Employees Sales and marketing Store rental T-shirt purchases Paying artists	T-shirt sales in store T-shirt sales online

Points to Include in a Business Brief

• Description of the business idea (company overview)
• Value proposition that highlights the problem being solved or need being met
• Customer profile and market size
• Proof of market demand and future growth
• Description of the entrepreneur/team
• Actions taken to date and future actions planned
• Simple pro forma income statement (up to 3 years)

about the business. Table 10.2 lists the points to include in a business brief. Figure 10.2 is a sample business brief for an online meal service called India in a Box.

Feasibility Study

Feasibility study: a planning tool that enables entrepreneurs to test the possibilities of an initial idea to see if it is worth pursuing.

A **feasibility study** is an essential planning tool that enables entrepreneurs to test the possibilities of an initial idea to see if it is worth pursuing. It serves as a solid foundation for developing a business plan when the time comes. The feasibility study focuses on the size of the market, the suppliers, distributors, and the skills of the entrepreneur.

FIGURE 10.2

Sample Business Brief: India in a Box

COMPANY OVERVIEW

India in a Box is an online meal service (subscription and on-demand) delivering authentic Indian food that is healthy and can be prepared in 5 to 10 minutes. We are on a simple mission to bring a taste of India to every home in the U.S.

Through the India in a Box online store, customers receive their choice of curry and can add rice or naan. Curries are easily prepared by adding water, stirring, and heating.

VALUE PROPOSITION

Cooking a traditional Indian meal requires time, knowledge, and passion. We captured and simplified the essence of this process. By using a specialized dehydration process, we ensure that 95% of nutrients are preserved during packaging compared to 50% in our competitors' products. Each dish has a simple ingredient list, is 100% vegetarian and gluten-free, and contains no added preservatives, sodium, or sugar. We start with whole, fresh ingredients and slowly simmer to develop complex sauces and then naturally condense through dehydration to lock in flavor and nutrition. The shelf life of our products is nine months.

MARKET

Key trends supporting the startup and scale up of India in a Box:

- Ethnic food industry is $11 billion and growing at 15% Year on Year (YOY).
- Indian cuisine is the second fastest growing cuisine with a 20% YOY growth rate projected until 2018.
- Eighty-eight percent of people are willing to pay more for healthful, great-quality food (Nielson 2015 report).
- Over $750 million has been invested in just the first half of 2015 in food technology companies, including meal kits and subscriptions.

CUSTOMERS

Our target consumers are Indian food lovers and enthusiasts. There are over 5 million Indians and 130,000 Indian students in the U.S. Indians are now the largest international cohort of students residing in the U.S. Specifically, our customers are the following:

- **Urban Food Explorers:** Whole Foods shoppers (health conscious), time constrained, looking for convenience
- **Indian Americans:** Highly influential group who will be our brand evangelists, helping build brand credibility
- **Millennials:** Young yet particular about food consumption and their current and future wellness

ACTIONS TAKEN

We have product. With the help of a professional chef and our head of nutrition, Sucheta Gehani, we have created five delicious recipes from scratch. We partnered with Spicebox, a state-of-the-art commercial kitchen in India, to create, iterate, and finalize our recipes.

We have co-packers. We have developed strategic partnerships for co-packing our products. Our food is created in a commercial kitchen and then dehydrated by a separate manufacturer—both in Mumbai, India. Both of these companies have the necessary FDA approvals and meet the production standards required.

We have a supply chain. Product is shipped by air freight from Mumbai, India, and warehoused by Ship Bob, which has two United States warehouses (New Jersey and Chicago).

We have sales. In May, India in a Box launched its first batch of five products and completely sold out, earning $1,200 in one day. After we launched our online platform www.indiainabox .us, we took in $6,000 in three months, fulfilling orders from eight different states.

(Continued)

FIGURE 10.2   (Continued)

OUR TEAM

Shyam Devnani, Founder and CEO:

Shyam is a Babson MBA 2015 alumni with an undergraduate degree in computer engineering. He has three years of experience as CEO of a startup garment textile manufacturing firm.

Sucheta Gehani, Head of Nutrition and Wellness:

Sucheta is a registered dietitian and brings to bear her expertise as a nutrition and health expert. Sucheta is passionate about health and wellness and is also a certified Yoga instructor.

Meet Kouchar, Operations Partner:

Meet is a serial food entrepreneur with companies such as SpiceBox (www.spicebox.in), Oye Kiddan, and the Bohri Kitchen in India. He is our new operations partner for food production and will help us set up our own kitchen and dehydration unit in India.

Vinayak Agarwal, Marketing Intern:

Vinayak is studying for his master's degree in international marketing from Hult University. He is a foodie and a passionate photographer who will bring to the company his digital marketing expertise to help us execute our social media strategies.

We are also looking at bringing on board a full time marketing/sales person and forming a board of advisors with industry experts.

FINANCIAL PROJECTIONS

Our revenue model is selling our meal boxes online at a price of $24 for 3 curries and 3 portions of rice or naan. Our second product line will be curated regional experience boxes, which will be priced at $35. We project our Year 1 revenue at $261,000. Our gross profit margin is 61%, and we project a net profit of $1 million in Year 3.

	YEAR 1	YEAR 2	YEAR 3
REVENUE	$261,000	$820,000	$2,540,000
EXPENSES	$132,000	$343,000	$980,000
GROSS PROFIT	$129,000	$477,000	$1,560,000
SG&A	$84,000	$225,000	$530,000
NET PROFIT	$45,000	$252,000	$1,030,000

FUTURE MILESTONES

We are currently looking to raise a $250K round of seed funding. This will enable us to bring the dehydration unit in house and also help expand our marketing and sales efforts to the west coast. With the addition of the new capital, we will grow our physical and online presence in highly Indian-populated regions with a demand for Indian food, such as New York, New Jersey, San Francisco, and Austin.

Spring 2016

- Bring operations of manufacturing in-house with partner in India.
- Raise a round of seed funding.
- Bring on board an experienced marketing person to push online sales strategies.
- Target sales in Boston and the Bay Area.

Summer 2016

- Launch curated regional subscription boxes.
- Increase product offerings to 15 with help of operations partner.
- Invest in our web platform and improve warehousing/fulfillment.

Source: Reprinted with permission from Shyam Devnani.

Every entrepreneur should conduct a feasibility study because it determines whether your idea is workable and profitable. It is typically created to assess the viability of a business concept.

The information you gather for your feasibility study will help you identify the essentials you need to make the business work: any problems or obstacles to your business, the customers you hope to sell to, marketing strategies, the logistics of delivering your product or service, your competition, and the resources you need to start your business and keep it running until it is established.

From the entrepreneur's perspective, the feasibility study is a useful way to assess whether you have the time, energy, abilities, and resources to get the venture off the ground. The conclusions you draw from the study will determine whether your venture is viable or not. Ultimately, the feasibility study is a valuable exercise in answering the question, Will my venture work? This feasibility study is for your eyes only, which means you need to be as honest as possible with the conclusions you draw from the study. If there are constraints, describe them and be realistic about whether your idea is worth further investigation.

The feasibility study is a written document of no more than 10 pages. It takes all of the action components we've been talking about in the book and places the learnings from the actions into a structure that can be used for decision making, such as "I do or do not want to move forward with this venture"—or, in short, a "Go/No Go" decision.

The feasibility study addresses the most critical elements entrepreneurs need to consider during the initial conceptualization of the venture (see Table 10.3). The key to the feasibility study is speed. It is a quick way to prompt you to zero in on what you need to know. It requires you to pursue answers to your questions and to gather real data from your interactions with potential customers, suppliers, distributors, and others. The feasibility study template (see Table 10.4) also prompts you to quickly find out the rules and regulations surrounding your startup, which could save you time and money.

To produce a feasibility study, there must be action, testing, information gathering, and analysis in order to reduce uncertainty and gain greater confidence about the opportunity and your approach. For example, if you haven't talked to at least 50 potential customers, *you are not ready to decide whether the business idea is viable*. "Talking" can include contacts by phone, social networking, and other electronic "conversations," but don't overlook the value of interviewing prospective customers face-to-face.

Though there is no one best format for a feasibility study, Table 10.4 gives a sample template that can be used to organize all the data you have collected from the idea generation and business model stage, allowing you to clearly articulate where you are and where you want to go.

Talking to people face-to-face is a valuable way to test the viability of your business idea.

TABLE 10.3

Critical Elements of Feasibility Study

• Does the idea fulfill a need or solve a big problem?
• Is there both short- and long-term market potential?
• Who are the customers, and what are they willing to pay?
• Does the opportunity provide competitive uniqueness?
• Is the business model feasible (can it be done) and viable (can it be sustainable)?

Source: Kelley, D., Ceru, D., George, B., & Neck, H. (2014). *Feasibility blueprint guidelines.* Wellesley, MA: Babson College.

TABLE 10.4

Sample Feasibility Study Template

Need Identification	Describe why there is a need for your business to exist
Venture Concept	Have a clear, concise description in 2–3 sentences.
Value Propositions	What makes you unique and why is this valuable for the customer? Prove that the customer wants what you are providing.
Market	Discuss the market size, potential market size, and target market size. Is the market large enough to meet your goals? Discuss trends and growth estimates.
Competitive Environment	Identify and compare your venture against the competition. By understanding the competition, you will have a better understanding of the dynamics of the industry in which you are competing and how you are differentiated. Are there specific laws or regulations you should be aware of?
Revenue Model	Describe your revenue model in terms of the revenue streams and the key factors that will influence those streams. You will also need to examine your cost model and determine the key drivers of your costs. Overall, you are assessing your potential profitability. Provide a simple income statement.
Startup Requirements	Identify the resources needed to start the business. What is absolutely essential before a sale can be made? What don't you have, but need?
Team	Critically assess your current team, its fit with the venture, and your ability to act (or not).
Decision	Based on the analysis laid out in the feasibility study, do you want to move forward? Why or why not?

Source: D. Kelley, B. George, D. Ceru, H. Neck. Babson's Feasibility Blueprint Assignment for MBA students, Babson College, 2013.

Using a gourmet food cart venture as an example, suppose you want to offer mayonnaise as a condiment and grated cheese as a topping for your featured menu items. If you conduct a proper feasibility study before you progress with your plan, you will find that most health departments do not allow food carts to sell dairy-based or edible-oil-based condiments. This is useful information to know before you go out and buy dozens of bottles of mayonnaise and packets of cheese.

One of the main aims of the feasibility study is to establish whether your idea is a "go" or a "no go." Is your idea feasible and worthwhile, or should you just draw a line through it and move on?

Whether your decision is a "go" or "no go," you will need to state the reasons why. For example, if it's a "go," then you will need to develop and test prototypes, carry out due diligence, find a management team, try to get some early customers, seek funding if necessary, and prepare a launch plan.

While a "no go" may feel disappointing, remember that a decision not to go ahead is also a valid and valuable result of a feasibility study. It has saved you the time, effort, and expense that you may have spent on a concept that does not have the potential to succeed in the market.

Knowing your constraints can also lead to doors opening in other areas you might not have imagined. Take Jorge Heraud and Lee Redden, the founders of Blue River

Robotic mower by Blue River Technology

Technology, for instance.[3] They had an idea to build robotic mowers for commercial spaces. Having spoken to 100 customers over a period of 10 weeks, they learned that their original target market—golf courses—did not think their solution was viable.

However, during their market research, the two entrepreneurs discovered a huge demand from farmers for an automated way to kill weeds without chemicals. This gave the two entrepreneurs the "go" they were looking for. They built and tested the prototype and received $3 million in venture funding less than a year later. In 2017, agricultural equipment manufacturer John Deere acquired Blue River Technology for $305 million.[4]

The more data you gather during the feasibility study, the more evidence you will have to show investors when the time comes to develop your pitch deck or write a business plan.

The Pitch Deck

The pitch deck is a presentation of varying lengths highlighting many of the essential elements found in a feasibility study and a business plan. Some call this the launch plan. Let's briefly discuss the specifics of the deck here. (An example pitch deck can be found in Supplement B.)

The pitch deck has replaced the formal business plan in most venues. A pitch deck is needed for collegiate competitions, applications to accelerators and incubators, and for angel and venture capital funding. There are many variations on the "ideal" pitch deck depending on your audience, so we encourage you to do your own research before preparing. The purpose of the pitch is to describe your product and get interest. In the case of using your pitch deck in front of professional investors, the goal is to get to the next meeting!

A pitch deck is essential for an investor meeting.

©iStockphoto.com/PeopleImages

There are no strict rules for the length or style of pitch decks. Author and entrepreneur Guy Kawasaki advises keeping pitch deck slides to a maximum of 10, while Mathilde Collin, founder of email app Front, used a 25-slide presentation that earned her $66 million from investors after only 5 days of pitching.[5]

The Business Plan

The **business plan** is considered the most formal of planning tools. It is typically a lengthy written document discussing the business concept, product mix, marketing plan, operations plan, development plan, and financial forecast.

As stated earlier, the business plan has been replaced by the pitch deck in most venues, but traditional investors and bankers are likely to require a traditional business plan. The business plan needs to show that you are serious and that you've done your homework, given the level of detail that is necessary to complete a strong business plan. However, there is an ironic angle to this: When a business plan is created, it must be thought of as a work in progress because nothing goes according to plan. It is important to realize this ahead of time, as some entrepreneurs struggle when things don't go according to plan because so much energy has been put into creating the actual business plan.

A traditional business plan usually consists of 20 to 40 pages, plus additional pages for appendices. It also includes the organization's mission, strategy, tactics, goals, financials, and objectives, together with a 5-year forecast for income, profits, and cash flow.[6] This information is divided into three main parts.[7]

The first part is the business concept, where you discuss the industry, business structure, products and services, and how you plan to make your business a success. The second part is the market section, where you describe potential customers and the competitors in

Business plan: the most formal of planning tools. It is typically a lengthy written document discussing the business concept, product mix, marketing plan, operations plan, development plan, and financial forecast.

your market. The third part describes how you intend to design, develop, and implement the plan and provides some detail on operations and management. Finally, the financial section includes details of income and cash flow, balance sheets, financial projections, and the like. In addition to these components, a business plan also has a cover, title page, and table of contents (see Table 10.5).

It can be a complex task to start writing a business plan too early, especially for a startup when there are still so many questions to be answered. Business plans are useful for established companies with a history of data and operations because this data will help the business to plan and forecast more accurately, but startups have no such history. Startups are not just smaller versions of bigger companies—a startup begins with guesswork and untested assumptions. Nevertheless, in order to get later-stage funding, a business plan will likely be needed.

In the order of entrepreneurial activities, business plans come after idea generation, business model canvas, feasibility study, and pitch deck. Figure 10.3 illustrates the path from idea generation to business plan.

By following the steps of the Entrepreneurship Method, which we introduced in Chapter 1, you have a better chance of creating a solid, evidence-based business plan to present to potential investors when the time comes. By gathering, testing, and analyzing

TABLE 10.5

Components of a Business Plan

BUSINESS PLAN OUTLINE

1. **Cover**

2. *Table of Contents*

3. *Executive Summary* (2–3 pages)
   - Brief introduction and description of the opportunity
   - Company overview
   - Product or service description
   - Industry overview
   - Marketplace and target market
   - Competitive advantage
   - Business model (with summary of financials)
   - Management team
   - Offering

4. *Company Overview* (1–2 pages)
   - Company description
   - History and current status (stage of development)
   - Products and service description
   - Competitive advantages
   - Entry, growth, and exit strategies

5. *Industry, Marketplace, and Competitor Analyses* (3–6 pages)
   - Industry analysis
   - Marketplace analysis
   - Competitor analysis

6. *Marketing Plan* (1–4 pages)
   - Target market strategy
   - Product/service strategy
   - Pricing strategy
   - Distribution strategy
   - Advertising and promotion strategy
   - Sales strategy
   - Marketing and sales forecasts
   - Marketing expenses

7. *Operations Plan* (2 pages)
   - Operations strategy
   - Scope of operations
   - Ongoing operations
   - Operations expenses

8. *Development Plan* (1–2 pages)
   - Development strategy
   - Development timeline (milestones)
   - Development expenses

9. *Management* (1–2 pages)
   - Company organization
   - Management team
   - Ownership and compensation
   - Administrative expenses

10. *Critical Risks* (1–2 pages)
    - Market, customer, financial risks
    - Competitor retaliation
    - Contingency plans

11. *Offering* (up to 1 page)
    - Investment requirements
    - Offer

12. *Financial Plan* (up to 2 text pages, including financial statements)
    - Detailed financial assumptions
    - Pro forma financial statements
    - Breakeven analysis and other calculations
    - Do include statement within this section; do not place statements in the appendix.

13. *Appendices* (no maximum)
    - Customer survey and results
    - Other items to include may be menus, product specifications, team résumés, sample promotions, product pictures.

FIGURE 10.3

Path From Idea Generation to Business Plan

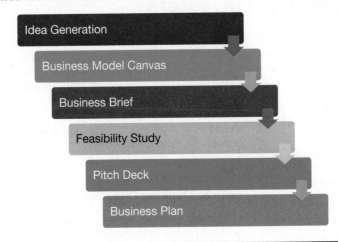

real data, you will be more able to illustrate your passion to create, the resources you have used, the actions you have taken to get your business on the move, the risks you have taken (and the ones you are prepared not to take), the people who have been enrolled in your journey, the experiments you have carried out to test what works and what doesn't, and where you would like the business to go next. In short, you will be able to prove that your product works, a real market exists, and your financials are not based just on guesswork.

Summary of Different Types of Plans

Although we are not advocating one type of plan over another, we believe it's important that entrepreneurs understand what is available to them and for what purposes. Table 10.6 summarizes the different types of plans we have outlined for entrepreneurs.

TABLE 10.6

Summary of Different Types of Plans

TYPE OF PLAN	PRIMARY AUDIENCE	PURPOSE	OUTPUT
Business Model Canvas	Team members, advisors	Identify gaps and critically evaluate each part of the business and how the components integrate	Completed and tested business model canvas
Business Brief	Friends and family, investors, advisors, other interested stakeholders	To have something in writing to show anybody interested in the business; also good practice for describing the business in a concise way	2- to 3-page typed document that is well formatted and professional looking
Feasibility Study	Team members, maybe early investors	Assess the potential of a new concept; can act as proof that the venture has market potential	10-page typed document that is well formatted and professional looking
Pitch Deck	Early investors, judges of venture competitions, incubators, accelerators	To get the next meeting with a potential investor; to apply to an incubator program; win a competition; get funding	10 to 20 slides, depending on length and purpose of the presentation
Business Plan	Banks, investors	Get funding	25+ page document plus appendices

When to Be Transparent With Investors

In the process of creating a concise, well-thought-out business plan, entrepreneurs can learn quite a bit about their own business. Planning helps to maintain focus on a project and get all people working on the venture on the same page.

A business plan or extensive pitch deck must highlight the projected financials of the venture, including projected revenue and profit over a three to five year period. Investors will require financial projections because this is one way they analyze the potential success of the venture.

With such reliance on the projected and planned financials, it might be tempting for an entrepreneur to exaggerate some numbers or hide some information that may harm the chances of receiving funding. However, for the most part, investors will discover this eventually, and transparency leads to trust. If the entrepreneur is not transparent from the start, then future funding will be scarce.

In the book *Discovering Phi: Motivation as the Hidden Variable of Performance,* a thorough study of investment management leaders and other investment professionals concluded that about 28% of investors are in the industry to help clients. A further 36% of investors said that career

risk comes from acting in the clients' best interest. If a good chunk of investors are not necessarily in the industry to help entrepreneurs, then how much does an entrepreneur owe an investor? If the entrepreneur cannot be certain that the investor has her best interests at heart, then that raises the question about how transparent she should be with the investor. This also suggests that the entrepreneur should work hard to ascertain the motives and strategies of the investor.

Critical Thinking Questions

1. Are there certain "white lies" that entrepreneurs can tell to potential investors?

2. Is transparency the same thing as truthfulness in business?

3. What if an investor does not have the right intentions? Should an entrepreneur maintain her principles in dealing with this investor? ●

Sources:

Guardian Sustainable Business. (2014, August 4). Corporate transparency: Why honesty is the best policy. *The Guardian.* Retrieved from https://www.theguardian.com/sustainable-business/corporate-transparency-honesty-best-policy

McSwain, P. (2017, March 20). Transparency: Do we protest it too much? *Enterprising Investor.* Retrieved from https://blogs.cfainstitute.org/investor/2017/03/20/transparency-do-we-protest-it-too-much/

In addition to the plans we've outlined here, there are other options used by entrepreneurs to showcase their businesses. Among them are the following:

- LeanLaunchLab, which allows you to test hypotheses and refine your business model;

- Lean Stack, a paid service that compresses the essential parts of your business down to one page to send to investors who have little time to read through a large document; and

- Plan Cruncher is a free tool that, like Lean Stack, allows you to summarize your idea in one page.

How do you know what plan to create? Depending on your business, you may use a different type of plan in the beginning from other entrepreneurs. The best plan for you is the one that helps give you the clarity and direction to take action to create your future venture. Use the Entrepreneurship Method to take action and get out of the building, just as our featured entrepreneurs have done: test your ideas, get market feedback, generate momentum, revise assumptions, make continuous iterations, use your social network, make contacts, and get potential customers interested in your product or service.

Most of the successful entrepreneurs featured throughout this book started out by testing their ideas in the real world to see if they really had wings and if they could make them into a business, long before they sat down to write their formal business plan—and many never wrote a formal business plan at all. They also used the time to equip themselves with the basic skills required for a successful venture—financial management, production capabilities, and marketing and sales—either by learning the skills themselves or partnering with other people. When you, too, have proved your concept, and gathered the data to go with it, then you will be able to produce a solid, credible business plan.

10.4 QUESTIONS TO ASK DURING PLANNING

>> **LO 10.4**   **Describe the questions to ask during planning.**

Regardless of what type of plan you are working on, you must ask the following questions. Not all plans require lengthy, complex answers, but it is important to ask the right questions before you put your plan into action.

What Is Your Business and How Does It Add Value?

A useful way to gain clarity on the type of business you are setting up, and the value it brings to your customer base, is to write a **concept statement**, which is a one sentence to one paragraph description of your vision for your product or service. The statement should include all the features of your product or service, potential problems that it solves, and the target market. It doesn't have to be long, but it does need to be clear and easy to understand. Here is a brief example of a concept statement for a tea company that is introducing a new in-cup tea brewing system:

> While there are lots of tea-drinkers in the world, not all of them are happy about the environmental impact of discarding teabags (many of which are made from nonbiodegradable materials). Although there are loose-leaf tea options, some people are put off with the time it takes to brew, and the special equipment it requires.
>
> The Tea-in-One product combines the tea mug and the strainer into one. The product addresses environmental concerns as it is partly ceramic (the mug) and silicone (the strainer). It is dishwasher safe and designed to keep the tea warm through extra insulation. The mug comes in 12 different colors and is marketed primarily toward women who often drink tea at home or at work.[8]

Concept statement: a written representation of your vision for your product or service.

Who Is Your Customer?

In Chapter 6, we explored the different types of customers and how to find your target market. Write down who your target customers are (end users, distributors, retailers), their defining characteristics, and why they will buy your product or service. Remember to include all this information in the plan you are writing as it will help you gain clarity on the right customer segments for your business.

How Big Is the Market?

Once you have a clear idea of your target customers, you will be able to conduct market sizing analyses to establish the size of your market and the share of the market you intend to capture. Chapter 6 includes more information about market sizing.

How Will You Enter the Market?

Write down your strategy for entering the market. This involves describing the needs your product or service fulfills for your customer, the problems you are solving for them, and any evidence you have to show that your potential customers will want to buy your offering.

What Do You Know About the Industry?

The more knowledge you have about your industry, the more likely you will be able to find ways to differentiate your ideas. Write down any research you have carried out that supports your ideas and make sure it is correct and up to date.

What Do You Know About Your Competition?

Entrepreneurs make lots of mistakes and they learn from just about all of them. But there is one mistake that is too often made and is a clear indication that you haven't done your homework. The mistake? When an entrepreneur says, "We have no competition." *Every* venture has competition. Even Uber had competition from taxis, and now it has competition from Lyft. The iPhone had competition from BlackBerry. There is always competition. Sometimes it's direct (when businesses are selling the same products and services) and sometimes it's indirect (when businesses are selling different products but solve the same problem or meet the same need), but it's always there.

For this Mindshift, you must complete a competitive analysis chart comparing your venture to *at least* one direct competitor and one indirect competitor. Use the competitive analysis template below as your guide, but feel free to change categories, especially in the "other information" category.

		COMPETITIVE ANALYSIS TEMPLATE	
		YOUR COMPANY	COMPETITOR 1 NAME	COMPETITOR 2 NAME
			DIRECT COMPETITOR	INDIRECT COMPETITOR
Company Highlights	Company Offering			
	Age of Company			
	Competitive Advantage			
Market Information	Target Market			
	Market Share			
	Marketing Strategy			
	Online Reviews/ Influencers			
Product Information	Products and Services			
	Benefits and Features			
	Pricing			
	Distribution Channels			
Other Information	Company Strengths			
	Company Weakness			
	Online Presence			
	Media Mentions			
	Future Opportunities			

Critical Thinking Questions

1. What did you learn about your competition that you did not already know?

2. Are you positioning yourself in a unique way relative to the competition?

3. Can you effectively compete in the market(s) you have chosen? Do you need to shape your idea further? ●

Who Is Your Competition? Why Are You Better?

Every startup has competition, and yours will be no exception. Preparing a competitive analysis is the best way to find out more about your competition and establish the reasons why your business is better.[9, 10] The "What Do You Know About Your Competition?" Mindshift provides a competitive analysis template that enables you to compare your venture with other competitors.

Who Is on Your Team and What Do They Bring to the Table?

Note down the different members of your team, their key duties and responsibilities, and the unique skills they bring to the venture. If you are planning to add people to your team, write those down too, and add any details of when they will start work.

What Are Your Financial Projections?

Include in your plan a concise forecast of your future revenues and expenses. This is a good exercise for taking stock of where your company is right now, the targets and milestones you hope to achieve, and any obstacles that you may need to overcome. Supplement A: Financial Statements and Projections for Startups provides more information on how to work out your company's financial projections.

10.5 THE BUSINESS PLAN DEBATE

>> **LO 10.5**   **Debate the value of writing business plans.**

Of all the types of plans presented in this chapter, the business plan is the most complex and time-consuming document to create. There is considerable debate on the value of spending the time writing a business plan. Proponents of writing a business plan say it helps you gain clarity, keeps you organized, establishes the core message, and creates alignment among team members.[11] It also helps establish legitimacy because, if nothing else, you have a business plan.

Some entrepreneurs in the very early stages find the practice of writing a simple business plan *just for themselves* a great exercise in thinking about things they may not have thought of before. It ensures that you truly understand the components of the plan and the best way to communicate these details to your team and investors. Practicing your plan also helps you to question the validity of your ideas, the markets you intend to target, and the customers you would like to attract.

Others point out that many ideas are pursued but may not be opportunities. The process of writing a business plan helps you vet the idea and shape it into an opportunity. As a result, spending time writing a business plan could help save the entrepreneur a lot of time and money down the road. For example, it can take up to 200 hours to write a comprehensive business plan. That's about a $10,000 investment, assuming you might get $50 per hour for writing a plan ($50 x 200). However, launching a poor idea and unproven concept could cost you millions.[12]

A business plan can be useful at the stage when you have partners or team members on board. It allows everyone to articulate a vision and strategy and ensures that everyone is aligned with current and future plans for the business. It is also a valuable benchmarking tool, as it forces you to be honest about your company's performance by showing not only areas where your business exceeded expectations but also those instances when your strategies didn't work out and the lessons you learned.

Nevertheless, there is growing support for *not* writing a business plan.[13] Those against writing a business plan say that the plan is old as soon as it comes off the printer, it's based on untested assumptions, financial projections are too far out to have validity, and the actual writing and compiling discourages action and gathering real data.[14] As just mentioned, it can take 200 hours to write a comprehensive business plan. Opponents of the business plan feel these hours could be spent on actual activities that can help shape the business idea, get customer input, make early sales, and so on.

Can We Think Ourselves Into (and out of) Planning?

Planning helps entrepreneurs face uncertainty and also helps them deal with the fact that they do not have all information they need to make decisions. According to researchers Brinckman and Kim, business planning is "an activity that is directed to predict the future and develop an appropriate course of action." They also suggest that given the future orientation of planning, new entrepreneurs may not want to engage in planning activities because the lack of information leads to fears, doubts, and decisions not to push forward. The researchers suggest that entrepreneurs tend to avoid planning for two main reasons: they prefer to focus on the present or the task of planning seems too time-consuming and daunting. This suggests that entrepreneurs feel they can use their time better on things other than planning.

Brinckman and Kim hypothesized that first-time entrepreneurs trying to get new ventures started would be more likely to undertake more business planning activities if they had entrepreneurial self-efficacy and entrepreneurial perseverance. Entrepreneurial self-efficacy (ESE) is one's belief in one's ability to perform entrepreneurial roles and tasks. ESE consists of five skills needed to be successful entrepreneurs: marketing, innovation, management, risk-taking, and financial control. Entrepreneurial perseverance (EP) refers to one's ability to continue entrepreneurial efforts regardless of setback, hurdles, and uncertainty. It's really the entrepreneur's ability to push through despite the highs and lows of starting a new business.

The researchers looked at 479 single-owner ventures to test their hypothesis. In other words, they only looked at ventures that were started by one person instead of a team. Additionally, all of the entrepreneurs in the sample were nascent entrepreneurs—those who are in the process of starting a new venture.

The researchers found the following:

- Founders with very high ESE developed more formal business plans than founders with low levels.

- Founders with high EP were more likely to engage in business planning activities, but they were not necessarily formal business plans.

- Founders with low EP were less likely to engage in business planning because it may be perceived as an overly challenging activity and takes too much time.

- Entrepreneurs with a bachelor's degree were more likely to have a formal, written plan.

This was the first study that used cognitive factors, ESE and EP, as variables to determine who does and who does not write formal business plans and why.

In sum, although formal business plans have their place, they may not necessarily be relevant to the new entrepreneur. Entrepreneurs are explorers—they take action to find answers, rather than basing their assumptions on speculation. They are also experts in using social capital—the people and connections you need to make your business a success. No entrepreneur is an island.

So, what should come before the business plan? As we have pointed out many times, at the early stages it is essential to follow the Entrepreneurship Method, to take action, and get out of the building. And make sure you have mastered the basic skills required for a successful venture—financial management, production capabilities, and marketing and sales. When you have proved your concept and gathered the data to go with it, then you will be able to produce a solid, credible business plan.

Critical Thinking Questions

1. Think about your own ESE and EP. What does your self-analysis say about your propensity for writing a formal business plan?

2. Given the findings from this research, why are business plans less popular today than they were 20 years ago?

3. Explain the difference between "planning" and "the plan" as it relates to this research. ●

Sources:

Brinckmann, J., & Kim, S. M. (2015). Why we plan: The impact of nascent entrepreneurs: Cognitive characteristics and human capital on business planning. *Strategic Entrepreneurship Journal, 9,* 153–166.
Chen, C. C., Greene, P. G., & Crick, A. (1998). Does entrepreneurial self-efficacy distinguish entrepreneurs from managers? *Journal of Business Venturing, 13*(4), 295–316.

The idea that the business plan—the most formal and complex of plans—is the first step for an entrepreneur is an outdated view. The business plan is more often used for bank loans and professional investment, but many other types of plans should be generated prior to the formal business plan.

Eric Ries, author of *The Lean Startup,* argues that one reason startups fail is due to "the allure of a good plan, a solid strategy, and thorough market research." Ries hints that corporate strategic planning led us to the conundrum that if a business plan works for the greatest corporations in the world, then it must be good for startups too! Ries notes, "Planning and forecasting are only accurate when based on a long, stable operating history and a relatively static environment. Startups have neither."[15]

10.6 TIPS FOR WRITING ANY TYPE OF PLAN

>> **LO 10.6**   **Implement the tips for writing business plans.**

When you feel you need some type of plan on paper, whether a feasibility study, pitch deck, or even a formal business plan, keep in mind what you put on paper represents *you*.

Remember, different audiences require different plans, and each plan should be tailored accordingly. For example, potential investors will be keen to know more about the financials because they will want to know details of the return on their investment, as well as a time frame for when there is an exit event.

The key to any written plan is knowledge—showing that you have done your homework through exploration, experimentation, and market research is one of the best ways to impress your audience. If your plan does not have a solid basis in fact and research, then do not waste time writing one. Following are some tips for writing formal business plans.[16] Keep in mind, though, that these tips are good for all types of plans we have discussed!

Remove the Fluff

Decorative language can sound nice, but do not be tempted to use it in a business plan. Too much wordiness or jargon can detract from the main message. For example, opening with "In our current environment of fast food, hot dogs are still a much sought-after food enjoyed by people all over the U.S." is purely a waste of space. Most people will know that hot dogs are a popular fast food, and they don't need to be reminded of this.

A better introduction to your business is to describe what it is, its current location, and the target market. For example, "Harry's Gourmet Hot Dogs is a food truck located in southwest Washington that offers 25 different hot dog varieties to satisfy the discerning tastes of local office workers, residents, and seasonal tourists." Here, instead of fillers and unnecessary detail, you have used direct language to quickly and clearly convey a description of your company without taking up too much space.

Define Your Target Audience

It might sound obvious, but many people neglect to properly define their target audience. Remember, there is no business in the world that will appeal to everyone. This is why it is so important to specify your target market, present how and why you have drawn these conclusions, and explain how you intend to target that particular customer segment.

Be Realistic

Outline the challenges ahead, potential risks, lessons you have learned, and opportunities to progress. A strong idea will stand on its merit when you are realistic about it. Everything you write or present must be based in fact or well-researched assumptions.

Focus on Your Competition

There is no such thing as no competition, regardless of how unique you think your business is. Focus on what your business does, but explain what differentiates your product or service from the competition and how you plan to compete now and in the future.

Understand Your Distribution Channels

Make sure you know how your product or service will be delivered to your target customers. Any vagueness around your distribution channels will cause investors to second guess you and your business.

You should always proofread, accuracy-check, and spell-check materials before showing your business plan to investors.

Avoid the Hockey Stick Projection

Ask any entrepreneur about "hockey stick projections" and they will smile and roll their eyes at the same time! A hockey stick projection is one that shows very few sales in Year 1, then suddenly, perhaps in Year 3 or 4, sales skyrocket. When you graph the growth in sales from Year 1 to Year 5, the line looks like a hockey stick, and it's typically unrealistic. Even though it can be difficult to establish solid financial projections, be conservative in your approach to financials. You may feel certain that your business will capture 50% of the market next year, but it is better to present a more plausible percentage, for example 10%. There is no use presenting figures based on guesswork or blown wildly out of proportion. If possible, back up your projections with examples to show investors that you are at least in the right ballpark. Remember, investors want a realistic picture of where your business is now and where you hope it will end up in the future. Overly optimistic projections are sure to put your investors off.

Avoid Typos, Grammatical Mistakes, and Inconsistencies

Revise your plan thoroughly for any mistakes and inconsistencies before you show it to investors. For example, if your plan's summary includes the requirement for $60,000 in investment but your projection shows that you plan to have $70,000 in cash flow in the first year, you have clearly made a mistake. Careless mistakes like these will not impress investors. Ask other people to review your plan for you; a second pair of eyes is invaluable for picking up errors. Furthermore, avoid exaggerated language like "hottest" and "greatest"—these words will not validate your product or service and will certainly not endear you to investors.

Be Honest About Your Weaknesses

Every business has its weaknesses, but it's better to be upfront about them rather than hide them. You don't need to go into too much detail about weaknesses, but you do need to include a well-thought-out strategy explaining how you plan to address these issues.

TABLE 10.7

Business Plan Resources

WEBSITE ADDRESS	DESCRIPTION
https://www.sba.gov/writing-business-plan	The U.S. Small Business Administration guide to writing a business plan
http://www.entrepreneur.com/landing/224842	*Entrepreneur* magazine's "How to Write a Business Plan"
http://www.entrepreneur.com/formnet/form/561	A free template for writing a business plan from *Entrepreneur* magazine's Business Form Template Gallery
http://www.caycon.com/resources.php?s=4	A collection of business plan resources in the Entrepreneur's Library—Startup Resources From Cayenne Consulting
http://www.businessnewsdaily.com/5680-simple-business-plan-templates.html	Eight simple business plan templates for entrepreneurs from *Business News Daily*

Use Visuals

Visuals are a good way to break up the text, help the plan flow better, and bring your idea to life. However, be careful not to crowd the plan with too many graphs, charts, and images. Use adequate white space for optimal legibility and a clean, uncluttered look.

The right time to write a business plan is when your business is more established, you have a fully functioning team involved, and you have the data to prove your concept. If you are considering expanding the business and seeking funding, now would be a good time to write a business plan. Table 10.7 lists some useful resources for writing a business plan when the time comes. ●

$SAGE edge™

Get the tools you need to sharpen your study skills. SAGE edge offers a robust online environment featuring an impressive array of free tools and resources.

- Access practice quizzes, eFlashcards, video, and multimedia at
  edge.sagepub.com/neckentrepreneurship2e

SUMMARY

10.1 Examine "planning" from an entrepreneurial perspective.

From an entrepreneurial perspective, planning helps clarify the entrepreneurial vision and helps the entrepreneur articulate where the business is going and how it can succeed. Entrepreneurs can use alternative planning methods, including simplified plans, planning with preparation, and planning with imagination.

10.2 Explain vision as an important part of planning.

All planning starts with a vision. The vivid vision exercise is a good way to present your vison in writing or as sketch or video. It should describe what the future looks like rather than detailing how you're going to get there.

10.3 Explain the different types of plans used by entrepreneurs.

Different types of plans include the Business Model Canvas, the business brief, the feasibility study, the pitch deck, and the business plan.

10.4 Describe the questions to ask during planning.

Regardless of what type of plan you are working on, you must ask the following questions: What is your business and how does it add value? Who is your customer? How big is the market? How will you enter the market? What do you know about the industry? Who is your competition and why are you better? Who is on your team and what do they bring to the table? And, what are your financial projections?

10. 5 Debate the value of writing business plans.

Experts disagree on the value of spending the time writing a business plan. Some see a business plan as complex, time-consuming, and based on untested assumptions, while others believe it is a useful way to crystallize and organize ideas. Formal business plans have their place, but they may not necessarily be relevant to the new entrepreneur.

10.6 Implement the tips for writing business plans.

Tips for writing business plans include use visuals; remove any fluff; define your target audience; understand your distribution; focus on your competition; avoid typos, grammatical mistakes, and inconsistencies; avoid the exaggerated hockey stick; be honest about weaknesses; and be realistic.

KEY TERMS

Business plan 243

Concept statement 247

Feasibility study 238

Planning 233

CASE STUDY

Boyd Cohen, cofounder, IoMob

Boyd Cohen is the cofounder of IoMob, a decentralized mobility network and platform built on blockchain technology. IoMob democratizes access to the mobility marketplace, both public and private. "In other words, if you are a user and want to get from point A to point B, then we'll give you a solution for the most optimal route, keeping in mind all mobility solutions available like public transport, bike shares, or taxi cabs. Any mobility service, even an individual provider, could be accessible by users through IoMob. We are not trying to be Uber. We are the anti-Uber," Boyd explains.

Boyd Cohen, an expert in smart cities and shared mobility, got his PhD in Entrepreneurship, Internet, and Sustainability from the University of Colorado in 2001. It was around this time that he read a book on profitable, environmentally responsible business practices called *Natural Capitalism,* by Amory Lovins, Hunter Lovins, and Paul Hawken. Being a die-hard capitalist at the time who worked for a big multinational consulting firm, Accenture, Boyd also enjoyed being in nature—mountain biking in the summers and snowboarding in the winters. *Natural Capitalism* inspired Boyd to view and use entrepreneurship as a medium to propagate positive change and bring these two worlds of capitalism and nature together. He dedicated his career both as an academic and an entrepreneur to this cause. Since then, Boyd has had a plethora of experiences, from starting companies, to consulting, to academia.

In 2011, Boyd wrote his first book, *Climate Capitalism,* as a sequel to *Natural Capitalism* along with one of the original authors, Hunter Lovins. At the time, the world was optimistic about Barack Obama's administration making real progress on climate change at the 2011 UN Climate Change Conference in Durban, South Africa. Frustrated with lack of action at both the national and international levels, Boyd started to view cities as potential agents for change. However, Boyd has been involved with making cities smarter since long before 2011. "Technically, I would say I've been in smart cities for over 12 years now. My first startup (2006), was a SaaS (Software as a Service) solution for cities to transparently track, monitor, and report their sustainability performance. Maybe we would've called them a smart cities project now, but in 2006 nobody was calling it that!"

In 2014, he and his colleague Jan Kietzmann wrote one of the most frequently cited peer-reviewed academic papers on shared mobility. Shared mobility refers to transportation services and resources that are shared among users, either concurrently or consecutively. This includes public transit; taxis and limos; bike sharing; car sharing (round-trip, one-way, and peer-to-peer); ride sharing (i.e., noncommercial services like carpooling and vanpooling); ride sourcing or ride hailing; shuttle services and "micro transit"; and more. Boyd believes that he has come full circle in his worldviews. Funnily enough, after writing a book (*Climate Capitalism*) that propagates using capitalism to tackle climate change and another book *(The Emergence of the Urban Entrepreneur,* 2016) that focused on innovation, entrepreneurship, and smart cities, his third book, *Post-Capitalist Entrepreneurship: Start-Ups for the 99%* (2017), was geared toward what steps can be taken beyond capitalism to make the economy more inclusive. For the book, he interviewed an entrepreneur, Jamie Burke, cofounder and CEO of Outlier Ventures, a venture fund well known for investing in blockchain. As they started to talk, Jamie told Boyd that if he were to start a blockchain company, Jamie would help him incubate the company. "At first I wasn't so sure. I mean, I was getting close to 50 and I've done several startups. I was sort of, kind of, enjoying my life as an academic. It's not so easy being an entrepreneur. But the blockchain bug got me."

Boyd knew that blockchain technology was a disruptive technology. As Boyd notes, "Digital currencies created through blockchain remove nation states and dilute the power of lobbyists and banks that are too big to fail. An alternative currency enables peer-to-peer transaction without involving its national governments. Similarly, blockchain can mediate peer-to-peer economies without the Ubers and the Airbnb's in the middle." Boyd feels that companies like Airbnb and Uber are platform companies that are not really sharing their "platform capitalism." This prompted Boyd to research and think about business models that support a truer, peer-to-peer sharing economy.

Burke told Boyd that they were doing a lot of work on a newer type of peer-to-peer model called *platform cooperativism,* a cooperative ownership of the platform. For instance, Airbnb would not be owned by Airbnb but by the homeowners and users. Boyd started to look into creating a blockchain-enabled platform for the few taxi cooperatives in Boulder and Denver, Colorado, his hometown. These taxi co-ops were not big enough to compete with the likes of Uber and therefore could not expect the customer to download three (or more) different apps for each taxi service. So Boyd created an app called Coopify that focused on building tech stacks for these co-op businesses that did not have the expertise or confidence to invest in technology. However, Boyd noticed a bigger opportunity, which had the potential to disrupt the market. Every city has its own bike sharing, car sharing, and public transport services that use closed networks to compete with each other. Boyd saw a powerful opportunity to use blockchain to connect them all. He pivoted the business idea in November 2017 and started reaching out to advisors. IoMob was born.

Boyd leveraged his extensive network to find the best people to invite to be IoMob advisors. The first one to join was Susan Shaheen from UC Berkeley, one of the world's leading experts on shared mobility and also sometimes called the "mother of shared mobility." Knowing that he did not have the ability to do blockchain computing, Boyd started looking for a cofounder/CTO for the company. "To me, one of the most important success factors for an entrepreneur is to identify where you're weak, where your team is weak, and convincing really good people who can fill that gap to join your team." He soon found Josep Sanjuas, a PhD in computer science, for the role of the CTO and got Victor Lopez, another computer science PhD, to join as the third cofounder. In late 2018, he resigned from his role as the dean of research at EADA Business School in Barcelona, Spain, to pursue IoMob full time. The company now has eight full-time people and two part-time people working on IoMob.

IoMob, as Boyd explains it, "is a decentralized mobility aggregation platform. IoMob stands for Internet of Mobility (inspired by IoT, or Internet of Things). Just like IoT, where different devices connected to the Internet can also be seamlessly connected together, IoMob does the same for mobility services through a digital layer. We connect every mobility service, public and private, into an open marketplace so that the end user has seamless access to discover, get multimodal routing, book, and pay for any mobility service you want through one open application connected to our marketplace." A mobility startup that wants to enter a market crowded with players that already have big private network effects can use IoMob's platform to reach out to customers.

IoMob leverages the blockchain ecosystem to create smart contracts between users, a function unique to blockchain. A smart contract allows any service provider to connect with customers (in this case, connected to the IoMob protocol) and charge whatever fees they deem fit, without the hassle of negotiating with the platform. Likewise, the customer can choose to accept the offer or not. This way, companies that offer their own mobility solutions can link to the IoMob platform to provide alternative modes of transport in case their services are unavailable. This might retain an existing customer base and help the other service provider monetize a customer he or she could not have had before. For example, if a bike sharing company has run out of bikes, it can link to the IoMob platform, which will then provide alternative transport solutions to the bike sharing company's customers. Today, IoMob's primary customers are governments and private operators. Boyd believes that mobility services such as Uber and Lyft would be the last ones to join IoMob's platform, and even if they did, they would be providing the service of fulfilling the requests of customers who could not find another mobility option.

Instead of writing a business plan in the beginning stage of the company, Boyd and his colleagues wrote three white papers explaining the concept behind Coopify and, later, IoMob. Because the company is in the pre-revenue stage, Boyd and his team are now focusing efforts on testing the proof of concept in real-world settings. Apart from being a semi-finalist in the City of Tomorrow, Ford Motor Company Pilot Competition in Pittsburgh, IoMob has scheduled test sprints with the Public Transit Authority in Portland, Oregon, and is in talks with the Netherlands, Singapore, and big brands such as Hyundai.

Boyd feels that one of the challenges they might face relates to the mindsets of business providers. "Capitalists are likely to take more time to come to terms with a completely open marketplace where your competitors could potentially know your inventory. On the other hand, smaller players love this openness. It is a way for them to feel like they've overcome the barrier to entry in a market," he says.

Boyd believes that mobility could either become monopolized by the likes of Uber or become a completely open mobility marketplace. A few multibillion-dollar OEMs, and car manufacturers who "see the writing on the wall," want to partner with IoMob for the future that depends less on private vehicle ownership. Another challenge that Boyd has faced with IoMob is communicating the vision of the company to potential stakeholders like public transit authorities. Because both the technology and concept are new, governments sometimes have a hard time grasping the context and IoMob's potential impact. However, over time, Boyd has tweaked the messaging to focus on the value proposition of IoMob as opposed to making it sound overly technical. "It's been an evolution of our own understanding of how to tell the narrative and how to share it with different audiences," says Boyd.

Boyd hopes to be able to leverage the billions of dollars being invested into blockchain technology to be able to scale up his operations successfully. To date, he has raised $700,000. And it's not just about immediate scale, but also about preparing for the future. The mobility market is changing every day. Boyd believes that he has a strong team that can tackle these changes and adapt accordingly.

Early in March 2019, Boyd and his IoMob team were one of 10 startups selected out of 360 to join the Techstars Accelerator Program in Amsterdam. "Techstars has taught us we have not been disciplined enough with ourselves as founders and as a team to ensure that everyone knows what their priorities are and is tracking their progress on a weekly basis. After going through this process the past few weeks, we are going to do a similar exercise every week with our own team." Additionally, Techstars introduced Boyd to a group of almost 90 mentors during the first 3 weeks of the Techstar program—it's referred to as the "Mentor Madness" phase. Mentor Madness forced Boyd and his team to be more open than ever to tough, constructive feedback. "This type of tough feedback is essential to achieving our global ambitions," said Boyd.

Boyd says that he has learned a lot of lessons through all his startup experiences. He reflects, "Don't fall in love with your cofounder. Dedicate less time to fundraising and more time to create a quality product or a service. Do not outsource competitive advantage. Media attention is great, but it is very difficult to convert this attention into monetary sales."

Critical Thinking Questions

1. How do you begin planning for a venture when the technology is so new?

2. What evidence in the case did you see of Boyd Cohen planning?

3. IoMob is in its beginning. What do you think its future holds? Would you invest today?

Sources:

Boyd Cohen (interview with Babson MBA graduate assistant Gaurav Khemka, November 7, 2018)

Cohen, B., & Kietzmann, J. (2014). Ride on! Mobility business models for the sharing economy. *Organization & Environment, 27*(3), 279–296. Retrieved from https://www.researchgate.net/publication/267757539_Ride_On_Mobility_Business_Models_for_the_Sharing_Economy

Maxwell, L. (2018). An interview with Susan Shaheen. *UC Berkeley Institute of Transportation Studies.* Retrieved from https://tsrc.berkeley.edu/news/interview-susan-shaheen-%E2%80%9Cmother%E2%80%9D-shared-mobility

What is shared mobility? (2019). *Shared Use Mobility Center.* Retrieved from https://sharedusemobilitycenter.org/what-is-shared-mobility/

11 Anticipating Failure

"Failure is fuel. Fuel is power."

—Abby Wambach, retired soccer star

Chapter Outline

Learning Objectives

11.1 Describe failure and its effect on entrepreneurs.

11.2 Identify several reasons for failure.

11.3 Describe the consequences of fear of failure for entrepreneurs.

11.4 Explain the different ways entrepreneurs can learn from failure.

11.5 Describe the significance of "grit" and its role in building tolerance for failure.

11.1 FAILURE AND ENTREPRENEURSHIP

>> LO 11.1   Describe failure and its effect on entrepreneurs.

In Chapter 1, we explained the ill-defined, unstructured, unpredictable, chaotic, and complex nature of entrepreneurship. We also presented some daunting statistics showing that not all attempts to grow a business will be successful, especially when many of the attempts end in bankruptcy. The reality is that many startups fail; therefore, it is important to include the topic of failure when discussing entrepreneurship.

A business failure is generally conceived as the termination of a commercial organization that has missed its goals and failed to achieve investors' expectations, preventing the venture from continuing to operate and resulting in bankruptcy or liquidation. Any type of failure, however, can intensify the cognitive processes involved in learning, resulting in improvements in future performance and increasing the probability of future success. For this reason, many entrepreneurs see failure as part of the journey. In the case of business failures, having learned from failure, entrepreneurs often feel more confident, prepared, and motivated to attempt another startup venture.

Despite these perceived benefits, the failure of a venture can be not only financially costly but also emotionally painful, even traumatic. The experience is not that different from ending a long relationship or losing a loved one, resulting in feelings of grief and loss, leaving the entrepreneur feeling guilty and even ashamed while wondering what exactly went wrong and how it could have been avoided.

Big failures in business are the ones we hear about the most. Bankruptcy or forced sale is probably the biggest failure for a startup. California-based peer-to-peer used car startup Beepi is a good example of an epic fail.[1] Beepi had raised more than $150 million from investors, but it burned through the money too quickly—reports showed that the founders were overspending on their own salaries and expensive office furniture—and ended up laying off almost 200 employees before closing its doors for good in 2017. Or take Juicero, the home juice maker that had received almost $120 million in funding from Google Ventures, Kleiner Perkins, and Campbell Soup Company.[2] Although the device seemed like an efficient way to make juice at home, the startup folded after a Bloomberg article reported that the pre-packed packets of juice and vegetables to be transformed into juice by the machine generated the same amount of liquid as if the packets had been squeezed by hand. The company was shut down shortly after the negative marketing exposure.

Poor money management caused the downfall of Beepi and a badly researched product was to blame for Juicero's closure. We can usually find many reasons behind the closure of a startup. Contributing factors often include lack of market need, poor marketing, and loss of focus. Figure 11.1 lists the most common reasons behind the failure of startups.

Master the content at
**edge.sagepub.com/
neckentrepreneurship2e**

David James, K12 Landing

Photo courtesy of David James

David James, founder of K12 Landing

David James holds the record at his high school for most magazines sold during a fundraiser. He found out the record was 74 so he sold 75! What does this have to do with entrepreneurship? Keep reading.

David earned an MBA from Babson College and a bachelor's in business administration from Bucknell University. During college, he interned with a large investment bank in New York City, and upon graduation transitioned into education as a corps member with Teach for America (TFA). There he was a founding member of the Boston region of TFA and taught 8th-grade science.

After completing his 2-year commitment with TFA, he helped restart a low-performing middle school in South Boston. Later he cofounded UP Academy Oliver, a public school for 6th–8th graders in Lawrence, Massachusetts, as part of a state-led district reform effort. During his time in education, he noticed that teachers didn't have enough high-quality training and development programs to choose from. He knew that teachers were required to participate in training every year, but the teachers didn't have a way to find something relevant and worthwhile. As a result, he

started to think about a new venture. He wanted to start a service to connect K–12 teachers to relevant training and development programs across the country. David called the service K12 Landing.

During his MBA program, David refined the idea for K12 Landing, raised a small amount of startup capital, hired a web development firm to build out a website, and even hired an employee to lead marketing. But by the time David finished his MBA, K12 Landing had not met expectations; the business model wasn't working and revenue wasn't generated. K12 Landing failed. Reflecting on his K12 Landing experience, he explained, "While I had strong knowledge of the K–12 education landscape, my lack of experience working with technology developers and sales led me to underestimate the barriers of starting the business." He added, "I was often frustrated by the slow rate of progress and lack of communication with developers. I fired my first developer and had to find a new one to rebuild the entire website.

Rather than looking at the experience of K12 Landing as a failure, David took away valuable lessons that led him to "pivot" his business and focus on higher education. "I now recognize the importance of leaning on your network and relying on people you know well, especially when starting a new venture." As David closed K12 Landing, he simultaneously began building a new venture called Beacon Instructional Partners that is focused on providing personalized instructional coaching to college professors. He recognized that he needed to pursue a venture that more closely aligned with his instructional background and would allow him to better leverage his network in the world of education.

His experience with K12 Landing and learning the nuances of starting a business paid off when he secured his first paying client soon after completing his MBA program. "With Beacon Instructional Partners I have more realistic expectations," said David, "and I am more intentional about how I manage things so that we set ourselves up for incremental growth." He also admits that after the K12 Landing failure he is more accustomed to the pressures of entrepreneurship as well as the need for sales skills and a keen understanding of the customer.

Beacon Instructional Partners has quickly expanded to four team members. After this initial success, David says that entrepreneurship in professional services often comes down to "being able to define exactly what you do and what value you can provide in language that clients understand and resonate with." But he's not all in just yet. David still has a full-time job with a national education consulting firm. "I will go full time when I have the confidence that it can support me and my family. This is the type of personal decision that varies for everyone." Ultimately, David provides great evidence that entrepreneurship is about learning as you go. With this mentality, failure doesn't exist. It's just part of the Entrepreneurship Method.

Critical Thinking Questions

1. What is a pivot? How did pivoting positively affect David's career?

2. What can you learn about lack of ability from David's ventures with K12 Landing?

3. How would you handle the failure of a business venture? ●

Source: David James (interview with the author, December 15, 2018)

FIGURE 11.1

The Top 20 Reasons Startups Fail

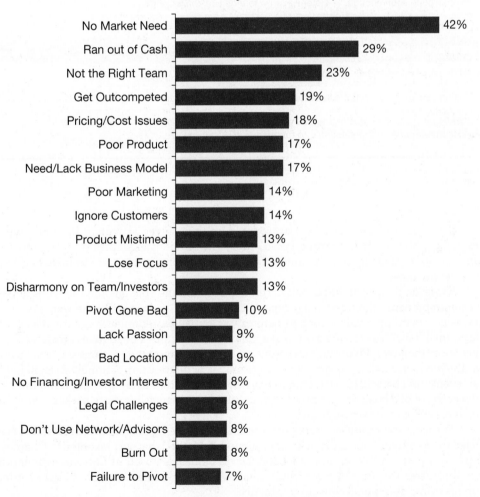

Based on an Analysis of 101 Startup Post-Mortems

Reason	Percentage
No Market Need	42%
Ran out of Cash	29%
Not the Right Team	23%
Get Outcompeted	19%
Pricing/Cost Issues	18%
Poor Product	17%
Need/Lack Business Model	17%
Poor Marketing	14%
Ignore Customers	14%
Product Mistimed	13%
Lose Focus	13%
Disharmony on Team/Investors	13%
Pivot Gone Bad	10%
Lack Passion	9%
Bad Location	9%
No Financing/Investor Interest	8%
Legal Challenges	8%
Don't Use Network/Advisors	8%
Burn Out	8%
Failure to Pivot	7%

Source: CB Insights https://www.cbinsights.com/blog/startup-failure-reasons-top/

TABLE 11.1

Entrepreneurs Share Their Reasons for Failure

PSYCHE "MISTAKES"
"Fear." —Philip Rosedale, founder, *High Fidelity, Inc.,* and *Second Life*
"Letting opinions cloud your purpose." —Scott Lewallen, founder, *Grindr*
"Trusting by default." —Jay Adelson, chair and founder, *Opsmatic*
"Not believing in myself was the biggest mistake I made as an entrepreneur." —Sam Shank, cofounder/CEO, *HotelTonight*
"Spending too much time worrying about competition and not enough time making what I'm building amazing." —Brenden Mulligan, founder/CEO, *Cluster Labs*
"Thinking that entrepreneurship was the most meaningful part of my life." —Mick Hagen, founder, *Zinch.com, Spatch, Undrip.com,* and *Mainframe*
WAITING TOO LONG MISTAKES
"My biggest mistake as an entrepreneur was waiting too long to start." —Jason Nazar, founder, *Docstoc.com*
"Not pivoting soon enough." —Peter Kazanjy, founder, *TalentBin*
"Waiting to see if a problem would resolve itself." —Joshua Forman, cofounder, *Inkling*
HIRING MISTAKES
"Hiring too fast and firing too slow." —Dan Yates, cofounder/CEO, *OPOWER*
"Hiring bad fits." —John Battelle, cofounder/CEO, *NewCo, Federated Media, Web 2.0 Summit, Wired*
"Getting the wrong people on the bus was the biggest mistake I made as an entrepreneur." —Hooman Radfar, partner, *Expa,* and founder, *AddThis*

Source: Carman. E. R. (2015, June 25). Successful entrepreneurs reveal their biggest mistakes. *FounderDating.* Retrieved from http://founderdating.com/successful-entrepreneurs-reveal-biggest-mistakes/

Pivot: a change in business direction.

It is also useful to hear how entrepreneurs themselves articulate the underlying reasons as to why their startups failed. Table 11.1 provides examples of entrepreneurs who attribute their failures to three main causes: their psyche, people mistakes, and market mistakes.

However, there is an important difference between the epic fail and the types of failure entrepreneurs should actually expect, embrace, and leverage. No one wants or even expects catastrophic failure such as bankruptcy, but all entrepreneurs experience countless small "fails" that require a quick reaction and sometimes a change in direction, often known as the **pivot**. Pivots for entrepreneurs include changing directions on such things as the product, customer segment, revenue model, or distribution channel.[3] A small fail is an event—an obstacle to overcome to get through the other side—whereas a big fail like the collapse of a business is a process that unfolds over time; it is more personal and can be more difficult to recover from.

The most successful entrepreneurs embrace and leverage failure and pivot when they need to—a key component of the Entrepreneurship Method that we presented in Chapter 1 and have built on throughout this book. David James, featured in Entrepreneurship in Action, made a successful pivot from his education marketplace K12 Landing to setting up his own instructional consulting practice.

Small failures are considered the "valleys" in the entrepreneurial journey that include the setbacks, the missteps, the ill-planned experiments, the misplaced decisions—all manageable events that can help you build on what you learn. Small, reversible, informative failures along the way can highlight key issues and set you on a better path to success. The point is that if we can expect and embrace the learning from the small failures, then perhaps we can mitigate the risks of the big failures.

11.2 THE FAILURE SPECTRUM

>> **LO 11.2 Identify several reasons for failure.**

Amy Edmondson, a professor of leadership and management at Harvard Business School, believes that failures range from big to small along a failure spectrum (see Figure 11.2). Although many of us link the admission of failure with taking the blame, Edmondson believes that not all failures are blameworthy; her spectrum of failures runs from blameworthy to praiseworthy. Some of the reasons for failure on the spectrum are indeed blameworthy. For example, entrepreneurs who intentionally violate certain rules and regulations ("Deviance," at the top of the spectrum) are more likely to have failed businesses as well as a tarnished reputation. However, not all of the failures in the spectrum are bad—in fact, many of them are at least preventable or even praiseworthy. Someone who doesn't have the skills to do a job can receive more training; processes can be monitored and refined; and "failed" hypotheses and exploratory testing can be opportunities to expand knowledge, iterate, and set the scene for different, better approaches.[4]

Despite our misgivings about failure, it is not always bad. The failure spectrum describes situations that may be perceived as failures, yet can sometimes have positive rather than negative outcomes. Let's look at the failure spectrum in greater depth.

Startup company Juicero collapsed due to poor product research.

© Michael Kovac/Contributor/Getty Images

FIGURE 11.2

The Failure Spectrum

| **Deviance** | • The entrepreneur defies legal and ethical boundaries leading to mismanagement of the venture. |

| **Inattention** | • The entrepreneur gets sidetracked from the core business—either in a new business direction or by delegating too much too soon without following up. |

| **Lack of Ability** | • The entrepreneur is overextended and lacks the skillset to get the job done. |

| **Process Inadequacy** | • The wrong (or lack of) processes are set up in the organization such that communication breaks down among employees and things begin to fall through the cracks. |

| **Uncertainty** | • The entrepreneur takes unreasonable actions due to a lack of clarity about future events. |

| **Exploratory Experimentation** | • The entrepreneur conducts market tests to get early feedback and acquire important learning and information. |

Source: Adapted from Amy C. Edmondson, Strategies for learning from failure, *Harvard Business Review*, April 2011. https://hbr.org/2011/04/strategies-for-learning-from-failure

Blood-testing startup Theranos collapsed under the weight of false claims and fraudulent charges.

Deviance: when an entrepreneur defies legal and ethical boundaries, leading to mismanagement of the venture.

Inattention: when an entrepreneur becomes sidetracked from the core business.

Lack of ability: the lack of skillset to get the job done.

Process inadequacy: wrong (or missing) processes set up in the organization, causing communication breakdown.

Deviance

Deviance occurs when an entrepreneur defies legal and ethical boundaries, leading to mismanagement of the venture. Blood-testing startup Theranos is a good example of a company that demonstrated deviance from social norms, as well as defiance of legal and ethical boundaries. Founded in 2003 by then-19-year-old Stanford drop-out Elizabeth Holmes, this startup promised to take the trauma out of blood testing by using just a single drop of blood that would run through the Theranos machine called the Edison. The company claimed that the Edison could run 240 different blood tests, but in fact, only a few could actually be done on the Edison.[5] The remaining tests were done on machines that were competitors of Theranos. The deviance was that customers, board members, and investors thought the Edison was actually running 240 tests using a single drop of blood. In 2018, Elizabeth Holmes and former company president Ramesh Balwani were charged with fraud for making false claims about the effectiveness of the blood-testing product.[6]

Inattention

An entrepreneur gets sidetracked from the core business by **inattention**—either by moving in a new business direction or by delegating too much too soon without following up. Entrepreneur Siouxsie Downs became sidetracked from her main business, STEM education accelerator IQ Co-Op, by trying to manage too many different projects at once.[7] When her colleagues called her out for her lack of follow-through, Downs stepped back from some of the projects and appointed a trusted colleague to help her manage her deadlines. While she admits that letting go can be difficult, this incident made her realize that "If you don't, you will be done with the startup world," she says. "You will stretch yourself thin and give 0% to 15% effort on 20 things instead of 100% on three things. Know what you value the most and give that your all."

Lack of Ability

With **lack of ability**, the entrepreneur is overextended and lacks the skillset to get the job done. He or she may have been good at the start, but as the business grew, more skills were needed. It is very common for companies to outgrow their founders because the founders lack the skills and abilities to get the company to the next level. In some cases, the founders either can't or won't develop the necessary skills to develop the organization, and they may have to step aside as a result.[8]

For example, Eddie Lou, founder of workforce technology company Shiftgig, stepped down as CEO in favor of new CEO Wade Burgess.[9] Although Lou had the most suitable skills to set up the company, raise capital, and bring it to market, Burgess had a better skillset for growing the company to its next stage.

Process Inadequacy

Process inadequacy means the wrong processes are set up in the organization, so communication breaks down among employees and things begin to fall through the cracks. Paul Biggar and Nathan Chong are the founders of NewsTilt, a news website for independent, professional journalists. Biggar believes lack of communication was one of the reasons why the startup lasted only 2 months: "When Nathan and I signed up together, we had not spent any time working together, and that was a big mistake.[10] Nathan is certainly a great coder, but when we didn't share a vision, and we found it so difficult to communicate, there was no way we were going to get this built. You need a cofounder who gets you and whom you work together well with."

Uncertainty

Uncertainty or lack of clarity about future events can cause entrepreneurs to take unreasonable actions. Keith B. Nowak, founder of social media instant messaging company Imercive, believes that company failed because it stuck to the wrong strategy for far too long. Nowak said, "If we had been honest with ourselves earlier on, we may have been able to pivot sooner and have enough capital left to properly execute the new strategy.[11] I believe the biggest mistake I made as CEO of Imercive was failing to pivot sooner."

Uncertainty: the lack of clarity about future events that can cause entrepreneurs to take unreasonable actions.

Exploratory Experimentation

Market tests are conducted to get early feedback and acquire important learning and information. Some of these tests may fail miserably, but **exploratory experimentation** is crucial for learning. Joelle Mertzel, founder of countertop butter dish Butterie, tested the market for her prototype by interviewing more than 1,000 people waiting to board flights in airports all over the United States.[12] The results showed that 67% of the respondents agreed they would use the butter dish, which was enough proof for Mertzel to develop it into a viable product. Butterie now sells in Bed Bath & Beyond and is profiled on the shopping channel QVC.

Exploratory experimentation: a method whereby market tests are conducted to get early feedback and acquire important learning and information.

As Figure 11.2 illustrates, there are different kinds of failures. Some failures are small, adjustable, informative, linked to bigger goals, and designed to highlight key issues. Others involve rigid thinking, discouragement, and may result in reputational damage.[13] Although the reasons behind failed businesses are varied, it might surprise you that none of these count as the number one reason for startup failure. A study carried out by CBI Insights analyzing 101 startup postmortems found that 42% of startups failed because they didn't solve a big enough problem.[14] For instance, visual configurator platform company Treehouse Logic failed because its customers didn't have the time, desire, and patience to use its customization tools. Being able to customize just wasn't a big enough pain point for Treehouse Logic's target market.

Whatever the type of or reason for the failure, the most important thing for entrepreneurs is the lessons they learn.

11.3 FEAR OF FAILURE

>> LO 11.3   **Describe the consequences of fear of failure for entrepreneurs.**

Despite the learning and opportunities that may arise from perceived failures, many of us view failure in a negative way and try our best to avoid it. This is because the concept of failure provokes an emotional reaction or antifailure bias that inhibits us from learning from the experience. This causes us to put the failure out of our minds rather than tackling the reasons behind it.[15]

It is not surprising that we never hear much about the emotions of failure (pain, humiliation, shame, guilt, self-blame, and anger—often associated with grief) that entrepreneurs experience when their businesses go under. As serial entrepreneur Meggen Taylor said, "Your ego will be crushed. Your faith will be tested. And if work is your identity you will feel completely lost and soulless."[16] Expressing these emotions is often too much to bear, as admitting our failures can be emotionally unpleasant and can damage our self-esteem.

However, it is only by managing these emotions that entrepreneurs can begin the process of learning from failure. But this is not an easy process; sometimes we would rather blame others or external events for failures in order to maintain our self-esteem and sense of control.

Meggen and Peter Taylor, co-founders of FindEverythingHistoric .com

From Tech Hero to Zero Net Worth

A company's ultimate failure may come at any time, before a first round of seed funding or as the company holds a billion-dollar valuation. Elizabeth Holmes, American entrepreneur and founder of medical testing company Theranos, learned that lesson the hard way, losing her $9 billion–valued company as lies and deception caught up with her. In the course of 1 year, Holmes went from being a billionaire to being valued by *Forbes* as having a net worth of "nothing."

Holmes dropped out of Stanford University at the age of 19 to start Theranos, a company that claimed to revolutionize the blood-testing process by using a finger prick instead of the more traditional needle-based method. Holmes claimed that a single drop of blood could be used to run more than 200 different health tests on their proprietary machine called Edison—a claim that was set to revolutionize health care. A pair of angel investors helped Holmes kickstart her company, raising an initial $6 million in 2004. Theranos grew exponentially, striking lucrative deals with Walgreens and Safeway to run blood-testing clinics.

As Theranos and the Edison technology began to gain widespread recognition in the startup world, with Holmes appearing on the cover of *Fortune* magazine (among other public achievements), *Wall Street Journal* reporter John Carreyrou took a deep dive into the company's practices and testing in 2015. He interviewed several former employees, including a former lab director, who exposed the company's severely exaggerated product marketing. Theranos claimed to be able to perform 204 tests with the finger prick, but in reality, only a handful worked.

The technology clearly did nowhere near what it advertised. Theranos was actually using competitors' equipment to perform the tests behind the scenes.

The company quickly spiraled downward after the report, losing the deals with Walgreens and Safeway. Holmes was banned from the lab-testing industry for 2 years by the Center for Medicare and Medicaid Services. She is (at the time of this writing) awaiting a 2020 trial, which will decide whether she will land in prison for up to 20 years and possibly pay millions of dollars in fines. Theranos ceased operations in 2018, and it has since been liquidated.

Critical Thinking Questions

1. How much can a company exaggerate its product, yet still remain ethical?

2. Should advertisements be made for a product before that product is fully ready? When is the proper time to declare a product to the world?

3. What would you do if you were an employee of Theranos and knew what was happening? ●

Sources:

Carreyrou, J. (2015, October 16). Hot startup Theranos has struggled with its blood-test technology. *Wall Street Journal.* Retrieved from https://www.wsj.com/articles/theranos-has-struggled-with-blood-tests-1444881901

Clark, K. (2019, June 28). Theranos founder Elizabeth Holmes to stand trial in 2020. *Tech Crunch.* Retrieved from https://techcrunch.com/2019/06/28/theranos-founder-elizabeth-holmes-to-stand-trial-in-2020/

Herper, M. (2016, June 21). From $4.5 billion to nothing: Forbes revises estimated net worth of Theranos founder Elizabeth Holmes. *Forbes.* Retrieved from https://www.forbes.com/sites/matthewherper/2016/06/01/from-4-5-billion-to-nothing-forbes-revises-estimated-net-worth-of-theranos-founder-elizabeth-holmes/#2c1e97943633

For entrepreneurs, failure is especially difficult because it is hard to separate personal failure from professional failure, given how closely associated the identity of the business is tied to the identity of the entrepreneur.

What many successful entrepreneurs have realized is that it is acceptable and human to try and then fail. Feelings of doubt, uncertainty, frustration, and a yearning for help are all perfectly normal. Yet before entrepreneurs are able to move forward or even start their businesses, they need to first overcome their fear of failure.

Signs of Fear of Failure

As we have learned, fear of failure can be a major impediment to seizing opportunities and transforming entrepreneurial objectives into real action.[17] Although many of us have a degree of fear of failure, some have a higher level than others. Researchers have suggested that the origins of fear of failure may lie in parent–child relations. For example, a child is likely to have a higher fear of failure if he or she is punished for failures and receives little or neutral praise for successful achievements. Studies also suggest that there is a connection between high parental expectations and a child's fear of failure, as well as other factors such as maternal irritability and paternal absence.[18]

Overcoming the Stigma of Failure

As much as entrepreneurs should learn from and even embrace failure, the impact of failure can be harsh. In many areas around the world, in families, in communities, business failure can be a stigma. A stigma is "a quality of social dishonor: a market of degradation, loss of esteem, or loss of reputation."[19] Researcher Grace Walsh looked at how entrepreneurs who have failed can reenter entrepreneurship and avoid stigma. Recognizing the negative impact of stigma such as humiliation, guilt, pain, embarrassment, and shame, Walsh wanted to better understand how entrepreneurs avoided or overcame stigma and decided to engage in entrepreneurship again.[20]

Her sample included 15 first-time entrepreneurs in Ireland who started a business between 1997 and 2007 but ceased to exist within 5 years of starting. Additionally, these same entrepreneurs reentered entrepreneurship after their failure experience. Walsh found that entrepreneurs use detachment, acknowledgment, and deflection to overcome negative social repercussions associated with stigma. Detachment relates to the entrepreneur separating himself from the venture and subsequent failure, as well as limiting the importance of the failure. In other words, making it sound like the failure wasn't that big of a deal or rationalizing the failure. Acknowledgment relates to the entrepreneur's ability to openly discuss the failure with various stakeholders—owning up to the failure. Deflection is more like quieting a bully. The entrepreneurs would simply dismiss the naysayers or ignore the overly judgmental. By overcoming or avoiding stigma through methods such as detachment, acknowledgment, and deflection, these entrepreneurs were able to move on and engage in entrepreneurship once again.

Critical Thinking Questions

1. Have you ever practiced one of the methods of overcoming stigma? What was the outcome?

2. Why do you think detachment, acknowledgment, or deflection could help a failed entrepreneur want to try to start a business again?

3. Does the stigma of failure look or feel different around the world? Why or why not? ●

Overall, studies show that individuals who are raised to believe that failure is unacceptable and has negative consequences will go out of their way to avoid failure. This means that rather than seeing mistakes as opportunities to learn and improve skills, or to compete against others, they will view them as threatening and judgment-oriented experiences. Here, failure is associated with shame—a painful emotion that many of us will avoid, even if it means losing out on lucrative opportunities. Avoiding the potential to make mistakes stunts the growth and maturity of individuals with a high fear of failure, which leads only to more mistakes and failures over time.[21] Understanding that failure is an important part of growth and learning is a vital lesson for entrepreneurs who want to succeed in their personal and professional lives.

People with a strong fear of failure tend to be anxious, lack self-esteem, and demonstrate reluctance to try new things. Table 11.2 illustrates some symptoms of fear of failure.

Once you establish the extent of your fear of failure, you can begin to develop some coping strategies to deal with it.[22] First, you can reframe specific goals so they become more achievable; for example, rather than setting a goal of earning $100,000 from a new product launch, you can expand the goal to focus also on what you learn from launching a new product. That way, even if the product does not meets its monetary target, you will not feel you have failed, as you have already committed to learning something of value from the experience. This ties in with the concept of acceptable loss outlined in the Entrepreneurship Method.

Second, if the product failed to generate as much revenue as you would like, it is helpful to separate your personal feelings from facts. Instead of thinking, "I feel terrible because I have failed," you can ask yourself, "What did I learn from this experience?" and "What are the positive things about what happened?"

Third, many of us try to suppress the emotions associated with fear, but by deliberately allowing yourself to feel the fear, you are more likely to diminish the fear of failure. Taking deep breaths for 2 minutes is a useful exercise to shift negative feelings and trigger a calm response.

TABLE 11.2

10 Signs You Might Have a Fear of Failure

1.	Failing makes you worry about what other people think about you.
2.	Failing makes you worry about your ability to pursue the future you desire.
3.	Failing makes you worry that people will lose interest in you.
4.	Failing makes you worry about how smart or capable you are.
5.	Failing makes you worry about disappointing people whose opinion you value.
6.	You tend to tell people beforehand that you don't expect to succeed in order to lower their expectations.
7.	Once you fail at something, you have trouble imagining what you could have done differently to succeed.
8.	You often get last-minute headaches, stomach aches, or other physical symptoms that prevent you from completing your preparation.
9.	You often get distracted by tasks that prevent you from completing your preparation, which, in hindsight, were not as urgent as they seemed at the time.
10.	You tend to procrastinate and "run out of time" to complete your preparation adequately.

Source: Adapted from Winch, G. (2013, June 18). 10 signs that you might have fear of failure. *Psychology Today.* Retrieved from https://www.psychologytoday.com/blog/the-squeaky-wheel/201306/10-signs-you-might-have-fear-failure

Credit: Forbes.com

Entrepreneur Neil Patel (left) claims that living with his parents taught him to be careful with his money.

Finally, a good way to deal with your fear is to seek support from the role models in your life. For example, serial entrepreneur Neil Patel believes that living with his parents until the age of 23 gave him the emotional support he needed to recover from a series of failed business ventures.[23]

Global Fear of Failure

A strong fear of failure is often rooted in one's national culture. The Global Entrepreneurship Monitor report (GEM) measures fear of failure by country.[24] When you look at this on a map, you can also recognize regional differences (see Figure 11.3). The GEM failure rate is based on those who admit to perceiving opportunities to start a business but feel prevented from acting on those opportunities due to fear of failure. The lower the percentage shown on the map, the lower the fear.

Overall, different countries and the cultures associated with countries had different tolerances for failure, but perhaps not as much difference as you would think. In particular, fear of failure was lowest in Angola (16%) followed by Colombia at 23%. The highest is Morocco at 64%, Greece at 57%, and India at 50%. The United States is 35%.

How does fear of failure influence our ability to spot opportunities and act on them? To find the answer, GEM also assessed the personal perceptions about entrepreneurship experienced by people between the ages of 18 and 64 (see Figure 11.4).

FIGURE 11.3

Fear of Failure Rates Around the World, 2018

Percentage of 18–64 population perceiving good opportunities to start a business who indicate that fear of failure would prevent them from setting up a business

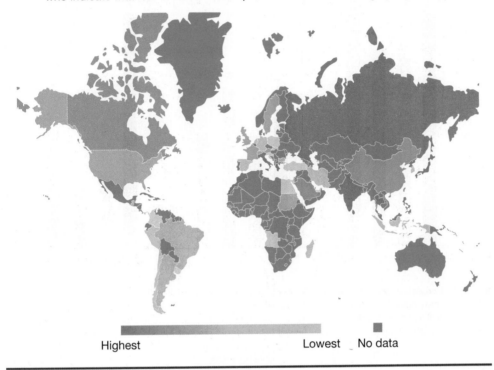

Highest   Lowest   No data

Source: Global Entrepreneurship Monitor Adult Population Survey 2018/2019

The GEM study focused on how people's personal perceptions in these three economies have influenced their decision to start a business. These perceptions include the extent to which people see opportunities around them to start a business (perceived opportunities); how capable they think they are of starting a business (perceived capabilities); how many people would feel constrained by their own fear of failing (fear of failure); and the degree to which those capable of starting a business may intend to do so over the next 3 years (entrepreneurial intentions).

As Figure 11.4 illustrates, people in Africa have the highest percentage of perceived opportunities, perceived capabilities, and entrepreneurial intentions. In contrast, while perceived capabilities rank high in Latin America and the Caribbean, the same countries (along with Asia and Oceania) score the highest for fear of failure. Finally, Europe and North America score the lowest for entrepreneurial intentions. People in these economies may perceive opportunities and score relatively high in perceived capabilities, but very few intend to take the next step into entrepreneurship. The reasons for this may lie in lack of confidence, cultural differences, types of skills, the level of entrepreneurship education, and different types of businesses that exist in the economy. For example, many businesses are started in Africa for sustenance and survival, whereas many businesses in the United States are high-tech. These different businesses require different levels of skills, which may account for differences in perceived capabilities.

Yet despite the differences between the economic regions, Figure 11.4 shows similar fear of failure rates across the different types of economies. The question then becomes, What makes some people act when others don't, even if their fear of failure is almost the same? The answer lies in how we manage failure and our ability and willingness to learn from it.

FIGURE 11.4

Self-Perceptions About Entrepreneurship

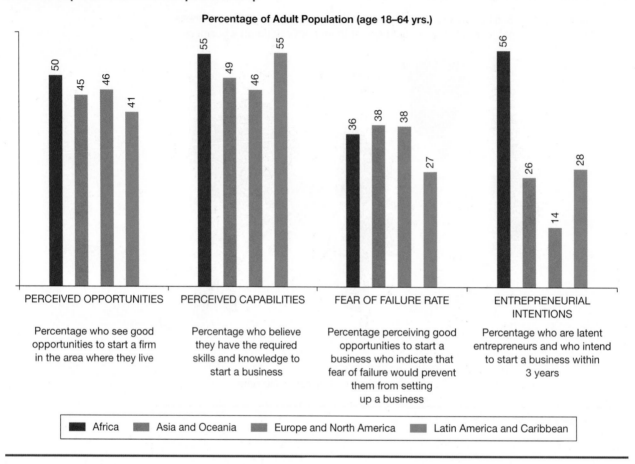

Source: GEM 2018/2019 global report. Figure 5. Retrieved from http://gemconsortium.org/report

11.4 LEARNING FROM FAILURE

>> **LO 11.4**   **Explain the different ways entrepreneurs can learn from failure.**

As shown by the statistics we presented in Chapter 1, the reality of entrepreneurship is that businesses do fail, which is why it is important for aspiring entrepreneurs to learn from others who have experienced failed businesses. Learning from others can help them take steps to prevent it from happening to them and also to understand how to take valuable lessons from failure. As we have explored, the use of the term *failure* evokes fear that discourages entrepreneurs from trying again or attempting new approaches.

In Chapter 7, we introduced experimentation and described how each "failed" experiment is an opportunity to build our knowledge and increase evidence.

Jeff Bezos, founder of Amazon.com, is a big believer in experimentation, especially when it comes to learning from failures. "I've made billions of dollars of failures at Amazon.com," he said. "Literally billions. . . . Companies that don't embrace failure and continue to experiment eventually get in the desperate position where the only thing they can do is make a Hail Mary bet at the end of their corporate existence."[25]

Experimentation is about trying something, seeing what happens, learning from it, and then moving forward, adapting or pivoting based on those findings. The goal of experimentation is not to conduct the "perfect" experiment, but to see it as an opportunity for further learning and better decision making, rather than a series of failed tests.

FIGURE 11.5

Intelligent Failure

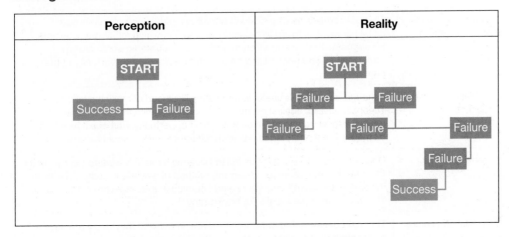

Source: https://sujanpatel.com/business/failing-fast-2/

In this context, perhaps it would be better to reframe the term *failure* as *intentional iteration*—a process that involves prototyping, testing, analyzing, and refinement. This may encourage entrepreneurs to perceive failure as simply a process of experimenting and learning from the setbacks, false starts, wrong turns, and mistakes, which will in turn help them develop the skills they need to tackle potential obstacles that may lie ahead.

This process of intentional iteration involves making intelligent failures—good failures that provide valuable new knowledge that can help a startup overcome hurdles and roadblocks (see Figure 11.5). Intelligent failures take place when experimentation is deemed necessary in order to find answers in situations that have never been explored before. Designing a new, innovative product or testing consumer reactions in an untapped market are tasks that may result in intelligent failures. With the right kind of experimentation, entrepreneurs can produce quick failures with positive results.[26]

For example, Sujan Patel, cofounder of marketing agency Web Profits, benefited from intelligent failure when he introduced his first marketing company, ContentMarketer.io. Patel said, "We tried to do way too much—both in terms of what the software did, and the work we had to put in to sustain it. We eventually ditched the bulk of the software, pivoted to providing only email outreach software (the part of ContentMarketer.io our customers used most), and rebranded as Mailshake. We're now making more money and putting in less hours doing it."[27]

Rather than giving up on his idea completely, Patel took the time to learn lessons from the failure and figure out what went wrong. This example shows how an entrepreneur can use failure in more productive ways.

Intelligent failures: good failures that provide valuable new knowledge that can help a startup overcome hurdles and roadblocks.

Lessons Learned by Successful Entrepreneurs

Kurt Theobald is the cofounder and CEO of the e-commerce firm Classy Llama—his 11th startup over the course of 5 years. Despite 10 failures behind him, Theobald learned valuable lessons and persevered until he achieved success. Table 11.3 lists some of the lessons he learned along the way.

Theobald learned some valuable lessons from his 10 failed businesses that helped him to finally succeed with his 11th new venture, a growing business that earns more than $8 million in annual revenue.[28]

Building a Blame-Free Environment

Many of us are guilty of playing the "blame game" when things don't go our way. After all, it's only human to blame other people or bad luck for our mistakes. However, a blame culture isn't healthy for you or your company, simply because you won't learn from the failure.

TABLE 11.3

Lessons Learned by Kurt Theobald

Beware of "shiny object syndrome"	Theobald admits he was guilty of pursuing multiple opportunities that came his way but failed to be strategic about it, which led to many failures. He suggests that all entrepreneurs need to be strategic about pursuing opportunities and understand how to identify the right opportunity at the right time.
Fail fast . . . but not too fast	Although failing fast is useful to reduce the likelihood of really big failures, Theobald advises against giving up to soon. He admits that he was sometimes too quick to let go and move on to the next opportunity. Perhaps if he was a bit more patient and tried things from different angles it would have worked out.
Find your formula	One of Theobald's businesses failed because he hadn't worked out the exact formula—the fundamental underlying method of why a business is viable. In the end, there wasn't enough revenue coming in to sustain the startup, and Theobald was forced to file for bankruptcy.
Know who you are	Theobald believes that entrepreneurs who know who they really are have a better chance at success as they are better equipped to deal with failure. He explains, "I wrote two things in my journal: One, when I fall, I am getting up. Every single time. And two, I get up because it's who I am as an entrepreneur. Therefore, to not get up is to betray who I am. And so that's what kept me going through all the failure. You can't stop. You don't really have a choice because if you choose that then you might as well sacrifice your whole life."
Find your deeper purpose	Theobald believes that entrepreneurs must have a deeper purpose to cope with failure—a deeper reason for starting and growing a business other than potential wealth and the freedom of working for themselves. He cites Steve Jobs's return to Apple (Jobs demanded only a $1 salary) as an example of an entrepreneur with a deeper purpose who prioritized changing the world with his products over money.
Focus on others	Being an entrepreneur is not about you, but about focusing on others—your customer, team members, suppliers, stakeholders—and helping them succeed. This is not about giving up control, but rather sharing it with others. Remember, the more value you give, the more you get back. By shifting your thinking to others, the people around you will be more likely to help you resolve problems and overcome obstacles.
Recognize when your approach is wrong	Many of Theobald's businesses failed because he was using the same approach every time. He quotes a mentor who advised, "Nothing's going to give if you keep doing the same thing you've been doing. If you keep banging your head against the concrete wall, the wall doesn't suddenly give way. Instead, you end up knocking yourself out. You need to pick a different approach."

Source: Wagner, E. (2013, October 22). 9 lessons from a 10-time startup failure. *Forbes.* Excerpted From Forbes.com. ©2013 Forbes. All rights reserved. Used under license.

Similarly, important lessons could be learned from failures that led to the demise of many startups by building blame-free cultures that encourage people to share, accept, learn from, and recover from failure. To do this, employees in a startup would also need to feel assured that they will not receive a negative reaction when they admit mistakes. When people feel comfortable enough to report failures, there is an opportunity for the team to work together toward understanding and analyzing what went wrong and to explore new approaches in order to prevent the same thing from happening again.

The key to building a blame-free culture is to communicate clearly what sorts of failures are acceptable and unacceptable. For example, lack of commitment, reckless conduct, violation of laws or standards, negligence, or wasting resources would be deemed unacceptable, whereas small fails that tend to occur through experimentation would be regarded as acceptable.

Your Failure Résumé

In this Mindshift exercise, your assignment is to craft a "failure résumé" that includes all of your biggest fails![29] These can be from school, work, or even in social relationships. For every failure you list, you must then describe what you learned from each fail (and, if appropriate, what others learned). By creating a failure résumé, you are forced to spend time reflecting on what you learned from those experiences. As tough as this sounds, it's also a very rewarding experience.

Want to go a step further? Share your résumé with a classmate and compare. Don't focus on comparing the failures; rather, focus on comparing and contrasting the learning that resulted from each failure experience.

Critical Thinking Questions

1. Was it easier than you expected, or more difficult, to list your biggest failures?

2. What emotions did you experience as you wrote your "failure résumé"?

3. How do you think you'll be able to take the lessons learned from your failures and use them to attain more success in the future? ●

Entrepreneurs also need to be open about their own knowledge limitations and admit the mistakes they have made in the past. This degree of openness encourages the rest of the team to be just as open and more willing to admit mistakes when they happen. Neha Motwani, founder of Fritternity, a fitness discovery and booking platform based in Mumbai, India, believes that accepting responsibility for failures is an essential part of being an entrepreneur: "As an entrepreneur you cannot find excuses or blame anyone else for any failure; you are in the driver's seat, whether you enjoy being there or not," she says.[30]

In essence, founders must give careful thought to making demands, giving orders, overruling thoughtful decisions, shooting the messenger, and assigning blame in order to build a culture in which people feel comfortable enough to share bad news and make the right choices.[31]

John Danner is an author and senior fellow at the Institute for Business Innovation in the Haas School of Business of the University of California, Berkeley. Like Motwani and others we have described earlier, Danner believes that failure in organizations should not be treated as a "regrettable reality," but rather as "a strategic resource—one that can help you make better decisions, create a more trusting and higher-performing culture, and accelerate your company's growth and innovation."[32]

Neha Motwani, founder of Fritternity

Photo: Abhijit Bhatlekar/Mint

11.5 GETTING GRITTY: BUILDING A TOLERANCE FOR FAILURE

>> **LO 11.5**   **Describe the significance of "grit" and its role in building tolerance for failure.**

Angela Lee Duckworth is a psychologist at the University of Pennsylvania who has spent more than a decade researching how character relates to achievement. Traditional

Grit: the quality that enables people to work hard and sustain interest in their long-term goals.

wisdom leads us to believe that talent—as measured by things like IQ, SAT, and GMAT scores—is a predictor of achievement. Yet Duckworth found something different. She identified "grit" as a trait that supersedes traditional methods of measuring talent.

According to Duckworth, **grit** is the quality that enables people to work hard and sustain interest in their long-term goals. Grit is also related to resilience, not just in the face of failure, but in perseverance to stick to long-term commitments and goals.[33]

One of the first studies Duckworth carried out to show the relationship between grit and high achievement took place at the United States Military Academy at West Point—one of the most selective and rigorous military training facilities in the United States and one with an infamously high dropout rate. Duckworth received permission to have incoming cadets complete a short "grit questionnaire," along with all the other evaluative methods employed by West Point such as The Whole Candidate Score (which includes SAT scores, class rank, etc.). Her intent was to find out what qualities would predict whether a cadet would remain at West Point through the "beast" summer program or would drop out.

Examples of the questions on Duckworth's grit questionnaire: "I have overcome setbacks to conquer an important challenge," "Setbacks don't discourage me," "I have been obsessed with a certain idea or project for a short time but later lost interest," "I have difficulty maintaining my focus on projects that take more than a few months to complete," and "I finish whatever I begin." Participants were asked to rate themselves on a five-point scale ranging from "very much like me" to "not like me at all."[34]

The findings showed that the cadets with higher levels of grit were more likely to stay until the end of the summer, and grit proved to be a better predictor than The Whole Candidate Score. Since the West Point study, Duckworth has found that grit predicts the effectiveness of sales agents, the survival of first-year teachers in tough schools, and even the identity of the finalists of U.S. National Spelling Bee contests.[35]

Duckworth's research on grit is also related to Stanford psychologist Carol Dweck's research on mindset, which we explored in Chapter 2. Dweck believes that people with a fixed mindset tend to believe that intelligence and talent are something we're born with, and they avoid failure at all costs, whereas people with growth mindset develop their abilities through dedication, effort, and hard work. They think brains and talent are not the key to lifelong success, but merely the starting point. They see failure as an opportunity to improve their performance and to learn from their mistakes. Despite setbacks, they tend to persevere rather than give up. Over the course of her research, Duckworth has found that children who have more of a growth mindset tend to have more grit.

Like Dweck, Duckworth also believes in the concept of deliberate practice, which is the conscious effort to practice things that we can't yet do. However, this type of practice does not involve doing the same thing over and over again; deliberate practice is a highly structured activity that must have a purpose and be carried out with an eye on long-term achievement. Deliberate practice can be frustrating, confusing, and even boring; but the fact is that we are supposed to feel confused when we are tackling the unknown—feeling frustrated can be a sign that we are on the right track.[36] In sum, deliberate practice allows us to refine our skills by making and accepting our mistakes in order to help us progress toward the achievement of long-term goals. This ties in with one of the key messages of this text—that entrepreneurship is a method that demands practice.

Building Grit

As defined in psychological studies by Duckworth and others, grit incorporates several different attributes. Let's examine each of these.

Courage

In the context of grit, people are courageous when they are not afraid to fail. They understand that failure is an important part of the learning process if they want to succeed. For example, Amy Freeman, founder of The Spice and Tea Exchange, overcame homelessness and lack of education by creating her own franchise business.[37] "Facing adversity

MINDSHIFT

Go Get Rejected

Author, blogger, and entrepreneur Jia Jiang has a TEDx talk that has been viewed by more than 5 million people. The topic? Rejection. And not just one rejection but 100 rejections. Jia Jang went on a 100-day journey to overcome his fear of failure and figure out a better way to handle the pain and shame that rejection brings. He talks about a game called "Rejection Therapy" that was invented by Canadian entrepreneur Jason Comely. The game requires you to look for rejection for 30 straight days. Jia Jang decided to take the game further and look for rejection for 100 days. Day 1 was "borrow $100 from a stranger." Day 2 was "request a burger refill." Another day was asking to plant a flower in a stranger's yard. The stranger said no, but suggested that he go to another person's house down the street. The flower was planted! His journey produced some great life lessons. He learned that sometimes with rejection come other gifts. The trick is not to run when first rejected, but rather ask why. You may learn something you didn't know and get something you didn't expect.

For this Mindshift, look for rejection for 3 days! You can do it . . . it's just 3 days. View Jia Jiang's TEDx talk, "What I Learned From 100 Days of Rejection", for inspiration (https://www.ted.com/talks/jia_jiang_what_i_learned_ from_100_days_of_rejection).

Critical Thinking Questions

1. What did you learn about yourself during the 3-day challenge?

2. Did your feelings about rejection change from Day 1 to Day 3?

3. Do you think these types of challenges can really help people overcome their fear of rejection and failure? ●

early on taught me that while it's okay to get mad or feel hurt, you need to resolve and move on before negativity and isolation take hold," she says.

Conscientiousness

Often, when we hear of someone being conscientious, we picture a person being meticulous in carrying out painstaking tasks. However, in the context of grit, being conscientious means working tirelessly in the face of challenges and toward the achievement of long-term goals.

Perseverance

Perseverance is the commitment to long-term goals through purposeful, deliberate practice. Serial entrepreneur Com Mirza, founder of multimillion-dollar company Mirza Holdings based in Dubai, Saudi Arabia, is a big believer in perseverance. The first eight companies he set up failed to take off, but he persevered nonetheless by writing down his goals and practicing his entrepreneurial skills. Mirza advises, "Start writing and continue practicing. You'll soon feel your brain rewiring to be equipped for real success. You'll feel more confident in your ability to carry through on what you tell yourself."[38]

Resilience

Resilience means the strength to recover from failure and overcome obstacles in order to persevere toward the achievement of long-term goals. Gritty people believe "everything will be all right in the end, and if it is not all right, it is not the end."[39]

Excellence

In the context of grit, striving for excellence means committing to activities that enhance skills, as well as prioritizing improvement over perfection. In other words, striving for excellence is an ongoing process, as each activity highlights new opportunities.

Removing the Stigma of Failure

Failure is still a topic that many of us would like to avoid, but that is changing. Initiatives are springing up to remove the stigma (feelings of shame and embarrassment) traditionally associated with failure.

Mobile technology nonprofit MobilActive runs an annual event called FAILFaire, which provides a forum for nonprofits all over the world to "openly, honestly, and humorously discuss [their] own failures." FAILFaire gives the opportunity for the participants to share their mistakes so others may understand and learn from them, in order to make better decisions in the future.

One failure that was openly discussed during the FAILFaire held in Bangalore, India, involved an initiative undertaken by Fiona Vaz, alumna of Amani Institute and Teach for India. Vaz attempted to set up a school with three other teachers as cofounders that failed because they couldn't all agree on important issues.

"It is tough for leaders to follow each other. We could not come to a consensus on key issues and did not know how to let go," she explained. "I realized that teachers help students overcome failure and pass exams—teacher-entrepreneurs should do the same for themselves as well," Fiona said.[40]

Similar to FAILFaire, the colorfully named F***up Nights is a global movement that holds events worldwide, giving entrepreneurs the opportunities to share their failure stories in front of a room full of strangers.[41]

DoSomething.org, a nonprofit set up to encourage people to take action on social change initiatives, holds a Pink Boa FailFest twice a year. The presenters wear a pink feather boa during a 10-minute presentation in which they discuss the history of their failure, what went wrong, and the lessons learned. Presenters allow 2 minutes of Q&A from the group at the end of the talk. They also employ fun, silly metaphors in discussing the lessons learned, such as a photo of a celebrity or a song lyric that takes the sting out of the failure.[42] If you are still unsure about sharing your failures in public, how about adjusting your physiology to better cope with failure? Improvisation teacher Matt Smith developed the "failure bow," which consists of raising your hands in the air, saying "I failed," grinning submissively, and moving on. Smith reports that athletes who use the failure bow find it helps them get over the fear of making a mistake. When they adjust their physiology, it helps them to change their mindset from embarrassment and shame to a more positive state that welcomes learning opportunities.[43] ●

---

⑤SAGE edge™

Get the tools you need to sharpen your study skills. SAGE edge offers a robust online environment featuring an impressive array of free tools and resources.

- Access practice quizzes, eFlashcards, video, and multimedia at
  edge.sagepub.com/neckentrepreneurship2e

SUMMARY

11.1   Describe failure and its effect on entrepreneurs.

Learning and further opportunities often come with failure. Failure does, however, come with extreme costs (financial and emotional) that need to be well managed to enable success down the road. If failure is seen as an acceptable step on the path to success, it is much more likely that failure may serve to hone the business and the entrepreneurs behind it.

11.2   Identify several reasons for failure.

Failures come in all shapes and sizes. Common types of failure include deviance, inattention, lack of ability, process inadequacy, poor business process flow, communication uncertainty, and exploratory experimentation.

11.3   Describe the consequences of fear of failure for entrepreneurs.

Fear of failure makes the entrepreneur less likely to pursue and achieve the transformative power of learning from failure.

11.4   Explain the different ways entrepreneurs can learn from failure.

Failure often goes hand-in-hand with experimentation, with each iteration bringing a product or service nearer to the state necessary for market success. Something can be learned from any failure, and it's important that the firm and its founders establish a blame-free climate in which learning can be maximized.

11.5   Describe the significance of "grit" and its role in building tolerance for failure.

Grit is that "special something" that enables people to persevere though prolonged hardship to maintain commitment and achieve long-term goals.

KEY TERMS

Deviance   262

Exploratory experimentation   263

Grit   272

Inattention   262

Intelligent failures   269

Lack of ability   262

Pivot   260

Process inadequacy   262

Uncertainty   263

CASE STUDY

Emily Lagasse, founder, Petwell Supply Co.

Emily Lagasse was working with the U.S. Peace Corps as a small-business development volunteer in a rural village in West Africa in 2008, and that is where she met her dog, Fenway. As soon as she and her new best friend came back to the United States, Fenway got very sick from eating traditional, U.S. dog food. This prompted Emily to cook for Fenway and her all-natural, homemade dog food worked! Fenway quickly got better! Emily concluded that the low-quality dog food available in pet stores was contributing to Fenway's poor health. "Traditional dog food had over 50 ingredients. Most of these were synthetic, most I couldn't pronounce, most of these I would not even eat myself." She realized that there must be other pet owners struggling with the same issue of having low-quality pet food. This prompted her to start her own pet food company, Fedwell Pet Foods, in early 2014 while pursuing her MBA at Babson College.

Fedwell was the first pet food on the market that did not have synthetic vitamins. Most dog food is extruded—made under high heat and pressure. This allows dog food producers to make product fast, but the downside is that food is then stripped of important nutrients. Emily was emulating the recipes she was using to cook at home for her dog—fresh wholesome ingredients that were friendly to a dog's natural diet. Her first product was oven-baked lamb kibble that had only meat, fruits, and vegetables and no synthetic vitamins. "We used the highest quality ingredients that you and I can eat. You can even pronounce everything that's on the label. Moreover, our food is baked, like crackers. This allows all the nutrients to be retained in the food." She started to sell in local pet stores and farmers markets in New England and online, but 80% of her revenue came from online sales. Some early national press coverage helped her direct traffic directly to her website.

"I had a lot of bumps in the road with getting the product made and distributed. It is a very competitive market," recalls Emily. "Things with my manufacturer got quite bad. I was trying to make a product that was better than existing ones, but manufacturers wanted to keep doing what they always did and were only interested in volume." Without scale Emily did not have leverage with the manufacturer to demand the quality levels she wanted. "After a lot of back and forth, I found out that the manufacturer broke the contract and was making the product differently than agreed upon. The manufacturer then got acquired by a bigger company who really didn't want to work with me. Being someone who did not expect to go back on their word, this caught me by surprise." It took Emily a year to find another manufacturer, and in 2016, she found a more supportive and willing manufacturer, but eventually this arrangement fell through as well.

The pet food industry was getting increasingly competitive given that it is a $30 billion market and growing rapidly. The opportunity for Emily was there but she was stuck in a hard cycle of not being able to sell through the product fast enough. Every time she almost got a deal for national distribution, it would fall through because of the intense competition. Even though the product was differentiated, it had a higher price point and distributors were not willing to take a risk. Even smaller distributors sold around 1,000 SKUs so there was little incentive to add a new brand. This meant that most of Fedwell's cash was tied up in inventory. Therefore, she didn't have the resources to spend on marketing, branding, and product development—the activities that could build her customer base and attract stronger distribution. Overall, she found it difficult to stand out in a crowded marketplace where most pet owners don't like switching food.

Emily, however, understood that most of her customers had pets with health issues. Additionally, she felt that veterinarians were diagnosing health issues and providing medications but not offering any type of holistic solution for preventative and long-term health. She started to experiment with health supplement bundles for dogs, such as a hip and joint bundle and a senior dog bundle. Through testing she learned that there was a market for local stores where pet parents could get medication and holistic products for their pets that were not easily available with other retailers. This prompted Emily to pivot away from Fedwell Pet Food products to Petwell Supply in 2018. Petwell Supply is a boutique pet store that sells food, treats, and medical remedies for pets in Somerville, Massachusetts. As Emily describes, "The store is set up in a way to help support different issues that dogs and cats face. You can find products that support your pet's allergies, kidney issues, cancer and we run education programs based around these issues as well!"

The idea of Petwell Supply was happening at about the same time that the relationship with her current dog food manufacturer was going sour. Emily decided to stop the manufacturing of Fedwell products and focus on getting the store up and running. "Most of my customers' pets are usually seeing the vet for some health issue or the other and thus Petwell aims to work in tandem with these vets to help provide a more well-rounded approach for the well-being of the pet," notes Emily. Petwell provides supplements like fish oil or probiotics that the vets prescribe but usually don't carry. Most of the remedies that Emily offers at Petwell are actually made by vets she met at trade shows, reflective of her focus on creating a great product.

Emily is working on engaging in conversations with local vets in the community to ensure that Petwell carries the products that they recommend. For example, instead of potential customers ordering a probiotic from a national marketplace like Chewy.com and waiting to get the product, Emily is working with vets so that they will recommend her store instead, where owners can walk in and get what they need on the same day. "There is a movement to support local neighborhood businesses in my area, so this approach is working for me." She is also in the process of connecting with social media influencers and bloggers to drive traffic and have online conversations with dog and cat owners all over the country to understand the different problems that these pet parents face regarding the health of their pets. Emily is taking a community-based approach to marketing her store. She was featured by the local press and has participated in community events, tagged sidewalks (spraying the sidewalk with chalk in the shape of PetWell's logo during the summer), and reached out to local dog walkers to help spread the word to the dog owners.

Emily is most concerned by not knowing what drives customer behavior. "Some days at the store are crazy busy and sometimes the store is empty, but this behavior cannot be traced back to anything." However, in order to help steady the demand and steady the revenue stream, Emily has added a lot of "regular" pet store services to her store, such as dog walking and grooming. She also conducts regular social events at the store as a way to engage with the local community. "I believe that customers do not necessarily react well to something completely new. They want the comfort of familiarity and this is one reason I offer the usual products such as pet food and treats along with supplements and prescription medication. That way customers will remember my store and come when the need arises. I can actually see some of that happening now!"

As Emily notes, "The store is an amazing touchpoint to directly interact with the customer and get real-time feedback and market trends on a regular basis." The store also gives Emily a sense of control over how she would like to react to this information and make changes if needed, almost immediately. This was in contrast with her experience with Fedwell, where she was heavily dependent on the manufacturers for her operations.

Her longer-term plan is to franchise the store nationally and also reformulate the food she used to produce at Fedwell to act as the natural alternative to a prescription diet. Because Emily is somewhat of an expert in pet food through her experience, she is looking forward to leveraging that expertise and getting back into reformulating food. However, Emily says that she now knows how exactly she wants her products manufactured and that all her not-so-positive experiences have been great lessons in themselves. She feels like she would be wasting an opportunity if she doesn't get back to reformulating the food and setting up a distribution channel for her products. Emily would like to leverage her knowledge on running an e-commerce company to grow her distribution channel once she introduces a reformulated product into the market. Although she believes that both distributors and online sales are important, she personally likes playing around with the data that online sales can generate. For instance, one insight that she learned through Fedwell sales was that her customers were usually married, with both partners working but without children. These were people who would travel with their pets everywhere. This love for data also prompted her choice of location for the store. She chose Somerville because it has the highest per capita millennial population in the United States.

The journey for Emily has not been easy. At the early stages of the business, she spent all of her time and effort growing the business. She missed social occasions like parties, birthdays, weddings, and even compromised on health and sleep at an unsustainable pace to help get her company off the ground. Now, however, she believes in the importance of having a well-rounded lifestyle and makes a point to take a little time off to do other things that make her happy, like hitting the gym. She feels she is the best version of herself when she is the healthiest. "It may sound cheesy, but I believe that the level of stress is directly related to your level of self-care."

When asked about what she would do differently with Fedwell, Emily said that she would find buyers and distributors for her product *before* manufacturing it. Emily credits her success to the strength of her network of seasoned entrepreneurs, professors, and investors who became advisors, especially when she was starting her first company. "When I was new to entrepreneurship, I lacked the confidence to get things going, and my mentors really helped me focus." However, she feels like she has grown as an entrepreneur. Today she is a lot more confident and relies on her network only for certain specific areas of guidance. If an expert is not available in her network, she starts asking around until she is connected to someone who can help. "My advice to young entrepreneurs is: Fail fast. That's a big one. And if you fail in one model, doesn't mean it's over. My story is an example of just that!"

Critical Thinking Questions

1. How did Emily Lagasse learn from and rebound from failure?

2. Do you believe Petwell will be an ongoing success given the setbacks she had with Fedwell?

3. How can you fail fast with your own venture?

Sources:

Emily Lagasse (interview with Babson MBA graduate assistant Gaurav Khemka, December 7, 2018)

Petwell Supply. (2014). The FedWell pet foods story [Video file]. *YouTube*. Retrieved from https://youtu.be/JhZRGUReSZk - T

Petwell Supply (2019). Retrieved from https://www.petwellsupply.com/

Radio Entrepreneurs. (2017). Emily Lagasse July 2017 [Video file]. YouTube. Retrieved from https://www.youtube.com/watch?v=ZuU7xUZ4lPc

PART IV

Supporting New Opportunities

©iStockphoto.com/AndreyPopov

12 Bootstrapping and Crowdfunding for Resources

"What's a bootstrapper to do? You have to go where the other guys can't. Take advantage of what you have so that you can beat the competition with what they don't."

—Seth Godin, author of *The Bootstrapper's Bible: How to Start and Build a Business with a Great Idea and (Almost) No Money*

Chapter Outline

Learning Objectives

12.1 Define bootstrapping and illustrate how it applies to entrepreneurs.

12.2 Identify common bootstrapping strategies used by entrepreneurs.

12.3 Explain the difference between crowdsourcing and crowdfunding.

12.4 Describe the effects of crowdfunding on entrepreneurship.

12.5 Define the four contexts for crowdfunding.

12.6 Describe 10 ways in which entrepreneurs can conduct a successful crowdfunding campaign.

12.1 WHAT IS BOOTSTRAPPING?

>> **LO 12.1** **Define bootstrapping and illustrate how it applies to entrepreneurs.**

One of the most common beliefs held by prospective entrepreneurs is that vast amounts of money are needed to start a business: "I can't start a business because I don't have any money—how do I get money?" Looking at entrepreneurship from the outside, it's common to believe that the key to success is to raise as much capital as possible in the beginning, but this is simply not the case. Very few entrepreneurs manage to get formal funding for their new ventures, especially in the early stages—bank loans are notoriously difficult for newly emerging businesses to access, and investments from "angels" or other investors aren't as common as people would like to believe because entrepreneurs often have difficulty proving to potential investors the value of a business that hasn't gotten off the ground yet. It can be incredibly risky to bet on the unproven and the unknown.

Almost 8,500 new companies in the United States received formal equity investment in 2018.[1] Considering that an average of 627,000 businesses are started every year, the likelihood of a new business getting formal investment is very, very small.[2] Some research has reported that a third of small businesses have begun with less than $5,000.[3] This method of starting a business is so well established that its name is borrowed from the old expression "pull yourself up by your bootstraps" (the small fingerholds used to pull on the entire boot), meaning to lift yourself by your own efforts. In entrepreneurship, **bootstrapping** is the process of building or starting a business with no outside investment, funding, or support.[4]

Bootstrapping is all about finding creative ways to access every resource you have available to launch your venture while minimizing the amount of cash you spend.[6] This means applying the eight components of the Entrepreneurship Method, as described in Chapter 1. Here is a quick reminder:

1. Identify your desired impact on the world.

2. Start with the means at hand.

3. Describe the idea today.

4. Calculate affordable loss.

5. Take small action.

Bootstrapping: the process of building or starting a business with no outside investment, funding, or support.

Master the content at
**edge.sagepub.com/
neckentrepreneurship2e**

Bryanne Leeming, Unruly Studios

Photo courtesy of Bryanne Leeming

Bryanne Leeming, founder of Unruly Studios

Bryanne Leeming bootstrapped her business, Unruly Studios, by raising $42,000 through Kickstarter and winning startup competitions. Many of the world's most successful businesses began as bootstrapped ventures, such as Coca-Cola, Apple, and Microsoft. It took only $1,000 for Michael Dell to start Dell Computers.[5]

Bryanne's career background is in marketing, with degrees in cognitive science and art history from McGill. After college, she began pursuing an MBA at Babson College in Massachusetts. At the time, Bryanne wasn't totally set on starting her own business, stating that "starting a company is a pretty crazy thing to do." In the end, though, Bryanne saw a problem that needed solving and she had an idea how to solve it.

Bryanne started her company, Unruly Studios, while she was pursuing her MBA at Babson College. The goal of her company is to combine physical activity and STEM education in order to expose children aged 6–12 to coding in a fun and playful way. Children learn how to code by using a series of floor tiles called "Unruly Splats," each of which contains lights resembling "spilled milk." The tiles light up and make sounds when kids jump on each one. The Unruly Splats are programmable floor tiles that pair with a tablet preloaded with lots of recess-style games. Kids first play the preloaded games, then they change the code, ultimately learning how to code their own games.

To get to this point has required plenty of iteration, attention to detail, and bootstrapping. She built a successful Kickstarter campaign, raising more than $42,000 with an average pledge of $140. She received awards from Amazon's Alexa fund and has quality advisors hailing from Disney, Mattel, and the MIT Media Lab.

Additionally, winning venture competitions has helped her get early startup funding.

Although the current iteration of the Unruly Splat looks very impressive, it didn't start this way. Bryanne points out that "ideas are ugly when they start out, and the prototypes are especially ugly." She emphasizes that the first iteration doesn't have to be pretty, and it shouldn't be. The current iteration of the Unruly Splat is a sleek data collection marvel, whereas the first iteration was a 4' × 4' wood surface with integrated electronics that she could barely fit inside the back of her car. Bryanne stresses this point as an important principle behind entrepreneurship: to not stress about the first version of an idea. Starting a business is hard enough; worrying about how an idea/prototype looks, in the beginning, is adding an unnecessary level of worry.

Even before launching her Kickstarter campaign, Bryanne had to engage her users—the kids. She watched kids make their own games, and they gave her feedback on what they liked or didn't like about the product or system. This required a lot of testing, something that she and Unruly Studios put a lot of emphasis on. Thousands have tested Unruly Splats in schools and have made many of the recommendations in design and function for the product. This enabled the product to get better faster. Then, once she achieved the best product, the Kickstarter campaign was launched so she could get resources for greater production.

The key for Bryanne and her Splats has been a focus on making the product as good as it can be through constant testing and refining so that funding finds them as often as they seek it. They have had great support from many different sources because they are so focused on that 6-year-old's experience with the product. As Bryanne notes, "As long as we continue to do this, we will have something that people want, something that makes a positive impact on future generations of kids."

Critical Thinking Questions

1. Why does Bryanne advocate for ugly prototypes?

2. How does Bryanne iterate so frequently?

3. What draws investors' attention to Unruly Studios, in Bryanne's eyes? ●

Source: Bryanne Leeming (interview with the author, December 11, 2018) https://www.unrulysplats.com/

6. Network and enroll others in your journey.

7. Build on what you learn.

8. Reflect and be honest with yourself.

The Entrepreneurship Method, as reflected in the components above, will enable you to think creatively about starting a business with little or no money. Take Sophia Amoruso, founder of American retailer Nasty Gal.[7] Amoruso started off buying vintage clothing in second-hand stores and selling them on eBay. She then used her profits to secure a warehouse for her stock and hire some staff. Thanks to some clever marketing over social media, Amoruso was able to build a loyal following and attract millions in investment.

Amoruso used a small amount of her own money to get her business off the ground, but other entrepreneurs go down different paths to find the money they need. For example, rather than seeking formal investment, it is more likely that entrepreneurs will turn to friends, family, and fools (sometimes called "the 3 Fs") for financial assistance. Many entrepreneurs have borrowed money from friends and family or people who are just simply won over by an idea and are willing to invest some cash in the business. Although borrowing from these sources can be an easier and quicker way to get the cash you need, it is better to treat the arrangement as a formal loan or investment with terms agreed by both parties. Many families have fallen out over arrangements like this due to lack of understanding or broken promises. You do not want this to happen to you.

Bootstrapping or External Financing?

Bootstrapping is fundamentally an entrepreneurial approach to acquiring resources without accessing long-term external financing sources such as raising equity from venture capitalists or borrowing from banks. Reasons for bootstrapping can include complementing current traditional financing sources, reducing reliance on them, or eliminating them entirely. More often than not, entrepreneurs just can't get or don't have access to traditional forms of financing because they don't have a business history, proven track record, or simply don't have enough customers. Additionally, entrepreneurs may voluntarily choose self-funding or funding from family and friends for all or most of the venture's financing to maintain most or complete control and autonomy over business decisions. Not every business needs a lot of capital, and not every investor wants to invest in you! Bootstrapping is a way of getting started with very little.

Although it is more difficult to acquire funding from more formal channels such as venture capital firms or angel investors, there are some real benefits to the formal route. Not only do you get the money you need, but you also gain advice and guidance from people who are far more experienced than you, as well as their contacts and connections that will, ultimately, help your business become more profitable. However, most entrepreneurs choose not to seek out, or can't get access to, angel investors or other external investors—at least not in the beginning. The truth is that most entrepreneurs appreciate the degree of independence and control they acquire by funding the business themselves. It keeps them focused and determined and allows them to grow the business the way they want to—on their own terms. They have the freedom to test their products and services and make decisions without having to explain themselves to outside investors. By not relying on outside investors, the business does not share ownership by giving away equity. There is also no pressure to repay bank loans or any other debt. In addition, any cash flow or income from the business goes straight to the entrepreneur or back into the business rather than to the investors.[8]

Marketing information platform Mailchimp has been heralded as one of the most successful bootstrapped startups of all time. Mailchimp founder Ben Chestnut explained how seeking investment just didn't seem like the right thing for the company: "Every time we sat down with potential investors, they never seemed to understand small business. Something in our gut always said that didn't feel right."[9] So how did Chestnut bootstrap one of the most successful email marketing service companies in the world? First, he used his severance check when he was laid off from a media company in 2000; Chestnut's wife was a pediatric nurse, and her steady income gave him the support he needed to build the business; and finally, he saved money by hiring low-cost artists and creatives who learned on the job rather than expensive programmers and coders.[10]

The hard reality, however, is that in the beginning most new ventures are simply not ready for investment. Outside investors are more likely to invest in a business that has been bootstrapped from the beginning, as it showcases the entrepreneur's level of commitment and resourcefulness as well as the market reaction to and demand for the product or service. Conversely, an entrepreneur who bootstraps a business with a good product–market fit, a committed team, and a decent customer base is in a much better negotiating position with investors should they express an interest in the business.

The Bootstrapped Startup

Most new ventures begin as marathon, not a race. This means that you are better off starting off at a steady pace and achieving desired milestones than trying to launch your dream business as quickly as possible. Beginning a business on a shoestring is the norm. By spending the time to build up the business piece by piece, you are more likely to generate a larger customer base as well as a steady stream of income. Once these building blocks are in place, there is a better chance of rapid growth and scalability.

As law firm president and author Jack Garson says, "You don't need to open your dream business on the first day. It's better to start with a successful hot dog stand than to get halfway through the construction of a full-service restaurant and run out of money."[11]

Furthermore, you don't need to quit your day job to start bootstrapping. In fact, many entrepreneurs use their own salaries to fund their startups until they feel secure enough to leave their full-time jobs. For example, Aytekin Tank, founder of online form builder Jotform, juggled both his full-time job and his startup for several years: "I'd wake up at 6 am, answer customer questions, and then go to work. It took me another 5 years to quit my job and start my own company—even though I already had a successful product."[12] Table 12.1 showcases some quotes from more entrepreneurs who bootstrapped themselves to success.

There are several different ways to bootstrap your new venture. You can use cash from your savings, carefully use certain credit cards, fund your startup out of your salary from your existing job (like Jotform founder Aytekin Tank), or take equity out of your home if you are a homeowner. However, all these methods require careful thought—you need to consider how far you are willing to risk your own personal finances before getting yourself into debt.

Once you have a cutoff point in mind, then you will be able to gauge whether you need to move beyond bootstrapping to additional financial resources or to end the business altogether. This ties in with the concept of affordable loss discussed in Chapter 1—how much are you willing to lose to take the next step to bring your venture to life?

Whatever your chosen bootstrapping strategy (discussed next), it is certain that you will put in a huge amount of effort to get your business up and running. In the entrepreneurial context, this is called **sweat equity**: a non-monetary investment that increases the value or ownership interest created by the investment of hard work for no compensation. For example, if you have decided to renovate houses for a living, you might save on the cost of hiring laborers by doing some of the work yourself and adding value to the properties at the same time. Or you might build your own prototype of a product, again creating value while saving the cost of hiring a designer or manufacturer. Even Bryanne, founder of Unruly Studios (see Entrepreneurship in Action, above), spent countless hours developing her crowdfunding campaign. This is also a type of sweat equity. But beyond sweat equity, let's take a look at a range of strategies entrepreneurs can use to bootstrap their businesses.

Sweat equity: a non-monetary investment that increases the value or ownership interest created by the investment of hard work for no compensation.

TABLE 12.1

Entrepreneurs Share Their Views on Bootstrapping

Bootstrapping is a force function for creativity and breakthrough. It'll challenge you to think outside the box and to do things differently. Bryan Johnson, founder of Braintree, OS Fund, and Kernel
Bootstrapping is the best guarantee that you can run your business the way you want. Laura Roeder, founder and CEO of MeetEdgar
By self-funding you have the ability to control your own destiny. Nathan Chan, CEO of Foundr Magazine
When you bootstrap, you have to care about every potential customer, client, and fan. John Lee Dumas of EOFire
Having limited resources means you won't survive unless you only focus on what brings the most value. Oleg Shchegolev, CEO and cofounder of SEMrush
Hire people that are on board with your vision, share similar values, and are prepared to work hard. Steve Shelley, chair and cofounder of Deputy
Will spending this money help me acquire or keep a customer? If the answer is no, don't spend it. Kate Morris, CEO and founder, Adore Beauty
Bootstrapping for as long as I did set me up for success down the road. Chris Strode, founder of Invoice2go
Bootstrapping forces you to relentlessly prioritize things that are actually going to move the needle. Christopher Gimmer, cofounder at Snappa
When you're bootstrapping, make sure to think about your customers, revenues, and profitability first. Greg Smith, CEO and cofounder at Thinkific

Source: Chan. J. (2019). 11 bootstrapping entrepreneurs share how they found business success without funding. *Foundr.* Retrieved from https://foundr.com/bootstrapping-entrepreneur

12.2 BOOTSTRAPPING STRATEGIES

>> **LO 12.2**   **Identify common bootstrapping strategies used by entrepreneurs.**

The key to successfully bootstrapping your business is to look for creative ways and use whatever resources you have to save money while you are getting your business off the ground.[13] These "penny pinching strategies," illustrated in Table 12.2, will not only help minimize the costs of running your business but will also delay or alleviate the need for external funding through investments or bank loans.

Above all, remember the old saying, "cash is king." Rather than spending too much time fretting over balance sheets, forecasts, and profit and loss, focus on the amount of cash you have to keep your business operative. How long can you keep your business afloat with the cash you have? Weeks? Months? It's important to be mindful of your cash flow: cash in, cash out, and overall cash needs.

12.3 CROWDFUNDING VERSUS CROWDSOURCING

>> **LO 12.3**   **Explain the difference between crowdsourcing and crowdfunding.**

As new entrepreneurs quickly learn, formal investment is very difficult to get, and traditional bootstrapping methods can take you only so far. The emergence of

TABLE 12.2

Common Bootstrapping Strategies

- Work from home to save on renting an office; or if you need an office, use coworking spaces instead.

- Never buy new what you can borrow, lease, or get for free; for example, borrow or lease office equipment such as computers, printers, and so on.

- Take as little salary for yourself for as long as possible.

- Use your network of friends and family to get what you need at a reduced rate or for free.

- Educate yourself on basic legal and accountancy matters before paying high fees to a lawyer or accountant.

- Reimburse advisors and consultants with equity and goodwill where possible.

- Be frugal with your travel—drive rather than fly, and choose cheap accommodation.

- Hire help if you need it, but keep in mind that some employees may agree to work temporarily for an equity share in the business rather than a cash payment.

- Attend every possible networking event to make connections and get introductions to people who may be able to contribute to or enhance your business.

- Offer discounts to early customers to ensure a consistent cash flow. Not only will this help to cover overhead, but it will also help you build a loyal customer base.

- Negotiate payment terms with suppliers (if you have them), and explain how they will benefit when your business takes off.

- Outsource some tasks if you are struggling to keep up with the workload. For example, 99designs and Elance are good examples of websites that can provide you with the services you need, allowing you more time to focus on the parts of the business that generate the most income.

- Don't give up your day job until the business is being productive and making proper money.

Source: Based on information from Sharp, G., (2014). *The ultimate guide to bootstrapping: How you can build a profitable company from day one* [Kindle ed.]. Real. Cool. Media; Victor, A. (2018). Bootstrapping strategies for building successful business. *Medium.* Retrieved from https://medium.com/@agvictorsblog/bootstrapping-strategies-for-building-successful-business-8fc0b1f65513

Crowdfunding: the process of raising funding for a new venture from a large audience (the "crowd"), typically through the Internet.

crowdfunding—the process of raising cash for a new venture from a large audience (the "crowd"), typically through the Internet—has been a new pathway for many entrepreneurs. People who use crowdfunding to raise money are known as "crowdfunders," and people who contribute financial support to crowdfunding ventures are known as "backers."[14] Usually, crowdfunding works by drawing on small contributions from a large number of people to fund entrepreneurial ventures.[15]

MINDSHIFT

Bootstrapping for Your Business

By now you should have a pretty good understanding of the different ways to bootstrap a business, from working out of your home, to using free resources from your network, using personal credit cards, crowdsourcing, and crowdfunding. Think about the idea or venture concept you are working on and identify at least 10 strategies you can use to bootstrap your venture idea. If you can't think of 10, then ask people, "How can I start this ["this" being your idea] with virtually nothing?" You will be surprised what others will say!

Critical Thinking Questions

1. Do you think you can really start a business with little to no formal outside help from investors or bankers?

2. Can you describe the mindset of a bootstrapper?

3. Did anything surprise you in your list of 10 strategies? What and why? ●

Crowdfunding is often confused with crowdsourcing, but the two are not the same. Crowdfunding focuses on raising cash for new projects and businesses, whereas **crowdsourcing** involves using the Internet to attract, aggregate, and manage ostensibly inexpensive or even free labor from enthusiastic customers and like-minded people. Thus, crowdfunding is a resource for money, and crowdsourcing is a resource for talent and labor. Like crowdfunding, crowdsourcing is a form of bootstrapping because it is a valuable method of saving money by utilizing the expertise and knowledge of the crowd to bring your ideas to life.

Throughout this text we have emphasized the importance of information as a critical and valuable resource, and finding ways to access this information is key to the success of your business. However, sometimes it can be difficult or even costly to acquire information. Crowdsourcing is a means of obtaining information that is contributed and shared by the members of a given crowdsourcing platform. Companies have capitalized on information resources by tapping into crowdsourcing social media platforms and social networking sites. Let's take a look at three different ways in which crowdsourcing has been used to gain knowledge and information.

> **Crowdsourcing:** the process of using the Internet to attract, aggregate, and manage ostensibly inexpensive or even free labor from enthusiastic customers and like-minded people.

Crowdsourcing to Improve Medical Treatment

In 2011, the University of Washington's department of biochemistry challenged a group of gamers to produce an accurate model of a retrovirus enzyme (that came from an AIDS-like virus) by playing an online science game called Foldit.[16] The players managed to produce an accurate model in just 3 weeks, beating the experts who had been struggling to find the solution for more than a decade. Since that event, the WHO Special

---

ENTREPRENEURSHIP MEETS ETHICS

When to Proclaim a Product Is Ready

With the advent of crowdfunding websites, the process of investing in startups has become democratized. No longer are entrepreneurs needing the help of bigger investors; they can amass small investments from a vast number of individuals. The newness of this style of investment system means that there is still a significant amount of uncertainty on both sides of the venture.

Because it can be easier to gain small amounts of funding from a large number of individuals, instead of a large amount of money from one or a few sources, the constraints on entrepreneurs to provide a conclusive and realistic business plan are lessened.

This raises the questions of whether or not it is right to look for investments when the product is not finished and whether the entrepreneur can say the product is finished when they know they just need the additional crowdfunding to get the product ready for market.

Business sense says that it is helpful to market a product before it is fully finished, as it will make the process significantly easier. For example, software companies have used this strategy for some years now—what many refer to as "vaporware." They hold significant marketing campaigns before the software is completely finished.

This is obviously the best route for an entrepreneur, as money will come more swiftly and allow for the completion of an idea. But, is this strategy fair to the consumer?

If a consumer feels cheated by an entrepreneur's lack of fulfillment on a desired product, that negative feeling could have a rippling effect. It may seem that it is just one customer or small investor lost, but bad reviews and a troublesome reputation are sure to follow in any future ventures.

Critical Thinking Questions

1. Can an entrepreneur lie about the readiness of a product to consumers or investors?

2. Does crowdfunding require enough accountability from investors?

3. Should an entrepreneur be absolutely certain a product will appear as marketed before looking for funding? ●

Sources:

Burkus, D. (2013, December 25). Sell your product before it exists. *Harvard Business Review.* Retrieved from https://hbr.org/2013/12/sell-your-product-before-it-exists

Fuld, H. (2018, February 23). How to hype up your product before it's ready for the market. *Inc.* Retrieved from https://www.inc.com/hillel-fuld/if-your-marketing-activity-begins-when-product-is-ready-you-missed-boat.html

Katai, R. (2016, April 11). How to launch a product before it's ready. *Bannersnack.* Retrieved from https://blog.bannersnack.com/launch-product-before-ready/

Programme for Research and Training in Tropical Diseases has set up a crowdsourcing initiative that involves groups of experts and nonexperts who solve health problems and then share the solution with the public. For example, WHO launched a contest to design a video to encourage HIV testing in China. The winner of the contest was not a professional videographer, but he won a cash prize for his educational and engaging video detailing the benefits of testing for gay men and their partners. Thanks to these crowdsourcing initiatives, WHO is achieving a number of medical breakthroughs worldwide.

Crowdsourcing to Reduce Labor Costs

Many companies use crowdsourcing to save on labor costs. For instance, say you wanted to find a designer to create a new logo for your startup. This might cost you $400 if you were hiring a traditional designer, but by harnessing creative talent through crowdsourcing or websites like Upwork, you will likely pay half that figure.[17]

On a much larger scale, consider the benefits of crowdsourcing to the XPRIZE Foundation. The foundation focuses on finding solutions to complex problems such as air and ocean pollution and adult illiteracy. XPRIZE launched a competition to challenge teams from all over the world to build a spaceship for a $10 million reward. Although this seems like a lot of money, it would likely have cost the foundation much more, as it would have had to fund research and development teams to generate the idea and pay enormous labor costs to build the spaceship. By using crowdsourcing, XPRIZE succeeded in saving on labor costs as well as inventing creative ways to build a new type of spaceship.

© Pool/Pool/Getty Images

One of the XPRIZE contenders for the $10 million prize, SpaceShipOne

Crowdsourcing Through Technology

Technological advances are greatly reducing the costs of design, manufacturing, and sales. What's especially exciting for entrepreneurs with product companies is the low cost of 3D printing and other tools that enable small companies to become microfactories. For example, free software tools like Google's Sketchup enable users to create a sketch of a 3D model of their own invention; this can then be turned into a 3D physical prototype using a specialized desktop printer like the MakerBot, which costs less than $1,000.

Once you're happy with your prototype, you can have it manufactured in China or similar countries. Chinese manufacturers have become efficient enough to manufacture in small batches (as small as a batch of one) while maintaining low costs—something that was previously impossible. Now small companies and even individuals have access to manufacturing lines that had been previously reserved for large factories.

Websites like Alibaba.com list China's manufacturers, products, and capabilities.[18] You can search the site to find companies that make items similar to yours. When you've selected your top choices, you can instant-message the factory using Alibaba's real-time English–Chinese instant-messaging system. Within two decades, Alibaba has earned revenue of $40 billion.

Where does crowdsourcing come in to 3D printing? Plastic is not the only material used by 3D printers—other materials like wood can be used. Wikihouse, for example, designs and builds houses through a form of 3D printing without involving a construction team.[19] Thanks to crowdsourcing, Wikihouse blueprints are submitted by the crowd that has created plans and designs of any type of house imaginable. These blueprints are freely available online for anyone who fancies building an affordable custom-built home. Aspiring homeowners can get the parts digitally printed before assembling the parts themselves, much in the manner of an IKEA furniture pack kit.

12.4 CROWDFUNDING STARTUPS AND ENTREPRENEURSHIPS

>> LO 12.4   Describe the effects of crowdfunding on entrepreneurship.

Just as crowdsourcing is a useful way to acquire valuable feedback and information, crowdfunding can be an effective way of getting the funds needed to start a business or, at least, show proof of concept. Crowdfunding is rapidly gaining momentum and shows no signs of slowing down. Crowdfunding has helped raise billions for all types of businesses: art, theater, photography, charity, retail, fashion, gaming, real estate, and much more.

Crowdfunding makes all types of entrepreneurship accessible to those who want to start their own business. In a time when banks have become more nervous about lending money and investors are more cautious than ever before, crowdfunding has become a democratized method of raising money for many budding entrepreneurs.

An estimated market value of $34 billion was raised globally through crowdfunding campaigns in 2017, with North America and Europe dominating the industry. Table 12.3 provides some additional statistics on the crowdfunding industry.

Many crowdfunding projects seek small amounts of money (often under $1,000) to fund one-off occasions like community or arts events, with family and friends being the main contributors. However, more and more projects are becoming a valuable source of funding for entrepreneurial ventures.[20] California-based Pebble Time, which makes smart watches, holds the record for the largest amount of money raised on a crowdfunding platform. Since the Pebble Time launch in 2012, backers have given more than $20 million through crowdfunding platform Kickstarter.[21] In 2016, digital health platform Fitbit acquired Pebble, but it phased out the watches in June 2018.[22] Similarly, strategic card game Exploding Kittens was heralded as Kickstarter's most-backed project of all time, with almost 220,000 people supporting the campaign.

What kind of people tend to back crowdfunding campaigns? According to the 2012 American Dream Composite Index,[23] crowdfunding backers tend to be between the ages

View Pictures/Luke Hayes/VIEW/Newscom

Wikihouse designs and digitally prints the parts of a house for later assembly.

TABLE 12.3

Key Crowdfunding Statistics

Number of U.S. crowdfunding platforms	191
Number of jobs created by crowdfunding	270,000
Amount that crowdfunding has added to the global economy	$65 billion
Average global success rate for crowdfunding campaigns	50%
Amount raised by average successful crowdfunding campaign	$7,000
Length of time it takes to prepare a successful campaign	11 days
Duration of average campaign	9 weeks
Average campaign donation	$88

Source: Fundly. (n.d.). *Crowdfunding statistics.* Retrieved from https://blog.fundly.com/crowdfunding-statistics

of 24 and 35, are more likely to be men, and have an income of more than $100,000 per year. This is a basic demographic snapshot of people who are most likely to invest in your startup through crowdfunding. Let's explore the different types of crowdfunding sites used by entrepreneurs and participants today.

Types of Crowdfunding Sites

Launched in 2009, U.S.–based Kickstarter is the most established crowdfunding site, as well as the largest platform for creative projects in the world. Kickstarter makes its money by charging a percentage of the funds collected from each successful project, in addition to payment processing fees.[24] It does not accept projects associated with charitable donations, loans, or general business expenses.[25] The expectation is that the money raised will be used to further develop or complete a project and that backers will receive some reward for contributing. As of April 2019, more than $4 billion had been pledged to more than 160,000 projects by more than 16 million backers on Kickstarter.[26]

North American entrepreneurs can join the Kickstarter community for free and start their own campaign by pitching ideas directly to a huge worldwide audience of potential online backers. There are three basic rules:

- Projects must create something to share with others.

- Projects must be honest and clearly presented.

- Projects can't fundraise for charity, offer financial incentives, or involve prohibited items.[27]

Each Kickstarter project is set up to run during a set period of time with a set fundraising goal. Project creators can build web pages that describe the projects they are looking to fund and the specific goals they would like to reach and broadcast their ideas through promotional videos, photos, and other information. Kickstarter also includes a facility to get feedback before the page is launched, notifies you of funds donated, allows you to track funds and the number of backers, includes a way to notify backers of progress, and includes a mechanism to reward backers for their support. Although campaigns are allowed to last from 1 to 60 days, it is worth keeping in mind that the most successful campaigns tend to last 30 days or less, with the most contributions coming in during the first and the last week.[28]

When setting a funding goal, Kickstarter crowdfunders must be aware that a project must be fully funded by the time the period of the campaign ends, or they get nothing. For example, if you decide to set a funding goal of $10,000 and receive pledges of only $5,000 within your specified funding period, then you will not receive anything. In contrast, if you surpass your funding goal early on, you will still be able to receive contributions right up until the campaign comes to an end. Yet in most cases, potential backers are less likely to fund a project once it has reached its original goal.[29]

Rewards tend to come in many different forms; for example, if you are looking to put on a play, you might offer potential backers free tickets on opening night, front row seats, or the chance to meet the actors backstage after the event. Similarly, in the case of a clothing line, you might give away some items of clothing for free or for a discounted price to your early backers. However, as noted in the basic rules, Kickstarter does not allow monetary rewards or equity in a company. Recent studies have shown that backers who are promised to be first to receive a certain product when it is launched, alongside the reward, tend to give larger amounts of money.[30]

Coolest Cooler

The Coolest Cooler, which broke Kickstarter's funding record.

Not all Kickstarter projects are successful, of course—and some have had unexpected twists and turns. One of the most infamous Kickstarter campaigns is the Coolest Cooler, a modern take on the ice cooler, which not only keeps drinks and food cool but also features a USB charger, a battery-powered blender, Bluetooth speakers, cutting board, and easy rolling tires. Oregon-based entrepreneur Ryan Grepper was initially looking for $50,000 in donations from the online community and ended up receiving more than $13 million from more than 60,000 backers. However, despite the huge amount of money raised, the Coolest Cooler suffered from a range of setbacks, including delayed production and selling the cooler on Amazon before fulfilling its promise to deliver to its backers first. These "growing pains" led some of its supporters to lose faith in the product.[31] As of June 2018, 40,000 coolers have been delivered to 60,000 backers, with 20,000 still waiting for their product.[32]

There are several alternatives to Kickstarter. Another crowdfunding platform, Indiegogo, is the largest global fundraising site in the world. Anybody on Earth, regardless of their geographic location, can use Indiegogo. Although it has a smaller community of backers than Kickstarter, it has a larger international presence. Unlike the Kickstarter model, on Indiegogo almost anything goes. For example, a male couple who wanted to become parents requested more than $75,000 from backers to pay for gestational surrogacy.[33]

Other crowdfunding sites that are popular with entrepreneurs include RocketHub, which focuses on science-related projects; Peerbackers, which funds creative, civic, and entrepreneurial projects; and Quirky, which helps inventors raise funds. Quirky might be considered both a crowdfunding and crowdsourcing platform as it involves collaboration with backers on the development of a product or prototype. Also worth examining are iFundWomen, a platform designed for female entrepreneurs, , and GoFundMe, which focuses solely on fundraising for nonprofits. Table 12.4 lists a number of crowdfunding platforms relevant to entrepreneurs. It is important to note that depending on the crowdfunding site, startups will be charged a transaction processing fee between 3% and 5%.

TABLE 12.4

Crowdfunding Sites for Startups and New Projects

SITE	CAMPAIGN TYPE	INDUSTRY FOCUS	CAMPAIGN/FUNDING FEES
CircleUp	Equity and credit	Early-stage consumer goods	Not available
GoFundMe	Reward, donation	People, charity, causes	0% of personal campaigns, 5% of charity campaigns
iFundWomen	Reward	Women-led businesses	5% of the total funds raised
Indiegogo	Reward, equity	Tech and innovation, creative works, community projects	5% of all funds raised
Kickstarter	Reward	Creative arts	5% of the total funds raised
Patreon	Reward, subscription	Artists and creators	5% of successfully processed payments
Peerbackers	Reward	Entrepreneurs and businesses	5% of successful campaigns
Republic	Reward, equity	Nonaccredited investing for startups with a focus on diversity	6% of the total cash funds + 2% "Crowd Safe" security
RocketHub	Reward	Science, arts, education, business, social good	4% of fully funded campaigns, 8% of partially funded campaigns
SeedInvest	Equity	Accredited investing for new startups	7.5% of the total amount raised in a successful round

Source: Adamson-Pickett, J. (2018). Best crowdfunding for startups: How to fund your small business. *Business.org.* Retrieved from https://www.business.org/finance/loans/best-crowdfunding-sites-for-startups

Equity Crowdfunding

For startups that are seeking investment in return for shares or equity, there is a new form of crowdfunding called equity crowdfunding—a form of crowdfunding that gives backers the opportunity to become shareholders in a company. In 2012, President Obama showed his support for this type of funding by signing the JOBS Act, which legalizes equity crowdfunding in the United States.[34] U.S. sites like Crowdfunder, AngelList, Fundable, and Circle Up provide investors with the opportunity to invest in companies in exchange for ownership or the promise of future returns.

The equity crowdfunding model is also gaining popularity all over the world. Crowdcube, a leading equity crowdfunding platform based in Britain, attracted almost $66 million from investors in 2017. Or what about OurCrowd, which exclusively focuses on investment in Israeli startups? It recently announced that it has reached $1 billion in funding commitment in just 6 years.[35] These are only two examples of many international equity crowdfunding sites that are changing the way people invest.

12.5 THE FOUR CONTEXTS FOR CROWDFUNDING

>> **LO 12.5** Define the four contexts for crowdfunding.

As we have explored, different crowdfunding sites offer different things to both crowd-funders and backers. We have already taken a look at some entrepreneurs who have raised funds through crowdfunding, but what about the backers themselves? What sort of reasons do people have for donating, lending, or investing in a startup? To answer this question, we need to explore four different contexts or circumstances in which people fund a project through crowdfunding: patronage model, lending model, reward-based crowdfunding, and investor model (see Figure 12.1).[36]

Patronage Model

The patronage model describes the financial support given by backers without any expectation of a direct return for their donations. Crowdfunding platform Patreon allows its patrons to fund illustrators, authors, podcasters, musicians, and other independent

FIGURE 12.1

Four Types of Crowdfunding

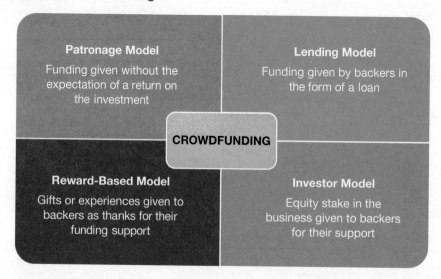

The Informational Value of Crowdfunding to Music Entrepreneurs

It's well known that crowdfunding brings much-needed financial resources to startup entrepreneurs. Now that crowdfunding is part of mainstream entrepreneurship, research has uncovered additional advantages for entrepreneurs. Researcher Jordana Viotto da Cruz wanted to know how entrepreneurs respond to information obtained from backers gathered during a crowdfunding campaign. Specifically, will entrepreneurs release their products to the market even if the crowdfunding campaign was not successful?

Crowdfunding protocol is very clear. If you reach your funding goals, the funds are released to you. If you do not reach the goal and even if you have a significant number of backers, you still do not get the funds. The only way to get funds is to reach your stated campaign goal. An entrepreneur is faced with an important decision when she has a significant number of backers, positive feedback, but did not reach her goal. Does she continue? Does she still try to bring her product to market?

Viotto da Cruz evaluated 1,505 U.S.-based projects on Kickstarter that aimed to produce a music album. Then she selected those whose albums were being sold elsewhere (such as Amazon or iTunes) after the campaign end date. This resulted in a final sample of 707 music entrepreneurs. Interesting results emerged regarding those music entrepreneurs with failed campaigns. First, contributions made by backers signal a possible market.

If the contributions were significant, and even though the goal wasn't reached, the musician could conclude there is a potential market. Second, the musicians gave increased attention to the feedback from backers and they were able to adapt their product (album) before release. Finally, many musicians used the failed campaign as a rationale for not continuing with the project. In other words, the market had spoken and it said "no"!

Viotto da Cruz summarized, "We empirically show that when not successful on crowdfunding, thus not accessing capital, project owners may decide to release the product in the market if contributions suggest positive valuation from the 'crowd.'"

Critical Thinking Questions

1. This research focused on music entrepreneurs. What type of information do you think other entrepreneurial types are seeking to gather from crowdfunding? Give examples.

2. What is crowdfunding protocol? Do you agree with the approach?

3. Are music entrepreneurs a good research sample? Why or why not? ●

Source: Viotto da Cruz, J. (2018). Beyond financing: Crowdfunding as an informational mechanism. *Journal of Business Venturing, 33*(3), 371–393.

creators. As of January 2019, Patreon has more than 3 million patrons supporting artists from many different fields.[37]

Lending Model

In the **lending model**, funds are offered as loans with the expectation that the money will be repaid. Lending models can take different forms; for example, some backers will expect interest to be paid on the loan, while other backers might expect to be reimbursed only if and when the project starts generating revenue, or if it begins to make a profit. There can also be elements of the patronage model within the lending process; for example, in the case of microfinanced loans, where small amounts of money are loaned to impoverished people in developing countries, backers might waive any expectation of repayment because the loans are promoting the social good.

Lending model: a crowdfunding model where funds are offered as loans with the expectation that the money will be repaid.

Reward-Based Crowdfunding

Reward-based crowdfunding involves rewarding backers for supporting a project. As in the example of Kickstarter, this is the most popular form of crowdfunding today. Rather than giving away precious equity or a large share in the profits, entrepreneurs give

Reward-based crowdfunding: a crowdfunding model that involves rewarding backers for supporting a project.

rewards to their backers, which can often take the form of more unique offerings such as product samples or experiences.

For example, Mamu Thai Noodle Truck rewarded its backers by hosting a cooking class featuring all their favorite recipes from the food truck menu.[38]

The Investor Model

Investor model: a crowdfunding model that gives backers an equity stake in the business in return for their funding.

The **investor model** involves giving backers an equity stake in the business in return for their funding. This model takes a few different forms; for example, investors can either buy shares in the company, which means they would be given a degree of ownership or certain rights in a project, or investors can take a share of the future revenue or profits of a company without taking ownership. In 2014, veteran-owned Bottle Breacher, which sells custom-engraved bottle openers made from .50-caliber bullets, gave away a 20% stake in their business to *Shark Tank* investors in exchange for $150,000 in order to grow their bottle-opening enterprise. By 2018, the company had generated more than $17 million in sales.[39]

The Advantages of Crowdfunding for Global Entrepreneurs

There are many benefits to crowdfunding for entrepreneurs all over the world. Not only will crowdfunding provide the money you need to get your business off the ground, but it also provides you with an idea of the level of enthusiasm and interest in your product or service before launch. This saves you money on expensive marketing as well as enabling you to gather valuable customer feedback and to test ideas at very little cost.

Crowdfunding also enables you to build early relationships with customers who have a keen interest in your product and who will most likely purchase it when it is launched. When backers choose to fund a project, they become emotionally invested—not only in the development process but in the product itself when it comes to fruition. The point is that committed, emotionally invested customers are more likely to spread the word about your offering and help to promote it through their own social networks.

Another major advantage to crowdfunding is that there are different options to choose from. Just because you have a backer does not mean you have to give away ownership or an equity stake in your venture. In many cases, you will be able to keep your equity and your independence. Most types of crowdfunding websites offer different things, and an entrepreneur is in the fortunate position of being able to choose which crowdfunding method to use.

Finally, crowdfunding is an exciting process. It is an excellent way for you to make new contacts, build your brand, attract customers, raise awareness for your products, and create a buzz before your product even hits the market. However, do not be fooled into thinking that crowdfunding is a quick and easy process. By setting up a crowdfunding campaign, you are exposing your business idea to the world, so it is important to ensure that it's ready for that level of scrutiny. To succeed in crowdfunding, you need to plan ahead; think deeply about the type of customers you would like to attract, consider how to reach them, clearly communicate your vision, and convince your online audience that your product or service is worth investing in. You must also gather support from your friends, family, and other contacts, not only to donate or invest in it through your chosen crowdfunding model, but also to help promote your product with *their* friends, family, and other contacts.

12.6 A QUICK GUIDE TO SUCCESSFUL CROWDFUNDING

>> **LO 12.6**   **Describe 10 ways in which entrepreneurs can conduct a successful crowdfunding campaign.**

Crowdfunding may seem like a temptingly easy way to get your hands on the funds you need for your new venture. However, like anything worthwhile, it involves a lot of thought,

Kickstarter Assessment

Kickstarter has projects in 15 different categories—from games to music to food. For this Mindshift exercise, go to the Stats area of Kickstarter (https://www.kickstarter.com/help/stats) and choose a project category that interests you. Then, identify what you believe to be the top five reasons for successful *and* unsuccessful campaigns in that category.

Critical Thinking Questions

1. What conclusions can you draw about the project category you chose? In what ways is it typical or atypical of Kickstarter projects?

2. Of the top five reasons for success, which do you think are most attainable for your entrepreneurial idea?

3. Of the top five reasons for failure, which do you think your entrepreneurial idea is most vulnerable to? ●

commitment, and hard work. The following tips have been provided by entrepreneurs who have successfully raised funds through crowdfunding sites such as Kickstarter and Indiegogo.[40]

1. Make Sure Your Product or Service Solves a Real Problem

Many of the entrepreneurs described in this text have become successful through their ability to solve a problem—they have managed to create something that people want to buy. If you think you have identified a product that provides a solution to a problem, then you will need to convey this message to your prospective backers. See if you can communicate your idea to your audience in no more than two sentences—if you can't, then spend time getting a clearer sense of the essence of your product.

2. Test and Refine Your Idea

Don't waste your time setting up a crowdfunding campaign and presenting an idea that is half-baked. The most successful crowdfunding efforts are a result of testing, refining, and planning. For example, the first time Ryan Grepper, inventor of the Coolest Cooler, launched his product on Kickstarter, he failed to get the funding he was looking for.[41] In response, Grepper went back to the drawing board and refined the cooler to produce a much sleeker model with additional features. Eight months later, Grepper put his product on Kickstarter for a second time, only to earn more than $13 million in pledges from enthusiastic backers. Grepper's crowdfunding campaign success shows the merit in refining and testing your idea until it is ready for launch.

3. Be Prepared

You launch your product on a crowdfunding site, and hopefully the pledges start pouring in. Suddenly, thousands of people want your product! Exciting though this is, many entrepreneurs make the mistake of failing to plan for how they will deliver their product to such a large group of consumers. Successful entrepreneurs prepare for this possibility in advance by setting up links with their suppliers, distributors, and warehouses before launching their products on a crowdfunding site, to ensure they are able to deliver as promised.

Industry watchers have noted a number of common crowdfunding mistakes (see Table 12.5). Review those so that you are clear on what *not* to do; then read the rest of this section for more tips on what you *should* do to achieve success in crowdfunding.

TABLE 12.5

Common Crowdfunding Mistakes

• Choosing the wrong crowdfunding platform
• Setting an unrealistic funding goal
• Not having enough presence on social media
• Lack of updates or communication with your backers
• Failure to get feedback and advice from the "crowd" and other crowdfunders
• Insufficient media coverage
• Failure to deliver product or rewards post-campaign

4. Seek and Accept Advice

It is always useful to seek guidance from other entrepreneurs who have been through the crowdfunding process and have either succeeded or failed. You can ask the successful entrepreneurs for advice about how they did it, as well as requesting feedback on your idea. It is also very important to talk to entrepreneurs who have failed at crowdfunding, so you can learn about the type of things to avoid. Not all advice you get will be useful, of course, but listen with an open mind and think critically about how you can constructively apply the lessons others have shared.

5. Get Your Campaign Started—Now!

Don't rely on crowdfunding sites alone to broadcast your product and attract an audience. Successful entrepreneurs have already started to build their customer base by spreading the word through social media and other outlets, before they even sign up to crowdfunding. For example, Danish entrepreneur Jonas Gyalokay, founder of wireless dongle Airtame, and his team each sent out 100 personal emails to their respective contacts explaining the importance of their idea and how meaningful it was to them. They ended the note by asking for support.

Even if your product isn't ready before your crowdfunding launch, you can release drawings or post a photo of the prototype on sites like Facebook or Twitter so your audience can provide feedback. People who are already familiar with your product will be more likely to pledge when it is officially launched on a crowdfunding site.

6. Money Matters

There are very few successful crowdfunding entrepreneurs who have launched a product without some kind of financing beforehand. Whether you use your own money, max out credit cards, or seek an investor, you will need some cash not only to manufacture your product but to cover delivery costs should your product be a hit.

When you are setting a funding goal, be aware of how much money you will actually *need* rather than how much you would *like*. Many projects fail because of crowdfunders setting unreasonable funding targets. If your goal is perceived by potential backers to be "too high," then they will not support you. By the same token, setting a target that is too low might attract backers but leave you with insufficient funds to deliver your product. It is important to do your financial homework to make sure the amount you set is realistic and conservative enough to attract backers, while also high enough to cover all your manufacturing and delivery costs.

7. Focus on the Pitch

In a crowdfunding campaign the video pitch is everything (see Figure 12.2). Remember, you are launching a product to people from all over the world, most of whom you've never met and who don't know you. Your job is not to just sell them your vision but also to earn their trust. The way to do this is to be totally transparent about your idea. Why do you truly believe your product will change/improve their lives? How are you solving a problem? If you have competitors, why is your product better than theirs? One of the best ways to get your message across is to make a video. Although 33% of Kickstarter projects have been successfully funded without videos, that figure increases to 66% when a video is included; this means that you are 50% more likely to achieve funding if you include a video as part of your launch.[42] You can even shoot on your phone if you have a tight budget. The goal is to let your potential backers see who you are.

In many cases, backers invest in a project based on their impression of the person as well as the product. If you are making a video, make sure your video is high quality and free of sound and signal problems. Also, when you are writing the description of your project, it is important that it be free of grammatical and spelling errors. As recent studies have shown, projects with spelling mistakes are 13% less likely to be successful than projects without.[43]

8. Make the Most of Crowdfunding Opportunities

Crowdfunding isn't just a money-making operation—it comes with additional perks. You get important feedback from backers, which can lead to more ideas and opportunities, and if you're successful, you also get the added benefit of press coverage, which can open lots of doors into other industries. For example, within a few days of launching its Kickstarter campaign, smart video doorbell startup SkyBell was featured on Engadget and TechCrunch, which led to an increase in exposure and a lucrative deal with companies like American multinational conglomerate Honeywell.

9. Commit to Your Campaign

Successful crowdfunders commit to managing the campaign.[44] If your idea proves to be popular with backers, you will need to reply to a lot of emails and potentially send out surveys to gain valuable feedback.

FIGURE 12.2

Example of a Kickstarter Campaign Site

In the first week of launching his product on Indiegogo, Canary home security device founder Adam Sager replied to 3,000 emails. Overwhelming as this may sound, never underestimate the importance of engaging with your audience. Once you have made this connection, then you can continue the dialogue after the campaign is over, which can lead to all sorts of exciting opportunities. For example, smart kitchen company Anova Culinary originally raised more than $2 million through Kickstarter, only to be later purchased by Electrolux for $250 million.[45]

10. Avoid the Crowdfunding Curse!

Delays and setbacks in product delivery, and failure to deliver the promised rewards, are the biggest problems experienced by successful crowdfunders, who are often unprepared for the extent of the demand. Research has shown that more than 75% of products are delivered later than expected.[46] In addition, funded projects sometimes fail altogether to deliver what they promised, which causes bad feeling among those who have been generous enough to donate.

If your product is not ready to be shipped and you know you are going to miss your initial deadline, then be honest about it. Make sure you update your backers via email and through the crowdfunding site. The worst thing you can do is to not communicate with your backers. Frustrated, impatient backers can destroy an entrepreneur's reputation and a product. They have put their faith in you by pledging to fund your idea, and they deserve to know what is happening. Don't let them down. If you are honest with them about the situation, and they are enthusiastic about your product, then many of them will cut you some slack. The lesson is to make a good-faith effort at all times to fulfill your promises.

Figure 12.3 summarizes the 10 tips we have presented in this section in the form of a checklist; you can track your stage of completion in carrying out the advice given in each tip.

If your first crowdfunding campaign does not succeed, it doesn't mean that all is lost. Small changes can go a long way to ensuring your chances of success next time around. ●

FIGURE 12.3

Crowdfunding Checklist

1.	Make sure your product or service solves a real problem.
2.	Test and refine your idea.
3.	Be prepared.
4.	Seek and accept advice.
5.	Get your campaign started—now!
6.	Money matters.
7.	Focus on the pitch.
8.	Make the most of crowdfunding opportunities.
9.	Commit to your campaign.
10.	Avoid the crowdfunding curse!

SUMMARY

12.1   Define bootstrapping and illustrate how it applies to entrepreneurs.

Entrepreneurs use their own sweat equity in combination with other bootstrapping strategies to make enough progress to get in a better position to attract more formal types of funding.

12.2   Identify common bootstrapping strategies used by entrepreneurs.

The list of common bootstrapping techniques is extensive. It includes ideas like using the home as the office, renting or leasing before buying, minimizing personal salary initially, developing and reaching out to contacts, offering equity reimbursement, and maintaining low operating inventories.

12.3   Explain the difference between crowdsourcing and crowdfunding.

Crowdfunding involves raising funds from a large audience, typically through the Internet. Crowdsourcing involves using the Internet to attract and manage low-cost or free labor generated by enthusiasm for the product or service.

12.4   Describe the effects of crowdfunding on entrepreneurship.

The crowdfunding movement has provided a democratic means of funding that has never before existed on the scale it exists today. Equity crowdfunding has emerged as a popular crowdfunding alternative, where ownership stakes (stock) are issued in exchange for funding.

12.5   Define the four contexts for crowdfunding.

Crowdfunding largely falls into one of four types: patronage model, lending model, reward-based model, and investor model. There are many benefits to crowdfunding for entrepreneurs: It provides you with the money you need to get your business off the ground, enables you to attract early customers, and allows you to test your ideas at very little cost.

12.6   Describe 10 ways in which entrepreneurs can conduct a successful crowdfunding campaign.

Crowdfunding is flexible and exciting but not without its challenges; it's not free money. Entrepreneurs still need to make sure their product/service addresses a real business need, a benefit to customers that is being under-addressed or unaddressed. Successful campaigns start as early as is feasible, maintain commitments, and do not overpromise.

KEY TERMS

Bootstrapping 281	Equity crowdfunding 292	Patronage model 292
Crowdfunding 286	Investor model 294	Reward-based crowdfunding 293
Crowdsourcing 287	Lending model 293	Sweat equity 284

CASE STUDY

Daymond John, founder, FUBU

FUBU is an American hip-hop apparel company started in 1992 by Daymond John, a current investor on *Shark Tank*, along with Keith Perrin, J. Alexander Martin, and Carl Brown. FUBU currently sells T-shirts, rugby shirts, hockey and football jerseys, baseball caps, and accessories, all embroidered with the now-popular FUBU logo.

Daymond John grew up in the heart of a thriving hip-hop culture in an area of Queens, New York, called Hollis. Also out of the Hollis neighborhood came hip-hop legends such as Russell Simmons, LL Cool J, and all three members of Run-DMC. Daymond had a love for hip-hop and the culture that surrounded it, especially the clothes. Daymond explained how the idea for FUBU was sparked. "We started to hear rumors that clothing companies, apparel companies did not want rappers, African Americans, inner-city kids, anybody wearing their clothes. I started to get fed up hearing about all these types of brands and I wanted to create a brand that loved and respected the people that loved and respected hip-hop, and I called it FUBU: For us by us!"

Daymond tested and experimented with his concept from 1989–1992. He printed a few "FUBU" labels and attached them to Champion-branded T-shirts that he bought off the rack from local retailers. He wore the T-shirts himself to see if people noticed. He also tested a hat concept. He noticed that many rappers were wearing a particular kind of hat. It was a type of ski cap with a small piece of shoestring on top. These hats were mostly sold by street vendors for $20. He thought he could do better, so he bought $40 worth of fabric. He stitched 80 hats together, added the FUBU labels, and tried to sell them for $10 on a street corner outside a local mall. He sold out in 3 hours and made $800.

He was the consummate bootstrapper, and the word about FUBU started to spread around town. He started selling more and more hats and soon added T-shirts to his product line. He approached retail booths outside the malls whose street corners he would stand on and asked them to sell his goods on "consignment" for him. "I was trying to figure any and every way out that I can to increase my sales!" He was sourcing his T-shirts from companies that would provide high=quality T-shirts with no brand name. He would then sew or screen print or even embroider his logo on the T-shirt and sell it. While continuously improving the product, he was also testing the market to see what customer preferences were in terms of pricing, colors, and styles.

Daymond was working at Red Lobster in the early days of FUBU, so he would spend early mornings visiting potential printers and embroiderers and make the T-shirts at night. He even closed FUBU three times because he ran out of cash. "I would be walking around the blocks when someone would say, Hey! Aren't you that little kid that sells FUBU? I need some more; I've been looking for you! I had to keep opening the business back up because the business started to call me instead of me calling the business." Fortunately, a friend of Daymond's, J. Alexander, saw FUBU's potential and invested, but he brought more to the table than money.

J. Alexander came up with a very interesting marketing plan. "The big black guys in the neighborhood had little options on what they could have to be very stylish. They had to go to Rochester Big & Tall and get a big white shirt or a black shirt or they had to pay a lot of money to get this stuff custom made for them because nobody was really making them. We just found a place that made 4X, 5X, 6X shirts and we made around 20 of these shirts. We made 20 of those shirts because we knew that these guys are normally bodyguards. Not all of them, but the ones we gave T-shirts were bouncers and something like that. They would not just wear it once—not like some of the stylish kids who don't want to be seen wearing something twice. We knew that these guys would wear it forever." These early adopters were walking billboards for FUBU!

Soon hip-hop artists who visited the clubs noticed FUBU on bouncers and bodyguards and demand started to increase. FUBU T-shirts were also being worn by video music director Ralph McDaniels's bodyguards. Between 1985 and 1998, Ralph was well-known for bringing hip-hop music artists into the spotlight, and Daymond wanted a meeting with Ralph. Since his bodyguards were wearing FUBU, Ralph was familiar with the brand and agreed to the meeting. Daymond recollected, "We were scared to death but he was very sweet and told everybody that FUBU was the next best thing. I really owe Ralph so much as he was one of my mentors and he was also mentor to the community. He really put us out there and after that all the rappers, all of them, were ready to wear our stuff because Ralph gave us the thumbs-up!"

Daymond John brought in business partners to help get the work done. While the partners together had accumulated around $50,000 in credit card debt at the time, they decided to go to the 1995 MAGIC fashion trade show in Las Vegas. They couldn't afford a booth at the time, but Daymond made the best use of his limited resources. He and his partners wore their FUBU-branded apparel and approached like-minded brands, such as Timberland. "I would stand outside their booth and say, 'Hey! How are you doing? I got this new brand, FUBU' and people would say, FUBU? the For Us By Us stuff? Where is your booth? I'll walk over to your booth. I would say, Instead of walking into my booth, you want to hop into a cab and head to the Mirage Hotel. I have my booth in one of the rooms there and we worked it out. We wrote $300,000 in orders and that's when I realized how much capital I actually needed."

To fulfill the Las Vegas orders, Daymond approached banks for a loan but none would work with him. As a result, Daymond's mother gave FUBU a $100,000 loan to cover operating expenses. Daymond set up manufacturing inside the house. He and his partners brought in sewing machines and hired seamstresses, all with the objective of completing the Las Vegas order by hand. Since he was paying all salaries on time, and paying for raw materials in advance, and having stores take credit for 30, 60, or 90 days, Daymond ran out of money within 4 months after having completed only $75,000 of the $300,000 orders promised.

The stores were starting to lose trust in Daymond, and Daymond was worried about losing his mother's house. Daymond's mother knew he needed a strategic investor and placed a classified advertisement in a local newspaper asking people to fund the company. Thirty of the 33 people who answered the ad were loan sharks charging extremely high interest rates, but one legitimate inquiry emerged. It was Norman Weisfeld, the president of Samsung's textiles division. Samsung agreed to finance the operations of the brand but asked Daymond to commit to selling $5 million within the next 3 years. Daymond said yes and the deal with Samsung was done.

With Samsung's backing, FUBU reached $30 million in revenue in 3 months, and the big retailers started to show renewed interest. Daymond recalled the resistance and discrimination of some buyers. "Many of the big retailers wanted to jump in on the highly profitable hip-hop bandwagon. Some of them were scared because they didn't want 'those' type of people in the store or were afraid of shootouts or shoplifting. One large retailer also asked me to take off the picture of myself and my three partners because we apparently looked like a gang." Undeterred, FUBU reached $350 million after 2 years and today has sales in the billions thanks to product line expansion, licensing, and partnering.

Today, Daymond John is semi-retired from FUBU and is now a Shark on *Shark Tank*. He's invested more than $8M in *Shark Tank* entrepreneurs.

Critical Thinking Questions

1. Identify and evaluate all of Daymond John's bootstrapping methods.

2. If FUBU was being started today, would it be a good candidate for crowdfunding?

3. How does discrimination impact entrepreneurs? What evidence of discrimination was presented in the case? How did he handle the discrimination? What would you do?

Sources:

Feloni, R. (2018). Shark Tank investor Daymond John landed a deal that helped him make $30 million by taking out a newspaper ad. *Business Insider*. Retrieved from https://www.businessinsider.com/shark-tank-daymond-john-newspaper-ad-samsung-deal-2018-2

FUBU. (2019). Retrieved from https://fubu.com/

Raz, G. (2018, April 8). FUBU: Daymond John [Podcast]. *Stitcher*. Retrieved from https://www.stitcher.com/podcast/national-public-radio/how-i-built-this/e/54019004

Shark Tank cast: Daymond John. (n.d.). Retrieved from https://abc.go.com/shows/shark-tank/cast/daymond-john

©iStockphoto.com/Ta Nu

13

Financing for Startups

"There are two times for a young company to raise money: when there is lots of hope, or lots of results, but never in between."

—George Doriot, American Venture Capitalist

Chapter Outline

Learning Objectives

13.1   Define equity financing for entrepreneurs and outline its main stages.

13.2   Illustrate the basics of business valuation.

13.3   Describe angel investors and how they finance entrepreneurs.

13.4   Explain the role of venture capitalists and how they finance entrepreneurs.

13.5   Describe how investors carry out due diligence processes.

13.1 WHAT IS EQUITY FINANCING?

>> LO 13.1   Define equity financing for entrepreneurs and outline its main stages.

In Chapter 12, we explored bootstrapping, the different ways in which entrepreneurs can get ventures started without formal external funding. We also explained how many entrepreneurs sometimes use bootstrapping to retain control, grow their business the way they want to, and keep hold of the company's equity.

Although bootstrapping may be ideal, if not necessary, in the beginning, as the company gains traction and shows evidence of potential, many entrepreneurs begin to look at the possibility of **equity financing**, which is the sale of shares of stock in exchange for cash. It gives entrepreneurs capital, which are financial resources to run the business including producing and selling the product. In other words, equity financing is a way to get capital from investors to start or grow a business. Most student entrepreneurs are not in a position to seek investment just yet; still, it is important to at least be familiar with the language of entrepreneurial finance for the future.

It's important to recognize that not all opportunities are investment worthy, but those that are face significant challenges. Sometimes it seems that entrepreneurs spend more time trying to raise money than actually working on the business. It becomes another full-time job for the founders. Additionally, balancing growth while preserving equity is a challenge, and entrepreneurs need to give serious thought as to whether—or at what point in time—they really need outside investment to grow. The general rule of thumb is to avoid seeking investment for as long as possible, to give your enterprise time to grow and build value so that you can secure a better deal with investors later on. However, sometimes competition will drive you to seek investment as early as you can, and some businesses are more capital-intensive than others. For example, if you have proprietary technology that has a proven market but you need additional funds to get the next version of the technology produced to reach a larger market, then equity financing is a logical next step.

Equity financing: the sale of shares of stock in exchange for cash.

Splitting the Ownership Pie

The idea behind equity is similar to splitting a pie. When you are the only owner of the company, you own 100% of a small pie. When someone invests in your company to enhance growth, then your pie becomes bigger. As you need to give away equity in exchange for the investment, the company is no longer fully yours. However, if the company does well, then your smaller slice of the bigger pie will be much larger than the original smaller pie.

There is no magic formula telling you how much equity to keep or give away. Google gave up the majority of its ownership, so cofounders Larry Page and Sergey Brin

$SAGE edge™

Master the content at
**edge.sagepub.com/
neckentrepreneurship2e**

Joel Barthelemy, GlobalMed

Virtual health care platform GlobalMed has provided health solutions for the U.S. Department of Veterans Affairs.

For Joel Barthelemy of GlobalMed, entrepreneurship started at "5 years old selling vegetables and flowers out of the back of a wagon." If he didn't have something one of his customers wanted, he would do everything he could to get it. This same commitment to customer needs has enabled him to build multiple successful companies. Joel says, "You have to make an impact." And he feels impact is about looking ahead and seeing the shifts before they happen.

Joel serves as the founder and CEO of GlobalMed Telemedicine, a health care technology company that is "the platform of platforms for virtual health" and provides hardware and software for virtual health solutions. He and his team developed the first lightweight, true HD video examination camera and the first cloud-based Image Management Exchange for Telemedicine. GlobalMed has been recognized as one of *Inc. Magazine*'s and Deloitte Technology's 500 fastest-growing private companies as well as one of the best places to work in Arizona. GlobalMed is the outcome of Barthelemy's 25 years in high-tech health care and his 14 years specifically in visual collaboration and connected health care.

GlobalMed has clients worldwide. For example, GlobalMed is helping U.S. military veterans access health care by providing the company's telehealth solutions to the U.S. Department of Veterans Affairs (VA). The VA operates the largest telehealth program in the United States, with 700,000 veterans receiving telehealth services for 50 different specialties. This allows providers to treat patients in remote locations via online, visual technology. Further, GlobalMed's Transportable Exam Station that provides a mobile, tablet-based telemedicine platform is used by health providers around the world. All in all, GlobalMed has delivered more than 15 million consults across 55 countries.

Joel's goal is to change the way people receive health care worldwide and to make sure it is available to all. There is a race to do this worldwide as populations age and more and more people need affordable, available health care. Joel leads this race with an innovative, future-focused platform aimed to help people globally in all types of environments. Barthelemy explains, "I'm focused on changing the way health care is delivered so that anyone can have access to health care anywhere."

Joel was a victim of the "dot com crash" of 2001 and lost a lot of money in the process. As he began GlobalMed, he "took on additional debt and reinvested himself." Now that the business is established, Joel has used an acquisition strategy to fund his later-stage growth. GlobalMed recently bought a competing, Miami-based company called TreatMD, which has expanded the functionality of GlobalMed's existing platform. Additionally, they bought an Oregon-based R&D company that has unique behavior modification software that has potential to help patients with chronic conditions.

As Barthelemy explains, "We're a debt-free company, we haven't taken outside investment, and we're profitable. . . . With all countries experiencing an aging population, there are few safer bets." For Joel, it's about building a profitable business related to something you love. He also believes in helping others do the same. One of Joel's favorite sayings is, "Ask me for money and I'll give you advice; ask for advice and I'll give you money." He spends a significant amount of his time nowadays "investing in companies that are run by people who love what they do." Joel's success has allowed him to be an angel investor and fund projects that he believes in.

Critical Thinking Questions

1.   Has Joel ever experienced failure? If so, how did he react to the failure?

2.   How does Joel remain a leader in his industry? ●

Sources:

Joel Barthelemy (interview with author, January 24, 2019).

AZBIO Board of Directors. Retrieved from https://www.azbio.org/az-bio-board-of-directors/joel-e-barthelemy

Robeznieks, A. (2017). Here's why GlobalMed acquired telemedicine startup TreatMD. Retrieved from https://medcitynews.com/2017/03/her-es-globalmed-acquired-telemedicine-startup-treatmd/

collectively own just 16% of Google stock. Though 16% for the founders may not sound like very much, think about it: 16% of an enormous Google-size pie is pretty lucrative.[1] At the time of this writing, Google was worth more than $800 billion, so 16% works out to almost $128 billion.

However, splitting the pie starts before investment, if there is a team involved. And splitting the pie in an early-stage company represents a unique challenge because what you are splitting is rather worthless.[2] The founders agree to a percentage of ownership of something that doesn't really exist, and the question becomes, How do you determine who should get what percentage of the pie in the beginning? Does everyone get an equal share? Entrepreneur Mike Moyer, who wrote the book *Slicing the Pie*, uses a common example of four students working on a venture in an entrepreneurship course. They split the "equity" four ways and each gets 25%. They even incorporate the business. The class ends and one student really takes the idea forward and the other three are slackers, yet they all want to keep their 25% stake in the company. What do you do? Legally, they may have a right to that 25%, but it's not really the right thing. Moyer says new entrepreneurs make two mistakes: "The first is to divide the pie *before* you build the company. This is quite common, and founders often wind up where my hapless student did. The other mistake is dividing up the pie *after* you build the company, which often leads to internal battles that can cripple a startup team."[3] Moyer suggests creating a process for allocating equity based on contribution, including time, money, intellectual property, and other resources. This will help later when formal financing, such as what we talk about next, is warranted.

Stages of Equity Financing

There are several stages of investment,[4] but for the purposes of this chapter we focus on the initial stages of equity financing usually provided to young companies: seed-stage financing, startup financing, and early-stage financing. **Seed-stage financing** usually consists of small or modest amounts of capital provided to entrepreneurs to prove a concept. **Startup financing** is the money provided to entrepreneurs to enable them to implement their idea by funding product research and development; and **early-stage financing** consists of larger amounts of funds provided for companies that have a team in place and a product or service tested or piloted, but as yet show little or no revenue. Florida-based augmented reality (AR) startup Magic Leap is a good example of an early-stage company that managed to raise more than $2 billion in funding before releasing its Magic Leap One AR headset.[5]

One of the most important factors to consider when you are seeking investment is to find investors who are most suitable for your stage of the company. Timing is also a factor. There is no use trying to raise funds when the venture is down to its last dollar. For one thing, it can take at least 6 months to raise money; in addition, a desperate early venture may give away far too much equity to investors, which can seriously dilute the position of its founders.

As the business grows and starts to take in more revenue, entrepreneurs may seek second-stage or later-stage financing. Even further down the road, a profitable company looking to expand and go public through an initial public offering (IPO) may seek investment through the third or mezzanine stage of financing. Finally, entrepreneurs may need bridge financing to cover the expenses associated with the IPO. These stages are displayed graphically in Figure 13.1.

Forms of Equity Financing

Depending on the stage of their venture, entrepreneurs have several equity financing options available to them. As we discussed in Chapter 12, entrepreneurs looking to raise initial funds tend to turn to friends, family, and fools (the 3 Fs). Typically, the 3 Fs either invest cash in exchange for equity in the business, provide a loan, or lend money in the form of a loan that can later be converted to equity (called convertible debt). Entrepreneurs may also use crowdfunding to raise money from their immediate network, as well as reaching out to a wider market. In general, entrepreneurs may raise from $1,000 to $100,000 through the 3 Fs.

However, entrepreneurs seeking more formal financial capital to fund a growing business may choose to seek an **angel investor**. They are investors who use their own money to provide funds to young startup private businesses run by entrepreneurs who are neither friends nor family.[6] Entrepreneurs may choose to seek a

Seed-stage financing: a stage of financing in which small or modest amounts of capital are provided to entrepreneurs to prove a concept.

Startup financing: a stage of financing in which the money is provided to entrepreneurs to enable them to implement the idea by funding product research and development.

Early-stage financing: a stage of financing that involves larger funds provided for companies that have a team in place and a product or service tested or piloted, but have little or no revenue.

Angel investor: a type of investor who uses his or her own money to provide funds to young startup private businesses run by entrepreneurs who are neither friends nor family.

FIGURE 13.1

Stages of Equity Financing

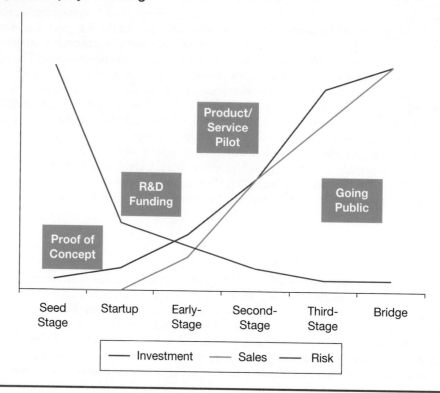

Source: https://www.marsdd.com/mars-library/angel-investors-seed-or-venture-capital-investors-that-depends-on-your-stage-of-company-development/

venture capitalist (VC) who is a professional investor who generally invests in early-stage and emerging companies because of perceived long-term growth potential.

Angel investors and VCs tend to be looking for the same types of opportunities, but there are differences between them, as illustrated in Table 13.1.

Seed-stage and startup entrepreneurs tend to seek out angel investors when they are initially trying to grow and scale the organization. VCs also invest in startups, but they are more likely to invest in companies in the early to third stage of business.

TABLE 13.1

The Differences Between Angels and VCs

ANGELS	VCS
Individuals worth more than $1 million	Funds consisting of limited partnerships
Invest from $25k to $100k in personal funds	Invest from $500,000 upwards in VC funding
Fund seed or early-stage companies	Fund from early- to late-stage companies
Carry out informal due diligence	Conduct formal due diligence
Responsible for own decisions	Decisions made with committee
Exit with returns on personal investment	Exit with returns to fund's partners

Source: Adapted from Adams, P. (2014, January 12). How do angel investors differ from venture capitalists? Retrieved from http://www.rockiesventureclub.org/colorado-capital-conference/how-do-angel-investors-differ-from-venture-capitalists/

Table 13.2 lists some other factors and key questions that investors take into account when making the decision to invest.

TABLE 13.2

Factors That Investors Take Into Account

FACTOR	KEY QUESTIONS
Market conditions	Is the market ready for your product/service? Is the market size big enough? Is the market reachable?
Competition	Who are the competitors in your industry? How does your product compare with similar items in the market? Is there a unique and compelling competitive advantage?
Market opportunity	What is the opportunity for your product? How many customers? What is the proof that there is a market?
Founders	Are they experienced in the industry? Have they done startups before? Can the investor work with them? Are they coachable?
Social proof	Is there evidence that others believe in the founders' vision as much as they do? Does the company have a board of advisors? What are their customers saying about the business?
Value add	How much value can investors bring to your business through their expert advice and guidance?
Potential for return	If an investor puts in $1 today, what will they get in 5 years? 10 years? Does the potential return match the potential risk?

Sources: What investors look for before investing in a small business. (n.d.). *Accion.* Retrieved from https://us.accion.org/resource/7-things-investors-look-investing/; Newlands, M. (2014). 5 things investors want to know before signing a check. *Entrepreneur.* Retrieved from https://www.entrepreneur.com/article/234536; What investors look for. (n.d.). *Fundable.* Retrieved from https://www.fundable.com/learn/resources/guides/investor/what-investors-look-for; Harroch, R. (2015). 20 things all entrepreneurs should know about angel investors. *Forbes.* Retrieved from http://www.forbes.com/sites/allbusiness/2015/02/05/20-things-all-entrepreneurs-should-know-about-angel-investors

13.2 THE BASICS OF VALUATION

>> **LO 13.2 Illustrate the basics of business valuation.**

Before entrepreneurs seek equity investment, it is essential for them to know the value of their company so that when the time comes to raise funds, they will understand how much of the business they will need to sell and at what price. That's what investment is: Entrepreneurs are selling part of their business in exchange for investment in the form of cash to operate and grow the business. Putting a value on a company that has very little or no financial history is not an exact science. However, when it comes to fundraising, most investors will expect to see an approximate valuation of your business. This is needed so both the entrepreneur and investor can negotiate the equity percentage and division of ownership. But how do you value a business without any financial history?

The valuation of a seed-stage, startup, or early-stage company is based on the anticipation of future growth. How much time will it take for the business to become profitable? What potential does it have to grow? How can you prove to investors that your business is worth investing in? What is the exit strategy so investors can see how they might realize a return on their investment?

How Can Entrepreneurs Value Their Companies?

As we have learned, there are very few overnight successes; entrepreneurs need to use the tools available to them to determine just how much their company is actually worth.

Typically entrepreneurs value their companies based on the firm's potential in their chosen market. The easiest way to do this is to check out similar companies operating in the same industry to see how they are being valued.

Sites such as BizBuySell and BizQuest will help you to find out how much businesses are worth in your industry and how much they have been valued at when they have reached profitability. For example, a company that's currently valued at $10 million after 5 years could mean that it was valued at a fraction of that price at the startup stage. You can also seek advice from lawyers and accountants who can help to determine the market rates for companies like yours.

However, be careful not to get too carried away by other valuations. Just because a similar company is worth millions doesn't mean your company is worth the same. Overvaluing your startup is dangerous—not only does it put investors off, but it puts the company and the entrepreneur's reputation at risk. Entrepreneurs typically have their valuation calculation and investors have their own. The true valuation falls somewhere in the middle!

How Do Investors Value Startups?

Expert investors do deals all the time, so they will have a very good idea of what your business is worth. There are a number of reasons investors fund startups, and their decisions are not necessarily just based on the numbers. By knowing the criteria that matter to them, you can better position your company to attract investors.

First, investors will want to know your experience and your team's past successes. Second, they will want to see how many people use your product or service. Even if your business is not currently profitable, showing that you have 100,000 users, for example, proves to the investor that you have a potentially scalable business if provided with the appropriate amount of funding.

Second, having a distribution channel already set up is also attractive to investors. In fact, distribution is so important that PayPal cofounder Peter Thiel believes that "Poor distribution—not product—is the number one cause of failure." For example, the founders of Morphcostumes, spandex costume manufacturer of the "morphsuit,"[7] attracted investment because they had already spent months perfecting their product, and they set up a website and a Facebook page that became distribution channels to customers all over the world.[8]

Simon Dack/Alamy Stock Photo

People wearing Morphsuits

Third, the industry in which you are operating might just be very popular at the moment. VCs are typically interested in investing in technology, as it usually means big business. For example, the top three industries invested in by VCs in 2018 were the Internet industry, health care, and mobile and telecommunications.[9] However, it often takes quite a bit of negotiation before entrepreneurs and investors agree on what they both consider a fair valuation of the company. Take the show *Shark Tank* in the United States (called *Dragon's Den* in the UK and Canada), where budding entrepreneurs get to pitch their ideas to angel investors in the hope of receiving investment. On any given episode, you will hear something like the following:

Entrepreneur: "We are asking for $150,000 for 10% of the company."

Shark: "Your pre-money valuation is too high at $1.35 million. I'll give you $150,000 for 30% of the company."

What does all of this mean? First, let's talk about two important definitions: pre-money valuation and post-money valuation. Pre-money valuation is the company's value before it receives outside investment, while post-money valuation is the company's value after it receives a round of financing. In the *Shark Tank* exchange above, what is the entrepreneur's valuation of the company before receiving funding?

The entrepreneur is asking for $150,000 for 10% of the company, which means that the post-money valuation is $1.5 million ($150,000 ÷ .10 = $1.5M). The pre-money valuation is simply the post-money valuation less the investment—in this case, $1.35M ($1.5M – $150K = $1.35M). The Shark, however, thinks that a $1.35 million valuation is far too high, so she counters with the new offer of $150,000 for 30% of the company. With this offer, the Shark believes the pre-money valuation of the company is really only $350,000.

It is with certainty that entrepreneurs and investors will always disagree on the valuation! The answers to the key questions will help investors determine an approximate value for your business before giving you an idea of how much they are willing to invest. This is why it is important to do your own homework in order to prove that your business is worth investing in. By providing an estimated valuation of your business before you meet with investors, you can display business savvy and commitment to growth.

TV show *Shark Tank*, where budding entrepreneurs get to pitch their ideas in the hope of receiving investment.

The Age of the Unicorn

A popular term in the venture capital industry is *unicorn*, originally coined by Aileen Lee, founder of Cowboy Ventures. A **unicorn** is a tech startup company that has received a $1 billion valuation, as determined by private or public investment.[10] Although unicorn startups are rare (there is a less than 1% chance of startups becoming one after raising venture capital), they are becoming more common. So far there are 35 unicorn companies in the United States. Table 13.3 lists the top 10. Though Epic Games was founded in 1991, the popularity of its Fortnite Battle Royale game, the company received substantial investment for growth in 2017.

Unicorn: a tech startup company that has received a $1 billion valuation, as determined by private or public investment.

TABLE 13.3

The Top 10 Unicorns in the U.S. (2018)[11]

COMPANY	WHAT IT DOES	VALUATION	YEAR FOUNDED
Juul Labs	Electronic cigarettes	$16 billion	2017
Epic Games	Video game developers	$15 billion	1991
DoorDash	Food delivery	$4 billion	2013
Snowflake	Cloud computing	$3.95 billion	2012
UiPath	Business task automation	$3 billion	2005
Circle	Cryptocurrency investment platform	$3 billion	2013
Roblox	Online game creation platform	$2.4 billion	2005
Bird	Electronic scooters	$2 billion	2017
Automation Anywhere	Robotic process automation (RPA)	$1.8 billion	2003
Discord	Voice, video, text app for gamers	$1.65 billion	2012

Source: Baston, N. (2018). 35 U.S. tech startups that reached unicorn status in 2018. *Inc.* Adapted from https://www.inc.com/business-insider/35-us-tech-startups-that-reached-unicorn-status-in-2018.html

Convertible Debt

Because valuation can be complicated when a business is new, entrepreneurs and investors often opt for **convertible debt** (also known as a *convertible bond* or *convertible note*), which is a short-term loan that can be turned into equity when future financing is acquired. Convertible debt is a middle ground between debt and equity financing.

For example, say you are running a startup and you fully believe that you need to attract a significant amount of venture capital to make your business succeed. However, you are aware that VC investment doesn't happen overnight, so you still need to raise money in the immediate future to get your business off the ground. In this early stage of business, you might first ask potential lenders such as friends, family, and angel investors to invest, but you will need to think about the terms to offer them in exchange for their investment.

In the context of seed financing, these early lenders will loan you the money to help you attract venture capital. But rather than get the money back with interest when you do receive investment from a VC, these lenders receive stock, instead. In other words, the initial debt converts to shares of stock after an agreed certain point, which is called a *conversion event*—for example, entrepreneurs and investors may agree to set the conversion after a product reaches $100,000 in profit or achieves $1 million in revenue.

Benefits and Advantages

One of the main advantages of issuing convertible debt is that it removes the need for valuation—in other words, you don't have to spend lots of time trying to figure out how much your company is worth to establish a stock share price. In fact, valuation becomes much easier after the first round of financing when there is a lot more data and information to work with.

Another benefit of convertible debt is that if your company succeeds, your investors may be entitled to a discount off the share price or bonus when converting the debt into equity, which can provide an incentive for your investors to commit. However, caution must be used when setting a discount—if the discount is too low, investors may not want to commit, and if the discount is too high, the investor may take this into account when pricing the stock, which may end up coming out of your own shares.

Finally, by issuing convertible debt, you the entrepreneur will remain the majority stockholder, with no interference from your lenders. Depending on the terms, they will have no control, no voting rights, nor any say over how you run your company.

Cautions and Disadvantages

However, there are also some disadvantages to convertible debt: Early lenders may not want to take the risk of having their money tied up until the debt is converted into equity. They may also be wary of losing money if the conversion event doesn't happen (i.e., if profits don't reach $100,000 or revenue does not reach $1 million) or if the company ends up filing for bankruptcy. However, a clause can be added to address the possibility of the conversion event not occurring. For example, the initial investment could remain as a debt (which the entrepreneur must repay).

For entrepreneurs, convertible debt can be a daunting prospect: Accumulating debt before the company takes off can be significantly risky. Similarly, if entrepreneurs fail to pay back the loan, they could be sued by the lenders. In addition, convertible debt requires a lawyer to draft the terms, which can be an expensive bill to pay early on in the life of a startup.

To summarize, entrepreneurs using convertible debt to gain financial support from early lenders such as friends, family, and angels can be condensed into the following: "I need money, and you have it. But I don't know how much my company is worth, so let's see if professional investors or the passage of time will set the value for us while giving you an upside that's more in keeping with the risk."[12]

In the following sections, we will explore how angel investors and VCs can help entrepreneurs grow their businesses.

13.3 ANGEL INVESTORS

>> **LO 13.3** Describe angel investors and how they finance entrepreneurs.

In the past, an "angel" in the context of investment was used to describe wealthy people who invested in Broadway theatrical productions.[13] Over the years, the term *angel* has evolved to mean anyone who uses personal capital to invest in an entrepreneurial venture. Angels are eligible to invest as long as they are **accredited investors**, which means they earn an annual income of more than $200,000 or have a net worth of more than $1 million. Research shows that startups that have received angel backing are more likely to survive. With angel investment, entrepreneurs are able to scale sooner, hire employees, and generate greater revenue, which all leads to great potential for later-stage investment. Apple, Google, and Netscape are just a few well-known companies that have benefited from angel funding in the early stages.[14]

Accredited investors: investors who earn an annual income of more than $200,000 or have a net worth of more than $1 million.

We may tend to think of angels as motivated by a pure spirit of goodness—so it's important to remember that the primary reason why an angel (or anyone else, for that matter) chooses to invest is to earn money. However, angel investment is not just about the money. Often experienced self-made entrepreneurs themselves, angel investors can add significant value by providing advice, skills, and expertise, as well as lucrative contacts. They typically enjoy the experience of mentoring others and the personal fulfillment of nurturing a new business and watching it grow. It is generally thought that the typical amount invested by angels can range from $25,000 to $100,000.[15] Angel investors usually look for opportunities in young startups that can be expected to return 10 times their investment in 5 years.[16]

Finding an Angel Investor

Angels used to be a notoriously elusive group, but thanks to sites like AngelList, today it is much easier to find a business angel. There are still some angels who will accept only referrals, but most angels will consider unsolicited submissions of ideas. Even so, when looking for an angel, it's always best to start with whom you know. Tap your network and think about who could provide you with an introduction to an angel. For example, Steve Jobs was introduced to his business angel through another investor, and Google's Sergey Brin and Larry Page found their angel through a faculty member at Stanford University.[17] Among those who can provide you with referrals to angels are attorneys, other entrepreneurs, work colleagues, university faculty, VCs, and investment bankers. Angels receive many unsolicited ideas every day, but having a professional vouch for you is always a good start.

Angels originally were wealthy patrons who supported theatrical productions.

© David M. Benett / Getty Images Entertainment

Table 13.4 outlines some reasons why angels and entrepreneurs can sometimes be a good match. The most successful working relationships are based on finding the right match for your business. The perfect match very much depends on the type of angel you are looking for.

Types of Angel Investors

Business angels have many different objectives and styles of operating.[18] They range from silent investors to those who want full involvement in the operations of the company, either as a consultant or as a full-time partner in the business.

As angels have gotten more sophisticated, different types of angels have emerged. There are five main types of business angels: entrepreneurial, corporate, professional, enthusiast, and micromanagement. Let's take a look at each of these.

TABLE 13.4

Why Angels and Entrepreneurs Are Good for Each Other

• After friends and family, angel investors provide up to 90% of outside equity raised by startups.
• Angels invested an estimated $25 billion in startups in 2018.
• Angels funded almost 70,000 early-stage ventures in 2018.
• Angel-invested early companies (less than 5 years old) over a 25-year period accounted for all of the net new jobs in the United States.
• Economic research shows that the largest growth comes from innovative startups, the kind angels fund.
• Angels provide entrepreneurs with mentoring, monitoring, and guidance.
• Angels provide entrepreneurs with connections and introductions to their widespread network.
• Angels teach entrepreneurs valuable business strategies that go beyond funding.

Source: Angel Capital Association. (n.d.). Angels and the entrepreneurial ecosystem. Retrieved from http://www.angelcapital association.org/about-aca/

Entrepreneurial Angels

Entrepreneurial angels are entrepreneurs who have already successfully started and operated their own businesses, which they may or may not still be running. Either way, they generally have a steady flow of income that allows them to take higher investment risks. Entrepreneurial angels are the most valuable to early ventures—not only are they knowledgeable about the industries in which they invest, but because of their personal experience, they are in a great position to advise and mentor entrepreneurs.

Corporate Angels

Corporate angels are individuals who are usually former business executives, often from big multinationals, looking to use their savings or current income to invest. Although they primarily seek profit, many corporate angels want to play a larger part in the company, often seeking a paid position in the venture. Because of their experience managing bigger corporations, corporate angels can often become frustrated with working in a small company with limited resources. As a result, corporate angels may be very controlling; in some cases, this can result in a clash of cultures, even leading ultimately to a breakdown of the investor–entrepreneurial relationship.

Professional Angels

Professional angels are doctors, lawyers, dentists, accountants, consultants, and the like, who use their savings and income to invest in entrepreneurial ventures. For the most part, they are silent investors, but some of them (the consultants, for example) may wish to be taken on by the company as paid advisors.

Enthusiast Angels

Enthusiast angels are independently wealthy retired or semiretired entrepreneurs or executives who often invest their personal capital in startups as a hobby. They tend to invest in several different companies and rarely take a role in active management.

Micromanagement Angels

Micromanagement angels are entrepreneurs who have achieved success through their own companies and want to be involved in the ventures they invest in. Many micromanagement angels demand directorship or a position on the board of advisors and expect regular updates on the running of the company. They will intervene in the running of the business if it does not perform to their expectations.

There are many types of angels, including the five principal types described above and summarized in Figure 13.2. The majority of them will be looking to invest in an entrepreneurial venture that meets the criteria outlined in Table 13.2. They will want to know your level of expertise in your chosen area of business, the extent of the market opportunity for your product or service, the estimated valuation of your business, the current state of your finances, and your expenses and projections for the future.

There are several reasons business angels will reject a pitch, some of which will be beyond your control. For example, sometimes business angels will reject a pitch for geographical reasons—in fact, most angels like to invest locally. Unless you are willing to move your company to their locale, then there's not much you can do in this instance. Another reason for rejection is that the angel does not operate in the same sector as you do—this is why researching the most appropriate angel for your business is paramount before you get in touch. Angels might also reject approaches that do not come via a trusted referral, so make sure to use your resources to find the right way to connect.

Angels will also reject entrepreneurs who do not come across as knowledgeable or passionate; they may decline to invest in a project because they believe the market is too small, the financial projections exaggerated/not believable, or there is very little need for your product or service at all. It is useful to review these reasons for rejection when you are preparing to meet with an angel investor, so that you can come prepared with excellent arguments that will convince him or her that your business is worth a shot.

FIGURE 13.2

Types of Angel Investors

Entrepreneurial Angels
- Experienced entrepreneurs
- Willing to take bigger risks
- Provide mentorship

Corporate Angels
- Commonly former business executives
- Looking for ROI or a paid position in the new venture
- May clash with startup culture

Professional Angels
- Professionals from other fields (doctors, lawyers, etc.)
- Commonly silent investors
- May want to become paid advisors

Enthusiast Angels
- Independently wealthy
- Retired entrepreneurs or executives
- Investing is a hobby

Micromanagement Angels
- Experienced entrepreneurs
- Looking for hands-on involvement in new ventures

Angel Groups

In recent years, angel investors have begun to form groups to evaluate and invest in startups. It's not uncommon for angels to pool funds to invest in a venture, and they work together to conduct due diligence, analyze financials, and learn more about the opportunity. Typically, angel groups meet regularly to hear pitches, ask the entrepreneurs questions, and decide if there is enough interest to hear more. Table 13.5 lists the top 10 angel groups in the United States, ranked by number of deals. These angel groups are spread all over the country and tend to specialize in specific areas. For example, Golden Seeds focuses solely on women-led startups, while Arizona-based Desert Angels looks for opportunities to invest in Southwest regional startups.

Yet the formation of angel groups has not been the only way angels have evolved over the last few years. Angel investing in entrepreneurs is also breaking barriers for women. There has been a major increase in the percentage of angel investors (many of whom are more likely to invest in women-led companies). In 2017, almost one in four angel-backed companies were led by women.[19]

Research also suggests that women are better investors than men, as they take more time researching potential entrepreneurial ventures, spot more market opportunities than men, and take on less risk.[20] Women-led angel funds such as Belle Capital, Golden Seeds, and the Texas Women Ventures fund are doing much to increase the visibility of women angels by showing the amount of value they can add to entrepreneurial ventures.

In stark contrast to the rise in women angels, there are very few minority business angels (defined as African American, Hispanic, Asian, or Native American), accounting for less than 13% of the angel population.[21] In an effort to address this imbalance, groups like TiE Angels, a South Asian funding community, have been set up for entrepreneurs seeking minority investors.[22]

The Angel Capital Association lists the following as the best time to seek angel investment:[23]

TABLE 13.5

Most Active Angels Groups in the United States, 2017

Top Angel Groups Ranked by Number of Deals
1. Keiretsu Forum
2. Houston Angel Network
3. Y Combinator[1]
4. Central Texas Angel Network
5. New York Angels
6. St. Louis Arch Angels
7. Desert Angels
8. Golden Seeds
9. Ben Franklin Technology Partner, Launchpad Venture Group[2]
10. 500 Startups, Pasadena Angels[3]

Source: Angel Resource Institute. https://angelresourceinstitute.org/reports/halo-report-full-version-ye-2017.pdf

1   Unique as an incubator, but very actively funding deals
2   Tied for 9th place
3   Tied for 10th place

- Your product is developed or near completion.

- You have existing customers or potential customers who will confirm they will buy from you.

- You've invested your own dollars and exhausted other alternatives, including friends and family.

- You can demonstrate that the business is likely to grow rapidly and reach at least $10 million in annual revenues in the next 3–7 years.

- Your business model is in top shape.

Angel investors get you over the hurdle that is referred to as the "valley of death," that stage when there is no steady stream of revenue and the company may be burning through cash (see Figure 13.3). There is a high probability that the "startup will die off before a steady stream of revenues is established."[24] Once you successfully navigate through the valley and your business is at a later stage, venture capital may be needed.

FIGURE 13.3

The Valley of Death

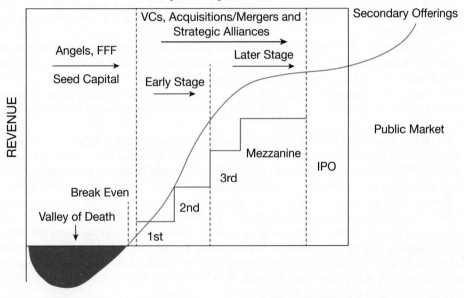

Source: http://www.eban.org/about-angel-investment/early-stage-investing-explained

---

13.4 VENTURE CAPITALISTS

>> LO 13.4   Explain the role of venture capitalists and how they finance entrepreneurs.

Like angel investors, VCs are often former or current entrepreneurs, but unlike angels, they are mostly professional money managers. Like angel investors, VCs look for opportunities that are likely to return 10 times their investment in 5 years.[25]

Typically, these venture capital money managers form a venture capital limited partnership fund that earns money through ownership of equity in different companies. The fund usually goes through a 10-year cycle before it dissolves and the assets are distributed to each of the partners. In terms of investment in early-stage to late-stage ventures, VCs investment generally starts at $1M, but in 2018, there were a number of "megadeals"

FIGURE 13.4

Venture Capital Investments by Stage

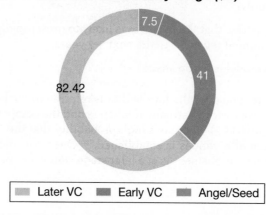

2018 U.S. VC Deals by Stage ($B)

Later VC   Early VC   Angel/Seed

Source: 2018 U.S. VC Deals by Stage chart—"NVCA 2019 Yearbook. Data Provided by PitchBook."

in excess of $100M.[26] Unlike angel investors, VCs are not really interested in smaller, seed-stage investments because it takes as much effort to monitor a small investment as it does a large one.[27]

The majority of VCs invest in businesses that have proved there is a significant market for their product and service. It is extremely rare for VCs to invest in the seed stage of business. In fact, it is commonly believed that seed-stage entrepreneurs have a better chance of winning $1 million or more in the lottery than getting venture capital investment.[28] As Figure 13.4 illustrates, VCs invested in only 7.5% of seed-stage companies in 2018.[29]

However, when considering an investment in a business, many VCs actually look for entrepreneurial ventures that have received seed funding in the early stages because it legitimizes the entrepreneur, helps to validate the idea, and shows an ability to stimulate belief among the entrepreneur's personal network.[30] Investors attract other investors.

Even if VCs do invest in young companies, their investment often comes at a price, as they tend to take more equity, more control, and may even take over the running of the company. However, although it is rare for seed-stage entrepreneurs to receive venture capital, it is not impossible. For example, online mobile photo-sharing, video-sharing, and social networking service Instagram received $250,000 VC seed investment that returned $78 million to the VC fund. It is widely regarded to be one of the most successful seed investments in history.[31]

Despite many success stories, the history of venture capital has been rocky, to say the least. Let's take a brief historical look at the highs and lows during the evolution of the venture capital industry.

A Brief History of Venture Capital

One of the most useful ways for entrepreneurs and VCs to succeed in the future is to reflect on, and learn from, mistakes made in the past. Venture capital traces its roots back to the early 20th century. Wealthy families such as the Rockefellers, Bessemers, and Whitneys were looking for ways to earn profits by investing in promising young companies.

Although venture capital was largely disorganized and somewhat informal at this stage, a more professional structure called American Research and Development (ARD) was created in 1946 by cofounder and Harvard Business School professor General George F. Doriot (considered the "father of venture capital"). Today, ARD is mostly recognized for its enormously successful investment in Digital Equipment Company (DEC) in 1957 when its initial investment of $70,000 was valued at more than $355 million when DEC went public in 1968.

The introduction of the Small Business Investment Act of 1958 furthered the progress of the venture capital industry, as it officially allowed small-business investment companies (SBICs) to finance entrepreneurial ventures seeking startup capital. During the 1960s, the United States experienced a mild boom in the number of young companies that went public, but a recession in the early 1970s hit the SBICs, and many ended up in liquidation and sank into obscurity.

However, the venture capital industry began to experience a new high thanks to a 1979 rule that allowed pension funds to invest in venture capital for the first time. This opened the door to pension fund managers who rapidly invested huge amounts of money into new venture capital funds with the expectation of enormous returns. Huge successes of DEC, Apple, Genentech, and many more spurred more and more investment as each venture capital firm vied for the next success story. However, despite billions of investment in startups by multiple venture capital firms during the 1980s, the returns declined. The firms had risked too much by overinvesting and had failed to nurture or monitor the companies properly. Because of these problems, VCs became more cautious and limited investment in early-stage companies. As a result, growth in the venture capital industry slowed down from the late 1980s to the first half of the 1990s.

RESEARCH AT WORK

Why Most Entrepreneurs Can't Access Capital

The Kauffman Foundation, a leading nonprofit organization supporting entrepreneurship, says that at least 81% of entrepreneurs do not access a bank loan or venture capital. Additionally, their research suggests that startups are at a generational low and much of this is due to lack of access to needed startup capital. By talking with thousands of entrepreneurs, Kauffman has identified three trends that prevent entrepreneurs from accessing capital.

The first trend relates to banks. Banks have become so large and the community bank is disappearing. On average, it takes $30,000 to start a business, but the large banks don't earn money when the loan is less than $100,000. If an entrepreneur gets a loan greater than $100,000 it's very difficult to pay back on a monthly basis.

The second trend relates to the types of businesses being started today. More and more businesses are service businesses that do not have physical assets that can be used for collateral, so banks are not interested.

The third trend relates to venture capital. Venture capital only serves a very tiny percentage of new businesses. Less than 1% of businesses ever raise venture capital, and it's very geographically focused, with much of the VC money concentrated in California, New York, and Massachusetts. According to Kauffman, less than 1% of VC funding touches rural areas, only 1% goes to minority-owned businesses, and less than 2% goes to female entrepreneurs.

The Kauffman Foundation concluded:

> Very little of the total capital flow to entrepreneurs is geared toward women and people of color. With 81 percent of funding coming through personal net worth, family wealth, or connections to networks, it's not a mystery why today's make-up of entrepreneurs is overwhelmingly white, older, and male.

> Going forward, we know communities need to build the mechanisms and networks that help more people start new businesses. With the nation's changing demographics, it is both a moral and strategic imperative to ensure inclusion and equity as communities seek to grow local economies.

Critical Thinking Questions

1. Why is there so much talk about venture capital in entrepreneurship when it's so difficult to access venture capital money?

2. Think about the examples discussed in this chapter that have received venture capital or angel financing. Do you see any patterns?

3. How can we create inclusion and equity for nontraditional entrepreneurs? ●

Source: https://www.kauffman.org/currents/2018/07/3-trends-that-prevent-entrepreneurs-from-accessing-capital

After this slow period, another boom was just around corner (known in retrospect as the dotcom bubble) as the Internet began to thrive and innovative Silicon Valley firms began to pop up. During the late 1990s, Amazon.com, America Online, eBay, Yahoo!, and Netscape were among the first tech firms that received venture capital funding. Blinded by the race to find the "next best thing," investors poured money into startup Internet companies without giving too much thought to how these companies would turn a profit, if ever.

The early dotcom businesses themselves made big mistakes. They had attracted venture capital because of the potential of the Internet—their whole theory relied on attracting huge numbers of people to their sites, without any clear strategies about how they could translate site visits into sales and sales into profits. These companies failed to plan properly, neglected research and development, and carried out limited promotion and advertising. As a result, hundreds folded.

When Internet stocks collapsed on the NASDAQ in 2000 (called the "dotcom crash"), so did the startups, leaving investors to deal with huge losses. Investors had overvalued the companies and had based their investments only on ideas without proving they had market potential. As a result, VCs lost large portions of their investments.

Since the crash, VCs have become a lot more cautious when investing in new ventures, and new ventures today have to do a lot more to prove themselves worthy of investment. But the momentum seems to be shifting in favor of VCs (see Figure 13.5): 2018 was a record year when VCs invested more than $130 billion in the U.S. compared to $82 billion in 2017, and 2019 numbers are expected to be similar to those in 2018. Interestingly, the number of deals done by VCs is down but investment is up, as depicted in Figure 13.6.

However, due to the gradual rise in venture capital investment in the years after recovery from the 2008 worldwide financial crisis, some experts predicted that another dotcom boom might be on the horizon. The rise of smartphones and tablets spawned the growth of a whole new generation of venture capitalist companies hoping to capitalize on this new market.[32] For example, messaging firm Snapchat received more than $500 million in venture capital in its first 5 years. But it's not just technology that has

FIGURE 13.5

Venture Capitalist Investment Over 20 Years

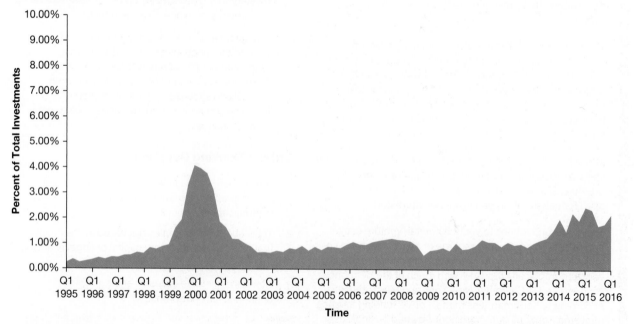

Source: Based on data from PricewaterhouseCoopers (2016) historical trend data. Retrieved from https://www.pwcmoneytree.com/HistoricTrends/CustomQueryHistoricTrend

FIGURE 13.6

The Rise of Capital Investment

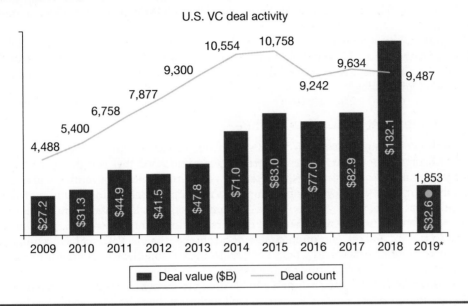

U.S. VC deal activity

Deal value ($B) ▬   Deal count ——

Source: National Venture Capital Association. (2019). *1Q 2019 Pitchbook–NVCA Venture Monitor* (p. 4). Retrieved from https://nvca.org/research/venture-monitor/

attracted VCs: The growing demand for healthier food has given rise to food companies like meatless plant-based burger maker Impossible Foods, which has raised $750 million in investment to date.[33]

How Venture Capital Works

There are many types of venture capital firms investing in businesses at different stages and across many sectors. Though there are about 1,000 active venture capital firms in the United States, they all operate very similarly.[34] So, let's take a look at how venture capital generally works. Today's VCs do not readily invest in seed-stage ventures as they once did, given the higher risk level. Yet there are many types of VCs out there, and the lines between informal and professional investors are blurring. It remains true, however, that professional VCs have the ability to catapult your venture from seed to high growth, so it's important to know how they operate.

Venture capital firms work within a specific investment portfolio, which means they have a defined list of the types of businesses in which they would like to invest. By narrowing these options, investors are often able to become experts in specific industries, which makes them better able to identify ventures that they think have the greatest potential.

VCs have very specific criteria for investing in an entrepreneurial venture, and these factors will very much influence the amount of investment made. Unlike banks, which seek return on capital through interest payments, VCs look for ventures that will earn them five to 10 times their original investment. They place a high value on quality management teams with excellent business skills who can deliver on their commitments.

One of the most important criteria for assessment is you, the entrepreneur, and your management team.[35] The VC will base its decision on how well you work together, the complementary skills you have, and your shared commitment to growing the business. VCs take an interest in entrepreneurs who surround themselves with smart, talented, well-respected people who support their ideas.

In relation to the industry, your company will be assessed for industry–market fit, its anticipated growth rate, the value-added potential, and the age and stage of development of your enterprise. The VC will also ensure that your goals for growth, control, and harvest (the stage at which they will cash in their investment) are aligned with their goals and strategies. The decision regarding the amount of investment will be based on these criteria.

In short, investors look for three main things: great teams, big markets, and unique and innovative ideas. However, they do not give them equal weight: The team trumps everything else. Most investors would rather have an "A" Team with a "B" idea than a "B" Team with an "A" idea.

Finding the Right VC for Your Venture

We've discussed how VCs decide whether a given venture is right for their investment; now let's explore how you, as an entrepreneur, can find a VC that is right for you. First, recognize that venture capital is a long-term investment. Typically, a venture will not see an exit event until 5 to 10 years after launch.[36] All going well, additional funding will be provided by the VC every year or two as the company grows. Because you're going to be dealing with one another over a number of years, it is important to make the right match between the VC and the entrepreneur. If a good choice is made, you will have a mutually rewarding working relationship both financially and personally. It's also not uncommon to have more than one VC firm as an investor.

The process of choosing a suitable VC is going to involve in-depth research on your part, and the first step is to find ways to get in touch with them. VCs are an elusive bunch, just as angels are; they prefer to be contacted through referrals from other VCs, angels, founders in their portfolio, or lawyers. It's not likely that you will reach a VC through an email! Investors rely on a trusted network, a tight circle, to send them deals. Once you have names and contact information, what information should you research and what kinds of questions should you ask? Table 13.6 lists some guidelines for this process.[37]

TABLE 13.6

Guidelines for Finding the Right VC for Your Startup

1. Look for a reputable brand of VC; securing investment from a credible company will encourage other investors to fund your startup.
2. Identify whether they are a good fit for your industry and have the connections to help grow your business.
3. Check their track record by taking three things into account: (1) their history of providing follow-up funding; (2) how they manage exits; and (3) how they treat their founders.
4. Find a VC partner that really believes in you and your business; getting mental and emotional buy-in is essential for a successful working relationship.
5. Make sure your goals are aligned with theirs in terms of building a brand, scaling a company, and planning a timeline.
6. Establish the levels of autonomy and availability; although you may value your independence, you will also need to check whether the VC will invest time in you when you need it.
7. Make sure the VC partner is someone you get along with who personally believes in what you are trying to achieve.
8. Carefully assess the agreement for fair terms; more VCs are tweaking agreements to benefit startups, so it pays to shop around for the best terms.
9. Check the location of your VC; keep in mind that a far-flung location can mean spending lots of time and money on travel to attend important meetings.

Source: Timmons, J., & Spinelli, S. (2008). *New venture creation* (8th ed.). Boston, MA: McGraw-Hill Irwin; Cremades, A. (2018). How to find the right VC for your startup. *Forbes.* Retrieved from https://www.forbes.com/sites/alejandrocremades/2018/12/11/how-to-find-the-right-vc-for-your-startup/#ca0ed188f24d

When you, as an entrepreneur, get the opportunity to meet with a VC, it is important to be prepared. You will be expected to explain clearly and concisely the market opportunity your business presents; the size and potential growth of your market; why customers will be attracted to your product/service; how your business makes money, or will make money in the future; how soon it is anticipated to reach profit; why you and your team are the right people for the job; and how your investor can exit the investment. By providing this information to the VC, you are displaying your confidence, knowledge, and commitment in your business, as well as reassuring the VC that you are in it for the long haul.

If the first meeting goes well, you will be invited for a second meeting that involves a formal presentation to several of the VC partners. This is the meeting that can either break or seal the deal, so it is crucial to allow yourself sufficient time to prepare. Following the second meeting, the VC partners will discuss whether they wish to invest in your company.

Why VCs Might Say No

VCs typically review more than 100 plans and proposals a month, but usually thoroughly read and review one or two of these. On average, a partner in VC firms will do only one to three deals per year. This means a couple of things: Your venture really has to stand out from the crowd, and you should not take it personally if your firm is turned down. However, you can boost your chances of success by knowing why a VC may be likely to say no.

One of the most common reasons why VCs do not choose certain companies for investment is that the opportunity presented does not fit in with the fund's criteria. For example, the fund might invest only in companies within a specific geographic location or industry sector, the deal might be considered too small/too big, or the business might not be quite mature enough for them to invest. As with angels and their criteria, some of these factors are beyond your control, but you can avoid wasting your time and the time of potential investors if you research their criteria ahead of time.

Another reason funds reject some applications is that they have a policy to review opportunities only via a referral. With such specific criteria, you need to carry out some

TABLE 13.7

Reasons VCs Might Say No to Your Business

Negative founder or team dynamics
The team is missing a key skillset
The founders don't have a clear mission
The team demonstrates a lack of focus (trying to do too many things at once)
Founders display negative behavior (racism, sexism)
Dishonesty
The founding team works in different locations
The VC receives negative references about the founding team
Investment needed is too much for the VCs
Poor-quality presentation or pitch
Licensing or IP issues
Unclear value proposition

Sources: Bamberger, B. (2018). 5 common reasons why VCs decide not to invest. *Fast Company*. Retrieved from https://www.fast company.com/40523247/5-common-reasons-why-vcs-decide-not-to-invest; Downey, S. (2018). The real reasons why a VC passed on your startup. Retrieved from https://entrepreneurshandbook.co/the-real-reasons-why-a-vc-passed-on-your-startup-917c30103ecb

careful research to find the most appropriate VC for your business and go through the proper channels in order to reach VCs. Table 13.7 lists some more reasons why VCs might say no to your business.

What About a Bank Loan?

Debt financing: borrowing money to start a business that is expected to be paid back with interest at a designated point in the future.

When equity financing is not an option, which for the majority of entrepreneurs it is not, then debt financing might be possible. **Debt financing** means borrowing money to start a business that is expected to be paid back with interest at a designated point in the future. Earlier we talked about convertible notes, a form of debt financing, but for many small businesses, bank loans are the "go to." However, only 18% of businesses (startups and beyond) ever access a bank loan.[38] The U.S. Small Business Association gives microloans to women, minorities, and veterans and the loans range from $500 to $50,0000 and carry interest rates between 8% and 13%.[39] Unfortunately, the demand is high and the process is long.

If an entrepreneur can't attract friends and family, angels, or VCs, then going to a bank may be a good option, but is it? Let's say you are starting a new business and you need a $300,000 loan to get the business operational. The bank say yes, but the loan is for a 5-year term at 12% interest. You may be thinking, "Yes! Where do I sign? At least the interest rate is lower than my credit card!" Well, you might want to think again. For a $300,000 loan at 12% interest for 5 years, your monthly loan payment would be $6,700 . . . starting just about now! Can you afford to make monthly loan payments of $6,700? Even if the loan was for 10 years, you would still have to pay $4,300 per month.

New business loans are very risky for banks, so they are not as common as you may think. Banks expect entrepreneurs to have the following:[40]

Capital: assets that can be used to create product that can then be sold and converted to cash to pay back the loan.

Collateral: personal assets (such as a home) to borrow against, so if the entrepreneur cannot pay back the loan, the bank can take the home and sell it in order to recoup the loan.

Capacity: a track record in business to prove the entrepreneur has the capacity to generate income to make loan payments.

Credit Rating: a poor credit rating will get you turned down immediately, but even a good credit rating is no guarantee you will get a loan.

The point is whether you approach an angel, a VC, or go directly to a bank, there is no easy way for you to acquire the money you need. The best way to secure funding is to build something that inspires people to invest in you in the long term.

Investors of all types, banks, and entrepreneurs go through a process to build a trusting relationship that will last a long time. Decisions and deals are not made overnight. If anyone is considering investing or loaning you money, the next stage is an intensive due diligence process.

13.5 DUE DILIGENCE

>> **LO 13.5** Describe how investors carry out due diligence processes.

Due diligence: a rigorous process that involves evaluating an investment opportunity prior to the contract being signed.

Due diligence is a rigorous process carried out to evaluate an investment opportunity prior to a deal being finalized. When considering an investment opportunity, both angel investors and VCs conduct a due diligence process, but typically, angel investors and groups do not carry out as much due diligence as VCs due to time, resource constraints, and a general lack of information given the early stage of the venture.

An angel or angel group generally conducts a proper analysis of the market opportunity to ensure it fits with investment goals and carries out background checks, legal checks, and financial analysis. Angels will also consider any personal conflicts that may

Find an Investor–Entrepreneur Pair

Investors and entrepreneurs usually have different perspectives. Sources of these differences include the size of the opportunity, the future growth potential of the business, appropriate business model, scalability, and company valuation, just to name a few. We often hear about the entrepreneur's side *or* the investor's side, but a lot can be learned from comparing the two perspectives.

Your Mindshift is to find an investor–entrepreneur pair. In other words, find an entrepreneur who had angel or venture capital financing and talk to the entrepreneur. Then talk to his or her investor. The order can be reversed; it doesn't matter whether you first talk to the investor or the entrepreneur.

Begin your conversation with a broad, open-ended question such as, "Tell me about the process of receiving funding from Investor X." Conversely, when talking to the investor, ask, "Tell me about the process of funding Company Y." Probe a lot, take notes, and then compare notes. What similarities and differences did you find?

Critical Thinking Questions

1. Was it easier than you expected to find an entrepreneur and investor to interview, or harder?

2. What obstacles or challenges did you encounter in your conversations?

3. Did you learn anything that surprised you or that ran counter to your expectations? ●

get in the way of the deal; different ways in which they can add value; and ultimately whether they want to establish a long-term working relationship with the entrepreneur.[41]

The Due Diligence Process for VCs

Like angels, VCs are very careful when it comes to due diligence, particularly because of their history of making impulsive, wild investments in young companies. In general, investing in early-stage companies is risky, especially when millions of dollars are at stake, and VCs need to identify any potential red flags to ensure they are making a sound investment. During this process, entrepreneurs, their teams, and the company itself will undergo a vigorous appraisal, which generally lasts several weeks or even months. During this period, the backgrounds of the entrepreneurial team will be verified; references thoroughly checked; and corporate compliance, employment and labor, intellectual property rights, and legal issues reviewed. Table 13.8 lists the steps taken by VCs when creating a due diligence plan.

During this time, it is important for the founding team to carry out its own due diligence on the VC. It is perfectly appropriate to ask VCs for the contact details of companies in their portfolio with whom they have achieved success, as well as those with whom the deals did not work out. Talking to others who have been involved with the VC is an invaluable way of garnering information that will help you decide whether or not you will be able to build a long-term successful relationship with them.

Exits/Harvesting

Part of the due diligence process involves the discussion of exit options. When VCs and business angels invest in a business, there is an expectation that they will receive a return on their investment when the firm exits the investment, within a certain time period, usually in around 5–10 years. Typically, this money is repaid through one of three types of exit strategies: an IPO, mergers and acquisitions, or buyback.

An **initial public offering (IPO)** is a company's first opportunity to sell stocks on the stock market to be purchased by members of the general public. Smaller companies are often bought by larger companies through *acquisitions,* which are ways for bigger companies to increase their profitability and, in some cases, swallow the competition.

Initial public offering (IPO): a company's first opportunity to sell stocks on the stock market to be purchased by members of the general public.

TABLE 13.8

Due Diligence Process for VCs

Founders	VCs need to like and trust the entrepreneurial team before proceeding with the investment. They tend to look for high-energy, mission-driven founders who are committed to building a successful organization. Given the changing business landscape, VCs need to know that the founders have the ability to react to customer demands, competitive threats, changing and new regulations, and more. VCs find out more by asking the following questions: • Who are the founders and what are their backgrounds? • Do they have relevant experience? • How well do the individuals function as a team? • Do they have a track record of success? • What critical resources do they have access to? • How well do they evaluate risk? • Are they detail oriented? • Do they exhibit a capacity for a sustained effort?
Market	VCs may conduct rigorous market analysis to establish the existence and size of the market for the product: • Who are the users of the product and how many of them are there? • What are the drivers that are fueling the growth? • How is the company positioned against competitive threats? • Describe the competition. • Is the customer, the supplier, and/or the competition fragmented? • Are there attractive substitutes? • What regulations govern this market space? • What are the barriers to entry? • What is the distribution channel and who controls it? • What are the market boundaries?
Product/Service	VCs will analyze the product or service by asking a number of key questions: • What customer problem is being solved? • What unique technology and/or knowledge does the company have? • How does this technology and/or knowledge create value for the customer? • Why is this product or service superior to the competition? • Are there any strategic relationships? • Does this product exhibit scalability? • What are the barriers to enter? IP protection?
Finance	VCs assess how a startup is going to make money by investigating key financial drivers: • How will the company sell its product or services? • How will the customer perceive value? • Are there comparable companies to benchmark? • Who are the key market influencers that the company needs to target? • What are the financial requirements, e.g., capital investment, cash? • Is the business model scalable? • What is the potential for recurring revenue? • What are the anticipated margins? • What is the exit strategy? Is it feasible?

For example, one of the biggest acquisitions of 2018 was when Amazon purchased doorbell-camera startup Ring for $1 billion.[42] Ring was founded by Jamie Siminoff, who had pitched his idea to *Shark Tank* investors in 2013 but walked away without a deal. Ring has grown to be the largest company ever to appear on *Shark Tank*. As Siminoff said about the reluctant *Shark Tank* business moguls, "Obviously, I think they wish they had invested."

A less common exit strategy is a *buyback*, which gives the entrepreneur an opportunity to buy back a venture capital firm's stock at cost plus a certain premium. However, buybacks are rare because the young company usually does not have the cash to buy out its investors, unless it has reached a highly profitable state.

Doorbell camera company, Ring.

The due diligence process is complete when all the issues have been resolved to the satisfaction of both parties. Getting through the due diligence process is the final step before contracts are signed and you finally receive capital. It is also an essential part of building a foundation of trust and commitment with your investor—and remember how important that foundation is because you will be in the newly forged relationship for years to come.

Rich or King/Queen? The Trade-Off Entrepreneurs Make

Very few entrepreneurs manage to make money and maintain full control of their businesses. Entrepreneurs who give up a bigger slice of equity to investors tend to build more valuable companies than those who give up less equity or none at all. Any investment comes with a price, and before you sign on the dotted line, you need to have a very clear idea of how you want to run your business and what matters to you most.

By giving away equity, you will have less control over your decisions and may even be at risk of losing your position of CEO. Why? Because once you give up equity, directors will join the board and will take over much of the decision making, including the decision to either keep you as CEO or move you to a different position, or even push you out of the company altogether.

For example, a study of 212 U.S. startups from the late 1990s and early 2000s showed that 50% of the founders were no longer the CEO after 3 years. In fact, the same research shows that four out of five entrepreneurs are forced by investors to relinquish their CEO roles.[43] One of the most famous examples of an entrepreneur pushed out of his own company was the late Steve Jobs, who was fired by Apple's board of directors less than 10 years after he cofounded Apple Computers with Steve Wozniak. More recently, Rob Kalin, the founder of the online crafts marketplace Etsy; Travis Kalanick, founder of Uber; and Jack Dorsey, founder of Twitter, have all been fired from their own companies. Being pushed out or moved to a "lesser" position can come as a real shock to entrepreneurs who have worked tirelessly on building their ventures from the ground up, as well as to employees who have worked alongside them. In fact, the way this leadership transition is handled by both the investor and the entrepreneur can make or break a company.

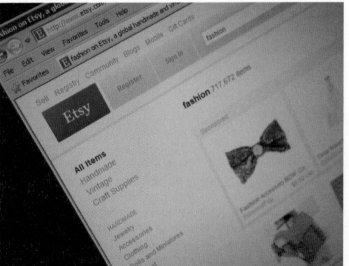

Online crafts marketplace Etsy, originally founded by Rob Kalin

Replacing the Founder CEO

It isn't uncommon for founder CEOs to be ousted from their own startups, but it is important that their investors have made this move for the right, ethical reasons. Silicon Valley startup lawyer Jose Ancer believes that there are usually two main motives behind the investors' decision to push out a CEO when a company is struggling: performance or power.

When VCs have good intentions, they will replace the CEO to improve the performance of the company to benefit all stockholders. However, if the reason is more focused on power, the VC will likely push out the CEO in favor of someone they can easily control and influence, which does not always benefit stockholders.

So, how can founders ensure that the VC has their best interests at heart? By holding frank discussions with the VC partners before a formal agreement has been signed. This involves the founder asking the VC about their philosophy on founder management and how they would manage the transition process if the CEO needed to be replaced. After the discussion, the founder should verify the VC's responses by talking to other teams that have worked with those particular partners before.

Once these facts have been confirmed, then the terms can be committed to paper to ensure that everybody is in agreement. These terms may include involving the CEO and other executive members to suggest suitable candidates as the replacement CEO, being part of the interview process, and making sure the process is as transparent as possible.

Although founders may never visualize being ousted from their own company, the reality is that it does happen. This is why it's important to make sure you choose the right VC with the best intentions for your company. As Ancer said,

> Save for the very, very small number of unicorns in which founders can keep strict control (think Facebook), reputable VCs will never tell a founder CEO that she/he will stay CEO as long as they want to. The job of a Board of Directors is to do what's best for all of the Company's stockholders as a whole, even if that means making a founder CEO unhappy.

Critical Thinking Questions

1. What would you do if you were forced to leave your own company?

2. How would go about choosing the right VC for your startup?

3. Can an entrepreneur really be picky when choosing investors? ●

Source: https://siliconhillslawyer.com/2018/03/26/replacing-founder-ceo/

One of the most common mistakes founders make is believing they can grow the business through inspiration, passion, and perspiration. Although these three key elements are helpful in getting a business off the ground, entrepreneurs need better resources to fully capitalize on future opportunities. As a company evolves, it needs different skills to grow into a more valuable business.

For example, a startup that has developed a product may not have the expertise or financial resources to market and sell it to customers or the know-how to set up after-sales service. This means relying on people with different skills, like financial executives, accountants, lawyers, and so on. More employees may need to be hired and a new organizational structure put in place. All these elements can be overwhelming for a founder and team who lack these skills.

Of course, it is entirely possible to remain in full of control of your business by keeping as much equity as you can. You may have less financial investment to increase the value of your business, but if you have more interest in being in control (i.e., being the "King/Queen"), then this is a viable option for you.

Thinking about what matters most to you—to be rich or to be all-powerful—is a useful exercise in how you define business success and what it means to you. As Figure 13.7 illustrates, maximizing control over wealth and vice versa can negatively impact success. Although the ideal would be to make tons of money and be completely in control, history shows that few entrepreneurs have managed to do both. ●

FIGURE 13.7

The Trade-Off Entrepreneurs Make

FINANCIAL GAINS

	WELL BELOW POTENTIAL	CLOSE TO POTENTIAL
LITTLE	Failure	Rich
COMPLETE	King/Queen	Exception

CONTROL OVER COMPANY

Source: Wasserman, N, The founder's dilemma. *HBR*, February 2008 issue. https://hbr.org/2008/02/the-founders-dilemma

Watch *Shark Tank* as an Investor

Google "Shark Tank Episodes" and watch one full episode of your choice. What is interesting about students who watch *Shark Tank* is that they are always more focused on the entrepreneur than the actual "Sharks." For this Mindshift, you need to practice the Shark mindset. In other words, focus more on the Sharks than the entrepreneurs. For each pitch, identify the following:

1. Body language of the Sharks

2. Questions they ask the entrepreneurs

3. How they respond to the answers given by entrepreneurs

4. What was the original ask by the entrepreneurs?

5. What were the offers made by the Sharks (if any)?

6. What was the final deal offered and accepted (if any)?

Critical Thinking Questions

1. Do you recognize patterns when a deal was successfully negotiated?

2. How different were the asks from the entrepreneurs and the offers from the Sharks?

3. Would you characterize the Sharks as angel investors or venture capitalists? Why? ●

$SAGE edge™

Get the tools you need to sharpen your study skills. SAGE edge offers a robust online environment featuring an impressive array of free tools and resources.

- Access practice quizzes, eFlashcards, video, and multimedia at **edge.sagepub.com/neckentrepreneurship2e**

SUMMARY

13.1   Define equity financing for entrepreneurs and outline its main stages.

Equity financing is the sale of ownership stake within the company in exchange for funding. Seed-stage financing, startup financing, and early-stage financing describe funds in support of different early-business objectives. As the organization grows, it may then seek out second- or later-stage financing through subsequent rounds of financing. Businesses may also choose to undergo an IPO, opening the firm to general market funding and offering an exit to early investors.

13.2   Illustrate the basics of business valuation.

Investors use a variety of factors to come to valuation proposals, including market conditions, opportunities, competition, comparables, and how much value a given venture can add to the mix.

13.3   Describe angel investors and how they finance entrepreneurs.

Angel investors are typically high-net-worth individuals who are accredited investors investing their own money in startup ventures. Other types of angels include corporate angels, professional angels, enthusiast angels, and micromanagement angels, each characterized by distinct goals and value-added capabilities.

13.4   Explain the role of venture capitalists and how they finance entrepreneurs.

Venture capitalists differ from angels in the sense that they are professional money managers. Entrepreneurs should also exhibit at least as much caution as venture capitalists when seeking VC funding; the owners are likely to concede a significant ownership stake in the venture, and need to be certain of both why venture capital is absolutely necessary and which firm would provide the best guidance.

13.5   Describe how investors carry out due diligence processes.

To ascertain the prospects of any potential investment, angel investors and venture capitalists alike conduct due diligence processes of the firm under consideration. Essential to this process is identifying a method and timing for the investors to recoup their capital at exit, such as completing an IPO.

KEY TERMS

Accredited investors 311	Due diligence 322	Seed-stage financing 305
Angel investor 305	Early-stage financing 305	Startup financing 305
Convertible debt 310	Equity financing 303	Unicorn 309
Debt financing 322	Initial public offering (IPO) 323	Venture capitalist (VC) 306

CASE STUDY

Rich Palmer, founder, Gravyty

Rich Palmer's venture, Gravyty, uses artificial intelligence (AI) to help make the process of fundraising a lot more effective. His startup journey is full of many twists and turns.

Rich worked with a company called Capital IQ in 2007, after earning his undergraduate degree in IT, computer science, and economics from Rensselaer Polytechnic Institute. At Capital IQ, he ran the portfolio analytics division and analyzed portfolios of stocks, options, and derivatives to help hedge fund managers decide whether to buy, sell, or over/underweight certain sectors the next day. He used data analytics to predict what factors in the economy or in a particular business sector might make the stock price rise or fall. Rich noted, "However, working on Wall Street didn't really fit with who I am or how I worked. So after about 4 years, I decided to quit and start my own company (not Gravyty)."

He pitched a business idea called OvenAlly to Y Combinator, a prestigious accelerator. OvenAlly was an online platform that Rich describes as "an Etsy for homemade food." The Y Combinator pitch was an enriching experience for Rich as he got to sit across the table from people like Paul Buchheit (founder of Gmail), Paul Graham (founder of Viaweb and Y Combinator), and Sarah Livingstone (author of the book *Founders at Work* and cofounder of Y Combinator). He recalls vividly, "I'm sitting across from these awesome, wonderful people. They looked at me and said, very poignantly, well, have you ever started or tried to sell your own food from your own kitchen? And I went [expletive deleted] . . . no! They said if you're going to start a company that does X, shouldn't you also try to do Y as well to understand all the issues around X? They ended up not funding it because they didn't think we could surpass some of the legal and operational hurdles!"

Being a self-proclaimed "scrappy guy," getting through Y Combinator rounds was enough validation for Rich Palmer to quit his Wall Street job and start OvenAlly with a friend in 2011. "The company failed fantastically,"! Rich exclaimed. "While I and my software engineer and cofounder sat in a room and coded for 3 months to come up with a beautiful website, things went south from Day 1. The chefs had questions on liability if the food was poisoned or had razors in it, and we weren't able to answer them." While Rich was trying to figure out the legal side of the business, his cofounder's father passed away, prompting the cofounders to shut down the company. Today, a quick look at ovenally.com leads you to a beautiful page that says, "The Kitchen is closed. OvenAlly was a marketplace for homemade food that allowed buyers and sellers to interact across the country. Unfortunately, we have shut our doors in pursuit of new opportunities."

Rich took a little time off to think about the advice he got at Y Combinator "about doing X" to solve a "first-person problem" and reflecting on his next entrepreneurship move. It was around this time an old friend from Capital IQ offered him a role in a company called Relationship Science, a New York City company dedicated to figuring out the route for one person to connect with someone they wanted to connect with. As Rich explained, "For example, if one wanted to connect with someone like Elon Musk, how would they do that? We raised $120 million, sourced data from 15,000 different public sources, and mapped out connections." Rich joined Relationship Science as a senior product manager and software engineer in October 2011. Although the pay was good, Rich again felt like he was solving a problem that he didn't have nor had experience with.

During this time, he met his wife, who got a job in Washington, D.C. Rich was able to follow her and work remotely for Relationship Science. Then, everything changed in an instant.

"I was down in D.C. for about a year, and I was working out in the gym that was in my building. I'm a relatively healthy guy. I drink socially. I don't smoke. I don't do drugs. None of that stuff! I ended up on one of the stationary bikes and had a brain aneurysm. Basically, a blood vessel burst in my brain and nearly f@#*ing killed me! I went from being this high-power dude to not being able to really walk or talk or think anymore. It was a pivotal moment for my entire world, my entire universe, and entire way of thinking!" After this incident and during his recovery, Rich decided his life needed a "reset." He took the GMAT to pursue an MBA at Babson College in order to start a company with meaning.

At Babson, Rich met Adam Martel (MBA alum from Babson) who was working in the development and fundraising office of the college. Adam developed relationships with donors of the college who would financially support such things as academic scholarships, new buildings, faculty chairs, and general college operations. Adam and Rich developed a great friendship and started exploring the prospect of starting a business together. After going through the process of coming up with some of their "worst business ideas" that included a hair gel company and a wine-based company, Rich reflected back on his experience at Y Combinator and how he should focus on the "X where he or his cofounder had experience." Soon enough, Adam and Rich were looking for things that they were good at and trying to find an overlap. Gravyty surfaced as their meaningful idea that fit with their life experience.

Rich had significant experience in predictive analytics, modeling, and AI while Adam had deep domain expertise related to fundraising and donations in the nonprofit world. Although Rich could predict who to talk to, Adam was able to give insight on how to talk to a potential donor. After a little brainstorming, the two came up with an MVP (minimum viable product) that used predictive modeling offered by AI to reach out to, create, and develop relations with potential donors. Services included drafting communications, developing donor guides, and recommending travel based on locations of donors. They pitched the idea to a few hospitals, colleges, and other nonprofit organizations. The initial response was good so they dove deeper into the idea to start Gravyty.

The startup process began in August 2015, and they had a working prototype used by early adopters by January 2016. Rich and Adam needed startup financing, and an early potential investor offered Gravyty $100,000, but the terms were not quite what Rich and Adam were looking for. Rich recalled, "We turned down the $100,000. It was one of the hardest decisions we ever had to make." A couple of months later, in March 2016, the founders pitched Gravyty during a competition at South by Southwest (SXSW), a large popular tech and music festival in Austin, Texas. They placed second in the pitch competition and that same investor reengaged with them. This time the group agreed on terms and Gravyty had its first investment of $100,000. Adam quit his job at Babson and they hired another developer. Gravyty then applied to and was accepted into Mass Challenge, a global, zero-equity startup accelerator based in Boston, Massachusetts.

After the initial $100,000, Gravyty raised additional funding from 29 investors, mostly angel investors. "We could go to one VC and raise the same amount, but each one of our investors donates to organizations or is on the board of a nonprofit or a school and so that helps us create a network effect." Rich's number one rule when looking for investment is to do your due diligence on the audience. "We had a chance to attend a board meeting of Babson trustees. Aware that a good percentage of the members on this board were potential investors or connected to prospects, we went to the Babson website, took everybody's name, their pictures, the list of boards they sit on, the things they've done, and created a bunch of note cards. One side had the picture and the other side had all the relevant information about that person." Rich familiarized himself so he could weave the person on the other side into the conversation. As Rich recalled, "One of the people we spoke to ended up being connected to a big nonprofit tech company (not on the postcard) and wanted to introduce them to the founder, who had started six prior nonprofit tech companies and was basically the Steve Jobs of the space." That person now sits on the board of Gravyty and his experience and expertise have helped shape the business.

Rich always wanted the funding at Gravyty to be done in a way that did not dilute equity too much and too quickly. Their first round of funding was only $300,000. After growing a little, and onboarding clients from top universities and hospitals, Gravyty raised another modest round of $300,000 that allowed the team to expand from three to eight. Over the summer of 2018, they raised $3 million, which has allowed them to grow strategically into a 20-member team and focus next-level efforts on sales and marketing. Today Gravyty works with some of the largest hospitals and schools in the United States (including Babson), and nonprofits such as the Cure Alzheimer's Fund, AARP, WGBH, Yale, City of Hope, and more.

Raising capital is a challenge for all entrepreneurs, and Rich learned that not all investors are the same. He explains:

> West Coast investors tend to accept more risk and look for certain types of companies and entrepreneurs. They are willing to let valuations go a little high as well. Conversely, those on the East invest in hardware and biotech companies, usually less risky propositions because they've had bad experiences with high valuations in the past. West Coast investors are more likely than East Coast investors to accept a convertible note. Look out for the "terms" of the deal. Understanding the terms will help ensure that money is not taken off the table in the event of a liquidation event. Also, entrepreneurs need to understand how dilution of their stake in the company will affect future payouts to investors and themselves. The investor–entrepreneur relationship is like a marriage; it will likely last many years and cover some heavy topics, so it is important to negotiate in good faith and with the right people. We entrepreneurs also need to remember that investors need us as much as we need them! If they're controlling the entire conversation or pushing lopsided terms, they're likely going to be bad partners.

Rich has two pieces of advice for aspiring entrepreneurs: "First, always look at problems on a first-person basis. How can your experience and understanding directly influence the solution to a problem you know about? Those problems are easier to iterate on since you already know many of the details. And second, I see my cofounder and my employees more often than I see my family, and picking the right people for these roles is very important. If you can work together in the hardest of circumstances there will be many points where you're going to love each other or you're going to fight with each other, but the only way you get through that is by talking to and understanding that person and getting to know that person better."

Critical Thinking Questions

1. Why was Gravyty a success for Rich when his other ventures failed?

2. Explain what Rich means by looking at problems on a first-person basis.

3. Not all companies need financing or are investor worthy. Why is Gravyty attractive to investors when OvenAlly was not?

Sources

Rich Palmer (interview with Babson MBA graduate assistant Gaurav Khemka, November 15, 2018)

Godfrey, R. L., Pulsipher, G. L., & Smith, H. W. (2011). *The 7 laws of learning: Why great leaders are also great teachers.* Springville, UT: Bonneville Books.

Godfrey, R. L., & Smith, H. W. (2009). *Home of the brave: Confronting and conquering challenging times.* New York, NY: Hachette.

Smith, H. W. (1994). *The 10 natural laws of successful time and life management.* New York, NY: Warner Books.

Smith, H. W. (2000). *What matters most: The power of living your values.* New York, NY: Fireside.

Smith, H. W. (2001). *The modern gladiator: Increasing productivity in the global age* [Audiobook]. FranklinCovey.

Smith, H. W. (2013). *The power of perception: 6 Steps to behavior change.* Juxtabook Digital Marketing.

SUPPLEMENT A
FINANCIAL STATEMENTS AND PROJECTIONS FOR STARTUPS

Angelo Santinelli

Chapter Outline

Learning Objectives

A.1 FINANCIAL PROJECTIONS FOR STARTUPS

>> **LO A.1** **Explain the purpose of financial projections for startups.**

As we have explained in this textbook, developing an entrepreneurial mindset, testing and experimenting, building business models, and planning are all elements of the Entrepreneurship Method, and now it's time to discuss another key element: financial projections. Through the iterative process discussed so far, entrepreneurs learn how to assess the problem–solution fit, product–market fit, competitive and industry fit, and now we will look at financial fit. Through action entrepreneurs develop assumptions, opinions, and a market perspective based on objective data and analysis. This primary data enables entrepreneurs to make a convincing case for financial projections, and prove that their startup is worth investment.

In Chapter 13: Financing for Startups, we touched on the topic of financial projections. Potential investors (angels, VCs) sometimes decline to invest in a project because they feel the financial projections are exaggerated or not believable. This is because financial projections are often built on a foundation of untested assumptions and third party data sources that are interpreted to portray market size and growth that exaggerates or distorts the revenue projections.

In many cases, entrepreneurs first develop pitch decks or other similar planning tools before testing the feasibility of their ideas to confirm whether or not the idea is indeed an opportunity. As result, they lack the necessary data to support their financial projections, which means the exercise is nothing more than guesswork.

Presenting carefully thought-out financial projections to investors is an exercise in lowering perceived risk in both you as an entrepreneur and your idea. When you are able to frame the opportunity from the perspective of the target market(s), understand

**Master the content at
edge.sagepub.com/
neckentrepreneurship2e**

the resources required to capitalize on the opportunity, and know how to allocate those resources under varying market conditions, investors will be more inclined to have serious investment discussions. Similarly, the confidence and knowledge that you have developed from building realistic projections should make the process of convincing others, employees and investors alike, a little easier.

A.2 THREE ESSENTIAL FINANCIAL STATEMENTS

>> **LO A.2   Describe financial statements as an essential part of financial projections.**

Income statement: a financial report that measures the financial performance of your business on a monthly or annual basis.

Balance sheet: a financial statement that shows what the company owes, what it owns, including the shareholder's stake, at a particular point in time.

Cash flow statement: a financial report that details the inflows and outflows of cash for a company over a set period of time.

Financial statements provide a window into the financial health and performance of a company. Every entrepreneur needs to understand the three essential financial statements: an income statement, a balance sheet, and a cash flow statement. The **income statement** (or profit and loss statement) is a financial report that measures the financial performance of your business on a monthly or annual basis. It shows sales and expense-related activities that result in profit or loss over a set period of time. The **balance sheet** is a financial report that shows what the company owes, and what it owns, including the shareholders' stake, at a particular point in time. The **cash flow statement** is a financial report that details the inflows and outflows of cash for a company over a set period of time. Each statement examines the company from a slightly different perspective, yet together they provide a holistic economic view of the company.

In the following sections, we will take a closer look at each of these three financial statements.

The Income Statement

The income statement measures the financial performance of your business on a monthly or annual basis. It subtracts the COGS (cost of goods sold) and expenses (administrative, marketing, research, and other operating expenses) from the total revenue to give you a net income figure, which will be either a profit or a loss. Using Table A.1 as a guide and assuming revenue of $10,000 as an example, let's explore the different line items of the income statement in further detail.

TABLE A.1

Income Statement

Revenue	$10,000
(-) Cost of Goods Sold	$4,000
Gross Profit	$6,000
(-) Sales, General and Administrative	$2,000
(-) Marketing	$1,000
(-) Research and Development	$500
(-) Depreciation and Amortization	$250
Operating Profit	$2,250
(-) Interest Expense	$100
(-) Taxes	$675
Net Income	$1,475

First, revenue is recorded on the income statement when the company makes a sale of a product or service and then delivers to the customer, thereby creating an obligation for the customer to issue payment to the company. It is important to note that there is a difference between a sale (revenue) and an order (bookings). An order may or may not become a sale. Orders become sales only when the product is shipped to and accepted by the customer. A sale is recorded on the income statement, while an order might only show up in a **backlog**—orders that have been received but not delivered to the customer. Also, the revenue number should be expressed net of any discounts offered. Table A.2 explains the distinctions between revenue, bookings, and backlogs.

Backlog: orders that have been received but not delivered to the customer.

COGS represents the total cost to manufacture a product. Costs are expenditures of raw materials, labor, and manufacturing overhead used to produce a product. For a service business, COGS may include the cost of service staff and associated overhead.

Subtracting COGS from revenue leaves you with three types of profit margins: gross margins, operating profit, and net income. A high gross margin percentage that remains consistently high over time can be an indicator of the company's long-term competitiveness.[1] It also shows that the company has sufficient funds for sales, marketing, product development, and other expenses.

Operating expenses are the expenditures that the company makes to generate income. These expenditures generally include sales, general, and administrative (SG&A); research and development (R&D); and marketing expenses. These expenses directly lower income.

As we explored in Chapter 9, the income statement also reflects depreciation and amortization of your company's assets. Recall that depreciation really means the cost of wear and tear of your physical assets such as machinery, equipment, and the building in which you operate. Amortization works similarly to depreciation; the main difference is that amortization relates to intangible assets such as patents, trademarks, copyrights, and business methodologies. Amortization matches the useful life of an intangible asset with the revenue it generates.

If you have studied accounting in the past, you might hear depreciation referred to as a "noncash" expense that is usually ignored when calculating free cash flow or EBITDA (Earnings Before Interest, Taxes, Depreciation, and Amortization). This is an accepted practice, but it avoids the obvious, which is that equipment and buildings eventually need to be replaced. From a short-term perspective, depreciation is a noncash charge to earnings, but in the long term, someone has to write a check for replacement. It is best to ask your accountant about the various rules for depreciating assets.

The second most important profit margin to monitor is **operating profit**, which is the amount left over from revenue once all costs and expenses are subtracted.

Operating profit: the amount left over from revenue once all costs and expenses are subtracted.

Another component of EBITDA is **interest expense**, which shows the extent of the company's debt burden as well as representing any interest owed on borrowed money. Taxes are the last expense item before net income. This line item captures federal, state, and sometimes municipal taxes due for the period. Sales taxes are not recorded here.

Interest expense: the extent of the company's debt burden as well as representing any interest owed on borrowed money.

The third profit margin item is **net income**, which indicates what is left after all costs, expenses, and taxes have been paid. It is important to note that there is a difference between income and cash; for instance, it is quite possible for a company to have positive net income, but have a negative cash flow, which causes it to struggle to pay its bills. We will explore this concept in more detail later.

Net income: indicates what is left after all costs, expenses, and taxes have been paid.

TABLE A.2

Revenue, Bookings, and Backlog

Revenue = Sale	Shown on the income statement net of any discounts when a customer receives and accepts an order
Bookings = Order	An order is a promise to purchase, which does not show up on the income statement until the customer receives and accepts the product or service
Backlog = Orders – Revenue	Orders that have been received but not delivered to the customer

The income statement alone does not reveal much about a company's long-term viability or financial health. It tells you little about how and when the company receives cash or how much it has on hand. For an accurate picture of financial health, the balance sheet and cash flow statements need to be analyzed.

The Balance Sheet

The balance sheet (see Table A.3) is a statement that shows a "snapshot" at a particular point in time of what the company has today (assets), how much it owes (liabilities), and what it is currently worth (shareholder equity). Numbers in Table A.3 are for illustrative purposes only.

As explained in Table A.4, the Balance Sheet gets its name from a basic equation, which must be equally balanced.[2]

Current assets: cash and other assets that can be converted into cash within a year.

Assets include cash, machines, inventory, buildings, and what you are owed and what you have the right to collect. **Current assets** include cash and other assets such as inventory, accounts receivable, and prepaid expenses that can be converted into cash within a year. Cash usually includes both cash and cash equivalents, or short-term, low-risk investments. Inventory represents what the company has to sell, as well as materials that are to be made into products. There are three basic types of inventory: raw materials, which include any goods or components used in the manufacturing process; work-in-process

TABLE A.3

Balance Sheet

ASSETS (WHAT THE BUSINESS OWNS)		LIABILITIES (WHAT THE BUSINESS OWES)	
Current Assets		**Current Liabilities**	
Cash	$36,000	Accounts Payable	$68,000
Inventory	$128,000	Accrued Expenses	$88,000
Accounts Receivable	$43,000	Short-Term Debt	$25,000
Prepaid Expenses	$16,000	Other Current Liabilities	$0
Fixed Assets		**Long-Term Debt**	$200,000
Property, Plant, and Equipment	$601,000	**Shareholder Equity** (what the business is worth)	
Accumulated Depreciation	($8,000)	Retained Earnings	$335,000
		Capital Stock	$100,000
Total Assets	$816,000	**Total Liabilities and Shareholder Equity**	$816,000

TABLE A.4

The Balance Sheet Equation

What You Own	=	What You Owe + What You Are Worth
Assets	=	**Liabilities + Shareholder Equity**
Both sides of this equation must always balance.		

(WIP) or semi-finished products, which are partially assembled items awaiting completion; and finished goods, which are ready to be sold (see Figure A.1).

Accounts receivable refers to money owed to the company for goods or services provided and billed to a customer. When the company ships a good or provides a service to a customer on credit and sends a bill, the company has the right to collect this money. **Prepaid expenses** represent payments the company has already made for services not yet received. These are usually things like insurance, deposits, and prepayment of rent. Prepaid expenses are considered current assets because the company has already paid for these services and will not have to use cash to pay for them in the near future.

Fixed assets might also appear on the balance sheet as property, plant, and equipment (PP&E). These are productive assets that are not intended for sale and are used over time to produce goods, store them, ship them, and so on. This commonly includes land, buildings, equipment, machines, furniture, trucks, autos, and other goods that have a useful life of 3 to 5 years, although the life of some assets, such as land and buildings, could be much longer. These assets are reported at cost less accumulated depreciation. Recall that depreciation is an accounting convention that appears on the income statement and represents the decline in value of the asset, due to age, wear, and the passage of time. Accumulated depreciation is the sum of all the depreciation charges taken since the asset was acquired.

Other Types of Assets

"Other assets" is a catchall category that includes items such as the value of patents, goodwill, and intangible assets. **Goodwill** represents the price paid for an asset in excess of its book value. You will see this on the balance sheet when the company has made one or more large acquisitions. **Intangible assets** represent the value of patents, software programs, copyrights, trademarks, franchises, brand names, or assets that cannot be physically touched. One important note is that only items that have been purchased can appear here. For instance, companies are not allowed to create a value for things like a brand name and place it on the balance sheet.

Another type of asset includes **long-term investments**, which refers to assets that are more than 1 year old and are carried on the balance sheet at cost or book value with no appreciation. Examples of long-term investments include cash, stock, bonds, and real

---

Accounts receivable: money owed to the company for goods or services provided and billed to a customer.

Prepaid expenses: the payments the company has already made for services not yet received.

Goodwill: the price paid for an asset in excess of its book value. You will see this on the balance sheet when the company has made one or more large acquisitions.

Intangible assets: the value of patents, software programs, copyrights, trademarks, franchises, brand names, or assets that cannot be physically touched.

Long-term investments: assets that are more than 1 year old and are carried on the balance sheet at cost or book value with no appreciation.

FIGURE A.1

Manufacturing Inventory

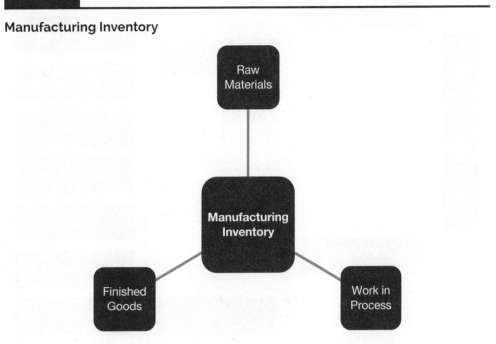

Liabilities: economic obligations of the company, such as money owed to lenders, suppliers, and employees.

Current liabilities: bills that must be paid within 1 year of the date of the balance sheet.

Accounts payable: money owed by a business to its suppliers.

Accrued expenses: costs incurred by the company for which no payment has been made.

Short-term debt: the portion of long-term debt that must be paid within a year.

Other current liabilities: short-term liabilities that do not fall into a specific category, such as sales tax, income tax, and so forth.

Long-term debt: obligation for debt that is due to be repaid in more than 12 months.

Shareholder equity: the money that has been invested in the business plus the cumulative net profits and losses the company has generated.

estate. It is possible that the assets are worth much more, or much less, than the original cost, but the convention is to carry them at cost.

Liabilities and Shareholder Equity

Let's turn our attention to the other side of the balance sheet: liabilities and shareholder equity. **Liabilities** are economic obligations of the company, such as money it owes to lenders, suppliers, and employees.

Current liabilities are bills that must be paid within 1 year of the date of the balance sheet. They are organized based on who is owed the money. **Accounts payable** is money owed by a business to its suppliers. **Accrued expenses** are costs incurred by the company for which no payment has been made. For example, wages and taxes may be indicated on the balance sheet to be paid at a future date, but that payment hasn't occurred just yet. **Short-term debt** is the portion of long-term debt that must be paid within a year. A common example of short-term debt is money owed to lenders such as bank loans. **Other current liabilities** are short-term liabilities that do not fall into a specific category; these will include sales tax, income tax, and so forth.

Long-term debt is an obligation for debt that is due to be repaid in more than 12 months. Bank loans, finance and leasing obligations are all examples of long-term debt.

Shareholder equity represents the money that has been invested in the business plus the cumulative net profits and losses the company has generated (see Figure A.2). This is a liability that is not usually repaid over the normal course of business. Subtracting

FIGURE A.2

Total Shareholder Equity

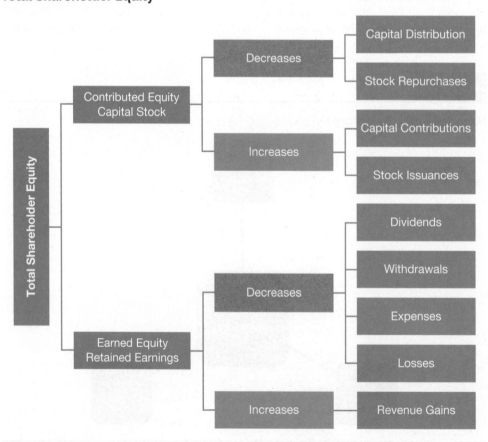

what the company owns (total assets) from what it owes (total liabilities) provides the percentage of its value to the owners, or its shareholders' equity.

There are two main components of shareholder equity. One component is **retained earnings**, the cumulative amount of profit retained by the company and not paid out in the form of dividends (a sum of money paid to shareholders from company profits) to owners. The other component is **capital stock**, which represents the original amount the owners paid into the company plus any additional paid-in capital to purchase stock in the company.

Shareholder equity increases when the company makes a profit (increase in retained earnings) or sells new stock to increase the capital stock. If the company has a loss, which lowers retained earnings, or pays a dividend, which also lowers retained earnings, these actions will result in a decrease in shareholder equity.

Retained earnings: the cumulative amount of profit retained by the company and not paid out in the form of dividends to owners.

Capital stock: the original amount the owners paid into the company plus any additional paid-in capital to purchase stock in the company.

The Cash Flow Statement

The cash flow statement tracks the movement of cash into (cash inflows) and out of (cash outflows) the company over a period of time. Cash inflows include loans, sales, interest, and shares; while outflows include payment to suppliers, wages and salaries, and dividends to shareholders (see Table A.5).

The cash flow statement is like a cash register for the company. It shows the cash that is available at the beginning of the period—in other words, cash that is already in the register. It also shows cash received during the period such as cash from the sale of a product or service, or cash received from investments, borrowing, or the sale of assets and stock, less the cash paid out in the period. This is cash actually paid out to support operations necessary to make and sell a product or service, or cash used to pay down loans, taxes, or the purchase of assets. This then leaves you with cash at the end of the period. Only cash transactions affect cash flow and are considered on the cash flow statement.

Cash flow statements are generally divided into two basic parts: cash generated from operations or profit-making activities, and cash generated from investment and financing activities. The first examines the profit-making inflows and expense outflows, while the second examines inflows and outflows of cash related to the purchase and sale of assets, and financing activities such as bank borrowing and stock sales. Together they form the full picture of cash moving through the company (see Table A.6).

The first line of the cash flow statement is net income. The first thing to do when examining cash flow is to add back depreciation and amortization that appear on the income statement. As you may recall, these are considered "noncash" charges related to the declining value of tangible and intangible assets. So, even though a write-down, or charge, may appear on the income statement, no cash actually left the company. Because we want to determine only cash in this statement, we add back both depreciation and amortization expenses.

TABLE A.5

Examples of Cash Inflows and Outflows

CASH INFLOWS	CASH OUTFLOWS
Loans	Payments to Suppliers
Sales	Wages and Salaries
Interest	Dividends to Shareholders
Shares	Taxes on Profits
Receipts from Debtors	Loan Payments

The next step is to examine the changes in the balances of current assets and current liabilities on the balance sheet. If a current asset balance increases, we are using cash. If a current asset balance decreases, we are adding cash. Conversely, an increase in a current liability balance adds cash, while a decrease in a current liability balance uses cash (see Table A.7).

Initially, it is best to understand the inflows and outflows of cash related to the operating activities of the company by determining the sources (inflows) and uses (outflows) associated with current assets and current liabilities to arrive at the degree of cash flow from operations.

Next, we shift our focus to cash changes stemming from investment and financing activities. One option might be to simply stockpile cash on the balance sheet, but this isn't the most productive use of cash. Another option might be to return cash to shareholders in the form of dividends, or to pay down any debt that the company may have amassed. And still another option might be to invest in productive assets such as machinery and equipment, or to acquire all or part of another business. This may show up as a separate line item in the cash flow as "Investments in Fixed Assets" or something similar.

TABLE A.6

Cash Flow Statement

Net Income	**$50,000**
(+) Depreciation and Amortization	$1,000
(+) Sources: Decrease in Assets or Increase in Liabilities	$12,000
(-) Uses: Increase in Assets or Decrease in Liabilities	($15,000)
Increase/(Decrease) Cash from Operations	**$48,000**
(-) Net Property Plant and Equipment	($8,000)
Increase/(Decrease) Cash from Investments	**$40,000**
(+) Increase in Net Borrowing	$0
(+) Sale of Stock	$0
(-) Paying of Dividends	$0
Increase/(Decrease) Cash from Financing	**($4,000)**
Increase/(Decrease) in Cash *(Should be equal to cash on the Balance Sheet)*	**$36,000**

TABLE A.7

Inflows and Outflows of Cash

SOURCES (INFLOWS) OF CASH	USES (OUTFLOWS) OF CASH
• Decrease in Assets	• Increase in Assets
• Increase in Liability	• Decrease in Liability
• Increase in Shareholder Equity	• Decrease in Shareholder Equity
• Profit from Operations	• Loss from Operations

Finally, you must examine cash inflows and outflows from financing activities such as selling stock, borrowing, or paying dividends. Borrowing money increases the amount of cash on hand. Conversely, paying down your debt lowers the amount of cash on hand, while the sale of stock by a company increases the amount of cash coming into the company.

Adding the cash flow from operations to the cash flow from investing and financing leaves us with either a cash increase or decrease for the period. If a company has either cash in the bank or access to additional cash, it can withstand negative cash flow for several periods. It is good business practice for entrepreneurial managers to strive to achieve profits and convert those profits into cash.

Net Income Versus Cash Flow

Although net income (or profit) and cash flow are both crucial to the success of the business, there are important differences between the two.

Net income, as it appears on the income statement, is determined by accounting principles and includes accruals and noncash items such as depreciation and amortization. In other words, there are items on the income statement that determine net income for a period that do not represent actual cash coming in or going out of the company for that period. For instance, in respect of how revenue is recorded on the income statement, the credit sales are captured as an obligation to pay (asset) in the balance sheet as an account receivable. Even though no cash has changed hands, the revenue on the income statement still reflects the sale. This treatment also applies to expenses and capital expenditures on the income statement.

Cash flow, in contrast, deals only with actual cash transactions. A company's operating policies, production techniques, and inventory and credit-control systems will influence the timing of cash moving through the business; and this is what the entrepreneurial manager must master in order to convert profit into cash.

A.3 LINKAGES BETWEEN THE THREE FINANCIAL STATEMENTS

>> **LO A.3**   **Clarify the relationship between the three financial statements.**

The power of financial statements lies in the linkages. It is important to understand how the three financial statements are linked to one another and how decisions with regard to the operations of a company will impact its financial performance. A company's pricing and credit policies will have a direct impact on revenue, an income statement item; and accounts receivable, a balance sheet item. Although each financial statement provides a different view of the company, each statement is also related to the other.

For instance, net income on the income statement is added to retained earnings on the balance sheet. The ending cash balance on the cash flow statement is equal to the cash on the balance sheet. Every entrepreneur needs to understand how cash and goods and services flow into and out of the company.

Figure A.3 shows what happens when a sale is made, the product or service is delivered, and the cash is collected. When a sale is made and the product or service is accepted by the customer, revenue on the income statement increases. Assuming that credit is extended for the sale, accounts receivable on the balance sheet also increases. Once the obligation to pay is met by the customer, accounts receivable decreases and the amount paid becomes a cash inflow on the cash flow statement. Additionally, when a sale is made, the value of the product is moved from inventory (a balance sheet item) to cost of goods (an income statement item).[3]

As with the *sales* cycle explained above, these types of connections between the various statements can be charted in similar fashion for the *expense* cycle, the purchase of fixed assets, and investments. When you understand how cash moves through the company, you begin to understand how policies related to credit, inventory, and payables can affect the time it takes for cash to be converted into products and returned back to the company at a profit.

FIGURE A.3

Income Statement/Balance Sheet/Cash Flow Statement

Income Statement

Revenue	$$$$
(-) Cost of Goods	$$
Gross Profit	$$
(-) Sales, General and Administrative	$
(-) Marketing	$
(-) Research and Development	$
(-) Depreciation and Amortization	$
Operating Profit	$$
(-) Interest Expense	$
(-) Taxes	$
Net Income	$$

> When a sale is made, Revenue increases on the Income Statement and an obligation to pay is incurred by the customer, which increases Accounts Receivable on the Balance Sheet.

> When a sale is made, Revenue increases on the Income Statement and an obligation to pay is incurred by the customer, which increases Accounts Receivable on the Balance Sheet.

> When a sale is made, Revenue increases on the Income Statement and an obligation to pay is incurred by the customer, which increases Accounts Receivable on the Balance Sheet.

Balance Sheet

Assets (What You Own)		**Liabilities (What You Owe)**	
Current Assets		Current Liabilities	
Cash	$$	Accounts Payable	$$
Inventory	$$	Accrued Expenses	$$
Accounts Receivable	$$	Short-Term Debt	$$
Prepaid Expenses	$$	Other Current Liabilities	$$
Fixed Assets		**Long-Term Debt**	$$
Property, Plant and Equipment	$$	**Shareholders' Equity (What You Are Worth)**	
Accumulated Depreciation	$$$	Retained Earnings	$$
		Capital Stock	$$
Total Assets	**$$$$**	**Total Liabilities and Shareholders' Equity**	**$$$$**

> When Net Income on the Income Statement increases, Retained Earnings on the Balance Sheet increases. The opposite is also true. A decrease in Net Income will decrease Retained Earnings.

Cash Flow Statement

Net Income	$$$
(+) Depreciation and Amortization	$
(+) Sources: Decrease in Assets or Increase in Liabilities	$
(-) Uses: Increase in Assets or Decrease in Liabilities	$
Increase/(Decrease) Cash from Operations	$$$
(-) Net PP&E	$
Increase/(Decrease) Cash from Investments	$$
(+) Increase in Net Borrowing	$
(+) Sale of Stock	$
(-) Paying of Dividends	$
Increase/(Decrease) Cash from Financing	$$
Increase/(Decrease) in Cash	$$
(Should be equal to cash on the Balance Sheet)	

A.4 THE JOURNEY OF CASH: THE CASH CONVERSION CYCLE

>> LO A.4   Describe the journey of cash through the cash conversion cycle.

Cash is used to purchase materials, which are then made into products. This creates obligations to make payments to certain suppliers of those materials, which is captured on the balance sheet in accounts payable. These products are stored, which appears on the balance sheet in inventory, and are eventually sold and delivered to customers. Then the company has the right to collect cash for the selling price of the products, which appears on the balance sheet in accounts receivable. Once collected, this cash has now returned to the company. You hope that this journey produces more cash that is returned to the hands of the company. This journey is called the **cash conversion cycle (CCC)**, and it refers to the number of days a company's cash is tied up in the production and sales process. CCC can be calculated using the equation shown in Figure A.4.

Cash conversion cycle (CCC): the number of days a company's cash is tied up in the production and sales process.

FIGURE A.4

Cash Conversion Cycle

Calculated in days, this equation shows how long the journey is for cash from the point of leaving the company to the point of return.

Days sales outstanding (DSO) is a measure of the number of days that it takes to collect on accounts receivable. Remember, if you do business in cash then your DSO is zero, but if you sell on credit, then this will be a positive number. DSO is calculated using the following equation:

Days sales outstanding (DSO): a measure of the number of days that it takes to collect on accounts receivable.

DSO = Average Accounts Receivable/Revenue per day

Average Accounts Receivable = (Beginning Accounts Receivable + Ending Accounts Receivable)/2

Revenue per day = Revenue/365

Days of inventory (DOI) is a measure of the average number of days it takes to sell the entire inventory of a company. DOI is calculated using the following equation:

Days of inventory (DOI): a measure of the average number of days it takes to sell the entire inventory of a company.

DOI = (Average Inventory)/COGS per day

Average Inventory = (Beginning inventory + Ending inventory)/2

COGS per day = COGS/365

Days payable outstanding (DPO) is a measure of the number of days it takes you to pay your bills. DPO is calculated using the following equation:

Days payable outstanding (DPO): a measure of the number of days it takes you to pay your bills.

DPO = Average Accounts Payable/COGS per day

Average Accounts Payable = (Beginning Accounts Payable + Ending Accounts Payable)/2

COGS per day = COGS/365

To calculate CCC, you need to include several items from the financial statements:

▸ Income statement

▸ Revenue and COGS

▸ Balance sheet

- Beginning and ending inventory
- Beginning and ending accounts receivable
- Beginning and ending accounts payable

Note that because balance sheet items capture a snapshot in time, you want to use an average over the period of time that you are investigating. So if you are looking at 1 year, then you need to look at the ending period for the current year and the same ending period for the previous year.

Let's use an example to explore this equation in more detail. Suppose you are making men's shirts and selling them through a retail channel. The DOI is 80 days. You purchase enough cotton material to make a shirt. This purchase creates an obligation for the shirt maker to pay (account payable) for this material in 30 days (DPO). The raw material arrives (inventory) and the manufacturing process begins.

At the end of 80 days, the completed shirt is sold to the retailer (DOI). The retailer now has an obligation to pay the shirt maker (account receivable) and takes 40 days to pay for the completed shirt. This means that from the time cash left the shirt maker 30 days after the purchase of raw material, it took 90 days for cash to make its way back to the shirt maker. In this case the formula would be:

$$CCC = DSO + DOI - DPO$$

$$= 80 + 40 - 30$$

$$= 90$$

Figure A.5 illustrates this process.

The CCC, or days that it takes for cash to return to the business, must be funded. Any increase in sales usually results in an increase in working capital necessary to support this higher level of sales. Therefore, you must be able to fund the growth of the company.

FIGURE A.5

Cash Conversion Cycle

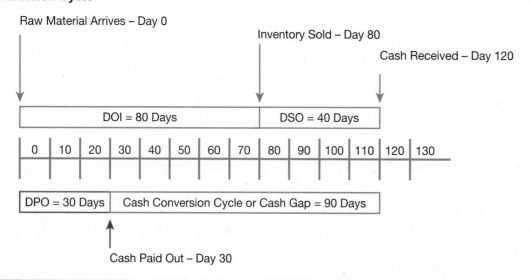

As a stand-alone number the CCC doesn't tell you much. Like many other metrics and ratios it must be compared over time and to other competitors in the industry. In general, a decreasing CCC is a good thing, while a rising CCC should motivate you to look a little more deeply into the management policies of the business to try and find the cash necessary to fund the company.

A.5 BUILDING PRO FORMA FINANCIAL STATEMENTS

>> LO A.5   **Discuss how to build a pro forma financial statement.**

Now that you have a better understanding of the three financial statements, it's time to turn our attention to developing projections or forecasted financial statements. When entrepreneurs are assessing the long-term viability of a business it's important to make projections and develop pro forma financial statements. Rather than looking at financial statements from what has happened, as we have been discussing, we must now look at how to project what could happen. Pro forma financial statements give an idea of how the actual statement will look if the underlying assumptions hold true.[4]

The pro forma financial statement should include at least three scenarios of your financial forecast—each containing an income statement, the balance sheet, and the all-important cash flow statement. Each of these three scenarios should manipulate the various revenue and cost drivers in an attempt to determine where there is leverage in the business model to deal with what may go right and what may go wrong. All of your assumptions and estimates should be carefully documented and built into the model so that you can dynamically change them to conduct "what if" analyses in real time.

Although there are many preexisting, dynamic, pro forma models on the Internet,[5] be mindful not merely to insert estimates randomly without corresponding backup for every assumption. Anyone who has been through this process knows that the numbers are estimates that will change over time. Nevertheless, you must be able to defend every assumption, and the components must logically support one another. In the end, the pro forma financial plans must be strategically compelling and operationally achievable, and they must convey both confidence and realism to investors.

Your goal is to determine how much absolute cash is required to get to cash flow break-even and how this cash might be logically staged so that you can achieve a step-up in valuation at each stage. It is worth noting that items will emerge that you have not considered and that items that you have considered will be magnified to either the positive or negative.

Creating pro forma statements can be a time-consuming process, but there are major benefits to doing so. First, it gives investors a degree of comfort that you understand how to build a business and execute the business model. Second, it shows that you have a good understanding of how the market may evolve and how to respond to these changes. Finally, it is a useful way of providing structure and discipline as operating decision points arise.

The Mechanics and Research

All too often, entrepreneurs begin the process with an existing model or business planning software and, before long, find themselves tweaking elements of the model to "make the numbers work." Instead, it is best to set the spreadsheet models aside and thoroughly research various business model elements that drive revenue and costs. This process requires both primary and secondary research. Figure A.6 outlines the overall process, or mechanics.

Research

Much of your research should focus on the customer and market size and growth potential. A common beginner mistake is to assume that an exceedingly large population is your market and all you will need to do is get 1% of that market to be successful.

The Mechanics

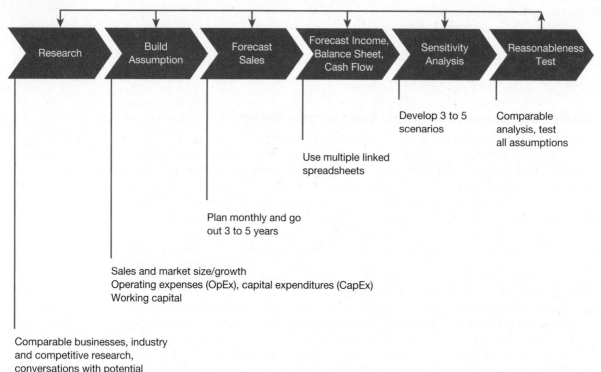

Research

Comparable businesses, industry and competitive research, conversations with potential customers, competitors, suppliers, experts

Build Assumption

Sales and market size/growth
Operating expenses (OpEx), capital expenditures (CapEx)
Working capital

Forecast Sales

Plan monthly and go out 3 to 5 years

Forecast Income, Balance Sheet, Cash Flow

Use multiple linked spreadsheets

Sensitivity Analysis

Develop 3 to 5 scenarios

Reasonableness Test

Comparable analysis, test all assumptions

Although understanding the aggregate market size is useful, it is recommended that you segment your market in greater detail to better understand the various subgroupings and their respective buying habits and behaviors. Understand how they differ and how they are similar in terms of needs, expectations, price sensitivity, amount, and frequency of purchase, to name a few.

For the purpose of forecasting, it is also useful to understand how each subgroup is growing and changing over time. In general, the more you know about your primary and secondary target markets, the more reliable your forecasts will be.

Primary research refers to data gathered by yourself through sources such as focus groups, interviews, and surveys. **Secondary research** refers to data gathered from external sources: industry publications, company websites, government agencies, and the like. Secondary source articles and research reports can be useful as a means to get smart about an industry but, given the pace with which markets develop today, the data can get stale rather quickly. It is more beneficial to use primary data gathered in real time through observation, conversation, and rapid prototyping.

One useful approach is to first determine the questions that need to be answered about your target market, channels of distribution, required resources, cost drivers, and revenue drivers. Next, consider the data required to answer these questions. When you have gathered that data, then think about the primary and secondary sources of the data.

Remember to document the source of every assumption so that you can reference it if asked. Let's say that you want to start a pizzeria restaurant. Let's call it Town Pizza. Table A.8 lists some of the critical questions that you will want to answer before even opening a spreadsheet.

In addition to fundamental market research, it is also useful to find some yardsticks, or generally accepted rules of thumb for your industry. The best source of this information can usually be found by examining businesses that are comparable to yours in terms

TABLE A.8

Key Spreadsheet Questions

KEY QUESTIONS	SOURCES		
	DATA REQUIRED	PRIMARY	SECONDARY
Customer and Market • What is pizza consumption in the U.S.? Is it growing? • Who eats pizza, how much and when? • When is pizza consumed most? What days of the week? Time of year? • What is the population and composition of households in the area? What is the college population? What is the working population? • What percentage of these people will be likely diners? (lunch, dinner) • How can you estimate the traffic to the pizzeria and typical purchase order? **Revenue Drivers** • What else is sold at the typical pizzeria restaurant? (sandwiches, salads, pasta, beverages) • What is the consumption of these items relative to pizzas? • What is the average order? What are the average prices for each item? • What is the contribution margin? • What are breakeven points? **Cost Drivers** • What does it cost to make a pizza? A sandwich? A salad? etc.? • What is the average size of a pizzeria? • What does build out cost? • What are the typical operating expenses? (monthly, yearly) • What costs are fixed? Which are variable? • What fixed assets are needed? (equipment) What does it cost? Should you buy new or used? • What are the working capital requirements?	• U.S. pizza consumption data • Census data • Traffic patterns • Demographics • Typical pizza restaurant menu and pricing • Average pizzeria statistics • Ingredients cost • Real estate data • Construction estimates • OpEx and CapEx for typical pizzeria	• Pizzeria owners, managers, and employees • Various customer segments of the pizzeria dining market • Associations • Consultants and experts • Accountants, lawyers, real estate agents • Suppliers • Contractors	• Industry research reports • Association research • Town census • Periodicals • News articles • Websites/blogs • New and used equipment sites • Annual reports

of industry and business model. There are numerous approaches to finding this information. Secondary sources are readily available on the Internet and include everything from historical data from public companies to industry associations and publications.[6] Similarly, primary data can be gathered through interviews with experts, business owners, potential customers, and observation. The comparable data will be extremely useful in both forming and validating your assumptions. In other words, everything covered in this text so far will help you build your assumptions.

Building Assumptions: Forecasting Sales

Forecasting sales can be a complex process. One useful way to estimate sales is the **bottom-up (or build-up) method**, a technique that involves first estimating revenue and costs from the smallest unit of sales and building up from there.

Let's apply this method to the Town Pizza example. As you can see from the revenue worksheet (Table A.9), Town Pizza sells pizza, sandwiches, salads, and drinks. By using the build up method you can present the assumptions gathered from your research to estimate revenue for a typical day, and then extrapolate what that revenue might be for a typical month and year.

Bottom-up (or build-up) method: estimating revenues and costs from the smallest unit of sales, such as a day.

TABLE A.9			

Revenue Worksheet

PRODUCT DESCRIPTION	SUGGESTED PRICE	EST. UNITS PER DAY	AVERAGE DAILY REVENUE
Pizza	$13.00	42	$546.00
Sandwich	$8.00	21	$168.00
Salad	$8.00	11	$88.00
Beverage	$2.00	37	$74.00
Total Average Daily Revenue			$876.00
Total Average Monthly Revenue @ 30 days/month * **Does not account for seasonality spikes**			**$26,280.00**

Assumptions:

U.S. Pizza Market

- Average traffic: 370 customers per month
- Average daily pizza sales = 42
- Sandwich sales are 50% of pizza sales
- Salad sales are 50% sandwich sales
- Beverages are 100% of pizza and sandwich sales
- Seasonal spikes: Super Bowl (Feb), Halloween (Oct), Thanksgiving (Nov), Christmas (Dec)
- Typical pizzeria average annual sales = $396,594.00
- 94% of Americans eat pizza; Average = 46 slices or 5.75 pizzas per year
- Pizza market is growing approximately 2% annually

Market Size/Growth

- Population = 27,982 (Households = 8,594), College Students = 5,974, Business employees = 1,050 (Total Pop 35,006)
- 62% of households < 45 years old (does not include college students and business employees)
- Growth 1% per year
- Currently 5 pizza restaurants in town

As Table A.9 shows, the monthly revenue has been estimated at $26,280 or $315,360 per year before accounting for seasonal spikes. This fits pretty closely to the national average of $396,594, which does include seasonal spikes, so our bottom-up approach appears to be feasible.

Furthermore, you can examine the market data to see if there will be sufficient demand for our pizzeria by using a top down approach. As you can see in the assumptions, the town comprises 8,594 households, of which 62% are age 45 and younger. Just to be conservative, let's assume that your primary target market is people aged 45 and younger, and likely to be either college students or families. That would leave 16,517 people in town under the age of 45. Add to that the college students and workers who come into town each day and the figure becomes 23,541. So, if 94% of these people eat pizza and the average person eats 5.75 pizzas in a year, that means approximately 127,000 pizzas are eaten by this population yearly. If the average pizzeria serves 14,400 pizzas per year and there are currently only five pizzerias in town, then there should be room in the market for our Town Pizza.

The process of gathering the data and formulating the assumptions helps you better understand the business model and the levers that might be used to generate more revenue. For instance, will spending more on advertising and promotions bring more people to the store? This type of scenario or sensitivity analysis can be explored in more detail once you have completed building the integrated pro forma financial statements.

Now that you have this baseline to work with, you can plot out what the first 2 or 3 years of revenue might look like on a monthly, quarterly, and yearly basis. This would also allow you to make estimates for seasonal spikes or lows.

Building Assumptions: Cost of Goods and Operating Expenses

With a firm estimate on top line revenue, you can now turn your focus to estimating costs. The first cost item on the income statement is COGS (Table A.10). Recall that COGS includes the cost of raw materials and direct labor in the production of the product. Here you can once more use the buildup method to estimate the exact costs for each product, or as a first cut, you might want to use comparable data from a typical pizzeria.

Say you have found that the average raw materials and labor cost for a typical independent pizzeria is 30%. Given your estimated monthly revenue of $26,280, COGS would be $7,884, leaving you with a gross margin of $18,396 or 65%. Once again, our estimates are close to the average.

Businesses also incur operating expenses (see Table A.11), such as salaries, rent, advertising, marketing, and possibly research and development. These costs can also be estimated and validated through primary and secondary research. Reliable estimates can be accomplished through Internet research and validated through conversations with pizzeria owners, associations, accountants, lawyers, real estate brokers, and government officials, to name a few. It is worth sweating the details to get these estimates as close to the actual expenses as you possibly can. Once again, the buildup method is employed to round these numbers up to the monthly or yearly costs.

As you can see from the worksheet, the estimated operating profit is $6,022.00. This is not to be confused with net profit, which is profit after interest, depreciation, and taxes have been paid.

Labor Estimates

A more complex business that might involve research and development of a product and a greater number of employees would require a more detailed approach to structuring new hires. In many types of business people can account for 75% to 85% of operating costs. Therefore, the schedule of new hires must be carefully thought out and matched to product development and sales requirements and milestones.

Given the time and cost involved in screening, hiring, and onboarding new employees, a plan that takes these items into consideration should be constructed for each department. A common mistake is to hire people too quickly and terminate poor performers too slowly. However, regardless of the size or complexity of your business, it is good practice to build a simple table to estimate this expense separately (Table A.12).

TABLE A.10

Cost of Goods Worksheet

PRODUCT DESCRIPTION	SUGGESTED PRICE	EST. COGS (%)	EST. UNITS PER DAY	COGS ($)
Pizza	$13.00	30%	42	$163.80
Sandwich	$8.00	31%	21	$52.08
Salad	$8.00	25%	11	$22.00
Beverage	$2.00	13%	37	$9.62
Total Daily COGS				$247.50
Total Monthly COGS				**$7,425.00**
Total Monthly Gross Margin **(Total Monthly Revenue – Total Monthly COGS)**				**$18,855.00**

TABLE A.11

Operating Expense Worksheet

OPERATING EXPENSE TYPE	ESTIMATED MONTHLY EXPENSE
Rent	$2,333.00
Labor	$7,925.00
Outside Services	$275.00
Credit Card Processing (1.9% of Sales)	$500.00
Utilities	$525.00
Advertising and Coupons	$100.00
Maintenance and Contingency	$500.00
Repair and Maintenance	$100.00
Insurance	$250.00
Office Supplies	$75.00
Equipment Rental	$250.00
Total Monthly Expenses	$12,833.00
Total Monthly Operating Profit **(Gross Margin – Operating Expense)**	**$6,022.00**

Assumptions:

Rent: 1,000 ft^2 at $28/year = $62,500.00

Labor: 1 Mgr, plus 3 hires

Fringe Rate: 15%

CC Processing: 1.9% of sales

TABLE A.12

Labor Estimates

POSITION	EST. ANNUAL/HOURLY WAGES	MARCH	APRIL	MAY
Manager	$31,200.00	$2,650.00	$2,650.00	$2,650.00
Hourly Employees				
Kitchen Staff	1 @ $13 per hr.	$2,297.00	$2,297.00	$2,297.00
Counter/Wait Staff	2 @ $11 per hr.	$1,944.00	$1,944.00	$1,944.00
Benefits	15%	$1,033.00	$1,033.00	$1,033.00
Total Monthly Cost		$7,924.00	$7,924.00	$7,924.00

Assumptions:

- 1 Manager
- 1 Kitchen Staff
- 2 Counter Staff

TABLE A.13

Capital Equipment and Other Expenditures Worksheet

EXPENDITURES	ESTIMATED COST
Pizza Ovens	$21,995.00
Walk-in Refrigerator	$10,500.00
Pizza Table/Work Tables	$13,000.00
Mixer	$3,500.00
Prep Sink/Dishwasher	$1,350.00
Pots and Pans	$500.00
Phone, POS, Coolers, CC Machine, Misc.	$1,000.00
Restaurant Build Out	$33,500.00
Signage	$1,250.00
Total Expenditures	**$95,595.00**

Assumptions:
- All prices assume new purchases; best efforts will be made to purchase used equipment in good repair.
- Build out estimate provided by contractor for 1,000 sq. ft. including restroom. (Carpentry, electrical, plumbing labor included. Fixtures broken out separately.)

With your top line revenue and operating expense worksheets completed, you can now turn your attention to expenditures necessary to build out and run the business (see Table A.13). These expenditures, or capital expenses, will not appear as a line item on your income statement. Because the expenditures will be used over a period of time, usually more than a year, they will appear on your balance sheet as an asset and on your cash flow statement as an outflow. What will appear on your income statement is depreciation, which reflects the annual decrease in value of these assets over their useful lives.

A.6 BUILDING ASSUMPTIONS: OPERATING POLICIES AND OTHER KEY ASSUMPTIONS

>> **LO A.6** **Explain how to apply assumptions when building pro forma statements.**

As we saw earlier when describing the CCC, operating policies can greatly affect the speed at which cash makes its journey back to the company. In constructing pro forma financial statements, these policies need to be carefully considered and enforced by the company. Some of the more critical policies are as follows.[7]

- **Purchasing Policy:** the price and timing of raw materials, and other goods and services necessary to build, sell, and support products

- **Pricing Policy:** how pricing will be determined for your products and services

- **Compensation Policy:** the level of compensation and benefits for each type of position in the business

Purchasing policy: the price and timing of raw materials and other goods and services necessary to build, sell, and support products.

Pricing policy: how pricing will be determined for your products and services.

Compensation policy: the level of compensation and benefits for each type of position in the business.

Credit policy: the process and timing in which obligations to pay for products and services sold will be billed and collected.

Payables policy: the process and timing in which obligations to pay for goods and services received by the business will be paid.

Inventory policy: the level of various types of inventory (e.g., raw materials, work-in-process, finished goods) maintained and the speed with which inventory moves from the business to the customer.

- **Credit Policy:** the process and timing in which obligations to pay for products and services sold will be billed and collected

- **Payables Policy:** the process and timing in which obligations to pay for goods and services received by the business will be paid

- **Inventory Policy:** the level of various types of inventory (e.g., raw materials, work-in-process, finished goods) maintained and the speed with which inventory moves from the business to the customer

Other critical assumptions can affect the timing of cash flows both into and out of the business. For instance, when do you expect to make the first sale, and how long will it take for the business to ramp up to full capacity? In our pizzeria example, it may take several months to obtain permits and complete a build out of the restaurant before the grand opening. Then it may take several more months before advertising efforts begin to bring in the traffic that you anticipated would be necessary to achieve peak sales. This logic can also be extended to the productivity of new hires. Be sure to take into account the time and training it may take before new hires hit their stride and begin achieving the established sales quota.

Assumptions must also be considered for local, state, and federal taxes; interest; and inflation. Understand how your various expense-related items might increase over time as well. It is important to carefully document the source of every assumption made because it may be necessary to revisit it, or to defend it during due diligence.

Building Integrated Pro Forma Financial Statements

With your research and analysis completed and assumptions made, you are now ready to build integrated pro forma financial statements. The logical place to begin is with the income statement. Using the validated assumptions from the revenue worksheet, build out a monthly pro forma income statement, balance sheet, and cash flow statement for a minimum of 2 years, followed by Years 3 through 5 on an annual basis. This time horizon will give you a good sense for the value-producing ability of the business.

When building your pro forma statements, remember the linkages between the three financial statements described earlier. Also ensure you understand how changes on one statement can affect the other statements. Understanding these linkages and especially how cash makes its journey through the business can mean the difference between success and failure. It is essential that you understand how the growth in your business will be funded and the amount of funding you will need until your business is producing enough cash to survive without constant external funding.

The cash flow statement is used to determine when and how much funding is required to get the business off the ground and support growth in the earlier years. This can be achieved by leaving the third section, financing activities, blank to determine the cumulative amount of cash needed. View a set of sample financial statements on the companion site for this text.

Sensitivity Analysis

With the first full set of pro forma financial statements completed, you can now begin to address critical assumptions related to the revenue and cost drivers to test what your business might look like in different scenarios relating to customer traffic and seasonality, or cost of raw materials. For instance, if the restaurant were to open in the summer, might customer traffic be lighter due to vacationing college and high school students? If so, how might that affect revenue? Alternatively, what costs might need to be adjusted during peak selling months, and how might that affect cash flow and profitability?

During this analysis, a minimum of three scenarios is recommended: best case, worst case, and likely case. Thinking through the drivers and operating policies and understanding what can go right, what can go wrong, and what you would do to mitigate any controllable circumstances is probably the greatest benefit to building pro forma financial statements.

Reasonableness Test

Using comparable data that you gathered during your research, compare your statements to those of similar businesses. Unless you have an entirely new and disruptive business model, your numbers should not be too different from businesses of similar size and scope.

Specifically, take a look at your top line revenue and determine whether sales ramp too quickly or too slowly. Have you accounted for seasonal changes in demand? Does the rate of sales growth level off at some point in time? Do expenses continue to rise in lockstep with sales, or should you expect to achieve scale effects that allow COGS and other operating expenses to grow at a slower rate as sales increase? Are there other efficiencies to your business model that are reflected in your operating policies?

Consider all of the questions that a potential investor may have about your business model and its effects on your financial model, and be prepared to answer those using data from your research and comparable analysis. If certain numbers do not pass the reasonableness test, revisit your assumptions until you are comfortable and confident that you can defend the model. ●

$SAGE edge™

Get the tools you need to sharpen your study skills. SAGE edge offers a robust online environment featuring an impressive array of free tools and resources.

- Access practice quizzes, eFlashcards, video, and multimedia at
  edge.sagepub.com/neckentrepreneurship2e

SUMMARY

A.1   Explain the purpose of financial projections for startups.

Financial projections enable the entrepreneur to frame the opportunity from the perspective of the target market(s), understand the resources required to capitalize on the opportunity, and know how to allocate those resources under varying market conditions.

A.2   Describe financial statements as an essential part of financial projections.

The three essential financial statements are the income statement, the balance sheet, and the cash flow statement. The income statement measures performance on a monthly or annual basis. The balance sheet shows what the company owns and what it owes at a given point in time. The cash flow statement assesses the inflows and outflows of money over a period of time.

A.3   Clarify the relationship between the three financial statements.

Although each financial statement provides a different view of the company, they are all needed to provide a complete picture. For example, a company's pricing and credit policies will have a direct impact on revenue, an income statement item; and on accounts receivable, a balance sheet item.

A.4   Describe the journey of cash through the cash conversion cycle.

The cash conversion cycle is the number of days a company's cash is tied up in the production and sales process. The number of days in the cycle is calculated by adding the days sales outstanding (DSO) to days of inventory (DOI), then subtracting days payable outstanding (DPO).

A.5   Discuss how to build a pro forma financial statement.

The pro forma financial statement should include at least three scenarios of your financial forecast, each containing all three types of financial statements. Each scenario should manipulate revenue and cost drivers to show how the business can deal with what may go right and what may go wrong. It should show a best case, a worst case, and a likely case.

A.6   **Explain how to apply assumptions when building pro forma statements.**

Assumptions include operating policies, which determine the speed of the cash conversion cycle, as well as taxes, interest, inflation, and the time it will take to ramp up the business. When assumptions are applied, integrated financial statements can be created and sensitivity analysis and reasonableness test applied.

KEY TERMS

Accounts payable   336

Accounts receivable   335

Accrued expenses   336

Backlog   333

Balance sheet   332

Bottom-up (or build-up) method   345

Capital stock   337

Cash conversion cycle (CCC)   341

Cash flow statement   332

Compensation policy   349

Credit policy   350

Current assets   334

Current liabilities   336

Days of inventory (DOI)   341

Days payable outstanding (DPO)   341

Days sales outstanding (DSO)   341

Goodwill   335

Income statement   332

Intangible assets   335

Interest expense   333

Inventory policy   350

Liabilities   336

Long-term debt   336

Long-term investments   335

Net income   333

Operating profit   333

Other current liabilities   336

Payables policy   350

Prepaid expenses   335

Pricing policy   349

Primary research   344

Purchasing policy   349

Retained earnings   337

Secondary research   344

Shareholder equity   336

Short-term debt   336

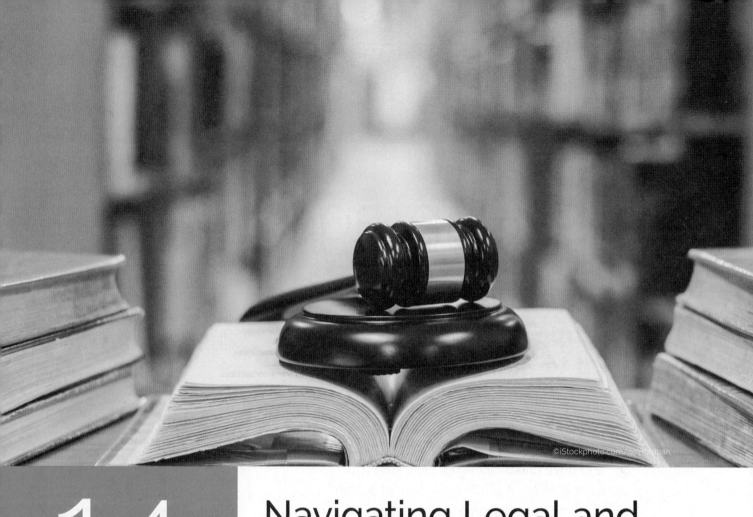

14

Navigating Legal and IP Issues

With Contributions From Richard Mandel, JD

"The law serves many purposes and functions in society. Four principal purposes and functions are establishing standards, maintaining order, resolving disputes, and protecting liberties and rights. The law is a guidepost for minimally acceptable behavior in society."

—Judy Kanarek, Quora contributor and YouTuber

Chapter Outline

Learning Objectives

14.1 Discuss how legal considerations can add value to entrepreneurial ventures.

14.2 Explain the most common types of legal structures available to startups.

14.3 Outline the most common legal errors made by startups.

14.4 Define IP and how it affects entrepreneurs.

14.5 Assess the global impact of IP theft.

14.6 Describe the common IP traps experienced by entrepreneurs.

14.7 Explain the legal requirements of hiring employees.

14.1 LEGAL CONSIDERATIONS

>> **LO 14.1 Discuss how legal considerations can add value to entrepreneurial ventures.**

Typically, when entrepreneurs start a company, they tend to focus on building and developing the product or service, attracting a customer base, and finding the right people to help with the launch. All these activities are essential to get early startup ventures off the ground, but focusing on the legal side should also take priority. John Suh, CEO of online legal solutions company LegalZoom, calls these "the necessary evils."

"When you think of law and tax, they're the necessary evils," Suh said. "Entrepreneurs just want them to be taken care of as quickly and efficiently as possible, so they can get back to the real business of building the company."[1]

It may not sound as exciting as building a new product, but dealing with the law is an essential part of the process. Seeking expert legal advice is essential. Most entrepreneurs either lack the skills to understand the legalities of setting up a business or neglect the legal side altogether. Facebook cofounder Mark Zuckerberg made several big legal mistakes in the early startup stage, including setting up Facebook as the wrong business structure. Zuckerberg may excel at anticipating user needs, but he was certainly no expert in legal matters.[2]

Before you meet with a legal expert, it is important to be prepared by knowing a certain amount of information in order to ask the right questions and make the best decisions for your new venture. Legal experts are in a great position to add value to your business if they are the right fit. And that "if" is important: Although some lawyers may be great at drawing up contracts and preparing documentation, not all can work with startups and small businesses. Because startup companies face a variety of unique legal issues and funding challenges that are simply not experienced by more established companies, one of the most important things to look for in a lawyer is familiarity with and comfort in working with startups. You will also want to look for one who understands the industry you are in. For example, if you are in the fashion industry, you will need a lawyer who has some experience in the many areas that are likely to affect your business, including textile production, international trade, manufacturing law, and e-commerce.

How much does it cost to hire a lawyer? Startup legal costs vary widely, depending on the type of business you are setting up. A simple, home-based cupcake-baking business may cost only a few hundred dollars in legal fees, whereas a larger, more complex enterprise is likely to cost a good deal more. In general, a business attorney will charge

$SAGE edge™

Master the content at
**edge.sagepub.com/
neckentrepreneurship2e**

Cameron Herold, 1-800-GOT JUNK? and COO Alliance

Photo courtesy of Cameron Herold

Cameron Herold, 1-800-GOT JUNK? and COO Alliance

"It has less to do with the idea and much more to do with execution and focus." This is Cameron Herold's motto that brought him great entrepreneurial success, built a consulting business, and enabled him to publish five books. Currently based in Scottsdale, Arizona, Cameron moves between the U.S. and Canada, and is a graduate of Carleton University in Ottawa, the capital city of Canada. He operates three businesses. First, Cameron runs the COO Alliance—a network for leading Chief Operating Officers. Second, for the past 12 years, Cameron has coached entrepreneurs and executives globally, which has led to his third business as a paid speaker, having given lectures and talks at events in 28 countries on six continents. Cameron has an expertise in "simplifying business problems and guiding business leaders to previously unimagined success." He consults with businesses that have at least $2 million in revenue and the intention of growing to $200 million. He estimates that he has actively consulted for more than 120 companies, and many of them have raised hundreds of millions of dollars to continue scaling.

Cameron worked on a number of projects while he built, tested, and proved valuable core beliefs about entrepreneurism. Like many founders, Cameron got his entrepreneurial bug in college when he had a house painting business and 12 employees. This business was a learning laboratory for him because he could practice in the real world what he was learning in the classroom. "For example, it is one thing to learn concepts and theories about the hiring process, and it is another to hold your own interview for a new employee; doing both at once creates excellent business leaders," according to Cameron. "Start something. This allows you to practice doing something. You can learn how to run a company regardless of its product or service."

For Cameron, being an entrepreneur is about creating your own value and creating something from nothing. In one of his larger successes, Cameron joined 1-800-GOT-JUNK?, a massive Canadian franchisor and full-service junk removal company, as its 14th employee and COO. In that entrepreneurial environment, he oversaw growth from

14 employees to thousands, alongside massive increases in revenue. Once he helped 1-800-GOT-JUNK? scale, he left the company because his passion is in growing entrepreneurial companies. However, even today, Cameron coaches the CEO of 1-800-GOT-JUNK?

Business law addresses the challenges that all businesses face regarding legal matters such as intellectual property (IP) and hiring and firing employees. Cameron is an expert in growing revenue, so naturally he confronts these issues from a revenue perspective. For example, he advises some clients to "spend most of your money in the early days on sales and marketing instead of operations and legal issues because revenue solves many problems. In your early days, you should beg and borrow in order to scale." There are products and services that require serious IP protection for profitability, but Cameron believes that should never detract from a focus on sales.

Yet Cameron has not underestimated the importance of hiring the right people. He has developed tried-and-true knowledge on employee hiring. He says, "The old phrase, 'hire for attitude; train for skill,' is outdated. You can find people with both—people with an attitude for growth, but with some relevant practical experience and a skillset." In consulting with clients, Cameron expounds, "Always raise the bar. Any time you bring on a new employee, make sure they are better than the average of your group!"

Cameron offers key advice for aspiring entrepreneurs in a few areas. Primarily, he has a simple formula that he shares with every client and leader: "Focus multiplied by Faith multiplied by Effort equals Success." Faith is the confidence in your abilities and vision. "So someone who is only 50% dedicated in all three categories, focus, faith and effort, has a 12.5% chance of success. Even someone who is 80% dedicated in all categories has only a 51.2% chance of success," according to Cameron. He uses this to remind entrepreneurs that success is much more dependent on the process than the idea. He says, "The people who really make it eat, sleep, and breathe their product and employees. Most people think that it's because there is a great idea, but it is much more about the formula."

Critical Thinking Questions

1. Have you worked for a company or started your own? If so, what did you learn about running a company?

2. Do you agree with Cameron's claim that success depends more heavily on the work put in than it does the business idea?

3. What is the formula for success Cameron shares with business leaders? ●

Source: Cameron Herold (interview with author, January 2, 2019)

at least $200 per hour, but a simple startup may only need 1 or 2 hours of work to draw up the required documents. Some legal practices provide a free 1-hour consultation for new clients and/or payment plans for startups. Before you decide on a lawyer, do some research and compile a list of four or five possible candidates, their qualifications, and their rates. Like anything else worthwhile that you need to buy for your business, it pays to shop around.

Of course, there are a wide range of free resources regarding legal issues and documents available through the Internet to entrepreneurs looking for advice. However, be careful using these resources as they may not be strictly accurate or relevant to the type of business you are trying to set up. Using certain sites online (see Table 14.1) is a good way to gather research and identify the type of legal counsel you might need. Although legal advice can be expensive, the expense far outweighs the risk of attempting to do it all yourself with the help of free, potentially inaccurate information online.

Entrepreneurs can also receive legal support from clinics operated at law schools all over the United States. For example, second- and third-year law students at Santa Clara University in California provide affordable legal services to entrepreneurs looking to set up a business or for advice on the legal issues that may arise from running a business.[3] Apart from clinics, law school websites can also be useful for legal information, as they may provide certain forms or documentation for no charge. Washburn University of Law, in particular, provides a wide range of forms and information, which can be accessed for free.[4]

The United States government also provides resources for entrepreneurs. One such resource is the United States Patent and Trademark Office (USPTO), which provides a pro bono legal program to support entrepreneurs. The Small Business Administration also sponsors the SCORE association, a network of volunteer business counselors throughout the United States and its territories who are trained to serve as counselors, advisors, and

TABLE 14.1

Useful Online Legal Resources

United States Patent and Trademark Office	You can learn about patent and trademark basics, search existing patents, and register trademarks. https://www.uspto.gov/
Quora	A question-and-answer website on thousands of topics but also a good place to ask legal questions. There is an area devoted to startup law. https://www.quora.com/topic/Startup-Law-1
Docracy	Free, open-sourced site for contracts and other legal documents. Documents are free to download and edit. https://www.docracy.com/
U.S. Small Business Administration	A comprehensive site for entrepreneurs that offers free guides for legal compliance in starting and running a business. https://www.sba.gov/
Startup Company Lawyer	Good sources for answers to frequently asked legal questions such as "When do I need to incorporate a company?" and "What state should I incorporate in?" and "What type of entity should I form?" http://www.startupcompanylawyer.com/
LegalZoom[*]	Provides legal services to help start and run a business as well as file trademark applications. https://www.legalzoom.com/
NOLO[*]	Offers low-cost DIY kits for setting up business entities. https://www.nolo.com/
Rocket Lawyer[*]	Helps you draft legal documents to start a business, manage employees, or rent property. https://www.rocketlawyer.com/

*Note: The authors are not advocating or promoting any paid services. We have no relationship with any site promoting products for a fee.

mentors to aspiring entrepreneurs and business owners. These resources can be incredibly useful in finding out the different legal requirements for your venture. Armed with this information, you will have a better chance of finding the right legal help when the time comes.

The best lawyers not only will be able to provide legal counsel but will also add value for many years as your business grows.[5] They will have experience with early-stage startups, know the industry, and be up front with their fee structure. They may also have an impressive list of contacts, which can be very useful in connecting you with investors and advising you on fundraising. What's more, a good lawyer will be a person you can actually relate to. The best way to hire legal experts is the same way you would hire an employee. When the time comes, ask yourself, "Is this the right person to advise and represent my company?"

14.2 TYPES OF LEGAL STRUCTURES

>> **LO 14.2**   **Explain the most common types of legal structures available to startups.**

One of the most important choices entrepreneurs make when starting a business is choosing the right type of legal structure for their company. The type of structure affects the authorities you need to notify regarding your business, tax and other contributions you may have to pay, the records and documentation you will need to maintain, and how decisions are made about the business.

As legal structures vary from state to state (and country to country), it is essential that entrepreneurs do as much research as possible before deciding on a particular form of organization. Depending on your situation, there are several structures to choose from, and it is important to understand the differences among them. If, after researching the question, you are still not sure which one best suits your business, then paying a few hundred dollars for a legal consultation can be a worthwhile investment. Let's examine some of the most common legal structures used in the United States.

Sole Proprietorship

Sole proprietorship: a business owned by one person who has full exposure to its liabilities.

A **sole proprietorship** is a business owned by one person who has not formed a separate entity to run it. This is the simplest and most inexpensive form of legal structure for startups, but it is rarely the correct choice. It means the business is completely managed and controlled by you, the owner, and that you are entitled to all the profits your business makes. However, it also means you are personally exposed to all the risks and legal responsibilities or liabilities of the business. But many large organizations began as sole proprietorships; for example, eBay was a sole proprietorship owned by founder Pierre Omidyar for 3 years before he joined with other partners.[6]

The main reason sole proprietorship is the most common choice of business structures is that forming a sole proprietorship is quite simple. In many jurisdictions and industries, there is no legal filing at all to set yourself up as a business owner.[7] If your business is in an industry and/or a location where licenses or permits are necessary, you may just need to pay a nominal fee to obtain the right license or permit. For example, for a painting business you might need a home improvement contractor license; for any retail business you will likely need a sales tax permit. Because you and your business are treated as one entity, you have to file only one personal tax return outlining your income and expenses. (You do, however, have to use a separate form, Schedule C, to report your business income.)[8] The business's income is added to whatever other income you (and your spouse) may have and is taxed at your personal income tax rate after a 20% deduction is allowed.

However, as previously mentioned, you are also held personally liable for any debts the business incurs (see Figure 14.1). There can be quite a lot of pressure to running a sole proprietorship, especially when it comes to fulfilling all your financial obligations. For example, say you have borrowed money to run your business, but you lose a major customer, which leaves you unable to repay the loan. Or say an employee of yours is

FIGURE 14.1

The Sole Proprietor

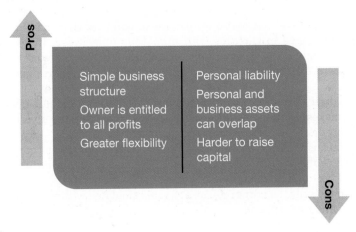

Pros

- Simple business structure
- Owner is entitled to all profits
- Greater flexibility

- Personal liability
- Personal and business assets can overlap
- Harder to raise capital

Cons

involved in an automobile accident while on the job and injures another driver; you, as sole proprietor, are fully responsible for dealing with the injured person's claims. Either of these scenarios could potentially mean having to sell personal assets such as your car, your investments, or even your house to raise the money. You could even be driven to personal bankruptcy. Some of the other business structures we will discuss provide at least a minimal level of protection against such personal losses.

General Partnership

A **general partnership** involves two or more people who have made a decision to comanage and share in the profits and losses of a business. Like a sole proprietorship, setting up a general partnership is relatively low cost and straightforward. As each partner reports profits and losses on individual tax returns rather than corporate returns, a process called pass-through taxation, taxes are also paid at your personal income tax rates (after the previously mentioned 20% deduction).

For example, say you and your business partner decide to open a café. To qualify for general partnership legal status, you and your partner must be involved in the business and contribute toward setting up and paying the costs of running the café. You and your partner will split the profits and losses between you.

Although partnership arrangements can be quite flexible, it is wise to have a formal agreement drafted by a legal expert to lay out the terms of the partnership. Typically, this agreement will cover the percentage of shares you are each entitled to, your individual rights and duties, and the consequences of one of you leaving the business for any reason.

Sharing the burden of running the business with someone else can be a great asset to a startup. However, like the sole proprietorship legal structure, in a general partnership each partner is still personally liable for the company's financial obligations. In a worst-case scenario, this means that if one partner is responsible for running the company into the ground, the other partner will still be liable. And if the offending partner cannot pay, the other partner would be liable for the full amount. Therefore, before entering into a general partnership it is essential that the partners know each other well and establish a high degree of trust.

General partnership: a business owned by two or more people who have made a decision to comanage and share in the profits and losses.

C Corporation

A **C corporation** (sometimes known as a "C-corp") is a separate legal entity created by the state government and owned by an unlimited number of shareholders. This means that the corporation, not the shareholders, is legally liable for its actions. The most money that shareholders can lose is their personal investment—the value of their stock.

C corporation: (sometimes known as a "C-corp")—a separate legal and taxable entity created by the state government and owned by an unlimited number of shareholders.

Another advantage to the C corporation is transferable ownership, which means it can issue shares of stock to investors in exchange for capital. In addition, because the corporation is a separate entity, it benefits from continuous existence, which means that it will still survive after the demise of its owners. This allows the corporation to plan for the future.

Many people believe that corporations are so complex that they are reserved for larger, more established businesses with numerous employees. In reality, however, corporations normally are not very time-consuming or expensive to set up. Many corporations are owned by only one or a few stockholders who elect themselves as directors and officers.

An alleged disadvantage is double taxation: The corporate profit is taxed twice—first on the profit it makes, and second, the shareholders are taxed on the dividends. However, in a startup, corporate profits are often paid out to the owners as additional compensation (which means that corporate tax is eliminated on nonexistent corporate profits). Otherwise these profits are often retained to fund the growth of the startup, thus eliminating any current tax on dividends (the sum of money paid to shareholders from company profits) and leaving only the corporate tax at a rate calculated without adding the income of stockholders and their spouses.

S Corporation

S corporation: (sometimes known as an "S-corp")—a type of corporation that is eligible for, and elects, special taxation status.

An **S corporation** (sometimes known as an "S-corp") is a corporation whose stockholders elect special treatment for income tax purposes. For all other purposes, it is identical to a C corporation. In order to qualify as an S-corp, the corporation must be a U.S. domestic corporation. In addition, it must have no more than 100 shareholders, who in most cases must be individual U.S. citizens or legal immigrants (not corporations, partnerships, or trusts), and all of whom must own only one class of common stock (ordinary shares).

Unlike the C-corp, the S-corp does not have to deal with double taxation, as there is only one level of tax to pay. Similar to a partnership, the income and losses are passed through to the company's shareholders' tax returns and taxed at the individual rates, after a 20% deduction. This is especially attractive for corporations expecting to lose money in the short term, as such losses will offset other income earned by shareholders, acting as a so-called "tax shelter." S-corps often consider a later switch to C-corp status because their growth may be limited by the restricted number and types of shareholders permitted. Another reason for switching to C-corp status is the fact that an S-corp's future retained earnings would be taxed to stockholders as so-called "phantom income"—earnings are taxed but not received by the individual.

Limited Liability Company

Limited liability company (LLC): a business structure that combines the taxation advantages of a partnership with the limited liability benefits of a corporation without being subject to the eligibility requirements of an S-corp.

A **limited liability company (LLC)** is a business structure that combines the pass-through taxation aspects of a partnership with the limited liability benefits of a corporation without being subject to the eligibility requirements of an S corporation.

This means that profits and losses are reported on individual tax returns in the same manner as other pass-through entities; therefore, double taxation does not apply, and there is potential tax sheltering from losses while personal assets are protected. Modern limited liability company statutes allow LLCs to have continuous existence, similar to corporations. And just as with partnerships and corporations, it is advisable for the LLC's owners (called "members") to enter into ownership agreements, often contained within an operating agreement that serves the combined purposes of bylaws and stockholder agreements in corporations. LLCs are rapidly replacing S corporations as the entity of choice for many startup businesses.

Limited Partnership and Limited Liability Partnership

There are a variety of other forms of business entity that may be used in certain circumstances. One example is the limited partnership (LP), a pass-through tax entity made up of two kinds of partners: general partners who manage the business but have personal exposure for its liabilities, and limited partners who are essentially silent investors but are protected from liability.

Recently, however, the LP has been largely replaced by the LLC. It acts as a pass-through entity, grants limited liability to *all* members, and does not prohibit any member from getting involved in management.

Another example is the limited liability partnership (LLP). This is essentially a general partnership that, in exchange for registering with the state and paying an annual fee, gets a form of limited liability for its partners. However, the partners are still not protected from the consequences of wrongful acts committed by themselves and, in some cases, by their employees. Generally, this form is popular only among firms of licensed professionals, such as lawyers and accountants, who want to avoid classifying their partners as employees of the business. This means that these employers do not have to comply with employment laws and regulations (such as mandatory or enforced retirement) with regard to their partners.

The principal types of legal structures we have described are summarized in Table 14.2.

Benefit Corporation

In Chapter 1, we mentioned a benefit corporation (or B-corp) as a form of organization certified by the nonprofit B Lab, which ensures that strict standards of social and environmental performance, accountability, and transparency are met. B Lab certification ensures that the for-profit company fulfills its social mission. It is available to businesses operating as any one of the business entities mentioned above (not just corporations).

In addition to the B Lab certification, many states have enacted statutes creating a new form of business entity also called a B or Benefit corporation that is not subject to the fiduciary obligations of other business corporations. Most business corporations must justify all their actions as contributing ultimately to increased shareholder wealth.[9]

On the contrary, a statutory B corporation declares in its charter one or more social benefit goals. This protects it and its managers from lawsuits from shareholders claiming that the company is spending more time or resources on social issues than on maximizing profit.

TABLE 14.2

Types of Legal Structures

BUSINESS ENTITY	STRUCTURE	LIABILITY	TAXATION	NOTES
Sole Proprietorship	One owner	Unlimited	Pass-through	
General Partnership	Two or more partners	Unlimited Joint and Several	Pass-through	
C Corporation	Stockholders, directors, officers	Limited	Taxable entity	Potential double tax on dividends
S Corporation	Stockholders, directors, officers	Limited	Pass-through	Subject to eligibility requirements
Limited Liability Company (LLC)	Members, optional board of managers	Limited	Pass-through	May elect to be taxable entity
Limited Partnership	General partners, limited partners	General partners: Unlimited Limited partners: Limited	Pass-through to all partners	Limited partners largely prohibited from management
Limited Liability Partnership (LLP)	Two or more partners	Limited with some restrictions	Pass-through	Generally used only for professional practices
Benefit Corporation (under corporate law)	Stockholders, directors, officers	Limited	May be either C-corp or S-corp, if eligible	Charter sets forth social purpose(s)

A statutory B corporation is similar to a corporation as it also has shareholders and employees. However, the main difference lies in the fact that managers in a statutory B corporation are held responsible for ensuring the right balance is met between pure profit and its declared social benefit goals.

Not-for-Profit Entities

Not-for-profit: a tax status granted to companies performing functions deemed by Congress to be socially desirable that exempts them from income tax and, in some cases, allows them to receive tax-deductible donations.

Not-for-profits are not technically a different form of business entity. **Not-for-profit** is a tax status available to corporations, LLCs, trusts, and other structures that meet specific criteria set out in the Internal Revenue Code.

All not-for-profits are exempt from income tax on their profits (so-called "surplus"), and some are also eligible to receive donations that are tax deductible to their donors. Only those companies described in Section 501(c) of the tax code are eligible; these include charitable organizations, business leagues, civic leagues, labor organizations, chambers of commerce, social clubs, fraternal organizations, cemetery companies, and the like.

Those also eligible to receive tax-deductible contributions are the smaller list of organizations in Section 501(c)(3), including religious, educational, scientific, and charitable institutions. One important condition applicable to all not-for-profits, however, is that none of the organization's earnings are permitted to benefit individuals. In other words, although not-for-profits can pay reasonable compensation to employees, they cannot have shareholders; all profit must be reinvested in the business and used for the organization's exempt purpose.

14.3 LEGAL MISTAKES MADE BY STARTUPS

>> **LO 14.3**   **Outline the most common legal errors made by startups.**

It is very common for entrepreneurs to make mistakes at the very beginning of their ventures.[10] Even the most successful entrepreneurs have fallen into legal traps in the early stages of setting up. As we mentioned, one of the best ways to avoid costly mistakes is by hiring the right legal counsel. Some entrepreneurs rely on friends and family who offer free advice or steep discounts. Although it is always useful to get input from people you know or through contacts, never let that be a substitute for seeking professional guidance from a lawyer experienced in startups and expert in the legal areas that are most relevant to your business.

As mentioned in the previous section, it is vital to choose the right business structure for your company. Choosing the wrong entity could incur higher taxes than necessary or expose you to significant personal liabilities. It is also important to be aware that business structures differ from state to state; setting up the wrong structure puts you at risk for financial penalties. In California and Nevada, for example, licensed professionals such as doctors, lawyers, architects, and accountants are legally permitted to form an LLP but are not allowed to operate as an LLC.

Keep in mind that experienced investors generally invest only in C corporations, so if you want to seek immediate external funding, you might be better off forming a C corporation rather than an LLC or an S-corp. However, if you don't plan to seek external financing until sometime down the road, be aware that it is normally relatively easy and inexpensive to convert to a C corporation from any of the pass-through entities.

It is essential that you enter into a formal written agreement with your cofounders early on that formalizes the terms of the business. This is necessary regardless of the form of entity you have chosen. It may be a partnership agreement in a general or limited partnership, a stockholder agreement in an S or C corporation, or an operating agreement in an LLC, but the purpose of the agreement is the same. Failing to enter into this agreement is almost certain to cause problems later on.

The Founders' Agreement

Founders' agreement: a clear agreement between founders on a number of key issues that their business might face.

In addition to formal agreements, entrepreneurs may also sign a shorter, less technical contract call a **founders' agreement**, which is a clear agreement between founders

TABLE 14.3

What Goes in a Founders' Agreement?

The Basics	• Name of cofounders • Name of the business • How long the agreement is valid for
The Business	• What business are you in? • What products do you offer? • What are your goals? • What are the company's values?
Roles and Responsibilities	• What is each founder responsible for? • What is the unique contribution of each? • What is each called (his or her title)? • How do decisions get made?
Ownership Breakdown	• How are you splitting the equity? • Is there a vesting schedule?
Salary and Compensation	• What's the baseline for all involved? • How can founders use company money? • Who approves investments or debts?
Termination	• What happens when a cofounder underperforms? • What happens when one wants to leave the business? • What happens if one of the founders dies?

Source: Prakash, P. (2019). Why a founders' agreement is important for every small business. *Fundera*. Retrieved from https://www.fundera.com/blog/founders-agreement

on a number of key issues that their business might face.[11] The founders' agreement usually comes before the formal written agreements and helps founders answer the tough questions before entering into legal contracts. Although the founders' agreement may not be legally binding, it provides a useful overview of how your cofounder relationships will work, how the business will be structured, and how you and your cofounders intend to tackle problems in the future. Table 14.3 summarizes the type of information that is commonly included in a founders' agreement. You can also check out https://www.pandadoc.com/founders-agreement-template/ for an example of a founders' agreement template.

It is also important to ensure you have the right vesting schedule in place to protect the other cofounders. **Vesting** is the concept of imposing equity forfeitures on cofounders over a certain period of time on a piecemeal basis should they not stay with the company. Without a formal vesting schedule in place, it is possible for a cofounder to walk away from the company at any time with a chunk of the equity, leaving the remaining cofounders working to increase the wealth of a noncontributing owner. A similar concern arises when including equity in a compensation package for an employee. Vesting is discussed in more depth later in this chapter.

In the next section, we explore the issue of intellectual property ownership, which can also cause legal complications if not handled correctly from the outset.

Vesting: the concept of imposing equity forfeitures on cofounders over a certain period of time on a piecemeal basis should they not stay with the company.

14.4 INTELLECTUAL PROPERTY (IP)

>> **LO 14.4**   **Define IP and how it affects entrepreneurs.**

Intellectual property (IP) is intangible personal property created by human intelligence, such as ideas, inventions, slogans, logos, and processes. IP law includes the copyright, trademark, trade secret, and patent protections for physical and nonphysical property that is the product of original thought and that can, in some sense, be owned. IP is a valuable asset for which entrepreneurs need to create an IP strategy that supports

Intellectual property (IP): intangible personal property created by human intelligence, such as ideas, inventions, slogans, logos, and processes.

Companies that depend on intellectual property

and evolves with the business. Intellectual property rights legally protect inventions.[12] IP is the backbone of innovation all over the world because it plays a significant role in economic growth and development.

Many startups are dependent on IP protection, regardless of industry or line of business; from manufacturing to tech enterprises to restaurants, IP protection is essential to the survival of small businesses. Without it, powerful companies like Amazon, Google, eBay, or Staples would never have gotten off the ground.[13]

Entrepreneurs and small businesses are becoming increasingly dependent on protecting their IP in order to bring their products and services to market. In fact, protecting IP has become more important to entrepreneurs than ever before.[14] The late Steve Jobs realized the importance of protecting IP early on: "From the earliest days at Apple, I realized that we thrived when we created intellectual property. If people copied or stole our software, we'd be out of business."[15]

IP is one of the most valuable assets for startups when it comes to transforming ideas and innovations into real market value. It is also one of the major assets that investors look for in a startup. A 2018 article in *Forbes* magazine asserted that out of 100 questions investors ask startups, 10 of them will relate to IP.[16] If the IP is usable and owned by the startup, investors will be more comfortable in investing, and it can increase the valuation of the new venture. Protecting your IP also prevents competitors from trying to copy your products and services.

However, IP law can be complex, confusing, and entirely misunderstood. In the flurry of setting up new ventures, many entrepreneurs neglect the issue of IP protection and fail to seek advice from experts. Yet, if the IP protection isn't in place, the whole venture can collapse.

Determining IP ownership is not straightforward. For instance, say you create IP for a venture while still employed at another company, or when you have just left a job. In many employment contracts and under the law of most jurisdictions, the rights to inventions that substantially relate to the employee's old job description belong to the company.[17] This means that your IP is owned by your former employer—not you. It is fundamental in the early stage of a startup that you seek legal advice from an IP attorney and review employee contracts and applicable law to determine whether there is anything that might prevent you from obtaining IP ownership.

Furthermore, a startup may use an independent contractor or a third party to help develop an innovation or trademark. Without a formal agreement in place, that third party may have a right to a portion of any IP that results from her contribution, even though she may have been paid to create it. Table 14.4 outlines some more resources for IP information.

Finally, be aware of the relationship between IP and hackathons—events where software and hardware developers intensively collaborate to generate new ideas and inventions. A number of popular innovations, such as the ideas for Twitter and GroupMe, arose from hackathons.

When organizations hold internal hackathons whose participants are their own employees, they automatically own the IP of whatever creative innovations arise. However, taking part in an external hackathon is not so clear-cut, especially if you are already an employee at a tech organization. Developing a proof-of-concept prototype product at a hackathon and then disclosing it could destroy any chance of patenting it in the future. Even worse, with so many people involved, it is not clear who can claim IP ownership of the innovation.[18] Similar issues can arise in the context of group projects in college classwork. In summary, it behooves you as an entrepreneur to educate yourself about IP and to seek legal guidance whenever appropriate.

TABLE 14.4

Resources for IP Information

U.S. Patent and Trademark Office	The site offers a wealth of information about patents, trademarks, and IP law and policy. https://www.uspto.gov/
U.S. Copyright Office	The authoritative source for information about copyright. https://www.copyright.gov/
World Intellectual Property Organization (WIPO)	An all-encompassing site to help navigate the world of copyright, patent, trademarks, and industrial designs. https://www.wipo.int/about-ip/en/
Managing Intellectual Property	A source of the latest news and updates on IP-related issues around the globe. https://www.managingip.com
LegalTemplates	Download free nondisclosure agreement template. https://legaltemplates.net
Pat2PDF	A web-based tool that finds patents and downloads them as PDFs. https://www.pat2pdf.org/
Inventors Digest	An online hub loaded with inventor and IP developer news, as well as IP trends and tips. Referred to as the magazine for "idea people." https://www.inventorsdigest.com/
PatentWizard	Designed by a patent attorney, the site helps you take the critical first steps toward filing an early provisional patent. https://www.neustelsoftware.com/patentwizard/

The Four Types of Intellectual Property

IP is an essential asset to a company as it provides opportunities for others to invest or collaborate and allows the founders to license, exchange, or even franchise their IP. In order to protect their IP, entrepreneurs need to be very knowledgeable about the different types during the early days of their business. There are four types of IP that fall under the protection of U.S. law: copyright, trademark, trade secrets, and patent.[19]

Many types of innovations have arisen from hackathons

epa european pressphoto agency b.v. / Alamy Stock Photo

Copyright

Copyright is a form of protection provided to the creators of original works in the areas of literature, music, drama, choreography, art, motion pictures, sound recordings, and architecture. It is important for tech entrepreneurs to be aware that computer code is classified as a literary work for purposes of copyright protection.[20] Another crucial thing to remember is that copyright does not protect ideas; it protects the tangible expression of the idea, such as written materials or recordings. Generally, U.S. copyright lasts for the duration of the author's life plus 70 years.

Copyright infringement cases can prove costly. For example, in 2018, music publisher Wixen brought a $1.6 billion lawsuit against Swedish music streaming platform Spotify for copyright infringement. Wixen alleged that Spotify had used thousands of songs from its artists without a proper license.[21] In the end, the parties agreed to settle the case for an undisclosed amount.

Copyright: a form of protection provided to the creators of original works in the areas of literature, music, drama, choreography, art, motion pictures, sound recordings, and architecture.

Some limited uses of copyrighted material are allowed without the permission of the copyright owner; this is called "fair use." Generally, it must be shown that the work is of a type meant to be copied, the use is for a noncommercial purpose, it constitutes only a small portion of the work, and/or it won't have a negative effect on the market for the work. Fair use is a "gray area" in U.S. law; there are no absolute rules or boundaries around what is and is not fair use.

Trademark and Service Mark

Trademark: any word, name, symbol, or device used in business to identify and promote a product. Its counterpart for service industries is the service mark.

Any word, name, symbol, or device used in business to identify and promote a product is a **trademark**; its counterpart for service industries is the service mark. Although the law affords some limited protection to trademarks without registration, a federally registered trademark generally lasts 10 years and, if still in use, can be renewed every 10 years thereafter. Trademarks and service marks are the legal basis of most branding campaigns.

Under Armour, the third-largest sports apparel company in the United States, has sued apparel company Armor & Glory, fishing apparel firm Salt Armour, shock-absorbing shorts retailer Ass Armor, and sports drink company Bodyarmor Superdrink for trademark infringement due to the use of "armour" or "armor" in their company names. In the case of Armor & Glory, the lawsuit stated, "Armor & Glory's name is likely to cause confusion, mistake and deception as to the two companies' connection, which would dilute the distinctiveness and further damage and irreparably injure Under Armour's brand." Armor & Glory has since changed its name to AG365.[22]

Trade Secret

Trade secret: confidential information that provides companies with a competitive edge and is not in the public domain, such as formulas, patterns, compilations, programs, devices, methods, techniques, or processes.

A **trade secret** is any confidential information that provides companies with a competitive edge and is not publicly known or accessible, such as formulas, patterns, customer lists, compilations, programs, devices, methods, techniques, or processes. Trade secrets last for as long as they remain secret; they are protected from theft under federal and state law. Companies can protect their trade secrets by having their employees and contractors sign nondisclosure, work-for-hire, and noncompete agreements or clauses. Famous examples of trade secrets allegedly include the recipe for Coca-Cola's beverages, KFC's ingredients, and the formula for WD-40.[23]

Patent

Patent: a grant of exclusive property rights on inventions through the U.S. and other governments.

A **patent** is a grant of property rights on inventions through the U.S. government. It excludes others from making, using, selling, or importing the invention without the patent owner's consent. In order to be granted a patent, the product or process must present a new or novel way of doing something, be nonobvious, or provide some sort of solution to a problem.

In the United States, the invention must not have been made public in any way before 1 year prior to the filing application date (the 1-year grace period does not exist in most other countries). Laws of nature, physical phenomena, mathematical equations, scientific theories, the human body or human genes, and abstract ideas cannot be patented. However, it is possible for a mobile app to be patented if it meets the criteria of the USPTO.

The duration of a patent is generally 20 years from the filing date of application, and it can be costly to file a patent. The Dog Umbrella and Leash (Patent No. 6,871,616) is an example of a novel and arguably useful invention, which is designed to keep a dog dry on a wet day.[24] It may not be a scientific breakthrough, but it qualifies for patenting.

It is important to note that although copyright protects artistic expression and trademark protects brand, there is no way to protect or patent an idea. Of course, the whole innovation must begin with an idea, but an idea must be turned into an invention before it can qualify for patenting.[25] This does not necessarily mean creating a prototype, but you must be able to meaningfully describe the invention, how it is made, and how others could use it. For example, the dog umbrella would have started out as an idea, but the inventors would have needed to flesh out the concept and create a sketch of it in order to explain its intended use.

MINDSHIFT

Patent Search

What is the coolest product that you own or would like to own? This can be anything from the stylus you may use on a tablet computer to a Frisbee you would play with in a park.

Your Mindshift task is to find the patent for this item. Use the "quick search" function on the United States Patent and Trademark Office website (http://patft.uspto.gov/). While you are searching, pay attention to the sections and content you see in patents: the abstract, the description, the patent's claim, and so on.

Once you have a good idea of what a patent looks like, try to find a patent that pertains to one of your own ideas.

Critical Thinking Questions

1. How easy or difficult was it to think of a cool product for your patent search? What factors came into play?

2. Did you find many other patents for products related to the one you were searching for?

3. What did you learn that surprised you or contradicted your expectations? ●

In summary, IP rights are the basis for every single business; without them, entrepreneurs would be less likely to risk bringing new innovations to the marketplace; investors would not invest; and customers would end up with less choice. Fewer businesses means more unemployment and less economic growth.[26] The importance of IP protection cannot be overestimated—this is why it can be so devastating to businesses of any size when IP is compromised.

Nondisclosure Agreement

One way for a startup to protect its IP is through a **nondisclosure agreement (NDA)** or confidentiality agreement, which is a legal contract that outlines confidential information shared by two or more parties.[27] This means that neither party has the right to share this information with competitors, the general public, or anyone else outside those involved in the agreement.

Adam Bornstein, founder of marketing and branding agency Pen Name Consulting, learned about the importance of a comprehensive NDA during the early stages of his business. Rather than spending the money on a lawyer to create a detailed NDA, Bornstein used a basic file he found online—which, as he was to find out, didn't cover the right information about his company, nor did it prevent people from sharing it. Bornstein said, "I discovered my error after a business meeting, where I mentioned a potential client and what they needed help with.[28] The person I was meeting with (who signed my weak NDA) then went after that client themselves—ultimately stealing work from me. There was nothing I could legally do. It probably cost me $30,000 in potential revenue."

Bornstein advises that all entrepreneurs should invest in a strong NDA for their business. As he found out, the cost associated with paying for an NDA that protects your company and ideas far outweighs the price of someone else poaching business from you.

As an entrepreneur, you will come across several situations where you will be required to share confidential information with another person or company. When should you ask them to sign an NDA? Usually, when you have something of value to share about your business and you want to make sure the other party does not steal it. Table 14.5 outlines some guidelines for when an NDA is required.

However, NDAs should not be used when you just have a half-baked idea with no resources. If you place an NDA in front of someone, especially an early investor, she may not sign it. As seasoned entrepreneur Gary Bizzo notes,

Investors are shrewd people, and many I work with won't sign an NDA for any reason.[31] One told me that by signing an NDA with one entrepreneur, it could

Nondisclosure agreement (NDA): a legal contract that outlines confidential information shared by two or more parties.

force him to abandon or severely limit him from accepting a really good idea down the road from another source. A couple of investors have actually told me they were already involved in ventures similar to the one presented to them and were surprised the entrepreneur had not done their due diligence.

Although you may not need an NDA in the very early stages of your business when you haven't really cemented your idea yet, when the right time comes, NDAs are essential to entrepreneurs, especially to protect against the growing threat of IP theft.

TABLE 14.5

Guidelines for When to Use an NDA

1. When talking to your competitors	In some situations, you will likely find yourself in conversation with your competitors. Without an NDA in place, they could copy your business and you could copy theirs. Signing a mutual nondisclosure agreement is the best way protect both parties.
2. When disclosing patent information	If you have invented something and patented the information, never disclose the patent information to outsiders until after the NDA has been signed by all parties involved.
3. When discussing trade secrets	Always use an NDA to protect your trade secrets, and even then, make sure that you only disclose them on a need-to-know basis with people you trust the most.[29]
4. When taking on a partner or an investor	When you're considering taking on a new partner or investor, make sure the information you share, such as business financials, personal information, and so on, is protected by an NDA. Bear in mind, however, that most investors will refuse to sign NDAs for startups in the very early stages.
5. When discussing the sale or licensing of a product or technology	When in discussions about licensing or selling your product, you need to make sure that the potential buyer does not disclose the details of your product or, indeed, any information about your company to a competitor. A signed NDA will protect all sensitive company information.
6. When employees have access to confidential and proprietary information	Without a strong NDA in place, there is nothing to stop your employees from accessing valuable information (client lists, supplier agreements) and using these data to set up a competing business after they have left your company. Make sure that every employee signs an NDA at the time of hire.
7. When sharing business information with a prospective buyer	If you are considering selling your business, then you will need to disclose every single detail of your financial and operations information to that acquiring company. An NDA will ensure all your information stays protected.[30]

14.5 GLOBAL IP THEFT

>> **LO 14.5** **Assess the global impact of IP theft.**

Any business that has a trademark, trade secret, patent, or copyright is dependent on IP protections. Consider this scenario: You have just launched your T-shirt business with a trademarked brand, and sales are really taking off. A few months later, you come across another website set up in a different country that is selling counterfeit versions of your T-shirts for a fraction of the price. You start losing sales, your brand becomes tainted, investors think twice about investing in your company, and your reputation becomes damaged—and all because someone has stolen your unique trademark and copied it for financial gain.

Millions of people all over the world violate IP laws every day. Recent statistics show that global online piracy is rife in the area of digital content such as movies, music, software, games, and e-books. More than half of global Internet users aged 16 to 24 have streamed music illegally, with the number highest in Spain and Brazil.[32] Ignoring copyright by downloading your favorite song from a peer-to-peer website without paying for it is similar to going into a music store and stealing a CD, yet people who would otherwise characterize themselves as law-abiding do it all the time. IP theft costs the United States between $225 and $600 billion every year, and it has a huge negative impact on legitimate businesses.[33]

Why does IP protection sometimes fail? IP rights are territorial, which means that although your rights may be protected in the United States, they are not necessarily protected in other countries. Countries such as the United States impose strict IP laws, but countries like China and India have a rich history of IP rights violations. However, according to the U.S. Chamber of Commerce's 2018 International IP Index, out of the 50 countries assessed for their commitment toward protecting IP, China ranks 25th—a marked improvement from where it ranked just a few years ago.[34]

RESEARCH AT WORK

Patent Trolls

U.S. patents have encouraged innovation, but they have also become subject to patent trolls—individuals or firms who own patents but have never actually produced useful products of their own.[35] Patent trolls issue legal complaints against alleged patent infringers in an effort to extract a licensing fee for the life of the patent. AT&T, Google, Verizon, Apple, and BlackBerry are only a few of the thousands of companies being sued every year by patent trolls. Yet, the biggest impact of patent trolls is on small startups. One survey of software startups reported that because of this issue, 41% were forced to either exit the business or change strategy.

According to a study by Santa Clara University professor Collen Chien, 50% of these patent trolls target companies that make an annual revenue of less than $10 million. They do this because they know that startups have limited resources and are more than likely to settle out of court, rather than risk a lengthy, costly suit.

Needless to say, the endless patent litigation has led to significant damage to innovation. Research findings have shown that it reduces VC investment in startups; it also decreases research and development, as the more research firms carry out, the more likely they are to be sued for patent infringement. Although the impact of patent trolls on startups may not look good, positive change is happening. The Patent Trial and Appeal Board, set up as a result of the America Invents Act of 2011, has rejected a number of bad patent claims. The process has been gradual, but it is certainly a step in the right direction.

"It probably hasn't made patent trolls go away, but it's changed their demands," noted Mark Lemley, a law professor at Stanford University. "Now they sue and ask for $50,000 rather than sue and ask for $1 million."

Even for startups with limited resources, there are protections against patent trolls. First, it is necessary to leverage a network. A good example of this is the LOT Network (www.lotnet.com), which is free for any company that makes less than $25 million per year. The mission of the LOT Network is to fight patent trolls. Companies that join LOT pledge that if they sell a patent to a company that's in the business of patent trolling, all LOT members will automatically get a free license to that patent. This ensures that patent licenses cannot solely fall into the hands of the patent troll. The LOT Network is growing in popularity, as evidenced by its membership of more than 300 companies, including Amazon, Slack, Canon, and Tesla.

Critical Thinking Questions

1. How would you protect your startup against patent trolls?

2. Do you think individuals or firms have the right to hold patents without producing any useful products of their own? Why or why not?

3. What are the effects of patent trolls on startups? ●

Sources:

Borenstein, N. (2018, April 10). More patent trolls are targeting startups. Here's what you can do. *Entrepreneur.* Retrieved from https://www.entrepreneur.com/article/310648

Chien, C. (2012, September 13). Startups and patent trolls. *Santa Clara Law Digital Commons.* Retrieved from https://digitalcommons.law.scu.edu/cgi/viewcontent.cgi?article=1554&context=facpubs

AP Photo/Nati Harnik

Thousands of counterfeit Rolex watches seized during an investigation in Philadelphia, PA

Nevertheless, there is still a strong market for counterfeit goods in the United States. In 2017, U.S. Customs and Border Protection officials seized almost 35,000 shipments containing counterfeit goods. Nike, Rolex, and Louis Vuitton are among the most counterfeited items.[36]

Major corporations can afford to wage massive legal battles and get compensation for IP theft, but how can a startup or a small business protect its IP in different territories? Entrepreneurs who are seeking to sell their innovations abroad must first conduct a search to ensure their company's name and brand can be used in the foreign country. Then, they must register for local IP ownership in that country or extend U.S. registrations to foreign countries at the beginning of the process. Also, it would be wise to seek proper IP counsel to protect IP rights abroad.

Finally, don't depend wholly on your patent for your business strategy. Building customer relationships, promoting your trademarked brand, providing quality products and services, and implementing rapid innovation will also help you defend your business against the effects of IP theft.

14.6 COMMON IP TRAPS

>> **LO 14.6**   **Describe the common IP traps experienced by entrepreneurs.**

IP can be a minefield, and many inventors fall into common traps that hamper the potential of exciting innovations.[37] Patenting can cost thousands of dollars, and some inventors find that they earn less than the cost of registering the patent. In a classic example, Robert Kearns, the inventor of the intermittent windshield wiper, sued car manufacturers Chrysler and Ford for copying the technology he had patented. Following a court battle that spanned decades, Kearns was finally granted a total of $40 million in compensation, which may sound like a lot, but it is nothing in comparison to what Kearns would have made if he had been credited with his invention from the beginning. Let's explore the common IP pitfalls and how entrepreneurs can avoid them.

Publicly Disclosing Your Innovation

You might be bursting to tell the world about your discoveries, but don't. Disclosing your new product or service in public before you have filed a patent application means that in most countries you will not be permitted to patent it at all. (We've mentioned

Patent Battle

A patent battle started between Apple and Samsung in 2011. After many years of countless court appearances, settlements, and appeals, the battle finally ended in 2018. At issue was the claim from Apple that Samsung copied the iPhone and infringed on many of Apple's patents.

For this Mindshift, play the role of a law student, dig into the Apple and Samsung dispute, and apply your learning from this chapter to answer the Critical Thinking Questions.

Critical Thinking Questions

1. What are the central IP issues associated with this case?

2. What, specifically, did Apple claim that Samsung copied?

3. What was Samsung's response?

4. How was the dispute finally resolved in 2018? ●

the 1-year grace period in the United States.) For example, a professor at Imperial College London, Robert Perneczky, discovered a protein that had the potential to significantly improve the chances of spotting the onset of Alzheimer's disease. However, Perneczky failed to qualify for a patent because of a detailed article he had written about his discovery that had been published in an academic journal. Because Perneczky's idea had been disclosed to the public, he was prevented from patenting it.

It is impractical to avoid disclosing anything at all about your discoveries, but try to refrain from revealing every single step. One way of protecting your IP that works in the United States is to file a provisional patent application before you make your idea public. This secures your rights as the inventor and gives you 12 months to complete the research and develop your idea into a working prototype. However, you will have to file a full patent application as soon as the 12 months are up; otherwise, the knowledge it holds will become publicly available. Also, your invention cannot have changed substantially from the date of the initial filing. Bear in mind that the United States has changed from being a "first to invent" to a "first to file" country, which means that if an inventor waits too long to file a patent application, he or she may lose out to someone else who is working on a similar innovation.

The intermittent windshield wiper, invented by Robert Kearns, who sued Chrysler and Ford for copying the idea

Failure to Protect Product and Processes

As Robert Kearns learned, it is easy for innovations to be copied by others. This is why it is important for entrepreneurs to ensure their products and processes are fully protected. Some inventors and other scientists protect their products by building unique markers into them; for example, a unique chemical "thumbprint" can reveal through a simple test whether someone else has copied their product. Another option some entrepreneurs use is to license their innovation to a larger organization that has all the tools already in place to protect and commercialize the invention. The inventor then profits through a stream of royalties.

Inability to Determine Originality

Entrepreneurs often build on existing products, tools, and techniques to create their innovations. However, the outcome must be considered both novel and useful if it is to qualify for IP protection. This means ensuring that products and services contain enough features to significantly improve the way they are used by others, with the intention of solving a problem. For example, when Jeffrey Percival and his research team developed the Star Tracker 5000—a low-cost device that determines a space rocket's altitude and tracks stars—the concern was it was not original enough, as it was mostly formed of standard components. To make his product more original, Percival added an algorithm that rapidly transmits digitized images. By enhancing the features of the product, Percival was able to license it to NASA for its space missions.

Failure to Assign Ownership

In the early stages of a startup, a number of people may be formally involved in contributing to the innovation process. This is why it is best to make formal agreements regarding IP ownership prior to any further development, in order to decide who owns and controls the innovation and who doesn't. Ownership can even vest in people you haven't paid, people you have paid but who haven't signed a formal assignment of ownership, or people who have otherwise made a valuable contribution to the innovation.

For example, InBae Yoon invented a medical device called the trocar, used to withdraw fluid from a body cavity, which he subsequently licensed to a larger organization.

However, Yoon had originally collaborated with electronics technician Young Jae Choi to create the product. Yoon failed to pay Choi for his work or obtain an assignment of his rights. Some years later, a competitor discovered the technician's involvement, amended the patent to assign him partial ownership, and won a court case to secure a separate licensing agreement with Choi to allow them to use the product. The same kinds of problems can arise with people who may have coauthored copyrighted material or helped to design a logo for a company's trademark.

Failure to Protect IP in Global Markets

As we mentioned earlier, IP rights are territorial, which means that although your rights may be protected in the United States, they are not necessarily protected in other countries. For example, in China, Apple Inc. lost a court battle with Chinese technology firm Proview International Holdings, which claimed it owned the iPad trademark in the Chinese market.[38] The case seriously threatened Apple's ability to sell the iPad in China. Apple finally agreed to pay $60 million in 2012 to settle the 2-year dispute.

Entrepreneurs hoping to sell in other territories need to get the right legal advice and carry out due diligence before even starting their business, in order to understand how to navigate any obstacles up front. Otherwise, they risk running into some major difficulties along the way.

14.7 HIRING EMPLOYEES

>> LO 14.7   Explain the legal requirements of hiring employees.

There may come a time when you need to hire some help when your business takes off. Yet there's more to the hiring process than interviewing and selecting the best person for the job. As an employer, you need to understand federal and state labor laws in order to protect both your business and your employees. In this section, we describe some of the regulatory steps you need to consider when hiring your first employee.[39]

Equal Employment Opportunity

Employers in the United States need to be aware that federal laws prohibit discriminating against employees on the basis of race, sex, creed, religion, color, national origin, or age. Workers with disabilities are also protected, though employers can refuse to hire on the basis of a disability if it prevents the worker from fulfilling job tasks. Some states forbid discrimination on the basis of sexual orientation.

Globally, the rules are not the same. For example, the global rights index provided by the International Trade Union Confederation (ITUC) shows that Austria, Finland, the Netherlands, Norway, and Uruguay score the highest for equality at work; however, the level of inequality in other countries is rising. The report showed that China, Belarus, Egypt, Colombia, and Saudi Arabia are among the worst in the world for equal opportunities and workers' rights.[40]

Employer Identification Number

Before you hire your first employee, make sure you get an employer identification number (EIN). You will need to use this on documents and tax returns for the IRS. It is also necessary when reporting employee information to state agencies. There is also a regulatory requirement to register your newly hired employee with your state directory within 20 days of the hire date. You can apply for the EIN online.

Unemployment and Workers' Compensation

Register with your state's labor department to pay state unemployment compensation taxes, which provide temporary relief to employees who lose their jobs. Depending on the size of your business, most states will require you to register for workers' compensation insurance to protect against any work-related injuries. (Some states make exceptions for very small businesses.)

ENTREPRENEURSHIP MEETS ETHICS

The Danger of Going on *Shark Tank*

Since 2009, a whole host of budding entrepreneurs have pitched to the business moguls on *Shark Tank* in the hope of receiving investment. Many of the contestants benefit from the exposure they receive from showcasing their ideas on such a popular show, but others have not fared so well. For instance, just 6 months after Nicki Radzley, cofounder of Doddle & Co., appeared on *Shark Tank* to introduce her colorful Pop pacifiers (the pacifiers pop closed when they hit the ground), she noticed several imitation products online. Radzley managed to persuade Amazon to take down some of the products, but she has not sought legal action against the imitators, as it would be a costly process for a new startup with only one full-time employee. Another *Shark Tank* contestant, Lani Lazzari, founder of skin-care line Simple Sugars, also discovered that someone online was mimicking her brand and even thanking customers for watching the show. Finally, entrepreneur Lori Cheek, who created online dating social network Cheek'd Inc., was accused of stealing the idea by a man who claimed that he had passed on information to his social worker, who had then told Cheek. During the lawsuit, Lori Cheek said that she had never met the man or his social worker before.[41]

It may not be illegal to steal an idea off a TV show, but is it ethical? One point of view is that the entrepreneurs have waived their rights to confidentiality by showcasing their ideas on a show that attracts millions of viewers. But is it fair that everyone who appears in public with a new idea is at risk of their idea being copied or stolen?

Many contestants have had many positive experiences on *Shark Tank*, but there is clearly a downside to being in the public eye. As Simple Sugars entrepreneur Lazzari said, "*Shark Tank* has been such a positive thing for us . . . but any time you get that much visibility for something, people see it and there are negative things that happen."

Critical Thinking Questions

1. Do you think it is ethical to steal or copy an idea from a TV show like *Shark Tank*? Why or why not?

2. How would you feel if you shared an idea on *Shark Tank* and someone else exploited that idea?

3. Do you think there should be laws to prevent people from stealing or copying ideas from TV shows? Why or why not? ●

Withholding Taxes

To comply with IRS regulations, you will need to withhold part of your employees' income and keep records of employment taxes for at least the most recent 4 years. You will need to report these wages and taxes every year. There may also be a requirement to withhold state income taxes, depending on the state in which your employees are located.

Employee Forms

Make sure you set up personnel files containing important documents for each employee that you hire. Each employee must fill out a W-4 form that lets you, as the employer, know how much money to withhold from their paychecks for federal tax purposes. You can ask employees to fill out this form every year if they wish to change the withholding amount. This form does not have to be filed with the IRS. The Form 1-9 is another form you need to complete within 3 days of hiring your new employee; this requires employers to verify the new employee's eligibility to work in the United States. In addition, you must file IRS Form 940 every year to report federal unemployment tax, which provides payment of unemployment compensation to employees who have lost their jobs.

Benefits

As an employer, you will need to decide what sorts of benefits you will provide your employees. The law requires you to pay and withhold Social Security taxes and an additional rate for Medicare and to pay for unemployment insurance. Businesses with more than 50 employees must also provide family and medical leave and health insurance. In a few states, employers must provide a certain number of paid sick days. You are not required by law to provide life insurance, retirement plans, or paid vacation leave, but by offering a competitive benefits package, you will have a better chance of attracting high-caliber employees. If you choose to provide these optional benefits, be aware that they are subject to many regulations; consultation with an accountant experienced in such benefits is a worthwhile investment.

Safety Measures

All employers have a responsibility to their employees to maintain a safe and healthy workplace environment. This means training employees to do their jobs safely, ensuring the workplace is free from hazards, maintaining safety records, and reporting any serious accidents at work to government administrators. You should also have provisions in place such as medical treatment and rehabilitation services to support employees who are injured on the job.

The key to complying with legal requirements is being organized. Maintaining payroll records, filing tax returns on time, keeping your employees informed, and ensuring you are up to speed with federal reporting requirements go a long way toward running an efficient business. Table 14.6 outlines 10 steps to setting up a payroll.

Hiring a Contractor or an Employee?

When hiring people, it is important to distinguish between contractors and employees.[42] Many startups and small businesses use independent contractors because of the advantages they bring. For example, it generally saves money to hire contractors because they don't require contributions toward health care, compensation insurance, or any other benefits. In addition, there can be cost-saving benefits when it comes to office space and equipment, as contractors will usually provide their own.

Furthermore, working with independent contractors gives employers greater flexibility in hiring and letting go of workers. For example, you could hire contractors for a specific project, and then let them go when the job is finished. Equally, if you do not like their work, you never have to see them again. There can also be valuable cost savings in hiring contractors who are experts in their field and are ready to hit the ground running, which means saving time and money on training.

TABLE 14.6

Ten Steps to Setting up a Payroll

1.	Get an Employer Identification Number (EIN)
2.	Find out whether you need state or local tax IDs
3.	Decide if you want an independent contractor or an employee
4.	Ensure new employees return a completed W-4 form
5.	Schedule pay periods to coordinate tax withholding for IRS
6.	Create a compensation plan for holiday, vacation, and leave
7.	Choose an in-house or external service for administering payroll
8.	Decide who will manage your payroll system
9.	Know which records must stay on file and for how long
10.	Report payroll taxes as needed on a quarterly and annual basis

Source: U.S. Small Business Administration. (n.d.). *Hire and manage employees.* Retrieved from https://www.sba.gov/business-guide/manage-your-business/hire-manage-employees

Independent contractors are not protected by the same laws as employees, which means there is less chance of dealing with the same legal claims that could be brought by employees. However, there are some disadvantages to hiring independent contractors. Because contractors have autonomy in what, when, and how they perform their job duties, you may feel you have less control over them. Also, independent contractors may be present for only a short period of time before leaving again, which might be disruptive to the other employees.

Finally, it is important to be aware that the classification of workers as independent contractors or employees is not your choice. The classification is dictated by the facts of the relationship. State and federal agencies are very strict on workers who are classified as contractors versus employees, and you may risk facing government audits as a result.

Misclassifying independent contractors and employees could have costly legal consequences. For example, if the individual you thought you were hiring as an independent contractor actually meets the legal definition of an employee, you may need to pay back wages, taxes, benefits, and anything else an employee would receive in your company—health insurance, retirement, and so on. Table 14.7 outlines some of the main differences between employees and contractors.

Whether the person you hire is a contractor or an employee depends on all of the factors listed above, but the most significant factor is the amount of control the employer has over the work being carried out.[43] For example, if you expect the person to show up at the same time every day and work a set period of hours, and you expect to closely oversee her duties, then you will have hired an employee rather than retained a contractor.

Compensating Employees

It is often the case that a startup's need for additional employees outstrips the company's ability to pay in cash. When faced with this resource constraint, entrepreneurs often come up with alternative ways to compensate employees, such as giving them flexible hours, additional days off, and small perks such as gift cards or a lunch paid for by the company.

TABLE 14.7

Differences Between Employees and Contractors

EMPLOYEE	CONTRACTOR
Duties are dictated or controlled by others	Decides what, when, and how duties are performed
Works solely for employer	Provides services to other clients
Uses tools or materials provided by employer	Supplies own tools or materials
Working hours set by employer	Sets own working hours
Tax, benefits, and pension paid by employer	Pays own tax, benefits, and pension
Expenses paid for by employer	Pays own expenses
Tasks must be performed by the employee	Can subcontract work to others
Employer provides annual and personal leave	Not provided with annual and personal leave
Paid regularly (weekly, monthly, etc.) as per employee contract	Provides an invoice when work is performed and the task is completed
Provided with training	Does not receive training

Source: "Hire a Contractor or an Employee." US Small Business Association https://www.sba.gov/content/hire-contractor-or-employee retrieved on August 2, 2015.

Compensation in the Form of Equity

Entrepreneurs often attempt to obtain services from employees and contractors in exchange for a share of the business. This raises two legal issues.

First, in the context of issuing shares to friends and family, issuance of shares to employees and contractors risks noncompliance with securities laws. Although the workers are not investing cash in the business, their time and labor is considered an investment under the law, triggering the protection of securities regulation. Therefore, just as much care must be paid to having the right processes in place when issuing shares to employees and contractors as when issuing shares to traditional investors.

Second, it is important to note that income tax is triggered any time an individual receives any form of property in exchange for performing services, not just when he or she is paid in cash. Therefore, the receipt of shares as compensation for work can result in an unexpected tax bill. This may not seem much of a problem in the early days of a startup when the shares may not be worth very much, but it could become an issue later on.

However, if the shares are subject to a vesting schedule, the problem becomes magnified as the tax may not apply until the shares have vested (when, it is hoped, they will have greatly increased in value). This same problem exists when founders' stock is made subject to a vesting schedule, since by doing so, you are tying the retention of stock to the performance of services. There are tax techniques available to mitigate, and in some cases eliminate, this unwelcome tax issue, so be sure to consult competent tax professionals before agreeing to pay compensation in the form of equity.

Unpaid Internships

The thought of receiving the services of enthusiastic young interns looking for work experience rather than financial compensation can be very attractive to the resource-constrained startup. However, bear in mind that such arrangements may be illegal. The Fair Labor Standards Act provides a minimum wage, overtime pay, and other protections to most workers. Putting an intern to work in your business might require compliance with these requirements. In 2018, the U.S. Department of Labor addressed the issue of unpaid interns and adopted a "primary beneficiary" test, allowing this practice if the benefits of the internship flow primarily to the intern and not to the employer. The Department of Labor has published a list of seven factors it will consider in determining the "primary beneficiary," including whether the internship is tied to the intern's formal education program and the extent to which the intern's work complements, rather than displaces, the work of paid employees.[44] ●

$SAGE edge™

Get the tools you need to sharpen your study skills. SAGE edge offers a robust online environment featuring an impressive array of free tools and resources.

- Access practice quizzes, eFlashcards, video, and multimedia at
  edge.sagepub.com/neckentrepreneurship2e

SUMMARY

14.1   Discuss how legal considerations can add value to entrepreneurial ventures.

Understanding the legal considerations applicable to the business is as important as understanding user needs. Taking legal considerations into account may add value to the firm. Whether it is a lawyer, free website content, or some form of legal expert, obtaining competent legal advice will certainly help improve the performance of the venture.

14.2   Explain the most common types of legal structures available to startups.

The most common types of legal structures are sole proprietorship, general partnership, C corporation, S corporation, limited liability company (LLC), limited partnership, limited liability partnership (LLP), and benefit corporation. In addition, most of these business structures can be run as a not-for-profit provided the company complies with IRS section 501(c).

14.3 Outline the most common legal errors made by startups.

Startups may make some common mistakes that could be expensive. The most common mistakes they make are in choosing the legal structure of the venture, not having a written agreement defining the many parameters of their relationship, and not paying close enough attention to drafting the right vesting schedules. To protect their business ideas, entrepreneurs can also sign a founders' agreement, which is a clear agreement between founders on a number of key issues that their business might face.

14.4 Define IP and how it affects entrepreneurs.

IP is intangible personal property created by human intelligence, as a result of creativity such as inventions, trade secrets, slogans, logos, and processes. The four main types of IP are copyright, trademark/service mark, trade secret, and patent. It behooves entrepreneurs to understand IP because startups are, by definition, innovative and likely to involve the creation of IP. One way for a startup to protect its IP is through a nondisclosure agreement (NDA) or confidentiality agreement, which is a legal contract that outlines confidential information shared by two or more parties.

14.5 Assess the global impact of IP theft.

Millions of people all over the world violate IP laws every day by ignoring copyright. IP theft costs the United States between $250 and $600 billion every year.

14.6 Describe the common IP traps experienced by entrepreneurs.

Entrepreneurs often make mistakes in the following areas:

- Public disclosure of an invention or innovation;
- Failure to protect products, processes, brands, and so on;
- Inability to determine originality;
- Failure to allocate ownership; and
- Failure to protect IP in global markets.

14.7 Explain the legal requirements of hiring employees.

Legal requirements related to hiring employees include registering employees with the state labor department, keeping records of employee tax history, preparing the appropriate legal documentation, and complying with safety regulations.

KEY TERMS

C corporation 359

Copyright 365

Founders' agreement 362

General partnership 359

Intellectual property (IP) 363

Limited liability company (LLC) 360

Nondisclosure agreement (NDA) 367

Not-for-profit 362

Patent 366

S corporation 360

Sole proprietorship 358

Trade secret 366

Trademark 366

Vesting 363

CASE STUDY

Matthew Vega-Sanz, cofounder, Lula

When he came to Babson College in early 2016, Matthew Vega-Sanz did not want to start his own company; he wanted to go to Wall Street instead. He started a student consulting firm with his brother and two of his best friends. It was a branch of one of the biggest student consultancy organizations in the world, 180 Degrees Consulting. Through this consulting experience, Matthew got the chance to work with tech companies and started to think to himself, "Wow! Startups are cool." Two years later, Matthew found himself dropping out of Babson because his own startup, Lula, was growing and he couldn't do college and entrepreneurship at the same time. The business was getting too big.

During a crisp spring evening in 2016, Matthew and his brother were craving pizza. "We didn't want Domino's; we were sick of it already and none of the Papa John's around would deliver. I tried calling them and bribing them but none of them would deliver to Babson," Matthew laughed. When he realized that Uber would charge him $30 to deliver an $8 pizza, he decided to stick with Domino's. While waiting for his pizza to be delivered, Matthew walked outside and saw the parking lot filled to capacity and thought, "Wouldn't it be cool if I could take one of these cars and go pick up the food?" The idea of Lula was born.

Lula is a first of its kind peer-to-peer car sharing platform where college students can rent out cars from their peers and others registered on the platform. While companies like Turo focus on drivers above the age of 25, Lula targets college students. When the brothers look back, the story of its origins is quite entertaining.

After the infamous pizza spark, Matthew mentioned the idea to friends, who liked it but didn't inspire him to take action. A few months later, Matthew's brother, Michael, was hanging out in his dorm and told Matthew about Babson's BETA Challenge. BETA stands for Babson Entrepreneurial Thought and Action. It is an action-based challenge in which new ideas are judged on actions taken and milestones achieved between the semi-final stage and final stage of the competition.[45] Even though the application deadline had passed, the link was still live and the brothers decided to apply. Matthew recalls, "I go to Michael's room and we draft up probably the world's worst executive summary and submitted it. I had forgotten about it and was already planning to do an internship in a company like J. P. Morgan. Around the first week of April 2016, I'm walking out of the library and one of my friends comes up to congratulate me on getting through to the semi-finals."

The brother duo had the only business idea in the competition that had not generated any revenue. They lost the competition that year; however, they received a lot of positive feedback and concluded they "were on to something." Michael asked Matthew if he was interested in working on the concept of Lula over the summer break. That summer they raised some seed money, started developing the app, and ultimately launched a pilot in early 2018. The pilot was 8 weeks long and targeted Babson and a few other campuses around Babson. The conclusion? Users liked the app! There was customer validation.

The positive feedback and early traction from the pilot helped the brothers raise $620,000 to develop a newer version of the Lula app. They launched the app in September 2018 and were aiming to be in 30 campuses in five states and have about 90 registered on the platform. However, within the first week of the launch, they were in 200 campuses and surpassed all projections that they had for Year 1. Within the first 2 weeks of the launch, they were listed in the top 100 apps in the iOS App Store and even getting ahead of Zipcar in the ranking. As Matthew explained, "The only marketing we were doing was a couple of $100-a-day on Instagram. It was mostly word of mouth. We realized that kids need cars and there was not really much competition since car rental companies prefer people aged 25 and up." Today Lula is in more than 400 campuses across all 50 states in the United States.

Matthew credits a lot to his advisors in the extended Babson network. Lula won the SoFi Entrepreneur Pitch Competition at Babson and went to California to be part of the program. There they developed a relationship with the founder of SoFi, the leading provider of student loan refinancing, who then came on board as an advisor and, later on, an investor in the company. Matthew and his brother were also able to leverage the services of the law firm that visited the Babson campus on a regular basis, and this free legal advice saved the brothers and the company "a bunch of money."

Lula, as a company, had to resolve significant challenges if the business was going to truly start. Their greatest challenge was insurance. The brothers were at a legal crossroad: The app was ready to launch, but they couldn't launch the app because they didn't have insurance. If they didn't have insurance, they could not legally operate.

Initially, Matthew and Michael thought that they would just need regular car insurance, but they quickly realized that companies like Geico or Progressive did not want to insure a startup—especially one that caters to young, high-risk drivers. Insurance experts suggest they speak to brokers that focus on specialty insurance lines.[46] "We were rejected by over 40 insurance brokers over 16 months because nobody wanted to listen to a company that wanted to provide rental services to people below the age of 25," said Matthew. Although some companies provided rentals to people ages 21 to 24 at a premium, asking for insurance for students 3 years younger than 21 sounded "crazy" to insurance companies. Insurance experts advised the brothers to stop working on Lula because it was not possible.

It was a frustrating period for the startup. As Matthew recollected, "Even the companies that were willing to listen to us were only providing us insurance in case the *company* got sued and not insurance on physical damage to the car. We were in legal battles because insurance companies would try to use confusing language, hoping we would not catch onto the fact that they weren't going to give us physical protection. We had to call our lawyers because what they were stating in the email was completely different than what was offered in the policy. Not just that, they were pushing us to sign, saying they wouldn't accept the deal otherwise. Luckily, we were able to catch them." In other words, Matthew quickly learned that the insurance they were being sold only protected Lula in the case of a lawsuit.

To resolve the ongoing insurance battle, Matthew decided to treat the insurance companies as their investors and made a pitch deck for them. He sent out emails saying that if they would invest in and work with Lula, they could potentially generate $55 million in revenue over the next 5 years. Within 2 weeks, they got positive responses from insurance companies and three firm offers. "The first insurance company to bite gave us probably the worst insurance coverage. If I was a student and knew what the insurance policy covered, I would not rent a car. We basically had no protection. Thankfully, we didn't have any crashes and we took this data to other insurance companies showing that 18-year-olds aren't as bad they thought." Lula is now partnering with the same insurance company that works with Lyft and Airbnb, with a multimillion-dollar protection policy. They now have 20 times the coverage for half the price. The major hurdle to the successful startup of Lula was overcome.

Other issues arose. One of Lula's competitors, Getaround, had filed for a patent on the peer-to-peer car-sharing model. The patent was loosely based on renting a car through a mobile device, and if that patent had been granted, it would have killed Lula as a business. Because Getaround was a heavily funded company, potential investors in Lula were scared of the potential patent being a huge roadblock. The Getaround patent was rejected because it was too general, which opened up investment doors for Lula.

Lula encountered pushback by college campus administrators who wanted Lula to operate on college campuses only after getting official permission from the university. Matthew believes that this was because of their previous interactions with companies like Zipcar that needed to rent a parking spot at the college. Matt explained, "Lula, unlike Zipcar, was a peer-to-peer model that allowed anybody to download and rent the car. When the college administrators asked us how they got parking spots on campus, we explained that the students that already had a parking space were renting their cars out. We also explained that the Lula service was similar to Uber or Lyft and they didn't need permission to operate on campus."

Matthew learned that raising money isn't as easy and glamorous as it seems on shows like *Shark Tank*. "Only 3–5% of startups ever get funding. There are hundreds of companies trying to get funding, and getting funding on an average takes around 6 months. What is not portrayed in movies (or on *Shark Tank*) is how it is a full-time job in itself and how much time it takes away from running the business." The journey so far has also taken a toll on Matthew's personal life. His parents hate that he and his brother are barely home, and he has lost a bunch of friends because of not having the time to spend with them. However, Matthew is excited about where Lula can go as a company.

Matthew's advice to aspiring entrepreneurs is that "When you're starting a company, listen to who your customer is going to be. When we started, we thought investors such as venture capitalists knew all this stuff, but at the end of the day they don't know nearly as much as you think they do. We had parents, professors, and investors telling us that there wasn't a need for this or that this wasn't a very good idea. So many people, who we thought were credible, gave us what we can call, in hindsight, bad advice. But every time we spoke to our target demographic, college students, they told us, 'Yes, there is a need for this!' So, my advice is don't launch a business unless you have random people across the target demographic telling you they need this."

Critical Thinking Questions

1. With the early legal challenges faced by Lula, what do you think kept the founders pushing forward?

2. Where do you think Lula will be 5 years from now? It's early in the life of the startup; would you invest today?

3. Look up the status of the company today. Are you surprised? Why or why not?

Source: Matthew Vega-Sanz (interview with Babson MBA graduate assistant Gaurav Khemka, November 30, 2018)

15

Engaging Customers Through Marketing

"The best marketing doesn't feel like marketing."

—Tom Fishburne

Chapter Outline

15.1 What Is Entrepreneurial Marketing?

15.2 The Basic Principles of Marketing

15.3 Building a Brand

15.4 Entrepreneurial Marketing

15.5 Creating Your Personal Brand

Learning Objectives

15.1 Discuss entrepreneurial marketing and explain how it is different from traditional marketing.

15.2 Explain the principles of marketing and how they apply to new ventures.

15.3 Describe branding and the importance of building a brand.

15.4 Discuss the different types of marketing tools available to entrepreneurs.

15.5 Practice marketing yourself.

15.1 WHAT IS ENTREPRENEURIAL MARKETING?

>> LO 15.1 Discuss entrepreneurial marketing and explain how it is different from traditional marketing.

Not too long ago, there were only three main ways to draw attention to your product or service: Invest in expensive advertising, persuade the mainstream media to tell everyone about you and your company, or hire dozens of salespeople to try and attract new customers. But times have changed and the old rules no longer apply. Thanks to technology, there is a new form of marketing on the scene that is available to any entrepreneur. **Entrepreneurial marketing** is a set of processes adopted by entrepreneurs based on new and unconventional marketing practices to gain traction and attention in competitive markets.[1]

Most entrepreneurs suffer constraints associated with money, people, and time, but the good news is that entrepreneurial marketing actually requires fewer resources. Just a few years ago, traditional marketers suggested that depending on word-of-mouth was a risky strategy and that you needed to spend lots of money to control and manage the message. Today, word-of-mouth is called "social media marketing," and if one person says something about your business or product, thousands, if not millions, hear about it almost instantaneously. If you want traditional marketing, take a marketing class. If you want to learn more about entrepreneurial marketing, stay right here!

Entrepreneurial marketing today is not about chasing sales; it's about chasing reputation, credibility, and buzz. The sales then follow. Methods for building reputation, credibility, and buzz have moved mostly online. The Internet has changed the rules of marketing.

How Entrepreneurial Marketing Is Different

Marketing today is really about proving to customers that you can solve their problem or fulfill a need they have. It's about delivering a clear message in a very noisy marketplace. It's about storytelling, building community through social media, content, and interactivity.[2] Furthermore, with so much information available through websites, reviews, and social channels, the buyer is in more control than ever. Marketing is more challenging for all businesses, so you can imagine it's even a bigger challenge for a startup that no one has ever heard of. This is why entrepreneurial marketing is not traditional marketing. Table 15.1 explains the differences between traditional marketing and entrepreneurial marketing.

Innovation, risk taking, resourcefulness, value creation, and proactivity are some of the main features of entrepreneurial marketing. For the entrepreneur, marketing and sales are not separate units. Until there is enough traction and enough customers, marketing and sales are very much about finding, acquiring, and keeping customers. Entrepreneurial marketing focuses on building trust, finding out customer preferences,

Entrepreneurial marketing: a set of processes adopted by entrepreneurs based on new and unconventional marketing practices in order to gain traction in competitive markets.

Master the content at
edge.sagepub.com/
neckentrepreneurship2e

TABLE 15.1

Traditional Marketing Versus Entrepreneurial Marketing

TRADITIONAL MARKETING	ENTREPRENEURIAL MARKETING
• Big cash investment • Main focus is on the product • Goal is to maximize profit • Short-term relationship with customer • Delivers marketing message as a monologue • Sales focus through interruption and coercion • Reaches the masses • Intermittent communication • Uses advertising to communicate to customers	• Investment of time, energy, creativity, commitment • Main focus is on the customer • Goal is to meet and satisfy customer needs • Long-term interactive relationship with customer • Delivers marketing message as a dialogue • Relationship-focused through content and participation • Reaches underserved, niche markets • 24/7 communications • Communicates directly with customers

and creating ongoing value. It also provides the entrepreneur with the opportunity to highlight the company's strengths while showcasing the different ways the product adds value.

Unlike traditional marketing, which is mostly centered on the product and how it can make money, entrepreneurial marketing requires an interactive approach. Entrepreneurs create a dialogue and build long-term relationships, adapting the business to meet their customers' needs. To paraphrase Seth Godin, the goal is not to find customers for your products, but to find products for your customers.[3]

To illustrate this point further, think of the Internet as a city and social media as a cocktail party. If you were at a cocktail party, would you do any of the following?

- March into the party filled with a mix of people you do and do not know, and shout "BUY MY PRODUCT!"

- Ask people for a business card before you agree to speak with them

- Try to get around to everyone in the room, rather than having fewer but higher-quality conversations

- Talk over people rather than listening to what they have to say

- Provide valuable information solely on the basis of getting something tangible in return

- Avoid cocktail parties altogether because this type of social interaction makes you feel uncomfortable

The point is that people tend to do business with people they like, and when someone likes you, he or she is keen to introduce you to others. The same concept applies to social media. It is the place where people gather to exchange information and discuss things they are interested in. Making yourself likeable by interacting with your customers directly and providing them with important information takes you one step closer to building lasting relationships and making valuable business connections.

Maine-based surfboard manufacturer Grain Surfboards is an excellent example of a company that does a great job engaging its customers. It applies boatbuilding techniques to make hollow, wooden, eco-friendly boards. Not only does the website share the history of wooden board building, but it provides details of how the boards are made—something that most companies are wary of for fear competitors will steal their ideas. However, sharing information to educate is one of the best ways to build customer loyalty and grow your business. In addition to selling surfboards, the company offers workshops where you can build your own surfboard and regularly shares content and images on Facebook and Instagram. Equally delighted with the high level of engagement, Grain Surfboards'

Charlie Regan, Nerds on Site

Photo courtesy of Charlie Regan

Charlie Regan, CEO of Nerds on Site

Charlie Regan is an owner and the CEO (capability expansion orchestrator) of Nerds on Site, a technology solutions company headquartered in London, Ontario. Established in 1995 by a pair of self-proclaimed "nerds" (John and David), Nerds on Site expanded rapidly in the local London, Ontario region. Initially, the problem to solve was a simple one: Computers were too bulky for it to make sense for people to shuttle them into a repair shop, yet people did it because they didn't have other choices. Large companies can afford to have departments devoted to remedying issues, but what about a small to medium-sized company? Making the repair person mobile was the idea that led to Nerds on Site. Today, Nerds on Site has franchise locations in more than 10 countries, including South Africa, UK, Australia, Bolivia, and Mexico, and has serviced more than 100,000 clients. Furthermore, it has a client satisfaction rating of 96.5%.

Nerds on Site is a global brand, but they operate the entire company with fewer than 15 full-time employees. They manage this thanks to their constantly improving franchise tools and back-end support for each of their "Nerds." Nerds on Site corporate headquarters functions as a partner to each of their Nerds on Site franchisees. Each Nerd is supported by the corporate infrastructure but is empowered to grow and build at their own pace.

This strategy is part of Charlie's vision to support and grow as many small and medium-sized enterprises (SMEs) as he can. Charlie wants Nerds on Site to be the best franchise partner possible in order for the brand to grow and the SME model to spread.

All Nerds are private franchisees, which allows individual franchise owners to sell and market services on their own, with their own creative capital behind it. "They are marketing themselves and their talents," Charlie says, "and when clients ask where the corporate office is, our Nerds can point to their cars and say 'that is my world headquarters right there.'" The franchise model allows Nerds to maximize their creativity as they are only responsible to themselves and their own local client base. "You need to market your business better than anyone else and to do that, you have to believe in it more than anyone else."

Nerds on Site operates a bit differently from most franchises. Charlie believes in letting Nerds control their own marketing, whereas most franchisors are all about consistency—consistency in messaging, consistency in approach, consistency in design, and consistency in types of advertising used—because franchisors are trying to create a brand, and strong brands are built on repetitive and consistent messaging. But, perhaps Charlie has cracked the code by allowing his franchisees a bit more freedom. The Nerds are more likely to be able to tell a personal story, build authentic relationships with clients, and think and act more entrepreneurially.

Charlie wants there to be more startups, with people taking more risks creating more impactful organizations worldwide: "Just try. You didn't learn how to walk by understanding the locomotion of muscles . . . you fell, bumped into sharp objects, and you learned how to walk by doing." He wants as many people as possible to be entrepreneurs, and he thinks everyone can own small businesses that serve specific needs.

Critical Thinking Questions

1. What was the "problem" that small and medium-sized companies faced that led to the creation of Nerds on Site?

2. What is unique about Nerds on Site's marketing strategy at both the corporate and franchisee level?

3. Why does Charlie want more SMEs? ●

Source: Charlie Regan (interview with the author, August 30, 2018)

Wooden surfboard

fans also help spread the company's ideas through their own social media, which has helped to cement its number one position in the marketplace. Thanks to its innovative and entrepreneurial approach to marketing, Grain Surfboards has achieved something that would have been considered impossible in the past: a way to reach its buyers directly without investing in expensive ads, hiring teams of salespeople, or begging the media to showcase the company.

Entrepreneurial marketing tools are not just reserved for entrepreneurs; more and more large, established companies are using the same tools in different ways to draw attention to their products. Although these industry giants may have a bigger budget and enormous resources, that should not stop new entrepreneurs from waging their own successful campaigns. Entrepreneurial marketing tools level the playing field: With a bit of knowledge, imagination, and ingenuity, entrepreneurs can make their products and services be heard and seen in very noisy marketplaces.

15.2 THE BASIC PRINCIPLES OF MARKETING

>> **LO 15.2** **Explain the principles of marketing and how they apply to new ventures.**

The rules may have changed, but the traditional principles of marketing still hold some value, and it's important to know them.[4] **Marketing** for entrepreneurs still involves showing how a product meets customer needs, pricing the products in a way that accurately represents the value perceived by the customer, promoting products in innovative ways to reach customers, implementing delivery of the products, and maintaining the relationship with the customer even after the sale is made.[5]

Getting all these elements to balance is tricky. It requires a lot of research and commitment to ensure your product is in line with your marketing vision. This is why it helps to use an established marketing framework to help develop your marketing strategy.

The basic principles of marketing are grounded in the **marketing mix**, a framework that helps define the brand and differentiate it from the competition. This framework helps companies crystalize their offering and how they intend to take it to market.

The marketing mix is made up of four main elements, known as the 4 Ps: product, price, promotion, and place (see Figure 15.1). It is important to be familiar with the 4 Ps, as they are still relevant to entrepreneurs with limited resources, but do bear in mind that they don't apply as well to entrepreneurial marketing as they do to traditional marketing. Each of the 4 Ps should be considered in relation to the others, in order to build the best overall marketing strategy for your offering.

The **product** is anything tangible or intangible (such as a service) offered by the company. This includes the features, the brand, how it meets customer needs, how and where it will be used, and how it stands out from competitors. A good way of assessing your product is to look at it objectively—as if you were someone seeing it for the first time. Then ask yourself some critical questions, such as, "Is this product or service suitable for my target market?" and "Is this something today's customers will want or need?" and "How can I market this product better than my competitors?" By repeatedly asking these questions, you will have a better understanding of your product or service and how it fits into the marketplace.

The **price** covers the amount that the customer is expected to pay for the product, its perceived value, and the degree to which the price can be raised or lowered depending on market demand and how competitors price rival products. Again, get into the habit of continually examining the pricing structure of your products and services to ensure it is appropriate for your target market. Depending on changes in the market, you may need

Marketing: a method of putting the right product in the right place, at the right price, at the right time.

Marketing mix: the combination of product, price, promotion, and placement of what a company is offereing.

Product: anything tangible or intangible (such as a service) offered by the company.

Price: the amount that the customer is expected to pay for the product.

FIGURE 15.1

Elements of the Marketing Mix

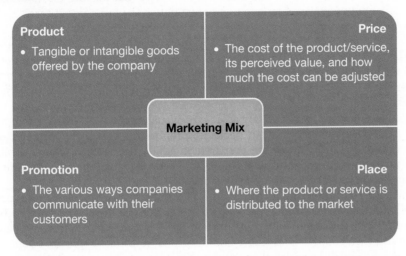

to raise or lower your price. Make a point of frequently examining competitors' pricing in order to price your products accordingly.

The third element of the marketing mix is **promotion**: all the ways in which companies tell their customers about their offering. This may involve advertising online, through social networking, direct mail, in the press, or even on TV if you have the budget. It also includes public relations such as being featured in blogs, newspapers, magazines—all free aspects of promotion. Both large and small companies need to continually experiment with finding ways to promote their products and services in order to find out what works and what doesn't. A promotional tactic that works one day may not work the next, so continuous development of new strategies is essential to retaining and increasing your target customer base.

Finally, **place** is where the product is actually distributed to your target market: trade fairs, retail stores, catalogs, mail order, online, and so forth. You can always revisit where you sell your product. For example, if you're selling retail products, you might start off selling online and then also decide to rent a retail space in order to make your company more visible to your target market. Ask yourself where else you could sell your products and what changes you need to make in order to reach your target market. Wherever you choose to sell, it is essential that your customers receive the best buying information on your product or service to help them make a buying decision.

Any type of marketing requires a discussion of who the customer is and how you are going to reach them; therefore, it is a good idea to use the 4 Ps framework to evaluate the strength and completeness of your marketing approach. Important questions can be answered using the 4 Ps framework:

- What are the benefits and features of my product? (Product)

- What is the value of my offering, and what are customers willing to pay? (Price)

- How will they know my business exists? (Promotion)

- How will the customers be reached? Where will they buy my product or service? (Place)

The marketing mix is constantly changing; you don't simply develop it and move on. By continually reviewing and tweaking your marketing mix, you will be better able to adjust to an ever-changing competitive environment.

Although the 4 Ps model is arguably the most recognized, newer marketing models have been developed to enhance the traditional model. Some of them extend

Promotion: all the ways in which companies tell their customers about their offering.

Place: where the product is actually distributed to your target market; for example, trade fairs, retail stores, catalogs, mail order, online.

People: the people who are responsible for every aspect of sales and marketing.

Packaging: every single visual element of the external appearance of an offering, as viewed through the eyes of your customer.

Positioning: a marketing strategy that focuses on how your customers think or talk about your product and company relative to your competitors.

the 4 Ps to 7 Ps, including **people**, which refers to the people responsible for every aspect of sales and marketing; **packaging**, which is a process that explores every single visual element of the external appearance of an offering through the eyes of your customer; and **positioning**, which is a marketing strategy that focuses on how customers think or talk about your product and company relative to your competitors.[6]

Your people are an important part of the marketing mix and the marketing strategy. They are responsible for enforcing every aspect of your sales and marketing activities. Hiring the right people with the right skills and abilities to market your products effectively is at the core of any marketing strategy. Often, in the early days of a startup the entrepreneur is wearing many hats and is playing the role of chief marketing officer and salesperson.

It is also important to objectively assess the visual element of the packaging of your product or service. Remember, your packaging represents you and your company, and first impressions count. Always be prepared to adjust elements of your packaging to encourage potential buyers to buy your product. Packaging is also an important part of branding, which we will discuss in the next section.

Positioning is something that should be at the forefront of every entrepreneur's mind. What are people saying about you, your company, and your product when you're not present? What are the words that people use about you to describe you and your offerings to other people? Knowing what other people think of you and your product determines the extent to which they will buy from you and how much they are willing to pay. Be vigilant in monitoring what other people think about you, especially on social media, and be sure to make the changes you need to enhance interaction with your target customer because positioning is at the heart of branding.

15.3 BUILDING A BRAND

>> LO 15.3   Describe branding and the importance of building a brand.

Branding: the process of creating a name, term, design, symbol, or any other feature that identifies a product or service and differentiates it from others.

Branding is the process of creating a name, term, design, symbol, or any other feature that identifies a product or service and differentiates it from others. Your brand is a promise to your customers, letting them know what they can expect from your offering and how it differentiates you from among your competitors. The face of your brand is your logo, which should also be integrated into your website, packaging, and promotional materials to communicate your brand message. People are more likely to invest in brands that are trustworthy, are worth spending money on, are fashionable, are adept at meeting their needs, and that they have an emotional connection to.

Brand strategy: a long-term plan to develop a successful brand; it involves how you plan to communicate your brand messages to your target customers.

A **brand strategy** is a long-term plan to develop a successful brand. It involves how you plan to communicate your brand messages to your target customers. This brand message can be channeled through your advertising, distribution, and packaging.

Two of the most classic and powerful brands are Coca-Cola, which has managed to differentiate itself from other sodas through its consistent strategic branding, and Nike, which involves famous athletes as part of its branding strategy, encouraging people to buy its products through the transfer of the emotional attachment they may feel for these star athletes. Over the years, both of these brands have evolved their branding strategies to appeal to generations of customers. See Figure 15.2 for the world's 10 most powerful brands.

While there isn't one "right" way to guarantee brand success, you can start defining the brand you would like for your company by answering the following questions:

- What is the primary goal of your company?
- What are the best features and benefits of your products or services?
- What are your customers and prospective clients already saying about you and your company?
- What sorts of qualities do you want them to associate with your company?

Your responses will help you to create a brand name that resonates with your target customers.

FIGURE 15.2

Top 10 Most Powerful Brands in the World

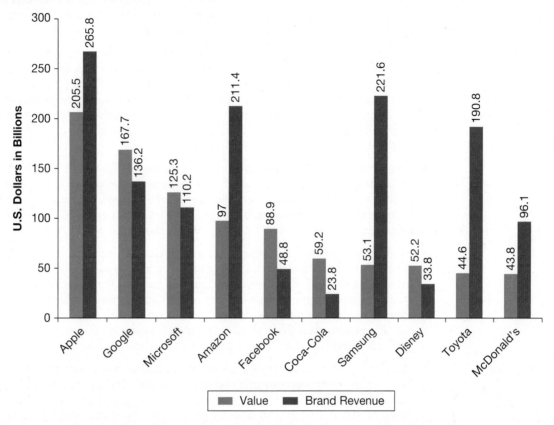

Source: The world's most valuable brands. (2019). *Forbes.* Retrieved from http://www.forbes.com/powerful-brands/list/#tab:rank

How to Build a Brand

Building a brand helps your customers understand what your product is in the simplest way possible and helps build an emotional connection to your product. Follow the steps below to build a successful brand.[7]

- *Choose a name.* A successful brand starts with a name. It could be a family name, which can add credibility to the business, or an obscure name that has nothing to do with the actual product. For example, the Starbucks name and logo have incredible brand recognition around the world, but they have no relationship to coffee whatsoever. Or you could go with an edgy name that carries shock value, such as UK-based clothing retailer FCUK (which actually stands for French Connection UK). Whatever name you choose, make sure it passes the SMILE test first (see Table 15.2).[8]

  Some experts believe that a strong brand can be created by just using one word—a concept first introduced by marketing professional and author Al Ries, who believed it made the brand easier for consumers to remember. Many top companies, such as Google, Salesforce, Uber, and Hubspot, have adopted this approach.[9] In fact, as Figure 15.2 shows, most of the world's most powerful brands consist of only one word. The key to defining your brand is knowing what your customers think of you and acting on that knowledge to build a successful brand. Alexandra Watkins, founder of San Francisco–based Eat My Words, a company that specializes in creating catchy brand names, believes that brand names should make people smile rather than scratch their heads. On this basis, she devised the Eat My Words® SMILE and SCRATCH Test™ (see Table 15.2)—a fun way to test your company or product name to see if you should keep it or scratch it off the list. Some of the names Watkins claims have passed the test include SPOON ME for a chain of frozen yogurt stores; BLOOM, a natural energy drink for women; and NEATO for a home-cleaning robot.

- *Design a logo.* Your logo is the gateway to your overall brand image. It triggers people's emotions and perception of the brand and answers questions such as, Who are you? What do you do? and What's in it for me? When designing a logo, make sure it shows up well in different types of media, its design and message are clear, and it is instantly recognizable. Put your logo everywhere you can—on your company website, social media, packaging, email signature, and all written communication.

- *Spread the word.* Get your brand out into the world. Social media is a great way for cash-strapped entrepreneurs to spread the word about their brand. Keep track of your online followers, and listen to what they have to say about your brand. Engage with your followers, be responsive to their needs, and reward them for following your brand.

- *Know your customer.* Knowing what your customer wants is key to building a successful brand. In order to achieve brand success, you need to know how your brand is perceived—who loves it, who hates it, and who would recommend it—what would make it stronger, how customers feel about competitor brands, and the extent to which customers will emotionally connect with your brand. You can find out this information through surveys and by keeping an eye on your followers and observing how they behave over a certain time period.

- *Become your brand.* Incorporate your brand into every aspect of your business. In an office environment, this includes how you greet people over the phone and what you and your employees wear. For example, if your aim is to promote sophistication through your brand, then you may want your employees to choose a polite yet formal manner over the phone and to dress smartly.

TABLE 15.2

Eat My Words® SMILE and SCRATCH Test™

SMILE, the qualities of a powerful name:
Simple—one, easy-to-understand concept
Meaningful—your customers instantly "get it"
Imagery—visually evocative, creates a mental picture
Legs—carries the brand, lends itself to wordplay
Emotional—empowers, entertains, engages, enlightens
SCRATCH it off the list if it has any of these deal-breakers:
Spelling-challenged—you have to tell people how to spell it
Copycat—similar to competitors' names
Random—disconnected from the brand
Annoying—hidden meaning, forced
Tame—flat, uninspired, boring, nonemotional
Curse of knowledge—only insiders get it
Hard-to-pronounce—not obvious, relies on punctuation

MINDSHIFT

One Sentence, Clear Message

Because entrepreneurs are so close to their ideas, you can easily fall into the trap of assuming everyone else understands what you are saying about what you are doing! Entrepreneurs have to develop a habit of quickly communicating their core offering—the essence of the business—so people want to hear more. What you believe is very clear in your head may not reach the same level of clarity for the listener, whether in person, on your website, or on social media. If we want our product or service or business to be shared by word of mouth, then we really need to get it down to one compelling sentence. That sentence should lead with the most important benefit or the need you are fulfilling.

For example, in 2011 Uber's slogan was "You push a button and in five minutes a Mercedes picks you up and takes you where you want to go." Later this was shortened to "Tap a button, get a ride."

For this Mindshift you must do two things: First, write your one sentence that describes your business idea. Second, share that sentence with at least five people and see if they get it. Of course, if they don't get it, you should rewrite it and try again!

Critical Thinking Questions

1. How difficult was it to create one sentence that clearly communicates your idea?

2. When you shared your sentence with others, did they get it? Why or why not?

3. Can you identify any other business that has been able to get their description down to one sentence? ●

Source: Bailey, D. (2017). The art of describing a product in one sentence. *Inc.* Retrieved from https://www.inc.com/dave-bailey/the-art-of-describing-a-product-in-one-sentence.html

- *Write a tagline.* Although it can be difficult to capture the essence of a brand in one succinct statement, a tagline is important for communicating your brand message. Keep your tagline short, simple, clear, and memorable. (See Table 15.3 for some approaches.)

- *Always deliver on your brand promise.* Customers are more likely to buy into your brand if it consistently meets and exceeds their expectations.

- *Be consistent with your brand.* It is possible to tweak a logo or a tagline, but make sure you always retain the brand voice and deliver on your brand promise.

Marketing Trends

Successful brands only stay successful when they stay on top of their marketing. This involves keeping a close eye on the current and future marketing trends, such as virtual

TABLE 15.3

Slogan or Tagline Approaches

APPROACH	EXAMPLE
Stake your claim	Death Wish Coffee: "The World's Strongest Coffee"
Make it a metaphor	Red Bull: "Red Bull gives you wings."
Adopt your customer's attitude	Nike: "Just do it."
Leverage labels	Cards Against Humanity: "A party game for horrible people"
Describe it literally	Aritzia: "Women's Fashion Boutique"

Source: Kumar, B. (2017). How to build a brand. *Shopify.* Retrieved from https://www.shopify.com/blog/how-to-build-a-brand

reality, artificial intelligence (AI), influencer marketing, experiential marketing, marketing through education, and honesty.[10]

1. Virtual Reality

   Integrating virtual reality (VR) into marketing strategies is becoming more and more popular; in fact, 75% of the world's biggest brands have launched VR campaigns. One of these brands is California-based for-profit shoe company TOMS Shoes, which gives away a pair of shoes for every pair purchased. Thanks to a VR tool set up in stores, customers can experience what it is like to gift the shoes to someone in Peru. Offering an immersive, exciting experience is a powerful way to build an emotional connection with their customers.

2. Artificial Intelligence (AI)

   The demand for more AI tools, such as voice-enabled devices like Amazon Echo with Alexa, is growing.[11] Many companies are using AI technology as a "live" chat tool (Chatbots) on their websites, to enable their customers to receive faster responses and save the cost of hiring customer support staff.

ChameleonsEye/Shutterstock

Realistic image of Domino's pizza

3. Honesty

   This low-tech approach may look a little out of place among all the latest technological advances, but honesty is more than just a passing craze. Being honest about your products and services by addressing any flaws or areas for improvement adds integrity to your brand, which may also translate into loyalty and sales. For example, pizza restaurant chain Domino's is on track to overtake its rivals by adopting a marketing strategy based on transparency.[12] Rather than posting "artistic," well-lit photos of its food online, it publishes realistic images of food—what you see is what you get. As Dennis Maloney, Domino's chief digital officer, says, "A lot of customers are out photographing their food. They know, depending on where you take it and the light you're under, food looks different. It feels much more honest and transparent when the images are imperfect."

4. Influencer Marketing

   Many brands are seeking the help of influencers on Instagram, Facebook, Snapchat, Twitter, YouTube, and Pinterest. For instance, pet foods company Pedigree used a group of influencers to promote its "Buy a Bag, Give a Bowl" campaign to showcase their mission to give a bowl of food to a dog in need in exchange for each bag of dog food bought at the store.[13] These influencers spread the word over blogs, posts, and video content, leading to a huge surge in media value. Celebrities are strong influencers. Singer and actress Selena Gomez is one of the most-followed people on Instagram, with more than 135 million followers. As a paid influencer for companies, she gets $550,000 per post.[14]

5. Experiential Marketing (Engagement Marketing)

   Experiential marketing, or engagement marketing, is a marketing strategy that provides people with a hands-on experience of what the company stands for. Whiskey company Glenfiddich has used experiential marketing to turn the concept of tasting sessions on its head.[15] To market their new Glenfiddich Experimental Series, the whiskey company set up a tasting event that invites customers to log into an app and answer questions about themselves. They are then matched with a drink that corresponds to their personality profile.

Sarah Ingle's partnership with Pedigree in their "buy a bag, give a bowl" campaign.

6. Marketing Through Education

The explosion of data has left many consumers a little world-weary and harder to engage. This means that marketers must also be educators and must offer easy-to-understand, engaging content to provide the information consumers are looking for. Exploring new ideas, sharing information, and providing value are key to building your brand and fostering customer engagement. As salesperson and motivational speaker Zig Ziglar once said, "You can have everything in life you want, if you will just help enough other people get what they want."[16]

These are just a few examples of marketing trends that brands need to pay attention to, especially in this era of social media, when savvy consumers tend to hold all the cards.

Reframing the 4 Ps

A 5-year study conducted by Harvard Business School, involving 500 managers and customers across numerous countries, presented the argument that because of the new relationships businesses have with customers, the traditional 4 Ps model is narrow and outdated and is not strictly relevant in a modern business environment.[17]

According to this research, the 4 Ps model overemphasizes product technology and quality, understates the necessity of explaining the value of the product and why customers need it, and distracts businesses from promoting themselves as important sources of information and problem solving. Researchers believe that a solutions-focused approach is needed when it comes to marketing products. Today's customers have far more input into the business–customer relationship, which necessitates a new framework that better reflects what the customer wants and cares about.

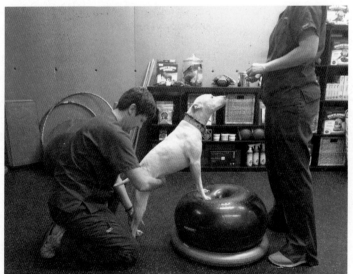

FlowDog physical therapy for dogs

FIGURE 15.3

The S.A.V.E. Framework

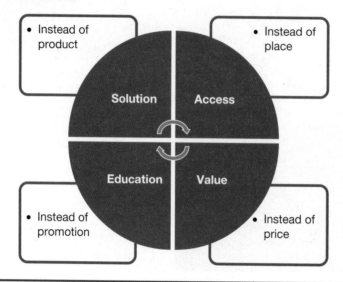

The study inspired the S.A.V.E framework—Solution, Access, Value, Education—which reinterprets the 4 Ps model by transferring the emphasis from products to *solutions*, place to *access*, price to *value*, and promotion to *education* (see Figure 15.3). Let's examine these factors one by one.

Solution rather than product: Researchers argue that businesses tend to get caught up in the features and functions of their product, when all customers really want to know is how the product solves their problems. S.A.V.E. advocates marketing a product based on how it meets customer needs, rather than emphasizing its features.

Access rather than place: Here, the focus is on how accessible your company is to your target customer. The exact location where someone can purchase your product is not so important. This approach considers the customer's journey from when they first hear of your company to when they actually make the purchase. Customers want to see that businesses care about customer feedback and are available if they need advice and support.

Value over price: Customers are drawn to value more than to price. This means that entrepreneurs need to build a strong case for showing customers why their product offers superior value to the competition, rather than focusing on the actual price tag.

Education rather than promotion: Today's businesses are in a good position to educate customers by providing information that they want to read that is up to date and relevant. This helps to build a relationship of familiarity and trust before a purchase is even made.

Figure 15.4 compares the message of FlowDog, a Boston-based physical therapy facility for dogs, with the 4 Ps on one hand and the S.A.V.E. model on the other.

Regardless of how many marketing models there are out there, the lesson is to take a broad approach to encompass all the elements that are relevant to your business. Then, test them, tweak them, and adjust them where needed.

15.4 ENTREPRENEURIAL MARKETING

>> **LO 15.4** **Discuss the different types of marketing tools available to entrepreneurs.**

Entrepreneurs who are just getting started always have one eye on the budget. It can be difficult to reach your chosen audience at the right time without compromising the quality of your marketing efforts. However, there is a wide range of entrepreneurial marketing

FIGURE 15.4

FlowDog: The 4 Ps Versus S.A.V.E.

4 Ps	S.A.V.E.
Product FlowDog provides the following: • Physical therapy for orthopedic and neurological conditions • Hydrotherapy for therapeutic swimming in a pool heated 84–89 degrees Fahrenheit • Fitness swimming for weight loss, weight management, and cross training • Massage to increase blood flow and relieve muscle tension • Reiki for stress reduction • Acupuncture for pain and tension relief • Physical therapy products to supplement service (e.g., special harnesses, toys to improve cognition)	**Solution** FlowDog brings peace of mind to the dog owner by providing an array of therapeutic services for a complete solution that increases the quality of life of postsurgical, injured, and aging dogs. By providing hands-on treatment, owner education, and products to use at home, FlowDog gives dogs every opportunity to fully recover, prevent injury, and even prolong life.
Place FlowDog is located in Waltham, MA. The facility is located in an office park area and is zoned for a dog-related business. There is ample parking.	**Access** FlowDog is conveniently located to dog owners in both Boston and the surrounding area for suburbs. With strong relationships with Boston-area vets, customers are often referred to FlowDog by their primary veterinarian or specialty/surgical hospital.
Price An initial evaluation for physical therapy is $185/hour and follow-up appointments are $110. Other treatments (massage, reiki, acupuncture) range in price from $40 to $80. FlowDog rates are competitive with other facilities in the Boston area.	**Value** Physical therapy reduces recovery time after surgery and reduces prolonged medication usage. It is often used as an alternative to surgery or as a way of preventing surgery. On average, dog owners can expect to pay $2,500 to $3,500 for a common knee surgery such as an ACL tear. Overall, FlowDog's focus is on prolonging the dog's life.
Promotion FlowDog advertises in local dog newsletters, vet offices, and online. The company uses Facebook to communicate with customers about upcoming events.	**Education** The FlowDog website offers case studies of dogs who have recovered from or better managed various medical conditions such as arthritis, cruciate tears, and spinal injuries. Because each dog is unique, a special treatment plan is created after the initial evaluation that meets the needs of both dog and owner.

tools that don't have to cost the Earth, such as guerrilla marketing, social media marketing, designing a website, and building a fan base. But success does depend on patience, consistency, and ingenuity.

Guerrilla Marketing

One form of entrepreneurial marketing is **guerrilla marketing**, which is a low-budget strategy that focuses on personally interacting with a target group by promoting products and services through surprise or other unconventional means. A successful guerrilla marketing campaign enhances the customer's perception of value, inspires word of mouth, and increases sales.

Guerrilla marketing: a low-budget strategy that focuses on personally interacting with a target group by promoting products and services through surprise or other unconventional means.

Snapple's World's Largest Popsicle campaign

RICHARD B. LEVINE/Newscom

Guerrilla marketing strategies are almost limitless: email, interactive poster campaigns, advertisements on cars, T-shirts, street branding (writing marketing messages with paint or chalk on pavements or walls), characters in costume, flash mobs (a large group of people that seemingly comes out of nowhere to perform an act in a public place), projecting images/videos/messages in public areas, and even YouTube videos that can go viral in minutes.

When guerrilla campaigns go viral, they can reach a huge audience. For example, to heighten awareness of its company and prove its blending expertise, global blender provider, Blendtec, posted a video on YouTube called "Will It Blend?" where viewers were asked for suggestions for items to blend.[18] The campaign was an instant hit, gathering 6 million views in 6 days. Since its launch, Blendtec has uploaded more than 150 videos blending everything from marbles, glow sticks, and Bic lighters, to Apple products, golf balls, and magnets. Thanks to the success of the Blendtec campaign, its founder, Tom Dickson, has been propelled into the media spotlight, making several TV appearances, including on the *Today Show* and Discovery Channel.

There is even a guerrilla marketing technique called snow branding, which involves making imprints of the product's name and brand during the night on snow-covered pavements, walls, cars, and the like.[19] When people emerge the next morning, they are surprised by these novel images that are aimed to create a good feeling, a sense of awareness, and a positive memory of the company's brand.

Guerrilla marketing strategies are also used by major companies. In an effort to promote the new Colgate Max Night toothpaste, Colgate partnered with various local pizzerias, which were supplied with special Colgate-branded boxes for pizza deliveries.[20] When customers opened the box, they were greeted with a design of the inside of a mouth. The message? To remind people to use Colgate to brush their teeth at night, so that their "dinner breath" doesn't turn into "morning breath."

Guerrilla marketing can be a creative and affordable way to reach your desired target market, but it has its limitations. In order to conduct a successful guerrilla campaign, you need to have a good understanding of your target market and where the high traffic exists; for example, subway, mall, university campus, and so on. You also need to get the timing right: Should you conduct the campaign during business hours, at weekends, or morning, or night?

Guerrilla marketing success can be difficult to measure: How do you know the good feeling or memory you're giving your customer is going to translate into sales? Monitoring the media (newspapers, radio) for mentions of your campaign and taking the time to scout blogs, forums, and social networks to see who is talking about your company and your product is a good start in measuring the campaign's impact on sales.

Finally, you need to have a good sense of the community and any legal, social, or moral restrictions that may cause a negative reaction to a campaign. In a classic example of guerrilla marketing going wrong, fruit drinks company Snapple came under fire when it attempted to create the world's largest popsicle in the middle of Manhattan—on a sunny day in June.[21] Inevitably, the 25-foot-tall popsicle began to melt, flooding the surrounding streets. Streets were closed off as firefighters were called in to clean the streets of the sticky goo. Snapple learned a valuable lesson that day: Always prepare for the unexpected!

Planning a guerrilla marketing campaign requires commitment, creativity, consistency, patience, and a true understanding of your target market. Getting it right could have big payoffs. Guerilla marketing can be considered a bootstrapping technique because many guerrilla efforts can be done quite inexpensively, so what do you have to lose? Take action, test, and see what works with your customer base.

Marketing Through Social Media

Social media has become an essential business tool for entrepreneurs to market their products and services and themselves. When used properly, social media can launch businesses to new levels of success. For example, fine artist Iris Scott is on track to exceed $1 million in revenue thanks to her creative use of social media to market her art.[22] From early on, Scott engaged in two-way communication with her followers by sharing her art on Facebook and Instagram, taking on board their suggestions, and offering her works for prices as low as $50. Through the support of her followers, Scott decided to try finger painting, which created a real spike in interest and more demand for her works. Several years after she started to market her art on social media, some of Scott's paintings now hang in the Filo Sofi Arts Gallery in New York, one of which has a price tag of $45,000.

Artist Iris Scott used Facebook and Instagram to promote her finger painting artwork, which is now worth up to $45,000.

As the Iris Scott example shows, social media is the most powerful way of spreading word of mouth about your products and services. Social media is also a valuable way of following market trends, finding new employees, and building and maintaining relationships with customers. It is also a useful way to find potential stakeholders. Social media sites like Twitter, LinkedIn, Facebook, Instagram, and YouTube all provide ways to connect with people who are experts in the field or fellow entrepreneurs—anyone who can potentially help you develop, build, and grow your venture. Some of these people may become self-selected stakeholders or may even become part of your founding team.

This is why it is so important for entrepreneurs to create their own social media strategy. Figure 15.5 lists some of the most popular forms of social media.

Getting the Most From Social Media

Anyone can engage in social media, but it takes a smart, dedicated entrepreneur to use social media wisely and productively. Here are some tips:

Start With Research

The most successful social media strategies start with solid research. Take a look at how your competitors use social media. What kind of content do they share with their customers and followers? What sort of language do they use to engage their followers? It also helps to read blogs and join discussions about subjects that are relevant to your business. Contributing to conversations helps you learn more about what is important to your customers, and it helps to boost your profile and showcase your knowledge about a particular area.

Think About Your Goals

After conducting your research, think about the goals you would like to achieve. Do you want your social media presence to attract customers, increase recognition of your brand, or both? Many companies use social media to provide efficient customer service; for example, online food ordering company Seamless provides round-the-clock customer service on Twitter, and American Airlines tweets if there are airline delays and responds quickly to tweets from frustrated passengers. Considering that more than 70% of Twitter users surveyed expect a response from a brand within an hour, it is very much worthwhile for companies to make the effort to provide excellent customer service over social media, especially as it could increase customer satisfaction by almost 20%.[23]

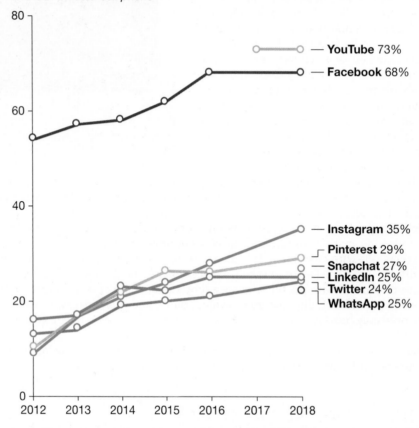

FIGURE 15.5

Popular Forms of Social Media

Majority of Americans now use Facebook, YouTube

% of U.S. adults who say they use the following social media sites online or on their cell phone

Source: Survey conducted Jan. 3–10, 2018. Trend data from previous Pew Research Center surveys.

Design Your Strategy

Next, think about ways in which you can measure your online presence. For example, you can catalog the number of visits to your site, the number of followers, the types of comments people make about your business, and who they share them with. It also helps to design your strategy around your target audience—how do you engage them? What media platforms do they use the most? Choose one or two social media sites to begin with that fit in with your industry and your target market.

Post Regular Updates

Once you have launched your social media campaign, make sure you post regular updates. Followers will expect to see quick messages on Twitter several times a day and longer blog posts or articles on Facebook at least a couple of times a week. New York City shop Squish Marshmallows posts images on Instagram twice per day, which owner Katherine Sprung credits for the increase in foot traffic into the shop.[24]

Monitor Your Social Media

Be vigilant about monitoring your social media—every day, check for new followers, any feedback, questions, or complaints. Then make sure you address them all. In addition, check out who your new followers are and how many of them have retweeted your posts.

Who has viewed your LinkedIn profile? How many people have viewed or subscribed to your YouTube channel? Also, keep a close watch on your competitor's sites—what are people saying about them? Is your business mentioned in customer reviews on their site?

Posting interesting content online on a regular basis is one of the best ways to get feedback from your followers and grow your online community. If you are a confident public speaker, then videos are also a powerful way to build trust with potential customers by letting them get to know you before they buy from you. You can choose to share videos or images on sites such as YouTube, Vimeo, Flickr, Slide Share, and Instagram.

Creating Content That Drives Sales

As we have learned, marketers must also be educators—ready to provide easy-to-understand, engaging content that appeals to their target audience. Whether you are using up-to-the-minute social media or traditional media such as magazines, newsletters, and other print collateral, the content matters. Let's take a closer look at how you can create interesting, engaging content online that ultimately translates into sales.

For many of us, the word *sales* evokes images of the pushy salesperson using hard-sell tactics to pressure us into buying stuff we don't need. So, it's time to let go of that outdated image and realize that today, most of us spend 40% of our time at work "selling" in one way or another: persuading, influencing, and convincing others in ways that don't necessarily translate into an immediate purchase.[25] In this sense, we are all salespeople, whether we realize it or not.

Sales has evolved from using hard-core sales techniques to a soft sell through engaging content that is genuine and creative, adds value, and builds relationships. Creating content is not about advertising your business or self-promotion. Instead, it aims to educate, inspire, and entertain people enough that they will grow to trust you and your brand. It is a way for your customers to get to know the human side of your business by injecting personality and authenticity into everything you produce. Here are some more tips to help engage your consumers:[26]

1. **Make your content about them, not you.**

   Most people, including your customers, don't like it when other people talk about themselves. When presenting content, make sure it is relevant to your audience: 90% about them and 10% (or less) about you.

2. **Develop a fresh point of view.**

   Rather than just talking about the industry in which you operate, try and broaden your scope to other areas. For instance, Trulia, the real estate search service, expands its content beyond the real estate market to provide novel geographic data based on social trends and demographics.[27]

3. **Pick your battles.**

   It is important to share your own point of view, but make sure you still come across as being likeable. Using inflammatory language, becoming overly political, or taking divisive standpoints may put off some of your customers. In 2017, an activism-themed ad from Pepsi featuring model Kendall Jenner triggered a massive backlash on social media. As a result, the ad was pulled and an apology was made by Pepsi for "missing the mark."[28]

4. **Be authentic.**

   Social media is about building long-lasting relationships, which means being authentic from the get-go. This involves participating in your customers' conversations, commenting on their content, and sharing your own thoughts and opinions. As *Unmarketing* author Scott Stratten says, "Setting up an automated Twitter program to tweet for you and automatically add followers is a great way to say to people 'We don't actually care what you're saying, just buy from us.' It would be like sending a mannequin to a networking event with your company logo on it. Yeah, creepy."[29]

♀trulia

MENU +

TRULIA RESEARCH | LIVABILITY

Best Places to Live to Avoid Natural Disasters

By Jed Kolko, Former Chief Economist | Aug 15, 2013 5:00AM

Today, Trulia added three new hazard maps – for wildfires, hurricanes, and tornadoes – to the two hazard maps we introduced earlier this summer, featuring earthquakes and floods. As part of your home search, you can now check Trulia to find whether the neighborhood of your dreams puts you in the eye, at the epicenter, or in the path of a natural disaster. You'll see that California is high risk for wildfires, Florida for hurricanes, Oklahoma for tornadoes, and more.

Donna - Sept 1960
Category One Hurricane
Avg wind speed: 95 mph

Trulia's website showing the best places to live to avoid natural disasters.

5. **Use your gut.**

   When reading over your content, ask yourself who it best serves, you and your company or the reader? If the answer isn't "the reader" then have another go. The effort will pay off in additional business and loyalty from your customer.

The key to good content is quality. If you can create content that is meaningful to your audience, they will share it through their own social networks—think tweets, retweets, likes, comments, reviews. It also helps to get in touch with people in a similar market who already have a large number of followers, and build a relationship with them. For example, if you have a product designed for mothers of young children, then you could get a list of the top mommy bloggers, send them the product, and get them talking about it. All going well, the product will be picked up by a company that will have heard of it through your more high-profile mommy bloggers. Over time, they may even share some of your content with their audiences, which gives your business an even larger platform to promote itself. In return, you can share some of their content in order to develop a mutually beneficial relationship.

It is important to be available to your online community. Publishing content regularly through blogs, infographics, videos, tweets, and taking part in conversations is essential if you want to maintain a loyal following. Getting your users involved is an even better way of spreading the word about your company.

Philadelphia-based mobile app and web development company Chop Dawg has discovered a unique way to engage its 500,000 followers over social media.[30] Currently writing a book, company founder Joshua Davidson live-streams his meetings with his publisher on Twitter to provide his Chop Dawg audience with an inside view of the book-writing process. Thanks to live-streaming, Davidson has gained an average of more than 1,000 people watching him create his book as it happens.

Building Your Website

However you choose to market your content, it is always important to build a decent platform that showcases you, your company, and your content. This is where a good-quality website can make a real difference in attracting customers.

Websites with crisp, clean designs and a clear description of your product or service, together with simple, uncluttered pages that flow well in relation to each other, tend to be the most successful. It is particularly important that your website be quick and easy to navigate on both a large computer screen and a mobile device. Recent studies show that smartphones are the most popular way to browse the Internet in the UK.[31] Remember, it's all about participation and content, not coercion and persuasion!

Site builder tools like Wix, Duda, and Squarespace and content management systems like WordPress have made it easier for entrepreneurs on a tight budget to build their own sites. Whatever method you choose, do seek guidance to ensure you are using the best possible search engine optimization. This is what enables people to find you online via Google or other search engines, so it is worth the investment. Because Google search results also take into account the number of times websites are shared on social media, it is also important that your site includes links to your social media pages and vice versa, in order to boost Google search rankings.

Remember that the act of building a website will not encourage visitors to flock immediately to your site. Attracting an audience takes time and patience. It won't be perfect from the very start, but it will evolve over time in line with industry fluctuations and the response you get from your audience. Table 15.4 contains 10 tips to help you avoid mistakes in building your first website.

Building a Fan Base

True fans: people who will buy anything you produce; they will wait in line for your products, drive for hours to attend one of your events, and preorder your next product without even knowing what it looks like.

Regardless of which marketing technique you use, it all comes down to one main goal: to attract enough people to your company to make what you are doing financially worthwhile. But how many people do you really need for your business to thrive? According to cofounder of *Wired* magazine Kevin Kelly, building a lasting, sustainable business is based on 1,000 true fans.[33] **True fans** are people who will buy anything you produce; they will wait in line for your products, drive for hours to attend one of your events, and

What "About Us"?

Did you know that the "About Us" page is one of the most visited pages for any new business website? This section of a website helps you build trust, legitimacy, and connection with your customers. Follow these basic steps to create your own "About Us" page. Keep in mind that the content created in this Mindshift can be used anywhere at any time! Create your own "About Us" story using the steps below. Our example is based on www.yellowleafhammocks.com.

Start with a quick introduction that explains the concept of your business.

Example: Yellow Leaf Hammocks offers ridiculously comfy hammocks with impeccable craftsmanship and transformative impact.

Describe what you stand for as a business. Communicate your why.

Example: Our motto is "Do Good. Relax." In addition to sustainable social change, we believe passionately in travel, naps, good food, great friends, long talks, broadened horizons, and a spirit of adventure. We are also 100% positive the world would be a better place if everyone spent 15 minutes a day in a hammock.

Describe what you specialize in or talk about the work you love doing.

Example: Each perfectly engineered Yellow Leaf Hammock directly empowers our artisan weavers and their families. We train mothers to weave the world's best hammocks, then spread good times and relaxation around the world, then break the cycles of poverty and build a brighter future.

Tell a quick story about why you started your business.

Example: Our artisan weavers and their families were previously trapped in extreme poverty and debt slavery. Now they are empowered to earn a stable, healthy income through dignified work. We call this a "prosperity wage." This is the basis for a brighter future, built on a hand up, not a handout.

Give a glimpse into your goals.

Example: Yellow Leaf Hammocks is breaking the cycle of extreme poverty through sustainable job creation.

Make it easy for the customer to take action.

Example: Join the community, live the lifestyle, and spread "Do Good. Relax."!

Now create a one-paragraph "About Us" description or a web page. Share it with 10 people and see if you can get some fans! Take a look at www.yellowleafhammocks.com/pages/about-us to see their engaging design.

Critical Thinking Questions

1. What was the most difficult part of your "About Us" to develop? Why?

2. What did you learn from those you shared your "About Us" with?

3. What other places can use your "About Us" content? ●

Source: Adapted from https://www.beamlocal.com/how-to-write-a-powerful-business-description-for-your-website/

---

preorder your next product without even knowing what it looks like. For instance, more than 400,000 Tesla fans have signed up for the much-anticipated Model 3 electric car, most of whom ordered it sight unseen.[34]

But of course, you don't need half a million fans to make a living when you first start your business; besides, 1,000 seems like a more realistic number. If you added only one true fan a day, it might only take a few years to reach 1,000. You might calculate the value of a true fan by assessing the amount their support generates; for instance, 1,000 fans paying $100 for your product or service on an annual basis amounts to $100,000. With 1,000 fans in tow, the possibilities are endless. Imagine being able to persuade 1,000 people to come and dine at the restaurant you just opened, or holding a seminar for which 1,000 people have signed up and paid $200 to hear you speak.[35] Given that there are more than 7 billion people in the world, doesn't capturing 1,000 of them seem achievable?

But like everything worthwhile, the path to gaining your true fan base is not easy. It requires patience, consistency, and a keen focus on building long-term relationships. Entrepreneur and blogger Yaro Starak is a good example of someone who successfully garnered 1,000 true fans. He started his blog Entrepreneurs-Journey.com in 2005, with the intention of using it as a platform to share his own experiences of being an Internet

TABLE 15.4

Top 10 Mistakes to Avoid When Building Your First Website

Inaccessibility	Make sure your website is available to everyone, including those with a disability. Can the size of the text be easily changed to cater to the visually impaired? Does your color scheme provide the right contrast between text and background design so the content can be easily viewed?
Difficult-to-find contact information	Some sites bury their contact information, which can be frustrating for people trying to get in touch. Easy-to-find contact information including a phone number and address is essential to new businesses, as it gives your site visitors the confidence that they are dealing with a genuine business, rather than a fraudulent one.
Overusing the "wow" factor	Flash can add pizzazz to your site but don't overdo it—not everyone has flash or even has enough bandwidth to support it. The same goes for graphics—use them sparingly as too many will slow down the functionality of your site. Similarly, don't go to town on audio and never let it play automatically—always let your visitors choose if they want to hear it or not.
Slow load times	We are an impatient bunch. A recent study by Akamai Technologies showed that on average, online shoppers will wait only 4 seconds for a website to load before doing their shopping elsewhere.[32] If your website is not loading within 4 seconds, then identify the elements that are slowing it down (Flash, large images, etc.) and remove them.
Not getting picked up by search engines	If you want to achieve higher rankings, you need to do at least the basics. These include a site map, concise and relevant content, use of standard mark-up tags that are recognized by search engines as well as meta tags such as keywords. Seek professional advice on this if you have the budget.
Long sections of text	A wall of text is difficult and frustrating to read online. Visitors want to see text in digestible chunks that they can scan quickly. To break up the text and to make it more user friendly, include subheads, bulleted lists, **highlighted keywords,** and short paragraphs—all written in jargon-free simple language.
Poor navigation	There is nothing more off-putting for online visitors than a disorganized, poorly structured site. The user experience should be as smooth as possible and populated by links and menus, all of which should work and should be frequently tested. Ask yourself how many clicks a visitor will need to access a piece of information on your site. Make their journey as easy and speedy as you can.
Not monitoring your site	There is no excuse for not keeping an eye on your site. There are many free tools available. They provide valuable insights into the type of visitors that your site attracts, including factors such as where they come from, what content they read the most, and what links are the most popular.
Not updating your content	Don't be one of those people whose site displays outdated information or creates blogs once in a blue moon. Frequently published fresh, new content is a way of building credibility with your audience.
Failing to link to social platforms	Your business will most likely have its own Facebook page, a Twitter and LinkedIn account, and maybe a Pinterest board. Visitors to your website should be able to move from your site to your social media presence as smoothly as possible, and vice versa. Connecting your social media to your website is essential to drive traffic to your site.

Source: Scocco, D. (2007). 43 web design mistakes you should avoid. Retrieved from www.dailyblogtips.com

entrepreneur (Starak used to run a proofreading business and a card game website). Yet, more than a decade later, it has become his main source of income, generating more than a million dollars. Because of his commitment to sharing information, thousands of people have learned how to make a living out of blogging part time, and they have become loyal followers as a result. Table 15.5 outlines Starak's tips for building a fan base.

The point is that it's not only giants like Apple and Tesla than can generate a diehard fan base. In fact, many of the classic megabrands such as Levi, Gap, and Lee Jeans have either slowed down or are on the decline.[36] This phenomenon is known as the long tail theory, first introduced by journalist Chris Anderson (see Figure 15.6). The theory holds that the focus is shifting from mainstream products and services offered by big brands, positioned on the vertical axis at the head of the tail, toward a wide variety of smaller niche markets at the horizontal axis at the bottom of the tail. Why is this happening? Because the Internet has given rise to unlimited numbers of retail sites offering easily accessible, cheaper products. Fewer than a few decades ago, the big brands operating in all sorts of industries needed to create bestsellers and blockbusters mainly because the cost of distribution was high and the shelf space limited. But in today's economy, the

TABLE 15.5

How to Build Your Fan Base

1.	From the day you start your business, always have an email and newsletter opt-in form; the more people who join your newsletter, the more chance you will have of converting them into true fans.
2.	Make sure you have the right mindset about the business you're going into; prepare to live and breathe your subject area every day and be confident about the content you are creating.
3.	Watch other people in your industry and study the types of information they are sharing to keep up to date with your competition.
4.	Maintain an ongoing dialogue with your audience; don't give them a reason to stray elsewhere.
5.	Share your own unique stories and use those messages to build a community of followers.
6.	Build relationships with other people who are willing to promote whatever you're selling. They could be journalists, bloggers, and other influencers.
7.	When you're writing blogs, make sure you have an engaging headline. Also make sure to check out Facebook to find the most popular shared blogs.
8.	Remember that people learn in different ways, so be prepared to use different types of social media such as Podcasts, imagery, and videos to promote your message and build a strong personal connection.
9.	Stay in control of your content; your blog and your email list are two things that you own—they are the best ways to generate a buzz and garner your true fans.
10.	When things don't work out, learn from your mistakes and keep moving forward. Perseverance is key to finding and maintaining your true fan base.

Source: https://www.easyspace.com/blog/2014/10/01/interview-with-yaro-starak-founder-of-entrepreneurs-journey-com/

FIGURE 15.6

The Long Tail Chart

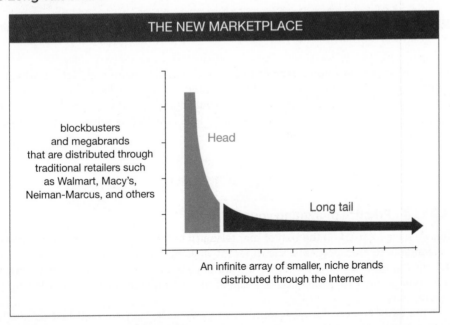

Source: https://www.forbes.com/sites/robinlewis/2016/05/31/the-long-tail-theory-can-be-reality-for-traditional-megabrands/#7fe46b4f6372>

Internet solves both problems, providing small businesses with a chance to take some market share away from the megabrands. Examples of today's most successful businesses that took advantage of the long tail include Amazon, which makes thousands of books available that otherwise wouldn't be found in bookstores; iTunes, which provides

How Social Media Can Provide Marketing Headaches

As social media has only been around since the turn of the millennium, and new platforms pop up every year, the field of social media marketing is relatively new. Although it is easier than ever for companies to communicate with current and potential customers, social media marketing has also given rise to a number of horror stories. If a company's social media account becomes overly political, suggestive, or ill-humored, the repercussions can destabilize that company's credibility and hurt customer relations.

Social media is a new way for companies to market, and as such, it carries with it a number of ethical quandaries. First, is marketing to consumers healthy for them? According to a study from the journal *Psychological Reports: Disability and Trauma*, addictions to technology and social media share similar traits with substance and gambling addiction. Social media marketing, especially in a very engaging manner, can cause some harm to those who have difficulty controlling their relationship with social media.

However, there is a line to be drawn, and social media is quite often too valuable a tool to pass up. Creating an enticing social media presence can stray away from traditional marketing tactics, but how far can you take your marketing? Different brands like to stay conservative in the online, social sphere, while others attempt more

intimate interactions. The decision on what path to take is up to the entrepreneur, and riskier campaigns can be pulled off. For example, Eggo teamed up with Netflix's *Stranger Things* to promote waffles and the show, tapping into audience interests. But, the pitfalls of taking a chance on social media campaigns can be dire. Playing politics in advertisements can be a dangerous game, and that only highlights the fact that all social media posts must be carefully considered.

Critical Thinking Questions

1. Is it fine to play politics with social media marketing, even if you know it caters to the target audience?

2. How do companies create social media disasters? How much does a mistake impact the brand?

3. Should a company have a strict review process in place before any social media posts are made live? ●

Sources:

Bergstrom, B. (2018, February 1). 24 creative social media campaign examples to boost your inspiration. *CoSchedule*. Retrieved from https://coschedule.com/blog/social-media-campaign-examples/
Conick, H. (2017, April 6). Marketing's ethical line between social media habit and addiction. *American Marketing Association*. Retrieved from https://www.ama.org/publications/MarketingNews/Pages/marketings-ethical-line-between-social-media-habit-addiction.aspx

niche music to people who prefer not to follow the mainstream; and Netflix, which has expanded the world of movies beyond the restrictions of a bricks-and-mortar retailer.[37] What does all this mean for entrepreneurs? That regardless of your product or service, there is a market for it, and if you can get 1,000 true fans to buy it from you, then you're well on your way to making a decent living.

15.5 CREATING YOUR PERSONAL BRAND

>> LO 15.5   **Practice marketing yourself.**

So far, we have focused on the role of marketing in entrepreneurship and the marketing tools available to entrepreneurs, the different ways of marketing new ventures through social media, and the importance of building your fan base. In this section, we will explore one of the most fundamental parts of marketing your business: marketing you, the entrepreneur.

At the early stages of a new venture, you are marketing yourself just as much as you are marketing a product, service, or company. This is why it is important for you to recognize that, from the beginning, you and your business are one. Most investors will invest in you first and foremost and not just in your idea. Investors will want to see that they can build a long-term relationship with you over a period of years and that you are capable of collaborating to build the business. This is why it is worth spending time figuring out how you're going to market yourself, and not just your company, before you pitch anything. Remember that when the time comes, pitching is a huge part of marketing yourself. In fact, the pitch is so important to "marketing the idea" that we've created an entire supplement on it! (See Supplement B: The Pitch Deck.)

As we learned in Chapter 8, research shows that people will unconsciously decide whether they like you or not within one-tenth of a second. People decide in fewer than 90 seconds whether they want to hear more about an idea or not, and it takes between 7 and 20 seconds to create a first impression.[38] So we have fewer than 20 seconds to make a good first impression and fewer than 90 seconds to engage our audience in our ideas. How you market yourself really matters.

Research shows that we have fewer than 20 seconds to make a good first impression.

Researchers conducted an experiment that compared first impressions with assessments built over a period of months. They compared the ratings given to college professors by students at the end of the semester with ratings of the same professors given by another group of students based on three 10-second video clips, which they were shown before the lectures. The results showed that both groups of students had pretty much the same opinions of the professors. This experiment indicates that a 10-second first impression gleaned from the second group of students was almost as powerful as the impressions the other students had derived while interacting with professors over the course of an entire semester. Such is the power of first impressions.[39]

Although we can train ourselves in what to say, we are often ill-prepared for how to say it. It is essential that you focus on other factors that could get in the way of conveying a positive first impression. For example, slouching while standing or sitting, avoiding eye contact, frowning, relying on technical jargon, reading slides, speaking too fast or too slowly, untidy physical appearance, and gesturing too much are all actions that can put off your audience. Research has shown that 93% of our communication is nonverbal:

- 55% of the message is conveyed through facial expression
- 38% of the message is conveyed through tone of voice
- 7% of the message is conveyed through words[40]

Another factor in nonverbal communication is the nonvisual dimension. We all see the world differently, so it pays to be aware of the different sensory learning styles of your audience in order to build a rapport. Numerous studies have shown that people learn information in different ways. For example, some are visual learners, while others are auditory or kinesthetic learners.[41] You can use these learning preferences to your advantage by using various kinds of media. For example, you might present a slide show with images. Ensuring that you describe your ideas and concepts clearly and confidently will appeal to auditory learners. If available, bring a prototype of your product along to give your audience something to touch and feel.

How to Build Your Personal Brand

Creating a strong first impression is essential to building a sustainable personal brand (see Table 15.6). More and more often, we look at the people behind the companies rather than the companies themselves. For example, we associate Jeff Bezos with Amazon, Microsoft with Bill Gates, and Arianna Huffington with *The Huffington Post*. We know so much about them because they have such strong personal brands, which they leverage to attract more customers to buy their products and services. The point is that personal branding is always a part of a company's success. As growth marketer Kevin Payne said, "As an entrepreneur, by now you should know that business isn't conducted based solely on the products and services you provide, but by your character, integrity, and personal relationships you build with others. Remember people don't buy from businesses, they buy from people that they like."[42]

How a Pitch Can Help Build Your Brand

What is the relationship between trust and early-stage investors' interest in investment during an entrepreneurial pitch? Is trust really a factor when it comes to investing, or do investors focus primarily on economic gains?

These are the questions Lakshmi Balachandra, a professor at Babson College, sought to answer. Balachandra carried out an experiment by studying 101 videos of entrepreneurs pitching to a network of angel investors from the Tech Coast Angels (TCA) in California—the largest angel group in the country. The results showed that trustworthiness displayed by entrepreneurs during the pitch had a direct impact on whether the angels would invest or not. In fact, angels who perceived trustworthiness were 10% more likely to invest. Angels were also more likely to rate "coachability" three times more important than competence during the trustworthiness assessments. For instance, investors will have more confidence that they can help "coach"—or make up any skills that are lacking—if the entrepreneur comes across as being trustworthy.

Other factors that led to an assessment of trustworthiness included the number of meaningful social network connections; the ability for entrepreneurs to accept suggestions, critique, and feedback; and commonalities between the angels and the entrepreneurs, such as background and expertise. It is clear from this research that entrepreneurs need to demonstrate trustworthiness while pitching.

Critical Thinking Questions

1. Give some reasons why trustworthiness is so important to potential investors.

2. Explain the relationship between trustworthiness and coachability. How can an entrepreneur demonstrate coachability during the pitch?

3. What are some ways you can demonstrate trustworthiness during a pitch? ●

Sources:

Balachandra, L. (2011). *Pitching trustworthiness: Cues for trust in early-stage investment decision making* (Unpublished doctoral dissertation). Carroll School of Management, Chestnut Hill, MA.
How venture capitalists really assess a pitch. (2017). *Harvard Business Review*, May-June, 25–28.

TABLE 15.6

Tips for Building Your Personal Brand

• Be authentic: Be honest about your attributes and qualities. Think about your strengths, passions, values, and beliefs and use them to promote a strong brand foundation.
• Be visible: Focus on increasing your visibility internally and externally. In addition to publishing content on your own online platform, increase your exposure to more people by guest speaking on podcasts, guest blogging, and applying to speak at conferences.
• Build a brand vision: Think about what you want to be an expert on; what you want to be known for.
• Write down your brand mission: Note why you want to build a personal brand, the people you want to influence, and what you want to accomplish.
• Consider your brand personality: Think about the personal characteristics you can draw on to build your brand. For instance, do you want to be seen as quirky and humorous or more formal and businesslike?
• Learn to influence: Draw on whatever personal power or network you have and use your influence in a positive way to promote your personal brand.
• Be unique: Don't be tempted to copy someone else's personal brand, even if it is someone you admire. Remember, it is your uniqueness that will differentiate you from your competitors.

Sources: Basu, T. (n.d.). How to build a personal brand (complete guide to personal branding). *Thinkific*. Retrieved from https://www.thinkific.com/blog/personal-branding-guide/; Payne, K. (n.d.). *Personal branding for entrepreneurs*. Retrieved from https://kevintpayne.com/personal-branding-for-entrepreneurs/

Successful entrepreneurs build a personal brand based on trust and authority, attract more customers, gain more media exposure and attention, and create a lasting platform that secures a loyal following of people they want to impact most. ●

⑤SAGE edge™

Get the tools you need to sharpen your study skills. SAGE edge offers a robust online environment featuring an impressive array of free tools and resources.

- Access practice quizzes, eFlashcards, video, and multimedia at
  edge.sagepub.com/neckentrepreneurship2e

SUMMARY

15.1   Discuss entrepreneurial marketing and explain how it is different from traditional marketing.

Entrepreneurial marketing is a set of processes adopted by entrepreneurs based on new and unconventional marketing practices to gain traction and attention in competitive markets.

In the past, marketing was largely based on interruption and coercion. Today's marketing is really about building relationships, engaging with people, and creating a community. The new marketing rules focus on participation and content to build a successful business.

15.2   Explain the principles of marketing and how they apply to new ventures.

The right product, in the right place, at the right price, at the right time. For entrepreneurs, this extends to identifying needs, serving those needs, communicating the value proposition, supplying the product or service, and supporting the customer relationship from then on.

15.3   Describe branding and the importance of building a brand.

Branding is the process of creating a name, term, design, symbol, or any other feature that identifies a product or service and differentiates it from others. Branding is important because people are more likely to invest in brands that they have an emotional connection to, are trustworthy, are worth spending money on, are fashionable, and are adept at meeting their needs.

15.4   Discuss the different types of marketing tools available to entrepreneurs.

There is a wide range of entrepreneurial marketing tools available to budget-conscious entrepreneurs. Some of these tools include: building a brand, guerrilla marketing, social media marketing, designing a website, and building a fan base.

15.5   Practice marketing yourself.

Creating a strong first impression is essential to building a sustainable personal brand. Successful entrepreneurs build a personal brand based on trust and authority, attract more customers, gain more media exposure and attention, and create a lasting platform that secures a loyal following of people that they want to impact most.

KEY TERMS

Brand strategy   386

Branding   386

Entrepreneurial marketing   381

Guerrilla marketing   393

Marketing   384

Marketing mix   384

Packaging   386

People   386

Place   385

Positioning   386

Price   384

Product   384

Promotion   385

True fans   398

CASE STUDY

Justin Real, founder, Realplay

The Realplay story is evidence that an entrepreneur markets himself before marketing his company. Realplay is a LinkedIn-style platform for amateur baseball and softball players that connects players, coaches, and recruiters through automatically generated video and statistics. The platform, consisting of on-field cameras and an image-recognition system, is designed as an easy-to-use amateur sports solution that edits a game and uploads every at-bat video to a player's profile page through a machine learning algorithm. Players have access to their own videos, coaches use videos to help players improve, and recruiters have a larger pool of prospects.

Every kid wants to make it to the majors and Justin Real was no different. As Justin explained, "I played college baseball, been playing baseball my whole life. My first job was working at a batting cage for 3 years teaching kids how to play baseball. *This* is my life." And so Realplay was born in 2016 out of a deep love for baseball, past experiences, a fascination with the possibilities of AI, a rock-solid financial model, and a problem that wasn't being solved very well. Players liked watching themselves play; parents wanted to preserve memories; coaches wanted to develop the best players; and recruiters wanted to find those players. The solution before Realplay? Low-quality video, unconnected video, no data, and video storage issues. Realplay became a high-quality, user-friendly solution for different stakeholders with different needs who all wanted access to the same information—the information that Justin could automate, tag, and post.

Justin Real thought he was going to be a successful consultant. He liked working on different projects and different companies in different industries. "The idea of dedicating your life to one job, one product was not something I saw myself doing," said Justin. One consulting project he worked on involved the potential development of a brainwave scanner helmet for baseball players that could measure the neurological effects of the "chess match" between a pitcher and a batter. Justin was hired to test the market, see how customers would react to the product, and what go-to-market strategies would be effective. As Justin recalled, "I kept getting the 'why are you doing this?' questions. I learned that why and how pitchers and batters react was not as important as the data and the visualization. I also learned a lot about how it was currently being done." What players and coaches wanted were statistics based on pitches and at-bats, but more than anything, the most important thing was literally *seeing* how they react and the patterns in those reactions. "How much they could see mattered," noted Justin. The helmet never went anywhere, but Justin identified an opportunity to do something that was sort of being done, but do it better, faster, and using innovative business structures that hadn't been tried yet.

Realplay installs proprietary camera systems at high school fields and multifield sport complexes. Baseball and softball combined are the most popular sport being played in the United States. Additionally, as Justin recalls, "High school and summer travel ball were the markets that were the least served by other video companies and seemed like the right market to be in for Realplay." The camera systems are installed at the beginning of the season so video can be captured at every home game. Unlike other camera solutions, Realplay cameras provide video footage from three different angles of specific players, tailored to the time they spend on the field. Using AI and machine learning, the cameras track a player by his or her jersey number, which makes the process of video editing more efficient. "What used to take 9 hours of human labor per game, we can do in 15 minutes."

Justin's experience in baseball outweighed his experience in technology. However, he had several jobs in technology where he learned the invaluable skill of taking a high-tech product and "dumbing it down so that I could explain it to people who needed to use it but didn't want to hear the technical jargon behind it. I was also then able to communicate what their needs were to the people who were actually designing the technology." While earning his MBA at Babson, he took technology courses and also enrolled in online courses at MIT to better understand computer vision, machine learning, and AI. Through networking, Justin eventually found his CTO, Andreas Randow, an ex-pat German who could bring the technology from Justin's whiteboard to the real world. According to Justin, "He is an expert in data visualization and machine learning the way that I am an expert in baseball. He has never played a day of baseball in his life. But the two of us came up with a solution that is unmatched by any technology company or baseball company!"

As Justin worked to raise capital to develop the platform and camera systems, he also learned the importance of developing the perfect pitch. He knew in the early stages that he was working to sell himself as a trustworthy and committed entrepreneur just as much as he was trying to sell his solution and vision. "The easiest pitch in the world is to describe an existing business. The more far away from reality the description of the business is, the lesser it will be believed and less you can back that pitch up as an entrepreneur."

Justin gives the example of running a bagel business to elaborate on the need to build reality into your pitch. "Let's say your business claims to sell the best bagels in the world. Someone will ask you how you do it. That question really means 'what is your business?' The answer to this question needs to be unflinchingly based in reality because any deviation from that will make it sound exponentially worse. If someone answers that question saying, 'We put the most love into our bagels, and we care deeply about our customers' that only answers why the business is good but *not* how it operates. That does not answer *why* the business works. So, taking that approach, what I've been doing is cutting off what we want to do and replacing it with what we actually do and why it works." For Justin, this recipe has impressed all those he meets because he is believable, authentic, and very much understands and is able to communicate what makes Realplay work.

Justin stresses that it is not the job of the pitcher to sell what the business is trying to do, but rather what it can do now. "Any information that focuses on the opportunity of a business should be based on fact and not conviction," says Justin. The pitch should clearly articulate operations and in a way that helps investors envision the bigger picture and potential impact of the business. If they understand the traction you have now, they can understand the potential in the future.

The focus of the pitch should also be on why the entrepreneur is so excited about the opportunity because it's difficult to separate the opportunity from the entrepreneur in the beginning. For Justin, it was important to build a story of what he has done, the customers he has acquired, the testing that was done, the feedback received. What work is still needed to do? All of this ties back to the facts of the business as well as the reality of who is running the business. "No one is going to back your idea if you don't have a business. It's really simple: If you can't answer how do you make your money, how much money do you need, and how much money the investor will get in 5 years, all in one sentence each, you don't have a business; you might have an idea, but you don't have a business."

Testing the pitch led Justin to create numerous iterations of the pitch. With each iteration, he added more clarity, more facts, more evidence, more realistic financial projections. With each new day of operational experience came stronger evidence of how the business operates. "When people poke holes in your pitch, they are probably right. Acknowledge that and the only way one can overcome that is by irrefutable evidence that you are right in what you're saying." Over time, his pitch became very comprehensive, so much so that he didn't feel the need to keep changing the pitch for different audiences. According to Justin, "The only time the pitch actually changes is if the ask of the pitch changes."

The following anecdote illustrates how effective Justin is in marketing himself before his business. He held a meeting for a group of investors so they could all be together in the same room while he made a formal pitch to all of them at the same time. He did this because he felt that people are likely to poke holes in the argument and question the execution of the project. He wanted to have a formal event that would allow him to get through a full pitch. Not just that, he wanted prospective investors to meet people who had already invested in Realplay. This would create an opportunity for current investors to be more candid with potential investors and tell them why they had already invested. After a lot of coordination and communication over LinkedIn, Justin organized the event in downtown Boston for this group of investors in the fall of 2018. As Justin recalled, "One thing that the event was able to showcase was that I have the capability to get a group of very qualified people in a room to listen to what I have to say. I also believe that pitching in a setting like this where the social effect, the business side of things, and the full story come together is more effective."

In May 2019, after 4 years of bootstrapping, Justin received $750k investment in a round led by LaunchPad Ventures and is using that money for operations and scaling. Time will tell whether Realplay succeeds in the long term. It's still early. But one thing is for certain: Justin Real is a success because he focused on building a business that reflects who he is, what he values, and what he loves. That makes selling Realplay very easy.

Critical Thinking Questions

1. Why is selling yourself just as important as selling your concept, in the early stages of a venture?

2. How is a pitch part of marketing your venture?

3. What is the difference between a good pitch and a good idea?

4. Would you invest in Realplay today? Why or why not?

Sources:

Justin Real (interview with Babson MBA graduate assistant Gaurav Khemka, January 18, 2019)

Realplay. (2019). *Crunchbase*. Retrieved from https://www.crunchbase.com/organization/realplay

Chapter Outline

Learning Objectives

B.1 TYPES OF PITCHES

>> LO B.1   Describe the pitch process and different types of pitches.

Every entrepreneur must have a pitch, and it can take many forms. However, what's common across all forms are two outcomes: (1) the receiver of the pitch understands your business and (2) the receiver is compelled to learn more. Whether you have 30 seconds or 30 minutes to pitch, these two outcomes are essential. Some pitches are more informal, without any presentation material besides yourself, while others are formal and require a pitch deck. A pitch deck is a presentation in PowerPoint (or a similar presentation software) that describes in detail the nature of the business, the need, the customer, the business model, profit potential, team, and call to action. But before getting to the pitch deck, let's look at the different types of pitches.

Dan Pink, in his book *To Sell Is Human,* gives a description of the first elevator pitch ever! He shares the story of Elisha Otis, who founded Otis Elevator Company in 1853. Contrary to popular belief, Otis didn't invent the elevator, but he did invent a much safer elevator. Before Otis, elevators were used to move materials from one floor to another, rather than people. The problem was that elevators were unreliable because the ropes would break, the platform would fall, and all contents would be destroyed. During the World's Fair in New York in 1854, Otis was looking to spread the word and get interest in his invention. So he gathered attendees and gave them a demonstration. With Otis standing on a platform common to most elevators at the time, his team hoisted him three stories into the air. Otis then abruptly took an axe and cut the ropes that were holding the platform in place. The platform started to fall, but Otis's invention, the safety brake, engaged and prevented the platform from falling to the ground. This demonstration of how his product worked is the most important take away from the concept of an elevator pitch. According to Dan Pink, "It was a simple, succinct, and effective way to convey a complex message in an effort to move others."[1]

Since the days of Otis, "elevator pitch" has evolved into a metaphor for a short pitch. For the past few decades, the elevator pitch was the standard way to pitch an idea. This meant that if you happened to find yourself in an elevator with someone important, you would be able to pitch your idea from the time of the doors closing to when they opened again. The idea was to use this short amount of time (less than 1 minute) to explain why your business was exciting and unique. Today, thanks to a more democratic working

$SAGE edge™

Master the content at
**edge.sagepub.com/
neckentrepreneurship2e**

structure that allows us easier access to influential people, and new technology that provides us with a whole set of tools to get in touch with others, the elevator pitch has evolved into several different forms. What's interesting now is that speed and brevity are even more important than ever. Table B.1 identifies pitch approaches that are even shorter than an elevator ride.[2]

Spend some time trying to apply the approaches in Table B.1 to your own business idea. The work done here will only help you when it's time to create your full pitch deck. For each of these approaches, and really any type of pitch you do, you need to answer three questions in advance:

What do you want the receiver of the pitch to know?

What do you want the receiver of the pitch to feel?

What do you want the receiver of the pitch to do?

Most of the pitch types described in Table B.1 are self-explanatory, but the Pixar pitch deserves a bit more explanation because it's a "storytelling" approach and the ability to tell a story is an essential skill of all entrepreneurs.

The Storytelling Approach

Regardless of your audience, it is essential that you articulate your idea clearly and tell a compelling story. Indeed, storytelling is part of our nature, and it is a powerful way of engaging and connecting with people.[4] Many of us make decisions based on stories that move or inspire us. Opening a pitch with "I have a story to tell" immediately alerts the audience that you have something to say that is interesting, personal, compelling, dramatic, and complete.

TABLE B.1

Pitch Types Shorter Than an Elevator Ride!

TYPE	DESCRIPTION	EXAMPLES
The one-word pitch	Identify the one word that describes the business	Google: Search Obama U.S. presidential campaign: Hope
The question pitch	Ask one question that can evoke emotion and compel people to respond	Uber: Are you tired of filthy taxis that you have to flag down in the middle of a rainstorm?
The rhyming pitch	Rhymes help the message stick	Five Guys: Five Guys burgers and fries
The subject-line pitch	The email subject line that is useful, specific, and evokes curiosity	Venture Blocks: Your students can learn how to interview customers in 30 minutes
The Twitter pitch	A message that is 140 characters or less	Babson College: Come join the only college that educates entrepreneurial leaders who generate economic and social value—EVERYWHERE
The Pixar pitch	Tell a complete story in six sentences	Toy Story: *Once upon a time,* there was a boy named Andy who loved to play with his toys. *Every day* when Andy wasn't around, the toys would come to life. *One day,* Andy got a new toy, Buzz Lightyear, that became his and all the other toys' favorite. *Because of that,* Woody became jealous and tried to get rid of Buzz Lightyear. *Because of that,* Buzz ended up at Sid's house and was almost destroyed. *But then,* Woody and the other toys rescued Buzz, and they all became friends.[3]

Most stories are based on a three-part narrative arc, which can be traced back to ancient Greece and the stories of the philosopher Aristotle. Aristotle's arc still applies to storytelling today: an introduction that presents the characters and ideas; the climax that outlines the problem at its height and how your solution can overcome the most complex of issues; and the resolution that explains how you expect things to work out.[5]

A story will be successful only if it is authentic and is told with genuine enthusiasm and energy. Starbucks founder Howard Schultz is known as an excellent storyteller who has used examples drawn from his personal life to ignite passion in others. According to Schultz, the philosophy behind Starbucks was based on his father's failure to find any meaning or fulfillment in his work. When his father ended up with a work injury and no compensation or health insurance, Schultz vowed that he would create the type of company that he could feel passionate about—one that both inspires and takes care of its staff.[6]

The Pixar pitch can be useful for explaining business ventures, even though this approach was designed to tell the story of a movie in six sentences.[7] Every movie made by Disney Pixar follows a narrative structure that can be summed up by the six chronological sentences outlined in Table B.2.

Let's now apply the Pixar pitch to a business called Attack! Marketing. Attack! is a marketing agency that provides experiential strategy and activation to lifestyle brands.[8] In other words, it takes the human approach to marketing by offering opportunities for people to taste, touch, and smell the products to inspire brand loyalty.

- Once upon a time, advertising agencies and brands in the United States were focusing solely on the concept of the campaign.

- Every day, millions of dollars would be spent on data collection, giveaways, and logistics, which neglected to engage the customer in a meaningful way, resulting in low trial rates and conversion numbers.

- One day, we developed a business called Attack! that revolutionized the consumer experience by introducing the human element, allowing consumers to taste, touch, and smell the products during live marketing events.

- Because of that, more consumers fell in love with the brand.

- Because of that, agencies saw a significant increase in the number of people who tried out the products and services and more conversions.

- Until finally, the Attack! philosophy became so widely accepted we were labelled as the pioneers in this approach.

The longer the pitch, the more important it is to tell a good story. The key to telling a good story is to tell the right story to the right audience. This involves understanding what type of people they are. Do your research. Who are they? What are their wants and needs? What is the best way of moving them? Don't be afraid to make your pitch

TABLE B.2

Six-Sentence Pitch Structure

1. Once upon a time, . . .
2. Every day, . . .
3. One day, . . .
4. Because of that, . . .
5. Because of that, . . .
6. Until finally, . . .

interactive by asking your audience for input—this makes them feel part of the story, and it will encourage them to become more engaged with your idea.[9]

In fact, successful pitches all have to do with drawing people in and moving them in some way. A study of the Hollywood pitch process conducted by Kimberly Elsbach of the University of California and Roderick Kramer of Stanford University showed that when pitchers invited studio executives to collaborate on an idea, there was a better chance of the project being green lit.[10] However, pitches were unsuccessful when the pitcher didn't listen or was unwilling to accept feedback or constructive criticism. Bringing people into your story and allowing them to participate is a powerful way of getting the buy-in you need. Everybody wants to be a part of something new and exciting, and everybody wants to feel like they had a part in its creation. That is why entrepreneurship is so enticing for so many—entrepreneurs, advisors, investors, employees, and even customers.

B.2 OVERVIEW OF THE PITCH DECK

>> **LO B.2** **Describe the pitch deck and its importance to potential investors.**

As mentioned above, a pitch deck is a presentation in PowerPoint (or a similar presentation software) that describes in detail the nature of the business, the need or problem it solves, industry characteristics, the customer, the market size, the business model, profit potential, team, and call to action. Keep in mind that it's usually impossible to get everything into a pitch, so your goal is to make sure the receiver is intrigued and interested enough to want to know more—to want to meet again. As highlighted in Chapter 10, there are many types of plans, and a pitch deck has become a visual and oral plan. In the past decade, the pitch deck has become one of the most valuable tools an entrepreneur can have when trying to raise startup capital or find other types of resources. A pitch deck is a good way to describe your business to a potential investor; it can also be used for meetings with potential partners, advisors, employees, or even a reporter who might be doing a story on your startup! Any stakeholder who has a vested interest in your business could be an audience for your pitch.

There are no strict rules for pitch deck length or style. For example, some people suggest that the pitch deck should have only 5 slides while others recommend 6, 10, 11, 12, 15, or even 30 slides.[11] Regardless of the slide count or style, all pitch decks need to answer the same fundamental questions:

- What is the problem/need?
- How will you solve the problem or meet the need in a unique way?
- Who is the customer, and are there enough customers to build a viable venture?
- What is the size/extent of the market for this product/service idea now and in the future?
- How will you reach, acquire, and keep the customer?
- Whom will you compete with, and how are you different?
- What is the revenue/expense model?
- What capabilities does your team have to execute the venture?
- What have you done so far?
- What is your call to action?

Typically, an initial meeting with a possible investor will be 30 minutes to 1 hour, but you should not use all of this time to present. Generally your pitch should not exceed 20 minutes, but different situations call for different pitch lengths. For this reason, we suggest being prepared to give a 1-, 3-, 10-, 15-, and 20-minute version. Whatever time is allotted for your pitch, it's important to leave room for questions. One of the biggest mistakes entrepreneurs make during a pitch is failing to leave time for questions at the end of the pitch.[12] If you can anticipate the questions in advance, it is also smart to create some backup slides with the answers to show that you have done your homework.

B.3 THE PITCH DECK

>> **LO B.3**   **Explain the content of pitch deck slides.**

While there is no one "right" pitch deck format, we have provided you with a basic template to follow that will help answer the essential questions. We use the company India in a Box, introduced in Chapter 10, as a pitch deck example. If you recall, India in a Box uses a subscription model to deliver authentic Indian meals that can be prepared by customers in minutes.

Slide 1: Title

The title slide should include the name of the company, logo, your name, and contact information (see Figure B.1). This is the first slide your audience will see and will likely be on screen the longest while they wait for you to present. Don't be boring here. Pay attention to slide design. In addition, consider putting your name and company on every slide so your audience will remember you and your company.

Slide 2: Company Purpose/Description

The purpose or vision slide is a quick overview of your company (see Figure B.2). Why does your company exist? Develop one sentence that describes what your company does. For example, it is a useful exercise to fill in the following blanks:

_____ [company] is _____ [product/service] for

_____ [target market] that _____ [problem].

For example: FlowDog *is* an aquatic and rehabilitation center *for* dogs *that* suffer from physical injuries.

_____ [company] sells _____ [product/service] to _____ [target market] in order to _____ [solution].

For example: VentureBlocks *sells* computer-based simulations *to* educators *in order to* help teach core topics related to entrepreneurship.

FIGURE B.1

Example Title Slide

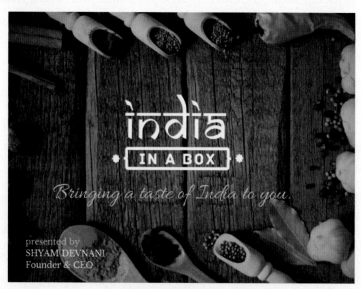

FIGURE B.2

Example Company Purpose/Description Slide

Source: Shyam Devnani

You could also include a comparison with a widely known brand, which will help the listener to immediately grasp the concept. For example, "We are the Uber for pets" or "we are the Netflix for video games."[13] Remember from Table B.1, these short pitches could come in handy as you prepare the opening for your pitch deck.

Slide 3: The Problem/Need

Describe the problem that your company is solving or how you are addressing a customer need (Figure B.3). Additionally, you should describe how the problem is currently being solved by other companies, and point out any inefficiencies in how it is being solved, or why the existing solutions are insufficient. Keep in mind that you need to prove to your audience that the problem is a big one. As venture capitalist Skylar Fernandes says, you need to solve the customer's #1 problem—not the #10 problem![14]

Slide 4: The Solution

The solution is really your value proposition, because if you can solve the customer's problem or fulfill their need in a unique way, then you are already creating value. Don't just type the solution on a slide, as in Figure B.4. If possible, offer a live demonstration. If the product or service is not yet fully developed, show a prototype or a picture of a prototype. If the solution is web-based, a mockup landing page is a must.

Another option is to show a **use case**—a methodology used in the software industry to illustrate how a user will interact with a specific piece of software.[15] Figure B.5 illustrates a use case to show how easy it is to prepare a meal from India in a Box. For entrepreneurs, use cases are also a good way of showing an audience how customers will interact with their products or services and how their lives are made easier through the interaction.

Use case: a methodology used in the software industry to illustrate how a user will interact with a specific piece of software.

Slide 5: Why Now?

There is a window of opportunity for many new ventures. You need to convince your audience that the time is now for your new product or service. This means pointing out trends or changes that prove that your company is timely (see sample slide in Figure B.6).

FIGURE B.3

Example Problem/Need Slide

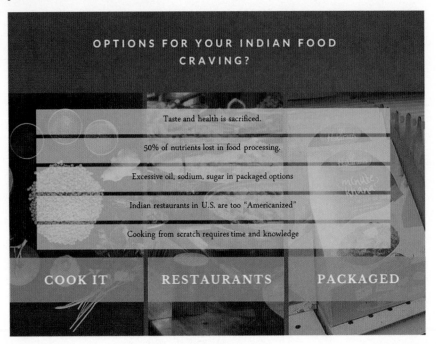

Source: Shyam Devnani

FIGURE B.4

Example Solution Slides

Source: Shyam Devnani

FIGURE B.5

Use Case Highlighting Cooking Instructions

Source: Shyam Devnani

FIGURE B.6

Example Why Now? Slide

Source: Shyam Devnani

Slide 6: Market Opportunity

As we discussed in Chapter 6: Developing Your Customers, the solution is powerful only if there is a market of customers willing to pay for the product or service. When it comes to creating your market opportunity slide, it is important to think about the three sub-groups of the market: TAM, SAM, and SOM (see 6.7: Market Sizing in Chapter 6). As a brief reminder:

- **TAM**, or total available market, refers to the total market demand for a product or service.

- **SAM**, or serviceable available market, is the section of the TAM that your product or service intends to target.

- **SOM**, or share of market, is the portion of SAM that your company is realistically likely to reach.

It is important for investors to see that you have thought through TAM, SAM, and SOM, so they have a better idea of the fraction of the market you intend to target. If you cannot prove that you have a good chance of penetrating the local market, then they will be unable to see the growth potential of your business.

Slide 7: Getting Customers

After depicting the market size and showing the target market, it is essential that you demonstrate an understanding of your customers—who they are and how you will reach them (see Chapter 6). This is where you talk about your interactions with customers and what you have learned about them during the planning process.

Using the café and donut example above, it's not enough to simply describe that your target market consists of 125,000 people living in a particular geographic area within the city of Baton Rouge. You also need to show that you have done your homework to better understand what kinds of people are likely to go to a café that serves high-end coffee and funky, gourmet donuts!

FIGURE B.7

Example Getting Customers Slide

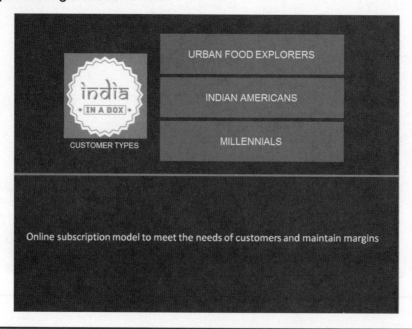

Source: Shyam Devnani

Additionally, you need to articulate how you will reach those customers, what they are willing to pay, and how you intend to keep them coming back (Figure B.7). Here you can begin to really build a market size number in terms of dollars using a simple calculation:

number of customers × price × frequency of purchase = market size $

You can do this calculation for a day, week, month, or year, and it should connect to your overall financials. Let's think about this for a single day. On an average day you may anticipate that 300 customers will enter the café and the average receipt based on 1 coffee and 1 donut is $7.50. Three hundred customers x $7.50 x 1 purchase = $2,250 total receipts for an average day. If there are 30 days in a month, then total monthly receipts could be $67,500. As a result the annual revenue could be $810,000.

Slide 8: Competitor Analysis and Differentiation

The competitor analysis shows how your company differentiates itself from others providing similar solutions, or how it has carved out a unique space that fulfills unmet needs. Competition is a good thing because it shows that there is a market for products and services. The key is to show how you are doing something better, different, and more compelling. A strong analysis will show the audience your competitive advantage—the source of why or how you will outperform others.

The competitive grid analysis compares your company to your most significant competitors and details their strengths and weaknesses relative to your own business. Figure B.8 illustrates an example of a competitive grid analysis for a new business called Best Cuts, comparing it to two different competing hair salons in terms of pricing, capacity, location, and other attributes.

FIGURE B.8

Example of Competitive Grid Analysis

Competitive Grid

Competitor	Bobo Salon and Styling	Johnny's Hair	BEST CUTS
Offerings	Men's/women's cut/styles/color perms	Men's cuts only	Men's/ women's cut/ style/ color/ perms
Service Prices	Starts at $38	Starts at $50	Starts at $30
Retail Prices	100% markup	100% markup	75% markup
Location	High traffic, highly visible	Moderate traffic, highly visible	High traffic, not visible
Expertise	20+years, up-to-date trends	15+ years, young hairstylists	13+ years, up-to-date trends
Service	Set hours, little schedule flexibility	Manager never there	Custom hours to suit clients needs
Turnover	Low	High	Sole stylist
Capacity	11 active chairs	8 active chairs	1 active chair
Client Base	Over 4000	?	Over 300

Source: http://www.slideshare.net/smarty23b/sample-business-plan-presentation2)

Another way to compare your company with the competition is to use a positioning matrix illustrating how you intend to position your business relative to the competition. Figure B.9 illustrates this concept with the Gourmet Donut Co. example.

The competitive matrix positions your company relative to the competition on selected variables. In Figure B.9, we look at the competition for the Gourmet Donut Co. based on price and flavors. Other possible variables could be price and quality or flavors and healthfulness of ingredients such as processed versus all natural. But in the example here, we will stick with price and flavors. After analyzing the competition in the Baton Rouge market, you can see that there are five donut shops that offer basic flavors of donuts at a low price, such as Dunkin' Donuts and Krispy Kreme. Their coffee is priced low as well. Starbucks and CC's offer expensive donuts, though basic flavors, and high-end coffee. You can see from the matrix that Gourmet Donut Co. is positioning itself very differently with its gourmet flavors.

Showing that you have done your homework on the competition is essential. One of the worst mistakes entrepreneurs can make in a pitch is claiming they have no competition. You will always have competition, and how you define that competition is important (see Figure B.10). Remember when you acquire customers you are taking them away from someone or something else. Who is that someone or something else? For example, before there was iTunes, there were music stores. Though iTunes was a great innovation, it still had competition.

Slide 9: Traction

Traction describes all the work you've done to date to build your venture. Your audience, especially investors, want to see the actions you have taken to construct your venture and the milestones you have achieved. Examples of traction include the following:

- Early customer adoption and showing you have revenue

- Completion of customer research

- Working website

- Working prototype or minimum viable product

FIGURE B.9

Gourmet Donut Co. Competitive Positioning

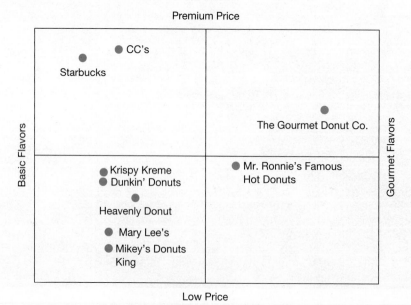

FIGURE B.10

Example Competitor Analysis and Differentiation Slide

Source: Shyam Devnani

- Submission of patent application
- Formation of team
- Product testing
- Contracting of suppliers
- Creation of first batch of product
- Successful crowdfunding campaign (where relevant)
- Securing of space (in the case of retail)
- Securing of investment or loans

Other evidence of traction includes recognition and press. For example, if you have won pitch competitions or been mentioned in blogs, magazines, TV shows, or other media, then you can talk about it here.

You could also include your future milestones or planned next steps. These could include expansion into new locations or overseas, the number of customers you intend to reach, or hiring more staff and employees. See Figure B.11 for an example of a traction slide.

Slide 10: Financials

In Chapter 13: Financing for Startups, we explored some options for financing. Your financials need to demonstrate that you have a clear understanding of potential profit and loss. It's important to highlight the key drivers of revenue and expenses, but keep it at the highest levels for now. In other words, you should not present a detailed income statement, cash-flow statement, and balance sheet (see Supplement A for further explanation), but you do need to show at least 3 years of revenue projections. Be realistic with these projections, and explain the assumptions underlying the projections. Have backup slides of detailed financials in case you are asked about them during the question and answer period.

In Figure B.12, Shyam shows 3-year profit potential for India in a Box. You may also want to consider showing three different scenarios, such as best case, worst case, and likely case. This shows investors and others that you are trying to be as realistic as possible with your projections.

FIGURE B.11

Example Traction Slide

Source: Shyam Devnani

FIGURE B.12

Example Financials Slide

	YEAR 1	YEAR 2	YEAR 3
FINANCIALS			
REVENUE	$261,000	$ 820,000	$ 2,540,000
EXPENSES	$ 132,000	$ 343,000	$ 980,000
GROSS PROFIT	$ 129,000	$ 477,000	$ 1,560,000
SG&A	$ 84,000	$ 225,000	$ 530,000
NET PROFIT	$45,000	$252,000	$1,030,000

61% GROSS PROFIT MARGIN | $1 Million PROFIT YEAR 3

Source: Shyam Devnani

Slide 11: Team

Showing you have a strong team with the right skillsets is more important than you might think. Your audience may not be convinced that the opportunity is there, but if the team is strong, then it's more likely that the team will be able to pivot as necessary to give the business the best possible chance for success.[16] The team slide should include a list of all team members, providing photos, their experience and education, and their role in the company (see Figure B.13). It's important that the team slide makes the audience think to themselves, "Yes, the team can actually do this. And, if they can't, they have the ability to pivot if necessary." If you have an advisory board, then include those names as well. Talent attracts other talent. So if you have an amazing team, you might even consider moving this slide to the beginning of your presentation. See Chapter 8 for more on building quality teams.

Slide 12: Call to Action

The call to action is the most often-forgotten slide! It doesn't matter if you are pitching to a venture capitalist, an angel investor, an audience in a pitch competition, your professor, a friend, your class, or your grandmother, you must always have a call to action (Figure B.14). By this point, you've likely spent about 15 minutes presenting your idea. So now it's time to ask for something.

What you ask for depends on your audience. If you are presenting to an investor, you are probably asking for money. If this is the case, then you need to say how you plan to use the money. For example: "I'm asking for $200,000 for 20% of the company. The money invested will primarily be used for . . . (e.g., building out the sales channel, customer acquisition through marketing, packaging, redesign, hiring)." If you are pitching to your classmates, you might be asking for feedback on the idea. If you are pitching to your professor, you might be asking him or her to act as an advisor. If so, then tell your professor what you are looking for in an advisor. If you need team members, ask for them, but be specific in the skillsets you are looking for. The bottom line is, don't ever pitch without asking for something at the end because you could be missing a major opportunity.

FIGURE B.13

Example Team Slide

Source: Shyam Devnani

FIGURE B.14

Example Call to Action Slides

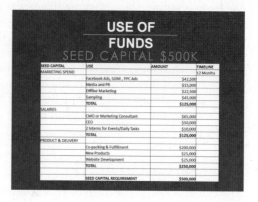

Source: Shyam Devnani

B.4 THE QUESTION AND ANSWER PERIOD

>> **LO B.4**   **Anticipate and prepare for the types of questions that may be asked during the question and answer period.**

During the question and answer period (Q&A) at the end of your presentation, the title slide should be showing. As we mentioned earlier, it is also useful to have a series of backup slides that can help you answer the most anticipated questions. In addition, you will likely pitch to more than one audience, so remember to incorporate answers to new questions that may have arisen in previous meetings.

For pitches in front of investors, or applications to incubators, or pitch competitions, you can be sure that some of the following questions will be asked.[17]

Team Questions

- Why is the team capable of executing what you have proposed today?
- How do you divide up responsibilities among the team members?
- What is the equity split among team members?
- How are decisions made among the team members?
- Who is the boss?
- Who came up with the original idea?
- Who else do you need to add to your team in the short term?
- What obstacles have you faced, and how did you overcome them?
- Are you open to changing your idea?

Product/Customer Questions

- What makes customers try your product/service?
- What is the technology behind your product?
- How does your product work in more detail?

- What are the risks?
- What is the next step in your product evolution?
- Where do most of your customers come from today?
- How many customers do you have today?
- Who is going to be your first paying customer?
- How are you understanding customer needs?
- How do you really know people want this?

Competition Questions

- Which competitor do you fear the most?
- Are the barriers to entry high or low? In other words, is it easy for competitors to enter the same market?
- How much money have your competitors made?
- Why do you think you are unique among your competitors?
- Can the competition do what you are doing if they want to?
- Why hasn't this already been done?

Financial Questions

- How did you calculate your market size?
- What are the assumptions behind your revenue projections?
- Are your numbers comparable to those of your competitors?
- What happens if you don't achieve your projected revenue?
- If I invest, what exactly are you going to do with the cash and what impact will it have on your business?
- What is the typical cycle between making initial customer contact and closing the sale?
- How much does it cost to acquire one customer?

Growth Questions

- If your startup succeeds, what additional areas might you be able to expand into?
- Are there other applications for your product/service/technology?
- How are you defining success?
- How big do you want to grow?
- What is a likely exit strategy for this business?
- What competition do you fear most?
- Where do your growth projections come from?

Regardless of how prepared you are, there may be some questions that still take you by surprise. Two-time technology entrepreneur Caroline Cummings, who raised $1 million for her startup, wrote a blog post on the 10 most unexpected questions she was asked during her pitch to a venture capitalist (see Table B.3). These questions show that investors are interested in who you are as a person and how you think, just as much as they are interested in the opportunity you present to them!

TABLE B.3

Ten Most Unexpected Questions

Who believes in you, and how can I get in touch with them?
What entrepreneurs do you admire and why?
How do you track trends in your market?
Can you tell me a story about a customer using your product?
How do you know how much money you need, and could you scale your business with less?
How can I connect with five customers who have used your product?
What will your market look like in 5 years as a result of using your product or service?
What mistakes have you made thus far in this business, and what have you learned?
What if 3 to 5 years down the road we think you are not the right person to continue running this company—how will you address that?
Have you ever been fired from a job? Tell us about it.

Source: Cummings, C. (2013, February 22). The 10 questions I didn't expect to be asked by investors. *Bplans Blog.* Retrieved from http://articles.bplans.com/the-10-questions-i-didnt-expect-to-be-asked-by-investors/

The pitch deck process is essential to engaging an audience in order to generate interest, and to secure commitment and, where appropriate, investment. The key to a good presentation is preparation. By creating the number of slides that succinctly outline the nature of your company, presenting with passion and knowledge, and taking the time to prepare the responses to questions you might be asked, you will have a better chance of engaging the right people to join you on your journey to entrepreneurial success.

B.5 PUBLIC SPEAKING TIPS

>> **LO B.5   Illustrate the importance of public speaking skills to entrepreneurs.**

With all this talk about the pitch, we still need to address pitching! You can have the greatest slide deck in the world with amazing content and beautiful design, but none of it matters if *you* can't *deliver* the message. How are your presentation skills? Do you fear or embrace public speaking? Here are some tips to help you overcome nerves and anxiety.

- **Practice but don't memorize**. If you memorize your pitch, it becomes more evident when you go off script. Practice enough that your pitch sounds more conversational than overly rehearsed. Know the flow of your pitch, outline the essentials, but don't script out every single word. Did we say practice? Practice, practice, practice until it becomes no natural that it becomes virtually impossible to mess up!

- **Pay attention to time restrictions**. If you are given 3 minutes, do not go over. Don't assume that if you are given 3 minutes, that the receivers will give you an additional minute. Usually they will not even give you an additional 10 seconds, especially if you are pitching in some type of competition.

- **Don't hold anything in your hands**. Don't hold notes, a tablet, your phone, or anything because if you are nervous, it will be obvious. An entrepreneur pitching with index cards that are shaking in his or her hands does not scream, "Hey, invest in me!"

- **Don't read slides.** Slides are there to complement the entrepreneur, not replace the entrepreneur. Looking back at your slides or, in some cases, to the back of the room at a confidence monitor, prevents you from engaging with your audience. Reading slides is not much different than reading those index cards shaking in your hands. Furthermore, if you have to read your slides then there is too much text on your slides. The focus needs to be on you, not your slides. If your story can be told without you and with the slides alone, you do not have a good pitch.

- **Dress the part**. Use your best judgment here. A business suit is not always required and the world of entrepreneurship is less formal. If you are pitching in a competition, see what others are likely to wear. Also consider *what* you are pitching. If you are pitching a clothing line, you should be wearing your product. If you are pitching a new golf product, you would likely wear a golf shirt with your company logo. Though Mark Zuckerberg's hoodie is not necessarily good judgment, the point that a business suit is not always required should be clear.

- **Drink water**. TED speaker coach Gina Barnett suggests you start drinking water 15 minutes before your pitch to avoid dry mouth.[18] Dry mouth leads to pronunciation errors, which increases nervousness, which will increase the likelihood of you messing up even more!

- **Eye contact cannot be faked**. Nervous speakers look above their audience, to the back of the room, or as just mentioned, at their slides. They may think the audience doesn't notice, but they do. Take time to look audience members in the eye as you pitch. This will increase your connection with the audience as well as give you immediate feedback. Eye contact will tell you if your message is resonating, if they are confused, or if you are boring them to tears!

- **Learn to improvise**. Stage actors are trained in theatrical improvisation so the audience would never be able to tell when the actor forgot their lines. The actor was so skilled that she or he could create new lines on the spot that would not disrupt the flow or change the direction of the story. Public speakers need to do the same. Improvisation is needed when you forget where you want to go next and when that eye contact just talked about reveals that your audience is just not with you for one reason or another.

- **Move but don't pace**. Don't stand behind a podium. Stand boldly in front of your audience but don't move too much around the room and certainly don't pace. Your body movement can be your greatest asset as a speaker or your worst liability. Movement is bad when it's annoyingly repetitive such as playing with change in your pocket, putting your weight on one foot forcing you to lean or move from side to side, or using the same hand movements over and over. Using your body movements, however, can help you tell your story and also encourage people to focus on you rather than your slides. To emphasize points, use a hand gesture or step forward. Wherever you begin your presentation, think about an imaginary box around you that extends 3 feet in each direction. Move inside that box with intention and purpose!

- **Practice crisp articulation**. Poor diction can destroy a first impression, but poor diction typically results from inappropriate stretching prior to your talk! Usually before a presentation we are a bit nervous and tight. Public speaking coach Gary Genard offers a few warmup exercises in Table B.4.

- **Vary your voice to avoid the monotone trap**. It's important to vary the pitch of your voice to keep the attention of your audience. In general, the average speaker has a high voice, middle voice, and low voice. Unless you are actor James Earl Jones, we generally speak in our high or middle voice. The high voice comes from the head and our middle voice comes from our gut area. The high voice is best used to show enthusiasm but can be a bit annoying if an entire pitch is in a high voice. The middle voice is where you get the most resonance, forces you to slow down, and to articulate. Always start in your middle voice. To get there take a deep breath and begin speaking from your diaphragm area between your chest and abdomen.

TABLE B.4

Exercises to Improve Diction

EXERCISE	HOW TO DO IT
The Lion	Make a "lion face": widen your eyes, open up your mouth fully, and stick out your tongue.
Scrunch-Face	Now do the opposite, scrunching your face up into a tight little ball. Go back and forth between The Lion and Scrunch-Face.
Invisible Gum	Chew a gigantic imaginary wad of bubble gum. Keep your teeth apart but lips together. Really move that thing around in your mouth. Blow imaginary bubbles if you like!
Rubber Face	Imagine that your face is made of rubber, and manipulate it with your hands. Move it all around. Danger: this might make you yawn (which is good).
Jaw Relaxer	With the balls of both hands, apply medium pressure to the sides of your face just below the temples. Move slowly downward, allowing your hands to pull your face downward until you're making a "horror comic" face.
Exaggerated Diction	Recite aloud any passage you know by heart. Over-articulate each sound, working your mouth into exaggerated shapes.

Source: Genard, G. (2018). *Speak for success! How to dramatically improve your voice for public speaking.* Retrieved from. https://www.genardmethod.com/blog/how-to-dramatically-improve-your-voice-for-public-speaking

- **Choreograph your rhythm.** Practice in advance where you will have pauses, what words or sentences you really want to emphasize, where you will slow down, and where you will speed up. Even think about when you want to smile or when you want to be serious. Think about when and how you should move in the imaginary box talked about above.

- **Embrace your nervousness.** That nervous feeling, those butterflies in your stomach, and shaking knees will not likely go away even with practice. The nerves will actually keep you focused and help you. The trick is not to let the nerves overpower and paralyze you. By employing some of the techniques above, you will control the nerves! ●

Get the tools you need to sharpen your study skills. SAGE edge offers a robust online environment featuring an impressive array of free tools and resources.

- Access practice quizzes, eFlashcards, video, and multimedia at **edge.sagepub.com/neckentrepreneurship2e**

SUMMARY

B.1 Describe the pitch process and different types of pitches.

Preparing a pitch involves thorough understanding of the audience, deliberate framing of the problem and solution, the resources required (the "ask"), and the method by which all of this will be communicated. Some popular pitches include the elevator pitch, the storytelling pitch, the Pixar pitch, the question pitch, the one-word pitch, the rhyming pitch, the subject-line pitch, and the Twitter pitch.

B.2 Describe the pitch deck and its importance to potential investors.

A pitch deck is a presentation in PowerPoint (or equivalent) that describes in detail the nature of the business, the need or problem it solves, industry characteristics, the customer, the market size, the business model, profit potential, team, and call to action.

B.3   Explain the content of pitch deck slides.

While there are no strict rules for length or style, your slides should include the following information: title, company purpose/description, the problem/need, the solution, why now?, market opportunity, getting customers, competitor advantages and differences, traction, financials, team, and call to action.

B.4   Anticipate and prepare for the types of questions that may be asked during the question and answer period.

When it comes to the question and answer period, expect the unexpected. In this regard, it is useful to prepare a series of backup slides that can help you answer the most anticipated questions.

B.5   Illustrate the importance of public speaking to entrepreneurs.

Public speaking is an essential part of pitching. Tips include practice, but don't memorize, pay attention to time restrictions, dress the part, learn to improvise, and drink water.

KEY TERM

Use case   413

16 Supporting Social Entrepreneurship

"Social entrepreneurs are not content just to give a fish or teach how to fish. They will not rest until they have revolutionized the fishing industry."

—Bill Drayton, *Leading Social Entrepreneurs Changing the World*

Chapter Outline

16.1   The Role of Social Entrepreneurship

16.2   Social Entrepreneurship and Wicked Problems

16.3   Types of Social Entrepreneurship

16.4   Capital Markets for Social Entrepreneurs

16.5   Social Entrepreneurs and Their Stakeholders

16.6   Differences Between Social Entrepreneurship and Corporate Social Responsibility

16.7   Social Entrepreneurship and Audacious Ideas

16.8   Global Entrepreneurship

Learning Objectives

16.1   Describe the role social entrepreneurship plays in society.

16.2   Explain how social entrepreneurship can help resolve wicked problems around the world that are connected to the United Nations Sustainable Development Goals.

16.3   Identify the different types of social entrepreneurship.

16.4   Explain how social entrepreneurs can use capital markets to fund their ventures.

16.5   Identify the primary attributes of stakeholders and how stakeholders can help or hinder a social entrepreneur.

16.6   Distinguish between corporate social responsibility and social entrepreneurship.

16.7   Explore audacious ideas being pursued by social entrepreneurs today.

16.8   Illustrate the global diversity of entrepreneurship.

16.1 THE ROLE OF SOCIAL ENTREPRENEURSHIP

>> **LO 16.1   Describe the role social entrepreneurship plays in society.**

In Chapter 1, we introduced social entrepreneurship as the process of sourcing innovative solutions to social and environmental problems. What's the difference between social entrepreneurs and traditional entrepreneurs? Social entrepreneurs and business entrepreneurs share some similarities: Both types found new organizations, identify opportunities, create and implement innovation solutions or services, find information and resources, form connections, and create marketing initiatives to promote offerings.[1]

However, the main difference between traditional and social entrepreneurship lies in its intended mission. Traditional entrepreneurs create ventures with a goal of making a profit, and they measure performance by the profits they generate. In contrast, social entrepreneurs create ventures to tackle social problems and bring about social change; they measure performance by advancing social and environmental goals. Some also desire profit, in the case of for-profit ventures, while others are less concerned about profit. The great number of new nonprofit and nongovernmental organizations (NGOs) being started around the globe attests to this second category. In this chapter, we celebrate all types of social entrepreneurs—those who are mission-based and solving social problems—regardless of the nature of their profit motives. Organic Valley is a good example of a for-profit organization that does good by supporting family farmers and providing healthy organic food for consumers.

In this chapter, we discuss the different types of social entrepreneurship, explore the global social and environmental challenges facing us today, and share some stories of social entrepreneurs who have acted on opportunities to build scalable businesses. With the right entrepreneurial skills and a strong sense of empathy, compassion, and commitment, entrepreneurs are preserving and protecting future generations.

Master the content at
**edge.sagepub.com/
neckentrepreneurship2e**

Organic Valley

Picture Source: Organic Valley (with permission)

The Organic Valley Team

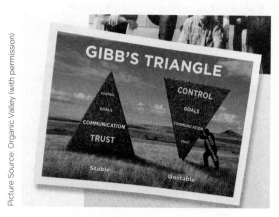

Picture Source: Organic Valley (with permission)

Organic Valley's organizational culture framework, Gibb's Triangle

In 1988, seven Wisconsin farmers set out to change the way that organic farmers in the United States would be rewarded economically for their stewardship of the land, animals, and earth. It was a revolutionary idea. Historically and to this day, American agriculture operates predominantly as a commodity market with heavy government subsidies fueling what was grown where, and at what scale. The seven farmers decided that they had had enough. They wanted out of the commodity game.

They organized themselves into the Coulee Region Organic Produce Pool (CROPP), parent to the now nationally recognized billion-dollar brand Organic Valley. Thirty years later, CROPP is the largest fully organic, fully farmer-owned dairy cooperative in North America, selling milk, cheese, butter, yogurt, cream, eggs, and both fresh and processed meats. The cooperative has grown from seven entrepreneurs to more than 2,000 family farmers across 35 states. No small potatoes: CROPP represents more than 14% of all organic farmland in the United States and in 2017, it pulled in $1.1 billion in revenue.

From day one, Organic Valley's mission has been to keep family farmers on the land and to give consumers better food without chemicals. The cooperative is committed to many social and environmental issues, yet it is structured as a for-profit enterprise.

"I'd never been a very profit-oriented person," reflected founding farmer and recent CEO George Siemon. "But I realized that a profitable company allows a mission to flourish. You may start out with noble values, but if you don't have a viable business plan, the values don't carry the water."

As a cooperative, Organic Valley is owned by its farmers, and the farmers make the decisions. With so many owners, this means a lot of meetings, and a somewhat chaotic process that can move very slowly. But "None of us are as smart as all of us" is a foundational tenet for them, and they adhere to it.

Gibb's Triangle is a framework they use to defend their organizational culture. "It compares two potential paths," explained Siemon. "The first is built on prioritization that begins with trust in human goodness, then sharing common goals and communicating them effectively. This path minimizes rules and controls. In contrast, the other path relies heavily on rules and controls, while minimizing trust. Over the years, the Gibb's Triangle has kept our cooperative viable. We must choose Gibb's first path and avoid the kind of tempting rigidity that wants to control everything that's human."

As a successful business with a nationally recognized brand, CROPP is sometimes accused of being yet another corporation profiting off the organic movement. But its missions remain front and center: saving family farms; providing meaningful work; proving that partnership is better; providing consumers with delicious organic food that is good for them, their families, the farmers, and the land.

Any time the question of "Are we getting too big?" comes up, the next question is always: "What is more important: size or mission?" Mission always wins. When it stops winning, CROPP is committed to stopping growth until the cooperative can regain its footing and its focus.

Logistically, Organic Valley is structured around regional pool points. So if you are standing in the dairy aisle in a grocery store in Boston, for instance, the Organic Valley products in that case came from family farmers living, working, and stewarding the land right around you in New England.

Critical Thinking Questions

1. Should entrepreneurs exist to make money? Solve social and/or environmental problems? Or both? Explain your answer.

2. Explain how trust plays a central role in the longevity of Organic Valley.

3. What social or environmental problem would you like to solve? ●

Source: This feature was written by Rachel Greenberger, Director of Food Sol at Babson College. Material was sourced from CROPP Cooperative (2013). Roots: The first 25 years. LaFarge, WI: Organic Valley.

16.2 SOCIAL ENTREPRENEURSHIP AND WICKED PROBLEMS

>> **LO 16.2** **Explain how social entrepreneurship can help resolve wicked problems around the world that are connected to the United Nations Sustainable Development Goals.**

In the 1960s, scholars coined the term **wicked problems**—large, complex social problems where there is no clear solution; where there is limited, confusing, or contradictory information available; and where a whole range of people with conflicting values engage in debate. More recently, Jeffrey Conklin, director of the Cognexus Institute, provided broader and more practical applications of the term (see Table 16.1).[2]

Issues relating to the environment, poverty, sustainability, equality, education, child mortality, sanitation, terrorism, and health and wellness are all examples of wicked problems, whether on a global, national, or local scale (see Figure 16.1).

The dramatic increase in life expectancy—an issue affecting many countries, particularly in the Western world—is an example of a wicked problem to which there are no easy answers. An aging population is likely to result in rising health care costs, an increase in the number of people claiming pensions, and potentially higher taxes for those supporting the nonworking retirees.

Wicked problems: large, complex social problems where there is no clear solution; where there is limited, confusing, or contradictory information available; and where a whole range of people with conflicting values engage in debate.

TABLE 16.1

Conklin's Defining Characteristics of Wicked Problems

1.	The problem is not understood until after the formulation of a solution.
2.	Wicked problems have no stopping rule.
3.	Solutions to wicked problems are not right or wrong.
4.	Every wicked problem is essentially novel and unique.
5.	Every solution to a wicked problem is a "one shot operation."
6.	Wicked problems have no given alternative solutions.

Credit: Conklin, J. (2006). *Dialogue mapping: Building shared understanding of wicked problems.* Chichester, UK: Wiley Publishing. Reprinted with permission from John Wiley & Sons.

FIGURE 16.1

Global Wicked Problems

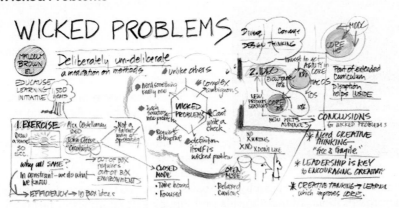

Source: David Sibbet, CEO of The Grove. Retrieved from http://redarchive.nmc.org/news/communique-2013-future-education-summit. Reprinted with permission of David Sibbet.

United Nations Sustainable Development Goals

Sustainable Development Goals

Source: United Nations Sustainable Development Goals website: https://www.un.org/sustainabledevelopment/. The content of this publication has not been approved by the United Nations and does not reflect the views of the United Nations or its officials or Member States.

In 2012, world leaders came together at a UN conference to adopt the Sustainable Development Goals (SDGs), a set of universal goals to tackle environmental, political, and economic challenges. The SDGs have been called the strategic plan for the planet given the importance of protecting the future of the planet and its inhabitants—us! The SDGs were a replacement for the Millennium Development Goals (MDGs), which made great strides in reducing poverty, increasing access to water and sanitation, improving child mortality rates, and providing greater opportunities for free primary education. Although there were many impressive achievements

made by the MDGs, there is still much to be done. The SDGs continue the objectives of the MDGs while incorporating some new goals—17 in total. Each goal is interconnected; for instance, tackling climate change leads to better management of our natural resources; promoting health and well-being helps eliminate poverty; and campaigning for peace and inclusiveness reduces gender inequality and cultivates economic prosperity. Based on the principle "of leaving no-one behind," the SDGs cover issues that impact us all, encouraging us to work together toward building a safer, more sustainable, better future for generations to come. Entrepreneurs around the world are creating new businesses to tackle one or more of the goals. Further evidence that the lines between social entrepreneurship and other forms of entrepreneurship are blurring, which suggests that all entrepreneurship is social.

Critical Thinking Questions

1. Which SDG do you most resonate with personally, and why?

2. Why do you think the SDGs are labeled as the "strategic plan for the planet"?

3. How can the SDGs be used to create economic and social value at the same time?

4. Do you agree or disagree that "all entrepreneurship is social"? ●

AP Photo/ Manish Swarup

The International campaign End Water Poverty (EWP)

Problems such as these are usually managed by policymakers who are responsible for creating ways to find solutions, but the path is fraught with obstacles. These problems are so complex that traditional linear problem-solving methods do not generally work. The nature of wicked problems poses significant challenges to social entrepreneurs, but also provides huge opportunities to make a real difference in their own countries and around the world.

The global water crisis is a good example of a wicked problem. According to the international campaign End Water Poverty (EWP), more than 600 million people worldwide have no access to clean, safe water. In addition, for at least 1 month a year, two-thirds of the world's population suffer from water scarcity. U.S.-based Planet Water Foundation is one of many nonprofit organizations addressing this problem by setting up water filtration systems, called Aqua Towers, in the world's most impoverished communities.[3] These systems kill harmful bacteria and provide thousands of people with clean water every day.

How Entrepreneurship Is Saving the Planet

The UN Sustainable Development Goals (SDGs) can be considered the strategic plan for the planet! Irina Bokava, former director-general of UNESCO, summarized the UN Sustainable Development goals with the following powerful quote:

> There is no more powerful transformative force than education—to promote human rights and dignity, to eradicate poverty and deepen sustainability, to build a better future for all, founded on equal rights and social justice, respect for cultural diversity, and international solidarity and shared responsibility, all of which are fundamental aspects of our common humanity.

Pick one of the 17 SDGs that you feel personally connected to in some way, and find four startups or entrepreneurial companies that are working in the space related to your chosen goal. Two of your examples must be for-profit businesses and two must be nonprofit organizations. For each example, answer the following questions:

- What is the business or organization?
- How is your example connected to your chosen SDG?
- What is the mission of the business or organization?
- Who are the most important stakeholders?
- Who is the customer?
- Assess impact. How are success and value measured?

Critical Thinking Questions

1. Compare and contrast your four examples. Do you see patterns?
2. Do you see differences or similarities between for-profit and nonprofit examples?
3. What do you now know that you didn't know before completing this Mindshift? ●

Source: #TeachSDGs (http://www.teachsdgs.org)

Whereas many of us avoid wicked problems because of their complex nature, these companies see wicked problems as a challenge to think differently or as an opportunity to break through constraints and develop creative solutions. Their focus lies in using their social entrepreneurs to generate the best alternative ideas.

Let's take a look at how two surfers, Alex Schulze and Andrew Cooper, created their own solution to a complex social problem. In 2015, college graduates Schulze and Cooper flew to Bali, Indonesia, for a surfing vacation. But instead of crystal-clear waters and pure white sand, they found piles and piles of plastic. When they made a few enquiries, they found that the local fishermen were catching more plastic in their nets than fish—something that threatened the fishermen's livelihood and the environment itself. This gave Schulze and Cooper an idea: What if the fishermen could be paid to collect the plastic as well as the fish? Determined to see their idea through, the two friends created 4ocean—a for-profit business that pays fishermen all over the world to catch plastic. The fishermen are funded by the sale of 4ocean bracelets made from recycled materials. To date, 4ocean has removed almost 4 million pounds of trash from the ocean and coastlines all over the world.

Companies like 4ocean are even more important when it comes to tackling the growing threat of climate change. A recent study conducted by the University of Hawaii shows that plastic releases greenhouse gases—gases that contribute to global warming—when exposed to direct sunlight.[4] In 2018, the Intergovernmental Panel on Climate Change warned that the world has less than a decade to reduce greenhouse gas emissions to prevent harmful droughts, floods, and other extreme weather events.[5]

This climate crisis has given rise to many other entrepreneurial ventures set up to find the solution to different aspects of climate change. For example, California-based Impossible Foods was set up to address the issue of animal farming—one of the biggest contributors to climate change—by creating a meatless burger made from plant-based products.[6] Fast-food chain White Castle was among the first to introduce the burger in 2018.

Koe Koe Tech, the app that helps mothers track their pregnancies and learn how to care for their children, is an example of a social purpose venture.

Social purpose ventures: businesses created by social entrepreneurs to resolve a social problem and make a profit.

Social consequence entrepreneurship: a for-profit venture whose primary market impact is social.

16.3 TYPES OF SOCIAL ENTREPRENEURSHIP

>> **LO 16.3** **Identify the different types of social entrepreneurship.**

There are different models of social entrepreneurship. Figure 16.2 illustrates the territory of social entrepreneurship.[7] As we have described the differences between traditional and social entrepreneurship, let's take a look at (1) social purpose ventures, (2) social consequence ventures, and (3) enterprising nonprofits and their relationship to social entrepreneurship.

Social Purpose Ventures

The aim of social purpose ventures is to resolve a social problem and make a profit. Koe Koe Tech is a good example of a social purpose venture: It was founded by Michael Lwin, a Myanmar American lawyer, in response to the shockingly high infant mortality rate in Myanmar. Lwin created the Koe Koe Tech app to help mothers track their pregnancies and learn how to take care of their children for the first 2 years of life. Within 3 months of launching, 40,000 people in Myanmar had signed up to the app.

Social Consequence Entrepreneurship

Social consequence entrepreneurship describes a for-profit venture whose primary market impact is social. A good example of a for-profit venture with a social impact is Sword & Plough, a startup founded by sisters Emily and Betsy Núñez. Sword & Plough hires army veterans to recycle surplus military materials such as parachutes, sleeping bags, and tents into fashionable bags and accessories. The company was launched in 2013, benefiting from $312,000 in funding, thanks to a powerful Kickstarter campaign. It donates 10% of its profits to veterans' organizations.

FIGURE 16.2

Typology of Ventures

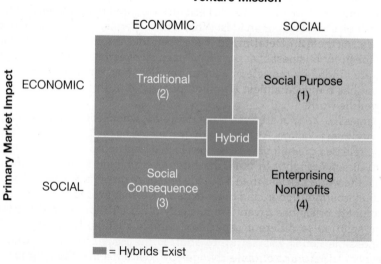

Source: Neck, H. M., Brush, C., & Allen, E. (2009). The landscape of social entrepreneurship. *Business Horizons, 52,* 13–19.

Since its founding, Sword & Plough has created almost 65 jobs for U.S. veterans and has recycled more than 30,000 pounds of discarded military material into thousands of products.[8] Through their innovative products, the founders aim to bridge the gap between civilians and the military by raising public awareness of veterans and the challenges facing servicemembers every day. Sword & Plough is just one of many for-profit companies in existence today that "does well [i.e., makes money] by doing good."

Enterprising Nonprofits

Enterprising nonprofits are a form of social entrepreneurship in which both the venture mission and the market impact are for social purposes. This means that any profits made must be channeled back into the organization. Unlike social purpose ventures, profit may not be distributed to the owners of the enterprising nonprofit. There are more than 1.5 million nonprofit organizations in operation in the United States today, including charities, foundations, and others (see Table 16.2).

Compared to traditional nonprofit startups, enterprising nonprofits are more likely to survive in business after the first 5 years. This may have to do with revenue resources: Typically, enterprising nonprofits have better access to revenue streams from universities, hospitals, and foundations. Table 16.3 illustrates the differences between traditional nonprofit entrepreneurs and enterprising nonprofits.

Credit: AP Photo/Bartley Young

Emily and Betsy Núñez, founders of Sword & Plough

Enterprising nonprofits: a form of social entrepreneurship in which both the venture mission and the market impact are for social purposes.

TABLE 16.2

Quick Facts About Nonprofit Organizations in the United States

1,571,056	tax-exempt organizations
1,097,689	public charities
105,030	private foundations
368,337	other types of nonprofit organizations, including chambers of commerce, fraternal organizations, and civic leagues

Source: NCCS Business Master File 12/2015. Retrieved from http://nccs.urban.org/statistics/quickfacts.cfm

---

TABLE 16.3

Differences Between Traditional Nonprofit Entrepreneurs and Enterprising Nonprofits

	TRADITIONAL NONPROFIT ENTREPRENEURS	ENTERPRISING NONPROFIT ENTREPRENEURS
Survival rate of business for the first 5 years	50%	84%
Gender breakdown	41% women/59% men	60% women/41% men
Average age of founders	40	53
Education level	31% have a college degree	89% have a college degree
Previous experience	55% of founders start nonprofits in industries other than those they have been working in	67% of nonprofit founders had more than 10 years' experience working in the private sector

Source: http://www.kauffman.org/blogs/growthology/2015/03/six-ways-non-profit-entrepreneurs-are-distinct-from-traditional-entrepreneurs

Although there may be some differences between nonprofit entrepreneurs and traditional for-profit (also called enterprising) entrepreneurs, both types create their own ventures out of a desire to fill a gap and meet a need. There are two types of enterprising nonprofits: earned-income activities and venture philanthropy.

Earned-income activities involve the sale of products or services that are used as a source of revenue generation. For example, American retailor nonprofit ABLE sells women's clothing and accessories manufactured by women living in impoverished conditions in deprived countries.[9] By empowering women with new skills, ABLE provides a new opportunity to break the cycle of poverty in their communities.

In contrast to the earned-income model, **venture philanthropy funding** combines financial assistance such as grants with a high level of engagement by the funder. Venture philanthropists share their experience with nonprofit entrepreneurs to help grow and scale the company to drive social change. This might take the form of marketing and communications, executive coaching, human resources, or providing access to other contacts and potential funders. Typically, financial support is provided for 3 to 5 years, with the goal of enabling the nonprofit to become financially independent by the end of this period (see Table 16.4).

The poverty-fighting nonprofit Robin Hood foundation is a good example of a venture philanthropy fund.[10] Every year, the foundation funds more than 200 programs across New York City to help feed and offer job opportunities to more than 200,000 New Yorkers. Over the last 30 years, it has raised $2.5 billion for impoverished, neglected communities.[11]

Like many venture capital (VC) firms, venture philanthropists look for nonprofits whose social impact can be definitively measured and that demonstrate the potential to develop and grow. Venture philanthropy organizations include BonVenture in Germany, Impetus Trust and CAN-Breakthrough in the United Kingdom, d.o.b. Foundation in

Earned-income activities: the sale of products or services that are used as a source of revenue generation.

Venture philanthropy funding: a combination of financial assistance such as grants with a high level of engagement by the funder.

TABLE 16.4

Features of Venture Philanthropy

CHARACTERISTIC	DESCRIPTION
High Engagement	Venture philanthropists have a close, hands-on relationship with the social entrepreneurs and ventures they support, driving innovative and scalable models of social change. Some may take board places on these organizations, and all are far more intimately involved at strategic and operational levels than are traditional nonprofit funders.
Multiyear Support	Venture philanthropists provide substantial and sustained financial support to a limited number of organizations. Support typically lasts at least 3–5 years, with an objective of helping the organization to become financially self-sustaining by the end of the funding period.
Tailored Financing	As in venture capital, venture philanthropists take an investment approach to determine the most appropriate financing for each organization. Depending on their own missions and the ventures they choose to support, venture philanthropists can operate across the spectrum of investment returns.
Organizational Capacity Building	Venture philanthropists focus on building the operational capacity and long-term viability of the organizations in their portfolios, rather than funding individual projects or programs. They recognize the importance of funding core operating costs to help these organizations achieve greater social impact and operational efficiency.
Nonfinancial Support	In addition to financial support, venture philanthropists provide value-added services such as strategic planning, marketing and communications, executive coaching, human resource advice, and access to other networks and potential funders.
Performance Measurement	Venture philanthropy investment is performance based, placing emphasis on good business planning, measurable outcomes, achievement of milestones, and high levels of financial accountability and management competence.

Source: John, R. (2006). *Venture philanthropy: The evolution of high engagement philanthropy in Europe.* Skoll Centre for Social Entrepreneurship Working Paper. Oxford, UK: Oxford Said Business School.

the Netherlands, Good Deed Foundation in Estonia, Invest for Children in Spain, Oltre Venture in Italy, and NewSchools Venture Fund, Social Venture Partners, and Venture Philanthropy Partners in the United States.

It is possible for enterprising nonprofits to use both earned-income activities and venture philanthropy. For example, Embrace is a nonprofit set up by Stanford graduate Jane Chen in an effort to improve the survival of low-birthweight babies, particularly in developing countries where incubators are too expensive to purchase. The organization originated with a class project in which students were tasked with designing a device to prevent neonatal hypothermia that cost less than 1% of a standard incubator.

The result was the Embrace Warmer—a miniature sleeping bag that maintains the baby's body temperature without the need for electricity. It costs just $25, in stark contrast to the $20,000 cost of a typical hospital incubator. So far, the Embrace Warmer has saved the lives of 200,000 premature babies. To support its humanitarian effort, Embrace has created Little Lotus, a brand that sells temperature-adjusting blankets and swaddles in the United States.[12] Drawing on the one-to-one giving model popularized by TOMS shoes, Bombas Socks, and Warby Parker glasses, an Embrace Warmer is shipped to every premature baby in need abroad for every sale of a Little Lotus item.

Another enterprising nonprofit is Goodwill, which operates more than 3,000 donation clothing stores across the United States. Funds from the sale of these donations are used to empower people from diverse backgrounds, such as youth, seniors, and people with disabilities or criminal histories, to become economically self-sufficient by providing job training programs in a variety of different areas. In 2017, Goodwill provided almost 300,000 people with the training they need to find employment. According to the 2018 Brand World Value Index, Goodwill is considered to be one of the top five most inspirational brands for consumers.[13]

Hybrid Models of Social Entrepreneurship

Through the typology of ventures illustrated in Figure 16.2, we have described several types of social entrepreneurship, but there are emerging forms of social entrepreneurship that do not fit as neatly into this four-part typology. A **hybrid model of social entrepreneurship** describes an organization with a purpose that equally emphasizes economic and social goals.

To further explain the hybrid model, let's take a look at two organizations with the same goal: to solve the problem of poor eyesight in developing countries. The first organization is the Centre for Vision in the Developing World, a traditional nonprofit that channels donations toward self-refraction glasses that enable the wearer to make simple adjustments at a low cost to increase vision quality. The product eliminates the need for an optometrist or prescriptions.

The second organization, VisionSpring, aims to solve the same problem but has a network of more than 20,000 salespeople to sell glasses to people in their local communities who have limited access to eye care. Unlike the Centre for Vision in the Developing World, the VisionSpring model sustains itself financially through the sales of the glasses, rather than through donations.

As a result, VisionSpring is classified as a hybrid social venture model because it combines a nonprofit's concern for social issues with the for-profit goal to make money. Although hybrid models can be an excellent way of exploiting the advantages of both for-profit and nonprofit models, they are less likely to receive VC funding or philanthropic donations because they sit in a gray zone between business and charity. As Harvard doctoral candidate Matthew Lee, who is studying hybrid organizations, explains, "It's much harder to get started and be successful if you don't fit into a well-defined form that people understand." Lee adds, "Creating a new

Hybrid model of social entrepreneurship: an organization with a purpose that equally emphasizes economic and social goals.

Better World Books drop box, where people can drop off unwanted books

TOMS Shoes is an example of a for-profit social entrepreneurial company doing good in the world.

hybrid is difficult to explain as a rational choice taking this limitation into account."[14]

However, if entrepreneurs can get it right, the hybrid model could have big social and economic payoffs. Better World Books is another example of a hybrid model, which earns money by taking donations of new and unwanted books and selling them online. The venture was originally begun in 2002 by three students at the University of Notre Dame who wanted to sell their textbooks online to earn extra money. The students then decided to donate a portion of the sales from each book they sold to literacy campaigns.

Since then, Better World Books has set up relationships with almost 4,000 libraries to collect unwanted books of many different types and genres. It has also launched an initiative that provides drop boxes in certain locations, allowing people to drop off unwanted books. The collection bins even come with sensory technology that tells Better World staff when the bins are full, so they can empty them quickly.[15]

In its book-for-book program, Better World Books has learned from other organizations. One example is TOMS Shoes, a for-profit company based in California that operates a "buy a pair of shoes, give away a pair of shoes" initiative (often shortened to Buy One Give One, or BOGO). Since it was set up, Better World Books has donated more than 26 million unwanted books and raised more than $28 million in funds for literacy and libraries.[16]

16.4 CAPITAL MARKETS FOR SOCIAL ENTREPRENEURS

>> **LO 16.4**   **Explain how social entrepreneurs can use capital markets to fund their ventures.**

Traditional entrepreneurial ventures need capital in order to survive, and so do social entrepreneurs running for-profit, nonprofit, or hybrid operations. For example, social entrepreneur Genny Ghanimeh, founder and CEO of Pi Slice, a Dubai-based online microfinance social platform for entrepreneurs across MENA (Middle East and North Africa), sought capital from all different types of funding channels, including angel investment and philanthropists, to help get her startup off the ground.[17] Ghanimeh and her team also took part in different entrepreneurship competitions and partnered with other businesses to improve her chances of funding. Since setting up in 2013, Pi Slice has funded microloans to hundreds of micro-entrepreneurs across MENA, starting from as low as $20.[18]

For-profits can also seek investment from social venture capitalists (SVC), also known as impact-investment funds. These funds look both for a return on investment and to make a specific social/environmental impact. For example, thanks to SVC, clean energy provider BBOXX has transformed lives by developing technology to provide pay-as-you-go solar power to hundreds of people living in remote areas in Africa and Asia.[19]

In fact, the SVC market has increased over the last few years, with some estimating that it could grow to $3 trillion in the future, mainly because of the rise of more socially conscious entrepreneurs looking for impact investment opportunities.[20] Table 16.5 lists a few examples of impact-investment funds.[21]

Another type of fund is the "community" fund, and its goal is to invest in economic development and job creation in impoverished areas.[22] Venture Philanthropy Partners (VPP), for example, is based in Washington, D.C., and focuses on helping youths and children from low-income families in the national capital region. Since its inception in 2000, VPP has raised more than $100 million to help children and youths in the greater Washington area.[23] SJF Ventures operates as a traditional VC fund but also allocates a percentage of the fund to companies seeking investment to make a positive social or environmental impact across areas such as waste reduction, heath advancement, education, and natural resource conservation. One of these social enterprises is Living Earth,

How Social Entrepreneurs Can Be Unethical

Although social entrepreneurs are generally a big-hearted breed, and should be supported as much as possible, they do not have complete ethical immunity in going about their business. There are ways that a sincere effort to do good in the world could be skewed the other way around.

First, if a social entrepreneur does not have a realistic business plan, he or she could end up doing more harm than good. If a socially geared company does not focus on raising some amount of money and growing the business, then they could very well be a failure story, among the many in the world of entrepreneurship. A failure by a company could produce a stronger negative effect on society, rather than positive. Not only are employees out of work, but the goodness intended at the outset of launching the company will remain unfulfilled.

Furthermore, there is a preconceived notion that a social entrepreneurial venture must be a nonprofit in order to work properly. However, a for-profit social entrepreneurial company could do just as much good, as it ensures the company has the finances to continue moving forward with ease.

Then, there is the issue of running the company in an ethical manner. A company must have an ethical framework, and if money is tight at a social entrepreneurial company, then employees could bear the cost. Although companies can have a valiant purpose, it would do no good to have disgruntled employees who are severely underpaid and without enough benefits. Also, serious questions must be asked in business dealings, as aspects like raw material could be acquired in an unethical manner.

Critical Thinking Questions

1. Could a social entrepreneurial venture be unethical in its business practices? Can the end justify the means?

2. Is it fair to pay employees of a nonprofit less money than they could be making elsewhere?

3. How important should finances be to a social entrepreneur? ●

Sources:

Chell, E., et al. (2014, November 20). Social entrepreneurship and business ethics: Does social equal ethical? *Journal of Business Ethics*. Retrieved from https://link.springer.com/article/10.1007/s10551-014-2439-6
Fitzgerald, P. (2011, December 27). The social entrepreneur's dilemma. *Huffington Post*. Retrieved from https://www.huffingtonpost.com/patrick-fitzgerald/the-social-entrepreneurs-dilemma_b_1171080.html

a leading composting and organic material products company that provides a more sustainable solution to Texas landfills by collecting yard waste, tree trimmings, and other organic materials and mixing them to provide a range of high-quality composts, which are then sold to landscapers, retailers, and residents.[24]

In the area of health care, SJF also invests in digital diabetes coaching platform Fit4D, which uses a combination of technology and diabetes experts to empower people with diabetes to live healthy and fulfilling lives.

Finally, SJF raises funding for Jopwell, a career advancement platform, which connects leading companies with black, Latino, and Native American professionals to help those companies fulfill their diversity recruitment objectives.

In fact, a whole range of clean energy startups are emerging, offering products and services that challenge how we use power. For instance, California-based veteran-owned company Constructis builds kinetic energy systems for roads that harvest electricity every time cars drive over a hidden road device (similar to a small speed bump). The excess electrical power is sent to power poles, a nearby building, or a car charging system. Startup Breezi also promotes clean energy through its audio sensors for air conditioning systems. The sensors troubleshoot errors in the system to make it more energy efficient.[25]

Microfinance as a Source of Social Financing

Microfinance is a term used to describe financial services (such as loans, insurance, savings) to people considered ineligible to receive traditional banking services. One of the earliest pioneers of microfinance is Nobel Peace Prize winner Muhammad Yunus. Yunus founded

TABLE 16.5

Examples of Impact Investment Funds

Sustainable Trade Financing
A UK-based $65 million fund invests in sustainable trade and targets high-impact, submarket rate returns for investors. The fund has provided more than $200 million in loans to 300 small and growing businesses is across Latin American and Asia, with borrower repayment rates surpassing 98%.
Example investment: The fund has invested in a fair trade and certified organic coffee cooperative in Ecuador. The cooperative's 300 active members are smallholder farmers who cultivate shade-grown coffee. The trade finance loan allowed the cooperative to cover operating costs and invest in new processing equipment. Additional revenue gained from fair trade coffee sales are used to sponsor projects in reforestation, education, and community-based health clinics in the community where smallholder farmers live.
Low-Income Housing
A private equity fund based in Brazil closed with $75 million in assets. Investments target market-rate financial returns and social benefits to rural communities in South America. The fund's investors include large financial institutions, private family offices, development organizations, and large-scale foundations.
Example investment: The fund has made an investment of $4 million to a provider of affordable homes designed for low-income families in rural settings. More than 10,000 homes have been constructed in three South American countries, focusing particularly in areas affected by natural disaster.
Clean Energy Access
A EUR 150 million European private equity fund invests between EUR 2–10 million in companies that provide clean electricity to rural communities in developing countries with limited access to energy. The fund targets competitive private equity returns and has made five investments in Asia and Africa.
Example investment: The fund made a EUR 2 million equity investment in a company that provides solar energy for lighting and refrigeration in rural Indian households, schools, and hospitals that have limited access to the main electricity grid. Enabled by this investment, the company has installed more than 40,000 systems and currently offsets 25,000 tons of carbon dioxide emissions.
Clean Drinking Water
An India-based impact investing fund manager started investing in microfinance institutions more than 10 years ago. After delivering 14% returns to investors, the fund manager decided to raise a second fund to target businesses across a broader set of sectors, including renewable energy, agriculture, health, and education. The fund provides risk capital and support to early-stage ventures, with investments averaging $50,000.
Example investment: The second fund invested in a company that sets up water purification plants in rural villages. The plants are owned by the local community and operated by the installation company, which sells the purified water to the village at affordable rates. The installation company also trains local entrepreneurs to develop businesses that deliver water to neighboring villages.

Source: http://www.impactbase.org/info/examples-impact-investment-funds

Microloan: a very small, short-term loan often associated with entrepreneurs in developing countries.

the Grameen Bank in Bangladesh in the 1970s, offering **microloans**, or small short-term loans, to impoverished villagers to enable them to start their own businesses. He placed borrowers, mostly women, into small groups but not all group members could borrow at once. One borrower may receive a loan for $40, but the other members only become eligible for their own loans when the original borrower begins to pay back her loan. Such a process created motivation, accountability, and empowerment. Yunus made his first loan of $27 in 1976 to a group of women who wanted to expand their bamboo business.

To date, the Grameen bank has extended credit to more than 7 million people, mostly in Bangladesh, who were in the past at the mercy of local money lenders who charged cripplingly high interest rates.[26] Through his revolutionary ideas, Yunus has not only proved that the poor are credit-worthy, but he has crossed social boundaries to give the people of Bangladesh an opportunity to be entrepreneurs themselves.

Since the founding of the Grameen Bank, other microlending providers have sprung up to extend Yunus's mission of eliminating exploitation of the poor by moneylenders and create self-employment opportunities for the disadvantaged.

For example, nonprofit organization Kiva has enhanced the microfinance concept even further by enabling anyone to loan as little as $25 to entrepreneurs in developing countries who lack access to traditional banking systems. The hundreds of entrepreneurs are profiled on the Kiva website, and people can choose whom they would like to fund based on this information. Kiva does not charge interest or take a cut of the loan—the entire amount goes to the entrepreneur. When the entrepreneur repays the loan, the individual can decide if he or she wants to use it to make another loan to support a different entrepreneur.

Social enterprises like the Grameen Bank and Kiva have revolutionized many lives and businesses in developing countries. Nevertheless, Shivani Soroya, founder of Tala, spotted a gap. Although the informal microloans certainly helped people to start their own businesses, when it came to growing those businesses, they still had no access to formal banking institutions. Because they had no credit score, they were perceived as too risky for formal loans. Soroya's aim was to break down these barriers by providing mobile and web tools so that entrepreneurs could save business data in order to build up a credit score, to prove to formal institutions that the business is growing and worth the risk of small-business loans. Tala operates in markets where millions of people have no credit score, such as Tanzania, Kenya, and the Philippines. Soroya said, "It made me realize that there are billions of people around the world who are not even seen and don't even have an identity. That felt really wrong."[27] However, none of the social entrepreneurs profiled in this chapter carried out their mission all by themselves. They had a number of people to help them. In the next section, we will take a look at how people can help or hinder a social venture.

16.5 SOCIAL ENTREPRENEURS AND THEIR STAKEHOLDERS

>> **LO 16.5** **Identify the primary attributes of stakeholders and how stakeholders can help or hinder a social entrepreneur.**

As we have learned, social entrepreneurs cannot resolve wicked problems in isolation. To gain support for their mission, social entrepreneurs need to think about how their actions affect their **stakeholders**, who are the people or groups affected by or involved with the achievements of the social enterprise's objectives.

Stakeholders: the people or groups affected by or involved with the achievements of the social enterprise's objectives.

Stakeholders include employees, volunteers, investors, customers, suppliers, and manufacturers, leaders in nonprofit organizations, community leaders, the government, sponsors, board members, and other entrepreneurs. By identifying your stakeholders, you will be able to better understand the impact of your enterprise's activities on others; give your stakeholders a platform to provide feedback, information, advice, and direction; and allow them to raise any concerns or obstacles that may stand in the way of achieving your objectives.

Linking all these stakeholders will help you get the best out of your social enterprise. A good way to identify your key stakeholders is to draw your own stakeholder map, as illustrated in Figure 16.3.

Building relationships with key stakeholders is an important way to gain support, but you must also prove to your key stakeholders how you intend to generate value for them. Although "doing good deeds" is a worthy objective, your stakeholders will want to understand the value of being involved with the venture.

When you create a social innovation, it is unlikely that all your stakeholders will be in immediate agreement. So it is your responsibility to communicate to stakeholders not only the value to be derived but also the potential for loss or consequences of your activities and suggest alternative solutions. There are two questions you need to ask yourself: (1) What is at stake for your stakeholders? This question will enable you to assess the level of risk for your stakeholders and force you to think about how you can reduce their risks. (2) How are you creating value for each stakeholder? Every stakeholder will see value in a different way.

With the potential for so many stakeholders, how do you decide which ones are the most important? Whom do you need to prioritize, and what level of attention should you give? The salience model helps social entrepreneurs select the most suitable communication approach for each group of stakeholders by classifying stakeholders based on their salience (or significance) in the social enterprise. There are three primary attributes

FIGURE 16.3

Example of Stakeholder Map

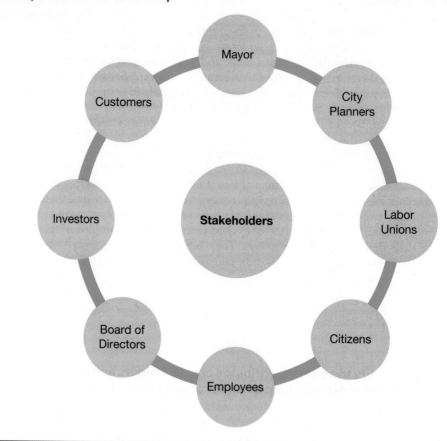

of stakeholders to consider when you are trying to achieve your objectives: power, legitimacy, and urgency.[28]

A stakeholder in a position of power has the ability to either help or hinder your social objectives. For example, labor unions have the power to prevent or hinder organizational objectives, particularly when certain initiatives may lead to job loss and unemployment. Legitimate stakeholders are those whose actions are appropriate, proper, and desired in the context of the company, organization, or community.[29] For example, if you have a problem or need some advice, you may consult with the stakeholders you feel have the most legitimacy.

The third attribute is urgency, which describes the extent to which stakeholders demand your attention. For example, in a case where there are last-minute questions that need to be answered by your investors during the due diligence process, you would need to prioritize the needs of your investors over other stakeholders until the situation has been resolved.

These three attributes are not necessarily independent of one another; in fact, a stakeholder may have both power and legitimacy, or a combination of all three. However, by identifying the different types of stakeholders, you will be better able to assess which ones are the most salient in a particular context.

Types of Stakeholders

In the 1990s, Ronald K. Mitchell and colleagues proposed a model of seven different types of stakeholders (see Figure 16.4). The model is based on the three factors of power, legitimacy, and urgency; note that each type of stakeholder occupies a position relative to these three overlapping circles. Let's examine each of these seven types using the

FIGURE 16.4

Mitchell Stakeholder Typology

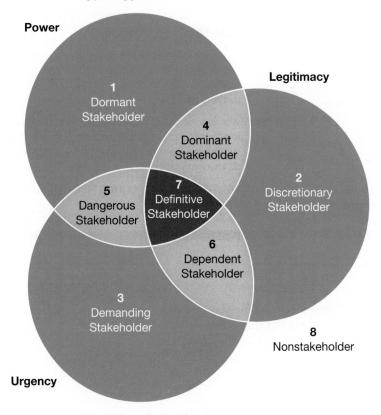

Source: Mitchell, R., Agle, B., & Wood, D. (1997). Toward a theory of stakeholder identification and salience: Defining the principle of who and what really counts. *Academy of Management Review, 22,* 853–866.

example of nonprofit organization familiar to many young entrepreneurs—the Collegiate Entrepreneurs Organization (CEO). CEO has chapters across 200 colleges and universities in North America. Its mission is "to inform, support and inspire college students to be entrepreneurial and seek opportunity through enterprise creation."[30]

Dormant Stakeholders

Dormant stakeholders are "sleepers"—they hold power but do not tend to use that power unless they are given a reason to do so. However, dormant stakeholders may become significant when they begin to utilize their power; for example, a disgruntled member may complain about CEO on social media. The key to ensuring these stakeholders are satisfied is to be transparent and keep them informed at all times. Just because they are "sleeping" doesn't mean they will never wake up.

Discretionary Stakeholders

Discretionary stakeholders have no power to influence and no urgent claims, but they have legitimacy. They may come in the form of philanthropists who donate to your organization and are willing to support social causes. For example, CEO provides visitors with the opportunity to donate money on its website to support the organization.

Demanding Stakeholders

Demanding stakeholders possess the urgency attribute. They have no power or legitimacy and may be the only dissenting voice in the room. For example, persons protesting

Practice Being "Other-Centered"

In this Mindshift, your challenge is to practice being "other-centered" for 1 week. Many of us live in a "me-centered" world, where events and relationships are measured by how much, and in what ways, they affect us. Being "other-centered" means stepping outside ourselves and shifting the focus onto serving others for the good of the greater community.[31]

For example, instead of getting frustrated at an older adult taking forever to put away her change at the checkout line, give her a reassuring smile, and maybe offer to help her with her bags of groceries. Think about different ways in which you can cheer up others. Make someone else's day.

Critical Thinking Questions

1. To what extent do you feel you are already "other-centered" in your life? Give some examples of your actions and decisions in this regard.

2. Was it easier than you expected, or more difficult, to focus for an entire day on being other-centered? Would you want to continue this focus for a second day running?

3. What did you learn from this Mindshift that surprised you? ●

outside the CEO national conference because they believe entrepreneurs create income inequality in the economy, but they do not have the power to enforce their claims. These stakeholders don't really impact CEO, and not a lot of time and energy should be devoted to them.

Dominant Stakeholders

Dominant stakeholders have both power and legitimacy, which gives them strong influence in your organization. Dominant stakeholders of CEO include college presidents or deans of business schools where CEO chapters are located. Communicating with them regularly and responding to queries efficiently and accurately will help you maintain a good relationship with these stakeholders and keep the chapter on campus!

Dependent Stakeholders

Dependent stakeholders have both urgency and legitimacy but lack the power to influence. These stakeholders are the most passionate, and their passion is likely to attract dominant stakeholders. For example, the student members of CEO are the most enthusiastic and passionate stakeholders connected to the organization, but they may not have the power necessary to effect change with the leaders of the national organization.

Dangerous Stakeholders

Dangerous stakeholders possess both power and urgency but may use this power to coerce or even resort to violence. Social issues can be emotive, and power and urgency exercised against your objectives can be a significant hindrance. For example, a competing organization may emerge that could use false advertising or slander to get members from CEO to move their membership to the new organization.

Definitive Stakeholders

Definitive stakeholders are the only ones who possess all three attributes of power, legitimacy, and urgency. These stakeholders have a significant role to play in your organization and must be given priority when it comes to handling their claims. In the case of CEO, the most definitive stakeholders are the foundations that fund CEO—the Kauffman and Coleman foundations.

Conclusions From the Mitchell Stakeholder Typology

Remember that stakeholders are not static—they can evolve, and through that evolution, they may either gain or lose attributes. Social entrepreneurs must continuously monitor the internal and external stakeholder environment to maintain relationships with stakeholders and ensure support for their social mission.

Stakeholders are vital to social entrepreneurship, and communities of stakeholders are emerging all over the world to share knowledge, collaborate on ideas, and build and grow social ventures. Ashoka, Social Venture Network, Investors Circle, Echoing Green, Net Impact, and Social Enterprise provide forums to connect with and learn about other stakeholders. Connecting and collaborating with others is the key to resolving wicked problems.

16.6 DIFFERENCES BETWEEN SOCIAL ENTREPRENEURSHIP AND CORPORATE SOCIAL RESPONSIBILITY

>> **LO 16.6** **Distinguish between corporate social responsibility and social entrepreneurship.**

Corporate social responsibility (CSR) describes the efforts made by corporations to address the company's effects on environmental and social well-being in order to promote positive change. Although social entrepreneurship may sound similar to the CSR model, they are not the same (see Table 16.6).

The difference lies in the primary objective. In essence, CSR adds social objectives while still pursuing the main goal of making a profit. In contrast, many social entrepreneurship models, including the hybrid model, place equal emphasis on social and economic goals. An organization with a CSR strategy could reduce spending on its CSR program if it is struggling to meet revenues, whereas a social enterprise would prioritize its social goals even in the face of a reduction in profits.

Together, the biggest global firms spend more than $20 billion on CSR, and recent research suggests that some of these companies reap financial rewards as a result.[32] For example, consumers may be attracted to these companies because the CSR spending may indicate high-quality products; they also may want to buy the products as an indirect way to donate to the causes the corporation supports; and they may also look on the organization favorably (the "halo" effect) because of its good deeds.[33]

On the legal side, research also suggests that if a firm is sued and prosecuted, it may tend to receive more lenient penalties if it has a record of CSR activities. For example,

Corporate social responsibility (CSR): the efforts made by corporations to address the company's effects on environmental and social well-being in order to promote positive change.

TABLE 16.6

Corporate Social Responsibility Versus Social Entrepreneurship

CORPORATE SOCIAL RESPONSIBILITY	SOCIAL ENTREPRENEURSHIP
Peripheral to mission	Core to mission
Side show	Main event
A department	The entire organization
Seeks to reduce harm	Measures social impact
Feel and look good	Do good
Stakeholder is the observer	Stakeholder is the customer
Consequence-driven	Purpose-driven
Image-motivated	Opportunity-motivated

FIGURE 16.5

CSR Makes Good Business Sense

Good CSR helps to:

- engage more customers, especially if your firm is helping to support good causes
- lead to real innovations, such as environmentally safe products
- decrease costs by cutting packaging, travel, and energy expenses
- increase public image through the company's efforts to do good deeds
- bring people together by holding charity events such as sponsored walks and bake sales

Source: Adapted from Mitchell, R., Agle, B., & Wood, D. (1997). Toward a theory of stakeholder identification and salience: Defining the principle of who and what really counts. *Academy of Management Review, 22*(4), 853–866.

organizations with a focus on labor rights issues such as eliminating child labor or companies who increase CSR spending by 20% tend to be treated more leniently if they are prosecuted.[34]

Additional research also shows that CSR initiatives relating to sustainability, corporate foundations, employee volunteer programs, and donations to charity tend to attract and motivate employees.[35] However, if employees believe that companies are investing in CSR for the wrong reasons, such as boosting productivity or purely for financial gain, then they will disengage with the company and become less motivated.

A 2018 study lists corporations with the best CSR reputations, including Google, Microsoft, IKEA, Bosch, Natura, and LEGO.[36] One of Google's main principles is "doing good." For instance, the Google Green and Google Energy initiatives focus on investing more than $1 billion in renewable energy to reduce the costs of energy consumption of the Google Group of companies. Another example of its commitment to "doing good" is Google Person Finder, which helps track people down in the aftermath of major disasters.[37]

Although CSR has been mostly associated with large companies, it is also important to small to medium-sized companies. As Figure 16.5 shows, good CSR makes good business sense for small companies.

Smaller companies can also build a good reputation in the local community by volunteering at local libraries, hospitals, and schools and by supporting local sports teams or local charities. Being connected with ethical suppliers with positive CSR is also a bonus for a small company as it builds trust with new customers. Building trust and being socially responsible is important for all companies—big or small.

16.7 SOCIAL ENTREPRENEURSHIP AND AUDACIOUS IDEAS

>> **LO 16.7** Explore audacious ideas being pursued by social entrepreneurs today.

It's tough to be a social entrepreneur; they may have groundbreaking ideas to save lives or improve the environment, but they still need funding to achieve their goals. This involves endless rounds of pitches to philanthropists or investors who may be hesitant to take the risk on a newly formed startup. Media organization TED is trying to narrow the gap between social entrepreneurs and philanthropists through a new model called The Audacious Project: Collaborative Philanthropy for Bold Ideas.[38] The Audacious Project invites social entrepreneurs to submit their ideas for creating global change, then carefully vets the ideas before choosing the ones with the most potential. These social entrepreneurs are given a platform to present their ideas to some of the most well-respected names in philanthropy.

More than $250 million has been raised to fund these ideas by a group of leading organizations including Virgin Unite, the Skoll Foundation, and The Bridgespan Group. Here are some of the 2018 Audacious Project awardees:[39]

The Bail Project

The Bail Project is an organization set up to address the injustice of automatic imprisonment for those who can't afford bail, which typically affects low-income communities, women, and minorities. With the support of The Audacious Project, The Bail Project aims to post bail on behalf of 160,000 people over the next 5 years by working with public defenders and the impacted community members. The bail returned at the end of each case will be used to fund other affected people. If it proves successful, this idea could help to end mass incarceration and combat racial disparity.

Robin Steinberg, CEO of The Bail Project, said, "Pretrial detention is a key driver of mass incarceration in the United States, accounting for all of the net jail growth in the last 20 years. Thanks to The Audacious Project, we have an incredible opportunity to help turn the tide on this crisis. We have a proven model, strong local partners, and a growing team ready to give it their all until our work is no longer necessary."

Environmental Defense Fund

Environmental Defense Fund (EDF) is a nonprofit environmental advocacy group that aims to reduce methane, a powerful greenhouse gas responsible for global warming. Although it is commonly known that the oil and gas industry is a major contributor to the tons of methane in our atmosphere, there hasn't been a way to measure the level of methane on a global scale or its original source.

With the support of The Audacious Project, EDF aims to build and launch low-cost satellite MethaneSAT, which tracks and measures emissions. The information gathered by MethaneSAT will provide companies and countries with the data they need to take steps to reduce and track their emissions.

"Cutting methane emissions from the global oil and gas industry is the fastest thing we can do right now to put the brakes on climate change," said Fred Krupp, EDF president. "MethaneSAT gives us the power to map and measure the problem, identify reduction opportunities, and track that progress over time."

GirlTrek

GirlTrek is a health movement with a goal to improve the health and well-being of African American women through daily walking. Because of underemployment, lack of community safety, and chronic poverty, African American women are more likely to die of preventable diseases and at younger ages than any other groups of women in the United States.

With the support of The Audacious Project, GirlTrek aims to tackle poor health, including obesity, by training 10,000 people as public health activists to reach their goal of 1 million GirlTrek members.

"We are not a workout group. We are an army of women who, in the iconic words of Fannie Lou Hamer, are 'sick and tired of being sick and tired,'" said Vanessa Garrison, cofounder of GirlTrek and Chief Operating Officer.

Sightsavers

Sightsavers is a UK-based nongovernmental international charity working to prevent avoidable blindness with a goal to combat the bacterial infection trachoma, which causes irreversible blindness. The charity aims to eliminate the disease by promoting the SAFE strategy (surgery, antibiotics, face-washing, and environmental improvements) endorsed by the World Health Organization (WHO), largely targeting people living in impoverished countries.

Dr. Caroline Harper, CEO of Sightsavers, said, "Trachoma traps the most vulnerable people in a vicious cycle of poverty. Together we can consign this awful disease to the history books, where it belongs. We'll free millions of people, today and for generations to come, from this scourge of the world's poorest communities."

One Acre Fund

One Acre Fund is a nonprofit social enterprise working to provide African farmers with the opportunity to grow more food by offering access to agricultural training, tools, and asset-based financing. By learning the techniques to increase their produce, the farmers will be able to earn a higher income to support their families.

"The world's smallholder farmers are some of the hardest working people on the planet," said Andrew Youn, cofounder and executive director of One Acre Fund. "By working together and increasing access to financing, tools, and training, we envision a future where all farmers can achieve big harvests, healthy families, and rich soils."

Social entrepreneurs use the fundamental principles of entrepreneurship to build businesses of economic and social value. They improve the lives of whole communities by providing employment; they save the lives of premature babies; they educate people so they can make a living; they utilize our "trash" to create businesses that improve the lives of others; they offer loans to excluded members of society and give them confidence and a sense of purpose. There is no such thing as waste or hopelessness in the mind of a social entrepreneur. Social entrepreneurs bring hope and change lives. They are making the world a better place.

16.8 GLOBAL ENTREPRENEURSHIP

>> **LO 16.8   Illustrate the global diversity of entrepreneurship.**

Entrepreneurship is taking off on a global scale. Let's explore some data provided by The Global Entrepreneurship Monitor (GEM), a global research study founded by Babson College and the London Business School in 1999. Today the study is conducted by a consortium of universities around the world and measures entrepreneurial activity across 112 economies.[40]

According to the 2018/19 GEM report, more than 15% of Americans are entrepreneurs—the highest percentage on record. In fact, there are almost 500 million entrepreneurs worldwide, making entrepreneurship a global phenomenon.

The GEM study gathers its data according to different phases of entrepreneurship (see Figure 16.6). The process begins with **potential entrepreneurs**, who are individuals who believe they have the capacity and know-how to start a business without being burdened by the fear of failure. The next phase focuses on **nascent entrepreneurs**, who are individuals who have set up a business they will own or co-own that is less than 3 months old and has not yet generated wages or salaries for the owners. The third phase is the study of **new business owners**, who are former nascent entrepreneurs who have been actively involved in a business for more than 3 months but less than 3.5 years. The final phase explores **established business owners**—those who have been active in business for more than 3.5 years. Interestingly, the study found the reason that many of the established business entrepreneurs had discontinued the business after 3.5 years was not necessarily because they had failed; in fact, in many cases, the entrepreneurs had instead become serial entrepreneurs or joined other companies to become inside or corporate entrepreneurs.

The GEM study also looks at opportunity-based entrepreneurs and necessity-based entrepreneurs. **Necessity-based entrepreneurs** are individuals who are pushed into starting a business because of circumstance. Layoffs, threat of job loss, and inability to find a job are some factors that drive people to start a new business. In contrast,

Potential entrepreneurs: individuals who believe they have the capacity and know-how to start a business without being burdened by the fear of failure.

Nascent entrepreneurs: individuals who have set up a business they will own or co-own that is less than 3 months old and has not yet generated wages or salaries for the owners.

New business owners: individuals who are former nascent entrepreneurs and have been actively involved in a business for more than 3 months but less than 3.5 years.

Established business owners: the people who have been active in business for more than 3.5 years.

Necessity-based entrepreneurs: individuals who are pushed into starting a business because of circumstance such as redundancy, threat of job loss, and unemployment.

FIGURE 16.6

Global Entrepreneurship Monitor Measuring Entrepreneurial Activity

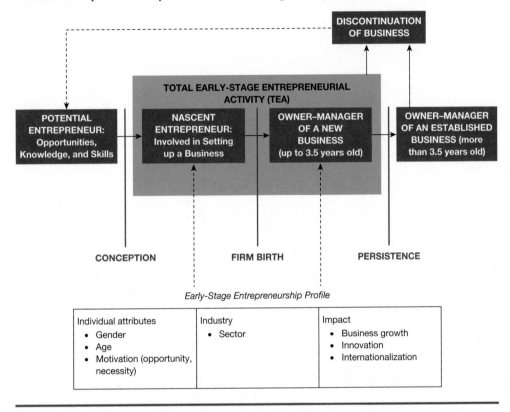

Early-Stage Entrepreneurship Profile

Individual attributes	Industry	Impact
• Gender • Age • Motivation (opportunity, necessity)	• Sector	• Business growth • Innovation • Internationalization

Source: GEM Report 2018-9: pg 16, GEM Consortium. http://www.gemconsortium.org/. Reprinted with permission.

opportunity-based entrepreneurs are individuals who make a decision to start their own businesses based on their ability to create or exploit an opportunity, and whose main driver for getting involved in the venture is being independent or increasing their income, rather than merely maintaining their income. Unlike necessity-based entrepreneurs, opportunity-based entrepreneurs freely make their own choice to get involved in a business.

One of the main focuses of the GEM study is the level of **Total Entrepreneurial Activity (TEA)** in different countries, which is the percentage of the population of each country between the ages of 18 and 64 who are either nascent entrepreneurs or owner—managers of a new business. For example, the early-stage TEA in the United States is just over 15% (Table 16.7). This means that just over 15% of the U.S. adult population from 18 to 64 years old is involved in some type of entrepreneurial activity, such as being in the process of starting a new business or owning and managing a business less than 3 years old.

Let's take a closer look at the age ranges of entrepreneurial activity in early stages of business across the world. North America is certainly perceived as being one of the most buoyant environments for entrepreneurship, but other geographical regions, such as Africa, Latin America, and the Caribbean, appear to have higher rates of entrepreneurial activity in certain age groups. Europe displays the lowest TEA rates over all, with Cyprus, Italy, Germany, and Poland, in particular, showing the lowest rates—5% or less of working adults begin or run new businesses. The low rates in some countries, particularly among the younger population, may be a consequence of compulsory military service or high college attendance.

Despite sub-Saharan Africa being a less well-developed region of the world than the United States, people living in some African countries tend to see opportunities to start their own businesses, have confidence in their own skills and abilities, and have less fear

Opportunity-based entrepreneurs: individuals who make a decision to start their own businesses based on their ability to create or exploit an opportunity, and whose main driver for getting involved in the venture is being independent or increasing their income, rather than merely maintaining their income.

Total Entrepreneurial Activity (TEA): the percentage of the population of each country between the ages of 18 and 64 who are either a nascent entrepreneur or owner—manager of a new business.

TABLE 16.7

Total Early-Stage Entrepreneurial Activity (TEA) Rates Among Adults (ages 18–64) in 49 Economies, in Four Geographic Regions

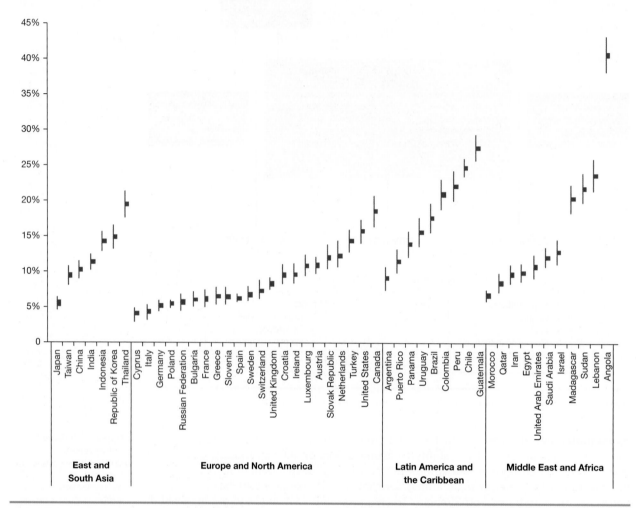

Source: GEM Report 2018-9: pg 16. GEM Consortium. http://www.gemconsortium.org/. Reprinted with permission.

of failure. These statistics prove that early-stage entrepreneurship is possible in poorer countries if the people are given the opportunity and support to grow their own businesses.

Gender and Entrepreneurship

One of the greatest myths concerning entrepreneurship is that it is a male-only profession. As Table 16.8 shows, nothing could be farther from the truth.

Most countries studied have a similar proportion of men to women early-stage entrepreneurs, with the percentage of women in Vietnam, Panama, Qatar, Madagascar, Thailand, Angola, and Indonesia being equal to or exceeding their male counterparts. This shows that these countries are providing support for women-owned ventures.

Why do women want to become entrepreneurs? For the same reasons as men: to support themselves and their families, to attain the fulfillment of having started something on their own, and to satisfy their desire for financial independence.[41] Just like their male counterparts, women not only create jobs for themselves and others, but also work toward growing their businesses and constantly innovating new products and services.

However, in certain countries, there are some differences in what drives women to be entrepreneurs. For example, women in less-developed countries with higher rates of unemployment, poverty, and lack of choice in work are more likely to be driven by necessity, whereas women in more developed countries tend be more motivated by opportunity and innovation.

TABLE 16.8

Total Early-Stage Entrepreneurial Activity (TEA) Rates Among Men and Women (ages 18–64) in 49 Economies, in Four Geographic Regions

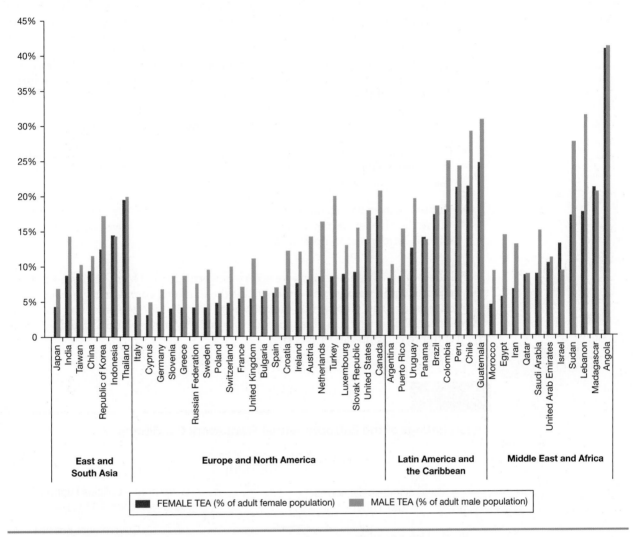

Source: GEM Report 2018-9: pg 16. GEM Consortium. http://www.gemconsortium.org/. Reprinted with permission.

What Makes a Country Entrepreneurial?

What makes one country more entrepreneurial than another? The following are certain conditions that need to be put in place for small and medium businesses (SMEs) to flourish. Together, these conditions form the Entrepreneurship Ecosystem (Figure 16.7).

- Financial resources: Entrepreneurs need access to appropriate financing such as grants and subsidies, loans, private equity, angel investors, VC funds, and so on.

- Support from government: Entrepreneurs need support from government policies that incentivize entrepreneurship by tax incentives, lower interest rates, loans, and the like. Some countries also offer government entrepreneurship programs that provide entrepreneurs with access to tools, mentors, and educational resources.

- Entrepreneurship education: Certain countries provide entrepreneurship courses and training at primary and secondary levels and at higher education such as colleges, business schools, and other institutions.

- Research and development (R&D) transfer: The extent to which scientists and research will pass on their knowledge to entrepreneurs involved in innovation. Many SMEs do not have their own R&D department so it is important that they have the opportunity to access knowledge from other resources.

- Commercial and legal infrastructure: Entrepreneurs should be supported by a secure commercial and legal framework assisted by experts and advisors in property rights, accounting, law, investment banking, and technology.

- Entry regulation: Entrepreneurs should be able to meet the regulatory costs of starting a new business as well as undergoing administrative procedures. The extent of these costs and procedures is dependent on two factors: market dynamics—the annual rate of change in markets; and market openness—the degree to which new businesses have the freedom to enter new markets.

- Physical infrastructure: Entrepreneurs should be able to easily access or purchase at a reasonable price vital resources in the areas of communication, land, office space, and transportation.

- Cultural and social norms: Entrepreneurs tend to thrive more in an environment where they feel encouraged enough to start a business or have the confidence to choose entrepreneurship as a career path.

All these factors interact to create a very powerful force: New businesses are created, employment increases, new products hit the markets, competition is intensified, and productivity rises, all of which makes a huge contribution to social and economic development. This is why it is essential for every country in the world to build a climate where entrepreneurship can thrive. ●

FIGURE 16.7

Expert Ratings of the Entrepreneurial Framework Conditions

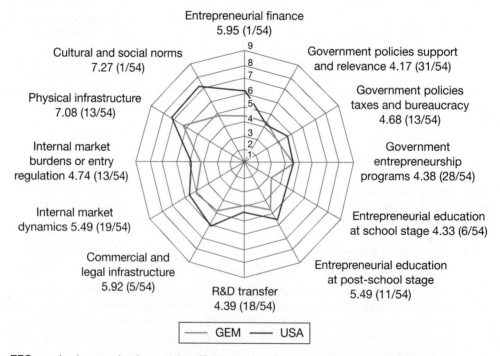

EFCs scale: 1 = very inadequate insufficient status, 9 = very adequate sufficient status
Rank out of 54 recorded in brackets

$SAGE edge™

Get the tools you need to sharpen your study skills. SAGE edge offers a robust online environment featuring an impressive array of free tools and resources.

- Access practice quizzes, eFlashcards, video, and multimedia at
  edge.sagepub.com/neckentrepreneurship2e

16.1 Describe the role social entrepreneurship plays in society.

Social entrepreneurship is the process of sourcing innovative solutions to social and environmental problems. Many companies strive simply to maximize shareholder value, but social entrepreneurs are often more committed to causes centered on preserving and protecting future generations.

16.2 Explain how social entrepreneurship can help resolve wicked problems around the world that are connected to the United Nations Sustainable Development Goals.

Social entrepreneurship can help resolve wicked problems such as those related to water shortages, education, health care, poverty, energy, forced migration, and global warming by creating innovative solutions that make a real impact on the lives and livelihoods of others.

16.3 Identify the different types of social entrepreneurship.

There are three primary types of social entrepreneurship: social purpose ventures, social consequence entrepreneurship, and enterprising nonprofits.

16.4 Explain how social entrepreneurs can use capital markets to fund their ventures.

Social entrepreneurs can seek funding from social venture capitalists (SVC) and community-funded VC to support operations. Microlending is another source of capital available for social entrepreneurs.

16.5 Identify the primary attributes of stakeholders and how stakeholders can help or hinder a social entrepreneur.

Stakeholders are all those involved in and affected by the activities of a social venture. Building relationships with key stakeholders is typically important for any entrepreneur, social or otherwise, but often social issues need additional support to gain traction with the majority of stakeholders.

16.6 Distinguish between corporate social responsibility and social entrepreneurship.

Corporate social responsibility and social entrepreneurship differ in one critical sense: the primary objective of the enterprise. Corporations seek to incorporate social initiatives into broader strategic and tactical objectives, while social entrepreneurs put those social issues front and center. To many corporations, social responsibility causes may just be another means to a successful business end.

16.7 Explore audacious ideas being pursued by social entrepreneurs today.

The Audacious Project: Collaborative Philanthropy for Bold Ideas is an initiative launched by media organization TED that provides social entrepreneurs with a platform to present their ideas to some of the most well-respected names in philanthropy.

16.8 Illustrate the global diversity of entrepreneurship.

There are hundreds of millions of entrepreneurs worldwide. Known as one of the most entrepreneurial nations on the planet, the United States is eclipsed by many world regions in terms of the percentage of the population engaged in entrepreneurship. Though entrepreneurs may be born out of necessity or to exploit opportunities, they all benefit from education, financial resources, accessible knowledge, and government support providing infrastructure that will enable the fledgling businesses to achieve success.

Corporate social responsibility (CSR) 445

Earned-income activities 436

Enterprising nonprofits 435

Established business owners 448

Hybrid model of social entrepreneurship 437

Nascent entrepreneurs 448

Necessity-based entrepreneurs 448

New business owners 448

CASE STUDY

Brandale Randolph, founder and CEO, 1854 Cycling Company

Before the 1854 Cycling Company started making state-of-the-art bicycles for law enforcement, Wharton graduate and founder Brandale Randolph was working as a commodities broker for a hedge fund in Los Angeles, California. When the financial crisis hit in 2008, Brandale's hedge fund lost 90% of its value in 48 hours. Brandale was interested in looking at PhD programs and attended a conference in Chicago called the PhD Project. Though he did not pursue a PhD, he met his future wife, Angela, at the conference. He followed her to Lubbock, Texas, where she started her PhD at Texas Tech University. Brandale started looking for work but could not find a brokerage house in Texas that could accommodate a seasoned broker. So, he started looking for something else to do.

Brandale took a low-wage job at Home Depot in Lubbock. As part of his job, he had to open the store, sometimes at 6 a.m. Because Lubbock was quite cold early in the mornings, he would stop at a fast-food restaurant to grab a cup of coffee. During one of these coffee runs, he saw a man throw a sandwich at a young man sitting outside the shop. A sandwich was thrown because the man felt that any money given would be used for alcohol or drugs. The sandwich hit the young person on his chest and fell to the ground. Brandale recalled, "I exchanged a few polite words with the gentleman but then starting talking to the young man sitting outside the coffee shop, and I learned that the boy was just a college student who needed money to get on a bus to get back home. Nobody knew that because nobody asked." This incident impacted Brandale and prompted him to do something for the poor people around Lubbock.

He started a nonprofit called Project Poverty that aimed to improve the lives of the poor. "I like numbers and created an algorithm that used 30 sets of data to discover pockets of poverty that were otherwise hidden." He identified the three most vulnerable groups in Lubbock: (1) soon-to-be-released incarcerated, (2) the chronically unemployed, and (3) at-risk young adults who don't have a stable home life. He started teaching these groups financial literacy and other life skills, yet he started to see the same people repeatedly. Brandale realized he was doing the same thing the man did outside the coffee shop—throwing the sandwich. "I was trying to beat poverty without fully understanding what the people wanted," said Brandale. "Upon revisiting the data and researching the problem, we realized that there were 30-odd internal and external factors that determined how much money a poor person had and how likely he or she was to keep it. Not just that, these people wanted different things. Soon-to-be-released offenders want to learn how to keep a job for more than 90 days and soon-to-be-released emancipated children wanted to learn how to make their money last longer. We started to teach them these things," Brandale says.

Through his experience, Brandale also learned it was very difficult to sustain a new nonprofit as it did not attract donations that were required to sustain the organization's activities. Although money was available, it usually went to bigger and older nonprofit organizations. Meanwhile, Brandale was reading about for-profit social organizations that were well positioned to provide well-paying jobs to people. He was inspired by Homeboy Bakery, a bakery that employs individuals who were previously incarcerated or gang-involved.

Brandale moved to Framingham, Massachusetts, in 2015 with his wife and kids when his wife took a faculty position after receiving her doctorate. Brandale began looking for a job. He submitted 82 job applications and got two interviews and zero job offers. His wife pointed out to him that if someone like him, with an Ivy League degree, found it difficult to get a job, the formerly incarcerated had it a lot tougher. He decided to apply the same algorithm he had developed for Project Poverty in Texas to the population in Framingham, Massachusetts. He discovered that Framingham had a disproportionate number of households led by formerly incarcerated women who had incomes below the poverty line. These women were also likely to have children under the age of 18. This was also the group that was least likely to revert to crime. Although women were less likely to revert to crime than men, they were more likely to live in poverty, with an average income of $11,500 per year. Brandale knew that if he wanted to make a lasting impact, he had to look for a for-profit model to tackle this problem.

At the same time, Brandale was looking to buy a new bike, and he couldn't find anything in the market that interested him. He then surfed the Internet and saw a number of beautiful bicycles that were being built in Europe. He decided to have a bike custom-made by Francisco Cornelio Jaquez of N+1 Cyclery in Framingham and custom leather maker Amar Sauza near Boston. Between the three of them, "The Garrison," the first bicycle by the 1854 Cycling Company, was born.

Through his research on the biking industry, Brandale discovered that bike mechanics at the time earned $13 an hour, which was above the minimum wage. On doing more research, he realized that there was also a demand in the market for master bike mechanics. Master bike mechanics are those that are "certified" to repair bicycles. Brandale saw the potential for a social, for-profit enterprise in the bike industry. He wanted to employ formerly incarcerated women he had identified in Framingham as master mechanics. Brandale believes that fair and stable employment is a good deterrent to crime. He would like to measure his company's success by the number of children of his employees who come from poverty and find their way to college. He believes that if the story is strong enough, people will not only pay for a world-class product but will also pay a premium, if they believe that their dollars are going to be used to help someone else.

To test the concept, he made a bike and tried to sell it. "We put this awesome bike on the market and sold exactly none of it. The lean business model that we used is based on creating a prototype to find market feedback before investing in unsellable inventory. We dodged a bullet because the unit cost for each bicycle was around $2,500." Talking with biking enthusiasts and retailers, attending local cycling events, and reading a trade publication called *Bicycle Retailer and Industry News*, he found out that he had not understood the Massachusetts cycling market at all. Most cyclists were vegan and anti-leather or felt that the weather in Framingham would crack the leather.

The company incorporated these learnings and started making bikes that customers wanted. They introduced single-speed bikes (called "The Craft") and cargo bikes (called "The Truth Cargo Bike"). In early 2018, they diversified into making electric bikes. "The demand for certified e-bike mechanics is very high and of the mechanics that were available, only 5% were women," he says. Brandale is now mostly focused on working with law enforcement officers to supply bikes equipped with the same technology in a squad car. Law enforcement—police—is now his primary target market. These bikes include radios and license plate scanners and enable the officers to ride the bikes on the street and do more community policing.

Brandale is also considering launching a motorbike by 2021. Apart from bikes, The 1854 Cycling Company now has its own set of merchandise that includes T-shirts, sweatshirts, hoodies, caps, and tank tops. The idea behind The 1854 Cycling Company is to create a brand that stands for a company that employs formerly incarcerated people and works toward reducing recidivism. They currently employ five women and produce 20 bikes a month.

The 1854 brand started off positioned as one of the first African American bike companies. "One of my best customers are white soccer moms. They buy my product, the merchandise, and also talk to their friends about the company. For every soccer mom customer, I get at least one more customer. In contrast, over the last 2 years, I've had only two white male customers, both of whom are my friends." Other customers include social activists, members of the #MeToo and the Black Lives Matter movements, and likewise. Today his primary customer is law enforcement. Brandale explains that his bikes are special to law enforcement because they see them as a way to give back to the community for some of their lapses of judgment toward African American people in the past.

Brandale is building a compelling story around the 1854 brand. He drew inspiration for the name of his company, The 1854 Cycling Company, from the first anti-slavery protest of the United States that happened in July 1854, at Framingham, Massachusetts. William Lloyd Garrison, a prominent abolitionist, burned the U.S. Constitution to protest the hypocrisy of celebrating independence while practicing slavery. This flame of the burning Constitution is part of their logo. He relates this protest to his company's fight against the "revolving doors of the criminal justice system where approximately 76.6% of all released prisoners will be rearrested within 5 years of their release." The brand stands for an opportunity for those people who did not have stable jobs and incomes to put food on the table and educate their children.

His advice to entrepreneurs who are planning on starting something that is potentially groundbreaking is "Do it slowly. Minimize and calculate your risk, but don't move too quickly because the industry is built to stomp companies like this into the ground."

Critical Thinking Questions

1. What is the social mission of 1854 Cycling?

2. Does 1854 connect to any of the Sustainable Development Goals discussed in the chapter?

3. Articulate the story behind the company and evaluate its potential as a brand.

Sources:

Brandale Randolph (interview with Babson MBA graduate assistant Gaurav Khemka, October 25, 2018)

The 1854 Cycling Company. https://www.1854cycling.com/bicycles-2

Entrepreneurship for All. (2018). EforAll Summit 2018 Brandale Randolph full keynote [Video file]. *YouTube*. Retrieved from https://www.youtube.com/watch?v=sq-XSHBQ1d4

TEDx Talks. (2014). Stop throwing breakfast sandwiches at the poor [Video file]. *YouTube*. Retrieved from https://www.youtube.com/watch?v=v6ZWKSbeD9w

GLOSSARY

Accelerator: an organization that provides tailored support in order to help new ventures scale and grow.

Accounts payable: money owed by a business to its suppliers.

Accounts receivable: money owed to the company for goods or services provided and billed to a customer.

Accredited investors: investors who earn an annual income of more than $200,000 or have a net worth of more than $1 million.

Accrued expenses: costs incurred by the company for which no payment has been made.

Advertising revenue model: generating revenue by advertising products and services.

AEIOU framework: acronym for *activities, environments, interactions, objects,* and *users*—a framework commonly used to categorize observations during fieldwork.

Alertness: the ability some people have to identify opportunities.

All-benefits: a type of value proposition that involves identifying and promoting all the benefits of a product or service to customer segments, with little regard for the competition or any real insight into what the customer really wants or needs.

Analytical strategies: actions that involve taking time to think carefully about a problem by breaking it up into parts, or looking at it in a more general way, in order to generate ideas about how certain products or services can be improved or made more innovative.

Angel investor: a type of investor who uses his or her own money to provide funds to young startup private businesses run by entrepreneurs who are neither friends nor family.

Backlog: orders that have been received but not delivered to the customer.

Balance sheet: a financial statement that shows what the company owes, what it owns, including the shareholder's stake, at a particular point in time.

Behavior-focused strategies: methods to increase self-awareness and manage behaviors, particularly when dealing with necessary but unpleasant tasks. These strategies include self-observation, self-goal setting, self-reward, self-punishment, and self-cueing.

Benefit corporation (or B Corp): a form of organization certified by the nonprofit B Lab that ensures strict standards of social and environmental performance, accountability, and transparency are met.

Bonds: the connections with family, friends, and others who have a similar cultural background or ethnicity.

Bootstrapping: the process of building or starting a business with no outside investment, funding, or support.

Bottom-up analysis: estimating potential sales using calculations in order to arrive at a total sales figure.

Bottom-up (or build-up) method: estimating revenues and costs from the smallest unit of sales, such as a day.

Brand strategy: a long-term plan to develop a successful brand; it involves how you plan to communicate your brand messages to your target customers.

Branding: the process of creating a name, term, design, symbol, or any other feature that identifies a product or service and differentiates it from others.

Bridges: the links that go further than simply sharing a sense of identity; for example, making connections with distant friends or colleagues who may have different backgrounds, cultures, and so on.

Brokers: the people who organize transactions between buyers and sellers.

Bundled pricing: a pricing strategy whereby companies package a set of goods or services together and then sell them for a lower price than if they were to be sold separately.

Business model: describes the rationale of how a new venture creates, delivers, and captures value.

Business model canvas (BMC): a one-page plan that divides the business model into nine components in order to provide a more thorough overview.

Business plan: the most formal of planning tools. It is typically a lengthy written document discussing the business concept, product mix, marketing plan, operations plan, development plan, and financial forecast.

Buyer personas: profiles or representations of ideal customers based on information and market research.

C corporation: (sometimes known as a "C-corp")—a separate legal and taxable entity created by the state government and owned by an unlimited number of shareholders.

Capital stock: the original amount the owners paid into the company plus any additional paid-in capital to purchase stock in the company.

Cash conversion cycle (CCC): the number of days a company's cash is tied up in the production and sales process.

Cash flow statement: a financial report that details the inflows and outflows of cash for a company over a set period of time.

Cognitive comprehensiveness: a process in which team members examine critical issues with a wide lens and formulate strategies by considering diverse approaches, decision criteria, and courses of action.

Compensation policy: The level of compensation and benefits for each type of position in the business.

Competition-led pricing: a pricing strategy that matches prices to other businesses selling the same or very similar products and services.

Concept statement: a written representation of your vision for your product or service.

Constructive thought patterns: models to help us to form positive and productive ways of thinking that can benefit our performance.

Consumers: Customers who actually use the product or service.

Convergent thinking: a thought process that allows us to narrow down the number of ideas generated through divergent thinking in an effort to identify which ones have the most potential.

Convertible debt: (also known as convertible bond or a convertible note)—a short-term loan that can be turned into equity when future financing is issued.

Copyright: a form of protection provided to the creators of original works in the areas of literature, music, drama, choreography, art, motion pictures, sound recordings, and architecture.

Corporate entrepreneurship (or intrapreneurship): a process of creating new products, ventures, processes, or renewal within large organizations.

Corporate social responsibility (CSR): describes the efforts taken by corporations to address the company's effects on environmental and social well-being in order to promote positive change.

Cost of goods sold (COGS): the direct cost of producing a product.

Cost-led pricing: a pricing strategy that involves calculating all the costs involved in manufacturing or delivering the product or service, plus all other expenses, and adding an expected profit or margin by predicting your sales volume to get the approximate price.

Creation logic: a form of thinking that is used when the future is unpredictable.

Creativity: the capacity to produce new ideas, insights, inventions, products, or artistic objects that are considered to be unique, useful, and of value to others.

Credit policy: The process and timing in which obligations to pay for products and services sold will be billed and collected.

Crowdfunding: the process of raising funding for a new venture from a large audience (the "crowd"), typically through the Internet.

Crowdsourcing: the process of using the Internet to attract, aggregate, and manage ostensibly inexpensive or even free labor from enthusiastic customers and like-minded people.

Current assets: cash and other assets that can be converted into cash within a year.

Current liabilities: bills that must be paid within 1 year of the date of the balance sheet.

Customer: someone who pays for a product or service.

Customer journey map: a visual representation that captures customer experience across multiple touchpoints.

Customer value proposition (CVP): a statement that describes why a customer should buy and use your product or service.

Customer-led pricing: a pricing strategy that asks customers how much they are willing to pay and then offers the product at that price.

Customers: people who populate the segments of a market served by the offering.

Data revenue model: generating revenue by selling high-quality, exclusive, valuable information to other parties.

Days of inventory (DOI): a measure of the average number of days it takes to sell the entire inventory of a company.

Days payable outstanding (DPO): a measure of the number of days it takes you to pay your bills.

Days sales outstanding (DSO): a measure of the number of days that it takes to collect on accounts receivable.

Debt financing: borrowing money to start a business that is expected to be paid back with interest at a designated point in the future.

Decision makers: customers similar to economic buyers who have even more authority to make purchasing decisions as they are positioned higher up in the hierarchy.

Deliberate practice: carrying out carefully focused efforts to improve current performance.

Demand: prospective customers' desire for the goods and services available.

Design pathway: a pathway that can uncover high-value opportunities because the entrepreneur is focusing on unmet needs of customers, specifically latent needs.

Design thinking: a human-centered approach to innovation that brings together what people need with what is technologically feasible and economically viable.

Development strategies: actions that involve enhancing and modifying existing ideas in order to create better alternatives and new possibilities.

Deviance: when an entrepreneur defies legal and ethical boundaries, leading to mismanagement of the venture.

Direct cross-subsidies: pricing a product or service above its market value to pay for the loss of giving away a product or service for free or below its market value.

Divergent thinking: a thought process that allows us to expand our view of the world to generate as many ideas as possible without being trapped by traditional problem-solving methods or predetermined constraints.

Diversified market: two or more customer segments with different needs and problems that bear no relationship to each other.

Dramatic difference: the uniqueness of your product or service in relation to other available options.

Due diligence: a rigorous process that involves evaluating an investment opportunity prior to the contract being signed.

Early-stage financing: a stage of financing that involves larger funds provided for companies that have a team in place and a product or service tested or piloted, but have little or no revenue.

Earned-income activities: the sale of products or services that are used as a source of revenue generation.

Economic buyers: the customers who have the ability to approve large-scale purchases, such as buyers for retail chains, corporate office managers, and corporate VPs.

Effectuate pathway: a pathway that involves using what you have (skills, knowledge, abilities) to uncover an opportunity that uniquely fits you.

Effectuation theory: an entrepreneurial approach to taking quick action using resources you have available to get early traction on new ideas.

End users: the type of customers who will use your product. Their feedback will help you refine and tweak the product.

Enterprising nonprofits: a form of social entrepreneurship where both the venture mission and the market impact are for social purposes.

Entrepreneur: an individual or a group who creates something new—a new idea, a new item or product, a new institution, a new market, a new set of possibilities.

Entrepreneurial marketing: a set of processes adopted by entrepreneurs based on new and unconventional marketing practices in order to gain traction in competitive markets.

Entrepreneurial mindset: the ability to quickly sense, take action, and get organized under uncertain conditions.

Entrepreneurial self-efficacy (ESE): the belief that entrepreneurs have in their own ability to begin new ventures.

Entrepreneurs inside: entrepreneurs who think and act entrepreneurially within organizations.

Entrepreneurship: a way of thinking, acting, and being that combines the ability to find or create new opportunities with the courage to act on them.

Equity crowdfunding: a form of crowdfunding that gives investors the opportunity to become shareholders in a company.

Equity financing: the sale of shares of stock in exchange for cash.

Established business owners: the people who have been active in business for more than 3.5 years.

Evidence-based entrepreneurship: the practice of hypothesizing, testing, and validating to create a business model.

Experiment: a method used to prove or disprove the validity of an idea or hypothesis.

Exploratory experimentation: a method whereby market tests are conducted to get early feedback and acquire important learning and information.

Fair pricing: the degree to which both businesses and customers believe that the pricing is reasonable.

Family enterprise: a business that is owned and managed by multiple family members, typically for more than one generation.

Feasibility study: a planning tool that allows entrepreneurs to test the possibilities of an initial idea to see if it is worth pursuing.

Feedback interview: an interview conducted to get feedback on an existing product or service.

Financial viability: defines the revenue and cost structures a business needs to meet its operating expenses and financial obligations.

Find pathway: a pathway that assumes that opportunities exist independent of entrepreneurs and are waiting to be found.

Fixed mindset: the assumption held by people who perceive their talents and abilities as set traits.

Founders' agreement: a clear agreement between founders on a number of key issues that their business might face.

Founding team: a group of people with complementary skills and a shared sense of commitment coming together in founding an enterprise to build and grow the company.

Franchise: a type of license purchased by a franchisee from an existing business called a franchisor to allow them to trade under the name of that business.

Franchising revenue model: earning revenue by selling franchises of an existing business to allow another party to trade under the name of that business.

Freemium revenue model: mixing free (mainly web-based) basic services with premium or upgraded services.

General partnership: a business owned by two or more people who have made a decision to comanage and share in the profits and losses.

Goodwill: the price paid for an asset in excess of its book value. You will see this on the balance sheet when the company has made one or more large acquisitions.

Grit: the quality that enables people to work hard and sustain interest in their long-term goals.

Groupthink: a phenomenon in which people share too similar a mindset, which inhibits their ability to spot gaps or errors.

Growth mindset: the assumptions held by people who believe that their abilities can be developed through dedication, effort, and hard work.

Guerrilla marketing: a low-budget strategy that focuses on personally interacting with a target group by promoting products and services through surprise or other unconventional means.

Habit: a sometimes unconscious pattern of behavior that is carried out often and regularly.

Habit-breaking strategies: actions that involve techniques that help to break our minds out of mental fixedness in order to bring about creative insights.

Heterogeneous team: a group of people with a mix of knowledge, skills, and experience.

Homogenous team: a group of people with the same or similar characteristics such as age, gender, ethnicity, experience, and educational background.

Hybrid model of social entrepreneurship: an organization with a purpose that equally emphasizes both economic and social goals.

Hypothesis: an assumption that is tested through research and experimentation.

Ideation: a creative process that involves generating and developing new ideas to address needs.

Imagination-based strategies: actions that involve suspending disbelief and dropping constraints in order to create unrealistic states or fantasies.

Implementation: a process involving the testing of assumptions of new ideas to continuously shape them into viable opportunities.

Impression management: paying conscious attention to the way people perceive you and taking steps to be perceived in the way you want others to see you.

Improvisation: the art of spontaneously creating something without preparation.

Inattention: when an entrepreneur becomes sidetracked from the core business.

Inbound marketing: bringing potential customers to your business by creating online content that addresses their needs, in order to build trust and brand awareness.

Income statement (or profit and loss statement): a financial report that shows revenue, expenses, and profit for a period of time, typically a month, quarter, or year.

Incubator: an organization that helps early stage entrepreneurs refine ideas, build out technology, and get access to resources.

Influencers (or opinion leaders): customers with a large following who have the power to influence our purchase decisions.

Infrastructure: the resources (people, technology, products, suppliers, partners, facilities, cash, etc.) that an entrepreneur must have in order to deliver the CVP.

Initial public offering (IPO): a company's first opportunity to sell stocks on the stock market to be purchased by members of the general public.

Insight: an interpretation of an observation or a sudden realization that provides us with a new understanding of a human behavior or attitude that results in the identification of a need.

Inspiration: the first phase of design thinking, when you develop the design challenge and acquire a deeper understanding of users.

Intangible assets: the value of patents, software programs, copyrights, trademarks, franchises, brand names, or assets that cannot be physically touched.

Intellectual property (IP): intangible personal property created by human intelligence, such as ideas, inventions, slogans, logos, and processes.

Intelligent failures: good failures that provide valuable new knowledge that can help a startup overcome hurdles and roadblocks.

Interest expense: the extent of the company's debt burden as well as representing any interest owed on borrowed money.

Intermediation revenue model: the different methods by which third parties such as brokers (or "middlemen") can generate money.

Interpersonal strategies: actions that involve group members generating ideas and building on each other's ideas.

Introductory offer: a pricing strategy to encourage people to try a new product by offering it for free or at a heavily discounted price.

Inventory policy: the level of various types of inventory (e.g., raw materials, work-in-process, finished goods) maintained and the speed with which inventory moves from the business to the customer.

Investor model: a crowdfunding model that gives backers an equity stake in the business in return for their funding.

Lack of ability: the lack of skillset to get the job done.

Latent needs: needs we don't know we have.

Lean Canvas: an adapted version of the BMC that was created to better address the needs of startup entrepreneurs.

Lending model: a crowdfunding model where funds are offered as loans with the expectation that the money will be repaid.

Liabilities: economic obligations of the company, such as money owed to lenders, suppliers, and employees.

Licensing revenue model: earning revenue by giving permission to other parties to use protected intellectual property (patents, copyrights, trademarks) in exchange for fees.

Limited liability company (LLC): a business structure that combines the taxation advantages of a partnership with the limited liability benefits of a corporation without being subject to the eligibility requirements of an S-corp.

Linkages: the connections to people or groups regardless of their position in an organization, society, or other community.

Long-term debt: obligation for debt that is due to be repaid in more than 12 months.

Long-term investments: assets that are more than 1 year old and are carried on the balance sheet at cost or book value with no appreciation.

Loss leader: a pricing strategy whereby a business offers a product or service at a lower price in an attempt to attract more customers.

Market: a place where people can sell goods and services (the supply) to people who wish to buy those goods and services (the demand).

Market opportunity: the degree of customer or market demand for a specific product application.

Market sizing: a method of estimating the number of potential customers and possible revenue or profitability of a product or service.

Marketing: a method of putting the right product in the right place, at the right price, at the right time.

Marketing mix: the combination of product, price, promotion, and placement of what a company is offereing.

Mass market: a large group of customers with very similar needs and problems.

Metacognition: our ability to understand and be aware of how we think and the processes we use to think.

Microloan: a very small, short-term loan often associated with entrepreneurs in developing countries.

Multiparty business: giving one party product or service free, but charging the other party (or parties).

Multisided markets: markets with two or more customer segments that are mutually independent of each other.

MVP (minimum viable product): a version of a new product that allows a team to collect the maximum amount of validated learning about customers with the least effort.

Nascent entrepreneurs: individuals who have set up a business they will own or co-own that is less than 3 months old and has not yet generated wages or salaries for the owners.

Natural reward strategies: types of compensation designed to make aspects of a task or activity more enjoyable by building in certain features or by reshaping perceptions to focus on the most positive aspects of the task and the value it holds.

Necessity-based entrepreneurs: individuals who are pushed into starting a business because of circumstance such as redundancy, threat of job loss, and unemployment.

Need: a lack of something desirable, useful, or required that is uncovered through the design process.

Need-finding interview: an interview conducted to better understand the problems or needs of people or validate what you think a need or problem may be.

Net income: indicates what is left after all costs, expenses, and taxes have been paid.

New business owners: individuals who are former nascent entrepreneurs and have been actively involved in a business for more than 3 months but less than 3.5 years.

Niche market: a small market segment that consists of customers with specific needs and requirements.

Nondisclosure agreement (NDA): a legal contract that outlines confidential information shared by two or more parties.

Not-for-profit: a tax status granted to companies performing functions deemed by Congress to be socially desirable that exempts them from income tax and, in some cases, allows them to receive tax-deductible donations.

Observation: the action of closely monitoring the behavior and activities of users/potential customers in their own environment.

Offering: what you are offering to a particular customer segment, the value generated for those customers, and how you will reach and communicate with them.

Operating expenses: the costs of running your business, including your rent, utilities, administration, marketing/advertising, employee salaries, and so on.

Operating profit: the amount left over from revenue once all costs and expenses are subtracted.

Opportunity: a way of generating profit through unique, novel, or desirable products or services that have not been previously exploited.

Opportunity-based entrepreneurs: individuals who make a decision to start their own businesses based on their ability to create or exploit an opportunity, and whose main driver for getting involved in the venture is being independent or increasing their income, rather than merely maintaining their income.

Other current liabilities: short-term liabilities that do not fall into a specific category, such as sales tax, income tax, and so forth.

Outbound marketing: promoting your product or service through traditional activities such as advertising, trade shows, and cold calling.

Overt benefit: the one big benefit for your customer.

Packaging: a process that explores every single visual element of the external appearance of an offering through the eyes of your customer.

Passion: an intense positive emotion, which is usually related to entrepreneurs who are engaged in meaningful ventures, or tasks and activities, and which has the effect of motivating and stimulating entrepreneurs to overcome obstacles and remain focused on their goals.

Patent: a grant of exclusive property rights on inventions through the U.S. and other governments.

Patronage model: a crowdfunding model where backers do not expect any direct return for their donation or investment..

Pattern recognition: the process of identifying links or connections between apparently unrelated things or events.

Payables policy: the process and timing in which obligations to pay for goods and services received by the business will be paid.

People: the people who are responsible for every aspect of sales and marketing.

Pilot experiment: a small-scale study conducted to assess the feasibility of a product or service.

Pitch: the act of clearly presenting and describing a product or service to others.

Pivot: a change in business direction.

Place: the location where the product is actually distributed to your target market; for example, trade fairs, retail stores, catalogs, mail order, online, and so forth.

Planning: a process of envisioning the future for a business, including what one plans to do and how one plans to do it.

Points-of-difference: a type of value proposition that focuses on the product or service relative to the competition and how the offering is different from others on the market.

Positioning: a marketing strategy that focuses on how your customers think or talk about product and company relative to competitors.

Potential entrepreneurs: individuals who believe they have the capacity and know-how to start a business without being burdened by the fear of failure.

Predictive logic: a form of thinking that sees entrepreneurship as a linear process in which steps are followed and outcomes are—ideally—predictable.

Prepaid expenses: the payments the company has already made for services not yet received.

Price: the amount that the customer is expected to pay for the product.

Pricing policy: how pricing will be determined for your products and services.

Primary research: refers to data gathered by yourself through sources such as focus groups, interviews, and surveys.

Prior knowledge: the information gained from a combination of life and work experience.

Process inadequacy: wrong (or missing) processes set up in the organization, causing communication breakdown.

Product: anything tangible or intangible (such as a service) offered by the company.

Product application: goods or services created to meet a demand, thereby providing a solution to a customer problem.

Product–market fit: an offering that meets the needs of customers.

Professional revenue model: earning revenue by providing professional services on a time and materials contract.

Promotion: the activities that involve all the ways in which companies tell their customers about their offering.

Psychological pricing: a pricing strategy intended to encourage customers to buy on the basis of their belief that the product or service is cheaper than it really is.

Purchasing policy: the price and timing of raw materials and other goods and services necessary to build, sell, and support products.

Real reason to believe: provides evidence to the customer that you will do as you promise.

Recommenders: people who may evaluate your product and tell the public about it, such as bloggers or experts in an industry.

Relationship-seeking strategies: plans of action that involve consciously making links between concepts or ideas that are not normally associated with each other.

Resonating-focus: a type of value proposition that describes why people will really like your product and focuses on the customers and what they really need and value.

Retained earnings: the cumulative amount of profit retained by the company and not paid out in the form of dividends to owners.

Revenue: the income gained from sales of goods or services.

Revenue model: a key component of the business model that identifies how the company will earn income and make profits.

Reward-based crowdfunding: a crowdfunding model that involves rewarding backers for supporting a project.

Royalties: a share of the income of a business paid by a franchisee to the franchisor.

S corporation: (sometimes known as an "S-corp")—a type of corporation that is eligible for, and elects, special taxation status.

SAM: serviceable available market; the section of the TAM that your product or service intends to target.

Search pathway: a pathway used when entrepreneurs are not quite sure what type of venture they want to start, so they engage in an active search to discover new opportunities.

Search strategies: actions that involve using a stimulus to retrieve memories in order to make links or connections based on personal experience that are relevant to the current problem.

Secondary research: refers to data gathered from external sources such as industry publications, websites, government agencies, and so on.

Seed-stage financing: a stage of financing in which small or modest amounts of capital are provided to entrepreneurs to prove a concept.

Segmented market: a market divided into groups according to customers' different needs and problems.

Self-cueing: the process of prompting that acts as a reminder of desired goals and keeps your attention on what you are trying to achieve.

Self–goal setting: the process of setting individual goals for ourselves.

Self-leadership: a process whereby people can influence and control their own behavior, actions, and thinking to achieve the self-direction and self-motivation necessary to build their entrepreneurial business ventures.

Self-observation: a process that raises our awareness of how, when, and why we behave the way we do in certain circumstances.

Self-punishment (or self-correcting feedback): a process that allows us to examine our mistakes before making a conscious effort not to repeat them.

Self-reward: a process that involves compensating ourselves when we achieve our goals. These rewards can be tangible or intangible.

Self-selected stakeholders: the people who "self-select" into a venture in order to connect entrepreneurs with resources in an effort to steer the venture in the right direction.

Serial entrepreneurs (or habitual entrepreneurs): entrepreneurs who start several businesses, either simultaneously or consecutively.

Shareholder equity: the money that has been invested in the business plus the cumulative net profits and losses the company has generated.

Short-term debt: the portion of long-term debt that must be paid within a year.

Skimming: a high pricing strategy, generally used for new products or services that face very little or even no competition.

Social capital: personal social networks populated with people who willingly cooperate, exchange information, and build trusting relationships with each other.

Social consequence entrepreneurship: a for-profit venture whose primary market impact is social.

Social entrepreneurship: the process of sourcing innovative solutions to social and environmental problems.

Social purpose ventures: businesses created by social entrepreneurs to resolve a social problem and make a profit.

Sole proprietorship: a business owned by one person who has full exposure to its liabilities.

SOM: share of market; the portion of SAM that your company is realistically likely to reach.

Stakeholders: the people or groups affected by or involved with the achievements of the social enterprise's objectives.

Startup: a temporary organization in search of a scalable business model.

Startup financing: a stage of financing in which the money is provided to entrepreneurs to enable them to implement the idea by funding product research and development.

Storyboard: an easy form of prototyping that provides a high-level view of thoughts and ideas arranged in sequence in the form of drawings, sketches, or illustrations.

Subscription revenue model: charging customers to gain continuous access to a product or service.

Supply: the sellers who compete for customers in the marketplace.

Sweat equity: a non-monetary investment that increases the value or ownership interest created by the investment of hard work for no compensation.

TAM: total available market; the total market demand for a product or service.

Target-return pricing: a pricing method whereby the price is based on the amount of investment you have put into your business.

Top-down analysis: determining the total market using demographic data and then estimating your share of the market.

Total Entrepreneurial Activity (TEA): the percentage of the population of each country between the ages of 18 and 64, who are either a nascent entrepreneur or owner—manager of a new business.

Trade secret: confidential information that provides companies with a competitive edge and is not in the public domain, such as formulas, patterns, compilations, programs, devices, methods, techniques, or processes.

Trademark: any word, name, symbol, or device used in business to identify and promote a product. Its counterpart for service industries is the service mark.

True fans: people who will buy anything you produce; they will wait in line for your products, drive for hours to attend one of your events, and preorder your next product without even knowing what it looks like.

Uncertainty: the lack of clarity about future events that can cause entrepreneurs to take unreasonable actions.

Unicorn: a tech startup company that has received a $1 billion valuation, as determined by private or public investment.

Unit sales revenue model: generating revenue by the number of items (units) sold by a company.

Use case: a methodology used in the software industry to illustrate how a user will interact with a specific piece of software.

Utility and usage revenue model: a pay-as-you-go model that charges customers fees on the basis of how often goods or services are used.

Value-based pricing: a pricing method that involves pricing a product based on how it benefits the customer.

Venture capitalist (VC): a type of professional investor who generally invests in early-stage and emerging companies because of perceived long-term growth potential.

Venture philanthropy funding: a combination of financial assistance such as grants with a high level of engagement by the funder.

Vesting: the concept of imposing equity forfeitures on cofounders over a certain period of time on a piecemeal basis should they not stay with the company.

Wicked problems: large, complex social problems where there is no clear solution; where there is limited, confusing, or contradictory information available; and where a whole range of people with conflicting values engage in debate.

NOTES

CHAPTER 1

1. Blank, S., & Dorf, B. (2012). *The startup owner's manual: The step-by-step guide for building a great company.* Pescadero, CA: K&S Ranch.

2. Neck, H. M., Greene, P. G., & Brush, C. B. (2014). *Teaching entrepreneurship: A practice-based approach.* Northampton, MA: Edward Elgar.

3. Sarasvathy, S. D. (2008). *Effectuation: Elements of entrepreneurial expertise.* Northampton, MA: Edward Elgar.

4. Sarasvathy, *Effectuation.*

5. Morris, M. H. (1998). *Entrepreneurial intensity: Sustainable advantages for individuals, organizations, and societies.* Westport, CT: Quorum.

6. Neck, H. M., & Greene, P. G. (2011). Entrepreneurship education: Known worlds and new frontiers. *Journal of Small Business Management, 49,* 55–70.

7. Brown, P. (2013, November 6). Entrepreneurs are "calculated" risk takers—The word that can be the difference between failure and success. *Forbes.* Retrieved from www.forbes.com/sites/actiontrumpseverything/2013/11/06/entrepreneurs-are-not-risk-takers-they-are-calculated-risk-takers-that-one-additional-word-can-be-the-difference-between-failure-and-success/

8. Schlesinger, L., Kiefer, C., & Brown, P. (2012). *Just start: Take action, embrace uncertainty, create the future.* Cambridge, MA: Harvard Business School Press.

9. Costello, C., Neck, H., & Williams, R. (2011). *Elements of the entrepreneur experience.* Babson Park, MA: Babson Entrepreneur Experience Lab. Retrieved from http://elab.businessinnovationfactory.com/sites/default/files/pdf/BabsonBIF-eLab-NVE-V1-2012rev.pdf

10. Rosen, A. (2015, May 7). *Why collaboration is essential to entrepreneurship.* Retrieved from https://www.entrepreneur.com/article/245599

11. Spors, K. K. (2007, January 9). Do start-ups really need formal business plans? Studies find often time wasted gathering data with no link to success. *Wall Street Journal.* Retrieved from http://www.wsj.com/articles/SB116830373855570835

12. Costello, Neck, & Williams, *Elements.*

13. Covin, J. G., & Miles, M. (1999). Corporate entrepreneurship and the pursuit of competitive advantage. *Entrepreneurship: Theory and Practice, 23*(3), 47–63.

14. Elkins, F. (2018, September 17). *The Corporate Entrepreneur Awards 2018: Recognizing the best in corporate innovation.* Retrieved from https://www.marketgravity.com/cea-celebrating-the-best-in-corporate-innovation/

15. Costello, C., Neck, H., & Dziobek, K. (2012). *Entrepreneurs of all kinds: Elements of the entrepreneurs inside experience.* Babson Park, MA: Babson Entrepreneur Experience Lab. Retrieved from http://elab.businessinnovationfactory.com/sites/default/files/pdf/babsonBIF-elab-EI-V2-2012rev.pdf

16. Ibid.

17. Judd, R. J., & Justis, R. T. (2007). *Franchising: An entrepreneur's guide* (4th ed.). Stamford, CT: Cengage Learning.

18. Retrieved from https://www.entrepreneur.com/franchises/500/2017

19. Mazareanu, E. (2019). Number of franchise establishments in the United States from 2007 to 2018. *Statista.* Retrieved from https://www.statista.com/statistics/190313/estimated-number-of-us-franchise-establishments-since-2007/

20. U.S. Small Business Administration. (n.d.). *Buy an existing business or franchise.* Retrieved from https://www.sba.gov/content/buying-existing-business

21. Chris Cranston, interview with the author.

22. Neck, H. M. (2010). Social entrepreneurship. In B. Bygrave & A. Zacharakis (Eds.), *The portable MBA in entrepreneurship* (pp. 411–436). Hoboken, NJ: Wiley.

23. Neck, H. M., Brush, C., & Allen, E. (2009). The landscape of social entrepreneurship. *Business Horizons, 52,* 13–19; Mair, J., & Marti, I. (2006). Social entrepreneurship research: A source of explanation, prediction and delight. *Journal of World Business, 41,* 36–44.

24. B Lab. (2019). *About B corps.* Retrieved from https://bcorporation.net/about-b-corps

25. Clifford, C. (2012, June 11). B corps: The next generation of company. *Entrepreneur.* Retrieved from www.entrepreneur.com/blog/223762

26. Smithers, R. (2016, January 22). Raise a toast and help tackle the problem of food waste. *The Guardian.* Retrieved from https://www.theguardian.com/uk-news/2016/jan/22/toast-ale-beer-surplus-bread-feedback-food-waste

27. Habbershon, T. G., Williams, M., & MacMillan, I. C. (2003). A unified systems perspective of family firm performance. *Journal of Business Venturing, 18,* 451–465.

28. Mars, V. (2017, April 19). *How does a family business survive?* Retrieved from https://insights.som.yale.edu/insights/how-does-family-business-survive

29. Ibid.

30. Featherstone, E. (2017, January 11). The women-led startups smashing the glass ceiling. *The Guardian.* Retrieved from https://www.theguardian.com/small-business-network/2017/jan/11/women-led-startups-smashing-glass-ceiling-investment

31. Blank & Dorf, *The startup owner's manual.*

32. McIntyre, G. (2019, March 20). What percentage of small businesses fail? (And other need-to-know stats). *Fundera.* Retrieved from https://www.fundera.com/blog/what-percentage-of-small-businesses-fail

33. Neck, H. M., & Greene, P. G. (2011). Entrepreneurship education: Known worlds and new frontiers. *Journal of Small Business Management, 49,* 55–70.

34. Neck, H. M., Greene, P. G., & Brush, C. B. (2014/2015). Practice-based entrepreneurship education using actionable theory. In M. Morris (Ed.), *Annals of entrepreneurship education and pedagogy* (pp. 3–20). Northampton, MA: Edward Elgar.

35. Blank & Dorf, *The startup owner's manual.*

36. Lehrer, J. (Host). (2006, November 22). Banker to the poor [Television broadcast]. In *The NewsHour With Jim Lehrer.* Arlington, VA: PBS. Retrieved from http://www.skaggsisland.org/sustainable/muhammadyunus.htm

37. Read, S., Sarasvathy, S., Dew, N., & Wiltbank, R. (2011). *Effectual entrepreneurship.* New York, NY: Routledge.

38. Mask, C. (2014, November 4). The 4 reasons why people start their own businesses. *The Business Journals*. Retrieved from http://www.bizjournals.com/bizjournals/how-to/growth-strategies/2014/11/4-reasons-why-people-start-their-own-businesses.html; Wells, C. (2015, May 26). Why some entrepreneurs feel fulfilled—But others don't: Money is only part of the equation; The latest research offers surprising insights into the path to satisfaction. *Wall Street Journal*, p. R.1.

39. Sarasvathy, *Effectuation*.

40. The concept of affordable loss is based on the previously cited words of Saras Sarasvathy.

41. Baron, R. A., & Henry, R. A. (2010). How entrepreneurs acquire the capacity to excel: Insights from research on expert performance. *Strategic Entrepreneurship Journal, 4*, 49–65.

42. Ibid.

43. Duvivier, R. J., van Dalen, J., Muijtjens, A. M., Moulaert, V., van der Vleuten, C., & Scherpbier, A. (2011). The role of deliberate practice in the acquisition of clinical skills. *BMC Medical Education, 11*, 101–108.

44. Clear, J. (2018). *The beginner's guide to deliberate practice*. Retrieved from https://jamesclear.com/beginners-guide-deliberate-practice

45. Ibid.

46. Ibid.

47. Wasserman, N. (2014, August 25). How an entrepreneur's passion can destroy a startup. *Wall Street Journal*. Retrieved from http://online.wsj.com/articles/how-an-entrepreneur-s-passion-can-destroy-a-startup-1408912044

48. Shen, J. (2017, May 31). The complete guide to deliberate practice. *Better Humans*. Retrieved from https://betterhumans.coach.me/the-complete-guide-to-deliberate-practice-3a70319be3af

49. Sarasvathy, *Effectuation*.

50. Dew, N., Read, S., Sarasvathy, S. D., & Wiltbank, R. (2009). Effectual versus predictive logics in entrepreneurial decision-making: Differences between experts and novices. *Journal of Business Venturing, 24*, 287–309.

CHAPTER 2

1. McKean, E. (Ed.). (2005). *New Oxford American dictionary* (2nd ed.). New York, NY: Oxford University Press.

2. Walker, H. (2019, February 1). Is Cory Booker for real? Retrieved from https://www.huffpost.com/entry/cory-booker-real_n_5c54a758e4b08710475356a8

3. Taghavi, A. R. (2018, December 4). Cory Booker's mentor, Virginia Jones on being optimistic in the hardest times. Retrieved from https://medium.com/swlh/cory-bookers-mentor-virginia-jones-on-being-optimistic-in-the-hardest-times-9f3d4830755e

4. Dweck, C. (2006). *Mindset: The new psychology of success*. New York, NY: Random House.

5. Bronson, P. (2007, August 3). How not to talk to your kids. *New York Magazine*. Retrieved from http://nymag.com/news/features/27840/

6. Ibid.

7. Dweck, C. (2016). *Mindset: The new psychology of success* (2nd ed.). New York, NY: Random House.

8. Dweck, C. (2010). How can you change from a fixed mindset to a growth mindset? *Mindset*. Retrieved from http://mindsetonline.com/changeyourmindset/firststeps/

9. Ireland, R. D., Hitt, M. A., & Simon, D. G. (2003). A model of strategic entrepreneurship: The construct and its dimensions. *Journal of Management, 29*, 963–990.

10. Cardon, M. S., Vincent, J., Singh, J., & Drnovsek, M. (2009). The nature and experience of entrepreneurial passion. *Academy of Management Review, 34*, 511–532.

11. Warren, R. (2013, September 7). 101 best inspirational quotes for entrepreneurs. *Business Insider*. Retrieved from http://www.businessinsider.com/101-best-inspirational-quotes-for-entrepreneurs-2013-9

12. Cardon et al., The nature and experience.

13. Brännback, M., Carsrud, A., Elfying, J., & Krueger, N. (2006). *Sex, [drugs], and entrepreneurial passion? An exploratory study*. Paper presented at the Babson College Entrepreneurship Research Conference, Bloomington, IN.

14. Baron, R. A. (2008). The role of affect in the entrepreneurial process. *Academy of Management Review, 33*, 328–340.

15. Cardon et al., The nature and experience.

16. De Witte, M. (2018, June 18). Instead of "finding your passion," try developing it, Stanford scholars say. *Stanford News Service*. Retrieved from https://news.stanford.edu/press-releases/2018/06/18/find-passion-may-bad-advice/

17. Duhigg, C. (2012, February 27). How you can harness the power of habit. *NPR*. Retrieved from http://www.npr.org/2012/02/27/147296743/how-you-can-harness-the-power-of-habit

18. Information in this section taken from D'Intino, R. S., Goldsby, M. G.,

Houghton, J. D., & Neck, C. P. (2007). Self-leadership: A process for entrepreneurial success. *Journal of Leadership & Organizational Studies, 13*(4), 105–120.

19. Manz, C., & Neck, C. (2004). *Mastering self-leadership: Empowering yourself for personal excellence* (3rd ed.). Saddle River, NJ: Pearson Prentice Hall.

20. Neck, H. M. (2010). Idea generation. In B. Bygrave & A. Zacharakis (Eds.), *Portable MBA in entrepreneurship* (pp. 27–52). Hoboken, NJ: Wiley.

21. Kang, H. (2018, April 27). *Behold the winners of the 2018 Cartier Women's Initiative Awards*. Retrieved from website https://www.prestigeonline.com/sg/people-events/behold-winners-2018-cartier-womens-initiative-awards/

22. Hamidi, D. Y., Wennberg, K., & Berglund, H. (2008). Creativity in entrepreneurship education. *Journal of Small Business and Enterprise Development, 15*(2), 301–320.

23. Neck, Idea generation, 34–35.

24. Adams, J. (2001). *Conceptual blockbusting* (4th ed.). Cambridge, MA: Perseus.

25. Hayton, J., & Cacciotti, G. (2018, April 3). How fear helps (and hurts) entrepreneurs. *Harvard Business Review*. Retrieved from https://hbr.org/2018/04/how-fear-helps-and-hurts-entrepreneurs

26. Pink, D. H. (2005). *A whole new mind: Why right-brainers will rule the future*. New York, NY: Riverhead Books.

27. Nielsen, J. A., Zielinski, B. A., Ferguson, M. A., Lainhart, J. E., & Anderson, J. S. (2013). An evaluation of the left-brain vs. right-brain hypothesis with resting state functional connectivity magnetic resonance imaging. *PLoS ONE, 8*(8), e71275. doi:10.1371/journal.pone.0071275

28. Right brain, left brain? Scientists debunk popular theory. (2013, August 8). *Huffington Post*. Retrieved from http://www.huffingtonpost.com/2013/08/19/right-brain-left-brain-debunked_n_3762322.html

29. Csikszentmihalyi, M. (1996). *Creativity: Flow and the psychology of discovery and invention*. New York, NY: HarperCollins.

30. Hmieleski, K., & Corbett, A. (2008). The contrasting interaction effects of improvisational behavior with entrepreneurial self-efficacy on new venture performance and entrepreneur work satisfaction. *Journal of Business Venturing, 23*, 482–496.

31. Gotts, I., & Cremer, J. (2012). *Using improv in business*. Retrieved from http://iangotts.files.wordpress.com/2012/02/using-improv-in-business-e2-v1.pdf

32. Tutton, M. (2010, February 18). Why using improvisation to teach business skills is no joke. *CNN*. Retrieved from http://edition.cnn.com/2010/BUSINESS/02/18/improvisation.business.skills/

33. White, S. (2018, January 31). How an improv class can help develop essential business skills. *Financial Management*. Retrieved from https://www.fm-magazine.com/issues/2018/feb/improv-class-helps-develop-business-skills.html

34. Zagorski, N. (2008, Fall). The science of improv. *Peabody Magazine*. Retrieved from http://www.peabody.jhu.edu/past_issues/fall08/the_science_of_improv.html

35. Schwartz, K. (2014, April 11). Creativity and the brain: What we can learn from jazz musicians. *Mindshift*. Retrieved from http://blogs.kqed.org/mindshift/2014/04/the-link-between-jazz-improvisation-and-student-creativity/

36. McGee, J. E., Peterson, M., Mueller, S., & Sequeira, J. (2009). Entrepreneurial self-efficacy: Refining the measure. *Entrepreneurship Theory & Practice, 33*, 965–988.

37. Godwin, J. L., Neck, C. P., & D'Intino, R. S. (2016). Self-leadership, spirituality and entrepreneurial performance: A conceptual model. *Journal of Management, Spirituality, and Religion, 13*(1), 64–78.

38. DeMers, J. (2017, December 14). 5 entrepreneurs who started with nothing—and 3 lessons to learn: Sam Walton. George Soros. Kevin Plank. Jan Koum. What can these successful entrepreneurs teach you? *Entrepreneur*. Retrieved from https://www.entrepreneur.com/article/305990

39. Schwarzer, R., & Jerusalem, M. (1995). Generalized self-efficacy scale. In J. Weinman, S. Wright, & M. Johnston (Eds.), *Measures in health psychology: A user's portfolio. Causal and control beliefs* (pp. 35–37). Windsor, UK: NFER-NELSON. Scale retrieved from http://userpage.fu-berlin.de/~health/engscal.htm

CHAPTER 3

1. Baron, R. A. (2006). Opportunity recognition as pattern recognition: How entrepreneurs "connect the dots" to identify new business opportunities. *Academy of Management Perspectives, 20*, 104–119.

2. Sheffield, H. (2017, July 26). Bios Urn: The startup that lets you grow a tree from human ashes. *The Independent*. Retrieved from https://www.independent.co.uk/Business/indyventure/startup-biodegradable-urn-grow-tree-human-remains-business-a7852446.html

3. History timeline: Post-it notes. (2014). *Post-it*. Retrieved from https://www.post-it.com/3M/en_US/post-it/contact-us/about-us/

4. From Crystal Pepsi to Colgate lasagna: Big companies' biggest product failures. (2019). *MSN*. Retrieved from https://www.msn.com/en-gb/money/companies/from-crystal-pepsi-to-colgate-lasagna-big-companies-biggest-product-failures/ss-BBSq6XA?li=AAnZ9Ug#image=13

5. Nguyen, T. C. (2018, March 29). 5 weird inventions that were surprisingly successful. *Liveaboutdotcom*. Retrieved from https://www.thoughtco.com/weird-inventions-4150072

6. Nova, A. (2017, December 11). 10 unlikely products that made millions of dollars. *CNBC*. Retrieved from https://www.cnbc.com/2017/12/11/10-unlikely-products-that-made-millions-of-dollars.html

7. Ibid.

8. Bizarre inventions that made serious bucks. (2016). *Business Management Degrees*. Retrieved from http://www.business-management-degree.net/bizarre-inventions-that-made-serious-bucks/

9. Thompson, D. (2012, June 15). Forget Edison: This is how history's greatest inventions really happened. *The Atlantic*. Retrieved from http://www.theatlantic.com/business/archive/2012/06/forget-edison-this-is-how-historys-greatest-inventions-really-happened/258-525/

10. Ibid.

11. Smith, G. F. (1998). *Quality problem solving* (pp. 133–135). Milwaukee, WI: ASQ Quality Press.

12. Climbing Mount Everest is work for supermen. (1923, March 18). *The New York Times*. Retrieved from http://graphics8.nytimes.com/packages/pdf/arts/mallory1923.pdf

13. This section is heavily sourced from four primary works: Alvarez, S. A., & Barney, J. B. (2007). Discovery and creation: Alternative theories of entrepreneurial action. *Strategic Entrepreneurship Journal, 1*, 11–26; Neck, H. (2018, August 22). Entrepreneurial intelligence [Video file]. Retrieved from https://www.youtube.com/watch?v=91APSwO9urc; Neck, H. M., Brush, C., & Corbett, A. C. (2018). *Entrepreneurial intelligence: Beyond the mindset* (Paper presented at Babson College); Townsend, D. M., Hunt, R. A., McMullen, J. S., & Sarasvathy, S. D. (2018). Uncertainty, knowledge problems, and entrepreneurial action. *Academy of Management Annals, 12*(2), 659–687.

14. Schumpeter, J. (1934/2004). *The theory of economic development: An inquiry into profits, capital, credit, interest and the business cycle*. Cambridge, MA: Harvard Business School.

15. Brush, C. B., Greene, P. G., & Hart, M. M. (2001). From initial idea to unique advantage: The entrepreneurial challenge of constructing a resource base. *Academy of Management Perspectives, 15*(1), 64–78.

16. Baron, Opportunity recognition as pattern recognition.

17. Fiet, J. O. (2000). The theoretical side of teaching entrepreneurship. *Journal of Business Venturing, 16*, 1–24; Fiet, J. O. (2002). *The systematic search for entrepreneurial discoveries*. Westport, CT: Quorum Books.

18. Marx, R. (2009). For Liddabit's Jen King and Liz Gutman, life is sweet. *Village Voice*. Retrieved from https://www.villagevoice.com/2009/11/16/for-liddabits-jen-king-and-liz-gutman-life-is-sweet/

19. Wilson, J. (2016). Liz Gutman & Jen King, Liddabit Sweets, women entrepreneurs. *Gotham Gal*. Retrieved from https://gothamgal.com/2016/02/liz-gutman-jen-king-luddabit-sweets-women-entrepreneurs/

20. Alvarez & Barney, Discovery and creation.

21. Kirzner, I. M. (1973). *Competition and entrepreneurship*. Chicago, IL: University of Chicago Press; Kirzner, I. M. (1997). Entrepreneurial discovery and the competitive market process: An Austrian approach. *Journal of Economic Literature, 35*, 60–85.

22. The invention of football—The story behind the ball we all know. (2015). *The Inventions Handbook*. Retrieved from http://www.inventions-handbook.com/invention-of-football.html

23. The concept of optimism and persistence is pervasive in entrepreneurship research. See Shane, S., Locke, E. A., & Collins, C. J. (2003). Entrepreneurial motivation. *Human Resource Management Review, 29*(2), 257–279; Cardon, M. S., & Kirk, C. P. (2015). Entrepreneurial passion as mediator of the self-efficacy to persistence relationship. *Entrepreneurship Theory and Practice, 39*(5), 1029–1050; Hmieleski, K. M., & Baron, R. A. (2009). Entrepreneurs' optimism and new venture performance: A social cognitive perspective. *Academy of Management Journal, 52*(3), 473–488.

24. Baron, Opportunity recognition as pattern recognition.

25. Shane, S. (2000). Prior knowledge and the discovery of entrepreneurial opportunities. *Organization Science, 11*, 448–469.

26. McKelvie, A., & Wiklund, J. (2004). How knowledge affects opportunity discovery and exploitation among

new ventures in dynamic markets. In J. E. Butler (Ed.), *Opportunity identification and entrepreneurial behavior* (pp. 219–239). Greenwich, CT: Information Age.

27. Glauser, M. (2016). 3 types of experiences that will help your startup succeed. *Entrepreneur*. Retrieved from https://www.entrepreneur.com/article/275091

28. Baron, Opportunity recognition as pattern recognition. The concept of pattern recognition comes from a rich research stream in cognition. See, for example, Matlin, M. W. (2002). *Cognition* (5th ed.). Fort Worth, TX: Harcourt College.

29. Baron, Opportunity recognition as pattern recognition.

30. Cutrin, M. (2018). 42 percent of startups fail for this 1 simple reason (it's not what you think). *Inc*. Retrieved from https://www.inc.com/melanie-curtin/the-no-1-reason-most-startups-fail-dont-make-this-mistake.html

31. Cohen, D., Shinnar, R. S., & Hsu, D. K. (2019). *Enhancing opportunity recognition skills in entrepreneurship education: A new approach and empirical test*. 2019 Babson College Entrepreneurship Research Conference, Babson Park, MA; Cohen, D., Pool, G., & Neck, H. (in press). *The IDEATE method: An empirically proven approach to generate high potential entrepreneurial ideas*. Thousand Oaks, CA: SAGE.

32. The great Pacific garbage patch. (2019). *The Ocean Cleanup*. Retrieved from https://www.theoceancleanup.com/great-pacific-garbage-patch/

33. Center for Disease Control and Prevention. (2017). *A look inside food deserts*. Retrieved from https://www.cdc.gov/features/fooddeserts/

CHAPTER 4

1. Vredenburg, K. (2016). *Design vs design thinking explained*. Retrieved from https://www.karelvredenburg.com/home/2016/8/29/design-vs-design-thinking-explained

2. Design thinking defined. (n.d.). *IDEO*. Retrieved from https://designthinking.ideo.com/

3. Liedtka, J., & Ogilvie, T. (2011). *Designing for growth: A design thinking toolkit for managers*. New York, NY: Columbia University Press. [location 168 of 3511, Kindle.]

4. Brown, T., & Katz, B. (2009). *Change by design: How design thinking transforms organizations and inspires innovation* (p. 17). New York, NY: HarperCollins.

5. Neck, H. (2012, March 8). What is design thinking and why do entrepreneurs need to care? *BostInno*. Retrieved from http://bostinno.streetwise.co/2012/03/08/what-is-design-thinking-and-why-do-entrepreneurs-need-to-care/

6. Berger, W. (2012, September 17). The secret phrase top innovators use. *Harvard Business Review*. Retrieved from https://hbr.org/2012/09/the-secret-phrase-top-innovato/

7. IDEO's human-centered design process: How to make things people love. (2018). *UserTesting*. Retrieved from https://www.usertesting.com/blog/how-ideo-uses-customer-insights-to-design-innovative-products-users-love/

8. A game-changing approach to sleep for athletes. (2016). *IDEO*. Retrieved from https://www.ideo.com/case-study/a-game-changing-approach-to-sleep-for-athletes

9. Hasso Plattner Institute of Design at Stanford. (n.d.). *An introduction to design thinking: Process guide*. Retrieved from https://dschool.stanford.edu/sandbox/groups/designresources/wiki/36873/attachments/74b3d/ModeGuideBOOTCAMP2010L.pdf

10. Ibid.

11. Brown, T., & Katz, B. (2019). How great design could fix the world's "wicked problems." *Fortune*. Retrieved from http://fortune.com/2019/02/15/change-by-design-new-excerpt-tim-brown/

12. MIT AgeLab. (2019). *AGNES (Age Gain Now Empathy System)*. Retrieved from http://agelab.mit.edu/agnes-age-gain-now-empathy-system

13. Chion, J. (2013). What it's like to work at IDEO. *Medium*. Retrieved from https://medium.com/@jimmmy/what-its-like-to-work-at-ideo-6ca2c961aae4

14. The ladder example is borrowed from Dev Patnaik, cofounder of Jump Associates.

15. Patnaik, D. (2009). *Wired to care: How companies prosper when they create widespread empathy*. Upper Saddle River, NJ: FT Press.

16. Wheeler, R., & Osborn, A. F. (n.d.). The father of brainstorming. *RussellAWheeler.com*. Retrieved from http://russellawheeler.com/resources/learning_zone/alex_f_osborn/

17. Bell-Mayeda, M. (2018). 3 tips to help you prototype a service. *IDEO*. Retrieved from https://www.ideo.com/blog/3-tips-to-help-you-prototype-a-service

18. Mockplus. (2019, February 25). *What is rapid prototyping? A full guide for beginners*. Retrieved from https://www.mockplus.com/blog/post/what-is-rapid-prototyping

19. IDEO. (2015). *The field guide to human-centered design*. San Francisco, CA: Author, 159. Retrieved from http://d1r3w4d5z5a88i.cloudfront.net/assets/guide/Field%20Guide%20to%20Human-Centered%20Design_IDEOorg_English-ee47a1ed4b91f3252115b83152828d7e.pdf

20. Gray, S. (2010, May 4). Insights—What are they really? *Quirk*. Retrieved from http://www.quirk.biz/resources/article/4878/insights

21. Ibid.

22. Williams, L. (2011, April 11). The key to design insights: See the world differently. *The Atlantic*. Retrieved from http://www.theatlantic.com/business/archive/2011/04/the-key-to-design-insights-see-the-world-differently/237117/

23. Sauro, J. (2015). 4 types of observational research. *MeasuringU*. Retrieved from https://measuringu.com/observation-role/

24. AEIOU framework. (n.d.). Retrieved from http://help.ethnohub.com/guide/aeiou-framework

25. Tool, K. (2011, March 28). Design thinking and three ways to improve our observation skills. *Design Due*. Retrieved from https://designdue.wordpress.com/2011/03/28/design-thinking-and-three-ways-to-improve-our-observation-skills/

26. Brown, T. (2012, November 27). One design thinking tip you can use right now. *Design Thinking*. Retrieved from http://designthinking.ideo.com/?p=784

27. Constable, G. (2014). *Talking to humans: Success starts with understanding your customers*. Retrieved from https://www.talkingtohumans.com/

28. Stocker Partnership. (2014). Innovation tools: Empathy mapping [slideshow]. *Slideshare*. Retrieved from http://www.slideshare.net/stockerpartnership/innovation-tools-empathy-mapping

29. Stanford Design School. (n.d.). *Empathy map*. Retrieved from http://dschool.stanford.edu/wp-content/themes/dschool/method-cards/empathy-map.pdf

30. Liedtka & Ogilvie. *Designing for growth*.

31. Design Sprints. (n.d.). *Transform the way your team works*. Retrieved from https://designsprintkit.withgoogle.com/introduction/overview

32. Liedtka & Ogilvie. *Designing for growth*.

CHAPTER 5

1. Osterwalder, A., & Pigneur, Y. (2010). *Business model generation: A handbook for visionaries, game changers, and challengers*. Hoboken, NJ: Wiley.

2. Amit, R. (2014, November 18). The latest innovation: Redesigning the business model. *Knowledge@Wharton*. Retrieved

from http://knowledge.wharton.upenn.edu/article/redesigning-business-model/

3. Nunes, K. (2018). Product innovation central to General Mills' growth plans. *Food Business News*. Retrieved from https://www.foodbusinessnews.net/articles/12141-product-innovation-central-to-general-mills-growth-plans

4. Johnson, M., Christensen, C., & Kagerman, H. (2008, December). Reinventing your business model. *Harvard Business Review*, 1–11; Osterwalder & Pigneur, *Business model generation*.

5. Info entrepreneurs. (n.d.). Price your product or service. Retrieved from https://www.infoentrepreneurs.org/en/guides/price-your-product-or-service/

6. Shoot, B. (2018). How do you innovate a barbershop? Ask Great Clips franchisees. *Entrepreneur*. Retrieved from https://www.entrepreneur.com/article/306749

7. Turn a 'no' into a winning solution [slideshow]. (n.d.). *Entrepreneur*. Retrieved from https://www.entrepreneur.com/slideshow/281277#1

8. Amit, The latest innovation.

9. Anderson, J., Narus, J., & van Rossum, W. (2006, March). Customer value propositions in business markets. *Harvard Business Review*, 91–99.

10. Amit, The latest innovation.

11. Johnson et al., Reinventing your business model, 3.

12. Johnson, M. W. (2010, February 3). A new framework for business models strategy and innovation. *Innosight*. Retrieved from http://www.innosight.com/innovation-resources/a-new-framework-for-business-models.cfm

13. Hall, D. (2005). *Jump start your business brain: The scientific way to make more money*. Cincinnati, OH: Eureka! Institute.

14. Milne, R. (2018). IKEA vows "transformation" as it reshapes business model. *Financial Times*. Retrieved from https://www.ft.com/content/1a66c838-3cc1-11e8-b7e0-52972418fec4

15. Johnson et al., Reinventing your business model.

16. Osterwalder & Pigneur, Business model generation, 129.

17. Sundelin, A. (2009, December 10). Tata Motors—Inexpensive cars for modular distribution. *The Business Model Database*. Retrieved from http://tbmdb.blogspot.com/2009/12/business-model-example-tata-motors.html

18. Sundelin, Tata Motors; Fogarty, J. (2009, April 7). Tata's Nano: How'd they do it? *Seeking Alpha*. Retrieved from http://seekingalpha.com/article/129832-tatas-nano-howd-they-do-it

19. No production of Tata Nano for third month in row, no sales in March. (2019). *Livemint*. Retrieved from https://www.livemint.com/auto-news/no-production-of-tata-nano-for-third-month-in-row-no-sales-in-march-1554219198846.html

20. Ghosh, K. (2018). It's time to say ta-ta to the world's cheapest car. *Quartz India*. Retrieved from https://qz.com/india/1326635/tata-nano-the-slow-death-of-the-worlds-cheapest-car/

21. Ibid.

22. Freyer, F. (2015). It costs you $43 every time you wait for the doctor. *Boston Globe*. Retrieved from https://www.bostonglobe.com/metro/2015/10/05/study-puts-dollar-value-time-spent-waiting-for-doctor/If7KB4aU9mkY5qK8CqDYUO/story.html

23. Wartzman, R. (2013). The real face of healthcare reform. *Time*. Retrieved from http://business.time.com/2013/10/09/the-real-face-of-healthcare-reform/

24. Shah, H. (2017). How Grammarly quietly grew its way to 6.9 million daily users in 9 years. *Medium*. Retrieved from https://medium.com/swlh/how-grammarly-quietly-grew-its-way-to-6-9-million-daily-users-in-9-years-88e417dbfbdf

25. Schroeder, J. (2018). How this 23-year-old college dropout built a $41m company. *Forbes*. Retrieved from https://www.forbes.com/sites/julesschroeder/2018/01/25/how-this-23-year-old-college-drop-out-built-a-41m-company/#4416a4733aa7

26. Anderson, J., Narus, J., & van Rossum, W. (2006, March). Customer value propositions in business markets. *Harvard Business Review*, 91–99.

27. Blank, S., & Dorf, B. (2012). *The startup owner's manual: Step-by-step guide for building a great company* (pp. 87–88). California: K&S Ranch.

28. Rosemesh. (2014, May 31). Business model canvas customer segments [Video file]. Retrieved from https://www.youtube.com/watch?v=VJdaCvviktk

29. Diet Coke vs. Coca-Cola Zero: What's the difference? (2017). *Huffington Post*. Retrieved from http://www.huffingtonpost.com/2012/01/11/diet-coke-vs-coca-cola-zero_n_1199008.html

30. Coke Zero ads aim clearly at the lads. (2006, July 8). *The Grocer*. Retrieved from http://www.thegrocer.co.uk/fmcg/-coke-zero-ads-aim-clearly-at-the-lads/111665.article

31. Osterwalder & Pigneur, *Business model generation*, 21.

32. Ibid.

33. This section borrows heavily from Osterwalder & Pigneur, *Business model generation*.

34. Ash Maurya adapted the Business Model Canvas to better meet the needs of startup entrepreneurs. His version has been popularized as the Lean Canvas. Maurya, A. (2012). *Running lean* (2nd ed.). Sebastopol, CA: O'Reilly Media; Maurya, A. (2012). Why Lean Canvas vs Business Model Canvas? *Medium*. Retrieved from https://blog.leanstack.com/why-lean-canvas-vs-business-model-canvas-af62c0f250f0; Canvanizer. (n.d.). *Business model canvas vs. lean canvas*. Retrieved from https://canvanizer.com/how-to-use/business-model-canvas-vs-lean-canvas; Inspire9. (2017). Lean canvas is the new business plan. *Medium*. Retrieved from https://medium.com/@inspire9/lean-canvas-is-the-new-business-plan-513dbfebbe8b

CHAPTER 6

1. Nijssen, E. (2014). *Entrepreneurial marketing: An effectual approach* (p. 29). London: Routledge.

2. Moore, G. A. (2006). *Crossing the chasm: Marketing and selling high-tech products to mainstream customers*. New York: HarperCollins.

3. The Honest Kitchen. Retrieved from https://www.thehonestkitchen.com

4. Nijssen, *Entrepreneurial marketing*, 17.

5. Scocco, D. (2006). Users, purchasers and influencers [Blog post]. *Innovation Zen*. Retrieved from http://innovationzen.com/blog/2006/12/06/users-purchasers-and-influencers

6. Blank, S., & Dorf, B. (2012). *The startup owner's manual* (pp. 87–88). California: K&S Ranch.

7. Baggs, M. (2019). Fyre Festival: Inside the world's biggest festival flop. *BBC*. Retrieved from https://www.bbc.co.uk/news/newsbeat-46904445

8. Blank, S. (2017). Everything you ever wanted to know about marketing communications [Blog post]. *Steve Blank*. Retrieved from https://steveblank.com/2017/04/05/everything-you-ever-wanted-to-know-about-marketing-communications/

9. Mullins, J. (2013). *The new business road test* (4th ed., p. 45). London, UK: Pearson.

10. Aulet, B. (2017). *Disciplined entrepreneurship workbook* (p. 49). Hoboken NJ: Wiley.

11. Berry, L. M. (2015). Know your customer [Blog post]. Retrieved from https://leahmberry.com/know-your-customer-walk-in-your-customers-shoes/

12. Nijssen, *Entrepreneurial marketing*, 37.

13. Aulet, B. (2014). Launching a successful start-up #3: The beachhead market. *MIT Sloan Executive Education innovation@work Blog*. Retrieved from https://executive.mit.edu/blog/launching-a-successful-start-up-3-the-beachhead-market

14. Aulet, Launching a successful start-up.

15. Ibid.

16. Dixon, C. (2010). The bowling pin strategy. *Business Insider*. Retrieved from http://www.businessinsider.com/the-bowling-pin-strategy-2010-8

17. Revella, A. (2015). *Buyer personas: How to gain insight into your customer's expectations, align your marketing strategies, and win more business*. Hoboken, NJ: John Wiley & Son.

18. Pruitt, J., & Grudin, J. (2017). Personas: Practice and theory. *Microsoft*. Retrieved from https://www.microsoft.com/en-us/research/wp-content/uploads/2017/03/pruitt-grudinold.pdf

19. Vaughan, P. (2015). How to create detailed buyer personas for your business. *Hubspot Blog*. Retrieved from https://blog.hubspot.com/marketing/buyer-persona-research

20. Salesforce UK. (2016). What is customer journey mapping & why is it important? *Salesforce Blog*. Retrieved from https://www.salesforce.com/uk/blog/2016/03/customer-journey-mapping-explained.html

21. Ellis, A. (2017). How any startup can create a customer journey map [Video]. *Forget the Funnel*. Retrieved from https://forgetthefunnel.com/customer-journey-maps-for-startups/

22. Boag, P. (2019). What is customer journey mapping and how to start? *Boagworld*. Retrieved from https://boagworld.com/usability/customer-journey-mapping/

23. Morasky, M. (2017). Customer journey mapping: How to understand each stage of your customer's experience. *Startup Nation*. Retrieved from https://startupnation.com/grow-your-business/art-opportunity-customer-journey-mapping/

24. Boag, What is customer journey mapping?

25. Ibid.

26. Fisher, Y. (2016). TAM SAM and SOM are not good enough—stop relying on them. *Medium*. Retrieved from https://medium.com/value-your-startup/tam-sam-and-som-are-not-good-enough-stop-relying-on-them-f7e378850f4

27. Parker, D. (2015). TAM, SAM, SOM and LAM—What's your launch addressable market? *Techstars*. Retrieved from https://www.techstars.com/content/entrepreneur-resources/tam-sam-som-lam-whats-launch-addressable-market/

28. Zhuo, T. (2016). 5 strategies to effectively determine your market size. *Entrepreneur*. Retrieved from https://www.entrepreneur.com/article/270853

29. Ibid.

30. Haden, J. (2013). Best way to do a market analysis? *Inc*. Retrieved from https://www.inc.com/jeff-haden/bottom-up-or-top-down-market-analysis-which-should-you-use.html

CHAPTER 7

1. Ries, E. (2011). *The lean startup* (p. 56). New York: Crown Business.

2. Dyer, J., Gregersen, H., & Christensen, C. (2011). *The innovator's DNA: Mastering the five skills of disruptive innovators* (p. 143/ibook). Boston, MA: Harvard Business Review Press.

3. Costa, R. (2019). 20 inspiring web and mobile wireframe examples. *Justinmind*. Retrieved from https://www.justinmind.com/blog/20-inspiring-web-and-mobile-wireframe-and-prototype-examples/

4. Kishfy, N. (2013). Button to nowhere. *Medium*. Retrieved from https://medium.com/@kishfy/button-to-nowhere-77d911517318

5. McCloskey, M. (2014). Turn user goals into task scenarios for usability testing. *Nielsen Norman Group*. Retrieved from https://www.nngroup.com/articles/task-scenarios-usability-testing/

6. The world's first monthly journal for living a great story. (2018). *Kickstarter*. Retrieved from https://www.kickstarter.com/projects/liveagreatstory/the-worlds-first-monthly-journal-for-living-a-grea

7. Buchenau, M., & Suri, J. F. (2000). Experience prototyping. In *DIS '00: Proceedings of the 3rd Conference on Designing Interactive Systems: Processes, practices, methods, and techniques* (pp. 424–433). doi:10.1145/347642.347802

8. Ries, E. (2011). *The lean startup: How today's entrepreneurs use continuous innovation to create radically successful businesses*. New York: Crown Business.

9. Chebanova, A. (n.d.). What is MVP and why is it necessary? *Steel Kiwi*. Retrieved from https://steelkiwi.com/blog/what-mvp-and-why-it-necessary/

10. Artemyan, M. (2018). What is the difference between a wireframe, mockup, prototype, and mvp? *Develandoo*. Retrieved from https://develandoo.com/blog/what-is-the-differencebetween-a-wireframe-prototype-and-mvp/

11. Dam, R., & Siang, T. (2019). Prototyping: Learn eight common methods and best practices. *Interaction Design*. Retrieved from https://www.interaction-design.org/literature/article/prototyping-learn-eight-common-methods-and-best-practices

12. Storyboarding. Retrieved from http://www.instructionaldesign.org/storyboarding.html

13. Bourque, A. (2012). 4 powerful reasons to storyboard your business. Retrieved from http://www.socialmediatoday.com/content/4-powerful-reasons-storyboard-your-business-ideas

14. Thorn, K. (2011). The art of storyboarding. Retrieved December 27, 2014, from http://elearnmag.acm.org/featured.cfm?aid=2024072

15. Bourque, 4 powerful reasons.

16. The Common Craft Blog. Retrieved from https://www.commoncraft.com/explainer-tip-creating-simple-storyboards

17. https://www.renttherunway.com/pages/about#about-definition

18. Roam, D. (2008). *The back of the napkin: Solving problems and selling ideas with pictures*. New York, NY: Penguin Books.

19. Blank, S. (2014). Keep calm and test the hypothesis. Retrieved from http://steveblank.com/2014/06/23/keep-calm-and-test-the-hypothesis-2-minutes-to-see-why/

20. Dyer et al., *The innovator's DNA*, 143.

21. Thomke, S., & Manzi, J. (2014, December). The discipline of business experimentation. *Harvard Business Review*, 70–79, at 72.

22. Steps of the scientific method. (2014, December 27). *Science Buddies*. Retrieved from https://www.sciencebuddies.org/science-fair-projects/science-fair/steps-of-the-scientific-method

23. Anderson, M. (2016). *The scientific method of entrepreneurship*. Retrieved from https://lassonde.utah.edu/the-scientific-method-of-entrepreneurship/

24. Buffer's 2018 in numbers (2019). *Buffer*. Retrieved from https://buffer.com/2018

25. 6 entrepreneurs share the brilliant, crazy ways they took their companies from pennies to profit. (2018). *Entrepreneur*. Retrieved from https://www.entrepreneur.com/article/311861

26. Anderson, E. T., & Simester, D. (2011, March). The step-by-step guide to smart business experiments. *Harvard Business Review*, 98–105.

27. Ibid.

28. Boehl, D. (2015). Why I ignored conventional wisdom and hired family members for my startup. *Forbes*.

Retrieved from https://www.forbes
.com/sites/theyec/2015/05/11/
why-i-ignored-conventional-wisdom-
and-hired-family-members-for-my-
startup/#46f7b419d58c

29. Lemley, P. (2018). I launched a tech
     startup in 2017: Here's everything I
     felt important enough to write down.
     Medium. Retrieved from https://
     medium.com/swlh/i-launched-a-
     tech-startup-in-2017-heres-every
     thing-i-felt-important-enough-to-
     write-down-4feb328b821f

30. Ries, *The lean startup*, 56.

31. Heller, C. (2018). *The intergalactic
     design guide: Harnessing the creative
     potential of social design* (pp. 71–82).
     Washington, DC: Island Press.

CHAPTER 8

1.   Tashakova, O. (2018). How networking
     can increase your business' net
     worth. *Entrepreneur.* Retrieved from
     https://www.entrepreneur.com/
     article/314496

2.   Cope, J., Jack, S., & Rose, M. (2007).
     Social capital and entrepreneurship:
     An introduction. *International Small
     Business Journal, 25,* 213–219, at 213.

3.   Ibid., 216.

4.   Tsai, W., & Ghoshal, S. (1998). Social
     capital and value creation. The role
     of intrafirm networks. *Academy of
     Management Journal, 41,* 464–476.

5.   Coleman, J. S. (1988). Social capital
     in the creation of human capital.
     *American Journal of Sociology:
     Supplement, Organizations and
     Institutions: Sociological and Economic
     Approaches to the Analysis of Social
     Structure, 94,* 95–120.

6.   Al Muniady, R., Al Mamun, A.,
     Mohamad, M. R., Permarupan, P. Y.,
     & Zainol, N. R. B. (2015). The effect of
     cognitive and relational social capital
     on structural social capital and micro-
     enterprise performance. *Sage Open.*
     Retrieved from http://sgo.sagepub
     .com/content/5/4/2158244015611187

7.   Uzzi, B. (1996). The sources and
     consequences of embeddedness
     for the economic performance of
     organizations: The network effect.
     American Sociological Review, 61,
     674–698.

8.   Covey, S. (2004). *The 7 habits of highly
     effective people.* New York: Free Press.

9.   Ibid.

10. Al Muniady et al., The effect of
     cognitive and relational social capital.

11. Keeley, B. (2007). *Human capital: How
     what you know shapes your life.* Paris:
     OECD. Retrieved from http://www
     .oecd.org/insights/37966934.pdf

12. Ibid.

13. Uzzi, B., & Dunlap, S. (2005, December).
     How to build your network. *Harvard
     Business Review,* 52–60, at 53.

14. Cope et al., Social capital and
     entrepreneurship, 2–14.

15. Casson, M., & Della Giusta, M. (2007).
     Entrepreneurship and social capital:
     Analyzing the impact of social
     networks on entrepreneurial activity
     from a rational action perspective.
     International Small Business Journal, 25,
     220–244, at 221.

16. Hoehn-Weiss, M., Brush, C., & Baron, R.
     (2004). Putting your best foot forward?
     Assessments of entrepreneurial social
     competence from two perspectives.
     Journal of Private Equity, 7(4), 17–26.

17. Guerrini, F. (2016). Study: For
     78% of startups, networking is
     vital to entrepreneurial success.
     Forbes. Retrieved from https://
     www.forbes.com/sites/
     federicoguerrini/2016/11/10/
     study-for-78-of-startups-networking-
     is-the-key-to-entrepreneurial-
     success/#6f1ecc434195

18. Uzzi & Dunlap, How to build your
     network.

19. Science quotes by Linus Pauling. (n.d.).
     Today in Science History. Retrieved from
     https://todayinsci.com/P/Pauling_
     Linus/PaulingLinus-Quotations.htm

20. Murphy, W., & Kram, K. (2014). *Strategic
     relationships at work.* New York, NY:
     McGraw-Hill.

21. Neck, H. (2001). *An ethnographic study of
     entrepreneurship education: Trajectories
     connecting the classroom to the real
     world.* Unpublished working paper.

22. Willis, J., & Todorov, A. (2006). First
     impressions: Making up your mind
     after a 100-ms exposure to a face.
     Psychological Science, 17(7), 592–598.

23. Pentland, A., & Heibeck, T. (2009,
     October 31). Great ideas vs. confidence:
     Which counts more? *Psychology
     Today.* Retrieved from http://www
     .psychologytoday.com/blog/reality-
     mining/200910/great-ideas-vs-
     confidence-which-counts-more-0]

24. Hoehn-Weiss et al., Putting your best
     foot forward?

25. Understanding implicit bias. (2015). *The
     Kirwan Institute.* Retrieved from http://
     kirwaninstitute.osu.edu/research/
     understanding-implicit-bias/

26. Payne, K., Niemi, L., & Doris, J. (2018).
     How to think about "implicit bias."
     Scientific American. Retrieved from
     https://www.scientificamerican.com/
     article/how-to-think-about-implicit-
     bias/

27. Understanding implicit bias.

28. Ibid.

29. Which leading entrepreneurs met their
     business partners at school? (2013,

May 14). *Nerdwallet.* Retrieved from
http://www.nerdwallet.com/blog/
loans/student-loans/entrepreneurs-
college-alumni-networks/

30. Sarasvathy, S. D. (2008). *Effectuation:
     Elements of entrepreneurial expertise.*
     Northampton, MA: Edward Elgar.

31. Loyd, T. (2018). Beyond autism
     awareness, Thorkil Sonne,
     Specialisterne. Retrieved from
     https://tonyloyd.com/beyond-
     autism-awareness-thorkil-sonne-
     specialisterne/

32. Senge, P. M. (1990). *The fifth
     discipline: The art and practice of the
     learning organization.* New York, NY:
     Doubleday/Currency.

33. Uzzi & Dunlap, How to build your
     network, 58.

34. Roberts, G. (2019). Runway East stories:
     How did you meet your co-founder?
     Runway East. Retrieved from https://
     runwaya.st/blog/how-did-you-meet-
     co-founder/

35. Extremely shy—Looking for friends.
     (n.d.). *Meetup.com.* Retrieved from
     http://www.meetup.com/extremely-
     shy-looking-for-friends/

36. Rahul, F. June 28, 2018. Decoding
     entrepreneurial meetups and their
     relevance in 2018. Entrepreneur
     India. Retrieved at https://www
     .entrepreneur.com/article/315905

37. Cremades, A. (2018). 10 startup
     accelerators based on successful
     exits. *Forbes.* Retrieved from
     https://www.forbes.com/sites/
     alejandrocremades/2018/08/07/top-
     10-startup-accelerators-based-on-
     successful-exits/#13ed6a84b3b9

38. Ibid.

39. Murphy, B. (2015, October 19). 9 smart
     habits of highly effective networkers.
     Inc. Retrieved from http://www.inc
     .com/bill-murphy-jr/9-smart-habits-
     of-highly-effective-networkers.html

40. Spencer, S. (2011, December 14).
     Business networking that works. It's
     called quid pro quo. *Forbes.* Retrieved
     from http://news.yahoo.com/
     business-networking-works-called-
     quid-pro-quo-190953397

41. Anderson, K. (2013, July 17). Pay it forward
     with the five-minute favor. *Forbes.*
     Retrieved from http://www.forbes.com/
     sites/kareanderson/2013/07/17/pay-it-
     forward-with-the-five-minute-favor/

42. Murphy, 9 smart habits.

43. Misner, I. (2009, January 14). You never
     know whom they know. *Entrepreneur.*
     Retrieved from http://www.
     entrepreneur.com/article/199542

44. Rollag, K. (2015). *What to do when
     you're new.* New York, NY: Amacom.

45. Kawasaki, G. (2015). *The art of the start*
     (p. 199). New York, NY: Penguin.

46. McClanahan, A. (2017). 6 entrepreneurs on why mentorship is the key to success. *Fundera*. Retrieved from https://www.fundera.com/blog/entrepreneurs-mentorship

47. Three famous billionaire entrepreneurs and their mentors. (2015, February 12). *Small Business BC*. Retrieved from http://smallbusinessbc.ca/article/three-famous-billionaire-entrepreneurs-and-their-mentors/

48. McClanahan, A. (2017). 6 entrepreneurs on why mentorship is the key to success. *Fundera*. Retrieved from https://www.fundera.com/blog/entrepreneurs-mentorship

49. Deutschman, A. (2004, December 1). The fabric of creativity. *Fast Company*. Retrieved from http://www.fastcompany.com/51733/fabric-creativity

50. Interview: Elizabeth Holmes. (2014). *The Academy of Achievement*. Retrieved from http://www.achievement.org/autodoc/page/hol0int-6

51. Branson, R. (2012, July 24). Network early, network often. *Daily Monitor*. Retrieved from http://www.monitor.co.ug/Business/Prosper/Network-early--network-often-/-/688616/1461204/-/1028mhh/-/index.html

52. Singh, N. (2018). How entrepreneurs can leverage LinkedIn to grow their business. *Entrepreneur India*. Retrieved from https://www.entrepreneur.com/article/310531

53. Koehn, E. (2017). 20 entrepreneurs to follow on Instagram in 2017. *Smart Company*. Retrieved from https://www.smartcompany.com.au/marketing/social-media/twenty-entrepreneurs-to-follow-on-instagram-in-2017/

54. VC4A. (n.d.). Connecting African startups to opportunities. Retrieved from https://vc4a.com/

55. Nsehe, M. (2015, March 1). Angel investors invest $27 million in African startups listed on VC4Africa. *Forbes*. Retrieved from http://www.forbes.com/sites/mfonobongnsehe/2015/03/01/angel-investors-invest-27-million-in-african-startups-through-vc4africa/

56. Uzzi & Dunlap, How to build your network.

57. Aldrich, H. E., & Kim, P. H. (2007). Small worlds, infinite possibilities? How social networks affect entrepreneurial team formation and search. *Strategic Entrepreneurship Journal, 1*, 147–165, at 149.

58. Timmons, J. A. (1994). *New venture creation: Entrepreneurship for the 21st century* (4th ed. p. 19). Burr Ridge, IL: Irwin; Cooper, A. C., & Daily, C. M. (1997). Entrepreneurial teams. In D. L. Sexton & R. W. Smilor (Eds.), *Entrepreneurship 2000* (pp. 127–150). Chicago, IL: Upstart.

59. Blank, S. (2013, July 29). Building great founding teams. Retrieved from http://steveblank.com/2013/07/29/building-great-founding-teams/

60. Cooper & Daily, Entrepreneurial teams.

61. Cooney, T. M. (2005). Editorial: What is an entrepreneurial team? *International Small Business Journal, 23*, 226–235, at 228.

62. Aldrich & Kim, Small worlds, infinite possibilities? 149.

63. Vozza, S. (2014, July 2). The only 6 people you need on your founding startup team. *Fast Company*. Retrieved from http://www.fastcompany.com/3032548/hit-the-ground-running/the-only-6-people-you-need-on-your-founding-startup-team

64. Houser, J. (2011, June 21). How to build an insanely great founding team. *Inc*. Retrieved from http://www.inc.com/articles/201106/how-to-build-an-insanely-great-team.html

65. Williams, G. (2017). It's a dirty job (and these entrepreneurs are doing it). *Success*. Retrieved from https://www.success.com/its-a-dirty-job-and-these-entrepreneurs-are-doing-it/

66. Rampton, J. (2019). 10 popular myths about leadership and how to overcome them. *Entrepreneur*. Retrieved from https://www.entrepreneur.com/article/330198

67. Rampton, J. (2016). 8 ways my ego killed my business. *Entrepreneur*. Retrieved from https://www.entrepreneur.com/article/278901

68. Spors, K. (2009, February 23). So, you want to be an entrepreneur. *Wall Street Journal/Small Business Reports*. Retrieved from http://www.wsj.com/articles/SB123498006564714189

69. Sommers, S. R., Warp, L. S., & Mahoney, C. (2008). Cognitive effects of racial diversity: White individuals' information processing in heterogeneous groups. *Journal of Experimental Social Psychology, 44*, 1129–1136.

70. Surowiecki, J. (2005). *The wisdom of crowds* (p. 36). New York, NY: Anchor Books.

71. Schwenk, C. R., & Cosier, R. A. (1980). Effects of the expert, devil's advocate, and dialectical inquiry methods on prediction performance. *Organizational Behavior and Human Performance, 26*, 409–424.

72. Chowdhury, S. (2005). Demographic diversity for building an effective entrepreneurial team: Is it important? *Journal of Business Venturing, 20*, 727–746.

73. Ibid.

74. Patrick Lencioni presentation at the World Business Forum, Oct. 6, 2009. For summary, see http://www.vault.com/blog/pink-slipped-make-your-layoff-pay-off/world-business-forum-building-winning-teams-with-patrick-lencioni/; see Lencioni, P. (2002). *The five dysfunctions of a team*. San Francisco, CA: Jossey-Bass.

75. Eisenhardt, K., Kahwajy, J., & Bourgeois, L. J., III. (1997, July–August). How management teams can have a good fight. *Harvard Business Review, 75*, 77–85.

76. Ibid.

77. The Keynote Group. (2016). Playing devil's advocate: Pushing your team to find solutions. Retrieved from https://thekeynotegroup.com/playing-devils-advocate/

78. Boulding, K. (1964). Further reflections on conflict management. In R. Kahn & E. Boulding, (Eds.), *Power and conflict in organizations*. New York, NY: Basic Books.

79. Eisenhardt et al., How management teams can have a good fight.

CHAPTER 9

1. This section is adapted from Laniado, E. (2013). Revenue model types: The quick guide. *BMN!*. Retrieved from http://www.bmnow.com/revenue-models-quick-guide/

2. Chrisos, M. (2019). Razor and blades model: What is it and what benefits does it possess? *Techfunnel*. Retrieved from https://www.techfunnel.com/martech/razor-and-blades-model-what-is-it-and-what-benefits-does-it-possess/

3. Vanian, J. (2018). Amazon is now the 3rd largest digital ad platform in the US. *Fortune*. Retrieved from http://fortune.com/2018/09/19/amazon-facebook-google-digital-ads/

4. Jolly, W. (2019). The 6 most effective types of social media advertising in 2019. *Bigcommerce*. Retrieved from https://www.bigcommerce.co.uk/blog/social-media-advertising/#1-facebook-advertising

5. Melendez, S., & Pasternack, A. (2019). Here are the data brokers quietly buying and selling your personal information. *Fast Company*. Retrieved from https://www.fastcompany.com/90310803/here-are-the-data-brokers-quietly-buying-and-selling-your-personal-information

6. Wong, J. (2019). The Cambridge Analytica scandal changed the world, but it didn't change Facebook. *The Guardian*. Retrieved from https://www.theguardian.com/technology/2019/mar/17/the-cambridge-analytica-scandal-changed-the-world-but-it-didnt-change-facebook

7. Key, S. (2018). How this novelty gift company gets open innovation right. *Inc*. Retrieved from https://www.inc.com/stephen-key/love-to-create-fun-products-consider-novelty-gift-licensing.html

8. Starr, R. (2019). 10 weird franchises to stand out from the crowd. *Small Business Trends*. Retrieved from https://smallbiztrends.com/2017/09/weird-franchises.html

9. Laniado, Revenue model types.

10. Ibid.

11. The five best freemium business services. (n.d.). *Tech Donut*. Retrieved from https://www.techdonut.co.uk/business-software/essential-business-software/the-five-best-freemium-business-services

12. The concept was popularized by Anderson, C. (2009). *Free: The future of a radical price*. New York, NY: Hyperion.

13. Greenslade, R. (2011 January 26). Profitable Metro can't stop making money, but we still need 'proper' newspapers. *The Guardian,*

14. Osterwalder, A., & Pigneur, Y. (2010). *Business model generation: A handbook for visionaries, game changers, and challengers* (p. 104). Hoboken, NJ: Wiley.

15. The information in this section is heavily drawn from Zacharakis, A., & Santinelli, A. (2014). *Finance and financial models* [Working paper].

16. London's quirkiest cafes: in pictures. (2014, November 6). *The Telegraph*. Retrieved from http://www.telegraph.co.uk/travel/destinations/europe/united-kingdom/england/london/galleries/Londons-quirkiest-cafes/ziferblatcafe/

17. Carter, D. P. (2011, June 7). *The four fundamental drivers of revenue*. Retrieved from http://www.davidpaulcarter.com/2011/06/07/the-four-fundamental-drivers-of-revenue/

18. Clark, D. (2014, October 6). How to determine what you should charge customers. *Entrepreneur*. Retrieved from http://www.entrepreneur.com/article/238086

19. StartUpMe. (2010, January 29). 9 pricing rules for entrepreneurs [Video file]. *YouTube*. Retrieved from https://www.youtube.com/watch?v=redLOAIkEvI

20. Team, Y. S. (2010, July 27). *10 pricing strategies for entrepreneurs*. Retrieved from http://yourstory.com/2010/07/10-pricing-strategies-for-entrepreneurs-2

21. Evans, L. (2014). Inside five businesses that let customers name their own price. *Fast Company*. Retrieved from https://www.fastcompany.com/3024842/inside-five-businesses-that-let-customers-name-their-own-price

22. Riley, J. (2012, September 23). Pricing strategies (GCSE). *Tutor2u*. Retrieved from http://www.tutor2u.net/business/gcse/marketing_pricing_strategies.htm

23. Ibid.

24. Berry, T. (n.d.). What is a break-even analysis? *Bplans*. Retrieved from https://articles.bplans.com/break-even-analysis/

CHAPTER 10

1. Brown, J. (2014). The top 10 dare devil entrepreneurs who embrace risk. #9 Elon Musk. *Addicted to Success*. Retrieved from http://addicted2success.com/entrepreneur-profile/the-top-10-dare-devil-entrepreneurs-who-embrace-risk/; An introduction to business plans. (2015). *Entrepreneur*. Retrieved from http://www.entrepreneur.com/article/38290

2. Herold, C. (2011). *Double double: How to double your revenue and profit in three years*. Austin, TX: Greenleaf Book Group Press.

3. Blank, S. (2013, May). Why the lean start-up changes everything. *Harvard Business Review*, 65–72.

4. Kolodny, L. (2017). Deere is paying over $300 million for a start-up that makes 'see-and-spray' robots. Retrieved from https://www.cnbc.com/2017/09/06/deere-is-acquiring-blue-river-technology-for-305-million.html

5. Kim, L. (2018). How this pitch deck raised $66 million in VC funding. *Inc*. Retrieved from https://www.inc.com/larry-kim/how-this-pitch-deck-raised-66-million-in-vc-funding.html

6. Berry, T. (2012, August 9). Should you create your business plan on Pinterest? *Entrepreneur*. Retrieved from http://www.entrepreneur.com/article/224157

7. Blank, S. (2013, May). Why the lean start-up changes everything. *Harvard Business Review*, 65–72.

8. Peterson, L. (2019). Example of a product concept statement. *Houston Chronicle*. Retrieved from https://smallbusiness.chron.com/example-product-concept-statement-13051.html

9. A guide to competitive analysis: It's not just about competitors. (n.d.). *Smartsheet*. Retrieved from https://www.smartsheet.com/competitive-analysis-examples

10. How to write a competitive analysis. (2017). *Expert Program Management*. Retrieved from https://expertprogrammanagement.com/2017/01/competitive-analysis-template/

11. Weinberger, J., & Hughes, L. (2014, March 2). Stay-at-home mom makes millions from pretzels. *CNBC*, 1.

12. Young Entrepreneur Council. (2013, January 13). The 10 reasons why you should write a business plan. *Small Business Trends*. Retrieved from http://smallbiztrends.com/2013/01/10-reasons-write-business-plan.html

13. Timmons, J., Zacharakis, A., & Spinelli, S. (2004). *Business plans that work: A guide for small business*. New York, NY: McGraw-Hill.

14. Zwilling, M. (2013, November 6). The 10 reasons not to write a business plan. *Entrepreneur*. Retrieved from http://www.entrepreneur.com/article/229804

15. Neck, H. (2013, May 21). What comes before the business plan? Everything. *Forbes*. Retrieved from http://www.forbes.com/sites/babson/2012/05/21/what-comes-before-the-business-plan-everything/

16. Henricks, M. (2008). Do you really need a business plan? *Entrepreneur*. Retrieved from http://www.entrepreneur.com/article/198618

CHAPTER 11

1. Hough, K. (2012, April 25). 10 greatest startup failures of all time. *Techli*. Retrieved from http://techli.com/2012/04/10-greatest-startup-failures/#

2. MacKay, J. (2017). 5 lessons to learn from the 10 biggest startup failures so far in 2017. *Inc*. Retrieved from https://www.inc.com/jory-mackay/5-lessons-to-learn-from-10-biggest-startup-failures-of-2017.html

3. Blank, S. (2014). *Do pivots matter?* Retrieved from https://steveblank.com/2014/01/14/whats-a-pivot/

4. Edmondson, A. C. (2011, April). Learning from failure. *Harvard Business Review*. Retrieved from https://hbr.org/2011/04/strategies-for-learning-from-failure

5. Stieg, C. (2019). What exactly was the Theranos Edison machine supposed to do? *Refinery29*. Retrieved from https://www.refinery29.com/en-us/2019/03/224904/theranos-edison-machine-blood-test-technology-explained

6. Solon, O. (2018). Theranos founder Elizabeth Holmes charged with criminal fraud. *The Guardian*. Retrieved from https://www.theguardian.com/technology/2018/jun/15/theranos-elizabeth-holmes-ramesh-balwani-criminal-charges

7. Vozza, S. (2015). Six millennial entrepreneurs share their lessons from early failure. *Fast Company*. Retrieved from https://www.fastcompany.com/3049841/six-millennial-entrepreneurs-share-their-lessons-from-early-failure

8. Cancialosi, C. (2015, April). 5 signs your organization has outgrown

you. *Forbes*. Retrieved from http://www.forbes.com/sites/chriscancialosi/2015/04/27/5-signs-your-organization-has-outgrown-you/#1faa91d6b917

9. Burgess, W., & Lou, E. (2018). This growing company realized it was time for the founder to step aside. Here's how they made it work. *Entrepreneur*. Retrieved from https://www.entrepreneur.com/article/308498

10. ReferralCandy. (2017). Why startups fail: 12 founders, and advice moving forward. *Medium*. Retrieved from https://medium.com/the-mission/why-startups-fail-12-founders-and-advice-moving-forward-edbcba80c522

11. CB Insights. (2019). 298 startup failure post-mortems. Retrieved from https://www.cbinsights.com/research/startup-failure-post-mortem/

12. Zissu, A. (2017). This founder created a genius way to do market testing on the cheap. *Entrepreneur*. Retrieved from https://www.entrepreneur.com/article/289144

13. Sastray, A., & Penn, K. (2014). *Fail better: Design smart mistakes and succeed sooner* [p. 1 Kindle]. Cambridge, MA: Harvard Business Review Press.

14. Curtin, M. (2018). 42 percent of startups fail for this 1 simple reason (It's not what you think). *Inc*. Retrieved from https://www.inc.com/melanie-curtin/the-no-1-reason-most-startups-fail-dont-make-this-mistake.html

15. Shepherd, D. A. (2003). Learning from business failure: Propositions of grief recovery for the self-employed. *Academy of Management Review, 28*, 318–328; McGrath, R. (1999). Falling forward: Real options reasoning and entrepreneurial failure. *Academy of Management Review, 24*, 13–30.

16. Taylor, M. (2018). Confessions of a recovering entrepreneur. *Forbes*. Retrieved from https://www.forbes.com/sites/meggentaylor/2018/03/18/confessions-of-a-recovering-entrepreneur/#6ac71681618f

17. Singer, S., Amoros, J. E., & Moska, D. (2014). *Global Entrepreneurship Monitor 2014 global report*. Retrieved from http://www.gemconsortium.org/report

18. McGregor, H. A., & Elliot, A. J. (2005). The shame of failure: Examining the link between fear of failure and shame. *Personality and Social Psychology Bulletin, 31*, 218–231, at 219.

19. Spicker, P. (1984). Stigma and social welfare. Oxfordshire: Taylor & Francis.

20. Walsh, Grace. S. (2017) Re-entry following firm failure: Nascent technology entrepreneurs' tactics for avoiding and overcoming stigma.

In J. A. Cunningham and C. O'Kane (Eds.), *Technology-based nascent entrepreneurship* (pp. 95–117). London: Palgrave Advances in the Economics of Innovation and Technology.

21. Ibid., 229.

22. Loder, V. (2014, October 30). How to conquer the fear of failure—5 proven strategies. *Forbes*. Retrieved from http://www.forbes.com/sites/vanessaloder/2014/10/30/how-to-move-beyond-the-fear-of-failure-5-proven-strategies/

23. Patel, N. (2016). Why every entrepreneur should live with their parents. *Forbes*. Retrieved from https://www.forbes.com/sites/neilpatel/2016/11/10/why-every-entrepreneur-should-live-with-their-parents/#422a07e96200

24. Heber, A. (2015, July 13). Chart: The fear of failure rates for entrepreneurs around the world. *Business Insider Australia*. Retrieved from http://www.businessinsider.com.au/chart-the-fear-of-failure-rates-for-entrepenuers-around-the-world-2015-7

25. Griffith, E. (2014, December 2). Amazon CEO Jeff Bezos: "I've made billions of dollars of failures." *Fortune*. Retrieved from http://fortune.com/2014/12/02/amazon-ceo-jeff-bezos-failure/

26. Edmondson, A. C. (2011, April). Strategy for learning from failure. *Harvard Business Review*, 48–55.

27. Patel, S. (2017). What "failing fast" really looks like. Retrieved from https://sujanpatel.com/business/failing-fast-2/

28. Temple, C. (2018). From dream to day job: Classy Llama Studios LLC. Retrieved from https://sbj.net/stories/from-dream-to-day-job-classy-llama-studios-llc,60603

29. Seelig, T. (2009, July 28). Fail in order to succeed. *CreativyRulz*. Retrieved from http://creativityrulz.blogspot.com/2009/07/fail-in-order-to-suceed.html

30. Avlani, S. (2018). Entrepreneurs cannot blame others for failures. *Livemint*. Retrieved from https://www.livemint.com/Leisure/pfrGN5YtX1joJMgWtwab4L/Entrepreneurs-cannot-blame-others-for-failures.html

31. Porter, M. E., Lorsch, J. W., & Nohria, N. (2004, October). Seven surprises for new CEOs. *Harvard Business Review*, 62–72.

32. Danner, J. (2015, May 11). How to make the other 'F' word work for you (not against you). *Fortune*. Retrieved from http://fortune.com/2015/05/11/how-to-make-the-other-f-word-work-for-you-innovation/

33. Perkins-Gough, D. (2013, September). The significance of grit: A conversation with Angela Lee Duckworth.

Educational Leadership, 71(1). Retrieved from http://www.ascd.org/publications/educational-leadership/sept13/vol71/num01/The-Significance-of-Grit@-A-Conversation-with-Angela-Lee-Duckworth.aspx

34. Del Giudice, M. (2014, October 14). Grit trumps talent and IQ: A story every parent (and educator) should read. *National Geographic*. Retrieved from http://news.nationalgeographic.com/news/2014/10/141015-angela-duckworth-success-grit-psychology-self-control-science-nginnovators/

35. Perkins-Gough, The significance of grit.

36. Del Giudice, Grit trumps talent and IQ.

37. Fox, M. (2018). 5 entrepreneurs on how facing adversity helped them build successful businesses. *Forbes*. Retrieved from https://www.forbes.com/sites/meimeifox/2018/12/21/5-entrepreneurs-on-how-facing-adversity-helped-them-build-successful-businesses/#798ba0cc2469

38. The Oracles. (2017). Never quit: Strategies on perseverance from 6 seasoned entrepreneurs. *Entrepreneur*. Retrieved from https://www.entrepreneur.com/article/299071

39. Perlis, M. (2013, October 29). 5 characteristics of grit—How many do you have? *Forbes*. Retrieved from http://www.forbes.com/sites/margaretperlis/2013/10/29/5-characteristics-of-grit-what-it-is-why-you-need-it-and-do-you-have-it/

40. Rao, M. (2018). Eight lessons in failure from Amani Institute's Fail Faire 2018. *Your Story*. https://yourstory.com/2018/05/eight-lessons-failure-amani-institutes-fail-faire-2018

41. Fuckup Nights around the globe. (n.d.). Retrieved from https://fuckupnights.com/blog/fuckup-nights-around-world/

42. Kanter, B. (2013, April 17). Go ahead, take a failure bow. *Harvard Business Review*. Retrieved from https://hbr.org/2013/04/go-ahead-take-a-failure-bow&cm_sp=Article-_-Links-_-End%20of%20Page%20Recirculation

43. Ibid.

CHAPTER 12

1. National Venture Capital Association. (2019). 2019 yearbook. Retrieved from https://nvca.org/wp-content/uploads/delightful-downloads/2019/03/NVCA-2019-Yearbook.pdf

2. Dinlersoz, E. (2018). Business formation statistics: A new Census Bureau product that takes the pulse of early-stage U.S. business activity. Retrieved from https://www.census.gov/newsroom/blogs/research-matters/2018/02/bfs.html

3. Mansfield, M. (2019). Startup statistics: The numbers you need to know. Retrieved from https://smallbiztrends.com/2019/03/startup-statistics-small-business.html

4. Sharp, G. (2014). *The ultimate guide to bootstrapping* [Kindle ed., LOC 173]. Real. Cool. Media.

5. Ibid., LOC 155.

6. Ibid., LOC 182.

7. Pilon, A. (2018). Don't have money? 17 entrepreneurs who bootstrapped their startups from nothing. Retrieved from https://smallbiztrends.com/2016/03/entrepreneurs-who-bootstrapped.html

8. Sharp, *The ultimate guide to bootstrapping*, LOC 147.

9. Mese, A. (n.d.). How to build a startup empire without selling your freedom. *Growth Supply*. Retrieved from https://growthsupply.com/build-bootstrapped-startup-without-investors/

10. Gooding, D. (2017). 16 bootstrapping tips and techniques from MailChimp. Retrieved from https://fourcolorsofmoney.com/16-bootstrapping-tips-techniques-mailchimp/

11. Garson, J. (2010). *How to build a business and sell it for millions.* New York, NY: St. Martin's Press.

12. Mese, How to build a startup empire.

13. Sharp, *The ultimate guide to bootstrapping*.

14. Steinberg, S. (2008). *The crowdfunding bible* [Kindle ed., LOC 78]. read.me Press.

15. Mollick, E. (2014). The dynamics of crowdfunding: An exploratory study. *Journal of Business Venturing, 29*, 1–16, at 2.

16. Yau, E. (2018). The ordinary people making medical breakthroughs via crowdsourcing: Solving problems that have doctors beat. Retrieved from https://www.scmp.com/lifestyle/health-wellness/article/2157627/how-crowdsourcing-helped-find-solutions-serious-health

17. Cohn, C. (2016). How crowdsourcing can help you with ideas, content and labor. *Entrepreneur*. Retrieved from https://www.entrepreneur.com/article/253959

18. Anderson, C. (2010, February). Atoms are the new bits. *Wired*, 59–67.

19. Owen, J. (2014, September 12). 3D-printed Wikihouse 4.0. *The Independent*. Retrieved from http://www.independent.co.uk/incoming/3dprinted-wikihouse-40-the-50000-house-you-can-download-from-the-internet-9727424.html

20. Mollick, The dynamics of crowdfunding, 3.

21. Zipkin, N. (2015, December 28). The 10 most funded Kickstarter campaigns ever. *Entrepreneur*. Retrieved from http://www.entrepreneur.com/article/235313

22. Goode, L. (2018). Fitbit will end support for Pebble smartwatches in June. Retrieved from https://www.theverge.com/2018/1/24/16928792/fitbit-smartwatch-pebble-end-support-date-june

23. Fundable. (n.d.). *Crowdfunding statistics.* Retrieved from https://www.fundable.com/crowdfunding101/crowdfunding-statistics

24. Kickstarter. (n.d.). *Kickstarter basics.* Retrieved from https://www.kickstarter.com/help/faq/kickstarter+basics?ref=footer

25. Kuppuswamy, V., & Bayus, B. (2014, January 29). *Crowdfunding creative ideas: The dynamics of project backers in Kickstarter.* (UNC Kenan-Flagler Research Paper No. 2013-15).

26. Kickstarter statistics listed on https://www.kickstarter.com/help/stats. These statistics change daily.

27. Kickstarter. (n.d.). *Our rules.* Retrieved from https://www.kickstarter.com/rules

28. Buck, S. (2012, May 13). 9 essential steps for a killer Kickstarter campaign. *Mashable*. Retrieved from http://mashable.com/2012/05/13/kickstarter-tips/

29. Kuppuswamy & Bayus, *Crowdfunding creative ideas*, 22.

30. Belleflamme, P., Lambert, T., & Schwienbacher, A. (2014). Crowdfunding: Tapping the right crowd. *Journal of Business Venturing, 29*, 585–609, at 589.

31. Statt, N. (2015, November 18). The Coolest Cooler is turning into one of Kickstarter's biggest disasters. *The Verge*. Retrieved from http://www.theverge.com/2015/11/18/9758214/coolest-cooler-amazon-kickstater-shipping-production-delay

32. Rogoway, M. (2018). Kickstarter fiasco Coolest Cooler has new plan to pay for 20,000 undelivered coolers. Retrieved from https://www.oregonlive.com/business/2018/06/kickstarter_fiasco_coolest_coo.html

33. Szabo, A. (2015). Two beards and a baby. *Indiegogo*. Retrieved from https://www.indiegogo.com/projects/two-beards-and-a-baby

34. Mollick, The dynamics of crowdfunding, 2.

35. Raphael, R. (2019). Equity crowdfunding platform OurCrowd has raised $1 billion in commitments. Retrieved from https://www.fastcompany.com/90316637/equity-crowdfunding-platform-ourcrowd-has-raised-1-billion-in-commitments

36. Mollick, The dynamics of crowdfunding.

37. Gomez, B. (2019). Patreon CEO says the company's generous business model is not sustainable as it sees rapid growth. Retrieved from https://www.cnbc.com/2019/01/23/crowd-funding-platform-patreon-announces-it-will-pay-out-half-a-billion-dollars-to-content-creators-in-2019.html

38. Benovic, C., & Oriando, S. (2015, April 16). Need some reward ideas? Here are 96 of them. Retrieved from https://www.kickstarter.com/blog/need-some-reward-ideas-here-are-96-of-them

39. Isbell, F. (2018). Veteran-owned Bottle Breacher cracking open $17M in sales after "Shark Tank." Retrieved from https://www.bizjournals.com/dallas/news/2018/08/15/veteran-owned-bottle-breacher-cracking-open-17m-in.html

40. Diallo, A. (2014, January 24). Crowdfunding secrets: 7 tips for Kickstarter success. *Forbes*. Retrieved from http://www.forbes.com/sites/amadoudiallo/2014/01/24/crowdfunding-secrets-7-tips-for-kickstarter-success/

41. Dewey, C. (2014, August 28). Ryan Grepper, inventor of the 'Coolest' Cooler, failed many times before raising $13 million on Kickstarter. *Washington Post*. Retrieved from http://www.washingtonpost.com/news/the-intersect/wp/2014/08/28/ryan-grepper-inventor-of-the-coolest-cooler-failed-many-times-before-raising-11-million-on-kickstarter/

42. Tarcomnicu, F. (2017). How to make a crowdfunding video people actually watch. Retrieved from https://www.entrepreneur.com/article/287665

43. Mollick, The dynamics of crowdfunding, 8.

44. Robinson, R. (2017). 5 crowdfunded side projects that became million-dollar companies. Retrieved from https://www.forbes.com/sites/ryanrobinson/2017/09/18/crowdfunded-side-projects-that-became-million-dollar-companies/#6af5241e3f1d

45. Flaherty, J. (2017). Despite billions in crowdfunding, only three "venture scale" exits. Retrieved from https://hackernoon.com/what-startups-can-learn-from-the-top-100-kickstarter-campaigns-6a0baf5bc31b

46. Mollick, The dynamics of crowdfunding, 2.

CHAPTER 13

1. Mathisen, T. (2014, April 29). The list: CNBC first 25. *CNBC*. Retrieved from http://www.cnbc.com/2014/04/29/25-google-team--sergey-brin-larry-page-eric-schmidt.html

2. Moyer, M. (2012). Slicing pie: A guide to dividing up early-stage start-up equity. Retrieved from https://slicingpie.com/slicing-pie-a-guide-to-dividing-up-early-stage-startup-equity/

3. Ibid.

4. Venture capital. (n.d.). *Small Business Notes*. Retrieved from http://www.smallbusinessnotes.com/business-finances/venture-capital.html

5. Page, H. (2018). A timeline of investor interest in AR startup Magic Leap, which has raised $2.3B. Retrieved from https://news.crunchbase.com/news/a-timeline-of-investor-interest-in-ar-startup-magic-leap-which-has-raised-2-3b/

6. Shane, S. (2008, September). *The importance of angel investing in financing the growth of entrepreneurial ventures* (a working paper for the Small Business Association). Retrieved from http://www.angelcapitalassociation.org/data/Documents/Resources/AngelGroupResarch/1d%20-%20Resources%20-%20Research%2019%20Angel_Investing_in_Financing_the_Growth_of_Entrepreneurial_Ventures.pdf

7. Retrieved from https://www.morphsuits.com/

8. Bailey, D. (2017). The secret formula for go-to-market. *Medium*. Retrieved from https://medium.dave-bailey.com/how-to-create-a-genius-go-to-market-strategy-89469ad9106d

9. Value of venture capital investment in the United States in 4th quarter 2018, by industry (in million U.S. dollars). Retrieved from https://www.statista.com/statistics/277506/venture-caputal-investment-in-the-united-states-by-sector/

10. What does unicorn mean? Retrieved from https://www.divestopedia.com/definition/5114/unicorn

11. Baston, N. (2018). 35 U.S. tech startups that reached unicorn status in 2018. *Inc*. Retrieved from https://www.inc.com/business-insider/35-us-tech-startups-that-reached-unicorn-status-in-2018.html

12. Asheesh, A. (2006, May 15). Raising money using convertible debt. *Entrepreneur*. Retrieved from http://www.entrepreneur.com/article/159520

13. Prive, T. (2013, March 12). Angel investors: How the rich invest. *Forbes*. Retrieved from http://www.forbes.com/sites/tanyaprive/2013/03/12/angels-investors-how-the-rich-invest/

14. Stengel, G. (2018). How women angels are good for innovation and the economy. *Forbes*. Retrieved from https://www.forbes.com/sites/geristengel/2018/06/06/women-are-different-and-thats-good-for-innovation-and-the-economy/#3985bcd1a3c5

15. Adams, P. (2014, January 12). How do angel investors differ from venture capitalists? [Rockies Venture Club blog.] Retrieved from http://www.rockiesventureclub.org/colorado-capital-conference/how-do-angel-investors-differ-from-venture-capitalists/

16. Hayden, B. (2015, March 20). Entrepreneurs can pay it forward through angel investing. *Entrepreneur*. Retrieved from http://www.entrepreneur.com/article/243759

17. Bygrave, W. (2010). Equity financing: Informal investment, venture capital, and harvesting. In B. Bygrave & A. Zacharakis (Eds.), *Portable MBA in entrepreneurship* (pp. 161–195). New York, NY: Wiley.

18. This section is sourced from: Finding an angel. (n.d.). *Small Business Notes*. Retrieved from http://www.smallbusinessnotes.com/business-finances/finding-an-angel.html

19. Stengel, How women angels are good.

20. Ibid.

21. Soper, T. (2017). Who are U.S. angel investors? Study shows 78% male; 87% white; 17% in California. *Geekwire*. Retrieved from https://www.geekwire.com/2017/u-s-angel-investors-study-shows-78-male-87-white-17-california/

22. Robehmed, N. (2013, October 16). There are few minority entrepreneurs, and they rarely get funding. *Forbes*. Retrieved from http://www.forbes.com/sites/natalierobehmed/2013/10/16/there-are-few-minority-entrepreneurs-and-they-rarely-get-funding/

23. Angel Capital Association. (n.d.). FAQ for angels & entrepreneurs. Retrieved from https://www.angelcapitalassociation.org/faqs/#How%20many%20angel%20investors%20are%20there%20in%20the%20U.S.

24. Kenton, W. (2017). Death Valley curve. *Investopedia*. Retrieved from https://www.investopedia.com/terms/d/death-valley-curve.asp

25. Timmons, J., & Spinelli, S. (2008). *New venture creation* (8th ed., p. 457). Boston, MA: McGraw-Hill Irwin.

26. Companies are raising bigger rounds across every investment stage. (2019). Retrieved from https://www.cbinsights.com/research/mega-rounds-venture-capital-2018/

27. Hadzima, J., Jr. (2005). All financing sources are not equal. *Boston Business Journal*. Retrieved from http://web.mit.edu/e-club/hadzima/all-financing-sources-are-not-equal.html

28. Frazier, D., Franklin, B., & Taylor, J. (2014). *National Venture Capital Association yearbook* (p. 13). New York, NY: Thomson Reuters.

29. Bygrave, Equity financing, 176.

30. Reich, D. (2014, January 4). Raising money from friends and family. *Forbes.com*. Retrieved from http://www.forbes.com/sites/danreich/2013/01/04/raising-money-from-friends-and-family/

31. Singerman, B. (2012, July 29). The paradox of VC seed investing. Retrieved from http://techcrunch.com/2012/07/29/the-paradox-of-vc-seed-investing/

32. Colombo, J. (n.d.). The dot-com bubble. *The Bubble Bubble*. Retrieved from http://www.thebubblebubble.com/dotcom-bubble/

33. Moon, A., & Franklin, J. (2019). Exclusive: Impossible Foods raises $300 million with investors eager for bite of meatless burgers. *Reuters*. Retrieved from https://www.reuters.com/article/us-impossible-foods-fundraising-exclusiv/exclusive-impossible-foods-raises-300-million-with-investors-eager-for-bite-of-meatless-burgers-idUSKCN1SJ0YK?il=0

34. Tyabji, H., & Sathe, V. (2010). Venture capital firms in America: Their caste system and other secrets. Retrieved from https://iveybusinessjournal.com/publication/venture-capital-firms-in-america-their-caste-system-and-other-secrets/

35. Timmons & Spinelli, *New venture creation*, 456.

36. Retrieved from http://www.angelblog.net/Venture_Capital_Exit_Times.html

37. Timmons & Spinelli, *New venture creation*, 458.

38. Jacob, L. (2018). 3 trends that prevent entrepreneurs from accessing capital. Retrieved from https://www.kauffman.org/currents/2018/07/3-trends-that-prevent-entrepreneurs-from-accessing-capital

39. Turits, M. (2018). 10 sources of financing for a startup or new small business to explore. Retrieved from https://www.fundera.com/blog/sources-of-financing-for-a-startup

40. Murray, J. (2018). Why do banks say no to business startup loans? Retrieved from https://www.thebalancesmb.com/why-do-banks-say-no-to-business-startup-loans-398025

41. Prithivi, S. (2011, August 24). Angel investing series part II: Due diligence, sealing the deal and post-investment relationship. *Tech.co*. Retrieved from http://tech.co/angel-investing-series-part-ii-2011-08

42. Lagorio-Chafkin, C. (2018). The 9 biggest—and most fascinating—startup acquisitions of 2018. *Inc*. Retrieved from https://www.inc.com/christine-lagorio/the-9-biggest-and-most-fascinating-startup-acquisitions-of-2018.html

43. Wasserman, N. (2008, February). The founder's dilemma. *Harvard Business Review*. Retrieved from https://hbr.org/2008/02/the-founders-dilemma

SUPPLEMENT A

1. Buffet, M., & Clark, D. (2008). *Warren Buffet and the interpretation of financial statements* (p. 33). New York, NY: Scribner.

2. Ittelson, T. R. (2009). *Financial statements: A step-by-step guide to understanding and creating financial reports* (pp. 15–17). Pompton Plains, NJ: Career Press.

3. Ittelson, T. R. (2009). *Financial statements: A step-by-step guide to understanding and creating financial reports* (pp. 79–82). Pompton Plains, NJ: Career Press.

4. http://www.businessdictionary.com/definition/pro-forma.html

5. EZ Numbers website, http://www.eznumbers.com; Lonee Corporation website, http://marketing.lonee.com

6. Bizminer website, http://www.bizminer.com; IBISWorld website, http://www.ibisworld.com; Statista website, http://www.statista.com

7. Smith, R. L., & Smith, J. K. (2004). *Entrepreneurial finance* (pp. 144–146, 2nd ed.). Hoboken, NJ: Wiley.

CHAPTER 14

1. Marinova, P. (2016). LegalZoom CEO: These are the biggest legal mistakes a startup can make. *Fortune*. Retrieved from http://fortune.com/2016/01/21/startup-legal-mistakes/

2. Abramowitz, Z. (2015, March 23). How lawyers can add value for startups *Above The Law* http://abovethelaw.com/2015/03/how-lawyers-can-add-value-for-startups/ retrieved on August 2, 2015.

3. Santa Clara University. (n.d.). The Entrepreneurs' Law Clinic. Retrieved from http://law.scu.edu/elc/

4. Source for legal research on the web. Retrieved from http://www.washlaw.edu/

5. Abramowitz, Z. (2015, March 23). How lawyers can add value for startups. *Above the Law*. Retrieved from http://abovethelaw.com/2015/03/how-lawyers-can-add-value-for-startups/

6. Successful entrepreneurs who started out as sole proprietors. (n.d.). *Gaebler.com*. Retrieved from http://www.gaebler.com/Successful-Entrepreneurs-Who-Started-Out-As-Sole-Proprietors.htm

7. http://www.inc.com/guides/2010/10/how-to-start-a-sole-proprietorship.html

8. http://www.moneyedup.com/2010/08/how-sole-proprietorship-works/

9. See, e.g., California Corporations Code Sections 2500, et seq., and Massachusetts General Laws Ch. 156E.

10. This section is heavily based on http://www.forbes.com/sites/allbusiness/2013/10/03/big-legal-mistakes-made-by-startups/

11. Prakash, P. (2019). Why a founders' agreement is important for every small business. *Fundera*. Retrieved from https://www.fundera.com/blog/founders-agreement

12. Intellectual property rights for innovative entrepreneurship. (n.d.). *The Innovation Policy Forum*. Retrieved from https://www.innovationpolicyplatform.org/content/intellectual-property-rights-innovative-entrepreneurship

13. Keating, R. J. (2013). *Unleashing small business through IP: Protecting intellectual property, driving entrepreneurship* (p. 36). Vienna, VA: Small Business & Entrepreneurship Council. Retrieved from http://www.sbecouncil.org/wp-content/uploads/2013/06/IP+and+Entrepreneurship+FINAL.pdf

14. Ibid.

15. Isaacson, W. (2011). *Steve Jobs* (p. 396). New York, NY: Simon & Schuster.

16. Cremades, A. (2018). 100 questions investors will ask entrepreneurs seeking funding. *Forbes*. Retrieved from https://www.forbes.com/sites/alejandrocremades/2018/08/14/100-questions-investors-will-ask-entrepreneurs-seeking-funding/#73bc397c4d81

17. McKenna, C. (2015, April 3). Do you really own all your intellectual property? *The National Law Review*. Retrieved from http://www.natlawreview.com/article/do-you-really-own-all-your-intellectual-property

18. Steele, A. (2013, June 11). Who owns Hackathon inventions? *Harvard Business Review*. Retrieved from https://hbr.org/2013/06/who-owns-hackathon-inventions

19. Purvis, S. (n.d.). The fundamentals of intellectual property for the entrepreneur. Presentation, U.S. Patent and Trademark Office, Department of Commerce. Retrieved from http://www.uspto.gov/sites/default/files/about/offices/ous/121115.pdf

20. Retrieved from www.copyright.gov/circs/circ61.pdf

21. Spotify settles $1.6bn lawsuit over songwriters' rights. (2018). *BBC*. Retrieved from https://www.bbc.co.uk/news/business-46646918

22. Miller, C. (2018). Clothing wars: Apparel giant Under Armour sends a cease and desist to local business. *Bendsource*. https://www.bendsource.com/bend/clothing-wars/Content?oid=8127194

23. Halligan, R. M., & Haas, D. (2010, February 19). The secret of trade secret success. *Forbes*. Retrieved from http://www.forbes.com/2010/02/19/protecting-trade-secrets-leadership-managing-halligan-haas.html

24. Quinn, G. (2009). Obscure patent: The dog umbrella & leash. *IPWatchdog*. Retrieved from https://www.ipwatchdog.com/2009/01/20/obscure-patent-the-dog-umbrella-leash/id=1634/

25. Quinn, G. (2014, February 15). Protecting ideas: Can ideas be protected or patented? *IPWatchdog*. Retrieved from http://www.ipwatchdog.com/2014/02/15/protecting-ideas-can-ideas-be-protected-or-patented/id=48009/

26. Keating, *Unleashing small business through IP*.

27. Twin, A. (2019). Non-disclosure agreement (NDA). *Investopedia*. Retrieved from https://www.investopedia.com/terms/n/nda.asp

28. Bornstein, A. (2018). Why you need to use NDAs to protect your business. *Entrepreneur*. https://www.entrepreneur.com/article/319362

29. Ibid.

30. Zwilling, M. (2017). How and when to pitch your idea without a signed NDA. *Inc*. Retrieved from https://www.inc.com/martin-zwilling/how-when-to-pitch-your-idea-without-a-signed-nda.html

31. Bizzo, G. (2017). Making non-disclosure agreements (NDA's) work for you. *Startups*. Retrieved from https://www.startups.com/library/expert-advice/making-non-disclosure-agreements-ndas-work-for-you

32. Watson, A. (2018). Media piracy: Statistics & facts. *Statista*. Retrieved from https://www.statista.com/topics/3493/media-piracy/

33. Sherman, E. (2019). One in five U.S. companies say China has stolen their intellectual property. *Fortune*. Retrieved from http://fortune.com/2019/03/01/china-ip-theft

34. Clark, G. (2018). What is intellectual property, and does China steal it? *Bloomberg*. Retrieved from https://www.bloomberg.com/news/articles/2018-12-05/what-s-intellectual-property-and-does-china-steal-it-quicktake

35. Bessen, J. (2014, November). The evidence is in: Patent trolls do hurt innovation. *Harvard Business Review*. Retrieved from https://hbr.org/2014/07/the-evidence-is-in-patent-trolls-do-hurt-innovation

36. Suneson, G. (2019). 10 most counterfeited products in America. *USA Today*. Retrieved

from https://eu.usatoday.com/story/money/2019/04/14/10-most-counterfeited-products-in-america/39327933/

37. Most of this section is based on Kotha, R., Kim, P. H., & Alexy, O. (2014, November). Turn your science into a business. *Harvard Business Review, 92*(11), 106–114.

38. Lococo, E. (2012, July 2). Apple pays Proview $60m to resolve iPad trademark dispute. *Bloomberg Business.* Retrieved from http://www.bloomberg.com/news/articles/2012-07-02/apple-pays-60-million-to-end-china-ipad-dispute-with-proview

39. U.S. Small Business Administration (n.d.). *Hire and manage employees.* Retrieved from https://www.sba.gov/business-guide/manage-your-business/hire-manage-employees

40. Burrow, S. (2015, June 10). Top ten worst countries for workers' rights: The ranking no country should want. *Huffington Post.* Retrieved from http://www.huffingtonpost.com/sharan-burrow/top-ten-worst-countries-f_b_7553364.html

41. Simon, R. (2019). The real danger of going on "Shark Tank": Copycats. *Wall Street Journal.* Retrieved from https://www.wsj.com/articles/the-real-danger-of-going-on-shark-tank-copycats-11556357401

42. U.S. Small Business Administration, *Hire and manage employees.*

43. See, e.g., Internal Revenue Service Publication 15-A, Employer's Supplemental Tax Guide 2016.

44. Wage and Hour Division (WHD). Retrieved from https://www.dol.gov/whd/regs/compliance/whdfs71.htm

45. See http://www.babson.edu/academics/centers-and-institutes/the-arthur-m-blank-center-for-entrepreneurship/john-e-and-alice-l-butler-launch-pad/beta-challenge

46. The specialty lines insurance market is the segment of the insurance industry where the more difficult and unusual risks are written. The specialty lines insurance market focuses on two types of products: unusual or difficult insurance and higher risk accounts.

CHAPTER 15

1. *Entrepreneurial marketing.* (n.d.). Retrieved from http://www.marketing-schools.org/types-of-marketing/entrepreneurial-marketing.html

2. Egan, K. (2017). 11 things that make marketing in 2017 different from 2007. Retrieved from https://www.impactbnd.com/blog/11-things-that-make-marketing-in-2017-different-from-2007

3. Godin, S. (2009). First, organize 1,000. *Seth's Blog.* Retrieved from https://seths.blog/2009/12/first-organize-1000/

4. Much of this section is based on Manktelow, J. (n.d.). The marketing mix and the 4Ps of marketing. *MindTools.* Retrieved from http://www.mindtools.com/pages/article/newSTR_94.htm

5. Crane, F. G. (2012, September 12). *Marketing for entrepreneurs: Concepts and applications for new ventures,* p. 3. Thousand Oaks, CA: SAGE. [Kindle ed.]

6. Retrieved from http://www.entrepreneur.com/article/70824

7. Williams, J. (n.d.). The basics of branding. *Entrepreneur.* Retrieved from https://www.entrepreneur.com/article/77408

8. Retrieved from https://www.entrepreneur.com/article/219314

9. Pono, M. (2016, May 3). How industry leaders create strong brands. *Medium.* Retrieved from https://www.linkedin.com/pulse/how-industry-leaders-create-strong-brands-myk-pono

10. 12 marketing trends to take advantage of this year. (2018). *Forbes.* Retrieved from https://www.forbes.com/sites/forbescommunicationscouncil/2018/02/14/12-marketing-trends-to-take-advantage-of-this-year/#208dfca87401

11. Teitelman, M. (2018). 18 artificial intelligence marketing trends for 2018. *Medium.* Retrieved from https://medium.com/trapica/18-important-marketing-trends-for-2018-64922e2daff4

12. Wilson, M. (2017). Domino's Instagram is gross. That's by design. *Fast Company.* Retrieved from https://www.fastcompany.com/90138198/dominos-could-win-the-pizza-wars-by-being-grosser-than-everyone-else

13. 11 Influencer Marketing Campaigns to Inspire You to Start with Influencer Marketing in 2018. (2018). *Influencer Marketing Hub.* Retrieved from https://influencermarketinghub.com/11-influencer-marketing-campaigns-to-inspire-you-2018/

14. Meet the 25 highest-paid social media influencers. (2018). *Izea.* Retrieved from https://izea.com/2018/04/05/highest-paid-social-media-influencers/

15. Brenner, M. (2018). 4 creative experiential marketing examples that are raising the bar. Retrieved from https://marketinginsidergroup.com/strategy/4-creative-experiential-marketing-examples-raising-bar/

16. Ritchie, J. (2017, January 26). Five simple ways to educate your customers through content. Retrieved from https://www.forbes.com/sites/forbesagencycouncil/2017/01/26/five-simple-ways-to-educate-your-customers-through-content/#1697e35ad991

17. Ciotti, G. (2013, July 23). The new 4Ps of marketing. *Help Scout.* Retrieved from http://www.helpscout.net/blog/new-4ps-of-marketing/

18. Blendtec celebrates 10 years of viral marketing success. (2016). Retrieved from https://globenewswire.com/news-release/2016/11/07/887174/10165944/en/Blendtec-Celebrates-10-Years-of-Viral-Marketing-Success.html

19. MyLoupus. (2010, January 17). Guerrilla marketing by Loupus—Snow branding in Leipzig [Video file]. *YouTube.* Retrieved from https://www.youtube.com/watch?v=_JcuDxT88_Y

20. Botticello, C. (2018, July 18). 10 creative guerrilla marketing tactics to boost your brand, company, or cause. Retrieved from https://medium.com/side-hustle/10-creative-guerilla-marketing-tactics-to-boost-your-brand-company-or-cause-8dc02e43f02d

21. Pinegar, G. (2018). What is guerrilla marketing (+16 ideas and examples for innovative brands). Retrieved from https://learn.g2crowd.com/guerrilla-marketing

22. Pofeldt, E. (2018, July 8). How a fine artist built a million-dollar, one-person business that's true to her vision. Retrieved from https://www.forbes.com/sites/elainepofeldt/2018/07/08/how-a-fine-artist-built-a-million-dollar-one-person-business-thats-true-to-her-vision/#6c3a33617ddf

23. Agrawl, A. J. (2017, February 24). How to have rock star customer service on Twitter. Retrieved from https://www.forbes.com/sites/ajagrawal/2017/02/24/how-to-have-rockstar-customer-service-on-twitter/#6f08a7c3d918

24. Wertz, J. (2018, April 24). 4 entrepreneurs share which social media outlet garners the most business. Retrieved from https://www.forbes.com/sites/jiawertz/2018/04/24/4-entrepreneurs-share-which-social-media-outlet-garners-the-most-business/#7c2c479f4a21

25. Pink, D. (2012). *To sell is human* (p. 21). New York, NY: Penguin.

26. Black, W. (2013). Marketers, stop creating content and develop a point of view. Retrieved from https://e-m-marketing.com/blog/2013/12/marketers-stop-creating-content-and-develop-a-point-of-view/

27. Ibid.

28. Pepsi advert with Kendall Jenner pulled after huge backlash. (2017).

Independent UK. Retrieved from https://www.independent.co.uk/arts-entertainment/tv/news/pepsi-advert-pulled-kendall-jenner-protest-video-cancelled-removed-a7668986.html

29. Black, Marketers, stop creating content and develop a point of view.

30. Davidson, J. (2017, January 3). 3 ways how I get my followers to meaningfully engage with me. Retrieved from https://medium.com/startup-grind/3-ways-how-i-get-my-followers-to-meaningfully-engage-with-me-1fe886d9edc4

31. Hern, A. (2015, August 5). Smartphone now most popular way to browse internet—Ofcom Report. *The Guardian.* Retrieved from http://www.theguardian.com/technology/2015/aug/06/smartphones-most-popular-way-to-browse-internet-ofcom

32. Mintzer, R. (2014, May 27). The 10 most deadly mistakes in website design. *Entrepreneur.* Retrieved from http://www.entrepreneur.com/article/234129

33. Kelly, K. (2008). 1,000 true fans. *The Technium.* Retrieved from https://kk.org/thetechnium/1000-true-fans/

34. Welch, D. (2018, December 20). Musk's brother finds good use for Tesla Model 3 shortage. Retrieved from https://www.bloomberg.com/news/articles/2018-02-20/musk-s-brother-finds-good-use-for-tesla-model-3-shortage

35. Godin, First, organize 1,000.

36. Lewis, R. (2016). The long tail theory can be reality for traditional megabrands. Retrieved from https://www.forbes.com/sites/robinlewis/2016/05/31/the-long-tail-theory-can-be-reality-for-traditional-megabrands/#453fa026372b

37. Scott, D. M. (2017). *The new rules of marketing & PR* (p. 32). Hoboken, NJ: Wiley.

38. Gregoire, C. (2014, June 12). How to make the perfect first impression. *Huffington Post.* Retrieved from http://www.huffingtonpost.com/2014/05/30/the-science-and-art-of-fi_n_5399004.html

39. Mackay, J. (n.d.). The weird science behind first impressions. *Crew.* Retrieved from http://blog.crew.co/weird-science-first-impressions/

40. *Body language for entrepreneurs.* (n.d.). Retrieved from Udemy.com Course.

41. Ibid.

42. Payne, K. (n.d.). Personal branding for entrepreneurs. Retrieved from https://kevintpayne.com/personal-branding-for-entrepreneurs/

SUPPLEMENT B

1. Pink, D. (2013). *To sell is human: The surprising truth about moving others.* New York, NY: Riverhead Books.

2. Ibid.

3. Clark, N. (2016). How Pixar can help you craft your 30-second pitch. Retrieved from https://www.linkedin.com/pulse/how-pixar-can-help-you-craft-your-30-second-pitch-nicholas-clark/

4. Monarth, H. "The irresistible power of storytelling as strategic business tool," Harvard Business Review.org (March 11, 2014) https://hbr.org/2014/03/the-irresistible-power-of-storytelling-as-a-strategic-business-tool/ retrieved on September 20, 2015

5. Neck, H. The entrepreneurial skillset of storytelling, *Forbes* (2015, July 14) http://www.forbes.com/sites/babson/2015/07/14/the-entrepreneurial-skillset-of-storytelling/ retrieved on September 20, 2015

6. Gallo, C. What Starbucks CEO Howard Schultz taught me about communication and success, *Forbes* (2013, December 19) http://www.forbes.com/sites/carminegallo/2013/12/19/what-starbucks-ceo-howard-schultz-taught-me-about-communication-and-success/ retrieved on September 20, 2015

7. Pink, D. (2012). *To sell is human*, New York: Penguin Group, p. 171.

8. Experiential Marketing and Event Staffing! Retrieved from https://www.attackmarketing.com/

9. Zwilling, M. Entrepreneurs who master storytelling win more, *Forbes* (2013, January 25) http://www.forbes.com/sites/martinzwilling/2013/01/25/entrepreneurs-who-master-storytelling-win-more/ retrieved on September 20, 2015

10. Pink, *To sell is human.*

11. See http://techcrunch.com/2010/11/02/365-days-10-million-3-rounds-2-companies-all-with-5-magic-slides/ (5 slides); http://avc.com/2010/06/six-slides/ (6 slides); http://guykawasaki.com/the-only-10-slides-you-need-in-your-pitch/ (10 slides); http://articles.bplans.com/what-to-include-in-your-pitch-deck/ (11 slides); http://www.forbes.com/sites/chancebarnett/2014/05/09/investor-pitch-deck-to-raise-money-for-startups/#5dcf25b84863 (12 slides); https://www.entrepreneur.com/article/240065 (15 slides); http://www.slideshare.net/Sky7777/the-best-startup-pitch-deck-how-to-present-to-angels-v-cs (30 slides).

12. http://techcrunch.com/2010/11/02/365-days-10-million-3-rounds-2-companies-all-with-5-magic-slides/

13. http://articles.bplans.com/what-to-include-in-your-pitch-deck/

14. http://www.slideshare.net/Sky7777/the-best-startup-pitch-deck-how-to-present-to-angels-v-cs

15. http://www.bridging-the-gap.com/what-is-a-use-case/

16. Sampson, M. (2011, March 23). Invest in people, not ideas. Retrieved from https://michaelsampson.net/2011/03/23/invest-people/

17. Question list was compiled from author experience, but some questions may be found at http://techcrunch.com/2012/04/27/be-concise-the-top-questions-asked-at-a-y-combinator-interview/; http://www.forbes.com/sites/allbusiness/2013/06/10/65-questions-venture-capitalists-will-ask-startups/#50987df18202

18. Behind the Scenes of TED Presenters. Retrieved from https://blog.powerspeaking.com/behind_the_scenes_of_ted_presenters

CHAPTER 16

1. Sharir, M., & Lerner, M. (2006). Gauging the success of social ventures initiated by individual social entrepreneurs. *Journal of World Business, 41,* 6–20, at p. 7.

2. Churchman, C. W. (1967). Wicked problems. *Management Science, 14*(4), B-141 & B-142; Conklin, J. (2006). *Dialogue mapping: Building shared understanding of wicked problems.* Chichester, UK: Wiley. See also http://www.cognexus.org/id17.htm

3. Escher, A., Kolodny, L. (2017). Causes of the global water crisis and 12 companies trying to solve it. Retrieved from website https://techcrunch.com/2017/03/22/causes-of-the-global-water-crisis-and-12-companies-trying-to-solve-it/

4. Does Plastic Contribute to Global Warming. (2018) Retrieved from website https://www.envirotech-online.com/news/water-wastewater/9/breaking-news/does-plastic-contribute-to-global-warming/46942

5. Harvey, F. (2018). World must triple efforts or face catastrophic climate change, says UN. Retrieved from website https://www.theguardian.com/environment/2018/nov/27/world-triple-efforts-climate-change-un-global-warming

6. Schaffrath, M. (2018). 5 startups that prove tech can solve the world's biggest problems. Retrieved from website https://www.forbes.com/sites/maikoschaffrath/2018/06/17/5-startups-that-prove-tech-can-solve-the-worlds-biggest-problems/#1a81460512fd

7. Neck, H. M., Brush, C., & Allen, E. (2009). The landscape of social

entrepreneurship. *Business Horizons, 52*, 13–19.

8. Sword & Plough website https://www .swordandplough.com/pages/social-impact

9. Clark, M. (2018). Empowering women to be ABLE to thrive. Retrieved from website https://socialenterprise .us/2018/02/16/empowering-women-able-thrive/

10. Robin Hood website https://www .robinhood.org/

11. Harris, E. (2017) Robin Hood, favorite charity on Wall Street, gets new leader. *New York Times.* Retrieved from https://www.nytimes .com/2017/04/25/nyregion/robin-hood-foundation-charity-wes-moore.html

12. Luna, J. (2017). Jane Chen: Be courageous because you will fail. Retrieved from Stanford Business website https://www.gsb.stanford .edu/insights/jane-chen-be-courageous-because-you-will-fail

13. Retrieved from Goodwill website http://www.goodwill.org/about-us/

14. Blanding, M. (2013, August 12). Entrepreneurs and the "hybrid" organization. *Forbes Blog.* Retrieved from http://www.forbes.com/sites/ hbsworkingknowledge/2013/08/12/ entrepreneurs-and-the-hybrid-organization/

15. Sistare, H. (2013, February 28). Better World Books continues to innovate. *Triple Pundit.* Retrieved from http:// www.triplepundit.com/2013/02/ better-world-books-continues-to-innovate/

16. Retrieved from Better World Books website https://www.betterworld books.com/go/book-for-book

17. The Staff of Entrepreneur Media, Inc. (2017). How social entrepreneurs can land funding. Retrieved from website https://www.entrepreneur.com/ article/290808

18. Pi Slice Celebrates its second year. Retrieved from website https://www .pi-slice.com/en/news-from-the-field/article/pi-slice-celebrates-its-second-year

19. Gilber, J. (2017). Putting the impact in impact investing: 28 funds building a credible, transparent marketplace. Retrieved from https://www.forbes.com/sites/ jaycoengilbert/2017/10/09/putting-the-impact-in-impact-investing-28-funds-building-a-credible-transparent-marketplace/#2caf84523e5f

20. Cohen, R., & Bannick, M. (2014, September 20). Is social impact investing the next venture capital?" *Forbes.* Retrieved from http://www.forbes.com/sites/ realspin/2014/09/20/is-social-impact-investing-the-next-venture-capital/

21. Examples of impact investment funds, *Impactbase* Retrieved from http:// www.impactbase.org/info/examples-impact-investment-funds

22. VPP website. Retrieved from http:// www.vppartners.org/about-us

23. Retrieved from Venture Philanthropy Partners website http://www .vppartners.org/about/history/

24. https://sjfventures.com/our-portfolio/

25. Fehrenbacher, K. (2018). Meet 5 startups working on big energy ideas. Retrieved from website https:// www.greenbiz.com/article/meet-5-startups-working-big-energy-ideas

26. Yunus, M., & Jolis, A. 2007. *Banker to the poor: Micro-lending and the battle against world poverty.* New York: Public Affairs

27. Klich, T. (2018). The founder of Tala on her leap from finance to fundraising for her mission-driven startup. Retrieved from https://www.forbes .com/sites/tanyaklich/2018/07/18/ tala-founder-shivani-siroya-on-her-leap-from-finance-to-fundraising-for-her-mission-driven-fintech-startup/#2852129056f7

28. Mitchell, R., Agle, B., & Wood, D. (1997). Toward a theory of stakeholder identification and salience: Defining the principle of who and what really counts. *Academy of Management Review, 22*, 853–866.

29. Suchman, M. C. (1995). Managing legitimacy: Strategic and institutional approaches. *Academy of Management Review, 20*, 571–610.

30. Retrieved from http://www.c-e-o.org/ about-us

31. Rao, S. (2010, April 14). Moving from a "me" to an "other-centered" universe. *Huffpost Healthy Living.* Retrieved from http://www.huffingtonpost.com/ srikumar-s-rao/how-to-be-happy-moving-fr_b_570730.html

32. Meier, S., & Cassar, L. (2018). Stop talking about how CSR helps your bottom line. Retrieved from website https://hbr.org/2018/01/stop-talking-about-how-csr-helps-your-bottom-line

33. The halo effect. (2015, June 27). *The Economist.* Retrieved from http:// www.economist.com/news/ business/21656218-do-gooding-policies-help-firms-when-they-get-prosecuted-halo-effect

34. The halo effect. (2015, June 27). *The Economist.* Retrieved from http:// www.economist.com/news/ business/21656218-do-gooding-policies-help-firms-when-they-get-prosecuted-halo-effect retrieved on October 30, 2015.

35. Meier, S., and Cassar, L. (2018). Stop talking about how CSR helps your bottom line. Retrieved from website https://hbr.org/2018/01/stop-talking-about-how-csr-helps-your-bottom-line

36. Valet, V. (2018). The world's most reputable companies for corporate responsibility 2018. *Forbes.* Retrieved from https://www.forbes.com/ sites/vickyvalet/2018/10/11/the-worlds-most-reputable-companies-for-corporate-responsibility-2018/#3940c0003371

37. Half, R. (2017). 3 awesome CSR initiatives by top tech companies. Retrieved from website https://www .roberthalf.com.au/blog/employers/3-awesome-csr-initiatives-top-tech-companies

38. Anderson, C. (2018). Introducing . . . The Audacious Project, a new model to inspire change at scale. Retrieved from website https://ideas.ted.com/ the-audacious-project-a-new-model-to-inspire-change-at-scale/

39. TED. (2018). The Audacious Project [Press release]. Retrieved from https:// www.prnewswire.com/news-releases/ the-audacious-project-a-new-model-for-philanthropic-collaboration-announces-first-ever-recipients-live-from-the-ted-conference-300628424. html

40. Retrieved from https://www .gemconsortium.org/report

41. Kelley, D., Singer, S., & Herrington, M. (2015). *Global Entrepreneurship Monitor 2016 global report.* Retrieved from http://www.gemconsortium.org/ docs/download/3106

NAME INDEX

SUBJECT INDEX

1989

Technical C

Rebecca

University of I

Wadsworth Publishing Company
Belmont, California
A Division of Wadsworth, Inc.

English Editor: John Strohmeier
Special Projects Editor: Judith McKibben
Production Editor: Leland Moss
Designer: Andrew H. Ogus
Print Buyer: Barbara Britton
Art Editor: Catherine Aydelott
Copy Editor: Tom Briggs
Technical Illustrator: BS&M
Compositor: Thompson Type
Cover: Andrew H. Ogus
Signing Representative: John Moroney

The part openers are details from the drawings of Leonardo da Vinci,
© Alinari/Art Resource, New York.

Printed in the United States of America
1 2 3 4 5 6 7 8 9 10—90 89 88 87 86

ISBN 0-534-06180-X

Library of Congress Cataloging-in-Publication Data
Carosso, Rebecca Burnett, 1947–
    Technical communication.

    Includes index.
    1. Technical writing. I. Title.
T11.C327 1986   808'.0666   85-20315
ISBN 0-534-06180-X

Contents in Brief

Contents

Preface

LEONARDO DA VINCI'S mechanical drawings are precise, detailed, functional, and focused. Because good technical writing also has these attributes, da Vinci's drawings—used throughout *Technical Communication*—emphasize the text's concern with these attributes. The text maintains the established conventions of technical communication while incorporating new issues.

Technical Communication has evolved from the author's experience in a variety of academic and industrial environments, working with both traditional and adult students as well as with technical professionals. The author's work with these groups has had an impact on the text's content and organization, resulting in a balance of academic, industrial, and professional concerns.

In order to ensure a balanced approach, the text incorporates ten key features.

- **Process and Product:** Educators tend to focus on the recursive writing process; people in government, business, industry, and the professions focus more often on the writing product. *Technical Communication* shows how the process creates the product. The text discusses ways to approach a writing problem, explains options available to a writer, offers suggestions about logical organization, and illustrates appropriate language use.

- **Writing for Readers:** *Technical Communication* provides in-depth coverage of audience analysis. The text moves from a theoretical to a practical level by providing specific suggestions for adjusting material to different audiences. This concern with audience analysis and the subsequent adjustment of material continues throughout the text. Because *Technical Communication* recognizes the increasing importance of science writing for general audiences, one chapter is devoted entirely to this subject.

- **Rhetorical Base:** The text uses rhetorical reality—constraints of the subject, needs of the readers, purposes of the writer—initially to define the field of technical communication and then to guide a writer through the process of producing documents. This analysis of subject, audience, and writer establishes a sound framework for presenting information verbally and visually. Early in the text, traditional organizational patterns are introduced, forming the basis for all the documents presented and making the text rhetorically consistent.

- **Visuals and Document Design:** *Technical Communication* is unique in that it identifies and illustrates the rhetorical base of visual material and establishes parallels between visual and verbal presentations. The text also incorporates discussion about recent research in document design, recognizing the impact of format on audience reaction. *Technical Communication* encourages a practical combination of visual and verbal elements.

- **Awareness of Technology:** Because technical communication often takes place in a rapidly changing environment, this text discusses the impact of technology on both the writing process and the resulting document. *Technical Communication* also stresses that creating effective technical documents demands a blend of communication skill and technical expertise.

- **Examples:** *Technical Communication* includes a broad spectrum of writing examples from students as well as working professionals in science, technology, and the professions—agriculture, astronomy, electronics, forestry, manufacturing, metallurgy, music, pediatrics, and robotics to name a few. In addition, historical examples provide another perspective. The varied and interesting examples illustrate different stages of the writing process and demonstrate how to create effective technical documents.

- **Style:** *Technical Communication* directly addresses its readers—technical students and working professionals—in a straightforward style that is appealing and readable. Clear and detailed explanations accompany the examples. Throughout, the text itself maintains a tone appropriate for most technical communication.

- **Case Situations:** The complexity of technical communication is presented in real-world case situations that are an ongoing feature of the exercises. In addition, one chapter offers an extended case situation that demonstrates how a single industrial problem generates a series of memos and letters, following the case from its inception to its resolution.

- **Exercises:** End-of-chapter questions, exercises, and assignments offer ample opportunity to discuss ideas and apply the principles and practices advocated in *Technical Communication*. The discussion questions focus attention on issues and problems that must be confronted in professional work. Individual and group exercises simulate the collaborative problem solving and writing that so often occur in actual professional situations. The assignments result in documents that use the principles of effective technical communication.

- **Professional Reference:** Busy professionals need a book they can refer to long after a course is over. *Technical Communication*'s key points are summarized in figures and checklists that can be used throughout the writing process. Questions and format outlines guide writers through the preparation of technical documents. The *Handbook* provides a practical survey of usage and conventions. Sentence and paragraph exercises offer practice with material from actual technical documents.

Technical Communication would not exist without the personal and professional support from these friends and colleagues: Elizabeth Foster wrote the documentation for both Chapter 8 and the endnotes, read numerous drafts of the text, and gave unwavering assistance; Muriel McGrann provided very necessary food for body and soul; Judith Dupras Stanford acted as a sounding board for my crystalizing ideas; Marcia Greenman Lebeau read outlines and chapter drafts and stimulated the inclusion of creative problem solving in Chapter 2; Leon Somers provided encouragement and plenty of provocative questions; Elizabeth Carros Keroack read numerous drafts; Steven Meidell added to both the interviewing section in Chapter 7 and the apparatus in several chapters; Arline Dupras gave invaluable advice about chapter organization; Geraldine Branca offered recommendations for revision; Christopher Burnett made suggestions about proposals and feasibility reports; Nancy Irish developed many of the examples for Chapters 7 and 8; Bernard DiNatale kept my computer and printers working.

The following people at Wadsworth Publishing Company have been instrumental in the publication of this text: Kevin Howat first convinced me of Wadsworth's concern for the people behind the books; Cedric Crocker provided enthusiasm and direction; John Strohmeier encouraged the final segments; Judith McKibben offered incisive criticism and productive suggestions; Leland Moss directed the text's production with careful attention to detail; Cathy Aydelott supervised the text's art; and Andrew Ogus created an appealing and usable design.

I am grateful to the following students from university classes and industrial seminars whose writing appears in *Technical Communication*: Kate Barton, Deb Beaudry, George Buchanan, Kim Buckingham, Suzanne Champion, Dean Cocozziello, Dennis Donahue, Robin Farwell, Lee Foster, Gail Greenough, Marty Hiltz, Elizabeth Howard, Tom Mansur, Chuck Mengin, Bob Musgrove, Jim Neroda, Crystal Novack, Karen Poisson, William Skoglund, Carolyn Stanhope, Robert Wamsley, Craig Wilder, Anne Marie Wilson.

Reviewers' often detailed and practical suggestions were instrumental in the revisions of the text. I appreciate the efforts of the following people who reviewed the manuscript in its various stages: Professors Joyce Buck, Pennsylvania State University; James Davis, Ohio University; Sam Dragga, Texas A&M University; John Eckman, John Tyler College; Carol E. Garrard, Communications Consultant; Claude Gibson, Texas A&M University; Dixie Elise Hickman, University of Southern Mississippi; Ken Ricks, University of Minnesota; Kenneth Risdon, University of Minnesota; Scott Sanders, University of New Mexico; Gilbert Storms, Miami University; Fred White, University of Santa Clara; and Thomas Willard, University of Arizona.

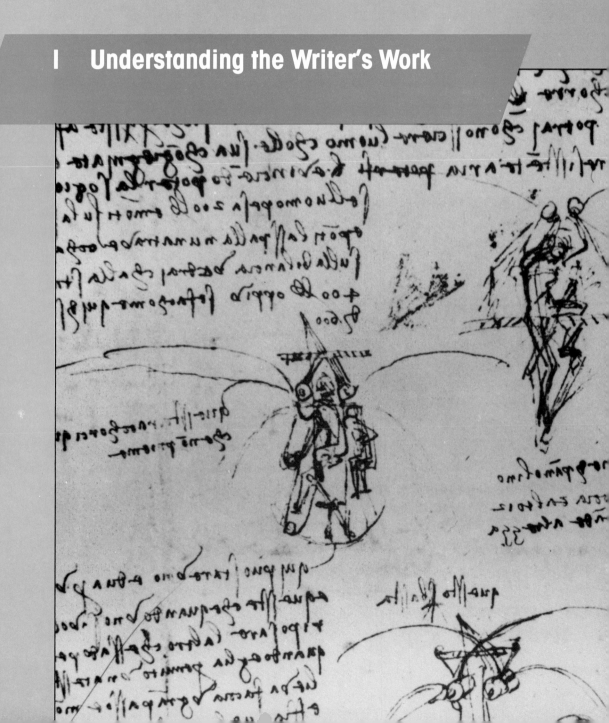

I   Understanding the Writer's Work

1   Technical Writing:
Subject, Audience, and Writer

WHAT DO THE MOONS of Jupiter, in vitro fertilization, silicon chips, wetlands conservation, soybean crops, flutes, and foals have in common? All are subjects in technical writing. What do astrophysicists, obstetricians, electrical engineers, ecologists, farmers, musicians, and veterinarians have in common? All read and write technical documents. Technical writing is a broad field that touches nearly every subject and profession through a vast array of documents; it defines, describes, and directs activities in business and industry, government and research institutions, hospitals and farms.

Although technical writing has traditionally focused on engineering, nearly any subject can be the topic of a technical document. For example, detailed information about sound formation is important for both a speech pathologist and an engineer designing a voice synthesizer. Knowledge about muscle conditioning is equally relevant to physical therapists, ballet dancers, and veterinarians. Data about weather changes are crucial to the meteorologist and the commercial fisher.

Technical subjects frequently appear in writing outside the technical world. Many major daily newspapers have science writers who make technical subjects interesting and accessible to the general reader. (Chapter 17 introduces you to popular science writing.) Writers of fiction often use technical concepts and details to authenticate and enliven their writing. Science fiction is based on a writer's ability to make the fantastic seem factual. In fact, what was science fiction twenty or more years ago is often now science fact: Jules Verne's fantasies in *Twenty Thousand Leagues Under the Sea*, written in 1870, have proven to be almost prescient in many of their details.

Writers of good fiction depend on technical accuracy and precise diction just as much as writers of effective technical documents. Sometimes fiction writers are so technically accurate that readers have a difficult time distinguishing fact from fiction. For example, when the Manhattan Project was developing the atom bomb during World War II, several science-fiction writers were investigated by government security and intelligence groups. The reason? These writers had included in their stories technical details gleaned from public documents and elementary physics texts. Government investigators were afraid a leak about the Manhattan Project would endanger United States security.[1]

So, if good writing—whether in journalism or fiction or technical documents—is concerned with technical accuracy and precise diction, what differentiates technical writing from other forms of writing? This text starts with the basic premise that all good writing has more similarities than differences. Good writing is logically organized, honest, and interesting; it is also mechanically and grammatically correct—and says something worth reading. To discover the special characteristics of technical writing, let's take a brief look at its history.

Historical Development of Technical Writing

Technical writing has not been created by the high tech generation of the 1980s. However, neither is it a product of the war industry of the 1940s, the explosion of the Industrial Revolution in the eighteenth and nineteenth centuries, nor even the scientific breakthroughs of the Enlightenment in the eighteenth century. Technical writing, in some form or another, has existed as long as people have been able to write.

The earliest examples of writing of any kind—some as much as 6000 years old—record technical information. Clay tablets and papyrus scrolls preserve agricultural yields, shipping and trading tallies, mathematical information, astronomical changes, and medical practices as part of Babylonian, Phoenician, and Egyptian cultures. In fact, many archaeologists believe that writing was created in order to record technical information.

Documents from ancient Greece, some dating as early as 500 B.C.E., show a skillful organization of technical details. Existing documents include a wide range of material—from detailed medical manuals to descriptions of the construction and operation of weapons, from explanations of architecture to descriptions of animal anatomy.

Technical writing continued in the Middle Ages; perhaps the most widely read document of this period is Chaucer's manual on the operation of the astrolabe, a valued astronomical and navigational instrument that had the added benefits of telling time and casting horoscopes. Chaucer's manual, written in the fourteenth century, is an important example of effective technical writing, boasting a personal style, everyday comparisons, careful organization, and technical detail.

During the Renaissance, successful scientific inquiry resulted in numerous documents written by broadly educated scientists who described their discoveries and investigations. Leonardo daVinci wrote treatises on topics ranging from aeronautics to anatomy, and Nicolaus Copernicus upset the Ptolemaic astrological system by proposing a heliocentric system in his *Hypothesis on Heavenly Motions*.

Then, beginning with the scientific revolution and expanding to the present day, the number of technical documents has multiplied. Modern technical documents—ranging from correspondence and manuals to analytical reports and proposals—have a strong heritage. The examples in this text as well as the writing you produce during the course reflect an evolving concern about the accurate presentation of technical information.

Defining Technical Writing

Although technical writing has existed as long as people have recorded information, technical writing as a profession has evolved tremendously during the second half of the twentieth century. Technical writing was defined initially as writing that dealt primarily with scientific and technical fields; but subject matter—although certainly relevant—proved to be insufficient to define technical writing. Later attempts to describe technical writing focused on its linguistic nature, which is usually stylistically conventional; but even in concert with subject matter, this approach failed to create a workable definition.

A more recent definition has focused on the purpose of technical writing, stressing that good technical writing conveys one and only one meaning, so the reader interprets the material in only one way.[2] This definition comes much closer to identifying the nature of technical writing, yet it still falls short of the mark.

Figure 1.1   Characteristics of Technical Writing

Characteristic	*Explanation*
PURPOSE	informs or persuades
SUBJECT MATTER	conveys technical aspects of any field, thus frequently uses a specialized vocabulary; usually verifiable
AUDIENCE	usually addresses specific, identified reader(s); material adjusted to meet reader needs
NEED	fulfills a specific, identified need
TIMELINESS	becomes dated because of changes
INTERPRETATION	presents a single meaning
VISUALS	convey content; fully integrated in the report
APPROACH	maintains an objective, impartial perspective and tone
STYLE	uses short-to-medium sentences; subject-verb-object word order; stylistically varied, but simple
FORMAT	uses standard forms to take advantage of audience expectation

The rapid growth of technical writing as a discipline and profession has extended the traditional definitions. Today, identifying a document as "technical" means examining collectively such characteristics as purpose, subject matter, approach, and audience; however, containing one or two of these characteristics is not sufficient to label writing as "technical," nor must technical writing have all these characteristics. Figure 1.1 summarizes the major characteristics of technical writing.

The situation of Jon Baliene, a manufacturing supervisor, illustrates each of the characteristics presented in Figure 1.1:

PURPOSE
inform and persuade

SUBJECT MATTER
technical

Division manager Sandy Schaeffer asks Jon Baliene to prepare a report about production problems in his department. Although Jon presents facts about the variables contributing to the problem, he also wants to persuade Sandy to accept the analysis presented in the report. Because Sandy's background is in business, Jon adjusts the technical material by adding explanations of the highly specialized information. In addition, Jon includes an appendix with calculations and specifications appropriate for secondary readers who have more technical experience than his manager.

AUDIENCE
identified

NEED
identified

Beyond identifying the problem, Jon includes recommendations, which, he stresses, are based on current projections and costs; in six months he would have to write a different report. He hopes the background facts along with his persuasive arguments convince Sandy to accept these recommendations. Because Jon has prepared an effective report, it contains another characteristic of technical writing: the information allows only a single interpretation. To ensure this, Jon checks the text as well as the visuals to make sure nothing is ambiguous or confusing.

TIMELINESS
current

INTERPRETATION
single meaning

Because he knows that information can get muddled if presented only in a narrative style, Jon has organized a great deal of numerical data into a table; he has also created a graph to show the trends he has identified from the data. He places these visuals in the text immediately following his references to them.

VISUALS
integrated

APPROACH
objective

Despite Jon's enthusiasm for his recommendations, he writes about the problems and proposes his solution objectively. He realizes that although his readers are intelligent and well educated, they have little time to read unnecessarily complex material. He checks his sentences for length and clarity. Following the format recommended in his company's style guide, Jon finds that his writing task is simplified and his report fulfills his readers' expectations.

STYLE
clear and direct

FORMAT
standard

Types of Technical Documents

If you identified every type of technical document, the list would extend for pages, both because so many types exist and because the terminology is not standardized. The easiest way to differentiate technical documents is by audience and genre; each technical genre has its own distinctive characteristics:

- *Correspondence* includes all notes, memos, letters, and forms of electronic mail. Notes and memos are intended for internal readers, while letters and electronic mail are generally for external readers. Correspondence is discussed in detail in Chapter 18.

- *Sales, marketing, and promotional material* is intended for external readers (the customers) or for sales representatives who work with customers. The kind of precise diction and specific technical detail needed to make these documents successful is presented in Chapters 5, 10, 11, and 12.

- *Directions and manuals,* prepared for both internal and external readers, standardize everything from the operation of manufacturing equipment to procedures for personnel practices. Every product, whether for the commercial or consumer market, should be accompanied by technical documents to direct assembly, guide operation, recommend maintenance, and troubleshoot common problems. Chapter 13 discusses directions and manuals in detail.

- *Reports*, for both internal and external audiences, may be brief and informal or extend to lengthy, formal documents. Reports fall into several broad categories: research, periodic activity, finance, personnel, decision making, and so on. General guidelines for short reports are presented in Chapter 14, while formats for formal reports are discussed in Chapter 15.

- *Proposals* written for internal audiences are often brief and informal, providing recommendations for anything from equipment purchase to staff reorganization. Lengthy, formal proposals are most frequently for external audiences, asking for approval or acceptance of a variety of services and products. Chapter 16 introduces guidelines for preparing proposals.

Who Are Technical Readers?

The reader of a technical document might be the person in the office next to yours, a first-year chemistry student, the general manager of a manufacturing company, a technician repairing the heating system, a dairy farmer, or a nurse-practitioner—in fact, a technical reader might be anyone.

However, the reader of the technical documents you write will seldom be a person just like you, a person whose education, experience, and responsibilities are identical to yours. Because the backgrounds of most of your readers will differ from yours, you need to identify and assess your audience, to guarantee that your content, organization, and diction communicate most effectively.

Motivation, reading level, education, experience, role, and environment affect readers who fit into any one of the following categories: experts, technicians, professional nonexperts, students, general readers, and children. All of these factors are discussed in detail in Chapter 3.

The Writer's Role

Technical writers fall into two broad categories:

- professional technical writers, whose primary job is writing
- technical professionals, who write as part of their job

Ideally, these people have dual expertise, as writers and as subject specialists. More frequently, however, professional writers are hired because they write well and have the ability to learn the technical background. Conversely, technical professionals are hired because of their subject expertise, with the hope that they know (or can learn) something about writing. This book has been written for both kinds of writers.

Most people in professional positions write as part of their job. Managers and supervisors need to write effective letters, memos, and reports. Technical experts who cannot communicate effectively are not an asset to any organization. They need to be able to prepare memos, procedures, and a variety of reports. Successful professionals see writing as an integral part of their job, not as something extra that they have to fit in. They assume responsibility for their own writing, from organizing ideas to final proofreading of documents.

In large organizations as well as in fields that expect publication of ongoing research, people's reputations may be built largely on their writing. Technical expertise is not sufficient. Indeed, technical expertise sometimes takes a back seat to effective communication: the higher a person is promoted, the more writing and public speaking are required.

People who work as professional technical writers are part of an important network that supports the products or services of an organization. The roles of professionals vary from organization to organization, but generally fall into one of three broad models:

- In some organizations, a professional writer is totally responsible for a writing project, from collection of data through publication of the document.
- Sometimes professional writers work as members of a team that includes technical experts, all of whom collaborate on one long-term project at a time.
- Other organizations assign writers to sections of projects—several chapters in a manual or one book in a series—with a managing or supervising editor overseeing the project.

Writers who are totally responsible for a project must be able to work with the support personnel who fulfill the responsibilities of editing, graphic design, word processing/typing, and publication. In a very small company, a writer may take on many of these support functions. In a team model, writers regularly coordinate their work with other members of the team, with the writer usually assuming primary responsibility for working with editors, designers, word processing (wp) operators, and printers. Sometimes a project or communications group manager takes care of some of these tasks. In the third model, writers have little responsibility beyond completing their own assignment and sometimes working with editors. Group supervisors and managers coordinate work with the designers, wp operators, and printers.

Professional technical writers are generally responsible for creating new documents; compiling, organizing, and editing technical notes into a publishable form; and updating existing documents. In order to do these tasks well, not only should they have the aptitude for understanding and explaining technical information, but they should also be able to establish friendly working relationships with the organization's technical experts. Technical professionals who communicate effectively usually achieve more career success and have greater job satisfaction than those who have only technical expertise.

In 1982 *Technical Communication* published results of a study about the importance placed by technical professionals on effective communication skills:

- An overwhelming 91% stated that their writing was either "important" or "very important" to their jobs. . . .
- More than 28% of the respondents spend between 40% and 100% of their time writing, and 42% spend between 20% and 40% of their time writing. . . .
- 73% responded that they have spent more time writing [as their responsibilities increased]. . . .
- About 80% said that the ability to communicate has helped in their advancement. . . .
- Almost all (97%) of the respondents rated speaking skills either "very important" or "important" to their jobs.[3]

As this survey shows, you gain tremendous professional advantages if you write and speak effectively. The discussions and assignments in this text are designed to help you develop these important skills.

Inquiries and Assignments

Discussion Questions

1. What are the most common types of technical writing in your career area?
2. How frequently in your work or study do you read technical materials? Select and bring to class specific examples of materials that you define as technical. What characteristics of technical writing can you find in the materials?
3. What has been the focus of your own on-the-job writing or the technical writing in your academic field: the quality of writing, the accuracy of technical content, audience awareness, or speed in preparing material?

4. What have been the attitudes toward writing and writers in organizations or companies where you have worked?

5. What areas of your own technical writing would you like to improve? Explain why.

Individual and Group Exercises

1. With a group of classmates who have the same academic major, take an informal poll of faculty members in your department. What policies, practices, and attitudes do department faculty have toward students learning to write well? Are technical assignments evaluated on the clarity and effectiveness of communication or just on their technical merit? What do faculty members write as part of their professional responsibilities? Create additional questions to ask. Compile your results for a brief oral or written presentation.

   If several disciplines are represented by the groups in your class, you can compare the policies, practices, and attitudes among departments.

2. a. Read the following piece of historical technical writing and identify any aspects that you believe are and are not characteristic of contemporary technical writing.

THEATER ACOUSTICS

Vitruvius (A.D. First Century)

Voice is a flowing breath of air, perceptible to the hearing by contact. It moves in an endless number of circular rounds like the innumerably increasing circular waves which appear when a stone is thrown into smooth water, and which keep on spreading indefinitely from the center unless interrupted by narrow limits or by some obstruction which prevents such waves from reaching their end in due formation. When they are interrupted by obstructions, the first waves, flowing back, break up the formation of those which follow.

In the same manner the voice executes its movements in concentric circles; but while in the case of water the circles move horizontally on a plane surface, the voice proceeds horizontally but also ascends vertically by regular stages. Therefore, as in the case of the waves formed in the water, so it is in the case of the voice: the first wave, when there is no obstruction to interrupt it, does not break up the second or the following waves, but they all reach the ears of the lowest and highest spectators without an echo.

Hence the ancient architects [i.e., the Greeks], following in the footsteps of nature, perfected the ascending rows of seats in theaters from their investigations of the ascending voice, and by means of the canonical theory of mathematicians and that of the musicians, endeavored to make every voice uttered on the stage come with greater clearness and sweetness to the ears of the audience. For just as musical instruments are brought to perfection of clearness in the sound of their strings by means of bronze plates or horn sounding boards, so the ancients devised methods of increasing the power of the voice in theaters through the application of the science of harmony. . . .

In accordance with the foregoing investigations on mathematical principles, let bronze vessels be made, proportionate to the size of the theater, and let them be fashioned that, when touched, they may produce with one another the notes of the fourth, the fifth, and so on up to the double octave. Then, having constructed niches in between the seats of the theater, let the vessels be arranged in them, in accordance with musical laws, in such a way that they nowhere touch the wall, but have a clear space all round them and room over their tops. . . . On this principle of arrangement the voice, uttered from the stage as from a center and spreading and striking against the cavities of different vessels as it comes in contact with them, will be increased in clearness of sound and will make a harmonious note in unison with itself. . . .

Somebody will perhaps say that many theaters are built every year in Rome and that in them no attention at all is paid to these principles; but he will be in error, from the fact that all our public theaters made of wood contain a great deal of boarding, which must be resonant. . . . But when theaters are built of solid materials like masonry, stone, or marble, which cannot be resonant, then the principles of the resonator must be applied.[4]

    b. What modern technical professionals would be concerned with theater acoustics? How could you determine whether the concepts presented in this explanation are accurate? Would modern technical experts be interested in other ancient methods for improving theater acoustics?

3. a. Identify at least two technical aspects for each of the following subjects.
    b. Identify a realistic audience for an article about each technical aspect of the subject. Explain why this audience would want or need to read the information.

rainbows	tricycles	daisies	dreams
golf balls	Renaissance paint	trout	perfume
hot dogs	poetry	pup tents	wire cable
light bulbs	eggs	coffee	tires
jogging shoes	ballet	peanut butter	plastic film

4. Examine the following abstract from a scientific article. Identify characteristics that distinguish this material as a sample of technical writing intended for expert professionals.

FIRE AND NUTRIENT CYCLING
IN A DOUGLAS-FIR/LARCH FOREST
NELLIE M. STARK
School of Forestry, University of Montana,
Missoula, Montana 59812 USA

Abstract. Twenty control burns performed with a wide range of fuel loadings and moisture conditions were used to study the effectiveness of old fuel reduction under standing Douglas-fir/larch forest. This paper reports the influence of burning on nutrient retention and loss from the soil. Sixty % of the fires were successful in reducing residual fuels with no accelerated loss of nutrients below the root zone. Net losses of Ca^{+2} and Mg^{+2} occurred below the root zone when soil surface temperatures exceeded 300°C, but were insignificant when soil surface temperatures remained below 200–300°C. No other elements were lost (net) from the soil as a result of burning. Precipitation on control soils delivers as much Ca^{+2} as is normally lost below the root zone in the absence of fire. Iron concentration in the soil water is a good indicator of the intensity of burn. The hotter the fire, the less iron in the soil water as a result of the alkaline pH. Ash shows a definite pattern of nutrient release under the influence of precipitation. Homogeneous subsamples of litter showed predictable nutrient losses when ignited at different temperatures. Overland flow and surface erosion are of little significance on this soil type. Decomposition of Douglas-fir litter was only slightly more rapid on hot burned substrates than on control (unburned) substrates. When the biological life concept was applied to this soil, it showed that this soil is young and capable of withstanding many years of cyclic intensive burns.

Key words: Ash; biological life concept; decomposition; Douglas-fir/larch; fire; nutrients; Montana.[5]

5. The memo displayed in Example 1.1 was submitted as a weekly progress report about project activities. It is typical of the reports and memos produced by William Jackson, associate engineer. Because Mr. Jackson is always extremely careful to doublecheck his content for accuracy, he is surprised that his semiannual review identifies his writing as a block to rapid advancement. Examine the memo and explain whether you agree with the assessment by Mr. Jackson's supervisor. What advice would you give Mr. Jackson?

Example 1.1

September 26, 1986

```
TO:       Mark Hager
FROM:     William Jackson WJ
SUBJECT:  Project Update


     We're on schedule except for setting up
the grinding wheels because they haven't
been recieved yet and calibrating the tools
'cause new master blocks haven't been uncrated
and Joe Simons has been out all week with
the flu.

     Next week everything should be done.

     The electrician is scheduled on Tuesday
to install new lines and wire the equipment.
```

Assignments

1. Locate samples of technical and creative writing about the same subject. The following examples offer suggestions:

   | Gothic architecture | architecture textbook | *The Hunchback of Notre Dame* |
   | white sharks | ichthyology journal | *Jaws* |

   Prepare a compare-and-contrast paper, oral presentation, or visual that identifies and illustrates the primary distinctions.

2. Locate samples of technical writing from your career area that fulfill most or all of the characteristics of technical writing discussed in this chapter. Prepare an analytical paper that identifies and illustrates the nature of technical writing in your career area.

3. Individually or in small groups, prepare a brief questionnaire to survey technical writers in local companies to compare publication processes. (*Note:* Chapter 7 introduces practical suggestions about constructing a questionnaire.) You might want to focus on the publication process itself or on the relationship between various individuals who have roles in the publication process—writers, wp operators, engineers, artists, editors, managers.

   With other students in your class, decide who will contact which companies (so local firms are not inundated with requests). If you attend a school that has several sections of technical writing, your instructor might suggest that your class focus on one company.

   Compile the data you collect and organize an oral or written presentation to share your results.

2   Communication Model and Writing Processes

YOU ALREADY KNOW from the discussion in Chapter 1 that the major elements in any writing situation are *subject*, *audience*, and *writer*. One thing that distinguishes technical writing from other types of writing is the relationship among these three elements. As a writer explaining technical subjects, you have an obligation to make the subject clear. You are usually writing to inform, through definition and explanation. Only occasionally do you insert your own opinions—when you are making recommendations or writing a proposal. Even then, your feelings about either the subject or the audience should be subordinate to your concern that the reader understand the material. Persuasion does exist as an element of technical writing because the design and organization of the document should encourage the audience to read it.

One way to learn more about your own writing process involves examining relationships among the subject, audience, and writer. Figure 2.1 illustrates the complex connections. Initially a writer establishes the relationship with the subject by asking, "What do I know about the subject? What is my purpose?" Nearly simultaneously the writer asks, "What does the reader need to know?" The response to this question leads the writer to think about other characteristics of the intended audience: education, employment experience, attitude. The writer can then select content and begin organizing the material by asking, "What is the most appropriate format for the document?" The answer helps determine the format and presentation of the document.

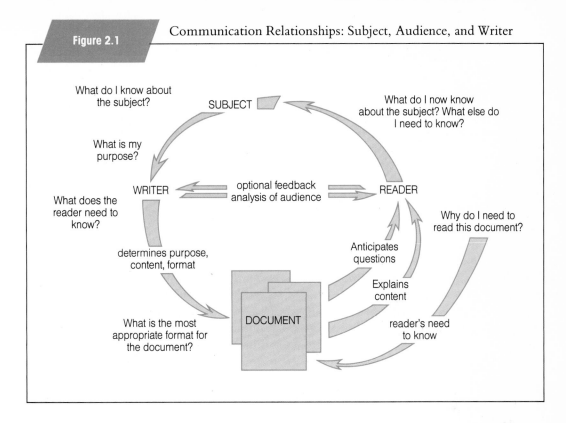

Figure 2.1 — Communication Relationships: Subject, Audience, and Writer

When a document is completed, a prospective reader will ask, "Why do I need to read this?" The reader needs a purpose: to gather information or to complete a task. After reading the document, a reader should be able to answer, "What do I now know about the subject? What else do I need to know?" At this point, a reader can give feedback to the writer that might influence future documents or correspondence.

The Writer's Process

What do writers do when they write? The writing process used to be described as three linear stages: prewriting, composing, and revising, as shown in Figure 2.2. Researchers who study the writing process used these linear stages to describe what happened when a person sat down to write, but they knew the stages were an inadequate and oversimplified model of what actually happened.

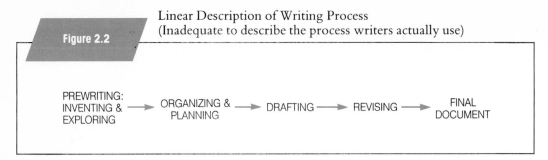

Linear Description of Writing Process
(Inadequate to describe the process writers actually use)

Figure 2.2

PREWRITING: INVENTING & EXPLORING → ORGANIZING & PLANNING → DRAFTING → REVISING → FINAL DOCUMENT

However, improved research techniques have been able to chart a writer's actions and ideas throughout the writing process. Carefully watching and listening to writers while they write has dispelled any notion that the process is linear. Researchers listen to writers talk about their own writing process and pay attention when they say things like this: "Yes, I do all those things, but I usually do them more than once." "You know, lots of times while I'm in the middle of writing, I'll get a terrific idea—something I've never thought of before, something that's not part of my outline." "I'll write one word and immediately know it's not quite right so I'll scratch it out and write a new one." These people are saying that the stages do not happen consecutively; rather, they recur and overlap in a multistrand spiral process, as shown in Figure 2.3.

The Stages of Writing

Let's explore what actually happens in each of these stages.

Inventing and Exploring. During the initial stages a writer engages in a period of problem solving: a series of mental activities to identify and investigate the subject as well as to consider the audience. Writers really do talk to themselves sometimes, listening to how something sounds or trying another way to solve a problem. During this stage writers may assess their knowledge, read and review available background references, ask questions and discuss ideas, conduct experiments, and take notes. Thinking about options and pondering the approach are part of this stage, one that writers return to many times while preparing a document.

Organizing and Planning. Planning begins when a writer reaches some decisions about the content and organization of the document. Initially, a writer

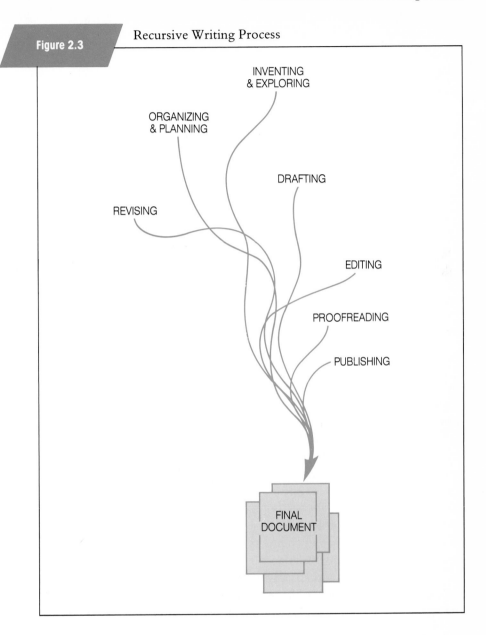

Figure 2.3   Recursive Writing Process

INVENTING & EXPLORING

ORGANIZING & PLANNING

DRAFTING

REVISING

EDITING

PROOFREADING

PUBLISHING

FINAL DOCUMENT

defines the subject and determines the document's scope. A writer also examines the document's objective and carefully analyzes the intended audience. Decisions are tested in outlines and diagrams to determine if the selection and sequence of material are logical, suitable for the audience, and faithful to the purpose of the document.

The first two stages are intertwined: A writer thinks, makes a decision, then thinks some more. These elements remain the same, but there are some other variations. Sometimes the exploration and problem solving are more productive when done with other people; brainstorming with someone else often generates ideas and approaches that an individual might not come up with alone. Decision making, especially on lengthy projects, also sometimes involves others. The amount of time a writer spends in exploring and planning also varies. Exploration for a short letter or memo may take only a few minutes before a writer begins to make decisions.

Writers preparing brief, rapidly written notes appear to use a linear process, but even though the exploring, planning, and revising take place inside their heads, they still use all the steps in the recursive process. For a lengthy document such as an operation manual, a writer may take days—working with the equipment, interviewing engineers, examining schematics and procedures, and reviewing the company style guide. The recursive nature of writing is more evident in a longer and more complex project.

Technical writers are almost always under time pressure. Despite temptations to jump right into the actual drafting, they should not skimp on exploring and planning. Before drafting, writers should have made decisions about content, organization, visuals, and overall design. Time thus spent reduces both drafting time and changes during revising and editing.

Drafting. The next stage involves writing the text and preparing the visuals. Writers have many different ways of approaching this stage. Some write bits and pieces of the draft during the planning stage, recording key sentences they don't want to forget. When their planning seems to be done, they take these ideas, develop them, and fill in the spaces between. A few writers sit down and compose the draft from beginning to end without interruption. Others study their outlines and notes, then set them aside and start to write, checking their planning materials only when they seem to get stuck. For other writers, the outlines are the framework of their draft, and they follow those outlines closely. Some writers work slowly, pondering and polishing every phrase and sentence and paragraph as they go along.

Drafting used to be done with pens and pencils on pads of legal-sized yellow paper. Now you're more likely to see writers producing their drafts on a computer. Does using a computer for writing have advantages? Yes, if a writer realizes that there are also constraints. A computer does not make someone a better writer; however, word processing can save significant time in both drafting and revising. While revising, a writer can move chunks of text to other locations in the document and material can easily be inserted or deleted, enabling a writer to capture fleeting ideas and polish word choices. Most people find that revising even that first, very rough draft (called

Q.A.D.—quick and dirty) from a typed copy is much easier than working from scratched-up handwritten pages. Word processing also gives the writer a clean, corrected copy, without the burden of retyping the entire document.

Drafting is not an isolated stage. Writers are involved in ongoing exploration for just the right words and phrases. Because writers also replan as they see a draft evolving in a different direction from their original plan, drafting overlaps with the next stage, revising.

Revising. During the revision stage, a writer reads and rereads a draft critically to examine choices in content, structure, organization, and design. A writer can add, delete, and rearrange material in order to produce a more effective document. Many writers begin revising almost as soon as they start their draft. Ideally, a writer composes the draft and then sets it aside for a while before thoroughly revising it.

Some computer software programs aid revision by scanning a document and giving data that a writer can use to make revision decisions. For example, by identifying overuse of passive voice or calculating readability scores, a computer can help a writer to eliminate some passive constructions or adjust factors such as sentence length that may affect readability.

Some writers like computer software that uses the initial sentence of each paragraph in a document to create the draft of a summary for the document. The summary will be accurate if the initial topic sentence in each paragraph reflects the content—*and* if the paragraphs themselves are in a logical sequence. If the subjects in the summary don't have the same focus, the document may not be unified. Likewise, if the flow from one idea to the next in the summary is not smooth, the coherence may need improvement. Even writers without sophisticated software can check their work using the same technique.

Beyond the benefits of word processing, using computer software to identify problems in spelling or syntax is smart, primarily because it frees a writer to do the kind of revising and editing that computers cannot yet do. But computer software cannot do the most important thing that writers do: think. A writer, not a computer, must deal with the critical analysis and substantive editing that focuses on content and organization.

Editing. Editing generally refers to the identification—and sometimes the correction—of inconsistencies and errors in a draft. Writers can edit their own drafts; in these situations, editing and revising have many similarities. However, editing is a broader function than revising and is frequently done by someone other than the writer. Many organizations have full-time editors who perform various levels of editing. Sometimes these editorial functions are lumped together in the single role of "editor." Large organizations often separate the editorial function into discrete tasks that can be performed by different people according to their respective levels of experience and expertise.

One of the most complete edit systems identifies nine separate types of editing that technical documents may need:

- substantive edit—reviews the content for organization and consistency
- policy edit—assures that institutional policies are enforced
- screening edit—corrects language and figure errors to minimal level of acceptance
- language edit—corrects grammar, punctuation, usage, sentence structure
- integrity edit—matches text references to corresponding figures, tables, references, footnotes, appendixes
- format edit—establishes consistency in "macro" physical elements such as headings, fonts, page design
- mechanical style edit—establishes consistency in "micro" physical elements such as symbols, citations, numerals
- copy clarification edit—provides clear instructions to the compositor and graphic artist
- coordination edit—deals with the administrative aspects in publishing technical documents[1]

In a very small organization, a writer is responsible for all of these levels of edit. A writer in such a situation includes screening edit, language edit, and substantive edit as part of revision and designates coordination edit as an administrative task.

In many organizations, as you can see in the nine levels of edit above, editors are not necessarily responsible for the technical accuracy of a document. Accuracy is the responsibility of the writer. In situations in which the editor does make changes in content, final approval for the changes usually remains with the writer.

Proofreading. The proofreading stage is primarily mechanical, checking a document for typographical inconsistencies and errors. In a single-writer organization, this stage includes integrity edit.

Differences between Writing Processes

Although the writing process divides into broad general stages of inventing and exploring, organizing and planning, drafting, revising, editing, proofreading, and publishing, individual writers differ in the time they spend in various stages, in the sequence of the stages, and in their thought processes. When you find a writing process that works for you, examine it, use it, develop it. Once you're confident of an approach, branch out and try another one. If it works, integrate it with your writing practices.

Writers demonstrate a variety of habits, concerns, and working procedures that identify them as skillful. Research during the past decade has delineated differences between skilled and unskilled writers, as summarized in Figure 2.4. Remember that different rhetorical situations—the influences of subject, audience, and writer—place different demands on a writer.

Unskilled writers frequently fail to recognize the integrated nature of the writing process. They don't know what the writing process involves, and they often see writing as linear instead of recursive. Unskilled writers tend to spend insufficient time in exploring and planning; instead they rush directly to drafting. They seldom sufficiently consider the reader or the complexities of purpose and audience. They think of revision as error correction, focusing primarily on mechanics and grammar.

In contrast, skilled writers recognize the importance of exploring and planning, using this time to investigate the subject and organize the information. For skilled writers, revising is recursive, occurring both during the drafting and again when the draft is complete. They are concerned with accuracy of the material as well as suitability of the presentation for the intended audience.

Constraints in the Technical Writing Process

Even skilled technical writers have constraints that seldom affect writers who do not work with technical subjects in business, industry, government, or research. These restrictions affect the process of creating a document as well as the actual content.

Time Constraints

Technical writers work within time limits, which are often set by people unaware of the demands of either the writing or the technical aspects of the project. Time considerations and deadlines limit every stage of the writing process. Technical writers acknowledge that levels of professionally acceptable work exist, and they develop priorities in deciding which projects deserve

Figure 2.4	The Composing Processes of Unskilled and Skilled Writers

Stage	Unskilled Writers	Skilled Writers
INVENTING AND EXPLORING	Do not consider exploring useful or important	Consider exploring activities useful and helpful
	Spend little time exploring	Spend more time considering, contemplating
ORGANIZING AND PLANNING	Typically make no plans before they write	Accompany their planning with note-taking, sketching, diagramming
	Prefer not to outline	
	Develop plans as they write	
DRAFTING	Write in a way that imitates speech	Write in a way that is less like speech
	Write without concern for the reader	Show sensitivity to reader
	Are preoccupied with mechanical matters	Spend more time in drafting
	Do not pause very much	Frequently stop to rescan, reread, reflect
	Do not rescan or reflect	Respond to all aspects of writing situation—audience, purpose, content, organization
	Focus on topic alone, not the entire writing situation	
REVISING AND EDITING	Either revise very little or only at the surface and word level	Either revise very little or revise extensively at sentence/ paragraph levels
	See revising mainly as "error hunting"	Are more concerned with accuracy and reader appeal
	Stop revising when they feel they have not violated any rules	See revising as recursive and ongoing
	Spend so much time and energy on changing spelling and punctuation that they lose sight of larger problems	
	Often see revising as "making a clean copy"	
PROOFREADING	Often overlook errors	Proofread with care

Source: Modified from Allan A. Glatthorn, *Writing in the Secondary Schools: Improvement through Effective Leadership* (Reston, Virginia: National Association of Secondary School Principals, 1981), 5. Used with permission of NASSP.

the most time. Some projects may require extensive exploring and planning or time-consuming revising and editing, while others may need no more than cursory revisions, incorporated as the drafting proceeds.

Subject and Format Constraints

The subject for a technical document is usually predetermined. However, technical writers face the challenge of focusing on details appropriate for the intended audience and presenting what may be uninspiring information in an interesting, or at least useful, manner.

Technical writers are seldom provided with a specific approach for a document. Rather, they must narrow the subject, select and organize content, and then determine the limitations of the document. In order to do this, technical writers must assess the audience's needs and identify their purpose for reading the document.

Within this seeming freedom, however, technical writers often must present information in a prescribed format, one specified by the organization or expected by readers. Prescribed formats ease some of a writer's decisions about the organization of a document.

Considerations of Audience

Sometimes a technical document is prepared for an audience in which everyone has similar education, experience, and expectation. Frequently, however, the readers of a document have varied backgrounds as well as different reasons for reading the document.

Technical writers also must write for audiences who have discrepancies between their organizational role and their technical knowledge. For example, a business manager might have an advanced degree in management but have little expertise in the technical field of the company.

Both these constraints—multiple audiences and discrepancies between organizational role and technical knowledge—impose restraints on technical writers. As a result, they have to make decisions about the level of technical complexity, organization, diction, and design, attempting to respond to the needs of a variety of readers.

Composite Authorship

A single document may be prepared by a "composite" author—several writers who work on the same document, each responsible for a section. Occasionally composite authorship requires two writers to collaborate on the same section. Writing as a member of a group or team is usually much more difficult than writing as an individual because people approach writing in different ways.

When you work with a partner on a writing project, you need to work closely at certain stages of the process. You will probably find the exploring stage easier to do individually. Then meet with your partner to discuss your perceptions and plans. Your joint planning will save a great deal of later work and avoid the problem of trying to combine two drafts into one document. Most writers draft a document individually, although some writing teams do work together at this stage. The revising, however, should be a joint effort, requiring more compromise on style than on content or organization (if the planning was done carefully). The extra effort required in team writing will result in a document that is consistent in format, amount of detail, and style.

A group leader or manager is important in any major collaborative writing project because disagreements may arise about everything from the selection and sequence of content to the structure of individual sentences. At least one person needs to have an overview of the project to avoid duplication of effort and inconsistencies in format and style. A group leader can also run meetings that help establish a unified perception of the task and provide a sense of how one part relates to the project as a whole.

Composite authorship requires good listening skills. You need to listen to what others in the group have to say, examining ways to produce the best possible document. Collaboration and compromise are essential. Problems resulting from composite authorship—and possible solutions—are summarized in Figure 2.5.

Constraints in Data Collection

Technical writers are often dependent on other people not only for the time constraints imposed on a writing project but also for the information needed to prepare a document. Consequently, technical writers must be skillful in interviewing as a primary method of collecting data. (Chapters 7 and 20 provide guidelines for conducting successful interviews.)

Figure 2.5 Composite Authorship: Problems and Solutions

Problems from Composite Authorship	*Ways to Avoid or Eliminate Problems From Composite Authorship*
Varying perceptions in interpreting the subject	Group meetings, with decisions by project manager
Duplication of effort	Careful assignment, supervision, and monitoring of tasks
No sense of how individual task relates to overall project; no sense of overall progress	Regular progress reports distributed to all project members accompanied by update from project manager
Inconsistencies in style	Overall editing of entire document using standardized style guide

In many situations, writers prepare documents about prototype equipment and brand-new procedures. In these situations, writers often role-play the end user, collecting information by learning to operate the equipment before writing about it.

Approaching the Writing Process

Writing is easier for you to draft and for your reader to understand if you use a process that provides the best opportunity for producing effective documents.

The following stages, part of the recursive process discussed earlier in this chapter, provide a way to overcome the constraints faced by many technical writers:

1. Inventing and exploring
   - define the problem in context
   - examine creative alternatives

134.251

2. Organizing and planning
   - establish the document's purpose and scope
   - assess the reader's needs
   - organize information

3. Drafting
   - write reader-based documents
   - design reader-based visuals
   - verify draft

4. Revising and editing
   - revise
   - proofread

5. Publishing
   - disseminate final draft
   - solicit reader response

You investigate a problem, identifying possible solutions and even creating new approaches. This section of the chapter focuses on creative thinking and problem-solving strategies that enable you to generate these fresh approaches.

Problem solving, like writing, is a recursive process that has overlapping stages:[2]

- recognizing and defining the problem

- formulating possible solutions (hypotheses) that may differ from traditional or conventional approaches; defer judgment

- gathering information and asking questions to support possible solutions

- testing and evaluating these solutions

- selecting and implementing the most appropriate, efficient solution with consideration for technical as well as interpersonal factors

Technical writers use two approaches in creating a document. In one, the writer works independently, assuming responsibility for exploring, planning, drafting, and perhaps even editing and publishing a document. In the other, the writer is a member of a group, a collaborator who shares the responsibility for one or more stages of the process. Figure 2.6 illustrates the broad spectrum between these two extremes. Realistically, the actual role of a writer in preparing any given document probably falls somewhere between the isolation of working independently and the pressure of working collaboratively. Regardless of the approach, writers benefit from interaction with others, exploring and testing ideas, theories, and assumptions.

Figure 2.6	Models for Dividing Responsibilities of Producing a Document

Writing Process	*Responsibilities of A Single Individual*	*Responsibilities of Many Individuals*
INVENTING AND EXPLORING	Writer originates ideas	Technical collaborator originates ideas
ORGANIZING AND PLANNING	Writer determines the content and organization	Technical and writing collaborators determine content and organization
DRAFTING	Writer drafts document	Writing collaborators draft the document
REVISING AND EDITING	Writer revises document independently; document must satisfy only the writer and intended audience	Revision is a collaborative process; document must satisfy writer, intended audience, technical collaborators, and writing collaborators
PUBLISHING	Writer oversees publication of the document	Collaborators and/or enablers oversee the publication of the document

Developing Questions and Dialogues

Whether writing independently or collaboratively, a writer needs to develop effective questioning techniques because nearly all problem solving involves questions directed either to the writer or to collaborators. Questions can be divided into two broad categories: convergent questions, which have only one correct answer, and divergent questions, which are open-ended and therefore more useful in problem solving.

Interacting with and questioning other people often help produce better documents. Each person approaches problems in a slightly different way; thus, divergent thinking provides a broader base for problem solving. Therefore, working in groups is sometimes more productive than working individually because the interaction stimulates suggestions that might not otherwise be made.

The following general guidelines will make your questioning more successful:

1. Identify in advance key topics for questions.
2. Ask direct, unambiguous questions, using simple language.
3. Allow sufficient time for answers.
4. Build on a respondent's answers by asking follow-up questions.

Writers can design questions with the help of a traditional taxonomy, a formal method of classification. Incorporating questions from each taxonomic level increases your chances of obtaining all the relevant information necessary to produce an effective document. One particularly well-known taxonomy developed by Benjamin Bloom[3] suggests six levels of questions:

1. *Knowledge* questions emphasize the recall of both specifics and abstractions. Such questions require recall of specialized terminology and symbols, quantifiable facts, conventions of organizing information, awareness of trends, knowledge of classification systems, evaluative criteria, methodology, principles, and theories.

Example   What conditions often mimic the symptoms of Alzheimer's disease, resulting in misdiagnosis?

2. *Comprehension* questions require responses that incorporate knowledge as well as understanding. Responses to comprehension questions can involve translation, interpretation, or extrapolation.

Example   Based on the symptoms and progress of the disease in this patient, what is your prognosis?

3. *Application* questions require specific applications of principles or theories.

Example   How can treating Alzheimer's disease patients with conventional and antidepressant drugs often postpone institutionalization?

4. *Analysis* questions emphasize the separation of objects, mechanisms, systems, organisms, operations, or ideas into the constituent parts, clearly establishing the relationship between these parts.

Example   Explain how the lack of an enzyme for synthesizing acetylcholine, a neurotransmitter, accounts for many characteristic symptoms of Alzheimer's disease.

5. *Synthesis* questions expect the response to focus on organizing or structuring the parts to form a unique whole. The response may either serve as an overall plan or explain a particular phenomena.

Example   Explain how the interplay of the cortex, the basal nucleus, and the region next to the hippocampus affects the progress of Alzheimer's disease.

6. *Evaluation* questions require responses that judge something's qualitative and quantitative value. Such questions examine internal elements for logic and consistency as well as external comparisons to establish the relation-

ship of the subject with accepted principles, theories, and works of recognized excellence.

Example   What areas of research into the causes for and treatments of Alzheimer's disease appear to be the most promising?

Although questions are useful for exploring a subject, dialogues are often more valuable, whether your documents result from individual or collaborative efforts. You can stimulate your writing with a series of real or imagined dialogues with a variety of people, as shown in Figure 2.7.

Using Problem-Solving Strategies

The questions and dialogues you use to identify and define your subject may raise additional questions and problems. In order to prepare an effective technical document, you need to focus on each specific problem so that you can solve it or at least offer possible alternatives. One way to approach problems is to borrow techniques from other successful problem-solving processes.

Quality Control Circles is a group problem-solving process used in many companies. Small groups of people doing similar work go through a training period and then meet regularly to identify, analyze, and solve problems connected to the work they do. Many companies have established Quality Control Circles, using work pioneered in Japan to improve productivity as well as employee involvement.

One of the initial strategies used in Quality Control Circles is also a formula frequently associated with journalism: 5W's plus H. These questions are effective for approaching any problem you're investigating:

WHO	Who is involved? Who should be involved?
WHAT	What is involved? What should be changed? What should remain the same?
WHEN	When should it be done? When is the most appropriate or convenient time?
WHERE	Where should it be done?
WHY	Why should it be done?
HOW	How should it be done?

This section of the chapter identifies several practical problem-solving strategies that you can use at any time during the writing process.

Brainstorming. A problem-solving technique that encourages you to suggest as many ideas as possible about a given problem or situation, brainstorming

Figure 2.7   Partners and Appropriate Questions for Dialogues
That Help Writers

Dialogue With . . .	First Know . . .	Then Ask . . .
YOURSELF	What do I already know about the subject and audience?	What is the purpose of the document? What aspects of the subject should I include?
INTENDED READERS	Who are the readers?	What do you want to know about the subject? Why are you reading this document?
REFERENCE SOURCES	What do I need from reference materials? What are the most current and reliable sources?	What are the key facts? What different views exist?
ENABLERS	Who are the enablers? How much help do I need from them?	Who is willing to brainstorm with me? Listen to my ideas? React to my drafts? Provide support (assuming part of work load, helping with background research, typing, reviewing)?
TECHNICAL COLLABORATORS	Who are my technical collaborators? Are they willing to work with me?	Is the document accurate? What is the best way to integrate different approaches and ideas?
WRITING COLLABORATORS	Who are my writing collaborators?	Who is responsible for which parts of the document? How will we integrate our different writing styles?
EDITORS	Who are my editors? What experience and expertise do they have?	Is the document well organized? Grammatically and mechanically accurate? Stylistically consistent?

emphasizes the quantity rather than the quality of ideas generated. You can brainstorm either independently on paper or in discussion with other people. For brainstorming to be successful, you should defer evaluation of the suggestions until all the ideas have been recorded.

Example   How will we save time and money by installing a word processor in every individual office?

- no erasing
- easy revisions
- writers can directly keyboard their own thoughts without going through another medium (handwriting, dictating)
- saves paper—no crumpled sheets fired into the wastebasket in frustration
- readable drafts—no trying to decipher hastily scratched handwriting
- if writer is a competent typist, the keyboarding can almost keep pace with thoughts so they are captured before they disappear

Enumeration. Listing specific characteristics about a subject is always helpful. Specialty enumeration identifies unique characteristics. Defect enumeration identifies faults or weaknesses. Desire enumeration identifies imaginative improvements. All three of these provide the basis for suggesting *functional improvements.*

Example   How does our current word processor compare with the updated model?

	Current *Word Processor*	*Improved* *Word Processor*
unique characteristics	user defined keys (limited to 10)	glossary function—unlimited entries
faults or weaknesses	slow scan in "search" function	easy to make mistakes in "merge" function (for form letters)
imaginative improvements	"sort" function (alphabetizing) clumsy; involves three documents	simplify print menu

Attribute listing. A problem-solving method that improves something by combining and/or adapting existing characteristics, attribute listing creates something new from something old. The process begins with listing the properties of the object that needs improving. Generally a matrix or chart is used to organize the attributes.

Example   How can a word processor be improved?

Item	*Attribute*	*Improvement*
keyboard	flat; attached to screen; foreign language and scientific symbols missing	raise to angle of 20°; make freestanding; add to alpha keys in conjunction with "control key" function
screen	reflects glare	make adjustable; use non-glare surface; consider various colors

Morphological analysis. Another problem-solving technique, morphological analysis, combines all kinds of attributes into a totally new solution or product. Just as in attribute listing, a matrix or chart is necessary to keep track of all the ideas. Morphological analysis usually involves the partition of a problem into its components. The solutions arise from entirely new combinations of these components.

Example   What factors should you consider when designing a storage case for floppy disks?

Material	*Shape*	*Opening*	*Internal Design*
plastic	cube	top	adjustable dividers
metal	rectangle	side slide	tabs or ears for labels
glass	cylinder	front slide	slots to hold disks separated and upright

Cause and effect analysis. A strategy recommended by Quality Control Circles, cause and effect analysis focuses on the causes of a particular problem. The initial causes are separated into four categories: machine, employee, material, and method. The causes can be expanded with additional headings.

Example   What causes the sector errors on the floppy disks?

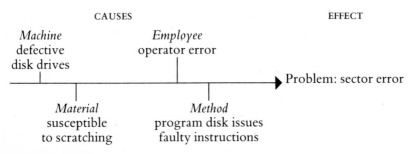

The problem-solving strategies discussed so far provide approaches to specific questions. Sometimes, however, not even the questions are clear and the problem needs a fresh approach. Three problem-solving strategies stimulate creative thinking that often results in entirely new perspectives. The first two strategies, tagmemics and bionics, are often used individually. The third strategy, synectics, is frequently used in group problem solving.

Tagmemics. Based on the idea that things are best understood when viewed from various perspectives, tagmemics provides a way to examine a problem as a particle (a thing in itself), as a wave (something that changes over time), and as part of a field (a component within a larger context).

Example	a particle (a thing in itself)	A word processing program is software that allows a writer to input, revise, print a document.
	a wave (a thing changing over time)	A flexible word processing program can be changed to meet the needs of individuals by the addition of user-selected glossaries and spelling lists.
	a field (a thing in its context)	A word processing program is one part of the involved process of publications.

Bionics. If you try to answer the question, "How would this problem be solved in nature?" you would be using bionics. For example, overproduction in a manufacturing environment is comparable to overpopulation in nature, where the concept of survival of the fittest assures the continuation of the most suitable or adaptable organisms. A comparable solution in manufacturing would raise quality control standards to assure survival of the fittest.

Example The following problems that could be approached through bionics illustrate the flexibility of this technique.

- How can word processors be simplified so the transition from typewriter to word processor will not deter purchases by insecure operators (especially small office and home users)?
- How should a neo-natal incubator be designed?
- How can a house maintain a constant temperature without mechanical HAC (heating/air conditioning)?
- What is the best nutrient or fertilizer for lettuce grown on a hydroponic farm?

Synectics. Synectics involves combining two unrelated ideas as a means of analyzing a particular problem. Utilizing a variety of techniques—including metaphors, analogies, role-playing, and simulations—synectics requires that you first define a particularly difficult problem. Then you put yourself into the problem by creating a metaphor or an analogy or by acting out a component of the problem.

Synectics encourages fantasy analogies—searching for the ideal solution; personal analogies—imagining you're the subject; direct analogies—comparing the subject to something concrete; and symbolic analogies—comparing the subject to an abstraction. Synectics establishes an understanding of the elemental nature of the problem.

You can, of course, return to any of these problem-solving strategies at any time during the writing process, knowing that you can develop effective solutions or at least alternatives for problems.

Before you begin planning and organizing the document, you need techniques to eliminate possible problems in the actual document.

Eliminating "Noise" in the Communication Process

A simple communication model, originally developed to describe the mechanics of telephone communication, depicts the elements of the communication process. It identifies "noise" or interference that affects a writer. A modified version of the model, in Figure 2.8, is valuable because it indicates areas that you as a writer can control.

The model identifies three types of "noise": semantic noise, mechanical noise, and psychological noise. Here's where your control comes in. Semantic noise results from incorrect choices in diction, sentence and paragraph structure, or overall organization of content in the document. You have control over all these elements of semantic noise. The second type of noise is mechanical, which refers to problems with the physical reproduction of the document. This includes errors in the mechanics of writing, such as punctuation, spelling, symbols, and capitalization. It also includes problems with layout and design that affect the document's appearance. You have direct or indirect control over all these elements of mechanical noise.

The third type of noise is psychological, the often unpredictable interference experienced by readers that reduces their ability to understand or respond to your message. You cannot possibly control all psychological noise because sometimes readers react in unexpected, unanticipated ways. However, you can reduce potential problems arising from psychological noise. For example, if you carefully analyze your readers, you will make a decision about whether they are positive, neutral, or negative toward the content of your document. If they are neutral, and particularly if they're negative, you should defuse their opposition before they have a chance to think of objections themselves; thus,

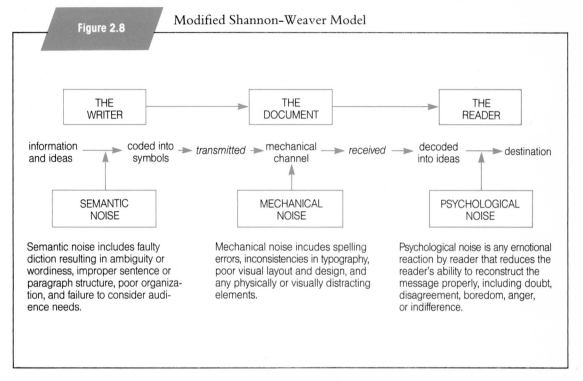

Figure 2.8   Modified Shannon-Weaver Model

Source: Modified from C. Shannon and W. Weaver, *The Mathematical Theory of Communication*
(Urbana, Illinois: University of Illinois Press, 1949).

you reduce some of the psychological noise. (Chapters 14–16, dealing with proposals and reports, discuss this idea in detail.) You can also avert another aspect of psychological noise, reader boredom, by making your writing stylistically interesting.

Since you can entirely control a document's semantic and mechanical noise and partially control the psychological noise, you are largely responsible for that document's success or failure.

Once you feel confident about the ideas you're working with, you can begin planning and organizing the document, moving toward drafting and then revising. Of course, you need to assess the readers' experience or knowledge about the subject, their attitudes, and their specific needs for the information in your document. Chapter 3 deals with audience analysis in detail. Details you will need to organize information are presented in Chapter 4. Suggestions to aid in revising appear in Chapter 5 as well as in the Handbook at the end of the text. Chapter 6 presents information useful for preparing visuals as well as the final version of the document.

Inquiries and Applications

Discussion Questions

1. Explain in which stage or part of the communication process you are most effective. Where do you need the most improvement?
2. During a recent in-house seminar on writing, employee participants were asked to identify one of their writing strengths. One woman said, "I pride myself on never rewriting anything. I get it right the first time." React to her statement.
3. What problem-solving strategies have you personally found useful in your writing?
4. Case situation: Marion Greene has just been assigned as project coordinator for the group update of a manual. The deadline for printing is in three weeks. What problems should she anticipate because the revisions will be made by several people and because of the time crunch?
5. What "psychological noise" would a writer have to anticipate in each of the following circumstances?
   a. a progress report to your section manager for a month when you failed to reach your quota
   b. a proposal for a new packaging design for your best-selling product to the director of marketing
   c. a grant proposal to a federal agency from a wealthy community

Individual and Group Exercises

1. Create a set of guidelines that "composite" authors could follow to avoid a piecemeal document.
2. Jennifer Allen, a technical writer, faces a problem in the production of a manual. The equipment prototype keeps changing; however, the engineers don't think it is their responsibility to inform her about the continuing changes, which obviously affect the operating manual. How should Ms. Allen approach the problem?
3. Choose a product that all the members of your group are familiar with—car tire, door lock, toaster oven, hair dryer. Then propose one change or improvement. Have each person in the group select a different problem-solving strategy and then develop a way to present your modifications.
4. Write a manual for operating a simple, everyday product—can opener, flashlight, bank automatic teller, hammer, screwdriver, recliner chair, alarm clock. When you have finished, analyze the *process* used to create this short manual.

Assignments

1. A personal error file is a notebook, file box, or computer file in which you record and categorize the types of errors you make in your own writing. Concentrate on the errors that appear regularly. Perhaps you often neglect to organize material in a logical manner or forget to define your subject before analyzing it. Maybe you habitually misspell a few particular words or use strings of prepositional phrases. Once you know the errors you are likely to repeat, make an index card (one card per error) with the correct spelling, the rule, or whatever, and post it above your desk.

2. Arrange to interview a professional technical writer or a technical professional who writes frequently. During the interview, inquire about both the person's approach to problem solving and the techniques used to control various types of "noise" that interfere with communication. Present your information in a brief written report.

3. Work with a group of classmates to develop a questionnaire and/or series of interview questions to ask of two groups: those who use typewriters and those who use word processors. Present your findings in a report in which you compile your data, discuss it, and draw conclusions.

4. Think about the way you go about writing and then describe your own writing process.

3   Writing for the Readers

"The manual is perfectly clear. We just need customers who can follow it."

Naturally this section of the report is difficult to understand; the concepts are complex. Anyway, it's intended for experts who are used to reading this stuff."

"Nothing is wrong with my memos. You should hire smarter employees who can understand what I write."

No one could get away with saying these things. Who is at fault when a reader doesn't understand a document—the writer or the reader? Rather than blame the reader, the solution is to improve the writing.

Whom you write for influences everything about the document—purpose, content, and manner of presentation. Nearly anything can be the subject of a technical document, but the treatment changes for different readers. For example, although the same polymer resin that is used to make baby bottles is also used for media storage disks, parents and pediatricians, media librarians and managers, chemists and production supervisors are interested in different aspects of the resin. A writer would have distinct reasons for addressing each audience and would adjust the document to particular readers.

Identifying the Purpose

As part of document planning, a writer identifies the *purpose*—both writer's and reader's. Having a clear sense of purpose helps a writer to decide about content and format as well as to focus on the intended audience. Generally, primary purposes of a document fall into these categories:

- to provide information for background or decision making
- to persuade to a particular thought or action
- to specify steps to complete a task

Writer's Purpose

Unlike a writer of imaginative stories or feature articles, a technical writer usually has narrow, clearly defined goals—to convey information in a simple and straightforward manner or to persuade through facts and logical comparisons. To identify the document's purpose, you need to ask these questions during the planning stage:

1. What information do I want the reader to gain?
2. What ideas or actions of the reader do I want to influence? What information will sway the reader?
3. How much detail will the reader require to complete a task?

The responses clearly identify the document's aim and help shape content. Next, you naturally consider why a reader wants or needs to use the document.

Reader's Purpose

The reader needs technical information for one of three primary reasons, although these may overlap:

- to gather information
- to make a decision
- to complete a task

For example, a journal article may provide an engineer with background information about a process that a competing firm is using. A division manager proposes a new product line after reading a report about market trends. A maintenance supervisor learns how to repair a piece of equipment by reading the manual that identifies step-by-step trouble-shooting procedures.

In order to determine the reader's purpose, you can role-play and ask several questions:

1. Why do I (the reader) need to read the document? What do I already know about the subject?
2. What background information do I expect to learn?
3. What information do I need to aid in decision making?
4. What facts and logical arguments can persuade me?
5. How much detail do I need in order to complete a task?

People may have both primary and secondary reasons for reading. For example, a reader's primary purpose might be to approve or reject a proposal; the secondary purpose might be to gather information about important areas for future research.

Once you have determined the document's purpose, you can identify and then analyze the reader. Knowing details about readers helps you adjust the document so that it responds to their needs.

Identifying the Readers

Before you analyze an audience, you must identify it. Every piece of technical writing has an *intended audience*—a specific individual (Elizabeth Jones, research and development [R and D] director) or a category of users (operators of the PDP-11 computer)—each with identifiable needs. Readers of technical documents address specific issues rather than general interests, so they usually can be more precisely identified than readers of most other types of writing. For example, people who read newspapers come from many professions and backgrounds; in contrast, those who read an operating manual probably have jobs that require them to operate the equipment.

Not only are the characteristics of a technical audience easier to identify than those of a general audience, but the technical audience is usually smaller. However, even when an intended technical audience is large (for example, people who control their diabetes through diet or students studying stress factors in engineering materials), the readers interested in the same document share goals.

Characteristics of Readers

To make matters more complex, different categories of readers often use the same document. A proposal for new product development could be read by people on various levels in several areas—finance, marketing, engineering, manufacturing. As a result, writers have to create material that simultaneously meets the needs of several categories of readers. This is most easily accomplished by directing different readers to particular sections of a report. For example, managers or executives would be most interested in the summary and the major recommendations, while engineers would be more interested in the application of these recommendations.

Frequently, writers must do more than identify individual or group readers; they must distinguish reader roles: initial reader, primary reader, and secondary reader. The *initial reader*, often a supervisor, directs the material to the appropriate primary reader(s). The *primary reader* is the person for whom the communication is intended, the one who will actually use the information. The *secondary reader* has an indirect interest in the communication, often being affected by the information or by decisions based on it. For example, a general contractor could be the initial reader of a request for a quotation on wiring a condominium's new community center. The primary reader would be the electrical contractor. The secondary readers might be the condominium's board of directors. In addition, many documents have *external readers* who are outside the immediate organization. In this case, the external reader might be a local building inspector.

Categories of Readers

All readers have two characteristics in common. First, they read technical documents for a specific reason; each of the purposes identified in the preceding section applies to each category of readers. Second, readers appreciate clear, direct writing far more than the fancy language some writers use to impress a reader or to inflate the importance of the ideas.

Technical writing is often intended for experts in technical fields; historically, experts have been the only audience. Today, however, technical writing also responds to a range of less specialized readers. These readers differ in their technical and general knowledge, which affects the concepts they understand, and in their reading ability, which affects the vocabulary as well as sentence and paragraph structure they can understand.

Experts have a theoretical as well as practical background that enables them to understand the most technical information in their own field. For example, engineers, ecologists, and economists all read technical material to maintain awareness of new theories and practices in their professions. These readers seldom have trouble with technical content or terminology in their own field. They are comfortable with abbreviations, jargon, and complex abstractions. They expect a straightforward presentation unencumbered by anecdotal examples. These readers usually have undergraduate or graduate degrees or equivalent experience in specialized fields. Because of their education and experience, they do not need detailed explanations of simple concepts and procedures. Experts are interested in both theory and practical application.

Technicians and *equipment operators* are important readers. Technicians frequently work in highly specialized fields and read complex material as part of their jobs, which often involve calibrating equipment or completing a process. Although their work is most often practical, many technicians have a theoretical understanding as well. In one company, chemical technicians helping to develop new applications for carbon fibers were able to contribute to the project because of their theoretical background in polymer chemistry. Technicians usually have less formal education than experts in the same field, perhaps a degree from a two-year or four-year college or on-the-job training.

Operators are concerned primarily with having clear procedures to follow. They seldom require background information and theory. For instance, the productivity of production workers in a corrugated paperboard plant would probably not increase by expanding the operation manual to include the rationale for material selection or the composition of surface treatment. Operators usually don't have a college education, but they do have on-the-job training. If operators understand how their role in the operation fits into the larger process, they'll often do a better job, but such information is usually communicated orally. Commonly, operations manuals include too much technical information. For example, wp operators need to know which keys to touch to get a desired function, but they do not need a description of microchips or binomial theory.

Professional nonexperts include many people who are interested in and required to read technical material that is outside their own professional specialty. Managers, supervisors, and executives most often fit this description. Sometimes these readers have technical backgrounds in fields related or peripheral to those they must read about. For example, a department manager in a computer firm may have a degree in business but little specialized knowledge of computers; however, much of the job-related reading may deal with computers. A manager of an engineering department may have earned an engineering degree twenty years ago or have a degree in industrial management, not engineering. These readers are often decision makers, so they must have a basic understanding of facts and concepts, even though they may not have an expert's level of knowledge.

Students, from those in advanced high school courses to those majoring in technical subjects in college, have a particular interest in technical material. They read as part of their academic preparation or their cooperative work-study programs. They are interested in learning facts and forming opinions to gain a broad background and eventually to become professionals in a specialized field. Subjects range from metal optics and metal fabricating to biomedical research and oceanography.

General readers, who read the daily paper as well as weekly and monthly news magazines, are also interested in science and technology. Many publications have special science writers who adapt technical information for the general reader, often someone lacking advanced formal education in the area an article is about, but who has an interest in how and why things happen. Recent science and technology articles in one large metropolitan daily newspaper have discussed plant genetics, ulcer treatments, and results of the Viking mission to Mars. (Chapter 17 focuses on writing for the general public.)

Children are seldom considered by technical writers in business and industry; however, children enthusiastically read science books and science magazines adapted to their level. Computer manuals, models, video games—many come with technical documents written especially for children. Children are also intrigued by answers to such questions as, Why do teeth get cavities? What makes thunder and lightning? How do computers work? A quick trip through a children's science museum suggests that children are legitimate technical readers.

These categories of readers or audience are not absolute; an individual reader often fits into more than one grouping. A polymer technician who is comfortable reading reports about composite materials may be a general reader or a professional nonexpert when reading about learning disabilities, astronomy, or kidney failure. A company vice-president is an expert in business matters, but may be a student reader in a flying class and a general reader regarding agronomy or microwaves.

Analyzing the Readers

Once you have identified the readers and fit them into a broad category, you can then analyze them more precisely. The classification of reader or audience falls under six broad, often interrelated headings:

1. Audience *attitude and motivation* establish how the reader feels about the subject and about using the document.
2. Audience *education* indicates how much formal knowledge the reader has.
3. Audience *experience* indicates how much on-the-job experience the reader has.
4. Audience *reading level* estimates the level of material the reader can handle without difficulty.
5. Audience *role* identifies the reader's position in an organization.
6. Audience *environment* for using the material identifies possible distractions.

The worksheet in Figure 3.1 focuses your audience analysis by asking specific questions about the audience and providing a summary of the responses. Initially, you will find it helpful to fill in the worksheet. The more frequently you use it, the more familiar you will become with the categories. Eventually, the audience analysis process, except for lengthy documents, will be entirely mental.

To understand how the audience analysis worksheet can help establish reader characteristics, let us examine a report prepared by Kate Greenough recommending a process camera for the graphics arts department in Industrial Imaging, Inc. A process camera (also called a graphic arts camera or a stat camera) performs various tasks regularly required in a graphic arts department. Ms. Greenough is asked by Sean Sullivan, her supervisor in the graphic arts department, to prepare this report for the manager of technical sales support, Marguerite Juarez. As part of her planning, Kate completes each section of the audience analysis worksheet:

Example

Document Subject and Purpose: *Purchase of a process camera*

Readers	Name	Category of Reader	Audience Purpose for Reading
initial reader	*Sean Sullivan*	*technician*	*information*
primary reader(s)	*Marguerite Juarez*	*expert*	*decision making*
	Henry Damon	*prof. non-expert*	*decision making*
secondary reader(s)	*Dan Lebeau*	*technician*	*information*

The report has no external readers, so Kate crosses out this category. She will submit the report to the initial reader, Sean Sullivan. However, he will pass it on to the primary reader, Marguerite Juarez, who will decide whether or not to follow the report's recommendation. The company treasurer, Henry

Audience Analysis Worksheet

Figure 3.1

Document Subject and Purpose: _____

Readers	Name	Category of Reader	Audience Purpose for Reading
initial reader	_____	_____	_____
primary reader(s)	_____	_____	_____
secondary reader(s)	_____	_____	_____
external reader(s)	_____	_____	_____

Audience Attitude and Motivation

     ▱ = initial   * = primary   △ = secondary   + = external

enthusiastic   negative and
and motivated   unmotivated

   ○ _____ ○ _____ ○ _____ ○ _____ ○

How can I persuade the primary audience to accept the recommendations
in this document? _____
_____

Education

	Highest Grade	Major or Specialty	Probable Focus of Education: theory	practice	both
primary reader(s)	_____	_____	_____	_____	_____
secondary reader(s)	_____	_____	_____	_____	_____
external reader(s)	_____	_____	_____	_____	_____

Professional Experience and Organizational Role

	Job Title	Years of Experience	Familiarity with Document Subject
primary reader(s)	_____	_____	_____
secondary reader(s)	_____	_____	_____
external reader(s)	_____	_____	_____

Environment Where Material Is Most Likely to be Used

	Location	Distractions	Time Constraints
primary reader(s)	_____	_____	_____
secondary reader(s)	_____	_____	_____
external reader(s)	_____	_____	_____

Damon, who approves all purchases over $5,000, is also a primary reader. Secondary readers include other staff members in the graphic arts department, such as Dan Lebeau.

Attitude and Motivation

Knowing about reader attitude and motivation helps you adjust the tone and organization of a document. For example, writers who are sensitive to reader attitude prevent or eliminate psychological noise (discussed in Chapter 2) that interferes with a reader's reception of information. An unmotivated reader may need more explanations and justifications than a highly motivated one, who needs less encouragement from the writer.

Assessing audience attitude helps you make adjustments in a document's organization to help the reader understand and agree with your reasoning. If the reader is enthusiastic about a project, you can feel confident in presenting recommendations initially and then supporting them in subsequent sections of the document. By contrast, if the reader might be opposed to possible recommendations, you can present the problem, discuss the alternatives, and then lead to the most appropriate and feasible solution, hoping the reader is swayed by your interpretation.

Analyzing reader attitude and motivation is relatively easy if you know the intended audience—individual or group—personally. However, many technical documents are prepared for groups of people the writer does not know. In these situations, you assess the probable attitudes and motivations of the readers by projecting their need for the information. A technician would be motivated to read a well-designed, accurate operations manual. However, the same technician would be less enthusiastic about a manual that discussed history of the equipment or theory of operation because such sections do not relate to the reader's purpose; the technician will not be motivated to read excess or peripheral material.

Because attitude and motivation are abstract qualities, and thus hard to quantify, your judgment and experience can best guide you. Estimating the primary and secondary readers' attitudes and motivation about a specific piece of written material can be recorded on a scale.

How do you make this assessment? Imagine an actual reader in your intended audience. How will this reader feel about the document—pleased, neutral, or negative? For example, a repair technician may be highly motivated in referring to the repair manual when equipment breaks down, but feel neutral-to-negative about having to look up repair procedures. A manager may feel neutral about the proposal he has to read and be completely unmotivated to begin.

When you are analyzing your audience, use the worksheet to record your perceptions:

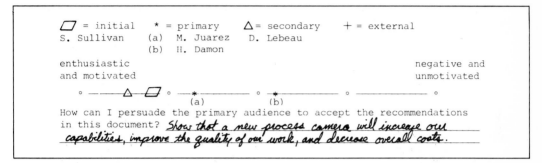

Note that as Kate Greenough planned her report recommending a process camera, she thought about how her various readers would react. Kate was most concerned with the attitude of the decision maker, Marguerite Juarez. She was also concerned with the attitude of Henry Damon, who approves all major expenditures. She was less interested in the attitude of Dan Lebeau because he isn't central to the decision making. Readers are more enthusiastic about material that is relevant to specific goals—gathering information, completing a task, or making a decision. If you can anticipate and successfully meet readers' needs, they will approach your material with a more positive attitude.

Education

If you can estimate a reader's level of knowledge, which is largely the result of formal education, you will be able to determine the appropriate vocabulary and content.

The reader's education indicates whether the intended audience has a practical understanding (acquired in vocational-technical training) or a theoretical understanding (acquired in professional or academic training). Some readers might have gained all their background through apprentice programs or on-the-job training. The following example includes several categories of readers with different educational backgrounds, yet all are interested in the subject of medicine:

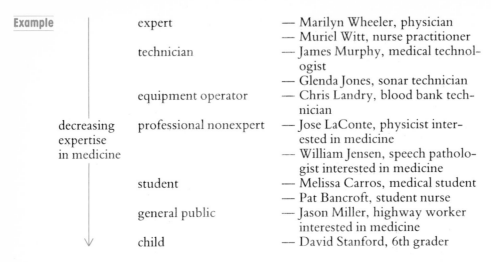

Example

	expert	— Marilyn Wheeler, physician
		— Muriel Witt, nurse practitioner
	technician	— James Murphy, medical technologist
		— Glenda Jones, sonar technician
	equipment operator	— Chris Landry, blood bank technician
decreasing expertise in medicine	professional nonexpert	— Jose LaConte, physicist interested in medicine
		— William Jensen, speech pathologist interested in medicine
	student	— Melissa Carros, medical student
		— Pat Bancroft, student nurse
	general public	— Jason Miller, highway worker interested in medicine
	child	— David Stanford, 6th grader

Writers should be able to identify the minimal education necessary for particular jobs. While completing the audience analysis worksheet, estimate three characteristics about the reader's education: highest grade completed, program major, and focus—theoretical or practical—to help you select material that is appropriate for the reader.

In preparing her recommendations about the process camera, Kate Greenough summarizes what she knows about her readers' education: Marguerite Juarez has a B.A. in graphic design and an M.B.A. in marketing; Henry Damon has both a B.S. and an M.S., in accounting; Dan Lebeau has an associate degree in commercial art.

Example

	Highest Grade	Major or Specialty	Probable Focus of Education: theory	practice	both
primary reader(s)	18	design/marketing			✓
	16	accounting			✓
secondary reader(s)	14	art		✓	

Professional Experience

A reader's professional experience indicates degree of awareness of factors that may influence reactions to a memo, letter, report, or manual. Some factors involve knowledge of day-to-day activities and operations at an individual company, such as delays in manufacturing or changes in personnel.

An experienced professional is more likely to be aware of corporate policies and to understand the influence of different personalities in support or opposition of a document's recommendations. A more important part of professional experience, however, involves the reader's level of expertise in the subject of the document. This includes the reader's level of responsibility, years of professional experience, and familiarity with the field, including new developments.

Although estimating professional experience—and thus, the reader's ability to understand the information and its practical application—is difficult, you can generalize about the amount needed to hold a job. The primary benefit of such information is the confidence the writer derives from selecting appropriate vocabulary, technical complexity, and format.

The audience analysis worksheet helps you summarize what you know about the readers. For example, Kate Greenough realizes that because of their graphics backgrounds, Marguerite Juarez and Dan Lebeau have a thorough understanding of the capabilities of process cameras. Henry Damon, however, knows virtually nothing about these specialized cameras except their price. This reminds Kate that she has to include information for both experts and nonexperts.

Example

	Job Title	Years of Experience	Familiarity with Document Subject
primary reader(s)	*manager*	5	*knowledgeable*
	treasurer	12	*minimal*
secondary reader(s)	*artist*	3	*extensive*

Reading Level

Reading level refers to the degree of difficulty of material a person is able to comprehend. Writing for the audience's level is important; if a reader cannot understand and act on the written information, it is useless. Technical accuracy, completeness, logical organization—all are irrelevant if the intended audience cannot comprehend the material.

Knowing an audience's reading ability helps you adjust content and approach. For example, readers with low reading ability generally feel less comfortable with abstractions than do more capable readers; thus, they prefer concrete terms. Remember that using concrete rather than abstract language increases the comprehension of all readers. When you accurately estimate the reading level, you can more easily select vocabulary and the number and type of supporting examples to use.

Writers sensitive to audience needs do not automatically assume, however, that the smarter the reader, the more difficult the material should be. A very intelligent person may not have a high reading level; another person may be able to read complex material in one subject area but not in another specialized field. Someone capable of reading nearly any material might be constrained by lack of time or interest, and thus prefer short, easy-to-read information. Your writing should be as easy as possible to read without oversimplifying, condensing, or distorting the content.

The assumed reading level of your audience is usually an estimate based on your knowledge of the person's education and experience; less frequently, it may be the result of a standardized reading test. The military, for example, tests service members to specify the reading levels of various groups of military personnel. Reading experts also have established standardized reading levels for students in each grade through college. The levels are expressed in two ways: (1) able to read easy, average, or difficult material, or (2) able to read material appropriate for seventh, ninth, twelfth, sixteenth grade level. Practically speaking, few technical writers can administer a reading test to intended readers, so a writer's estimate of reading level is most often based on common sense.

On the audience analysis worksheet, the categories of audience education and experience are generally accurate, though not failsafe, indicators of a person's reading level. For example, in estimating the reading level of her audience, Kate Greenough decides that because they all have college degrees, she can use vocabulary and sentence structures appropriate for formally educated readers.

Organizational Role

Identifying the organizational roles of the readers is important because each position carries its unique professional responsibilities. Readers justifiably expect documents to respond to their needs. If you identify the organizational roles of your readers, you are more likely to include information they need in a document.

Organizations are generally categorized as *hierarchical* or *nonhierarchical*. A hierarchical organization has a vertical structure, with the bosses at the top, managers in the middle, and workers at the bottom. A nonhierarchical organization has a horizontal structure, with everyone contributing equally to the productivity of the organization. Roles within these two types of organiza-

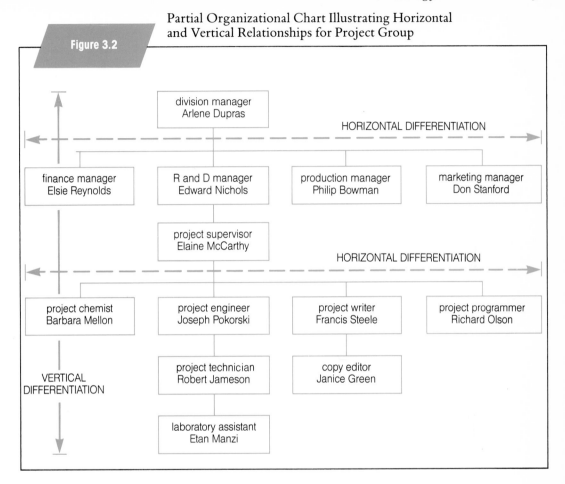

Partial Organizational Chart Illustrating Horizontal
and Vertical Relationships for Project Group

Figure 3.2

tions differ because of inherent assumptions about the purpose of an organization and the relationship among its employees. Hierarchical organizations generally assume that people work best when directed; nonhierarchical organizations regard people as most productive when they participate in decision making. Many organizations incorporate both hierarchical and nonhierarchical characteristics.

A hierarchical organization can be analyzed both vertically and horizontally. Vertical assessment requires knowing where a person fits into the organizational structure of the company—who reports to whom, who is a decision maker, who holds ultimate responsibility for a project. Such an assessment also requires sensitivity to and awareness of any subtle differences between the formal structure and the actual working structure. This information is particularly important to a writer who has to prepare reports for multiple audiences.

Figure 3.2 illustrates part of a hierarchical organization. Project writer

Frances Steele prepares a status update report for a variety of readers. Project supervisor Elaine McCarthy, who would be the initial reader, passes the document on to the primary reader, R and D manager Edward Nichols. Nichols determines immediate support for the project's funding and staffing. Secondary readers include Nichols' counterparts in other departments—the managers of finance, production, and marketing—as well as the division manager. These people will be part of the decision-making process as soon as the project moves from R and D into production, so naturally they want to be aware of progress. The report will also be available to members of the project, who have varying levels of experience and responsibility—engineer, chemist, programmer, technician, copy editor, and lab assistant.

Knowing people's roles in an organization helps you distinguish primary and secondary readers as well as estimate probable levels of knowledge for readers on different vertical levels in an organization. Vertically differentiated readers usually have obvious distinctions in their purpose for reading, amount and type of education, and organizational experience and role. Figure 3.2 illustrates this vertical differentiation of lab assistant, technician, engineer, project supervisor, R and D manager, and division manager. Such an awareness of audience helps a writer adjust the difficulty of content by changing vocabulary and number and type of details.

Horizontal assessment of an audience is equally important, for it identifies people on the same organizational level who are performing different functions, often in different departments. For example, readers on the same horizontal level might be the engineer, chemist, writer, and programmer on the same project or the managers of different departments—finance, R and D, production, and marketing—as shown in Figure 3.2. Horizontally differentiated readers usually vary in their reasons for reading and in type of education although their level of education, organizational experience, and role may be similar. Documents for horizontally differentiated readers take into account the differences in expertise and purpose, with necessary adjustments in content and focus.

Some organizations have a nonhierarchical structure in which all employees have an equal say in management and operation. Nonhierarchical organizations function on the principle that varying job positions should not create superior or subordinate roles and that consensus is more productive than mandated direction. Writers preparing materials for nonhierarchical organizations can think of readers as an extended horizontal audience, people with different responsibilities but with equivalent corporate rank.

So far, the discussion has focused on internal readers—those within the writer's organization. Frequently, however, readers are external, belonging to another organization. Such readers might be customers or a funding agency. They would not know many of the things that are apparent to internal readers, so the writer needs to provide more background information than may be customary for an internal reader.

This background can include definitions, a brief history, the relation of the subject to the overall operation, and so on. An external reader may need such information to give perspective to the material in the document. In addition, an external reader will probably not be familiar with the operation of another company, so a document might need to include information about its organizational policies, practices, and sometimes even personnel.

Also, the tone used for external readers is often more formal than the tone for internal readers. As a result, the word choices are generally more formal. However, *formal* does not mean *pompous*; rather, the document just does not include casual language common in internal memos. For example, an internal memo might say, "I'll get back to you by Monday about the revised schedule," while a document for an external reader would be more likely to say, "I will send you information about the revised schedule by Monday, October 22" or "Information about the revised schedule will reach you by Monday, October 22."

Environment

An often ignored but vital consideration for technical writers is the constraint a reader's physical environment may impose on a document's format and organization. Regardless of a person's reading ability or knowledge of the subject, if the environment is distracting or noisy, reading difficult material may be nearly impossible. A writer might adjust elements such as paragraph division, headings, page design, type and size of illustrations, and binding to make the document easier to use. For example, a repair manual used by technicians while they are troubleshooting equipment needs a sturdy cover, pages that lie flat, a detailed, easy-to-read table of contents and index, and headings and visuals that scan easily. A report read by a busy executive needs an accurate, concise abstract, clear headings, an initial statement of conclusions and recommendations, and brief explanations and justifications.

Another constraint is the available time the audience has to read the material. Because time is valuable, documents should be designed so that readers can understand and use the information as quickly and comfortably as possible. Technical writers use any organizational or graphic devices that ease the reader's task. The following devices are particularly helpful:

- subheadings
- use of descending order so the most important information comes first
- definition of terms, if necessary
- summaries for the entire document and sections of the document
- page layout that is not crowded or cluttered

When Kate Greenough prepares her recommendations about the process camera, she considers the environment of her readers.

Example

	Location	Distractions	Time Constraints
primary reader(s)	*office*	{ *people walking in* / *telephone*	*very busy*
secondary reader(s)	*office* / *open art area*	*telephone* / *talking at other desks*	*very busy* / *very busy*

With this information summarized in front of her, Kate sees that her readers have little time and lots of interruptions. She recognizes the necessity of including a brief abstract (summary) and section subheadings.

Adjusting to the Readers

After you have identified and analyzed your readers, you can use the information to prepare documents that respond to their reasons for reading as well as to their attitude, knowledge, experience, position, and time. You can adjust the following four factors in order to tailor a document to a specific audience:

- content complexity
- diction choices
- sentence structure
- paragraph structure

In addition, Chapter 6 discusses design format and visuals that influence readers.

Content Complexity

Writers can adjust material by changing the content for vertically or horizontally differentiated readers by either adjusting the complexity of the material or shifting its focus.

Vertical differentiation. Vertically differentiated readers vary either in their level of technical knowledge (expert to uninformed) or in their organizational role (top to bottom). Adjusting material for vertically differentiated readers involves changing the complexity of the concepts, simplifying the language, and making changes in details and examples.

The following two paragraphs are about the same subject—why stars twinkle—but are intended for different audiences. Primarily because of changes in content complexity, the first paragraph is easier to read than the second.

Example A   The stars twinkle because the earth's air scatters the light that comes from them. So during windy weather, stars appear to twinkle more than when it is calm. Also, stars near the horizon twinkle more than stars higher in the sky because the light has a thicker layer of air to go through. Observed from the moon, stars do not appear to twinkle at all because the moon does not have any air. Planets do not appear to twinkle as much as most stars because planets usually appear much brighter than most stars, making it harder for their light to be scattered.

Example B   Stars twinkle because of atmospheric diffraction, the scattering of light caused by the earth's atmosphere. Stars appear to twinkle much more when the atmosphere is extremely turbulent, as it is just before a weather front passes through. Stars near the horizon appear to twinkle much more than those near the zenith because light has to pass through a thicker layer of atmosphere and has more of a chance to be diffracted. The moon's lack of an atmosphere causes a very small amount of diffraction. The light from planets is not diffracted as much as that from stars because planetary disks subtend a much larger area than do stellar disks (40 arc seconds as compared to .001 arc seconds). This larger area causes the light to be more intense and results in less diffraction.

Example A assumes the reader has little knowledge about stars; the vocabulary is simpler—"air scatters the light" rather than "atmospheric diffraction"—because an uninformed reader would not know technical terms. Example B assumes the reader understands more complex information and includes more detail, such as information about the comparative differences of light from stars and planets.

Example 3.1

MARLBOROUGH SCIENCE, INC.

October 11, 1986

TO: Assembly Personnel
FROM: Marty Holmann MH
SUBJECT: EREM Hand Cutters

Each assembler on your production line has evaluated three styles of EREM ergonomic hand cutters from September 23, 1986 to October 10, 1986. The three styles are similar in size and shape and contrast only in the metals that they are made from.

The line preferred cutter style 711E-BH. This cutter was selected for its comfort, versatility, and durability. The cutter was also found to reduce operator fatigue, which is a factor in our processes.

If these cutters are approved, we would be purchasing 400 cutters for a one-time purchase price of $9,200 or $23.00 per cutter. Therefore, it is imperative that each employee controls the use and security of his or her cutters.

Horizontal differentiation. Although the level of technical complexity of documents usually remains the same for horizontally differentiated audiences, the emphasis is on different aspects of the same subject. The following four memos are about the same subject, the purchase of hand cutters for assembly workers; the focus shifts because of the readers' different organizational roles.

The memo in Example 3.1 addresses line workers. The first two paragraphs summarize the workers' evaluation of three styles of hand cutters. The supervisor who wrote the memo added the last paragraph containing pricing information to impress on the workers the impact of their decision and to reinforce the importance of caring for the tools.

Example 3.2

MARLBOROUGH SCIENCE, INC.

October 11, 1986

TO: Charles Faria
            PCB Manufacturing Engineering
FROM: Marty Holmann M⊬
SUBJECT: EREM Hand Cutters

From September 23, 1986 to October 10, 1986, the SPS assembly personnel evaluated three styles of EREM ergonomic hand cutters. The assemblers prefer cutter style 711E-BH to cutter styles 511E-BH and 512E-BH.

Nine line assemblers as well as six post solder operators had the opportunity to use the three styles of cutters. The 711E-BH cutter was the most comfortable, durable, and versatile. The padded handles and quick-action internal spring reduce the fatigue factor experienced by the assemblers with their current cutters. The cutters were used to cut leads varying from 0.019 inches to 0.050 inches and showed little sign of wear, even after being used to cut soldered leads.

In summary, the assemblers strongly prefer the EREM hand cutters to the Lindstrom or Utica cutters. They are still willing to evaluate any new cutters that you may consider equivalent or applicable to their needs.

The memo in Example 3.2 is directed to an engineer in manufacturing. The reader wasn't involved in arranging or performing the on-line tests, so he needs a summary of who performed the test and what types of cutters were considered. Because the reader is particularly interested in the function and capability of the cutters, the writer focuses primarily on specifics of operation. The workers' recommendation is presented at the end of the memo.

Example 3.3

MARLBOROUGH SCIENCE, INC.

October 11, 1986

TO: Diane Martin
            Finance Representative
FROM: Marty Holmann MH
SUBJECT: EREM Hand Cutters

PCB Manufacturing Engineering and PCB Management are requesting approval from the Finance Department to purchase 400 EREM hand cutters for the assembly line workers for a one-time purchase price of $9,200.

From September 23, 1986 to October 10, 1986, three styles of EREM hand cutters were evaluated by the assembly line workers and the manufacturing engineer of the department. The three styles are similar in size and shape and contrast only in material and price.

style #	unit price	discount price (over 100)
711E-BH	**$30.00**	**$23.00**
511E-BH	$31.00	$25.00
512E-BH	$32.00	$25.00

The line preferred cutter style 711E-BH. This cutter was selected for its comfort, versatility, and durability. The cutter was also found to reduce operator fatigue, which is a factor in our processes.

The third memo, presented in Example 3.3, is written to a finance representative. Unlike the workers and engineers, she is not interested in specific information about function or capability. Instead, her primary concern is cost—initially, total expenditure, then cost comparison. Least important to her is the reason for the choice, so this information is placed at the end of the memo.

Example 3.4

MARLBOROUGH SCIENCE, INC.

October 11, 1986

TO: Jim Wabash
PCB Manufacturing Manager
FROM: Marty Holmann MH
SUBJECT: EREM Hand Cutters

From September 23, 1986 to October 10, 1986, three styles of EREM hand cutters were evaluated by the assembly line workers and the manufacturing engineer of our department. The three styles are similar in size and shape and contrast only in their material.

All line assemblers as well as those performing post solder operation had the opportunity to use the three cutters.

The line preferred cutter style 711E-BH for its comfort, versatility, and durability. The padded handles and quick-action internal spring are favorable aspects. The same cutters were used to cut various size leads of components and showed little sign of wear, even after being used to cut soldered leads.

In summary, the line strongly prefers EREM hand cutters to the Lindstrom or Utica cutters. We are still willing to evaluate any new cutters that the manufacturing engineering department may be considering.

Marty Holman addresses a fourth memo, presented in Example 3.4, to his direct supervisor. After summarizing critical information, Marty ends with a statement indicating his department's cooperative attitude.

These four memos have approximately the same level of content difficulty, yet the focus shifts in each one to emphasize the content that is relevant to each reader.

Diction

Diction is your manner of expression or choice of words. In technical writing, the diction you use must be precise, but it must also be understood by your audience. You can write for different audiences by adjusting the word length and complexity and controlling acronyms in your documents.

Word length and complexity. Effective writers use the simplest word that accurately and concisely conveys their meaning. Generally, if you have a choice between a short or a long synonym, choose the short one because the reader will comprehend it more quickly.

However, shortness is not always a measure of reading ease, for short words do not necessarily have simple meanings. For example, *quark* and *erg*, although short, are more difficult words than *satellite* or *occupation*. Also, word length decreases as a factor influencing comprehension if the words are familiar to the intended audience. While some technical words are long and appear complex to the general reader, they are easily understood by experts in the field. In many cases the technical term is exactly the correct word; an explanation comprised of shorter, more recognizable terms would be less precise. The following sentence might not make sense to a general reader, but to a plastics engineer it is both accurate and easy to understand:

Example

Polysulfones comprise a class of engineering thermoplastics with high thermal, oxidative, and hydrolytic stability, and good resistance to aqueous mineral acids, alkali, salt solutions, oils and grease.[1]

As a technical writer, you should choose words that the reader will comprehend. Be concerned initially with accuracy and then with word length.

Acronyms. Acronyms are terms made by using the first letter of each word in a phrase. They are useful as a kind of shorthand that is recognized by people in the same field. However, indiscriminate use of undefined acronyms causes confusion because most acronyms are unfamiliar to almost everyone outside a particular speciality.

Acronyms fall into several overlapping categories:

- Words so common that many people do not even realize they are acronyms are appropriate for use in any document although nonexperts may need to have the term explained. A simple definition of such acronyms won't help a person understand a concept such as *laser*.

Examples

SCUBA   self-contained underwater breathing apparatus
LASER   light amplification by stimulated emission of radiation

- Acronyms that most people recognize as words while still realizing that they are acronyms are also appropriate for any document. Often, people know what the term means but cannot identify the specific words from which the acronym is constructed.

Examples

NASA	National Aeronautics and Space Administration
BASIC	beginner's all-purpose symbolic instruction code

- Acronyms accepted in specific industries and recognized by most professionals in that field can be used in documents written for all levels of readers in a particular academic or industrial specialty. Outside these fields, however, such acronyms should be used sparingly.

Examples

ANSI	American National Standards Institute
PVC	polyvinylchloride

- Acronyms that would be familiar only to a specific organization and recognized by few others should be used with caution.

Examples

VISSR	visible/infrared spin/scan radiometer
HAC	Hughes Aircraft Company

Writers who use an acronym should first decide whether the reader is likely to be familiar with the term. In any case, the first time the term is employed, the entire phrase should be spelled out, followed by the acronym in parentheses. The second time the term is used, the reader should recognize the acronym. If the second use follows within a few sentences, the reader can look back to check the meaning. If the second use is several paragraphs or pages later, the reader would probably benefit from an explanatory phrase in parentheses. After that, the acronym alone will suffice. Acronyms are also appropriate entries for a glossary if a document needs one.

Sentences

Sentence length can affect material's readability. Generally, shorter sentences are easier to read than longer ones unless content complexity varies greatly from one sentence to another. Sentences with no more than 8 words are easy to read. Increasing the sentence length increases the reading difficulty to the point that sentences with 29 or more words are judged very difficult.

Comprehension is affected by a combination of content complexity and sentence length. The more difficult the content, the lower the comprehension; similarly, the longer the sentences, the lower the comprehension. However, simple ideas in a long sentence may be easier to understand than difficult ideas expressed in a short sentence. Particularly when the content is difficult, writers avoid long sentences that compound the difficulty in reading.

The following sentences illustrate the relationship between sentence length and ease in reading. The content does not vary much in difficulty because all the sentences are from the same article in *Aviation Week and Space Technology*, a magazine for professionals and experts in aerospace-related industries. The examples show the increasing difficulty that comes with longer sentences.

very easy **8 words or less**	The cockpit instrumentation is well designed. (6 words)
easy **11 words**	This aircraft is equipped with combined dual navigation and communication systems. (11 words)
fairly easy **14 words**	All controls are within easy reach of the pilot and have readily discernible functions. (14 words)
standard **17 words**	The DO 228 has easy access to cockpit seats by an optional door located on either side of the cockpit. (19 words)
fairly difficult **21 words**	The aircraft's fuel, electrical, deicing and starting systems controls are color coded and shown in clearly styled flow diagrams on the overhead panel. (23 words)
difficult **25 words**	The front instrument panel is not cluttered, partly due to the large center console located between the pilots that contains most of the avionics controls. (25 words)
very difficult **29 + words**	Dornier's DO 228-200 commuter and utility twin-turboprop offers operators a versatile-mission aircraft with short-field performance combined with excellent flight performance characteristics and easily maintained aircraft systems. (28 words)[2]

Just as critical as sentence length for ease in reading is variety of sentence lengths in the same article. An article or document with all the sentences the same length quickly becomes repetitious and boring. Variation maintains reader interest and increases comprehension. Although a single document might not have the tremendous variety shown in the previous examples, effective technical writers generally try to vary sentence length.

Sentence type as well as sentence length affects reader interest and comprehension. Simple sentences are often easier to understand than compound, complex, or compound-complex sentences because the relationships among the ideas are simpler. However, a series of simple sentences is not only boring but may not convey the relationships the writer intends; thus, the reader is left to make independent and potentially erroneous interpretations. (Sentence relationships are discussed in more detail in Chapter 5.)

Paragraphs

The length and organization of paragraphs affect the audience's ability to read and comprehend. Most traditional guidelines stress that paragraphs develop a single idea. This works well most of the time, but sometimes a single idea can be developed at great length, often running a page or more. In such cases, the single idea should be divided into several paragraphs.

Writers recognize additional reasons to begin a new paragraph. For instance, paragraph breaks provide visual relief from dense pages of type. Most readers approach a document with a more positive attitude if they see three or four paragraphs rather than one paragraph filling the entire page. Paragraphs also separate information into manageable portions so that readers can take a mental breather. Finally, paragraphs provide variety in page layout that makes a document more visually appealing.

The paragraph's organization is equally important as length. Just as some sentence patterns are easier to comprehend, so are some paragraph structures. Paragraphs that use simple organizational patterns (chronological order, spatial order) are easier to read than those with more complex structures (contrast, cause/effect). Also, paragraphs that use initial topic sentences are generally more readable because they provide clues about the paragraph's content and organization. Transitions within a paragraph reinforce the relationships among the ideas, helping the reader to follow the writer's train of thought. (Chapter 4 discusses paragraph organization and provides useful examples.)

Readability

To many professional writers and reading experts, the term *readability* has developed a specialized meaning, referring to aspects of writing that can be measured. In an attempt to define what makes documents easy to read, many people have tried to quantify various aspects of writing, to measure readability with formulas (also called scales, indexes, or equations). Common formulas—Fry, Flesch, Fog, and Kincaid—are reproduced in the appendix. Readability formulas are accessible and convenient and are widely used in government, industry, and education, partly because of their availability on computer software. The question is whether they do what they claim.

How Readability Formulas Work

Readability formulas are based on the relationships between average word length (number of syllables per word) and average sentence length (number of words per sentence). The theory states that both the higher the average number of syllables per word and the greater the average number of words per sentences, the more difficult the document is to read. The formulas yield a ratio between word length and sentence length that estimates a document's readability in one of two ways: level of difficulty (easy to difficult) and grade level (first grade to postgraduate study).

Readability formulas can benefit technical writers by calculating whether all sections of a long report or a series of related manuals maintain a consistent level of difficulty. This is particularly valuable when several writers are preparing separate sections of a lengthy report or a series of manuals. In addition, readability formulas may allow writers to tailor material for audience ability by identifying word and sentence length.

They also help writers identify and analyze reasons for the ineffectiveness of reports or manuals for specific audiences. Formula scores may show the material to be excessively difficult (thus ignored) or unnecessarily simple (thus boring and insulting).

Restraints in Using Readability Formulas

Readability formulas are valuable tools—if used properly and with other methods of assessing the suitability of writing for a particular audience. A writer can best determine whether material is understandable by giving it to representative readers in the intended audience. If these readers comprehend and act on the information, a writer can assume the information is appropriate.

If readability formulas are employed, a writer should be aware of their weaknesses and avoid restricting word choice or sentence structure inappropriately. Because readability formulas are based on a quantifiable ratio, several elements of writing are not adequately addressed, including variations in the scales themselves, overgeneralizations about word and sentence length, poor format, and content.

Readability formulas do not consider difficulty of content. For example, a paragraph may be labeled "seventh grade readability" because of relatively short words and sentences; however, a 12-year-old seventh grade child would not necessarily be able to understand it. Highly technical or abstract material can be easy to read, but the ideas extremely difficult to comprehend. For example, this sentence has only fifteen words: "Boards with tight lines and spaces required reworking due to shorts caused by solder bridging." According to the criteria presented in the previous section of the chapter, the sentence falls between fairly easy and standard to read because most of the words are short and the sentence has a total of only 21 syllables. However, the terminology is unfamiliar to the general reader and the sentence not easy to understand—despite formulas that indicate otherwise. Or consider what grade level you would assign for "I think; therefore, I am"?

Another problem is that the formulas differ from expert to expert. The appendix presents the common formulas and shows their differences. Lack of consistency leads to confusion because results from different formulas are not comparable. For example, three passages analyzed by a computer using both the Flesch Index and the Kincaid Index produced the following results:

	Kincaid Grade Level	*Flesch Grade Level*
passage 1	7.4	9.4
passage 2	9.4	11.2
passage 3	7.4	8.9

Readability formulas also ignore the important function of subordination in increasing comprehension. Writers recognize that for most readers, a series of short, separate sentences that treat all ideas equally may be more difficult to comprehend than sentences that have subordinate and main ideas clearly established. Two versions of the same information illustrate this point.[3]

Example   A decayed woven linen robe was found in 1981. The robe dated from c. 1000 B.C.E. It is the oldest known piece of cloth found in Greece. The robe was found by a Greek-British excavation team. The team was digging on the island of Euboeoa. Euboeoa is about 40 miles from Athens.

Revision   A decayed woven linen robe from c. 1000 B.C.E., the oldest known piece of cloth found in Greece, was unearthed in 1981 during a Greek-British excavation on the island of Euboeoa, 40 miles from Athens.

Although readability formulas indicate that the first version is easier to read, most adults prefer the second version because relationships are established clearly and repetition is eliminated.

Readability formulas equate short words with simplicity, without regard to word meaning or audience knowledge. Actually, some very long (and sometimes technical) words have a high recognition factor. For example, some multi-syllable medical and chemical terms are easily and immediately recognized by all professionals in their respective fields. Likewise, a fourth-grade child recognizes the words *Mississippi* or *Massachusetts*. Such multi-syllable, high-recognition words can give a false high grade-level equivalency (compared with the difficulty of the content) when evaluating readability for adult professionals.

Finally, readability formulas do not consider document design. Closely spaced, small printing with little visual relief is more difficult and takes longer to read and comprehend—regardless of the content—than carefully designed, visually pleasing pages. (Chapter 6 discusses document design in detail.)

Appealing to the Readers

Technical writers not only have to craft accurate and readable documents, they also have to create a pleasing writing style. Readers annoyed by the tone or bored by the style pay too little attention to content. Figurative language and inclusive (nonsexist) language contribute to the appeal of the writing.

Figurative Language

Figurative language creates comparisons and images that make your writing more interesting. Additionally, figurative language helps explain difficult ideas by giving the reader a familiar comparison. Figurative language that reflects the thought process is especially beneficial, giving the reader insight into the origin of the idea.

The most frequently used types of figurative language in technical communication are *analogy* (a comparison of two things that are similar in most respects) and *metaphor* (an implied analogy). Analogy makes the unfamiliar easier to understand by comparing it with something familiar to the reader. Metaphor suggests that the unfamiliar *is* the familiar, but the reader understands that the comparison is not literal.

Carl Sagan uses the analogy of a calendar year to explain the chronology of life since the creation of our universe. The "Big Bang" occurred on January 1. The origin of our solar system occurred on September 9. Earliest life began about September 25. Dinosaurs began to roam the earth on December 24. The first human evolved on December 31, about 10:30 P.M. The Renaissance started about 11:59:59 P.M.[4] Such an analogy helps readers place events in chronological perspective and comprehend relative time spans.

Frequently, figurative language is not dramatic. Rather, it blends in with the rest of the document, maintaining reader interest, clarifying information, and creating images, as in this sentence describing a Brain Electrical Mapping (BEAM) display:

Example   Within the oval shape divided into quarters, jagged waves of bright red and blue exploded and pulsed, blossomed and ricocheted from one side of the screen to another.[5]

While "quarters," "exploded," "pulsed," and "ricocheted" are technically descriptive, "jagged waves" and "blossomed" are not. The latter terms create a visual image that helps the reader understand exactly what is displayed on the screen during a BEAM display.

The metaphor in this next example is less flamboyant, but the word choices cause a response in the readers:

Example

It's a small dam against a torrent of chemicals, diverting only a trickle out of America's annual industrial deluge of 40 million tons of acid sludges, toxic solvents, and herbicides and pesticides. But the equipment . . . is at the forefront of an accelerating effort to harness hazardous waste. . . .[6]

The excerpt employs an extended metaphor of "dam," "torrent," "deluge," "harness" [as dams harness energy]. The deluge is not a literal flood, but the comparison impresses on the reader the effect of hazardous waste.

There are two purposes for figurative language in technical communication. First, problem solving is often metaphoric; new ideas are born when scientists gain insight about a problem by seeing it in a new way. An effective writer uses metaphoric language to describe what is often a metaphoric process. Famous examples abound. Kekule formulated the benzene molecule after picturing a snake swallowing its own tail. Alexander Graham Bell developed the telephone after examining the membrane and bones of the human ear and visualizing a similar membrane to move the metal plate in his invention. Second, figurative language is particularly appropriate for nonexpert readers because the unfamiliar is explained in familiar terms.

The example below illustrates how effectively figurative language can be incorporated into a technical description. The excerpt from United Technologies' *Technology in Brief* uses analogy and metaphor, as well as personification and simile, to describe a turbofan engine.

Example

personification
analogy

A turbofan engine develops propulsive thrust by accelerating the mass of air that flows through it. At takeoff, for example, a P&WA JT8D-9 turbofan, the parent engine of the Dash 209, gulps 318 pounds of air every second—roughly the volume of air inside a typical two-story house—and increases its velocity about 1,000 miles an hour to produce 14,500 pounds of thrust.

Part of the air flows through the engine's core to emerge as a high-velocity jet exhaust stream. The balance bypasses the core and is boosted to moderate velocity by a high-speed fan driven by the hot gases generated within the core.

personification

Noise is an inevitable consequence of making air move faster. A turbofan engine sings a cacophony of different sounds, but the most annoying are:

simile

- *jet roar*—a blow-torch-like noise produced aft of the engine as the jet exhaust merges with still air.

metaphor

- *combination-tone fan noise*—a strident buzz-saw whine broadcast ahead of the engine by shock waves leaving the tips of the fan blades.

simile

- *interaction-type fan noise*—a siren-like wail generated when the intake air stream is "chopped" by the fan blades and deflected by other internal structures.[7]

Inclusive Language and Visuals

Because you need your reader's attention unencumbered by psychological noise (referred to in Chapter 2), your language and visuals should be accurate and inclusive—nonsexist and nonracist—to avoid prejudice and insensitivity. Equally important, inclusive language and visuals are essential for accuracy: Today's workforce is nearly 54 percent women; over 32 percent of managers are women.[8]

Sexism is any verbal or visual reference that presents men and women as unequal or excludes one group in favor of another. Sexism can take several forms, some of them subtle. For example, one company displayed a new manual that balanced examples of men and women in the workplace. The initial idea was commendable; however, the presentation was not because in the manual all operator errors were made by women and all repairs by men. Despite gender balance, the manual was sexist.

Similarly, racism is any verbal or visual reference that presents racial or ethnic groups as unequal or excludes one group in favor of another. Racist language in documents is rare; however, visuals often do not show the same sensitivity. People in visuals used in documents, in-house publications, technical advertising, and articles should be portrayed in representative racial balance.

Because noninclusive (exclusionary) language is more often sexist than racist, the remainder of this section deals with types of sexist language and ways to avoid it. In many cases, sexist language may be thoughtless, as in this notice sent to all company employees:

Example Your request for reimbursement for a membership fee, subscription, or technical books has been approved. At your convenience, please ask the girl handling petty cash in the accounting department for your reimbursement.

Or, sexism may be a misdirected attempt at humor:

Example Thermistors are temperature sensitive semiconductors which exhibit a large change in electrical resistance when subjected to a relatively minute change in body temperature. Negative temperature coefficient thermistors decrease in resistance when subjected to an increase in body temperature. For this reason it has been stated that they might be renamed "Thermisses."

Sometimes the sexism in technical documents is visual, particularly in advertising of technical products for industrial and business markets. For example, many ads by computer companies depict a woman as typist (document copier) and a man as document originator. This stereotype repeats itself frequently throughout the industry. Other instances of visual sexism involve women in ads for products that do not use a human operator—male or female. For example, some companies have women display products such as ball bearings and printed circuit boards. Even more sexist are ads in which women are shown in clothing or poses totally inappropriate to the product. By contrast, men are generally attired in suitable business or work clothes.

Inclusive communication creates good will and conveys a strong, self-confident image, which reflects the attitude of the individual and, by implication, the company. Such positive communication requires an organizational attitude and policy that shuns sexist policies and practices. To avoid offensive sexist language, writers should follow these general guidelines:

1. Select words and phrases that do not imply or encourage sexist (or racist) stereotypes. For example, instead of writing "conference participants and their wives," write "conference participants and their spouses."

2. Select generic terms that are not gender specific. Instead of writing, "Theory X managers believe that men are generally hard working," use an inclusive—and more accurate—term: "Theory X managers believe that people are generally hard working."

3. Avoid sexism in compound words. Instead of a memo saying, "Too many man-hours of overtime have been used this month because of the poor utilization of manpower available," rephrase it to say, "Too many hours of overtime have been used this month because of poor use of available personnel."

4. Instead of using the pronouns *he, him,* and *his* as generic terms, rewrite sentences to consistently use plural constructions, avoiding the sexist as well as the awkward he/she and him/her. "The man pursuing a career as a technical writer will be in great demand if he has a dual background in technology and communication" can easily become "People pursuing a career in technical writing will be in great demand if they have dual backgrounds in technology and communication." Or, "Any employee who needs new safety glasses should bring his/her old glasses to the nursing station" can be changed to "All employees who need new safety glasses should bring their old glasses to the nursing station." If singular pronoun references are necessary, consider varying the examples, in one section using men and in the next, women.

5. Use inclusive salutations in business correspondence. Instead of "Dear Sir" or "Gentlemen," write "Dear Personnel Director" or "Dear Department Manager." (Using the person's name is the best choice.) And for unisex names and ever-present initials—as in Pat Munson or C. H. Smith—write "Dear Pat Munson" or "Dear C. H. Smith." "Ms." is now a widely accepted form of address for women; use it unless you know a woman specifically prefers "Miss" or Mrs." An emerging but not yet widely accepted letter style eliminates the salutation altogether and substitutes a subject line. (In this style, the complimentary closing is also omitted.)

6. Plan company titles carefully to avoid the sexism that can creep in just

because the job happens to be done by men or women at the present time. For example, one large machine tool catalogue company called their new women employees "person-to-person-gals" (the actual job title!) because they made personal telephone contact with customers. The company could have selected any number of more descriptive and inclusive job titles: telephone representative or customer service representative.

The goal of every writer should be to communicate effectively, guiding the reader to focus on the content. The reader should not be distracted by sexist language or imagery or even by self-conscious attempts at inclusive language. The most effective inclusive language does not draw attention to itself; no one will ever even think that you have made an effort to avoid biased language or visuals.

Inquiries and Applications

Discussion Questions

1. All companies value time. Why not, then, save the reader's time? Discuss whether a writer should prepare separate documents for the variety of audiences who need the same information.
2. What are the benefits, for you and your organization, of using inclusive salutations in business correspondence?
3. Explain why you think it appropriate to use single-gender references in career fields dominated by men (machinists) or women (nurses). Why not?
4. Why do you think readability formulas are so popular if they consider only a few of the factors that influence the difficulty of a document? Is their use justified? Beneficial?
5. Reading reports and technical documents is part of a job. Since people have to read the material whether they want to or not, why should a writer consider the reader's attitude and motivation?
6. Why is the organization of material important to persuade a neutral or negative reader to agree with the writer's recommendations?

In-Class Exercises

1. Suggest inclusive terms for the following sexist terms:

   man-hours   wives' program
   manpower   serviceman

workmen's compensation   salesman
policeman   fireman
gal Friday   stock boy

2. After examining the differences in the following sets of sentences intended for different audiences, answer these questions:

- Who are possible audiences for these sentences?

- How has the writer adjusted for the different audiences?

- What information did the writer need in order to make these adjustments?

- Why are the changes necessary if all the sentences convey essentially the same information?

- Why not just express the information in the most simple manner?

Set 1 (vertical differentiation)

The sun damages many human-made materials.

The sun causes degeneration and weakening of any synthetic fibers.

Ultraviolet radiation causes polymer degeneration by attacking links in the polymer chain and reducing the molecular weight of the material.

Set 2 (horizontal differentiation)

The shipment was delayed because of manufacturing equipment malfunction and misjudgment about the resulting delays.

Because your shipment has again been unavoidably delayed, we will credit your rental fee for 14 days—the anticipated length of this second delay.

Occasional brief delays in shipping have a minimal impact on attaining projected third-quarter goals.

3. a. Editing exercise: Rewrite the following paragraphs to lower the difficulty.

A new concept that greatly improves the economics of outdoor storage of grain and other free-flowing bulk materials includes a self-erecting cover and new method of aeration. The cover is laced together from triangular sections of vinyl-coated nylon fabric and raised to the top of a central filling tower before the filling operation is begun. During filling, it is lifted and spread by the growing grain pile and provides a form-fitting cover that completely encases the pile during all stages of fill.

This form-fitting cover is highly resistant to lifting effects of high winds and protects the pile against rainfall. This protection allows the filling operation to be continued during the heaviest downpours. It also completely contains dust particles that would otherwise be carried into the atmosphere to settle on the surrounding countryside.

When full, the covering, tightly fitted to the finished pile, is held in place without need of the usual tires or cable tie-downs and provides long-term protection against crusting and other surface spoilage effects caused by the weather. This protection is obtained at a very low cost, as the cost of the cover can be completely paid off by the spoilage eliminated by a single year of the cover's use.

b. Calculate the "before" and "after" readability using one of the formulas in the appendix.

c. Calculate the readability levels again, this time using a different formula. Prepare a simple table to display the results.

d. In accompanying discussion, identify and try to account for any differences.

4. a. Rewrite the following sentence for a machinist and a company comptroller, changing the emphasis for the different audiences. You may need to change or add words.

The purchase order for 125 complete systems, increasing third-quarter gross income by $250,000, requires our immediate acquisition of a new lathe and new tooling and inspection equipment costing $40,000.

b. Rewrite the following sentences to reduce their length.

A 35-mm SLR (single lens reflex) camera is a camera (a light-tight box that uses a physical means of reproducing an image and a chemical means of preserving it) that uses film of 35-mm width and allows the photographer to see the image to be photographed through a single lens, the one used to expose the film, rather than through a second one used only for viewing the image. (72 words)

A single-lens method of viewing the image to be photographed is preferable to the viewfinder or rangefinder method, in which the user "finds the view" through a separate lens, because it eliminates the problem of parallax error, or not seeing precisely what will be photographed. (46 words)

5. Carefully read the document in Figure 3.3. Identify the intended audience. How appropriate do you think it is for them? Select an entirely different group of readers and rewrite the paragraph for them.

Assignments

1. Write three separate paragraphs about the same subject for three horizontally or vertically differentiated audiences. Some examples are listed:

E.M.T. (emergency medical technician)	athlete
nurse	trainer
physician	coach
patient	equipment manufacturer

Figure 3.3

The inner ear's vestibular cavity is the point of entry for signals that tell us where we are and how we move. Linear motion and the constant force of gravity are sensed by the inner ear's otolith ("ear stone") organs which contain calcite crystals that lie like a carpet on a sensory membrane in the labyrinth of the inner ear. If you sit motionless, the otolith registers gravity alone; linear movement (forward, backward or up and down) and acceleration cause the crystals to shift and move the hair cells on which they sit. These send signals to cerebellum and brain stem, which perform the complex job of making sense of these signals. Another element of our internal guidance system consists of three tubes in the inner ear called the semicircular canals. These narrow pipes contain fluid that moves through the canals when you rotate your head, and signals rotational or angular movement.   —C.J.

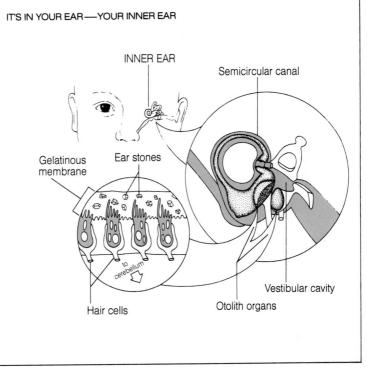

IT'S IN YOUR EAR—YOUR INNER EAR

INNER EAR

Semicircular canal

Gelatinous membrane

Ear stones

to cerebellum

Hair cells

Otolith organs

Vestibular cavity

Source: Christopher Joyce, "It's in Your Ear—Your Inner Ear," *Psychology Today*, May 1984, p. 32. Reprinted with permission from *Psychology Today* magazine. © 1984 (American Psychological Association).

Make appropriate adjustments in content focus and complexity, diction, sentence structure, and organization. Label each paragraph to indicate the intended audience. Select one of the readability formulas in the appendix to evaluate the reading level of each paragraph. Consider one of the following suggested topics or select your own:

treatment for hangovers	capability of computer software
shifting sand barriers	setting a fractured bone
propagation of house plants	safety standards in paint shop
operation of microwave oven	cable TV operation
fetal alcohol syndrome	new treatment for cavities
effect of cigarette smoking	gene splicing
manufacture of plastic film	weather tracking
effect of aerobic exercise	hybrid seed development
construction of road bed	artificial insemination
development of photographic film	conformation of show animal

2. Select an article from *Science Digest* or *Science News* and then locate the original article from which it was abridged. Identify and comment on the changes the editors made in shortening and simplifying the article.

3. Select one of the following questions to answer for three different audiences: a ten- to twelve-year-old child, a general reader without any technical expertise, and a college student majoring in the appropriate technical field. Incorporate appropriate visuals.

- Why do leaves change color?
- Why do some people get white hair?
- Why do people get a fever when they are sick?
- What makes people burp?
- Why is the sky blue?

II   Developing the Writer's Tools

4   Organization of Information

THE MANUFACTURE of rubber supports for rooftop solar modules is causing problems for Charlie McCray, an engineer at Customized Extrusion, Inc. Charlie decides to organize his knowledge about the process and the problem. He writes the sequence of steps in production, charts the flow of material movement during production, identifies the frequency of problems that occur, compares this production process with a similar established process that has no problems, and lists probable causes of problems arising from materials, methods, machines, personnel, or environment. Using various patterns to organize his thinking helps Charlie define the problem and then specify causes in a clear, cause-and-effect organization.

As the manufacturing problem above illustrates, organizing information is a useful strategy for thinking about and planning work. In arranging his data, Charlie uses standard organizational patterns which are discussed in this chapter:

Organizational Pattern	*Charlie's Application of the Pattern*
chronological order	— sequence of steps in production
spatial order	— flow of material movement during production
descending order	— frequency of problems that occur
comparison	— similarities between this production process and a similar established process that has no problems
cause and effect	— probable causes from materials, methods, machines, personnel, or environment

In addition to organizing ideas and information while exploring a subject, you also organize the final document in order to communicate effectively with someone else. If a sender does not arrange information so that a receiver can easily understand and follow it, the receiver imposes a structure so that the information makes sense. Unfortunately, the structure may not be the one the sender intended. Letting the receiver infer the structure might be as disastrous as letting a color-blind person adjust the color on your television; the person cannot guarantee accuracy. No sender should assume that ideas and information are perceived in the way the sender intends unless easily recognized signposts are provided. Organizational patterns represent the bridge between the writer's intent and the reader's understanding.

Good ideas and accurate information deserve a well-organized presentation. This chapter focuses on making information accessible to readers, viewers, and listeners through organizational patterns, visuals, outlining strategies, unity, and coherence. These patterns and strategies operate on all levels—from structuring paragraphs to sections of reports and entire documents.

Organizational Patterns

Many writers and teachers of writing believe that the organizational patterns you use in writing mirror your thought processes. In other words, ideas in a document are not arranged in arbitrary patterns; rather, they reflect your thinking about the subject. This section of the chapter examines ways to analyze ideas and information and then presents patterns that work equally well to organize paragraphs and entire documents. Decisions about patterns are affected not only by your own thinking on the subject but also by the purpose of the document and the intended audience.

Analyzing Ideas and Information

Initially, a writer should identify the "whole" of the subject and then differentiate the "parts" of the whole. An effective strategy involves identifying the parts/whole patterns that exist:

- *Partition* separates a single item into individual components.
- *Division* identifies related types of an item.
- *Classification* identifies the broad category to which something belongs.

Figure 4.1   Car Key

Sometimes partition, division, or classification of a subject suffices, and a writer does not have to use an additional organizational pattern. But even if further organization is necessary, a writer first should know the parts of the subject and their relationship to the whole.

Partition. Most simple objects, mechanisms, and organisms can be partitioned in three standard ways: structural parts, functional parts, and materials. Partitioning involves separating a single item into its parts. You need to make sure readers define "part" the same way you do; their job influences the interpretation of part. For example, a manufacturing engineer is most concerned with the structural parts that require separate manufacturing steps, while a materials engineer focuses on physical composition.

Try a simple experiment: Ask several people how many parts comprise a simple metal car key, as shown in Figure 4.1. You may get answers ranging from one part to more than 20, depending on how each person defines part. The person who says the key has one part views it as a single piece of metal. The person who identifies multiple parts lists the head, chain hole, shank, words and code numbers, and the various grooves and notches. This information can be organized in several patterns: sequence of manufacture, relative physical location of parts, relative importance of parts, comparison of this key's parts with those of other keys, explanation of how notches work to unlock and start the ignition.

The more complex the subject, the more ways to partition it. For example, even on a superficial level, several ways exist to partition a person: structural parts—muscle system, skeletal system, digestive system, circulatory system, reproductive system, lymphatic system, and so on; materials—blood, lymphatic fluid, bone, muscle, and so on; self—physical self, emotional self, spiritual self, intellectual self, and so on.

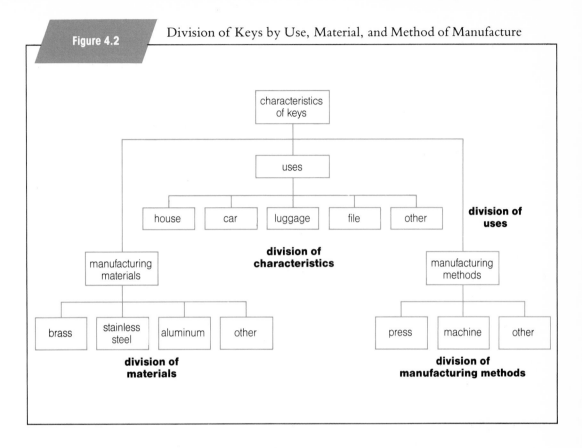

Figure 4.2   Division of Keys by Use, Material, and Method of Manufacture

Division. The second method of determining parts/whole relationships involves division—identifying related subcategories not of a single item but of
a group or category. Objects, mechanisms, organisms, ideas, and situations
can be divided in many ways. Keys, for example, might be divided by material, function, and method of manufacture. Each of these categories can be
further divided: material—brass, stainless steel, aluminum; function—house,
car, luggage, files; and manufacture—pressed, machined, as illustrated in
Figure 4.2.

Information about keys could be further organized along several lines:
differences in key design based on use, advantages of various materials, comparisons of manufacturing methods, structures of key copiers, reasons why
master keys work in multiple locks. Ideas for these topics could be stimulated
by examining the relationship between parts and the whole.

Classification. The third method of determining parts/whole relationships is
classification—the identification of the broad category to which something
belongs. Information can be classified only if the writer knows about more

Figure 4.3   Classification of Keys

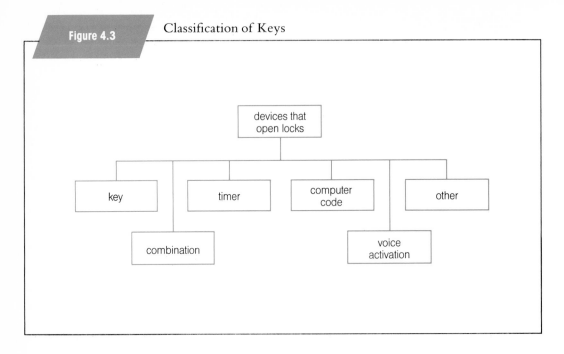

than just the primary object or situation. For example, keys are one of several devices that open locks, as shown in Figure 4.3. Identifying the larger whole to which an object, mechanism, organism, idea, or situation belongs gives the receiver a clearer understanding by placing the parts in a logical context.

Sometimes, accurate classification bears little relationship to complexity of subject. For instance, it is easier to classify some complex organisms than many microscopic organisms. Few would argue with the classification of humans as primates, mammals, animals, and living organisms. However, scientists are unsure of whether certain microscopic organisms should be classified as plants or animals.

As part of data gathering during exploring and planning, you should get into the habit of examining the various parts/whole relationships of your subject. This process does more than familiarize you with the subject. Your parts/whole analysis might turn out to be the structure for your paragraph or document. More frequently, it provides the basic information that you present using various organizational patterns.

Using parts/whole analysis. Conducting a parts/whole analysis also helps pinpoint the concrete aspects of your subject. Generally, a partition, division, or classification chart deals with concrete material at the bottom and abstract at the top. Because readers respond more quickly to concrete rather than abstract information, a writer benefits from identifying concrete aspects of a

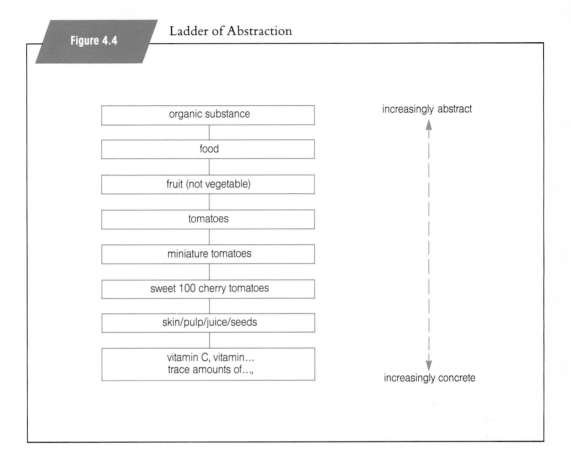

Figure 4.4

Ladder of Abstraction

subject. For example, the ladder of abstraction in Figure 4.4 is actually part of a chart presenting classification, division, and partition.

The abstract organic substance includes everything living and dead (as opposed to inorganic, or never alive). Food is a specific type of organic substance although this is still a broad category. Consider the range: Salmon are food for bears, larvae food for moles, plankton food for whales, mosquitoes food for bats. Fruit is a specific kind of food, tomatoes a type of fruit. The terminology seems much more concrete—until you remember the many varieties of tomatoes. Miniature tomato narrows the field, and a particular variety, sweet-100 cherry tomatoes, makes the identification as precise as possible—until you partition an individual tomato into skin, pulp, juice, and seeds. The tomato can be further partitioned into its nutritional components.

Parts/whole relationships can be used with more relevant subjects than keys or cherry tomatoes. For example, if you wanted to write about floppy disks, you could partition, divide, and classify them. Each of these analytical techniques can be carried out in several ways.

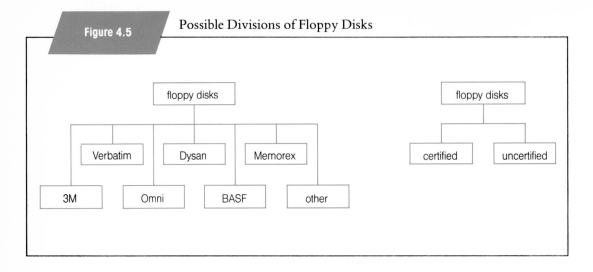

Figure 4.5   Possible Divisions of Floppy Disks

Partition identifies the parts of an individual floppy disk:

Version 1: **Structural Parts**	**Version 2:** **Materials**	**Version 3:** **Functional Parts**
label(s)	printing ink	label(s)
storage envelope	glue	storage envelope
sealed casing	paper	sealed casing and
antistatic cloth	mylar	holes in casing
mylar film	cloth	antistatic cloth
electronic data	electronic impulses	mylar disk and
		holes in disk

Division identifies categories or types of disks. Possible ways to divide categories of floppy disks include size and type of computer for which the disks are designed. Additional ways to divide floppy disks consist of the following three versions:

Version 1: **Brands**	**Version 2:** **Cost/Disk**	**Version 3:** **Function**
3M	$1–$2	certified
Omni	$2–$3	uncertified
Dysan	$3–$4	
Verbatim	$4–$5	
BASF	$5–$6	
Memorex	$6–$7	
other	over $7	

Categories that do not overlap can be presented in charts, as in Figure 4.5.

Classification identifies the broader category—methods of storing elec-

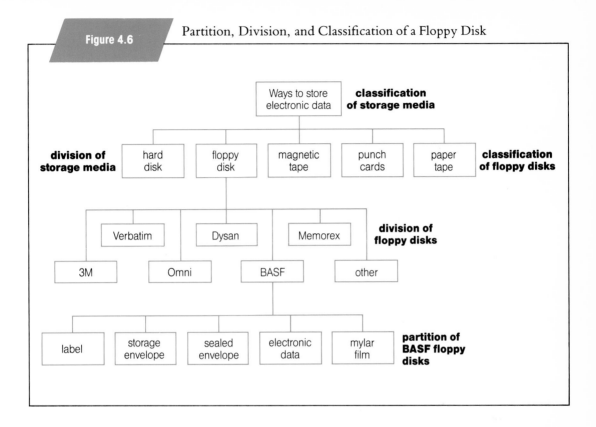

Figure 4.6   Partition, Division, and Classification of a Floppy Disk

tronic data—to which floppy disks belong. The most common way to depict this information is presented in Figure 4.6. The chart illustrates that classification and division are part of the same process. Partition separates the components of a single object, in this case a BASF floppy disk.

So far, this section has used only three charts to partition, divide, or classify information. You have access to a variety of additional visual techniques that work equally well, depending on the subject. For example, Figure 4.7 partitions a floppy disk in a modified phantom view that lifts the vinyl jacket, rather than making it transparent, to reveal the friction-free liner and the magnetic disk. The simple drawing presents the structure far more effectively than a verbal description. In some cases, the same technique can be used for more than one analytical strategy, reinforcing the idea that partition, division, and classification are often just different views of the same subject. Examples of some common techniques are presented in Figure 4.8.

The analytical steps of partitioning, dividing, or classifying a subject form the groundwork for planning a paragraph or document. Based on the analysis, a writer selects information, employing one or more of the organizational patterns discussed in the next section.

Figure 4.7   Floppy Disk

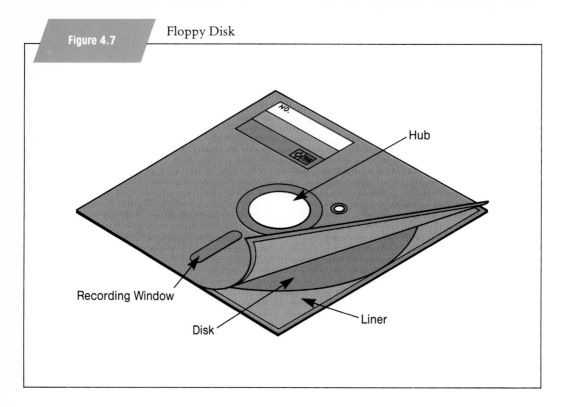

Selecting Organizational Patterns

Technical writers use patterns to organize ideas and information that have already been logically partitioned, divided, or classified. These organizational patterns are particularly important because they make ideas and information clear and accessible to the reader. Although some partitioned, divided, and classified material requires no additional organization, the patterns help to establish the relationships among various pieces of information. Because a pattern reflects thought processes, it can be presented either verbally or visually. Some common organizational patterns are chronological order, spatial order, ascending/descending order, comparison/contrast, and cause/effect.

Chronological order. Chronological order arranges material by sequence or order of occurrence, to give instructions, describe processes, or trace the development of objects or ideas. Chronologically arranged information about floppy disks might include a description identifying each step of the manufacturing process or an explanation of the historical development of electronic

Figure 4.8	Visual Techniques for Partition, Division, and Classification

Analytical Strategy	*Visual Technique*	*Example*
Partition	exploded view	parts of engine in order of assembly
	percent graph	percent components of blood
	schematic	electronic circuit for television
	cutaway view	interior of insulated water heater
	cross section	structure of leaf (enlarged view)
	phantom view	interior of smoke alarm (through transparent surface)
	parts list	components of humidifier
	diagram	electron configuration of aluminum
	architectural drawing	view of proposed addition to a building
	blueprint	floorplan of new manufacturing area
Division	organizational chart	employees in the marketing section of company
	family tree	relatives and ancestors of Morrow family
	percent graph	percent of profit from each product
	species chart	identification of types of salmon
	histogram	distribution of types of fertilizer according to impact on yield per acre
	bar graph	amount of production in each department
	Pareto diagram	same bar graph arranged in descending order
	line graph	rate of infant growth during three-month period
	fish-bone chart (cause and effect)	contributing causes of contamination of specimens for laboratory testing
	trouble-shooting chart	list of possible causes for furnace malfunction
Classification	species chart	relation of salmon to other species of game fish
	periodic table	identification of heavy metals
	photo	Physician's Desk Reference to identify medication
	Venn diagram	overlapping groups of species competing in the same habitat
	nutrient table	relation of B-complex vitamins to other essential vitamins
	organizational chart	relation between line workers, supervisors, and managers
	fish-bone chart (cause and effect)	categories of causes for cracks in new gas pipes

	Visual Forms for Chronological Order

Figure 4.9

Visual Technique	*Example*
flow chart	sequence of manufacturing process
time line	development of synthetics for medical use
genealogy chart	history of family with Huntington's disease
sequential photos	embryo development
sequential drawings	steps in resuscitation of drowning victim
story board	public service ad urging water conservation
time-lapse photos	emergence of butterfly from cocoon
line graph	increase in restlessness during REM sleep
calendar	production schedule for new product
chart	stratification of rock layers according to geologic periods

storage media, from paper tape to mylar disks. If the information were presented visually, you could use any of the forms in Figure 4.9, which also lists an example of each technique.

Spatial order. Spatial order—arrangement by relative physical location—describes the physical parts of nearly anything, from cellular structures to the orbital path of a satellite. Spatial organization could explain parts of a floppy disk or location of the disk drives in relation to the other parts of the computer. Figure 4.10 identifies and gives examples of several visual techniques. Visual presentations are particularly effective for spatially arranged material because they help the reader see the actual physical relationships.

Ascending/Descending Order. Ascending and descending orders arrange information according to quantifiable criteria. The most frequent orders of this type are:

appeal	durability
authority	ease of manufacture, operation, repair
benefit	frequency
cost	importance
delivery	size

Descending order uses a most-to-least-important order; ascending order, a least-to-most. Descending order is found in technical and business writing more frequently than ascending order because most readers want to know the

Figure 4.10	Visual Forms for Spatial Order

Visual Technique	*Example*
map	identification of migration stopovers
blueprint	specification of dimensions for machined part
navigational chart	location of sand bars and buoys
celestial chart	sequence of moons around Jupiter
exploded view	assembly of disk brake
cutaway view	interior components of pool filter
wiring diagram	wiring of alarm system
floor plan	work flow in busy area
set design	arrangement of furniture/props for *Equus*
architectural drawing	appearance of building with solar modifications

Figure 4.11	Visual Forms for Ascending/Descending Order

Visual Technique	*Example*
numbered list	priority of options for treating breast cancer
bull's-eye chart	population affected by nuclear explosion
percent graph	percent of different economic groups receiving balanced nutrition
Pareto diagram	productivity using different methods (bar graph arranged in descending order)
line graph	increasing success for breeding endangered species in captivity over 20-year period

most important points first. In business and industry, readers generally form opinions and make decisions based on what they read initially; they expect descending order in nearly all technical documents. Descending or ascending order would be appropriate for organizing the relative convenience of various forms of electronic data storage or for identifying the disk specifications in various price ranges. If you wanted to arrange information visually, one of the forms illustrated in Figure 4.11 would work.

Figure 4.12   Visual Forms for Comparison and Contrast

Visual Techniques	*Example*
paired photos or drawings	before/after of patient treated for scoliosis
	before/after of factory renovated into apartments
multiple or paired bar graph	expenditures for utilities for each quarter of the fiscal year
multiple or paired percent graphs	distribution of corporate income (every ten years)
	utilization of food nutrients with and without coconut oil to increase absorption
line graph	changes in toxicity of emissions since installation of scrubbers
multiple or paired gauges	illustration of danger/no-danger in training manual for pilots
table	data collected on species size of bats according to age, gender, and location
dichotomous key	distinction of edible wild plants
Pareto diagram	distinction between major and minor causes of delays in shipping
histogram	women, grouped by age, affected by lung cancer
columned chart	physical symptoms of substance abuse

Comparison/Contrast. Comparison and contrast arrange information according to similarities and differences. Comparison identifies the similarities of various ideas, objects, or situations; contrast, the differences. A comparison and/or contrast organization could present the advantages and disadvantages of certified versus uncertified disks or the ease or difficulty of various methods of storing electronic data. Any of the techniques in Figure 4.12 could visually present information that you want to compare and contrast.

Cause/Effect. The cause-and-effect pattern arranges information according to precipitating factors and results. You can move from cause to effect or from effect to cause. For example, you could carry the disk through an electronic surveillance scanner and then trace the effects—the various disk errors that appear. Or, beginning with the effect—a damaged disk—you could then investigate the causes of the damage. Figure 4.13 identifies and illustrates various visuals that are effective for presenting cause-and-effect relationships.

One type of cause and effect—*inductive reasoning*—moves from specific

Figure 4.13	Visual Forms for Cause and Effect

Visual Technique	*Example*
paired photos or drawings	effects of two different treatments for removing facial birth marks
weather maps	impact of cold front on majority of Midwest
bar graph	efficiency of various methods for harvesting cranberries
line graph	destruction of American chestnut by blight during this century
cause-and-effect diagram	identification of multiple contributing factors to contamination of drinking water
Pareto diagram	identification of major causes in low birth weight

instances to broad generalizations, forming the basis for the "scientific method" used in research and experimentation. You begin by collecting data in support of an unproved hypothesis. After you have organized and examined a sufficient body of data, you draw a conclusion. When your conclusion proves consistently to be valid, it is considered a generalization. Most scientific principles and theories are based on this method of inquiry.

Because there is no way to test every instance, induction has a certain risk, and researchers must be careful to avoid basing their reasoning on invalid assumptions. They must not assume chronology is the same as causality, and they must examine a large sample before drawing a conclusion.

The first of these problems, equating chronology with causality, represents an error in reasoning. Just because B follows A does not mean that A causes B. Because inductive reasoning moves from specifics to a generalization, an investigator should not assume that sequence of events alone causes the effect. (Such an error in reasoning is called *post hoc, ergo propter hoc,* Latin for "After this, therefore because of this.") For example, Kevin Wilson may become ill the day after donating blood to the Red Cross, but he cannot logically conclude that donating blood caused him to become ill. Guard against fallacious reasoning by examining all possible causes.

You also need to examine a large number of instances before drawing a conclusion. For example, before a new drug is allowed on the market, the Food and Drug Administration (FDA) requires extensive tests with a broad segment of the target population. As a result of testing, a powerful painkiller such as darvon, when taken according to directions and under a physician's care, is certified as safe, even though all darvon tablets and capsules have not

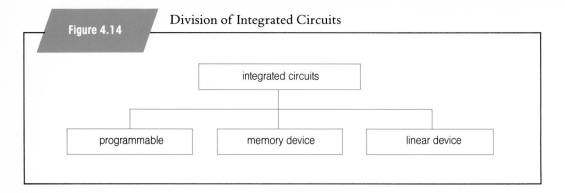

Figure 4.14   Division of Integrated Circuits

been individually tested. Unfortunately, errors occur, although rarely, causing some people to suspect all inductive reasoning. So make sure your methodology is sound, your sample large, and your analysis free from bias or distortion.

When a generalization is widely accepted, you can use it as a base from which to predict the likelihood of specific instances occurring. This process is called *deductive reasoning*—moving from general premises to specific causes. A patient taking darvon trusts that the pills are safe, even though those particular ones have not been tested.

Using Organizational Patterns

Not only do organizational patterns reflect a writer's thought processes, they also help organize information so the reader receives it with less chance of misinterpretation. The arrangement of material influences the way the reader thinks about and reacts to the information. The following examples demonstrate that the same subject—integrated circuits—can be presented in different ways by using several organizational patterns.

Example A presents a straightforward *division* of integrated circuits. During her planning, the author charted the information and divided integrated circuits into three types, as shown in Figure 4.14. In Example A the initial parts/whole analysis suffices; the writer doesn't have to use any additional organizational pattern.

Example A   Integrated circuits are divided into three categories, depending on their function and capability in the final product. The first type is a programmable integrated circuit, a multi-functional component designed to be programmed by the supplier or by in-house technicians. The second type of integrated circuit is the memory device, used to store memory in an end product. The third type is a linear device designed to do many specific predetermined functions and used in conjunction with other components to operate computers.

Example B explains the *chronology* of incoming inspection that integrated circuits go through. The reader easily follows the process because of the transitional phrases or words: "the first stage," "then," "next," "after this," "the final step." The chronological pattern highlights each step of the sequence.

Example B   Integrated circuits received at incoming inspection go through a five-step process. The first stage of inspection ensures that the parts have been purchased from a predetermined qualified vendor list. The parts are then prioritized according to daily back order quantities and/or line shortages assigned by the production floor. Next the parts are moved into the test area where a determination is made as to which lots will be tested at 100 percent and which will be sample tested. After this, the parts are electrically tested for specific continuity and direct current parameters using M.C.T. handlers. The final step of incoming inspection is distributing the parts according to need on the production floor.

Example C uses *spatial order* to describe the in-coming inspection of an integrated circuit. Transitions such as "through the test area," "aligned," and "upper left" signal relative physical location.

Example C   The movement of the I. C. (integrated circuit) chip through the test area is very efficient. The chips arrive from the supplier, already set—24 at a time—into a removable channel within a clear tube. The chips are aligned in the same direction within the tube. This tube is inserted by the operator into the M. C. T. handler so that pin 1 of the first chip, marked by a small dot, is in the upper left. The tube slides through a slot, into the testing compartment, where each chip is tested individually. Automatically, the good chips are placed in one channel, the rejects in another. The channels are moved so the operator can slip on the protective tubes. The good chips are sent to the manufacturing area; the rejects are sent to another engineering station for further testing.

Example D used *descending order* to identify the priorities for testing circuits. Relative importance is shown by the transitional phrases: "most important," "further separated," "all other integrated circuits." Descending order is common in technical writing because readers often want to know the most important idea first.

Example D   Integrated circuits received at incoming inspection are processed according to priorities. The most important integrated circuits are those that fill line shortages on the production floor. These parts take first priority at incoming inspection and are handled according to frequency of use and critical demand. These priority parts are further separated according to how fast they can be accurately tested and sent to the production floor. All other integrated circuits are then prioritized by back order demand and the availability of open test equipment.

The next two examples use *comparison and contrast* to differentiate the responsibilities of incoming inspection and in-process inspection of integrated circuits. Comparison and contrast can be organized in two different ways. The first pattern, in Example E, shifts back and forth between incoming inspection and in-process inspection, explaining how each deals with specific responsibilities.

Example E   Integrated circuits are inspected and/or tested by two separate quality control departments: incoming quality control and in-process quality control. Incoming quality control is responsible for ensuring that all integrated circuits sent to the production floor meet all electrical standards set by the Component Engineering Department. In-process quality control is only responsible for ensuring that the parts are properly mounted on the printed circuit board. Incoming quality control also has to verify the markings on the integrated circuits in order to do proper testing and make certain that the company has purchased a qualified product. In contrast, in-process quality control only has to do random inspections of the circuit markings to ensure that qualified parts are being used in the manufacturing process. Although incoming and in-process inspection are two different areas, they do share the same goal of building a quality product.

topic sentence

incoming inspection

in-process inspection

incoming inspection

in-process inspection

mutual goal

Example F takes the same paragraph and rearranges the information to present all the information about incoming inspection first and then discuss the in-process inspection.

Example F   Integrated circuits are inspected and/or tested by two separate quality control departments: incoming quality control and in-process quality control. Incoming quality control is responsible for ensuring that all integrated circuits sent to the production floor meet all electrical standards set by the Component Engineering Department. Incoming quality control also has to verify the markings on the integrated circuits in order to do proper testing and make certain that the company has purchased a qualified product. In-process quality control is only responsible for ensuring that the parts are properly mounted on the printed circuit board.

topic sentence

incoming inspection

incoming inspection

in-process inspection

In-process quality control only has to do random inspections of   in-process
the circuit markings to ensure that qualified parts are being used   inspection
in the manufacturing process. Although incoming and in-process
inspection are two different areas, they do share the same goal of
building a quality product.   mutual goal

Example G uses *cause and effect* to organize information about I. C. testing.
In this example, the cause and effect transitions indicate the descending order
of the reasons an I. C. chip can be rejected.

Example G Reasons for rejection of I. C. chips during in-coming inspection
fall into three categories. Most often, rejections occur because of
some flaw in the chip itself. For example, a chip may have a short
in the circuitry or fail to perform at the specified voltage or current. A second reason for rejection occurs when the supplier sends
the wrong parts or a mixed batch of parts. The final reason, which
happens infrequently, occurs when the automatic test equipment
has the wrong program or a program with a bug, so the contacts
for the electrical testing are misplaced.

The organizational patterns discussed here are equally useful in structuring
sentences, paragraphs, sections of a report, or entire documents. Although
information may be presented in a single organizational pattern, more frequently a combination of patterns is used—perhaps two within a single paragraph and several within a report. For example, a paragraph describing a
redesigned engine component could use partition to identify the separate parts
of the new component and spatial order to explain the physical relationship of
the parts. Additional organizational patterns might be used in a short progress
report:

- descending order   — to summarize most important achievements
- chronological order   — to trace weekly activities
- comparison   — to compare progress with projected time line
- cause and effect   — to explain unexpected problems
- division and   — to separate tasks in revised time line
  chronological order

These patterns are easy to recognize in published material, as the following
example illustrates.

Example It is not generally realized that 70 species of entirely marine mammals—the whales and porpoises—play as crucial a role in oceanic
ecosystems as the terrestrial mammals do on land. The broad success of the land mammals at the end of the Mesozoic era (some 65

million years ago) was due in large part to their high-energy way of life, including such features as warm-bloodedness and an expanded central nervous system. When some of these terrestrial mammals later filled a marine ecological niche, they evolved further adaptations of the same high-energy type.

CHRONOLOGY

How have the whales and porpoises—the Order Cetacea—overcome the many physiological obstacles presented by living in the ocean? Consider, for one thing their severely stressed life cycle. Initially expelled from a submerged birth canal into water that can be close to the freezing point, the newborn calf must struggle to the surface unaided before it can even take its first vital breath of air. To be suckled by its mother the calf must hold its breath and return underwater. When eventually it can feed itself, it may have to develop an entirely new behavioral repertory: diving in order to find its prey. Finally, once the cetacean is an adult, it must master a further repertory of complex gymnastics before it can reproduce and thereby give rise to the offspring that initiate the next life cycle.

SPATIAL DISTRIBUTION

CLASSIFICATION

Consider also the surprising diversity of the cetaceans, both in geographic distribution and in size. Whales and porpoises are plentiful in all the oceans, from the Tropics to the edge of the polar ice, both north and south. Many species even migrate seasonally from cold seas to warm ones and back again. The largest adult blue whale is some 20,000 times heavier than the smallest newborn porpoise, yet both large and small species are found in tropical and polar seas. The toothed whales—the odontocetes—include small porpoises such as the harbor porpoise at one end of their size range and the great sperm whale at the other. How is it that the sperm whale is the cetacean that dives the deepest and stays submerged the longest? How does it avoid the "bends" and other physiological problems human beings encounter when they dive to much shallower depths? The porpoises, being smaller than the smallest of their larger toothed-whale cousins, have a much higher surface-to-volume ratio. How do they manage to stay warm in cold water? Questions of this kind led us to the first of several investigations: the thermal physiology of porpoises.

Our observations of captive porpoises at Marineland in Florida showed us that the animals were able to maintain a stable internal temperature close to the human one and similarly well regulated. Since water removes heat from an object much faster than air does, we found this observation intriguing. We had thought these thermally stressed mammals might exhibit the more variable body temperatures typical of terrestrial hibernators. This not being the case, we were led to calculate the stringency of the thermal problem faced by a small porpoise living in the cold waters of high latitudes.

SPATIAL (BODY STRUCTURE)

For the purpose of heat-flow calculations a cetacean may be regarded as a uniformly warm fleshy core surrounded by a surface layer of insulating blubber. The outward flow of heat from the core, encountering the thermal resistance of the blubber layer, must be great enough to maintain the temperature difference between the surrounding water and the warm inner core. It is known that this difference is equal to the product of the thermal resistance of the blubber times the outward flow of metabolic heat generated in the core. When the insulation is insufficient, more body heat must be generated if the animal is to maintain a constant core temperature. For example, if the core temperature of a terrestrial mammal falls by as little as .5 degree Celsius, the mammal will begin to shiver in order to increase its metabolism. Over longer periods any such imbalance can be corrected by increasing the amount of insulation. The land mammal grows a winter coat and the whale in polar waters develops a thicker layer of blubber.

CHRONOLOGY

When the animal is active, such an increased thermal barrier may actually be too much of a good thing. For example, when a whale swims fast, the increase in its metabolic activity will cause its core to overheat. The whale then has recourse to a circulatory stratagem. An increase in blood flow near the body surface, particularly through the flippers and flukes, thermally bypasses the insulating blubber and returns the core temperature to normal. In cetaceans generally a steady body temperature is mainly achieved by such changes in blood flow. The same is true of human beings: when they are too warm, more blood is shunted to the surface of the body, producing the flushed appearance that is the opposite of being "blue from the cold."

CAUSE AND EFFECT

COMPARISON and CAUSE & EFFECT

There are fundamental differences, however, between the physiology of human beings and the physiology of whales. For example, cetaceans have no sweat glands; evaporative cooling in an aquatic environment is impossible. By the same token, for their surface insulation human beings have only a very poor equivalent of blubber. Human divers have now learned to imitate whales by wearing insulation in the form of foam rubber suits. Ashore human beings overcome the handicap of their essentially tropical origins by covering themselves with, among other things, winter insulation grown by other terrestrial mammals.[1]

CONTRAST

You can make a paragraph or document more understandable, as well as overcome some of the psychological noise that interferes with a reader's acceptance or comprehension of information, by organizing appropriately. For example, processes, procedures, and directions are best arranged in chronological order. Descriptions of physical objects, mechanisms, organisms, and locations frequently employ spatial order. Reasons and explanations most often are presented in descending order. Problems are often solved using comparison/contrast and cause/effect.

You should also consider the intended audience's abilities and attitudes because some organizational patterns are easier to understand than others. Generally, chronological, spatial, and descending orders are easier for readers than comparison/contrast or cause/effect. If the subject is very complicated and also requires the use of comparison/contrast or cause/effect, consider introducing the subject with one of the simpler patterns.

You can adapt your material to the reader's attitudes by taking advantage of what you know about induction (specific to general) and deduction (general to specific). If you think the reader might be reluctant to accept your conclusions or recommendations, you can organize the material inductively, moving from various specifics to your conclusion. Thus, the reader can follow your line of reasoning and, perhaps, be persuaded by your analysis. If you think the reader will agree with your conclusions, you can organize the information deductively, presenting the conclusion initially and then following it with the specifics that led to it. This deductive organization is more commonly used.

Outlining

Because organizing information in a verbal or visual format is usually easier if you outline your ideas, outlining is a valuable planning strategy. Outlines come in innumerable forms, but two of the most helpful are informal outlines and Warnier-Orr diagrams. These working outlines are flexible and easy to change as you rearrange ideas, add new information, and delete unnecessary material. Outlines are not intended to restrict you; rather, they are tools to help you manage the material for a document. Think of outlines as document blueprints that show overall structure and primary features. As with buildings that exist only on paper, changes in documents are easier to make before drafting.

Outlines are logical extensions of parts/whole analysis. An outline divides a subject and then subdivides and sometimes partitions it. As you plan your material, you can ask yourself these questions to check whether your working outline will be useful:

- Are the main headings arranged according to some organizational pattern (chronological, spatial, descending order, comparison/contrast, or cause/effect)?
- Is the organizational pattern most appropriate for your purpose?
- Does the sequence of the main headings accurately summarize your document? Would reading the main headings give a reader an accurate overview of your document?
- Do the main headings reflect the major divisions of the document?
- Are main headings written in parallel grammatical form?
- Are the items in the subsections arranged according to some organizational pattern?

- Are these organizational patterns most appropriate for your purpose?
- Are the items in the subsections complete and accurate?
- Does the detail in each subsection reflect the appropriate emphasis for that main heading in relation to the rest of the document? Do you use few details for unimportant sections and more details for important sections?
- Is all important information included?
- Is all information in the correct place?
- Is all unnecessary information omitted?
- Are items within each subsection written in the same grammatical form?

If you can answer yes to all these questions, your outline will be useful in planning, organizing, and drafting your document. Like the parts/whole charts in the previous section, outlines give you a chance to examine the content and structure of a paragraph or document without being burdened by sentences. In a long document, the outline main headings often provide ready-made subheadings. Outlines can also be modified for use as a table of contents. They can provide the phrases for headings and subheadings within a document. Sometimes outlines actually form the body of a document, as in the excerpt from an article, "External and Internal Parasites—Causes, Symptoms, Treatment, and Control."

Example

INTRODUCTION

Dairy goats, like other animals, wild or domestic, have their share of parasites (both external and internal) and effective parasitic treatment, prevention and control play an integral part in milk and meat production. . . .

There are two main types of parasites in most domestic animals including the dairy goat. In this article, basic information will be presented on the common signs and symptoms of the most prevalent external and internal parasites along with their treatment, prevention and control.

1. EXTERNAL PARASITES
A. Lice

Lice are the most common external parasites of dairy goats. The two primary types of lice which affect goats are:

1. Biting louse—Bovicola caprae
2. The sucking louse—Linognathus stenopsis

The biting louse, red in color, feeds on the skin and burrows into the hair follicles causing severe itching. The blood-sucking louse, blue in color, is larger and more visible. It pierces the skin to feed and is prevalent on the sides of the neck, underline and around the udder.

Symptoms.

a. Excessive scratching against the sides of the barn, fence post and wire.
b. Weight loss.
c. Decreased milk production.
d. The appearance of dry, crusty or scabby areas on the back, side of the face and underside of the neck.

Treatment and Control. The best time to control and treat lice is in the fall. Dipping or spraying using "Coral" (coumaphos) is the drug of choice even in lactating animals. Good control is obtained if spraying is repeated once or twice at least 10–14 days apart to kill all the lice which hatch from eggs. Lice must live on their host to survive, thus neither barns nor bedding need be treated.

B. Mange

Two types of mange are common in dairy goats:

1. Sarcoptes scabei, var. caprae
2. Demodectic spp

Sarcoptic mange, *Sarcoptes scabei var. caprae* is seen mostly around the neck, the underline, and face, while demodex is generalized but can be commonly found in the flank and udder areas. Demodex, the more prevalent of the two, is caused by *Demodex caprae.* The mites which burrow into the hair follicles leave blebs (or small raised welts) which are mainly detected by shaving the hair close, or passing the hand over the areas involved.

Symptoms.

a. In addition to excessive scratching, sarcoptic mange exhibits a relative thickening of the (epidermal) layer of skin in the areas of irritation.
b. With demodex, when the hair is shaved, the blebs or subcutaneous swellings laden with mites are seen. These swellings or nodules, ranging in size from pin head to hazel-nut, contain thick grayish material of waxy consistency, which can be easily expressed. Numerous demodectic mites are found in this material.

Treatment. Frequent dips with an insecticide are necessary, and "Coral" (coumaphos) does an effective job even with lactating animals.

C. EAR MITES

Ear mite infestation in the dairy goat is a common problem and is easy to misdiagnose. The infestation is caused by a mite of the genus Psoroptes spp.[2]

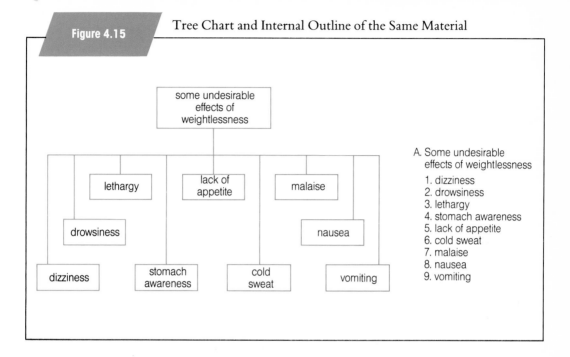

Figure 4.15   Tree Chart and Internal Outline of the Same Material

A. Some undesirable effects of weightlessness

1. dizziness
2. drowsiness
3. lethargy
4. stomach awareness
5. lack of appetite
6. cold sweat
7. malaise
8. nausea
9. vomiting

Informal Outlines

One way to organize a document is to make a parts/whole chart into an informal outline, as Figure 4.15 illustrates.

Outlines can help you arrange and examine collected information. They do not have to be formal, complete-sentence outlines. Initially you can just jot information and later rethink, rearrange, and reorganize it in an outline. For example, in reporting the findings of a Harvard ethnobotanist attempting to explain the zombies of traditional Haitian voodoo,[3] a writer could list points of information without organizing them:

- natives believe in zombies (walking dead); fertile ground for mind control
- natives believe in power of a *bocor*, malevolent voodoo priest
- zombies created by a *bocor*; sophisticated knowledge of pharamacology and psychology
- poisons from puffer fish contain powerful neurotoxin, tetrodotoxin
- initially produces hypothermia, nausea, respiratory difficulties, hypertension, hypotension, paralysis

- long-term control maintained with hallucinogenic plant containing daturas; causes disorientation, amnesia
- *bocor* have variety of poisons, all with same main ingredient
- tetrodotoxin reduces metabolic functions to deathlike state

This list can be developed into a preliminary outline to help the writer determine whether the information is complete and parallel—equivalent in importance, sequence, and wording. While constructing an outline, a writer arranges the information, in this case using division, chronology, and cause and effect:

- division—separates the list into physical and mental control
- chronology—sequences the information; first poison with tetrodotoxin, then control with daturas
- cause and effect—identifies the drug, then presents the symptoms and effects

The preliminary outline presented has incomplete information, needs reordering, and isn't parallel. But without the outline, the writer might not see these inadequacies.

Example

Topic: Folk myth about zombies possible through combination of pharmacology and psychology

wording not parallel; complete sentence—all other entries are phrases

I. Physiological control is initiated and maintained through drugs given by a *bocor*, malevolent voodoo priest
    A. Poison from puffer fish containing tetrodotoxin

missing information: need to identify type of poison

        1. Symptoms
           a. Hypothermia
           b. Nausea

illogical structure with only one subheading

           c. Respiratory difficulties
           d. Sequence of hypertension, hypotension, and finally complete paralysis

not parallel wording in subsections a, b, c, d, and e

           e. Reduced metabolic functions create deathlike state
    B. Maintain control with plant containing daturas

not parallel with structure under A

        1. Causes disorientation and amnesia

subsections in wrong order

        2. Hallucinogenic
II. Mental control through psychological manipulation
    A. Native belief in zombies
    B. Belief in own death
    C. Surrender of personality and soul

out of sequence; should be A, not D

    D. Susceptible because of poison and hallucinogenic drugs

The writer has corrected the problems in the following revised version of the same outline. The changes are more than cosmetic. First, expressing ideas in parallel structure demonstrates that the writer intends to treat them equally, as shown in the revision of section I-B. Next, the sequence of entries must be logical, as shown in the revision in the order of entries in section II. Here, indicating native susceptibility logically comes first; instances of their beliefs resulting from this susceptibility follow. Finally, essential information must not be inadvertently omitted, as shown by the omission of the type of poison in section I-A. In each case, changing the outline is easier than changing the draft of the paper.

Revision

Topic: Folk myth about zombies possible through combination of pharmacology and psychology

I. Physiological control through drugs by a *bocor*, malevolent
  voodoo priest   phrase now
                       parallel with II
  A. Poison from puffer fish containing tetrodotoxin   added type of poison
    1. Powerful neurotoxin
    2. Symptoms
      a. Hypothermia
      b. Nausea
      c. Respiratory difficulties
      d. Sequence of hypertension, hypotension, and finally
        complete paralysis   parallel structure
      e. Deathlike state from reduced metabolic functions with other subsections
  B. Maintain control with plant containing daturas
                    order corrected
    1. Hallucinogenic   A and B now parallel
    2. Symptoms
      a. Disorientation
      b. Amnesia

II. Mental control through psychological manipulation
  A. Susceptible because of poison and hallucinogenic drugs
  B. Native belief in zombies
  C. Belief in own death
  D. Surrender of personality and soul

Warnier-Orr Diagrams

Another organizational strategy is based on the Warnier-Orr diagram, which some writers believe presents the relationships between ideas more effectively than a traditional outline. The Warnier-Orr diagram places equal emphasis on organization and content development.

The diagram separates the main points at each level of a document into columns, grouping and aligning one-, two-, and three-level elements. As a result, a writer can better examine the overall structure as well as the development of a series of primary or subordinate ideas. When examining the

Figure 4.16   Warnier-Orr Diagram Compared to a Traditional Outline

i	ii	iii	iv
			[1]
		[A]	[2]
	[I]		[1]
		[B]	[2]
			[1]
		[A]	[2]
[Title]	[II]		[1]
		[B]	[2]
			[1]
		[A]	[2]
	[III]		[1]
		[B]	[2]

Source: Henry R. Harrington and Richard E. Walton, "The Warnier-Orr Diagram for Designing Essays," *Journal of Technical Writing and Communication* 14 (1984): 193–201.

columns, a writer focuses primarily on the organization of any level of the proposed document. When examining the diagram horizontally, a writer focuses on development of content. Flaws in the organization and inadequately developed content of writing become obvious in a Warnier-Orr diagram.

A Warnier-Orr diagram can be used instead of a traditional outline or as a supplement. It provides an alternative method for examining the organization and content during the planning stage. Although a Warnier-Orr diagram is no easier to construct than a traditional outline, it is more effective for quickly identifying potential weaknesses in a document. Figure 4.16 shows how the diagram uses spatial organization to display relationships between ideas.

The following Warnier-Orr diagram, which outlines a section of an article, shows how to determine if the information is well organized and complete. A quick scan indicates that in column iii the development of the third main topic is not parallel to the first two.

Example

i	ii	iii	iv
		—Warm blooded	—environmental-monitoring temperature-regulating brain centers —internal thermostat shuts down so body heat, respiration, metabolism fall rapidly, resulting in unconsciousness
	—Triggered by seasonal changes in temperature	—Cold blooded	—no internal thermostat — bodies respond to seasonal cold
Hibernation	—Protection against freezing	—Warm blooded	—breathe faster — fluff fur; shiver
		—Cold blooded	—careful burrow selection —dehydration in some species to avoid ice crystals in organs and blood vessels
	—Benefits of hibernation	—no food needed during winter —resistance to illness —drop in infection and parasite levels —rise in antibody levels	

A revision of this section clarifies that benefits apply equally to both warm- and cold-blooded animals.

Revision

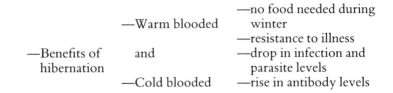

Such a change can be more difficult to make in a traditional outline because the lack of development wouldn't have been as obvious.

Organizational Strategies

Effective organization of information alone will not make the material immediately clear to the reader. Just as outlines and diagrams are important during the planning stage, three other strategies are necessary for the actual draft: *topic sentences* to establish subject and organization, *unity* to limit the subject, and *coherence* to assure continuity.

Topic Sentences

One of the easiest ways to establish a strong paragraph is to start it with a topic sentence. An effective topic sentence identifies both content and organization of the paragraph, so the reader begins the sentence with definite expectations.

Chronological order. A topic sentence conveying chronological order includes words or phrases that indicate a process or a sequence of actions, as illustrated in the following sentences.

Examples   Seven operations are necessary to fabricate sheet metal. . . .

Most poultry farms are vertically integrated, from breeding to egg to packaged product. . . .

The reader justifiably expects the paragraph that follows the first topic sentence to identify and explain the seven steps of sheet-metal fabrication. The paragraph that follows the second topic sentence should identify each stage in the process of poultry production.

Spatial order. Because spatial order deals with the relative physical location of objects, the topic sentence suggests their placement, as seen in these examples.

Examples   Unnecessary or damaged inventory that is scheduled to be scrapped is placed on skids in one of six bin locations in the Defective Stockroom. . . .

Sound is a ripple of molecules and atoms in the air that travels from its source to our ears. . . .

The reader of the first sentence anticipates the identification of each bin's location according to type of scrap material. The second topic sentence indicates to the reader that the paragraph will track the sound as it moves through the air from source to listener.

Descending/ascending order. Unlike topic sentences for paragraphs using other organizational patterns, those beginning descending or ascending paragraphs do not give an immediate clue about the subsequent pattern. The reader understands that the paragraph will present a series of related ideas, but the specific relationship is not clear until the second sentence. The topic sentence in the next example begins a paragraph about the master station in Beijing, presenting the characteristics of the Beijing antenna in descending order.

Example   The largest earth station in China is a 15-to-18-meter-diameter dish antenna in Beijing for domestic satellite communications.

A paragraph using descending order to identify the various sized antennas in China begins with a general statement before going on to identify each type of station.

Example   Three types of earth stations are planned for domestic satellite communication in China. The largest is a 15-to-18-meter-diameter dish antenna of the master station in Beijing. . . . Regional stations are equipped with a 10-to-13-meter-diameter antenna. . . .[4]

Comparison/contrast. The reader expects comparison and contrast sentences to present ideas dealing with similarities and differences, or both, as illustrated by the following two sentences.

Examples   The Honey Bee Lens, with three telescopic lenses for each eye, is patterned after the compound eye of a bee.

Computers can now analyze measurable differences between the cries of healthy newborns and high-risk infants. . . .

The first sentence introduces a paragraph that compares new lenses to the compound eyes of bees. The second sentence leads the reader to expect that the paragraph will deal with characteristics that differentiate cries of healthy and high-risk infants.

Cause and effect. In paragraphs that show cause and effect, both should be identified in the topic sentence, as seen in the next examples.

Examples   One hypothesis about the formation of mineral-rich marine nodules suggests that marine bacteria break down organic material into free-floating minerals that eventually collect to form nodules. . . .

The Zephinie Escape Chute (ZEC) can rapidly evacuate people from 10-story burning buildings because of its unique construction. . . .

The reader of the first sentence expects the information in the paragraph to explain how minerals form marine nodules. The second sentence develops a paragraph that explains how the ZEC's unique construction aids rapid evacuation.

Will every paragraph in a document have a topic sentence? Not necessarily. Some paragraphs are transitional, connecting one main paragraph or section to the next. Occasionally, an excessively long paragraph will be separated into two or more to reduce the visual density of solid type and give the reader a chance to breathe. Usually, however, the paragraphs in a well-constructed report will have clear topic sentences, which can be separated from the document and listed together. If the message from this topic sentence summary is clear and logical, then the document is probably well constructed.

Unity

An effective topic sentence provides the subject for a unified paragraph. *Unity* is a quality of writing that subordinates each sentence in a paragraph to that topic sentence. A paragraph that is not unified has information that does not relate to the topic sentence, as illustrated in the following example.

Example   Quality Control Circles is a program that brings together the techniques of Quality Control and the philosophies of the behavioral scientists. Doctors Deming, Juran, and Ishikawa have been leaders in the statistical quality control field and some of their teachings are included in QC Circles training. But QC Circles are useful to more than quality control departments. Also brought into the program are the findings of such behavioral scientists as Douglas McGregor and Frederick Herzberg. For instance, McGregor

attaches a "Y" label to the style of managerial behavior that recognizes the intellectual potential of every member of the workforce—not just that of the management. Another important theory
included in the QC Circle philosophy was developed by Frederick
Herzberg: employees are better, more contributing employees if
they are given responsibilities for having some influence over how
they go about doing their work. Supervisors and managers are
introduced to QC Circles in a seminar.

Two sentences in this paragraph do not directly relate to or support the topic
sentence; the paragraph is better unified if these sentences are omitted.

Revision Quality Control Circles is a program that brings together the techniques of Quality Control and the philosophies of the behavioral
scientists. Doctors Deming, Juran, and Ishikawa have been leaders
in the statistical quality control field and some of their teachings are
included in QC Circles training. ~~But QC Circles are useful to more
than quality control departments.~~ Also brought into the program
are the findings of such behavioral scientists as Douglas McGregor
and Frederick Herzberg. For instance, McGregor attaches a "Y"
label to the style of managerial behavior that recognizes the intellectual potential of every member of the workforce—not just that of
the management. Another important theory included in the QC
Circle philosophy was developed by Frederick Herzberg: employees are better, more contributing employees if they are given responsibilities for having some influence over how they go about
doing their work. ~~Supervisors and managers are introduced to QC
Circles in a seminar.~~[5]

Closely related to the concept of unity of thought within a paragraph is
unity of terminology. One of the most confusing things a writer can do is to
refer to the same object, process, or idea by more than one name, causing the
reader to think another subject has been introduced. In the following sentences, how many types of tubing are identified?

- Formula S-50-HL tubing is clear, flexible, and nonaging, important
  characteristics for hospital and surgical applications.
- Tygon surgical tubing is made for use with heart/lung machines.
- Modified PVC tubing is used with peristaltic pumps, artificial kidneys,
  and similar surgical apparatus.
- U.S.P. class VI tubing that also meets Federal Specifications L-T-790 A,
  Type I is appropriate for many surgical applications.

All four sentences describe identical tubing; to avoid confusion, the writer
should select one term for consistent reference. Technical writing does not
benefit from the practice used in fiction and feature writing that encourages
the use of various synonyms for the same object, process, or idea. (The need

for consistent terminology is discussed in "Appropriate Diction" in Chapter 12.)

Of course, each paragraph in a document should be unified, but that alone does not produce a unified document. Two other strategies are useful. First, make an informal outline of points to be included in a document; you'll see whether the sequence of ideas is related. Second, just as each unified paragraph develops and supports a topic sentence, each paragraph in a unified document develops and supports a purpose statement. This purpose statement, developed by the writer during the planning stage, identifies the primary intent of informing, directing, or persuading the audience. This purpose statement is usually incorporated into the introduction of a document.

Coherence

While unity assures that all the ideas relate to the same subject, *coherence* assures that the ideas follow logically, one after the other. A writer creates coherent documents in several ways. By logically analyzing and organizing the information, as already discussed in this chapter, a writer establishes patterns for the audience to follow. A writer also uses appropriate transitions to establish relationships among ideas. If too many ideas are lumped together and the material is too dense to read, transitions and explanations can ease the problem. Or a writer can employ "known-new" strategies to rearrange information.

Transitions. Transitions are one of the most important techniques in achieving coherence. Acting as the glue that connects one idea to the next, transitions can be words, phrases, sentences, or even short paragraphs. Transitions connect ideas and sentences within a single paragraph, link one paragraph to another, and even relate one section of a document to the next section.

A writer best uses word and phrase transitions by matching them with various organizational patterns, as shown in the following samples. *Chronological transitions* indicate the sequence of events or the passage of time:

Transition	*Application*
while	while the sample cools
before	before the injection
final	the final stage
seconds	10-second delay
minutes	within two minutes

Additional Chronological Transitions	
first	immediately
initially	next
second	sporadically
third	after
in turn	momentarily
then	later

Spatial transitions suggest the relative physical location of components or objects:

Transition	Application
above	above the horizon
perpendicular	perpendicular to the roof line
mm	extend within 6 mm of the base
parallel	set parallel to the heating coil
beneath	beneath the membrane

Additional Spatial Transitions	
below	horizontal
next to	extended 30°
behind	at the next level
2″ apart	internally
overhead	running diagonally
36″ roadbed	adjacent to

Descending and ascending transitions indicate the relative priority of points in the paragraph or document:

Transition	Application
highest	the highest cost factor
increasing	of increasing concern
easiest	easiest to use of all models tested
fewest	fewest repairs during 12-month period
lower	selected for its lower cost-to-benefit ratio

Additional Ascending/Descending Transitions	
the most significant	least necessary
smallest	least utilized
of minor interest	frequent
of least consequence	less durable
most helpful	slightly
more likely	somewhat

Comparison and contrast transitions identify various similarities and differences:

Transition	Application
comparable	comparable to the less expensive model
distinctive	distinctive in three significant features
commensurate	commensurate with competitors' benefits
unlike	unlike the automatic ejection
analogous	analogous to the production of the XM-374

Additional Comparison/Contrast Transitions	
similarly	also
like	not only, but also
resembling	conversely
proportional	in opposition
correlative	on the other hand
in contrast	dissimilar to

Cause and effect transitions signal the relationship between an action and its result:

Transition	Application
evolving from	evolving from work done by earlier geneticists
since	since the hatch cover is warped
therefore	therefore the report will be delayed
consequently	consequently the department needs new collets

Additional Cause/Effect Transitions	
based on	as a result of
following that	generated by
caused by	brought about by
due to	resulting in
because of	necessarily
it follows that	if, then

Density. Transitional elements do more than give the reader clues about organization of information. Sometimes a paragraph appears to focus on a single topic, has correct sentence structure, yet is difficult to read. Such a paragraph can suffer from "density"; the ideas are packed so tightly that connections are omitted, and the reader has trouble following the reasoning. Several techniques help make writing less dense:

- separate information into several sentences
- develop important points in separate paragraphs
- use direct diction

- use visual devices to highlight key ideas: lists, bullets, tables, underlines, italics, boldface
- illustrate objects and concepts to aid understanding
- add examples to illustrate points
- add explanations for important points
- use headings and subheadings to identify key sections
- add transitions within paragraphs and between paragraphs and sections of a document

In the following paragraph about a three-fingered robot hand, the information is so dense that the reader has trouble absorbing it. The sentences are long and wordy, with few transitions to establish relationships among the ideas; in some places, additional information is needed.

Example   A robot hand can perform rapid, small motions by humanlike finger actions—independently of its manipulator arm, be attachable to many different manipulators without any modifications to the arms, and has the potential as a prosthesis for humans. The hand employs three opposed fingers, each one with three joints and a cushioned tip on the outer segment, controlled by four sheathed cables running to motors on the forearm. The motor drives on the forearm impose no loads on the hand actuators, and the drives are more easily accommodated on the forearm and have a much smaller effect on its response than they would if located on the hand. The robot-hand fingers can provide more than three contact areas since more than one segment per finger can contact an object; thus, the robot hand can move objects about, twist them, and otherwise manipulate them by finger motion alone.

Revision of this paragraph uses some of the devices recommended above— writing shorter sentences, separating information into several paragraphs, adding a clarifying figure, and including transitions to signal relationships.

Revision   A robot hand currently under development performs rapid, small motions by humanlike finger actions—independently of its manipulator arm. Without modification, the robot hand attaches to many different arms. The hand even has the potential as a prosthesis for humans.

As shown in the figure, the hand employs three opposed fingers. Each has three joints and a cushioned tip on the outer segment. Each finger is controlled by four sheathed cables running to motors on the forearm.

The new hand eliminates some problems with previous designs. Its motor drives are on the forearm (rather than on the hand itself), where their weight and inertia impose no loads on the hand actuators. The drives are more easily accommodated on the forearm and have a much smaller effect on its response than they would if located on the hand.

Like the fingers on the human hand, the robot-hand fingers provide more than three contact areas since more than one segment per finger contacts an object. Thus, like the human hand, the robot hand moves and manipulates objects by finger motion alone.[6]

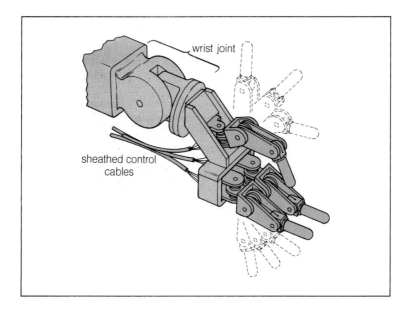

"Known-new" analysis. Another way to achieve coherence in some paragraphs is to apply "known-new" analysis. The theory of known-new states that new information should be connected to what the reader already knows, either from background knowledge or from immediately preceding reading. Three variations of known-new are possible, with A, B, C, and so on representing pieces of information:

- Variation I
  sentence: known A tagged with new B
  sentence: known A tagged with new C
  sentence: known A tagged with new D
  sentence: known A tagged with new E

Example   The ink of a squid [A] is brown or black viscous fluid [B], which is contained in a reservoir. The ink [A] is ejected through the siphon when a squid is alarmed [C]. This ink [A] not only forms an effective screen behind which the animal can escape [D], but it [A] contains alkaloids that paralyze the olfactory senses of the enemy [E].

- Variation II
  sentence: known A tagged with new B (so now B is known)
  sentence: known B tagged with new C (now C is known)
  sentence: known C tagged with new D (now D is known)
  sentence: known D tagged with new E (now E is known)

Example   All squids [A] propel themselves by taking in and forcibly expelling water from the mantle cavity through the siphon [B]. The force and direction of the water expelled [B], plus the undulation of the fins and body, determine the direction and rapid movement [C] of the animals. The rapid movement [C] is always in the opposite direction of the water ejected from the siphon [D]. The ejection of the water [D] also oxygenates the gills, located in the mantle cavity [E].

- Variation III (a combination of I and II, with the sentence sequence variable)
  sentence: known A tagged with new B
  sentence: known B tagged with new C
  sentence: known A tagged with new D
  sentence: known B tagged with new E
  sentence: known B tagged with new F

Example   The unusual coloration [A] of squid is caused by the presence of integumental pigment cells [B]. These cells [B], called chromatophores, contain red, blue, yellow, and black pigment [C]. Coloration [A] is specific to each species [D]. The chromatophores, color cells, [B] are controlled by muscles that expand or contract in relation to visual or olfactory stimuli, thus changing the color of the animal [E]. The pigment cells' [B] release of color into the flesh of a dead animal indicates the onset of spoilage [F].[7]

Known-new analysis aids revision by giving you a quick, effective way to check whether you introduced material that the reader wouldn't expect. The following paragraph is technically accurate but difficult to read because the writer pays little attention to coherence; some of the new ideas that pop up do not connect to what the reader already knows. Too much new information in too short a space lessens the reader's chances of understanding and retaining the information. Known-new analysis quickly illuminates why the paragraph seems difficult—the subject shifts too many times.

Example   (1) Hot Isotatic Processing [A] makes metal more dense [B]. (2) Dense metal [B] is more durable [C]. (3) Metal parts [D] cannot be cast without unavoidable small cracks and air pockets [E]. (4) Imperfections [E] lead to wear and breakage [F]. (5) These flaws [E] can be eliminated with Hot Isostatic Processing [A]. (6) The parts [D] are heated in special units, then pressurized with gas to minimize flaws [G]. (7) A controlled cooling process [H] ensures that the parts retain their original shape [I]. (8) Hot Isostatic Processing [A] produces stronger parts, able to withstand greater pressures for a longer span of time [J].

(1) A : B (2) B : C
(3) D : E (two new subjects)

(4) E : F
(5) E : A
(6) D : G

(7) H : I (two more new subjects)

(8) A : J

The first revision of this paragraph uses a consistent subject for all the sentences. Because each sentence relates new information to what is already known, readers follow ideas more easily.

Revision 1   (1) *Cast metal parts* can be made more durable if they undergo Hot Isostatic Processing to eliminate flaws that occur during casting. (2) *Metal parts* cannot be cast without small cracks and air pockets, imperfections that lead to wear and breakage. (3) During the Hot Isostatic Process, *cast metal parts* are heated in special units, then pressurized with a gas to minimize these casting flaws. (4) The *parts* are able to retain their original shape because of a controlled cooling process. (5) Stronger *parts*, able to withstand greater pressures for longer periods, result from Hot Isostatic Processing.

(1) A : B

(2) A : C

(3) A : C

(4) A : D
(5) A : E

A second revision also results from known-new analysis.

Revision 2   (1) *Hot Isostatic Processing* makes *cast metal parts* more dense and, thus, more durable. (2) *Metal parts* cannot be cast without *small cracks and air pockets*, imperfections that lead to wear and breakage. (3) These *flaws* can be eliminated with *Hot Isostatic Processing*. (4) The *cast metal parts* are heated in special units, then pressurized with gas to *minimize flaws*. (5) The *parts* retain their *shape* because of a controlled cooling process. (6) *Hot Isostatic Processing* produces *stronger parts*, able to withstand greater pressures for longer periods.

(1) A : B
(2) B : C

(3) C : A
(4) B : D
(5) B : E
(6) A : F

Inquiries and Applications

Discussion Questions

1. In what ways do topic sentences make technical information easier to read?
2. Paragraph density and lack of coherence result partly from infrequent use of transitions, but for a reader who is an expert in the subject, why are transitions necessary? Won't an expert understand the relationships among the ideas?
3. What are the advantages of using either an informal outline or a Warnier-Orr diagram? Which do you prefer?
4. Biological researcher Lance Stewart is preparing a report about the results of his work during the past six months. He wants his readers to follow the progress of his experiments step by step, not knowing the results until they read the conclusions and recommendations at the end of the report. He says he worked hard to get the results; he wants the readers to appreciate all his work. What is wrong with Lance's reason for placing conclusions and recommendations at the end? What would you say to persuade him to reconsider his plan?
5. Identify the organizational pattern indicated by each of these topic sentences:
   a. The CAT Scan creates an image resembling a "slice" that clearly visualizes anatomical structures within the body.
   b. The fetus is in the birth position by the ninth month of a normal pregnancy.
   c. The routine use of drugs in labor and delivery sometimes has adverse effects on otherwise healthy, normal infants.
   d. The stages of normal labor and delivery begin at term when the fetus reaches maturity and end with the expulsion of the placenta.
   e. Two major forms of leukemia—chronic myelocytic and acute myelocytic—have distinct differences.
   f. Improper downstroke and follow-through can cause the golf ball to either hook and fade to the left or slice and fade to the right.
   g. Three main types of parachutes are used for skydiving. The most widely used parachute has a round, dome-like canopy. . . .
   h. A square parachute provides more maneuverability and a better overall ride than a conventional round parachute.
   i. Two methods of disinfecting treated wastewater are chlorination and ozonation.
   j. The chlorinator room contains the evaporators, chlorinators, and injectors, three of each. The evaporators are used only when liquid chlorine is being drawn from the containers. . . .

Individual and Group Exercises

1. Identify the combined organizational patterns used in the following excerpt from an article entitled "Modern Pork Production." Discuss whether the writer has selected the most appropriate organizational patterns for the information.

Example   The pig lingers in the memory of many people as a farmstead animal that roots in the ground for various edibles, wallows in mud and is fed slop and swill, meaning the liquid and semiliquid leavings from the farmer's kitchen and the operation of the farm. That is not the pig of modern agribusiness. Such a pig lives indoors for its entire brief life: born and suckled in a farrowing unit and raised to slaughter weight in a nursery and later in a growing-feeding unit. It is fed a computer-formulated diet based on cornmeal and soybean meal with supplements of protein, minerals and vitamins. Unless it is destined for breeding, it is sent to market at five or six months of age, having reached the slaughter weight of 220 pounds or more from its birth weight of about two pounds. In the U.S., which is one of the leading countries in the production of pork, some 97 million pigs with a value of $8.9 billion went to market in 1980.

It is best to be precise about terminology. All pigs, wild and domestic, are swine, members of the family Suidae, which in turn is a member of the mammalian order Artiodactyla (even-toed ungulates). In the U.K. all domestic swine are called pigs, but in the U.S. the term applies technically to young swine weighing less than about 120 pounds; the others are called hogs. One hears also of boars (uncastrated males), barrows (castrated males), gilts (virgin females), sows (females that have bred) and shoats (newly weaned piglets.)

The domestic pigs of today are descended from the European wild pig (*Sus scrofa*), which is also known as the European wild boar. Pigs living in the wild are still found in many regions of the world. Except for old males, which are solitary, wild pigs live in groups. They are nocturnal and omnivorous, digging for edible roots and tubers, gathering fruits and nuts on the ground and also eating a large variety of insects, reptiles, birds and small mammals. The wild pig stands about 90 centimeters (35 inches) tall at the shoulder and has a thick coat of bristly hair. It is a fast runner and a good swimmer.

The time of domestication of the pig is lost in history. One study has it that the earliest known domestication of pigs was in what is now Iraq in about 6750 B.C. A Chinese scholar has asserted that domesticated pigs were to be found in his country by 2900 B.C. Probably the attractiveness of the pig as a domestic animal originally was that it is an efficient scavenger and will eat a wide variety of foods. This is still its role in many developing countries.

In modern agribusiness the pig is attractive because of its efficiency in converting feed into food. Today's pig gains a pound of weight for each three or 3.5 pounds of food it eats. Fifty years ago it took more than four pounds of food to achieve the same result. In terms of the pig's yield of edible energy per calorie consumed it outdoes cattle, lambs and poultry. Indeed, the production of pork, like that of beef, lamb and poultry, is based on the economic advantage for the farmer of selling his crops through animals at a higher profit than he would realize by selling the crops directly for human food.

From the consumer's point of view the meat of the pig has high nutritional values. A four-ounce serving of lean pork supplies about three-fourths of the adult's daily need for thiamin and iron, from a fourth to a third of the need for niacin, vitamin B-6 and vitamin B-12, half of the need for protein and most of the requirement for trace minerals. In North America and Europe the annual consumption of pork is about 60 pounds per capita; the worldwide average, however, is less than 20 pounds per capita. Since the demand for animal protein in the diet increases linearly with average per capita income in a country, the geographic disparities in the consumption of pork largely reflect the huge disparity in per capita income among countries.

Modern Practices

The trend that took the pig out of the pigpen and into a carefully controlled environment resulted from high labor costs, the rise in land values, the fact that it became more profitable to raise crops on productive land than to keep animals on it, the ability to keep the pig's diet under closer control indoors and the possibility for more effective control of diseases and parasites. On a farm that raises pigs from birth to marketing age, which is a strong modern trend, a typical physical arrangement includes a unit housing pregnant sows, a farrowing unit where the sows give birth, a nursery and a growing-finishing unit. They all have slatted floors for easier removal of wastes. In Temperate Zone farms each unit (except sometimes the growing-finishing unit) has a heating system.

The main task of husbandry is feeding the pigs, an operation that accounts for from 55 to 85 percent of the total cost of the commercial production of pork. The variations result from the relative costs of feed, labor and housing between one farm and another or from one season to the next. The economics of feeding swine depend on the local availability and price of feedstuff, competition for a particular foodstuff for consumption by people or by other domestic animals and the prices of the protein, mineral and vitamin supplements.[8]

2. Editing Exercise: Revise the memo in Example 4.1 by deleting sentences that do not directly support the topic sentence. The intended audience is interested in information that will help decrease rejects during manufacturing. They are not particularly concerned with personnel or cost.

Example 4.1

⟩⟩ Stanford Engineering, Inc.

February 14, 1986

TO: Quality Control Supervisor
FROM: R. Hood, Engineer *R.H.*
SUBJECT: Increased scrap and customer
              rejects

The Engineering Department is recommending the purchase of an Internal glue line inspection system to strengthen standard visual inspection. Machine operators will not be slowed down by the addition of this new glue line inspection system. The system will detect breaks in the glue line and eject a carton from the run before it reaches shipping. If the system detects more than five consecutive rejects, it will automatically stop the machine.

Purchasing this International system is a better solution than purchasing a new glue pot for $6,500. The savings in purchasing the $4,000 International system will allow us to rebuild the existing glue pot.

3. Editing Exercise: Revise the following paragraphs by adding topic sentences.

Buss bars, the smallest of the parts the Sheet Metal Fabrication Shop produces, are made of grade A copper and are tin-plated before being used for internal grounding. Paper deflectors, used in printers, are made of stainless steel and do not require any plating or painting. Deflectors guide the paper through the printer and usually measure 4″ in width and 15″ in length, depending on the size of the printer. A larger boxlike structure, made of aluminum and requiring plating in the enclosure chassis, is designed to hold a variety of electronic devices within an even larger computer main frame. A steel door panel requiring cosmetic plating and painting is the largest of the parts produced by the Sheet Metal Fabrication Shop.

The fetal causes for abortion are infectious agents: protozoa, bacteria, viruses, particularly rubella virus. Drugs such as thalidomide cause fetal abnormalities. When radiation is given in therapeutic doses to the mother in the first few months of pregnancy, malformation or death of the fetus may result.

4. Editing Exercise: Revise the following paragraph to eliminate density. You may separate the material into shorter paragraphs, use lists, and add or delete material. This information was part of a memo informing employees about changes in procedures dealing with scrapped parts.

Several steps must be taken to separate and stage inventory to be scrapped. The first step is to locate and stage all excess parts. The white tag on each part will identify the part as either EXCESS, GOOD or EXCESS, DAMAGED. Parts tagged EXCESS, GOOD should be staged in bin #020185. Parts tagged EXCESS, DAMAGED should be staged in bin #020186 for further sorting and staging by code. The code is etched into the frame of each part: 1A—defective consumable, 1B—unidentified damage, 1C—vendor return/unrepairable, 1D—identifiable damage. Parts labeled code 1A, defective consumables, are staged in bin #020188, to be automatically scrapped without further investigation. Parts labeled code 1C, vendor return/unrepairable, are staged in bin #020189; these parts can also be automatically scrapped. If a part is labeled code 1B, additional information is required. Code 1B parts should be visually examined for signs of damage such as broken chips or split jumper cables. Parts with observable damage should be placed on a skid in bin #020187. Parts with no observable damage should be hand carried to the Repair Center where each part will be tested to determine the extent of damage. Parts the Repair Center determines cannot be repaired are staged in bin #020187. Parts the Repair Center believes are repairable are placed in the Repair Stockroom and scheduled for repair. Parts labeled with code 1D are staged in bin #020190. When ten or more skids have accumulated, the manager should be notified to check the accumulated parts and fill out a justification form to scrap each part.

Assignments

1. Select a single topic that will be the subject for five paragraphs, each using a different organizational pattern. Identify the specific audience for whom you are writing. When a parallel visual form could be used to present the information, include it with the paragraph, clearly referring to it in the text. Each paragraph should have a topic sentence that reflects both the organization and the content. Transitions should be appropriate for the organizational pattern.

   You may approach the assignment in one of two different ways:

   a. Use the same information (or as close as possible) for all five paragraphs so that you gain experience in writing about the same aspect of a subject in a variety of ways. The five paragraphs will not form a unified, cohesive paper, but will serve as a rigorous exercise.

   b. Use the same subject for all five paragraphs, but select material so that the paragraphs form a unified, coherent paper.

2. Jim Smith knows something is wrong with an important section of a report. He recognizes that the paragraphs are confusing because they are so full of numeric data. Suggest and then create alternate ways for Jim to present the same information.

5　Sentence Structure and Diction

THE FOLLOWING PASSAGE cites relevant state laws for the general sports enthusiast.

Example　*Lake or Pond Partly in Another State.* If, in the case of a lake or pond situated partly in this state and partly in another state, the laws of such other state permit fishing in that part thereof lying within such other state by persons licensed or otherwise entitled under the laws of this state to fish in that part of such lake or pond lying within this state, persons licensed or otherwise entitled under the laws of such other state to fish in the part of such lake or pond lying within such other state shall be permitted to fish in that part thereof lying within this state, and, as to such lake or pond, the operation of the laws of this state relative to open and closed seasons, limits of catch, minimum sizes of fish caught and methods of fishing shall be suspended upon the adoption and during the continuance in force of rules and regulations relative to those subjects and affecting that part of such lake or pond lying within this state, which rules and regulations the director is hereby authorized to make, and from time to time add to, alter and repeal.[1]

The revised version conveys the same message but in far more understandable terms.

Revision　If the legal boundary between two states runs through a pond or lake, licensed fishers from either state can fish in the pond or lake, following the standard fish and game laws of their own state unless these laws are superseded by special regulations for that specific pond or lake. The laws deal with open and closed seasons, limits of catch, minimum sizes of fish caught and methods of fishing.

What makes the first sentence virtually incomprehensible and the revised version fairly easy to understand?

The differences between the two versions result from choices in sentence structure and diction (word use). The first version uses language that the writer imagines to be impressive and legally airtight. The second version is no less legally precise, but it's certainly more understandable. Knowing more about sentence structure and diction will help you in drafting a document; this knowledge and the skill to use it is even more important in the revision process.

Sentences

No matter how carefully organized and important ideas are, they mean little to a reader if they're not presented in effective sentences. Effectiveness refers to far more than grammatical correctness. In a broad sense, effective sentences use active and passive voice appropriately, match sentence structure with ideas, and combine sentences for desired emphasis.

Active/Passive Voice

Voice determines whether a sentence emphasizes the person who acts or the receiver that is acted upon. In active voice, the person who acts—the "actor"—is the subject of the sentence.

Active
Voice

subject

Dactylography experts identify fingerprints.

In passive voice, the receiver that is acted upon becomes the subject of the sentence, and the agent is relegated to a prepositional phrase or, in some cases, even omitted entirely.

Passive
Voice

subject

Fingerprints are identified by dactylography experts.

Writers have several reasons for preferring active voice in most situations. Material presented in active voice is more interesting to read, in part because the subject of the sentence is responsible for the action. Active voice is more direct; the reader does not have to work as hard to figure out who does what. Active voice is less wordy because the "to be" verb form necessary to form a passive construction is omitted. In general, use active voice unless there is a specific reason not to. While you might not think a great deal about active and passive voice while you're drafting a document, voice becomes more important during revision.

The agent in active voice does not always have to be a person, or even a living organism, as the following example illustrates.[2]

Example Solid-state computer scanners maintain a file of fingerprints. When a fingerprint is put into the file, the computer scanner identifies the characteristic "points" of a fingerprint (up to 150 points, though only 12 are needed for legal identification) and then converts them to a series of numbers that are stored on a computer disk file. When a fingerprint from a crime scene is digitized in a similar manner, the scanner attempts to match the "numbers." Each disk drive stores up to 90,000 fingerprint cards, each card with 10 prints. The computer can riffle through 1200 such points every second. The computer can increase arrest rates based on fingerprints 10 to 15 percent above the current levels.

Passive voice does have appropriate uses. When the receiver is more important than the agent, passive voice is correct. In this example, the agent ("by Hollywood") is less important than the concept ("the fingerprint").

Passive Voice The fingerprint is overrated by Hollywood lore as a way to catch criminals.

Passive voice is also appropriate when the agent is unknown or insignificant.

Passive Voice Fingerprints are collected only between 25 and 30 percent of the time, even though they are usually the most prevalent form of physical evidence at the scene of a crime.

In this sentence the agent is not identified—"Fingerprints are collected [by unknown detectives] only between 25 and 30 percent of the time"—so passive voice is not only correct but necessary.

Passive voice distances the reader and also masks the agent of action. The paragraph below is unified in subject but could be improved by the use of active voice.

Example   Argon lasers and household "Super Glue" are now used by some dactylography experts to collect fingerprints. A small, highly concentrated, single wavelength light beam is produced by the laser. Fluorescence is induced by the laser in such fingerprint chemicals as riboflavin. Prints—even old ones—can be lifted from paper, something that has been impervious to traditional dusting, by the laser. The benefits of "Super Glue" were discovered by accident. The fumes from the glue interact with the animo acids and outline the print. A fingerprint is raised and preserved by "Super Glue" on just about any surface. The glue is used on smooth surfaces such as skin, plastic, coarse metal, and leather.

Just changing the passive constructions to active makes the paragraph easier to read.

Revision   Some dactylography experts now use argon lasers and household "Super Glue" to collect fingerprints. The laser produces a small, highly concentrated, single wavelength light beam that can induce fluorescence in such fingerprint chemicals as riboflavin. The laser can lift prints—even old ones—from paper, something that has been impervious to traditional dusting. Experts discovered the benefits of "Super Glue" by accident. The fumes from the glue interact with the print in a way that raises and preserves it on just about any surface, including skin, plastic, coarse metal, and leather.

Sentence Structure

Understanding sentence structure is valuable to writers because structure gives them the flexibility to express a single idea, coordinate equal ideas, and subordinate unequal ones. This flexibility comes from arranging independent and dependent (or subordinate) clauses in various combinations.

A clause is simply a group of words that expresses a relationship between subject and verb, and sometimes a complement. An *independent clause* expresses an idea that makes sense by itself; a *dependent clause* must be complemented with an independent clause in order to make sense.[3]

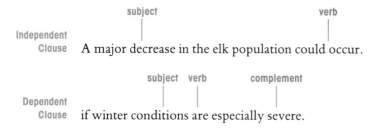

The dependent clause must be connected to the independent clause.

Examples   If winter conditions are especially severe, a major decrease in the elk population could occur.

OR

A major decrease in the elk population could occur if winter conditions are especially severe.

When the dependent clause introduces the main idea, a comma often separates it from the independent clause, as if to say, "Okay, the main idea is about to start." However, no comma is needed when the independent clause comes first and is followed by the dependent clause.

All sentences represent various combinations of independent and dependent clauses. A *simple sentence* contains one independent clause and no dependent clauses.

Simple Sentence   Natural fires in national parks have benefits.

Simple sentences are not necessarily short. Compound subjects, verbs, or complements and the addition of phrases can result in simple sentences that are quite long.

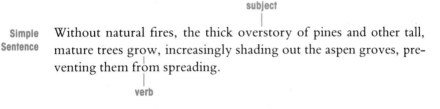

Simple Sentence   Without natural fires, the thick overstory of pines and other tall, mature trees grow, increasingly shading out the aspen groves, preventing them from spreading.

Simple Sentence   Natural fires encourage a diverse arboreal woodland suitable for a broad range of wildlife and less susceptible to insect infestations than the current monoculture of lodgepole pine.

A *compound sentence* joins two independent clauses into a single sentence by using a *coordinate conjunction, correlative conjunction*, or *conjunctive adverb* between the two clauses. Coordinate conjunctions connect words, phrases, or clauses of equal (or parallel) grammatical rank:

and   but   or   for   nor   so   yet

Correlative conjunctions are simply pairs of coordinate conjunctions that connect independent clauses or other grammatically equivalent units:

either . . . or   neither . . . nor
though . . . yet   both . . . and
not only . . . but also

Common conjunctive adverbs also connect independent clauses in a compound sentence:

also   likewise
hence   still then
instead   thus
otherwise   furthermore
therefore   indeed
consequently   moreover
however   nevertheless

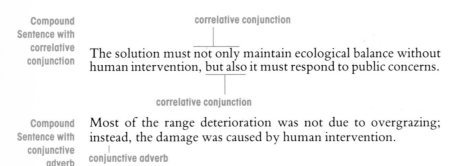

Compound Sentence with coordinate conjunction

The elk herd in Yellowstone was outgrowing its habitat, —— first independent clause

coordinate conjunction — so park officials considered the traditional solutions of trans- _ second independent planting and hunting. clause

Compound Sentence with correlative conjunction

correlative conjunction

The solution must not only maintain ecological balance without human intervention, but also it must respond to public concerns.

correlative conjunction

Compound Sentence with conjunctive adverb

Most of the range deterioration was not due to overgrazing; instead, the damage was caused by human intervention.

conjunctive adverb

A comma before the coordinating conjunction properly separates two independent clauses in a compound sentence. Whenever a conjunctive adverb connects two independent clauses, it is preceded by a semicolon and often followed by a comma.

A *complex sentence* contains both a dependent and an independent clause. Adverbial dependent clauses are often introduced with one of the following subordinate conjunctions:

- Time   after, before, until, when, whenever, while, since
- Reason/Cause   as, because, whereas, since
- Purpose   that, in order that, so that
- Condition   if, unless, in case, provided that
- Concession   although, though, even though
- Result   so that
- Place   where, wherever, everywhere
- Manner   as, as if, as though

subordinate
conjunction

Complex Sentence   A good fire is better than trees dying out because nutrients are cycled back into the soil.

subordinate
conjunction

Complex Sentence   After severe fires killed some of the tall trees in the lower elevations where the elks live, the aspens below spread and flourished.

A *compound-complex sentence* contains two independent clauses and one or more dependent clauses.

Compound -Complex Sentence   Because managers have tools such as elevated boardwalks, campgrounds, and restricted areas, national park managers have the flexibility to limit human interference; therefore, terrain can recover from years of use.

conjunctive adverb

Understanding sentence structure allows writers to establish relationships among ideas by appropriate use of coordination and subordination. Clearly, important ideas belong in independent clauses while less important ideas should be expressed in dependent clauses or even in phrases.

Sentence Combining

Sentence combining gives a writer tools to connect and rearrange independent and dependent clauses so that sentences are direct and expressive, establishing relationships to make reading easier. Judicious sentence combining usually clarifies the content and improves the style.

Sentence combining helps writers eliminate excessive use of short sentences. While short, simple sentences are easier to understand than longer, structurally complex sentences, they can be overused, resulting in a primer writing style that often insults and annoys the reader. A primer style contains unnecessary repetition and may, in fact, significantly lower comprehension because subordination is seldom employed; thus, relationships among the ideas in sentences are not clear.

As a reader, how do you react to this paragraph?

Example   High acidity kills fish. Fish in the lakes of the Northeast and Canada are dying. Coal-burning plants produce sulfur dioxide. Some clouds retain this sulfur dioxide. Rain combines with sulfur dioxide. Weak sulfur dioxide is formed from rain and sulfur dioxide. Coal-burning plants produce nitrogen oxides. Some clouds retain this nitrogen oxide. Rain combines with nitrogen oxide. Coal smoke is produced in the Ohio Valley. Some snow and rain originate in the Ohio Valley. This rain and snow sometimes fall in the Northeast and in Canada. Canada blames the Ohio Valley for the high acidity levels in lakes.

Each idea is presented in a separate sentence, with no attempt made to establish relationships among the ideas. When you compare this choppy, primer version to the paragraph below (as it was originally published), you can see the importance of combining and subordinating ideas.

Revision   High acidity levels are killing fish in the lakes of the Northeast and Canada. When rain combines with sulfur dioxide from a coal-burning plant it forms weak sulfuric acid, and when the cloud contains nitrogen oxides the product is nitric acid. Canada blames rain and snow originating in the smoky Ohio Valley for its problem.[4]

Because the relationships the writer intends are clearly expressed, the second version is easier to read than the first, which forces the reader to make assumptions about these relationships that may be different from what the writer intended.

Writers use four strategies to combine sentences: adding, deleting, embedding, and transforming. Combining sentences by *addition* involves connecting sentence elements with punctuation (comma, semicolon) and either coordinate or subordinate conjunctions. In the following example, three separate sentences can be combined.

- The multiple layers of fossil-bearing deposits indicate that early humans first took shelter in the cave 460,000 years ago.
- The last of them did not abandon the site until 230,000 years ago.
- They were forced out by the filling of the cave with rubble and sediment.

In this case, combining requires absolutely no changes to the sentences themselves. The original article about "Peking Man" in *Scientific American* combined them by adding the coordinate conjunction "and" along with a comma and the subordinate conjunction "when."[5]

Example   The multiple layers of fossil-bearing deposits indicate that early men first took shelter in the cave 460,000 years ago, and the last of them did not abandon the site until 230,000 years ago, when they were forced out by the filling of the cave with rubble and sediment.

When combining sentences, skillful writers often use *deletion* to eliminate redundant words or phrases. Pronouns are sometimes substituted for deleted elements. The remaining parts are combined into a series or a compound element:

- The skull of the Peking man was much thicker.   (and)
- ~~The skull of the Peking man was much~~ flatter.   (and)
- ~~The skull of the Peking man~~ had protruding brows.   (and)
- ~~The skull of the Peking man had~~ a marked angle at the rear.

By deleting the repetitious "The skull of the Peking man," the writers have produced a clear sentence that is easier to read.

Example   The skull of the Peking man . . . was much thicker and flatter and had protruding brows and a marked angle at the rear.

A more sophisticated method of sentence combining involves *embedding*—placing elements of one sentence into another sentence. This example of embedding takes the key concept in the first sentence and places it in apposition within the second sentence:

- One technique was called anvil percussion.
- In the technique a large flat stone (the anvil) was placed on the ground and forcefully struck with a piece of sandstone.
- ~~One technique was~~ <u>called anvil percussion</u>
- In the technique   a large flat stone (the anvil) was placed on the ground and forcefully struck with a piece of sandstone.

By deleting repetitious phrases and combining the two sentences into one, the writer has produced a smoother, more effective sentence.

Example   In the technique called anvil percussion a large flat stone (the anvil) was placed on the ground and forcefully struck with a piece of sandstone.

The final combining strategy is called *transformation*, in which the form and order of words, phrases, and even clauses may be changed. In this example, combining makes one sentence subordinate to the other.

- The stone artifacts produced by the Peking man are primarily made of vein quartz, rock crystal, flint and sandstone.
  (suggesting that)
- He did not rely exclusively on water rounded pebbles for tools.

The second sentence is made subordinate to the first with the addition of "suggesting that."

Example   The stone artifacts produced by the Peking man are primarily made of vein quartz, rock crystal, flint and sandstone, suggesting that he did not rely exclusively on water rounded pebbles for tool material.

In combining sentences emphasis is as important as grammatical correctness and accuracy of content. The most effective way to change the emphasis in a sentence is to change word order. The beginning of a sentence is the most prominent location; information presented first is assumed to be most important. The end of a sentence is the second best location for emphasizing information. Placing information in the middle of a sentence gives it the least emphasis.

The importance of location is demonstrated by revising the following sentence in several different ways to emphasize a different idea. The first example is a formal definition.

Example   Hydrocephalus is a condition in which increased amounts of spinal fluid within the ventricles of the brain cause an enlargement of the head.

Revisions

- Emphasis on "an enlargement of the head":
  An enlargement of the head, resulting from increased amounts of spinal fluid within the ventricles of the brain, is a primary characteristic of hydrocephalus.

- Emphasis on "ventricles of the brain":
  The ventricles of the brain collect increased amounts of spinal fluid, resulting in an enlargement of the head in the condition called hydrocephalus.

- Emphasis on "spinal fluid":
  Spinal fluid increases within the ventricles of the brain cause an enlargement of the head in victims of hydrocephalus.

Awareness of audience is important for writers who are revising ideas and sentences through combining. The primer sentences in the next example all deal with the same subject, but they have no relationship established among them. They can be combined in different ways, depending on the needs of the reader.

- Plastic pails are used in industry.
- Plastic pails are often made of high density polyethylene.
- Polyethylene pails cost 40 to 50 percent less than steel pails.
- The cost of polyethylene pails has risen.
- The cost of steel pails has risen faster than the cost of polyethylene pails.

One version is suitable for an expert or technican who wants accurate information supported by specific facts:

Example   Although the cost of plastic pails for industrial use has risen, the cost for comparable steel pails has risen faster. Now, pails made of high density polyethylene cost 40 to 50 percent less than comparable steel pails.

Another version is more appropriate for a reader who is interested in general information but does not need specific details:

Example   Plastic pails for industrial use, frequently made of polyethylene, cost less than comparable steel pails.

Precise Diction

After a writer determines the relationships between ideas in a document, attention focuses on precision and accuracy of words and phrases. A writer must know the meaning of words, apply them accurately, and use plain language. A writer must also pay attention to the needs of the audience; what is considered "simple" diction depends on the particular reader. No word is inherently right or wrong until the audience is taken into account. For example the simple word *feel* would be appropriate in a pamphlet for women on breast self-examination that stated, "If you feel a lump, contact your doctor." However, in a document for medical personnel, *palpate* would be a better choice than *feel*.

Plain language in all forms of technical communication—documents, formal presentations, conversations, and commentary accompanying visuals—

results in more effective writing. Plain language is often a matter of common sense, insistence on directness, and, especially, precise diction, which requires writers to do several things:

- eliminate wordiness
- revise noun strings
- use direct diction
- use concrete details
- use positive phrasing

Writers who ignore these areas often produce ambiguous, distorted writing.

Eliminate Wordiness

Wordiness can make writing difficult to understand because readers are forced to plow through unnecessary words to read essential information. Readers may lose patience with a document that uses redundant or ambiguous language. Precise and direct writing shows that you are sensitive to your readers and have carefully edited information so that it is easily understood.

The most effective way to reduce wordiness is to avoid redundancy—the unnecessary repetition of concepts, words, or phrases. Sometimes the readers cannot discern the point because it is hidden underneath layers of language. At other times redundancy is so annoying or time consuming that readers give up without completing a document.

The memo in Example 5.1 has numerous instances of redundancy. Section manager Catherine Saunders typed the memo directly into her word processor and read the copy after it was printed.

When Ms. Saunders proofread her draft, she was appalled by its redundancy. She edited the draft, crossing out unnecessary terms and making minor changes in wording. Producing a new copy constituted very little work on the word processor; within a few minutes, she printed the revision (Example 5.2).

We will discuss several redundant elements from Ms. Saunders' first memo as well as examples you may encounter in other business and technical documents.

Redundant Pairs. Some common terms contain two words, both of which mean the same thing. Some writers use such redundant pairs to give their writing what they think is an air of elegance. Because both terms mean the

Example 5.1

August 3, 1986

TO: Production Supervisors
FROM: Catherine Saunders
           Section Manager
SUBJECT: Weekly Staff Meeting

The staff meeting will start at 10 a.m. Tuesday morning.

First and foremost, our primary goal of the meeting will be to reach a consensus of opinion about the best way to utilize the high degree of expertise of the consultant we brought in. The consultant advised us about future plans for implementing new state-of-the-art developments in production techniques.

At this point in time, we must prioritize in order of importance those basic and fundamental changes we believe are most important to modify in our production system.

same thing, only one is necessary. You could correctly write "first" or "foremost," but using both terms is repetitive. Sometimes, as in Ms. Saunders' memo, neither term is necessary because there is only one stated goal. Examples of pairs of redundant terms to avoid are:

basic and fundamental	issues and concerns
full and complete	first and foremost
thorough and complete	null and void
simple and elementary	final and conclusive
each and every	

Example 5.2

TM Taranto Manufacturers, Inc.

August 3, 1986

TO: Production Supervisors
FROM: Catherine Saunders
           Section Manager
SUBJECT: Weekly Staff Meeting

The staff meeting will start at 10 a.m.
Tuesday.

Our goal is to reach a consensus about the best
way to use the consultant's advice about production
techniques.

At this time, we must prioritize changes to our
production system.

Redundant Modifiers. Phrases in which one of the terms implies the other are known as redundant modifiers. For example, "collaborate" implies "together," so "collaborate together" is redundant. Some examples of redundant modifiers to avoid include:

true facts	finally in conclusion
consensus of opinion	collaborate together
new state-of-the-art	most unique
future plans	end result
initial preparation	circulate around
mandatory requirement	completely eliminated
totally unified	actual experience
positive benefits	optional choice
absolutely essential	personal opinion
prioritize in order of importance	three different people

Ms. Saunders' memo contains the phrase "high degree of expertise of the consultant brought in," which has three redundant features. A consultant is assumed to have expertise and is also brought in from outside the company; saying a consultant has expertise and is brought in is doubly redundant. Also, expertise assumes a high degree of competence; repeating high degree is unnecessary.

Redundant Categories. When one term in a phrase is in the general category to which the other term belongs, it's known as a redundant category. For example, the expression *bitter taste* is redundant because bitter is one of four tastes; the word *bitter* is sufficient. In Ms. Saunders' memo, the initial "a.m." implies the category stated in the second term, so "morning" is unnecessary. You could correctly write "at 10 A.M. Tuesday" or "at 10:00 Tuesday morning." Some examples of redundant categories to avoid are:

10 A.M. Tuesday morning	bitter taste
at this point in time	seven in number
red in color	unstable nature
rectangular in shape	hot temperature
rough in texture	small size
dull in appearance	manufacturing process
inspection procedure	reliability factor
excessive degree	promotion activity

The following examples show how eliminating redundant categories makes sentences less wordy.

Examples   The *reliability factor* of the equipment was guaranteed.
The *reliability* of the equipment was guaranteed.

The marketing manager explained current *promotional activities*.
The marketing manager explained current *promotions*.

Revise Noun Strings

Imprecise diction also results from noun strings, a series of two or more nouns in which the first nouns modify the later ones. For example, in the string "circulation pump filter," both *circulation* and *pump* modify filter. Noun strings are distinguished by the absence of both apostrophes and connecting words that show relationships (such as *of, for, in*).

Problems result from using noun strings, particularly when the reader is unable to determine exactly how the nouns relate to each other. Strings that are only two words long seldom present difficulties. For example, "data analysis" is easily understood; saying "the analysis of data" is unnecessary. When the strings are three words long, the reader can usually figure out what is meant, as this example shows, but reading may be slowed slightly.

Original   standardization blending control
Revision   controller that standardizes blending

When the strings reach four words, extra time is required to figure out the relationship among words. Although the reader probably will correctly interpret the string, this takes unnecessary time and effort, which may distract and annoy the reader. The next example illustrates the problems inherent in four-word noun strings.

Original   test module specification review
Revision   the specifications review for the test module

Original   scanner head motion control
Revision   control of the scanner head's motion

Strings that are five or more words long are open to multiple interpretations and can be undecipherable, as seen in the next example. The reader may never guess exactly what the writer intended.

Original   coordinated pasteurization processing sequence logic (part of a mechanized system in the dairy industry)
Revisions   the logic that coordinates pasteurization [processing]

or

the coordinated logic of the sequence in pasteurization [processing]

or

logic of a coordinated sequence of pasteurization [processing]

Revisions of noun strings usually require additional words to clarify the relationships; however, these extra words eliminate ambiguity.

Use Direct Words

A great deal of poor writing results from attempts to use formal language in situations that require direct, straightforward wording, as in the following request for maintenance.

Example   It has come to my attention that the lights in my office have not been working.

The writer should have just written, "Replace the light bulbs in my office." Indeed, most memos, letters, and documents would be improved by direct, precise language; technical writing has little need for inflated, pompous language.

One way to be direct is to use straightforward terms. Figure 5.1 lists substitutes for common but complex words. Writers who use direct wording express their ideas simply, concentrating on content rather than impressing the reader with their extensive vocabulary.

The revisions of the following sentences substitute simple diction for the needlessly ornate language of some writers.

Inflated   Your conceptualization of our aggregate capability may enhance our marketing position.

Revision   Your ideas about our capability may improve our marketing.

Inflated   Subsequent modifications will be disseminated to all users.

Revision   Later changes will be sent to all users.

A guaranteed shortcut to eliminating pompous, incomprehensible writing involves changing abstract nouns, which make writing less personal and more difficult to understand, into verbs. Some common examples are listed in Figure 5.2, but many others appear in technical documents.

Changing abstract nouns back to verbs and deleting words that add nothing to the meaning greatly improves writing, as these examples show.

Abstract   The judge *provided the required authorization* for the search.

In this example, "provided the required authorization" is changed to "authorize"; the revised sentence is more direct because "authorize" identifies the action.

Direct   The judge *authorized* the search.

Another revision works for sentences that begin with expletives such as "there is" or "there are" followed by abstract nouns.

Abstract   *There is a need for identification* of all areas of noncompliance.

The expletive is eliminated, the noun is changed back to a verb, and a new subject is chosen.

Direct   The quality control inspectors must *identify* all areas of noncompliance.

One of the major problems with abstractions is that the sentences use passive voice and, thus, do not identify who is responsible for the action.

Figure 5.1   Substitutes for Inflated Words

	Inflated, Obscuring Words	*Simple, Direct Words*
VERBS	ascertain	discover, find out
	communicate	talk, write
	consolidate	combine
	construct, fabricate	make
	disseminate, transmit	send
	effectuate	carry out
	endeavor	try
	enhance	improve
	establish	show, create
	expedite	speed up
	formulate	design, create
	initiate, activate	begin, start
	interface	talk with, connect
	modify, redesign	change
	terminate	end, fire
	utilize	use
NOUNS	capability	ability
	compensation, remuneration	pay
	compilation	list
	conceptualization	idea, plan
	conflagration	fire
	designation	name, label
	discrepancy	error
	implementation	start
	modification	change
	predisposition	tendency
	ramification	result, impact
ADJECTIVES	advantageous	useful
	aggregate	total
	erroneous	wrong
	expeditious	fast
	explicit	plain
	initial	first
	numerous	many
	optimum	best
	subsequent	later
	sufficient	enough

Figure 5.2	Abstract Nouns Changed to Active Verbs

Abstract Nouns	*Direct, Active Verbs*
allocation	allocate
assessment	assess
assignment	assign
avoidance	avoid
compliance	comply
comprehensibility	comprehend
conservation	conserve
conversion	convert
coordination	coordinate
decision	decide
deterioration	deterioriate
determination	determine
discussion	discuss
distribution	distribute
documentation	document
evaluation	evaluate
expiration	expire
explanation	explain
exposure	expose
formation	form
implementation	implement/use
information	inform
intention	intend
justification	justify
maintenance	maintain
promotion	promote
redemption	redeem
reliance	rely
specification	specify
transmission	transmit
utilization	use
verification	verify

Abstract   *Continuation of the conservation effort* for the environment often takes place at the town government level.

This example has been revised by adding a subject that is responsible for the action.

Direct   Many town governments *continue to conserve* the environment.

Understanding ideas is even harder when the sentence has more than one abstract noun. In this example, using abstract terms creates an impersonal tone. Furthermore, the sentence is difficult to understand because it doesn't state who did what.

Abstract   The *deterioriation of her condition* led to the *determination* [by whom?] that surgery was necessary.

The revision changes "deterioration of her condition" to specify the action, saying instead, "her condition deteriorated"; "determination" becomes "doctors determined," providing a human decision maker.

Direct   Her *condition deteriorated*, so *doctors determined* surgery was necessary.

Use Concrete Details

Concrete words, which refer to tangible objects, are usually easier to understand than abstract words. Thus, they generally make writing more precise. If abstractions must be used, they should be supported and explained with specific details and examples.

An effective technique for reducing abstract writing is to insert specific details in place of vague or general statements. The list in Figure 5.3 identifies some of the ways you can make abstract statements precise and concrete, providing the statement is quantifiable and verifiable.

Use Positive Phrasing

Effective writers often employ positive phrasing for several reasons. Psychologists and linguists know that readers and listeners understand positively phrased sentences more quickly and accurately than negatively phrased sentences, which the human brain takes slightly longer to process. Also, positive phrasing generally is more direct and appealing because eliminating negatives eliminates words.

Figure 5.3	Selecting Concrete Details

Abstract		*Concrete*
important client	WHO?	Jean Thompson, PPI president
a new development	WHAT?	development of blight-resistant chestnut
schedule early	WHEN?	schedule before 9 A.M.
ideal location	WHERE?	Southfield, MA
a substantial profit	HOW MUCH?	a 37 percent profit
a broken part	WHICH ONE?	a broken camshaft
limited leg mobility	WHAT PERCENTAGE?	lift her leg 40 percent of normal extension
operates in high-temperature environments	WHAT DEGREE?	operates in temperatures up to 2000°F
a small wingspan	WHAT SIZE?	a 7.0 mm wingspan
few changes in the procedure	HOW MANY?	three changes in the procedure
corrosion-resistant metal	WHAT KIND?	stainless steel

The most obvious negative words, which include *no, not, none, never,* and *nothing,* are added to a positive sentence to negate the idea. During revision, a phrase with a negative word can be replaced by a less overtly negative term, often an antonym for the word in the "not" phrase:

not many	→	few
do not accept	→	reject
do not succeed	→	fail
do not approve	→	deny

Other negative words are created by adding a common negative prefix to a word. The words with the prefixes are less overtly negative, and thus easier to read. However, when you want to emphasize a negative point, use "not":

*in*efficient	→	not efficient
*im*possible	→	not possible
*un*reliable	→	not reliable
*ir*revocable	→	not revocable

*il*logical   →   not logical
*dis*functional   →   non functional
*non*renewable   →   not renewable

While one negative word or phrase only slightly delays a reader, multiple negatives in a sentence significantly decrease reading speed and inhibit comprehension. Also, possible confusion results from multiple negatives. The following sentences illustrate how replacing negative wording with positive lessens the chances of confusion arising from multiple negatives.

Negative   If the policy is not effective, it is not irrevocable.
Positive   If the policy is not effective, it can be changed.

Negative   When the inspector did not accept this data, claiming it was unreliable, we were not so inefficient as to reject suggestions for alternative testing methods.
Positive   When the inspector rejected the data as unreliable, we sought alternative testing methods.

Negative   The production line change-over will not be ready on time.
Positive   The production line change-over will be delayed.

Another way to eliminate negatives is to reword the sentence so that it is positive.

Negative   The manager could not approve the decentralization of the tool crib because there would be no inventory control or centralized maintenance checks.
Positive   The tool crib provides a regular inventory control and maintenance checks.

The shift in emphasis stresses the positive aspects of the current method without criticizing the idea of decentralization.

In some situations, however, positive phrasing is inappropriate because it is not emphatic enough. The following set of directions presumes that many users will do the wrong thing unless specific "do not's" are presented.

Negative   Failure to follow standard procedures in using a disk will have detrimental results. Follow these guidelines:
- Do not turn drive on or off with disk in the drive.
- Do not bend disk.
- Do not touch disk surfaces with fingers or objects.
- Do not store out of protective envelope.
- Do not expose to heat, magnets, or photoelectric beams.

Such phrasing cautions computer operators to treat disks carefully. Although the wording is negative, experience has led manual writers to realize that some readers ignore cautions that use positive wording.

Consider Plain Language

Because some writers pay too little attention to sentence structure and diction, many documents in government, law, medicine, education, insurance, and numerous other areas abound with language that is not easily or quickly understood by the intended audience. Sometimes the problem results from the inappropriate use of jargon—specialized language for people within a particular field. Other times, problems result from careless or inaccurate use of language. In both situations, the principle of plain language is ignored.

Jargon itself is not bad; however, its frequent misuse has given it a bad reputation. Used to communicate with people who have knowledge or skill in specialized areas, jargon is precise and saves time. Used inappropriately, jargon inhibits communication by alienating the reader or listener. Deciding whether to use jargon requires careful analysis of the audience. If you have any question about whether to use jargon in a particular document, substitute plain language instead. If technical accuracy precludes the use of any other term, include parenthetical definitions, footnotes, or a glossary to assist the reader. The following article discusses both the advantages and annoyances of jargon.

IF YOU WANT TO INTERFACE, BEWARE OF USER ERROR

At Home Box Office headquarters in New York, the sales operatives are constantly seeking new ways to sell their cable television service to those people who don't seem to want it, a group they call "the untouchables." They refer to their unceasing efforts to bring these hard-core unsold into the fold as "re-marketing to the untouchables."

At the Pentagon, a defense consultant frequently discusses "retrograde motion" with his Army clients. He says they much prefer this term to the word "retreat."

In Silicon Valley, where the impenetrable lingual thicket called computerese first flourished, an employee of a computer component company didn't just "interface" with her boss, she "core-dumped" on the poor man.

In case you haven't noticed, the hills are alive with the sound of strange new locutions. A bumper crop of jargon is being harvested, and not just in the traditional fields of business, bureaucracy and academia. The computer engineers and technicians are getting into the act in a big way, generating "nouvelle" gibberish even faster than the sociologists in their heyday (remember "ex-urban" and "other-directed"?).

All of this raises some essential questions that you might want "to access."

Why do people use jargon, anyway? Why do they coin such words as "interface" when there are such perfectly serviceable ones as "talk" in stock? Why did that woman in Silicon Valley convert the act of voicing grievances into an Anglo-Saxon atrocity like "core-dumping?"

And more to the point for us, why do people in specialized fields such as computers inflict their jargon on us laymen? Even worse, why do we outsiders pick up so many of these new words and put them into general use?

Several experts in linguists and psychiatrists have a number of answers to these questions, some of them rather obvious, some of them fascinating.

Jargon, they agreed, is indigenous to any vocational field, and frequently serves as a useful, time-saving shorthand for the people in the business. As William Labov, a linguistics professor at the University of Pennsylvania, observes, "Jargon is used inside a field to get information across faster and, secondly, to identify members of that (professional) group. I'm not kidding when I tell students that learning the right jargon is the first step to becoming a professional."

But when jargon is used on laymen and by them, it begins to take on psychological baggage. For example, the computer expert who shovels technical jargon on laymen might be trying to impress them, to make himself seem superior by using words and terms they can't understand.

In the extreme, adds Dr. Philip Mechanick, a professor of psychiatry at Penn, using jargon on laymen can be a "very hostile" way of "demeaning or diminishing the listener."

Then again, adds Labov, its use simply could mean that the speaker cannot express his specialty in lay terms, either because he's not accustomed to doing so, or because he really doesn't have a good enough grasp of his discipline. Labov suggests that it is no accident that the best minds in a field usually can discuss it in clear, everyday language.

"It's the people with the firmest grip on their subject matter who can relate it in the simplest terms," he contends. "If a person really knows the meaning of his professional jargon, he probably has no problem translating it into plain language. It's the people who don't know their own terms, they're the ones who can get into trouble."

When laymen adopt jargon, these experts agree, it is because they want to seem sophisticated and informed. They want to be "in," not left out.

"Certainly, all of us like to present ourselves as competent, educated, intelligent and alert to what's going on," Mechanick observes. And because science and technology are "what's going on" at the moment, he feels there is a particular propensity to borrow jargon from them.

"Because of the premium on science, there is a temptation to use what we feel is relatively scientific language," he says. "Words like 'interface' (a computer term) have a scientific ring that is reassuring."

Apart from its vocational and psychological uses, jargon has considerable utility as euphemism.

The government and military are past masters at this, of course. During the Vietnam War, the army didn't destroy villages, it "pacified" them. More recently, the Marines didn't retreat from Beirut to their ships. President Regan "redeployed" them. (If Reagan had been president in the years after the Civil War, would we now be talking about Custer's Last Redeployment?)

In the military, according to the Washington defense consultant, the use of such euphemistic jargon is often obligatory. "The Pentagon has no such word as retreat," he says. "It's retrograde motion. The people there think it's bad, psychologically, to talk about retreat, even though it is something you have to do every once in a while."

The military, the consultant adds, drops jargon just as easily as it makes it up. "In the mid-70s," he recalls, "the Navy referred to its aircraft carriers as 'high-value units,' or HVUs. Later, the chief of naval operations decided that that made the people on other kinds of ships feel bad because theirs weren't regarded as high-value. So he decreed that the term HVU should no longer be used, and within a year it had dropped out of existence."

Jargon's development usually follows a literal-to-figurative path, experts say. It begins as a literal, technical term, and then takes on figurative meaning. Thus interfacing, which originally meant computers conversing, came to mean people conversing as well. Core-dumping, which means to drain a computer's central memory, is now also used to mean getting everything off your chest.

Similarly, the term "read-only memory," meaning a computer element that cannot be altered by the user, has taken on figurative utility. If you want to tell someone he has limited learning ability, you can tell him he has a "read-only memory."

The computer folks, incidentally, have added a novel twist to jargon creation. They have this aesthetically nasty habit of turning a normal noun ("access") into a verb ("to access") and then back into a noun ("accessing").[6]

Careless use of language persists, however, despite the growing number of writers who advocate "plain English." Primarily, plain English connotes simplicity in diction and sentence structure. The simplest word that accurately conveys meaning is often your best choice, unless the audience, purpose, or style of the document requires variation. Writing with simple words is much like reducing a fraction to its lowest common denominator in math. It is easier to understand, but the meaning does not change.

The proliferation of verbal garbage has led to federal statutes mandating "plain English." In addition, many states have passed laws that require documents such as insurance policies, consumer contracts, and even state agency guidelines to be written in plain language. Many companies also now require their internal and consumer documents to be written in language understood by general readers.

Plain language should not be confused with boring language. Plain language is easy to understand and gracefully constructed, and it benefits from well-chosen figurative language that clarifies ideas without burying them under inappropriate and ornate terms, as in this example.

Example   The most recent discrepancy compilation demonstrates the origin of the dysfunction, resulting in the immediate implementation of corrective action.

"Discrepancy," "compilation," "demonstrate," "dysfunction," "originate," "implementation," and "corrective action" are perfectly good terms—but they don't convey a clear, direct message. The writer could have written two simple statements with much less effort and much better results:

Revision   The new list of errors shows where the breakdown begins. The errors must be corrected immediately.

The revision is effective because the writer has substituted simple, precise words and divided the lengthy sentence.

Inquiries and Applications

Discussion Questions

1. Why would a writer purposely obscure meaning in writing?
2. Identify several appropriate uses for jargon.
3. Explain how "plain English" can be easily understood by a general audience and yet be written in an interesting style. Explain how writing style influences a reader's understanding or interest.
4. Based on your knowledge about the effectiveness of sentence combining, what questions are raised about the value and validity of readability indexes (discussed in Chapter 3)?
5. One rule of punctuation says, "After introductory adverbial clauses, a comma is used." A textbook for high school shorthand students offers this simplification: "Sentences that begin with *if, as,* or *when* always require a comma." The textbook goes on to state that there are other similar constructions that should also be followed by a comma.
   a. Why might the first rule be difficult to apply for people unfamiliar with grammatical terms?

b. Do you approve of the second version? Can you see ways people might be led astray by relying on it?

6. Discuss whether directions are more effective with or without negative wording. In what situations might you choose to word directions positively? Negatively?

7. Explain whether you agree or disagree with this statement: Plain English is the result of lower standards in education and increased inability to use our own language.

Individual and Group Exercises

1. Develop an accurate, usable definition of "plain English."

2. Correct the problems of wordiness, phrasing, and unnecessary expletives in these sentences:

   a. It is clear that we must hire another technician.

   b. The work-in-progress (WIP) report serves as the primary tool for fulfilling the dispatching function or role.

   c. The vertical and horizontal alignment must be designed according to the design criteria so that safety is insured when determining stopping and braking distances.

   d. The purpose of the tripod is to hold the camera completely still during film exposure.

   e. The elevator crank, with a total length of 6 inches, is a gear-driven metal device that is attached to the pan and tilt head.

   f. There are many problems that can occur with a single lens reflex camera.

   g. Please do not attempt any repairs not covered under "Operator Maintenance."

   h. At the present time among manufacturing managerial personnel, there is a problem of being unaware of the current scope of jobs in the fabrication department.

   i. There are five different types of contact lenses currently on the market. These five types are hard lenses, soft lenses, gas permeable lenses, silicone lenses, and extended-wear lenses.

   j. The bridge plate assembly is rectangular in shape with a length of 3.5 inches and a width of 1 inch. It is mass produced from stainless steel and is silver with a smooth surface. It has six holes to allow the passage of strings and a seventh hole to accommodate the insertion of the tremolo arm.

3. Editing exercise: Revise the following statement, part of a news article about labor problems in a local company.

   Mansfield employees will disband the picket lines, states the company president of this area's largest employer, as both the employees and the company have reached a tentative agreement to end the four-day work stoppage, but the five-year contract will not be voted on until Thursday afternoon of the next week, and a package probably has a slim chance of passage as the employees are dissatisfied with the proposals regarding money and working conditions that the company has previously offered, and thus raises the possibility of another walkout by the employees late Thursday night, but the company president is confident that this will not be the case when the employees are presented with the company's new financial offer.

4. List (a) common pairs of redundant terms, such as "first and foremost" or "willing and able"; (b) phrases that are constructed from repetitive terms, such as "end result" or "circulated around"; (c) phrases in which one term is a specific example of a general category also identified, such as "red in color" or "reliability factor." You should be able to identify at least 12 common phrases not already presented in this chapter.

5. Use the following information to create sentences that are appropriate for different audiences:
   - subject: toxic shock syndrome
   - occurs during or just after menstrual period
   - tampon use alone doesn't cause syndrome
   - tampon makes it easier for causative bacteria, *Staphylococcus aureus*, to enter bloodstream
   - initial symptoms vague—headache, vomiting, fever, diarrhea
   - red rash on palms and soles of feet; later peeling
   - within 48 hours, toxin produced by *Staphylococcus aureus* causes severe hypotension
   - severe hypotension leads to kidney failure
   - rare; strikes 3 in 100,000 women/year; four times greater risk for women under 30
   - recurrence common; repeat episodes reduced by prophylactic use of antibiotics[7]

6. Rewrite these sentences to establish clear and logical relationships between ideas. The combined sentences should form a unified, cohesive paragraph. Will the nature of the final paragraph change depending on your intended audience?
   a.   The taste of food is important to Americans.
   b.   The cost of food is important to Americans.
   c.   The nutrition of food is not important to most Americans.
   d.   The "Environmental Nutrition Newsletter" published a report.
   e.   One group of people is most concerned with nutrition.
   f.   People over 50 believe nutrition is important.
   g.   People over 50 are concerned about their food's ingredients.

h.   They check salt.
i.   They check sugar.
j.   They check choresterol.
k.   They check fat.
l.   They check artificial additives.
m. Two groups are least concerned with nutrition.
n.   Young people are not concerned with nutrition.
o.   Young people are interested in convenience foods.
p.   Single people are concerned with convenience foods.

7. Editing exercise: Rewrite the following information about digoxin, one of several drugs that may be used as part of the therapy for patients suffering from congestive heart failure. The intended audience is registered nurses involved in the care of cardiac patients.

> Digoxin or lanoxin is a positive inotropic drug that can be given intravenously or PO; a loading dose of 1 mg IV or 1.5 mg PO in divided doses and 0.125–0.5 mg daily (normal dose usually 0.25 mg) to increase heart contractions and lower the rate, but in cases of renal failure and debilitating disease the dosages may be required to be lowered as the patient may become hypokalemic, risking digoxin toxicity that is evidenced by rhythm irregularities (atrial and functional tachyarrhythmias, ventricular bradarrhythmias, atrioventricular block, or the combination of tachycardia or block) so it is necessary to monitor the pulse, but nausea and vomiting may be observed before or in conjunction with the irregular rhythms, so notification of the physician is important so that he or she may follow the plasma digoxin level(s) (1–2 ng/ml—reasonable level; 2.6 ng/ml toxic risk) plus low serum potassium levels, and digoxin should be withdrawn in the presence of toxic level, slow apical rate (i.e. below 60), and/or low potassium level.
>
> PO—per ora (by mouth)
> IV—intravenous
> mg—milligrams
> ng—nanograms
> ml—milliliters
> hypokalemic—low potassium levels

8. Make a list of the jargon most frequently used in your professional/academic field. Indicate why each term is necessary. Select non-jargon substitutes that would be appropriate when communicating with a non-expert audience.

6   Design and Visual Forms

EVERYONE KNOWS the sinking feeling of turning to a page filled with tiny print and virtually nonexistent margins. Unquestionably, a document's appearance affects a reader's attitude as well as ease and speed of reading. While Chapters 4 and 5 discuss selection and organization of information, from document and paragraph down to individual sentences and words, this chapter deals with the visual presentation of information, focusing on how the design of a document affects both readability and the reader's response.

Design Elements of a Document

Numerous factors beyond content and its organization influence the overall impression that any document makes. The following factors can be used to create effective documents: page layouts, typeface variations, typographic devices, white spaces, justification.

Page Layout

Writers need to be attentive to the overall design of a document because the appearance of the text on a page influences both reader comprehension and affective response. You do not need to depend on the expertise of artists and printers to create visually effective documents. Knowing a few basic elements of design in addition to your own judgment enables you to produce appealing, readable materials.

One of the options available to a writer/designer is a full-page or two-column layout, with either justified or ragged right margins. Figure 6.1 displays different page designs so that you can compare them to the full-page, justified format of the rest of the text.

Figure 6.1   Page Designs

FULL-PAGE, RAGGED RIGHT:

What do the moons of Jupiter, in vitro fertilization, silicon chips, wetlands conservation, soybean crops, flutes, and foals have in common? All are subjects in technical writing. What do astrophysicists, obstetricians, electrical engineers, ecologists, farmers, musicians, and veterinarians have in common? All read and write technical documents. Technical writing is a broad field that touches nearly every subject and profession through a vast array of documents; it defines, describes, and directs activities in business and industry, government and research institutions, hospitals and farms.

Although technical writing has traditionally focused on engineering, nearly any subject can be the topic of a technical document. For example, detailed information about sound formation is important for both a speech pathologist and an engineer designing a voice synthesizer. Knowledge about muscle conditioning is equally relevant to physical therapists, ballet dancers, and veterinarians. Data about weather changes are crucial to the meteorologist and the commercial fisher.

Technical subjects frequently appear in writing outside the technical world. Many major daily newspapers have science writers who make technical subjects interesting and accessible to the general reader. (Chapter 17 introduces you to popular science writing.) Writers of fiction often use technical concepts and details to authenticate and enliven their writing. Science fiction is based on a writer's ability to make the fantastic seem factual.

Historical Development of Technical Writing

Technical writing has not been created by the high-tech generation of the 1980s. However, neither is it a product of the war industry of the 1940s, the explosion of the Industrial Revolution in the eighteenth and nineteenth centuries, nor even the scientific breakthroughs of the Enlightenment in the eighteenth century. Technical writing, in some form or another, has existed as long as people have been able to write.

Figure 6.1   *Continued*

TWO-COLUMN, JUSTIFIED:

What do the moons of Jupiter, in vitro fertilization, silicon chips, wetlands conservation, soybean crops, flutes, and foals have in common? All are subjects in technical writing. What do astrophysicists, obstetricians, electrical engineers, ecologists, farmers, musicians, and veterinarians have in common? All read and write technical documents. Technical writing is a broad field that touches nearly every subject and profession through a vast array of documents; it defines, describes, and directs activities in business and industry, government and research institutions, hospitals and farms.

Although technical writing has traditionally focused on engineering, nearly any subject can be the topic of a technical document. For example, detailed information about sound formation is important for both a speech pathologist and an engineer designing a voice synthesizer. Knowledge about muscle conditioning is equally relevant to physical therapists, ballet dancers, and veterinarians. Data about weather changes are crucial to the meteorologist and the commercial fisher.

Historical Development of Technical Writing

Technical writing has not been created by the high-tech generation of the 1980s. However, neither is it a product of the war industry of the 1940s, the explosion of the Industrial Revolution in the eighteenth and nineteenth centuries, nor even the scientific breakthroughs of the Enlightenment in the eighteenth century. Tech-

TWO-COLUMN, RAGGED RIGHT:

What do the moons of Jupiter, in vitro fertilization, silicon chips, wetlands conservation, soybean crops, flutes, and foals have in common? All are subjects in technical writing. What do astrophysicists, obstetricians, electrical engineers, ecologists, farmers, musicians, and veterinarians have in common? All read and write technical documents. Technical writing is a broad field that touches nearly every subject and profession through a vast array of documents; it defines, describes, and directs activities in business and industry, government and research institutions, hospitals and farms.

Although technical writing has traditionally focused on engineering, nearly any subject can be the topic of a technical document. For example, detailed information about sound formation is important for both a speech pathologist and an engineer designing a voice synthesizer. Knowledge about muscle conditioning is equally relevant to physical therapists, ballet dancers, and veterinarians. Data about weather changes are crucial to the meteorologist and the commercial fisher.

Historical Development of Technical Writing

Technical writing has not been created by the high-tech generation of the 1980s. However, neither is it a product of the war industry of the 1940s, the explosion of the Industrial Revolution in the eighteenth and nineteenth centuries, nor

Some of the guidelines that work to produce appealing documents merely apply common sense to page design:

- balancing the appearance of individual and facing pages
- incorporating visuals in appropriate places
- signaling shifts in subject and providing visual variety with headings

Individual and facing pages in a document should look balanced—neither crowded, top heavy, nor "stretched" to look longer. The path the readers follow through the text and visuals should be clear.

Readers appreciate not having to constantly turn back and forth between the page they're reading and visuals placed in an appendix. A recent survey of management and nonmanagement engineers and scientists concerning the format of NASA technical reports indicated that 80 percent preferred visuals integrated into the text rather than placed in an appendix. The only exceptions noted were if several consecutive pages of visuals interrupted the flow of the text and thus distracted the reader.[1]

The page position of headings and subheadings identifies their relative importance in a document. Headings not only establish the subject of a section; they also give the reader a chance to take both a literal and a mental breath while previewing the upcoming content. Some writers try to use a heading or subheading every three to five paragraphs to avoid visual monotony and keep the reader focused. Although you may find such breaking too frequent, the concept is important. As noted in Chapter 4, a well-designed outline can serve as the structure for the table of contents and also provide headings and subheadings that make a document easier to read.

Figure 6.2 shows two common variations in headings. Importance is signaled not only by page position but also by capitalizations, underlinings, and changes in typeface and type size.

Figure 6.2

TITLE OF THE DOCUMENT	TITLE OF THE DOCUMENT
MAIN HEADING I	MAIN HEADING 1
Subsection A	SUBSECTION A
Subsubsection 1	Subsubsection 1
	Sub-subsubsection a

Typefaces

An associate software consultant for a company that designs and manufactures typesetting systems for business and industry wrote the paper displayed in Figure 6.3 for her fellow students in a technical writing class, to introduce them to typography. The paper also provides general background information for you.

Figure 6.3

```
                   Definition of Typography
                            for
                  Technical Writing Interns


    Typography is the art of producing words and symbols from type.  The

word type refers to the individual letters, numbers, and symbols that

make up the words on a printed page.  Typography also involves the precise

layout of words on a page and the creative design of the page using

different typefaces.  A typeface is the style or design of letters.  (1: 1)

    Typography is a craft that has been developing for over 500 years.

About 1440, Johann Gutenberg of Germany devised a method of mechanically

reproducing manuscripts that were handwritten by monks and scribes.  He

cut the individual letters in the form of a metal punch and then drove

this punch into a bar of soft metal to form what is known as a matrix.

From this matrix, he cast a mold that gave each character uniform width

and height in an adjustable mold.  Each letter and number had two parts,

which allowed the typesetter to move the type in innumerable ways.  (2: 3)
```

Figure 6.3   *Continued*

Typesetting did not change significantly until 1886, when Ottmar Mergenthaler invented an automatic typecasting machine called the Linotype. This machine cast a line of type at a time using a keyboard similar to a typewriter. For about 100 years, hot composition was the only method available for setting type. The term *hot* is used because molten metal is used. In 1960, cold composition was developed through phototypesetting machines. These devices produce typography on film or photographic paper by the use of master photographic type negatives rather than casting matrices. The cost of the equipment needed to go from hot to cold composition is costly. Therefore, hot composition is still used by some typesetters in the United States and by many typesetters in European countries such as Germany. (3: 163-173)

In the past twenty years, phototypesetters have become substantially more sophisticated. The equipment has been developed into computer systems that allow larger storage capacity, increased speed, and the ability to interface with other computers and word processors. The computerized typesetters of the 1980s allow an operator to change important typesetting specifications with a few keystrokes. Common changes made to typeset copy are point sizes, justification or quadding modes, and typefaces. Below are examples of these parameters changed on a Linotron 202 Composition System. Each of these changes required computer codes that could be accessed with only two extra keystrokes for each paragraph.

Figure 6.3 *Continued*

Point Size:

This copy has a point size of 10. Notice the height of the characters.

This copy has a point size of 20. Notice the height of these characters.

Justification:

These lines have been justified. Notice how the left and right margins are aligned. This style of typesetting is often used in books and has been   used   for   most   of   this   paper.

These lines have been quadded left. Notice
how the left margin is aligned, but
the right margin is uneven,
sometimes referred to as "ragged right."

Typefaces:

This typeface is called Bembo and is usually used for typesetting books, letters, and reports.

This typeface is called Cochin Black Italic and is sometimes used for typesetting wedding invitations or other announcements.

One of the advantages of typesetting text is to convey different moods. Changing any of the above parameters has an effect on the message of the copy. Therefore, the type should be consistent with the purpose of the text. (3: 165) For example, typesetting a serious warning in Bembo Bold in a point size of fourteen can be effective.

WARNING! Ingestion of this chemical could be fatal!

If that same message were set in Cochin Black Italic in a point size of ten, the reader might not notice the warning or be affected by it.

WARNING! Ingestion of this chemical could be fatal!

Figure 6.3   *Continued*

When having copy typeset, keep in mind that styles of typesetting may help
or hinder the effectiveness of a message.

References

1. Compugraphic Corporation. *Personal Composition System*.   Wilmington,
MA: Technical Product Support, 1983.

2. Huss, Richard E. *The Development of Printers Mechanical Typesetting
Methods*. Virginia: University Press of Virginia, 1973.

3. Schlemmer, Richard M. *Handbook of Advertising Art Production*.
Prentice-Hall, Inc., 1976.

Paper reprinted courtesy of Deb Beaudry.

Typewritten Versus Typeset. Ordinary typewritten material looks different
from typeset material because typewriters generally use monospacing while
typeset material is spaced proportionally. Monospacing gives all characters
the same width of space, regardless of actual character width; proportional
spacing employs different widths based on actual width of the character.

Example

Typewriting—monospacing	Typeset–proportional spacing
Mm Aa Ii million	Mm Aa Ii million
This is an example of a typewritten sentence that uses monospacing.	This is an example of a typeset sentence that uses proportional spacing.

Office equipment available to technical professionals is rapidly changing.
For example, many electronic typewriters now offer proportional spacing.
More significantly, word processors can now interface with office-size typesetters to produce typeset documents as rapidly as a printer with a word
processor can produce a printed copy. (The only restriction is price.) Such
technological advances benefit writers tremendously because readers can be
so positively influenced by the appearance of a document. As a result, writers

Figure 6.4   Examples of Different Typewriter Typefaces

This is a proportional spacing type face called Arcadia.
abcdefghijklmnopqrstuvwxyz ABCDEFGHIJKLMNOPQRSTUVWXYZ

This is a proportional spacing type face called Boldface.
abcdefghijklmnopqrstuvwxyz ABCDEFGHIJKLMNOPQRSTUVWXYZ

This is a proportional spacing type face called Boldface Italic.
abcdefghijklmnopqrstuvwxyz ABCDEFGHIJKLMNOPQRSTUVWXYZ

This is an elite (12-pitch) type face called Prestige Elite.
abcdefghijklmnopqrstuvwxyz ABCDEFGHIJKLMNOPQRSTUVWXYZ

This is an elite (12-pitch) type face called Courier.
abcdefghijklmnopqrstuvwxyz ABCDEFGHIJKLMNOPQRSTUVWXYZ

This is an elite (12-pitch) type face called Script.
abcdefghijklmnopqrstuvwxyz ABCDEFGHIJKLMNOPQRSTUVWXYZ

This is a pica (10-pitch) type face called Delegate.
abcdefghijklmnopqrstuvwxyz ABCDEFGHIJKLMNOPQRSTUVWXYZ

THIS IS A PICA (10-PITCH) TYPE FACE CALLED MANIFOLD.
ABCDEFGHIJKLMNOPQRSTUVWXYZ ABCDEFGHIJKLMNOPQRSTUVWXYZ

need to be familiar with the typographic options available to them. Readers, of course, have to be careful not to let a visually attractive document influence their assessment of content.

Typeface Variations. A document's typeface, whether typewritten or type-set, can create a variety of impressions as well as contribute to ease in reading. The student paper introducing typography identified several different type-faces. Several standard typewriter typefaces are highlighted in Figure 6.4.

Various typographical devices, including capitalization, boldface, and italics, are used to emphasize headings, set off examples, and highlight key words and phrases.

Using ALL CAPS for emphasis can be effective; however, your use of ALL CAPS should be limited to headings and single words or short phrases in the text. WHEN YOU USE ALL CAPS FOR ENTIRE SECTIONS OF TEXT, THE READER IS NOT ABLE TO RAPIDLY DIFFERENTIATE THE WORDS BECAUSE ALL THE LETTERS ARE THE SAME HEIGHT. THUS, READING IS SLOWED. YOUR INTENT TO EMPHASIZE A POINT IS LOST IN THE VISUAL MONOTONY OF CONSISTENT CAPITALIZATION.

Visual emphasis can be created by using **boldface** or **ALL CAP BOLDFACE**. These techniques are usually reserved for signaling warnings, cautions, and dangers and for calling attention to important points and terms.

Visual emphasis can also be created by selective use of *italics*. Key terms and foreign terms are frequently italicized. Occasionally, examples are italicized to draw special attention to them.

Another typeface variation is typesize, which refers to the size of the letters. Small type enables you to fit more into a space; however, if the type size is too small, the material looks crowded and may be difficult to read. Slightly larger type can make the material look more appealing; however, type that is too large may create an elementary rather than professional image.

Generally, flexibility in type size differs depending on whether you are typing, using a computer printer, or typesetting material.

Most typewriters are set at either 10 characters per inch or 12 characters per inch, although some have the capability of printing in either size type. A few typewriters can be set at 15 characters per inch. Typewriters that have a variety of type elements give the user the ability to adjust typeface as well as type size. Figure 6.4 shows the same material typed at 10 and 12 characters per inch.

Type size can be affected by typeface, as the two type styles in Figure 6.5 reveal.

Computer Printers. Computer printers can be separated into two broad categories—dot matrix and letter quality. These terms refer to the appearance of the output—the printing—not to the method of printing, which ranges from impact and ink-jet to laser. Dot matrix printers frequently can vary type sizes if the writer types special print codes when preparing the document. Letter-quality printers in homes and offices can also use different type sizes as well as different type styles; however, the operator must not only type special print codes into the document but also usually stop to change the print element, much the same way a type element is changed in an electric typewriter. A writer should consider that documents prepared on letter quality printers are usually visually more appealing and easier to read than those prepared on dot matrix printers (see Figure 6.6).

Most people consider 10 point type easy to read although type ranging

Figure 6.5

Bembo

Avant Garde Bold Condensed

6 point
The quick brown fox jumped over the lazy white dog. The quick
ABCDEFGHIJKLMNOPQRSTUVWXYZ
abcdefghijklmnopqrstuvwxyz   1234567890

7 point
The quick brown fox jumped over the lazy white dog. The
ABCDEFGHIJKLMNOPQRSTUVWXYZ
abcdefghijklmnopqrstuvwxyz   1234567890

8 point
The quick brown fox jumped over the lazy white
ABCDEFGHIJKLMNOPQRSTUVWXYZ
abcdefghijklmnopqrstuvwxyz   1234567890

9 point
The quick brown fox jumped over the lazy
ABCDEFGHIJKLMNOPQRSTUVWXYZ
abcdefghijklmnopqrstuvwxyz   1234567890

10 point
The quick brown fox jumped over the
ABCDEFGHIJKLMNOPQRSTUVW
XYZ
abcdefghijklmnopqrstuvwxyz
1234567890

11 point
The quick brown fox jumped over
ABCDEFGHIJKLMNOPQRSTU
VWXYZ
abcdefghijklmnopqrstuvwxyz
1234567890

12 point
The quick brown fox jumped
ABCDEFGHIJKLMNOPQRST
UVWXYZ
abcdefghijklmnopqrstuvwxyz
1234567890

6 point
The quick brown fox jumped over the lazy white dog. The quick brown
ABCDEFGHIJKLMNOPQRSTUVWXYZ
abcdefghijklmnopqrstuvwxyz   1234567890

7 point
The quick brown fox jumped over the lazy white dog. The quick
ABCDEFGHIJKLMNOPQRSTUVWXYZ
abcdefghijklmnopqrstuvwxyz   1234567890

8 point
The quick brown fox jumped over the lazy white dog.
ABCDEFGHIJKLMNOPQRSTUVWXYZ
abcdefghijklmnopqrstuvwxyz   1234567890

9 point
The quick brown fox jumped over the lazy white
ABCDEFGHIJKLMNOPQRSTUVWXYZ
abcdefghijklmnopqrstuvwxyz   1234567890

10 point
The quick brown fox jumped over the lazy
ABCDEFGHIJKLMNOPQRSTUVWXYZ
abcdefghijklmnopqrstuvwxyz
1234567890

11 point
The quick brown fox jumped over the
ABCDEFGHIJKLMNOPQRSTUVWXYZ
abcdefghijklmnopqrstuvwxyz
1234567890

12 point
The quick brown fox jumped over
ABCDEFGHIJKLMNOPQRSTUVWXYZ
abcdefghijklmnopqrstuvwxyz
1234567890

from 8 point to 12 point is comfortable. Combinations of type size and type-face provide visual appeal and variety. For example, the body of this book is set in 10/13 point Bembo with 12 point Avant Garde Bold Condensed main headings; 10/11 point Bembo is used for the examples.

Figure 6.6   Examples of Dot-Matrix and Letter-Quality Printing

```
     This is an example of a            This is an example of a
single-spaced paragraph that       single-spaced paragraph that
is printed on a dot-matrix         is printed on a letter-quality
printer.  All drafts of the        printer.  All drafts of the
manuscript for this text           manuscript for this text
were all printed on a              were all printed on a
dot-matrix printer.                dot-matrix printer.
```

If particular material must fit into a prescribed and limited amount of space, you can use type size to make minor adjustments. For example, information for a resume could fit attractively on a single 8½- by 11-inch sheet if typed using 12 characters per inch, whereas the information might take up 1¼ sheets if typed using 10 characters per inch.

Typographic Devices

Sometimes you need to emphasize information by separating it or visually distinguishing it from the text. Effective devices include numbered lists, bulleted lists, underlinings, boxes, shading or tints, and colors. As with any devices, their impact diminishes with overuse. Too many visual devices make a page look so cluttered that the reader cannot concentrate on content.

Numbered lists suggest one of three things to the reader:

- sequence or chronology of items is important
- priority of items is important
- total count of items is important

When all items in the list are equivalent, then a *bulleted list* is preferable, as illustrated in the preceding lines. The bullets (made on your typewriter by a lower-case letter "o" neatly filled in) draw attention to each item in the list but infer no priority or sequence.

Underlined words or phrases in typing are converted to italics when the material is typeset. If you type most of your documents, you need to be familiar with these conventions. The following elements that occur in technical writing are generally underlined or italicized:

- material that deserves emphasis

Examples
```
Each type of anesthesia available has specific risks.
General anesthesia holds the greatest risk for the
patient. . . .                          (underline in typing)
```

Each type of anesthesia available has specific risks. *General anesthesia* holds the greatest risk for the patient. . . .
(italicize in typesetting)

(In such a discussion, each type of anesthesia could be underlined or italicized as it is introduced. Emphasis through underlining or italics should be used cautiously or it loses its effectiveness.)

- book titles

Examples
```
Edgerton's work in stroboscopy and electronic flash
photography is illustrated in Moments of Vision.
                        (underline in typing)
```

Edgerton's work in stroboscopy and electronic flash photography is illustrated in *Moments of Vision.*   (italicize in typesetting)

- periodicals, newsletters, and newspapers

Examples
```
Aviation Week and Space Technology is an important
trade publication.              (underline in typing)
```

Aviation Week and Space Technology is an important trade publication.   (italicize in typesetting)

- legal citations

Examples
```
In Technicomp v. Chemco, industrial safety was
established as the mutual responsibility of . . . .
                        (underline in typing)
```

In *Technicomp v. Chemco,* industrial safety was established as the mutual responsibility of . . . .   (italicize in typesetting)

- letters

Examples
```
the nth power         (underline in typing)
```
the *n*th power   (italicize in typesetting)
```
the p's and q's       (underline in typing)
```
the *p*'s and *q*'s   (italicize in typesetting)

■ algebraic equations

Example $a^2 + b^2 = c^2$

■ textual references to visual points

Examples   `Plot a course from `A` to `Y` as shown on the`
`navigational chart.`   (underline in typing)

Plot a course from *A* to *Y* as shown on the navigational chart.
                              (italicize in typesettting)

■ Latinate (usually scientific) names

Examples   `Eel grass (`Zostera marina`) can take over a small`
`pond if left unchecked.`   (underline in typing)

Eel grass (*Zostera marina*) can take over a small pond if left
unchecked.   (italicize in typesetting)

`Streptomyces griseus` ` is a fungus-like bacteria that`
`produces streptomycin, a commonly used antibiotic.`
                              (underline in typing)

Streptomyces griseus is a fungus-like bacteria that produces strepto-
mycin, a commonly used antibiotic.   (italicize in typesetting)

■ names of vessels—spacecraft, ships, aircraft

Examples   `The `Voyager` space probe sent back data about the`
`outer planets in our solar system.`
                              (underline in typing)

The *Voyager* space probe sent back data about the outer planets in
our solar system.   (italicize in typesetting)

Boxes can emphasize or separate material. Boxed material should be surrounded by white space so that the text does not run into the box. Sometimes
the boxed material relates directly to the text; other times it is supplemental.

Boxes are often effective in the following situations:
  ■ identify major headings
  ■ highlight key terms
  ■ emphasize formulas or equations
  ■ separate anecdotal material

Shading, like boxing, can highlight and emphasize material. Sometimes shaded areas are used in conjunction with boxing. Like all visual devices, too much shading diminishes its impact.

Color is an especially appealing visual device, often contributing significantly to the clarity of a document. Some technical materials require color. For example, anatomical diagrams need shading and color to differentiate muscles. Color-coded electronic components should be accompanied by color-coded trouble-shooting diagrams. In documents with difficult material, color can create visual interest, highlight section headings, identify examples, and emphasize important points.

Despite its value, the use of color is often restricted by cost. A separate printing run is needed for each color added to a page. Often, a well-designed document employing a variety of visual devices other than color will be as effective.

White Space

White space is the part of any page that is blank—no print or visuals. Not only does white space make documents more attractive, it also makes them easier to read. Although no hard and fast rules concerning the use of white space exist, several conventions have evolved that suggest white space be used for margins, between lines within a paragraph, between paragraphs and sections of a document, and around visuals. Generally, the amount of white space on a page approximately equals the amount of type on the page.

The impact of white space is illustrated by the two segments in Figure 6.7—the first with crowded printing and minimal margins, and the second with wider margins and more space between sections.

The four margins on a page are usually different widths. The top (head) margin is the narrowest. The inner margins are wider, to ensure that no words are lost in the binding; the outer margin is wider still. Type that runs nearly to the edge of the paper not only is unattractive but also leads readers' eyes off the page. Sometimes, outside margins are even wider to provide space for note taking or a *running gloss*, marginal notes that emphasize particular points. The widest margin should be at the bottom of the page.

The spacing between lines of type (called *leading* by photocompositors) improves legibility and, thus, increases ease and speed of reading. Generally, the line spacing easiest to read is one-and-one-half times the letter height. For typewritten material one-and-one-half spacing produces the most visually pleasing document, single spacing often being too dense and double spacing too widely separated.

Figure 6.7	Impact of White Space on Ease of Reading

> This paragraph is more difficult to read because little attention is given to physical features of the presentation. The single spacing creates greater eye strain. The tiny margins give an impression of crowding. The proportion of white space is much less than the amount of text.

This paragraph is easy

to read because the physical

features consider the reader.

The material is double-spaced

and is surrounded by margins.

The white space and text are

balanced.

White space between paragraphs and sections visually separates ideas. Typewritten papers that use double space or space-and-a-half do not need additional lines between paragraphs. Single-spaced typewritten papers should double space between paragraphs. All documents, whether typewritten or typeset, should distinguish major sections of a document with additional line spacing.

White space also sets off special elements in the text, such as quotations and visuals. Quotations that are not integrated into the text but instead presented in block form (usually those longer than three lines) should be preceded and followed by white space that is double the regular leading. Every visual should be surrounded by a border of white space to clearly separate it from text. This white space assures that the label, title, and caption of the visual do not run into the text.

Justification

If all the lines of type on a page are exactly the same length, the lines have been *justified*—adjusted to equal length by proportional spacing between words on each individual line. A justified right-hand margin gives a document a neat, clean appearance, as Figure 6.8 (left) illustrates; however, elimination of the ragged right margin does not increase ease of reading. If the lines all

Figure 6.8

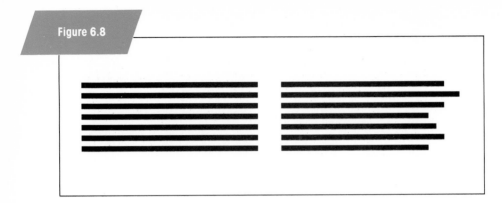

begin at the same left-hand margin, and the right margin is ragged, the lines are *quadded* left and *unjustified* on the right, as Figure 6.8 (right) shows. Readers may prefer unjustified right-hand margins because the lines are easier to distinguish, but the primary benefit of ragged right margins is that they are less difficult to revise in typing or typesetting and less expensive to typeset.[2] In addition, a recent survey in *Technical Communication* indicated that a clear majority of both managers and nonmanagers preferred documents with ragged right margins.[3]

Incorporation of Visuals

Technical visuals are not a recent addition to technical communication. As the cover of this text and the part divisions illustrate, Leonardo da Vinci produced a wide variety of technical art. His work exemplifies the accuracy and attention to detail found in all effective technical visuals. Figure 6.9 is another sixteenth-century technical drawing that precisely illustrates and labels the major components of a pair of mine pumps. Visuals have become an aid, and sometimes even a necessity, to understanding technical material.

Purpose and Value of Visuals

Visuals in technical reports should have a specific purpose and convey specific content. They should not be used simply for decoration, as in one report about the construction methods of eighteenth- and nineteenth-century covered bridges in New England. The report's centerfold was a long shot of New

Figure 6.9

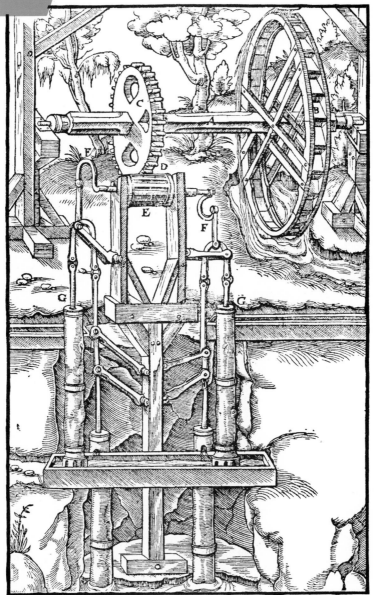

PAIR OF CRANKS driven by an overshot wheel rotating a two-gear train are converting rotary motion into linear motion in this illustration from *De re metallica*. The linear motion is being conveyed to pistons of two pairs of mine pumps. The lower pump of each pair lifts water from the mine shaft to a trough in the foreground for further raising by the upper pumps.

Source: Georgius Agricola, *De re metallica*, 1556, in Terry S. Reynolds. "Medieval Roots of the Industrial Revolution," *Scientific American*, July 1984, 127.

Figure 6.10   Variations of Visual and Verbal Integration

a. **Verbal Presentation with Words Alone**

```
Ad regum thalamos numine prospero qui caelum
superi quiquae regunt fretum ad sint cum populis
rite faventibus primum sceptriferis cola tonanti-
bus taurus celsa ferat tergore candido lucinam
nivei femina corpore
```

b. **Verbal Presentation with Visual Support**

```
Ad regum thalamos numine prospero qui caelum
superi quiquae regunt fretum ad sint cum populis
rite faventibus primum
sceptriferis cola tonan-
tibus taurus celsa fer-
at tergore candido
lucinam nivei femina
corpore intempta iugo
```

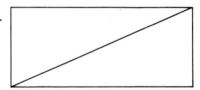

c. **Visual Presentation with Verbal Explanation**

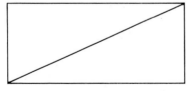

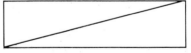

```
Ad regum thalamos          regunt fretum ad sint
numine prospero qui        cum populis rite faventi-
caelum superi quiquae      bus primum sceptriferis
                           cola tonantibus taurus
                           celsa ferat tergore
```

d. **Visual Presentation with Visuals Alone**

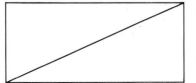

England fall foliage, with a covered bridge nestled in one of the valleys. More useful visuals for this report might have presented cutaway diagrams of joint construction.

In technical communication, visuals illustrate, explain, demonstrate, verify, or support the text. In fact, visuals are often more useful or appropriate than words. As a writer, you can combine words and visuals in several ways. Your choices are displayed along the continuum in Figure 6.10.

You need to select visual/verbal combinations that most effectively communicate to readers. In many situations visuals are more efficient than words, saving words, space, and reader time. Specific applications of visuals include:

- situations in which the reader's understanding is limited
- situations in which speed is of the utmost importance and reading would slow the process
- situations in which the process is more clearly illustrated visually

Visuals, like words, can be adapted to various audiences—in complexity of content, presentation, and sometimes color and size. Figures 6.11 and 6.12 illustrate this point. Both are published by the American Association for the Advancement of Science; both are about the same discoveries and hypotheses in the study of human evolution. Figure 6.11 is from *Science 83*, a monthly magazine for the educated nonexpert interested in science. Figure 6.12 is from *Science*, a weekly journal that updates professionals in science about new research.

A verbal explanation of the tabular information in Figure 6.13 would be confusing because the reader would not immediately see the relationships that the table makes clear. Imagine trying to convey this information in a paragraph.

Information that would be repeated in a paragraph explaining the relationship between alcohol consumption and blood level alcohol is simply presented as headings for the rows and columns. Because the numeric information is tabulated, the reader can easily see the impact of increased alcohol consumption on safe driving.

Visuals are also useful in illustrating definitions or explanations. Figure 6.14 describes the operation of an automobile seat belt. Although the verbal explanation alone is understandable, the addition of the visual clarifies the information.

Selecting the visual that best suits a particular situation depends on the same type of audience analysis as the verbal portion of a document. Because visuals have different purposes and varying levels of complexity, you need to be familiar with your options. Regardless of the situation, however, the visuals you select should be directly related to the information in the text.

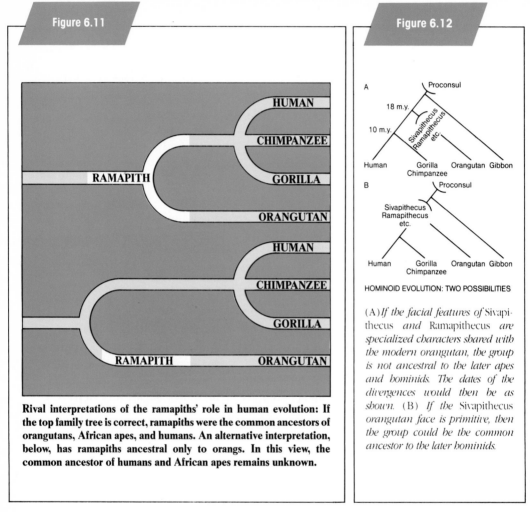

Figure 6.11

Rival interpretations of the ramapiths' role in human evolution: If the top family tree is correct, ramapiths were the common ancestors of orangutans, African apes, and humans. An alternative interpretation, below, has ramapiths ancestral only to orangs. In this view, the common ancestor of humans and African apes remains unknown.

Figure 6.12

HOMINOID EVOLUTION: TWO POSSIBILITIES

(A) *If the facial features of* Sivapithecus *and* Ramapithecus *are specialized characters shared with the modern orangutan, the group is not ancestral to the later apes and hominids. The dates of the divergences would then be as shown.* (B) *If the* Sivapithecus orangutan *face is primitive, then the group could be the common ancestor to the later hominids.*

Source: Illustration by Ellen Cohen in Allen L. Hammond, "Tales of an Elusive Ancestor," *Science 83*, November 1983, 43.

Source: Roger W. Lewin, "Is the Orangutan a Living Fossil?" *Science*, 222 (16 December 1983): 1223. Copyright 1983 by the AAAS. Reprinted with permission of the AAAS.

Visuals are valuable in themselves as definitions, as the drawings of types of screw heads in Figure 6.15 show. The drawings in this case are more accurate and efficient than a verbal description.

Visuals are applied in many other ways in technical writing. Knowing that ideas can be presented either verbally or visually gives a technical writer great flexibility. Figure 6.16 lists specific examples of visuals that are appropriate for definitions, summaries, descriptions of objects and mechanisms, explanations of processes, and directions. Each of these applications uses a specific organizational pattern (as discussed in Chapter 4).

Figure 6.13

KNOW YOUR LIMITS

CHART FOR RESPONSIBLE PEOPLE WHO MAY SOMETIMES DRIVE AFTER DRINKING!

APPROXIMATE BLOOD ALCOHOL PERCENTAGE

Drinks	Body Weight in Pounds								
	100	120	140	160	180	200	220	240	Influenced
1	.04	.03	.03	.02	.02	.02	.02	.02	Rarely
2	.08	.06	.06	.05	.04	.04	.03	.03	
3	.11	.09	.08	.07	.06	.06	.05	.05	
4	.15	.12	.11	.09	.08	.08	.07	.06	
5	.19	.16	.13	.12	.11	.09	.09	.08	Possibly
6	.23	.19	.16	.14	.13	.11	.10	.09	
7	.26	.22	.19	.16	.15	.13	.12	.11	
8	.30	.25	.21	.19	.17	.15	.14	.13	Definitely
9	.34	.28	.24	.21	.19	.17	.15	.14	
10	.38	.31	.27	.23	.21	.19	.17	.16	

Subtract .01% for each 40 minutes of drinking
One drink is 1 oz. of 100 proof liquor, 12 oz. of beer, or 4 oz. of table wine.

SUREST POLICY IS . . . DON'T DRIVE AFTER DRINKING!

Source: New Hampshire DWI Prevention Council, *Know Your Limits* (Dover, NH). Reprinted with permission of the New Hampshire DWI Prevention Council.

Figure 6.14

The Safety Belt: How It Works

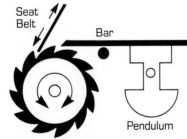

Normal Conditions

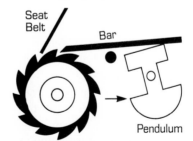

Emergency Conditions

Under normal conditions, the pendulum and bar are in their rest positions. The reel, which holds the belt, is free to rotate. As the occupant moves forward the belt moves unrestrained with the occupant.

Under emergency conditions, such as in a collision, the pendulum moves forward under the force of the impact causing the bar to engage the ratchet. The reel and seat belt now lock in place and the occupant is held firmly in place.

Source: From "The Safety Belt: How It Works," *The Lowell Sun,* 3 September 1983.

Figure 6.15

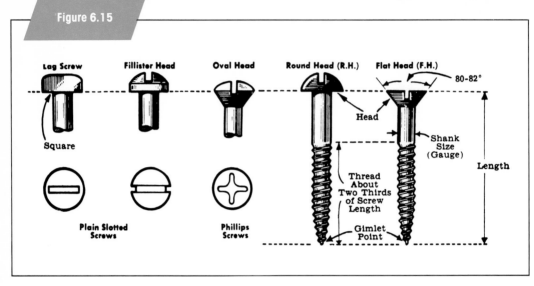

Source: "Screws," Sears Craftsman Master Shop Guide (Hearst Corporation, 1969), sheet 3. Reprinted with permission of Sears.

Figure 6.16   Visuals Appropriate for Technical Writing Applications

Applications	*Examples*
DEFINITION *Use:* Chronology Spatial order Partition Division	exploded view of floppy disk
	X-ray of beryllium block
	map of habitat for mountain lions
	periodic table segment identifying molybdenum
	time-lapse photos showing butterfly emerging from a cocoon
	chart of geological stratification showing age of fossil layers
	drawings of birds, mushrooms, flowers, insects, shells in field identification guide
SUMMARY *Use:* Descending/ ascending order Chronology	table identifying characteristics of wood used for carpentry
	list of safeguards against industrial pollution to residential neighborhoods
	chart of suggestions for trouble-shooting equipment malfunction
	certification list of master blocks
	percent graph of R and D expenses

Figure 6.16   *Continued*

Applications	*Examples*
ORGANISM OR MECHANISM DESCRIPTION *Use:* Spatial order Partition Division Classification Comparison/ contrast	schematic of micro chip; switch circuit diagram of rotary motor; DNA; zoom lens micrograph of aberrant cell; optical fibers phantom view of video cassette; extruder cutaway view of centrifuge pump; fossil exploded view of protective packaging X-ray of foot; mummy sketch of little brown bat wings
PROCESS EXPLANATION *Use:* Chronology Division Cause/effect	flow chart of steps in substance analysis time line of water purification in waste treatment plant sequential photos showing embryo development story board of training film tree diagram of genetic relationships series of changes in weather map, showing development of storm front
DIRECTIONS *Use:* Chronology Spatial order Partition Cause/effect	navigational chart of Cape Ann sequential photos/drawings showing steps for connecting new terminal chart of problems caused by improper installation of terminal exploded view of engine parts, showing order for reassembly calendar specifying dates for completion of project goals sketches of parts identified on parts list flow chart to document steps in computer program

Conventions in Presentation of Visuals

Visuals are generally most effective if they are placed as close as possible following the text reference. If a visual in a book requires an entire page, it should be located on the page facing the text reference and discussion. If a visual in a report (printed on only one side of the paper) requires an entire page, the visual should be located on the page following the text reference.

Visuals that the reader needs to refer to repeatedly should probably be placed near the end of the document. For example, they can be located after

Figure 6.17

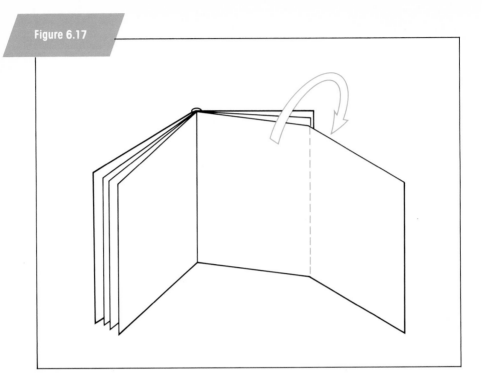

the final text reference or in the first appendix on a fold-out page, as shown in Figure 6.17.

Several general guidelines will help you use visuals in ways that will be most useful to the reader:

1. Accurately label each visual. Make sure to include complete identification, title, and caption.

Example   Table 1: Worker Fatigue Using Wire Cutters
Worker fatigue was compared using three different models of ergonomic cutters during a two-week period.

2. Include complete dimensions of each visual. Specify the units of measure or scale.
3. Whenever possible, spell out words rather than using abbreviations. If abbreviations are included, use standard ones and include a key.
4. Surround the visual with white space to separate it from the text of the document.
5. Include a complete textual reference. Do not assume that the reader will check the visual unless you refer to it. Your reference should include the number and title. Textual references can be accomplished in several ways:

■ . . . as illustrated in Figure 2.

■ . . . (see Table 3).

■ The effectiveness of the antitoxins tested is presented in Figure 4.

■ Table 5 shows the rapid increase of gas prices during a five-year period.

6. If a document has more than five visuals, include a List of Figures or List of Tables.

7. Identify the source of the data as well as the graphic designer.

8. Specify the focus or interpretation you want the reader to apply when examining the visual. Without a sentence to identify the significance of the visual, the reader may not understand its purpose.

Types of Visuals

Visuals can be separated into six broad categories, each with distinct advantages and disadvantages: tables, graphs, diagrams and charts, drawings, maps, and photographs. Each type of visual plays an important part in technical documents, explaining and clarifying content, providing sensory stimulation, and creating reader interest.

Tables

Numeric data identifying the characteristics of ideas, objects, or processes can be displayed in *tables*. The rows and columns of a table provide a system for classifying data that would be confusing if presented in sentences and paragraphs.

In addition to their obvious organizational benefits, tables present large amounts of data in an accessible format that takes far less space than would the verbal presentation of the same information. The table charting amino acids in Figure 6.18 is easy to read and understand. The same information presented in a paragraph would be difficult to follow and would force the reader to work unnecessarily hard to get the information.

If the data in a table is self-contained and self-explanatory, it is usually boxed as well as surrounded with white space to set it apart from the text. Such a table is labeled with a number and a title. Conventions that have been

Figure 6.18

AMINO ACID COMPOSITION OF RED MEAT AND POULTRY MEAT (PERCENT OF PROTEIN)

Amino acid	Pork	Lamb	Beef	Turkey	Chicken
Leucine	7.5%	7.4%	8.4%	7.6%	6.6%
Valine	5.0	5.0	5.7	5.1	6.7
Isoleucine	4.9	4.8	5.1	5.0	4.1
Methionine	2.5	2.3	2.3	2.6	1.8
Threonine	5.1	4.9	4.0	4.0	4.0
Phenylalanine	4.1	3.9	4.0	3.7	4.0
Arginine	6.4	6.9	6.6	6.5	6.7
Histidine	3.2	2.7	2.9	3.0	2.0
Lysine	7.8	7.7	8.4	9.0	7.5
Tryptophan	1.4	1.3	1.1	0.9	0.8
Glutamic acid	14.5	14.4	14.4	–	–
Aspartic acid	8.9	8.5	8.8	–	–
Proline	4.6	4.8	5.4	–	–
Tyrosine	3.0	3.2	3.2	1.5	2.5
Glycine	6.1	6.7	7.1	–	–
Serine	4.0	3.9	3.8	–	–
Cystine	1.3	1.3	1.4	1.0	1.8
Alanine	6.3	6.3	6.4	–	–

Source: Evan F. Binkerd et al., "Animal Protein from Meat, Poultry and Eggs," in *Protein Resources and Technology: Status and Research Needs,* Max Milner, Nevin S. Scrimshaw, and Daniel I.C. Wang, eds. (Westport, CT: AVI Publishing Company, Inc., copyright 1978), 393. Used with permission of AVI Publishing Company.

established for designing an effective table are listed here and shown in Figure 6.19:

- Place columns to be compared next to each other.
- Round numbers if possible.
- Limit numbers to two decimal places.
- Align decimals in a column.
- Label each column and row.
- Use standard symbols and units of measure.
- Use footnotes for headings that are not self-explanatory.
- Present the table on a single page whenever possible.

Figure 6.19

MODEL OF AN EFFECTIVE TABULAR FORMAT
Subtitle is an Optional Addition

rule

identifies
horizontal
line of data

rule

STUB	MULTIPLE COLUMN HEAD		SINGLE COLUMN HEAD	SINGLE COLUMN HEAD
	Subhead[a]	*Subhead[b]*		
Line Head	ww.w	xxx.x	y.y	zzz.z
Line Head	www.w	x.x	yy.y	zzz.z
Line Head	w.w	xx.x	yyy.y	z.z
Line Head	www.w	xx.x	yy.y	zz.z
Column Average				

rule

rule

rule

[a]*Footnote*
[b]*Footnote*

Less formal tables are integrated into the text. These shorter tables depend directly on the surrounding text to provide a context for the data. They are not numbered or titled, but they usually do have clear row and column headings.

Although tables generally present numeric data, the tabular format is also appropriate for some primarily and even completely verbal material. As with numeric tables, verbal tables can be economical and effective; explaining the information in Figure 6.20 in sentences and paragraphs would be time-consuming and difficult to read. Figure 6.20 also illustrates the close relationship between text and properly organized visuals.

Remember that tables present but do not interpret data. To make the information accessible to the reader, the text *must* discuss and evaluate the data. Because of their complexity, tables are usually reserved for technical audiences.

Figure 6.20

THE GLUE USED for any job should be a little stronger than the wood that forms the joint. *Polyvinyl (white)* glue is perhaps easiest to use, but is not as strong as some other glues. Don't use excessive pressure when clamping polyvinyl. *Plastic resin* is extremely strong, and leaves an almost invisible glue line, but it requires heavy clamping pressure. *Casein* is a good choice for oily woods such as teak and pitch pine, and shrinks very little in drying. *Resorcinol glue* is waterproof, but never apply it at temperatures lower than 70°. *Contact cement* is the choice for applying any sheet material to a wood base, but *don't spray it on!* It's highly flammable. *Epoxy* is not a good choice for wood joints (wood inhibits its curing) but may be useful in cementing metal or plastic to wood.

WOODWORKERS' GLUING CHART

TYPE OF WORK	GLUE FOR LOW-COST WATER-RESISTANT JOINT (In order of preference)	TYPE OF WORK	GLUE FOR LOW-COST WATER-RESISTANT JOINT (In order of preference)
All general gluing of hard and softwoods	Plastic resin glue Casein glue Polyvinyl glue	End-wood joints, mitered joints, scarf joints	Polyvinyl glue Casein glue (heavy mix)
Particle and chip boards to wood	Plastic resin glue Casein glue Contact cement Polyvinyl glue	Loose-fitting joints, relatively rough surfaces	Polyvinyl glue Casein glue (heavy mix)
Plywood to decorative plastic laminates	Casein glue Contact cement Plastic resin glue	Doweling	Plastic resin glue Polyvinyl glue
Laminating heavy framing members	Casein glue	Hardboard to plywood, wood or itself	Plastic resin glue Casein glue Polyvinyl glue Contact cement
Veneering, inlays, cabinet work	Plastic resin glue (extended) Polyvinyl glue	Porous materials, such as linoleum and canvas to wood	Plastic resin glue Casein glue Contact cement
Bonding oily woods (teak, pitch pine, osage, yew)	Casein glue (sponge surface with dilute caustic soda solution 1 hour before gluing)	Plastics, metal and foil to wood	Epoxy glue

Source: "Glues and Adhesives," Sears Craftsman Master Shop Guide (Hearst Corporation, 1969), sheet 16. Reprinted with permission of Sears.

Graphs

Relationships between two or more sets of data are displayed in *graphs*, including line graphs, logarithmic graphs, scatter graphs, pie graphs, circular graphs, bar graphs, and pictorial graphs.

Line Graphs. *Line graphs* show the relationship between two values represented by intersecting values projected from the abscissa (horizontal) and ordinate (vertical) axes on a coordinate grid. Line graphs usually plot changes in quantity, showing the exact increases and decreases over a period of time—minutes, days, decades, or centuries. Line graphs are one of the most commonly used forms of displaying relationships, so most categories of readers are comfortable with them.

In constructing line graphs, these conventions are usually followed:

- Use the horizontal axis to depict time.
- Limit the number of lines on one graph.
- When using more than one line, differentiate the lines by design or color.
- Use a key or label to identify each line.
- Keep the vertical and horizontal axes proportionate.

Figure 6.21 illustrates a series of four effective line graphs accompanied by a clear caption.

Logarithmic Graphs. A specialized form of line graph for comparing data in which rate of change is more important than quantity of change is known as a *logarithmic graph*. The numbers on the vertical scale of a logarithmic graph are not evenly spaced as they are on a conventional line graph. Instead, the numbers increase according to logarithmic factors; thus, the graph has a series of open and grouped vertical lines in which the top and bottom of each group of lines (called a cycle) is a decimal or multiple of ten.

Logarithmic graphs are frequently used to display the relationship between production figures and their rate of increase (or decrease). Logarithmic graphs are also helpful when the vertical range is so large that it is difficult to fit on a normal graph. However, nonexpert readers often are not familiar with a logarithmic scale, so logarithmic graphs should be reserved for professional and expert audiences.

Scatter Graphs. *Scatter graphs* use single, unconnected dots to plot instances where two variables (one on each axis) meet. Usually, scatter graphs are plotted on graphs where the X-axis and Y-axis are proportionate. However,

Examples of Line Graphs

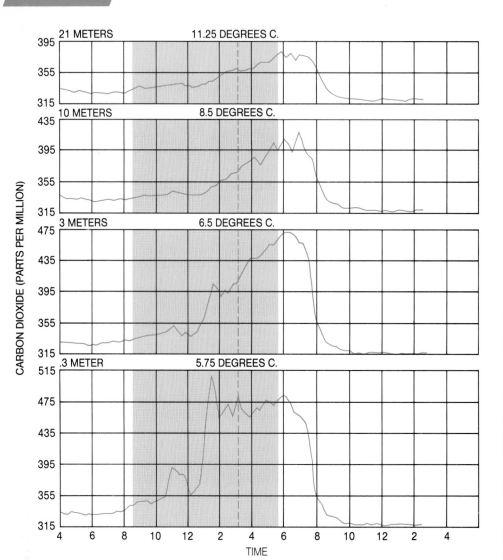

RATE OF RESPIRATION of the forest was determined by measuring the rate at which carbon dioxide, a product of respiration, accumulated during the nights when the air was still because of a temperature inversion. The curves give the carbon dioxide concentration at four elevations in the course of one such night. (Note that the temperature, recorded at 3:00 A.M., was lower near the ground than at greater heights.) The hourly increase in carbon dioxide concentration, which was calculated from these curves, yielded rate of respiration.

Source: George M. Woodwell, "The Energy Cycle of the Biosphere," in *The Biosphere* (San Francisco: W. H. Freeman and Company, 1970), 34. Copyright © 1970 by Scientific American, Inc. All rights reserved. Reprinted with permission of Scientific American, Inc.

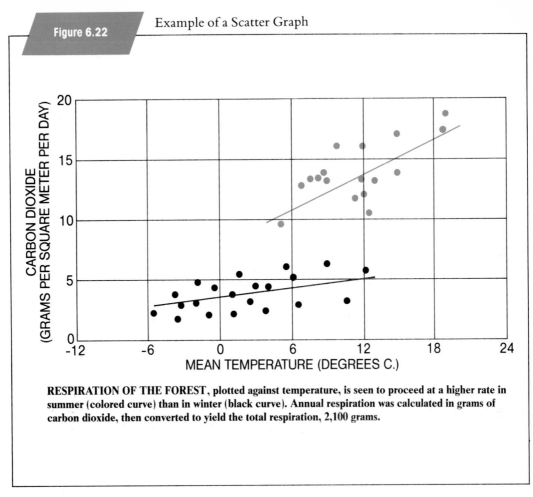

Figure 6.22

Example of a Scatter Graph

RESPIRATION OF THE FOREST, plotted against temperature, is seen to proceed at a higher rate in summer (colored curve) than in winter (black curve). Annual respiration was calculated in grams of carbon dioxide, then converted to yield the total respiration, 2,100 grams.

Source: George M. Woodwell, "The Energy Cycle of the Biosphere," in *The Biosphere* (San Francisco: W. H. Freeman and Company, 1970), 34. Copyright © 1970 by Scientific American, Inc. All rights reserved. Reprinted with permission of Scientific American, Inc.

if the range of data is very large, the data can be charted logarithmically to show more clearly the direction of the correlation.

The pattern of the dots expresses the relationship between variables, as illustrated in Figure 6.22. If the dots are randomly scattered, the two variables have no correlation. If the dots are primarily on a diagonal running from the lower left to the upper right, the correlation is positive. If the diagonal runs from the upper left towards the lower right, the correlation is negative.

The correlation between the variables is sometimes highlighted by shading the area on the graph. However, the significance of the correlation must also be discussed in the text. Because interpreting scatter graphs is often difficult, their use is generally limited to professional and expert audiences.

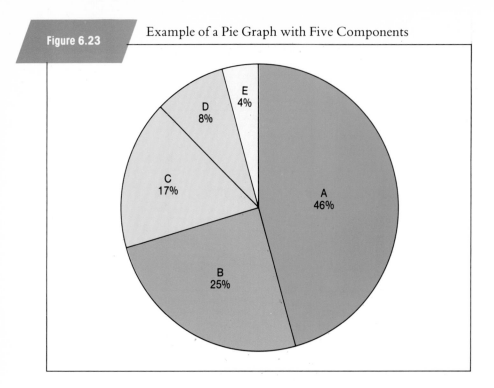

Figure 6.23   Example of a Pie Graph with Five Components

Pie Graphs. *Pie graphs*, also called pie diagrams, pie charts, percent graphs, or divided circle graphs, emphasize the proportionate distribution of something, frequently money or time. Pie graphs are 100-percent graphs, where each percent represents 3.6° of the circle, as shown in Figure 6.23.

Pie graphs can make a striking visual display, but the significance of the presented information must be discussed in the text. Pie graphs are popular attention-getting devices that focus the reader's attention for more detailed data; however, they are generally unsuitable for the comparison of more than five items. The primary problem is the impossibility of comparing areas. Additionally, the visual difference between areas representing similar percentages is minimal.

Circular Graphs. Curiously, pie graphs are not the same as *circular graphs*, which depict information in a circular rather than linear form, usually to maintain continuity. Values on a circular graph begin with a small bull's-eye circle representing zero and increase as the circles radiate outward. The key that accompanies the circular graph is critical for reader comprehension. The interpretation and significance of data must be included in the text when the graph is discussed. Because most people are not familiar with circular graphs, they have limited uses.

Bar Graphs. *Bar graphs* show comparisons, trends, and distributions. Like line graphs, bar graphs are drawn from a series of values plotted on two axes, but the values are represented by vertical or horizontal bars instead of points joined by a line. Because each bar represents a separate quantity, bar graphs are especially appropriate when the data consists of distinct units, such as tons of grain or megawatts of hydroelectric power produced over a specified period. The same general guidelines apply to any type of bar graph:

- Make bars the same width.
- Make the space between bars one-half the bar width.
- Label each bar.

Commonly used bar graphs include a simple bar graph, subdivided bar graph, subdivided 100-percent bar graph, multiple bar graph, sliding bar graph, and floating bar graph:

- In the *simple bar graph* in Figure 6.24, all the bars represent the same type of information, so the differences in magnitude among items are stressed.
- In the *subdivided bar graph* in Figure 6.25, each bar is subdivided to represent the magnitude of different components. Parts are differen-

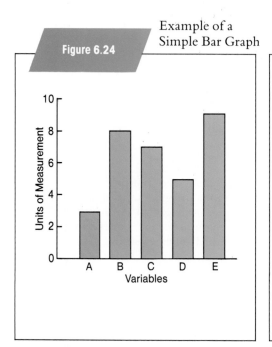

Example of a
Simple Bar Graph

Figure 6.24

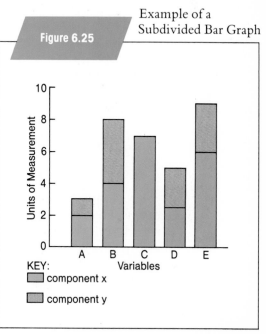

Example of a
Subdivided Bar Graph

Figure 6.25

Figure 6.26   Example of a Subdivided 100-Percent Bar Graph

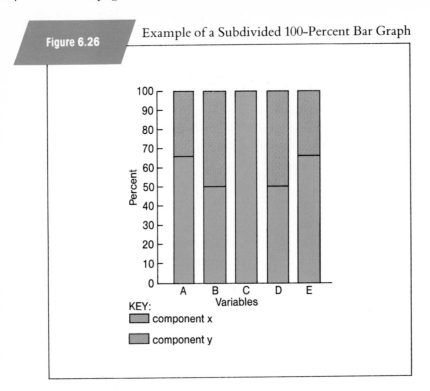

tiated by shading or crosshatching. Although the magnitude of each bar can be compared, as in a simple bar graph, the individual components are not easily compared.

- In the *subdivided 100-percent bar graph* in Figure 6.26, each bar extends to 100 percent, and the components of the bar are separated by percentage. While the relative size of the individual components can be easily compared, the magnitude of each bar cannot be compared. Note that Figures 6.24, 6.25, and 6.26 illustrate three ways to present the same information.

- Figure 6.27 illustrates a variation of a subdivided 100-percent bar graph—a subdivided 100-percent area graph. Imagine a series of 150 bars, each extended to 100 percent and each subdivided to show the percentage of types of fuel used during one year. The bars, representing the years from 1850 to 2000, are then pushed together so the overall effect is a continuous line for each type of energy source. The area under each bar is shaded to make the distinctions clear.

- The *multiple bar graph* in Figure 6.28 groups two or more bars to present the magnitude of related variables. The figure compares three variables during three different time periods.

| Figure 6.27 | Example of Subdivided 100-Percent Area Graph |

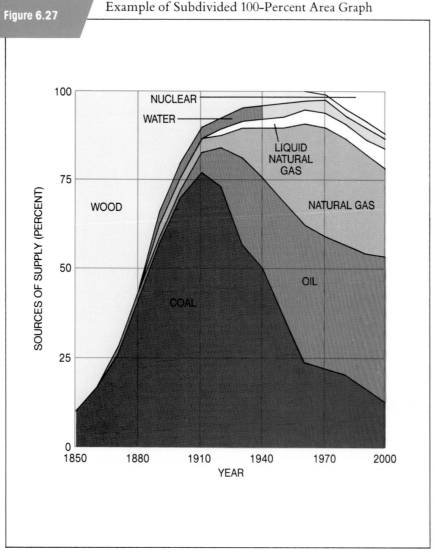

- The bars in the *sliding bar graph* in Figure 6.29 move along an axis that is usually marked in opposing values (active/passive, hot/cold) that extend on either side of a central point, such as values on a temperature scale.

- The *floating bar graph* in Figure 6.30 has bars that "float" in the area above the X-axis, which may extend below zero.

Figure 6.28

Example of a Multiple Bar Graph

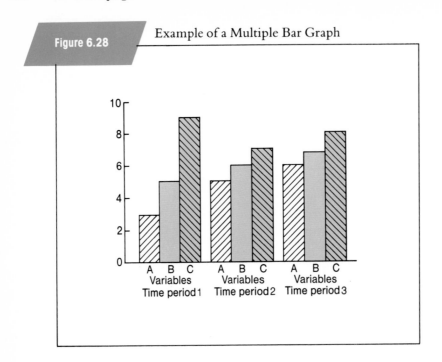

Figure 6.29

Example of a
Sliding Bar Graph

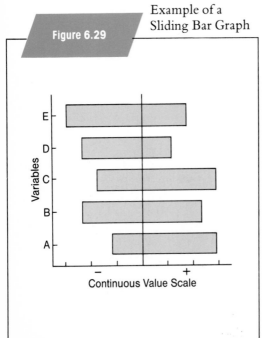

Figure 6.30

Example of a
Floating Bar Graph

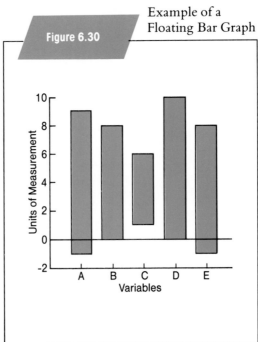

Pictorial graphs. An adaptation of the bar graph, called a *pictorial graph*, uses actual symbols to make up each bar. Each symbol (isotype) represents a specific number of people or objects. Pictorial graphs are very appealing and are widely used with all audiences. Problems arise, however, when depicting fractions (see Figure 6.31). To avoid these problems, these guidelines are generally followed when creating pictorial graphs:

- Round off numbers to eliminate fractions.
- Make all symbols the same size and space them equally.
- Select symbols that are clearly representative of the object.

Another version of a pictorial graph uses single isotypes of different sizes to represent the quantity or magnitude of each variable, as shown in Figure 6.32. In this graph, the increasing number of children allowed in day care groups is represented by increasingly large isotypes representing children in each age group. Such a graph is appropriate for attracting reader attention, but it should not be used to present technical data.

A third variation of a pictorial graph uses symbols to represent the actual quantity or magnitude of the variable, usually without an *x* or *y* axis. Figure 6.33 displays four blocks, the volume of each representing a specific volume of water. The significant differences in the volume (not just the surface area) of the blocks create a dramatic visual image.

Figure 6.31   Problems of Pictorial Graphs

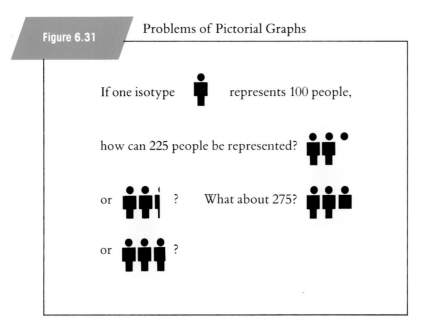

| Figure 6.32 | Example of a Pictorial Graph |

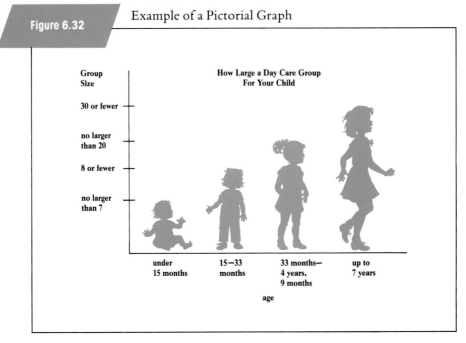

Source: "Consumer Alert: How to Choose Day Care for Your Child," *Masscitizen*, April 1985, p. 11. Reprinted with permission of the Massachusetts Public Interest Research Group.

| Figure 6.33 | Example of Pictorial Graph Showing Volume |

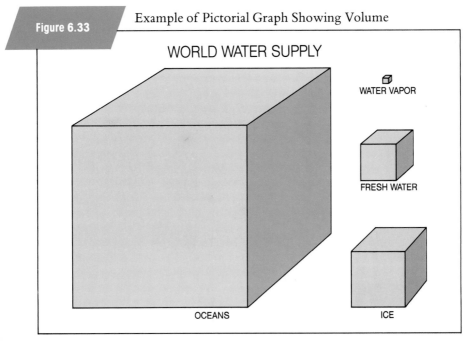

Source: H. L. Penman, "The Water Cycle," in *The Biosphere* (San Francisco: W. H. Freeman and Company, 1970), 40. Copyright © 1970 by Scientific American, Inc. All rights reserved. Reprinted with permission of Scientific American, Inc.

Charts

Charts can represent the components, steps, or chronology of an object, mechanism, organism, or organization. The most common charts are listed below:

▪ A *block components chart* (also called block component diagram and classification chart), illustrated in Figure 6.34, uses blocks to represent the components or subdivisions of the whole object or system. The example shows a teleconferencing system that uses regular telephone lines to transfer drawings, photos, and text between two conference sites.

Figure 6.34   Example of a Block Component Chart

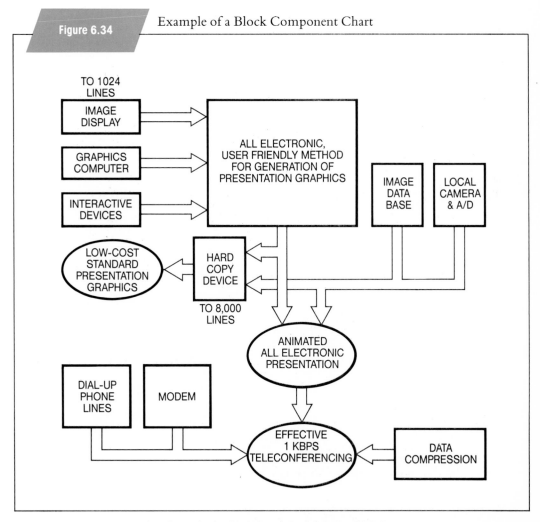

Source: "Low-Cost Teleconference System," NASA Tech Briefs 9 (Spring, 1985): 61.

Figure 6.35   Example of an Organizational Chart

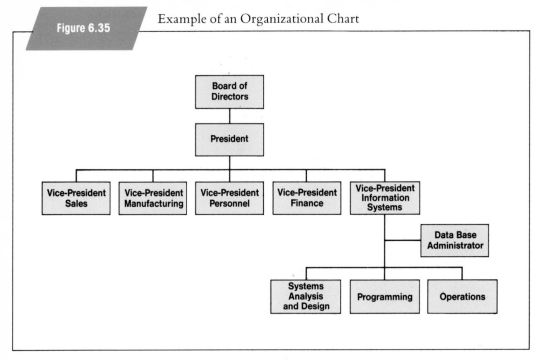

Source: Gary B. Shelly and Thomas J. Cashman, *Introduction to Computer and Data Processing* (Brea, CA: Anaheim Publishing Co., 1980), 10.19.

- An *organizational chart* portrays the hierarchy of an organization by putting each position in a separate block as in Figure 6.35. The chart shows the vertical and horizontal relationships in the organization (as discussed in Chapter 3).
- A *flow chart* (also called a route chart), shown in Figure 6.36, depicts the sequence of steps in a process, often indicating the amount of time each step takes.

Diagrams

Diagrams illustrate the physical components of objects, mechanisms, or organisms. Diagrams explain complex structures clearly; indeed, they are easier to understand than photographs or representative drawings because the reader is not distracted by unnecessary details.

The diagram in Figure 6.37 is particularly effective—the drawing is concise and comprehensible, but equally important, detailed text references accompany the diagram. Too many visuals are given no more than a "See Figure"

Figure 6.36   Example of a Flow Chart

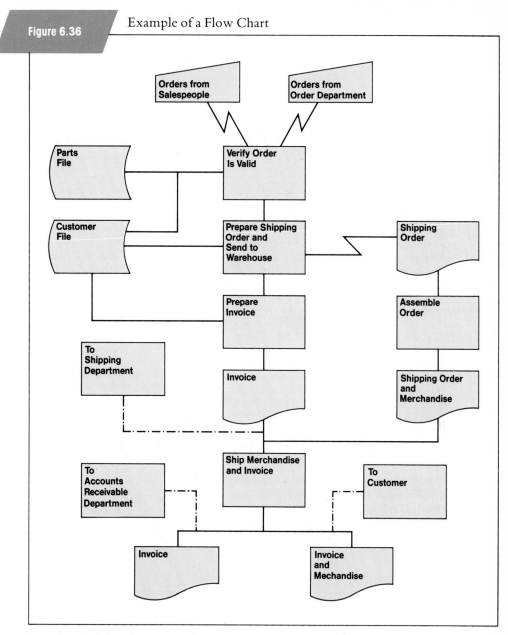

Source: Gary B. Shelly and Thomas J. Cashman, *Introduction to Computer and Data Processing* (Brea, CA: Anaheim Publishing Co., 1980), 10.19.

in the text; the reader must try to identify significant aspects. The explanation and diagram of the solar furnace are closely related; a significant part of the discussion refers directly to the labeled parts in the diagram.

Figure 6.37	Example of Solar Furnace Diagram

Temperature Controller for a Solar Furnace
An adjustable shield varies the amount of solar energy that reaches the receiver.

NASA's Jet Propulsion Laboratory, Pasadena, California

A relatively simple movable shield has been suggested for controlling the temperature of a solar furnace. The temperature modulator can be set to have the collected solar energy fully "on," fully "off," or at any intermediate level.

The solar furnace for testing materials at 3,000° F (1,650° C) is shown in the figure. A parabolic mirror concentrates Sunlight into the receiver. The shade plate that blocks insolation at the back of the receiver produces a shade zone in the center of the collector. No radiation is returned to the receiver from the shade zone; only rays falling on other areas of the reflecting surface are directed back toward the receiver.

The proposed solar-flux modulator would be interposed between the receiver and the reflector. The modulator is a circular plate with the same outside diameter as the shade plate and the same aperture diameter as the receiver. Three positions of the modulator plate are illustrated:

• At position 1, which is closest to the receiver, all of the rays from outside of the shade zone pass through the aperture of the modulator and into the receiver.

• At position 2, some of the rays that are reflected from the mirror are blocked by the modulator plate and thus are prevented from reaching the receiver.

• At position 3, where the modulator plate is farthest from the receiver, all rays are blocked from passing to the receiver aperture and cavity.

Any modulator position between 1 and 3 can be selected by operating an actuator mechanism, thereby controlling the solar power entering the receiver.

This work was done by Allan R. McDougal and Robert R. Hale of Caltech for NASA's Jet Propulsion Laboratory.

Source: "Temperature Controller for a Solar Furnace," *NASA Tech Briefs* 6 (Spring 1981): 26.

Schematics are diagrams that use symbols to represent the components of an object, mechanism, or system. Because of the specialized nature of the symbols, schematics are usually appropriate only for professional and expert readers, in fields such as electronics and engineering.

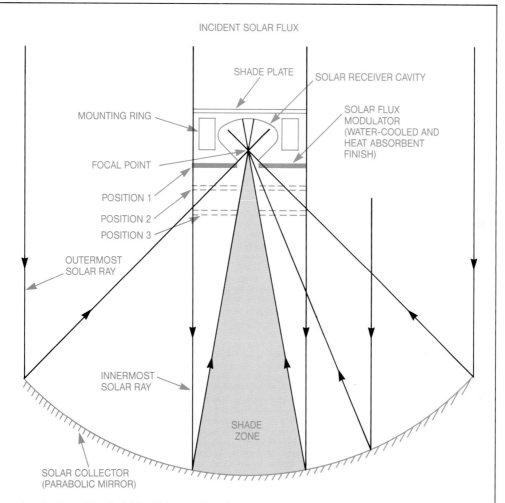

INCIDENT SOLAR FLUX

SHADE PLATE

SOLAR RECEIVER CAVITY

SOLAR FLUX MODULATOR (WATER-COOLED AND HEAT ABSORBENT FINISH)

MOUNTING RING

FOCAL POINT

POSITION 1

POSITION 2

POSITION 3

OUTERMOST SOLAR RAY

INNERMOST SOLAR RAY

SHADE ZONE

SOLAR COLLECTOR (PARABOLIC MIRROR)

The Position of the Modulator Plate would be adjusted to vary the flux into the receiver cavity from fully on (position 1) to fully off (position 3).

Drawings

Drawings depict the actual appearance of an object or organism. Unlike a photograph, a drawing can delete details and emphasize more important portions. Drawings are appropriate when you want to focus on specific characteristics or components of a subject.

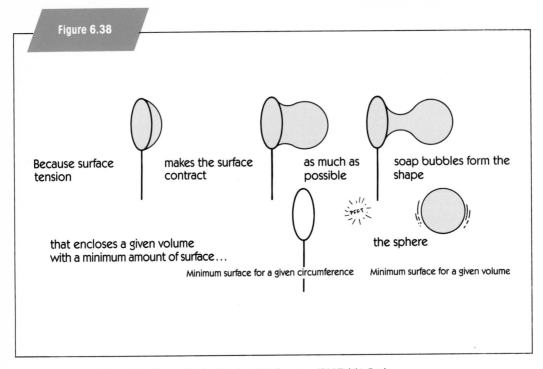

Figure 6.38

Because surface tension

makes the surface contract

as much as possible

soap bubbles form the shape

that encloses a given volume with a minimum amount of surface...

the sphere

Minimum surface for a given circumference

Minimum surface for a given volume

Source: Charles and Rae Eames, "Surface Tension," *Mathematics—IBM Exhibit Catalogue.*

To be effective, a drawing does not have to be complicated. Figure 6.38 illustrates just how well a simple drawing can illustrate an abstract concept.

Often more representational drawings are necessary, particularly when the drawing will be used to aid identification. Figure 6.39 presents three types of abdominal drains, each drawing accompanied by a brief explanation. These drawings are far more efficient than verbal descriptions in differentiating the drains for the readers of the nursing journal in which the drawings originally appeared.

Various components and aspects of objects, mechanisms, and organisms can be shown by different drawing views. Drawings that a technical professional might refer to include perspective drawings, phantom views, cutaway views, exploded views, and action views.

The versatility of drawings is demonstrated in a book for farriers. The series of three drawings in Figure 6.40 shows an external view of a hoof, followed by a phantom view and a cutaway view to reveal the internal structure.

Another common type of technical drawing is an exploded view, illustrated in Figure 6.41. An exploded view shows an entire mechanism or organism by separating or exploding the whole to provide a clear view of each

Figure 6.39 Effective Representational Drawings

TYPES OF ABDOMINAL DRAINS

The type of abdominal drain used for a patient depends on the size and location of his wound and on the type and amount of drainage expected. Since some drains may be used inter- changeably for different kinds of wounds, the surgeon's personal preference may also determine the choice of a par- ticular drain.

Here's a list of the abdominal drains you'll most often see in postoperative patients:

Penrose drain

The most common and oldest type of abdominal drain, the Penrose drain is a flat, short, single-lumen tube that works through capillary action. Used for uncomplicated draining wounds of moderate size, a Penrose drain doesn't damage surrounding tissues and causes little inflammation.

Sump drain

This is a stiff, double-lumen, silicone or plastic tube. The outer lumen has several openings through which air can enter; this helps to keep adjacent tissues from clogging drainage holes. Used primarily for large or infected abdominal wounds with sub- stantial fluid output, a sump drain can be connected to constant, low-pressure suction.

T tube

A very common drain, this is a thin, silicone catheter with a stem and perforated crossbar. Inserted during common bile duct exploration, it protects the suture line by diverting about one third of the 1,000 ml of bile secreted daily by the liver. The T tube is also used to remove small stones from the bile ducts.

Source: Sally Brozenec, "Caring for the Postoperative Patient with an Abdominal Drain," *Nursing 85* 15 (April 1985): 56. Copyright © 1985 Springhouse Corporation. All rights re- served. Reprinted with permission of the Springhouse Corporation.

Figure 6.40

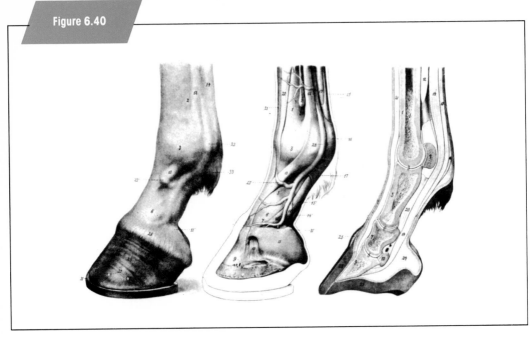

Source: D. M. Canfield, *Elements of Farrier Science*, 2nd ed., (Albert Lea, Minnesota: Enderes Tool Co., 1968), 10. Reprinted with permission of Donald M. Canfield.

Figure 6.41

repair parts

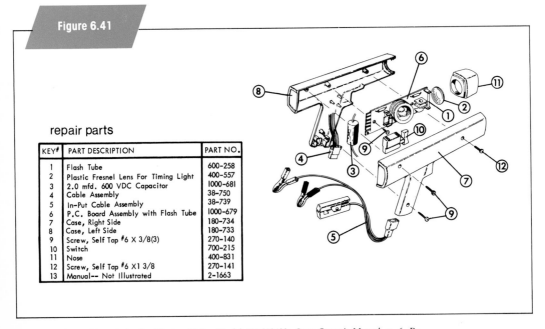

KEY#	PART DESCRIPTION	PART NO.
1	Flash Tube	600–258
2	Plastic Fresnel Lens For Timing Light	400–557
3	2.0 mfd. 600 VDC Capacitor	1000–681
4	Cable Assembly	38–750
5	In-Put Cable Assembly	38–739
6	P.C. Board Assembly with Flash Tube	1000–679
7	Case, Right Side	180–734
8	Case, Left Side	180–733
9	Screw, Self Tap #6 X 3/8(3)	270–140
10	Switch	700–215
11	Nose	400–831
12	Screw, Self Tap #6 X1 3/8	270–141
13	Manual-- Not Illustrated	2–1663

Source: From Inductive Timing Light, Model 161.213400, *Sears Owner's Manual*, p. 6. Reprinted with permission of Sears.

component. Exploded views are useful as part of an overall description of a mechanism or organism, but they are most frequently used in assembly and repair manuals. The timing light that is illustrated is accompanied by a numbered parts list that identifies each component by name and part number.

Sometimes a drawing can be effective by depicting only a portion of the subject. For example, Figure 6.42 shows part of a daisy wheel element for a computer printer. Although a daisy wheel has 96 arms, each with a character element on the end, the drawing shows only five of them. In operation, the daisy wheel of an impact printer spins until the desired letter aligns with the hammer and strikes against the ribbon and paper, as shown in the drawing only by arrows. Simple drawings often convey as much information as complex drawings. Additionally, they cost less to create than more detailed ones.

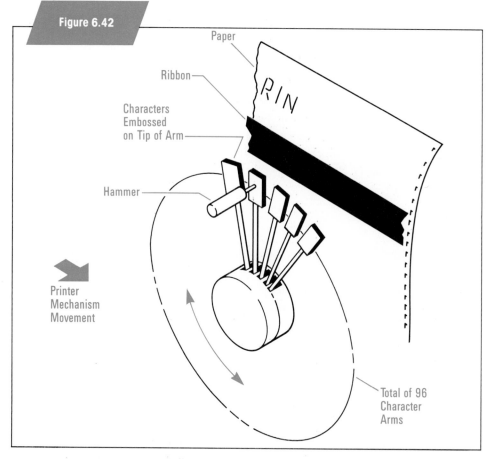

Figure 6.42

Source: Gary B. Shelley and Thomas J. Cashman, *Computer Fundamentals for an Information Age* (Anaheim, CA: Anaheim Publishing Co., 1984), 6.8. © 1981 Dataproducts Corporation. Reprinted with permission.

Figure 6.43

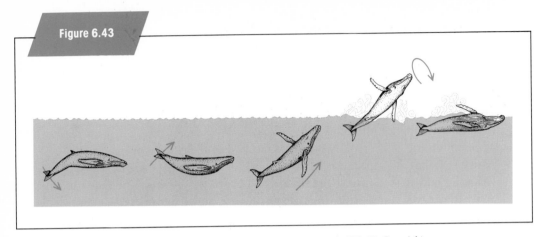

Source: Hal Whitehead, "Why Whales Leap," *Scientific American*, March 1985, 87. Copyright © 1985 by Scientific American, Inc. All rights reserved. Reprinted with permission of Scientific American, Inc.

Action views, drawings that illustrate a sequence, vary widely according to the process being presented. Figure 6.43 shows the breach of a whale, depicting the whale along with arrows that show the direction it takes at each stage of the breach. Although the action view is accompanied by a caption, it is supplemental rather than essential; the drawings can stand alone. Figure 6.44, however, displays an action of a very different type: the process of using an abacus. In this figure, the explanations are essential; neither the drawings nor the text would work alone.

Maps

Geographic information is displayed on *maps* (called charts, not maps, for air or water). To most people, maps mean road guides. But maps can also display topographic, demographic, argicultural, meteorological, and geological data. Maps show features of a particular area, such as land elevation, rock formations, vegetation, animal habitats, crop production, population density, or traffic patterns. Statistical maps can depict quantities at specific points or within specified boundaries. Data can be presented on maps in a number of ways: dots, shading, lines, repetitive symbols, or superimposed graphs.

Photographs

The actual appearance of an object, mechanism, or organism can be shown in a photograph. Because a photograph offers the most realistic view of a subject,

Figure 6.44

COUNTING ON THE ABACUS

 1 3 8 13 28 248

On a Japanese abacus, you count by pushing beads toward the crossbar. The value of a bead is determined by the column. Beads on the farthest right column beneath the bar count 1; on the next, 10; on the next, 100; and so on. Above the bar, corresponding values of the columns are, right to left, 5, 50, 500, and so on. In these drawings blue beads represent the numbers to the right of each abacus.

ADDING ON THE ABACUS

A. 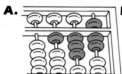 **B.** 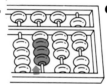 **C.** 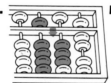 **D.**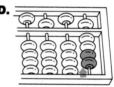

The sequence of drawings shows how to add 137 to 372. On the abacus, the Japanese add from left to right, totaling the 100's, 10's, and 1's. The blue beads in drawing A represent 137. In drawing B, you move up three 100's. Now you want to add 70, but you cannot add seven 10's because there are not enough beads in the 10's column. Nor can you add 100 and subtract 30 because all the 100's are up. Drawing C shows what you can do: add 500, subtract four 100's and three 10's. The final step is shown in drawing D; you add two 1's. The result is 509.

it's appropriate when you want to emphasize realism, particularly showing the subject in its natural setting.

However, even though photographs accurately depict their subjects, they often show too much detail. For this reason, callouts (small arrows superimposed on a photo) are used to draw attention to main features. Also, when a photo is printed, its appearance can be altered so that the primary subject is visually more prominent than the background, thus giving emphasis that's not possible if the photo is printed normally. Photos can also be reduced, enlarged, or cropped to stress a particular portion of the subject.

Distortion and Misuse of Visuals

Because visuals can distort a reader's perception of the material, you need to know how to avoid unintentionally misrepresenting information. Sometimes avoiding distortion rests with the data collection; other times it's with the presentation.

Careless Data Collection

Several traps that can cause you to distort your data are easily avoided. Positive responses to the following questions will let you know the data collection has not distorted the information:

1. Is the random testing sample sufficiently large? A nonprescription medication that relieves pain in 90 percent of the users sounds impressive, but the results don't mention that only ten people were in the sample.
2. Have questions been designed to elicit unambiguous responses? Do questions address all relevant aspects of the topic?
3. Has all of the available data been recorded? Has all data been included, even that which is unfavorable?
4. Is the data measuring what it purports to measure?
5. Are the cause and effect relationships logical? Does A logically result in B, or is the sequence of A and B merely coincidental?
6. Are measures of central tendency used correctly? For example, imagine that production runs of 100 during a given week result in rejection rates of 1, 2, 2, 2, 3, 5, 7, 8, 8, 19, 27—what is the average rate of rejection? The mean is 7.6, the median, 5, and the mode, 2. What can be said about the rejection rate? To be accurate, identify which measure of central tendency you're using. Know the difference between these measures of central tendency, then select the most appropriate one:

   - *mean* (arithmetic average)—the numerical result obtained by dividing a sum by the number of quantities added
   - *median*—the middle number in a series containing an odd number of items or the number midway between the two middle numbers in a series containing an even number of items
   - *mode*—the value or number that occurs most frequently in a series

Inaccurate Data Presentation

Even if you have collected accurate and complete data, the manner of presentation can be distorted. A few general observations about ways to avoid confusion or misrepresentation of data precede suggestions about some common problems encountered when constructing graphs.

Selecting the appropriate type of figure is important. Think of the purpose of the figure, and then select the type that most effectively conveys the significant information. For example, a line graph showing the increases in sales during the last fiscal year is better suited for an annual report than a table detailing the sales totals in each department for each month.

Percentages can distort information. Imagine that a monthly report from a group leader concludes that although production was down 30 percent during the first week of the month, it was up 10 percent during the next three weeks, so nothing was lost.

Example   week 1: 30% decrease, from 100 widgets/hour to 70 widgets/hour
week 2: 10% increase, from 70 widgets/hour to 77 widgets/hour
week 3: 10% increase, from 77 widgets/hour to 84.7 widgets/hour
week 4: 10% increase, from 84.7 widgets/hour to 93.17 widgets/
hour

Although the percentages are correct, the conclusion that "nothing is lost" is wrong, as simple calculations show. A careful writer makes sure the percentages and numbers match the conclusions.

Extending or projecting data cannot always be done merely by multiplying or dividing the numbers. For example, a company with 100 employees is not necessarily twice as productive as a company with 50 employees. Other variables besides the number of employees affect the productivity of a company. When extending or projecting data, consider all the variables involved.

The manner in which data is calculated or the hypothesis on which calculations are based significantly influences a graph. For example, Figure 6.45 shows three different ways to graph the same information about the relationship between radiation and cancer. General agreement exists about the relationship between high levels of radiation and cancer; however, experts disagree about the relationship between low-level radiation and cancer. The three different hypotheses—linear, quadratic, and supralinear—result in the three different dotted lines on the graph. Readers could be misled if only one of the dotted lines were used and the method used to establish the relationship between low-level radiation and cancer was not clearly identified. A careful writer should specify the source of data and the method of calculation.

Two types of graphs often unnecessarily distort data: line graphs and pictorial graphs. Following several standard practices eliminates most problems.

Figure 6.45   Insert Graphs That Show Distortion of Data

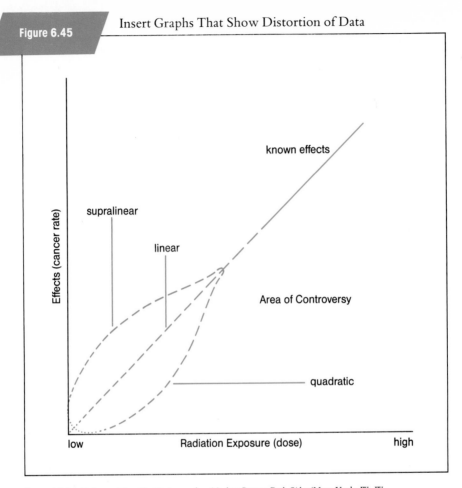

Source: Michio Kaku and Jennifer Trainer, eds., *Nuclear Power: Both Sides* (New York: W. W. Norton, 1983), 30. Copyright © 1982 by Michio Kaku and Jennifer Trainer. Reprinted with permission of W. W. Norton & Company, Inc.

Constructing an accurate line graph that does not manipulate or distort information requires attention to several aspects of the graph's construction:

- Begin the quantitative scale (usually the *Y*-axis) at zero. "Suppressing" the zero prevents the reader from seeing the true proportion of the graph.

- Differentiate lines on a graph by varying the type of line used. (Note the caution about misusing color. If the graph is photocopied, the color isn't reproduced, and thus the differentiation is lost. Professional printing costs escalate rapidly when color is added to a document because each added color means an additional press run.)

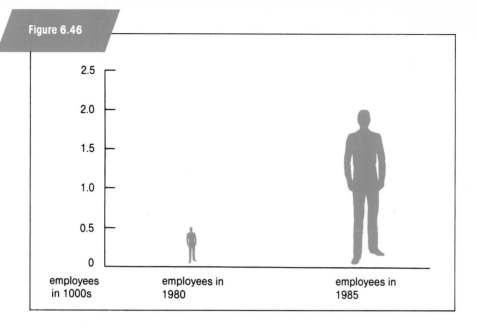

Figure 6.46

- Do not change the proportion of the grid by distorting the relationship between the vertical and horizontal scales.
- Change the width as well as the height of bars in a graph.

Even though a pictorial graph is designed for the impact it will make on the general reader, it must still be accurate. Its accuracy depends on two primary factors:

- Avoid using fractions of isotypes (the symbols on a pictorial graph).
- Use isotypes of the same size for the same graph. Changing more than one dimension of pictorial representations, for instance width as well as height, alters the meaning of the isotype. For example, Figure 6.46 has a ½-inch figure representing the 500 workers employed by company X in 1980, while the second isotype, a 2-inch figure, represents the 2000 workers employed in 1985. The problem is that a 2-inch figure is more than four times the size of a ½-inch figure, just as a 6-foot man is more than four times larger than a 1½-foot toddler.

To determine whether your visual presentation of information could mislead readers, ask yourself the following questions:

- Does the visual clarify, explain, or support the text?
- Will the reader know the source of the data?

- Is the source authoritative?
- Is the sample for collected data randomly selected?
- Is all the necessary collected data included?
- Is irrelevant data omitted?
- Is the visual completely labeled: number, title, caption?
- Are variables and scales accurately labeled?
- Is the quality of the visual—its design and presentation—the highest possible?
- Is the visual easy to understand?
- Does the conclusion logically follow from the data?
- Does the text refer to and discuss the visual?
- Is the significance of the information in the visual clear?

If you can respond positively to these questions, you can be fairly sure your visual is appropriately used.

Inquiries and Applications

Discussion Questions

1. In what situations might visuals be more appropriate and useful than words for conveying technical information?
2. In what situations might visuals be distracting or minimally helpful to a reader?
3. Discuss whether distortion of information, for example a pictorial graph in a daily newspaper, is justified to make a point.
4. One of the final cautions in this chapter explains distortion that can occur in pictorial graphs. Explain why the example of a pictorial graph in the chapter (Figure 6.32) is not an example of distortion, even though the isotypes are different sizes.

Individual and Group Exercises

1. In the following situations, why would you recommend a particular verbal or visual presentation? Justify your choice:

- verbal presentation alone in paragraph format
- verbal presentation with visuals
- visual presentation with verbal explanations
- visual presentation alone
  a. instructions for first aid emergency
  b. replacement of typewriter ribbon
  c. explanation of solution to manufacturing problem
  d. presentation of computer printer components
  e. changing oil and filter in car

2. Design a speed comparison table that presents the equivalents for kilometers per hour, miles per hour, and knots.
3. Examine the diagrams of splice and lap joints in Figure 6.47. Select one to describe verbally, without naming it and without an accompanying visual. Make the verbal description accurate enough that someone else can identify the joint when looking at the diagrams.

| Figure 6.47 | Splice and Lap Joints |

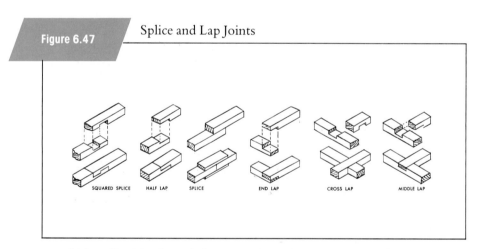

Source: "Splice and Lap Joints," *Sears Craftsman Master Shop Guide* (Hearst Corporation, 1969), sheet 12. Reprinted with permission of Sears.

4. Collect data from people in your class and work place on hair color, shoe size, preferred beverage, birthday, town and state of birth, car, and other categories agreed on by the class. Tabulate the data for easy reference. Then make a graph, using all the data in at least two categories, that establishes a correlation between two unrelated areas. For example, can your data support statements such as these: People who drink milk are born in the first quarter of the year. The larger a person's shoe size, the further west the person will have been born.

Figure 6.48

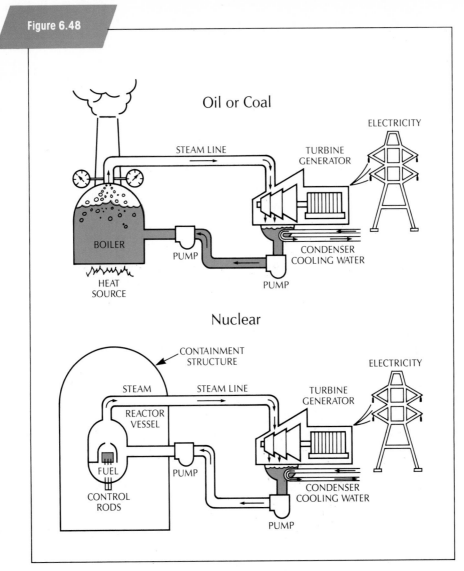

Source: Nuclear Information Committee of the Electric Council of New England, *Yankee Ingenuity*, 14.

5. Write a paragraph to accompany Figure 6.48, explaining the process of producing electricity and clarifying the differences between nuclear plants and conventional (oil-, gas-, or coal-fired) plants. Select an appropriate audience, such as consumers or first-year engineering students. Decide whether the paragraph should focus on the production of electricity or the differences between nuclear and conventional plants. Refer specifically to the figure in your paragraph. Also make sure to give the figure a title.

Assignments

1. Select an example of a particularly effective page design in a technical document that includes one or more visuals. Discuss the elements that make the page design effective and appealing.

2. Select an example of a technical report or manual that is difficult to read because of poor design or poor visuals.

   a. Write a memo that identifies the problems with the design and the visuals and recommends specific changes.

   b. Redesign the layout of a page in the report or manual.

3. Select a published graph and write a critique to determine if it presents the data effectively and accurately. Use four criteria for evaluation: Consider whether the appearance is appealing, the accompanying description/discussion complete, the type of visual appropriate for the data and purpose, and the presentation free from distortion. You may also evaluate other aspects of the graph.

4. The drawing in Figure 6.49 is effective because it combines a representational view of a computer system (monitor, disk drives, and keyboard) with a cutaway sideview of a critical internal component, the cathode ray tube, commonly called the CRT. Use the drawing in Figure 6.49 to explain the operation of a CRT, specifically as it relates to the computer. Write the section of a manual for a personal computer, explaining the theory and operation of a CRT. Although this section of the manual is primarily theoretical, include practical information for the readers.

Figure 6.49

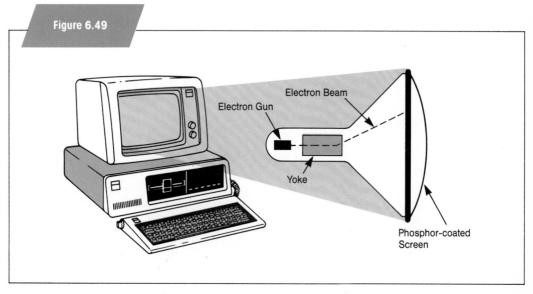

Source: Gary B. Shelly and Thomas J. Cashman, *Computer Fundamentals for an Information Age* (Brea, CA: Anaheim Publishing Co., 1984), 6.8.

7 Locating Information

YOUR RESEARCH AND WRITING intertwine because most documents require research to provide evidence that substantiates a position. These connections between research and writing affect you as both writer and reader. The quality of the evidence depends on the writer's thoroughness in conducting research. The credibility of this evidence affects readers' acceptance of information.

In your own technical writing, you will have to conduct research that moves far beyond that which you may have done for a freshman research paper. The following examples are typical of research you might conduct:

- Hollis Craig has spent several hours searching a computerized data base to locate materials about new techniques to strengthen carbon fibers.
- Pat Wilson is calculating the expected heat loss in a new passive solar office complex.
- Herb Kane has just designed a survey to use for market research about industrial degreasers.
- Gina Salmone is collecting water samples from a local brook running through an industrial park.
- Richard Minkoff has spent an hour reading abstracts in indexes such as *Pollution Abstracts* and *Water Resources Abstracts* to locate relevant research on contamination of ground water.

Frequently in major projects, both academic research and real-world research are necessary. For example, Nancy Irish, a nutritionist who has worked for government agencies as well as private groups, is investigating the ecological and nutritional benefits of soy protein and its potential for greater use in the diets of Americans. Her preliminary work involves academic research, using library resources to review available literature about soy proteins and tofu. Then she moves into real-world research, conducting interviews and surveys to determine people's attitudes toward tofu and obtaining tofu samples from local stores and food cooperatives to determine availability and quality. Some of the research techniques she uses are included as examples in this chapter.

Locating Primary and Secondary Sources

You can collect information from any of ten different categories of sources:

1. personal observations and activities
2. calculations
3. samples and specimens
4. experiments
5. internal records
6. interviews and letters of inquiry
7. surveys and polls
8. library resources
9. computerized data bases
10. government documents

Your selection of sources depends on the purpose of and audience for your document. If you intend to provide general background information for professional nonexperts, you can confidently employ summaries of calculations, experiments, or expert opinions. However, if you are writing an analysis of problems for experts who will implement the solutions, you need precise details rather than summaries. Refer to Chapter 3 to review the process of audience analysis.

The most credible documents incorporate a variety of types of evidence or data to support their positions. Even before selecting specific evidence, though, you need to consider the relative advantages of primary and secondary sources. Then, whether you decide on primary or secondary sources, check the credentials of the source, the sponsoring agency, and the date the information was obtained.

Primary source information is first-hand information, reported by people directly involved with an action or event. Because primary source information has not been filtered or interpreted through a second or third person, it is often considered particularly reliable. However, primary sources can be slanted or biased. For example, two firefighters who worked to put out a chemical fire in a warehouse could give first-hand reports about fighting chemical fires. But if one of the firefighters had been injured during the chemical fire, that firefighter might give a different account of the specific fire and have a different opinion about safety in firefighting.

Another problem with first-hand information is that a particular situation might be an exception. Evidence you cite should be representative, to ensure validity. For example, Nancy Irish would not assume that the experiences of one farmer or one supermarket manager are necessarily representative of all farmers or supermarket managers.

Secondary source information does not come directly from people involved in the action or event. Instead, the information is passed to a second or third person, who reports it. If Sidney Clark conducts an experiment and then reports his findings, the document is a primary source. However, if Sidney Clark is interviewed about his research by Joyce Perkins, and she writes the report, the document is a secondary source. The relationship of writer to subject determines whether the material is considered a primary or a secondary source. Secondary sources are sometimes considered less desirable than primary sources because the information is further removed from the source, and thus is believed by some people to have a greater chance of being distorted, incomplete, or misrepresented. This view does not consider the possible bias of the primary source. Figure 7.1 illustrates the relationship of writer to subject in primary and secondary sources.

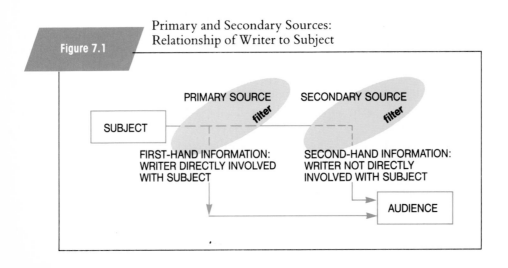

Figure 7.1

Primary and Secondary Sources:
Relationship of Writer to Subject

The ten types of sources are all accessible as both primary and secondary sources. They are arranged in order from those you can do most easily yourself, thus producing primary source materials, to those that are most difficult to produce as primary sources.

Personal Observations and Activities

Personal observations are legitimate primary sources if the observer is trained in the area of investigation. For example, botanists can identify a bog by observing and classifying the vegetation in a geographic area. Physicians can diagnose many illnesses by observing the symptoms of a patient. Opticians can make remarkably accurate judgments about the flatness of a mirror surface by observing light refraction. Veterinarians can determine when a mare is ready to foal by observing physical changes. Psychologists can observe changes in behavior that signal a patient's progress or decline.

Your own involvement—even if you're not a specialist—in completing a procedure is an important source of primary information. As a technical writer who operates a computer system, you are better equipped to explain its operation than another writer who merely hears about it. Similarly, if you are a supervisor who can actually run the equipment in a machine shop, you are better qualified to train new employees than a colleague who knows the theory but not the actual operation. A nutritionist experienced in dietary analysis is better equipped to teach such analysis than an inexperienced nutritionist. Do not underestimate the value of your hands-on experience.

If you choose to use your own or others' personal observations and experiences as evidence in a document, consider several guidelines to increase the likelihood that the data will be accepted as credible:

- Support generalizations with specific details and examples.
- Quantify observations whenever possible.
- Use standard terminology and notation.
- Differentiate between objective and subjective observations.
- Indicate the expertise of the observer.

Before the days of sophisticated test and measuring equipment, technical knowledge depended on recording the personal observations and experiences of trained experts. For instance, in 1628, William Harvey wrote *De Motu Cordis*, (*On the Motion of the Heart*), part of which is quoted below, based entirely on his personal observations and activities. Modern medicine, in fact, has derived in part from this method based on Harvey's observations made well over 300 years ago.

Example

In the motion, and interval in which this is accomplished, three principal circumstances are to be noted:

1. That the heart is erected, and rises upward to a point, so that at this time it strikes against the breast and the pulse is felt externally.
2. That it is everywhere contracted, but more especially toward the sides, so that it looks narrower, relatively longer, more drawn together. The heart of an eel taken out of the body of the animal and placed upon the table or the hand shows these particulars; but the same things are manifest in the hearts of small fishes and of those colder animals where the organ is more conical or elongated.
3. The heart, being grasped in the hand, is felt to become harder during its action. Now this hardness proceeds from tension, precisely as when the forearm is grasped, its tendons are perceived to become tense and resilient when the fingers are moved.
4. It may further be observed in fishes, and the colder-blooded animals, such as frogs, serpents, et cetera, that the heart when it moves becomes of a paler color; when quiescent, of a deeper blood-red color.

From these particulars it appeared evident to me that the motion of the heart consists in a certain universal tension—both contraction in the line of its fibers and constriction in every sense. It becomes erect, hard, and of diminished size during its action; the motion is plainly of the same nature as that of the muscles when they contract in the line of their sinews and fibers; for the muscles, when in action, acquire vigor and tenseness, and from soft become hard, prominent, and thickened: in the same manner the heart.[1]

Calculations

If you calculate information for a specific situation, the results constitute primary source information. Standard formulas exist for determining such things as heat loss in a house, strain on the foundation of a building, and quality of protein.

By using well-known, widely accepted formulas, you are more likely to produce error-free calculations. In the body of a document, the results of calculations are most important, but the actual formulas and calculations should also be included in a footnote or appendix. For example, a nutritionist applies a formula to calculate the biological value of protein, based on the amount of nitrogen absorbed.

Example $$BV = \frac{\text{Dietary N} - (\text{Urinary N} + \text{Fecal N})}{\text{Dietary N} - \text{Fecal N}} \times 100$$

BV = biological value
N   = nitrogen

A nutritionist doing case study research to determine the biological value of consumed protein in a group of patients suffering from gall bladder problems could use this formula to calculate the collected data. The resulting biological values might be presented in a table, with the formula itself placed in an information note. If the writer wanted to include the formula and the individual calculations, they could all be placed in an appendix.

Samples and Specimens

Actual objects or specimens can be primary sources. Geologists often take core samples of earth, ecologists take water samples, physicians take bioposies (tissue samples), and dairy farmers take milk samples. In her investigation of tofu in retail food stores, Nancy Irish collected samples—randomly selected packages of tofu—to determine type, quality, and freshness.

Obviously, samples themselves are not included in a document, but a description focusing on the significant characteristics of the sample should appear. For example, Nancy Irish assembled a trained tasting panel to rate samples of dishes made from the randomly selected packages of tofu. One of the dishes, tofu cheesecake, was given an average rating of 7.5 on a 10-point scale; this figure would be cited as a primary source in her report.

Experiments

You begin an experiment with a hypothesis, or supposition, and design a set of conditions to establish whether the hypothesis is true or false. A well-structured experiment has a control group and a test group, which have the same characteristics; results are measured by applying experimental treatments only to the test group, not to the control group.

Experiments are not always laboratory studies. In her soy protein research, Nancy Irish developed a hypothesis: Soy food (such as tofu and tempeh) consumption will increase in people who have witnessed cooking demonstrations, tasted tofu/tempeh dishes, and been educated about the ecological and nutritional benefits of soy foods. She designed experiments to test the tasting part of the hypothesis.

An experiment should be designed so that the results are both valid and reliable. *Validity* represents the extent to which the experiment produces the intended results—its capability to prove or disprove the hypothesis. *Reliability* represents the extent to which the experiment consistently produces similar results whenever it is used in testing the hypothesis. If an experiment is valid, it is also reliable; that is, if it substantiates what you want to prove or disprove, it does so consistently. However, an experiment can be reliable without being valid; it can produce consistent results that do not prove or disprove the hypothesis.

In experiments involving people, you must guard against two types of psychological interference: the Hawthorne effect and the placebo effect. Sometimes, when you tell people that you are testing them or that they are part of an experiment, they change their behavior, not because of the experimental conditions, but because of the attention paid to them. This is known as the Hawthorne effect. The placebo effect is easily observed in medical experiments. For example, patients who believe they are taking a beneficial medication sometimes report improved symptoms, when in fact they are taking sugar pills. This is known as the placebo effect.

Carefully run experiments protect against psychological interference. In many medical studies, for example, neither doctors and nurses nor patients know who is receiving the experimental pills and who is receiving the sugar pills. This double-blind testing produces more valid and reliable results because it negates the placebo effect.

Internal Records

Internal records—the data kept on company transactions in a business—often serve as supporting material in a document. Such records might provide facts and details about finances, personnel, manufacturing, marketing, or shipping. For example, in submitting a memo proposing the addition of three employees to his sheet metal department, Raphael LaCoste used a variety of data, including personnel information about salaries and benefits, monthly productivity sheets, backlogged orders, and projected sales figures. His proposal wouldn't have any impact if he merely said his department needed three additional workers. All of the evidence he needed to support his proposal was available in the files and internal documents of his own company.

If you are preparing a document, particularly one to circulate solely within your company, some of your strongest evidence may come from internal records. The research you do may include determining what kinds of data are available within the company. Often the problem is that you have too much information and need to eliminate all that is not essential to your central purpose.

Internal records sometimes have to be analyzed before you can use them. For instance, pages of computer printouts detailing manufacturing quotas and actual production figures first need to be compiled. Then the writer has to compare the quotas with actual production. Once the figures are accessible, the writer can evaluate, draw conclusions, and finally make recommendations.

Internal records are not always an appropriate source of information, even if the conclusions and recommendations are accurate. You must consider the legal and ethical implications of using internal records, particularly in a document intended for external readers. Many companies require key employees to sign statements (usually considered legally binding) to restrict the dissemination of proprietary information.

Interviews and Letters of Inquiry

Interviews provide first-hand information. The primary source material is not your interpretation of the interview, but the words and ideas of the expert. When you read information based upon interviews that someone else has conducted, the ideas have been filtered through another person; therefore, the interview material becomes a secondary source.

Interviewing is one of the most important skills a technical professional or technical writer can have. Often the information you need is not written in any book or article, but in the mind or indecipherable notes of another person. You have to ask the right questions in order to elicit this information.

Preparing effective questions for an interview requires some homework. What do you already know? What do you need to know? What do you expect this particular person to be able to tell you? The answers to these questions provide a focus for the interview. As a courtesy, learn to pronounce the name of the person you're interviewing as well as terminology you'll use during the interview. Be aware when you select the site that time and place can affect the quality of the interview.

Identify specific topics that you want to explore with the person. Listing topics rather than specific questions gives you more flexibility. The following guidelines, illustrated by some of the questions that Nancy Irish used in her interviews, will help:

- Design questions whose answers require a definition or an explanation rather than a simple Yes or No.

  Not: Are people's diets improved by using soy protein?

  Instead: In what ways are people's diets improved by using soy protein?

- If you must ask a yes/no question to establish a position, follow it with a question requiring some explanation.

  Not: Has there been an increase in the past five years in soy protein used in processed food for human consumption?

  Instead: Has there been an increase in the past five years in soy protein used in processed food for human consumption? What has contributed to this increase (or decrease)?

Generally, you should know the answers to basic questions as part of your preparation. Rewording the question shows your familiarity with the subject and gets more quickly to the meat of the interview. Don't waste interview time asking questions you already know the answers to.

  Better: What has contributed to the increase (or decrease) in the past five years in soy protein used in processing food for human consumption?

- Ask questions that require a focused response, not a broad, rambling discussion.

  Not: What do you think of the public attitudes about soy use?

  Instead: What specific strategies work to persuade the public to incorporate soy into regular means?

- Ask a single question at a time, not combined (complex) questions that require multiple answers.

  Not: Describe the progress that has been made in identifying those components responsible for undesirable flavors and colors and in developing processing technology to eliminate these from food products.

  Instead: Describe the progress that has been made in identifying those components responsible for undesirable flavors and colors.

  Then ask: What processing technology has been developed to eliminate these from food products?

■ Use terminology that narrows the area of response.

> Not: In what ways have soybeans been improved?
>
> Instead: In what ways has the nutritive value of soybeans been improved, specifically the amino acid profile and the digestibility?

■ Prepare questions to tactfully redirect a respondent who has begun to ramble.

> Not: Getting back to the subject, I'd like to ask you again to describe the ways in which soybeans have been improved.
>
> Instead: I'd be interested to hear more of the ways in which the nutritive value of soybeans has been improved.

■ Research other interviews in the field to avoid asking what have become cliché questions; instead find a new angle so that the respondent will be interested in what you ask and will know you have done your homework.

> Not: What are the ecological benefits of soy foods?
>
> Instead: How do you think the ecological benefits of soy foods could be used in marketing to increase the American public's interest in them?

■ Refer intelligently to the respondent's published work.

> Not: I liked your recent article on soybeans for human consumption.
>
> Instead: Your article in last month's *Soy Research Journal* effectively supports the importance of increasing human consumption of soybeans.

■ Prepare questions the respondent might perceive as hostile so that the respondent is not offended but, instead, answers.

> Not: How can you carry out objective research on soy foods when your research is funded by the National Soy Growers of America?
>
> Instead: I understand that your research is funded by the National Soy Growers of America. Does that make it difficult for you to conduct your research objectively?

What you ask is important. How you ask it is also important. Give the person time to respond. Don't interrupt unless the person strays off track or becomes too long-winded. Convey interest through tone of voice, facial expressions, and body language. Note the person's body language as a signal to how well the interview is going. (Body language is discussed further in Chapter 19.) Consider asking the person to prepare responses to statistical questions prior to or after the interview itself. Mechanical problems are a possibility whenever you use a tape recorder, and a recorder may increase tension, so be prepared to take notes, paraphrasing the person's comments.

If time is limited or distance a problem, a person may agree to be interviewed by telephone. This is a good alternative to an in-person interview, but despite the convenience, you should consider certain problems that result from not being able to see the person. Questions need to be particularly clear and focused because you cannot reword or clarify them based on the quizzical expression on the person's face. Also, determining a person's attitude is more difficult because you cannot see the body language and facial expressions. Pauses, an inevitable part of interviews while a person is thinking, are more disconcerting on the telephone.

Some conventions of courtesy apply to all interviews, whether in person or on the telephone. Confirm arrangements beforehand regarding the time, place, and duration of the interview. Arrive or call on time, and do not exceed the agreed-on length. If you want to record the interview, ask for permission; it's usually granted. Be attentive and courteous.

Sometimes it is not convenient or even possible to interview a person either in person or on the telephone. In such cases, a letter of inquiry is an appropriate vehicle for collecting primary source materials. In some situations, a person may even agree to record answers on a tape that you provide, so that he or she is spared writing detailed responses.

Example 7.1 displays a letter of inquiry that Nancy Irish wrote to Chris Morgan.

Whether you obtain your information through a personal interview, telephone interview, written questionnaire with taped response, or written response to a letter of inquiry, take the time to write a thank-you letter, acknowledging your appreciation for the time and effort the person took to assist you. You can give the letter a personal tone by mentioning one or two things that were particularly helpful. If the person is someone you regularly see in your company, you can write an informal note; even a person you see every day appreciates a brief thank you. If the person is someone you do not see every day, make the thank you more formal.

Surveys and Polls

Surveys and polls are usually considered secondary sources because they compile the opinions of many people into a single set of data. While such compiled

Example 7.1

```
                              310 West Washington Street
                              Urbana, IL  61801
                              October 30, 1986


Chris Morgan
Research Director
National Soybean Institute
731 Jefferson Street
Dubuque, Iowa  52086

Dear Chris Morgan:

I am conducting research on the role of soybeans in an
ecologically and nutritionally sound food system.  I am
particularly interested in the increased use of soybeans
in the American diet.

Could you please provide information on the following topics?

1.  Percentage of annual U.S. soybean crop consumed by humans
    vs. livestock? domestic vs. foreign markets?
2.  Percentage of U.S. arable land (acreage) planted in
    soybeans?
3.  Nutrient composition of traditional Asian soy foods?
4.  Resource efficiency of soybean products vs. grain-fed
    livestock production?
5.  Current research to develop new soy products for human
    consumption?

I appreciate your assistance.  If you wish, I will be glad
to send you a copy of the final report.


                              Sincerely,

                              Nancy Irish

                              Nancy Irish
```

data are often used to subtantiate a position, they can be misleading if care has not been taken in constructing the questions, selecting the test group, and compiling the results. If you are conducting your own survey, you need to be attentive to each of these areas. If you are using the data from the surveys by others, you need to investigate how carefully the survey was constructed and conducted.

Survey design is important. The questions should be both valid (the questions really ask what the survey takers intend to ask) and reliable (the questions mean the same thing to everyone). In order to determine the validity and reliability of questions, you need to test them with representative members of the survey group. If changes are necessary, you can make them before officially administering the survey. Without valid questions, a survey might not focus on important areas. Without reliable questions on a survey, responses cannot be accurately tabulated because people would interpret the questions differently.

Surveys can be designed using any of six different types of questions; each type has advantages and disadvantages you should consider when designing a questionnaire for a survey or poll:

- *Dual alternatives*, the simplest questions to tabulate, offer only two choices: yes/no, positive/negative, true/false, and so on. Such questions adequately address simple issues, but they often unrealistically limit the range of responses needed to portray an accurate view in a more complex situation. If you want to use this type of question, assure yourself that there really are only two possible answers, so that the respondent does not feel as if the choices are inadequate.

- *Multiple choice* questions are easy to tabulate and give respondents several alternatives, asking them to indicate preferences or opinions. Different formats either limit the respondents to a single answer or permit them to check all applicable answers. Because the survey designer provides all the choices, multiple choice questions may not offer an answer with which respondents agree. A well-designed multiple choice question does not have two or three choices that are obviously wrong, nor does it have choices in which the distinctions are so slight that the respondent must guess the correct answer. Ambiguous or misleading wording defeats your purpose.

- *Rank ordering* provides respondents with a series of items and asks them to order the items according to preference, frequency of use, or some other criteria. Tabulating rank ordering is easy, but distortion may occur if the mean (arithmetic average) differs significantly from the mode (most frequently occurring number). If the items in a particular grouping are similar, respondents will have a difficult time ranking them and may assign an arbitrary value rather than an actual preference.

- *Likert scales* provide a method for respondents to express their opinion by rating items either numerically or verbally on a continuum. As with rank ordering, tabulation is easy but may give distorted results if the mean and mode are significantly different. Scales are most effective if they have an even number of choices (usually four or six). If a scale has a middle choice (as occurs when the scale has an odd number of choices), respondents choose it a disproportionately large percentage of the time.

- *Completions* expect respondents to provide information, both fact and opinion, either in fill-in or open-ended responses. The answers are simple to tabulate if the responses are quantitative, such as age, frequency, or amount. But even short, open-ended opinion questions present problems in tabulation if respondents give a variety of answers; the evaluator must decide which terms respondents use are synonymous.

- *Essays* give respondents the opportunity to fully express themselves, presenting both facts and opinions, but the responses are difficult to tabulate. Essays are much more effective if they ask respondents to focus on specifics rather than requesting general opinions or reactions.

Do the types of questions really make a difference? Imagine that Nancy Irish read a claim that 23 percent of people questioned agreed they would include tofu in their diets. The statistic doesn't mean much unless she knows the question. It is possible to have the same answer to several variations of the question. Dual alternatives, for example, could elicit far more positive responses than completion questions. Figure 7.2 illustrates some of the possible questions that could have elicited such a response.

Figure 7.2   Variations of Questions that Could Produce the Same Response

```
DUAL              Would you include tofu in your meals   (23 percent)
ALTERNATIVE       if you knew good recipes?              yes ▱    no ▱


SINGLE            Tofu is a traditional Asian soybean food high in
MULTIPLE          protein and other nutrients and low in calories
CHOICE            and fat.  Considering the high nutrient value of
                  tofu, check the one item you most agree with.
    (14 percent)  ▱ willing to try tofu if I had a good recipe
    ( 9 percent)  ▱ use tofu regularly
                  ▱ tried tofu and didn't like it
                  ▱ not interested in trying tofu
                  ▱ never heard of tofu


RANK              Rank order the following soy food items in order of
ORDER             preference as additions to your current diet.
                  ___ soy sauce
                  ___ tofu        (23 percent ranked tofu second)
                  ___ miso
                  ___ natto
                  ___ tempeh


CONTINUUM         Mark your preference for each food item on the scale.
(Likert)
            Tofu    would not     might     would use     use
                    ever use      consider  if knew how   now

                  _____○_____○_____○_____○_____
                                        (23 percent)


COMPLETION        Which soy product are you most willing to include
                  in your meal planning? _____ (tofu—23 percent)
```

Designing an effective series of questions is only the first step. After you have designed and tested your questions, you need to administer the survey to a representative random sample of the target population. Compiling and reporting the results should not be difficult if your questions have been carefully designed.

Even when the questions are valid and reliable, the population sample random and representative, and the data compiled accurately, the results may be disappointing, particularly with mail-in surveys, which have a very low return rate.

Library Resources

Knowing how to locate information in an academic, public, or industrial library is invaluable to technical professionals and professional technical writers, who benefit from access to a variety of library resources:

- professional research librarians, who can ferret out information where those less well trained fail
- research tools such as periodical indexes and abstract indexes
- a large variety of technical journals
- a large variety of computer data bases
- audio-visual resources (audio tapes, video tapes, films, slide tapes)
- microforms (microfiche and microfilm)

The amount of library resources available is astounding. For example, the Library of Congress, which holds a copy of every book published in the United States, in 1983 had holdings of nearly 20 million books and over 60 million other holdings. This number increases every year since thousands of new books are published every year—over 41,000 in the United States in 1984 alone. In addition to books, in 1984 there were nearly 11,000 different periodicals published in the United States.

With these vast resources, you obviously must develop techniques to sort and select the information. This section of the chapter reviews the most common library services and references: professional librarians, reference resources, card catalogues, periodical indexes, abstract indexes, and newspaper indexes.

Professional Librarians and Their References. The best resources in any library—academic, public, or industrial—are professional librarians and trained staff members who know alternative approaches and can locate information often inaccessible to average library users. One of the reasons librarians are so effective is their familiarity with a variety of bibliographic references.

Several resources aid in locating books about almost any subject. The *Cumulative Book Index* (CBI), published monthly, with a bound cumulative volume published annually, provides the bibliographic details for any book published in English. Another valuable resource is the *Books in Print* (BIP) series, an annual publication that lists every book published in the United States (if the publisher supplies the information), beginning in its year of publication and continuing until it goes out of print. The author index lists books alphabetically by author and includes title, publisher, and price. The subject index lists books alphabetically by subject, using the Library of Congress subject headings. *Library of Congress Subject Headings*, a reference tool that offers alternative headings for a subject, helps by suggesting other terms to look up. More specialized resources of books in science and technology include *Scientific and Technical Books in Print* and *Technical Book Review Index*.

Three bibliographies of reference works are particularly important. Both Winchell's *Guide to Reference Books* with Sheehy's supplements and Walford's *Guide to Reference Material* are valuable. These volumes do not overlap in their coverage of various fields in science and technology, so you can benefit from using both; however, Walford has more than twice as many entries dealing with science and technology. A third resource, *American Reference Books Annual* (ARBA), covers a broad range of science subjects. The ARBA evaluates all reference books published in the United States in brief reviews (up to 300 words).

Reference Section. The reference section of a library provides easy access to a large collection of volumes containing a vast array of data. These resources include handbooks, specialized dictionaries, specialized encyclopedias, and business and industrial guides.

Handbooks are compact and carefully organized one-volume reference works, usually presenting information in tables, charts, diagrams, graphs, and glossaries. Handbooks seldom contain extensive theoretical explanations; rather, they contain factual information that is unlikely to become dated. Even so, new editions are published to include the most current information. Handbooks are available in astronomy, biological science, biomedical science, chemistry, computer science, engineering, environmental science, geoscience, mathematics, physics, and every other major field of technical and scientific inquiry.

Specialized dictionaries concentrate on providing precise, current meanings of technical terms. Having one or more specialized dictionaries on your private reference shelf will make your professional work easier. The most frequently used general technical dictionaries are listed:

- *Chambers Dictionary of Science and Technology*
- *Dictionary of Technical Terms*
- *A Dictionary of Scientific Units, Including Dimensionless Numbers and Scales*
- *The Penguin Dictionary of Science*

In addition, several other types of technical dictionaries are commonly used. For example, translators and technical professionals who work with international vendors and clients use a variety of specialized bilingual and foreign language dictionaries. Dictionaries of acronyms are often necessary to survive in government and business. Many companies create so many acronyms that they publish an acronym glossary of company-related terms for their own employees and customers. Common acronym dictionaries include:

- *World Guide to Abbreviations of Organizations*
- *Abbreviations Dictionary*
- *Acronyms and Initialisms Dictionary: A Guide to Alphabetic Designations, Contractions, Acronyms, Initialisms, and Similar Appellations*

Specialized encyclopedias are invaluable for an initial inquiry because the entries provide an overview, summarizing and discussing essential facts and theories about a subject. Beyond the discussion, the entries often present statistical data in various graphic forms, provide historical background, and list bibliographic references. Commonly used specialized encyclopedias are listed below:

- *Cowles Encyclopedia of Science, Industry, and Technology*
- *The Harper Encyclopedia of Science*
- *McGraw-Hill Encyclopedia of Science and Technology*
- *Van Nostrand's Scientific Encyclopedia*

The reference section of a library also usually houses a variety of *business and industry guides*. The most frequently used include these volumes:

- Daniell's *Business Reference Sources*
- Coman's *Sources of Business Information*
- Thomas' *Register of American Manufacturers*
- Poor's *Register of Corporations, Directors, and Executives*
- Moody's *Investor's Service*
- *Standard and Poor's Corporation Records*

■ *The Federal Reserve Bulletin*

■ *Survey of Current Business*

Other valuable references that are often overlooked include *annotated bibliographies* and *bibliographic essays*, available in every scientific and technical field. Annotated bibliographies not only identify authoritative sources but also provide a descriptive abstract of the material. Bibliographic essays go further; they categorize and discuss the relative merits of significant sources.

Card Catalog. The card catalog is an alphabetical file of all the books and audio-visual (a-v) holdings (films, records, audio and video tapes) in a particular library. Sometimes the card catalog also lists bound periodicals—a year's issues of a particular journal bound into a single volume. The card catalog may be actual files on three- by five-inch cards or a computerized catalog that displays information on a screen. You can use the card catalog to determine if the library has books, bound periodicals, or a-v materials relevant to your subject. You can also search for related material much more quickly and efficiently through a computerized catalog than through a manual one.

Each book or other item is assigned an individual number, based on one of two classification systems: the Dewey decimal system or the Library of Congress system. Public libraries generally use the Dewey decimal system, while university libraries use the Library of Congress system. The Dewey decimal system divides books into 10 categories, each identified by a range of numbers. The Library of Congress system divides books into 20 categories, each identified by a letter followed by specific numbers. The broad letter categories represent major subject areas.

In both the Dewey decimal and the Library of Congress systems, the broad categories are further subdivided until each book has an individual number— the *call number*—which helps you locate specific volumes in library stacks. Being familiar with call numbers enables you to go into the stacks and browse through the books in your specific field of interest. Browsing does not constitute efficient use of time, but you often find volumes of interest that you might have ignored had you only read the card.

In order to use the card catalog efficiently, you need to be familiar with the information it contains. Each book has at least three cards:

1. a card filed alphabetically by the book's *title*
2. one or more cards filed alphabetically by the book's *subject*
3. a card filed alphabetically by the book's *author*

Some libraries file all three types of cards together; others have a separate file for subject cards. Figure 7.3 illustrates these three types of cards.

The basic information on each card is identical, as shown in the annotations

Figure 7.3   Card Catalogue Cards for Title, Subject, and Author

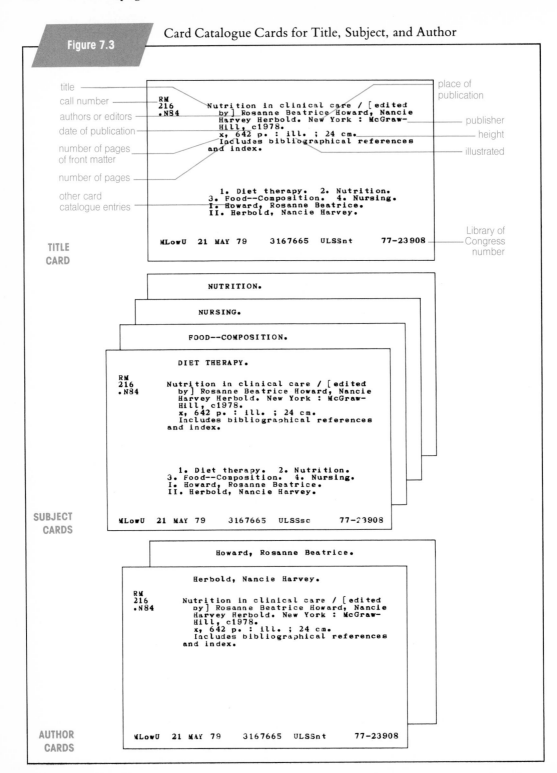

on the first card in Figure 7.3. The only differences appear on the first line of each card, which identifies the title, author, or subject. Notice in the example that the researcher could have located the book, *Nutrition in Clinical Care*, by looking up the title, the author (or in this case, editors), or any of four different subject entries: diet therapy, food—composition, nursing, nutrition.

Standard information appears on each card:

- identification: complete title, authors and/or editors
- call number: location of the book on the library shelves
- publication: publisher, place of publication, copyright date
- physical information: number of pages of front (prefatory) matter, number of pages, height
- supplements: bibliography, index
- cross references: other card catalogue entries for the same book
- library information: order or acquisition date, Library of Congress number

Many libraries have computerized their card catalogues. Figure 7.4 shows a series of three screens that Gerry Wilson used when conducting a preliminary search of the card catalogue.

1. The first screen shows the explanation Gerry receives when she presses H to receive help.
2. Screen two shows the circulation information for one of the books listed by the computer after Gerry entered *soybean*. This screen provides enough information for her to locate the book in the government documents section of the library.
3. Gerry decides to examine the bibliographic information that is shown on screen three. Here she gains valuable information about the book as well as alternative Library of Congress subject headings she can search next.

The *Library of Congress Guide to Subject Headings* is particularly valuable to use here. After one or two attempts at identifying the term(s) under which a subject is catalogued, check this *Guide* for alternative labels and related areas of study. Figure 7.6 reproduces a section of the *Guide* used by Nancy Irish during her research.

Periodical Indexes. Periodical indexes locate articles in magazines and journals. Several general references will help you determine what periodicals publish material in the fields you're investigating. You will benefit from using *Ayer Directory: Newspapers, Magazines, and Trade Publications* and *Ulrich's International Periodicals Directory: A Classified Guide to Current Periodicals, Foreign and Domestic* with its supplements. Two additional resources make locating microforms (microfiche and microfilm) easier: *Guide to Microforms in Print,*

1. Enter H and read HELP SCREEN

Figure 7.4

```
                        LOWELL CATALOG
                         Subject search

To begin a subject search enter S followed by a space and the term you wish to
search.  For example:
                Dichlorobenzenes would be :  S DICHLOROBENZENES
A subject is a description of the content of the material you are looking for.  It
can be a person, place, thing, event, or a concept.
Be brief but as specific as possible in your search.  For example:
                Sick children would be :  S SICK CHILDERN
                            or
                Niagara Falls would be :  S NIAGARA FALLS

Refer to the two large red books near the terminal entitled "LC SUBJECT
HEADINGS" for the official list of headings which the library uses.


If you need more help ask a member of the library staff.
To search a subject enter S and the term you want, then press return.
To go back to start, enter Q.


Enter search request:
```

2. Enter *S soybean* and read circulation information about a government
    document.

```
                        CIRCULATION INFORMATION
        AUTHOR:  Bahadur, Raj.
        TITLE:  Interaction of ozone and herbicides in soybeans /by Raj Bahadu
        EDITION:        PUBLISHER;  Corvallis EnvironmentaYEAR:  1978
                TOTAL COPIES:  1     TOTAL HOLDS:  0

                    DETAIL INFORMATION FOR LOWELL
   1.  CALL#:  EP 1.23:600/3-78-047                  MEDIA:  HARDBACK
        STATUS:  ON SHELF 7/15/85         LOCATION:  GOVT DOCS


    PRESS RETURN TO CONTINUE LIST.
    ENTER LINE NUMBER FOR CIRCULATION INFORMATION.
    ENTER B FOLLOWED BY THE LINE NUMBER (EX.B4) FOR BIBLIOGRAPHIC
    INFORMATION.
    REMEMBER YOU CAN ENTER H FOR HELP, Q TO START OVER, P TO PAGE BACK, R
    FOR OTHER RELATED TERMS -- OR BEGIN A NEW REQUEST FROM ANY SCREEN.
    ENTER:
```

3. Enter *B* Read detailed bibliographic information about the book.

LOWELL CATALOG
BIBLIOGRAPHIC INFORMATION

AUTHOR: Bahadur, Raj.

TITLE: Interaction of ozone and herbicides in soybeans / by
                   Raj Bahadur.

PUBLICATION INFO: Corvallis, Or. : Corvallis Environmental Research
                   Laboratory, Office of Research and Development, U.S.
                   Environmental Protection Agency ; Springfield, Va. :
                   available through the National Technical Information
                   Service, 1978.

PHYSICAL DESC: vi, 19 p. : ill. ;
                   28 cm.

SERIES: Ecological research series ; EPA-600/3-78-047

NOTES: "This report was submitted in fulfillment of contract
                   no. R-803072 by Mississippi Valley State University.
                   Under the sponsorship of the U.S. Environment Protection
                   Agency"--P. iv. May 1978.
                   Includes bibliographical references.

SUBJECT HEADINGS: Soybean Diseases and pests.
                   Herbicides.
                   Environmental aspects.
                   Plants, Effect of ozone on.
                   Plants, Effect of herbicides on.

Figure 7.5 — Excerpt from *Applied Science and Technology Index*

Soy sauce *See* Sauces
Soybean cheese *See* Soybean products
Soybean curd
  All-natural dairy-type products with a difference: they're dairyless [Brightsong Light Foods] il *Food Eng* 56:87 N '84
Soybean flakes *See* Soybean products
Soybean flour
  Testing
  Sensory characteristics and oxidative stability of soybean oil and flour extracted with aqueous isopropyl alcohol. K. Warner and E. C. Baker. bibl *J Am Oil Chem Soc* 61:1861-4 D '84
Soybean milk *See* Soybean products
Soybean oil
  Engine durability screening test of a diesel oil/soy oil/alcohol microemulsion fuel. C. E. Goering and B. Fry. bibl *J Am Oil Chem Soc* 61:1627-32 O '84
  Flavor stability of soybean oil based on induction periods for the formation of volatile compounds by gas chromatography. K. Warner and E. N. Frankel. bibl *J Am Oil Chem Soc.* 62:100-3 Ja '85
  Improving the fatty acid composition of soybean oil, E. G. Hammond and W. R. Fehr. bibl *J Am Oil Chem Soc* 61:1713-16 N '84
  Methyl and ethyl soybean esters as renewable fuels for diesel engines. S. J. Clark and others. bibl *J Am Oil Chem Soc* 61:1632-8 O '84
  Processing characteristics and oxidative stability of soybean oil extracted with supercritical carbon dioxide at 50 C and 8,000 psi. G. R. List and J. P. Friedrich. bibl *J Am Oil Chem Soc* 62:82-4 Ja '85
  Analysis
  Dectection of chlorophyll derivatives in soybean oil by HPLC. M. S. Fraser and G. Frankl. bibl diags *J Am Oil Chem Soc* 62:113-21 Ja '85
  Testing
  Oxidative stability of soybean oil at different stages of refining. T. W. Kwon and others. bibl *J Am Oil Chem Soc* 61:1843-6 D '84
  Sensory characteristics and oxidative stability of soybean oil and flour extracted with aqueous isopropyl alcohol. K. Warner and E. C. Baker. bibl *J Am Oil Chem Soc* 61:1861-4 D '84

Soybean products
  See also
  Soybean curd
  [American Soybean Association's 5th European Outlook Conference, London, Eng.] *J Am Oil Chem Soc* 61:1810-14 D '84
  Anaerobic pretreatment saves money and eases pressure on city sewers [Grain Processing's Anitron system] il *Food Eng* 57:128 F '85
  Is this beef/soy protein combo better than beef? [Tenderlean] il *Food Eng* 56:71 N '84
  Low-cost extruder promotes soy uses. B. F. Haumann. il *J Am Oil Chem Soc.* 61:1809 D '84
  Soyfoods entering mainstream U.S. diet. B. F. Haumann. il *J Am Oil Chem Soc* 61:1800-2 + D '84
  Soyfoods used in anti-hunger programs. B. F. Haumann. *J Am Oil Chem Soc* 61:1807-8 D '84
  Soymilk; new processing, packaging expand markets. B. F. Haumann. il *J Am Oil Chem Soc* 61:1784-93 D '84
  Soymilk packaging; aseptic packaging spurs increased sales. B. F. Haumann. il *J Am Oil Chem Soc* 61:1796 D '84
  Manufacture
  Development of a pilot plant process for the preparation of a soy trypsin inhibitor concentrate. E. C. Baker and J. J. Rackis. bibl diag *J Am Oil Chem Soc* 62:84-7 Ja '85
  Soymilk processing; how manufacturers try to reach Western market [Alfa-Laval's process] B. F. Haumann. *J Am Oil Chem Soc* 61:1794 D '84
  Soymilk worldwide; Shurtleff, Aoyagi chronicle soymilk industry. B. F. Haumann. *J Am Oil Chem Soc* 61:1798 + D '84
  Tomsun: largest East Coast soyfood factory. B. F. Haumann. *J Am Oil Chem Soc* 61:1806-7 D '84
Soybeans
  See also
  Soybean flour
  Comparative studies of three solvent mixtures for the extraction of soybean lipids. H. T. Khor and S. L. Chan. bibl *J Am Oil Chem Soc* 62:98-9 Ja '85
  More soybean surprises. D. Bartholomew. *J Am Oil Chem Soc* 62:61 + Ja '85

published annually, and *Microform Review*, published quarterly. Microforms enable a library to maintain large collections of newspapers and periodicals without the problems of bulky storage, damage, and loss.

As this list illustrates, most subject areas have periodical indexes:

  ■ *Applied Science and Technology Index*
  ■ *Accountants' Index*
  ■ *Bibliography and Index of Geology*

- *Biological and Agricultural Index*
- *Business Index*
- *Business Periodicals Index*
- *Cumulative Index to Nursing Literature*
- *Engineering Index*
- *General Science Index*
- *Index Medicus* and *Abridged Index Medicus*
- *Index of Economic Journals*
- *Index to Legal Periodicals*
- *Index to Scientific Reviews*
- *Natural History Index-Guide*
- *Social Sciences Index*
- *Pandex Current Index to Scientific and Technical Literature*

Each index includes an introductory section that clearly explains how to use that particular volume. These indexes are generally organized much like the commonly used *Readers Guide to Periodical Literature*. Figure 7.5 reproduces a section of the *Applied Science and Technology Index*.

An interesting and useful resource is the *Science Citation Index*, which indexes authors or sources cited in footnotes and bibliographies of periodical articles, government documents, and published reports. This resource is valuable in identifying significant and frequently cited documents that influence the direction of research.

Newspaper Indexes. Newspaper indexes are helpful, particularly to pinpoint dates of specific events and announcements. *New York Times Index* and *Wall Street Journal Index* are the most widely used newspaper indexes.

Abstract Indexes. Abstract indexes not only give author, subject, and title references, they also provide an abstract—a summary of each article. Abstract indexes can save a researcher a great deal of time. Imagine that you have identified the titles of 20 articles that appear to be relevant to your research. If the articles average 10 pages each, you have 200 pages of technical material to read. If you had initially read 20 abstracts, you could have selected the relevant articles without having to read the others.

Like indexes for periodicals and newspapers, abstract indexes have an introductory section that explains their use. The Library of Congress *Guide to the World's Abstracting and Indexing Services in Science and Technology* and Owen and Hanchey's *Abstracts and Indexes in Science and Technology* are excellent bibliographic resources. In some cases, several different abstracting indexes are available in a single area. For example, computer science abstracts are

Figure 7.6   Excerpt from *Library of Congress Guide to Subject Headings*

Soybean products   *(Indirect)*
    sa Bean curd
         Bean curd industry
         Miso industry
         Soy sauce
         Soybean flour
         Soybean glue
         Soybean meal
         Soybean milk
         Soybean oil
         Soybean processing
    xx Soybean processing
Soybean   *(Indirect) (Botany, QK495.L52;*
        Culture, SB205.S7)
    sa Cookery (Soybeans)
    x Glycine max
        Soja bean
        Soja max
        Soy-bean
        Soya bean
    xx Beans
         Forage plants
         Oilseed plants
  —Diseases and pests   *(Indirect)*
    sa Diaporthe phaseolorum
         Heterodera glycines
         Phytophthora sojae
         Soybean mosaic disease
Soybean as feed   *(SF99.S)*
    sa Soybean meal as feed
Soybean as food   *(TX558.S7)*
    sa Bean curd
         Bean curd industry
         Miso
    xx Food
Soybean chlorosis
    See Soybean mosaic disease
Soybean curd
    See Bean curd
Soybean cyst nematode
    See Heterodera glycines
Soybean flour
    x Soya flour
    xx Flour
         Soybean products
Soybean glue
    xx Glue
         Soybean products

Soybean industry   *(Indirect)*
        (HD9235.S6-62)
    sa Soybean oil industry
Soybean leaf curl
    See Soybean mosaic disease
Soybean meal   *(Indirect)*
    x Soybean oil meal
        Soybean oilmeal
    xx Meal
         Soybean products
Soybean meal as feed   *(SF99.S)*
    xx Soybean as feed
Soybean milk
    xx Milk
         Soybean products
Soybean mosaic disease   *(Indirect)*
        (SB608.S7)
    sa Soybean mosaic virus
    x Soybean chlorosis
        Soybean leaf curl
    xx Soybean—Diseases and pests
         Soybean mosaic virus
Soybean mosaic virus
    sa Soybean mosaic disease
    xx Plant viruses
         Soybean mosaic disease
         Viruses
Soybean oil   *(Indirect) (TP684.S)*
    x Bean oil
        Chinese bean oil
        Soy oil
    xx Drying oils
         Soybean products
Soybean oil industry   *(Indirect) (HD9490)*
    xx Soybean industry
    Example under Oil industries
Soybean oil meal
    See Soybean meal
Soybean oil mills   *(Indirect)*
    xx Soybean processing plants
Soybean oilmeal
    See Soybean meal
Soybean processing   *(Indirect)*
    sa Soybean products
    xx Soybean products
Soybean processing plants   *(Indirect)*
    sa Soybean oil mills
    xx Factories
         Food processing plants

catalogued in three different indexes: *Computer and Control Abstracts, Computer and Information Systems*, and *Computer Reviews*. In other cases, specialized abstract indexes that concentrate on relatively narrow subfields include material that is also available in a broader index. For example, the information in *Rheology Abstracts* and *Acoustics Abstracts* is also contained in *Physics Abstracts*. The following list, which is by no means inclusive, identifies some of the other commonly used abstract indexes in science and technology:

- *Abstracts on Health Effects of Environmental Pollutants*
- *Astronomy and Astrophysical Abstracts*
- *BioAbstracts*
- *Biology Digest*
- *Botanical Abstracts*
- *Chemical Abstracts*
- *Electrical and Electronics Abstracts*
- *Geological Abstracts*
- *Mathematical Reviews*
- *Microbiology Abstracts*
- *Nuclear Science Abstracts*
- *Oceanic Abstracts*
- *Personnel Management Abstracts*
- *Pollution Abstracts*
- *Psychological Abstracts*
- *Referativnyi Zhurnal* (printed in Russian, but abstracts are article's original language)
- *Sociological Abstracts*
- *Statistical Theory and Methods Abstracts*
- *Water Resources Abstracts*

Computerized Data Bases

Your university or industrial library may rent, lease, or own machine-readable tapes for various data bases, or it may have direct on-line access to any number of data bases. Computer data bases permit a literature search that usually far exceeds what you could do manually. Research librarians are trained to conduct database searches. Some of the data bases available in DIALOG Information Retrieval Services, a widely available method to access information with a computer, are listed on the next page.

Agriculture and Nutrition

AGRICOLA 79–present (File 10)
AGRICOLA 70–78 (File 110)
BIOSIS PREVIEWS 81–present (File 5)
BIOSIS PREVIEWS 77–80 (File 55)
BIOSIS PREVIEWS 69–76 (File 255)
CAB ABSTRACTS (File 50)
CRIS USDA (File 60)
FOOD SCIENCE & TECHNOLOGY ABSTRACTS (File 51)
FOODS ADLIBRA (File 79)

Energy and Environment

APTIC (File 45)
AQUACULTURE (File 112)
AQUALINE (File 116)
AQUATIC SCIENCES & FISHERIES ABSTRACTS (File 44)
BIOSIS PREVIEWS 81–present (File 5)
BIOSIS PREVIEWS 77–80 (File 55)
BIOSIS PREVIEWS 69–76 (File 255)
CA SEARCH 67–71 (File 308)[1]
CA SEARCH 72–76 (File 309)[1]
CA SEARCH 77–79 (File 320)[1]
CA SEARCH 80–81 (File 310)[1]
CA SEARCH 82–present (File 311)[1]
DOE ENERGY 83–present (File 103)[1]
DOE ENERGY 74–82 (File 104)[1]
ELECTRIC POWER DATABASE (File 241)
ENERGYLINE (File 69)
ENERGYNET (File 169)
ENVIROLINE (File 40)
ENVIRONMENTAL BIBLIOGRAPHY (File 68)
OCEANIC ABSTRACTS (File 28)

Social Sciences and Humanities

AMERICA: HISTORY & LIFE (File 38)
ARTBIBLIOGRAPHIES MODERN (File 56)
CHILD ABUSE AND NEGLECT (File 64)
FAMILY RESOURCES (File 291)
HISTORICAL ABSTRACTS (File 39)
INFORMATION SCIENCE ABSTRACTS (File 202)
LANGUAGE & LANGUAGE BEHAVIOR ABSTRACTS (File 36)
LISA (File 61)
MIDDLE EAST ABSTRACTS & INDEX (File 248)
MIDEAST FILE (File 249)
MLA BIBLIOGRAPHY (File 71)
PAIS INTERNATIONAL (File 49)
PHILOSOPHER'S INDEX (File 57)
POPULATION BIBLIOGRAPHY (File 91)
PsycALERT (File 140)
PsycINFO (File 11)
RELIGION INDEX (File 190)
RILM ABSTRACTS

Source: DIALOG® Information Services, Inc. Reprinted with permission.

Government Documents

The Government Printing Office in Washington, DC and the Congressional Research Service of the Library of Congress also compile useful documents on topics of special concern. You can read the *Congressional Quarterly* as well as the daily hearing transcripts. Also consider state and local hearings that might provide relevant testimony for a particular issue.

Two useful resources for identifying federal and state documents are available in the reference section of most libraries:

- *Monthly Catalog of United States Government Publications*
- *Monthly Checklist of State Publications*

Footnotes, Endnotes, and References

You can often identify valuable resources by reading the footnotes, endnotes, and references in articles and reports. In reading *Protein Resources and Technology: Status and Research Needs*, an anthology edited by three Massachusetts Institute of Technology professors, Nancy Irish found a reference to a mimeographed report, *National Soybean Research Needs*, that had not been mentioned in the periodical and abstract indexes or in her computerized data base search. The reason was obvious: it was an unpublished committee report from the University of Missouri. This resource would never have been part of her research base if she hadn't taken the time to read carefully the references listed at the end of relevant articles.

Inquiries and Applications

Discussion Questions

1. Imagine that you have prepared a report. What problems can result if you don't have information verified or authenticated?
2. Which repository of government documents is closest to you? What resources there are available to you?
3. Can you ever justify taking a "not for circulation" periodical or reference book from any library—public, academic, or corporate?

4. Can you justify the use of proprietary and/or confidential material if it ultimately benefits someone? For example, could you offer confidential company records about the hazardous use of chemicals to a research group developing a way to safeguard against industrial accidents?

5. Should you send questions for an interview in advance? Should you agree to submit material written from the interview for clarification? What are the pros and cons of giving the person interviewed approval of the resulting article before publication?

6. Which information is more reliable—primary or secondary?

Individual and Group Exercises

1. In small groups with others who share your academic major, design a hands-on library orientation for first-year technical majors to develop skills in using library references and resources. Go beyond the usual orientation by including information about the services of professional librarians, data base searches, periodical and abstract indexes, technical reference materials, government documents, microfilm and microfiche files, and audio-visual materials. Present the orientation in a guidebook that also serves as a convenient reference for students after the orientation.

2. Corita Muir is investigating the cost effectiveness of her company, Geo-Tech, Inc., instituting a longer lunch hour and flex-time with the goal of having company-sponsored fitness programs available to all employees from 6:00–8:00 A.M., 11:00 A.M.–1:00 P.M., and 4:00–7:00 P.M. She plans to use the following resources to prepare her proposal:

   ■ company records providing the number of sick days employees used in the past 24 months

   ■ recent articles in the local newspaper describing the benefits of regular exercise

   What additional resources would you recommend?

3. Identify the problems that might result in interviewing the following categories of people:
   a. supervisor
   b. scientist/mathematician
   c. public relations manager
   d. friend

4. You are trying to locate information about one of the following topics. Before looking in the *Library of Congress Guide to Subject Headings*, you brainstorm possible alternative labels and related areas with some other researchers. What terms can you come up with?
   a. midwives
   b. medical applications of lasers
   c. new coal mining techniques

Assignments

1. Compile and then annotate a list of reference books that are particularly helpful to a person in your career field.
2. Write a letter of inquiry that will help you in research you are currently conducting.
3. During your undergraduate and graduate work, the college or university library is important. Some colleges have cooperative arrangements with local businesses so that academic library facilities are available for practicing professionals. In small groups or as a class, design questions for a college librarian about services available to and interaction with local businesses and industries. Select class representatives to arrange and conduct an interview with a college librarian. Each group or representative should report the findings in a memo to the class.
4. Learning about corporate library resources is important for technical professionals and for technical writers. In small groups or as a class, design questions for a corporate librarian about differences between a university and corporate library, resources and services available in a corporate library, frequency of use, and types of professionals who use them. Select class representatives to arrange and conduct interviews with librarians at different local industries. Each group or representative should report the findings in a memo report to the class.
5. Design a hands-on library orientation to introduce new professional employees to the references and resources in a corporate library. Include information about services of professional librarians, available books and periodicals, loan privileges, data base searches, periodical and abstract indexes, technical reference materials, government documents, microfilm and microfiche files, and audio-visual materials. Present the orientation in a guidebook that will serve as a convenient reference for employees.

8   Recording, Examining, and Documenting Information

NO SINGLE METHOD for recording information is best; thus, you need to develop several techniques for recording data in different situations. In most cases, your choice of technique depends on the source of the original material as well as personal preferences in organizing a draft.

Recording Data

You should be familiar with various methods of recording data: field journals; lab notebooks; note cards; outlines; such visual forms as tracings, photographs, drawings, maps, video tapes, and films; and audio recordings.

Field Journals

Field journals are maintained by professionals who work literally in the "field": wildlife biologists recording feeding habits of deer; civil engineers noting rechanneling of a river where a new highway is planned; ecologists studying the impact of noise on the reproductive cycles of marsh animals. Field journals record activities and observations in chronological order—what, when, where, and how. The name of the investigator and the year are placed at the tops of pages, which are consecutively numbered. The exact location of each observation is noted—country, state, and county, as well as date, time, mileage, and direction relative to a permanent map feature.

Because of environmental hazards, professionals using field journals are selective in their materials for recording data. Ink should be waterproof and resistant to alcohol, formalin preservatives, grease, animal fluids, and ammonia. Also, the paper should be durable and resistant to water damage and age deterioration. Specially treated all-weather paper is available for field use, and loose-leaf binders enable you to remove field notes and keep them in a safe place.

A particularly useful type of field journal is a *parallel notebook*. One version places factual notes on one page and comments on the facing page, which allows you to clearly distinguish between facts and opinions; another has notes on one side and drawings on the facing page. Commenting on data when you collect it is very important because if you wait until all your data has been accumulated, you may well forget some of your insights.

Lab Notebooks

Experimental data and primary observations in laboratory situations are recorded in lab notebooks, which are intended as documentation of activities. In many cases, the notebook is bound so that pages cannot easily be torn out. Each page is usually numbered, dated, and signed after the information is recorded. Occasionally, such notebooks are used to establish proprietary rights in cases of patent infringement.

When these notebooks are used to record calculations in tables or graphs, you should be careful to provide essential identifying information: name, date, method or formula, and labels on the columns or axes. Equally important, write a few sentences about the significance of the calculated data.

Note Cards

Information from other sources that will later need to be reorganized can be recorded on note cards. For example, note cards are an effective technique for recording information from periodicals for a literature search to discover state-of-the-art developments for a new research and development project in a company. Note cards work equally well for collecting and organizing information for traditional academic research.

Note cards, usually 4 by 6 inches, are convenient because you can rearrange the cards (and thus, the information) in a variety of ways after collecting the data. Note cards are particularly useful if you follow these conventions:

- Record the source at the top of each card.
- Record the topic at the top of each card.
- Mark direct quotations clearly.
- Label/differentiate your comments and opinions about the source and/or information.
- Limit each card to one subtopic of information.
- Record biographical data about authors' expertise.
- Make a bibliography or source card for each source.

Outlines

Outlines list major and subordinate points and summarize ideas from either documents or speeches. Outlines are less useful than notebooks or note cards for recording data simply because written and oral material may not be sufficiently organized to permit a note-taker to make an effective outline. However, if you can easily and logically outline material, you can generally assume that it is well organized. (Chapter 4 identifies another use for outlines that you will find helpful for organizing your own documents and oral presentations.)

Tracings, Photographs, Drawings, Maps, Video Tapes, Films

In many situations data that cannot be fully recorded in writing, whether in notebooks, on note cards, or in outlines, is more accurately and efficiently recorded visually, by tracings, photographs, drawings, maps, video tapes, or films.

For example, such medical tests as electroencephalograms, such geologic data as seismographs, engineering materials' stress/strain tests, and chemical assays using chromotography all employ tracings to record information. These tracings can be directly interpreted by experts and then explained verbally to nonexperts.

Photographs, drawings, and maps provide accurate visual depictions of objects, processes, and locations. Photographs are appropriate when the overall physical characteristics are important. However, drawings are often preferable because they can focus on important components, whereas photographs may contain distracting details. Similarly, maps depict geographic and topographic features more effectively than photographs or drawings of the same area. Sometimes, a combination of photographs, drawings, and maps is particularly valuable. For example, a field biologist photographs the interior of a cave containing bats and then draws a map identifying the locations of various bat colonies. The photograph of a finished metal optic for a satellite becomes even more impressive when accompanied by a blueprint that specifies that dimensions on the actual part can vary from those on the print by no more than 0.0001 inch.

Video tapes and films are valuable when recording action is crucial. Business and industrial training is often most efficiently accomplished by taping or filming the required sequence and then showing it to new employees so that everyone sees the same material. For example, McDonald's has made extensive use of training films to ensure nationwide conformity to their standards.

Audio Tapes

Audio recordings are particularly effective for data where sound is essential. An environmental engineer uses audio tapes to record the highway noise that spills into adjacent residential areas. A speech pathologist records a client's progress. Without audio tape, the information could not be recorded as accurately or quickly.

Audio tapes are also useful for the technical professional who doesn't have the time to record observation notes or write the draft of a document. For example, many medical personnel use tapes to record clinical observations, and sales people use tapes while traveling to record information about customers and accounts.

Determining Accuracy and Logic of Data

After recording data, a writer examines it, draws conclusions, and makes recommendations. The material on which these recommendations are based must be accurate because the credibility of every document you prepare depends on the supporting evidence or data. The evidence should be from recognized authorities, giving your readers confidence in the accuracy of the data. Beyond this, readers should be able to follow your reasoning as you move from the facts of the evidence to inferences and then to the conclusions and recommendations.

Evidence takes several forms—statistics, facts, quotations from experts, case studies—and its logic affects not only the accuracy of the document but also the reactions of readers. Inaccurate evidence and fallacious reasoning make readers suspect the premises of the entire document. (Other aspects of credibility are discussed in Chapter 16.)

In presenting evidence in a document, you must first recognize potential problems in logic and then know how to correct them. Once you recognize these pitfalls, you are likely to judge your evidence more critically. The problems fall into four broad categories:

- using data derived from authorities
- presenting facts without drawing inferences
- drawing inferences
- establishing causal relationships

Using Data Derived from Authorities

Readers often respond more positively to evidence from a recognized authority in the field. However, the evidence loses its effectiveness if the expert's qualifications are suspect or if the expert has a vested interest. The experts cited must be recognized authorities in the field that they are discussing. People may comment as interested nonexperts about any subject, but only their opinions in their specialty should be presented as supporting evidence.

Similarly, if people or organizations have a vested interest, that is, a proprietary concern in supporting a particular position, their views might be more self-serving than objective. For example, the New England Soy Dairy prints a flier that states, "People everywhere are excited about the prospect of adding tofu to their diets." The business of the New England Soy Dairy is to market soy products, so it is in their interest to promote positive attitudes about soy products. Before accepting their word about the widespread excitement regarding soy products, you should verify the information with an unbiased source.

Presenting Facts Without Drawing Inferences

Writers often present facts in the form of statistics, quotations, or visuals intended to support points in a document. If these supporting facts are superficially accurate but in some way incomplete, out of context, oversimplified, or distorted, the reader will be misled. These four potential problems are defined, illustrated, and then revised.

Omitted or Incomplete Data. Omitted or incomplete data, whether done purposefully or accidentally, affects the accuracy and credibility of a document. If the reader needs more information than is provided, he or she will not be able to complete a task or make a decision. This problem sometimes results from failure to check and recheck facts, but it also occurs when a researcher hopes to influence a reader by omitting discrepant or conflicting data, as the following example shows.

Statement   Soy-based infant formula is generally the best food for infants with milk allergies.

Comment   The statement fails to mention that breast milk is the best food for infants and greatly reduces the likelihood that an infant will develop milk allergies.

Revision   When breast feeding is impossible or is not the feeding method of choice, soy-based infant formula is generally the best alternative for infants with milk allergies.

Out of Context Data. Out-of-context information may be accurate in itself, but relevant background or related information is omitted, thus giving the reader a distorted view. Out of context, even an undisputable fact can be misleading, as seen in this next example.

Statement   American farmers often prefer to plant corn instead of soybeans.

Comment   Although the statement is true, taking it out of context ignores both the important reasons that influence farmers' decisions and the relationship between soybeans and other major crops.

Revision   "Since the soybean crop competes with other major crops in the principal production areas, the amount of land planted to soybeans has depended on a complex interaction of factors which affect both soybeans and the competing crops. The most significant of these factors appears to be the price relationship between corn and soybeans in the major Midwest area, and between cotton and soybeans in the Mississippi Delta. This relationship is, in turn, dependent on world market factors, which most recently have tended to favor corn over soybeans and soybeans over cotton."[1]

Oversimplification of Data. Oversimplification reduces a complex situation or concept to a few simple issues or ideas, ignores relevant details, and gives the reader a distorted view, as this example illustrates.

Statement   Adding soy protein to a person's diet improves the quality of the diet.

Comment   Many factors determine the quality of a diet; the interrelationships of all dietary components must be considered. Adding soy protein to some diets may result in an excess protein intake, limit the intake of other necessary nutrients, and so on.

Revision   The inclusion of soy protein in a person's diet may have economic, nutritional, and sensory benefits.

Visual Distortion of Data. Visual distortion results from the accidental or purposeful presentation of data that misleads the reader. One of the primary types of visual distortion is the manipulation of scales on graphs, either through suppression of zero or the imbalance of the scales on the X-axis and Y-axis. After eliminating the possibility of distortion, be sure to comment in the text about the significance of your visual. (Refer to Chapter 6 for more detailed discussion of visual distortion.)

Figures 8.1A–F all plot the same data points (12, 16, 8, 10, 20, 18) during a 24-hour period. Figure 8.1A correctly displays the data. Figures 8.1B, 8.1C, and 8.1D distort the data by manipulating the scale on the Y-axis. Figures 8.1E and F distort the data by manipulating the scale on the X-axis. Such manipulation can mistakenly lead the reader to believe that the changes displayed on the graph are more or less significant than they really are.

Drawing Inferences

In general, documents present data and then the writer draws inferences based on that data. These inferences will be faulty if a writer makes hasty generalizations, assumes irrelevant functions, or falls prey to fallacies of composition and division.

Hasty Generalizations. A hasty generalization occurs when a particular case or situation is mistakenly assumed to be typical or representative of a group. This error usually takes place when the researcher has not examined enough cases to warrant a generalization, as seen in the following example.

Figure 8.1 Manipulation of Data on Graphs

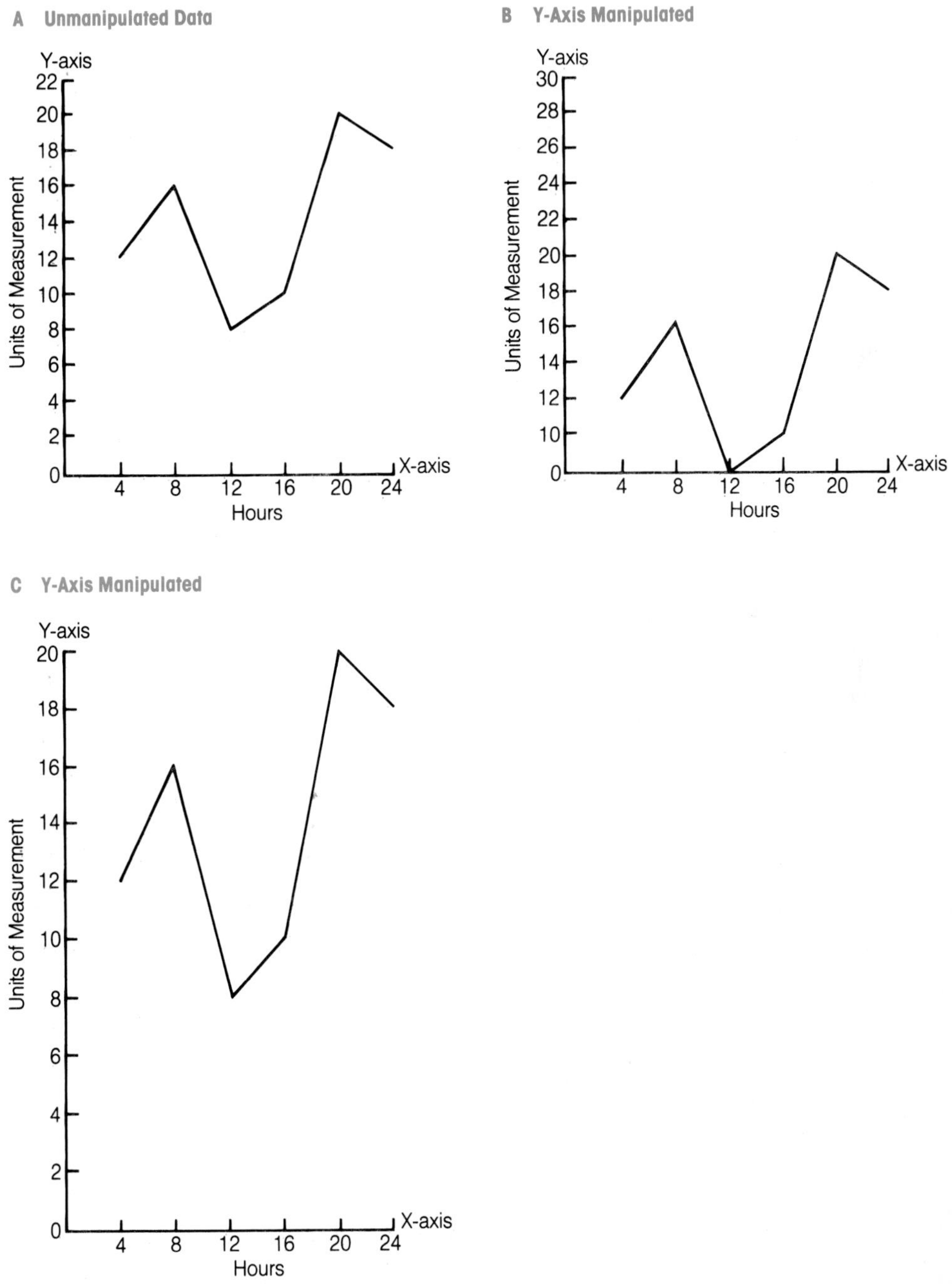

A   Unmanipulated Data

B   Y-Axis Manipulated

C   Y-Axis Manipulated

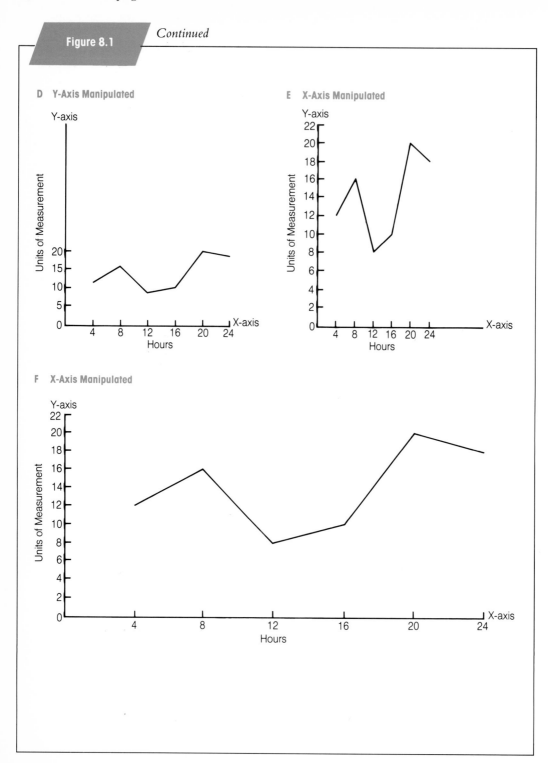

Figure 8.1 *Continued*

D   **Y-Axis Manipulated**

E   **X-Axis Manipulated**

F   **X-Axis Manipulated**

Statement In a survey of food cooperative members, 90 percent stated they would like to increase the amount of soy in their diets. Therefore, Americans are willing to eat more soy foods.

Comment Food cooperative members may not be representative of the greater population.

Revision The willingness of co-op members surveyed to increase soy food intake suggests that there is potential for increased soy food consumption in at least some segments of the American population.

Irrelevant Functions. When a writer assumes an irrelevant function, he or she is criticizing something for not having a characteristic it was never intended to have:

Statement Tofu and tempeh (a traditional Indonesian cultured soybean food) do not taste like meat.

Comment Tofu and tempeh, traditional foods in several cultures, should be appreciated for their own characteristics. They are not intended to taste like meat.

Revision Tofu and tempeh are alternative sources for protein for people who choose to eat less meat in their diet.

Fallacy of Composition and Division. The fallacy of composition assumes that the characteristics of the individual components can be attributed to the whole. The reverse occurs in the fallacy of division, in which the characteristics of the whole are attributed to each of the individual components comprising the whole. The following example illustrates the fallacy of division.

Statement Peanut butter on wheat bread is a protein dish of high biological value (it is a "complete protein"); therefore, peanut butter alone or wheat bread alone has a high biological value (is a "complete protein").

Comment In this example of the fallacy of division, the basic assumption is faulty: Nuts (peanut butter) and grain (bread) proteins complement each other to provide protein of high biological value.

Revision Peanut butter combined with wheat bread is a protein dish of high biological value.

Establishing Causal Relationships

One of the most frequent relationships employed in technical documents establishes causes and resulting effects. The reader can be misled by poorly drawn causal relationships in several ways, including a condition not being sufficient cause, variables not being correlated, and the fallacy of *post hoc, ergo propter hoc.*

Condition not a Sufficient Cause. An effect that results from multiple causes must have sufficient causes, and it may also have contributing causes. A sufficient cause is one that by itself can produce the effect. A contributing cause may help bring about the effect, but if all other causes are eliminated, any one contributing cause by itself cannot produce the effect. The following example demonstrates how poorly established cause/effect relationships can mislead a reader.

Statement	The patient's heart attack was caused because his diet contained too much cholesterol.
Comment	Heart disease is caused by a number of contributing factors, such as diet, obesity, smoking, heredity, hypertension, amount of exercise. Evidence has not yet shown that cholesterol alone is a sufficient cause, but it is usually a contributing cause.
Revision	The high cholesterol may have contributed to the patient's heart disease.

Correlation of Variables. This principle is based on the concept that even though a number of factors frequently occur in sequence, a cause/effect relationship does not necessarily exist:

Statement	In the 1970's, the U.S. production of soybeans rose, and soon after, Americans began eating more soybeans.
Comment	The increase in soy production was primarily to help the balance of trade. Most of the soy was exported and used as animal feed. Americans' increase in soy consumption has resulted from a number of factors such as increased awareness, marketing, and availability.
Revision	In the 1970s, the U.S. production of soybeans rose to help the balance of trade. At the same time, Americans began eating more soybeans in response to a combination of factors, such as increased awareness, marketing, and availability.

Post Hoc, ergo Propter Hoc. The line of reasoning that is known as *post hoc, ergo propter hoc* claims that because one event follows another, the first event must cause the second. The Latin translates as, "After this, therefore because of this." This example demonstrates how such fallacious logic can undermine a document's credibility:

Statement	Japanese women eat a high proportion of soy protein in their diets. Japanese women also have a low incidence of breast cancer; therefore, eating soy lowers the likelihood of breast cancer.

Comment   Even though eating soy precedes the low incidence of breast cancer, the chronology does not necessarily indicate a causal relationship. Japanese women also have a high intake of fish. Does fish also lower the risk of breast cancer?

Revision   Japanese women eat a high proportion of soy protein in their diets. Japanese women also have a low incidence of breast cancer. Emphasizing low-fat foods in the diet (such as soy and some types of fish) may be a contributing dietary factor in lowering the risk of breast cancer.

The following questions will help you evaluate your evidence to determine if it is logical. If you can answer affirmatively to each item in the first set of questions you can be fairly sure that your evidence will withstand hard scrutiny:

- Is all the evidence and data accurate?
- If you're using a single example or case, is it representative of the general condition(s) or situation(s)?
- Has the information been presented with related data so that it is meaningful to the reader?
- Has appropriate background been presented?
- Does a quoted source have expertise in the area being discussed?
- Are the qualifications or affiliation of experts referred to?
- Are visuals presented without distortion of any kind?
- Are parts/whole relationships treated accurately?
- Are chronology and cause/effect treated accurately?
- Are cause and effect clearly differentiated?
- Are causes necessary and sufficient for the effect?

Likewise, if any of these questions elicits a positive response, then you must reexamine the accuracy and logic of your data:

- Has any information been purposely or accidentally omitted?
- Could any of the statistical information be misinterpreted because it is incomplete or distorted?
- Is any of the information oversimplified?
- Are there other factors that should be considered?
- Does a quoted source have a special vested interest that could slant the position presented?
- Is the subject being criticized for something that is not part of its nature or function?
- Are scales on graphs expanded or compressed?
- Is a cause/effect relationship mistakenly assumed because of a common sequence of events?

Documenting Sources

The term *documentation* means different things to different groups of technical specialists. In this text, it refers to the recording by the writer of the source of nonoriginal facts and ideas.

Although careful documentation is time-consuming, it is a necessity for the serious investigator or researcher. Documentation can enhance a writer's credibility by noting original sources of information, but careful documentation represents far more than academic courtesy. Future researchers need to know the sources of ideas in a document to aid in their investigations. Even original or innovative ideas have to evolve from some combination of the writer's thoughts and nonoriginal material or information. And apart from its contribution to accurate research, careful documentation is a legal necessity.

The importance of complete and accurate citations is suggested by *Science Citation Index*, a reference volume that indexes the footnote and endnote citations in technical and scientific periodicals. Such a volume stresses that the sources a writer uses in preparing a document are as important as the document itself. Source citations enable researchers to refer to an original source both to determine its accuracy and to see if they agree with the interpretation. Researchers also use citations to develop ideas presented in a document but not explored in depth, thus providing the opportunity for new ideas to evolve from existing work.

Documentation can be separated into two major tasks: preparing a list of sources cited and preparing internal documentation, footnotes, or endnotes.

Sources Cited

Documents that are prepared with the help of other sources and that include references to these sources should have a list of *Sources Cited* following the last page of document or appendix text. This list is also called *Bibliography*, and occasionally, *References, Sources, Works Cited,* or *Literature Cited.* Whatever the title, the list contains the sources the writer quotes directly, takes original ideas from, and refers to in the document. Sources that the writer examines while preparing the document but does not quote from or refer to are not included in the list of sources cited.

Several variations exist for ordering the entries in *Sources Cited.* Usually, the entries are arranged alphabetically by the last name of the author. Less frequently, the entries may be arranged by order of citation in the document, by publication date, by primary and secondary sources, or by genre or subject of the source.

Books and journal articles listed in *Sources Cited* include, at the least, the author(s), the title, and publication information (place, name of publisher or journal, and date). The information usually appears in the following order:

1. *Author's name*—List the author's last name first, followed by a comma and then the first name or initials, however it appears on the title page.
2. *Title of (the part of) the book or periodical*—If only part of a book or periodical is used, for example, a single selection from an anthology, a part of the introduction, or a specific article, cite it after the author's name.
3. *Title of the work*—Give the full title of the work. If the book or article has a subtitle, follow the title with a colon and then the subtitle. Underline the entire title of a book or periodical.
4. *Name of the editor, compiler, translator*—Include the name of any editor, compiler, or translator identified on the title page or at the beginning of an article.
5. *Edition used*—Indicate that a book is a second or succeeding edition, a revised edition, or an annual edition if such information is listed on the title page.
6. *Number of volumes*—Identify the complete number of volumes in a multi-volume work.
7. *Name of series*—Cite the series and the arabic numeral identifying the work's place in the series.
8. *Place of publication, name of publisher, and date of publication*—Identify the city of publication, followed by a colon. If more than one city is listed on the title page, identify only the first city. Then give the name of the publisher, followed by a comma and the most recent date of the copyright or edition.
9. *Page numbers*—Identify the inclusive page numbers if you cite part of a book. Page numbers, usually the last item in an entry, are followed by a period.

Several sources exist for writers to check the proper format for documentation. The most frequently used general style guides include the following three:

- American National Standards Institute. *American National Standard for Bibliographic References* (Z39.29—1977). New York: American National Standards Institute, 1977.
- University of Chicago Press. *The Chicago Manual of Style*, 13th ed. Chicago: University of Chicago Press, 1982.
- U.S. Government Printing Office. *GPO Style Manual*, rev. ed. Washington DC: GPO, 1984.

Figure 8.2

Differences Between Chicago Style *A* and Chicago Style *B* Bibliography Formats

	Chicago Style **A**	*Chicago Style* **B**
names	Usually spells out the author's given name	Usually uses initials instead of author's given name
date of publication	Places book date after publisher, journal date after volume number	Places date after author's name
capitalization	Capitalizes all key words in titles	Capitalizes only the first letter of titles and subtitles and any proper nouns
titles	Uses full titles	Often omits subtitles and sometimes omits article titles
quotation marks	Uses quotation marks around article titles	Does not use quotation marks around article titles
abbreviations	Usually uses full names of publishers and journal titles	Often abbreviates publishers and journal titles

Many fields require certain formats for all professional publications within that area. Some of the most widely used include the following:

- American Chemical Society. *Handbook for Authors of Papers in the Journals of the American Chemical Society.* Washington, DC: American Chemical Society, 1978.
- American Institute of Physics, Publication Board. *Style Manual*, rev. ed. New York: American Institute of Physics, 1978.
- American Mathematical Society. *Manual for Authors of Mathematical Papers*, 5th ed. Providence, RI: American Mathematical Society, 1980.
- American Medical Association, Scientific Publications Division of the AMA. *Stylebook/Editorial Manual.* Littleton, MA: Publishing Sciences Group, Inc., 1976.
- American Psychological Association. *Publication Manual of the American Psychological Association*, 3rd ed. Washington, DC: American Psychological Association, 1983.
- Council of Biology Editors, Committee on Form and Style. *CBE Style Manual*, 4th ed. Washington, DC: American Institute of Biological Sciences, 1978.

- Engineers Joint Council, Committee on Engineering Society Editors. *Recommended Practice for Style of References in Engineering Publications.* New York: Engineers Joint Council, 1977.
- Modern Language Association. *MLA Handbook.* New York: Modern Language Association, 1984.
- U.S. Geological Survey. *Suggestions to Authors of Reports of the United States Geological Survey*, 6th ed. Washington, DC: 1978.

Of the style manuals listed here, two in particular illustrate the preferred formats of source citation. The *MLA Handbook* has long been favored by writers in the humanities, but recently some writers in technical fields are also using MLA's formats. *The Chicago Manual of Style* presents two styles of documentation: Style *A*, which is quite similar to the MLA formats, is generally recommended for writers in the humanities, whereas Style *B* is preferred by writers in technical fields. Figure 8.2 summarizes the differences between styles *A* and *B*.

The following models illustrate the formats of the Chicago *B* (science) and the MLA (humanities) styles. A space is left for you to add the citation format for each entry, using your own professional field's style guide.

Book—One Author

- Chicago *B*
  Lentz, K. W., Jr. 1985. *Design of automatic machinery*. New York: Van Nostrand Reinhold.

- MLA
  Lentz, Kendrick W., Jr. *Design of Automatic Machinery*. New York: Van Nostrand Reinhold, 1985.

Book—Two Authors

- Chicago *B*
  King, R. W., and J. Magid. 1982. *Industrial hazard and safety handbook*. London: Butterworth Scientific.

- MLA
  King, Ralph W., and John Magid. *Industrial Hazard and Safety Handbook*. London: Butterworth Scientific, 1982.

Book—Three or More Authors

- Chicago *B*
  Moore, J. H., C. C. Davis, and M. A. Coplan. 1983. *Building scientific apparatus: A practical guide to design and construction*. London: Addison-Wesley.

- MLA
  Moore, John H., Christopher C. Davis, and Michael A. Coplan. *Building Scientific Apparatus: A Practical Guide to Design and Construction*. London: Addison-Wesley, 1983.

Anthology

■ Chicago *B*
Hawk, G. L., ed. 1982.
*Biological/biomedical
applications of liquid
chromatography IV.*
New York: Marcel
Dekker.

■ MLA
Hawk, Gerald L., ed.
*Biological/Biomedical
Applications of Liquid
Chromatography IV.*
New York: Marcel
Dekker, 1982.

Journal—One Author

■ Chicago *B*
Helms, L. J. 1985. Errors
in the numerical
assessment of the
benefits of price
stabilization. *American
Journal of Agricultural
Economics* 67
(February): 93–100.

■ MLA
Helms, L. Jay. "Errors in
the Numerical
Assessment of the
Benefits of Price
Stabilization."
*American Journal of
Agricultural Economics*
67.1 (1985): 93–100.

Journal—Two Authors

■ Chicago *B*
Percy, K. E., and
S. A. Borland. 1985. A
multivariate analysis of
element concentrations
in *sphagnum
magellanicum* brid. in
the Maritime
Provinces, Canada.
*Water, Air, and Soil
Pollution* 25 (July):
331–38.

■ MLA
Percy, Kevin E., and
Susan A. Borland. "A
Multivariate Analysis
of Element
Concentrations in
*Sphagnum
Magellanicum* Brid. in
the Maritime
Provinces, Canada."
*Water, Air, and Soil
Pollution* 25 (July 1985):
331–38.

Journal—Three or More Authors

■ Chicago *B*
Rudnic, E. M.,
J. L. Kanig, and
C. T. Rhodes. 1985.
Effect of molecular
variation on the
disintegrant action of
sodium starch
glycolate. *Journal of
Pharmaceutical Sciences*
74(6) : 647–50.

■ MLA
Rudnic, E. M., J. L.
Kanig, and C. T.
Rhodes. "Effect of
Molecular Variation on
the Disintegrant
Action of Sodium
Starch Glycolate."
*Journal of Pharmaceutical
Sciences* 74.6 (1985):
647–50.

Edition

- Chicago *B*
  Washizu, K. 1982.
  *Variational methods in
  elasticity and plasticity.*
  3d ed. Oxford:
  Pergamon Press.

- MLA
  Washizu, Kyuichiro.
  *Variational Methods in
  Elasticity and Plasticity.*
  3rd ed. Oxford:
  Pergamon Press, 1982.

Volumes

- Chicago *B*
  Marshall, J. L. 1983.
  *Carbon-carbon and
  carbon-proton NMR
  couplings: Applications
  to organic stereochemistry
  and conformational
  analysis.* Vol. 2,
  *Methods in
  stereochemical analysis.*
  Ed. A. P. Marchand.
  Deerfield Beach, FL:
  Verlag Chemie
  International.

- MLA
  Marshall, James L.
  *Carbon-Carbon and
  Carbon-Proton NMR
  Couplings: Applications
  to Organic
  Stereochemistry and
  Conformational
  Analysis.* Vol. 2 of
  *Methods in
  Stereochemical Analysis.*
  Ed. Alan P. Marchand.
  20 vols. Deerfield
  Beach, FL: Verlag
  Chemie International,
  1983.

Proceedings

- Chicago *B*
  American Congress on
  Surveying and
  Mapping. 1984.
  *Technical papers of the
  44th annual meeting of
  the American Congress
  on Surveying and
  Mapping.* Falls Church,
  VA.

- MLA
  *Technical Papers of the
  44th Annual Meeting of
  the American Congress
  on Surveying and
  Mapping.* Proc. of
  ASP-ACSM
  Convention.
  11–16 Mar. 1984. Falls
  Church, VA:
  American Congress
  on Surveying and
  Mapping, 1984.

No Author Given

- Chicago *B*
  Improving road/rail
  interface. 1985.
  R T & S 81 (May):
  20–22.

- MLA
  "Improving Road/Rail
  Interface." *R T & S*
  May 1985: 20–22.

Reviews

- Chicago *B*
  Smith, D. T. 1985.
  Review of *Concrete
  Problems: Causes and
  Cures*, by J. C. Ropke.
  *Cement, Concrete, and
  Aggregates* 7(1): 53.

- MLA
  Smith, Dennis T. Rev. of
  *Concrete Problems:
  Causes and Cures* by
  J. C. Ropke. *Cement,
  Concrete, and Aggregates*
  Summer 1985: 53.

Newspaper Articles

- Chicago *B*
  Computerworld. July 8,
  1985.

- MLA
  Korzeniowski, Paul.
  "Users, vendors facing
  up to break-ins."
  Computerworld
  8 July 1985: 1 + .

Generally accepted formats for the documentation of computer materials
are being developed. *The Chicago Manual of Style* has suggestions for references to computer programs; the *MLA Handbook* includes examples for commercially produced software packages.

Source Notes

Source notes, which identify the source of material, are required in four
situations:

- direct quotations, even excerpts
- quantifiable data (facts and statistics)
- paraphrased presentation of original or unique ideas
- visual material, both content and design

Accurate documentation assists readers by identifying the original sources
as well as demonstrating the writer's awareness of authoritative material. You
can document your sources using one of the following three methods:

- parenthetical notes within the text of a document (internal documentation)
- endnotes, at the conclusion of a document
- footnotes, at the bottom of a page

Traditionally, documentation in the humanities has differed greatly from
that in technical fields: Humanities professionals typically use footnotes, and,

less frequently, endnotes; technical professionals primarily use parenthetical notes or endnotes. Recently, some common ground has been found, with professionals in both the humanities and technical fields using internal documentation or endnotes.

Internal documentation is the preferred method for many technical documents. In this style of documentation, a parenthetical reference immediately follows the quoted or paraphrased material, in one of two forms:

- (Marshall 1983) identifies the author and date.
- (Marshall 1983, 127) identifies the author, date, and page.

Complete citations for the sources are then listed at the end of the document.

Endnotes are especially useful when many different sources are cited. In such cases, complete endnotes provide the bibliographic information that would be duplicated in a list of works cited. Such a list of source citations would be more appropriate if numerous citations to a limited number of sources were made.

The formats for notes given in *The Chicago Manual of Style* and the *MLA Handbook* are essentially the same. Only these differences distinguish the two forms:

- *The Chicago Manual of Style* places the reference number on the same line as the text, followed by a period and a space; the *MLA Handbook* uses a raised numeral called a superscript.
- *The Chicago Manual of Style* single spaces all notes and aligns them with the left margin; the *MLA Handbook* double spaces notes and indents the first line five spaces.
- *The Chicago Manual of Style* uses a comma following the parentheses enclosing the publication information; the *MLA Handbook* omits this comma.

Because of the similarities between the two forms, only one example of each note is provided, following guidelines in *The Chicago Manual of Style*. Regardless of the style, notes are numbered sequentially, either througout the text or, as in this book, by chapter:

- Book—Single Author
  1. Kendrick W. Lentz, Jr., *Design of Automatic Machinery* (New York: Van Nostrand Reinhold, 1985), 36.
- Subsequent Reference
  2. Lentz, 47.
- Two Authors
  3. Ralph W. King and John Magid, *Industrial Hazard and Safety Handbook* (London: Butterworth Scientific, 1982), 125.

- Subsequent Reference
  4. King and Magid, 379.

- Multiple Authors
  5. John H. Moore, Christopher C. Davis, and Michael A. Coplan, *Building Scientific Apparatus: A Practical Guide to Design and Construction* (London: Addison-Wesley, 1983), 418.

  (Subsequent references to works with *more* than three authors may use the last name of the first author, followed by et al.)

- Anthology
  6. Gerald L. Hawk, ed., *Biological/Biomedical Applications of Liquid Chromatography IV* (New York: Marcel Dekker, 1982), 76.

- Edition
  7. Kyuichiro Washizu, *Variational Methods in Elasticity and Plasticity*, 3rd ed. (Oxford: Pergamon Press, 1982), 123–24.

- Volumes
  8. James L. Marshall, *Carbon-Carbon and Carbon-Proton NMR Couplings: Applications to Organic Stereochemistry and Conformational Analysis*, vol. 2 of *Methods in Stereochemical Analysis*, ed. Alan P. Marchand (Deerfield Beach, FL: Verlag Chemie International, 1983), 69.

- Proceedings
  9. *Technical Papers of the 44th Annual Meeting of the American Congress on Surveying and Mapping* (Falls Church, VA, 1984), 56.

- Journal—One Author
  10. Jay L. Helms, "Errors in the Numerical Assessment of the Benefits of Price Stabilization," *American Journal of Agricultural Economics* 67 (February 1985), 96.

- Journal—Two Authors
  11. Kevin E. Percy and Susan A. Borland, "A Multivariate Analysis of Element Concentrations in *Sphagnum Magellanicum* Brid. in the Maritime Provinces, Canada," *Water, Air, and Soil Pollution* 25 (July 1985), 333.

- Journal—Three or More Authors
  12. E. M. Rudnic, J. L. Kanig, and C. T. Rhodes, "Effect of Molecular Variation on the Disintegrant Action of Sodium Glycolate," *Journal of Pharmaceutical Sciences* 74, no.6 (1985), 649.

- No Author Given
  13. "Improving Road/Rail Interface," *R T & S* (May 1985), 22.

- Reviews
  14. Dennis T. Smith, review of *Concrete Problems: Causes and Cures*, by J. C. Ropke, *Cemet, Concrete, and Aggregates* 7 (Summer 1985), 53.

- Newspaper Articles
  15. Paul Korzeniowski, "Users, vendors facing up to break-ins," *Computerworld,* 8 July 1985, p. 15.

Figure 8.3   Combinations of Source Notes and Information Notes

Version A	*Version B*	*Version C*	*Version D*
internal source notes	internal source notes	combined footnotes for sources and for information	combined endnotes for sources and for information
footnotes for information	endnotes for information		

Information Notes

Information notes can be presented as footnotes on the appropriate page or as endnotes, either separately or in combination with source notes. The possible combinations are shown in Figure 8.3.

Generally, information notes are used to present the following kind of material:

- source(s) to verify or validate a point
- source(s) providing additional information
- formula and/or calculation of data
- definition of unfamiliar terms or concepts
- an aside—an interesting point not directly relevant to the primary discussion in the paragraph
- alternative opinion or interpretation
- anecdotal observation that is too casual for the style and tone of the body of the document
- alternative spelling and/or pronunciation
- translation of a foreign term
- explanation of an acronym

The examples listed above are indicative rather than inclusive.

Despite the frequent use of information notes by many writers, writing is more effective when relevant information is incorporated in the body of the document and irrelevant information is deleted.

Inquiries and Applications

Discussion Question

1. Your supervisor asks you to plot ten pairs of coordinates demonstrating the impact of increased temperature on the tensile strength of a new fiber. You plot the first six coordinates, which show a direct correlation between increased temperature and increased tensile strength. Discuss whether you can justify *not* testing the last four pairs of coordinates, merely assuming the direct correlation continues.

Individual and Group Exercise

1. Arrange the following information into the correct formats for the *Sources Cited* following a paper. Exclude any unnecessary information.

journal:	*Design News*
author:	David J. Bak
article:	Sprayed Metal Patterns Lower Casting Costs
visuals:	photos, cutaway views
date:	17 June 1985
pages:	124–125
volume:	41
number:	12
journal:	*Journal of Technical Writing and Communication*
author:	Dennis E. Minor
article:	Albert Einstein on Writing
date:	1984
pages:	13–18
volume:	14
number:	1
newspaper:	*The New York Times*
author:	Daniel Goleman
article:	New Evidence Points to Growth of the Brain Even Late in Life
date:	30 July 1985
pages:	C1 and C7
book title:	*Engineering Graphics and Design with Computer Applications*
authors:	David I. Cook and Robert N. McDougal
date:	1985
publisher:	Holt, Rinehart, and Winston
place:	New York
pages:	390

2. Identify the problems in logic in each of these situations. Explain why the situation is fallacious and how it could be corrected.

   a. The success of the Codex Training Program is proven by the 89 percent of certificate students who have jobs after training.
   b. Drafters who use the finest tools and the best CAD (computer-assisted design) software are going to produce only excellent drawings.
   c. Zeta Manufacturing Division of Delta Industries, Inc., consistently has the highest quarterly output of all the company's manufacturing divisions; therefore, Zeta Division must have the best workers.
   d. Dr. Ruben Thompson recommends that everyone take supplemental doses of vitamins every day.
   e. Industrial waste facility manager Eric Hanson affirmed that the compounds treated at his plant do not damage the ecological balance of the adjoining stream.
   f. Because the plans for the new building had been water damaged despite careful shipping in strong paperboard tubing, the architect vowed to sue the paperboard tube manufacturer for damages.
   g. Greenfield Mining Company has announced an agreement with 17 employees who have claimed medical disabilities from working conditions.
   h. Wind energy is a logical and economic alternative to heating with fossil fuels.
   i. For years Dan Madison drank large amounts of soft drinks and fruit juices, which must have caused him to develop diabetes.
   j. This batch of extruded cases made with brand XYZ filler is defective; therefore, all cases made with XYZ filler must be defective.
   k. The deer in the state forest starved last winter because of overpopulation.

Assignments

1. Locate the preferred documentation format for publications in your field. Write your citations in the space following the Chicago B and MLA models provided in the chapter.
2. Read the following article and take notes that you could use to study for a quiz about the material.

   Static electricity is everywhere. Lightning is the most spectacular and visible form of static electricity. A more common example is the small shock you occasionally feel when touching a door knob after walking across a carpet. Both types are referred to as an electrostatic discharge.

   Electrostatic discharge in the workplace, although a nuisance, is harmless to people and frequently goes undetected. However, just as lightning can damage or destroy a tree, electrostatic discharge that you emit can damage electronic components. This damage can occur in your everyday work with printed circuit boards and related components without your even being aware of it. Three situations can cause damage to electrostatic-sensitive devices:

1. sliding a printed circuit board into a plastic bag
2. picking up individual integrated circuits or transistors
3. unpacking printed circuit boards at an inspection station

Static charges can be generated and stored on all kinds of nonconductive and conductive surfaces. Examples of nonconductive surfaces are plastic bags, styrofoam cups, candy wrappers, and synthetic clothing. A common example of a conductive surface is the human body. You may not even be aware that a static charge is present, for the charge you are carrying must be at least 4000 volts before you feel a shock. Yet, only 100 volts are required to damage a component. Therefore, anyone can easily damage a component without being aware of it. A charge received by an electrostatic-sensitive component can degrade its performance, change its electrical characteristics, or even cause component failures.

Static discharge can be generated when two surfaces come into contact and then separate. A common example of generating a static charge on a nonconductive surface occurs when you pull tape off a roll. To show whether a static charge is present on the tape, hold it next to a pile of ashes; they will be attracted to the tape. How much static electricity is generated depends on the type of material, humidity in the air, and amount of friction between the tape and the roll. Thus, in the dry winter months, static is more of a problem than during the humid summer months.

3. Select a change that can be recorded on film—biological, meteorological, chemical. Record the changes in a sequence of photographs. Design and construct a display that presents the photos along with captions that explain the reason for the change. You may also add drawings that enhance your photos and explanations. Select one of the suggested subjects or choose one of your own:

horse jumping	seeds sprouting	photo developing
snake molting	storm front approaching	mold growing
flower blooming	egg coagulating (cooking)	egg hatching

III Applying the Writer's Techniques

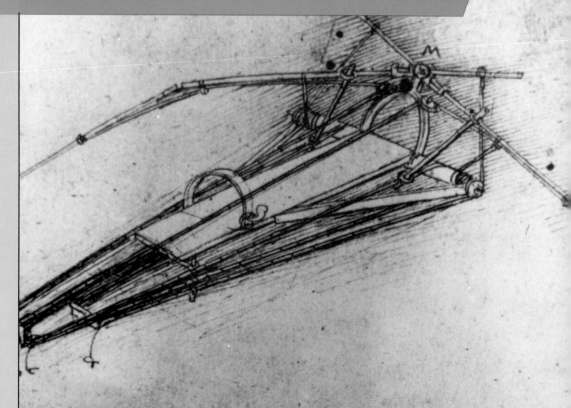

9 Definitions

THE MEANINGS OF WORDS change. The unusual histories of some words have influenced modern usage, and knowing a little about those histories can clarify the way in which multiple meanings have come about. In *Words of Science and the History Behind Them*, Isaac Asimov explores the circuitous etymology typical of many common technical terms. In this excerpt, he traces the path *vitriol* took to reach its modern everyday and technical meanings in English.

In ancient times, *transparent* objects (from the Latin "trans," meaning "across," and "parere," meaning "to appear"; light can, in other words, travel across a transparent object and appear on the other side) were unusual and names were derived from the fact.

The Latin word for "glass," for instance, is "vitrum," so things that are glassy in appearance are *vitreous.* The jellylike transparent fluid inside the eyeball is called *vitreous humor,* for instance. (*Humor* means "fluid," in this case.) The more watery liquid in front of the eye's lens is the *aqueous humor,* from the Latin "aqua" (water).

In the early Middle Ages, vitreous or glasslike minerals came to be called *vitriols.* The first mineral to be named so (in about 600 A.D.) was iron sulfate, which was called *vitriol of Mars,* Mars being the alchemical name for iron.

In time, a number of *sulfates* (minerals with molecules containing a sulfur atom and four oxygen atoms combined with any of various metal atoms) received the name, each being distinguished by color. Copper sulfate, for instance, forms beautiful blue, semitransparent crystals and is called *blue vitriol* (or simply *bluestone*); while zinc sulfate forms colorless crystals and is *white vitriol.* The original vitriol, iron sulfate, forms green crystals and is *green vitriol.*

If vitriols are heated strongly, vapors are given off. About 1200 it was discovered that if these vapors are trapped, cooled, and dissolved in water, an oily and very corrosive liquid is formed. It was called *oil of vitriol,* or sometimes simply *vitriol,* though its proper name today is sulfuric acid.

The term *vitriolic,* as applied nowadays to a caustic and cutting remark or to a sharp-tongued and bitter personality, refers to the strong and caustic sulfuric acid and not to the innocent glass from which all these names derive.[1]

As a technical writer, you need to correctly define your terms, whether you know the derivations or not. Nonexpert or general readers may be interested in your information but lack the requisite technical vocabulary. And technical readers will want precise meanings and definitions in order to understand distinctive details in your discussion.

An effective definition explains an unfamiliar term using vocabulary and concepts within the reader's grasp. A writer can tailor the sophistication of the definition for different audiences by adjusting technical details, technical vocabulary, and types of examples and explanations.

This chapter discusses problems that occur when you are searching for precise and appropriate definitions, examines the construction of various types of definitions, and presents specific uses for definitions.

The Need for Definitions

Inadequate definitions cause a variety of problems. The reader may recognize the term but not understand the specific use, or the reader may not comprehend technical jargon or unfamiliar symbols. Definitions are sometimes not used, which causes the reader to become confused by meanings, complexity of meanings, and technical jargon and symbols.

Multiple Meanings

Many words have multiple meanings—different definitions for the same word—that might mislead a reader. In technical communication, multiple word meanings can be a problem because readers might perceive unintended meanings. To ensure that the reader understands your intent, you must define terms. Sometimes meanings of even simple terms change entirely when the term is applied in a different field. The variety of meanings for the everyday word *focus* illustrates the range of possibilities. The use of a word in context helps, but unless a definition is provided, a biologist, geologist, and naval gunner would probably react differently to *focus*:

- in biology—the localized area of disease or the major location of a general disease or infection[2]
- in calculus—one of the points that, with the corresponding directrix, defines a conic section[3]
- in earth science—the location of an earthquake's origin[4]
- in photography—the adjustment of a camera lens to a particular image to ensure a sharp and clear picture[5]
- in physics—the small area of a surface that light or sound waves converge upon[6]
- in naval gunnery—the rotation and elevation of a gun to accurately hit a target[7]

Indeed, definitions are frequently necessary even for common words—if their application is ambiguous or unclear. Examples include such words as *limit, base, traverse, positive, stock,* and *cover.*

One of the largest groups of technical readers—nonexpert professionals—is often victimized by multiple meanings. Imagine a manager with a background in agronomy reading a memo from a graphic artist that includes the phrase *insufficient crop.* The context may make the meaning clear, but only after a moment or two of hesitation. To eliminate problems caused by multiple meanings, assess your audience and decide whether any of your terms have meanings that the reader might think of before discerning the correct technical definition. If there is the least possibility of confusion, include an unobtrusive parenthetical definition.

Complexity of Meaning

Your definitions can be simple or detailed, depending on the intended reader. The definitions for *volt* illustrate a range of complexity:

- *volt*—standard unit of electromotive force; after Alessandro Volta, an Italian electrician[8]
- *volt*—the unit of electromotive force. It is the difference in potential required to make a current of one ampere flow through a resistance of one ohm[9]

- *volt*—the meter-kilogram—second unit of electromotive force or potential difference, equal to the electromotive force or potential difference that will cause a current of one ampere to flow through a conductor with a resistance of one ohm[10]

- *volt*—a unit of electromotive force and potential difference; the absolute volt is the potential difference which forces a current of one ampere through a resistance of one ohm; named for Alessandro Volta (1745–1827), Italian physicist[11]

- *volt*—the derived SI unit of electric potential defined as the difference of potential between two points on a conducting wire carrying a constant current of one ampere when the power dissipated between these points is one watt. Also the unit of potential difference and electromotive force. 1 volt = 108 electromagnetic units. Symbol V (= W/A). Named after Alessandro Volta (1745–1827).[12]

Although the first definition would probably satisfy a general reader, all the others require some technical knowledge because of the vocabulary: *ampere, ohm, electromagnetic units.* The middle three definitions contain about the same amount of information; however, the second one is far easier to read than the third or fourth. The final definition is not any more complex than the others, merely more detailed. Curiously, the first and third definitions are from general dictionaries, those common in public schools and homes, whereas the others are from technical sources.

Whether to include definitions in a document depends on your analysis of the intended audience's education, knowledge, and experience. Once the decision is made to define a term, a writer determines the amount of detail and appropriate complexity of the definition by considering what information is needed to understand the term in the context of the document.

Technical Jargon

Definitions are frequently needed when technical rather than everyday terms are used. As a writer, you should assess whether the technical term refers to a concept, object, or situation familiar or unfamiliar to the intended audience. If the reader is familiar with the terms, no definitions are necessary. For example, the following paragraph contains technical vocabulary that the writer could be fairly certain the readers know; the specific magazine is a trade publication for the plastics industry, and the intended readers, professionals knowledgeable about plastics. The specialized technical terms, italicized here, were not italicized in the original.

Example   Ratios are indexed via a *digital thumbwheel. Reinforcement* is loaded into the emptied tank (by means of a *positive vertical auger conveyor*)

Figure 9.1 Incorporated Definitions

FINISH/FLATNESS CONCEPTS

SURFACE FINISH

The surfaces produced by machining and other methods of manufacturing are generally irregular and complex. Of practical importance are the geometric irregularities generated by the machining method. These are defined by height, width and direction, and other random characteristics not of a geometric nature.

The general term employed to define these surface irregularities is Surface Texture, the repetitive or random deviation from the nominal surface (Figure 1) which forms the pattern of the surface. It includes: roughness, waviness, lay and flaw.

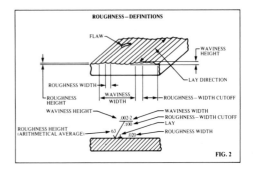

FIG. 2

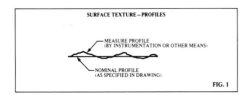

FIG. 1

- Roughness consists of fine irregularities in the surface texture produced by the machining process (Figure 2).

- Waviness is the widely spaced component of surface texture. It is of wider spacing than roughness (Figure 2). It results from cutting tool runout and deflection.

- Lay is the direction of the predominate surface pattern and it is determined by the machining process used in producing the surface (Figure 2).

- Flaws are irregularities which occur at scattered places, without a predetermined pattern. They include cracks, blow holes, checks, ridges, scratches, etc. (Figure 2).

Roughness is defined as the arithmetical average (AA) deviation of the surface roughness expressed in microinches from a mean line or roughness centerline (Figure 3). AA has been adopted internationally and is often referred to as CLA or c.l.a. (centerline average). Many instruments still in use employ an average deviation from the roughness centerline which

Source: Machinability Data Center, *Machining Data Handbook* (Cincinnati, OH: Metcut Research Associates), 3. Reprinted with permission.

and activated to achieve a uniform density; *polyol* is then added from bulk storage tanks and mixed with *reinforcement.* With initial production now under way, no requirement for *heat-tracing* of mixing tanks has been observed, and this is probably due to the effective but essentially *shearless mix action* of the *orbital auger principle* employed.[13]

Sometimes, however, technical terminology unfamiliar to the reader is necessary. For instance, a concept or process may be introduced that requires a technical explanation employing new terms. In such cases, the writer should

is the root mean square average (RMS) deviation of surface roughness, also expresssed in microinches. RMS, while used frequently, has actually been obsolete since about 1950. Roughness measuring instruments calibrated for RMS will read 11 percent higher, on a given surface, than those instruments calibrated for AA. The difference is usually much less than the point-to-point variations on any given machined surface.

on the type of grinding wheel, the method of wheel dressing, the wheel speed, the table speed, cross feed, down feed, and the grinding fluid. A change in any one of these factors may have a significant effect on the finish of the final surface produced.

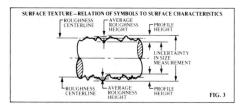

FIG. 3

SURFACE TEXTURE–RELATION OF SYMBOLS TO SURFACE CHARACTERISTICS

The commercial ranges of surface roughness produced by various machining processes are shown in the table. A range of finishes can be obtained by more than one process; however, the selection of a surface finish involves more than merely designating a particular process. The ability of a processing operation to produce a specific surface roughness or surface finish depends on many factors. In turning, for example, the surface roughness is geometrically related to the nose radius of the tool and the feed per revolution. For surface grinding the final surface depends

TYPE OF SURFACE	ROUGHNESS HEIGHT (Microinches)
Honed, lapped or polished	2
	4
	8
Ground with periphery of wheel	4
	8
	16
	32
	63
Ground with flat side of wheel	4
	8
	16
	32
	63
Shaped or turned	32
	63
	125
	250
	500
Side milled, end milled or profiled	63
	125
	250
	500
Milled with periphery of cutter	63
	125
	250
	500

define the terms for the reader. The following excerpt, from a short article about safety precautions necessary to protect workers who use industrial robots, defines the unfamiliar term *dwell-time.*

Example   Perhaps the most dangerous condition exists when people are unaware of a robot's dwell-time. (Dwell-time is the temporary period of inactivity between motions.)

Figure 9.1 illustrates longer definitions incorporated into an informational sales brochure for "diamond laps," instruments used to make metal surfaces flat. The definitions are given credibility because they are taken from *Machining Data Handbook*, a standard machinists' reference book. The company includes the definitions to educate its customers about the comparative benefits of its product.

Symbols

Technical language can be nonverbal, as in the symbolic language of mathematics, chemistry, and physics. For example, the equation explaining conservation of matter and energy—$E = mc^2$—is completely understandable to a physicist and, in fact, to most physics students. Yet it might be confusing to even highly educated people not trained in physics or a related field. A person familiar with these symbols would know that E = energy, m = mass, and c = velocity of light, and could translate the symbolic statement into a verbal statement.

Are the definitions of the symbols sufficient for the nonexpert to comprehend the content of either the symbolic or verbal statement? No. Clearly, then, the definitions a writer constructs need to do more than identify the unfamiliar terms. A writer must consider the reader's knowledge and adjust the definition to the appropriate level. The definitions in this list illustrate the range of possibilities available to the writer:

- $E = mc^2$ means mass-energy is conserved. The energy produced directly from the loss of mass during a nuclear fission or fusion reaction is equal to that mass loss times the square of the constant velocity of light.
- $E = mc^2$ means that mass can be converted to energy. The amount of energy produced is proportional to the amount of energy converted.
- $E = mc^2$ means that mass and energy are equivalent.

Furthermore, a writer needs to understand the concepts behind the definitions in order to provide an explanation appropriate for the reader's education and experience.

Construction of Definitions

Definitions are a valuable writing tool because they answer questions a reader has—or could have—*before* the reader verbalizes them. Recognizing the nature and variety of possible questions helps you construct your definitions, recognize when a definition is appropriate in a piece of writing, and determine the effectiveness of existing definitions when editing. After the initial What is it?, some common questions include:

- What is it similar to?
- What does it look like?
- What are its physical features?
- How is it classified?
- What are its distinguishing characteristics?
- What are its components?
- What does it do?
- How does it work (function, operate)?
- Who uses it?
- What is the relevant background in development or application?
- What are examples of its use?
- How does it differ from similar objects (theories, procedures, situations)?
- What is its value?

A variety of techniques is available to aid you in answering these questions when constructing definitions, which generally fall into four broad categories: informal, formal, operational, and expanded.

Informal Definitions

Informal definitions tend to be the type we insert in communications without realizing that we're defining a term. We integrate informal definitions casually and comfortably—and frequently out of necessity—into our normal writing and speech. Six types of informal definitions are particularly useful for technical writers: synonym, antonym, stipulation, negative, analogy, and illustration.

Synonym. A word that means essentially the same thing as the original term is a synonym. A synonym employed as a definition should be a simpler word than the original term so the reader immediately understands the approximate meaning:

Examples microbe—germ
helix—spiral

Synonyms can be used in an article or report, as these examples show.

Examples   Corrugated paperboard is the technical term for what is popularly known as cardboard.

The bellows in a thermostatic element is made of paper-thin, hardened (heat-treated) copper to make it strong, elastic, and corrosion resistant.

Notice that the synonym can be incorporated into the sentence or included parenthetically. Synonyms usually answer such questions as, What is it similar to? What do I know that it resembles?

Antonym. A word that is opposite in meaning to the original term is an antonym. As with synonyms, the antonym is easier to understand if it is a simpler term than the original.

Examples   deviating—direct
indigenous—foreign

Antonyms answer the obvious question, What is the opposite?

Stipulation. Stipulative definitions specify the meaning of a term for a particular application or situation. Stipulations frequently appear in introductory sections to eliminate ambiguity.

Example   When the term x [not necessarily mathematical, just any term] is used in this paper, it means. . . .

Such stipulation eliminates the confusion that can result from a common term not specifically defined, such as the "focus" example at the beginning of this chapter. Stipulations respond to such questions as, What are the limitations of use? Additionally, technical experts in many fields use stipulative definitions in assigning new names or applying existing terms in new ways to identify the products or processes of research.

Negative. Explaining what something is *not* represents an effort to provide the audience with accurate information. This excerpt from a paper about machine and equipment rivets demonstrates the value of using a negative for clarifying and narrowing a definition.

Example   Machine rivets, usually made from metals such as aluminum or titanium, are unlike the rivets used in iron work in that they do not need to be heated before insertion.

Negatives respond to such questions as, What similar things should I *not* equate with this object? What similar things might mislead me?

Analogy. An analogy compares the unfamiliar to the familiar to identify major characteristics of the unfamiliar term. An analogy is a specific comparison; indeed, the terms *analogy* and *comparison* are used interchangeably by some writers. For example, assume your audience knows nothing about kumquats. You could say a kumquat is a citrus fruit about the size and shape of a pecan. The skin is much thinner than that of a tangerine, and entirely edible. When fully ripe, the kumquat is a motley orange-green, much like an unprocessed orange. These analogies assume that your audience is familiar with a pecan and the general characteristics of citrus fruit.

An example from a paper about reduction gears revolves around an analogy based on the writer's assumption that most people have a basic understanding of how a car's transmission works.

Example   The reduction in speed of the steam turbine engine is necessary to achieve efficiency. The efficient speed for operating the turbine is higher than the speed of the shaft. The transmission of your automobile functions similarly by converting a high engine speed to a lower wheel speed.

Generally, an analogy responds to the same questions as a synonym: What is this similar to? What related object has characteristics I'm already familiar with?

Illustration. An actual drawing or diagram can illustrate a term. In many cases, a visual definition is far more efficient and accurate, and easier for the audience to understand, than a verbal definition. Imagine trying to write an image-evoking definition for aardvark. A simple sketch displays the general external features of an aardvark, as in Figure 9.2.

Figure 9.2

aard vark (ärd′värk), *n.* a burrowing African mammal with a piglike snout, a long, sticky tongue, and very strong claws; ant bear. It feeds on ants and termites. [< Afrikaans < *aarde* earth + *varken* pig]

aardvark
6 ft. long
including tail

Source: Scott Foresman Advanced Dictionary, s.v. "aardvark." Reprinted with permission of Scott Foresman.

Figure 9.3   Distilling Flasks from *American Scientific Products* Catalog

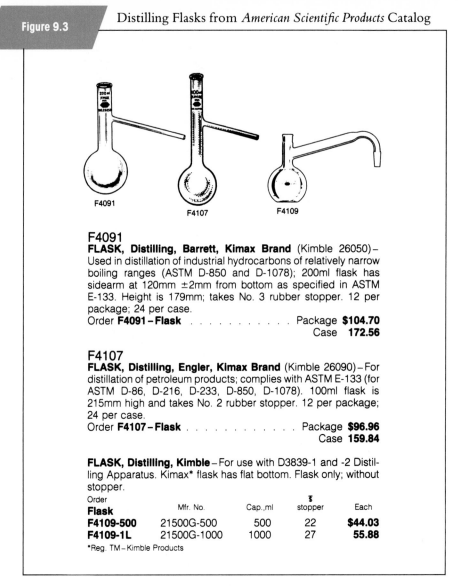

F4091

F4107

F4109

F4091
FLASK, Distilling, Barrett, Kimax Brand (Kimble 26050)–
Used in distillation of industrial hydrocarbons of relatively narrow
boiling ranges (ASTM D-850 and D-1078); 200ml flask has
sidearm at 120mm ±2mm from bottom as specified in ASTM
E-133. Height is 179mm; takes No. 3 rubber stopper. 12 per
package; 24 per case.
Order **F4091–Flask** . . . . Package **$104.70**
                                             Case   **172.56**

F4107
FLASK, Distilling, Engler, Kimax Brand (Kimble 26090)–For
distillation of petroleum products; complies with ASTM E-133 (for
ASTM D-86, D-216, D-233, D-850, D-1078). 100ml flask is
215mm high and takes No. 2 rubber stopper. 12 per package;
24 per case.
Order **F4107–Flask** . . . . Package **$96.96**
                                             Case **159.84**

FLASK, Distilling, Kimble–For use with D3839-1 and -2 Distilling Apparatus. Kimax* flask has flat bottom. Flask only; without
stopper.

Order **Flask**	Mfr. No.	Cap.,ml	⚗ stopper	Each
F4109-500	21500G-500	500	22	**$44.03**
F4109-1L	21500G-1000	1000	27	**55.88**

*Reg. TM–Kimble Products

Source: American Scientific Products: 1984–1985 Catalog (McGaw Park, IL: American Hospital
Supply), 460. Reprinted with permission of Corning Glass Works and Kimble Division of
Owens-Illinois, Inc.

More practically, visuals are a simple and direct way to present features
quickly. For example, in Figure 9.3 the *American Scientific Products* catalog's
sketches of various types of distilling flasks clarify the distinctions presented
in verbal descriptions.

In Figure 9.4, an annotated sketch accompanying a definition illustrates the

Figure 9.4

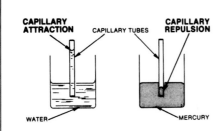

capillary attraction,   the force that causes a liquid to rise in a narrow tube or when in contact with a porous substance. A plant draws up water from the ground and a paper towel absorbs water by means of capillary attraction.

capillary repulsion,   the force that causes a liquid to be depressed when in contact with the sides of a narrow tube, as is mercury in a glass tube.

Source: Advanced Dictionary, s.v. "capillary attraction" and "capillary repulsion." Reprinted with permission of Scott Foresman.

Figure 9.5

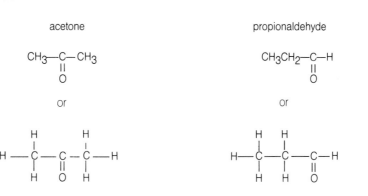

verbal information so the reader can readily understand the explanation of the terms *capillary attraction* and *capillary repulsion.*

Sometimes, visual definitions are not merely desirable but essential. For example, both acetone and propionaldehyde molecules contain three carbon atoms, six hydrogen atoms, and one oxygen atom. Although each molecule has the same number and kind of atoms, they are arranged differently, resulting in two compounds with different characteristics. The chemical formulas in Figure 9.5 state the differences verbally, but the addition of the diagrams brings those differences into focus.

Whatever the reason for using illustrations, the visuals respond to the question, What does it look like?

Formal Definitions

Because dictionaries use formal definitions in many entries, people often believe that is the only way to define a term. Formal definitions, with their prescribed, unvarying format, are valuable for identifying the broad category to which a term belongs as well as its distinctive characteristics. As a writer, you may be expected to construct clear and accurate formal definitions—for new products and processes when no definition exists and for existing products and processes when current definitions are inadequate. The format of formal definitions is always the same.

Example	SPECIES	equals	GENUS	plus	DIFFERENTIA
	the term		the class or		distinguishing
	being defined		category to		characteristics
			which the		which differentiate
			term (species)		this species from
			belongs		other species in
					the same genus

A simple example illustrates the structure and demonstrates the application of guidelines the writer should follow when constructing effective formal definitions.

Example	SPECIES	equals	GENUS	plus	DIFFERENTIA
	A robin	is	a bird	with	a red breast and yellow beak.

A writer should make the genus as narrow as possible. A robin is a bird, but can the category be more specific? Yes. A robin is a type of thrush, so the formal definition can be revised.

Example	A robin	is	a thrush	with	a red breast and yellow beak.

A writer should also take care to make the differentia as inclusive as possible to eliminate the possibility of mistakenly identifying one species with another. Are there characteristics other than a red breast and yellow beak that differentiate a robin from other thrushes? Again, yes. A robin has a distinctive black back and wing tips. A complete and accurate formal definition for robin can be constructed:

Example	A robin	is	a thrush	with	a red breast, yellow beak, and black back and wing tips.

The need to construct your own formal definitions arises when dictionary definitions are inadequate or nonexistent. The following examples of formal definitions were constructed by writers for specific reports. Formal definitions answer such questions as, How is it classified? How does it differ from similar objects? What distinguishes this from related objects? What are the identifying characteristics?

Example A lathe	is	a machine	in which the work piece is rotated and shaped by a tool that is either fixed or moved along one or more linear axes.
A distribution fuse link	is	an upgraded version of the household fuse	used on distribution circuits operating at voltages up to 35,000 volts.

Notice that in all these examples, the genus is purposely kept narrow and the differentia are inclusive.

Operational Definitions

Operational definitions define the functions or workings of an object or process. Naturally, many situations do not lend themselves to operational definitions—only those which require answers to such questions as, How does it work? An operational definition summarizes or outlines the primary steps involved in the function, usually in chronological order. A good operational definition can form the basis for a detailed process explanation. (Process explanations are discussed in detail in Chapter 11.) While an operational definition usually merely outlines the major steps in a procedure, a process explanation provides specific details of each step, often describing the relationships between steps as well as offering theoretical background.

The following examples show how useful an operational definition can be when defining a term.

Examples   A thermostatic element with a remote bulb is a temperature-sensitive instrument that converts a temperature change into a mechanical force. The instrument consists of three copper parts (bulb, capillary tube, and bellows) soldered together, with a liquid sealed inside. The bulb contains liquid that turns to a gas when heated. Since the gas requires more volume per unit weight than the liquid, the pressure in the bulb increases, forcing gas through the capillary tube and into the bellows. This increase in the volume of gas causes the bellows to expand. Just the opposite happens when the bulb is cooled. This loss of heat in the bulb causes some of the gas in the bulb to condense into its liquid state. Since the liquid has a much smaller volume per unit weight, the pressure drops, which pulls gas back from the bellows. A decrease in the volume of gas in the bellows causes the bellows to contract.[14]

When current through the fuse link exceeds the rating of the element, excessive heat is generated and the element melts. Strain wires in the strain type elements are heated and then separate. At this instant, an arc is established across the gap created in the element. The arc serves as a conducting path for current. The pretensioned spring in the spring type link ejects the leader from the auxiliary tube into the body of the fuse holder, drawing out the arc. An inert, nonconductive gas is generated when the heat of the arc attacks the lining of the fuse holder. The gas extinguishes the arc, interrupting the current flow and opening the circuit.[15]

Expanded Definitions

Expanded definitions take many forms, although all the different forms do provide detailed information about the term. Etymologies (the linguistic origins of a term) are appropriate for general readers who appreciate high-interest material. Histories of terms are also appropriate for general readers; even readers with technical expertise may need recent historical information. Examples have value for all audiences. The most widely used expanded definitions present information in one of the traditional organizational patterns.

Etymology. Etymologies anticipate such questions as, How did this object get its name? How old is this word? Where did this word come from? What are the historical precedents of this word? Presenting the linguistic derivation or origin of a term itself sometimes gives insight into its current meaning(s). Etymological information is found in dictionaries or in research books specializing in etymologies. In a dictionary entry, this information is most frequently presented in abbreviated form inside square brackets. Every dictionary contains a page near the front of the volume explaining the abbreviations.

Etymologies are a useful part of a definition if knowledge of the original meaning increases the reader's understanding of the modern meaning and usage. Such explanations are particularly appropriate in writing for general audiences, although they also add interest to definitions for more technical audiences.

The following examples demonstrate how etymologies can be used effectively as a technique for definition.

Examples   The word "lathe" is derived from the Middle English word *lath*, which came from the Old English *laett* and the Old High German *latta*, which refers to a thin, narrow strip of wood nailed to the rafters or joists of a building. The lathe was so named because the original lathes, used for wood turning, utilized two wooden springs boards and foot power to drive the wood piece.[16]

The word rivet comes from the Vulgar Latin word *ripare*, which means to make firm, or from the Middle French words *rivet* or *river*, which means to clinch.[17]

History. Presenting historical background about the development and use of the subject puts the current meaning into perspective. History can cover several thousand years (if the subject is chemistry and begins with the magicians in the pharaohs' courts) or decades (if the subject is lexan, which was invented in the 1960s). The use of historical background anticipates such questions as, What are the subject's origins? How long have such objects (concepts) existed? How has the history affected modern development? How were original objects (concepts) different from modern ones? The following example shows how history can be used.

Example   The process of making carbon black, though obviously not as sophisticated as the technology used today, has been known to man for a very long time. Records show that carbon black was made in China about 3000 B.C., and records indicate that China began exporting black to Japan about A.D. 500. The original process used by the Chinese consisted of burning purified vegetable oil in small lamps with ceramic covers. The smoke would gather on the cover; thus, deposits of carbon black would be on the covers and would have to be scraped off.

Commercial production of carbon black has been taking place in the United States for over 100 years. In the earlier days, it was used primarily as a pigment (powdered coloring), but as technology improved and expanded, so did the uses of carbon black. Prior to 1870, the only commercially produced blacks were made by the lampblack process, which is a process similar to that of the Chinese.

In approximately 1912, researchers discovered that carbon black has good reinforcing properties in rubber. With this discovery, carbon black production went from a small volume pigment to a large volume industrial chemical used in rubber products, particularly tires.

Because of the increased need, new methods of production were introduced. Thermal black and acetylene black processes were tried and in some locations are still in use. In the early 1940s, the oil furnaces process was invented; today this process accounts for nearly all of the world's production of carbon black because it is the most efficient of all the processes.[18]

Examples. Using specific examples to illustrate the application of a term effectively expands a definition. Examples are particularly useful in clarifying a formal or operational definition. As the following paragraph shows, they respond to such questions as, What are actual applications?

Example   The study of chemistry is the study of change. Man [sic] lives in a universe that is in constant motion and is continually undergoing transformations from one form to another. . . . Changes . . . such as the rusting of iron, the boiling of an egg, the lighting of a match, or the explosion of a stick of dynamite, are processes that are essentially chemical in nature. It is the study of these changes and the factors that govern them that comprises the field of chemistry.[19]

Organizational Patterns. In addition to using etymology, history, and examples to expand the definition of a term, a writer can use any of the organizational patterns presented in Chapter 4: chronological order, spatial order, priority (descending/ascending) order, comparison/contrast, and cause/effect.

Placement of Definitions

Writers of technical material have four basic choices for the placement and incorporation of definitions although the choices are not mutually exclusive:

1. glossary
2. information notes
3. incorporated information
4. appendix

Glossary

A glossary is a minidictionary located at the beginning or end of a technical document. Glossaries placed at the beginning are particularly useful when the reader is unfamiliar with the information and must know the terminology in order to comprehend the document. A glossary placed at the end of a document primarily provides occasional references rather than essential information.

Individual entries can employ any of the forms of definition: formal, informal, operational, or expanded. Traditionally, glossaries have appeared at the end of a document. When this is the case, terms as they occur in the body must be marked in some way (italics, asterisks) to let the reader know that the definition is in the glossary.

Example   The seat gaskets* are first removed from the plug. . . .

---

*All terms so marked are defined in the Glossary beginning on page 11.

Recently, however, manuals and reports have been placing the glossary at the beginning so that the reader can review the technical terms and then read. The disadvantage of this system is that without having read the document, a reader lacks a frame of reference and may not be able to judge which terms to focus on.

Information Notes

Information notes can be placed on the bottom of a page or collected at the end of a document along with source or reference notes. The information notes may simply define a term or concept; however, writers often use information notes to discuss related issues because that material would be a distraction if included in the text. Such notes give the writer the opportunity to define and provide examples, to cite related studies, to explain tangential concepts, to postulate possible explanations, and so on. Technical reports for business decisions usually restrict themselves to information notes that offer brief definitions or explanations since readers usually have little time. Technical documents for research or academic purposes may include more detailed information notes for readers who might want to investigate an idea in greater depth.

Incorporated Information

Frequently, definitions can be incorporated into sentences without the distraction of glossary entries or information notes, as shown in this excerpt from the article, "A Manager's Guide to Computer Systems."

Example   Every computer system has two types of components, hardware and software. Most visible is the hardware, or equipment, typically a *central processing unit* (CPU) and *peripheral equipment*—the input-output and storage devices. . . . Basically, the user communicates with the CPU by means of the peripherals.

Less visible, but usually even more critical, is the *software,* or programs that tell the equipment what to do with information. Too often both computer buyers and sellers focus on stylish, competent-looking hardware, rather than on the software that determines what a system can or can't do for a particular business. Software is so important that part two of this series will be devoted entirely to it.

Software is not only important; it can be expensive, often equaling or exceeding hardware costs. And it's only one of the factors that make estimating computer system costs so complicated. There are also "hidden costs" such as maintenance and supplies. Maintenance for a small microcomputer system can be as low as $50 per month; most of this is for the printer, whose moving parts take quite a beating. Yearly maintenance contracts for a large system can run from 8% to as much as 18% of the initial cost of the hardware.

Another often-overlooked expense is the *backup storage* equipment that's generally needed in addition to basic system components. It's usual at the end of each day to create back-up files— duplicates of the updated records—as a safeguard against loss or damage of magnetic disks, a common storage medium that resembles a phonograph record. Damage can result not only from disasters like fire, but from machine failure. The extra few thousand dollars spent on the backup equipment should be viewed as insurance. Lost programs can be difficult and expensive to replace; data files are often impossible to reconstruct.

The total cost of your computer system can be anything from a few thousand to a few hundred thousand dollars. Beware of those who claim to have simple formulas that determine the size and price of the computer you need by the size of your company. Today's diverse market, and the diverse needs of small companies, make reliable computer consultants wary of hard-and-fast rules. . . .

Regardless of what system you buy, be prepared for the impact the system will have on your company. First, one or more of your employees must learn to use it. This means sitting at a keyboard, entering identification codes or passwords, and responding to instructions displayed on the video screen or printer. This basic procedure—calling up programs and files by following a "menu" sequence, and entering data or commands—is commonly used in business tasks.[20]

The examples of definitions in this article illustrate several ways to incorporate definitions effectively into the text of a document.

Incorporated information consisting of a simple synonym or example can be separated by parentheses:

Examples   Computers carry out all computations using binary (base 2) arithmetic, which involves rapidly manipulating strings of bits according to fixed rules.

Because of the nature of computer storage procedures, a byte is the amount of storage space needed to represent a character (i.e., a numeral, letter, symbol, or blank).

A definition can also be separated by dashes—two hyphens if you're typing:

Examples   It's usual at the end of each day to create back-up files—duplicates of the updated records—as a safeguard against loss or damage of magnetic disks. . . .

This basic procedure—calling up programs and files by following a "menu" sequence, and entering data or commands—is commonly used in business tasks.

Incorporated definitions are separated by commas:

Examples   There are two basic kinds [of hard disks]: packs, which consist of several platters in a removable case, and cartridges, which usually contain one platter.

A modem, a device that couples a computer or terminal to a telephone line, is used for long-distance data transmission.[21]

Sometimes the formal definition incorporated into a paragraph is a direct quote from an authoritative source:

Example   Gifted behavior may also be affected by particular nonintellectual characteristics. The examination of locus of control (LOC), "the belief that reinforcements are contingent upon one's own behaviors, capabilities, or attributes (Internal LOC) or that reinforcements . . . are under the control of powerful others, luck, chance, or fate" (External LOC) . . . , is suggested by research that indicates a positive correlation between the acceptance of responsibility for one's successes and failures (internal LOC) and verbal fluency . . . , high IQ . . . , and high achievement via test scores. . . .[22]

So far, this section of the chapter has discussed the incorporation of relatively short definitions. Frequently, however, lengthy definitions are necessary. The following excerpt from an article, "A Componential Theory of Intellectual Giftedness," shows how important it is for a writer to be able to define concepts. The author identifies and defines the first metacomponent of intellectual giftedness. The definition effectively replaces the abstraction of "higher-order control processes" by relating a series of everyday examples.

COMPONENTS OF INTELLECTUAL GIFTEDNESS

Although all components are viewed as elementary information processes, these components can be of various kinds. In particular, components seem to perform five different kinds of important functions, which we consider now. The functions will be illustrated in the context of how gifted college students excel in their performance of these functions.

Metacomponents

Metacomponents are higher-order control processes that are used for executive planning and decision making in problem solving, both in academic situations and in everyday life. Taken together, these metacomponents are sometimes referred to as the "executive" or the "homunculus." Gifted individuals tend to excel in their access to and implementation of at least six metacomponents.

Decision as to just what the problems are that need to be solved. The most important part of problem solving is often recognition of the nature of the problem that needs to be solved. This recognition can be viewed as hierarchical. At the highest level, the college student is faced with what seem to be innumerable tasks to be accomplished. He or she may be faced with multiple assignments in each of four or five courses; demands from extracurricular activities such as campus newspaper reporting, dramatic performance, and the like; everyday chores such as doing the laundry and running errands; and the need for interpersonal contacts of a wide variety. The student needs to recognize as a problem the scheduling of the many activities demanded of him or her, rather than merely to plunge into these activities, hoping that there will be time for all of them. The complexity of the problem can scarcely be underestimated, since there is no one criterion against which the value of a particular activity, or all of the activities, can be matched. Different activities each contribute to the fulfillment of multiple goals, so that any individual's optimization criteria will of necessity be multidimensional. The ability to recognize the effective organization of one's time as a key problem to be solved is an important aspect of giftedness. Given that everyone has only the same 24 hours in a day to get things done, the ability to ration this time effectively will make a large difference in the quality and quantity of outcomes. Although there are large differences in how hard students work, there are even greater differences in the effectiveness with which they plan and organize the time in which they do work.

At a lower level of the problem-recognition hierarchy is the recognition of the nature of each individual problem within one's "problem space." Such individual problems include such things as specific assignments for papers and specific mathematical problems such as those found in calculus or physics homework. Very often students do a good job of solving the wrong problem, with disastrous results. For example, a good paper may be written on a topic other than the one assigned; or a physics problem may be solved, but one other than the one presented. Writers of standardized tests have long recognized students' proclivities to solve problems other than the ones presented. Hence, multiple-choice ability and achievement tests will often include distractors that are correct answers to incorrect interpretations of the given problems. Students frequently do worse on such tests than they thought they would do simply because they have given right answers to the wrong problems. Standardized tests thus indirectly tap problem-recognition ability by penalizing students who do not recognize the problems that are presented to them.[23]

Appendix

Lengthy documents intended for readers with widely varying backgrounds often confuse the nonexpert by jumping into the subject without sufficient explanation or by boring or even offending technical experts by including elementary material. One way to resolve this dilemma is to include a series of appendixes that provide both operational and expanded definitions of critical terms. Readers already familiar with the material glance at the reference to the appendix in the text and continue reading, virtually uninterrupted. Readers who need to review the background material appreciate the detailed, illustrated definitions and discussions.

Inquiries and Applications

Discussion Questions

1. Writers sometimes work hard to locate effective and accurate synonyms. How could synonyms in technical documents be misleading to the reader?

2. Where are definitions placed so they are most convenient for you as a reader? Where are you most likely to use them? Where are they least obtrusive?

3. Identify the types of definition below and discuss what audiences would respond to each type.

   a. The word for chemistry comes from the Middle East; long ago the sacred name for Egypt was "Chemia," which means black and probably referred to the fertile black soil of the Nile valley. In those ancient times almost any kind of change was mysterious, such as the change of wood to ash when it burns, or the transformation of sand into glass. Men who understood how to make some things change were considered to be magicians (at least we might call them that today). From their mysterious abilities to cause changes the word for the study of change was derived.[24]

   b. *chemistry*—The study of the composition of substances and of the changes of composition which they undergo. The main branches of the subject are inorganic chemistry, organic chemistry, and physical chemistry.[25]

4. A highly technical document is directed toward specific readers who should be familiar with the technical field. Why should a writer take the time and effort to define terms for such expert readers?

5. Some people argue that *analogies* and *illustrations* are not forms of definition. Support or refute their use as effective ways to define some terms.

In-Class Activities

1. Develop formal definitions for the following terms:

orange	bond	secretary	quality control
furlong	compound	engineer	technician

   Discuss the difficulties in developing acceptable formal definitions—even though people think they know what the words mean—because of multiple meanings and cultural bias.

2. The following words have multiple technical and general meanings:

limit	traverse	stock
base	positive	cover

Add at least six more to the list and then define them.

3. Case Situation: Imagine that your audience, managers of a rapidly expanding small business, may consider buying a computer. You are rewriting part of an article dealing with computer basics; you assume the audience knows little or nothing about computers. The article will contain a computer glossary, but you believe that brief definitions should be incorporated into the article itself so the readers don't have to regularly check the glossary while they're reading.

Rewrite the following paragraph incorporating necessary definitions.

> Every computer system has two types of components, hardware and software. Most visible is the hardware, typically a central processing unit (CPU) and peripheral equipment. Less visible, but usually even more critical is the software. Too often computer buyers and sellers focus on stylish, competent-looking hardware, rather than on the software that determines what a system can or can't do for a particular business. Another often overlooked expense is the backup storage equipment that generally is needed in addition to basic system components.[26]

Excerpts from the computer glossary:

- backup storage
- computer system
- CPU
- hardware
- peripheral equipment
- software

The necessary definitions from the original article are reproduced below.

Backup storage. Copies of data files, used as a safeguard against damage or loss. Usually *magnetic tape*, sometimes *floppy* or *hard disk*.

Computer system. A computer plus *software* plus one or more pieces of *peripheral equipment*.

CPU (central processing unit). The part of a computer that performs calculations and processes data according to the instructions specified by the *software*. CPU is sometimes used interchangeably with *computer*. See also *microcomputer*.

Hardware. The computer itself or any item of *peripheral equipment*.

Peripheral equipment. Input-output and data storage devices: printers, keyboards, *CRTs*, remote *terminals*, and tape and disk drives.

Software. The programs, or instructions, that tell the computer how to respond to specific user commands.[27]

4. a. Carefully read the following papers in Example 9.1 ("The Fugue") and Example 9.2 ("The Stall").

   b. Marginally annotate to identify all the types of definition the writers use.

   c. Identify the probable audiences for these papers.

Example 9.1

THE FUGUE

A fugue is a polyphonic form of music that is most easily recognized by several reappearances of a short melodic theme. Fugues are usually written in from two- to five-part harmonies. Each part blends with the other parts to form harmony, but it is also a melodic line as well. This characteristic of a fugue makes it unique. Writing a short melody with simple harmony is easy; however, if the supporting parts do not form a melody very similar to the melodic theme first stated in the fugue, then the composition cannot be called a fugue.

A fugue is similar to a canon or a round, but a canon usually has only two parts that are always exactly alike. One part begins the canon and the second part enters later, duplicating the first. An example of a canon is shown in Figure 1.

Figure 1   Canon

(By the way, can you name that tune?)

The fugue, however, always has the second part entering in a different key. This new key is called the dominant key and is five tones higher than the original key, the tonic key. (See Figure 2.)

Figure 2   Tonic–Dominant Relationship

There are, then, two important characteristics of a fugue:

1. The melodics are imitative.
2. The imitation occurs in related keys.

The fugue is commonly divided into three distinct sections:

1. Exposition
2. Development
3. Stretto

The exposition consists of the statement of the melodic theme and its answer in the dominant key. These statements and answers may occur several times, depending upon the number of parts written into the composition. Most frequently, fugues are written in four parts and require two statements and two answers.

The development is the most exciting and improvisational part of the fugue. Indeed, the fugue is so-named because of the action within the development. Fugue is derived from the Latin *fugere*, meaning to flee or run away. The development runs away from the straightforward statements and answers of the exposition and adds color and variety to the composition. The development uses the following techniques to achieve interest:

1. Countersubject—playing a new theme with the original theme
2. Augmentation—playing the theme more slowly
3. Diminution—playing the theme more quickly
4. Inversion—playing the theme upside down

The stretto section of the fugue is a restatement of the original theme by all the parts. They often overlap unexpectedly and reach a climax to provide a dramatic end to the fugue.

The fugue was a popular form of composition during the Baroque era. Most of the major composers have written fugues or parts of fugues in larger compositions. However, Bach remains the most famous and prolific writer of fugues.[28]

Example 9.2

STALLING AN AIRPLANE

Stalling an airplane is not the same as stalling a car, in which case the engine ceases to run. In an airplane, stalling is a loss of lift resulting in the wing no longer supporting the plane. (The aircraft engine can be humming like a top throughout the stall.) During a stall there is some lift but not enough to support the plane in a normal flying position. Understanding the stall requires understanding lift.

Lift is a force exerted by the wings, also known as airfoils. As the wings move through the air, either in gliding or powered flight, lift is produced. Because of the curved top of the wing, the distance the air must travel over the top is greater than the air under the bottom. As the air moves over this greater distance, it speeds up in an attempt to re-establish equilibrium at the rear top of the wing. This extra speed causes the air to exert less pressure on the top of the wing surface than on the bottom, and lift is produced. You can observe this principle by holding your hand out the window of a fast-moving car. The impact of the air on the bottom surface, when it is sharply inclined upward, creates a lifting force that is easily sensed. Figure 1 shows the wind approaching a wing. As air moves over and under the wing, the top air motion accelerates in contrast to the bottom.

Figure 1   Slight increase in speed on top of wing causes lift

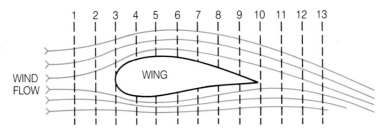

A pilot can, up to a point, increase the angle of the wings and increase the lift. However, if the wings are angled even steeper into the onrushing air, it becomes more difficult for the air to flow smoothly across the top of the wing. Then the air starts to separate from the wing and enters a burbling pattern. The angle at which air flow separation and burbling turbulence occur on the upper wing surface is called the critical angle of attack. The burbling results in a loss of lift in the area of the wing where it takes place. See Figure 2.

Example 9.2   *Continued*

Figure 2   Burbling results in loss of lift

The separation of air starts near the rear edge of the wing and progresses forward as the angle of attack is increased. Finally, the separation point moves so far forward that most of the wing loses its lift and a stall occurs. In other words, a stall is a loss of lift caused by too large an angle of attack.

Recovering from a stall in most airplanes requires a decrease in the angle of attack or lowering the angle of the wings to the normal flight position. If a full stall is desired, the pilot keeps increasing the angle of attack until the wing stalls, drops, and the plane rolls toward that wing. Pilots are encouraged to practice stalls at least 3000 feet above ground level to develop confidence and skill in recognition and recovery. Learning how a plane reacts when approaching a stall will prepare a pilot for early recovery of a stall at a potentially dangerous low altitude.[29]

Assignments

1. Locate at least three different levels of definition for the same term. Check dictionaries, texts, encyclopedias, handbooks, and professional journals in the reference and periodical section of your library. Photocopy the definitions you select, and document your sources, using the appropriate formats from Chapter 8. Identify the major distinctions among the various definitions and evaluate the effectiveness of each definition for the intended audience.
2. Locate a published technical article that incorporates various types of definition. Document your sources. Photocopy the article and marginally annotate the various types of definition used. Write a paragraph discussing whether you believe the definitions are necessary and effective.

3. Write an informal, formal, operational, and expanded definition for two of the following terms. Identify your intended audience for each definition.

    a. lens   eyes? cameras? spectacles?

    b. cane   walking stick? chair seat? sugar plant? medical term? beating a school boy?

    c. plate   dish? dentures? metal layer? baseball goal? dinosaur? ship's shell?

    d. scroll   movement on a computer screen? decoration on furniture? ancient manuscript?

    e. card   process in textile manufacturing? piece of still paper (business card, playing card)? list of players in athletic event? request for ID in a bar? colloquial expression for funny person?

    f. punch   device for making holes? beverage? physical blow? critical line of a joke?

    g. key   top stone in an arch? lock opener? musical notation? critical item or idea?

    h. post   bookkeeping process? part of a fence? horseback riding technique? mailing a letter? occupational assignment? military community? at a later date (as in post-war)?

    i. ream   quantity of paper? machinist's tool?

    j. lap   one circuit of an oval track? cat's drinking process? fold of material? where you can hold a child? finishing process for metal surfaces?

    k. play   looseness in a mechanical device? child's recreation? form of literature or stage performance? activate a record or tape? perform on an athletic team?

    Or try one of these terms:

accretion	matrix	oligarchy	surface tension
actuarial	spinnaker	ferment	cirrocumulus
odometer	heterodyne	kinesthetics	ergonomics
synthetic	lumens	penultimate	tensile strength
striae	detrius	peristalsis	prehensile

4. Write a multi-paragraph paper incorporating various forms of definition for a single term. Your paper should resemble the sample papers defining fugue and stall in the in-class exercises. Make sure to include visuals if they are appropriate for illustrating or clarifying the term. Document any sources used in preparing the paper.

10 Description

FOR CENTURIES SCIENTISTS have described their observations. In 1610, Galileo Galilei announced "the occasion of discovering and observing four planets, never seen from the very beginning of the world up to our own times, their positions, and the observations made during the last two months about their movements and their change of magnitude. . . ." Galileo carefully recorded his observations of the four satellites of Jupiter. These same four satellites were the object of intense scrutiny in 1980 by *Voyager 1*. *Voyager's* mission was to collect data about Jupiter's "miniature solar system," including the four Galilean satellites: Io, Europa, Ganymede, and Callisto. The detailed data collected by *Voyager 1* allowed scientists to describe the moons of Jupiter in far greater detail than Galileo had. The following excerpt from Galileo's journal shows that his description is general, establishing size as "greater than [another . . . that was] exceedingly small," luminescence as "very conspicuous and bright," and location as "deviated a little from the straight line toward the north."

> January 11. [My observations] established that there are not only three but four erratic sidereal bodies performing their revolutions round Jupiter. . . .
> January 12. The satellite farthest to the east was greater than the satellite farther to the west; but both were very conspicuous and bright; the distance of each one from Jupiter was two minutes. A third satellite, certainly not in view before, began to appear at the third hour; it nearly touched Jupiter on the east side, and was

exceedingly small. They were all arranged in a straight line, along the ecliptic.

January 13. For the first time four satellites were in view. . . . There were three to the west and one to the east; they made a straight line nearly, but the middle satellite of those to the west deviated a little from the straight line toward the north. The satellite farthest to the east was at a distance of 2′ from Jupiter; there were intervals of 1′ only between Jupiter and the nearest satellite, and between the satellites themselves, west of Jupiter. All the satellites appeared of the same size, and though small they were very brilliant and far outshone the fixed stars of the same magnitude.[1]

In vivid contrast to Galileo's brief comments, the *Voyager Bulletin* (a mission status report that regularly reported the discoveries of *Voyager*) describes the Galilean satellites in considerable detail. The following excerpt describes the moon Io.

Of all the satellites, Io generated the most excitement. As *Voyager 1* closed in on Io, the puzzle was why its surface, so cratered and pocked when viewed from a distance, began to look smoother and younger as the spacecraft neared. Theories of erosion due to intense bombardment from Jupiter's radiation were advanced.

But the mystery was solved with the discovery of active volcanoes spewing sulfur 160 km (100 mi) high and showering it down on the crust, obliterating the old surface. Infrared data indicated hot spots at the locations of the plumes identified in the photographs, confirming the find.

Io is undoubtedly the most active known surface in the solar system, surpassing even the Earth. If a spacecraft were to fly past Earth, it is unlikely that any volcanic activity would be visible despite the great number of volcanoes. But Io! As many as seven simultaneously erupting volcanoes have been identified.

Most of Io's volcanoes are extremely violent—similar to Vesuvius or Etna. Some evidence of Hawaiian-type volcanoes exists—vents through which the hot magma oozes rather than erupts. Infrared studies have observed lava lakes which may be as much as 400 degrees Fahrenheit warmer than the surrounding surface.[2]

Defining Technical Description

The excerpts both from Galileo's journal and from the *Voyager Bulletin* illustrate several characteristics of description that are discussed in this chapter.

Most important, the descriptions include specific focused details, presented in an organized manner for an identified audience.

Descriptions in technical communication are most frequently associated with mechanisms, but as the examples about the Jovian moons illustrate, this is a narrow view. Mechanisms do make up a large percentage of subjects for technical descriptions; however, you can also describe objects, substances, systems, organisms, and locations. Figure 10.1 lists the range of subjects about which you may be expected to write a technical description.

Descriptions summarize physical characteristics, answering questions about the appearance or composition of an object, substance, mechanism, organism, system, or location. Regardless of a description's length or subject, it is characterized by objective information that responds to assumed questions:

1. What is it? How is it defined?
2. What is its purpose?

Figure 10.1 — Range of Subjects for Technical Description

Objects	chain	plastic wrap
	drain pipe	tire
	thermal glass	stained glass
Substances	high protein supplement	interferon
	tofu	acrylic paint
	microbial insecticide	allspice
Mechanisms	faucet	rifle
	laser	harrow
	anchor	lawn mower
Systems	ignition system	immune system
	reproductive system	root system
	inventory system	alarm system
Organisms	little brown bat	gypsy moths
	highland gorilla	hybrid corn
	amoeba	plankton
Locations	Georges Banks	proposed site for a well
	Jovian moon, Amalthea	Mount St. Helens
	Lowell canals	wildlife refuge

3. What are the characteristics of the whole?
   - What does it look like (size, shape, color)?
   - What are its characteristics (material or substance, weight, texture, flammability, density, durability, expected life, method of production or reproduction, and so on)?

4. What are its parts?
   - What is the appearance of each part (size, shape, color)?
   - What are the distinctive characteristics of each part?

5. How do the parts fit together?

Which of these questions are answered depends on the depth of detail required by the description. Complex descriptions clearly answer more questions.

Sometimes, technical description constitutes an entire document. However, in many situations a technical description is limited to a single segment of a longer document detailing many facets of a subject. Descriptions range from a few lines included in a one- or two-page memo to several paragraphs in a longer report. For instance, a description of equipment would be just one part of a report about monitoring airport noise that is interfering with animals in an adjoining wildlife refuge. Or the description of equipment would take up one section in a proposal to purchase a new X-ray machine.

In another example, a technical brochure for a numerical control stamping machine for a machine shop contains information about the structure of the product. The brochure begins by giving the reader a general overview and presenting a photograph of the machine. Once the reader is familiar with the characteristics of the whole machine, the brochure explains physical characteristics in greater detail, including a description of the major components, exploded and cutaway views, and equipment capabilities. The brochure concludes by specifying materials, dimensions, and attachment options. Many different readers—buyers, group managers, engineers, manufacturing supervisors—read this brochure before making a decision about whether to purchase the equipment; therefore, the brochure anticipates readers' questions. What the readers do not need at this initial point in their decision making is information about how to operate, maintain, or repair the equipment.

Using Technical Description

Technical descriptions usually appear as part of larger documents. The following discussion identifies and illustrates some of the most common applications of technical descriptions: observation notes in medicine, orientation and training materials, field study and scientific research, reports, proposals, marketing and promotional materials, and manuals.

Observation Notes

Many situations require accurate first-hand descriptions, particularly in medicine, field study, and scientific research. The technical expert observes, selects, and records relevant data, often employing abbreviations and jargon specific to the field. The initial purpose of observation notes is accurate record keeping for the person taking notes. Later, the notes can be extended or transcribed so others can read them, or they can be used as the basis for a more formal document.

The *Manual of Pediatric Therapeutics*, a reference volume for pediatric practitioners, outlines the criteria for immediate evaluation of the newborn in the delivery room and nursery. This evaluation, based on observation by the medical professional, provides a detailed physical description of the newborn:

Example

I. EVALUATION OF THE NEWBORN

A. Delivery room Immediate assessment of the newborn infant by the Apgar scoring system should help to identify infants with severe metabolic imbalances. At 1 and 5 min after delivery (the times at which feet and head are both first visible), the infant is to be evaluated for five signs, namely, *heart rate*, *respiratory effort*, *muscle tone*, *reflexes*, and *irritability and color*, and given a rating of 0, 1, or 2 (as defined in Table 5-1). In the extremely compromised infant, prompt and efficient resuscitation is far more important than his exact Apgar score.

Table 5-1. Apgar Score (Score Infant at 1 and 5 Minutes of Age)

Sign	0	1	2
Heart rate	Absent	Slow, less than 100	100 or over
Respiratory effort	Absent	Weak cry, hypoventilation	Crying lustily
Muscle tone	Flaccid	Some flexion, extremities	Well-flexed
Reflex irritability	No response	Some motion	Cry
Color	Blue, pale	Blue hands and feet	Entirely pink

B. Nursery
   1. General
      a. **Activity** General level of activity, movement of extremities
      b. **Color** Cyanosis, jaundice, paleness
      c. **Measurements** Head circumference, crown-heel length, respiratory rate, pulse rate, blood pressure (flush is most accurate), temperature
      d. **Respirations** Rhythm, effort, rate
      e. **Head** Head circumference $= \dfrac{\text{crown-heel length}}{2} + 10$ cm; size of fontanelles, nonfusion of sutures
      f. **Eyes** Cataracts, red reflex; reaction to light; glaucoma; Brushfield spots; palpebral fissures
      g. **Ears** Position: posterior rotation denotes development abnormalities; preauricular sinuses
      h. **Nose** Patent bilaterally
      i. **Mouth** Size of tongue; size of mandible; cleft lip or palate
      j. **Neck** Broken clavicles; palpable thyroid; cysts. Pass a feeding tube to the stomach to establish that esophagus is patent
      k. **Chest** Retraction, auscultation
      l. **Heart** Point of maximal impulse (PMI); rhythm; murmurs
      m. **Abdomen** Liver, spleen, and kidneys are palpable in complete examination; umbilical cord: two arteries and one vein
      n. **Genitalia**
          (1) Male Testes descended or in canal; hypospadias
          (2) Female Vaginal discharge; enlarged clitoris
      o. **Extremities** Five digits on each extremity; hips; equal gluteal creases; no "click" on abduction of hip
      p. **Back** Spine in midline; pilonidal sinus; anus patent
      q. **Neurologic** Sucking; root and tonic neck reflexes; knee jerks; abdominal reflexes; withdrawal from pain; Babinski reflex present; transillumination of skull when indicated; palmar grasp; head-bobbing ability[3]

Orientation and Training Materials

Work-study students and new employees often need descriptions of the mechanisms and systems with which they'll work. Short technical descriptions, as part of their initial training, orient both students and employees. The description in Example 10.1 of a circular inspection mirror is used to introduce a basic piece of inspection equipment.

Example 10.1

CIRCULAR INSPECTION MIRROR

A circular inspection mirror is a tool used when visually inspecting general electrical and mechanical equipment for production flaws. The tool's appearance is similar to a hand mirror used by a dentist to inspect teeth, with one exception: the mirror swivels separately from the handle.

The inspection mirror shown in Figure 1 consists of three main parts: mirror, handle, and universal swivel joint. The mechanics incorporated in the swivel design allow a complete 360° spherical positioning of the mirror with no movement of the handle.

Using the circular inspection mirror helps a person observe areas that, because of the angled displacement within the unit, are normally hidden from view.

The 1⅛"-mirror reflects identical size figures. The mirror's durable stainless steel casing adds ⅛" to the overall diameter, making the total diameter 1¼".

Attached by spot welding to the inside of the casing back is a small stem extending ⅜" and concluding in the form of a round bearing. This bearing is positioned inside a two-bearing universal joint.

The simple universal joint uses two encloser plates held together by a nut-and-screw combination. Impressed in the plates are four concave pockets that prevent the bearings from leaving the joint, but allow maximum rotation to the attached handle or mirror. By tightening and loosening the screw, an operator can adjust the mirror to the desired tension.

Also located inside the universal casing and opposite the bearing attached to the mirror is the second bearing, which connects to a hard tempered-steel rod approximately 6" in length. The rough surface of the metal is covered for 3" with plastic orange insulating material that protects the user from electrical shock and possible electrocution.

An additional feature of the circular inspection mirror is a pocket clip, located towards the middle of the handle, which allows the tool to be carried in a shirt pocket like a pen.

Figure 1

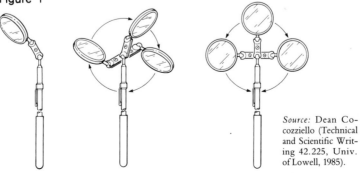

Source: Dean Co-cozziello (Technical and Scientific Writing 42.225, Univ. of Lowell, 1985).

Reports

Several types of reports incorporate descriptions. For example, a report about changes in the work flow in an assembly area because of new automatic insertion equipment could logically include a description of this equipment. The supervisor writing to the division manager would emphasize features of the equipment that have affected the work flow. Generally, any report justifying or recommending acquisition or modification of equipment or facilities will include a description.

Proposals

If a description helps a reader to understand and approve a proposal, it should be included. This type of description gives an overview and then provides details appropriate for the primary reader(s). For example, a proposal from a manager of research and development (R and D) to the company comptroller about an equipment purchase would logically include a description of the equipment. However, the description would not be detailed because the equipment's technical specifications and capabilities are not relevant for the reader. If secondary readers for the same proposal are familiar with R and D operations, an appendix could discuss technical details. In contrast, a proposal to a state's environmental control commission from a local community to preserve a wetlands area would include a detailed description of the geographic area as a main part of the proposal. The members of the commission would need the details to make an informed decision about the validity of the preservation plan.

Marketing/Promotional Pieces

Technical descriptions in marketing materials are usually both informative and persuasive. Positive (and, of course, subjective) terms are often incorporated into the initial description. The information presents an overview, identifying major components and characteristics. Additional information is often condensed on specification sheets (specs). Promotional/marketing materials frequently include visuals that first display the entire object or mechanism and then highlight its special features. For example, an ad for Penn Engineering and Manufacturing Corporation (PEM) displays a photo of a Coleman lantern, along with two smaller visuals. The first insert is a cutaway view of the lantern's mixing chamber assembly; the second is a photo of the PEM self-clinching stud. The ad copy and the small visuals both describe the self-clinching stud, the actual focus of the ad.

Manuals

Most manuals include a technical description of the mechanism or system that the manual deals with. The description usually appears in one of the manual's early sections, often providing a general overview and then more detailed information. The technical description introduces the user, operator, technician, or repair person to the physical characteristics of the mechanism or system. Technical descriptions in manuals are usually accompanied by a variety of visuals: the entire mechanism or system, exploded views, blowups, and phantom and cutaway views of individual parts and subparts.

Example 10.2, from the first section of an *ATEX Systems Manager's Reference Manual*, briefly introduces the hardware that comprises the system. The description provides only an overview, since details are presented in the rest of the manual.

Preparing a Technical Description

To prepare a technical description, you need to identify the audience and purpose, partition the subject (object, organism, location, and so on), choose precise diction, design effective visuals, and select an appropriate format.

Audience and Purpose

A technical description should address the intended audience. The only way to make sure the description meets reader needs is to conduct a careful audi-

Example 10.2

THE ATEX SYSTEM

Looking closer at the block in Figure 1-2 labeled "The ATEX System," we see it actually consists of two sections: hardware and software (as shown in Figure 1-3).

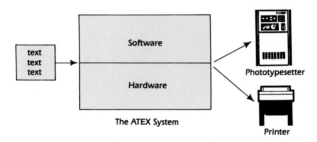

Figure 1-3   The ATEX System Consists of Hardware and Software

These two sections are interdependent; the software cannot do its job without electronic and mechanical help, and the hardware cannot process text without instructions that tell it how. It's kind of like an automobile: the machine is perfectly capable of performing certain functions, but without instructions and guidance from you, it just sits in the driveway.

Hardware
Figure 1-4 shows yet finer detail on the ATEX system. The central component in the hardware section is the computer itself: a Digital Equipment Corporation PDP-11. That is where the text is actually processed; i.e., within its memory are performed all the system's operations — editing, hyphenation, justification, line counting, etc.

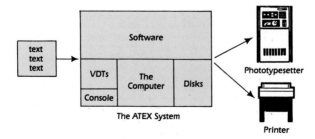

Figure 1-4   Within the Hardware Section

Source: ATEX, Inc. *System Manager's Reference Manual* (Bedford, MA: ATEX, 1981), I-1-3–I-1-4. Reprinted with permission of ATEX.

Example 10.2   *Continued*

Attached to each computer are a number of video display terminals (VDT's), at least one disk drive, and a system console. The VDTs allow users to give the system commands and enter, retrieve, display, and manipulate text. The system console allows you to start the central software programs (as described in the next section). The disk is the home of the data base; i.e., all the text that users process, as well as the software programs that make it all possible.

Usually an ATEX installation contains at least one *pair* of PDP-11s (each with its own disk drive(s) and VDTs), joined together through an electronic bridge called the multiprocessor bus (MPB — also called a Copy Management Processor, or CMP; see Figure 1-5). The MPB is nothing more than a messenger; it is this device that allows the perfect redundancy of data bases in an ATEX installation. That is, a user at a VDT is connected to only one of the computers in an installation, yet every time he/she stores a file on that system, the ATEX system automatically sends a copy of that file to one or more other systems via the MPB. Thus, each data base in an ATEX installation has an identical twin. The twin is connected to (and is accessed through) another computer (via the MPB), but it contains exactly the same data. Therefore, if one data base becomes corrupted in some way (e.g., if the disk drive for the system breaks down), users attached to that system can still access their files in the companion system's data base via the MPB. For example, in Figure 1-5, if the disk drive attached to System 1 develops a mechanical problem, the files in that system are not irretrievably lost or inaccessible. The users whose VDTs are attached to System 1's computer can still access their files in the duplicate data base on System 2 over the MPB.

As System Manager, you must be aware of the hardware you are using. More important, however, for everyday use, is your knowledge of the interactions possible between the hardware and the programs that govern it.

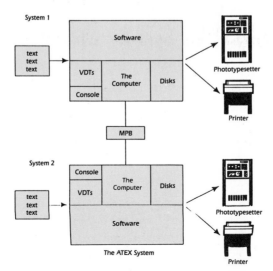

Figure 1-5   Sample ATEX System Configuration

ence analysis to determine their purpose in reading the document and identify the questions they expect to have answered. At this stage, you should ask several questions:

- Why do readers want or need the information?
- Are readers interested in a general overview or a detailed description?
- Do they need information in order to understand more detailed discussion that follows?
- Do they want to make a decision about purchase?
- What details do the readers need: Dimensions? Materials? Assembly? Function? Capabilities? Benefits?

Giving insufficient information leave readers with unanswered questions, but be equally wary of including unnecessary information; you may obscure facts you want to convey. For example, the person who uses a camera for family snapshots does not need (or want) the same information about the focusing screen as a professional photographer who needs interchangeable screens. The casual user wants a simple description that answers basic questions:

- What is a focusing screen?
- Where is it located on the camera?

Such information can be provided in a few sentences accompanied by a simple line drawing. Details about the focusing screen would be unnecessary, perhaps confusing or annoying, and possibly even intimidating to the casual user. Yet the professional photographer wants a detailed description to answer specific questions:

- What are the different types of focusing screens?
- What distinguishes each separate focusing screen?
- What are the specifications of a particular focusing screen?

One or more paragraphs and drawings of the different focusing screens would be necessary.

As you prepare a technical description, select information that responds to the audience's probable questions. The more removed the reader is from actually using the information in the description, the more general it can be. For example, the excerpt from the *Voyager Bulletin* is easy to read despite the inclusion of specific data; the readers of this status update report are generally interested nonexperts, not astrophysicists or aerospace engineers.

Precisely identifying the audience also helps you decide on such crucial aspects of the description as partition, diction, visuals, and format.

Partition

Before you can describe something, you must partition it—separate it into parts or components—because the description emphasizes the physical characteristics of each part. But people's concept of *part* differs greatly. For instance, should the Jovian moon Io be partitioned according to elements, geologic structures, or electromagnetic fields? Or consider the group of mechanical engineers asked to specify the number of parts in a simple house key. The answers ranged from 1 to 27, with the mode (the number occurring most frequently) being 5. Their answers differed because they did not define part in the same way.

Components of an object, mechanism, or system can usually be separated into structural parts and functional parts. Structural parts comprise the physical aspects of the device, without regard to purpose. For example, a simple house key is made of a single piece of metal. Functional parts perform clearly defined tasks in the operation of the device. Although the key has a single structural part, it has multiple functional parts. Another example concerns the hull of a sailboat, which may be molded from a uniform shell of fiberglass, and thus be considered a single structural part; however, parts of this single-unit hull include the transom and keel, which serve different functions.

An organism, whether decathlon athlete or experimental variety of corn, can be partitioned in a number of standard ways: by cellular composition, by body fluids such as blood, by structures such as muscles in animals or stems in complex plants, or by functions such as reproduction and respiration.

Substances also have components. Sometimes they're clearly identifiable components, such as those in granola; at other times they're identifiable only through analysis, as with soil, horse feed, blood, or ocean water. Every substance can be taken back to its elemental components, but this is seldom necessary except in detailed chemical investigations.

Locations can also be partitioned, often in several different but equally correct ways. For example, the site of a new building could be partitioned by typography displaying elevation or ground cover, by geologic cross section showing layers of soil, sand, gravel, and rock, or by dimensions and legal boundaries.

Applying your knowledge about the audience along with the partitioned information can help you decide whether one version of partition is more appropriate than another. Thinking about the audience also helps you decide whether you need to describe all the parts or only some of them.

Diction

The diction of a technical description should be precise, so that the information is verifiable and not open to interpretation. You can achieve this precision by choosing specific, concrete, and accurate words.

Whether a writer selects general or specific terms again depends on the needs of the audience. Generally, the greater the technical expertise of the readers, the more detail you will want to include in a description. Nonexperts need accurate information, but they do not require extraordinary detail. For example, a general description of a lawnmower might appear in an advertising flyer from a chain store. A more detailed description would be part of the specifications listed in a wholesale catalog. Figure 10.2 presents two lawnmower descriptions, which illustrate how characteristics can be described using general or specific diction, depending on audience needs. (*Note:* The initial discussion of abstract versus specific terms appears in Chapter 5.)

To ensure precision, a writer must use words that accurately differentiate two- and three-dimensional objects. How often have you heard someone mistakenly refer to a ball as round instead of spherical? The following list contains the geometric shapes most commonly misnamed:

- sphere/circle
- cube/square
- cone/pyramid/triangle

Careless diction is not only inaccurate, it also causes confusion. For example, if a three-dimensional object is described as triangular, how will the reader know if the solid form is really a cone or a pyramid? Figure 10.3 reviews the terminology of geometric shapes. Accurately applying the terms for these figures, solids, and surfaces will improve your descriptions.

Visuals

Precise visuals are as important in effective technical descriptions as precise diction. Appropriate visuals enable the reader to form a mental image of the subject being described. Different types of visuals illustrate the exterior, the interior, and individual components.

The introduction of a technical description often contains a *photograph* or a *realistic drawing* that gives the reader a visual overview of the external features. Similarly, *topographic* and *contour maps* show the surface features of geographic locations.

Figure 10.2 Gaining Precision in Technical Description

General, *Abstract Terms*		*Specific,* *Concrete Terms*
dependable mower	(specify brand)	Briggs and Stratton
powerful	(specify amount)	4 cycle, 3½ HP
self-propelled	(specify type)	rear-wheel belt to chain drive
wide blade	(specify size)	21″
adjustable height	(specify variation)	7 positions, 1–3″
powerful, dependable, self-propelled mower with wide blade adjustable to cut different heights		Briggs and Stratton mower with 4-cycle, 3½ HP engine; self-propelled by rear-wheel belt to chain drive; 21″ blade; 7 cutting heights from 1″–3″

A common way to present the assembled interior components is with a *phantom view,* a drawing that depicts the exterior surface as transparent so the inside structure can be viewed. Another way to display the parts and their relation to the whole is by a base drawing with attached transparent *overlays* that show additional parts. *Schematics* and *wiring diagrams* are also useful for presenting an overall view of interior components and structure. In geographic descriptions, *cross-section maps* show the depth and location of each layer.

The clearest way to present the individual parts in relation to the whole is with an *exploded view* that separates all the components and displays them in the proper sequence and relationship for assembly. Exploded views are the visual equivalent of partition in the text of a technical description. *Blue prints* also show the structure of the individual components. Another way to depict part of the interior is a *cutaway view* that slices a section out so that the reader can see a full or partial cross-section. Components can also be isolated and presented in individual photographs or drawings.

In organizing a typical technical description of a mechanism, your introductory section could contain a drawing that shows the exterior features, perhaps followed by an exploded view. In the rest of the description, you could use phantom or cutaway views to show the location of each part, and

Figure 10.3   Geometric Shapes

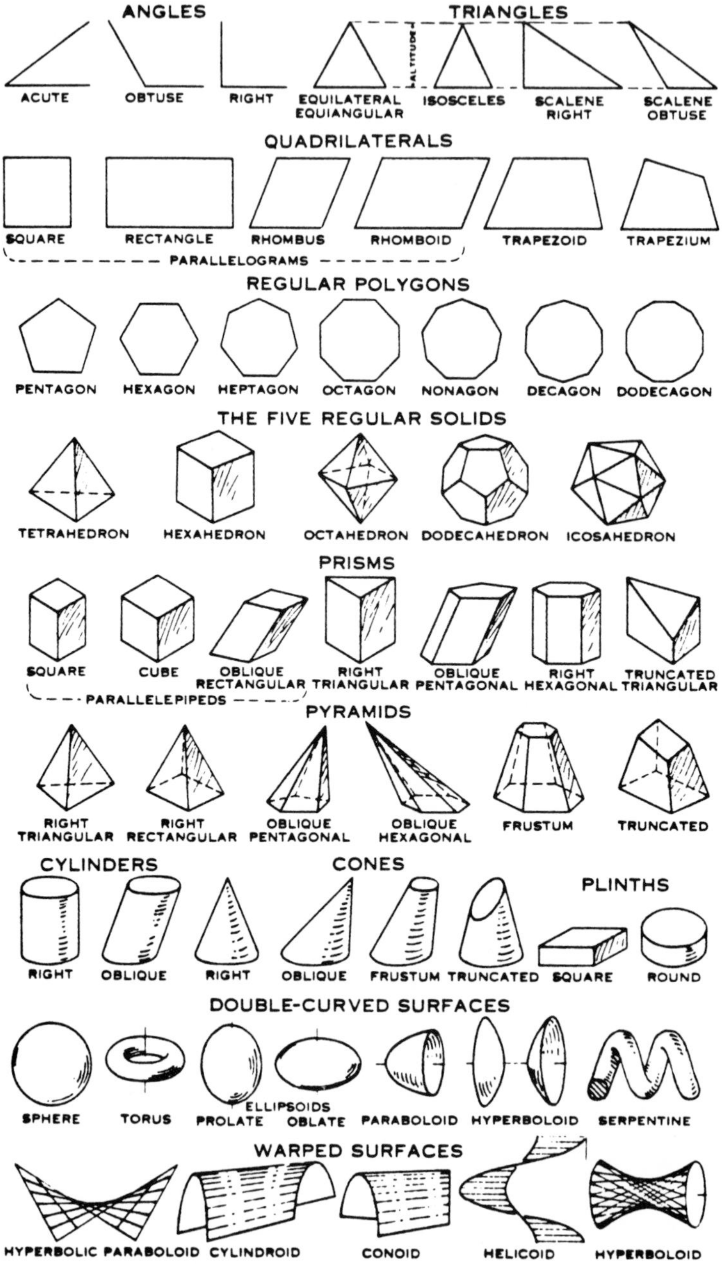

Source: Thomas E. French and Charles J. Vierck, *Graphic Science and Design* (New York: McGraw-Hill, 1970), p. 79. Reprinted with permission of McGraw-Hill Book Company.

Visuals Frequently Used in Technical Description

Figure 10.4

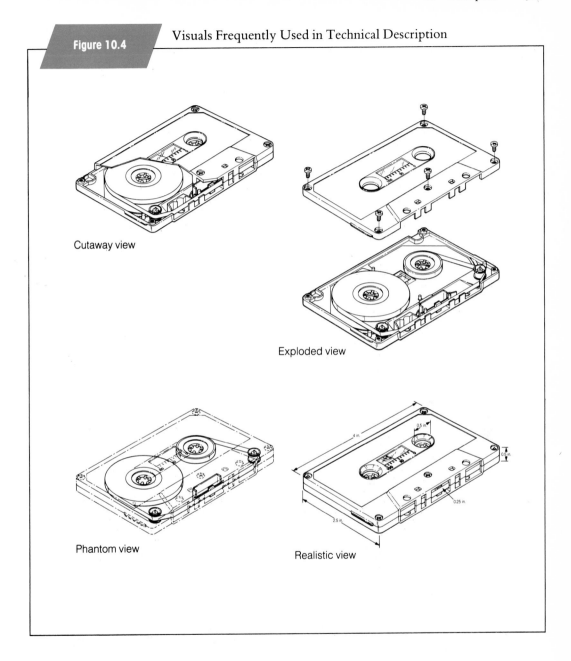

Cutaway view

Exploded view

Phantom view

Realistic view

then an enlarged drawing of the details of the individual part, placed adjacent to the text that describes it. All the visuals should be labeled and titled and referred to in the text. Dimensions are better presented in visuals so the text is not cluttered or difficult to read. Figure 10.4 shows the differences between various visuals most frequently used in technical descriptions.

Organization

When preparing a technical description, you have to make decisions about length, organization, and number and type of details.

The length of a technical description depends on the description's purpose. Often, a technical description is merely a few sentences or a paragraph incorporated into a larger document. Less frequently, a description requires a multi-paragraph document to detail information about individual parts and subparts.

A technical description organizes information in conventional patterns. It almost always uses spatial order to give the reader the clearest view of appearance and structure. Occasionally, a technical description may be organized in chronological order, describing the components in order of assembly, or it may use priority order, describing the components in order of importance. Figure 10.5 outlines the sequence of information in a detailed technical description.

Technical descriptions should have a title if they are printed as a separate document and a section heading if they are incorporated into one section of another document.

The introductory section usually begins with a definition suitable for the intended audience. The definition can include or be followed by a statement of the purpose or function of the document, as in this example.

Example   As the new owner of a wood-burning stove, you should be familiar with its structure and components. This information will help you safely maintain your stove as a supplemental source of home heat.

The introductory material presents an abbreviated version of the description. It includes characteristics of the whole: overall shape and major dimensions, primary color and texture, and any distinctive aspects. A photograph or realistic drawing often supplements this overall description. The final part of the introductory section partitions the whole into its major parts, in the order they will be described. This partition can be illustrated with an exploded or cutaway view.

To appeal to a particular audience, a writer may incorporate into the introductory material elements that increase reader interest and background knowledge but do not add substantively to the technical content. Keep in mind that expert readers are usually annoyed by the inclusion of what they consider extraneous information. However, if you are writing for a general or nonexpert audience, consider some of these elements that may add interest or appeal to the introductory section:

- Background information—What is the history? What are current developments?

Figure 10.5 Technical Description Format

TITLE

1.0 Introduction
   1.1 Definition
   1.2 Purpose
   1.3 Characteristics of the whole
   1.4 Visual
   1.5 Partition

2.0 Part-by-part description arranged in order of assembly, location, or importance
   2.1 Part one
      2.1.1 Definition
      2.1.2 Purpose
      2.1.3 General appearance
      2.1.4 Characteristics
      2.1.5 Visual
         2.1.5.1 General shape and dimensions
         2.1.5.2 Material
         2.1.5.3 Material characteristics
            (color, flammability, optical properties, solubility, density, conductivity, magnetism, and so on)
         2.1.5.4 Surface treatment, texture
         2.1.5.5 Weight
         2.1.5.6 Method of manufacture
         2.1.5.7 Subparts of part one
      2.1.6 Attachment to other parts
   2.2 Part two

      and so on

3.0 Conclusion
   3.1 How the parts fit together
   3.2 How the parts function together

- Division or classification—Where does the object fit in relation to similar ones?

- Qualitative distinctions—What separates it from similar objects?

The body of a technical description involves a part-by-part description arranged in order of location, assembly, or importance. Each section of the body follows the same format. Initially, the part, and sometimes its purpose, is defined. Then a description of the general appearance of the part, including shape, major dimensions, and material, follows, often accompanied by a visual presenting detailed dimensions. Specifics are added according to the needs of the audience. For example, an architect designing a passive solar house would want information about surface treatments, optical and insulating properties, and weights of specially treated glass. An interior designer would be more concerned with color and texture. Both would be interested in subparts and methods of attachment to other parts. The outline in Figure 10.5 identifies additional characteristics that are relevant for some audiences.

The conclusion explains how the parts fit and function together. Often a technical description does not have a concluding section, but simply ends when the last part has been fully described. Just as you can stimulate reader interest in the introduction, you can also create a more lively conclusion by including some of these elements:

- Applications—How is it used?
- Anecdotes or brief narratives—Who uses it?
- Advantages/Disadvantages—What are the benefits and/or problems?

Inquiries and Applications

Discussion Questions

1. Discuss ways you believe an operator's knowledge of equipment structure or function might influence ability to operate the equipment.
2. Choose an object in the classroom or an object familiar to all members of the class. Propose several ways in which it could be partitioned; identify your audience for each version.
3. Compile a list of words to avoid in descriptions, either words that project a negative image or words with vague or even inaccurate meanings (a *fat* patient, a *complicated* step, a *sharp* angle, a *cheap* replacement part, a *hard* surface).
4. Several kinds of visuals are described in this chapter (and also in Chapter 6). Which do you feel would be most appropriate to incorporate into a description of each of the following items?
   a. a human leg
   b. an apple—from bud to harvest
   c. a crankshaft
   d. a checkwriter
   e. a septic tank and leach field
   f. a silicon chip
   g. a ribbon carrier (or ribbon vibrator) on a typewriter

h. a reclining chair or geriatric chair
i. sprocket gears (as on a bicycle)
j. Mechineck (a toy creature whose neck extends and head turns when a lever in back is pressed)
k. an espresso coffee maker
l. a proposed condominium complex

In-Class Exercises

1. Identify the structural and functional parts of the following items:

baseball	pocket lighter	ballpoint pen	AA battery	light bulb
hand saw	comb	field daisy	scissors	flashlight

2. You work for a company that manufactures modular houses and sells directly to individual customers. Several publications are being prepared, and you have been assigned responsibility for the partitioning of the descriptions. How would you partition the descriptions of the modular houses for these audiences:
   a. lumber wholesaler
   b. government agency from which you want information about fuel-efficient construction methods
   c. prospective home owner
   d. municipal wiring and/or plumbing inspector
   e. architect
   f. production line manager

3. Bring to class examples of technical descriptions. Analyze them, considering the following points:

   ■ For what audience is each intended?

   ■ Has the writer accurately analyzed the audience?

   ■ Are the visuals appropriate and helpful?

   ■ Are additional visuals needed?

   ■ Does the format make the description easy to read?

4. Analyze and evaluate the description in this chapter of the ATEX system in terms of audience, partitioning, visuals, and organization.

Assignments

1. Write a technical description, following the format outlined in Figure 10.5. Modify the format so that it is appropriate for the audience and purpose of the description.

   Select an object, substance, mechanism, system, organism, or location from the following lists, or choose another subject that relates to your field:

Objects

drill bit	polarizing filter
shotgun shells	magnet
contact lenses	photographic film
mallet	golf club
candle	baseball
magnetic tape	box-end wrench
computer chip	daisy wheel

Substances

acetylene	plant fertilizer
baking powder	cough medicine
baby food	cleaning fluid
blood sample	effluent
measles vaccine	wine
yogurt	diesel fuel

hypoallergenic makeup
photographic developer and fixer
nonprescription cold medicine

Mechanisms

micrometer	safety pin
telephone	camera lens
wood lathe	combination lock
computer keyboard	clothes pin
solenoid valve	solar panel
generator	adjustable wrench
cider press	carburetor
pool filter	thermostat
spinning reel	smoke alarm
vaporizer	semicircular canals
spinning wheel	tape cassette
telescope	syringe
refrigerator	seat belt
gas chromatograph	transit

Systems

respiratory system   H/AC system
photovoltaic system   irrigation system
braking system   photocopying machine
electronic auto inspection system
scrubbing system (for removing contaminants)
planetary system

Organisms

seals   yeast
humans   tape worms
termites   mosquitoes
dolphins   fox gloves
algae   pumas
chickens   protozoa

Locations

a harbor mooring
geologic cross section of site for a well
R and D section of a plant
sections of forest marked for logging
layout for a vegetable or flower garden
geologic fault noted for seismic activity
archaeological excavation

2. Case Situation: Pat Dussault, manager of technical publications for Bio-Tech, Inc., has just come back from a seminar in which she heard about the development of a word processing system with typesetting capabilities. Her company manufactures prosthetic devices controlled by the user by means of a miniature computer. Currently, the company brochures, specifications, and manuals are prepared by a small staff of writers and artists and are typed in the company's word processing center. The material is then sent to an outside printer to be typeset and printed. This process is time consuming and expensive. Pat is sure that a system like the one she's just learned about could save time and money.

   The idea of a word processor that typesets material intrigues her, but she has lots of questions. What *is* this new system? Is it more a word processor or more a typesetter? Would it fit in the cramped publications area? What are the components of the system? How durable and reliable is it? What are its capabilities? She calls the manufacturer and asks them to send an information package describing the system. Pat depends on the accuracy of the description in the marketing material to answer her preliminary questions.

   After Pat reads the information sent by the manufacturing company, she decides the equipment is precisely what her department needs. However, because of the expense involved, she needs the approval of the division manager. Courtesy also requires that she inform the office manager and director of graphic design about the potential purchase of equipment After investigating such equipment, write three different mechanisms descriptions that she would include in her memo to each of these three people.

- Bob Cutcliffe, division manager—BS (biomedical engineering)
  MBA (finance)
  7 years professional experience
  18 months with Bio-Tech

- Kristin Marcks, office manager—AS (business management)
  15 years professional experience
  4 years with Bio-Tech

- Emily Hammond, director of graphic design—MA (art history)
  MFA (graphic design)
  10 years professional experience
  5 years with Bio-Tech

3. You have the responsibility of hiring a person whose major task will be writing descriptions of your company's products. List the questions you would ask during the interview and the qualifications, education, and experience you hope to find in an applicant.

   After completing the assignment, ask yourself: Would you hire yourself? What are your qualifications for such a job? What areas do you need to strengthen?

11 Process Explanations

PROCESSES PLAY an important role in technical communication—providing information about the sequence of steps in any action, from blood donation to operation of a jet engine. Generally, process explanations (also called process descriptions) provide an overview or background, regardless of the reader's specific purpose(s).

Because some managers read process explanations to help them make purchasing decisions, marketing brochures frequently contain such explanations. Supervisors often read process explanations, like those in many manuals, to gain an understanding of a process they're responsible for but don't actually do. Technicians and operators are usually encouraged to read a process explanation before following the directions to actually conduct a process. General readers find that process explanations satisfy their curiosity about many things—how wine is made, how hurricanes are tracked, how oil wells are drilled.

Defining Processes

Processes have distinctive characteristics, which are summarized in Figure 11.1. The most obvious characteristic is that processes explain sequential actions in chronological order. They are written in the indicative mood, a verb

Figure 11.1	Characteristics of Processes

DEFINITION	explanation of the sequential order of an action
SUBJECT	any action, natural or with human involvement
PURPOSE	to provide a general overview of an action
AUDIENCE	person who wants to know about the action
FOCUS/ FORMAT	explanation of the process; paragraphs often include theory or principle of operation
ORGANIZATION	chronological
AMOUNT OF DETAIL	includes general characteristics and a few selected details; often includes applications as well as discussions and explanations
VERB MOOD AND VOICE	indicative mood; usually more effective in active voice; also uses passive voice if appropriate
Example:	Routine maintenance involves changing the filter when it's dirty and making sure the heat exchanger and smoke pipe are clear of accumulated creosote.

form that makes statements about the operator or the action. Processes are usually more effective in the active voice, but they can switch to passive voice for variety or specific emphasis.

The most important characteristics involve audience and purpose. Audiences for processes include general readers, potential customers, supervisors or managers, and first-time or novice users. Subject matter ranges from natural or autonomic processes to industrial or business tasks and human actions.

Process explanations contain enough details to provide a complete understanding of an action, but not enough to enable a reader to complete the action. The following example of one step in mechanical inspection illustrates the difference between a process explanation and directions. The process explanation identifies the general nature of the task:

> A mechanical inspector's initial task is to assure that the labels on the packages are correct.

In contrast, this segment of the directions for the task is very specific:

Example   Assure that all the marking is typewritten and that the label contains all of the following information:

a. customer contract number
b. contract annex and line item
c. part number
d. nomenclature
e. NSN (national stock number)
f. quantity
g. date packaged
h. serial number (if applicable)

Process explanations are valuable precisely because they don't focus on the
details required to complete a task; rather, they introduce the process.

Using Process Explanations

Process explanations inform readers about a sequence of actions in a variety
of categories that have different degrees of human involvement:

- actions that are natural or autonomic (spontaneous)
- actions that involve a person but focus on a task
- actions that actively involve and focus on a person

Figure 11.2 identifies some specific actions within each category. These categories are not absolute; rather, they offer a way of thinking about the subject
when you are planning a process explanation.

Process explanations do not always require a verbal presentation. A primarily visual presentation in Figure 11.3 explains how acid rain is formed.
Although the term *acid rain* is familiar to most people, the complex natural
process by which it is formed is not. Figure 11.3 simplifies the process with a
drawing that includes the major elements of the cycle of acid rain formation.
Although based on detailed technical information, the figure provides a simple and appealing explanation appropriate for its intended audience—readers
of local daily newspapers.

While general readers most frequently appreciate a simple, uncluttered
process explanation, students need more detailed information because they
are expected to understand the reasons behind a sequence of actions. The
illustrated summary of a natural process in Figure 11.4 is given to students in
a seminar about bog formation; the article contains terminology, definitions,
and explanations that make the material inappropriate for a general reader.

Figure 11.2   Different Types of Processes

	Natural or Autonomic Focus	**Task Focus**	**Human Focus**
CHARACTERISTICS	no human involvement or intervention	minimal human involvement or intervention	major human involvement
APPLICATIONS	physical actions biological actions meteorological actions chemical actions	automated tasks manufacturing shipping mechanical operations	personnel actions creative tasks high-skill tasks hand assembly
EXAMPLES	mitosis solar flares fetal development decomposition digestion rusting	sludge treatment voice-activated locks mail sorting brewing beer CNC machine operation film development	embalming a body wiring a computer chip hiring an employee cutting a gem stone focusing a camera diagnosing a patient

Figure 11.3

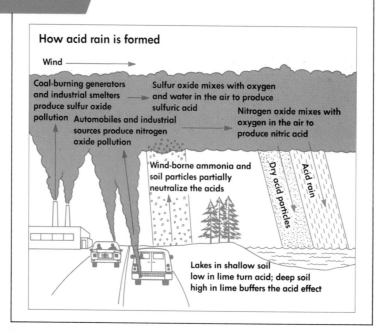

Source: "How Acid Rain is Formed," *Lowell Sun.*

Figure 11.4

BOG DEVELOPMENT

The characteristic bog develops over several thousand years in a relatively deep glacial depression, a "kettle," which is either poorly drained or has no outlet. Water is gained through precipitation alone and is lost by evapotranspiration. As flow through the pond in the depression is sluggish or nonexistent, there is no source for minerals, and the bog water is deficient in nearly all major plant and animal nutrients, especially nitrogen. Certain plants, particularly *Sphagnum* moss, may dominate the lower levels of vegetation, crowding out less well-adapted species. The *Sphagnum* also withdraws nutrients from the water, replacing them with acids. Bog water is, thus, acidic—especially beneath the *Sphagnum*-dominated zones.

Bog succession begins as horizontal growth over the surface of the water, since the bottom is generally too deep near the shore to allow plants to root as in a typical marsh or swamp. This lateral growth forms a dense mat of intertwining stems that supports all further growth. This mat characteristically grows out over the water, closing in on the pond center from all sides and eventually covering all open water. As there is still water beneath the mat, the mat is essentially floating; though it will generally support the weight of a person, the person gets the feeling that the earth is trembling. From this phenomena stems the term "quaking bog."

Growth proceeds upon the mat as vegetation builds up vertically, the accumulating mass forcing underlying vegetation downwards and below the static water level. This plant matter decays slowly, if at all, because the acidity of the water coupled with its coldness (it is, after all, well insulated from the warmer air above) inhibits bacterial action that causes decomposition. Thus, the basin becomes filled with partially decayed vegetation, and the mat eventually supports trees, which grow first over the landward, more "grounded" parts of the bog. Trees will advance out over the mat as the depression becomes filled, ultimately closing over the original open bog altogether. At this stage, the old bog may be difficult to recognize, though for some time to come, the acidity of the soil dictates which plants may survive there and which may not. The accompanying figure shows the cross section of a typical bog.

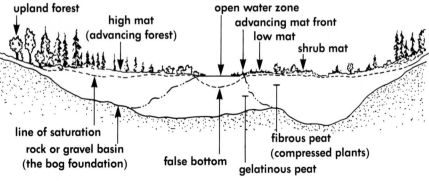

Figure 1 Cross Section of a Typical Bog

Source: Frederick M. Oltsch, "Bog Development" (Becket, MA, 1984).

The writer of the article makes a number of assumptions about the reader's background knowledge but still adheres to the format of an effective process explanation. The article begins with a broad definition of a bog before summarizing the sequence of its development; however, some technical terms are not defined. The writer uses chronology to explain the development but also orients the reader with precise spatial references.

Some actions are far easier to delineate than bog development. For instance, Figure 11.5 presents a process explanation with a human focus, written for apprentice carpenters. This explanation specifies the audience, identifies the purpose of saw sharpening, and lists the major steps. Each succeeding section of the explanation defines the individual step and discusses how and why it is done. The article uses the passive voice to focus attention on the action of saw sharpening itself, not on the carpenter's role. The explanation does *not* give sufficient detail for apprentice carpenters to sharpen their own saws. Instead, it provides a general overview.

Figure 11.6 is a development notice written primarily for professionals; it is a technical marketing document that presents information about new technology. Only about 10 percent of the text in this notice explains the sequence of actions in the new technique; the process explanation doesn't even appear until the second page. The majority of the text focuses on a task—applications and benefits of the new technique—with twice as much space devoted to the simplified figure illustrating the technique as to verbal process explanation. Considering the development notice's purpose and audience, the focus is understandable.

Many manuals incorporate process explanations, which are particularly important as part of the documentation accompanying new equipment that may be unfamiliar to either the user or manager. Manuals often place explanations of the process in an introductory section, sometimes incorporating background theory along with the explanation.

Figure 11.7 is from the *Systems Manager's Reference Manual* for the ATEX text procesing system. This excerpt from the first two pages of the manual presents no theory; instead, the pages review the editorial and production processes for system managers and then identify the ways the ATEX system changes these processes.

Preparing Processes

In preparing a process explanation you need to consider the audience and purpose, identify the steps in the process, select or design visuals, refine diction, and organize information.

Figure 11.5

SAW SHARPENING

Properly sharpened hand saws are a necessity for any professional carpenter interested in safe, accurate, and efficient work. Because sharpening saws by hand is tedious and eye-straining, most construction companies provide a saw sharpening service for their workers. Nevertheless, a professional carpenter should know the five basic operations involved in sharpening a saw: jointing, shaping, setting, filing, and dressing.

JOINTING

Firmly secured in a saw vise or clamp (see Figure 1), the saw is jointed with a flat file. The file is passed back and forth lengthwise over the cutting edge until all the teeth make contact with the file. Jointing assures that all the teeth are the same height. This step is necessary whenever the saw has any low or broken teeth. Contrary to the usual printed information about jointing, professional carpenters prefer not to have their saws jointed straight from heel to toe, but rather to have the saws jointed with a slight convex bow, allotting the middle teeth (which get more use) a slightly greater height.

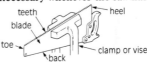

Figure 1 Saw Secured in Clamp

SHAPING

After the saw is jointed, the tips of some teeth will be blunt and wide. These teeth must be shaped back to a sharp formation, as shown in Figure 2. A triangular handsaw-file is applied, perpendicular to the saw blade at both sides of the blunt teeth. The front of each tooth is angled from 8 to 15 degrees, depending on the type of blade (cross-cut or rip), and the back of the tooth is shaped at from 45 to 52 degrees from vertical.

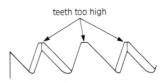

Figure 2 Shaping Saw Teeth

SETTING

After the saw blade is jointed and the teeth are shaped, each tooth must be "set" with a tool called a "saw set." Alternating teeth are punched or stamped slightly out of line in opposite directions to make a cut in the wood that is wider than the blade and to prevent the saw from binding in the wood. Care must be taken to make sure that all teeth are set to the same degree to assure that no tooth gets more pressure than the others.

FILING

The actual sharpening of the cutting edge of each tooth is done with the saw file applied at 65 degrees from the side of the blade. During filing, the square edges of the teeth that were produced in the shaping operation are honed to sharper cutting edges. By convention, the teeth set in one direction are sharpened first, from toe to heel; then the saw is reversed in the vise, and the teeth in the opposite direction are sharpened from heel to toe as illustrated in Figure 3.

Figure 3 Sharpening the Teeth

DRESSING

Dressing is a step that can be eliminated if, after sharpening, no burrs exist on either side of the blade. The burrs detected by manual inspection are removed or "dressed" by laying the saw on a flat surface and gently passing an oilstone or flat file over both sides of the cutting edge.

Source: Elizabeth Howard "Saw Sharpening" (Technical Writing EN–C–302–B, Merrimack College, 1981).

Figure 11.6

REMOVAL OF CO₂ FROM HYDROCARBON STREAMS

Introduction

Helix Processing Systems is developing a new, low temperature process for separating carbon dioxide (CO_2) from streams containing methane. This process, called the Ryan/Holmes process, produces a methane sales gas stream at up to 600 psia, a dry liquid or gaseous carbon dioxide stream at up to 500 psia and a liquefied hydrocarbon stream containing ethane and other higher hydrocarbons that were present in the feed. In addition, it removes H_2S from the methane sales gas, has low fuel/energy requirements, and is economically attractive when compared with sorption methods for removing CO_2.

Major Process Applications

The Ryan/Holmes process can be used on hydrocarbon streams containing up to 90% CO_2 in order to produce a carbon dioxide product gas in addition to a methane sales gas, thereby increasing the profitability of producing gas fields (see Tables 1 and 2). Currently, when natural gas streams are processed for the production of methane sales gas and natural gas liquids (NGL), a water-saturated CO_2 byproduct stream is produced at atmospheric pressure and is vented. With the Ryan/Holmes Process, a dry pressurized CO_2 stream can be produced as either a gas or liquid. This carbon dioxide can be either sold or used as an injection fluid for an enhanced oil recovery project, thus increasing the profitability of treating CO_2-containing natural gas streams.

Due to the flexibility which was designed into this process, the Ryan/Holmes Process is also uniquely suitable for treating "breakthrough" CO_2 in enhanced oil recovery floods. When CO_2 is injected into an oil field during an enhanced oil recovery flood, it will eventually be produced with casinghead gas. This results in altered gas compositions sufficient to jeopardize methane and NGL sales.

Process Description

The Ryan/Holmes Process is a proprietary, low temperature distillation which is carried out in two steps (see Figure 1). The first step produces a sales gas stream at up to 600 psia which meets pipeline CO_2 specifications and a bottoms stream containing virtually all the CO_2, C_2^+ and H_2S. The freezing problem generally associated with low temperature CO_2 processing is fully controlled and eliminated.

The bottoms stream from the first step is further processed in the second step to yield a liquid or gaseous CO_2 stream at up to 500 psia and a liquefied C_2^+ stream. The H_2S can appear in either the CO_2 or C_2^+ streams, depending on client specifications. With the Ryan/Holmes method of resolving the CO_2-ethane azeotrope, ethane is recovered in the NGL stream.

The flexibility of the Ryan/Holmes process provides several major benefits:

1. *The composition of product streams can be varied . . . in order to meet a client's specifications.*
2. *Changing feed volume and composition can be accommodated with relative ease while maintaining product specifications.*
3. *Changes in product specifications over time can be accommodated.*

Table 1. Major Process Benefits

- Produces CH_4 at up to 600 psia.
- CH_4 product contains less than 1% CO_2.
- Produces dry, liquid or gaseous CO_2 at up to 500 psia.
- Produces liquefied C_2^+.
- Low fuel/energy requirements.
- Requires no expensive chemicals.

Table 2. Major Process Applications

- Conditioning/processing for natural gas streams containing up to 90% CO_2.
- Production of CO_2 for sale or use in enhanced oil recovery CO_2 floods.
- Processing "breakthrough" CO_2 in an enhanced oil recovery flood.
- NGL recovery for natural gas streams containing up to 90% CO_2.

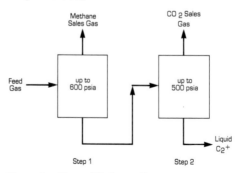

Figure 1   Ryan/Holmes Process

Source: "Removal of CO₂ from Hydrocarbon Streams," Development Notice (Westboro, MA: Koch Process Systems, 1980), 1–2. Reprinted with permission of Koch Process Systems, Inc.

Figure 11.7

INTRODUCTION

The publishing industry has as many facets as the number of companies that comprise it. Every firm that is in the business of processing and producing printed pages has a unique system for handling the flow of copy through its facilities. Regardless of the individual variations, however, producing a document, whether it is a newspaper story, a magazine article, a technical manual, or a law brief, involves repeated refinement of the text before it is ready. Text may be written, rewritten, edited, re-edited, cross-edited, reviewed, analyzed, and discussed many times before it is ready to be typeset. And once it's typeset, it may be proofread and edited again before it is finally printed. In Figure 1-1, all this is represented within the box labeled "The Editorial Process."

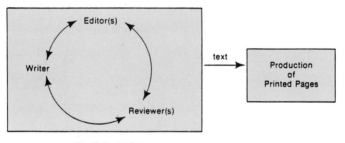

The Editorial Process

Figure1-1   Copy Flow

Starting at the left, drafts of stories/articles/documents are written. Sometimes this means that the author writes and rewrites his/her own material several times before submitting it. When the author is ready, he/she usually passes the resulting text on to one or more editors. Then, when the editor is done, the text may go back to the writer for further revisions, or to reviewers or advisors for their opinions, or straight into the production phase. In any case, each stage of the editorial process results in changes and additions to the original text; often this means that the text must be retyped many times in order to produce legible copy for the next phase. The ATEX system facilitates and expedites this process and makes everyone's job easier.

The ATEX system consists of a unique combination of specific hardware and software products that provide its users with full electronic text processing capabilities. The goal of the ATEX system is the same as that of a non-electronic system, but ATEX allows the editorial and production processes to function faster and more efficiently. The emphasis here is on *processing*; the ATEX system accepts letters, numbers, words, and sentences from many different sources simultaneously and *stores* them for easy, repeated access. This means that text can be entered into the system once and manipulated any number of times. Thus, once a writer's story is in the system, he/she can modify it as often as desired; when finished,

Figure 11.7   *Continued*

the text can be passed *electronically* to his/her editor. The editor, in turn, may use a video display terminal (VDT) to read and modify/correct the text, then use the system to send it either back to the writer for further work, or on to the reviewers or analysts (who, in turn, can manipulate the text and return it electronically to the editor). When the text is ready, the ATEX system allows people in either the editorial or production phases to format it as desired and send it out to a device (either a phototypesetter or printing terminal) that produces printed pages or galleys. Figure 1-2 shows the general flow of text through the system.

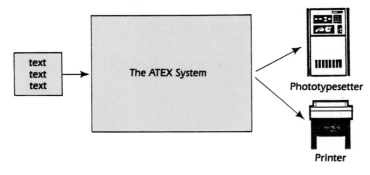

Figure 1-2   Copy Flow with an ATEX System

Source: ATEX, Inc., *System Manager's Reference Manual* (Bedford, MA: ATEX, 1981), I-1-1–I-1-2. Reprinted with permission of ATEX.

Audience and Purpose

As with so many phases of technical writing, identifying your audience and its purpose for reading a document helps you to prepare a process explanation. Most readers, including professionals, are more interested in an explanation of an action than the precise details necessary to actually complete that action. Readers who wish to complete a process themselves should not depend on a process explanation; instead, they need procedures or directions. (See Chapter 13.)

Your choice of visuals and diction is also affected by the audience. The less expertise the audience has in the subject, the simpler you should make the visuals and the text.

Identification of Steps

An essential part of preparing process explanations involves listing the steps of the action. If the time needed for each step or the time between steps is important, it too should be recorded. The sequence of steps forms the basis for the process explanation and also aids in designing visuals.

For example, a common procedure in a hospital pediatrics unit is setting up a croup tent. Both parents and young patients demonstrate anxiety about the tent, but parents seem to calm down (and thus the children relax) after they read an explanation about what the croup tent does, how it is set up, and how it operates. The brief outline in the following example identifies the basic steps the writer would use to prepare a process explanation.

Example
1. Defining a croup tent
2. Setting up a croup tent
   a. Metal frame attached to crib
   b. Canopy placed over the frame
   c. Water bottle filled and attached to frame
   d. Ice placed in chamber
   e. Valve inserted and hoses attached
3. Operating a croup tent
   a. Oxygen flow turned on to prescribed level
   b. Oxygen forced through water
   c. Oxygen enters tubing and passes through ice
   d. Moist, cooled oxygen enters tent

This outline gives the writer the basic structure for a clear process explanation.

Visuals

You can choose from several different visuals to illustrate the overall sequence. Most common are *flow charts* that give a visual overview, in the same way the introductory section of the text defines the action and identifies the major steps. The development notice in Figure 11.6 about removal of CO_2 from hydrocarbon streams employs a flow chart tracing the distillation to summarize the actions for potential customers. Other visuals that provide an overview of the entire sequence are *time lines* and *schedules*.

Step-by-step changes can be effectively illustrated in a variety of ways: *time-lapse photographs, sequential drawings, drawings with overlays of changes*, and *drawings showing the final product.* Such visuals are useful because they show the changes discussed in the text or demonstrate how the step is performed. Incorporated into the article for apprentice carpenters in Figure 11.5 are *drawings showing major steps* in the process of sharpening a saw. The figure of the bog accompanying the article for seminar students in Figure 11.4 uses a *single drawing showing each element in a process.*

Diction

Your choices of active or passive voice, verb mood, and person are all influenced by the audience for and purpose of the process.

Active or Passive Voice. Selection of active or passive voice depends on the subject of the process, the purpose and focus, and the audience. Active voice emphasizes the *doer* of the action and de-emphasizes the receiver. Such emphasis is appropriate when the reader is more interested in the doer or in the action itself than in the receiver or result of the action. For instance, the following paragraphs contain the same content. In the first example, the active voice stresses the role of the nurse because the paragraph is written for practicing nurses.

Active Voice The neonatal nurse can decrease the chances that a newborn will suffer from cold stress by following several standard procedures. The nurse should monitor the baby's temperature regularly and should not bathe the baby until the temperature is stabilized. A careful nurse coordinates all medical procedures that expose the baby to cool air and will be certain to remove all wet bedclothes and diapers that cool the skin by evaporation.

The use of passive voice emphasizes the receiver of the action and de-emphasizes the doer, especially when the receiver or the action itself is more important to the reader. In the following paragraph, the use of the passive voice emphasizes the baby; here, new parents would be an appropriate audience.

Passive Voice A newborn will not suffer from cold stress if the neonatal nurse follows several standard procedures. The baby's temperature should be monitored regularly. The baby should not be bathed until the temperature is stabilized. A baby should not be exposed to cool air while undergoing medical procedures and should not be left with wet bedclothes or diapers that cool the skin by evaporation.

	Figure 11.8	Active or Passive Voice in Process Explanations

	Active Voice	*Passive Voice*
when the action involves a person and . . .	you want to emphasize the operator or doer of the action	you want to emphasize the recipient of the action, or the person doing the action is insignificant or unimportant
Examples:	Dr. Hunt attended a seminar to learn about new techniques for treating kidney disease.	The marathon runner was treated for dehydration by the doctor on duty in the emergency room.
when the action does not involve a person and . . .	you want to emphasize the activating agent	you want to emphasize the recipient of the action
Examples:	Torrential rains weakened the dam.	The machine was activated by the automatic timer.

As discussed in Chapter 5, active voice results in stronger, more effective writing, whether the action involves a person or not. If the sequence of action itself does not involve a person, use active voice to stress the activating agent, and passive voice to stress the recipient. Figure 11.8 summarizes your choices.

Verb Mood. Mood is the form of the verb that expresses whether the action is a fact, command, condition, or wish. Because process explanations deal with facts, they are written in the *indicative mood.* For example, "A careful nurse coordinates all medical procedures" is indicative. Technical writers use indicative mood for nearly all situations except conditions contrary to fact (which require the subjunctive mood, rarely used) and directions (which require the imperative mood). The following example illustrates the difference between indicative and imperative mood.

Indicative Mood for Processes	*Imperative Mood for Directions*
The nurse uses a rectal thermometer to take the baby's temperature.	Use a rectal thermometer to take the baby's temperature.

Person. Choosing among first, second, or third person depends on the purpose and audience of the process. *First person* (I, we) is correct if the writer is narrating the events in a sequence in which he or she was involved. If the writer's role in the action was significant, the use of first person emphasizes this. *Second person* (you) is infrequently used in processes and is usually reserved for directions since the reader is being directed to complete a particular action. *Third person* (he, she, one, it, they) is most common in processes, allowing emphasis to be placed on the sequence of the action rather than on the writer or the reader.

Organization and Format

Processes are chronological, often using headings to distinguish the major steps. Section headings and subheadings can help the reader by signaling the movement from one part of the process to the next, as illustrated by the article for apprentice carpenters in Figure 11.5 and the development notice about CO_2 removal in Figure 11.6

Processes follow a format, summarized in Figure 11.9, that can be varied according to audience needs. The less expert the audience, the less complex the information should be. However, less informed nonexperts often need careful explanations, which may take more space than the highly technical explanations appropriate for experts.

Introductory section. The introductory section of a process explanation defines the process and identifies its purpose or goal. Occasionally you actually state the intended audience before you explain background information needed to understand the explanation. A flow chart or other visual provides an overview of the entire sequence. The relevant parts, materials, equipment, or ingredients are identified in this introductory section or as they arise in individual sections in the body of the paper. The introductory section closes with an enumeration of the steps, in the order that you will discuss them.

Body. In the body of the paper you explain each step in the sequence. The amount and type of details you include and your decision either to present the steps in paragraphs or enumerate them depends on the audience. Your chronological presentation may also include cause-and-effect explanations.

The presentation of each step in the sequence is the same. You define it and state its purpose or goal. If you haven't already identified the necessary parts, materials, equipment, or ingredients, you need to incorporate this information. The explanation will be clearer if you include a visual that shows the

Figure 11.9   Format for Process Explanations

TITLE

1.0 Identify the process in an introduction.
    1.1 Define the process.
    1.2 Identify purpose or goal.
    1.3 Optional: Explain necessary background needed by the intended audience.
    1.4 Optional: Identify the intended audience and the purpose.
    1.5 Optional: Identify the relevant parts, materials, equipment, ingredients, and so on.
    1.6 Optional: Design a flow chart or other visual to provide an overview.
    1.7 Enumerate the major steps.

2.0 Present a step-by-step explanation of the process in chronological order, including cause-and-effect explanations as necessary.
    2.1 Explain step one of the process.
        2.1.1 Define step one.
        2.1.2 Present the purpose or goal of step one.
        2.1.3 Optional: Identify the necessary parts, materials, equipment, or ingredients for step one.
        2.1.4 Optional: Illustrate step one.
        2.1.5 Present chronological details of step one, including any substeps.
        2.1.6 Optional: Present chronological details of the substeps if they're relevant to the audience.
        2.1.7 Optional: Explain the theory or principle of this step's operation or function if it's relevant to the audience.
        2.1.8 Explain how this step relates to the next step.
    2.2 Explain step two . . .

3.0 Optional: Present a conclusion if it will increase the reader's understanding of the sequence, its theory, or applications.
    2.3.1 Summarize the major steps ONLY if the action is long and/or complex.
    2.3.2 Discuss the theory or principle of operation if it has not already been incorporated in the primary discussion.
    2.3.3 Explain applications if they're not self-evident.

action or the result of a step. Any relevant substeps are also presented chronologically. Readers who want to know about more than the step-by-step operation benefit from an explanation of the background theory or principle. Transitions explain how one step relates to the next step.

Conclusion. Process explanations may omit a conclusion if the information is unnecessary or fits more comfortably in the body of the document. You should include a concluding section only if it increases the reader's understanding of the sequence, its theory, or applications. If you choose to include a conclusion, consider several possibilities. Briefly discuss the theory or principle of operation if it has not already been incorporated into the primary discussion. Explain applications if they're not self-evident. Summarize the major steps only if the action is long or complex.

Inquiries and Applications

Discussion Questions

1. If a process explanation does not enable a reader to perform a task, why bother with it? Why not simply write instructions?
2. Read carefully the article on bog development; identify the technical terms that are not defined. Does the lack of definitions hinder your understanding?
3. Discuss whether simplified process explanations such as the one in Figure 11.3 should be avoided because they may mislead readers by omitting key information.

In-Class Exercises

1. The following process is excerpted from an article in *Lapidary Journal*, a publication for gem enthusiasts and professionals. Design a visual that could replace this paragraph but still retain the chronology and details of the content.

> The cloisonné process involves bending and soldering thin, flat ribbons of precious gold, a thirtieth of an inch wide, to a metal base. When the gold wires or ribbons are soldered in place, the spaces in between are filled with a paste made of glass or vitreous powder and colored with various metallic oxides. The object is then fired at a high temperature until the gold and enamel are fused. Often the enamel shrinks during firing and the compartments must be refilled and refired several times to produce a level surface. When this is accomplished, the hard surface of the object is polished until perfectly smooth. The end result—a gleaming translucent pattern, highlighted by the timeless elegance of shining gold.[1]

2. Explain your choices of voice—active or passive—and person—first, second, or third—for each situation and audience:
   a. blood donation to a potential donor
   b. purification of water from sewage treatment plant for an ecologist
   c. grading of pearls for jewelry to a consumer
   d. professional dry cleaning of antique clothing for dry cleaner
   e. an operation to a child in hospital for surgery
   f. filling a claim to a new insurance adjuster
   g. a change in manufacturing procedures to a customer
   h. formation of sebaceous cysts for patient with cysts
   i. operation of a heat exchanger for a home owner

3. Locate an effective published example of a process. Photocopy it and, with a small group, determine the appropriateness of the following aspects:
   a. clarity of chronology or sequence
   b. transitions connecting each section
   c. headings and subheadings
   d. mood, voice, and person
   e. visuals

4. Examine the visual description in Figure 11.3 of the cycle that creates acid rain. Conduct the necessary research and then prepare an entirely verbal explanation of the process appropriate for a general reader.

5. Read the explanation in Figure 11.10 about pamphlet binding and book-binding. Identify the probable intended audience. Evaluate the effectiveness of the language choices (voice, person, mood), organization, and visuals.

Figure 11.10

Some printing like stationery, small posters, notices, etc. can be delivered as printed, but most printing must be converted from printed sheets to a finished printed piece, through various binding and finishing operations. The work required to convert printed sheets or webs into books, magazines, catalogs and folders is called *binding*. The operations to make displays, folding cartons and boxes, tags, labels, greeting cards, and a variety of special packaging and advertising materials are known as *finishing*.

PAMPHLET BINDING

This is a rather general term for binding folders, booklets, catalogs, magazines, etc., as opposed to bookbinding which will be discussed later. There are generally five steps in pamphlet binding: *scoring, folding, gathering* or *collating, stitching,* and *trimming*. Most printing requires one or more of these, but not necessarily all. For example, a printed folder, the simplest form of pamphlet binding, is trimmed to size and folded. When printed sheets are delivered to the bindery, the first step is to fold the sheets (in multiples of 4s) into sections or *signatures*. In the case of heavyweight or cover paper, folding is made easier by first scoring.

Scoring

A score is defined as a crease in a sheet of heavyweight or cover paper to facilitate folding. As a rule, only those methods which produce an embossed ridge on the paper will give good folding results. The fold should always be made with the ridge or hinge on the inside for minimum stretch *(see illustrations)*. Booklet or catalog covers must have a score wide enough to take the necessary number of pages without strain on the fold.

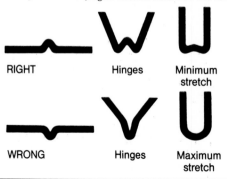

| RIGHT | Hinges | Minimum stretch |
| WRONG | Hinges | Maximum stretch |

Figure 11.10 *Continued*

The most common method of scoring is using a round face scoring rule locked in a form on a platen or cylinder press. The width of the rule varies with the thickness of the paper. A thicker paper requires a thicker rule which will give a wider crease to help make a cleaner fold.

Folding

Paper is usually folded on a *buckle type* folding machine. The sheet is carried on conveyor belts from an automatic feeder, and rollers force the sheet into a fold-plate, which is adjustable to the length of the fold. The sheet hits a stop in the fold-plate, buckles, and is carried between two other rollers which fold the sheet. There can be as many as 64 pages to a signature.

There are two kinds of folds: *parallel* and *right angle*. Parallel folding is just what the name implies, each fold is parallel to the other. An example would be a letter which requires two parallel folds for mailing. An *accordion* or *fan fold* is a type of parallel folding used extensively for computer printout forms. A right angle fold is two or more folds, with each fold at right angles to the preceding one. For example, most formal invitations are folded with two right angle folds.

Folding machines can be equipped with attachments for scoring, trimming, slitting, perforating and pasting. These are generally inexpensive and time saving.

In designing printing, the different types of folds and the limitations of mechanical folding should be considered at the planning level. Otherwise, one or more folds might end up being a costly hand-folding operation. The sketches on the following page illustrate the most common types of folds.

Types of Folders

1. Four-page folder Simplest type of folder, with only one fold, folding either on the (A) long or (B) short dimension. Used for bill stuffers, instruction sheets, price lists, etc.

2. Six-page folder Made with two parallel folds, either (A) regular or (B) accordion. Used for letters, circulars, envelope stuffers, promotional folders, etc.

3. Eight-page folder Illustrated in three ways, (A) one parallel and one right angle fold, also called *french fold* when printing is on one side of the paper, (B) two parallel folds and (C) three parallel accordion folds, for ease in opening. Also, (A) and (B) can be bound into an 8-page booklet.

4. Twelve-page folder Illustrated in two ways, both with one parallel fold and two right angle folds, either (A) regular or (B) accordion. Sometimes used as 4-page letter, with the two right angle folds, folding letter to fit mailing envelope.

Figure 11.10 *Continued*

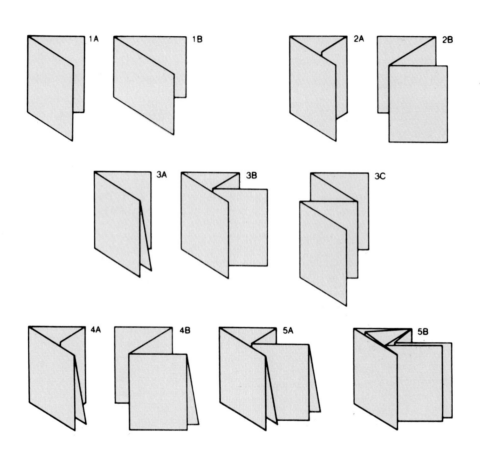

5. Sixteen-page folder Shown in two ways, (A) one parallel and two right angle folds and (B) three parallel folds, used for easy-to-open transportation schedules. Also, can be bound into a 16-page booklet.

Collating

Once folded, the next step is to gather or collate the signatures in a predetermined order. The collating order should be checked to be sure of the correct sequence. Collating can be done by hand or machine, depending on the size of the job.

Figure 11.10   *Continued*

Stitching

After the signatures are collated, they can be stitched together. There are two methods of stitching: *saddle-stitch* and *side-stitch*. The thickness or bulk of paper determines the style to be used. *Time* magazine is saddle-stitched; *National Geographic* is side-stitched.

In saddle-stitching, the booklet is placed on a saddle beneath a mechanical stitching head, and staples are forced through the backbone or spine of the booklet. This type of binding is the simplest and most inexpensive. Booklets will lie flat and stay open for ease in reading. Most booklets, programs and catalogs are saddle-stitched.

SADDLE-STITCH   SIDE-STITCH

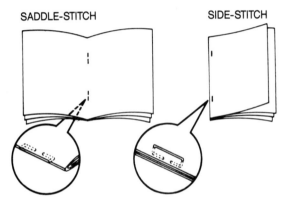

Side-stitching is used when the bulk is too great for saddle-stitching. The sections are collated, and then placed flat under a stitching head. Since the stitches are inserted about ¼″ from the back edge, the inside margin must be wider than in a saddle-stitched booklet. Side-stitched books cannot be completely opened flat and often have glued-on covers.

Trimming or Cutting

Three sides (top, bottom, right) of the booklet are trimmed on a guillotine-style paper cutter. For large-edition pamphlet binding, three-knife trimmers, which automatically trim three sides at one time are used. These are sometimes used as an attachment to the stitcher.

An automatic-spacing paper cutter is used for faster trimming of volume printing such as labels, leaflets, or any job printed in multiple form on the same sheet. This type of cutter automatically shifts to pre-set gauges after each cutting, resulting in greater uniformity and higher production.

Source: Pocket Pal, 13th edition (New York: International Paper Company), 146–151.

Assignments

1. Write a process description on a topic of your choice. Identify the intended audience and specify the purpose of the description. Analyze the audience to determine use of (a) active or passive voice, (b) first, second, or third person, (c) relevant visuals, and (d) headings and subheadings. Consider some of these topics:

birth of a calf, foal	inventory control (FIFO)
energy audit of house	production of maple syrup
depreciation	operation of a laser
creation of a silicon crystal	formation of kidney stones
function of kidneys	manufacture of carbon fibers
fabrication of metal optics	extrusion of polymer parts
welding or brazing	grafting of plants
formation of plaque on teeth	design of a dietary program
operation of a rotary engine	operation of a transit
formation of a weather front	packing a parachute
test/inspection procedure	thermal aging process
refinishing of a piece of furniture	
maintenance of a spinning reel	
operation of a septic tank, leach field	
self-regulating pain control (ex: biofeedback)	
installation of a wood-burning stove	
regeneration of tails in lizards	
development of hybrid varieties of corn	
breeding of genetically pure laboratory animals	

2. Design the visual and write the text material for an explanation of a process similar to "How Acid Rain is Formed." Identify the intended audience and specify the purpose of the description or procedure. Design the visual so that it appeals to the audience and also clearly presents the process. Analyze the audience to determine use of (a) active or passive voice and (b) first, second, or third person. The accompanying text should be direct and brief. Consider some of the topics listed in the preceding list.

12 Abstracts and Summaries

ABSTRACTS AND SUMMARIES are similar—they both represent abbreviated forms of longer works, and occasionally the terms are used interchangeably—but they are not identical. This chapter distinguishes between *descriptive abstracts*, *informative abstracts*, and *executive summaries*, which precede a document or appear independently. Figure 12.1 highlights the primary characteristics of these abstracts and summaries.

Abstracts, which frequently accompany journal articles and technical reports, condense the document to give readers essential information about subjects, methods, results, conclusions, and recommendations. Most abstracts are a single paragraph, and seldom more than one page.

Summaries are thorough but brief, though usually longer than abstracts. They are less concerned with condensing the document than with emphasizing results, conclusions, and recommendations. Independent or executive summaries precede documents; concluding summaries end a document.

Recommending a length for abstracts and summaries is difficult because to a large extent length depends on the complexity and scope of the specific document. Some organizations restrict the length of abstracts and summaries; for example, NASA limits abstracts to 200 words and summaries to 500 words. Such rigid guidelines may cause a writer to focus on length rather than meaning. However, condensing or summarizing in such a rigorous fashion forces most writers to identify the critical or central issues of a document.

	Figure 12.1	Characteristics of Abstracts and Summaries

	Descriptive Abstract	*Informative Abstract*	*Executive Summary*
usual length	one paragraph	one paragraph to one page	thorough but brief; may be one paragraph to several pages
location	preceding document or in abstract index	preceding document or in abstract index	preceding document or at end
purpose	to help reader decide whether to read the document	to provide an abbreviated basis for decision making; to give overview of document	to identify major points of document and present conclusions; provide information for decision making
relation to document	stands independently; may be published separately	stands independently; may be published separately	stands independently or concludes document
point of view	external perspective	document's point of view	document's point of view

Abstracts

Abstracts Preceding Articles and Documents

Many journal articles, reports, and papers for presentations are preceded by an abstract that highlights the main points. The most important function of an effective abstract is to provide an overview *without interpretation*. A well-written abstract maintains the tone and focus of the original document, presenting key points.

Abstracts from articles in two different technical journals, *Science* and *The New England Journal of Medicine*, show the amount of detail available to readers who want to know the contents of an article before starting to read it. Both abstracts provide the same information in the same sequence: purpose or rationale of study, methodology, results, and conclusions.

Example

POLLUTION MONITORING OF PUGET SOUND
WITH HONEY BEES

Abstract. *To show that honey bees are effective biological monitors of environmental contaminants over large geographic areas, beekeepers of Puget Sound, Washington, collected pollen and bees for chemical analysis. From these data, kriging maps of arsenic, cadmium, and fluoride were generated. Results, based on actual concentrations of contaminants in bee tissues, show that the greatest concentrations of contaminants occur close to Commencement Bay and that honey bees are effective as large-scale monitors.*[1]

The information is easily accessible to the reader:

1. *purpose or rationale of study:* determine if honey bees are effective biological monitors of environmental contaminants
2. *methodology:* collected pollen and bees for chemical analysis
3. *results:* kriging maps showing concentrations of arsenic, cadmium, and fluoride based on concentrations of contaminants in bee tissue
4. *conclusions:* (a) greatest concentrations of contaminants occur close to Commencement Bay, (b) honey bees are effective as large-scale monitors

Example

OSTEOPOROSIS IN WOMEN WITH ANOREXIA NERVOSA

Nancy A. Rigotti, M.D., Samuel R. Nussbaum, M.D., David B. Herzog, M.D., and Robert M. Neer, M.D.

Abstract   Because estrogen deficiency predisposes to osteoporosis, we assessed the skeletal mass of women with anorexia nervosa, using direct photon absorptiometry to measure radial bone density in 18 anorectic women and 28 normal controls. The patients with anorexia had significantly reduced mean bone density as compared with the controls (0.64 ± 0.06 vs. 0.72 ± 0.04 g per square centimeter, $P < 0.001$). Vertebral compression fractures developed in two patients, and bone biopsy in one of them demonstrated osteoporosis. Bone density in the patients was not related to the estradiol level ($r = 0.02$). Levels of parathyroid hormone, 25-hydroxyvitamin D, and 1,25-dihydroxyvitamin D were normal despite low calcium intakes.

The patients with anorexia who reported a high physical activity level had a greater bone density than the patients who were less active ($P < 0.001$); this difference could not be accounted for by differences in age, relative weight, duration of illness, or serum estradiol levels. The bone density of physically active patients did not differ from that of active or sedentary controls.

We conclude that women with anorexia nervosa have a reduced bone mass due to osteoporosis, but that a high level of physical activity may protect their skeletons. (N Engl J Med 1984; 311:1601–6.)[2]

Although the information in the abstract is more technical than in the previous abstract, readers can still identify the major points:

1. *purpose or rationale of study:* to determine whether women with anorexia nervosa are predisposed to osteoporosis
2. *methodology:* used direct photon absorptiometry to measure radial bone density
3. *result:* patients with anorexia nervosa had significantly reduced mean bone density
4. *conclusion:* women with anorexia nervosa have a reduced bone mass due to osteoporosis, but a high level of physical activity may protect their skeletons

The abstracts you prepare will follow the same basic sequence as the two you have just examined.

A short descriptive abstract assumes an external perspective, describing what the document is about. Descriptive abstracts identify the document's topic, methodology, major results, and conclusions. Readers often use a descriptive abstract to help decide whether to read an entire document. The following example of a descriptive abstract, which precedes a report titled "An Evaluation of the XC-2000 Display Failures," is typically brief.

Example

DESCRIPTIVE ABSTRACT

The failure rate of the XC-2000 display is identified as internal shorts of the 4305 driver components. The evaluation by Design Component Engineering has determined that the problem occurs between final system test and delivery to the customer site. The report recommends that the most effective and economical solution, placing two 1N7211 zener diodes across selected pins on the J1 and J4 connectors, should be used on the XC-2000.[3]

Just to complicate things, what this text refers to as a descriptive abstract is sometimes called something else. For example, *Science* calls it a summary, even though it takes an external perspective and describes the content of the article, as the following example shows.

Example

Summary. This article provides a brief look at the current status of supercomputers and supercomputing in the United States. It addresses a variety of applications of supercomputers and the characteristics of a large modern supercomputing facility, the radical changes in the design of supercomputers that are impending, and the conditions that are necessary for a conducive climate for the further development and application of supercomputers.[4]

Your concern should be to learn the purpose and structure of various types of abstracts and summaries rather than worrying about inconsistencies in labeling from journal to journal or organization to organization.

A longer informative abstract (sometimes simply called a summary) assumes the same perspective as the document and includes actual content from the document. An informative abstract identifies the topic and emphasis but concentrates on the results, conclusions, and recommendations—the likely results if the organization adopted the document's recommendations. People who need an informative abstract want a clear, straightforward presentation that answers their questions about the subject, as you can see from the following informative abstract dealing with the same report as the descriptive abstract above.

Example

INFORMATIVE ABSTRACT

The XC-2000 display, suffering from a 20 percent field failure rate since July, has been held from shipment. This delay is due to the concern for customer reaction to the smoke produced when the 4305 driver components short internally.

Both the 4305 driver and the 4503 receiver failures have been evaluated by Design Component Engineering. The failure evaluation included pin-to-pin electrical testing, external and internal visual inspection, and failure mode duplication testing in and out of the application. The cause of failure noted is a 10,000-volt transient on the 12-volt supply (pin 8) of the 4305, and a similar transient on the input (pin 5) of the 4503 receiver. The transient damage occurs between final system test and delivery to the customer site. Because of the difficulty encountered in locating the exact cause of the transient, efforts were channeled toward protecting the parts rather than removing the cause.

XC-2000 display driver/receiver boards were tested with several bypass protection techniques. The most effective and economical method is the placement of two 1N7211 zener diodes across selected pins on the J1 and J4 connectors. Three hundred reworked units have been shipped through normal methods and have arrived in working order at the customer sites. Therefore, a corrective action has been identified and should be used on the XC-2000.[5]

Occasionally, a lengthy or complex document requires both a descriptive abstract and an informative abstract. In such situations, the descriptive abstract helps readers decide whether to read the document and the informative abstract stands as an abbreviated version of the document, including details for decision making that save the busy professional the trouble of reading the entire document.

Abstract Indexes for Research

Abstracts of important published articles and documents may be reproduced in an abstract index, which catalogs abstracts (but not the articles themselves) in broad fields such as biology or chemistry. Abstract indexes, available in academic and industrial libraries, provide easy access to overviews of current research in many fields—academic, professional, business, and industry. (Types of indexes and search techniques are discussed more fully in Chapter 7.) For example, people interested in artificial intelligence could find abstracts of research in several abstract indexes. An investigator could first look up artificial intelligence (AI) in the subject index of a monthly or annual volume of *Biology Digest.* The January 1985 volume lists two entries on artificial intelligence:

- 84/85-1936 ARTIFICIAL INTELLIGENCE, EXPERT SYSTEMS, FIFTH GENERATION PROJECT, JAPAN, PARALLEL PROCESSORS
- 84/85-1941 ARTIFICIAL INTELLIGENCE, EXPERT SYSTEMS, HEURISTICS, KNOWLEDGE ENGINEERS, NATURAL LANGUAGE, ROBOTICS USAGE, THREE-DIMENSIONAL SCENE ANALYSIS, VISUAL SYSTEMS

A quick examination of these abstracts reveals that the articles appear to be general, introductory discussions of artificial intelligence. Rather than reading either of these articles, the investigator moves to another abstract index that is likely to have more technically sophisticated material.

Summaries

The executive summary (also called an independent summary) preceding a lengthy document identifies the subject and then focuses on results and conclusions. While most details, examples, facts, definitions, and explanations are omitted, the recommendations—the benefits and limitations of accepting the conclusions of the document—are definitely included.

A summary provides an overview of the document, but it does not include additional opinions of the writer that are not also included in the document. Additionally, an effective summary presents information without jargon. Finally, the summary does not necessarily order information in the same way it is presented in the document (or either version of the abstracts), but rather as it is needed for decision making.

The following summary for "An Evaluation of the XC-2000 Display Failures" presents information very similar to that in the informative abstract earlier in the chapter, but the sequence is different, since the executive summary, after identifying the subject, concentrates on results and conclusions.

Example

EXECUTIVE SUMMARY

The XC-2000 display, suffering from a 20 percent field failure rate since July, has been held from shipment since October 20, because of worry about customer reaction to the smoke produced when the 4503 driver components short internally. Field service technicians can restore the system on site by replacing either or both the 4305 driver and the 4503 receiver integrated circuits, but the expense of employee time and replacement parts is high.

Because the damage occurs between final system test and delivery to the customer site, protection of the XC-2000 system during transient is the best solution.

Both the 4305 driver and the 4503 receiver failures have been evaluated by Design Component Engineering, including pin-to-pin electrical testing, external and internal visual inspection, and failure mode duplication testing. The cause of failure is a 10,000-volt transient on the 12-volt supply of the 4305 driver and a similar transient on the input of the 4503 receiver. The most effective and economical protection is the placement of two 1N7211 zener diodes across selected pins on the J1 and J4 connectors.

Three hundred reworked units have been shipped through normal methods and have arrived in working order at the customer sites. This corrective action should be used on the XC-2000.[6]

Another type of summary, the concluding summary, appears at the end of a document. Unlike an executive summary that is independent of the document, a concluding summary is the part of the document that reviews the major points.

For some documents, however, concluding summaries are definitely the wrong way to end. A short document presenting a simple, straightforward discussion (such as those in Chapter 14) does not need a concluding summary: Who wants the major points of pages 1, 2, and 3 summarized on page 4?

A concluding summary should begin with an abbreviated restatement of the document's thesis or purpose. Then the individual points can be presented in a paragraph or, preferably, in a numbered or bulleted list. In either case, the summary should include a statement that condenses each major point of the document but omits supporting details, examples, facts, definitions, and explanations.

Because a concluding summary reviews the document, it should include only information and conclusions that are actually in the document, without additional evaluative comments. Additionally, a concluding summary should present major points, without jargon, in the same order as they are presented in the document.

Preparing Abstracts and Summaries

Preparing an effective abstract or summary requires several stages. You can apply the same process for descriptive abstracts, informative abstracts, and summaries. Since more people read the abstract or summary than the document itself, it is obviously important. As a stand-alone section of a document, it must be clear and accurate.

Good abstracts and summaries are difficult to write for several reasons. First, writing an accurate, effective abstract or summary requires good *reading* skills—high comprehension and an understanding of relationships among ideas. A writer has to be able to differentiate main ideas from subordinate ideas. Second, a writer has to avoid the temptation to include too much information. Finally, an abstract or summary usually requires a great deal of revision to accurately represent the original document.

With few exceptions, abstracts and summaries maintain the tone and focus of the original document. One specialized form of abstract includes an evaluation or commentary, but that section is clearly labeled to distinguish it from the summary of the content. Preparing an abstract or summary generally requires several recursive steps: planning, drafting, and revising.

Planning

You should be familiar with the particular abstract format preferred by your discipline because the selection and sequence of information vary from field to field. If you are unable to locate an example of an abstract appropriate for your field, the following sequence, one often used for scientific abstracts, works well:

1. What you did
2. Why you did it
3. How you did it
4. How it turned out (results)
5. Recommendations (if applicable)

As always, assessing the audience's purpose for reading the abstract is important. If the purpose is to provide help in deciding whether to read the document, a descriptive abstract is appropriate; if the reader wants information to aid in decision making, an informative abstract is preferable. In some cases, a single document will have both a descriptive abstract and an informative abstract or an executive summary. The complete documentation of the material being abstracted is essential, so investigators know where to locate the document.

In order to identify the main points of a document, you need to read it carefully, highlighting, underlining, or marginally annotating key issues, facts, relationships, and primary conclusions and recommendations.

Drafting

These highlighted, underlined, or annotated portions of the document become the basis for your abstract or summary. Begin by trying to summarize each major point of the document in a single sentence. Unless you have another format to follow, use this sequence of information:

1. purpose or rationale of study
2. methodology
3. results
4. conclusions

Be sure to connect these separate sentences with logical transitions.

Revising

Revision can take place at any stage of writing an abstract or summary, practically as soon as you begin drafting. Each time you revise, focus on a specific area. For example, you need to ensure the logical sequence of content and the inclusion of essential information. Then you need to eliminate any repetition and unnecessary detail, at the same time checking the accuracy of the content. You also need to eliminate jargon because some readers of the abstract or summary will not have up-to-date expertise in the subject. Finally, you should proofread to locate any grammatical or mechanical errors.

Inquiries and Applications

Discussion Questions

1. What would be the advantages and disadvantages of an informative abstract or executive summary prepared by:
   a. the author of the document
   b. an expert in the field other than the author

2. Many top-level managers indicate they frequently read only the executive summary or abstract that precedes a report. What assumptions must a manager make about the quality of the summary in order to follow this practice safely?

3. When is it acceptable and responsible to read only the abstract or executive summary of a document? Does your opinion remain the same for documents in business and industry as well as for documents in science research?

Individual and Group Exercises

1. Read the following article, "Pollution Monitoring of Puget Sound with Honey Bees"; you read a descriptive abstract of this article earlier in the chapter. Now prepare an informative abstract and then a summary of the article.

POLLUTION MONITORING OF PUGET SOUND WITH HONEY BEES

Honey bees have been used as monitors of a variety of environmental contaminants, including trace elements, low-level radioactivity, and pesticides. However, most work has emphasized deleterious impacts to bees rather than the use of bees as chemical monitors. An averaged sample of pollutants can be obtained from an area of more than 7 km^2 with honey bees. Because bees have low tolerance to many toxic chemicals, they provide a potentially sensitive indication of pollutant-induced harm. Pollination services and bee products such as wax, pollen, and honey can be affected by environmental contamination. Bees are thus a rather unusual biological monitor since they are of considerable economic value. In 1981, U.S. bees provided $124.6 million worth of honey and wax while pollinating $8 billion to $40 billion of crops.

Pollutants may reach honey bee colonies by several routes. Contamination of the body, mouth parts, and spiracles during flight is possible, and bees may mistake dust for pollen. Our observations indicate that some particulate pollutants may become intermixed with pollen grains, since particles can readily be seen with a light microscope. Electrostatic charges on the surface of the bee body may contribute to the insect's ability to gather pollen. We speculate that this may partially account for the gathering of other small particles.

Nectar and pollen may become contaminated by atmospheric deposition of pollutants onto plants as well as by plant uptake of these substances from soil. Uptake dynamics from food have been studied with radiotracers. Feeding tests in which a uranium tracer was used resulted in high concentrations in bee tissues, with lower levels in comb, larvae, and honey. These findings are consistent with field studies, which indicate that levels of trace elements tend to be highest in or on bees and pollen.

Pollutants, which are likely to be encountered either in a gaseous form or a water-soluble form, such as fluoride, appear to be taken up by both the hard external and soft internal body tissues by ingestion, inhalation, or absorption. Regardless of pollutant form, colonies may become contaminated not only through foraging activities but also by forced-air circulation and evaporative cooling employed by bees to control hive temperature and humidity. Contaminant levels in the environment may be reflected in the bees themselves or in hive components, including wax, pollen, and honey.

How best to use the potential of bees as environmental pollution monitors on a large geographic scale has been the subject of considerable debate. The several million existing bee colonies in the United States provide an in-place and accessible monitoring network from which beekeepers can take samples. We implemented this concept in 1982 in the Puget Sound region of Washington where a large number of beekeepers keep bees in rural and urban locations. The region, although large, is clearly bounded by the Pacific Ocean and the Cascade Mountains. Over 130 pollutant sources are routinely monitored by regulatory agencies. These sources include smelters, chemical plants, and other large industries, but the actual distribution and extent of emissions has never been adequately established.

From July through mid-September 1982, 64 beekeepers collected samples and performed measurements at 72 sites over approximately 7500 km². Each volunteer was asked to (i) establish at least one sampling site, (ii) measure the percentage of brood survival, (iii) collect forager bees, and (iv) trap pollen. The methods employed were developed and tested during a study of a lead smelting complex in Montana.

For the brood-survival test, dressmaker pins were used to mark six rows of 20 cells on a brood comb, and two independent determinations were made. An initial record was made of eggs and young larvae, and a follow-up scoring of cell contents by developmental stage was performed 13 to 17 days later. Observations were scored on a standardized data sheet and later processed by a computer program that we had developed. Pollen was trapped at the hive entrance through a tube of polyvinyl chloride (PVC) with a grid of 5-mm holes. As bees passed through the holes, pollen was scraped off the legs into the tube. Pollen traps were left on hives for 6 to 10 hours. Blocking the hive entrance with a strip of fiber glass screening allowed collection of bees returning to the hive. These bees were aspirated into a polyethylene sample bag with a PVC and acrylic aspirator attached to a 12-volt vacuum. Pollen traps and nozzles were washed with acid before use. Bee and pollen samples were placed into Whirl-Pac bags and frozen.

Samples, in acid-washed beakers, were covered with a clean

watch glass and dried in a forced-air oven at 45°C. For fluoride measurement, samples were dry-ashed at 600°C and analyzed by an Orion 601 ion specific electrode. For arsenic and heavy metal measurements, samples were dissolved in Instra-analyzed nitric acid in a sealed-tube pressured system for 3 hours at 175°C. Analyses were performed with a Varian AA 275BD and an Instrumentation Laboratories IL 251 atomic absorption spectrophotometer, the former equipped with a model 65 vapor generator for the introduction of arsenic as arsine and the latter with a model 555 flameless atomizer, which was used for some of the cadmium analyses. Vapor generation, flameless atomization, and flame aspiration were done as described. Performance was monitored by standard additions and National Bureau of Standards reference materials (SRM orchard leaves 1571 and SRM bovine liver 1577), as well as our own standard bee tissue.

Kriging, a weighted moving average technique in which point estimates or block averages can be calculated over a specified grid, was used to map the distribution of pollutants. The derivation of the kriging weights takes into account the proximity of the observations to the point or area of interest, the "structure" of the observations (that is, the relation of the squared difference between pairs of observations and the intervening distance between them), and any systematic trend or drift in the observations. Kriging also provides a variance estimate for constructing a confidence interval for the kriging estimate. From the grid of estimates, contour maps can be obtained. From the confidence intervals for the kriging estimates, confidence bands for individual isopleths can be obtained. For the analysis natural logarithms were used.

Over 64 percent of the colonies tested displayed low brood viability; 40 percent sustained a 75 percent or greater loss of eggs and larvae. At some locations, colonies lost 97 to 100 of the brood.

Kriging maps of arsenic, fluoride, and cadmium, based on actual concentrations from bee tissues, display distinct distributional patterns. . . . The highest arsenic concentrations occur northwest of Tacoma and apparently are rather smoothly disbursed by atmospheric forces, at least to the Lake Sammamish Plateau. In contrast, cadmium seems to follow a similar pattern but for a much shorter distance, and fluoride appears to be concentrated east of Tacoma. Measured levels of arsenic and fluoride for bees near Commencement Bay were as high as 12.5 and 182 ppm, respectively, whereas bees from Whidbey Island generally contained less than 0.5 ppm arsenic and 4 ppm fluoride.

Arsenic, cadmium, lead, zinc, copper, and fluoride concentrations in pollen were of little use for mapping, both because too few pollen samples were received and because no patterns could be identified. Cooper, zinc, and lead concentrations in or on bees showed no patterns related to pollutant distribution. However, high lead values tended to be associated with highways, and individual pollen samples displayed values for heavy metals comparable to those for bees.

Arsenic and fluoride concentrations in bees near Commencement Bay were higher than any we have previously observed [that is, 8.2 ppm arsenic and 123 ppm fluoride]. Our kriging maps of arsenic and cadmium in bee tissues show patterns similar to isopleth maps developed by regulatory agencies (based on measured soil concentrations) and to deposition isopleths produced by the industrial source complex long-term model. However, these other maps describe an area circumscribed by our 5 and 6 ppm arsenic isopleth (soil map) and our 3 and 4 ppm isopleth (dispersion model). Thus, our maps cover a more extensive area. Further, our map suggests long-range transport of arsenic from Commencement Bay to the Lake Sammamish Plateau. This observation may explain reports of somewhat elevated arsenic levels occasionally observed at distant monitoring stations.

There were no statistical differences for arsenic or fluoride for bees collected during July or September at similar sites. However, limited data were available so that the power of the test was low. The same result was obtained in a follow-up experiment conducted in 1983. Bees sampled weekly for 10 weeks at two sites near Commencement Bay displayed temporal coefficients of variation of about 20 percent.

Kriging errors for arsenic show that estimated error is related to data density (that is, the number of sites sampled in a given area). Error was relatively small in the urban areas of Seattle and near Tacoma where many beekeepers obtained samples. In contrast, errors were larger in the rural areas, where sample locations were more scattered. Largest errors occurred at the perimeter of the study area and in those places where a section of the kriging grid encompassed a large mass of water. Kriging error is not synonymous with a standard deviation determined from replicate hives at a single location. Results from our studies indicate that coefficients of variation of about 20 percent with a range of 1.7 to 43 percent can be expected, depending on time of year, proximity to source, and other factors.

The predicted fluoride concentration map suggests a different source and dispersion mechanism. On the basis of our studies in Montana, we predicted that fluoride concentrations in nearby vegetation would also be proportionately high. Data provided by the Washington State Department of Ecology show that levels in grasses near the tide flats area of Commencement Bay contained up to 100 ppm, whereas background levels for grass should be about 1 to 6 ppm. In much of the area of high concentrations of arsenic and cadmium in bees, levels are also so high in vegetables that the Pierce County Department of Health has advised against consumption.

Our results show that beekeepers can effectively use colonies of bees as a self-sustained system for environmental monitoring over large geographical areas. Honey bees provide a spatially integrated sample of all three (gas, liquid, and particulate) modes in which pollutants may be transported. Moreover, our experience indicates that this monitoring system is less expensive than, for example, high volume air samplers that only monitor particulate pollutants. To determine how bee colonies can most effectively contribute to monitoring needs, especially in terms of integrating the information obtained with decision-making and regulatory processes, will require better understanding of the extent and limitations to which colonies of bees can be used in other places and for other pollutants.

J. J. Bromenshenk
S. R. Carlson
Gordon Environmental Studies
Laboratory, University of Montana, Missoula 58912
J. C. Simpson
J. M. Thomas
Statistics and Quantitative Ecology Sections,
Pacific Northwest Laboratory, Richland, Washington 99352[7]

2. Select a partner, then agree to watch a PBS television program that deals with science or technology—NOVA, a National Geographic special, a wildlife show. Take notes on the show and then prepare a summary that does not exceed one typewritten page. During the next class, compare your notes and summaries and discuss the similarities and differences.

Assignments

1. Select and photocopy an article from *Science* or some other periodical that regularly uses abstracts. Skip over the abstract, but carefully read the article. After reading the article, write an abstract and then compare your version with the one preceding the article. Marginally annotate your paragraph to identify differences with the published abstract. Write a paragraph that discusses the differences between the two abstracts.
2. Conduct a search (manually or using a computer data base) in *Biological Abstracts* or other appropriate abstract index(es) to compile a list of recent research relevant to an area you are investigating.
3. Select one or more of the first seven chapters of this text to summarize. Both the process of summarizing and the resulting summary should give you greater understanding of the material.
4. Prepare a bibliography of current articles from professional journals and trade magazines about some subject that interests you in your professional work or about some specific area of technical communications related to your work. After you have read each article, decide if it fits in with your selected focus for the bibliography. For each article you choose to include in the bibliography, write a descriptive abstract. The result will be an *annotated bibliography*, useful for academic or industrial research.
5. Use the annotated bibliography you have compiled as the basis for a discussion that summarizes prevailing views about the subject, a state-of-the-art update. Use internal documentation to cite the sources.

IV   Completing a Document

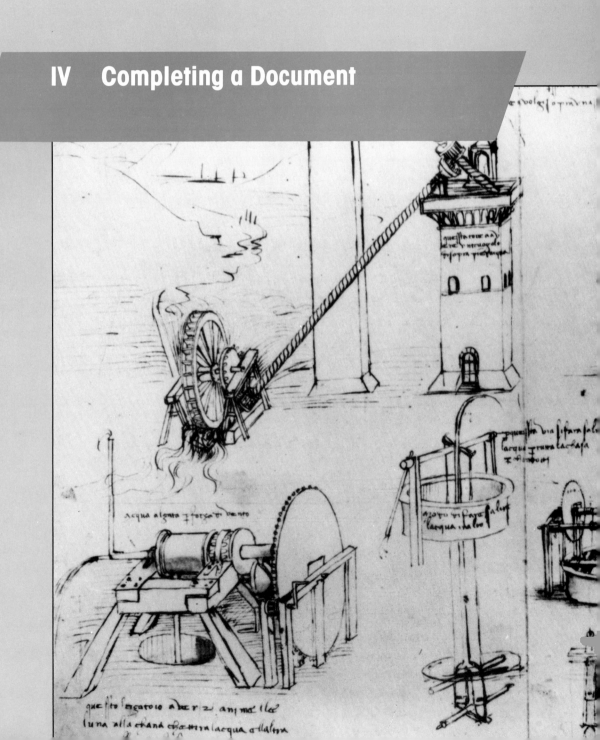

13 Procedures, Directions, and Manuals

PROCEDURES AND DIRECTIONS are everywhere—from the arrow painted on the lid of a peanut butter jar that indicates the way the lid twists off to multi-volume manuals detailing every step in the operation of field artillery. In practice, the terms *procedures* and *directions* are often used interchangeably. However, they do have distinctions, which this text recognizes, so you do have a choice about which form to use.

Distinguishing Procedures and Directions

Procedures and directions perform similar functions—both trace the steps of some process involving a person, whether the process has a task focus or a human focus—but they are not identical:

- Procedures provide detailed, step-by-step *explanations* of what is done in a process.
- Directions provide the step-by-step *instructions* necessary to complete a process.

Figure 13.1 summarizes the essential characteristics of and distinctions between processes, procedures, and directions.

As Figure 13.1 suggests, the primary distinction between procedures and

Figure 13.1   Distinctions Between Process Explanations, Procedures, and Directions

	Process Explanations	*Procedures*	*Directions*
SUBJECT	any process, natural or with human involvement	limited to processes that have direct or indirect human involvement	limited to processes that have direct or indirect human involvement
PURPOSE	to provide a general overview of the process	to provide a step-by-step explanation of the process	to provide step-by-step instructions to perform the process
AUDIENCE	person who wants to know about the process	person who wants to know about the process and may also want to complete the process	person who wants to complete the process
FOCUS/ FORMAT	explanation of the process; paragraphs	enumeration of the steps in the process	enumeration of the steps in the process
AMOUNT OF DETAIL	includes general characteristics and a few selected details	includes all specific details necessary to understand and complete the process	includes all specific details necessary to complete the process
VERB MOOD AND VOICE	indicative mood; active or passive voice	indicative mood; active or passive voice	imperative mood; active voice
Example	Routine maintenance involves changing the filter when it's dirty and making sure the heat exchanger and smoke pipe are clear of accumulated creosote.	Routine Maintenance 1. Filter is checked regularly and cleaned when necessary. 2. Heat exchanger and smoke pipe should be cleaned to eliminate accumulated creosote.	Routine Maintenance 1. Check the filter and clean it when necessary. 2. Clean heat exchanger and smoke pipe of accumulated creosote.

directions is that procedures are written in indicative mood ("Filter is checked") while directions are written in imperative mood ("Check the filter"). Furthermore, procedures can employ either active or passive voice, whereas directions generally are restricted to active voice. The choice of which to use is dictated by stylistic preference and company policy.

Types of Procedures and Directions

Regardless of format, procedures and directions are extraordinarily important; according to some surveys, they make up the majority of technical communication. Procedures and directions in business and industry can be separated into four broad categories:

- actions/behavior of personnel
- assembly of objects or mechanisms
- operation of equipment
- implementation of a process

Figure 13.2 identifies the focus within each category, with emphasis on the person decreasing as the process becomes more complex. The first category

Figure 13.2   Focus in Different Types of Directions

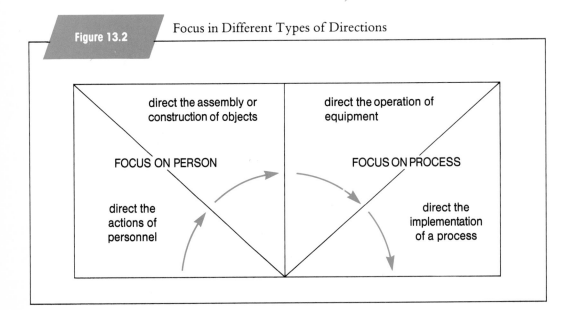

focuses on human behavior because the directions manage or regulate personnel. Consistent action or behavior is the goal. If you want to standardize office or shop procedures, you need to write directions that result in consistent action by each person.

The second category directs a person to make (assemble, construct) something. Again, the person is the focus although the end result is the object or mechanism itself.

The third category directs a person to operate tools or equipment in order to complete a task or process. The person is still important, but the focus is on the correct sequence of steps to operate the equipment, which in turn accomplishes a particular goal.

The fourth category focuses even less on the person and concentrates instead on the implementation of a process. A person is necessary to carry it out, but the process is more important than the person doing it. Labeling these four types of directions is convenient for discussion purposes, but in practice they tend to overlap rather than remain as distinct types.

Figure 13.3 identifies some specific examples that fall within each category. Note that in many instances one set of procedures or directions spans more than one category, for example the assembly and operation of a component stereo system or the detailed and interrelated steps in a surgical procedure.

Although the categories identified in Figure 13.2 and illustrated in Figure 13.3 have distinct functions, the broad purpose of each category of procedure and direction is to help a person understand and then perform an action accurately and efficiently. Knowledge about the specific audience can help you design effective procedures and directions.

Audience Analysis

Procedures and directions are distinct from other forms of technical communication in that they specifically address individual users who actually *do* something. For example, the directions in the *User Reference Manual* that came with the word processing software used to type the manuscript for this text approach the novice user in a direct, friendly manner:

Example   To enter text, just start typing. Each non-control character typed is entered into the text of your document. If you type beyond the right margin, notice that WordStar moves the word that wouldn't fit inside the margin to the next line, positioning the cursor after the word to allow you to continue typing. This is word wrap.[1]

Figure 13.3   Examples of Procedures and Directions in Four Categories

Type of Direction	*Examples of Common Use*
Direct the actions/ behavior of personnel	complete work-in-process form specify incoming inspection procedures implement new payroll-error reporting procedures recommend approaches for dealing with delinquent accounts specify tool requisition procedure change official communication channels for weekly/monthly reports specify questions for preliminary interviews respond to survey
Direct the assembly or construction of objects or mechanisms	install automatic washing machine assemble a jungle gym install built-in vacuum system assemble build-it-yourself stereo assemble traverse drapery rods construct prefab tool shed assemble cable TV unscrambler construct a portable cold frame for vegetable seedlings
Direct the operation of equipment	operate injection molding machine operate video display terminal (VDT) use syringe for diabetes injection use micrometer to determine size operate a telephone switchboard calibrate electronic inspection equipment use a pasta maker operate a Rototiller
Direct the implementation of a process	identify trees for logging draw blood from a patient install chips on a circuit board perform CPR conduct random-sample survey install a solar rooftop panel conduct a dietary analysis conduct a health-care needs assessment

The *Installation Manual* for the same software, although dealing with far more complex content, also speaks directly to the technician:

Example   PATCH "RUBFXF" BELOW TO NON-ZERO. THE CONTENTS OF "RFIXER" WILL THEN BE OUTPUT IMMEDIATELY AFTER A "DELETE" IS INPUT; THIS CHARACTER, RATHER THAN THE NEXT CURSOR POSITIONING STRING, SHOULD THUS BE REPLACED WITH BACKSPACE-SPACE-BACKSPACE, REDUCING THE CONSEQUENCES OF YOUR SYSTEM'S MACHINATIONS. TRY NULL (ZERO) IN RFIXER FIRST; IF THIS DOESN'T WORK, TRY BACKSPACE (08) OR SPACE.[2]

To a greater extent than any other type of technical writing (excluding correspondence), directions attempt to establish a direct relationship between writer and reader. Your understanding of this relationship—and the implicit emphasis on careful audience analysis—can help you to avoid problems that often plague procedures and directions. Such problems include inappropriate vocabulary and visuals and overly complex or simple explanations. Most of the problems result from assumptions about what the reader knows or doesn't know. For example, a user manual for a word processor written by a software engineer who infrequently uses word processing may be a less than satisfactory document. The software engineer may overestimate the user's knowledge of and interest in the technical aspects of the word processing program, incorporating unnecessary material and using terminology that confuses rather than clarifies. Careful audience analysis, emphasizing the user's needs, could eliminate many of the problems.

When preparing procedures or directions, you already know several things about your audience. For example, usually only a primary audience—the user—exists. Also, the purpose is defined—to accomplish a task. Furthermore, you can assume that the user is motivated to complete the task, though not necessarily motivated to read the procedures or directions. The answers to the other questions in the modified audience analysis worksheet in Figure 13.4 help you construct and present effective procedures or directions.

The user's attitude affects the likelihood of the user initially consulting the procedures or directions and then reading and following them. A person with a positive, enthusiastic attitude will be more likely to follow them than a person with a less than positive or even a negative attitude, who may need to be convinced that they are useful. Your assessment of the user's attitude influences your decision to justify the steps. A justification involves an explanation as to why a step should be done or why it should be done in the prescribed manner. Some people are likely to complete a task more efficiently if they know why they're doing it. For other people, any information beyond the actual step is confusing and slows the task.

Figure 13.4	Audience Analysis Worksheet for Directions

Title of directions _____

Specific purpose/objective of directions _____

_____

Primary reader—user of directions

Name _____ and/or Job Title _____

User attitude

   enthusiastic   negative

   ■_____■_____■_____■_____■

User education

highest grade reached _____

academic major or professional specialty _____

probable educational focus: theory ☐ practice ☐ both ☐

User professional experience

experience in immediate or related position _____

probable familiarity with similar procedures _____

familiarity with subject of directions _____

Environment where directions will most likely be used

physical location _____

environmental distractions _____

time constraints in using directions _____

frequency user may consult directions _____

The user's education and professional experience affect the level of the vocabulary and the need for explanations. A user with more education and/or experience is likely to understand industry-specific jargon, whereas a less educated and/or experienced user needs to have terms defined and concepts explained.

The environment in which the procedures or directions are to be used influences their design. If the environment is full of distractions, the procedures or directions need brief explanations, clear markers for locating (and relocating) one's place, and summaries or reviews. If the procedures or directions are to be used frequently, the binding needs to be secure and sturdy.

Most writers find this modified audience analysis worksheet useful in designing procedures and directions. Initially, actually completing the sheet is beneficial. As you become more experienced, you will probably complete the audience analysis in your head, except for complex or lengthy procedures and directions. The following list identifies specific benefits of the analysis:

Analysis Factor	*Impact on Directions*
user attitude	need to justify individual steps or entire directions use of attention-getting devices
user education	level of vocabulary definition of terms types of visuals
user experience	expectations of prior knowledge amount and type of detail to use
user environment	physical characteristics of directions including page design, typography, and binding (if any)

Who Writes Directions

Procedures and directions should be written by a person with specific qualifications:

- experience in completing the task
- awareness of the audience's skills, attitudes, and experience
- ability to present information clearly, adjusting the steps and explanations to the audience

Obviously, the person who writes procedures or directions must know how to complete the particular task or process. The greater the intended user's knowledge and experience, the more familiar the writer must be with all aspects of the task. But procedures and directions may be written either by a person who has long-term experience with the task or by someone who has just learned.

An experienced person knows every nuance and variation needed to complete the task correctly and efficiently; however, this person often assumes too much about the user's knowledge or uses unfamiliar terminology.

A person who recently learned how to perform the task often has more sensitivity to the problems the user might have in following the procedures or directions; however, this person might not know the theory of operation, every necessary detail, or possible dangers or problems that would require cautions and warnings.

Constructing Procedures and Directions

Several factors are crucial to construct effective procedures and directions. This section of the chapter identifies these factors and provides suggestions for implementing them.

For many people, procedures and directions have a tarnished reputation. How many times have you heard the adage, "When all else fails, check the directions." In spite of this sentiment, properly constructed procedures and directions inspire confidence in users. The following elements were compiled by business and industry professionals during a recent technical communication seminar; checking your procedures and directions against this list helps you produce the kind of documents that users refer to *before* problems occur:

1. Content Elements
   - title and purpose/goal/objective identified
   - necessary components included: parts list, equipment list, definitions
   - chronology consistent and accurate
   - time factors included
   - wording clear and direct
   - terminology used consistently
   - details adequate and accurate
   - justifications appropriate
   - warnings and cautions present
   - stylistic and grammatical conventions followed

2. Visual Elements
   - visuals appropriately used
   - visual and verbal content balanced
   - sufficient visuals to illustrate steps
   - key parts or similar parts illustrated
   - visuals juxtaposed with relevant text
   - visuals labeled
   - visuals accurately drawn
   - scales included on visuals

3. Design Elements
   - sequence on page easy to follow
   - print easy to read
   - sufficient space for notes

- manual easy to handle or refer to while completing job
- manual withstands frequent use

4. Quality Control
   - directions tested for accuracy
   - directions updated as needed

Content Elements

The content elements of procedures and directions include the title, essential components such as parts and materials, appropriately ordered steps, and necessary warnings and cautions.

Title/Purpose. Procedures and directions need a precise title and a clear identification of purpose, goal, or objective. This identification can be achieved in a variety of ways, applied separately or in combination:

- title may imply or state purpose:
  Operation Manual for Garden Tractor
- title may be accompanied by visual that illustrates final objective
- title may be supplemented by separately stated objective:
  Objective: To use mail-merge with word processing software.

Necessary Components. Most cookbook recipes identify ingredients and amounts before listing the steps to prepare a particular dish. Likewise, many technical procedures and directions would benefit by listing parts and equipment. For example, kits (for hobbyists who build model rockets or industrial assemblers who build electronic monitors) should come with both a list of the parts and a list of tools or equipment needed to complete the assembly. Many recipes include or refer to definitions of terms unfamiliar to the cook; technical directions should also define terms accurately and concisely.

A *parts list* identifies the enclosed or necessary parts by name and part number (if needed for verifying or reordering) as well as the quantity provided or needed. In addition, parts may need to be identified by a description or diagram if several are very similar or if the user may be unfamiliar with part names. For example, a parts list that identifies "washers" and "lock washers" may need a diagram to differentiate the types; a list that identifies several capacitors may need labeled diagrams to distinguish them. Even on parts lists that have no similar parts, diagrams benefit inexperienced users.

A *material and/or equipment list* specifies what tools the user will require to complete the task. Such a list is helpful because the user can order special tooling or materials and organize the work area.

Most novice users appreciate definitions of unfamiliar parts and processes. Definitions can be presented in several ways—as parenthetical definitions directly in the steps, as a glossary in a preliminary section, or as an appendix. (For a more detailed discussion about definitions, refer to Chapter 9.)

Chronological Order. Procedures and directions should be presented in chronological order. Steps are easiest to follow if they are enumerated and separated. Examine the difference in the two sets of directions in Example 13.1. The content in each is identical; however, Version A, the paragraph without enumerated steps, is more difficult to read and follow than Version B.

Not only should the overall sequence of steps in procedures and directions be chronological, but each individual step should be in order, as the following examples show.

Not Chronological   Anodize the aluminum housing after the surfaces have been deburred.

Chronological   After the surfaces have been deburred, anodize the aluminum housing.

The second version is logical because the steps are identified in the order in which they are done.

Effective procedures and directions also specify factors dealing with time. The examples in the following list illustrate the benefit of including these chronological details:

Without Chronological Details	*With Chronological Details*
Pump the lever to prime the lantern.	Pump the lever for 15–20 seconds to prime the lantern.
Stir the pesticide until it dissolves in the water.	Stir the pesticide until it dissolves in the water, usually about 2–3 minutes.
Apply a second coat when the first is completely dry.	Add a second coat when the first is completely dry, at least 24 hours later.

Appropriate Diction. Procedures and directions are useful only if the user can read them. As a general guideline, select the simplest term that accurately conveys the information.

Example 13.1   Directions in Paragraph and Enumerated Form

VERSION A
OPERATOR INSTRUCTIONS FOR A MAGNETIC TAPE RECORDER

Inspect the heads, guides, capstan, and pinchroller for accumulation of foreign material. Place the supply reel on the left reel hub. Place the take-up reel on the right reel hub. Thread the tape through the tape-threading guide. Press POWER ON-OFF pushbutton switch. The white indicator light will illuminate. If all other pushbuttons are released, press STOP to unlock other pushbuttons. Set the meter function switch to PEAK position. Establish record level: set monitor selector to RECORD and choose channel desired; adjust the level control for a panel meter reading of 100% peak. To record, press PLAY and RECORD buttons simultaneously; the red light will illuminate. To replay the tape, press STOP; then press PLAY.

VERSION B
OPERATOR INSTRUCTIONS FOR A MAGNETIC TAPE RECORDER

1. Inspect the heads, guides, capstan, and pinchroller for accumulation of foreign material.
2. Place the supply reel on the left reel hub. Place the take-up reel on the right reel hub.
3. Thread the tape through the tape-threading guide.
4. Press POWER ON-OFF pushbutton switch. The white indicator light will illuminate.
5. If all pushbuttons are released, press STOP to unlock other pushbuttons.
6. Set the meter function switch to PEAK position.
7. Establish record level: set monitor selector to RECORD and choose channel desired; adjust the level control for a panel meter reading of 100% peak.
8. To record, press PLAY and RECORD buttons simultaneously; the red light will illuminate.
9. To replay the tape, press STOP; then press PLAY.

One way to make writing more direct is to eliminate noun forms of verbs by turning nouns into verbs, as the following list shows:

Noun Form	*Verb Form*
Determine the calculation	Calculate
Make an estimation	Estimate
Begin the removal	Remove
Take a measurement	Measure
Establish synchronization	Synchronize
Place in juxtaposition	Juxtapose

Another way to make writing clearer is to use a word consistently as the same part of speech, even though some words can easily be used as two or three parts of speech.

Examples   Filter the solvent.   (verb)
Wash the filter.   (noun)
Order a filter frame.   (adjective)

Base the design on current cost.   (verb)
Adjust the base.   (noun)
Seal with a base coat.   (adjective)

In such cases, correct usage is not so much a matter of right and wrong as one of consistency. The conscientious writer tries to employ the same word or phrase the same way within one set of procedures or directions.

Writers also need to be consistent with terminology. Do not refer to a part as the "5 mm tubing connector" in one place and the "Y connector" later in the same document. Once the term for a part or a step is established, use it throughout.

Appropriate Details. Generally, the procedures or directions you construct should be as simple as possible without sacrificing accuracy. Those that are overly detailed show little sense of audience needs and are as difficult to use as those that skimp on information and leave the user unable to complete the task.

Justification of Steps. Should procedures and directions only specify the required action, or should the action be explained or justified? The amount of detail you include depends on both the audience and the nature of the step. Explanations are essential in situations when personal injury, equipment damage, or procedure malfunction might otherwise occur, but they are probably unnecessary if the audience is predisposed to comply with procedures. However, if including an explanation will encourage the audience to complete the procedure correctly, without risk of personal injury or equipment malfunction, then do so.

In order to determine whether justifications are necessary, ask yourself several questions:

1. Is the user/operator more likely to complete the step if a justification is included?
2. Does the inclusion of a justification influence the user's precision or accuracy?
3. Will the justification delay or interfere with the user's immediate understanding and implementation of the step?

The responses to these questions should guide your decision to include or omit justifications as part of the steps. If the user is more likely to complete the step, and with greater accuracy, then the justification will be beneficial. If the justification interferes with the user's understanding or implementation of the step, then it should be omitted.

The following example from "Thermal Measurements of Building Envelope Components in the Field," specifies seven steps for determining building component R values. Each step includes an explanation that enables the engineer to perform the evaluation with greater understanding and accuracy.

Example   Step 1. Establish the type of building component to be analyzed. This determines the length of testing and a choice of environmental conditions. A southerly wall may require testing early in the morning, after a cloudy day, or several days of recording. A window sash may only require a few hours to determine its R value.

Step 2. Estimate the time constant of the component to be analyzed. This gives some guidance on test duration based on expected capacitive effects of the component. Quick time constant calculations can be accomplished as shown in Eq. 2. A finite difference numerical analysis can also be used for complex systems that may involve phase changes.

Step 3. Choose the appropriate weather conditions for the test and be prepared to test as soon as these conditions appear imminent. On the West Coast and in the Southwest, periodic temperature excursions may exceed 40 F (22°C). These conditions require testing over several diurnal cycles to isolate the capacitive effects. In the Midwest, there may be several days during the winter when ambient temperature variations are less than 10 F (6°C) for several days with no solar radiation. In this case, a highly heat-capacitive wall may be analyzed in a relatively short period of time.

Step 4. Upon arrival at the test site, assess the thermal state of the building component by using a thermal scan or other thermographic means. This tells the uniformity of the wall so that representative areas can be marked for point readings. It also determines if solar effects are still present, if there is significant damage due to moisture, or if infiltration or exfiltration will cause measurement error.

Step 5. Install instrumentation at indicated locations and start recorders. Measure inside surface heat flow, outside surface heat flow, outside temperature, inside temperature, outside component surface temperature, inside component surface temperature, outside air velocity, and inside air velocity. A measurement inside the component between the inside and outside surfaces is useful.

Step 6. Periodically calculate R value bounds for the component based on interior and exterior heat flow meters. The R value bounds are the variability ranges of R value due to stochastic inputs, such as wind speed and instrument error. Interior heat flow meters are inherently more stable due to less air velocity fluctuation. Outside meters usually vary significantly due to the rapidly changing air film resulting from wind. Variations in temperature and heat flux readings should be incorporated in the calculation of R value using probabilistic methods. Although the variation of Q and T may be represented by a Gaussian (Normal) distribution, the variation in Ra is non–Gaussian at small values of Q or highly oscillating values of Q.

Step 7. If the apparent mean R value does not vary more than plus or minus 15 percent for at least three component time constants, and the inside and outside mean heat flows are within 10 percent, then acceptable data have been taken within the range of variability stated by the mean R value and standard deviation computed from Q and T. These criteria have been successfully utilized in the field, but the ultimate acceptance number depends on the accuracy desired. Obtaining Ra within a bound of plus or minus 5 percent may require more time and expense than obtaining a value with a bound of plus or minus 15 percent.[3]

Necessary Warnings and Cautions. Because of product liability laws, writers as well as manufacturers and sometimes distributors can be held legally liable for damage or injury caused by faulty procedures and directions and defective products. Technical writers must alert users to possible damage to equipment or injury to themselves if the steps are not followed.

Grammatical and Stylistic Conventions. The individual steps in procedures and directions are written in *parallel structure,* with each statement using the same grammatical structure.

The two sets of instructions in the following examples show how confusing nonparallel directions can be:

Example	NOT PARALLEL STRUCTURE	PARALLEL STRUCTURE
	Always Observe Safety Rules	***Always Observe Safety Rules***

NOT PARALLEL STRUCTURE

Always Observe Safety Rules
1. Wearing of safety glasses
2. Proper tool for the job
3. Use only tools that are functioning tools
4. Maintain a clean and organized work area
5. Questions relating to procedures or the proper handling of tools should be presented to your group leader

PARALLEL STRUCTURE

Always Observe Safety Rules
1. Wear safety glasses.
2. Select proper tool for the job.
3. Use only properly functioning tools.
4. Maintain a clean and organized work area.
5. Ask your group leader questions about procedures and tool handling.

Directions most frequently use the imperative mood because individual steps are commands to the user, not statements about the process. Procedures most frequently use the indicative mood because the individual steps explain or describe the sequence of actions. The next example illustrates the difference between imperative mood and indicative mood.

Imperative Mood for Directions
Clamp the specimen onto the flat plate.

Indicative Mood for Procedures
The specimen is clamped onto the flat plate.

Directions that employ second person, referring to the user as *you*, are the most concise and effective. Sometimes the *you* is not stated, but the readers (or listeners) understand that they are being directly addressed.

Second Person for Directions
Use only properly functioning tools.

Make sure you don't type anything after the target drive name, not even a space.

Procedures are more often written in third person, addressing the user impersonally as *he, she, one, the operator,* or *the technician.* In procedures the step is described rather than written as an order. However, third person is more removed from the reader, so the response may not be as immediate as with directions that use second person.

Third Person for Procedures
Technicians should use only properly functioning tools.

Operators should not type anything after the target drive name, not even a space.

Directions written in active voice have the stated or implicit subject of the sentence as the doer of the action. Procedures can be written in either active or passive voice, depending on the desired emphasis.

Active Voice,   [You] Wear safety glasses.
Second Person
for Directions

Active Voice,   Technicians wear safety glasses.
Third Person
for Procedures

Passive Voice,   Safety glasses must be worn [by all technicians].
Third Person
for Procedures

Additional elements of grammar and style are discussed in Chapter 5 and in the Handbook.

Visual Elements

This section of the chapter discusses selecting and incorporating visuals into procedures and directions, including identifying appropriate uses for visuals, correctly balancing verbal and visual portions of procedures and directions, maintaining accuracy of visuals, determining effective placement, and deciding on the option of a totally visual presentation.

Appropriate Visuals. Visuals play an important role in many kinds of procedures and directions. The combination of verbal and visual components conveys information in a particularly accurate and efficient manner.

Visuals can be used to illustrate a variety of elements:

- parts, tooling, equipment
- sequence of steps
- positioning of the operator and/or equipment
- development or change of object or equipment

A diagram often identifies a part or tool more accurately than a verbal description. For example, sketches of different kinds of screws for assembling a cabinet help the assembler. A series of illustrations can effectively trace the movements in a process. In directions for knitting, the most efficient way to demonstrate hand or body position is through illustrations. Changes that occur as a result of following the procedures or directions are often more clearly illustrated visually than explained verbally.

Making the decision about whether to include visuals must be balanced by space requirements and production costs. The following checklist can help you determine whether visuals are appropriate for a particular set of procedures or directions. An affirmative answer to any of these questions indicates that visuals should be integrated:

- Will a flow chart or series of visuals clarify the overall process for the user?
- Will visuals enable the user to clearly understand the end result?
- Will visuals help the user correctly identify parts?
- Will visuals help the user understand and implement individual verbal steps?
- Will including visuals emphasize safety and decrease the likelihood of danger?

Visuals are often essential in illustrating and clarifying a process that someone is trying to duplicate. Imagine trying to follow procedures or directions for electronic trouble-shooting, botanical identification, or celestial navigation without visual support. The visuals eliminate ambiguity by providing diagrams or maps wherever appropriate in the text.

The writer who wants to incorporate visuals has to make a decision about the kind of visuals to employ. (Chapter 6 discusses types of visuals in detail.) Generally speaking, keep the visuals as simple as possible to still convey the information. For this reason, drawings are often preferred over photographs, which can present unnecessary and distracting detail.

Visual and Verbal Balance. Some processes are more easily understood through a visual presentation than a verbal one. For example, suppose that you are eating in a restaurant when you choke on a piece of chicken. You give the international sign of choking, hands to your throat. Your friends have put off learning the Heimlich maneuver, but they see a "Choke Saver" poster on the restaurant wall. Which version of the poster would you want them to check?

1. entirely verbal—well-organized chronological paragraphs with causal elements, clear topic sentences, and good chronological transitions
2. verbal and visual—sequence of captioned photographs showing a choking victim being saved by a trained person
3. verbal and visual—sequence of clear, captioned sketches showing a choking victim being saved by a trained person
4. entirely visual—sequence of clear sketches showing a choking victim being saved by a trained person, with arrows and inserted enlargements of critical positioning

No doubt you would select version 3 or 4, and probably version 4. Version 1 would take too long to read, and without the sketches the saver would not be sure of correctly positioning hands on the victim's body. Version 2 would be an improvement, but photographs frequently show too much detail; also, people's clothing would obscure correct positioning. Version 3 would be a good choice, as long as the saver took the time to read necessary information in the captions. But, assuming the sketches and enlargements were accurate, version 4 would assure the fastest and most accurate response.

Most procedures and directions require a logical balance of verbal steps and visual support. Visuals should be included when they help the user complete the task more quickly or accurately and with less anxiety.

Accurate Visuals.   Accuracy is of the utmost importance in any type of visuals in procedures and directions. Visuals that can not be easily understood, whether drawings, diagrams, photographs, or maps, are not much help to the user. Many problems can be eliminated if writer and artist consider visuals as an integral part of the directions, not just a decorative addition.

The accuracy and appropriate use of each visual must be double-checked by both the artist and the writer. How helpful is a wiring diagram that omits some of the circuits? How can a user confidently follow a step that reads, "Add two drops of oil in all set-screw holes, locations shown in the diagram," when the diagram does not label the set screws? How can a user be expected to follow directions that say, "Calibrate by turning the middle knob to zero," with a diagram that shows only two knobs? Accuracy means completeness of the visual itself, inclusion of accompanying labels, and visuals and text that go together.

The quality of visuals is reflected in their careful execution and reproduction. Imagine the frustration of a laboratory technician who reads this step, "Scan the slide for the distinctive aberration shown in the accompanying diagram," with a diagram that is too blurred to be useful. Or consider the technician trying to follow a set of procedures that verbally identify electronic components by colored bands but contain black-and-white drawings.

Visuals are not necessarily prepared by a writer, but a writer is responsible for determining whether they will work for the user. For example, a writer can replace references to color with references to crosshatching or dots and then have an artist make the appropriate changes.

The size of visuals can affect the user's ability to interpret them accurately. If a drawing is too small, the user won't be able to identify the important parts of the subject. Occasionally, a full-view drawing or photograph is accompanied by an insert showing an enlargement of a crucial part. A drawing or photograph may have small parts identified by arrows, circles or boxes, or highlighted portions. Visuals should always be labeled with an indication of the scale (actual size, ½ scale, ⅕ scale, 1 inch = 1 foot, 1 inch = 10 miles, and so on) so that the user can accurately interpret them.

Placement of Visuals. Visuals in technical communications are usually placed as close as possible following or next to the text reference. The visuals should always be referred to in the text, by figure number or title, so that the user is led to look at the correct visual for each step.

Total Visuals. In response to the problems raised by international and multi-national users as well as American users who find visual steps faster or easier, several companies have experimented with totally visual procedures and directions.

It is not easy to create totally visual procedures or directions because pictures, signs, and symbols do not all have universal meanings. For example, could the up-arrow sign on shipping cartons be misinterpreted? Should the carton be placed with the arrow pointing up to indicate the top of the carton? Or, should the carton be placed with the arrow pointing down, indicating the carton's most stable position? The answer depends on a person's perception.

In the development of nonverbal directions, color coding can be very important. Coloring parts of drawings often effectively replaces verbal emphasis and is also valuable for differentiating similar elements in a drawing. Problems arise, however, if directions are to be reproduced (perhaps photocopied) in a manner that ignores the color. For this reason, color coding is often combined with a variety of design patterns on matte acetate film, as illustrated in Figure 13.5. Symbols for materials are also available on matte acetate film, as illustrated in Figure 13.6.

Figure 13.5 Design Patterns in Visuals

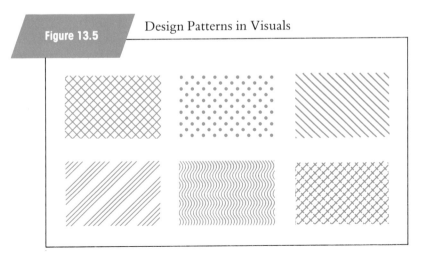

Figure 13.6   Symbols for Materials

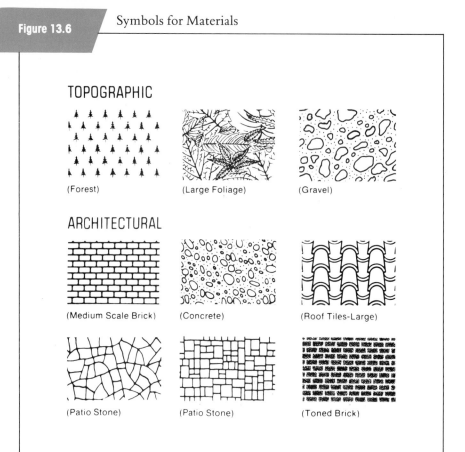

TOPOGRAPHIC

(Forest)   (Large Foliage)   (Gravel)

ARCHITECTURAL

(Medium Scale Brick)   (Concrete)   (Roof Tiles-Large)

(Patio Stone)   (Patio Stone)   (Toned Brick)

Design Elements

Appealing, Usable Format. In designing the physical layout of procedures and directions, a writer makes sure the steps and visuals are clear and easy to read. The layout should not discourage the user with small print, haphazard page design, or insufficient differentiation of steps, explanations, and examples.

The white space (the part of the page without text or visuals) should enhance the readability of procedures and directions—text and visuals should not be crowded or bunched together. Steps should be enumerated, with white space between each entry. Explanations or justifications that follow the steps should be physically set off, so that the steps clearly stand out and the explanations are seen as subordinate. Particularly in directions and manuals that will be used frequently, the page layout should leave enough white space, perhaps even a column, for personal notes by the user.

Visual devices are valuable in procedure and direction writing. For example, boldfaced or boxed information alerts the user to cautions and warnings. Bullets (small solid circles, usually emphasizing listed information) or type variations such as italics identify justifications that are not part of the actual step. Shading signals major sections in a process, with steps to complete that process listed below.

User's Needs and Environment. A writer helps meet the user's needs by considering the situation in which the directions will be used. How will the user react to the directions? Will the directions be too much trouble to use because they are too detailed or physically inconvenient?

Procedures and directions should address the needs of both first-time and experienced users. For example, lengthy procedures with detailed explanations should include a summary page that lists only the steps, without explanation, so that the experienced user can skip over explanatory information.

The quality of paper for procedures and directions should suit the frequency of use and the user's needs. Directions that probably will be used only once, perhaps for the installation of an air conditioner or the assembly of a Rototiller, need not be printed on high quality paper. However, directions that will be referred to often should be able to withstand frequent handling.

The binding of multi-page procedures and directions is also important. The document should lie flat, so the user can work and refer to it at the same time. The pages should turn easily yet be secure in the binding. If the directions might sometime be updated, a loose-leaf binder will enable revisions to be inserted in the appropriate places. If revisions are relegated to a separate binder, they may not be checked.

Quality Control

Quality control in procedure and direction writing involves several phases. Content editing and copy editing take place in all good technical and business writing. Procedures and directions need to be checked to ensure that verbal and visual material corresponds. If the material has been translated, it must be checked for idiomatic accuracy. Two additional steps are testing and updating.

Testing. In order to determine if the procedures and directions are accurate and clear, they must be tested by sample users. As writer, you are not qualified to be a tester because you might assume things that are inadvertently omitted.

One example clearly shows the problems that result if procedures and directions are not properly tested. Recently, a nationally known high tech company that manufactures circuit boards in one of its facilities had a serious problem with assembly workers who were not following new inspection procedures at each work station. The detailed instructions, written and tested by engineers who supervised the production assembly, were intended for assembly line workers, many of whom had not finished high school, and whose only training was received on the job. The communications consultant called in to analyze the situation identified the problem: The line workers couldn't understand the directions because users' knowledge was miscalculated, multiple operations were presented as single steps, and vocabulary level and sentence structure were too difficult.

These problems (as well as the frustration and expense) could have been prevented if the engineers had initially tested the directions with the user audience.

Updating. A company that uses long-range planning tries to coordinate research and development, manufacturing, and publication cycles for the same product. Such coordination ensures that the procedures and directions reflect the most recent version of the product. Updating of procedures and directions takes place during initial product development, when new versions of the product are released, and when errors or omissions in the directions themselves are noted.

Product developers and writers need frequent two-way communication. Key people in each group should regularly exchange progress reports. Writers should feel comfortable and confident in working directly with the product as well as in approaching the developers to ask questions and clarify information. The developers should feel equally comfortable in giving feedback to the writers about the accuracy and practicality of procedures and directions.

In some small companies, the developer may also function as writer. In such a situation, the developer-writer needs to give careful attention to documentation and not focus exclusively on product development. A product that can't be easily used because of inadequate documentation is often passed over for products accompanied by clear procedures or directions.

Even procedures and directions that are carefully written and edited may have errors in content, visuals, text, or design. (Refer to the detailed list earlier in this chapter.) Whether the publication group is a single writer in a small company or a self-contained division in a large company, a formal process for identifying and correcting errors in published material should be standard practice. All published material should be reviewed by people other than the writers. Users should be encouraged to identify errors, and an error file for each document should be maintained.

Manuals

Manuals are just very long procedures or directions, with a few sections added to provide background and to answer possible questions. Although manuals are written for audiences with a variety of technical backgrounds, most manuals have the same basic structure, whether they are user manuals, repair manuals, operation manuals, or procedure manuals.

The effectiveness of manuals is as important as the effectiveness of the product they accompany. Recently, the partners in a medium-sized law firm purchased a computer system to handle all the business functions of the office, with software for word processing and accounting and a data base for cases. After three days of training and six weeks operating the system, it was re-crated and returned. According to the office staff, the accompanying manuals were virtually useless—incomprehensible in some places, inaccurate in others. They never had a chance to evaluate the capability of the computer system fairly because the manuals were inadequate. In short, the best engineering design cannot overcome poor directions.

Sections of a Manual

Title Page and Table of Contents. Most manuals are long enough to have a title page and a table of contents. When a manual has more than a single section and more than five pages, a table of contents aids the user in locating information.

Pagination. Double page numbering in manuals, while not mandatory, is convenient, especially when sections of a manual will be updated at some point. For example, page 6.7 refers to page 7 in section 6; page 8.7 to page 7 in section 8. If pages are subsequently revised, only the page numbers in the affected section require changing, which saves the time and expense of re-paginating the entire manual. When double page numbering is used, the table of contents follows the same numbering system.

Introduction. The introduction of a manual usually contains several sections. One section tells how to use the manual. Another section provides an overview, including a general definition and description of the equipment or process. Some manuals include a history or development of the equipment or process as part of the general background information, and some summaries list major steps.

Glossary. The glossary of the manual may be presented as one of the early sections, or it may comprise an appendix. In either case, it is a minidictionary defining key terms that appear in the manual. Entries may also contain examples or explanations that clarify or support the formal definition. A carefully done glossary boldfaces or italicizes terms within a definition that are defined elsewhere in the glossary; entries may also include a "See . . ." reference.

Theory of Operation. Many introductory sections describe the theory of operation—information that is included for users who might want to know the *why* of things, not just the what. The theoretical explanations should be written with as little jargon as possible and with clear definitions and appropriate diagrams.

Training Section. Some manuals have a training section that takes first-time users through an introductory lesson, including basic operations, terminology, and sample applications. Sometimes the manual provides the entire lesson; other times, it supports a recorded or computerized lesson.

Part of the introductory section of *Differential Diagnosis of the Electrocardiogram,* a reference manual for practicing physicians presented in Figure 13.7, carefully lists, discusses, and illustrates the technique for taking an electrocardiogram. This excerpt is a particularly good example of a set of procedures. The intent is not to direct the operation of the equipment, but to give the physician a thorough understanding of the technician's task.

Justifications. Individual sections or chapters within a manual usually include discussion that provides the user or operator with justifications explaining reasons for each step. Manual writers try to anticipate possible questions users might have. The explanations in manuals often take the form of examples, demonstrations, samples, or illustrations to clarify processes for the user.

Tone. The tone in most effective manuals is conversational, giving the user the feeling that the writer is a friendly voice. The term *user-friendly* implies that the writer is taking a personal interest in the user. The imperative is reserved for step commands; manuals are usually written in second person, with the resulting tone suggesting a seminar between manual writer and user.

Summary of Steps. Lengthy manuals often present a summary of steps and then a detailed explanation. The inclusion of this summary is convenient for the user who wants to refer to the steps occasionally but does not need a detailed presentation.

Figure 13.7

TECHNIQUE FOR TAKING
THE ELECTROCARDIOGRAM

The electrocardiograph is a very sensitive recorder of the differences in voltage between two points. This voltage is inscribed on a strip of paper moving at a constant predetermined rate, usually 25 mm. per second. Therefore, the voltage is plotted as a function of time. There are many electrocardiographs available commercially. Almost all of them are entirely satisfactory for clinical purposes. Almost all are direct writing machines giving an immediate graph of the cardiac electromotive forces.

Precautions Necessary to Avoid Artifacts. Certain precautions should be taken in recording an electrocardiogram:

1. The instructions of the manufacturer should be followed precisely.
2. The patient's skin must be well prepared (salt paste is preferable in most instances, though alcohol is usually satisfactory).
3. Lead tips should be frequently cleaned with fine sandpaper.
4. The electrodes should be cleaned often. Use soap and water only and polish with fine sandpaper. *Never use steel wool.*
5. The connection of the wire tips of the patient cable to the electrodes should be tight.
6. The electrodes must be placed on the correct extremities. This should be double-checked every time an electrocardiogram is taken, since incorrect lead placement is the most frequent single source of serious error in the taking of the record (Fig. 1-33).

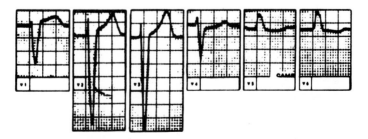

Fig. 1-33.   The right and left arm leads are reversed leading to an electrocardiogram that resembles situs inversus with a negative P, negative QRS, and inverted T in L1. But the horizontal leads show normal progression of the R and T waves from V1 through V6 thus ruling out situs inversus and suggesting right arm and left arm lead transposition.

Figure 13.7   *Continued*

7. The electrocardiograph should be properly and well grounded. This can usually be accomplished by proper orientation of the power plug in the wall socket. The new machines have three prong power plugs and if these are inserted in a corresponding three hole wall socket, the machines are always properly grounded.

   When taking electrocardiograms of a patient in bed in his own home, it is often necessary to ground the bed. This can usually be accomplished by a direct wire connecting the bed to the grounding post on the electrocardiograph or to a coldwater pipe. In an office set-up with a metal table, the table should be permanently connected to a good ground. Failure to properly ground the machine is a common cause of 60 cycle interference (Fig. 1-34).

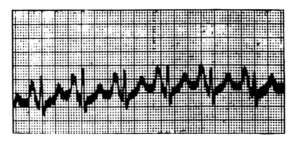

Fig. 1-34. The effect of 60 cycle interference on the electrocardiogram. Characteristically there are 12 spikes to each large box (0.20 sec.).

8. A standardizing impulse of 1 mv. should be recorded on every electrocardiogram taken. This provides three checks on the accuracy of the electrocardiogram: (1) It demonstrates that the machine is standardized correctly—1 mv. causing a 1 cm. deflection (Fig. 1-35A). (2) It provides a safeguard against a damping defect in the electrocardiograph. If the machine is overdamped, the mv. deflection will be distorted by undershooting (Fig. 1-35B). This technical error can cause artificial depressed or elevated S-T segments as well as other distortions on the electrocardiogram. (3) If the machine is underdamped, the standardizing deflection will be distorted by overshooting (Fig. 1-35C). This may cause excessive amplitude of the R waves (high voltage) and other distortions. If the damping of the machine is incorrect as in Figure 1-35B and C it is recommended that the machine be serviced by the manufacturer or his representative.

Figure 13.7 | *Continued*

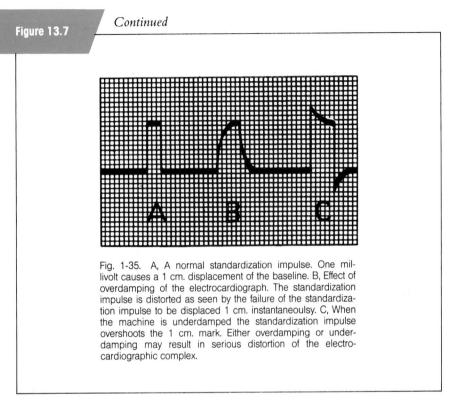

Fig. 1-35. A, A normal standardization impulse. One millivolt causes a 1 cm. displacement of the baseline. B, Effect of overdamping of the electrocardiograph. The standardization impulse is distorted as seen by the failure of the standardization impulse to be displaced 1 cm. instantaneoulsy. C, When the machine is underdamped the standardization impulse overshoots the 1 cm. mark. Either overdamping or underdamping may result in serious distortion of the electrocardiographic complex.

Source: Sidney R. Arbeit, M.D., Ira Lloyd Rubin, M.D., and Harry Gross, M.D., *Differential Diagnosis of the Electrocardiogram*, 2nd ed. (Philadelphia, PA: F. A. Davis Company, 1975), 15–18. Reprinted with permission of F. A. Davis Company.

Trouble-shooting and Maintenance. Most manuals also include a trouble-shooting section and a maintenance section. The trouble-shooting section says, "If this happens, this is what you did wrong." The maintenance section recommends basic upkeep. Both of these sections often save unnecessary service calls and give the user control over general operation of the equipment.

Index. A good index is invaluable to the user. All the concepts, terms, and processes are listed alphabetically with appropriate page numbers. Cross references increase the usefulness of any index.

Inquiries and Applications

Discussion Questions

1. Specify some of the poorest procedures or directions you have used. What features identified earlier in this chapter on the list of criteria for effective procedures and directions are omitted? What are the worst features? How could the procedures or directions have been improved?

2. In your response to each of the following questions, take a position that you can justify with a realistic example:

   ■ Is it necessary for an operator to understand *why* each step is included in a set of procedures or directions?

   ■ Does the operator's understanding ensure the procedures or directions will be more carefully followed?

   ■ Do reasons and explanations take up too much space, thus making the procedures or directions too long and cumbersome?

3. Should the documentation—the manuals—that comes with a product (for example, a computer system) influence the purchase of that product?

4. Instructions accompanying foreign-made products are sometimes written in stilted, nonidiomatic English. How do you react to this? Is your confidence in either the product or the accuracy of the instructions affected? If a product made by your company were intended for export, how would you avoid such problems in translation?

5. A four-volume user's manual, consisting of almost 300 pages, contained at the end of each volume a tear-out page requesting a user evaluation and a list of specific weaknesses or errors. One reader found about 20 such problems: some omissions, some ambiguities, some undefined technical terms.

   Do you think the reader should have returned the user evaluation form? With in-depth comments or generalities? Do you believe a reader should take the time and effort to upgrade another company's manual? Would your answer be different if the user expected to have future dealings with the company instead of being a one-time purchaser? Can you think of a way a company could reward user evaluations?

Individual or Group Exercises

1. Examine the variations in wording of a single step in the following three sets of directions. Identify audiences appropriate for each version. Which version would you respond most positively to? Explain if any of the versions are better than the others:

   - SET I
     - Version A Close the valve completely by turning the knob until the arrow points to the red dot.
     - Version B Close the valve completely by turning the knob until the arrow points to the red dot. Failure to close the valve completely will result in pressure loss, decreasing the efficiency of the system.
     - Version C So the system does not lose pressure, close the valve completely by turning the knob until the arrow points to the red dot.

   - SET II
     - Version D Lower the safety bar before turning on the machine. If you operate the machine without the safety bar in place, you might severely injure your hand.
     - Version E Lower the safety bar before turning on the machine to avoid personal injury.
     - Version F Lower the safety bar before turning on the machine.

   - SET III
     - Version G If the patient's pain persists, turn her on her side.
     - Version H If the patient's pain persists, turn her on her side in order to alleviate the pressure.
     - Version I If the patient's pain persists, turn her on her side. This change in position alleviates the pressure on the spine.

2. Case Situation: Karen Sidel has just hired a new but experienced employee to rework printed circuit boards. Below are the original directions Karen jotted down for the first job. She asks you to take responsibility for putting them into a more usable format.

Please use the following procedure for reworking all 218-200 Rev. Ø P.C. boards. On the component side, cut the etch that leads from I.C.-7-H, pin #2, to the nearby cap. C-29. Cut the etch near C-29 so it will be readily visible. On the circuit side of the board, cut the etch that leads from I.C.-7-H, pin #3, to I.C.-7-E, pin #2. Cut the etch twice, near both pins, so it will be readily visible. Then add jumper wires, 26 ga. green Kynar, between I.C.-7-H, pin #2, and I.C.-7-E, pin#2, and also between I.C.-7-H, pin #3, and I.C.-7-E, pin #3.

Assignments

1. Select a set of particularly poor directions and rewrite them so they will be effective.
2. Select a set of outdated directions and rewrite them so they will be accurate.
3. Select a procedure or activity that needs a set of effective directions. Write them.
4. Select a class representative to contact several local companies to determine (a) the various types of directions they produce both for in-house and external use and (b) the style guide or format they use. Write a memo presenting your findings. Include appendixes of sample directions and style guides if you have been able to obtain them.
5. Rewrite a process description as a set of directions.
6. Locate a manual. Establish criteria for evaluating manuals and determine whether your sample manual fulfills these criteria. Prepare a short report that identifies the manual's strengths and recommends specific changes to eliminate weaknesses.

14 Short Reports

SHORT REPORTS COMPRISE the majority of writing in academic institutions, nonprofit organizations, government, business, and industry. In fact, unless writing is your primary job, short reports and correspondence (discussed in Chapter 18) will comprise most of the writing you do. This chapter examines the purposes, characteristics, and organization of the most frequently used short reports:

- task reports (recommendation, justification, inspection, information, investigation)
- periodic activity reports (daily, weekly, monthly, quarterly)
- progress (interim, status) reports
- meeting minutes
- trip (conference) reports
- "to file" (archive) documents

The chapter concludes with a brief discussion of report formats and suggestions for preparing effective forms.

Functions of Short Reports

Short reports record, and sometimes influence, current operations and also information that may be needed in the future. How could you buy a computer printer without a report on comparative models? Why would you finance a business trip or conference attendance if you never were told what was accomplished? How could you plan a production schedule if you didn't know the current status—how much was finished, how much was yet to be completed, what supplies were on hand, what personnel were available? Short reports have several common purposes:

- justifying and recommending actions
- reporting information
- analyzing problems
- providing data for decisions
- recording daily activities
- reporting progress
- recording key aspects of meetings, trips, and conferences

Regardless of the type of report you are preparing, always consider *why* it is needed: Someone needs to make a decision or justify an action. The content, style, and format of your reports should simplify the work of the reader.

Readers are generally neutral or positive because most are willing to form opinions based on currently available facts rather than on previously held beliefs. Generally, the information in any short reports follows the same sequence, which is modified for each specific type of report:

1. *Overview:* This section states the purpose and/or problem that necessitates a report. (On a prepared form, the title and column heads may provide this information.) Sufficient information is provided for the reader to understand the context of the report.
2. *Background:* This optional section presents information dealing with methods of investigation as well as materials and equipment used.
3. *Recommendations:* This section identifies any conclusions and/or recommendations (usually in priority order). Placing the recommendations near the beginning saves the busy reader time. Some reports, such as information reports, do not need a section for recommendations.
4. *Evidence:* This section presents the results, both data and discussion. Sometimes the results are summarized preceding the detailed presentation. On a prepared form, this summary might be a final column showing net gain or good/fair/poor evaluation.
5. *Discussion:* This section explains or justifies the conclusions or recommendations, based on the supporting results. If the report does not contain recommendations, this concluding section can review or summarize the major points. In a short report, however, this section is often entirely omitted.

As discussed in Chapter 4, the organization of a document is affected by the attitude of the reader. If the reader is generally receptive and positive, or at least neutral, the material should be organized with the most important information—conclusions and/or recommendations—first, followed by supporting details. If the reader has a negative attitude toward the subject of the document, or might be opposed to its recommendations, the material should be organized with the recommendations at the end, to enable the reader to follow the logic of the writer.

To organize information for any kind of report, you will find the patterns introduced in Chapter 4 particularly useful. In some situations, a straight *chronological* listing of actions or activities is all that is required. For example, a report describing a new accounting procedure could easily list the revised steps. Occasionally, *spatial order* will help you describe physical characteristics of objects, mechanisms, organisms, or locations. *Cause and effect* is valuable for projections and estimates, *comparison and contrast* useful for reports surveying the similarities and differences between various equipment or services. Specific suggestions for content and organization are provided with the discussion of each type of report.

Types of Short Reports

This section discusses the function and organization of the most frequently used short reports: a variety of task reports, periodic activity reports, progress reports, meeting minutes, trip reports, and reports addressed "to file."

Task Reports

Technical professionals deal with a variety of tasks that often result in reports. Most common are recommendation or justification reports, inspection or examination reports, and information or investigation reports. Typical subject matter in these three broad categories of task reports is listed in Figure 14.1.

A *recommendation report* or *justification report* primarily presents or defends a specific suggestion or solution for a particular situation. (See Chapter 16 for more formal ways to present recommendations in feasibility reports and proposals.)

Figure 14.1   Typical Subject Matter of Task Reports

Category of Task Report	*Examples of Subject for Which Report is Needed*
RECOMMENDATION/ JUSTIFICATION	equipment purchase
	program change
	procedural change (design, manufacturing, inspection, marketing, shipping)
	personnel change (benefits, scheduling)
	policy change
INSPECTION/ EXAMINATION	object/mechanism
	organism
	location/site
	process
INFORMATION/ INVESTIGATION	equipment failure
	personnel problem
	safety record/accident
	traffic/parking
	new or existing site/facility condition
	cost estimate (personnel, materials, equipment, and so on)
	delivery schedule
	market expansion
	laboratory research
	survey (research literature, employee opinions)

An *inspection report* or *examination report* focuses on recording observable details, sometimes followed with recommendations. In some cases, an inspection report is completed on a prepared form, for example, when the task involves the inspection of mechanical parts.

An investigation results in an *informative* or *investigative report* that collects and evaluates information about some existing situation, but the writer need not always include a recommendation.

Although the audience, purpose, and content of each report determine its organization, the general guidelines presented at the beginning of this chapter

	Differences in Types of Task Reports		
Figure 14.2			

Report Component	*Recommendation or Justification Report*	*Inspection or Examination Report*	*Information or Investigation Report*
OVERVIEW	introduce circumstances that necessitate the change	identify or define the subject being inspected	introduce circumstances that necessitate the investigation
BACKGROUND	identify the criteria for selecting a change	describe the subject being inspected	identify the procedures, including method and materials, if necessary
RECOMMENDATIONS	recommend or justify a change	make recommendations, if necessary	make recommendations, if necessary
EVIDENCE	provide data to support recommended change	present data from inspection or evaluation, noting discrepancies	present the results of the investigation
DISCUSSION	explain the advantages or benefits of the change	discuss the impact of the discrepancies	explain the reasons for the results

apply to all types of task reports. Ways to modify these standard components—overview, background, recommendations, evidence, and discussion—to meet specific report purposes are shown in Figure 14.2.

Examples 14.1 and 14.2, both recommendation reports, illustrate the possible variety in reports, even those with the same purpose.

The first report, in Example 14.1, opposing the use of foam-in-place packaging, is written as a memo for a manager who has expressed some enthusiasm for this packaging system. Because the manager will not initially be receptive to the report's conclusion, the writer places his recommendation at the end rather than its usual place near the beginning. By the time the manager has read the points the writer makes, he will probably agree with the writer and be receptive to the negative recommendation.

Example 14.1

L.C. Meredith Manufacturing, Inc.
1473 Pepperell Drive
Alexandria, VA 22304-0993
703-555-5523

TO: Neil St. John   DATE: 08 April 1986
                                          FROM: George Buchanan
                                          DEPT: Quality Assurance
                                          EXT: 555-5597
                                          LOC/MAIL STOP: NQ/S09

SUBJECT: Recommendation about using foam-in-place (FIP) packaging

    We have been considering foam-in-place (FIP) packaging as an effective
alternative to our packaging problems. Since a number of companies in the
area have implemented FIP systems, we can benefit from their experiences.   OVERVIEW
Many have found that FIP creates as many problems as it solves and have since
turned to other packaging.

    While investigating FIP, I have read FIP promotional material and
discussed the product with representatives from three local FIP   BACKGROUND
distributors. I have also spoken with quality assurance managers and
packaging engineers at five local companies that have tried FIP.

    FIP has many pitfalls that affect its use. This memo highlights   EVIDENCE
information about material density, shipping, drop tests, costs, operator   AND
protection and health, and chemical disposal.   DISCUSSION

   1. Material density is very important in determining the "G" level or
       shock transmitted to a packaged product. The density of the foam
       in FIP is not uniform. Regardless of what the FIP suppliers
       advertise, the density varies from operator to operator.

   2. The effective static stress of FIP is from 0.04 to 0.2 pounds per
       square inch (psi), which means a large contact surface area is
       required to cushion a dense product properly. Other cushioning
       materials such as polyethylene have an effective static stress
       range of 0.3 to 1.0 psi, which means less surface area is required.
       In general, an FIP package is larger than the equivalent expanded
       polystyrene or polyethylene package, based on the same fragility
       level. This means that shipping charges are greater for FIP packages.

   3. FIP obtains its cushioning ability from its foam structure. FIP
       suppliers in our area show cushioning curves for only the first drop
       test. Second and third drops are less favorable because the cell
       structure breaks down during the first drop. Other cushioning
       materials such as polyethylene do not break down and are much more
       consistent according to ASTM's standard 10-drop test. The probability
       that a packaged product will be dropped more than once during
       transportation is very high.

Example 14.1   *Continued*

4. FIP has many hidden costs:

    a. Additional costs include continued maintenance and spare parts, gun cleaning solvents, nitrogen, protective clothing, and utilities.

    b. If the foam touches any part of a product, the product is damaged and must be reworked. Once the foam adheres to a surface, no chemical will remove it. If the person operating the FIP system is careful, most rework expenses can be avoided. However, many people working on the packaging line are the least skilled hourly workers; often they are not careful.

    c. On an annual basis, the cost is substantial for plastic film to cover the product before the foam is molded around the product.

    d. FIP chemicals are typically sold by weight. However, in every canister, some of that weight is not converted into foam. Chemicals that cannot be extracted are left in the bottom of the canisters. Additionally, a 15 to 20% weight loss occurs because of gasses that escape during chemical mixing.

    e. The largest initial cost is the FIP equipment. The cost of providing ventilation equipment must also be included.

5. Most FIP systems use an MDI form of isocyanate, which is an irritant to the human body. This means that FIP work areas must be well ventilated, operators must wear special clothing to protect their garments, and goggles are mandatory to prevent eye injuries.

6. Regardless of which FIP system--with operator safeguards--is installed, the health of the operators is still a concern. All FIP systems use urea formaldehyde isocyanate chemicals, which according to medical experts can cause cancer. OSHA regulations clearly specify that overexposure to the chemicals results in irritation to the respiratory tract. (See attached OSHA regulations.)

7. The biggest deterrent to using an FIP system is the fact that EPA regulations classify urea formaldehyde isocyanate as hazardous waste; any residual chemicals must be disposed of in accordance with local, state, and federal guidelines.

Because of the engineering, health, and environmental limitations of FIP systems, I recommend that we no longer consider installing such a system. Instead, we should investigate other alternatives for packaging our product.

RECOMMENDATION

George Buchanan
George Buchanan

GB/ml
Attachments

Source: George Buchanan, FIP Packaging (Technical Writing 42.225, University of Lowell, 1984).

Example 14.2

RECOMMENDATION FOR MAKING ARTWORK WITHIN WATSON SYSTEMS, INC.

BASED ON

ANALYSIS OF QUOTATIONS FROM INTERNAL AND EXTERNAL SOURCES

Submitted to

Blake Elliott, Director
Watson Systems, Inc.
261 Industrial Avenue
Lowell, MA 01851

Prepared by

Kim Buckingham, Manager
Watson Systems, Inc.
261 Industrial Avenue
Lowell, MA 02851

December 5, 1986

Example 14.2   *Continued*

RECOMMENDATION FOR MAKING ARTWORK WITHIN WATSON SYSTEMS, INC.
BASED ON
ANALYSIS OF QUOTATIONS FROM INTERNAL AND EXTERNAL SOURCES

OVERVIEW

The Paint Shop is responsible for silkscreening for Production and R & D
requirements. We currently have to rely on an outside vendor to supply artwork
necessary for the silkscreening process. By having a vendor supply artwork,
we have no control over the following areas:

1. Costs
2. Delivery
3. Quality

Because our workload is increasing, we have to meet more stringent schedules.
In order to maintain our schedules, the time has come to eliminate these
problems with the artwork.

BACKGROUND

To recommend a practical solution, I investigated three alternatives:

1. Purchase the necessary equipment to do the artwork ourselves in the Paint
   Shop.
2. Continue with the outside vendor to do the artwork.
3. Identify in-house groups with the capability and capacity to do the artwork.

RECOMMENDATIONS AND SUMMARY OF ANALYSIS

The Font Area should be responsible for preparing the artwork for the
Silkscreening Department for the following reasons:

1. Cost savings: I obtained quotations for the artwork for the same ten
jobs--approximately three weeks' work--from the Font Area in Watson's
Westford facility and from the present outside supplier of artwork, Lampert
Designs, Inc. The quotations differed by $688.00:

                in-house estimate $1500.00
                outside vendor estimate $2188.00

Figure 4 summarizes the in-house and outside vendor costs for preparing artwork
for the Silkscreening Department.

2. Control over delivery: Using Lampert Designs or another outside vendor, we
have little control over delivery. If a job is rushed, we send out for the
artwork; the vendor may take two weeks to turn the job around. If the artwork
is done within Watson, we can push to have the artwork completed.

3. Improved quality: We have Quality Control Inspectors within our area who
can monitor the quality of the artwork. If the job is sent outside, we are at
the vendor's mercy if the artwork is rejected.

4. Utilizing in-house capacity: By utilizing present in-house capacity, we
would be saving approximately $14,230, considering the purchase price
of new equipment.

Example 14.2   *Continued*

-2-

COLLECTED DATA

Equipment purchase

    To do the artwork ourselves, we would need to purchase the equipment as well as allocate approximately 1500 square feet to set up and operate it.

    Thompson Company, Inc., was asked to quote on the equipment necessary to produce the artwork. Their quotation for $14,230 follows in Figure 1.

1.	1 Camera	VV-2024-M2B1--24 x 20	$7,095.00
2.	1 Crating		200.00
3.	1 Processor	P2500	1,095.00
4.	1 Vaccumma	DSVF-5066--50 x 60	2,395.00
5.	1 Crating		100.00
6.	1 Gamma 920 Exposure Lamp		3,295.00
7.	1 Crating		50.00

$14,230.00

Figure 1: Quotation on Equipment from Thompson Company, Inc.

Outside vendor

    I requested a quotation from our current artwork supplier, Lampert Designs, Inc., on ten separate jobs. Their quotation in Figure 2 totals $2,188.00.

			Lampert Designs
1.	1 Silkscreen	06619-0098	$648.00
2.	1 Silkscreen	10078-5-32	516.00
3.	1 Silkscreen	10167-5004	148.00
4.	1 Silkscreen	6889-5003	156.00
5.	1 Silkscreen	6106-165	152.00
6.	1 Silkscreen	6626-4	112.00
7.	1 Silkscreen	10105-5003	112.00
8.	1 Silkscreen	10019-5018	96.00
9.	1 Silkscreen	6850-404	152.00
10.	1 Silkscreen	06621-0110	96.00

$2,188.00

Figure 2: Quotations on Ten Silkscreens from Lampert Designs, Inc.

Example 14.2   *Continued*

-3-

In-house <u>suppliers</u>

Two separate areas within Watson Systems could supply artwork to the Paint Shop: Publications and the Font Area in the Westford facility.

Although Publications has the capability, they do not have the capacity. Because of their combined workload from R & D and production, they are already working 15% overtime.

The Font Area supervisor in Westford, Peter Finlay, said they had the capability and the capacity. His quotation on the same ten jobs quoted by the outside vendor totals $1,500.00, as shown in Figure 3.

			Westford Font Area
1.	1 Silkscreen	06619-0098	$400.00
2.	1 Silkscreen	10078-5-32	400.00
3.	1 Silkscreen	10167-5004	160.00
4.	1 Silkscreen	6889-5003	160.00
5.	1 Silkscreen	6106-165	160.00
6.	1 Silkscreen	6626-4	80.00
7.	1 Silkscreen	10105-5003	40.00
8.	1 Silkscreen	10019-5018	40.00
9.	1 Silkscreen	6850-404	40.00
10.	1 Silkscreen	06621-0110	20.00
			$1,500.00

Figure 3: Quotations on Ten Silkscreens from Watson's Westford Font Area

DISCUSSION

Figure 4 summarizes the differences in quotations from the two suppliers, Lampert Designs and the Font Area.

			Lampert Designs	Westford Font Area
1.	1 Silkscreen	06619-0098	$648.00	$400.00
2.	1 Silkscreen	10078-5-32	516.00	400.00
3.	1 Silkscreen	10167-5004	148.00	160.00
4.	1 Silkscreen	6889-5003	156.00	160.00
5.	1 Silkscreen	6106-165	152.00	160.00
6.	1 Silkscreen	6626-4	112.00	80.00
7.	1 Silkscreen	10105-5003	112.00	40.00
8.	1 Silkscreen	10019-5018	96.00	40.00
9.	1 Silkscreen	6850-404	152.00	40.00
10.	1 Silkscreen	06621-0110	96.00	20.00
			$2,188.00	$1,500.00

Figure 4: Quotations on Ten Silkscreens from Lampert Designs and Watson's Westford Font Area

Example 14.2	Continued

-4-

The collected data shows significant differences in cost:

1. Purchase new equipment to do
    artwork in the Paint Shop $14,230.00

2. Continue with outside vendor
    (quotation on ten jobs) $ 2,188.00

3. Use Font Area for artwork
    (quotation on ten jobs) $ 1,500.00

Based on costs of equipment, outside vendor artwork, and in-house artwork, my recommendation is that the Paint Shop have the silkscreening artwork done by the Westford Font Area.

Source: Kim Buckingham, Recommendation for Making Artwork within Watson Systems, Inc., Based on Analysis of Quotation from Internal and External Sources (Technical Writing 442.225, University of Lowell, 1983).

The second recommendation report, in Example 14.2, is more formal. It also incorporates information from outside sources—the responses to inquiries the writer made. Because the director to whom the report is submitted is receptive to the idea, the recommendation is placed first, with supporting information following.

Periodic Activity Reports

Efficient organizations have developed reporting methods to keep track of ongoing activities within the organization. These reports, filed daily, weekly, monthly, or quarterly, are compiled by supervisors and managers to describe the work completed by their section or group. Typically, each engineer compiles weekly reports, which an engineering manager uses for a monthly report; a section manager turns the monthly reports into a quarterly report, as shown in Figure 14.3. Sometimes information from these reports is used as the basis for projections that anticipate changes in project design, scheduling, or budgeting.

When the work is routine, daily or weekly periodic activity reports can be recorded on prepared forms. However, non-routine activity reports require more than merely filling in the blanks. These reports, whether routine or not, should be factual and honest—exaggerating to make a particular time period look better than it really is is simply bad policy.

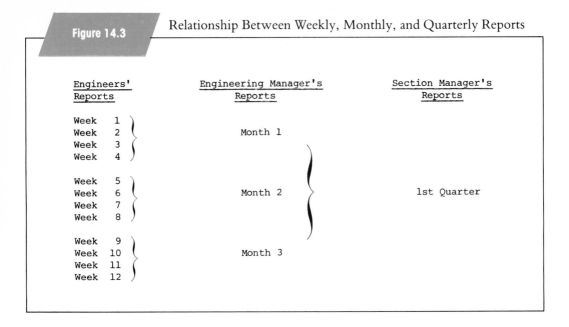

Figure 14.3   Relationship Between Weekly, Monthly, and Quarterly Reports

Organizations usually list information they expect a periodic activity report to contain:

1. *Overview:* Identify projects.
2. *Activities:* Specify project activities that are completed, in process, and planned.
3. *Recommendations:* Establish needed changes in scheduling, personnel, and budget.

Organizations also often have a required format (even if they don't have prepared forms) so that technical professionals don't have to spend much time selecting the information to include or organizing it.

In some situations, though, you may be given the criteria for the reports and then left on your own to organize and present the information in the activities section. Basically, you have two organizational choices—chronological order or priority order—which should depend on the expectations and needs of the readers. If the reader expects a straightforward listing of the activities, with no comment or evaluation, chronological order is appropriate. However, if the reader needs the report to rank order the completed and in-process work by importance, priority order is better.

For example, in preparing a monthly report, department head George Byron uses descending order, writing in great detail about the significant activities of the month and giving routine matters only cursory attention. But, hotel banquet manager Suzanne Juarez logically uses chronological order

Figure 14.4   Typical Project Master Schedule

PROJECT MASTER SCHEDULE

○ = planned start ▽ = planned completion
▢ = revised start △ = revised completion
● = started   ▼ = completed

#	WORK DESCRIPTION	ASSIGNED	WEEK ENDING			
			M T W T F	M T W T F	M T W T F	M T W T F

for her periodic activity reports because those reports must identify the daily use of the banquet facilities.

The recommendation section in a periodic activity report is used only if the writer needs to suggest changes based on the activities. The evidence and discussion sections are seldom included in periodic activity reports.

Job planning makes preparing a regular periodic activity report much easier. Figure 14.4 illustrates a typical project master schedule, which can be modified to meet the needs of most job situations. The schedule identifies the job and worker and provides space to note the time of start and completion. A planner regularly updates the master schedule, marking delays. Anyone preparing a periodic activity report can refer to this schedule to see the status of every job.

Progress Reports

Unlike periodic activity reports, which are prepared on a regular schedule regardless of current projects, progress reports summarize the progress, status, and projections related to a particular project. Progress reports (sometimes called status reports or interim reports) are part of almost all long-range projects and may also be expected in short-term projects.

Information about the *progress* of an activity answers a variety of reader questions:

- How's the project going?
- What has been accomplished during this phase of the project?
- How much time [or effort, money, and so on] did these tasks take?

Information about *status* answers additional reader questions:

- Where are we now?
- How do current activities relate to the overall project?
- How does this work affect other phases of the project?

Information about *projections* answers even more reader questions:

- Are we on schedule to meet our completion date?
- What plans need to be changed or altered?
- What will we do in the future?

A progress report generally follows this sequence of information:

1. *Overview:* Introduce the project.
2. *Progress:* Summarize the progress to date.
3. *Recommendation:* Identify major recommended schedule changes.
4. *Evidence:* Provide reasons for changes.
5. *Discussion:* Discuss the impact of the changes.

The overview of a progress report orients the reader to the project, identifying the purposes of both the project and the report. Additionally, the overview surveys the project and specifies the dates covered in the report. This section of the report is crucial, dealing with both specific times and number of tasks, but one or the other can be emphasized, depending on the desired focus. Some progress reports recommend changes necessitated by the progress—or lack of progress. Less frequently, additional reports establish and discuss reasons for these changes.

Like periodic activity reports, progress reports can be organized in either chronological or priority order. A chronologically ordered progress report emphasizes the time period, listing dates and then specifying the tasks that were completed during that period. If you prefer to emphasize the tasks, place them before the time period in your report; these tasks can be arranged in chronological or priority order, depending on the needs of the reader. The data should be clearly organized and presented in tables, graphs, and charts, a more effective method than placing the data in conventional paragraphs.

A progress report is particularly easy to prepare if the schedule with the

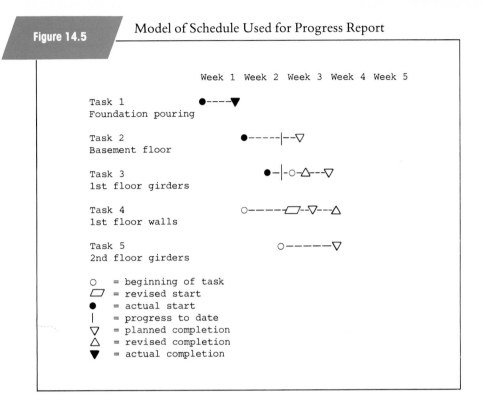

Figure 14.5   Model of Schedule Used for Progress Report

original project proposal is structured so that the progress of each task can be monitored. Figure 14.5 shows a progress summary prepared at the end of the second week of the project: Task 1 is completed, task 2 is on schedule, task 3 is slightly ahead, and task 4 is behind. Figure 14.6 illustrates your choices in organizing the information for a progress report.

The chart in Figure 14.5 would be accompanied by a narrative section in the report giving further details about the project, as shown in the following example. (In fact, in most documents, including textual discussion with every figure and table is expected.)

Example   Task 1 (foundation pouring) progressed right on schedule and is now completed.

Fortunately, the weather was in our favor, and we were able to beat our target date for task 2; the floor was almost finished by the beginning of week 3.

By using two trucks from the maintenance department, we were able to get task 3, the errection of the first floor girders, done ahead of schedule. We should complete that phase in the next day or two.

Unfortunately, shipping delays have caused us to fall behind schedule on the first floor walls. . . .

| Figure 14.6 | Ways to Organize a Progress Report |

Progress Report with Focus on Time

Time Period	**Tasks**
(day, week, month)	
time 1	task a
time 2	task b
time 3	task c
time 4	task d

OR

Progress Report with Focus on Tasks

Tasks	**Time Period**
(arranged by time)	
task a	time 1
task b	time 2
task c	time 3
task d	time 4

OR

Tasks	**Time Period**
(arranged by importance)	
task c	time 3
task b	time 2
task a	time 1
task d	time 4

Meeting Minutes

Minutes provide a record of the discussion and decisions that occur at meetings, serving as official (sometimes even legal) records. Beyond their function of official documentation, minutes provide a convenient review of the meeting for people who attended as well as for those who didn't.

Effective minutes generally adhere to the following guidelines:

- Provide accurate identification: date, time, location, organization, type of meeting, attending members, person presiding.

- Use chronological order:
  Committee reports (identify the committee and the reporter and abstract the main points)
  Old business
  New business

- Maintain an objective tone—no editorializing or subtle slanting of factual statements.

- Summarize rather than transcribe discussions.

- Express motions and amendments precisely, name the maker and seconder, and indicate the margin by which each motion passed or failed. If motions are long, complex, or legally binding on the organization, they should be submitted in writing.

- Record all parliamentary points: resolutions, points of order, and so on.

- Indicate time of adjournment (and time/date of next meeting if applicable).

- Attach a copy of the meeting announcements and agenda.

Preparing the minutes for a meeting requires both organization and attention to long-established conventions. The agenda for a meeting can provide you with a basis from which you can organize the information. If the meeting was recorded, you can use the tape to fill in details you may have missed while taking notes. The following excerpt from *Robert's Rules of Order* recommends the traditional format and sequence of information for meeting minutes.

The record of the proceedings of a deliberative assembly is usually called the *minutes*, or sometimes—particularly in legislative bodies—the *journal*. In an ordinary society, unless the minutes are to be published, they should contain mainly a record of what was *done* at the meeting, not what was *said* by the members. The minutes should never reflect the secretary's opinion, favorable or otherwise, on anything said or done.

CONTENT OF THE MINUTES. The *first paragraph* of the minutes should contain the following information (which need not, however, be divided into numbered or separated items directly corresponding to those below):

1. the kind of meeting: regular, special, adjourned regular, or adjourned special;
2. the name of the society or assembly;
3. the date and time of the meeting, and the place, if it is not always the same;
4. the fact that the regular chairman and secretary were present or, in their absence, the names of the persons who substituted for them; and

5. whether the minutes of the previous meeting were read and approved—as read, or as corrected—the date of that meeting being given if it was other than a regular business meeting.

The body of the minutes should contain a *separate paragraph for each subject matter*, and should show:

6. all main motions or motions to bring a main question again before the assembly—except any that were withdrawn—giving:
   a. the wording in which each motion was adopted or otherwise disposed of (with the facts as to how the motion may have been debated or amended before disposition being mentioned only parenthetically);
   b. the disposition of the motion, including—if it was *temporarily* disposed of—any primary and secondary amendment and all adhering secondary motions that were then pending; and
   c. usually, in the case of all important motions, the name of the mover;
7. all notices of motions, and
8. all points of order and appeals, whether sustained or lost, together with the reasons given by the chair for his ruling.

The *last paragraph* should state:

9. the hour of adjournment.

Additional rules and practices relating to the content of the minutes are the following:

■ The name of the seconder of a motion should not be entered in the minutes unless ordered by the assembly.

■ When a count has been ordered or the vote is by ballot, the number of votes on each side should be entered; and when the voting is by roll call, the names of those voting on each side and those answering "Present" should be entered. If members fail to respond on a roll call vote, enough of their names should be recorded as present to reflect that a quorum was present at the time of the vote.

■ The proceedings of a committee of the whole, or a quasi committee of the whole, should not be entered in the minutes, but the fact that the assembly went into committee of the whole (or into quasi committee) and the committee report should be recorded.

■ When a question is considered informally, the same information should be recorded as under the regular rules, since the only informality in the proceedings is in the debate.

- When a committee report is of great importance or should be recorded to show the legislative history of a measure, the assembly can order it "to be entered in the minutes," in which case the secretary copies it in full in the minutes.

- The name and subject of a guest speaker can be given, but no effort should be made to summarize his remarks.

THE SIGNATURE. Minutes should be signed by the secretary and can also be signed, if the assembly wishes, by the president. The words *Respectfully submitted*—although occasionally used—represent an older practice that is not essential in signing the minutes.[1]

Trip/Conference Reports

Trip and conference reports are important for several reasons. They force the traveler to review and evaluate the activities of the trip or conference and distinguish the major accomplishments from those less important. Such reports also provide an opportunity for the traveler to share activities and information with people who didn't make the trip or attend the conference. Of course, the report also justifies the time and expense of the trip or conference. In fact, trip reports can even be used to verify business trips for IRS inquiries and audits.

A trip or conference report is seldom completed on a prepared form. Instead, the information listed below is incorporated into a logically organized, clearly stated report:

Trip	*Conference*
purpose and date of trip	purpose and date of conference
primary task(s)	primary task(s)
personal role	personal role
people contacted	sessions attended
question(s) raised or resolved	information gained
conclusions	conclusions

As you can see, the information presented in trip and conference reports is very similar. Unlike periodic activity reports and progress reports, which frequently use chronological order, effective trip and conference reports employ priority order. Priority order gives you the opportunity to rank the tasks and information according to their value to your organization.

As Example 14.3 shows, a trip report does not have to be lengthy to be effective. Notice that the essential identifying information is presented in the memo heading rather than in the text itself.

Example 14.3

MEIDELL & ASSOCIATES, INC.

TO: Software Development Group
FROM: Suzanne Champion
DATE: April 8, 1986
SUBJECT: Trip Report
          Training for Automatic Instrumentation Corporation
          Glenview, IL
          April 3-5, 1986

This three-day course was an on-site introduction to our software. All 14 participants in my training group were new to computing, so the programming tasks focused on two areas:

1. top-level commands in procedures
2. elementary control structures (do loops, if-then-else. etc.)

The system manager, Tom Searson, was very cooperative and a good resource during the entire training period.

The following three concerns were raised:

1. A global DIRECTORY pathname variable would be very useful. In particular, the command

   ```
   DIRECTORY = HOME <RET>
   ```

   seems preferable to our current command

   ```
   DIRECTORY = '|' <RET>
   ```

2. Tom Searson wonders what sorting algorithm is used by the DIR command; it's about as slow as a bubble sort. Is there any way to make it more efficient?

3. Several class members were interested in multi-tasking--for example, simultaneously performing contour plots and editing a model.

We should discuss these concerns at next Monday's department meeting, so that we're ready for the second training course at Automatic Instrumentation Corporation, scheduled for the second week of May.

"To File" Reports

"To file" reports are prepared for the express purpose of documenting an idea or action. These reports, available for reference if questions ever arise about some aspect of a project, form an archival history of a project.

Frequently, such reports simply record oral conversations, discussions, directives, or decisions in a concise, permanent document. If the situation is appropriate, the name and title of any person(s) responsible for (or having authority to sponsor) actions that develop from the "to file" report are included. A copy of the report is sent to that person so the information in it can be verified or amended before it reaches the file. Because people occasionally retract, change, or forget positions they've taken, you can avert confusion by documenting discussions and commitments.

The problem with "to file" reports is that people sometimes spend an excessive amount of time documenting activities as a political protection. Accurate archive records are important, but they should not take an inordinate amount of time, effort, or attention.

Formats of Short Reports

In addition to serving multiple purposes, short reports also vary in format: memos, letters, reports, and prepared forms. The choice of format generally depends on a combination of factors: whether the document is routine or nonroutine, whether the audience is internal or external, and whether the tone should be informal or formal. Figure 14.7 indicates the most likely format for various short reports.

Memos and Letters. Routine information can be easily presented in *memos* and *letters*, accounting for the widespread use of form memos and letters, which were popular long before word processing made individualization possible. Often, though, memos and letters deal with nonroutine information, with memos going to internal readers (either an individual or a group) and letters going to external readers (a single individual, though copies may be sent to others). Both memos and letters range from informal to fairly formal. (Refer to Chapter 18 for a more detailed discussion of correspondence.)

Reports. Communication that does not fit neatly on a prepared form and requires a more formal tone and format than a memo or letter is placed in a *report*. Reports can be intended for both internal or external readers.

Figure 14.7   Formats for Short Reports

	TASK		AUDIENCE		TONE and FORMAT	
	Routine	Nonroutine	Internal	External	Formal	Informal
PREPARED FORMS	■		■	■		■
MEMOS	■	■	■			■
LETTERS		■		■	■	■
REPORTS		■	■	■	■	

Regardless of purpose, audience, or degree of formality, a short report should be easy to read and visually appealing. Even in a short report, headings and subheadings can facilitate reading. Data should be presented clearly and directly; often tables, charts, and graphs are used.

The organization and format of a report has a strong impact on the reaction of the reader. Examples 14.4 and 14.5 are different versions of the same memo report requesting that automatic garage doors be installed in a shop area constanly exposed to harsh weather. Both reports were accompanied by several attachments that are not included here. The second version of the report, in Example 14.5, is far easier to read because of its organization, subheadings, format, and awareness of the reader.

Prepared Forms.   An appropriate method for routine, informal communication for both internal and external readers is *prepared forms*. Accounts of day-to-day operations most frequently use prepared forms and memos, seldom formal reports. For example, inspection and evaluation reports are often done on prepared forms, whether the subject is a precision machined part or a patient admitted to a pediatric unit.

Forms can be a tremendous timesaver for both writers and readers. Forms assist writers by reminding them to include every essential item. And they assist readers by ordering information in the same sequence in each report of a series, so the readers can quickly locate whatever information they need.

Unfortunately, existing forms are often poorly designed or outdated. As part of your work as a technical professional or as a technical writer, you may

Example 14.4

R&D
1023 LINDEN
PAULI, TEXAS
69966

TO: Charles Malatesta

FROM: Tom Mansur *TM*

SUBJECT: Purchase and installation of automatic roll-up doors

DATE: September 27, 1986

The R & D Model Shop moved to its present location--next to the rear shipping
and receiving dock of the Colebrook facility--15 months ago. Since then, we have
been subjected to excessive heat in summer and extreme cold in winter. Most of
the day the loading doors are open, and the heat or air conditioning is lost
through the two connecting doorways. This is both expensive and a health risk.

One attempt to control the temperature was swinging metal doors, which kept out
the weather but was dangerously noisy. These doors banged loudly against the
chain link fence outside. Machinists would jump at the sound, presenting the
danger of severed fingers. Eventually these doors were knocked off their hinges,
leaving us no protection from the outside elements.

We next installed clear plastic strip doors, which flap in the breeze and offer
no protection from extreme temperatures. They also present a safety risk to
fork truck drivers, in that the flexible strips swing down from the fork truck
extensions and slap the drivers on the face and arms.

The approximate cost of the lost heat and air conditioning is $5,970.00 per
year. (See attached cost breakdown.) In human terms, in the summer when the
air conditioners are on, we are sweating; in the winter when the heaters are
blowing, we are shivering. These conditions are unacceptable.

We, therefore, recommend the purchase and installation of two electric garage
doors with both wall-mounted and pull-chain openers. These doors would be
equipped with pneumatic safety stops at the bottom to prevent injury. In
compliance with the fire safety egress requirements, we recommend the
installation of two regular doors, with pneumatic closers, as common entry/
exit ways. The total cost to purchase and install the equipment to correct
the situation in $4,262,00. This would account for $1,708.00 in savings at
the end of one year. Please refer to the attached estimates for prices of
the garage doors and regular doors. Refer also to the attached building
layout that identifies the recommended locations of the proposed doors.

We need these doors now, since winter is rapidly approaching.

TM/db
Attachments

Note: The figures that accompanied the original report are not included here.
Source: Tom Mansur, Justification for the Purchase and Installation of Automatic Roll-Up
Doors for the R & D Model Shop (Technical Writing 42.225 University of Lowell, 1983).

Example 14.5

R&D
1023 LINDEN
PAULI, TEXAS
69966

TO: Charles Malatesta
           Plant/Facilities Administration

FROM: Tom Mansur *TM*
           R & D Model Shop Group Leader

SUBJECT: Justification for the purchase and installation of
           automatic roll-up doors for the R & D Model Shop

DATE: September 27, 1986

OVERVIEW

Unacceptable Conditions: The R & D Model Shop has been in the Colebrook
facility, zone 5 (see Figures 1 and 2), for 15 months, adjacent to the
shipping and receiving dock. The dock's loading doors are open approximately 8-10 hours a day, so the heat or air conditioning escapes from the
R & D Model Shop through the two connecting doorways. The Model Shop
machinists are exposed to excessive heat during the summer and extreme cold
during the winter. This situation poses personnel problems as well as energy
losses.

BACKGROUND

Personnel Problems: Machinists working in the R & D Model Shop are exposed
to temperature extremes for up to 10 hours a day, causing discomfort and
decreasing resistance to colds and flu. Employee satisfaction with the
working conditions is low, influencing shop productivity. Additionally, use
of sick days by R & D Model Shop employees has increased 7% since we moved
to the Colebrook facility, costing the company money.

Energy Loss: Because the loading dock is open to the outside for up to 10
hours a day, the energy expended to heat or air condition the R & D Model
Shop is wasted.

RECOMMENDATION

Automatic Garage Doors: The purchase and installation of two electric garage
doors with both wall mounted and pull-chain openers would eliminate the
problem with temperature extremes. These doors would be equipped with
pneumatic safety stops at the bottom to prevent injury. In compliance with
the fire safety egress requirements, two regular doors (with pneumatic closers)
would be installed as common entry/exit ways.

Example 14.5   *Continued*

EVIDENCE

<u>Cost</u> <u>of</u> <u>Lost</u> <u>Energy</u>: The cost of BTU loss in zone 5--based on heating and air conditioning expenses for FY 85 and cost formulas (see Figures 3, 4, and 5)-- is approximately $5,970.00

<u>Purchase</u> <u>and</u> <u>Installation</u> <u>Costs</u>: The total cost to purchase and install the equipment to correct the situation is $4,262.00, based on quotations from Dempsey Door Company and Jackson Lumber Company. (See Figures 6 and 7.)

<u>Potential</u> <u>Savings</u>: The payback period would be less than one year.

Estimated annual cost of problem	$5,970.00
Estimated cost of solution	- 4,262.00
	$1,708.00

    Savings the first year

The recommended solution would account for more than $1,708.00 in savings at the end of one year. Please refer to the attached estimates for prices of the garage doors and regular doors. Refer also to the attached building layout that identifies the recommended locations of the proposed doors.

PREVIOUS ATTEMPTS TO SOLVE THE PROBLEM

<u>Swinging</u> <u>Metal</u> <u>Doors</u>: Swinging metal doors were in place for the first six months that the R & D Model Shop was in the present location. They kept out the weather but were dangerously noisy. When fully loaded fork trucks passed through, these doors banged loudly against the chain link fence that surrounds the shop. Machinists in the area would jump at the sound, presenting the danger of severed fingers or worse, not to mention the rattled nerves. The constant traffic of fork trucks eventually knocked these doors off their hinges.

<u>Plastic</u> <u>Flap</u> <u>Doors</u>: The swinging metal doors were replaced with clear plastic strip doors. These doors flap in the breeze and actually provide no protection at all from extreme temperatures. They also present a safety risk to fork truck drivers. As the fork trucks move through the doorway, the flexible strips swing down from the fork truck extensions and slap the drivers on the face and arms.

DISCUSSION

Implementing the recommendations in this report will benefit both the R & D Model Shop employees as well as the Colebrook operation in general. The comfort of the work environment and job satisfaction will increase for employees in the R & D Model Shop. Sick time should decrease. The impact on the heating and air conditioning expenses should be felt almost immediately.

This report has been approved by Raphael Calvo, Manager of the R & D Model Shop, and Max Freeport, Director of Colebrook Operations.

Example 14.5

```
So that work can begin immediately, a working print (Figure 8) and the
completed work request form (Figure 9) are attached.


ATTACHED FIGURES

Figure 1: Colebrook facility, zone 5 floor plan
Figure 2: Colebrook building layout
Figure 3: Colebrook heating expense report for FY 8
Figure 4: Colebrook air conditioning expense report for FY 8
Figure 5: Cost breakdown/conversion formulas
Figure 6: Dempsey Door Company quotation
Figure 7: Jackson Lumber Company quotation
Figure 8: Working print for Plant Facilities Department
Figure 9: Work Request
```

Note: The figures that accompanied the original report are not included here.
Source: Tom Mansur, Justification for the Purchase and Installation of Automatic Roll-Up
Doors for the R & D Model Shop (Technical Writing 42.225 University of Lowell, 1983).

need to design or redesign forms; the guidelines in Figure 14.8 should aid you in this task. Four areas of form design are highlighted: content, layout, visual elements, and stock. The more items in Figure 14.8 that you adhere to, the greater the likelihood that your form will be easy to fill out and provide the recipient with useful information.

Figure 14.8   Suggestions for Effective Form Design

Content

The purpose of the form is clearly identified by number and an accurate, descriptive title.

Content of the form is consistent with its stated purpose.

The instructions and labels are easy to understand.

No unnecessary information is requested.

The routing sequence is clearly identified.

Filing information is clearly labeled.

The necessary number of copies are provided and clearly named and numbered in the order each copy can be removed.

Figure 14.8 *Continued*

Layout

The form sections are not crowded.

The margins have sufficient space for binding.

The instructions are in a logical location, clearly labeled, and enumerated.

Right margin justification of items is used.

Example Correct

Name: _____
Address: _____
Telephone: _____

Incorrect

Name _____
Address _____
Telephone _____

The horizontal spacing is appropriate for a typewriter or computer printer (for example, the need for tab stops is minimized).

The vertical spacing is appropriate for a typewriter or computer printer.

Signatures and conditions for the form's validity are at the bottom of the form.

The address box is appropriately placed for a window envelope if the form is mailed.

Visual Elements

The printing on the form is easy to read.

Visual devices (boldface, type variation, shading, color variation, enumerated items) assist the user in completing and routing the form.

Thick (or double) rule lines set off the major sections of the form.

Check-off boxes are used to minimize filling in information.

Boxes identify areas for recording brief answers.

Lines (rather than boxed areas) or blocks of blank space provide areas for longer answers.

Stock

The paper stock is appropriate (weight, color) for the purpose of the form.

Multiple-copy forms use NCR (no carbon required) paper or inserted, easy-to-remove carbon.

Judicious placement of carbon and blanking out of areas for some information allows data to be omitted on some copies.

The form fits in standard envelopes, binders, and file folders.

Inquiries and Applications

Discussion Questions

1. Your supervisor requested you to attend a conference and went to considerable trouble to obtain approval for it. You found the meetings dull and unproductive. You did gather one or two useful ideas from other people attending the conference, but your overall judgment was that the meeting was a waste of time. How do you orient your report? Will you be brutally frank about the conference's general worthlessness?

2. Try to think of a report (not for an academic class) that you or someone you know had to prepare that, at the time, seemed unnecessary. Now take the point of view of the person who ordered the report or the person who received it. Can you uncover any justification for the time and effort expended?

3. Develop two or three scenarios that would prompt you to write a "to file" report.

4. In what circumstances would you prefer to submit reports on prepared forms? In narrative form? What are the limitations of each? Which do you think readers would prefer in each situation?

5. You are the production supervisor in a small company that does precision grinding of optical lenses. What types of reports might you request? What types of reports might you prepare?

Individual and Group Exercises

1. Design a form for reporting monthly progress on a prototype thermostat. Create your own details. Will you use chronological or priority order?

2. Compose a set of guidelines to be used by writers of progress reports in the printing plant.

3. Write a series of reports generated by a business trip—request for authorization to go, request for expense money, report of the trip, expense report, recommendation that your company adopt a procedure or product you learned about.

4. The local Civil Liberties Union has requested a report of your plant's accommodations—or lack of them—for handicapped workers. What reports would you need to obtain and what would you need to write? (You are not preparing the actual documents; rather, you are explaining their probable source, type, audience, and content.)

Assignments

1. Select a small piece of equipment or machinery you are familiar with. Assume you work for a company that needs to purchase 50 of them. Write a report that you hope will lead to the purchase of your chosen brand or model.

2. Select a short report (written by you or someone else) that you are not satisfied with—even if it has already been submitted for class or work. Revise it, much like the examples earlier in the chapter about the shop area that needed garage doors installed. Submit both the original and the revised versions of the report.

3. Select a prepared form that is particularly confusing or poorly designed. Following the guidelines presented in this chapter, redesign the form. Submit both the original and the revised versions of the form. Also include a page explaining and justifying the changes.

15 Formal Reports

WHILE CHAPTER 14 FOCUSED on short reports, which require straightforward presentation of information, usually in chronological or priority order, this chapter deals with more complex, or formal, reports. Like their shorter counterparts, formal reports not only record current operations but also influence future ones. After defining formal reports and differentiating them from short reports, the chapter deals with the process of planning and designing them.

Defining Formal Reports

Formal reports differ from short reports in function, organization, and format.

In general terms, formal reports provide background information and data for decisions, analyze problems, and describe empirical research. These technical reports usually combine the results of formal research or informal investigation with interpretations and recommendations. More specifically, formal reports in government, education, business, and industry usually fit one of three broad purposes, which may occasionally overlap:

- Analyze a problem, identify alternative solutions, then recommend and justify a solution.
- Present and interpret original research from laboratory or field studies.
- Examine current literature in a particular subject.

Formal reports are also distinguished from short reports by organization, format, length, and amount of detail. Formal reports can employ simple organizational patterns, such as chronology and priority when the subject requires little analysis. More frequently, however, the subject requires complex patterns, such as comparison/contrast and cause/effect.

Formal reports contain more front matter and end matter than short reports. The front matter in a short report is nearly nonexistent; just the heading on a memo or letter or occasionally a title page precedes the report. In contrast, the front matter in a formal report includes some or all of these elements: cover, title page, letter of transmittal, abstract, table of contents, and list of figures. While a short report may have attachments, a formal report often has a glossary (which may also precede the document), appendixes, and a list of sources.

Because of the extensive front matter in a formal report, it tends to repeat content, something that seldom occurs in a short report. However, this is usually an advantage rather than a disadvantage because the multiple audiences for formal reports read various sections for different purposes. For example, managers focus on conclusions and recommendations so they can make informed decisions. Technical professionals focus on the accuracy and feasibility of the technical details. Individual readers seldom go through an entire formal report from beginning to end; rather, they read the sections relevant to their jobs.

Planning a Report

The process of preparing a formal report is not as simple or straightforward as preparing a short report. For example, sometimes preparing a formal report involves analyzing a complex problem in order to determine possible solutions. The report presents these options and then recommends a particular solution. The process is illustrated by the situation of Kate Barton who was asked by her manager to identify the causes of the cracking problems of the bezel trim on the MV8000 central processing unit (CPU) cabinet. Her investigation is discussed in this chapter, and her report presented in Example 15.4.

When you begin to plan a formal report, you need to ask yourself a series of questions to identify the audience for and purpose and organization of the report:

- Who will read this report?
- What do they want to know?
- What is my goal as writer?
- What should be the scope of the report?
- What should be the balance of technical and nontechnical material?
- How should the report be organized?

Identify Audience

Knowledge about your report's audience helps you clarify the report's purpose and organization. One of the most difficult aspects of preparing reports is tailoring your material for readers with a variety of backgrounds and needs.

When you begin planning a report, the information in Chapter 3 about audience analysis will help you to identify the organizational relationship between you and your readers. Are you dealing with a *vertical* audience, with readers on a different organizational level than you? Is the audience *horizontal*, with the readers on the same organizational level, but with a different technical specialization? Or is the audience *external*, with the readers in an entirely different organization?

Once you identify the readers and place them in an organization in relation to you, concentrate on how they will use the report. *Primary readers* fall into one of two categories: those who will use the conclusions and recommendations for decision making and those who will be interested in the technical details, particularly the accuracy of data and the feasibility of the conclusions and recommendations, as they affect their work. *Secondary readers* are indirectly affected by the conclusions and recommendations of a document. For example, a report recommending reroofing and insulating a manufacturing plant would have the facilities manager as one of the primary readers. Department supervisors, whose work might be disrupted by the construction, would be secondary readers.

State Purpose

After you have identified the audiences for a report, focusing on the purpose is easier. In addition to having mixed audiences, formal reports also frequently have dual purposes—to inform or to persuade; you need to specify the purpose(s) of your report, both for yourself and for the readers. Writing a purpose statement gives you a clear focus for a report and provides a way for you to control content, format, and organization. The audience benefits from a purpose statement that focuses on the intent of a report and explains how it fulfills their need(s) for certain information.

The purpose, placed at the beginning of a report, should follow a specific pattern: State the problem, identify questions and activities related to the problem, and explain how the report responds to the problem and to related questions and activities.

Designing a Report

A formal report's audience and purpose influence not only the actual content of a report but also its organization. Writing for a mixed audience requires you to organize the material so that it serves all categories of readers, whatever their different needs.

In dealing with a mixed audience, one approach is to write a report that imagines the reader as a composite of decision makers and technical professionals. However, such a compromise does not fully address the needs of any group of readers. A second possibility is to write completely different reports for different audiences. One disadvantage to this is the amount of time required. Furthermore, separating reports in such a way eliminates the natural and necessary interaction between decision makers and technical professionals. Therefore, a single report, responsive to the needs of both decision makers and technical professionals, is the most realistic approach.

Knowing the audience plays an important role in the overall structure of a report. Recall from the discussion in Chapter 4 that inductive reasoning moves from specific to general, and deductive reasoning, from general to specific. Receptive readers appreciate reports that are organized deductively, giving the conclusions first and then providing the substantiating details; most reports are arranged this way. Sometimes, however, a report might be better received if arranged inductively, giving specifics first and letting them lead to general conclusions and recommendations.

The overall purpose of most reports is to state a position and then establish its validity. The usual organization for a deductively organized report uses a two-tier approach:

1. Give an overview of the problem and then summarize the preferred solution.
2. Cite evidence or support for the solution in descending order of significance, dealing with both positive and negative points.

You might assume that formal reports have a specific format that everyone follows. However, there is little agreement as to what constitutes the best format, nor is there any definitive list of what must be included, as the proliferation of style guides suggests. Further evidence for the disparity of report formats comes from NASA: "The preliminary findings of a [1981] NASA study revealed that (1) nearly one hundred components were used [in different technical reports], (2) there was an apparent lack of consistency in the terms used for the components, and (3) there was an apparent lack of consistency in the location of the components."[1]

This lack of consistency shows up in the dozens of style guides published by individual companies and professional associations. (Chapter 8 lists the most frequently used guide for organizing and documenting formal technical reports and articles.)

This text employs a generic report format that incorporates the standard elements of most reports; if your company prescribes its own format, use that instead. Figure 15.1 presents a list of the components in this generic format. Each component is first defined and then illustrated in the sample report reproduced at the end of the chapter.

Front Matter

The front matter in a report consists of the sections that come before the body of the document; however, not every formal report includes every section. These sections follow:

- cover
- letter of transmittal
- title page
- table of contents
- list of figures
- list of tables
- list of appendixes
- glossary (here or in end matter)
- list of symbols (here or in end matter)
- abstract (descriptive or informative) or executive summary

The *cover* secures the pages and presents a professional image. The weight of the cover should match the weight of report, so a brief report needs only a lightweight cover; a lengthy report requires a sturdy cover. For the convenience of the reader, the cover should lie flat when the report is open.

Figure 15.1   Standard Report Components

Cover

Front Matter
letter of transmittal
title page
table of contents
list of figures
list of tables
list of appendixes
glossary (here or in end matter)
list of symbols (here or in end matter)
abstract (descriptive or informative) or executive summary

Body (selection and sequence of elements depend on audience and purpose)

Part I
statement of purpose or problem
summary of findings
summary of recommendations

Part II
background to problem
literature search (of information relevant to problem)
approach, method, and materials
    (for reports of experiments, surveys)
available options (solutions)
results: collected data/findings
discussion
interpretation(s)
conclusion(s)
recommendation(s)

End Matter
appendixes
glossary (if not included in the front matter)
list of symbols (if not included in the front matter)
footnotes and references
    or
sources cited

Format Elements
headings and subheadings
pagination
figures and tables
information notes

Key identifying information is presented on the *title page*, which, at the very least, should include the following elements:

- title/subtitle
- author(s) and organization
- person and organization for whom report was prepared
- date

In addition, the title page may contain a descriptive abstract, project identification, and report numbers. (Example 15.3 shows a typical title page.)

Whether to include a *letter of transmittal* depends on company policy. Using a standard letter format (illustrated in Chapter 18), the author of the report uses a letter of transmittal to introduce the primary reader to the document. Generally, a letter of transmittal has three paragraphs. The first introduces the document's subject and purpose. The second usually focuses on one or two key points dealing with the document's preparation or content: problems, resources, additional work, conclusions, recommendations. The third paragraph is a courtesy that encourages the reader to contact the writer about any questions.

The *table of contents* identifies major sections and subsections of report, differentiating the sections both typographically and spatially. In Example 15.1, all capital letters are used for major headings, and indentation indicates subsections.

If a report uses a numeric outline, then the table of contents also does, as Example 15.2 shows.

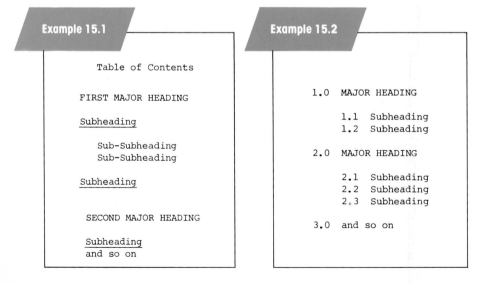

Example 15.1

```
        Table of Contents

FIRST MAJOR HEADING

Subheading

    Sub-Subheading
    Sub-Subheading

Subheading


SECOND MAJOR HEADING

Subheading
and so on
```

Example 15.2

```
1.0   MAJOR HEADING

      1.1   Subheading
      1.2   Subheading

2.0   MAJOR HEADING

      2.1   Subheading
      2.2   Subheading
      2.3   Subheading

3.0   and so on
```

Example 15.3

```
1.0  Problems in Treating Postoperative
     Lung Congestion

            NOT

1.0  Introduction
```

As Example 15.3 demonstrates, an effective table of contents uses content headings, not sections labels, so readers know what each section and subsection is about.

The *list of figures* serves as a table of contents for most of the visuals in a report: graphs, charts, drawings, maps, and photos. Such a list is optional if a report has fewer than three figures. Similarly, tables are listed in a *list of tables*. If a report has more than three of only one kind of visual—for example, maps—then they can be identified in a list of maps rather than a list of figures.

If a report has appendixes, these are included in the *list of appendixes*. If the report has only one or two appendixes, the listing can be included as a major section in the table of contents.

The *abstract* summarizes the major points, findings, or recommendations of the report. The abstract does *not* serve as the introduction to the report, but as an independent, entirely condensed version—the report in miniature. The abstract is frequently considered the most important part of report, especially if the primary reader is a busy manager. (Chapter 12 discusses abstracts in detail.)

Body

The selection and sequence of elements in the body of a formal report depend on audience and purpose. Usually some of the following elements are included:

Part I

- statement of purpose or problem
- summary of findings
- summary of recommendations

Part II

- background to problem
- literature search of information relevant to problem
- approach, method, and materials (for reports of experiments, surveys)
- available options (solutions)
- results: collected data/findings
- discussion
- interpretation(s)
- conclusion(s)
- recommendation(s)

Separating the body into two major segments responds to the needs of the two very different kinds of primary readers—decision makers and technical professionals.

Part I of the body states the purpose or problem and then summarizes the findings and recommendations, immediately giving decision makers the information they need without making them sort through myriad technical details.

Part II of the body provides details for technical professionals. The organizational patterns presented in Chapter 4 provide a variety of structures whose application depends on both purpose and content. The following list summarizes these patterns and suggests appropriate uses:

- *chronological order*—Chronology is used for explaining processes. A report in which this is appropriate might explain the process of setting up a new production line.
- *spatial order*—Descriptions of objects or locations are best arranged spatially. For example, such an organizational pattern would work in describing the physical facilities in a remodeled plant.
- *cause and effect*—Problem-solution situations are easily explained this way, often arranged in descending order of importance. For example, suggestions of ways to increase the acceptance ratio of items passing through quality control could be explained using cause and effect.
- *comparison and/or contrast*—Focusing on the similarities and differences, also often arranged in descending order, provides a reader with the basis for decision making. A report using comparison and contrast might advocate the lease/purchase of new equipment or recommend a change in vendors.

End Matter

The end matter of a report comes after the body. Any of the following elements could be included:

- appendixes
- glossary (if not included in the front matter)
- list of symbols (if not included in the front matter)
- footnotes and references
  or
  sources cited

Appendixes present useful information that might interrupt the flow of the report. Although no rules dictate what should be included, information in the appendix should increase the reader's knowledge or understanding. The decision as to what to include depends on the purpose and audience of the document. For example, a primary reader who has a technical background benefits from detailed technical data in the body of the document far more than a person who relies on the writer's technical expertise to summarize pertinent information. For a primary reader who is a manager with a background in business rather than a technical field, detailed data is appropriately placed in an appendix.

The following list identifies some of the items that you can consider placing in an appendix. Whether these are included in the body or the appendix, or are omitted entirely, is a decision that must be made for each individual document:

- formulas used in calculations
- complex calculations of which only the results are used in report itself
- survey forms
- interview questions
- transcripts
- correspondence related to the document subject
- detailed figures from which selected information is taken for report
- references for further reading

A *glossary*, which defines terms unfamiliar to the readers, constitutes an optional section of a document. You decide whether or not to include a glossary based on the expertise of the audience and the complexity of the content. Sometimes the glossary is placed with front matter if the primary reader is not likely to know the terms.

Information notes can be used instead of a glossary to define unfamiliar terms or concepts. These notes are appropriate if the report has only a few terms to define, making a full glossary unnecessary. Information notes are most convenient if placed at the bottom of the page on which the reference appears; occasionally, however, these notes are combined with the end notes.

A list of the *symbols* used in the report is often part of the end matter, particularly if any of the material is complex and the readers do not have expertise in the field.

The list of *sources cited* or source notes is the final section of the end matter. The formats for the entries are presented in the documentation section of Chapter 8.

Format Elements

In addition to the main section of a formal report, a writer needs to be attentive to several aspects of format:

- headings and subheadings
- pagination
- figures and tables

Headings and subheadings should match those listed in the table of contents—in typography, placement on page, and wording. These headings and subheadings do more than provide visual breaks for the reader; they also act as cohesive devices, identifying the movement from one topic to the next.

By convention, most reports identify the first page of the body as page 1 of the report, continuing sequentially until the final page of the end matter. The front matter of the report—those pages preceding the body—is usually numbered with lower case Roman numerals (i, ii, iii, iv, v, vi, and so on).

Visual material (figures, tables, and so on) should generally be incorporated into the report, closely following textual reference. Incorporating visuals makes more work for the writer in designing the layout of each page, but benefits the reader who can immediately refer to the appropriate figure or table without turning to an appendix.

Examining a Sample Report

Example 15.4 illustrates the components of a formal report. In the letter of transmittal, the writer (process engineer Kate Barton) introduces the report to the primary reader (division director Brooke DiNatale). This particular analytical report was written in response to the division director's request to investigate the cracking problem on the trim of the CPU (central processing unit) cabinet.

The report itself begins with a title page, followed by three pages of front matter: table of contents, list of figures, and abstract. The body of the report initially defines and presents the background of the problem, summarizes the

findings, and then lists the three recommendations. The collected data follows, separated into four subsections, corresponding to the four studies conducted during the investigation. The report concludes with the findings and
recommendations. Following the body of the report are ten pages of appendix
material, including blueprints, manufacturing tolerances, calculations. The
actual appendix material is not reproduced with the report, but it is identified
and referred to.

Example 15.4

> *Holsclaw and Moss, LTD.*
> *9669 Solomon Avenue*
> *Gannon, CA 94198*
>
> June 16, 1986
>
> Brooke DiNatale
> Division Director
> Holsclaw and Moss, Ltd.
> Manufacturing Division
> 415 Industrial Way
> St. Petersburg, FL   33709
>
> Dear Ms. DiNatale:
>
> Accompanying this letter is the analytical report on the cracking problem
> of the MV8000 that you asked me to investigate. The report examines the
> parts involved in the assembly and installation of the front bezel.
>
> After examining the results of the studies on the problem and talking with
> the manufacturer of the panel trim, I have concluded that there are two
> causes of the cracking problem. The first cause is the shrinkage of the
> panel trim, which occurs at the vendor plant. The second cause is that the
> equipment mounting rails in the CPU cabinet are set too low. The report
> includes the illustrations and technical studies supporting the conclusions.
>
> If you have any questions regarding this report, please feel free to discuss
> them with me at any time.
>
> Sincerely,
>
> *Kate Barton*
>
> Kate Barton
> Process Engineering
>
> KB:mm
>
> Enc.

Example 15.4   *Continued*

RECOMMENDED SOLUTION FOR THE

CRACKING PROBLEM

FOR THE MV8000 FRONT BEZEL TRIM

Kate Barton
Process Engineering
Holsclaw and Moss, Ltd.

June 16, 1986

Example 15.4   *Continued*

TABLE OF CONTENTS

> NOTE: The appendixes
> accompanying the original
> report are not included
> here.

Example 15.4   *Continued*

LIST OF FIGURES

Example 15.4   *Continued*

ABSTRACT

During the installation of the front bezel on the CPU cabinet, 50% of the bezels are cracking. Presently, ten bezels per week are cracking at a cost of $80.00 per bezel. This analysis discusses two causes of this costly problem:

1. The cracking problem is a result of shrinkage in the panel trim, which occurs in 50% of the panel trims produced by Polyform Inc.
2. The cracking results from the equipment mounting rails being set at an incorrect level.

Polyform Inc., has agreed to change its production methods to eliminate the shrinkage problem. Data General's incoming inspection has been supplied with a fixture to check for shrinkage so that equipment mounting rails are set at the specified height. If these recommendations are followed, the cracking problem will be eliminated.

Example 15.4   *Continued*

CRACKING PROBLEMS OF THE MV8000 FRONT BEZEL TRIM

Definition and Background

The panel trim (p/n 002-10881) MV8000 on the CPU cabinet is a plastic u-shaped trim piece that mates with the front panel (p/n 002-11249) to form the front bezel sub-assembly. The panel trim, made by Polyform Inc., costs $80.00.

The front bezel is designed to allow easy access to the MV8000 CPU; however, easy access has not been possible since the MV8000 was put into production. During the installation process, 50% of the panel trim pieces are cracking. Presently, ten front bezels per week are cracking, which is costing Data General $800.00 per week in material. This figure is expected to rise due to the increased demand for the MV8000.

The panel trim is breaking in two locations during two separate steps in the installation process. The cracking first occurs in the lower left or right corner (See figure 1). This cracking appears when the front panel is being secured to the panel trim. The cracking next appears in the upper left and right wings of the panel trim during the installation of the completed front bezel to the MV8000 CPU.

Summary of the Findings

This report analyzes the problems involved with the installation of the front bezel. Findings indicate there are two main causes for the cracking of the panel trim. Together, these problems are responsible for 100% of the cracked front bezels.

Summary of Recommendations

1. Incoming inspection should inspect 100% of panel trims received, using the new recommeded tool.
2. Equipment mounting rails must be set at the specified height. New tools are available to set guide pins on the equipment mounting rail.
3. An Engineering Change Order should be written to match the front panel to the front trim.

Scope

This report consists of four individual studies.
1. The first study is an analysis of the panel trim specification drawing to determine if the panel trims received from Polyform, Inc. meet the dimensions specified.
2. The second study analyzes the front panel to determine if the part is actually built to the specifications of the drawing.
3. The third study is a tolerance study to determine if the given dimensions and tolerances will allow the front panel to mate with the panel trim.
4. The fourth study is a tolerance study that investigates the dimensional tolerances between the front bezel and the CPU cabinet to determine if the two parts can be mated.

Example 15.4 *Continued*

COLLECTED DATA

<u>The Panel Trim (002-10881)</u>

On June 1, 1986 the panel trims were purged from stock. Three critical dimensions were checked against drawing 002-01088 rev. 02. (See figure 1.) Dimension A and B were found to be within the tolerances specified. Dimension C was found to be less than the dimensions specified on the drawing. Dimension C of the incorrect panel trims ranged from 719.0mm to 725.1mm.

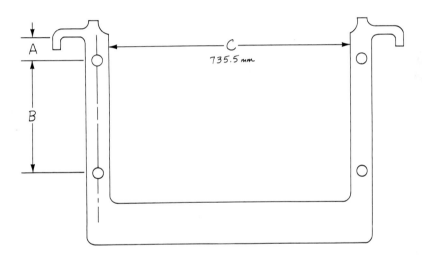

Figure 1. Critical Dimensions of the Panel Trim

The undersized panel trims were separated and checked for cracking. Cracking occurred during the sub-assembly portion of the installation at a rate of 43% cracked in the lower left and right corners. Cracking also occurred during the installation of the front bezel at a lower rate of 33%.

<u>The Front Panel</u>

The MV8000 front panels were purged from stock and inspected. The results showed that 100% of the front panels met the dimensions specified on drawing 002-11249 rev.04.

Example 15.4   *Continued*

-3-

Front Bezel Sub-Assembly: A Tolerance Study

    The specification drawings of the front panel (002-11249 rev. 04) and of the panel trim (002-10881 rev. 02) were checked to see if the parts could be assembled as they are specified on the drawings.

    Five major dimensions were checked for hold alignments. (See figure 2.) Dimension A was checked to insure the front panel would fit inside the panel trim. Dimensions B and C were checked to insure the screw holes would align during the assembly process. Dimensions D and E were checked to insure that the guide pins could be inserted into the holes provided.

    Dimension A was found to be correct and would allow the front panel to fit inside the panel trim. Dimensions B, C, D, and E were found to be unacceptable. The dimensions as specified would not allow the screw holes and the guide pin holes to align. (See Appendix 1.)

Tolerance Study: MV8000 Front Bezel vs. Cabinet

    This study was done to determine the possibility of the front bezel not fitting the CPU cabinet. The study was performed by looking at two critical dimensions as shown in Figure 2. The critical dimensions checked are from the top of the cabinet to the bottom of the guide pin (A) and from the bezel bearing surface to the bottom of the guide pin hole (B).

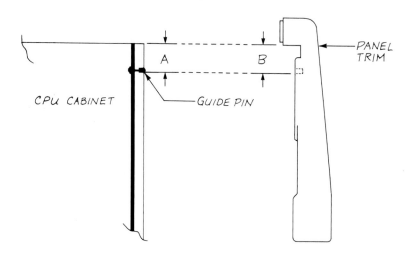

Figure 2. Critical Dimensions: Cabinet vs. Front Bezel

Example 15.4

-4-

For the MV8000 front bezel to fit the cabinet, dimension A must be less than or equal to dimension B. The attached tolerance study shows that with all the parts within the specifications, the bezel may not fit on the cabinet unless the adjustments in the equipment mounting rails are utilized. (See Appendix 2.) The study states that the maximum error possible is 2.31mm. Ten cabinets were checked, and all ten were found to have this error of 2.31mm.

On June 5, I traveled to Data General in Portsmouth, to investigate the cabinet rails being set 2.31mm lower than specified. I discovered that Portsmouth was supplied with a fixture to set the equipment mounting rails at the specified height. They refuse to use the fixture because it is very large, too heavy for one person, and damages the cabinet surface. I also discovered that when the equipment mounting rails were set at the proper height, the front bezel fit perfectly.

FINDINGS AND RECOMMENDATIONS
Comprehensive Interpretation of the Findings

The first cause of the cracking problem is a result of shrinkage in the panel trim. The shrinkage is occurring at the vendor plant (Polyform Inc.) in 50% of the panel trims produced. The shrinkage is responsible for the cracking in the lower left and right corners of the panel trim and is responsible for 40% of the cracking which occurs.

The second cause of cracking results from the equipment mounting rails being set too low. The rails are set in Portsmouth and are responsible for 60% of the cracking.

The problem discovered with the hole alignment between the front panel and the panel trim had no effect on the cracking problem. The front panel should be changed to match the panel trim.

Recommendations

Polyform Inc. has agreed to change their method of production to eliminate the shrinkage problem. However, incoming inspection should inspect 100% of panel trims received. Appendix 3 shows a recommended tool for inspection, which I have designed to accelerate the inspection procedure.

The equipment mounting rails must be set at the specified height. Appendix 4 shows a tool, which Portsmouth has agreed to use, that will set the rails accurately without the bulk of the previous fixture. Also included in Appendix 4 is a design for a tool that will set the guide pins on the equipment mounting rail to improve the accuracy of the installation process.

The front panel should be changed to match the trim panel. An Engineering Change Order (ECO) will be written.

With these recommendations implemented, the MV8000 front bezel cracking problem will be eliminated.

Kate Barton, Recommended Solution for the Cracking Problem for the MV8000 Front Bezel Trim (Technical Writing 42.225 University of Lowell, 1983).

Inquiries and Applications

Discussion Questions

1. Discuss any circumstances in which you believe the two-tier approach to the body of a formal report would be unnecessary.
2. A formal report often has a significant amount of repetition. Support or oppose the inclusion of sections that repeat information, such as the summary of findings and the summary of recommendations in the beginning and then a more detailed presentation of the material near the end of a report.

Assignments

1. Identify a problem that needs to be solved and then prepare a formal report that supports the most appropriate solution. Subjects can come from your personal or community life, your academic work, or your professional work. The list of verbs on the left may help you decide how to approach a report. Some possible topics are listed on the right.

analyze	water quality in local lake, river, reservoir
approve	toxic waste dump in your community
establish	corporate day-care facility
change	manufacturing, testing, marketing procedure
compare	over-the-counter cold remedies
eliminate	drainage problem
initiate	corporate physical fitness program
install	solar hot water heater
investigate	energy alternatives
institute	telemarketing program
justify	capital expenditure for equipment
organize	food co-op
recommend	program to eliminate electrostatic discharge
reorganize	management system for department, warehouse
	test and immunization program
	cable television
	machine or program X versus machine or program Y
	wetlands disruption
	insulation alternatives
	artificial insemination
	agriculture on marginal lands

16 Proposals and Feasibility Reports

PROPOSALS OCCUR in a variety of situations, as the following list suggests:

- Bayville, a seaport city, wants to select an architectural firm specializing in marine construction to restore and renovate the city's waterfront.
- Micro-Engineering, Inc., needs a vendor to supply precision parts for a communications satellite.
- The U.S. Department of Energy is willing to fund research that investigates the practicality of biomass as an energy source.
- The Kellogg Foundation is willing to fund research that works to improve nontraditional approaches to agriculture.
- Mark Garcia, a drafter for Richardson Technology, Inc., believes that a CAD (computer-assisted design) system would increase the productivity of the drafting department. The department manager, Warren De-Sola, is willing to hear what Mark has to say.
- Media Designs' warehouse for storing damaged and returned goods is overflowing. The manager, Judith Greene, mentions in a meeting that she wishes they could find a workable, inexpensive solution. Donald Ayers thinks he has a plan.

All of these cases result in the development and submission of proposals. Bayville, Micro-Engineering, the U.S. Department of Energy, and the Kellogg Foundation all solicit input through a published request for proposal (RFP). At Richardson Technology, Inc., and Media Designs, unsolicited proposals are submitted by employees. Mark Garcia writes an unsolicited proposal to use CAD equipment. Judith Greene receives an unsolicited proposal from Donald Ayers suggesting a way to deal with damaged and returned goods.

Defining Proposals and Feasibility Reports

As a form of persuasive writing, proposals attempt to convince an audience that a proposed plan fulfills a need while being workable, manageable, logically organized, and cost efficient. As the previous list indicates, proposals range from responses to formal requests for proposals to unsolicited proposals to solve perceived problems.

A type of report closely related to proposals is the feasibility report. Like a proposal, a feasibility report offers a solution to a problem. However, unlike a proposal's single solution, a feasibility report offers a range of possibilities, each evaluated according to the same criteria. For example, Electronic Designs, Inc., a manufacturer of multi-layer printed circuit boards for computers, was losing an average of $16,000 each month due to faulty handling of the boards during production. A feasibility study identified several possible ways to decrease this handling loss. Each possibility was evaluated according to the same criteria: ease, expense, and time of implementation. Then the feasibility report recommended immediate and long-range solutions to the handling problem.

Purposes

As these examples show, proposals can have one of several purposes:

- to solve a problem
- to investigate a subject
- to sell a product or service

The problems that proposals try to solve vary, from designing or manufacturing a mechanism to modifying a process or establishing a new procedure. An important part of technical writing in business and industry as well as in government and research institutions is investigative proposals, which range from formal and lengthy scientific inquiries to brief, informal documents. Sales proposals offer a service or product, providing the potential customer with information needed to make a decision.

Proposals for internal readers respond primarily to problems that need to be solved or changes that need to be implemented. Often, the writer of an internal proposal identifies and responds to a problem without a formal RFP (request for proposal). In contrast, proposals for external audiences usually respond to RFPs, offering to solve problems, investigate ideas, or provide services or products.

Like proposals, feasibility reports respond to problems that need to be solved or changes that need to be implemented. Any feasibility report defines the problem and then identifies and examines alternative solutions. The primary responsibility of a feasibility report is to establish valid criteria for the reliable evaluation of selected alternatives. Then the report recommends the alternative that best meets the established criteria.

Solicited and Unsolicited Proposals

A *solicited proposal* is written in response to an RFP. When an organization turns to an outside source to address a problem, it issues an RFP that identifies all the specifications the proposal must fulfill in order to be accepted. The requirements and restrictions in RFPs vary depending on the needs of the issuing organization. Since an RFP provides the specifications for the proposal, a successful proposal writer adheres to the RFP precisely. Some RFPs even indicate a point value assigned to each section, so a proposal writer can emphasize those sections most important to the organization that issued the RFP.

When the need that stimulated the RFP is actually a product or service, the solicited proposal may also be called an invitation to bid, a bid request, a purchase request, an invitation for proposal, or a request for quotation (RFQ).

Sometimes, a problem exists but no one issues an RFP. A person who identifies the problem and has the skill or experience to solve it may submit an *unsolicited proposal*. Thus, an unsolicited proposal is written not in response to an RFP, but in response to a perceived need.

Sources of RFPs

RFPs are not always sent to every organization or company that might want to respond, so an interested person might be unaware of a particular RFP. However, because approved proposals are a potential source of income for businesses and funding for human services organizations, an enterprising individual should seek RFPs pertinent to corporate or organizational objectives.

The acceptance of a proposal means the award of a contract or a financial grant.

RFPs are issued by several organizations:

- research and nonprofit foundations
- educational institutions
- government agencies
- private business and industry

You can locate funding agencies and RFPs from a variety of sources, including university grant offices, which list available RFPs as well as assist in preparing the proposals.

Public, university, and corporate libraries usually have reference volumes that can assist you. For example, the *Annual Register of Grant Support* provides listings of grant programs and requirements for applications. The *Foundation Directory* lists more than 2,500 foundations that fund research. Another useful reference is the *Foundation Grants Index.*

The *Grantsmanship Center News,* a bulletin published eight times per year (write to Grantsmanship Center, 1015 West Olympic Boulevard, Los Angeles, CA 90015), identifies grants for nonprofit organizations and provides helpful suggestions for writing effective proposals.

Other excellent resources that identify specific grant and contract announcements include these publications, available in most libraries or university grant offices:

- *Commerce Business Daily*
- *Research Monitor News*
- *Research Monitor Profiles*
- *Federal Grants and Contracts Weekly*
- *Catalog of Federal Domestic Assistance*
- *Federal Register*

You can also identify possible sources of funding through computerized data bases that use a key word system to help you locate grant announcements for research in specific areas. Most major university grant offices offer assistance in computerized searches.

Approaching Proposals and Feasibility Reports

To write effective proposals or feasibility reports, you need to understand persuasive techniques. Effective use of such techniques helps convince the nonprofit foundation, educational institution, government agency, or private business to approve or accept your proposal. Persuasive techniques are equally important in feasibility reports because you need to convince your reader that the solution you have selected is the most appropriate. In addition, preparing both proposals and feasibility reports is easier if you are aware of general guidelines and formats.

Persuasive Techniques

Traditionally, persuasion has been identified with emotion and, therefore, has often been viewed as inappropriate for technical writing. However, the reader who develops positive attitudes toward the subject of a proposal is more likely to accept that proposal, as is the reader who is receptive to the options in a feasibility report. Persuasion does not connote manipulation; rather, it applies credible, logical argument to convince the reader that the writer's view is correct. When you are preparing a proposal or feasibility report, you have an obligation to employ those writing tools that will most likely gain approval for your document.

Technical writers have a responsibility to produce proposals and feasibility reports that are credible, logical, and ethical. Three factors influence the success of persuasion: the needs of the reader, the credibility of the persuader, and the logic of the message.[1]

You can identify the needs of your reader by conducting a careful audience analysis. (Refer to Chapter 3 to review the elements of audience analysis.) Once the needs of the reader have been determined, you can take time to think about how you will meet reader needs.

The reader must have some sense of need in order to agree with the changes advanced by a proposal or feasibility report. Part of your job as writer is to identify this need for the reader. The more sweeping the changes you advocate, the greater the reader's need must be and the more completely the proposal or feasibility report must establish the need and then substantiate the validity of the changes.

Understanding why readers react the way they do to new material in a proposal or feasibility report helps you write more persuasively. Theorists in psychology and communication believe that *cognitive dissonance* creates anxiety and causes people to reject or at least devalue information that conflicts with their current beliefs. As a writer, you will find this principle of cognitive dissonance has important, practical applications. The more a reader adheres to existing beliefs, the less likely he or she is to accept proposed changes.

In your proposal or feasibility report, you can negate the effects of cognitive dissonance by suggesting to your reader why the change will be beneficial. After you identify elements that may cause anxiety in the reader, offer a solution that dissipates the anxiety. Explain how the solution meets the reader's needs and, thus, results in a decision that benefits the organization as well as the decision maker.

After you have established audience needs, you need to develop your credibility. If a reader believes that the writer is trustworthy and competent, then the writer has *credibility*. You gain credibility through a variety of qualities: technical expertise, favorable reputation, corporate status, values similar to those of the reader, and characteristics in your writing that show you to be understanding, well informed, carefully organized, articulate, and fair-minded.

The importance of a writer's credibility has been substantiated in research, clearly demonstrating that in many situations credibility is the single most important factor in awarding contracts. For example, some firms choose a vendor based on reliability for delivery and reputation for integrity—before they consider cost. Similarly, your credibility as a writer may be the deciding factor in the selection.

The more far-reaching or expensive the changes proposed, the more credibility a writer must have if the proposal or feasibility report is to be seriously considered. In fact, credibility is so important that gaining the support of a person with higher credibility than the writer increases the likelihood that a proposal or feasibility report will be accepted. Even though this is a political issue, as a writer you should be aware that it can affect the acceptance or rejection of your ideas.

After the reader's needs and your credibility are established, you should make sure a proposal or feasibility report is logical. First, your document must be based on sound assumptions. Then you should build a reasonable case that explains and relates audience needs to your proposed plan, supporting each point with valid, reliable evidence. In addition to presenting a logical case, you also need to acknowledge and respond to opposing views. (Chapter 8 identifies some other aspects of logic—common fallacies that are likely to infiltrate a technical document if the writer isn't aware of them.)

You can develop a sound argument and organize your ideas by reasoning, either inductively or deductively. Induction is reasoning from the particular to the general. You reach a conclusion about all the members of a group after examining a few representative examples (as in the Gallup poll or the Neilson ratings). Deduction is reasoning from the general to the specific. Traditionally, this reasoning takes the form of a syllogism: a major premise, a minor premise, and a logical conclusion. As a writer, you can apply the concepts of induction or deduction to organizing your documents. (Induction and deduction are discussed in Chapter 4.)

Developing a strong proposal or feasibility report that persuades readers is easier if they believe you have advanced the best plan to meet identified needs. Your analysis and response to audience needs, awareness of your own credibility, and attention to logic go a long way in building a case that wins approval.

General Guidelines

Regardless of the purpose and format of a proposal or feasibility report, it is more likely to be accepted if you follow some general guidelines:

- Learn everything you can about the subject and specifications.
- Be aware of deadlines. If possible, submit the proposal or feasibility report early.
- Know the review and evaluation procedure that will be used to assess the document.
- Know the evaluation criteria that will be used to determine acceptance or rejection.
- If an RFP exists, follow it exactly.
- Determine the content and information necessary to win approval of your preferred plan.
- Assess the reader's knowledge and experience.
- Anticipate and defuse objections, without definitely stating the potential objections. (There's no need to plant them in the reader's mind!)
- Support your generalizations with specifics.
- Establish parallel structure for each section.
- Make sure the sequence of points in the summary parallels the sequence in the proposal.
- Establish an achievable schedule and manageable budget.
- Use a you-attitude when possible and appropriate. A you-attitude emphasizes the attitudes and interests of the reader, instead of those of the writer. The emphasis moves from "I" to "you." Such an attitude requires that you identify with the reader, understanding his or her perspective. You need to be especially aware of using a you-attitude when proposals and feasibility reports are presented in memos and letters. (Chapter 18 discusses the advantages and disadvantages of the you-attitude.)
- Design a visually appealing document.

Formats

Proposals and feasibility reports can be presented in a variety of formats, ranging from an informal, one-page memo to a business letter to an extensive

| Figure 16.1 | Components for Formal, Less Formal, and Informal Proposals |

	Formal	*Less Formal*	*Informal*
TITLE PAGE	■	■	
TABLE OF CONTENTS	■	■	
LIST OF FIGURES	■		
ABSTRACT/EXECUTIVE SUMMARY	■		
INTRODUCTION state problem recommend solution present scope and plan of report	■	■	■
BACKGROUND discuss relevant background identify state-of-the-art work	■		
TECHNICAL SOLUTION define and discuss proposed plan discuss in relation to standards/specifications	■	■	■
MANAGEMENT explain how, who, when of management organization personnel	■	■	
BUDGET labor materials support services	■	■	
SCHEDULE planning implementation evaluation	■	■	■
EVALUATION measure objectives monitor progress	■	■	
ORGANIZATION CAPABILITIES facilities experience personnel proof of capabilities	■		
CONCLUSIONS	■	■	
SUMMARY	■		
APPENDIX	■	■	

| Figure 16.2 | | Variations in Content for Different Types of Proposals | |

Differences in Content	Proposal to Solve a Problem	Proposal to Investigate a Subject	Proposal to Sell a Service or Product
INTRODUCTION	identify and define the problem	identify and define the subject	identify and define the need
TECHNICAL SOLUTION	explain a workable solution that has clear benefits	justify the importance and benefits of the inquiry	explain a service or product that meets the need
	establish a connection between the problem and solution	establish the limits of the inquiry	establish a connection between the need and service or product
	provide a plan for implementing the solution	provide a plan for pursuing the inquiry	provide a plan to deliver the service or product

formal document of perhaps several hundred pages. Regardless of format, each generally follows a consistent sequence of information.

Figure 16.1 identifies components that are normally found in proposals. However, only the most formal proposals contain all of them; less formal proposals eliminate several components, informal ones even more. Also, a formal proposal contains more front matter, and it usually presents background information, organizational capabilities, and a summary, which are seldom included in less formal proposals. In contrast to the complexity of a formal proposal, informal proposals contain only essential material: an introductory statement, the technical solution, and a schedule.

The three general types of proposals mentioned earlier in the chapter—solving a problem, investigating a subject, and selling a product or service—have similar components, but the content varies in the introduction and the technical solution. Other sections, such as management, budget, and schedule, are less influenced by the type of proposal. Figure 16.2 highlights the primary distinctions.

Proposals in memo form are usually short, simple internal documents, often responding to an identified need rather than an issued RFP. Example 16.1 presents an internal proposal memo requesting approval to investigate solutions to maintenance problems for an Army Reserve missile system; in

Example 16.1

TO: Commander 187th Spt *RBF*
FROM: Robin B. Farwell
SUBJECT: Approval to investigate a maintenance program for the
           TOW missile systems in the 187th brigade

Statement of Problem
The 187th support unit [of the Army Reserve] has been directed to provide 30%
of the maintenance of the TOW [tactical, optically-guided, wire-linked] missile
systems. At the current time, no program exists to perform the periodic
maintenance necessary for the TOW system in the 187th brigade. This problem
is acute because without proper maintenance and support, the TOW systems could
be damaged and out of operation.

Proposed Solutions
Three possible solutions should be considered.
1. Increase the number of people trained to maintain the TOW systems, which
    would also necessitate an increase in tools and equipment.
2. Make more efficient use of the existing personnel and equipment. This
    option should be closely examined because the personnel and equipment to
    do a limited amount of maintenance does exist.
3. Turn over all the maintenance to the National Guard, which is currently
    capable of handling all the periodic maintenance for the TOW systems in
    the brigade.

Schedule
The following tasks will be completed in one week.

TASK	SOURCE	COMPLETED BY
1. Learn how the National Guard operates its maintenance system.	Sergeant First Class Joe Sacarelli	June 1
2. Examine the active army maintenance plan for TOW.	Warrant Officer Ronald Baker	June 2
3. Investigate maintenance systems recommended in private industry.	Raytheon	June 3
4. Compile cost estimates.	Internal records	June 4
5. Prepare feasibility report.		June 5

Source: Robin B. Farwell, Approval to Investigate a Maintenance Program for the TOW
Missile Systems in the 187th Brigade (Technical Writing 42.225 University of Lowell, 1983).

Figure 16.3	Components of a Feasibility Report

TITLE PAGE or HEADINGS	
TABLE OF CONTENTS	(if needed)
LIST OF FIGURES	(if needed)
ABSTRACT	(if needed)
INTRODUCTION	state purpose
	describe problem
	present scope of report
BACKGROUNDS	discuss relevant background
CRITERIA	
POSSIBLE SOLUTIONS	
CONCLUSIONS	
RECOMMENDATIONS	
APPENDIX	(if needed)

fact, this memo is actually proposing to conduct a feasibility study. This one-page memo includes the basic components of a proposal:

- Introduction: statement of the problem
- Technical solution: proposed solutions
- Schedule: dates for tasks to be completed

Although feasibility reports are similar to proposals, they evaluate two or more solutions to a problem. Feasibility reports generally adhere to the sequence identified in Figure 16.3.

The introduction gives an overview of the feasibility study (the work that results in the report) by stating the purpose of the study, describing the problem being investigated, and presenting the scope of report. The purpose of the feasibility report, to advocate the best solution for a problem, can usually be stated in one or two sentences. The description of the problem clearly states the various components as well as complications caused by the problem. The scope identifies the options the study considered and the criteria used to evaluate these options.

The optional background section can contain such information as the history of the problem, the possible long-range impact of not correcting the problem, and relevant work that has already been done in the field. This information is included when the audience is not likely to be familiar with the situation that necessitated the feasibility study.

The next two sections of the report, the criteria and the possible solutions, are the most important. The criteria allow you to evaluate the various solutions fairly, so their selection is important. Some of the following criteria are often used:

- cost of purchase, installation, maintenance
- ease and frequency of servicing
- ease of operation
- training required
- performance specifications
- dimensions
- compatibility with existing systems
- flexibility for expansion
- environmental impact

You should select only criteria that identify significant differences in the solutions, and the solutions you offer should be feasible. Including impractical or weak solutions as a way to make your preferred solution look better borders on the unethical, and it might destroy the credibility of the entire document.

The criteria and solutions are most efficiently presented using comparison and contrast as the organizational pattern. You have your choice of two different, but equally effective patterns. Imagine that you have three possible solutions (A, B, C) and three evaluative criteria (1, 2, 3). Both patterns enable you to use descending order, perhaps placing the solutions in order from most to least desirable according to the criteria, as in Figure 16.4. You can also arrange the solutions from most to least desirable within each criterion, as in Figure 16.5.

The final section of a feasibility report incorporates the conclusions and recommendations. These sections may be presented separately or together; in either case, the points are often bulleted or enumerated. Sometimes the conclusions in a feasibility report present both advantages and disadvantages of each solution, synthesizing rather than just summarizing the information. The recommendations identify the best solution based on the criteria used in the feasibility study. The recommendations should be clear, precise, unambiguous, and logical.

Other considerations also affect the process of writing proposals and feasibility studies: document design and team writing.

The visual appeal of a document is important; the design should be as neat and visually appealing as possible to attract and hold the attention of the readers. The overall layout should include clearly labeled sections with head-

Figure 16.4		

Pattern I

	Solution A evaluated by
A-1	Criterion 1
A-2	Criterion 2
A-3	Criterion 3
	Solution B evaluated by
B-1	Criterion 1
B-2	Criterion 2
B-3	Criterion 3
	Solution C evaluated by
C-1	Criterion 1
C-2	Criterion 2
C-3	Criterion 3

Figure 16.5		

Pattern II

	Criterion 1 as it applies to
A-1	Solution A
B-1	Solution B
C-1	Solution C
	Criterion 2 as it applies to
A-2	Solution A
B-2	Solution B
C-2	Solution C
	Criterion 3 as it applies to
A-3	Solution A
B-3	Solution B
C-3	Solution C

ings and subheadings to help the reader distinguish between major and subordinate points. Carefully prepared figures make a document easier to read and data more accessible. Enumerated or bulleted points also increase the ease with which the reader can understand the document. (Chapter 6 discusses the visual aspects of a document in greater detail.)

Team efforts are common, particularly if the proposal or feasibility study is a major project, sometimes hundreds of pages long, requiring a team of writers. The time restrictions because of deadlines make preparation by a single writer impossible, so individuals prepare various sections, with an editor, group leader, or manager supervising the process to assure consistency in style and coherence between sections.

Boilerplate is "canned," prewritten material that is often used to save time when preparing the standard sections of lengthy, formal proposals. Some sections change little or not at all, regardless of the proposal. Generally, boilerplate is used for these elements:

- structure and capabilities of the proposing organization
- fixed cost items in the budget
- resumes of key personnel to implement the proposal

This standard information is prepared and periodically updated so that it can be used as part of any proposal.

Knowing why a proposal can be turned down helps. The National Institute of Health, a federal organization that funds a great deal of research, has published a list of the ten most common reasons that proposals are disapproved. The reasons can be easily adapted for feasibility reports:[2]

- lack of new or original ideas
- diffuse, superficial, or unfocused research plan
- lack of knowledge of published relevant work
- lack of experience in the essential methodology
- uncertainty concerning the future directions
- questionable reasoning in the experimental approach
- absence of an acceptable scientific rationale
- unrealistically large amount of work
- lack of sufficient experimental detail
- uncritical approach

Referring to these reasons and making sure none apply to your proposals or feasibility reports may increase the chances that your document will be approved.

Ultimately, the format and content of a proposal or feasibility report are determined by the needs of the reader as specified in an RFP or by the writer's assessment. The suggestions offered in this chapter should be modified to meet the needs of the organizations involved as well as the specific circumstances that precipitated the document.

Preparing Proposals and Feasibility Reports

Preparing a proposal or feasibility report is easier if you are familiar with the preparation process. This section of the chapter reviews the process and then presents parts of a short formal proposal prepared for a company.

Like any writing task, preparing a proposal or feasibility report benefits from your awareness of the writing process—exploring, planning, drafting, evaluating, and revising—with exploring, planning, and revising taking the bulk of the time. (Review details of the writing process in Chapter 2.) The following list identifies the major tasks for each stage in the process. Although the steps are listed as if the process is linear, the process is in fact recursive, so a writer repeats some steps several times:

1. EXPLORING
   - Study invitation to bid, specifications, correspondence, and so on.
   - Collect background information.
   - Define the problem or area of inquiry.
   - Analyze probable competition.

2. PLANNING
   - Create a technical design.
   - Analyze the intended audience.
   - Make decisions about focus and emphasis.
   - Develop a plan with an outline or flow chart.
   - Consult with colleagues about the plan.
   - Use outline as table of contents.
   - Prepare a tentative schedule.

3. DRAFTING
   - Write rough draft.
   - Design graphics and layout.
   - Initially define, classify, describe, interpret.

4. EVALUATING
   - Determine if RFP/RFQ directions have been followed.
   - Know the criteria for evaluation.
   - Examine accuracy of technical content.
   - Examine selection and organization of content.
   - Study feasibility of management plan.
   - Review acceptability of cost.
   - Consult with colleagues about the draft.

5. REVISING
   - Add, modify, or delete information to meet evaluation criteria.

Proposals presented in a formal report are usually intended for upper management personnel or external readers and may range from five to several hundred pages. The following pages discuss the preparation process of a formal proposal, followed by an actual proposal in Example 16.2 (on p. 454).

In preparing a proposal to improve the efficiency of the mechanical assembly and final assembly areas at Cybertronics, Inc., industrial technology expert Craig Wilder followed the process just enumerated. During his initial *exploring*, he carefully studied the RFP, noting the constraints. Then he examined the company's internal documents and interviewed employees and managers to collect information about the size of the facilities, packaging and handling costs, and long-range manufacturing requirements. He identified a series of related problems:

1. ineffective use of plant facilities

    - mechanical assembly: uses 8,000 square feet of 14,550 square feet available
    - final assembly: uses 7,000 square feet of 13,000 square feet available
    - combining departments would eliminate duplication
    - both could fit into 13,000 square feet of current final assembly area

2. insufficient response to long-range market needs

    - major product: Model CY800 dot matrix printers
    - three years ago shipped 300 CY800 units each day
    - now shipping 100 CY800 units each day with 75 percent downward trend
    - two new products nearly ready for production

3. unnecessary overhead costs, excessive materials handling

    - double supervision overhead decreased with combined department
    - duplication of shipping facilities and crews
    - unnecessary materials handling

4. neglect of cross training and employee motivation

    - currently no use of "progressive assembly" with timed conveyor belt
    - little attention given to increased employee boredom and decreased motivation because of repetitive work

5. uneven work flow

    - without progressive assembly, no predictable way to determine productivity
    - wasted time for some employees

As he moved into the *planning* stage, Craig Wilder decided to focus on the consolidation of the mechanical assembly and final assembly areas into a single department. He developed a plan and drew floor plans that showed the design for the consolidated department. Then he met with the managers of the two departments involved and listened to their criticisms and suggestions.

Because of his careful preparation, Craig Wilder was confident while *drafting* the proposal. In the introductory section, he defined and described the problems before recommending his solution. He went on to provide the details of the plan for consolidating the departments, specifying how the plan responded to each one of the problems. Then he suggested a schedule for implementing the changes and summarized the anticipated expenses.

After the draft was completed, Craig spent some time *evaluating* it. Rechecking the RFP to make sure he had followed the specifications precisely, he then went through the proposal again, using the criteria for evaluation that would determine the acceptance or rejection of the proposal. Realizing that the primary readers had technical, not management, expertise, he decided to eliminate some of the jargon in the proposal. He also checked for technical accuracy, organization, and feasibility. As he checked the cost effectiveness in the budget, he decided the proposal would be more convincing if he extended the projections for 18 months, rather than the 12 months in his original draft.

Based on his evaluation of the draft, Craig started *revising*—eliminating the jargon and expanding the budget to 18 months. The proposal was now ready for the final draft and the addition of the support material—front matter and appendixes showing floor plans and changes in management.

Example 16.2

PROPOSED MERGER: MECHANISM ASSEMBLY WITH FINAL ASSEMBLY

Submitted to
Brian Donnelly
Manager, Production
Cybertronics, Inc.

Prepared by
Craig Wilder
Supervisor, Mechanical Assembly
Cybertronics, Inc.

October 27, 1986

Abstract

The cost and inconvenience of moving an entire department must always be
weighted against the long-term benefits to be derived from such a move.
Both the company and the employees would benefit from moving the Mechanical
Assembly line from its present building (M.C.B.) into the Final Assembly
area (P.A.B.).

Valuable work space would be better utilized, opening up the much needed
space for new products scheduled for production. The move would also
reduce handling and shipping costs, cross-train employees, reduce overhead
by 50%.

Example 16.2   *Continued*

Table of Contents

Example 16.2   *Continued*

PROPOSED MERGER: MECHANISM ASSEMBLY WITH FINAL ASSEMBLY

Statement of Problem

Two new products going into production need the space, tools, and equipment now used for older products.

Proposed Solution

Combining the Mechanical Assembly area and the Final Assembly area would free approximately 14,500 square feet.

Background

For the past seven years, Cybertronics has been a leader in the dot matrix printer industry. This success is largely because of the company's model 800 series printers. This product line has been the heart of the company's revenue growth and rapid expansion.

Three years ago Cybertronics was shipping 300 units per day of 800 series products alone. Today, however, Cybertronics is shipping only 100 series 800 printers per day, the forecast ramps down to 75 per day in three months, and the backlog for sales is soft for the next fiscal quarter.

Cybertronics should shift away from series 800 products and emphasize the new product lines that are ready to go into production.

Example 16.2   *Continued*

Solution

Space is being wasted in both the Mechanical Assembly and Final Assembly areas, as Table 1 shows.

AREA	SPACE		
	Available	Used	Unused
Mechanical Assembly	14,500 sq ft	8,000 sq ft	6,500 sq ft
Final Assembly	13,000 sq ft	7,000 sq ft	6,000 sq ft

Table 1
Allocation of Space in Mechanical Assembly and Final Assembly

Both the Mechanical Assembly and Final Assembly areas could fit into 13,000 square feet because some of the area now needed would not have to be used if the departments were combined. Most of this space saving comes from two areas:

1. Packing and shipping in Mechanical Assembly would be combined with receiving and unpackaging in Final Assembly.

2. Final Assembly could eliminate their entire storage location that is now being used to hold spare parts to fix defective mechanisms.

The packing area could be nearly eliminated. At present we use about 1500 square feet for packing mechanisms, holding them in a loading area while waiting for pickup. Final Assembly uses over 500 square feet to receive and unpack mechanisms received from stock. Nearly all of the 2000 square feet now allocated to packing, shipping, and receiving would be eliminated. A small area--less than 500 square feet--would still be needed for packing and shipping overseas and for occasional excess being moved into stock. In addition to the space savings, the overhead would be reduced.

The storage space in Final Assembly that is now used to store spare parts to repair defective mechanisms would be totally eliminated. If there were one department containing both the mechanism build and the final build, then all the mechanism parts would be already in the department.

-2-

Example 16.2   *Continued*

To further reduce the material handling requirements, we could join the two assembly line conveyors and make them into one continuous flow of production.

Supervision overhead would be cut in half because there would be only one line and a smaller total workforce; one supervisor could do an effective job.

Cross training requirements would be an advantage. According to a manual, <u>Modern</u> <u>Supervisory</u> <u>Techniques</u>, when people become bored with their jobs, they are unmotivated. However, cross training on new jobs sparks interest and, therefore, increases motivation. Additionally, the National Foreman's Institute's manual, the <u>NFI</u> <u>Standard</u> <u>Manual</u> <u>for</u> <u>Supervisors</u>, says that when employees understand the "big picture" of how their jobs affect the product and the company, they will have more pride in their work, improve the quality of their work, and increase their motivation. Combining the two assembly areas would provide many opportunities for cross training, so employees could understand the entire assembly operation.

At present, the two assembly areas are operated in different ways. The Mechanical Assembly area has a conveyor that is automatically timed to advance one unit every $3\frac{1}{2}$ minutes. The assembly line has nine different positions, each with a certain job on mechanisms as they pass through that station. After a mechanism reaches the end of the line, it is a finished unit. This "progressive assembly line"--one mechanism every $3\frac{1}{2}$ minutes--is a steady flow that is easily controlled and very predictable. It is efficient for two reasons:

1. The mechanism moves to the worker rather than the other way around.

2. Each worker becomes specialized by repeating the same job.

Workers are rotated from job to job on a weekly basis to avoid boredom and excess repetition.

In Final Assembly, on the other hand, mechanisms are unpackaged and put on a long conveyor line, about 20 at a time. Workers select (or are assigned) a task. Workers take the necessary tools, parts, and hardware and walk up and down the line doing their job. Each worker goes along at an individual rate; when all the jobs are done, the line is emptied and the process begins again. The process offers no incentive to work quickly because the mechanisms will stay on the line until everyone is done. A lot of time is wasted; a lot of effort is spent walking around and looking for tools and parts. The units are not finished one at a time but rather in batches of 20. This uneven flow makes predicting production speed nearly impossible; management has little control over the speed of the assembly area.

Example 16.2 *Continued*

Conclusions

The combination of Mechanical Assembly and Final Assembly into a single area that uses progressive assembly has distinct benefits:

1. frees space for new product lines
2. increases productivity in Mechanical and Final Assembly
3. increases employee motivation
4. increases management control of production
5. lowers overhead and management costs

-4-

Source: Craig Wilder, Proposed Merger: Mechanical Assembly with Final Assembly (Technical Writing 42.225 University of Lowell, 1983).

Inquiries and Applications

Discussion Questions

1. Discuss the ethics of using what are popularly called propaganda techniques (fallacious appeal to authority, appeal to pity, appeal to emotion, question begging, slanting, and so on) in preparing a proposal or feasibility report.

2. In a long, formal proposal, do you recommend placing supporting data—tables, figures, documentation—at the point of reference in the body of the proposal or in the appendixes? What types of information should definitely be reserved for the appendixes?

3. If you're interested in submitting a proposal, how far should you go to contact people who can discuss the RFP with you? After the proposal is submitted, should you take the initiative to make the contact again?

4. You are a six-month employee and think you have a plan that would eliminate a production bottleneck. Will you submit an unsolicited proposal? Will you discuss your idea with your supervisors? What if one of them subsequently presents your idea as an original proposal?

Individual and Group Exercises

1. Examine the following summaries for proposals. Develop criteria for selecting an effective proposal summary. Discuss which one you prefer.

"The On-Call program, a public health library accessible by telephone, has had a meteoric beginning. On-Call, a program of the Any County Medical Society, has disseminated the staggering sum of over 100,000 health messages to a grateful public during its first eleven months of operation. With its transplantation to two major urban areas already accomplished, and its impending adoption by several other urban areas, this program will conservatively dispense somewhere between 3 and 5 million health messages to the American Public during 1973.

"The goal of On-Call is to increase the capacity of the patient to care for himself and to enhance effective and appropriate utilization of physicians and other health care professionals.

"The purpose of this grant request is to seek funds to expand the size of the library, to evaluate its usefulness as an educational tool, and to assist other communities who wish to adopt the program.

"The long-range goal of this proposed program is to help students develop into adults who think creatively and independently, learn by observation, work together in inquiring teams, develop judgment and decision making abilities and most importantly, adults who can conceive of more satisfactory alternatives to social problems than passive acceptance or militant violence. In short—this program's aim is to help students to grow into adults who actively practice and participate in democratic citizenship."[3]

2. a. Working with a group of classmates who have the same academic major or who work together in the same department, identify a problem you *all* agree upon. Record the process or steps the group uses to identify the problem.

   b. Still working with the above group, attempt to propose a solution you *all* agree upon. Record the process or steps the group uses to evaluate the proposed solution.

3. You need to convince an engineering committee in your company to support and fund leaves of absence for employees to teach technical courses in City College. These four-month leaves enable the college to offer courses in state-of-the-art technology. Outline the proposal you could present to have the plan approved.

4. You work for a manufacturer of air conditioners. Your supervisor gives you an RFP from the city of Los Colatz, Arizona, for air conditioning units for all their public buildings: city hall, courthouse, library, schools, police and fire stations, and so on. Outline the procedure you would follow and the content you would select in preparing your proposal.

5. Jargon, technical terms, and buzz words can endanger the clarity of a proposal or feasibility report. On the other hand, sometimes such terms are unavoidable in technical writing. Examine the sample documents included in this chapter. Do you find any expressions you do not understand? How successful are the writers in insuring your comprehension? Are there any terms that are explained in a condescending tone?

Assignments

1. Safe disposal of industrial and human wastes is a widely publicized problem. Government and industries call for proposals to help them choose acceptable sites for storage, pending recycling. Identify a particular waste disposal problem in your community and prepare a proposal recommending a realistic solution.

2. Assume you represent a private foundation whose concern is to increase scholarship in and public support for foreign language capability (particularly for technical experts working for multi-national companies). Prepare an RFP and decide to whom you will send it.

3. You work for the manufacturer of orthopedic shoes. Your company's shoes are sold exclusively through retail stores. Prepare a proposal that would convince your company's officers to consider adding mail order distribution to increase sales.

17 Science Writing

SCIENCE WRITING REPRESENTS the branch of technical communication that explains technical and scientific information to nonexpert general readers. Concepts, theories, facts, mechanisms, processes, situations—all are presented with a special concern for clarity and appeal.

Think of science writing as a genre that integrates technical writing and journalism, whose direct purpose is nearly always to inform and educate rather than persuade. Through science writing, people learn about and appreciate technical and scientific advances. Discoveries and experiments are made relevant to everyday lives; indeed, emphasis is on the application of the information rather than its theoretical basis.

Science writing has a variety of forums. Most daily newspapers and general interest news magazines carry science columns. Some magazines, such as *Science 86*, *Science Digest*, and *Psychology Today*, are devoted entirely to presenting technical information to the general reader. Science news is also communicated to the general public in such formats as brochures, press releases, and advertisements. Beyond this, business and industry often use science writing in bulletins and in-house newsletters, called house organs.

Regardless of the medium and format, science writing has distinct benefits for the interested nonexpert:

- providing access to technical information
- eliminating misconceptions about science and technology
- creating awareness of science and technology's impact on daily lives

Science writing makes important information readily available to the public in a way most people can understand. An interested and informed public supports technological advances, thus stimulating research and encouraging relevant applications. For example, much of the support for NASA's space shuttle program exists because popular science articles about the space program have intrigued and educated the interested nonexpert.

The positive attitudes engendered by effective science writing also help bridge the gap between the "two cultures" that writer-scientist C. P. Snow wrote about—the schism between science and the humanities.

Despite the importance of science writing, some concerns exist. The *Wall Street Journal* article reproduced below expresses some of the criticism. The article acknowledges the benefits of science writing—a better educated public, a contrast to the fluff in other sections of the newspaper, increased readership. These benefits, however, do not eliminate what some critics see as problems with science writing. Critics point to articles that focus on sensational or even trivial aspects of science and technology. Some critics say that science writers cater to current interests—health, nutrition, exercise, medicine. Others point to the emergence of politics in science, saying that some scientists are using the popular press to gain support for controversial views that do not represent the mainstream scientific community. A more serious criticism is that science writing sometimes distorts meaning, downplaying or even eliminating qualifiers and restrictions that accompany the often ambiguous conclusions of research. The article points out that, despite these criticisms, science writing is an expanding field.

SCIENCE GETS BIG PLAY IN THE PRESS, BUT CRITICS QUESTION THE QUALITY

By DAVID STIPP

Staff Reporter of THE WALL STREET JOURNAL

Science is becoming a pop topic.

U.S. newspapers and magazines are scrambling to satisfy Americans' robust appetite for scientific, medical and technological information. Topics like artificial hearts and mysterious diseases, once found only in specialized journals, now appear regularly in newspapers and magazines.

"With all the science reporting going on now, a lot of adults are being better educated about science than their kids are in schools," says Jon D. Miller, a Northern Illinois University political scientist who researches science issues. "We have better science writing going on now than ever."

But the boom in science coverage hasn't escaped criticism. Many scientists complain that science journalists too often sensationalize, distort or trivialize scientific issues to make them more accessible to a general audience. Other critics charge that some scientists contribute to the problem by trying to promote their projects on their political viewpoints on such controversial public issues as nuclear power or biotechnology research.

"It often becomes just entertainment—cute science—and doesn't give the readers the idea that there are important public choices to be made," says Dorothy Nelkin, a Cornell University professor who studies science and the media. "We see a lot of dramatic stories about artificial-heart transplants, but rarely anything about the important issue of how long you can expect to live with one."

Public interest in science and technology has been high since the U.S. entered the space race in the late 1950s. But more recent developments have led to expanded science coverage. Fred Jerome of the Scientists' Institute for Public Information, a nonprofit concern, cites the widespread use of personal computers. He says the new science coverage also caters to the "me-generation's tremendous emphasis on health, nutrition, exercise and other medical subjects."

Many newspaper editors feel science sections help offset "all the puff and fluff sections on things like style and fashion that have been introduced in the past 10 years," says Mr. Jerome. Adds Ruby Scott, who edits the Chicago Tribune science section: "I think the section gives the paper a classier look."

The New York Times' "Science Times," introduced in 1978, is the acknowledged pacesetter for the nation's nearly 20 newspaper science sections, and many of its articles are reprinted in other papers' science pages. The general-audience magazines that boast science coverage include: "National Geographic," with 10 million subscribers, Time Inc.'s "Discover," with 850,000 subscribers and "Science 85," published by the American Association for the Advancement of Science, with 700,000 subscribers.

Despite the mushrooming audience, the media science boom is mostly a financial bust so far. Mr. Jerome found that among newspaper science sections, only the New York Times carries enough ads to be profitable. However, readership surveys show science sections have large audiences, and "even if a paper loses money on a section, it can attract readers that help it sell ads elsewhere," says Bruce Thorp, a newspaper analyst with John Morton & Co.

Several of the new science magazines also are losing money; last year, Time brought in a new management team for four-year-old "Discover" in an attempt to stem the magazine's losses.

Pressure to build circulation can lead to sensationalism and exaggeration, critics say. Newspaper science writers sometimes "hype" news to get prominent display for their stories, charges Jay Winsten, a researcher at the Harvard School of Public Health who recently completed a three-year study of science coverage. Moreover, he says editors striving "for the strongest possible statements" in stories also cause distortions.

Last October, for example, Mr. Winsten says the press ran stories about a new experimental treatment for Alzheimer's disease at Dartmouth-Hitchcock Medical Center in Hanover, N.H. The treatment for the disease, which causes mental deterioration, usually in older people, was tried on four patients and was evaluated by interviewing the patients' families.

Mr. Winsten blames the medical center, which had called a news conference on the treatment as well as the press for raising hopes for a cure before statistically meaningful studies were done to evaluate the treatment. The press, he says, should put more emphasis on "the limits of research."

But Milner E. Noble, a Dartmouth-Hitchcock spokesman, says it was the media that overplayed the research, not the medical center. "We went out of the way to state that the research was preliminary and not a treatment or cure," he says.

Gerard O'Neill, science editor of the Boston Globe, defends newspapers' decision to publish the story but concedes that his paper could have put the news in better context. "We stressed perhaps too (far down) in the story that it was a preliminary study and involved only four people," he says.

Harvey Brookes, a physicist who teaches government at Harvard, says much science coverage is sound, but that most journalists have a "low tolerance for ambiguity" and often leave out important details that might weaken a science story's conclusions. Mr. Brooks charges that press reports on the 1979 accident at the Three Mile Island nuclear power plant relied heavily on statements from a small group of scientists critical of nuclear power, while ignoring other scientific views of nuclear power, which, he says, 80% to 85% of scientists support. "There's too much weight given by the press to extremists in the scientific community, especially if they are articulate and helpful in a simple way," he says.

That assertion draws a sharp retort from James Naughton, a Philadelphia Inquirer editor who has worked on his paper's coverage of the Three Mile Island accident. "We would like to think that there is ample evidence by now," he says, that the press generally was more "deferential, if anything, than we should have been to government and industry spokesmen."

White House science advisor George A. Keyworth III voiced another criticism of news coverage of some science and technology issues in an interview last December with officials of the Scientists Institute for Public Information, says an institute spokesman. In the interview, Mr. Keyworth charged that the press "has done an irresponsible job of discussing important technical issues" and that the American press consists of a "relatively narrow fringe element on the far left." According to the institute's spokesman Mr. Keyworth specifically mentioned two areas of coverage in the interview: the Strategic Defense Initiative, or "Star Wars", and biotechnology.

Few science writers would agree. William Cromie, director of the Council for the Advancement of Science Writing, says, "I think Keyworth's comments on the press are typical of politicians who are mad at the press for not covering things the way they want it covered. There are problems with press coverage, but I don't think the press does nearly as bad a job as Keyworth says it does."

And Mr. Winsten of Harvard says scientists that publicize their research are also to blame for distortions. David Perlman, a veteran San Francisco Chronicle science reporter and editor, says publicity seeking in the science world has increased "an awful lot" as more academic scientists have entered business. He tells of a biotechnology meeting where he was badgered by public relations representatives saying things like "You must come and see our wonderful new cloning machine." "You have to fend them off," he says.[1]

Characteristics

Several elements in science writing differentiate it in tone from most other technical communication. As mentioned earlier, the purpose is nearly always to report or inform, not to persuade. Because science writing is intended for interested nonexperts, you need to be particularly aware of audience needs and interests. The audience analysis skills presented in Chapter 3 help you adjust vocabulary, sentence structure, content complexity, and organization of scientific material to levels appropriate for the nonexpert reader. Frequently, elements of human interest are added to make the information more relevant to the readers, relating the material to everyday life.

Popular Appeal. Science articles often begin with a human interest "hook"— an anecdote or other narrative device designed to interest the reader. Typical hooks include shocking facts, anecdotes, appeals to emotions, dramatic statistics, and apparent paradoxes. The following example, part of an article about stress, shows how the *lead* (opening paragraph of a news article) captures reader attention.

Example

Headline   Stress

Lead   Several years ago in Canada, researchers injected three laboratory mice with cancer cells, then gave two of them electric shock to test their reaction to stress. One of the shocked mice was allowed to escape, while his mate remained tied down.

Over a series of similar experiments, one of the three invariably developed tumors faster and died sooner than the others. Which one?[2]

Vocabulary. Science writing seldom employs technical jargon. When technical terms are necessary—often because they are the only accurate terms that exist—the terms are defined.

Sentence structure. The sentences in science writing, as in other technical writing, are usually short-to-medium length; however, they tend to be more varied stylistically. Occasionally, elliptical contructions (acceptable sentence fragments) are used for emphasis.

Complexity. Science writing almost always contains less detail, in both amount and degree of complexity, than a technical or scientific article for the business or industrial reader.

Organization. Science writing frequently places the most complex and technical information in the central part of the article.

Format. Science writing often uses dramatic design elements—full-page illustrations, bright colors, enticing subheadings. In addition, articles usually incorporate simple, eye-catching visuals. Occasionally, related information may be boxed, giving the reader a series of short articles rather than one lengthy article.

Technical sources. The ideas for science writing often come from highly technical sources. Science writers need to be technically knowledgeable in order to understand the material and rewrite it in a manner appropriate for the interested nonexpert.

The examples reproduced below illustrate how a technical article is modified. Example A presents a newspaper article, "Studies Link IUDs to Fertility Problems," based on two articles from the *New England Journal of Medicine*; Example B presents the first page from one of these articles. The most noticeable difference is that while the *NEJM* is cautious in its conclusions, using terms such as "suggests" and "remains to be determined," the newspaper article makes absolute statements.

Example A   STUDIES LINK IUDS TO FERTILITY PROBLEMS

Childless women should not use an intrauterine device for birth control if they ever want to have a child, particularly if they are young and have multiple sexual partners, researchers said yesterday.

That was the conclusion of two new studies that found the risk of infertility overall is about twice as high in users of IUDs as in nonusers.

Older women who have had at least one child and who have just one partner are at only a small increased risk of subsequent infertility if they use a copper-bearing IUD, one of two types on the market, said researchers who studied the issue in Boston and Seattle.

Of the IUDs studied, the Dalkon Shield, now off the market, was found to be the most likely to cause infertility, followed by the plastic Lippes loop, the Saf-T-Coil (also off the market), and copper-bearing devices. A newer type of IUD which releases a hormone was not evaluated in the studies.

"We have known since the mid-1970's that the IUD raises the risk of pelvic inflammatory disease, which can impair fertility," Dr. Bruce Stadel of the National Institute of Child Health and Human Development said yesterday. "But until now we haven't known just how often different types of IUDs lead to infertility."

The institute sponsored the studies of the issue, both of which were published today in the New England Journal of Medicine.

The research is the first directly to link IUD use not merely with pelvic inflammatory disease, an infection of the uterus and Fallopian tubes, but with the infertility that often follows such infection.

The likelihood of such infection increases, researchers said, with the number of sexual partners. The Boston team could find no evidence of increased risk of infertility associated with IUD use in women who reported having only one sexual partner.

Infertility can occur when bacterial infection, which can itself be sexually transmitted, spreads up a small string or "tail" from the IUD into the Fallopian tubes, thus blocking the passage of eggs from the ovary to the uterus. Only about 20 percent of women who contract pelvic inflammatory disease become infertile, doctors said yesterday, but many women have pelvic inflammatory disease without knowing it.

By the researchers' estimates, 88,000 women may have infertility problems caused by IUDs. IUDs are the fourth most common form of contraception after voluntary sterilization, birth control pills and condoms. An estimated 2.2 million American women use IUDs, according to the institute's figures. . . .[3]

Example B

Primary Tubal Infertility In Relation To The Use Of An Intrauterine Device

Abstract   *Women who use an intrauterine device (IUD) are at increased risk of acute pelvic inflammatory disease, but the relation of the IUD to subsequent infertility is not established. We interviewed 159 nulligravid women with tubal infertility to determine their prior use of an IUD. Their responses were compared with those of a matched group who conceived their first child at the time the infertile women started trying to become pregnant. The risk of primary tubal infertility in women who had ever used an IUD was 2.6 times that in women who had never used one (95 percent confidence interval, 1.3 to 5.2). The observed difference between cases and controls was not uniform for different types of IUD. The relative risk associated with use of a Dalkon Shield was 6.8 (1.8 to 25.2),* *and that associated with use of either a Lippes Loop or Saf-T-Coil IUD was 3.2 (0.9 to 12.0). The smallest elevation in risk was found among users of copper-containing IUDs (relative risk, 1.9 [0.9 to 4.0] for all women who had ever used a copper-containing IUD). The relative risk for women who used only a copper-containing IUD was 1.3 (0.6 to 3.0).*

We conclude that use of the Dalkon Shield (and possibly of plastic IUDs other than those that contain copper) can lead to infertility in nulligravid women. (N Engl J Med 1985; 312:937–41.)

Users of an intrauterine device (IUD) are at a greater risk than nonusers for the development of acute pelvic inflammatory disease, most cases of which represent the clinical manifestation of acute salpingitis.[1-7] In turn, acute salpingitis may predispose to the occurrence of infertility, most likely from occlusion or restriction of the fallopian tubes by postinflammatory fibrosis.[8-11] For example, among 415 women with laparoscopically verified salpingitis, 21.2 per cent were infertile through 9.5 years of follow-up,[9] in contrast to only 3 of 100 salpingitis-free controls. Also, of 52 infertile women whose tubes were abnormal in appearance, 50 per cent had a history of pelvic inflammatory disease.[12] Although there was no formal comparison group, this is a considerably higher figure than would be expected in most groups of women.

Nonetheless, although it is likely that users of an IUD have an increased risk of subsequent involuntary infertility (through their susceptibility to salpingitis), the data fall short of being conclusive. Acute salpingitis is a condition with multiple causes, and it may be that different ones have different implications for subsequent infertility. Thus, it is possible that salpingitis resulting from IUD use may have particularly benign (or particularly serious) implications for fertility.

In order to distinguish among these possibilities, it is necessary to examine the association between IUD use and infertility directly. From data collected in our case-control study of infertility in relation to contraceptive practices, we have been able to compare prior IUD use in women seeking treatment for tubal and other types of infertility with that of fertile women. . . .[4]

Techniques

Science writers use a number of techniques designed to make difficult technical information accessible and interesting to nonexpert readers. (*Note:* The examples in this section are all taken from the same article in an issue of *Science 83.*)[5]

- *Eye-catching titles and headlines* focus readers' attention and stimulate curiosity with such devices as alliteration and puns. The title of the article, "The Solid-State Parrot," juxtaposes a term generally associated with electronics, *solid-state*, with *parrot*, a term usually not considered part of the high-tech world. The subtitle, "Talking computers are sounding more natural as linguists and engineers come closer to understanding how people talk," suggests an intriguing connection between the "parrot" and the beginning of the article.

- *Rhetorical questions*, both at the beginning and in the body of an article, pose questions that readers themselves might ask, giving the article a conversational tone that make readers feel included. Sometimes these questions are a device to increase reader attention; other times they are part of a direct quotation or dialogue, as the example shows.

- In general, a variety of *concrete examples* makes the abstractions understandable. Although statistics are difficult for people to remember, a few startling facts to emphasize a point are effective. This highlighted example is effective for two reasons: First, the numerals themselves provide a contrast to the words that surround them; second, the difference between 45 phonemes and the more than 200,000 words they can create is dramatic.

THE SOLID-STATE PARROT

Talking computers are sounding more natural as linguists and engineers come closer to understanding how people speak.

Programming a Pavarotti

The future opera singers listened spellbound to the recording that their teacher, Berton Coffin, had brought in to their master class at Southern Methodist University.

"A vocal candidate for the singing program," said Coffin. "What do you think?"

The singer had a rich baritone that was truly miraculous. Even at the very bottom of his vocal range, the notes came without strain. Whoever he was, the students agreed, he should enter the program at the highest level. Coffin let them talk. Then he smiled.

"The singer you've just been listening to is a computer."

. . . English uses roughly 45 phonemes to create more than 200,000 words. (The spoken word *science*, for instance, is made up of five phonemes whose sounds can be represented as /s/ /ay/ /uh/ /n/ /s/.) Speech can be synthesized simply by linking strings of phonemes, and some speech scientists do this. But the result sounds stiff and machinelike.

One reason, according to Coker, is that "the phoneme is an imprecise unit made to catch a fairly wide range of sounds." Computer analysis shows that the same person . . .

■ The narrative nature of *anecdotes* and *case studies* makes them particularly effective as practical examples that readers can relate to. Almost all readers enjoy the story line that gives the article an informal tone. This example identifies several situations in which people respond more positively and quickly to a female voice.

■ *References to everyday and historical events* are another type of example that interested, nonexpert readers appreciate. In the same way that people respond positively to anecdotes and case studies, they enjoy references to events they know, as this example suggests. In fact, many readers tend to remember the anecdotes and references to everyday and historical events more clearly than the technical facts these elements are intended to support. Thus, these elements become memory tags that help readers recall the significant facts of an article.

■ Concepts are clarified by the use of *analogies,* which help define unfamiliar terms or concepts. Readers can grasp that a clarinet and oboe sound different because of their shape. It's a short step, then, to understand that people's voices differ because their vocal cords differ.

But as speech chips have talked their way out of the lab, manufacturers have put more pressure on chip designers to come up with equally inexpensive and natural-sounding female voices. Military psychologists, for instance, found that fighter pilots react faster in an emergency when the instrument panel barks out an order in a female voice. The Japanese reportedly prefer their public announcement systems to sound female; Mitsubishi's Technica, sold by Chrysler, comes with a polite female voice that urges the car's occupants to fasten their seat belts. But the messages on a Texas Instruments chip in several U.S.-built Chryslers ("Your engine is overheating—prompt service required") are male.

The most ubiquitous synthetic voices—those in Texas Instruments' line of talking toys, in the dashboards of 1983 Chryslers, and in nearly every home video game— are made by first recording a voice. Instead of storing the recording directly on a computer, scientists squeeze it down to fit on a . . .

Invented during World War II, the spectrogram led to extremely useful observations about the human voice. What makes two people sound different, scientists found, is far more than their vocal cords. It is also that the size and shape of each person's vocal tract boosts particular frequencies. A clarinet sounds different from an oboe because its contours reinforce certain overtones. In the same way, the vocal tract reinforces, or resonates at, certain frequencies.

■ Objects and abstractions are often explained through *personification* and *anthropomorphism.* One of the easiest ways to gain someone's attention is to give human characteristics to animals or inanimate objects. Everyone knows computer chips don't really talk, yet the phrase "talking chip" creates interest.

■ *Direct quotations* from interviews with experts or even excerpts of *dialogue* from conversations or transcripts add to reader appeal. The inclusion of such material in a science article gives readers a sense of actually listening to the people involved.

■ *Definitions of terms,* directly stated or incorporated parenthetically, help readers unfamiliar with specialized vocabulary. Because science writing deals with serious technical content, articles often must include technical terminology; sometimes simpler but still accurate synonyms simply do not exist. This example incorporates both parenthetical and formal definitions. (Chapter 9 identifies a variety of ways to approach definitions.)

■ *Simple graphics* are especially valuable for conveying complex ideas, which are often easier to understand

Most talking chips feature a male voice. For one thing, it is somewhat easier to duplicate. The frequencies in the female voice are higher than those in the male voice, and these higher frequencies must be painstakingly hand-encoded.

Ignatius G. Mattingly punches out instructions on a computer keyboard and fidgets impatiently. Several seconds tick by. Then, from a loudspeaker on a nearby table at Haskins Laboratories in New Haven, Connecticut, an odd but perfectly intelligible voice pronounces: *Emily Post says when two are served all may begin.* Mattingly smiles at the quaint intonation. "I imagine an avuncular old Swede who came to this country and never really mastered English," says the linguist, a leading researcher in the art of speech synthesis.

To come to terms with such subtleties, scientists and engineers begin by electronically splitting sound waves apart. Just as a single note on the violin is a fundamental tone (440 cycles per second for an A, for example) mixed with overtones, or multiples (880, 1,320, and so on), the sound wave of a single phoneme represents a fundamental frequency combined with many overtones. This waveform is highly complex, even though the fundamental frequency and individual overtones are simple. Not even researchers can listen to a sentence and describe the frequencies . . .

if illustrated. The X-ray reveals differences in the position of the mouth and tongue far more clearly than could a verbal description.

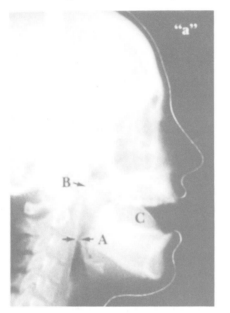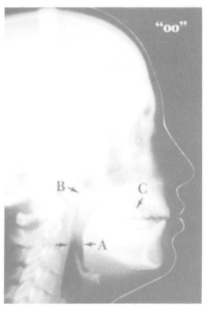

The young woman in these X rays pronounces a *as in* sad *(above left) and* oo *as in* sue *(above right). The vocal tract (A) opens wider for* a *than for* oo. *A small gap (B) between the soft palate and the back of the throat allows air to escape through the nose for the slightly nasal* a, *but it almost closes for the* oo *sound. The tongue (C) is positioned further forward for* a *than for* oo, *and the lips are parted for* a *but rounded for* oo.

- ■ *Detailed but easy-to-understand captions* accompany graphics. Many readers check captions before reading an article; some read only the captions. Thus, captions need to be informative and clearly relate the content of the visual to the discussion in the article.

A technique called Fourier transform, devised by a 19th-century French mathematician, allows any waveform to be dissected into a simple fundamental frequency and series of exact multiples, or overtones. The technique shows that the waveform below represents the combination of a fundamental frequency (F) and overtones that are two (2F), three (3F), and four (4F) times its frequency.

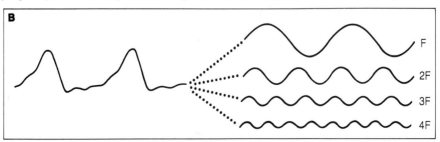

Headlines and leads from articles in the *Boston Globe* weekly Sci-Tech supplement illustrate some of these techniques that science writers employ to capture the interest and attention of the general reader from the beginning of an article.

Headline   Cloned Cows Beef Up Herds

Lead   Beneath the lenses of a powerful microscope, a small blade slices through a tiny, translucent embryo, neatly severing its thick hide and the scrambled clump of cells inside.

With one deft jab, Timothy Williams has just made twins.[6]

Headline   Tides Will Produce Electricity

Lead   Like a magical car that runs on air, it's an energy plant that runs practically by itself, using no Arabian oil or smoky coal or nuclear reactions with radioactive leftovers.

It's called tidal power and it's about to get underway in Canada.[7]

The following excerpts from student articles demonstrate the flexibility of some popular science writing techniques used as openings. The first example begins with a particular instance and a quotation from an expert in the subject—acid rain.

Example

HOW DANGEROUS IS ACID RAIN?

Hubert W. Vogelmann, a University of Vermont botanist, gazes wistfully at a slide projected on the screen. The slide is a picture of a thick, rich forest of fir and spruce that covers Camel's Hump Mountain. "I took this picture in 1963. See how green and healthy the vegetation is."

With a flick of the finger Vogelmann changes the image. The next slide is an up-to-date photo of Camel's Hump Mountain. The rolling mountain side is now covered with the skeletal frames of a once-beautiful forest. "It looks as if someone has taken a blow torch and swept through the trees."

This Vermont study shows that more than half the spruce trees have died since the 1960s. Botanists claim that the high acid content in fog and rain is causing this terrible destruction.[8]

In this next example, the writer begins with rhetorical questions that are answered in the article.

Example

NEW PLANTS THROUGH GENETIC ENGINEERING

Sunflowers twelve feet tall? Three-hundred pound pumpkins? Cucumbers three feet long? These may seem to be futuristic vegetables dreamed up in a Lucas-type mind; actually, they are examples of plant genetic engineering.[9]

You can use all of these techniques to produce accurate science articles for the interested nonexpert. An effective article conveys facts and explains concepts, but is also entertaining, thus encouraging readers to explore the subject further.

Inquiries and Assignments

Discussion Questions

1. Most newspapers have recently increased emphasis on science writing. Can you justify this editorial decision? Is the need for people to be technologically aware greater now than in the past?

2. The beginning of this chapter claims that science writing is primarily to inform, not persuade. Do you feel this is an accurate statement for all publications? For example, are industrial news releases not public relations pieces trying to change attitudes, overcome mind sets, and sell products and services?

3. What publications beyond those identified in this chapter contain science writing? Identify three that you believe are accurate, informative, and interesting. Discuss differences in their intended audiences, their selection of content, and their approach.

4. Explain why effective science writers need a solid technical understanding of the subjects they write about. In your opinion, which would be more helpful to a science writer, a degree in English or a degree in one of the natural or physical sciences?

5. Some people say that nonexperts so overreact to dangers that may exist from toxic wastes, airborne pollutants, food additives, and so on, that experts are justified in countering the paranoia by soft-pedaling the risks. Discuss the ethics involved in using persuasive techniques, euphemisms, and oversimplification to downplay possible dangers. How can technical professionals present a balanced view?

In-Class Exercises

1. Examine the following article, "The Brain Branches Out," reproduced from *Science 85*. Working individually or in a small group, identify elements in the article that clearly classify it as science writing.

THE BRAIN BRANCHES OUT

The phenomenon has long been known: a rat's cerebral cortex will grow larger and heavier when the animal lives in an enriched environment—a cage, for example, where numerous toys and other objects have been placed. Now, more than 20 years after the occurrence was first discovered, it is at the core of some exciting revelations about brain structure and function coming out of the University of Illinois laboratory of neurobiologist William Greenough.

The rat's brain grows heavier because it is developing more synapses, the tiny junctures between nerve cells across which impulses are transmitted. When a rat has more objects to see, to touch, to move around, Greenough and coworker Anita Sirevaag established, the number of synapses per neuron in the visual center of its cerebral cortex increases.

Greenough then asked, Is there a connection between enhanced brain capacity, represented by the addition of new synapses, and memory? The answer, according to results he reported last fall at the Conference on the Neurobiology of Learning and Memory held at the University of California at Irvine, appears to be an unexpected, Yes.

The brains of rats that had learned to master a series of mazes over a three-and-a-half-week period were examined microscopically. Their visual cortices showed an increase in dendrites, the filamentous branches of a nerve cell that harvest information from the various synapses and forward them to the main body of the cell. Control rats—which were simply removed from their cages periodically for brief handling sessions and feedings of sugar water—showed negligible change.

For the next step, a University of Illinois shop mechanic named Oskar Richter performed the unheralded task of fashioning tiny, opaque contact lenses out of acetate for the lab rats. By placing one of these eye patches over a rat's eye, Greenough was able to compare one side of the animal's brain with the other.

This experiment worked because in rats, as in other mammals, sensory input from the right side of an animal goes to the left hemisphere of its brain. With the fiber bundle that normally permits communication between the two brain halves severed, one-eyed rats scurried through their mazes, piling up new synapses along the way. What the Illinois researchers found was increased dendritic branching in the brain hemisphere opposite the functioning eye. More information, more synapses.

In a further refinement, "handedness" was tested. Rats usually prefer to use one forepaw over the other. However, as Greenough explains, "With partitions and a judicious use of expletives, you can train them to use their nonpreferred paw."

In the Illinois experiments, the forepaw was being trained to reach for bits of chocolate chip cookies. The learning progressed at a calorically astounding pace. "A good rat can reach in, grab the food, and get it to the mouth in 1.2 seconds," says Greenough. "We had one rat which ate 219 chocolate chip cookie pieces in 20 minutes."

When Greenough and company took a look at the brains of these rats, specifically at the areas controlling paw movements, they found that the hemisphere opposite the trained paw, regardless of which side it was on, showed a pronounced increase in dendritic branching. More learning, more synapses.

Until now, most research has suggested that organisms are born with an exceedingly detailed "printed circuit" of neurons. On this grid the connections, or synapses, are generated continually and randomly. But they are synapses with what Greenough calls a sunset law. If they are used, they become part of the "hardware" of memory. If insufficient information passes through them, they simply perish.

Greenough's recent work suggests, however, that an individual animal's experience can, in effect, provoke previously nonexistent neuronal connections to pop up systematically, precisely where they are needed: synapses on demand.

As even Greenough admits, the connection between synapses on demand and memory is "intriguing but far from compelling." It does, however, have possible practical implications for creatures higher up the mammalian ladder. It might, says Greenough, offer new hope of counteracting the effects of brain aging, mental retardation, learning disabilities, and brain damage in humans.

"We can offset and even reverse late brain aging in rats by providing changes in experience on a regular basis," says Greenough. "It's known that old rats lose synapses, and old people do, too. Are they lost because they're forming fewer connections? There's a good possibility that experience can govern the number of synapses that are born and the number of synapses that survive."[10]

2. Work with a group to create a headline and lead paragraph for a popular science article dealing with one of these subjects:

satellite antennas	cable television
natural vitamins	wireless telephones
microwaves	genetic counseling
out-patient surgery	wood stoves
high fiber diets	air bags in cars

Assignments

1. Newspapers as well as special interest and general news magazines often have science writers on their staffs or subscribe to a science news service. Interview a science news writer, a television science reporter, or a science wire service reporter. Inquire about their educational and professional background and their degree of interest in both science and reporting/ writing.

2. Select a magazine or newspaper that regularly publishes science and technology articles for the nonexpert. Examine at least eight issues of the publication that contain science articles. Identify the categories of the technical articles' subjects. Develop a hypothesis that explains the selection of subject matter for these articles. Discuss your hypothesis and support it with examples. Prepare a memo report for others in the class.

3. Business and industry publications and news releases sometimes want or need to explain information to the general public. Interview the editor of a corporate house organ. Inquire about the information the company releases to the public. Who selects it? Who writes it? How does it differ from the internal technical documents? How does it differ from the company's technical material prepared for experts? Report your findings in a memo to the class.

4. a. Select a local issue that has technical aspects. Prepare a science news article to interest and inform the general public.

   b. Contact a local daily or weekly newspaper or the college newspaper about publishing your science news article.

5. Select a technological issue of local or national concern—an issue that is not only misunderstood, but is technologically complex. Such issues include nuclear energy, acid rain, and fluoridation of water supplies. Work with a group to prepare a newsletter that has a series of short, high-interest articles and graphics that appeal to and educate nonexperts.

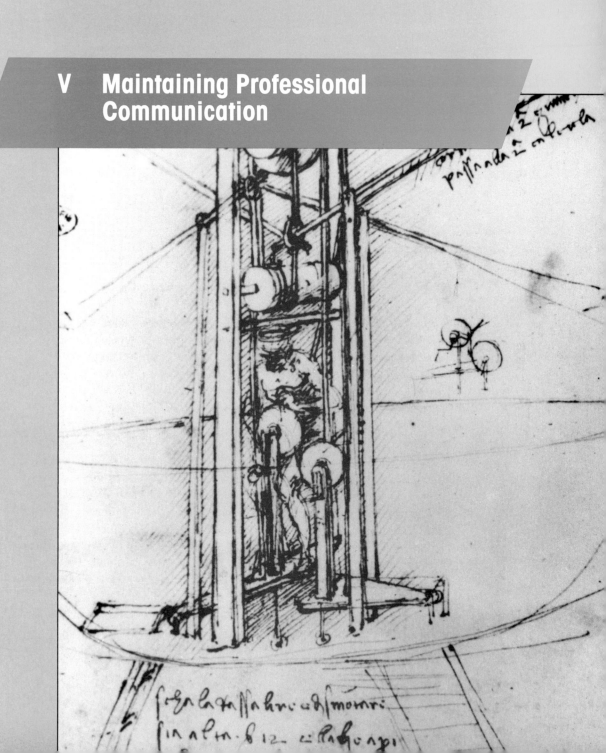

18 Correspondence

CORRESPONDENCE INCLUDES ALL types of notes, memos, and letters as well as electronic mail such as telex messages. Unlike face-to-face and telephone conversations, correspondence provides a record of daily transactions in business and industry that can be referred to and checked.

Correspondence is distinguished from other technical writing by its immediacy—generally, writers have little time for revision, often only one rewrite. Because correspondence usually responds to a current situation, it becomes outdated more rapidly than other forms of business and technical writing. Although the correspondent may not have the responsibility of maintaining files, he or she should authorize a file clerk to discard or transfer to dead files correspondence that is no longer pertinent to current operations, keeping only the correspondence for which a long-term record is needed.

The rapid generation of correspondence unfortunately often implies less attention to stylistic details than in such documents as procedures, reports, or articles. However, even though correspondence is often prepared quickly, a writer must always make sure that it is accurate and unambiguous. Letters especially represent the company to the public. Errors in mechanics, grammar, diction, or organization reflect negatively on the company image and encourage the reader to think either that accuracy and details don't matter to the company or that the reader isn't important enough to merit error-free correspondence.

More and more, telephone calls are displacing correspondence for all sorts of routine business. Typically, the following activities are handled by phone:

- inquiring about costs, deliveries, specifications
- responding to an inquiry
- placing purchase orders
- reminding colleagues about a meeting
- thanking a colleague for assistance

However, in the following cases, a written document is more appropriate than a telephone call:

- establishing a permanent record
- clarifying complex issues
- guaranteeing precise, unambiguous phrasing
- documenting a conversation
- making clear statements
- providing a reference for data
- lowering the cost of international telecommunication
- speeding the transmission of the same message to many people

Body of Letters and Memos

The core of any piece of correspondence is the body—the message itself. Strategies for composing the body of the document, whether letter, memo, or note, remain constant.

General Guidelines

The following general guidelines should help you construct an effective piece of correspondence:

- Analyze your audience.
- Include a subject line if appropriate.
- State objectives or ask questions initially; follow with explanatory material.
- Organize material in direct order (descending) if you anticipate a neutral or positive response.
- Organize material in indirect order (ascending) if you anticipate a negative response.

- Enumerate items that are clearer by being listed.
- Be specific about the action (if any) that you want the reader to take.
- End with a friendly comment.

Correspondence is generally organized in direct or descending order because readers want the most important information first. Within this broad organizational pattern, each type of correspondence has a generally accepted sequence of information. Good news—information to which the reader is receptive—is presented in descending order. Bad news uses ascending order, presenting the negative information indirectly. Bad news is easier to accept if the reader has an explanation to soften it.

Visual Displays

Because correspondence is read quickly, readers benefit greatly from visual devices that highlight, outline, or separate sections and identify main points. Any devices that increase comprehension are appropriate. (Chapter 6 discusses and illustrates visual devices in more detail.) Several visual devices that make your correspondence more effective are common to both memos and letters:

- precise subject line
- underlining or italicizing
- bulleting or enumerating
- section headings and subheadings

A *precise subject line* helps orient and prepare your reader for the content of the correspondence. Examine the difference in the example of two versions of a subject line for the same memo.

Example   SUBJECT: Shipping delay

Revision   SUBJECT: Shipment of P.O. #547-0331 delayed 2 weeks

The first subject line does not identify the shipment or the length of the delay; the revision is more effective because it specifies the purchase order number as well as the length of the delay.

You can *underline* or *italicize key terms*, as the following example illustrates, to emphasize the importance of the deadline.

Example   The proposal must arrive at our offices *no later than* February 15.

You can also effectively emphasize a series if you *bullet* or *enumerate* a list of items.

Examples

Milestones for the program are:
- May 1986
- July 1987
- June 1988
- December 1990

The top three energy resources in New England in 1982 were:
1. oil—68 percent
2. natural gas—12.3 percent
3. nuclear—11 percent

A lengthy memo or letter benefits from *section headings* that identify the main ideas. As Examples 18.1 and 18.2 show, you have a choice of more than one way to set up the subheadings.

Example 18.1

```
                    LETTERHEAD
                  June 4, 1986




      791 Balboa Drive
      San Diego, CA   ZIP

      Dear Ms. Jackson:

      SUBJECT:  Analysis of soundproofing for asbestos

      Problem:
            xxxxxxxxxxxxxxxxxxxxxxxxxxxxxxxxxxxxxxxx
            xxxxxxxxxxxxxxxxxxxxxxxxxxxxxxxxxxxxxxxxxxx
            xxxxxxxxxxxxxxxxxxxxxxxxxxxxxxxxxxxxxxxx

      Investigation:
            xxxxxxxxxxxxxxxxxxxxxxxxxxxxxxxxxxxxxxxxxxxxx
            xxxxxxxxxxxxxxxxxxxxxxxxxxxxxxxxxxxxx
            xxxxxxxxxxxxxxxxxxxxxxxxxxxxxxxxxxxxxxxxxx

      Recommendation:
            xxxxxxxxxxxxxxxxxxxxxxxxxxxxxxxxxxxxxxxx
            xxxxxxxxxxxxxxxxxxxxxxxxxxxxxxxxxxxxxxxxxxxx
            xxxxxxxxxxxxxxxxxxxxxxxxxxxxxxxxxx

      Sincerely,
```

William DeAngelis

```
      William DeAngelis
```

Example 18.2

```
                    LETTERHEAD
                    June 4, 1986




     791 Balboa Drive
     San Diego, CA  ZIP

     Dear Ms. Jackson:

     SUBJECT:  Analysis of soundproofing for asbestos

     Problem:  xxxxxxxxxxxxxxxxxxxxxxxxxxxxxx
     xxxxxxxxxxxxxxxxxxxxxxxxxxxxxxxxxxxxxxxxxx
     xxxxxxxxxxxxxxxxxxxxxxxxxxxxxxxxxxxxxxxxxxxx

     Investigation:  xxxxxxxxxxxxxxxxxxxxxx
     xxxxxxxxxxxxxxxxxxxxxxxxxxxxxxxxxxxxxxxxxxxx
     xxxxxxxxxxxxxxxxxxxxxxxxxxxxxxxxxxxxxxxxxx

     Recommendation:  xxxxxxxxxxxxxxxxxxxxxxxxxx
     xxxxxxxxxxxxxxxxxxxxxxxxxxxxxxxxxxxxxxxxxxxx
     xxxxxxxxxxxxxxxxxxxxxxxxxxxxxxxxxxxx

     Sincerely,
```

William DeAngelis

```
     William DeAngelis
```

Attitude and Tone

Some people know you only through your correspondence and form an opinion of your competence based on the content and style of your writing. While this may not seem fair, it is realistic. Because people do judge you by your correspondence, use a positive, sincere approach, avoid trite, outdated expressions as well as exclusionary language, and involve the reader by using the you-attitude. This section suggests ways to create a professional image in your correspondence.

Simple, Direct Language. One way you can create a positive, sincere approach is to use simple, direct language. Your readers are as busy as you are.

They don't have time to wade through the formal, pompous phrasing some people employ in a misguided attempt to enhance their image of competence.

Few people begin a telephone conversation or open a business meeting by saying, "This serves as notification of our agreement, as per our conversation of 10 October, that all orders processed on and following 12 October will meet the rev. 2 specifications." Why not just say, "Beginning on October 12, all orders will meet specifications of rev. 2"? To clarify your correspondence, avoid trite phrases such as the following:

Trite Phrases	Possible Revisions
attached please find	attached enclosed
in reference to said specification	in reference to the specification
re your claim	regarding your claim about your claim
under separate cover	separately mailed by air freight
each and every one of you	each of you all of you
If I can be of any further service to you, please do not hesitate to let me know.	You can reach me at 555-3941 if you have any questions or comments.

You-Attitude. Substitute the *you* attitude for the *I* or *we* attitude whenever possible. Focus on and emphasize the reader rather than the writer:

I or We Attitude	You-Attitude
I appreciate your hard work on this project.	Your hard work on this project has been valuable.
We need your crew to follow the new procedures.	Your crew will benefit from following the new procedures.
Our department is backlogged, so your order will be delayed a week.	Your order will be shipped on March 17, one week later than originally scheduled.

Your writing should be sincere; using the *you*-attitude helps achieve this tone by implying that you recognize the reader's perspective. However, overuse of the you-attitude results in writing that sounds insincere; be aware not only of the language in your writing but also of the image it projects.

Exclusionary Language. Exclusionary language (for example, assuming dieticians are women or engineers are men) causes several problems. First, it is often just inaccurate; technical professionals, who are seldom limited to a single gender in any particular field, pride themselves on precise, factual presentations. Second, a person's use of exclusionary language reflects badly on you as an individual. Third, exclusionary language reflects a negative corporate image, which certainly should be avoided. Fourth, exclusionary language has resulted in legal battles because corporate language is often assumed to reflect corporate policies.

Differences and Similarities Between Letters and Memos

Letters and memos differ mainly in audience addressed, degree of formality, and format. They are similar in their organization of information for different purposes.

Audience

Generally, letters and electronic mail are intended for external readers (those outside an organization), while memos and notes communicate to internal readers.

A writer should always identify by name or position the specific reader(s) of correspondence. Letters are usually directed to a single individual, memos to either individuals or specific groups. In some companies, distribution lists identify groups of readers who should receive memos about particular topics or from particular departments.

A writer identifies the recipient of correspondence and judges the reader's mind-set and anticipated reactions. More psychological noise can be eliminated in correspondence than in such documents as reports and proposals, which are written for broader audiences. (Chapter 3 provides detailed information about analyzing and adjusting to an audience.)

Format

There are literally hundreds of minor variations in the formats used for letters and memos, and with the advent of word processors, conventions are changing. You need to be familiar with formats and conventions for two reasons.

First, with the increasing acceptance of word processing, many document originators (who traditionally dictated or composed in longhand) are entering their own drafts of correspondence and documents directly into a computer. If you choose to write directly on a computer, you need to be familiar with conventions and formats of correspondence so that the memo or letter is correct. Second, when you sign a letter or initial a memo, you are acknowledging that it meets your standards of format as well as content.

In deciding which format to use, search in your organization's files for examples of previous correspondence that are pleasingly and logically arranged and that meet the approval of your supervisor. Also, many organizations have a corporate style guide that specifies preferred formats. If these avenues are closed to you, consult any good secretarial or business writing handbook. Composing your own letters lends a personal tone that can never be achieved with a form letter. However, if you are rushed or encounter a mental block, you can get ideas from books of form letters designed to meet hundreds of situations you might encounter in business or industry. For your reference, two common letter styles and a common memo style are included here.

Example 18.3 presents the standard block style letter; note that all lines start at the left margin.

Example 18.4 presents the standard modified block style letter. Here, date and closing lines start at the center, and all other lines begin at the left margin. Paragraphs may be indented or flush with the margin.

Memos follow a format so universally accepted that many companies have memo forms printed to eliminate having to write the headings. One of the most commonly used formats is presented in Example 18.5.

While memos and letters have distinct formats, they also have several common elements, as illustrated in Examples 18.3, 18.4, and 18.5: reference initials, enclosure notations, copy notations, subsequent page captions.

Reference Initials. Reference initials identify the document originator (the writer) and the document copier (usually the secretary). These initials appear near the lower left corner of a letter or memo; commonly, the document originator's initials are displayed in capital letters, followed by a colon, and then the document copier's initials in lower case letters. The notation DC:jm indicates that a person with the initials D.C. wrote the letter, and someone with initials J.M. typed it.

Signature or Initials. The signature or initials of the document originator indicates the person has read and approved the correspondence after it was typed.

Example 18.3

```
                              xxxxxxxxxxxxxxxxxxxxxxxxx   (printed letterhead)
                                xxxxxxxxxxxxxxxxxxxx     (If a printed
                              xxxxxxxxxxxxxxxxxxxxxxxxx   letterhead is not
                                                         used, type the
                                                         return address a
                                                         double space above
          xxxxxxxxxxxxxx   (date)                         the date line.)



          xxxxxxxxxxxxxxxxxxxxxxxx   (inside address)
          xxxxxxxxxxxxxxxxxx
          xxxxxxxxxxxxxxxxxxxxx

          xxxxxxxxxxxxxxxxxxxxxxxx:   (salutation)

          xxxxxxx:   xxxxxxxxxxxxxxxxxxxxxxxxxxxxxxxxxxxxxxxxx   (subject line)

          xxxxxxxxxxxxxxxxxxxxxxxxxxxxxxxxxxxxxxxxxxxxxxxxxxxxxxxxxxxxxxxxxxxxxxxx
          xxxxxxxxxxxxxxxxxxxxxxxxxxxxxxxxxxxxxxxxxxxxxxxxxxxxxxxxxxxxxxxxxxxxxxx
          xxxxxxxxxxxxxxxxxxxxxxxx   (body of message)   xxxxxxxxxxxxxxxxxxxxxxxxxxxxxxxxxxxx
          xxxxxxxxxxxxxxxxxxxxxxxxxxxxxxxxxxxxxxxxxxxxxxxxx.

          xxxxxxxxxxxxxxxxxxxxxxxxxxxxxxxxxxxxxxxxxxxxxxxxxxxxxxxxxxxxxxxxxxxxxxxx
          xxxxxxxxxxxxxxxxxxxxxxxxxxxxxxxxxxxxxxxxxxxxxxxxxxxxxxxxxxxxxxxxxxxxxxxx
          xxxxxxxxxxxxxxxxxxxxxxxxxxxxxxxxxxxxxxxxxxxxxxxxxxxxxxxxxx.

          xxxxxxxxxxxxxxx,   (complimentary closing)

          Signature   (signature)
          xxxxxxxxxxxxxxx   (name of writer)
          M/S xxxx-xx   (extension reference/mailstop)




          XX:xx   (identifying initials)
          enc.    (enclosure notation)
          c:  xxxxxxxxxxxxx   (copy notation)
```

Example 18.4

xxxxxxxxxxxxxxxxxxxxxxx
xxxxxxxxxxxxxxxxxxxx
xxxxxxxxxxxxxxxxxxxxxxxxxxx

xxxxxxxxxxxxxx
(date)

(printed letterhead)
(If a printed letterhead is not used, type the return address a double space above the date line, all lines beginning at the center.)

xxxxxxxxxxxxxxxxxxx
xxxxxxxxxxxxxx
xxxxxxxxxxxxxxxx

(inside address)

xxxxxxxxxxxxxxxxxxx: (salutation)

xxxxxxx: xxxxxxxxxxxxxxxxxxxxxxxxxxxxxxxxxxxx (subject line)

xxxxxxxxxxxxxxxxxxxxxxxxxxxxxxxxxxxxxxxxxxxxxxxxxxxxxxxxxxxxxxxxxxxxxxxxxxxx
xxxxxxx. xxxxxxxx (body of message) xxxxxxxxxx. xxxxxxxxx xxxxxxxxxxxx
xxxxxxxxxxxxxxxxxxxxxxxxxxxxxxxxxxxxxxxxxxxxxxxx.

xxxxxxxxxxxxxxxxxxxxxxxxxxxxxxxxxxxxxxxxxxxxxxxxxxxxxxxx. xxxxxxxxxxxxx
xxxxxxxxxxxxxxxxxxxxxxxxxxxxxxxxxxxxxxxxxxxxxxxxxxx.

(complimentary closing) xxxxxxxxxxxxxxx,

(signature)

(name of writer) xxxxxxxxxxxxxxxxxxx

(identifying initials)
(enclosure notation)
(copy notation)

XX:xx
enc.
c: xxxxxxxxxxx

Example 18.5

DATE: xxxxxxxxxxxxxx

TO: name, title
          xxx-xxxx ext xxx (extension reference/telephone)

FROM: name, title (initials or signature line
                       at the end)

SUBJECT: memo subject

xxxxxxxxxxxxxxxxxxxxxxxxxxxxxxxxxxxxxxxxxxxxxxxxxxxxxxxxxxxxxxxxxxxxxxxxxx
xxxxxxxxxxxxxxxxxxxxxxxxxxxxxxxxxxxxxxxxxxxxxxxxxxxxxxxxxxxxxxxxxxxxxxx
xxxxxxxxxxxxxxxx (body of memo message) xxxxxxxx. xxxxxxxxxxxxxxxxxxxxxxxxxxxxx
xxxxxxxxxxxxxxxxxxxxxxxxxxxxxxxxxxxxxxxxxxxxxxxxxxxxxxxxxxxxxxxxxxxxxxx
xxxxxxxxxxxxxxxxxxxxxxxxxxxxxx

xxxxxxxxxxxxxxxxxxxxxxxxxxxxxxxxxxxxxxxxxxxxxxxxxxxxxxxxxxxxxxxxxxxxxxx
xxxxxxxxxxxxxxxxxxxxxxxxxxxxxxxxxxxxxxxxxxxxxxxxxxxxxxxxxxxxxxx

XX:xx   (identifying initials)

enc.   (enclosure or attachment notation)

c: (copy notation)

Extension Reference. The extension reference is usually a telephone extension or mail stop that the reader can use to discuss or question information in the memo or letter.

Enclosure Notation. The enclosure notation—usually *Enc.* or *Encl.*—indicates that additional sheets beyond the letter or memo itself are included.

Copy Notation. The copy notation identifies names of people who have received copies of the correspondence. This notation is courteous as well as practical:

■ cc: for "carbon copy" (seldom used anymore)

■ c: for "copy" (used more frequently and accurately because of photo-copying and word processing) If the copy is a "blind copy," the original letter will not have a notation, but the copy will be clearly marked COPY. This "blind copy" procedure is used when, for whatever reason, it is not diplomatic for the receiver of the letter or memo to know that a copy has been sent to someone else.

Subsequent Page Caption. The second and succeeding pages of a memo or letter should be clearly marked in the upper right hand corner with the last name of the receiver, the page number, and date.

Content

The content of letters and memos—the message—falls into a relatively small group of categories. Memos are widely used for internal correspondence and most frequently consist of follow-ups to conversations and short reports (discussed in detail in Chapter 14). Notes are closely related to memos. For a very personal message such as a thank you or congratulations, a note is warmer and more casual. Letters commonly include requests or inquiries, positive or negative responses to requests or inquiries, complaints, and demands. Regardless of the format you use, content is usually organized so that the information can be read easily and quickly. This section suggests ways to effectively organize correspondence that disseminates internal information through directives, policy statements, announcements, requests or inquiries, and responses to requests or inquiries. These are not unbreakable rules; rather, they should be seen as guidelines that can be modified to suit specific situations.

Dissemination of Information Through Directives, Policy Statements, Announcements, and Press Releases. The standard formula used in journalism—who? what? when? where? why? how?—forms the basis for organizing information for readers within your own company, other companies, and the public. Internal information is commonly dispensed through memos, often posted on bulletin boards or delivered to a distribution list. These postings convey information about such diverse subjects as changes in insurance coverage, holiday party plans, and quarterly quotas. Correspondence with other companies or agencies may be addressed to a specific individual or to a particular department. For example, a company might announce to customers dates for the summer shutdown or changes in the price structure. Press releases within an industry or for the general public announce such things as new products, research successes, and outstanding employee achievements.

The organization of correspondence that disseminates such information varies depending on the receptivity of the audience:

Receptive or Neutral Audience	*Negative or Neutral Audience*
1. Identify the *who* (including individual and company).	1. State the relevant background (such as the problem or situation that necessitates the change).
2. Identify the *what*.	
3. Include details of when, where, why, how.	2. Identify the who and what.
4. Explain the impact.	3. Include details of when, where, why, how.
	4. Explain the impact.
	5. Provide a name and number for people to contact for additional information.

Requests or Inquiries. Routine requests and inquiries usually seek information; however, they may also ask for actual samples of a product or a specific action. Requests or inquiries usually contain the following elements, with amount of detail dictated by the requirements of the situation:

1. State the reason for the request.
2. State the request directly.
3. Explain the benefit of the information, sample, or action.
4. Assure confidentiality, if warranted.
5. Identify when the information, sample, or action is needed.
6. Thank the recipient.

Responses to Requests or Inquiries. Some routine requests can be handled by sending prepared information, such as a price list, catalog, spec sheet, or brochure. Other routine requests can be handled with a form letter that is personalized by using the inquirer's name and address. One of the many benefits of word processing is that it enables a company to generate original copies of form letters.

When a request or inquiry requires an original response, the letter or memo can be either positive or negative. A positive, nonroutine response not only answers the question(s) but also offers additional information if appropriate, and builds good will. Letters that deny a request, claim, or order usually follow a sequence that explains the negative response while maintaining good will:

Positive Responses

1. Acknowledge the request or inquiry.
2. Say "yes."
3. Include the information or identify an accessible source for the information.
4. Offer additional helpful suggestions, if appropriate.
5. Build good will.
6. Conclude in a friendly manner.

Negative Responses

1. Acknowledge the request or inquiry.
2. Explain what makes a refusal necessary.
3. Say "no" directly to avoid misunderstanding.
4. Offer an alternative.
5. Build good will.
6. Conclude in a friendly manner.

Other Types of Correspondence. Several other types of correspondence are discussed in other chapters of this text:

- proposals and feasibility reports in memo format—Chapter 16
- memos used for short and informal reports (trip/conference reports, field studies, progress reports, and so on)—Chapter 14
- cover letters (letters of transmittal)—Chapter 15
- letters of application—Chapter 20

When you need to write a memo or letter dealing with a situation not illustrated in this text, refer to that old standby—common sense.

Telecommunications

More and more, communication in business and industry is done electronically; thus, written correspondence can be transmitted almost instantly to many places around the world. Telecommunication services link a network of computer terminals, electronic mailboxes, telex terminals, and message services. A teleconference linking two or three offices in different parts of the country may use computers, video-display phones, and devices to send and receive graphic and verbal material.

Sending electronic messages requires good writing skills for the communication to be effective. Avoid being too cryptic or using too many abbreviations in an attempt to shorten a message. The message is more likely to be understood if your phrasing is direct and straightforward. Receiving a message such as the following one isn't much help to the reader/receiver.

Example   Delay on PO 376819. Reconf new date.

A few more words completely eliminates any ambiguity or confusion.

Revision   Shipment of PO 376819 delayed until March 17.

As more and more companies install electronic communication equipment, the telecommunications network will increase, and the cost of equipment, linkup, and message input will decrease. Typically, a one-page, 300-word correspondence takes 60 seconds to input at a cost of approximately 75¢.

The growth in telecommunications modifies the roles people have traditionally assumed. Specifically, the use of telexes, telecommunicating word processors, and electronic mail is significantly simpler and faster if document originators as well as document copiers (secretaries) know how to type. Additionally, telecommunications necessitates an electronic file system to keep track of documents. This system may be (or become) the responsibility of the document originator, particularly if that person is drafting documents directly on the computer. Finally, a distinct advantage exists for the document originator and receiver because the correspondence can be nearly instantaneous.

"Domino" Effect of Correspondence

No piece of correspondence exists in a vacuum; a single message can trigger a chain reaction of memos and letters. For example, a request for a price quotation generates a memo to the Sales Department and an answering letter to the customer. But that is an oversimplified example; consider instead the following, more realistic scenario.

In this case, a single piece of correspondence from a customer triggers a series of memos and letters, as the organizational chain reaction in Figure 18.1 illustrates. Here's what happens:

1. An important *customer* voices a complaint in letter.
2. As a result, *field service* initially sends two memos:
   - one memo to R and D, the group that designed the widget and is now working on a new similar version
   - another memo to engineering, the group that developed the specifications for the widget

   Field service also immediately writes a letter to the customer, indicating the problem will be resolved.

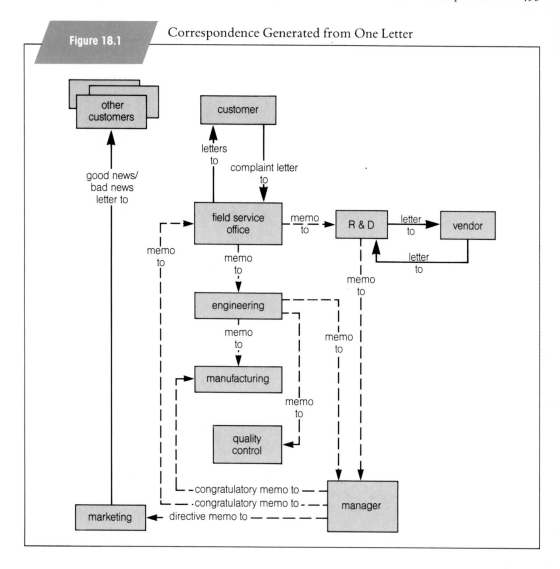

Figure 18.1   Correspondence Generated from One Letter

3. *R and D* studies how the complaint affects development of a similar product. They produce two pieces of correspondence:

   ■ a letter to a prime vendor informing them of a design change that affects an order, with the vendor acknowledging that the change can be made

   ■ a memo to the division manager, identifying a design change in the new product.

4. *Engineering* locates the problem, resulting in three pieces of correspondence:

   ■ an engineering change order (ECO), accompanied by a memo, to manufacturing

- a copy of the memo to manufacturing as well as another memo to the division manager, identifying the problem and resolution

- a memo to quality control informing them of changes in the specifications

5. The *division manager* examines the information from R and D and manufacturing and then writes three memos:

   - the first to the field service office, commending them for rapid handling of the complaint

   - the second, a directive to marketing, instructing them to contact all customers with the same equipment

   - the third to manufacturing, commending them on their rapid response

6. When the solution is developed, *field service* writes a follow-up letter to the customer.

7. *Marketing* contacts their customers, informing them that their equipment will be updated, with no expense to the customer.

The correspondence in this case situation follows general guidelines for presenting information. However, each individual piece of correspondence has adapted the guidelines to suit the specific circumstances. Originally, the *complaint letter* in Example 18.6, from James W. Crocker at Crocker Computers, Inc., is sent to John Quickstone, the Field Service manager for Tele-Robics, Inc.

John Quickstone, manager of Field Service for Tele-Robics, Inc., immediately responds to the customer complaint with the letter in Example 18.7.

John Quickstone, Field Service manager, then sends the memo in Example 18.8 to Sarah Bell, Tele-Robics' manager of Research and Development, to inform her about the recent complaints so that she can make appropriate changes in her current research.

John Quickstone also sends the "answer-gram" memo in Example 18.9 to Tom Watt, manager of Engineering at Tele-Robics, Inc. An answer-gram, or similar type of memo form, includes a space for the recipient's response.

Sarah Bell, manager of R and D for Tele-Robics, contacts her vendor responsible for coating the lenses, as seen in Example 18.10.

Chuck Thincoat of Optical Coatings, Inc., responds immediately to Sarah Bell's letter, in Example 18.11.

Sarah Bell sends the memo in Example 18.12 to Brian Brass, division manager.

Tom Watt in Engineering also sends a memo, in Example 18.13, to division manager Brian Brass.

Tom Watt in Engineering sends the memo in Example 18.14 along with the ECO to Manufacturing. Copies of the memo and ECO are sent to Quality Control.

The next week, Brian Brass, division manager, congratulates Field Service in a memo shown in Example 18.15 for their effective handling of a potentially serious problem with customers.

In Example 18.16, Brian Brass also thanks Mike Middleman, Manufacturing manager, for the overtime, which prevented delays in shipping.

In Example 18.17, Brian Brass contacts Shawna Sellers, Marketing manager, updating the situation and requesting her representatives to contact customers.

Shawna Sellers writes the letter in Example 18.18 that is individualized to each customer who purchased Lightening IV Illuminators and signed by the Marketing representative who handles the account.

The samples in this chapter are guidelines indicating the appropriate format and tone as well as suggesting possible sequences for the content in memos and letters. They are not rigid prescriptions. If your correspondence is accurate and easy to understand, chances are it is correct.

Example 18.6

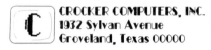

CROCKER COMPUTERS, INC.
1932 Sylvan Avenue
Groveland, Texas 00000

January 21, 1986

Mr. John Quickstone
Manager, Field Service
Tele-Robics, Inc.
799 Warren Avenue
Greenville, TX 00000

Dear Mr. Quickstone:

Our recently purchased Lightening IV Illuminator is a disappointment.
Instead of increasing our productivity, it has cost Crocker Computers, Inc.,
thousands of dollars in downtime.

Your field service office has sent three different technicians in the
past week to service this new illuminator, with no success. Either your
technicians do not know how to repair the Lightening IV Illuminator, or
your company cannot manufacture this illuminator to meet our specs.

I expect that you will correct this problem immediately.

Sincerely,

James W. Crocker

James W. Crocker

JWC:cd

Example 18.7

TELE-ROBICS, INC.
799 Warren Avenue
Greenville, TX 75933

January 23, 1986

Mr. James W. Crocker
Crocker Computers, Inc.
1932 Sylvan Avenue
Groveland, TX 00000

Dear Mr. Crocker:

Your field service representatives have filed reports detailing the energy
failure of the Lightening IV Illuminator reported by your company. Based
on this information, I have concluded that your illuminator contains lenses
that have defective coatings.

The engineering staff here at Tele-Robics, Inc., assures me that your energy
spec can easily be met once the original lenses are replaced. Our
manufacturing facility has already sent a new illuminator to you. Your
field service representative will contact you to install the replacement
this week.

The replacement illuminator will meet your specs, enabling you to increase
productivity.

Sincerely,

John Quickstone

John Quickstone
Manager, Field Service

JQ:jn

Example 18.8

TELE-ROBICS, INC.   MEMO   January 23, 1986

TO: Sarah Bell, Research & Development
FROM: John Quickstone, Field Service *JQ*
SUBJECT: Energy failure - Lightening IV Illuminator

I have recently been flooded by complaints concerning the output energy of the Lightening IV Illuminator. Enclosed is the suspected defective lens and an exposed silicon wafer. You may find this information useful in developing your current project.

If you need more detailed information, call me at extension 2437.

Example 18.9

TELE-ROBICS, INC.   MEMO   January 23, 1986

TO: Tom Watt, Engineering
FROM: John Quickstone, Field Service *JQ*
SUBJECT: Engineering failure with Lightening IV Illuminator

Tom, I'm sure you've already heard about our recent illuminator energy failures.

Enclosed are some suspected defective lenses and exposed silicon wafers. After your usual thorough investigation, could you please engineer a quick fix for the field?

I appreciate whatever you can do to ease the situation.

RESPONSE:

_____

_____

_____

Example 18.10

TELE-ROBICS, INC.
799 Warren Avenue
Greenville, TX 75933

January 28, 1986

Charles D. Thincoat
Optical Coatings, Inc.
536 Stevens Street
Crandell, TX 00000

Dear Chuck:

      SUBJECT: Revision of spec for lens' coating
                on Lightening IV Illuminator

    The engineering staff at Tele-Robics has informed me that the lens' coatings that Optical Coatings did for the Lightening IV illuminator are not adequate for long life. The coating degenerates with lens' use, allowing longer exposure times because of lowered energy output.

    This, of course, affects our work on the Lightening V. As a result, we're changing the specs for the coatings, which should eliminate any problem.

    Hold up on coating all Tele-Robics lenses you currently have in house.

    Coat the enclosed lens to the following revised spec:

        narrow band coating 405 nm 1/4   mag fluoride

How does this change affect the price and delivery schedule for the 25 lenses you've already quoted?

    Please let me know when you'll have the lens with the new coating ready for testing.

Sincerely,

Sarah Bell

Sarah Bell
Manager, Research and Development

SB:mj

Example 18.11

OPTICAL COATINGS, INC.

January 30, 1986

Sarah Bell
Manager, Research and Development
TELE-ROBICS, INC.
799 Warren Avenue
Greenville, TX   75933

Dear Sarah:

We will have no problems in coating the lenses to your new specs.

We currently have 10 lenses already coated to the old specs and another 15 lenses that have not yet been coated. Would you like us to strip the coating and recoat the lenses to the new specs? There is no charge in the per price piece for the new coating.

	per piece	x	# pieces	= net $
Cost experimental lens:	$33.00		1	$33.00
Strip lens coating:	$ 6.00		10	$60.00
Coat lens to new spec:	$27.00		15	$405.00

The coating on the one lens you sent will be ready on Tuesday morning. As soon as you contact me, we can begin the new coatings on the other 25 lenses.

Sincerely,

Charles D. Thincoat

Charles D. Thincoat

CDT:1p

Example 18.12

TELE-ROBICS, INC.   MEMO

January 30, 1986

TO: Brian Brass, Division Manager
FROM: Sarah Bell, R & D   *SB*
SUBJECT: Lightening IV Energy Failure

The R & D group is working on the problem of the energy
failure with the Lightening IV Illuminator so that it is not
repeated with the new product line.

We're working with Tom Watt in Engineering to correct the
problems with the Lightening IV.

I've contacted Chuck Thincoat of Optical Coatings, Inc., to try
an experimental coating that I believe will hold up longer in
our new system.

Example 18.13

TELE-ROBICS, INC.   MEMO

January 30, 1986

TO: Brian Brass, Division Manager
FROM: Tom Watt, Engineering *TW*
SUBJECT: ECO for Lightening IV Illuminator

Enclosed is the ECO for the lens coatings in the Lightening IV
Illuminator. I have informed Purchasing of the latest rev. and
asked them to contact the lens vendors. I've also had the
remaining stock of this lens purged from the stockroom and
sent for recoating.

Enc: ECO

Example 18.14

TELE-ROBICS, INC.   MEMO

January 30, 1986

TO: Mike Middleman, Manufacturing Manager
FROM: Tom Watt, Engineering *TW*
SUBJECT: ECO for Lightening IV Illuminator

In response to Field Service's situation, we have revised the coating specs for lens #01477.

The enclosed ECO is effective immediately. The Materials Group has already initiated a stock purge.

Please send all defective lenses (coated according to the old spec) that are now on the assembly floor or in OC receiving back to the Materials Group.

Enc: ECO
c: Q.C.

Example 18.15

TELE-ROBICS, INC.   MEMO

February 5, 1986

TO: John Quickstone, Field Service
FROM: Brian Brass, Division Manager *BB*
SUBJECT: Lightening IV Illuminator Servicing

Congratulations to you and your group on the way you handled the coating failure on the Lightening IV. Due to your quick response to a customer, the manufacturing plant was able to avert further shipment of defective illuminators. Good job!

BB:ft

Example 18.16

TELE-ROBICS, INC.   MEMO

February 5, 1986

TO: Mike Middleman, Manufacturing Manager
FROM: Brian Brass, Division Manager *BB*
SUBJECT: Lightening IV Illuminator

You and your manufacturing crew did a great job in handling the changes in the assembly of the Lightening IV Illuminator. The long hours you all put in to rebuilding the Lightening IV's eliminated shipment of defective illuminators. As always, the manufacturing group gets the job done!

BB:ft

Example 18.17

TELE-ROBICS, INC.   MEMO

February 5, 1986

TO: Shawna Sellers, Marketing Manager

FROM: Brian Brass, Division Manager *BB*

SUBJECT: Lightening IV Illuminators

Some defective Lightening IV Illuminators are still in the field. Since the introduction of the Lightening IV, we have shipped a total of 80 systems and 20 retrofits.

Please have your sales staff check their records to determine the customers who purchased the first 100 illuminators. Inform customers that a defective lens coating causes gradual reduction in the energy output. Naturally, Tele-Robics will absorb all costs involved in replacing the lenses.

The manufacturing plant is scheduled to build 100 sets of replacement lens cells, which can be installed by Field Service at each customer's facility. Field Service estimates that repair time will be 1/2 to 1 hour.

BB:ft

Example 18.18

TELE-ROBICS, INC.
799 Warren Avenue
Greenville, TX 75933

February 7, 1986

Leigh Ward, Buyer
Omnitech, Inc.
17 Industrial Park
Stoughton, PA 00000

Dear Ms. Ward:

SUBJECT: Lightening IV Illuminator Modification

Your Lightening IV Illuminator is designed for continual use. Recently,
we became aware of less than 100% operation with some of these systems.
Specifically, the original lenses coatings--after extended use--gradually
permit higher than normal exposure times due to lower energy output.

Your field service representative will contact you this week to arrange
a time to replace the original lenses, as part of the equipment's warranty.
Down time will not exceed one hour. This short interruption in your
production schedule will assure continued operation of your Lightening IV
Illuminator.

Sincerely,

Shawna Sellers
Shawna Sellers
Marketing Manager

SS:rg

Inquiries and Applications

Discussion Questions

1. Discuss whether it is necessary (or even appropriate) to write an employee a letter expressing thanks or acknowledging excellence for doing something that is part of the employee's regular job.
2. Agree or disagree with this statement: Readers tend to be much more affected by the tone of a one- or two-page letter or memo than by the tone in a multi-page report.
3. What circumstances might warrant a blind copy of a letter or memo?
4. Who should be responsible—the originator or the transcriber (secretary) of correspondence—for each aspect:
   - factual accuracy
   - grammatical precision
   - typographical correctness
   - clear and tactful wording
   - physical appearance (visuals, page layout)
5. Some organizations provide a portfolio of model letters for recurring tasks. What advantages do you see in this procedure? What dangers?
6. An innovative letter format that is receiving guarded acceptance omits the salutation and complimentary closing and incorporates the addressee's name in the first sentence. What is your reaction to this style? Can you find any reasons why a company should adopt it?

Individual and In-Class Exercises

1. You work for a wholesale grocery distributor. Within the past month you have received five complaints from retailers about damaged packages, poor quality, and spoiled contents.
   a. Write a letter to the wholesale supplier.
   b. Write a memo to the decision maker in your purchasing department.
   How will the tone of the two communications differ? Will you use chronological or priority order? What action do you expect from each person?

2. Rewrite the memo in Example 18.19 using visual displays to improve the clarity of the message. (Invent any missing details.)
3. Compose a response to the memo in Example 18.19. Assume the role of Carole Marcotte, general manager, writing to Richard Curtis in Marketing.

Example 18.19

October 3, 1986

TO: Carole Marcotte, General Manager
FROM: Richard Curtis, Marketing
SUBJECT: Major order for 024BL6 carrier

There is a possibility of our receiving an order for 200,000 nibs for the 024BL6 carrier, but it must be delivered before July 31. Do you think we have the production capability to accept such an order?

Here are some data to help you come to a decision: Last year in January we produced 150,000, in February 155,000, in March 145,000, in April 140,000, in May 143,000, in June 147,000, in July 90,000 (plant closed two weeks for vacations), in August 120,000, in September 160,000, in October 25,000 (strike), in November 120,000, and in December 153,000.

We have been very successful with this product. Some of our largest sales have been to Fortune 500 companies, although last month we shipped to many less well-known organizations. Lagassee, Inc., bought 10,000, Demonsthanes bought 16,000, P & C Company 22,000, Clairbridge Brothers bought 17,500, and Harpswell bought 8,250. We must not commit ourselves to one large order to the exclusion of these others.

One of my main concerns about accepting so large an order is the question of material supplies. Before coming to a decision, you might want to contact some of our more reliable vendors. Mr. Edwin Mundale of LaSol Iron Works, at 1125 Industrial Avenue in Tyngsboro, Missouri, is one suggestion. Another is Ms. Ramona Fitzdurwood who is the liaison officer for Abruters, Inc. Their plant is on Liatris Road in Chelmsville, Kansas.

Let me have your advice within two weeks. I hate to turn down such a plum, but I don't want to risk our reputation for reliability, either.

Richard Curtis

Assignments

1. Write a letter to congratulate an employee about the acceptance of her safety suggestion and her $600 award.

2. Write a letter to explain to a customer how you will respond to his concern about an unacceptable part your company manufactured. Make up whatever information you need to create a credible response.

3. An employee who has performed commendably over a period of 15 years has developed during the past three months a pattern of tardiness, excessive absenteeism, inaccurate and sloppy work, and disruptive behavior. Decide whether you want to discharge or rehabilitate him, then write a memo to him. (You may invent further details if you wish.)

4. Write two letters or memos incorporating the following facts. In the first one use priority order, and in the second one use chronological order. Which do you prefer? Explain why and justify your preference:

   - Our production of component Z43X has dropped.
   - A meeting of production supervisors will be held.
   - Two of our best customers have complained about late shipments.
   - Supervisors should bring to the meeting figures on costs, equipment, personnel, and so on.
   - One customer has cancelled his standing order and is buying his Z43X's from our competitor.
   - The meeting will be held on March 4 at 2:30 P.M..
   - Last month four machines had excessive down time.
   - The supervisors are to meet in Conference Room G in the administrative wing.
   - Two months ago our production of component AB22X also plummeted.

5. Bit–Byte Corporation Case Situation: Early this morning you found out that part of an already-delayed order for a major account (Bit–Byte Corporation) will not meet the new deadline and that the customer has serious complaints about some of the delivered portion of the order.

   Specifically, the production schedule for system XY-9 has been set back due to manufacturing backlogs, equipment malfunction, and duplicate scheduling. Your supervisor is busy sorting out another complex problem and asks you to write a detailed memo explaining how you have decided to handle the problems with manufacturing and with the customer.

   Meanwhile, the customer has serious complaints. The equipment that has been delivered is missing an I/O board for the CPU, has the wrong character set for the printer, and has broken prongs on the disk-drive plug. Beyond these problems, the shipment was five weeks late because it was originally delivered to the wrong customer. Bit–Byte Corporation demands an explanation and a guaranteed solution to the problems.

Help! You're due in Maynard for an important lunch meeting, but you must write a memo to your supervisor and then a letter to the customer before you leave. Answer the following questions:

- Can you send both the same information?
- What should you say to each?
- What tone should you take?
- How much of an explanation should you include?
- Should you make excuses?
- Should you make promises?
- What should you focus on or emphasize?

19 Oral Presentations

ORAL PRESENTATIONS PLAY an important part in professional communications. A positive correlation exists between a person's professional reputation (as well as promotions and raises) and a person's effectiveness in making oral presentations.

This chapter presents information and suggestions for improving oral presentations. Initially the chapter identifies purposes and types of presentations. Then the chapter discusses various factors you need to consider when preparing and giving oral presentations. Finally, the art of *listening* is examined, so that you can improve your listening skills and, even more important, so that you can get your audiences to listen to you.

Professional Presentations

Knowing the purposes of oral presentations helps you define primary and secondary goals for your own presentations. The nature of a presentation—informal or formal—influences the tone you establish and the expectations the audience has. This section of the chapter discusses purposes and types of oral presentations.

Purposes of Presentations

Oral presentations in business and industry have several purposes that may occur separately or in combination:

- *inform:* to give your audience factual information, usually for decision making or background
- *persuade:* to convince your audience about the advantages of accepting your proposal or position
- *demonstrate:* to show your audience how something is done
- *train:* to teach your audience how to do something, giving them the opportunity for hands-on experience and practice

Information. Informative presentations convey facts. Usually, the speaker offers objective, verifiable information rather than opinions. A status update report given by a project supervisor to other project supervisors in the same division of the company would probably be direct and factual. However, some informative presentations have a built-in bias. For example, a recent factual presentation about available options for packaging heavy equipment replacement parts was given by a sales representative for industrial packaging. Not unexpectedly, the presenter also suggested that his company's packaging was better at limiting corrosion and rust than the competition's. The presentation was primarily informative because it outlined the requirements for specialized packaging, but the presenter's sales pitch also gave it a persuasive element.

Persuasion. Indeed, some oral presentations are primarily persuasive, designed to convince an audience of the merits of the case presented. For example, a direct sales pitch for brand X solvents and reagents is persuasive. An oral proposal to restructure incoming inspection procedures is also persuasive. A speaker who wants to convince the audience to accept a proposal or position will initially establish common ground between the ideas of the speaker and the ideas of the audience.

An effective persuasive presentation provides facts and demonstrations illustrating the advantages and benefits of the presenter's purpose. A persuasive presentation may also identify the disadvantages of competing or opposing views. For example, medical laboratory technicians listening to a presentation about automated equipment that rapidly identifies foreign substances in blood might be strongly influenced by seeing the equipment in operation.

Demonstration. If the primary purpose of a presentation is to show the audience how something is done, the speaker uses a demonstration. Unlike informative or persuasive presentations, in which the speaker is the focus, in a demonstration the audience concentrates on the process being demonstrated. Demonstrators must guard against performing the process without talking; an effective demonstrator defines and describes the process as it happens, educating the audience without drawing attention to himself.

Generally, the audience viewing a demonstration is more interested in observing the process than actually doing it themselves. For example, auto designers and doctors may both witness a simulated auto crash with monitored robots in place of human passengers in order to study the effects of the impact on car and passengers. Supervisors might want a demonstration of how each piece of equipment in their department operates; however, they do not need to be trained in the actual operation of the equipment. Frequently, though, a demonstration precedes or is part of a training session.

Training. A training session gives the audience, or session participants, the opportunity to learn and practice a skill. Trainers have a double task: to teach concepts and techniques to the entire group and also to provide individual assistance. Even more than in a demonstration, the audience in a training session focuses not on the presenter but on the process and on themselves. Trainers are often surprised to discover such a high level of anxiety in some people who attend a training session: Will they be able to understand everything? Will they look foolish in front of co-workers? Will they forget what they are supposed to do? In addition to providing hands-on experience, a training session also presents information, includes persuasive points (to convince operators to follow standard procedures), and demonstrates each step before participants try it themselves.

Types of Presentations

Throughout your career, you will both participate in and give presentations in a variety of situations—business meetings, seminars, academic and industrial classes, and professional conferences. Both informal and formal presentations can be designed to inform, persuade, demonstrate, or train, or some combination of these four elements.

Informal Presentations. Informal presentations may take place in weekly department meetings, when you are asked to describe how you're solving an inventory control problem or to explain progress you've made redesigning a circuit board for a customer. The audience for informal presentations usually consists of your professional peers or your immediate subordinates or supervisors. Informality is appropriate because these people are probably familiar with you and your work. In addition, though they may include discussion, handouts, or visuals, informal presentations are often merely an extension of day-to-day professional activities and conversations.

Formal Presentations. Formal presentations frequently require more preparation than informal presentations. Because the audience for a formal presentation may not be your professional peer group, they are not immediately familiar with either you or your work. You usually need to provide more background information and adjust the material to the audience's needs. In a formal presentation you might justify departmental reorganization to corporate executives, introduce your company's manufacturing and inspection capabilities to international customers, or explain research findings at a professional society conference.

Sometimes the distinctions between informal and formal presentations are blurred. A project progress report about the development of a new aircraft engine might be submitted informally to other project managers in the same group; however, when the report is given to the customers who are officials from a foreign government, the presentation will certainly be formal.

Both informal and formal presentations may be effectively used in lengthy sessions. For example, a day-long seminar for independent farmers interested in the uses of marginal land might begin with a formal presentation about techniques to extend land use that includes research by the local university and results from experimental farms. This formal information session could be followed by an informal brainstorming to exchange ideas about ways to practically and profitably use marginal lands. Other formal sessions could deal with financial implications, ecological impact, and government support. Informal sessions would give participants a chance to express their own views and talk with other farmers with similar concerns and problems.

Class Presentations. Class presentations represent a valuable opportunity to strengthen oral presentation skills. The class audience provides reactions from a variety of academic and professional interests. In some situations the class can actually role-play a particular audience. For example, you might have developed an information session for summer interns in mechanical engineering. You could ask the class audience to imagine they are third-year mechanical engineering majors; their role-playing will give you a sense of how the presentation would be received by the actual intended audience.

Class presentations have another benefit that you seldom receive in the professional world. Members of the audience can give you honest, helpful criticism as well as identify areas in which you are particularly effective. Such feedback gives you the chance to maintain and develop your strengths while improving weaknesses.

Preparing a Professional Presentation

In order to give an effective professional presentation, you need to prepare carefully. This section of the chapter discusses steps in preparation, beginning with your identification of the purpose for the presentation and the research to collect necessary information. Then, as with any other technical presentation, you consider characteristics of the audience that will affect your selection and organization of material. After preparing your notes or outline, you will be able to practice presentations. Finally, this section of the chapter discusses how you can increase the likelihood that your audience will listen to your presentation.

Purpose

Preparation for your presentation begins as soon as you know you're going to speak. Initially, as with so many types of technical communication, you need to identify the audience and establish your goals for the presentation. Who is the audience? What is the purpose of the presentation? What do you want to accomplish? What does the audience need or want to know? You should be able to express the purpose of the presentation in one sentence, as the following example illustrates:

Example   This presentation introduces computer-assisted design (CAD) to apprentice drafters by demonstrating the CAD software and beginning the training with a simulation problem.

Research

To accomplish your stated purpose, you need specific information; obtaining it may require research, or at least the coordination of information you already have. Generally, the research separates into two categories: information you need to make the presentation and additional information the audience might ask about. The same primary and secondary research you do for a written report is useful for an oral presentation. (Refer to Chapter 7 for detailed discussion about locating information.)

Audience

The more you know about the audience you're speaking to, the more likely you are to tailor the presentation to their needs and interests and focus on information that is relevant to them.

Every audience appreciates components that make a technical presentation more appealing, credible, and useful:

- Indicate the purpose of the presentation.
- State and, if necessary, define the subject.
- Summarize what the presentation covers.
- Include clear transitions to mark movement from one topic to the next.
- Include specific examples and illustrations.
- Provide a conclusion that summarizes major points and indicates preferred action of audience.

Beyond these basic elements, you need to make adjustments for specific audiences in complexity of content, vocabulary, and amount of detail.

Professional Peers.   Your professional peers understand your field's jargon and can draw on relevant background knowledge to understand your points and follow complex ideas. They assume a high degree of technical expertise, expect facts to substantiate points, and will probably ask more difficult questions than any other audience. Your presentations to professional peers should be carefully organized, thoroughly documented, and supported by evidence.

Nonexpert Professionals.   Nonexpert professionals, another frequent audience for technical presentations, have similar expectations; however, they are less comfortable with technical jargon and less familiar with current theory and practice. This audience usually includes people in decision-making positions who have limited or outdated technical experience—corporate officers, government officials, military leaders. They want technical facts, but do not appreciate being overwhelmed by peripheral technical details. They will listen especially carefully to your conclusions and recommendations, and understand them more easily if you precisely define terms, clearly identify benefits as well as problems, employ visuals to stress key information, and provide a logical, easy-to-follow sequence of points.

International Audiences. Addressing an international audience, whether professional peers or nonexperts, requires additional skills; you need to be familiar with the customs of those you are addressing, for both courtesy and effectiveness. For example, an Asian or Eastern audience might hesitate to question you because in their culture that would publicly offend an expert. Eye contact and hand gestures mean different things in different cultures. People in some cultures react to business women differently than to business men. Even the way you organize your presentation should consider the culture of the audience; people in some cultures expect a formal opening that is not topic related. In short, respect the audience you are addressing and do your homework; it is neither good business nor good manners to adopt the attitude, "They're on our turf; they can do things our way." They might just go somewhere else.

An international audience greatly benefits from your use of well-designed visuals. Charts and transparencies clarify the meaning of terminology and make the sequence of a process understandable. Effective visuals give members of the audience confidence that they are following your presentation.

General Audiences. A nontechnical audience has needs and interests quite different from the professional peer or nonexperts. Such an audience might be a community group with people of varying backgrounds: auto mechanics, supermarket managers, Ph.D. biologists, kindergarten teachers, civil engineers, hair dressers, secretaries, dentists, highway department workers, and so on. (The mix is similar to the "general reader" category discussed in Chapter 3.) They come together for a common purpose, usually to learn more about your company's plans, products, or practices. As companies work to establish strong community relations, more corporate representatives will be asked to make presentations to local groups.

For a general, nontechnical audience, you should clearly state your purpose, define terms, make useful analogies, provide interesting examples, use effective visuals, and mark your shifts with clear transitions. Your presentation will be more effective if you are able to involve the audience whenever possible. You have several methods available:

- Ask rhetorical questions that the audience answers in their minds and relates to your presentation.
- Encourage responses to specific, easy-to-answer questions whose answers you incorporate into the presentation.
- Involve everyone in a simple activity.
- Get audience volunteers to help with a demonstration.
- Distribute copies of your visuals, which should have plenty of white space for notes.

Lengthy presentations should be scheduled in facilities that allow a variety of activities to change the pace and encourage audience participation. Following a presentation, you can separate the audience into small groups and apply several techniques that actively engage them with the subject:

- Provide a list of intriguing, problem-oriented questions that extend the ideas in your presentation.
- Provide case situations that encourage the groups to apply creative solutions.
- Develop a simulation that involves the groups in role-playing.

Organization

The way you organize your presentation determines its success. Your listeners need to be able to follow your ideas easily. The same patterns that you use in writing—chronological, spatial, priority, comparison/contrast, and cause/effect—can and should be used to organize your oral presentation. For example, if you are giving a status update, chronological order summarizes the weekly or monthly progress and descending order identifies the most significant gains or losses. A marketing presentation applies descending order to identify the features of your product and contrast to identify significant differences between your product and your competitor's.

Beyond these standard patterns, additional conventions of content and organization can make your presentation more successful. Such conventions include the following practices:

- Offer illustrations or examples to support generalizations.
- Incorporate brief anecdotes that provide insight and interest.
- Include figures of speech (metaphor, simile, personification) to clarify relationships and add appeal.
- Summarize after presenting each main idea.
- Intersperse difficult material with easy material.

Transitions are a very important aspect of oral presentations. As bridges linking ideas, transitions help guide the audience through your presentation. Listeners depend on them for several reasons. Most frequently, transitions signal the organization of information.

Example   First I'll summarize design changes in this component. Then I will identify problems these changes have caused and explain the steps we've taken to eliminate them.

Transitions also act as sign posts to indicate shifts in perspective.

Example   Now that I've identified the few disadvantages of the continuous assembly line, I will discuss the significant benefits this change in procedure could bring.

Finally, transitions identify complete changes in topic.

Example   As I said initially, Human Resources Development deals with three different areas. I've just explained the training function. Now I will talk about the second area, career counseling and planning.

Notes and Outlines

Unless you are a very lucky, gifted, or experienced speaker, you will not be able to give an effective presentation without referring to notes or an outline. These notes, written on index cards or sheets of paper, should contain the main points of the presentation and specific facts, details, or statistics that you can refer to during your presentation.

A topic outline is one of the most useful ways to organize main and subordinate ideas. Example 19.1 illustrates part of a topic outline for a presentation.

An outline is far more useful to you than a complete text of your presentation. If you write out the entire presentation, you might be tempted to memorize the material and then recite it as if giving a speech. Remember, an audience is interested in hearing you talk to them and with them—not read to

---

Example 19.1   Outline Excerpt for Oral Presentation

```
        Title:  Converting from Team Assembly to Line Assembly

        I.   Define current problems and emphasize need to
             eliminate these problems

        II.  Comparison of team assembly with line assembly
             A.   Cost
             B.   Job Training
             C.   Purchasing

        III. Advocacy of line assembly
```

them. Even if you prepare the complete text of the speech (perhaps for publication in an in-house newsletter or in conference proceedings), your presentation is far more appealing if you do not read the paper.

An outline or notecards should also include key quotations and statistical information you'll need during a presentation. Even an informal presentation is strengthened by specific facts; you'll find them easier to remember and locate if you have them as part of your notes.

Listening

As a speaker, you must encourage the audience to listen to your speech so that they recognize the purpose of your presentation, recall significant points, and then make a critical evaluation of the content. If research done on the listening patterns of college students is any indication, you have a challenging job. One recent study reported that at any given time only 20 percent of a college audience at a lecture are paying attention, and as few as 12 percent are actively listening.

Good Listening.   Most good listeners have developed specific techniques that help them listen more effectively—staying attentive, following the speaker's presentation, understanding the content—by engaging internally in a number of activities that increase their listening comprehension:

1. Determine own purpose for listening.
2. Identify the speaker's purpose.
3. Identify and follow the speaker's plan of organization.
4. Note transitional words and phrases.
5. Identify accurately the speaker's main points and ideas.
6. Keep track of main points by notetaking, use of outline in handout, or mental recapitulation.
7. Note accurately the speaker's supporting details and examples.
8. Distinguish between old and new material.
9. Distinguish between relevant and irrelevant material.
10. Note possible speaker bias.
11. Note emotional appeals.
12. Distinguish between facts and opinions.
13. Anticipate possible impact of speaker's remarks.
14. Recognize speaker inferences.
15. Predict outcome of presentation.
16. Delay criticism until the speaker is finished.
17. Draw conclusions from the presentation.

18. Ask questions (mentally or on paper) as talk proceeds.
19. Summarize and paraphrase the speaker's main points (mentally or on paper) after the presentation.
20. Relate the speaker's ideas to own.[1]

Organize for the Listener. Far more than in written reports, which the audience can reread, oral presentations need strong, obvious guideposts to indicate the organization and movement of the presentation. The following suggestions can make your presentations easier for the listener to comprehend:

- Use a standard organization and tell the audience how you are organizing the information.

Example   I will give a time line of the steps to eliminate the asbestos problem.

- Identify particularly important points.

Example   The most severe health problems will occur in two high-risk groups.

- Include previews or summaries.

Example   So far I have explained three common methods to eliminate exposed asbestos areas in your facility. Next I will present the cost breakdown of each method.

- Support your oral presentation with appropriate visuals that illustrate or reinforce your information. Visual aids increase most people's retention by approximately 20 percent.

The following list modifies the one used by good listeners. Ask yourself these questions about the audience listening to you speak. Affirmative answers to these questions ensure that you have given your listeners the opportunity to easily comprehend your message:

1. Will the audience believe you are responsive to their needs?
2. Will the audience be able to identify your purpose?
3. Is your plan of organization clear and easy to follow?
4. Do you use transitional words and phrases?
5. Will the audience be able to identify accurately your main points and ideas?
6. Will the audience be able to easily keep track of main points by notetaking, use of outline in handout, or mental recapitulation?
7. Do you use effective supporting details and examples?
8. Do you clearly distinguish between old and new material?
9. Do you omit irrelevant material?

10. Have you worked to eliminate your own bias?
11. Do you avoid dependence on emotional appeals?
12. Do you clearly label and distinguish facts and opinions?
13. Will the audience be able to draw conclusions from the presentation?
14. Are you receptive and responsive to questions?
15. Do you provide common ground so the audience can relate your ideas to their own?

Facing the Audience

Making an interesting, informative, well-organized presentation in a confident, appealing manner does not happen automatically. It takes the careful preparation just discussed as well as control of your voice and body, knowledgeable use of visuals, relevant handouts, the ability to respond effectively to questions—and lots of practice.

Vocal Characteristics

Your "voice print" represents a unique combination of vocal characteristics: volume, articulation and pronunciation, rate, and pitch. Everyone has a distinctive voice that can be used effectively in an oral presentation. Vocal characteristics are so closely intertwined that the improvement of one nearly always improves the others.

A speaker has to be heard. The speaker's voice needs sufficient volume to project throughout the entire room. If it's possible, try to practice your presentation in a room the same size as the one you'll make the presentation in. Speak in a voice that can be clearly heard by a person sitting in the back of the room. If you are speaking in a very large room, arrange to have a microphone available and practice with it before you speak.

Your audience will react more positively if you clearly articulate each word: Pronounce all the parts of each word, without dropping, adding, or slurring letters or syllables. Your presentation will go more smoothly if you are confident of the pronunciation of every word in your presentation; mispronouncing or stumbling over words makes you uncomfortable and lowers your credibility with the audience.

The rate at which you speak affects how the audience reacts and how well they can listen. The average speaking speed is approximately 150 words per minute. Variations in your rate of speech—your *pacing*—give you some control over the audience's attention. Rapid delivery demands the audience's full attention, and slow delivery allows carefully placed emphasis. Pauses do not detract from a presentation, but rather permit the audience (and you) time to collect thoughts.

Use your voice as a tool. Its pitch or tone, its highness or lowness, helps determine your credibility and appeal. Pitch is controlled by muscle tension, so relaxing helps your voice sound natural (and usually prevents the nervous squeak caused by tense muscles). An unvarying pitch creates a monotone, which is boring and difficult to listen to for very long. Your control of pitch allows you to inflect or emphasize important words and thus your speech.

Professional Appearance

Your professional image depends in part on your demeanor during the presentation. Your material can be accurate and interesting, and your voice can project to the back of the room, but if your behavior or appearance distracts from the presentation, its effectiveness is diminished. Some people do strange things when they are in front of a group, partly from nervousness, partly because they do not consider how the audience will react. This section of the chapter identifies some of the things people do, sometimes unconsciously in an effort to alleviate anxiety, that detract from professional presentations.

Creating a professional appearance is not difficult if you assess the situation and dress appropriately. Wear clothes that make you feel good and that you don't have to adjust and check. Avoid clothes and jewelry that distract from the presentation. Avoid wearing brand new clothes because you might be more concerned with your appearance than with the content of your presentation. Too many people wait until they are facing an audience to check and adjust their clothing and hair. Men checking zippers or adjusting trousers and women tugging at underwear can spoil an otherwise professional image. Make sure everything is in place *before* you get up to speak.

Fumbling with notes or shuffling pages of an outline lowers the professional credibility of any speaker. Managing the notes or manuscript is not difficult if you prepare for the speaking situation. Make sure to number the cards or pages; this proves particularly useful if you should accidentally drop them. If there is no podium, you should have a firm backing for your notes so that the sheets don't bend and shake.

Staring over the heads of the audience makes them uncomfortable or disinterested. American audiences, even large ones, expect direct eye contact; lack of such contact makes them doubt the credibility of the speaker. Looking directly at the audience helps to establish a rapport and also gives you the appearance of confidence. And people are unlikely to let their attention wander if you look, even briefly, directly at them.

Sometimes when presenters make mistakes, even barely noticeable ones, they make faces—they scrunch their lips, move their tongue inside their cheek, squint their eyes. Some people even laugh or giggle. If you make a noticeable error, simply apologize and continue with the presentation.

Shoving hands into pockets, clutching the podium, or waving wildly about—all are a distraction during a presentation. Many people are unsure what to do with their hands, the very hands that never seem to give them problems any other time. So, what do you do with your hands? Hold your notes. Rest your hands on the podium or lectern. Try one hand casually in your trouser or skirt pocket. Relax them by your side. Gesture naturally, as you normally would in a discussion. Hold the pointer for the flip chart or overhead projector. In other words, don't worry a great deal about your hands.

Standing on one foot or rocking from side to side distracts the audience. Stand on both feet during your presentation. Some people try to ease their nervousness by standing on one foot or even removing a shoe. Such movements may reduce the nervousness, but they look peculiar (and you may not be able to find your shoe).

Shoulder shrugs, stretches, knee bends—this body wiggling also distracts the audience. So does standing ramrod straight without moving. Try to move naturally and comfortably by focusing on what you are saying, not on how you look.

The podium can hold up or obscure a speaker. Leaning on a podium distracts from your presentation, especially if you clutch it to give your hands something to do. A tall speaker should be particularly careful to avoid leaning on a podium. A short speaker who barely reaches the podium should arrange to have a riser to stand on; otherwise, the audience may be able to see just his or her head.

Most distracting behaviors disappear when a speaker relaxes in front of an audience. To discover whether you have any of these habits, arrange for a presentation to be video-taped. You can view the tape and note the areas that need improvement. Then practice to eliminate the problems. Work with groups such as the Toastmasters, a professional organization with chapters throughout the country, whose purpose is the improvement of business presentations. Such a group often helps because you get immediate, constructive feedback from other people who also make professional presentations. Also consider utilizing your company's Human Resource Development staff. These people often are willing to arrange for practice sessions for an important presentation you have to give and may provide a staff member to help polish your delivery.

Visuals

Visuals are extremely valuable during an oral presentation. Because most people's visual memories are much stronger than their auditory (hearing) memories, visual aids are particularly useful for presenting facts and statistics. Many technical oral presentations contain a great deal of numeric data, which audiences will absorb better by seeing as well as hearing. Psychological research indicates that most people cannot simultaneously remember more than seven ideas presented verbally, so visuals help short-term memory. Also, most people retain only half of what they hear immediately after hearing it, so again, the visuals can reinforce the speaker's points.

Visuals can be used to:

- emphasize main points
- display data that is hard to follow or remember
- organize complex information
- provide humor
- illustrate or exemplify points
- provide sensory variety to stimulate interest
- vary the pace of the presentation
- move visual focus away from the speaker
- summarize points of presentation

When you are deciding what types of visuals and visual devices to select or design, refer to Chapter 6 for a detailed discussion. Types of visuals are separated into these categories: charts, diagrams, schematics, graphs, tables, maps, drawings, photographs. Devices that create visual interest include color, spacing and white space, typography, borders, and layout.

Visual information can be presented in many formats, depending on the audience, purpose of the visuals, art or graphic design facilities (your own talent or company artists), finances, physical limitations of presentation room, time available, equipment available, your familiarity with each format, and so on. Both benefits and problems exist with each type of visual; generally choices of visuals fall into the following categories:

- chalk boards
- flip pads (charts)
- transparencies or vu-graphs
- prepared charts
- slides (35mm transparencies)
- physical models

- demonstrations
- video tapes
- films (usually 16mm)

All take some time for preparation, from a few minutes for arranging for delivery of a flip chart to several months for filming, developing, and editing a 16mm production. All have expenses involved, from pennies for a piece of chalk or felt-tip marker to thousands of dollars for elaborate models or films. The ease of use varies also, from simple overhead transparencies to complicated demonstrations. Different visuals are also appropriate for audience of varying sizes. Charts work well with small audiences; transparencies and actual demonstrations are fine for average audiences; slides and films work well for large audiences.

Visuals that are part of an oral presentation are usually simpler than those integrated into a written document. In most cases, the visuals that support a presentation display only one or two ideas; often, too many elements are

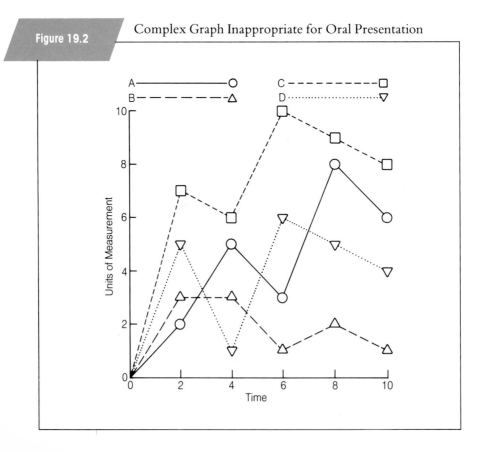

Figure 19.2   Complex Graph Inappropriate for Oral Presentation

incorporated into a single visual. For example, the graph in Figure 19.2 would be difficult for an audience to read. Instead, the presenter could prepare four separate graphs, as in Figure 19.3, each clearly showing the growth. If direct comparison is necessary, the presenter could follow the separate graphs with a composite. Some experts recommend no more than six pieces of information to convey an idea on a single visual. Therefore, a block diagram would have no more than six components, a slide no more than six words or phrases.

The size of visuals is important. Few things are more frustrating and annoying to an audience than visuals they cannot see. A good general guideline for presenters who use flip charts and posters displayed on easels allows 1 inch of letter height for every 10 feet of audience. So if there are 30 feet between the flip chart and the last row of the audience, lettering on charts should be approximately 3 inches high. Clearly, this guideline becomes impractical in a large room, where a presenter should switch from charts to overhead transparencies (vu-graphs) and 35mm slides, which can be projected even in an auditorium.

| **Figure 19.3** | Series of Simple Graphs Appropriate for Oral Presentation |

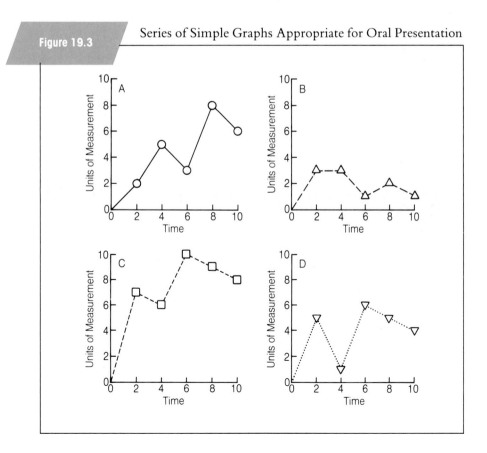

Handouts

Handouts can be a valuable asset for your presentation because they give the audience something to refer to after the presentation. Other uses for handouts include:

- listing primary visuals for future reference
- explaining complex terminology
- providing reading lists or bibliography references
- summarizing key points

In considering whether to utilize handouts, there are certain questions you have to resolve.

How Should Handouts Be Packaged? Handout material should be collated and bound, if only with a single staple. Loose pages create the impression of inadequate preparation and cause confusion; someone is always missing page 4, while someone else needs page 7. The packet should also have a cover page that gives the title of your presentation, your name and company, the meeting, the date, and the location. Sometimes you may also include an address, mail stop, and telephone number. This cover information enables the packet to be filed and also provides a way to contact you later for questions or discussion. If you are making an important presentation, consider putting the packet in a corporate folder.

When Should You Distribute Handouts? Depending on their purpose, handout packets can be distributed at the beginning or end of a presentation. If the packet is needed for reference during the presentation or contains a general outline, then the packet should be issued at the beginning of the session. You generally can keep people from riffling through the pages by saying, "Periodically during my presentation I'll refer to specific sections of your packet. I'll tell you what pages you need to refer to as they come up." If the packet contains sections that "give away" your presentation or if it is simply a review of the oral/visual information, tell people that a summary will be available after the presentation for those who need it for reference. If you do not plan to refer to the packet during the presentation, certainly it is not necessary to distribute it at the beginning.

How Much Detail Should the Handouts Include? Handouts usually do not just duplicate the presentation; rather, they highlight or outline key points and provide details of factual or statistical information that might be difficult to remember. Handout material is similar to visual material in that it supports the presentation. Particularly when the packet is distributed at the beginning of the presentation, the handout material referred to should illustrate the points in the presentation.

Visual material (copies of vu-graphs or flip charts) may be reproduced so that the audience can refer to them quickly. Reproducing visuals also safeguards against breakdowns of audio-visual equipment and eliminates problems from poor eyesight in the audience.

The only time a handout should exactly reproduce the presentation is in formal conferences where someone presents a prepared paper; copies of the paper are usually available after the presentation and are often published in a collection of conference papers.

How Should You Refer to the Handouts During the Presentation? If you distribute the packet at the beginning of the presentation, tell your audience that you will refer to the appropriate pages as you go along. Each page should have a heading and a page number for easy reference. In a packet with several sections, you will find references faster if you insert a sheet of colored paper between each section. Then you can say, "Turn to the page immediately after the blue page divider." Audiences seem to find this much easier than turning to page 9.

After you refer to a page in the packet, give the audience a few moments to locate the proper place. This slight pause eliminates most of the paper rustling.

Carefully assess what you want the audience to do during and after the presentation. Having them engaged in reading and notetaking may encourage attention—if the activities are necessary and enhance your presentation. If the activities do not contribute to the audience's understanding, omit them so the people can devote their full attention to you.

What Is the Real Value of Your Handouts? Take the time and effort to prepare a packet only if you refer to it directly during the presentation or if people in the audience would need to refer to it afterward. If the packet is never going to be used, spend your time elsewhere to ensure the presentation's succcess. If the packet will be used, make the information accessible and put it in a clear context. For example, a list of key words and phrases might be meaningful during or immediately after a presentation, but a week or two later, most people will have forgotten the context. A context defines the terms, identifies the situation to which they apply, or explains how they were interpreted in your presentation.

Questions

Members of your audience almost always ask questions, so you need to plan not only how but when to respond. Whether you permit questions during the presentation or after depends on your reaction to being interrupted, the nature of the presentation, and the size of the audience. If you prefer not to be interrupted, ask people to hold their questions until the question-and-answer session at the end. Questions are also usually held until the end in formal presentations, particularly with large audiences. However, if the session is small, informal, and you do not mind interruptions (and can easily get back on the track), tell the audience you will respond to questions as they arise.

You also need to consider problems that might result from questions. For example, if you don't know the answer to a question, don't panic. A presenter is not expected to know everything. An experienced, confident presenter will say, without embarrassment, "I'm sorry, I don't know, but if you'd like me to find out, contact me after the presentation."

A person may disagree with you, in which case you will at least know people are listening. In some cases, you may simply acknowledge the specific area of disagreement, noting that multiple views or interpretations are possible. In other situations, you may want to focus on the likely cause of the disagreement or restate your case, including a response to the person's disagreement.

Example   I understand your reluctance to commit to the expense of retooling an entire production line, but the market research shows first quarter sales of this product cover all equipment and tooling.

If one person monopolizes the questioning, you can ask if other people have questions, and then call on another person. If no one except the monopolizer has a question, suggest that the person meet you after the presentation to continue the discussion—and end the presentation.

Occasionally, someone will ask a seemingly stupid question or perhaps a question about something you have carefully explained. Act as if the question is legitimate. You can't tell what provoked the person to ask the question. Keep a straight face and give a straight answer.

Other times a person actually makes a statement rather than asking a question. In such situations, you can express interest in the person's view and then ask the person if he has a question (just like radio talk show hosts do when a caller tries to dominate).

If you or the audience can't hear the question, tell the questioner, and ask him to repeat it. If parts of the audience can't hear a question, you should repeat it so that everyone can hear. Repeating the question has the additional benefit of affirming that you understand what was asked.

When a person asks a question that has nothing to do with the topic or you don't understand the question, you can ask the questioner to *rephrase* the question; it may be just poorly worded. If you ask them to *repeat* the question, you might get a repetition of the very same one you didn't understand. If the rephrasing doesn't help, you might not be able to provide an answer.

Finally, if there are no questions, thank the audience for their attention and conclude the presentation.

Evaluating Presentations

Oral presentations are a regular part of academic and professional life. Most of the time you attend a presentation to acquire information. Sometimes, however, a classmate or colleague asks you to assess the presentation he or she has given. The following questions, though not inclusive, will help you with such an evaluation:

1. Is the presentation area set up before the presenter begins?
2. Is the presentation area arranged so that everyone in the audience has a clear view?
3. Does the presenter appear well prepared?
4. Does the presenter appear poised and confident?
5. Does the presenter handle notes unobtrusively?
6. Is the presenter dressed appropriately for the situation?
7. Does the presenter identify the purpose of the presentation?
8. Does the presenter make the opening interesting?
9. Has the presenter selected material appropriate for the audience?
10. Are the main points in the presentation clearly identified?
11. Is the information of the presentation logically organized so that the audience can follow the ideas easily?
12. Does the presenter provide clear transitions between the ideas in the presentation?
13. Does the presenter use examples to illustrate points?
14. Is the presenter's voice pleasant and professional?
15. Does the presenter's voice have sufficient volume for the size of the room and audience?
16. Is the presenter's inflection varied?
17. Is the presenter's pronunciation correct?
18. Is the pace of the presentation appropriate?
19. Does the presenter make direct eye contact with the audience?
20. Are the visuals used in the presentation sufficiently large to enable everyone in the audience to see?

21. Are the visuals appropriately selected?
22. In a demonstration, is the presenter able to speak clearly while demonstrating the procedure?
23. In a demonstration, is the audience able to see each step without an obstructed view?
24. In a demonstration, does the presenter handle equipment with knowledge and confidence?
25. In a demonstration, does the presenter perform and explain each step slowly enough that the audience can understand what is happening?
26. Does the presenter provide an appealing, appropriate conclusion?
27. Does the presenter provide helpful handout material?
28. Does the presenter respond directly to audience questions?
29. What are the areas in which the presenter needs most to improve?
30. What are the presenter's greatest strengths?

Inquiries and Assignments

Discussion Questions

1. What are some of the best things you have seen people do in oral presentations to keep your interest and assure your understanding?
2. What are some of the worst things you have seen people do when making an oral presentation?
3. What aspects of making an oral presentation make you the most anxious?
4. Explain how each of the following oral presentations has a persuasive element.
   a. Training session to teach use of new computer software to monitor inventory
   b. Informative presentation to justify a decision to change production procedures
   c. Sales talk explaining the control panel on ovens used to heat-treat metal parts
   d. Demonstration of precision capable using CNC (computer numerical control) machines

Individual and Group Exercises

1. Case Situation: Thelma Michelson is a staff chemist doing successful R and D work a year after her graduation. She has returned to college to

take an evening course in technical communication to upgrade her professional skills. The only assignment she is apprehensive about is an oral presentation near the end of the term. Throughout the semester, she has used various aspects of her research at work for class writing assignments. Frequently, she has been able to use completed class assignments for writing she is required to do as part of her job.

One paper describing an innovative analytical process is particularly important to her because when she showed it to the project manager, he added the names of the other project members and submitted it for presentation at the upcoming ACS (American Chemical Society) conference. Thelma was ecstatic when the paper was accepted for presentation at the conference and publication in the conference proceedings. Now she is panic-stricken; her project manager has suggested that she present the findings because she was instrumental in the process development.

Thelma has a list of reasons why she is the wrong person to represent her company by presenting the information: she'd turn red, her voice would crack or disappear, she'd forget her material, she'd put the vugraphs on the projector upside down, she'd forget to refer to the handouts, she'd be unable to answer questions. She is very anxious that her nervousness about talking in front of a group and her inexperience as a presenter will detract from her credibility as a chemist. Her manager has insisted: Thelma will make the presentation.

She has five weeks to prepare for a full dress rehearsal of her presentation for the upper management of her company. She believes if she can do well in this rehearsal, she will do well in the actual presentation. How should she prepare? Design a practical and effective plan for Thelma to follow. Be very specific. She will need a plan that identifies what she should do and when she should to it. Build in ways that will give her constructive feedback as well as build her confidence.

Assignments

(*Note:* For each presentation in this section, identify the intended audience. You may specify that the class audience role-play a particular group.)

1. Prepare an informative presentation that educates the audience about a product or procedure. Consider these topics:

   - start-up new manufacturing facility
   - alternatives to traditional burial
   - career options for social workers
   - polymer film used to cover food products
   - building of a micro-chip
   - selection of wine at a business dinner

2. Prepare a presentation to demonstrate how to use equipment or complete a process unfamiliar to the audience. Consider these topics:

- mountaineering equipment
- SIDS (sudden infant death syndrome) monitor
- air layering for plant propagation
- film or tape splicing
- computer keyboard
- quilting
- restringing tennis racquet

3. Prepare a persuasive presentation that convinces your listeners to accept your position. Consider one of these topics:

- tool crib versus individual tool boxes
- lowering industrial emissions standards
- hospices provide valuable medical care

4. Prepare a training session that teaches your audience to complete a task. Consider these topics.

- polishing an optical surface
- caning a chair
- air layering a plant
- inspecting a machined part

20 Career Concerns

WHEN YOU DECIDE to look for a new job, you can benefit from reviewing ways of approaching the search. The practice of blanketing the job market with a hundred or more identical resumes and letters, hoping to get a few responses, seldom results in a job. The traditional grapevine often works, but you have many other ways to learn about job possibilities.

Learning About Jobs

One of the most successful techniques is networking, a modification of the grapevine. Networking involves contacting people you know, as well as people they know, to gather leads for jobs. Networking produces useful information that you might not otherwise learn. For example, imagine that your next door neighbor is an engineer in a company that you might be interested in working for. She's not in a position to hire you; in fact, her department even has a six-month moratorium on hiring. However, she can suggest people you can talk with in another division of the company to learn more about the company—with the understanding that you are not looking for a job, but merely collecting information.

Such networking opportunities exist all around you because you know people in a wide variety of settings:

- classes (classmates, instructors)
- present jobs (full- and part-time; paid and volunteer)
- previous jobs
- professional organizations
- civic and political organizations
- neighborhoods
- social activities
- family gatherings
- religious organizations
- daily activities

People in any one of these settings might provide a lead to a possible job, but you have to let them know of your interest in other jobs.

Whether you know exactly the type of position you're looking for or are simply exploring a range of possibilities, networking can be effective, though it does require some effort. You need to talk with people, share your interests and experiences with them, get to know them so that they, in turn, know you. They may be comfortable offering you employment suggestions, and you should feel comfortable asking for their recommendations and even for introductions to other people.

Apart from networking, you can learn about possible jobs in some of the following ways:

- Work with your university placement office.
- Answer newspaper ads.
- Place newspaper ads.
- Respond to ads in professional journals.
- Attend job fairs.
- Read job lists at your state's Division of Employment.
- Attend company open houses.
- Mail blind letters and resumes.
- Sign with an employment agency.
- Contact a job clearinghouse.
- Read such publications as *National Business Employment Weekly* (published by the *Wall Street Journal*).

No single technique necessarily works best, so be receptive to any one, or even a combination, of these sources.

Once you have identified a job you think you'd like, you need to determine if your initial impressions, not only regarding the specific position you're interested in but also the company as a whole, are correct. You should begin your research before you send a letter and resume, to determine if you even want to apply for the position. Your investigation might include some of these lines of inquiry:

- Use publications by Dun and Bradstreet, Moody, and Standard and Poor in the library reference section to look up the company's vital statistics—corporate officials, size, services or products, financial position.
- Use the *Wall Street Journal Index*, *New York Times Index*, and *Business Periodicals Index* to locate articles about the company's people or products. Read articles in such periodicals as *Fortune, Forbes, Business Week, Inc.,* and *Electronic Business.*
- Read the company's annual report, which can be obtained from stockbrokers or the company itself.
- Call the company to request promotional literature about one of their major products.
- Talk with people who work for the company and listen to their impressions.

This information should give you a good idea if the company is one you want to pursue.

Preparing Application Letters

Your initial contact with a prospective employer usually consists of a resume and cover letter, so these are important. The letter should be sincere and informative, addressing the reader in the second person (the "you attitude"), the style of most effective business letters.

Ken King applied the following general guidelines for a letter of application in his response to the newspaper ad in Figure 20.1 for a procedures writer:

1. OPENING: Identify yourself.
   - State your overall qualification.
   - Identify the position applied for.
   - Identify source of information about job.

Figure 20.1

PROCEDURES WRITER

Northrop Precision Products Division, in Norwood, MA, manufactures sophisticated electromechanical precision devices and related guidance systems.

Working within the Data Processing Department, you will write and edit policies and procedure drafts; revise/update existing Policies and Procedures. Position will also involve writing and maintaining Program Standards Manuals, Systems Documentation and a Disaster Recovery Manual.

Requires a minimum of 1 year's writing experience and a Bachelors Degree in English, Computer Science or equivalent. Familiarity with IBM 4300 series highly desirable.

Northrop provides a competitive, comprehensive benefits package. Please send resume to: **Professional Employment, Dept. BG714, Northrop Corporation, 100 Morse Street, Norwood, MA 02062.**

Northrop is an Equal Opportunity Employer M/F/H/V.
U.S. Citizenship Required.

We're within your reach.

NORTHROP
Precision Products Division
Electronics Systems Group

2. BODY: Match your background to the job.
   - Determine priority of academic or professional experience.
   - Summarize key qualifications, without repeating resume.
   - Include specific examples rather than generalizations.
   - Include relevant supplemental information.
   - Refer to resume, if you've enclosed one.

3. CLOSING: Indicate your availability.
   - Express interest in an interview.
   - Indicate special considerations.

Ken's background does not exactly match the criteria in the ad, but he believes he has equivalent qualifications. Notice that in Example 20.1, his letter specifically identifies projects he has worked on.

In the job-search process, you will also need to write other types of letters. After an interview, you should write a thank-you letter, expressing your appreciation for the time given to you and restating your interest in the position. Sometimes after an interview, you won't hear from a company; if more than two weeks pass, you can write to inquire about the status of the selection process. If you receive a rejection, you should respond, thanking them for considering you; this courtesy could keep the door open for a job in the future. Finally, if you receive a job offer, you should respond in writing, indicating whether you accept or refuse.

Designing a Resume

One of the primary purposes of any resume is to procure an interview for yourself so that, in person, you can convince an organization to hire you. Unlike a job application form that has questions the employer wants answered, you design your resume to highlight your skills and experience.

A legitimate secondary purpose of a resume is organizing your background so that you keep track of your expanding professional experience. At least once a year, you should update your resume to include the additional responsibilities or skills that increase your options or make you a more effective professional. Even if you are not looking for a new job, updating your resume helps you summarize your recent work when preparing for your annual review and gives you a chance to view your achievements.

If, during the year that you are reviewing, you have done absolutely nothing that can be added to your resume, you should engage in careful personal

Example 20.1

176 Stevens Avenue
Nashua, NH 03060
July 22, 1985

Mr. Donald Grayson
Professional Employment
Department BG714
Northrop Corporation
Precision Products Division
100 Morse Street
Norwood, MA 02062

Dear Mr. Grayson:

   Your position for a procedures writer, advertised in the July 21 Boston
Sunday Globe, matches both my academic background and experience. I have a
B.A. in Technical Communications with a minor in Computer Science and
experience in writing technical manuals.

   As a co-op student at Northeastern University, with a 3.1 cumulative
average, I have had more than a year and a half of experience working for
Honeywell and Itek. At Honeywell, I assisted with writing system
documentation. One major project involved documentation for remote network
processing for the Honeywell Level 66 to Level 6. Recently, at Itek, I was
completely responsible for revising a quality assurance manual, incorporating
changes in DOD and ANSI specifications. Copies of these documents are
available for you to examine in my portfolio.

   My computer science minor has given me a working knowledge of BASIC,
COBOL, FORTRAN, and Assembler. My enclosed resume gives additional details
of my academic background.

   Because of my co-op positions, I am comfortable working with engineers
and enjoy a fast-paced, technical environment. My experience with both
mainframe and minicomputers makes me confident I can quickly learn new
computer systems.

   I look forward to meeting with you for an interview. I can be reached
at my home address or by telephone any day after 3:00 p.m. at 603-555-8140.

                              Sincerely,

                              Kenneth J. King

inquiry. Are you happy with the status quo? Do you enjoy your current status and responsibilities? Have you gained or maintained personal and professional fulfillment from your job? If you answer affirmatively, consider yourself lucky—and keep doing your job. If you are not satisfied, then examine those areas of your professional responsibility that you would like to change. Maintaining your resume can be an effective vehicle for reinforcing job satisfaction or signaling the time for a change.

There is no best way to organize your resume. A resume reflects your experience as you want others to perceive it, so you might have more than one resume, to emphasize different aspects of your background.

Because a resume not only records your experience but also reflects your character, you should be scrupulously honest in selecting and describing your experience. An inflated or enhanced resume misrepresents your background and abilities—and also says something negative about your self-image and your integrity. For example, if your job title is "receptionist," do not put "public relations liaison" on your resume.

How do you know what information is essential, desirable, optional, unnecessary, or inappropriate? Because styles of resumes change, what is appropriate in content and format? For example, several years ago people regularly attached a photograph and included personal information; such attachments are seldom expected today.

A resume begins with identifying information: your name, address, and telephone number, often followed by a summary of your education and work experience. However, your resume may include other information, generally that which will positively influence the reader to invite you for a job interview. What's appropriate for you may not be appropriate for a friend or colleague. In fact, what's appropriate for you for one job may not be appropriate for another job. For example, if you're applying for a staff position with an industrial magazine, your photography hobby could be relevant; it would probably be irrelevant for a position as a quality control inspector. Figure 20.2 separates your choices into essential, optional, and generally unnecessary items.

Essential Elements

Name, Address, Telephone Number. The heading of your resume can begin with your name, address, and telephone number. It does *not* need to begin with the word *resume*, any more than a business letter needs to be headed with

---

| **Figure 20.2** | Information for a Resume |

ESSENTIAL
name
address
telephone number
education (college, military, professional training)
job experience

OPTIONAL

goals or objectives	publications
skills	patents
hobbies	honors
community activities	awards
church/synagogue activities	sports
political activities	interests
military status	test scores
security clearances	civil service ranking
professional organizations	travels
offices held	volunteer work
citizenship	references

GENERALLY UNNECESSARY
marital status
physical characteristics (height, weight)
birth date or age
health
race or nationality
home ownership
social security number
personality traits
religion
family background
clubs
fraternal organizations

---

business letter. Example 20.2 shows two variations for arranging the essential identifying information.

Use your legal name, not your nickname, even if that's what you prefer being called. And do not put a nickname in quotation marks, such as Jason "Chip" Mason. If your name is particularly difficult to pronounce, consider

Example 20.2

```
                    CHERYL KIRK HARDING
                    1751 South Palm Drive
                    Santa Barbara, CA 93117
                     (805) 555-9764 (home)
                  (805) 555-1500 ext. 164 (work)




                      SEAN M. GREENE

College Address (until May 30):          Permanent Address:
Fields House, Room 421                    17 East Hill Road
University of Massachusetts               Sudbury, MA 01776
Amherst, MA 01002                         617-555-8841
413-555-4210
```

adding the phonetic spelling in parentheses, to make the person calling you for a job interview more comfortable.

Use your permanent legal address. If you also have a temporary address (summer home, college apartment), you need to include and clearly label both addresses, with ZIP codes. The only abbreviations should be the U.S. Postal Service two-letter capitalized abbreviation for each state.

Include your area code with your telephone number. If you currently have a job and do not mind being called at work, you can include this number as well as your home number, but label them.

Education. Whether you put your education or your job experience next depends on which will make a stronger impression on a prospective employer. Resumes should be organized in descending order, with the most important or impressive information coming first.

If you are entering the professional job market directly from college, you probably have stronger academic credentials than work experience. Exceptions to this might be students who have gained professional experience through a co-op work program or students who have found summer and part-time jobs related to their professional area. Entry level college graduates usually list their education before their work experience on a resume to emphasize their strength—current knowledge in the field.

Figure 20.3 Variations for Presenting College Education in a Resume

Version 1 school (and location if not obvious)
EDUCATION
University of Illinois, B.S. in Physics, 1983
Parks Junior College, A.S. in Aeronautics, 1981

Version 2 degree (if applicable)
EDUCATION
B.S.—University of Illinois, Physics, 1983
A.S.—Parks Junior College, Aeronautics, 1981

Version 3 academic major
EDUCATION
Physics, University of Illinois, B.S., 1983
Aeronautics, Parks Junior College, A.S., 1981

Version 4 date of degree or dates of attendance
EDUCATION
1983, University of Illinois, B.S. in Physics
1981, Parks Junior College, A.S. in Aeronautics

An experienced professional has both academic credentials and job experience. Such people often place their job experience before their education, particularly if the experience relates directly to the desired position. However, people changing careers often place their education first, especially if their academic background relates more closely to the new position than their recent jobs.

Employers are interested in four basic aspects of your college education: school, academic major, degree, and dates attended. You may provide additional information that reflects your level of achievement or breadth of knowledge by indicating specialized courses, high grade point averages, and academic honors. The order in which you present this information depends on what you want to emphasize, as shown in Figure 20.3, but separate items are always listed in reverse chronological order, from most recent to earliest.

You do not need to restrict information in the education section of your resume to colleges. Include relevant military education and training provided by companies. Also, be sure to mention attendance at a community or junior college as well as specialized technical or vocational training. Education skills you have acquired informally—electronics learned through a local community education program, computer languages you taught yourself—might be listed, if relevant. Generally, you needn't include high school education, unless it was specialized or highly prestigious, or unless you are entering the job market directly from high school. Some other elements of your education that might be placed in your resume include:

- additional coursework in areas outside your specialty or major
- specialized courses in your major area
- course concentrations outside of or complementary to major area
- thesis subject
- departmental honors project
- grade point average if above 3.0
- military training
- company seminars

How do you present yourself if you are in the working world and currently have or want a professional position but do not have a college degree? This situation is difficult if you work for a company that mandates a degree for recognition, raises, and promotions. Do *not* do what one person did: list school, academic major, dates, and then state, "Did not graduate." Instead, emphasize your job experience by placing it before the education section on your resume. If you are pursuing a college degree while working, consider one of these versions of presenting your current college work:

- Merrimack College, 1984–present, Division of Continuing Education
  78 credits of 120 required for B.S. in Accounting

- Accounting, Merrimack College, Division of Continuing Education
  B.S. in accounting anticipated next year
  112 credits accumulated of 120 required for degree

- Merrimack College, Division of Continuing Education, completed six
  semesters toward B.S. in Accounting

These versions express the nondegree status in a positive way, emphasizing ongoing education as well as indicating progress towards a degree. If you are not pursuing a college degree, focus instead on your on-the-job training and in-house seminar programs.

Experience. Resumes can be separated into three types, depending on the way the employment experience is presented:

- Chronological resumes present information according to dates you have worked.
- Organizational resumes present information according to the type or name of the organizations for whom you have worked.
- Functional resumes present information according to job titles or job skills you have.

Regardless of the format, each individual listing is often accompanied by an explanation of the job, focusing on a person's primary responsibilities, and sometimes including major accomplishments.

Job experience is commonly organized chronologically. Many people choose this familiar form because it effectively shows continuous employment and steady expansion of responsibility. Clearly, chronological resumes are not particularly useful for entry level people because they have little professional experience. Nor are chronological resumes appropriate for people who have had breaks in their employment (pregnancy, illness, layoff) or who have held a series of jobs for short periods of time; the chronology merely stresses what some employers might consider undesirable qualities.

Like education, jobs are always listed in reverse chronological order, with the most recent job first. Part of Mark Gordon's resume, shown below, arranges his work experience chronologically.

Example

```
1985-present   BAYLOR RESEARCH CORPORATION--Soren, VA
               Staff Chemist

1983-85        CHEMCOM, INC.--Wheeler, VA
               Chemical Technician

1980-82        ADDEX CHEMICALS--Leigh, VA
               Laboratory Technician
```

Organizational resumes stress the name or type of organization. Organizational resumes are useful for people who have worked for well-known and respected organizations. This form of presenting professional experience is also appropriate for people who have worked for short periods of time or have had unimpressive job titles. Before Mark Gordon was hired at Baylor Research Corporation, he presented his professional experience organizationally, like this:

Example

```
CHEMCOM, INC. (Wheeler, VA)--Chemical Technician, 1983-85

ADDEX CHEMICALS (Leigh, VA)--Laboratory Technician, 1980-82
```

In this way, he emphasized the companies, while at the same time giving less attention to his technician status.

An organizational resume can be used to tremendous advantage by people who want to stress the variety of their professional experience. When Jan Peterson applied for a job in the training and development division of a company specializing in bioengineering, she separated her professional experience into categories to highlight the breadth of her background, as illustrated in this example:

Example

```
TEACHING
     Physiology Instructor, Trinity College, 1985-present
     Biology Instructor, City Community College, 1981-84
     Biology Tutoring, Human Engineering Deparment,
          University of Bridgeton, 1977-80 (part-time)

MEDICAL RESEARCH
     Project Assistant, 1978-80
          Human Engineering Laboratory
          University of Bridgeton
     Laboratory Assistant, 1977-78 (part-time)
          Human Engineering Laboratory
          University of Bridgeton

INDUSTRY
     Quality Control Inspector, Medicus, Inc., 1976-77 (part-time)
```

A functional resume focuses on either job titles or skills. Organizing professional experience by job title is particularly useful when titles of jobs a person has held closely match those being sought. If Mark Gordon applies for a new job as a chemist, he could develop a functional resume, as shown below, because his background relates to the field in which he is applying.

Example

```
STAFF CHEMIST
     Baylor Research Corporation, Soren VA, 1985-present

CHEMICAL TECHNICIAN
     Chemcom, Inc., Wheeler VA, 1983-85

LABORATORY TECHNICIAN
     Addex Chemicals, Leigh VA, 1980-82
```

Sometimes, however, a particular way of organizing a resume can mask a person's experience. For example, without the organizational labels Jan Peterson's professional experience seems scattered rather than focused:

```
Physiology Instructor, Trinity College, 1985-present
Biology Instructor, City Community College, 1981-84
Biology Tutoring, Human Engineering Department,
     University of Bridgeton, 1977-80 (part-time)
Project Assistant, 1978-80
Laboratory Assistant, 1977-78 (part-time)
     Human Genetics Engineering Laboratory
Quality Control Inspector, Medicus, Inc., 1976-77 (part-time)
```

Another more sophisticated type of functional resume organizes professional experience by categories of skills. This format requires more analysis of your own background than the other forms of presenting professional experience. Such a resume is most appropriate for a person with a considerable amount of varied professional experience, often in widely differing fields. In his resume, Carl Lawlor includes first a job history that summarizes job title, employer, and dates, and then his professional experience. Because of his distinctive work history, in which each position he held required two functions, he separates it into two categories—training and engineering. A portion of this section of his resume is shown in the following example:

```
TRAINING         Conducted on-site training in state-of-the-art
                 electronics.
                 Produced training tapes, focusing on industrial
                 safety.
                 Instituted a three-tier retraining program for
                 electronics technicians.
                 Created self-paced, interactive software as
                 training supplement.

ENGINEERING      Developed and patented interface between
                 X-1700 series mainframe and X-17 minicomputers.
                 Designed circuitry for PC boards used in
                 telecommunications projects.
```

Optional Elements

You can decide whether to include any of the optional resume elements listed in Figure 20.2 by determining if the information creates a positive, professional image, advances your chances of being invited for an interview, or relates to the position for which you're applying. If the information does none of these things, omit it.

Including a *goal or objective* at the beginning of your resume is a common practice. An effective goal or objective identifies your job target and relates your experience, education, and skills to a particular position. It also suggests that you have thought about how your background suits the company's needs. Frequently, your cover letter is not duplicated and sent with your resume when it is circulated in a company, so a stated goal or objective lets a reader know what position interests you.

On the other hand, a vague or over-generalized goal or objective merely demonstrates your lack of knowledge about the company's needs and your inability to assess your own qualifications. For example, one major state university placement office actually advises engineering graduates to state an objective so generalized that one prospective engineer is indistinguishable from the next.

Example   Objective: Entry level engineering position that offers a challenge
               and a chance for advancement

If you have room on your resume, list your *publications, presentations, and patents*, especially if they demonstrate experience and skills related to the position for which you're applying. Such information lets a reader know that you have gained professional recognition for your achievements.

Another way to convey your qualifications is to identify skills outside your academic or career area. For example, an English major wanting to be a technical writer could indicate knowledge of computer programming and industrial photography. An engineer applying to a multi-national corporation might benefit from mentioning fluency in German and Spanish.

Whether you mention *church/synagogue, community, political, and volunteer activities* depends primarily on whether the experience you gained relates to the position for which you're applying or to the organization as a whole. For example, managing a political campaign, supervising a religious education program, chairing the finance committee in your community, and supervising March of Dimes volunteers all demonstrate experience that is relevant if you're applying for a managerial position, irrelevant if you're applying for a technical position.

List your *honors and awards* as well as *test scores* and *grade point* or *cumulative averages* if they relate to a potential job. For example, high scores on actuarial exams would be relevant for someone trained as a mathematician, accountant, financial analyst, or actuary.

Active military status should be noted, but *previous military experience* should be included only if you have an honorable discharge. Military experience is particularly important to include if your training and experience relate to the position for which you're applying.

A prospective employer appreciates knowing if you have a *security clearance* or *civil service ranking*, if either is necessary to the position. Similarly, indicate your *citizenship* or *nationality* if it might be relevant.

State your membership in relevant *professional organizations* or on *professional committees* because such involvements show an interest in and awareness of advancements in your field. Full-time students should consider the benefits of obtaining a student membership in the appropriate professional sociey; it may be the single factor that distinguishes you from other similarly qualified job seekers. Mentioning *offices held* is proper if you want to demonstrate professional recognition and managerial experience.

Like so many of the other optional elements, *hobbies, sports,* and *travel* should be included only if they are related to the position for which you're applying. For example, if you are an oceanographer, your interest in scuba diving and underwater photography is pertinent; but if you are an electrical engineer, it's not.

Finally, you need to consider whether to include *references* in your resume. Listing people's names, address, and telephone numbers (with their permission) is acceptable, but it takes up space that might better be spent in detailing your education, experience, and/or skills. An alternative is merely to state, "References available" or "References available upon request."

Unnecessary Elements

Some elements are unnecessary or inappropriate to incorporate into a resume, either because resume styles have changed or because privacy laws now exempt people from having to reveal personal information that is not directly connected to the job. (See Figure 20.2.) On a resume, you select the information to include, keeping in mind that gaining an interview is your goal. So, even though you seldom benefit from including such information, add it if it will help convince an employer to meet you in person.

When resumes are initially received, a worker in the personnel department sorts them into three piles: possible, questionable, and rejected. Your goal should be to land in the "possible" pile or, at worst, in the "questionable" pile. So, when planning your resume, exclude any information that might get your resume tossed in the "rejected" pile. Your resume can be rejected for any number of reasons: lack of appropriate training, insufficient experience, inconsistent work history, confusing layout, messy appearance.

You want to avoid having it rejected because you include a piece of unnecessary information to which the reader reacts negatively. There is no such thing as a composite of a perfect employee. Your age and height, your health and marital status, your religion and family background, your race and gender, your personality and social activities—whether they are "right" or "wrong" depends on who reads the resume. Generally, the items in this list are not needed on your resume:

marital status	social security number
physical characteristics (height, weight)	personality traits
	religion
birth date or age	family background
health	clubs
race	fraternal organizations
home ownership	salary history

Design Elements

The visual impression made by a resume is as important as the content. No matter how good the content of your resume, if its design does not invite attention, your qualifications may be overlooked. Some people may interpret a sloppy or carelessly prepared resume as a reflection of your attitude or work habits.

One important design factor of a resume is the length. An entry level applicant should prepare a one-page resume, whereas the resumes of experienced professionals can run to two pages. In some cases, a person may enclose attachments listing credits, such as patents, presentations, or publications.

Your reader is also influenced by the several visual factors. If you can answer affirmatively to each of the following questions, you probably have designed a visually appealing resume:

- *Balance:* Are the sections arranged to avoid a top-heavy or lopsided appearance?
- *White Space:* Does the amount of text approximately balance the amount of white space?
- *Typeface:* Is the typeface easy to read?
- *Stock:* Is the paper a high-quality stock? Is the color appropriate: white, ivory, tan, gray?
- *Accuracy:* Is the typing or typesetting completely accurate?

■ *Visual Variety:* Does the resume use two or three techniques for emphasis and variety?

Examples

```
Underline:  Job Titles, Company Names, Responsibilities.

CAPITALIZE AND UNDERLINE for greater emphasis.

Indent to differentiate
    Job Titles and
        Job Responsibilities (and especially to make
        subsections easier to read).

Box Major Headings.

Identify titles of publications, speeches, or jobs
in script or italic type.

Use bullets to
• align parallel points
• avoid repetition
• emphasize key elements
```

■ *Reproduction:* Is the copy clear, with dark ink and no smudges?

Examples 20.3 and 20.4 represent two versions of the resume of a college senior graduating with a B.S. in computer science and a significant amount of experience, based on the 25–40 hours per week she has worked throughout college, part-time during school and full-time during vacations and summers. Notice how much more difficult the first one is to read than the second, though the content is virtually identical. The difference lies in the format.

Interviewing

Informational interviews are conducted when you are collecting information about a company but do not necessarily want a job with them. Such interviews have several benefits:

■ You can learn about a company: policies, practices, products.

■ You establish new professional contacts.

■ You practice interviewing techniques for a time when you really do want a job.

■ You gain a sense of your value in the current job market.

Example 20.3

KARON P. POISSON
8 DIAMOND STREET
LAWRENCE, MA 01843
(617) 555-1299

GOAL
Technical and marketing support of computers and their related products for business clients

EDUCATION
B.S.--1982--Merrimack College, North Andover MA
Major: Computer Science
Concentration: Marketing (Business GPA 3.2)
Nominated for Who's Who in American College Students

COMPUTER LANGUAGE and SYSTEMS
BASIC, COBOL, FORTRAN, Wang Decision Processing, and DEC Assembly Language; DEC 11/70; WANG 2200VP, 2200VS, OIS, WP

BUSINESS COURSES
Marketing I, II; Industrial Marketing; Accounting I; Process of Management; Organizational Behavior; Business Policy

PROFESSIONAL WORK EXPERIENCE:

WANG LABORATORIES, INC.

Applications Specialist (September 1981-present)
Responsibilities: Designing, implementing, and writing programs for bids and proposal, word processing conversions, software support, and contract administration. Training a new programmer on the use of the system and channeling work for her.

RECENT PROJECTS:

Automatic Bid Writer   Configures a boiler plate bid for the home office bid group (14 people)

Invoice System   Handles all invoicing for two departments (25 people)

Programmer Trainee (April-September 1981)
Responsibilities: Supporting the departments of Contract Administration, Conversion Center, and Bids and Proposals, with program development and program maintenance; providing technical support to the field support, home office, and customers on the capabilities of the media conversions; training personnel to handle the programs developed for the conversion center

Conversion Operator (January 1978-April 1981)
Responsibilities: Answering customer question on technical material sent from the Conversion group; solving on-site problems with the conversion material; interfacing and training other operators; providing support for supervisor of conversion group regarding feasibility of projects

VOLUNTEER ACTIVITIES

Commuter Council Member (1978-1982) responsible for organizing forums and social functions as well as providing voice to administration for 75 commuters; served as the Council Coordinator

National Committee Chairperson (1977-1979) for Square Dance Convention--responsible for maintaining financial records, organizing fundraiser for local group

References available; Relocation possible

1982

Example 20.4

```
                          KARON P. POISSON
                          8 Diamond Street
                          Lawrence, Massachusetts  01843
                          (617-555-1299)

OBJECTIVE         A position providing technical and marketing support for
                  computer hardware and software users

EDUCATION         B.S.--Merrimak College, North Andover, Massachusetts
                  Major:  Computer Science--1982
                  Concentration:  Business (Business GPA 3.2/4.0)
                  Nominated for Who's Who in American College and Universities

                  Related Courses:    Marketing I, II; Industrial Marketing;
                                      Accounting I, II; Process of Management;
                                      Organizational Behavior; Business Policy

OTHER TRAINING    Languages:          BASIC, COBOL, FORTRAN, Assembly Language,
                                      Wang Decision Processing

                  Systems Used:       DEC 11/70; WANG 2200VP, 2200VS, OIS, WP

EXPERIENCE        Wang Laboratories Incorporated--Lowell, Massachusetts
1981 to present   Applications Specialist--Designing, implementing, and writing
                  programs that are used by marketing support staff in the areas
                  of media conversions, bids and proposals, software support, and
                  contract administration.  Designing and implementing a training
                  program for a new applications specialist

                  Recent Accomplishments:  Automatic Bid Writer--Configures a
                                           boilerplate bid for the home office
                                           bid group (14 people)

                                           Invoice System--Handles all invoicing
                                           for two departments (25 people)

    April 1981 -  Programmer Trainee--Supporting the departments of Contract
September 1981    Administration, Conversion Center, and Bids and Proposals with
                  program development and program maintenance; providing technical
                  support to the field support, home office, and customers on the
                  capabilities of the media conversions; training personnel to handle
                  the programs developed for the Conversion Center.

January 1978 -    Conversion Operator--Answering customer questions on technical
   April 1981     material sent from the conversion group; solving on-site
                  problems with the conversion material; interfacing and training
                  other operators; providing support for supervisor of conversion
                  group regarding feasibility of projects

ACTIVITIES        Commuter Council Member (1978 - 1982) responsible for organizing
                  forums and social functions and providing voice to administration
                  for 75 commuters; served as the Council Coordinator

                  National Committee Chairperson (1977 - 1979) for Square Dance
                  Convention--responsible for maintaining financial records,
                  organizing fundraiser for local group

PERSONAL          Willing to travel
                  References available
                  Willing to relocate

1982
```

If you want an informational interview, you first need to establish its specific purpose or goal. Then identify the person in the company best qualified to help you achieve the goal. By letter or telephone, arrange a convenient time to meet. The suggestions in Chapter 7 for interviewing will help you prepare.

Job interviews are different. You're not just collecting information; you're seeking employment. And whether or not you get the job you're applying for is usually decided in large part on the basis of the interview(s). You can prepare for an interview by doing some background investigation about the company and about the type of job you'll be doing.

Being nervous before an interview is normal; everyone gets nervous. You can allay some of your anxiety by practicing. Think of questions you'd like to ask, and practice saying them out loud. Anticipate questions you'll be asked, and practice possible responses. Consider how your skills and experience can specifically benefit the company, and plan how you'll convey that information to the interviewer.

You can also role-play an interview, with someone else acting as interviewer. If possible, video tape or at least tape record the mock interview, then view it or listen to it to determine what you'd like to change. Much of the same advice for giving an oral presentation applies to interviewing: Make direct eye contact, speak clearly, listen carefully, wear comfortable, professional clothes, relax.

Personnel, a journal published by the American Management Association, has published an article that identifies questions an interviewer might ask or be asked when interviewing executive candidates. The article is prepared for the personnel interviewer, but the questions are equally useful for a person being interviewed for any professional position.

Questions the Interviewer Should Ask

1. Which of your accomplishments at your present position or former positions are you proudest of?
2. Which personal accomplishments and attributes make you the proudest?
3. What are your goals or schedule for accomplishment at your present position for the next year, for the next two or three years?
4. What would you have liked to accomplish in your present position that you have not accomplished, in whole or in part? What prevented you from accomplishing these things?
5. Why do you want to leave your present position?
6. From what you know about this company and the position available, what characteristics and accomplishments should we expect in the six months from the individual we hire? During the first year? The first five years?
7. What do you think will be the toughest aspects of the job if you were to accept the position? What will be the most enjoyable aspects? The least enjoyable?

8. What do you think your greatest contribution to the job or to the company will be? Where and how do you think you would be able to make your greatest contribution?

9. What would your personal goals in this job be for the next year? For the next five or ten years? For the rest of your working career?

10. From what you have been able to learn of the company and the position, what short- and long-term problems do you think you will face, and how would you deal with them?

11. What problems do you think this organizatin faces in the next year? In the next two years? In the next five years? What do you think you can contribute to the identification and/or solution of those problems?

12. How long do you think the challenges of this job will excite and interest you? How would you deal with the problem many executives face after two to four years on the job when they have conquered most of the interesting problems or have set in motion a way to conquer them and their enthusiasm wanes? When will you be ready for your next job?

13. Assume we faced a significant cut in expenditures—for example, 10 to 20 percent within a year or two. How would you go about planning and implementing such a cut in the areas of your responsibility?

14. Assume that we expected significant growth in your area of responsibility and ask you to give us a plan for growth. How would you do that?

15. Assume that the company was going to be merged with or bought by another company. What kinds of things would you like in the merger agreement and in the administrative operations plan covering your own area of responsibility and the company as a whole as you know it?

16. I assume that at some point you were in head-on competition with an individual in your present company for promotion or for status or project managership or something of that type. What would your competitor say about you in terms of your strengths and weaknesses?

17. If you are selected for this position, how would you deal with individuals in the company who were competitors for the job for which you are being interviewed, and who may feel that they are better qualified? (Assume that some of them may then be your subordinates.)

18. If you were conducting the selection process for this position, what would you have done differently and why?

19. If you were promoted to the next higher position in the company, how would you select your successor and what would you be looking for?

20. What criteria would you (a) use in measuring your own performance over the next year and the following years, (b) like your performance measured by, (c) use in measuring your superior's performance and your relationship to him or her?

21. What criteria would you use in evaluating your subordinates' performance? How would you conduct an evaluation process? What philosophy and techniques do you use in motivating subordinates and energizing them and, when necessary, disciplining them? Do you vary your approach for subordinates who are outstanding, good, satisfactory, mediocre? If so, how?

22. What factors are: (a) most important to you personally in job satisfaction? (b) most important to your subordinates in job satisfaction?

23. How would you deal with a subordinate (a) who does not appear to measure up to increasing demands of the job, (b) whose enthusiasm, motivation, and performance seem to be going down, (c) who seems to be under some sort of personal stress or tension?

24. What skills or attributes do you think the following should have: an outstanding subordinate, an outstanding peer, an outstanding supervisor of someone at your level? What skills or attributes do you possess that you think others would regard as being outstanding as compared with other individuals of your rank, experience, and accomplishment?

25. How would your spouse and children feel about your changing position and relocating your home?

26. What gives you the most satisfaction during free or vacation time?

27. How do you motivate yourself? How do you deal with stress, tension, boredom?

28. How do you set priorities for your own time? For your subordinates' time?

29. What do you expect from the social and public relations demands of this job? How would they affect you and your family?

30. Do you belong to business, community, and social organizations? What business, community, and public policy issues interest you and why?

31. If a number of executive training sessions or continuing education sessions or conferences were to be scheduled, what types of sessions would you (a) care to attend and why? (b) feel competent to serve and interested in serving as a panelist, discussion leader, speaker, or teacher?

32. If you were able to do things differently from age 18 on, what would you do that differs from what you have done with your life during that period?

33. From whom have you learned the most in your management career? What have you learned and why is it valuable?

34. If you were able to meet with an outstanding management expert for (a) a one-to-one three-hour uninterrupted session and/or (b) an uninterrupted week or two, what kinds of things would you ask and what would you hope to learn from the experience?

35. Why do you want this job? Why should we hire you?

Questions the Applicant Might Ask
1. What specific responsibilities of the position do you regard as most important? What are the other responsibilities?

2. What criteria will my supervisor use for my performance evaluation, and what is the time schedule for performance evaluations?

3. How frequently, and in what manner, will I and my supervisor meet on a regular basis, and how will we deal with particular problems?

4. How do you, the supervisor, like to operate in terms of assignments, delegation of responsibility and authority, general operating style? What are characteristics that you like in a subordinate, characteristics you don't like?

5. What are the company's goals, the supervisor's goals for his or her own area and for the area I might be in charge of? What are the long- and short-term goals of you, my prospective supervisor?

6. What short- and long-term problems and opportunities do you think exist for (a) the company, (b) the supervisor's area, (c) the supervisor's superior's area?

7. What long- and short-term problems and opportunities do you think my prospective area faces? What will I face in the first week, month, three months, six months, one year, two years?

8. What do you and/or my prospective supervisor hope I would accomplish in three months, six months, twelve months, three years, five years, ten years?

9. What are the major frustrations, as you see it, of my job? Of your (the supervisor's) job? Of your superior's job? Of my subordinate's job?

10. What are the major challenges/rewards/stimulations of my job? Of my supervisor's job? Of his or her superior's job? Of my subordinate's job?

11. What are the strengths and weaknesses of my prospective subordinates, as you see them?

12. What are the responsibilities of my peers and what are their strengths and weaknesses?

13. With whom will I be interacting most frequently, and what are their responsibilities and the nature of our interaction? What are their strengths and weaknesses?

14. What are the limits of my authority and responsibility? What do I have to get permission for? Inform others about after the fact? Discuss prior to action?

15. What freedom do I have to act and what budget is available to me for (a) changes in staffing, promotion, salary increases, (b) use of consultants, requesting or purchasing software and hardware systems, venture capital for new ideas and approaches, implementing planned growth, implementing planned cutbacks, (c) changes within my area in regard to policies, procedures, practices, performance expectations?

16. How frequently, and on what matters, do you, my prospective supervisor, interact with your superiors on a regular basis, and how are particular problems or crises handled?

17. What contact on what issues will I have with my supervisor's boss, his or her superior, and others on a higher level?

18. What particular things about my background, experience, and style interest you? Make you think I'll be successful? Give you some amount of concern? What experience, training, attributes, operating style, accomplishments, and personality factors should the "ideal" candidate for this job have?

19. What opportunities are there for growth in my prospective area of responsibility and for advancement in the company? On what kind of timetable?

20. What social requirements does the job entail, for me personally and for my spouse and family?

21. What professional, industrial, community, or public policy involvement do you feel it necessary for me to have, and in what depth?

22. How do you think the company and its top leadership is perceived in the industry and in the local business community and why? What are its perceived strengths and weaknesses?

23. Why did my predecessor leave the position, what were her or his strengths, weaknesses, accomplishments, failures? (Or, if this is a newly created position, what factors led to the decision that this position should be created?)

24. Why did you come here? Why do you stay?

25. After 6 months, 1 year, 2 years, 5 years, how will you know you made the right decision in hiring the person for this position? If the position were offered, why should I accept it?[1]

Inquiries and Applications

Discussion Questions

1. Explain which resume form—chronological, organizational, or functional—you believe is most appropriate for you.

2. Who would probably want to place the education section of their resume before the experience section? Who would want to place the experience section first?

3. Read the following article that advocates *never* sending a resume. Explain whether you agree or disagree.

WHAT YOU CAN DO WITH YOUR RESUME

Somehow the idea that the job resume is a grand form of communication managed to slip out of the jar. Anyone who sends out resumes ought to have his head examined. Even though you may have been pushed, even though you may have jumped, even though you need a job, don't send a resume. Even though you read the string of desiderata strung out in the ads—late model car, self-starter, industrious, state salary requirements, and send a resume—don't send one.

Don't say anything about money either. Companies know perfectly well what the jobs pay, but when you ask they blush delicately, screw their toes into the ground, and clam up. Despite all their arguments to justify the secrecy, the fact is they hope to find someone willing to take less than the going rate and to keep old-timers from learning what newcomers are going to be getting. So you be businesslike too by keeping your mouth shut about pay.

Part of the popularity of the resume is that it compresses a lot of facts into small space. No bargain. What resume reviewers want are ones to throw out, so the neater you lay everything out, the quicker they can shoot it into the trash. So keep your counsel.

As the hymn says:

God moves in a mysterious way
His wonders to perform

and so do personnel departments. They seldom have the faintest of what makes for success in job applicants. Feeble as they used to be, tons of the pet sort-'em-out schemes that served in the past no longer are legal. So now the fashion is to ask for a resume, and the applicants obey like sheep, offering info that the company isn't legally even allowed to ask. And think about another point.

Why should you tell your whole life story to a stranger who so far has evidenced not the slightest interest in you? An applicant often has no idea what the company makes, does, or sells. For all you know it's collecting a prospect list of aluminum siding or magazine subscriptions. The applicant often has no idea whether he would want to be associated with the venture, let alone take the specific job it might offer (should he ever find out what it is). But there he is, spilling his guts.

The smart way to go is to write a letter mentioning that the ad attracted you, that you'd like to know more about the job, and that meanwhile you'll give them letter—like a few facts about yourself. Then do just that, briefly and attractively. Remember— you are shooting in the dark. You don't know exactly what they're after, and half the time they don't either. In short, write a nice come-on letter that shoots for an interview. No resume. Repeat: No resume.

Another thing—they make boring reading and they're risky. Consider again the person with a great stack of resumes to review. What's his temptation? To find some little thing that displeases and to drop the resume into the trashbasket. True enough, the reviewer might find something likeable, but why take a chance? If you interest the reviewer, he'll ask for more information. If he's not interested, you have the satisfaction of not having done a full prostration before someone lacking respect for your dignity and privacy.[2]

4. Read again the questions that interviewers frequently ask during job interviews. Identify five questions that you would feel most comfortable answering and five that you would feel uncomfortable answering. Create a group or class matrix of these questions to determine if there are patterns about what makes people feel comfortable or uncomfortable. Discuss what causes the comfort or discomfort in responding to particular questions.

Individual and Group Exercises

1. Editing exercise: Rewrite the following portion from the experience section of a resume in two different forms.

   Reaction Technician, Grade 4, 1976–77
   General Electric Company
   Polycarbonate Manufacturing
   Pittsfield, MA

   Research Technician, Grade 5, 1978–79
   General Electric Company
   Polymer Products Research and Development
   Pittsfield, MA

   Quality Control Technician, Grade 5, 1980
   General Electric Company
   Polymer Products Operation
   Pittsfield, MA

   Research Technician, Grade 6, 1981
   General Electric Company
   Chemical Development Operation
   Pittsfield, MA

   Specialist—Fiber Development, 1982–83
   General Electric Research and Development Center
   Schenectady, NY

   Process Development Engineer, 1984–present
   Stackpole Fibers Company, Inc.
   Lowell, MA

2. Editing exercise: Rewrite the following education sections from resumes in two different forms. You can rearrange as well as delete information.
   a. 1981 Northfield (MN) High School, diploma
      1985 University of Minnesota, B.S. in Mechanical Engineering
   b. Associate's Degree in Electronics
         Belleville (IL) Community College, 1980
      Bachelor's Degree in Electrical Engineering
         SIU—Edwardsville (IL), 1985
   c. 90 of 120 credits towards B.S. in Metallurgy, Rolla (MO) School of Mines, degree anticipated in 1987

3. Read the ads in newspapers and technical publications for various positions. Independently or in small groups, select an ad and write a letter of application for that position. Have members of the class role-play the recipient of each letter and discuss their responses to the letters' content and organization.

4. Conduct mock job interviews for the positions applied for in Exercise 3. After each interview, members of the class can identify the areas for improvement as well as the strengths of both interviewer and interviewee.

Assignments

1. Locate an ad or job description for a position you would like to have. Write a cover letter to accompany your resume.
2. Create two different resumes for yourself. Bring them to class and, in small groups, examine and discuss people's preferences.

Usage Handbook

Contents

Sentences

1.1 Sentence Fragments

A sentence fragment is an incomplete sentence. Every sentence must have a subject and verb; a fragment is missing one of these essential parts. Often, a fragment is a phrase or subordinate clause that should be part of another sentence. Other times, a fragment represents only part of a thought the writer wants to express.

Missing verb   Pain relievers with extra ingredients such as caffeine.

Missing subject   Offer no advantages over aspirin or acetaminophen.

Subordinate clause   Though they are more expensive.

These elements can be combined to create a sentence.

Example   Though they are more expensive, pain relievers with extra ingredients such as caffeine offer no advantages over aspirin or acetaminophen.

Sometimes a writer creates fragments by mistakenly separating a subordinate clause from the independent clause.

FRAGMENT   Starting diesel engines is difficult. *Because high pressures are required inside the cylinders.*

Even though the fragment has a subject (high pressures) and a verb (are required), "because" is a subordinate conjunction. The subordinate clause "because high pressures are required inside the cylinders" should be connected to the sentence that precedes this fragment.

SENTENCE   Starting diesel engines is difficult because high pressures are required inside the cylinders.

Other fragments are created when a writer begins but doesn't finish an idea.

FRAGMENT   Wild ducks harbor influenza viruses in their intestinal tracts, causing no illness in the ducks. *Spread influenza to many other species.*

"Spread influenza to many other species" is a fragment. It can be corrected when the writer completes the idea by adding a subject.

SENTENCES   Because ducks migrate great distances, *they* spread influenza to many other species.

Ducks spread influenza to many other species during their migration.

Some fragments are created by carelessness. Others are caused by a writer's indecision. The following examples illustrate both situations.

FRAGMENT   Judging from recent radar scans. Venus appears to have mountain ranges similar to earth's Appalachians and Himalayas. Parallel mountains formed by horizontal movements of the crust.

This example has two fragments, "judging from recent radar scans" and "parallel mountains formed by horizontal movement of the crust." The first fragment is a phrase that should be part of the sentence. The second fragment can either be connected to the sentence or have a verb added to make it a sentence itself.

SENTENCES   Judging from recent radar scans, Venus appears to have mountain ranges similar to earth's Appalachians and Himalayas, parallel mountains formed by horizontal movements of the crust.

Judging from recent radar scans, Venus appears to have mountain ranges similar to earth's Appalachians and Himalayas. Parallel mountains are formed by horizontal movements of the crust.

Exercises: Fragments

1. The access mechanism of the floppy disk drive contains two motors. One motor that rotates a floppy disk at 300 rotations per minute (rpm). Another motor is used to move the read-write head inward and outward on the tracks of the disk.
2. Modern strain gauges are manufactured by etching a very thin metal foil through a mask to obtain a grid pattern. The foil having been previously coated with a thin layer of epoxy to form the gauge backing.
3. Paperboard asceptic packaging has already revolutionized the beverage industry. Taking over a significant market share from metal cans and glass bottles. Developments in technology mean a rapid increase in production of more radical packaging. Plastic multi-layer, high-barrier containers.

4. A vendor evaluation system should increase the number of good vendors and decrease the number of bad vendors. The effect being the acquisition of quality parts on time and at a reasonable price, lowering the overall product cost.

5. The iris diaphragm, a circular, variable-size door inside the camera that controls the amount of light the reaches the film in a given time.

1.2 Comma Splices

Comma splices are caused by connecting two sentences with a comma. The independent clauses in the next example are incorrectly connected by a comma.

COMMA
SPLICE
Botulism requires immediate medical attention, the disease can be fatal.

The sentences can be correctly separated by a period.

REVISION
Botulism requires immediate medical attention. The disease can be fatal.

However, if the clauses should be connected because the ideas are closely related and of equal importance, a writer can choose one of three ways to do it:

1. Two independent clauses can be connected by a coordinate conjunction (*and, but, or, nor, for, so, yet*) that is preceded by a comma. The coordinate conjunction expresses the relationship between the two clauses. The ideas in the independent clauses must be of equal importance.

Examples
Botulism requires immediate medical attention, *for* the disease can be fatal.

Synthetic substances such as Teflon have been used to reduce hoarseness, *but* they may be rejected by the body as foreign material.

2. Two independent clauses can be connected by a semicolon if the ideas in the clauses are closely related and of equal importance.

Example
Collagen, a natural protein, offers hope for people unable to speak or cough normally; it can fill out missing tissue in vocal cords.

3. A conjunctive adverb that connects two clauses is usually preceded by a semicolon and followed by a comma. The most common conjunctive

adverbs include *accordingly, also, besides, hence, however, moreover, nevertheless, otherwise, therefore, thus, still.*

Examples   Botulism requires immediate medical attention; *otherwise,* the disease can be fatal.

Collagen may be useful for remolding delicate vocal cord areas; *however,* only preliminary research has been completed so far.

Exercises: Comma Splices

1. Some safety glasses have a sintered magnet molded into the temple portion of the frame, metal particles that float in the air in an industrial environment are attracted to the magnet, protecting the eyes from injury, a window exposes the magnet, both to attract the metal particles and to facilitate cleaning.

2. Financially, local companies are doing well. Spanner Associates is in excellent shape, sales for FY85 [fiscal year 1985] ended at $578 million with a net income of $37 million. Desktop Computer Corporation has done well until recently. Total sales for FY84 were $3.8 billion, net income was $417 million. FY85 was not as successful, sales were down 20 percent from the same period in FY84, FY86 should swing up.

3. Combustion toxicity of building materials and furnishings can be determined in laboratory tests, small quantities of materials are heated or burned in a miniature furnace, identifying the type and potency of toxic gases and materials, however, such tests do not consider ignition resistance, rate of flame spread, and extinguishability, therefore toxicity tests should not be the sole criteria for making fire safety decisions.

4. Many drugs can be absorbed through the skin, transcutaneous, or through-the-skin therapy, eliminates many problems associated with traditional treatments, transcutaneous application releases a constant amount of medication, reducing side effects, medication is distributed through a polymer pad that is bonded to a thin, flexible hypoallergenic foam and then to an adhesive bandage that is laminated with soft foil.

5. The solar pond project at Fort Benning, Georgia, covers 11 acres, 80 pond modules supply domestic hot water to 26 barrack buildings as well as the post laundry, each 15½ by 200-foot pond has concrete walls, insulated sand bedding, and a water bag under an arched glazing cover of translucent glass–fiber reinforced panels, panels transmit 89 percent of the available solar energy, enabling the black plastic water bags, each filled with 4 inches of water, to reach 140° Fahrenheit to 160° Fahrenheit on sunny afternoons, at peak temperature the heated water is pumped to the insulated 500,000-gallon storage tank for distribution during the night and next day, the system saves 11,300 barrels of oil each year.

1.3 Run-On Sentences

Run-on sentences (sometimes called fused sentences) result when two sentences are written as if they are a single sentence, without internal punctuation separating the clauses.[1]

RUN-ON   The diving reflex is the body's natural response to being immersed in water the heart rate slows dramatically and the blood supply to certain tissues and organs is restricted.

A run-on sentence such as this usually results from haste in writing the draft. The writer is working so quickly that punctuation is momentarily ignored. A correction produces two separate sentences.

REVISION   The diving reflex is the body's natural response to being immersed in water. The heart rate slows dramatically, and the blood supply to certain tissues and organs is restricted.

Another common run-on error occurs in compound sentences—two independent clauses connected by a coordinate conjunction. Sometimes the writer forgets to insert the requisite comma preceding the coordinate conjunction.

RUN-ON   Weddell seals have a larger-than-normal blood supply and the blood itself is richer in red blood cells.

The error is easy to correct by inserting a comma before the "and."

REVISION   Weddell seals have a larger-than-normal blood supply, and the blood itself is richer in red blood cells.

Writers do have to be careful not to indulge in "hypercorrection," inserting a comma every time they see an "and." Commas are only necessary when the "and" connects two independent clauses and when it connects the last of three or more items in a series.

Another type of run-on sentence probably results from the writer starting the sentence, getting distracted, and then finishing the sentence without re-reading the first part.

RUN-ON   Weddell seals in Antarctica dive to extraordinary depths even beyond 1500 feet they can hold their breath for an hour and fifteen minutes.

In this sentence, the phrase "beyond 1500 feet" can be part of the first sentence; however, it also fits as part of the second sentence. The result is a run-on sentence that can be corrected in two ways, depending on the writer's intent.

REVISION   Weddell seals in Antarctica dive to extraordinary depths, even beyond 1500 feet. They can hold their breath for an hour and fifteen minutes.

Weddel seals in Antarctica dive to extraordinary depths. Even beyond 1500 feet, they can hold their breath for an hour and fifteen minutes.

Exercises: Fragments, Comma Splices, and Run-Ons

A Pareto diagram is a special form of vertical bar graph or column graph data classifications are arranged in descending order from left to right. The only exception is a class referred to as "other." A composite of several very small categories. If it is used, "other" is always located on the far right of the diagram. Even when it is not the smallest of all the classes appearing on the diagram.

Pareto diagrams are useful in problem investigation, they show the priorities of a myriad of problems in a systematic manner. Particularly important when resources are limited. The analytical process has several steps. Selecting classifications, tabulating data, ordering data, and constructing the diagram. Employees who conduct this process often identify important relationships. Previously unnoticed.

Pareto diagrams are used in industrial settings in a variety of ways. They can analyze a problem from a new perspective, for example, rather than arranging manufacturing defects by frequency, the defects can be arranged by dollar losses. Which may change what is labeled as the most important defect. By arranging issues or problems in order of priority, Pareto diagrams differentiate major problems from minor ones and they also enhance communication because employees at all levels can see the same priorities. Another use for Pareto diagrams is to compare data changes during different time periods. Finally, Pareto diagrams provide a basis for the construction of a cumulative line. So that employees can determine the percentage of each prioritized item in relation to the overall problem.

1.4 Subject-Verb Agreement

The subject and verb of a sentence must agree in number—singular subject and singular verb or plural subject and plural verb.

ERROR IN SUBJECT-VERB AGREEMENT   Because of inexperienced workers and old equipment, the *costs* to build the assemblies *is* increasing.

Even when a word or phrase comes between the subject and verb, they must agree. The plural subject "costs" requires a plural verb. Or, the singular verb "is" requires a singular subject.

SUBJECT-VERB Because of inexperienced workers and old equipment, the *costs*
AGREEMENTS to build the assemblies *are* increasing.

Because of inexperienced workers and old equipment, the *cost*
to build the assemblies *is* increasing.

Errors in agreement also can result from using the wrong verb form with a compound subject. When two or more subjects are joined by *and*, they usually take a plural verb, even if one or more of the subjects is singular.

ERROR IN The Fahrenheit *scale* of temperature *and* the mercury *thermom-*
SUBJECT-VERB *eter was* invented by Daniel Fahrenheit in 1714.
AGREEMENT

SUBJECT-VERB The Fahrenheit *scale* of temperature *and* the mercury *thermom-*
AGREEMENT *eter were* invented by Daniel Fahrenheit in 1714.

When the subject of the sentence is an indefinite pronoun, it usually takes a singular verb. Indefinite pronouns do not refer to any specific person or thing. (See list of common indefinite pronouns on page 572 of the Handbook.)

SUBJECT-VERB Nearly 300 years later, *everyone* in this country *is affected* by
AGREEMENT Fahrenheit's invention.

When an indefinite pronoun functions as an adjective preceding a compound subject, the sentence uses a singular verb.

SUBJECT-VERB *Each* observation and experiment towards developing a ther-
AGREEMENT mometer *was reported* in a paper Fahrenheit wrote in 1734.

Some collective nouns can take either a singular or plural verb, depending on the meaning. When the collective noun refers to the group as a single entity, use a singular verb.

SUBJECT-VERB The research *team has reported* their experimental results in the
AGREEMENT next issue of *Science.*

When the group's members are being considered as individuals, use a plural verb.

SUBJECT-VERB The research *team have reported* differing versions of their re-
AGREEMENT search.

A common subject-verb agreement error results from making a linking verb agree with the complement rather than the subject of the sentence.

SUBJECT-VERB   An important *part* of cattle breeding *is* clones developed from
AGREEMENTS   embryo splitting.

Clones, developed from embryo splitting, *are* an important part of cattle breeding.

Exercises: Subject-Verb Agreement

1. Every engineering proposal, test plan, and test report written by the engineering staff are submitted to the engineering writer for copy editing.
2. The blade and rejection blade on a time-delayed fuse is soldered to the element assembly, a copper element soldered to a silver element.
3. The telecommunications system derive polled information from each store via EPOS (Electronic Point of Sale Registers), SATs (Store Administrative Terminals), and telephone lines.
4. Each time a customer buys something, the cash registers, which are small computers, remembers this information.
5. All government documentation are in the process of being classified or reclassified as confidential, secret, or top-secret.
6. The computer tape and the input that has been keypunched is given to the Internal Operations Department.
7. One benefit of running is that the number of red blood cells are increased, thus more oxygen can be carried per quart of blood.
8. The sinoauricular (SA) node is the key regulator of the electrochemical impulses that stimulates contractions of the heart muscles.
9. Two types of peptic ulcer is common: gastric ulcers in the stomach and duodenal ulcers in the intestine. Duodenal ulcers causes pain between the breastbone and navel, often relieved by food or milk. Gastric ulcers causes pain at a higher location, however, and is often brought on, rather than relieved, by eating. Diagnosis for both types of ulcers involve any combination of three basic procedures. The most common procedure are X-rays. Endoscopy uses a long fiberoptic instrument that light up the walls of the stomach and duodenum, take photographs, and even obtain samples for microscopic study. A third method, less frequently used, involves obtaining samples of gastric juices.
10. The result of the Sysgen procedure are program disks designed to load onto your computer. (Sysgen is a coined word, derived from System Generator.) Once the Sysgen is programmed into the terminal, a list of questions appear on the screen. The operator responds with the names of the source and destination drives. When all the system generation process are completed, the built-in commands and the operating system is on the new disk.

1.5 Pronoun-Antecedent Agreement

A pronoun substitutes for or replaces a noun; an antecedent is a noun or pronoun earlier in the sentence (or an immediately preceding sentence) to which a pronoun refers. A pronoun must agree with its antecedent in three ways:

- gender: feminine, masculine, neuter
- person: first, second, third
- number: singular, plural

Errors in pronoun-antecedent agreement cause awkward sentences that often confuse the reader.

Many errors result from the misuse of indefinite pronouns, which are pronouns that do not refer to a specific person, idea, or thing. The most common indefinite pronouns are:

all	both	many	no one
another	each	more	one
any	either	most	several
anybody	everybody	neither	some
anyone	everyone	none	somebody
anything	everything	nobody	someone
	few		something

With the exception of such obvious plurals as *all, few, many, more, most, several,* and *some,* indefinite pronouns are third-person singular. When indefinite pronouns are antecedents to other pronouns, they generally require singular pronouns.

ERROR IN   *Everyone* brought *their* bathing suit to the company picnic.
AGREEMENT

The error results because "everyone" is singular and "their" is plural. The correction can substitute "his" only if all the company employees are male, "her" only if all employees are female. To write, "Everyone brought his bathing suit to the picnic" would be inaccurate if both men and women employees brought bathing suits. However, to write, "Everyone brought his or her bathing suit to the company picnic" would be awkward. The most appropriate correction bypasses the stylistic problem of using *his/her* or *his or her* by making both the antecedent and pronoun plural.

AGREEMENT   *All* employees brought *their* bathing suits to the company picnic.

Collective nouns used as antecedents can take either a singular or plural pronoun, depending on the meaning. When the collective noun refers to the group acting together, the pronoun should be singular.

AGREEMENT The *staff* discussed changes in organizational structure at *its* monthly meeting.

When the individual members of the group are acting independently, the pronoun should be plural.

AGREEMENT The *staff* wrote *their* recommendations for changing the organizational structure.

1.6 Pronoun Reference

Pronouns can cause ambiguity and confusion for the reader if the antecedents are not clear. Most problems result from inappropriate use of these pronouns:

you	this	they	these
it	that	which	there

Reserve *you* for situations in which you directly address the reader. Use *it*, *this*, *that*, *which*, or *there* only when you can identify a specific, concrete antecedent. These pronouns usually do not present a problem in speech, but they make your writing unnecessarily wordy, vague, and sometimes confusing. You can easily rewrite common expressions that use pronouns ineffectively.

INEFFECTIVE It is believed . . .
PRONOUN USE There are several competitors . . .

REVISION Our committee believes . . .
Several competitors include . . .

Clear writing requires that pronouns have stated rather than implied antecedents.

UNCLEAR An air conditioner removes much of the humidity from the air. *It* either evaporates or runs off through a tube to the outside.

What is the antecedent of "it"? Air conditioner? Humidity? Air? "It" has no stated antecedent; rather, the antecedent is implied.

IMPROVED An air conditioner removes much of the humidity from the air. As the humidity condenses, the resulting water either evaporates or runs off through a tube to the outside.

Sometimes the reference is so general that the pronoun has no antecedent. Often *this, that,* or *these* is used, referring broadly to several preceding ideas, thus confusing the reader.

UNCLEAR   Holding your work in your hand when using a screwdriver can be dangerous. Place your work on a flat surface or secure it in a vise or clamp. Do not put your body in front of a screwdriver blade tip. The blade can cause a bad cut if it slips. *This* is a good practice for any pointed tool.

IMPROVED   Holding your work in your hand when using a screwdriver can be dangerous. Place your work on a flat surface or secure it in a vise or clamp. Do not put your body in front of a screwdriver blade tip. The blade can cause a bad cut if it slips. *These safety rules* apply to any pointed tool.

Another pronoun reference problem occurs when the pronoun is so far away from the antecedent that the reader can't be sure of the reference without rereading the passage.

UNCLEAR   The *generalization* usually holds true that the lifespan of a mammal can be correlated to its size. The larger the mammal, the longer the lifespan. Most mammals take approximately the same number of breaths and have the same number of heartbeats. A shrew compresses its biological functions into one or two years whereas an elephant spreads its activities over 60 or so years. *It* does not apply to humans.

The problem can be eliminated by substituting a noun phrase for the pronoun.

IMPROVED   The *generalization* usually holds true that the lifespan of a mammal can be correlated to its size. The larger the mammal, the longer the lifespan. Most mammals take approximately the same number of breaths and have the same number of heartbeats. A shrew compresses its biological functions into one or two years whereas an elephant spreads its activities over 60 or so years. *The relationship between longevity and body size* does not apply to humans.

Pronouns references also cause a problem if too many pronouns create confusion or ambiguity.

UNCLEAR   Owls have round eyes that are so large *they* cannot turn in *their* sockets so *they* must rotate *their* entire head in order to follow a moving object.

IMPROVED   In order to follow a moving object, an owl must rotate its entire head because its eyes are too large to turn in their sockets.

An owl has round eyes that are so large they cannot turn in their sockets, so the owl must rotate its entire head in order to follow a moving object.

Exercise: Pronoun-Antecedent Agreement and Pronoun Reference

1. During a heart–lung transplant, it is standard procedure to sever the trachea, aorta, and right atrium of the heart in order to remove the organs.

2. The committee voted their approval of proposed research.

3. Pregnant women can exercise vigorously as long as her doctor approves.

4. When stressed to the near breaking point, all material emits their own characteristic sound waves.

5. Everyone in the department is ready to donate their time to establishing an apprentice program.

6. It is now claimed that milk may be one of the worst foods for peptic ulcers. The fat and protein in it stimulate the production of gastric acid; the calcium causes additional acid production. They can be treated with several types of medication. Traditionally, they were treated only with antacids, but then anticholinergics were developed to control gastric production. Most recently they are treated with new antihistamines called H2-receptor blockers.

7. The type of evening exercise people do may affect the time it takes them to fall asleep. Dynamic exercise such as jogging or cycling tends to lengthen the time it takes to fall asleep because of the generalized stress that results. Static exercise such as push-ups or isometrics tends to bring on sleep sooner, the result of a static muscle contraction that triggers fatigue in some people. It may help certain types of insomnia.

8. Trobriand Islanders are matrilineal, tracing their ancestors through their mother's side of the family. The women hold high status in the society and are actively involved in ceremonial and economic functions. Their opinions are respected. This may be because, traditionally, men are thought to play no biological role in conception.

9. The point angle of a twist drill is approximately conical; it is the angle between the lips measured in the plane parallel to the drill axis and the lips. It ranges from 60° to 150°. The point deviates from the conical shape due to the lip relief angle. This is necessary to permit the drill to advance into the work. For the drill to perform effectively, it is essential that it be accurately sharpened.

10. It has recently been discovered that the Wave 3000 units, beginning with s/n (serial numbers) 78-100213 through s/n 78-100713 were shipped containing a faulty 64K PROM chip. It was found that the error was in a program that has already been corrected. These 500 units should not have left the factory with this problem. It is clearly stated on page 27 of the *Wave Test Manual* the procedure to follow to verify that the memory is correct. It is absolutely essential that all procedures are followed to ensure that we are shipping a quality product. Effective immediately, if any technicians are found to be leaving out test procedures, it will result in dismissal.

1.7 Dangling Modifiers

A dangling modifier is a word or phrase that appears to modify the subject of the sentence, but doesn't. The modifier dangles because there is no word in the sentence that it can logically modify. A dangling modifier should be corrected because it gives the reader inaccurate information and may cause unintended humor. Correction is easy: Sometimes you can eliminate the phrase entirely, you can add or change the subject of the independent clause, or you can change the dangling phrase into a subordinate clause. Occasionally, rewriting the entire sentence produces the best result.

Let's examine some examples of sentences in which the writer had good intentions and a definite idea, but still confuses the reader.

DANGLING MODIFIER　When in production, the engineer is responsible for keeping the production lines running smoothly.

Is the engineer being manufactured? Replicated? Assembled? The reader can figure out that the writer *means* the engineer works in the production department or is responsible for the production process—but that's not what the sentence says; it says the engineer is in production. Placing the questionable phrase immediately after the subject is a good test for some sentences. If the result is ridiculous or nonsensical, you know the sentence must be revised. The revision of the sample sentence is easy because "production" is repetitious; the dangling modifier is merely eliminated.

REVISION　The engineer is responsible for keeping the production lines running smoothly.

The next sentence has an unstated but understood *you* as the subject.

DANGLING MODIFIER　After 30 minutes at 250° Fahrenheit, raise the oven temperature to 300° Fahrenheit.

Whoever is adjusting the oven temperature is going to be mighty warm! A person cannot possibly spend 30 minutes at 250° Fahrenheit without being cooked. The sentence can be corrected by making the dangling modifier into a subordinate clause by adding a subject.

REVISION　After the oven has been at 250° Fahrenheit for 30 minutes, raise the temperature to 300° Fahrenheit.

Sometimes a dangling modifier can be eliminated by turning the phrase into a subordinate clause with a logical subject.

DANGLING
MODIFIER   After assembly, the index, middle, and ring fingers are inserted into the holes at the end of the control arm.

Have you ever heard of a manufacturer offering ready-to-assemble fingers?

REVISIONS   After you have assembled the control arm, insert your index, middle, and ring fingers into the holes.

After the control arm is assembled, insert your index, middle, and ring fingers into the holes at the end.

Often the confusion caused by a dangling modifier can be eliminated in more than one way.

DANGLING
MODIFIER   When investigating this problem, three major areas should be considered.

One way to correct this sentence is to add a logical subject.

REVISIONS   When investigating this problem, consider three major areas.

When investigating this problem, you should consider three major areas.

Another way to correct the sentence is to invert the phrase and the independent clause.

REVISION   Three major areas should be considered when investigating this problem.

A third way to correct this sentence is to rewrite it entirely.

REVISION   Three major areas should be investigated.

The next example illustrates the flexibility you have in revising dangling modifiers.

DANGLING
MODIFIER   With proper diet and exercise, the statistics on cardiovascular disease can be lowered.

The dangling modifier here makes "statistics" sound like they need proper diet and exercise. The phrase "With proper diet and exercise" actually modifies the omitted subject—people. Several revisions are possible.

REVISIONS   With proper diet and exercise, people can lower their chances of having cardiovascular disease.

People who eat a balanced diet and exercise regularly reduce the risk of cardiovascular disease.

Exercises: Dangling Modifiers

1. To compete in the CAD/CAM market, product quality must be assured.
2. When contemplating contact lenses as a means of correcting vision, both the advantages and disadvantages should be considered.
3. To develop the negatives, a combination of chemicals is poured into the tank.
4. If deemed necessary, our children will be sent to private schools.
5. When choosing a pair of pliers, a few things should be considered.
6. Through the use of gear reduction, the speed is reduced to 600 revolutions per minute.
7. When determining the internal temperature of the autoclave, the figure indicated by the thermometer should be carefully observed because the steam pressure gauge alone may be misleading.
8. Once established as a corporation, a preliminary operating fund will be necessary.
9. While changing the filter floss, the fish are not disturbed because the system is located on the back of the tank.
10. With a small amount of practice, a French curve makes an otherwise hopeless task easy to achieve.
11. To fully understand the air conditioning process, it is necessary to follow each step to see how the parts operate.
12. When taking a breath, the head rotates 90° to the side, keeping one ear in the water.
13. Plant cuttings can be rooted in water or in a mixture of sand and vermiculite. When using water, the stems are placed in a container filled with water up to the bottom of the leaves. The water should be changed regularly. Before using a mixture of sand and vermiculite, the roots should be lightly dusted with rooting powder. Roots need to be established on the cuttings before they're ready to plant.
14. A planimeter is an instrument used for measuring the area of a regular or irregular plane figure by tracing the perimeter of the figure. By using a planimeter, a result is easily obtained that is not in error more than 1 percent, except for very small areas. When using the planimeter, the anchor point is set at some convenient position on the drawing outside the area to be measured. To determine the area, the tracing point is then run around the perimeter of the area to be measured.
15. Silversmiths can use a torch to produce designs on various metals. By controlling such factors as metallic alloy proportions, thickness of protective surfaces, amount of heat, and flame size and direction, the roughened surface texture is produced. With much experience, a textural surface with a definite pattern can be produced. For example, by angling the torch in one direction on the first row and in another on the second, a herringbone pattern is created. Controlling the amount of heat and the size and direction of the flame, the interior of the copper-silver alloy can be partially melted. By melting only the interior of the metal alloy, a wrinkled surface is produced.

1.8 Misplaced Modifiers

Like dangling modifiers, misplaced words and phrases cause confusion—and sometimes unintentional humor.

Adverbs are particularly easy to misplace because they can be correctly placed in several locations in a sentence; however, changing the location of the adverb changes the meaning of the sentence. The following words can be particularly troublesome:

almost	exactly	just	nearly	scarcely
even	hardly	merely	only	simply

Notice how changing the location of "only" changes the meaning.

Examples *Only* the technician adjusted the valve.

The *only* technician adjusted the valve.

The technician *only* adjusted the valve.

The technician adjusted the *only* valve.

A good guideline is to place phrases and subordinate clauses close to the words they are intended to modify. Incorrectly placed modifiers can change the meaning.

MISPLACED MODIFIER Endorphin is released during labor when a woman is having a baby to dull her senses.

Motherhood might, in some situations, temporarily dull the senses, but no woman begins with this as a goal. The revision places the phrase "to dull her senses" close to the word it modifies, endorphin.

REVISIONS Endorphin is released to dull a woman's senses during labor.

Endorphin, which dulls senses, is released during labor.

MISPLACED MODIFIER In the technical journal, she read an article about insect reproduction *which verified her own field study.*

The sentence is illogical if "which verified her own field study" modifies "insect reproduction"; instead, it should be placed next to "article," the word it modifies.

REVISION In the technical journal, she read an article which verified her own field study about insect reproduction.

Exercises: Misplaced Modifiers

1. Differences?
   Just the manager approved the proposal this morning.
   The manager just approved the proposal this morning.
   The manager approved just the proposal this morning.
   The manager approved the proposal just this morning.
2. Differences?
   Our department has almost completed all of the investigation.
   Our department has completed almost all of the investigation.
3. Differences?
   Nearly everyone is ready for the quality control survey.
   Everyone is nearly ready for the quality control survey.
4. I ordered drills from the manufacturer with carbide tips.
5. The pilot sighted the missing fishing boat using a sonar scanner.
6. The personnel department recommended a candidate from a competitor who was already skilled in using CNC machines.
7. The buyer ordered a part from the distributor guaranteed for five years.
8. WANTED: Industrial site for precision manufacturing company with chemical drains and 220V.
9. The decision will only be made after all data is compiled.
10. The supervisor placed the damaged manual in the drawer of his desk with missing pages.

1.9 Parallel Structure

Parallel structure requires a writer to use equivalent grammatical structures for ideas or facts of equivalent importance.

This sentence identifies two results of accidents; both should be written in the same grammatical structure.

ERROR IN PARALLEL STRUCTURE   Accidents can be either personal injury producing or property damage.

The revision could be any of the following versions.

REVISIONS   Accidents can either *produce personal injury* or *damage property*.

Accidents can result in either *personal injury* or *property damage*.

Accidents can either *injure people* or *damage property*.

This second example is more difficult, partly because the sentence is longer and partly because the ideas are more complex.

ERROR IN PARALLEL STRUCTURE Conditions for a disaster loan include taking over property by a federally supported urban renewal program or when property displacement is caused by the federal government in projects such as highway construction.

The sentence identifies two of the conditions for disaster loans in a compound direct object. Notice that the two reasons have different structures:

- "taking over property by a federally supported urban renewal program"
- "when property displacement is caused by the federal government in projects such as highway construction"

This error in parallel structure can be corrected in more than one way.

REVISIONS Conditions for a disaster loan include *property takeover by a federally supported urban renewal program* or *property displacement caused by the federal government in projects such as highway construction.*

A disaster loan can be approved *when federally supported urban renewal programs take over* or *when property displacement is caused by federal projects such as highway construction.*

A disaster loan is justified in *the takeover of property by a federally supported urban renewal program* or *the displacement by federal projects such as highway construction.*

In the next example, the parallel error is in the subject of the sentence.

ERROR IN PARALLEL STRUCTURE Minimizing displacement of existing structures and avoidance of water bodies must be considered, or the cost of the roadway will increase.

Because the sentence has a compound subject, each part of the subject must have the same structure.

REVISIONS *Minimizing displacement of existing structures* and *avoiding water bodies* must be considered, or the cost of the roadway will increase.

Minimize displacement of existing structures and *avoid water bodies,* or the cost of the roadway will increase.

The last example shows that items in a list should be parallel. The following sign was posted in a shop to remind workers of safety guidelines.

ERROR IN PARALLEL STRUCTURE

ALWAYS OBSERVE SAFETY RULES:

  a. Wearing of safety glasses
  b. Proper tool for the job
  c. Use only tools that are functioning properly
  d. Maintain a clean and organized work area
  e. Questions relating to procedures or the proper handling of tools should be presented to your group leader

---

The items in any list should adhere to the same grammatical form. Because the sign instructs workers to follow guidelines, the items can all be in imperative mood, as the revision illustrates.

REVISION

ALWAYS OBSERVE SAFETY RULES:

  a. Wear safety glasses.
  b. Use proper tools for the job.
  c. Use only tools that are functioning properly.
  d. Maintain a clean and organized work area.
  e. Ask your group leader questions about procedures or proper tool handling.

Exercises: Parallel Structure

1. The work-in-progress report is used by a wide variety of employees, ranging from dispatchers to those at managerial levels.
2. Informal communication includes talking to the customer at the point of purchase, talking to peers, and directions by management to employees.
3. I judged the systems on price, effectiveness, special options, and how easily the alarm could be installed.
4. Major causes of electrical injuries include defective insulation on electrical power cords, loose connections or wiring, and improper or lack of grounding on home appliances and power tools.

5. The test procedure to determine expansion and contracting of PVC packaging film under abnormally high-temperature shipping conditions has been recommended by the quality control department.

6. Documentation includes how to load your program into the computer, any error messages from the computer, and limitations on your program.

7. The amount of thermal mass for a house depends on the total area of south glazing, where the mass areas are placed, how much sunlight they will receive, and the types of materials used.

8. A simple radar device operates by transmitting a particular type of wave form, such as a pulse-modulated sine wave, and detects the nature of the echo wave.

9. The amplitude corresponds to how loud a person is speaking, and the frequency is the pitch of the voice.

10. Three major steps are involved in adjusting the scales on the Vemco V Trackmaster: (a) setting up the machine, (b) construction of a reference line, and (c) scale alignment.

11. The first step is to measure the roll surface under ambient conditions. Second, place the test roll into a preheated 200° Fahrenheit oven for three hours. The last step is to remove the test roll from the oven and remeasure the roll surface.

12. The table of contents in a manual for assemblers lists these items:

    a. Air hook-up and disconnect
    b. Proper holding of air-driven tools
    c. Changing tips safely on air-driven tools
    d. How to avoid stripping the hardware

13. This bulleted list is from a report:

    - STEEL—This material can corrode and is magnetic.
    - STAINLESS STEEL—This material is noncorrosive and is nonmagnetic.
    - PLASTIC—Nonmetallic and nonconductive

14. a. The insulation for a home can be chosen according to the area for installation. In areas of the country where it is cold or if heating or air conditioning is used, the R-value should be raised. Typically, contractors recommend that walls and crawl spaces have insulation rated between R-11 and R-13. Insulation for floors that are unfinished and finished floors should be between R-11 and R-19. Insulation for ceilings can range from R-13 to R-30.

    b. The type of insulation determines whether it's fire resistant. Fiber glass blankets and batts are naturally fire resistant. Loose insulation can be made from cellulose, vermiculite, and it is also of fiber glass. Vermiculite and fiber glass are naturally fire resistant; cellulose can smolder or it burns unless chemically treated. Plastic foam insulation is made of urea formaldehyde or polyurethane. Both types are combustible but are chemically treated for safety. Rigid board insulation can be made polystyrene, polyurethane, or fiberglass. The polystyrene can be extruded or sometimes it is made of molded beads pressed together. Polystyrene and polyurethane, both combustible, are chemically treated for safety.

15. These definitions are listed in a reference manual glossary:

- LOCK NUTS—prevent the nut from becoming loose after being properly torqued.

- NUTS—are internally threaded fasteners designed to mate with bolts and screws. Nuts are two-sided. The flat side should be against the washer.

- POP RIVETS—A rivet is a headed fastener with the shank end designed to be expanded or spread in order to join the work pieces. Rivets are used for inseparable assemblies. Rivets are made of aluminum or steel and come in different sizes. They are fastened with a rivet gun or hand tool.

- RIVETS—Rivets that are solid, eyelet, or tubular should be fully seated. Stacking and rolling should be uniform.

- SEMS—Are preassembled screws and washers in one unit. These units expedite assembly operations and assure the presence of a washer in each assembly.

- STANDOFFS AND SPACERS—Standoffs and spacers are used to separate work pieces. They may be plastic, metal, ceramic, or phenolic.

- WASHER—A part, usually thin, having a centrally located hole of partial slot. The washer performs various functions when assembled between the bearing surface or a fastener and the part being assembled.

Cumulative Exercises

Exercise: Sentence Fragments, Comma Splices, Modifier Errors, and Parallel Structure

Using word processing (wp) software, a document is accessible to the writer for unlimited revisions. Revision becomes easier because a writer does not have the physical burden of entirely rewriting a document. Instead, a writer incorporates necessary changes in the appropriate places. For example, sections of a document can be moved to any other place in the document, you can delete material and insert new material. Automatically adjusting the remaining content to fill in the lines and meet the margins. A writer can revise directly on the screen attached to the terminal or getting a paper printout and revising on paper appeals more to some writers. After completing the revisions, the final copy of the document is printed.

Exercise: Sentence Fragments, Comma Splices, Subject-Verb and Pronoun-Antecedent Agreement, Pronoun Reference, Modifier Errors, Parallel Structure

Excessive amounts of scrap and customer rejects has caused us to recommend three solutions to this. One, a new glue pot at a cost of $6,500. A more favorable solution is repairing the existing glue pot for $1,500 and then to purchase an International Glue Line Inspection System, the price for this system is $4,000. The new glue line system will decrease scrap and customer rejects by 75 percent. The system will detect breaks in the glue line and ejects defective cartons from the run. If the system detects more than five consecutive rejects, it automatically stops the machine. In the first year of use, the cost savings will exceed $10,000. More than covering the cost of rebuilding the glue pot and the new inspection system.

Exercise: Sentence Fragments, Modifier Errors, Parallel Structure

Machinists must follow blueprints and operating precision equipment including lathes and machines that do milling work. Working to very tight tolerances, some machined parts are accurate to 0.0001 inches. At regular stages in the machining of a part, the blueprint is checked. Dimensions of the part must match the dimensions specified on the blueprint. The application of the part determines the accuracy required by the blueprint. Even for medical and aerospace applications, some blueprints allow the part dimensions to vary slight. Stating + (plus) or − (minus) the specified dimensions. Machinists must measure the part, determining that the dimensions are within the tolerances, and correct any errors. Because being undersized results in being scrapped, the machinists remove material from parts in extremely tiny amounts.

Exercise: Sentence Fragments, Comma Splices, Subject-Verb and Pronoun-Antecedent Agreement, Pronoun Errors, Modifier Errors, Parallel Structure

Although relatively high in initial cost ($50,000), a company using the pivoting arm industrial robot RX 784 will earn increased profit. Based on the salaries of the three workers it replaces, the payback period averages 16 months. By relying on hydraulic systems for movement, the manufacturer recommends the seals at the three main joints—hand, arm, and main rotary—be inspected and then only replace them if necessary every 400,000 hours.

The robot is more reliable than human workers and the noise and heat of the work place does not affect it. Operates in hazardous and harsh environments. The RX 784 is made of tempered steel alloy that operate in radiation and up to temperatures of 2000° Fahrenheit.

The RX 784 arm, which can extend from 500 mm to 1000 mm and has an overall arc of 270°, is attached to a solid base. Although the base is stationary, it can be adapted to work from a moving track. It can be programmed in four hours to perform a variety of repetitive functions.

After the robot is installed, the highest expense is for electricity they require to operate. This cost, however, is 50 percent less than the cost of heat and cooling required to keep workers comfortable in the same work area.

Punctuation

(*Note:* Conventions discussed in this section are based on the 13th edition of *The Chicago Manual of Style* and the 3rd edition of *Words into Type*.)

2.1 Apostrophe

2.1.1 Use an apostrophe to indicate possession.

Add an apostrophe plus *s* to singular nouns and indefinite pronouns to form the possessive.

Examples   Fire destroyed the company's data processing room.
The physician examined everyone's medical records.

Add an apostrophe plus *s* to plural nouns that do not end in *s*. Add only the apostrophe to plurals that end in *s*:

Examples   women's locker room (locker room of the women)
              schooners' crews   (crews of more than one schooner)

2.1.2 Use an apostrophe to indicate omission of one or more letters or figures.

Examples   doesn't = does not   '86 = 1986

2.1.3 Avoid a common misuse that confuses *it's* (it is) and *its* (possessive form of it), *you're* (you are) and *your* (possessive form of you).

     Do not use apostrophes with such possessive pronouns as *hers, theirs,* or *ours.*

2.2 Brackets

2.2.1 Use brackets to enclose comments or explanations inserted in a quotation.

Examples   "Production declined last month [May 1986]."
              "The section manager [Thompson] identified the problem."
              "Improper leveling [of the comparator] resulted in inaccurate data."

2.2.2 Use *sic* (meaning "so" or "thus") to indicate an error in the original document.

Example   "The shipment was made on 5-33-85 [*sic*]."

2.3 Colon

2.3.1 Use a colon as a convention in salutations, citations, time, titles.

Examples   Dear Mr. Ellis:
              (January 1986): 342
              5:30 a.m.
              Synectics: The Development of Creative Capacity

2.3.2 Use a colon to introduce a list or series when the words preceding the colon are a complete sentence.

Example   The machinist regularly works with five metals: aluminum, beryllium, molybdenum, stainless steel, titanium.

Do *not* use a colon if the words preceding the list or series are not a complete sentence.

Example   The machinist regularly works with aluminum, beryllium, molybdenum, stainless steel, titanium.

2.4 Comma

2.4.1 Use a comma as a convention in dates, numbers, addresses, informal salutations, and titles or degrees:

Examples   April 19, 1776 or 19 April 1776   Dear Kate,
317,554,203   Christopher D. Burnett, Ph.D.

1055 Thomas Jefferson, N. W.
Washington, DC 20007

2.4.2 Use a comma to separate two sentences connected with a coordinate conjunction—*and, but, or, for, so, yet.* Place the comma preceding the coordinate conjunction.

Example   The printer was too slow, and most of the programs were never delivered.

2.4.3 Use commas to separate items in a series. Place a comma following each item in the series, except the final one.

Examples   Health, self-confidence, and self-esteem usually improve as a result of a running.

To perform the test, an operator connects the coupler to the enclosure, evacuates the instrument, purges it with a reference gas, evacuates the system again, and then opens the coupler.

An automated coal-mining system would increase productivity, make mining safer, and protect the health of the mine workers.

Do *not* use commas to separate compound elements—two nouns, two verbs, or two modifiers.

Examples   The lenses✗and photodetectors are mounted on a plate.

Break-even costs vary widely with financing methods✗and tax structures.

The gas is noncorrosive✗and nontoxic.

2.4.4 Use a comma to separate introductory phrases and subordinate clauses from the main sentence.

Example   Because solar-cell arrays can be built on roofs, they have low structural costs and can displace some costs of conventional roofs in new homes.

2.4.5 Use a comma to separate nonessential elements from the rest of the sentence.

Examples   Before the IRAS (Infrared Astronomical Satellite), little could be learned about the formation of smaller stars, those like our sun, because of their faintness.

Scientists have discovered the worst-tasting substance ever discovered, a white powder so bitter it can be detected even when diluted to 1 part in 20 million.

2.5 Dash

Use a dash (made with two hyphens on your typewriter or computer keyboard) to signal a break in thought. Do *not* separate the dash with spaces.

Examples   The interpreter of ancient clay tablets failed to recognize that one sign—a small circular impression—did not always have the numeric value of 10.

2.6 Ellipsis

Use ellipsis points (three spaced dots) to indicate that something has been omitted. If the omission comes at the end of a sentence, the first dot is the period, followed by the three dots of the ellipsis.

Examples   Strokes in the temporal or parietal lobes of the left hemisphere of the neocortex characteristically result in the impairment of the ability to read, write, speak, and do arithmetic.

Strokes . . . characteristically result in the impairment of the ability to read, write, speak, and do arithmetic.

2.7 Exclamation Mark

Use an exclamation point at the end of a sentence to signal an extraordinarily startling idea or event. An exclamation point is seldom appropriate in technical documents.

2.8 Hyphen

2.8.1 Use a hyphen to signal the break of a word, showing that the word is carried over to the next line. Break words *only* at the end of a syllable.

2.8.2 Use a hyphen to create compound modifiers that precede a noun:

Examples
pollen-carrying hairs	word-length units
high-pressure valve	two-layer membrane
6-, 12-, and 16-foot fence	three-dimensional structure

2.8.3 Use a hyphen in all words that begin with *self-*:

Examples
self-examination	self-incrimination
self-regulatory	self-employed

2.8.4 Use a hyphen to avoid ambiguity.

Examples
coop:	The chicken coop was freshly painted.
co-op:	The food co-op has 200 members.
re-cover:	After the storm, the plants were re-covered with cheesecloth.
recover:	The plants would recover if protected from the sun.

2.8.5 Use hyphens in fractions and ratios that function as adjectives preceding a noun.

Examples

Committee rules require a two-thirds majority to pass resolutions.

The vote was carried by a three-to-one margin.

2.8.6 Use hyphens in compound numbers from twenty-one through ninety-nine.

Example

Twenty-seven bus routes will be added on January 1.

2.9 Parentheses

2.9.1 Use parentheses to separate supplementary information within a single sentence or to enclose one or more sentences.

Example   At short wavelengths (12 to 25 micrometers), the main contributor to infrared background is emission from zodiacal dust from the solar system.

2.9.2 Use parentheses to separate acronyms the first time they are introduced.

Example   The Infrared Astronomical Satellite (IRAS) was launched in a joint undertaking by the Netherlands Agency for Aerospace Programs (NIVR), the U.S. National Aeronautics and Space Administration (NASA), and the U.K. Science and Engineering Research Council (SERC).

2.10 Period

2.10.1 Use a period to signal the end of a statement or command.

2.10.2 Use a period (without parentheses) to follow the numbers or letters enumerating items in a list.

2.10.3 Use a period as a decimal point.

2.10.4 Use a period following some abbreviations. Most scientific and technical abbreviations no longer require periods. However, use a period if the abbreviation spells another word: in. (inches), no. (number), and so on.

2.11 Question Mark

Use a question mark at the end of a question.

2.12 Quotation Marks

2.12.1 Use quotation marks to indicate the titles of articles from periodicals and newspapers.

Examples   "Consumer Products Need Better Manuals" in *Simply Stated*
"Rolling-Contact Rheostat" in *NASA Tech Briefs*

2.12.2 Use quotation marks to enclose short direct quotations. Longer quotations (more than three lines) should be single spaced and indented from the regular margins.

Example   Gerontologist Lorraine Hiatt said, "Many of today's elders don't realize that the environment may be exaggerating and, in some cases, causing certain functional disabilities."

2.12.3 Place commas and periods inside quotation marks. Place colons and semicolons outside quotation marks. Place question marks, exclamation points, and dashes inside the quotation marks only if the punctuation is part of the quotation; otherwise, place them outside the quotation marks.

2.13 Semicolon

2.13.1 Use a semicolon to separate two closely related sentences.

Example   The world's earliest written records are inscriptions on clay tablets; they have been unearthed at the sites of two great ancient cities in Iran and Iraq.

2.13.2 Use a semicolon to separate two sentences connected by a conjunctive adverb. Precede the conjunctive adverb with a semicolon; follow it with a comma.

Example   Penny's is a retail outlet; therefore, it is essential that the information from their stores be polled daily.

2.13.3 Use a semicolon to separate items in a series if individual items themselves contain commas.

Example   The twist drill body contains the point, which is the cutting portion of the drill; the flutes, which convey the chips away from the cutting edges; and a number of other details.

2.13.4 Do *not* use a semicolon preceding a list; instead, use a colon.

Example   The system has two parts; Filecreate and Crosstab. (wrong)
The system has two parts: Filecreate and Crosstab. (right)

2.14 Slash

Use a slash to separate elements in dates, to indicate a fraction, and in place of *per*.

Examples 6/6/47   (6 June 1947)
2/3   (two thirds)
/order   (per order)

2.15 Underlining/Italics

2.15.1 Use underlining (italics if the material is typeset) to indicate titles of books, periodicals, newsletters, and newspapers.

Examples *Wall Street Journal*
Simply Stated

2.15.2 Use underlining or italics to indicate legal citations.

Example *Skillin v. Hall*

2.15.3 Use underlining or italics to indicate letters.

Example $p + q$

2.15.4 Use underlining or italics to indicate Latin scientific terms.

Examples *Rhododendron maximum*
Subularia aquatica

Capitalization

(*Note:* These conventions for capitalization are based on those suggested in the 13th edition of *The Chicago Manual of Style.*)

3.1 Capitalize Personal Names.

3.1.1 Names and initials of people

Example Edward H. Burnett

3.1.2 Civil, military, religious, and professional titles that immediately precede a name as part of the name

Examples   General Jones has arrived.
            The general has arrived.

3.2 Capitalize Academic Degrees.

Examples   The B.S. is awarded after four years of study.
            The bachelor's degree is awarded after four years of study.

3.3 Capitalize Nationalities—Racial, Linguistic, or Religious Groups of People:

Examples   German
            Hispanic
            Korean
            Navaho

3.4 Capitalize Place Names.

3.4.1 Parts of the world or a country:

Examples   Arctic Circle   Pacific Northwest   the Middle East
            Central America   Southeast Asia   Washington State

3.4.2 Countries, states, cities, counties:

Examples   Southfield
            New Marlborough

3.4.3 Topographic locations (rivers, lakes, islands, mountains):

Examples   Appalachian Trail   Penobscot Bay
            Berkshire Hills   Matinicus Island

3.4.4 Buildings, monuments, and public places:

Examples   Kenmore Square   Gateway Arch
            Merchandise Mart   Bunker Hill Monument

3.5 Words Derived from Proper Nouns are Lowercased:

Examples   curie   pasteurize
india ink   roman numerals
macadam surface

3.6 Capitalize Names of Organizations.

3.6.1 Governmental and judicial bodies

Examples   Department of Health and Human Services
Supreme Judicial Court

3.6.2 Institutions and companies

Examples   New Mexico State University
Digital Equipment Corporation or DEC

3.6.3 Associations:

Examples   American Association for the Advancement of Science
Society of Technical Communication

3.7 Capitalize Historical and Cultural Terms.

3.7.1 Numerical designation of a period is lowercased:

Examples   sixteenth century
nineteenth

3.7.2 Archaeological and cultural periods:

Examples   Renaissance   Stone Age
Industrial Revolution   Bronze Age

3.7.3 Acts, treaties, and government programs

Example   Declaration of Independence

3.7.4 Laws and legal citations

Examples   Sherman Antitrust Act
Wade v. Roe

3.7.5 Awards

Example   Nobel Prize

3.8 Capitalize Most Calendar and Time Designations.

3.8.1 Months and days of the week
Seasons are lowercased:

Examples   June   spring
            Monday   autumn

3.8.2 Holidays:

Examples   Christmas
            Passover

3.9 Scientific Terms

(For more detailed assistance, refer to the *Council of Biology Editors Style Manual* and the U.S. Geologic Survey's *Suggestions for Authors*.)

3.9.1 Capitalize names of genus, family, order, class, and phyla, not the species or subspecies:

Examples   *Iris prismatica* [genus and species]
            Chordata [phylum]

3.9.2 Common plant and animal names generally use the *down* style:

Examples   puffin   foxgloves
            gerbil   hemlock

3.9.3 Capitalize geological terms:

Examples   Tertiary period
            early Pliocene epoch

3.9.4 Capitalize astronomical terms:

Examples   North Star   Milky Way
            Ursa Major   Halley's comet

3.9.5 Medical terms are lowercased except for proper names within the term:

Examples   Hodgkin's disease
measles

3.9.6 Generic drug names are lowercased:

Example   propoxyphene

3.9.7 Infectious organisms are capitalized, but diseases based upon such names are lowercased:

Examples   *Giardia lambia*   *Trichinella spiralis*
giardiasis   trichinosis

3.9.8 Capitalize only proper names attached to laws and principles:

Examples   Boyle's law
first law of thermodynamics

3.9.9 Capitalize chemical symbols, but not the names:

Examples   sodium chloride   urea
NaCl CH_4ON_2

3.10 Registered Trademarks Should Be Capitalized, but Not the Generic Derivative of the Term:

Examples   Levi's   Bufferin   Xerox   Vaseline
jeans   aspirin   photocopier   petroleum jelly

3.11 Capitalize titles of works.

3.11.1 Capitalize first, last, and key words in a title of books, periodicals, pamphlets, newspapers, movies, television and radio programs, musical compositions, and works of art:

Technical Communication   PBS's *Nova*
American Journal of Nursing   *Amadeus*
Wall Street Journal   WGBH's "Morning Pro Musica"

3.11.2 Computer software is often in full capitals:

APL	COBOL	Assembler
BASIC	FORTRAN	Pascal

Numbers—Figures or Words

(*Note:* These conventions for use of figures and words are based on those suggested for scientific and technical use in the 13th edition of *The Chicago Manual of Style.* More specialized usage is presented in the United States Government Printing Office *Style Manual.*)

4.1 Generally, Use Words for Numbers One through Nine and Figures for All Other Numbers, Both Cardinal and Ordinal.

cardinal: The office suite has seven rooms.
The manufacturing facility has 22,000 square feet.

ordinal: The company was second in mass market sales.
She ranked 23rd out of the 300 applicants.

4.2 Use Words at the Beginning of a Sentence. If This is Awkward, Rewrite the Sentence.

Examples   Two thousand three hundred and fifty seedlings were delivered.
The delivery of 2,350 seedlings arrived.

4.3 Express Very Large Numbers (Over Six Digits) by a Figure Followed by *million, billion,* and so on.

Example   Sales figures for last year reached $7 million.

4.4 Use Figures For Physical Quantities—Distances, Lengths, Areas, Volumes, Pressures, and so on:

Examples
17 inches	12 picas
1,700 square feet	220 volts
3.2 liters	5 cubic yards

Use figures with symbols or abbreviations:

Examples
90°	latitude 39°20′ N
55 MPH	32 psi
35mm film	4″ × 4″

4.5 Use Figures for all Percentages and Decimal Fractions. Use the Symbol "%" in Technical and Scientific Material.

Examples   A rejection rate of 7% is too high.
The manual had a readability level of 10.2 on the Fry scale.

Decimal fractions less than one are set with an initial zero if the quantity expressed is capable of exceeding 1.00.

Example   ratio of 0.93

If the quantity never equals 1.00, no zero is used.

Example $p < .07$

4.6 Use figures to indicate age:

Examples
age 39	women in their 70s
2-year-old	18 months old

APPENDIX
Readability Indexes and Formulas

THIS APPENDIX PRESENTS the methods to calculate four standard measures of readability: Flesch Formula, Fog Index, Fry Graph, and Flesch–Kincaid Formula.

Figure A–1

Flesch Formula[1]

Step 1. *Pick your samples.* Unless you want to test a whole piece of writing, take samples. Take enough samples to make a fair test (say, three to five of an article and 25 to 30 of a book). Don't try to pick "good" or "typical" samples. Go by a strictly numerical scheme. For instance, take every third paragraph or every other page. (Ordinarily, the introductory paragraphs of a piece of writing are not typical of its style.) Each sample should start at the beginning of a paragraph.

Step 2. *Count the number of words.* Count the words in your piece of writing. If you are using samples, take each sample and count each word in it up to 100. Count contractions and hyphenated words as one word. Count numbers and letters as words, too, if separated by spaces. For example, count each of the following as one word: *1948, $19,892, e.g., C.O.D., wouldn't, full-length.*

Step 3. *Figure the average sentence length.* Figure the average sentence length in words for your piece of writing. If you are using samples, do this for all your samples *combined.* In a 100-word sample, find the sentence that ends nearest to the 100-word mark—that might be at the 94th word or the 109th word. Count the sentences up to that point and divide the number of words in those sentences in all your samples by the number of sentences in all your samples. In counting sentences, follow the units of thought rather than the punctuation: usually sentences are marked off by periods; but sometimes they

600

| Figure A-1 | *Continued* |

are marked off by colons or semicolons—like these. (There are three sentences here between two periods.) But don't break up sentences that are joined by conjunctions like *and* or *but*.

Step 4. *Count the syllables.* Count the syllables in your 100-word samples and divide the total number of syllables by the number of samples. If you are testing a whole piece of writing, divide the total number of syllables by the total number of words and multiply by 100. This will give you the number of syllables per 100 words. Count syllables the way you pronounce the word: e.g., *asked* has one syllable, *determined* three, and *pronunciation* five. Count the number of syllables in symbols and figures according to the way they are normally read aloud, *e.g.*, two for *$* ("dollars") and four for *1916* ("nineteen sixteen"). However, if a passage contains several or lengthy figures, your estimate will be more accurate if you don't include these figures in your syllable count; in a 100-word sample, be sure to add instead a corresponding number of words after the 100-word mark. If in doubt about syllabication rules, use any good dictionary. (To save time, count all syllables except the first in all words of more than one syllable; then add the total to the number of words tested. It is also helpful to "read silently aloud" while counting.)

Step 5. *Find your "reading ease" score.* Using the average sentence length in words (*Step 3*) and the number of syllables per 100 words (*Step 4*), find your "reading ease" score on the HOW EASY? chart.

You can also use this formula:

Multiply the average sentence length by 1.015 . . . .
Multiply the number of syllables per 100 words . . . .
   by .846 _____

                            Add

            Subtract this sum from _____ 206.835

        Your "reading ease" score is . . . .

The "reading ease" score will put your piece of writing on a scale between 0 (practically unreadable) and 100 (easy for any literate person).

Description of Style	Average Sentence Length	Average No. of Syll. per 100 Wds.	Reading Ease Score	Estimated School Grades Completed	Estimated Percent of U.S. Adults
Very Easy	8 or less	123 or less	90 to 100	4th grade	93
Easy	11	131	80 to 90	5th grade	91
Fairly Easy	14	139	70 to 80	6th grade	88
Standard	17	147	60 to 70	7th or 8th grade	83
Fairly Difficult	21	155	50 to 60	some high school	54
Difficult	25	167	30 to 50	high school or some college	33
Very Difficult	29 or more	192 or more	0 to 30	college	4.5

Figure A-1   *Continued*

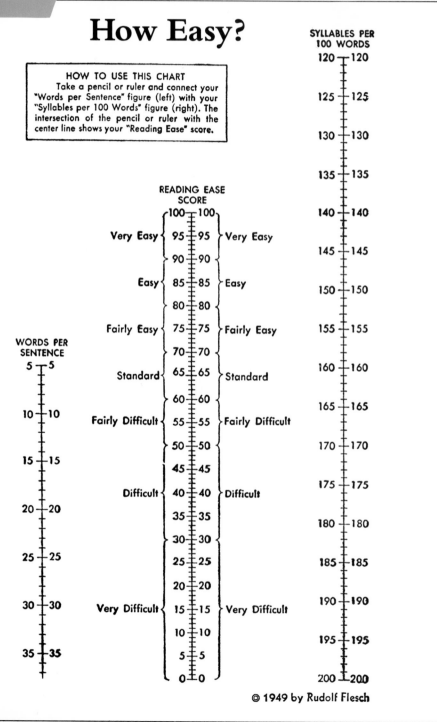

How Easy?

HOW TO USE THIS CHART
Take a pencil or ruler and connect your
"Words per Sentence" figure (left) with your
"Syllables per 100 Words" figure (right). The
intersection of the pencil or ruler with the
center line shows your "Reading Ease" score.

© 1949 by Rudolf Flesch

Figure A–2   Fog Index[2]

1. Find the average number of words per sentence. Use a sample at least 100 words long. Divide total number of words by number of sentences. This gives you average sentence length.
2. Count the number of words of three syllables or more per 100 words. Don't count: (a) words that are capitalized; (b) combinations of short easy words like "bookkeeper"; (c) verbs that are made three syllables by adding "ed" or "es," like "created" or "trespasses."
3. Add the two factors above and multiply by 0.4. This will give you the Fog Index. It corresponds roughly with the number of years of schooling a person would require to read a passage with ease and understanding.

Figure A–3   Fry Graph[3]

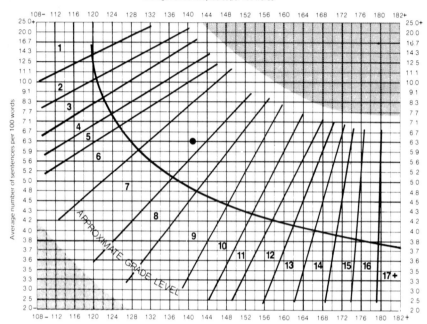

GRAPH FOR ESTIMATING READABILITY — EXTENDED

by Edward Fry, Rutgers University Reading Center, New Brunswick, N.J. 08904

Average number of syllables per 100 words

Expanded Directions for Working Readability Graph

1. Randomly select three (3) sample passages and count out exactly 100 words each, beginning with the beginning of a sentence. Do count proper nouns, initializations, and numerals.
2. Count the number of sentences in the hundred words, estimating length of the fraction of the last sentence to the nearest one-tenth.
3. Count the total number of syllables in the 100-word passage. If you don't have a hand counter available, an easy way is to simply put a mark above every syllable over one in each word, then when you get to the end of the passage, count the number of marks and add 100. Small calculators can also be used as counters by pushing numeral 1, then push the + sign for each word or syllable when counting.
4. Enter graph with *average* sentence length and *average* number of syllables; plot dot where the two lines intersect. Area where dot is plotted will give you the approximate grade level.
5. If a great deal of variability is found in syllable count or sentence count, putting more samples into the average is desirable.
6. A word is defined as a group of symbols with a space on either side; thus, *Joe, IRA, 1945,* and & are each one word.
7. A syllable is defined as a phonetic syllable. Generally, there are as many syllables as vowel sounds. For example, *stopped* is one syllable and *wanted* is two syllables. When counting syllables for numerals and initializations, count one syllable for each symbol. For example, *1945* is four syllables, *IRA* is three syllables, and & is one syllable.

Note: This "extended graph" does not outmode or render the earlier (1968) version inoperative or inaccurate; it is an extension. (Reproduction permitted—no copyright)

Figure A–4   Flesch-Kincaid Formula[4]

Grade level $= (\ 0.39) \times$ (average number of words/sentence)
$+ (11.8\ ) \times$ (average number of syllables/word)
$-\ \ 15.59$

Index

Notes

Chapter 1

1. Albert I. Berger, "The *Astounding* Investigation: The Manhattan Project's Confrontation with Science Fiction," *Analog—Science Fiction Science Fact* 104 (September 1984): 125–137.
2. W. Earl Britton, "What Is Technical Writing? A Redefinition," *College Composition and Communication* 16 (May 1965): 113–116.
3. Carol Barnum and Robert Fischer, "Engineering Technologists as Writers: Results of a Survey," *Technical Communication* 31 (Second Quarter 1984): 9–11.
4. Vitruvius, "Theater Acoustics," in *The Autobiography of Science*, eds. Forest Ray Moulton and Justus J. Schifferes, 2nd ed. (Garden City, N.Y.: Doubleday, 1960).
5. Nellie M. Stark, "Fire and Nutrient Cycling in a Douglas-Fir/Larch Forest," *Ecology* 58 (Winter 1977): 16. Reprinted with permission of The Ecological Society of America.

Chapter 2

1. Mary Fran Buehler, "Defining Terms in Technical Editing: The Levels of Edit as a Model, " *Technical Communication* 28 (Fourth Quarter 1981): 10–15. Based on a system developed and used at Jet Propulsion Laboratory, Pasadena, California.
2. The following sources were used as background material for the discussion of creative problem solving: John F. Feldhusen and Donald J. Tressinger, *Creative Thinking and Problem-Solving in Gifted Education* (Dubuque, Iowa: Kendall/Hunt Publishing Company, 1977), Chapter 4; Linda Flower, *Problem-Solving Strategies for Writing*, 2nd ed.

(New York: Harcourt Brace Jovanovich, 1985); Marcia Greenman Lebeau, *A Teacher's Guide to Creative Problem-Solving* (ESEA, Title IVC Project Grant, 1981), Chapter V; William J.J. Gordon, *Synectics: The Development of Creative Capacity* (London: Collier-Macmillan, 1961).
3. Benjamin S. Bloom, ed., *Taxonomy of Educational Objectives* (New York: David McKay, 1956).

Chapter 3

1. Joel R. Fried, "Polymer Technology—Part 7: Engineering Thermoplastics and Specialty Plastics," *Plastics Engineering* 39 (May 1983): 39.
2. Scale from Rudolf Flesch, *The Art of Plain Talk* (New York: Harper & Brothers, 1946), 38. Sentences from David M. Worth, "DO 228–200 Offers Mission Versatility," *Aviation Week and Space Technology* 119 (December 1983): 5.
3. Adapted from the *Boston Globe*, 5 July 1983.
4. Carl Sagan, *The Dragons of Eden* (New York: Random House, 1977), 14–17.
5. Richard A. Knox, "Brain Mapping Can Reveal Hidden Disease," *Boston Globe*, 18 July 1983. Reprinted with permission of *The Boston Globe.*
6. Jerry Ackerman, "Destroy It or Clean It Up," *Boston Globe*, 18 July 1983. Reprinted with permission of *The Boston Globe.*
7. Ron Benrey, ed., "Quiet Power: Technology for Quieter Jet Engines Moves from the Test Bed to the Flight Line," *Technology in Brief* 1 (1978): 1. Reprinted with permission of United Technologies Corporation.

8. "She's Come a Long Way—Or Has She?" *U.S. News and World Report*, 6 August 1984, 46–47.

Chapter 4
1. John W. Kanwisher and Sam H. Ridgway, "The Physiological Ecology of Whales and Porpoises," *Scientific American*, June 1983, 111. Copyright © 1983 by Scientific American, Inc. All rights reserved. Reprinted with permission of Scientific American, Inc.
2. A. B. Watkins, "External and Internal Parasites—Causes, Symptoms, Treatment, and Control," *Dairy Goat Journal* 61 (August 1983): 14, 16. Reprinted with permission of the publisher.
3. Modified from Nick Jordan, "What's in a Zombie," Review of *The Serpent and the Rainbow*, by Wade Davis, *Psychology Today*, May 1984, 6.
4. Modified from Jeffrey M. Lenorovitz, "China Plans Upgraded Satellite Network," *Aviation Week & Space Technology* 119 (21 November 1983): 71–75.
5. W. S. Rieker, *Quality Control Circles Study Guide*, Quality Control Circles, Inc., Saratoga, CA 95070, 1–4. Reprinted with permission of Rieker Management Systems.
6. "Three-Fingered Robot Hand," *NASA Tech Briefs* 8 (Fall 1983): 99.
7. Modified from John E. Bardach and Ernst R. Pariser, "Aquatic Proteins," *Protein Resources and Technology: Status and Research Needs*, ed. Max Milner, Nevin S. Scrimshaw, and Daniel I. C. Wang (Westport, CT: AVI Publishing, 1978), 461.
8. Wilson G. Pond, "Modern Pork Production," *Scientific American*, May 1983, 96. Copyright © 1983 by Scientific American, Inc. All rights reserved. Reprinted with permission of Scientific American, Inc.

Chapter 5
1. New Hampshire State Fishing Laws, 1983, 6.
2. Examples modified from Gary McMillan, "Fingerprinting Moves into the Computer Age—Science of Fingerprinting," *Boston Globe*, 30 January 1984.
3. Examples modified from Gary Blonston, "Where Nature Takes Its Course," *Science 83*, November 1983, 44–55.
4. Joanne Omang, "A Primer for Debate Looming on Clean Air," *Boston Globe*, 19 August 1981.

5. Examples modified from Wu Rukang and Lin Shenlong, "Peking Man," *Scientific American*, June 1983, 86–94.
6. Al Haas, "If You Want to Interface, Beware of User Error," *San Francisco Sunday Examiner and Chronicle*, 8 April 1984. © 1984. Reprinted with permission of *The Philadelphia Inquirer*.
7. "Tampon-Related Disease Can Be Fatal," *RN* 43 (October 1980): 21.

Chapter 6
1. Thomas E. Pinelli *et al.*, "Report Format Preferences of Technical Managers and Nonmanagers," *Technical Communication* 31 (Second Quarter 1984): 6–7.
2. Daniel B. Felker *et al.*, *Guidelines for Document Designers* (Washington, D.C.: American Institutes for Research, 1981), 85.
3. Pinelli *et al.*, "Report Format Preferences," 6–7.

Chapter 7
1. William Harvey, "On the Motion of the Heart and the Circulation of the Blood," in *The Autobiography of Science*, ed. Forest Ray Moulton and Justus J. Schiffers, 2nd ed. (Garden City, N.Y.: Doubleday, 1960), 106–107.

Chapter 8
1. Adapted from V. A. Johnson *et al.*, "Grain Crops," in *Protein Resources and Technology: Status and Research Needs*, ed. Max Milner, Nevin S. Scrimshaw, and Daniel I.C. Wang (Westport, CT: AVI Publishing Company, Copyright 1978), 244. Used with permission of AVI Publishing Company.

Chapter 9
1. Isaac Asimov, *Words of Science and the History Behind Them* (Boston: Houghton Mifflin, 1959), 243. Copyright © 1959 by Isaac Asimov. Reprinted by permission of Houghton Mifflin Company.
2. *American Pocket Medical Dictionary* (Philadelphia: Saunders, 1940), s.v. "focus."
3. George B. Thomas, Jr., *Calculus and Analytic Geometry*, 5th ed. (Reading, MA: Addison-Wesley, 1972), 479.
4. *Encyclopaedia Britannica*, 15th ed., s.v. "earthquakes."
5. Polaroid Corporation, *The Square Shooter* (Cambridge, MA: Polaroid Corp., 1974), 3.
6. Alan Semat, *Fundamentals of Physics* (New York: Holt, Rinehart, & Winston, 1966), 96.
7. Bureau of Naval Personnel, *Principles of Naval Ordnance and Gunnery*, NAVPERS 10783-A (Washington, DC: U.S. Navy, 1965), 4.
8. *Webster's New School and Office Dictionary*, s.v. "volt."

9. *Handbook of Chemistry and Physics*, 55th ed. (Cleveland, OH: Chemical Rubber Publishing, 1973), 3143.
10. *Random House Dictionary of the English Language*, s.v. "volt."
11. Siegfried Mandel, *Dictionary of Science* (New York: Dell Publishing, 1974), 355–56.
12. *Penguin Dictionary of Science*, s.v. "volt."
13. Joseph Sneller, "Mass Production of RRIM Parts Starts up on Automotive Lines," *Modern Plastics* 59 (January 1982): 48.
14. Chris Drake, "Operational Definition of a Thermostatic Element" (Technical and Scientific Writing 42.225, Univ. of Lowell, 1982).
15. William L. Skoglund, "Operational Definition of a Fuse Link" (Technical and Scientific Writing 42.225, Univ. of Lowell, 1983).
16. *Webster's Seventh New Collegiate Dictionary*, s.v. "lathe."
17. *Webster's New World Dictionary*, 2nd ed., s.v. "rivet,"
18. Lee J. Foster, "Brief History of Carbon Black" (Technical and Scientific Writing 42.225, Univ. of Lowell, 1982).
19. Lejaren A. Hiller, Jr. and Rolfe H. Herber, *Principles of Chemistry* (New York: McGraw-Hill, 1960), 3.
20. Edward Goldfinger, "A Manager's Guide to Computer Systems," *Inc.*, May 1980, 107. Copyright © 1980 by Inc. Publishing Corporation, 38 Commercial Wharf, Boston MA 02110. Reprinted with permission of *Inc.* magazine.
21. Goldfinger, 102–3, 107. Reprinted with permission of *Inc.* magazine.
22. Robert J. Sternberg, "A Componential Theory of Intellectual Giftedness," *Gifted Child Quarterly* 25 (Spring 1981): 86. Reprinted with permission of *Gifted Child Quarterly*.
23. Sternberg, 87. Reprinted with permission of *Gifted Child Quarterly*.
24. Alan Mandell, *The Language of Science* (Washington, DC: National Science Teachers Association, 1974), 23.
25. *Chamber's Technical Dictionary*, s.v. "chemistry."
26. Adapted from Goldfinger, "Manager's Guide," 107. Used with permission of *Inc.* magazine.
27. From "Computerspeak Glossary," *Inc.*, May 1980, 102–103. Copyright © 1980 by Inc. Publishing Corporation, 38 Commercial Wharf, Boston MA 02110. Reprinted with permission of *Inc.* magazine.

28. Carolyn Stanhope, "The Fugue" (Technical Communication EN 4676, Northern Essex Community College, 1980).
29. Crystal Novack, "Stalling an Airplane" (Technical Communication EN 4676, Northern Essex Community College, 1981).

Chapter 10

1. Galileo Galilei, "The Sidereal Messenger," in *The Autobiography of Science*, ed. Forest Ray Moulton and Justus J. Schifferes, 2nd ed. (Garden City, NY: Doubleday, 1960), 75–76.
2. NASA—Jet Propulsion Laboratory, *Voyager Bulletin* Mission Status Report No. 36, 23 February 1979, 3.
3. Robertson Parkman, "Management of the Newborn" in *Manual of Pediatric Therapeutics*, ed. John W. Graef, M.D. and Thomas E. Cone, Jr., M.D. (Boston: Little, Brown and Company, 1977), 99–100. Reprinted with permission of Little, Brown and Company.

Chapter 11

1. Linda Taylor, "Cloisonné: A Peek into the Past," *Lapidary Journal* 36 (December 1982): 1554.

Chapter 12

1. J. J. Bromenshenk, *et al.*, "Pollution Monitoring of Puget Sound with Honey Bees," *Science* 227 (8 February 1985): 632–34. Copyright 1985 by the AAAS. Reprinted with permission.
2. Nancy A. Rigotti, M.D., *et al.*, "Osteoporosis in Women with Anorexia Nervosa," *New England Journal of Medicine* 311 (1984): 1601. Copyright 1984 Massachusetts Medical Society. Reprinted with permission of *The New England Journal of Medicine*.
3. Chuck Megnin (Technical and Scientific Writing 42.225, Univ. of Lowell, 1984).
4. B. L. Buzbee and D. H. Sharp, "Perspectives on Supercomputing," *Science* 227 (8 February 1985): 591.
5. Megnin.
6. Megnin.
7. Bromenshenk, *et al.* Copyright 1985 by the AAAS. Reprinted with permission.

Chapter 13

1. MicroPro International Corporation, *WordStar Reference Manual* (San Rafael, CA: MicroPro, 1981), 2-2.
2. MicroPro International Corporation, *WordStar Installation Manual* (San Rafael, CA: MicroPro, 1981), E-13.
3. Inframetrics, "Thermal Measurements of Building Envelope Components in the Field" (Bedford, MA). Reprinted with permission of Inframetrics, Inc.

Chapter 14 1. General Henry M. Robert, *Robert's Rules of Order* (Glenview, IL: Scott Foresman, 1981), 389–91. Reprinted with permission of Robert's Rules Assn., John Robert Redgrave, Author's Agent.

Chapter 15 1. Freda F. Stohrer and Thomas E. Pinelli, "Marketing Information: The Technical Report as a Product," *Technical Writing: Past, Present, and Future*, NASA Technical Memorandum 81966 (March 1981), 14.

Chapter 16 1. The material on persuasive techniques is based on Roger Wilcox, "Persuading Your Reader or Listener," *Communication at Work* (Boston: Houghton Mifflin, 1977), 284–92.
2. Department of Health and Human Services, *NIH Peer Review of Research Grant Applications* (Washington, DC: Government Printing Office, 1983), 54.
3. Norton J. Kiritz, "The Proposal Summary," *The Grantsmanship Center News* 8 (October–November 1974): 9.

Chapter 17 1. David Stipp, "Science Gets Big Play in the Press, But Critics Question the Quality," *The Wall Street Journal*, 1 March 1985, Eastern edition. © Dow Jones & Company, Inc. 1985. All rights reserved. Reprinted with permission.
2. Judy Foreman, "Stress: Research Shows That Inability to Cope with Stressful Situations Affects All the Body's Systems," *Boston Globe*, Sci-Tech Section, 30 May 1983. Reprinted with permission of *The Boston Globe*.
3. Judy Foreman, "Studies Link IUDs to Fertility Problems," *Boston Globe*, 11 April 1985. Reprinted with permission of *The Boston Globe*.
4. Janet R. Daling, Ph.D., *et al.*, "Primary Tubal Infertility in Relation to the Use of an Intrauterine Device," *New England Journal of Medicine* 312 (1985): 937. Copyright 1984 Massachusetts Medical Society. Reprinted with permission of *The New England Journal of Medicine*.
5. Jeanne McDermott, "The Solid-State Parrot," *Science 83*, June 1983, 59–65. © 1983 by the American Association for the Advancement of Science. Reprinted with permission of *Science 83* Magazine.
6. Robert Cooke, "Cloned Cows Beef Up Herds," *Boston Globe*, Sci-Tech Section, 2 May 1983. Reprinted with permission of *The Boston Globe*.

7. Roy Bongartz, "Tides Will Produce Electricity," *Boston Globe*, Sci-Tech Section, 6 June 1983.
8. Robert Walmsley, "How Dangerous Is Acid Rain?" (Technical and Scientific Writing 42.225, Univ. of Lowell, 1983).
9. Dennis A. Donahue, "New Plants Through Genetic Engineering" (Technical and Scientific Writing 42.225, Univ. of Lowell, 1983).
10. Stephen S. Hall, "The Brain Branches Out," *Science 85*, June 1985, 72–74. © 1985 by the American Association for the Advancement of Science. Reprinted with permission of *Science 85* Magazine.

Chapter 19 1. Modified from Thomas Devine, *Listening Skills Schoolwide: Activities and Programs* (Urbana, IL: National Council of Teachers of English, 1982).

Chapter 20 1. Sigmund G. Ginsburg, "Preparing for Executive Position Interviews: Questions the Interviewer Might Ask—or Be Asked," *Personnel* 57 (July–August 1980): 32–36. © 1980 AMACOM, a division of American Management Associations, New York: All rights reserved. Reprinted with permission of the publisher.
2. David M. Kinsler, "What You Can Do with Your Resume," *Material Handling Engineering* (February 1980): 41. Reprinted with permission of *Material Handling Engineering*.

Handbook 1. Modified from Robert Cooke, "Understanding the Diving Reflex," *The Boston Globe*, 30 May 1981, 45.

Appendix 1. Rudolf Flesch, "How Easy?" chart, "How to Use the Readability Formula" (steps 1–4, 7), and table on p. 177 from *The Art of Readable Writing*, 25th Anniversary Edition, Revised and Enlarged by Rudolf Flesch, Copyright 1949, 1974 by Rudolf Flesch. Reprinted with permission of Harper & Row, Publishers, Inc.
2. Robert Gunning, *New Guide to More Effective Writing in Business and Industry* (Boston: Gunning-Mueller Clear Writing Institute, 1963), 2-15.
3. Edward Fry, "Fry's Readability Graph: Clarification, Validity, and Extension to Level 17," *Journal of Reading* 21 (December 1977): 249.
4. Philip J. Klass, "Software Augments Manual Readability," *Aviation Week & Space Technology* 116 (11 January 1982): 106.